F.V.

WITHDRAWN

Music in the Age of the
RENAISSANCE

Music in the Age of the
RENAISSANCE

Leeman L. Perkins

W · W · Norton & Company · New York · London

✔

Copyright © 1999 by W. W. Norton & Company, Inc.

The text of this book is composed in Galliard
with the display set in Castellar and Zapf Chancery
Desktop composition by Gina Webster
Music composition by Willow Graphics, Music by Design, and K. Yarmey
Manufacturing by Courier
Book design by Jack Meserole
Title page illustration: Detail from Nicolas Vallet, *Pseumes de David*
(Amsterdam, 1619), page 29 (2× original size)

✔

Library of Congress Cataloging-in-Publication Data

Perkins, Leeman L. (Leeman Lloyd), 1932–
Music in the age of the Renaissance / Leeman L. Perkins.
p.   cm.
Includes bibliographical references and index.
ISBN 0-393-04608-7
1. Music—15th century—History and critisism. 2. Music—16th century—History and criticism.
I. Title.
ML172.P47   1998
780'.9'031—dc21   98-28961
                                   CIP
                                   MN

W. W. Norton & Company, Inc., 500 Fifth Avenue, New York, N.Y. 10110
http://www.wwnorton.com

W. W. Norton & Company Ltd., 10 Coptic Street, London WC1A 1PU

1 2 3 4 5 6 7 8 9 0

*For my peerless partner
and our sons*

Contents

PART THREE ⁊ The Sixteenth Century:
The Established Genres and Stylistic Change

Preface

The accumulating fruits of scholarly labors dedicated to the music of the Renaissance have in a sense made this book increasingly difficult to write. Despite recent tremors and shifts affecting the paradigms of the musicological disciplines, studies in this area continue to appear at an accelerating pace. At present the sheer mass of historical data and musical material is far greater than a single volume of this kind could possibly accommodate. Consequently, its preparation has necessarily been primarily a process of selection. From the rich abundance of historical detail I have retained only that which appeared to me most relevant to the musical culture of the period. Of the many theoretical treatises written by authors of the fifteenth and sixteenth centuries I have included only those whose work seemed most pertinent to the music under discussion. And of the vast repertory of compositions that have reached us from those times, only a limited number could be examined closely.

These choices were often all the more difficult because of important work that is still in progress. As Gustave Reese brought his comprehensive survey of the music of the Renaissance to a close in 1954, he expressed regret that its completion could not be delayed a bit longer to include research the results of which were about to appear. At present the publications for which he might have wished to wait have of course long since seen the light, as has a great deal more, so that anyone at the same stage today must inevitably be prey to the same misgivings. At the same time, however, there are gaps in our knowledge that continue to be keenly felt. Despite the multifarious strands of history touching upon the music of the Renaisssance that can now be woven into a broad tapestry increasingly rich in detail, significant parts of the picture remain uncomfortably blurred. There are places even in the central foreground where the narrative fibers are too thin or too few to give a coherent picture. As a result, it has often been necessary to pick and choose details for presentation even where the overall design is still uncertain.

The process of selection thus made me acutely aware that the relative significance of many particulars could easily be either enhanced or diminished by discoveries yet to be made or fully understood. As a hedge against the imponderable, even the unknowable, I have attempted to focus as much on the historical processes as on the general picture as it appeared to me at the time of writing. Since the latter is unlikely ever to be definitive, I hoped to provide some basic paradigms for dealing with music in the particular historical context of the fifteenth and sixteenth centuries, approaches that would retain their usefulness even after present views as to what is central will have required revision. From my own particular methodological perspective, this has meant including enough of the political and social history to provide a context for the musical culture of that age. I have also tried to inform my own account of it from as many different vantage points as possible, drawing for example upon source studies, archival research, musical iconography, and theoretical discussions in addition to the musical repertories currently accessible in published editions.

Still, whatever the nature or the intrinsic interest of the ancillary material, I have endeavored to maintain at the heart of the overall design the music itself, introducing relevant findings from these various areas of study primarily to illuminate the works under discussion. My intention has been to explain in some measure, despite the distance in time and space that separates us from that age, the conceptual matrix from which a particular composition emerged, its liturgical, celebratory, and social uses, and its communal, ceremonial, and symbolic meanings for those who performed and heard it.

Although the book unfolds generally in a chronological sequence, there is considerable doubling back, most notably when it comes to the instrumental repertories. Moreover, mindful of the significant differences between local traditions at the time, I have often interrupted the chronology in order to organize the discussion around specific geographical regions and their distinctive intellectual and cultural traditions. In that connection the emphasis has been more on the development of musical institutions—ecclesiastical, courtly, and civic—than on the biographies of individual composers, and more on musical genres and their essential characteristics than on the personal compositional style of central figures such as Josquin, Palestrina, or Lassus. Such an approach seemed all the more justified now that excellent musical dictionaries, such as *The New Grove Dictionary of Music*, provide both life stories and stylistic profiles for all of the major masters of the age.

The secondary sources to which reference is made in the footnotes (and which are listed comprehensively in the bibliography) could have been multiplied in many instances by recourse to the musicological literature in European languages, especially French, German, and Italian. However, since the book is intended primarily for an English-speaking readership, I have preferred to cite first of all studies in that language whenever a choice was available.

I was guided in the selection of specific musical works for discussion by a number of factors, both personal and practical. In some instances I have simply taken pieces that I have learned to love whenever they seemed to serve well the didactic purposes for which they have been introduced. Others were chosen because they exemplify in a paradigmatic fashion a given genre—Mass, motet, or chanson, for example—or a particular subtype within a larger category—such as an antiphon motet or a combinative chanson. At the same time, since the examples are mostly relatively brief excerpts rather than complete pieces, I thought it prudent to consider as well the ready accessibility of the entire composition, not only in the collected and monumental editions found in specialized libraries but also in the various anthologies that are perhaps more widely available.

No project of this nature can be brought to completion without incurring a great many debts, both scholarly and personal. Whenever possible I have acknowledged my direct reliance upon the work of colleagues in the field by means of footnotes and bibliographical references. In some instances, however, I have undoubtedly assimilated ideas gleaned in a less formal way from papers heard, epistolary exchanges, or casual conversation, whose source is no longer easily identified. Some readers may therefore encounter on occasion a notion or viewpoint with a familiar ring of whose origins I may now be simply unaware. To them, and in fact to all those who have contributed in any way to the discovery of the facts and the formulation of the concepts that inform this study, I should like to express my deepest gratitude. By the same token I should like to absolve them of any errors that I have made and to take full responsibility for opinions that they may consider idiosyncratic, or even misguided.

Debts of a personal nature are perhaps even more difficult to define and to acknowledge, and in recognizing by name some of those to whom I owe the most, I should apologize in advance to anyone whom I have inadvertently missed. Two grants from the National Endowment for the Humanities, coupled with a sabbatical leave from Columbia University, provided the time to do much of the research required by this study and an opportunity to begin the writing as well. I should like to thank in this connection Professors Lawrence F. Bernstein, Herbert Kellman, and Lewis Lockwood, who kindly wrote in support of those grant applications. Professors Bernstein and Kellman also tried some of the material on their students at an early stage and shared with me their criticisms and suggestions. Professor Richard Taruskin, similarly, took the time to read portions of an early typescript and to comment upon them.

The staff of the Gabe M. Wiener Library of Music and Art at Columbia have been unfailingly helpful, in particular Elizabeth Davis and Nicholas Patterson, responding to every request quickly and with rare good humor. Cynthia Lemiesz, while a member of the departmental office staff, kindly used otherwise relaxed summer hours to key a number of chapters into the computer. William Atkinson provided invaluable assistance during the final stages of revision with bibliographical searches and the preparation of musical examples. I am especially grateful to Patrick T. Perkins, who provided indispensable counsel at a critical moment, and to Eric R. Perkins and Bruce P. Perkins for their advice and encouragement. Above all, I owe an incalculable debt to Marianne S. Contesse, who has advised me on innumerable historical and cultural issues and has been as well an unfailing source of inspiration and support.

I would also like to express my gratitude to the editorial and production staff at W. W. Norton for their extraordinary efforts over the past year. In the face of considerable obstacles—some of them of my own making—Ann Tappert sought, with unflagging energy, permission from widely scattered owners for the use of the images that enliven the pages of this text. David Severtson undertook the taxing chore of copyediting the original typescript, which he did with care and sensitivity. I am particularly indebted to Martha Graedel for responding cheerfully to my numerous requests, and for dealing efficiently with the problems that arose day-to-day while she was the assistant for music. Her promotion brought onto the scene in her stead Anne White, who, although new to both the job and the project, saw to the final details with good-natured efficacy. Lastly, I should like to acknowledge the contibution of Michael Ochs, who, as Norton's music editor, kept a vigilant eye on the preparation of the book for publication—a long and sometimes difficult process—doing his professional best every step of the way to make it as good as it could be.

Englewood, New Jersey
November 20, 1998

PART ONE

The Historical Perspective

CHAPTER 1

Music in the Historical
Renaissance

INTRODUCTION

Since this volume is intended as an introduction to the music of the Renaissance, readers will want to know how that evocative term is to be understood. Its inclusion in the title implies—as it does for many works dealing with the beginnings of the modern era, whether in music or some other field—a clearly distinguishable and generally recognized period of history. According to a well-established convention in the West, the Renaissance encompasses a period centered on the fifteenth and sixteenth centuries. This view owes much to the enduring influence of Jacob Burckhardt's brilliant study, *The Civilization of the Renaissance in Italy* (1860). More a static image of Italian culture frozen in time than a historical narrative, his book carefully distills the spirit of the age. Clearly differentiating the Renaissance from the Middle Ages, the author describes the people of that time as the "first-born among the sons of modern Europe."[1]

That historical view went virtually unchallenged for nearly fifty years, but now scholars question ever more frequently whether the Renaissance, as defined by Burckhardt, represents in fact a distinct historical period. Even those who believe that it does often disagree about its proper chronological limits and—even more strongly—about the events and conditions that mark most plainly its beginning and its end. These learned arguments should not surprise us. Every historical division can be viewed as somewhat arbitrary since continuity in human events and, even more, in cultural developments is usually more evident than are the springs and signs of incipient change. Conservative and innovative strands lie side by side in the patterns of history. The dissemination of established views stimulates, by its very nature, historical revision and the formulation of new interpretations of the evidence. Even

---

1. See Jacob Burckhardt, *The Civilization of the Renaissance in Italy*, 2 vols. (New York: Harper and Brothers, 1958), 1:143.

where a fundamental and far-reaching historical revolution is clearly discernible, its beginnings and its effect on the course of history will vary as it spreads to localities and circumstances that are farther and farther removed from its original context.

Similarly, the rhythm of change differs from one facet of human activity to another. A significant trend with general implications is not likely to make itself felt at the same moment or in exactly the same manner in political history as in economic or social history, or in literature and the arts. These variables are responsible for many of the scholarly disputes as to the precise span of time encompassed by the Renaissance, and they explain as well some of the resistance that has developed to the very notion of a historical "rebirth." Still, whatever the arguments raised against it, the idea of a renewal in human affairs—a *renovatio*, *restitutio*, or *rinascità*, to cite but a few of the terms by which it has been known—has the distinct advantage of having been born of the age to which it is traditionally applied. The way people of a given age think of themselves may be an illusion, but that illusion is already a significant historical reality. In the instance at hand, moreover, the vision of a cultural renaissance that first fired the imagination of those who stood on its threshold in the 1300s tended steadily and vigorously toward self-realization for more than two hundred years.

THE HISTORICAL CONCEPTION OF THE RENAISSANCE

The characterization of the fourteenth through the sixteenth centuries as a time of rebirth has been traced to the humanist scholars and writers of that period, the earliest of whom were Florentine.[2] These same authors, who played a major role in reviving a learning and culture modeled on Greek and Roman antiquity, also formulated an interpretation of history that reflected their own particular perspective and their professional interests. It is truly surprising that a point of view that was initially so local in character attained such widespread and enduring currency.

The "humanists," as they came to be called ever more commonly in the fifteenth century, were educated in the *studia humanitatis*, a curriculum that included grammar, rhetoric, poetry, history, and moral philosophy. They were usually lay members of the community, at least in Italy, even though humanistic studies were included ever more frequently in the training necessary for professions of all kinds, clerical and secular alike. They generally found employment in the chancelleries of princely courts and of urban communes, where they composed—as much as possible in a

2. The discussion that follows owes much to the informative and stimulating studies by Wallace K. Ferguson, *The Renaissance in Historical Thought* (Cambridge, Mass.: Riverside Press, 1948), especially chaps. 1–3, and by Erwin Panofsky, *Renaissance and Renascences in Western Art* (New York: Harper and Row, 1972), chaps. 1–2 and *passim*. Also useful is the article by Lewis Lockwood, "Renaissance," *The New Grove Dictionary of Music and Musicians*, 15:736–41; for a more recent review of the problem, see Jessie Ann Owens, "Music Historiography and the Definition of 'Renaissance,'" *Notes* 47 (1990): 305–30.

Latin of elevated style—letters, orations, and poems on behalf of their patrons or city governments. Consequently, they often took part in the commercial and political affairs of their day, but they also taught the disciplines in which they were expert at the local *studium* or university.[3]

Just such a one was Leonardo Bruni, an accomplished scholar who served the republic of his native Florence as chancellor.[4] It was he who first borrowed the term *humanitas* from Cicero and applied it to the new combination of disciplines, thereby helping to systematize an educational program that had no precedent in the schools of the Middle Ages.[5] When he died in 1444, he had been working for some years on a *History of the Florentine People* that is noteworthy for the historical vision upon which it is based. Gone are the assumptions of the medieval chronicler, who saw history as a working out of the divine will and equated the progress of civilization with the spread of Christianity. Gone, too, as a result, are the patterns of periodization that had been used earlier: six ages to correspond with the days of Creation or four monarchies in accordance with the biblical prophecies of Daniel (2:31–40).

Inspired instead by patriotic purpose and republican zeal for political liberty and civic virtue, Bruni saw the apogee of civilization in the Roman republic, the beginnings of its decline with the encroaching despotism of the emperors, and its nadir as an unfortunate consequence of the periodic barbarian invasions. The abyss into which the Western world had been plunged by those events contrasted sharply, in his eyes, with the flourishing vigor of the Italian communes in his own day, especially that of Florence itself. He interpreted their rise, their growth, and their struggle to maintain republican ideals as a recovery of what had been lost, a revival that had become possible only as the Carolingian Empire was gradually dismembered.

This view of history was a remarkable departure from the medieval tradition. Bruni's threefold division was not new, however. Neither was his assumption that civilization had reached in ancient Rome a high point that was followed first by decline and then renewal. These ideas had been current in Florence for nearly a century when Bruni wrote; it was his adaptation of them to Florentine history and his development of them in political terms that were radically new. Nor was it Bruni himself, but rather one of his contemporaries, who conveniently identified the beginnings of unmistakable decadence with the sack of Rome by the Goths. Flavio Biondo of Forlì, a learned cleric of the papal curia who was familiar with Bruni's work, took the year 412 in which the sack was thought to have occurred as the starting point for his *History by Decades from the Decline of the Roman Empire* (written between 1439 and 1453).[6] He thus provided an easily remembered historical landmark to divide the

---

3. The humanism of the fifteenth and sixteenth centuries has been carefully defined by Paul O. Kristeller in a series of essays; see his *Renaissance Thought* (New York: Harper and Row, 1961), especially 9ff., 102, and 110f., and *Renaissance Thought II* (New York: Harper and Row, 1965), chaps. 1–3.

4. See the essays edited by Paolo Viti in *Leonardo Bruni, Cancelliere della Repubblica di Firenze: Convegno di Studi*, Atti di Convegni, Istituto di Studi sul Rinascimento, vol. 18 (Florence: Olschki, 1990).

5. See Wallace K. Ferguson, *The Renaissance* (New York: Holt, Rinehart and Winston, 1940), 77–78; also Kristeller, *Renaissance Thought II*, 163–89.

6. The sack of Rome actually occurred in 410 A.D.

first two segments of the threefold system adopted by Bruni, one that would be retained by generations of historians to follow.

It was more difficult to fix the origins of political renewal, especially since Bruni's theory of history was contradicted by stark reality. His optimistic vision of a return to the liberties and civic virtues of republican Rome could not last long in what has been aptly called an "age of kings."[7] Even as Bruni wrote, Florence was being drawn under the yoke of the Medici—whose rule was to be institutionalized in the sixteenth century with the transformation of the republic into a duchy—and throughout western Europe the tendency was toward centralized governmental powers under a reigning despot. Only much later, and with an eye more to the development of Hellenistic studies than to the political events themselves, was the beginning of the Renaissance tied to the fall of Constantinople in 1453.

In fact, from its earliest inception, the idea of a Renaissance was defined primarily in cultural terms. Long before Bruni formulated his original interpretation of political events, Francesco Petrarch (1304–74) rejected the traditional Christian view

of history that had come to predominate during the Middle Ages (see Figure 1-1). Medieval chroniclers assumed a "steady progress from heathen darkness to the light that was Christ," which they saw as beginning with the Creation and continuing until their day. Petrarch's admiration for the civilization of ancient Rome gives him a much different perspective; he views the period following the conversion of the emperor Constantine to Christianity as one of decline into darkness when compared with the glorious age that had gone before, and he therefore hopes for a "revival under the influence of classical models."

Using the language of theology, he contrasts the cultural level of classical antiquity with that of his own

FIGURE 1-1.   Francesco Petrarch, as painted by Andrea del Castagno.

7. The term was coined by Denys Hay, who traced with a few telling strokes the political trends of the period in *The Italian Renaissance in Its Historical Background* (Cambridge: Cambridge University Press, 1961), 16ff.

times, vividly opposing the light of the past to present darkness, wakefulness to sleep, and sight to blindness. As he affirms hopefully in his most famous Latin poem, *Africa* (1338), "there is perhaps a better age in store; this slumber of forgetfulness will not last forever. After the darkness has been dispelled, our grandsons will be able to walk back into the pure radiance of the past."[8] Although Petrarch was both poet and scholar—a model for the humanists of subsequent generations—his concept of history embraces not only literature but also the visual arts, a reflection of whose ancient splendor he discovered in the ruins of Rome during his first visit there a year earlier.

THE CONCEPT OF REBIRTH SPREADS IN ITALY

It was Petrarch, then, who first posited a cultural rebirth as a significant stage in the development of the Western world. And even though that concept wholly contradicted the Christian traditions of his age, the idea of renewal was so inherently attractive that his revolutionary point of view spread from Italy over the whole of Europe and has survived in its essentials until the present day. His vision of history, particularly as it applied to literature and the visual arts, permeated the writings of Florentine humanists already during his own lifetime. Giovanni Boccaccio (1313–75), for example, asserts that Dante had recalled dead poetry to life, that Petrarch had purified it and spread its fame abroad, and that Giotto had brought back into the light the art of painting, "which had for many an age lain buried under the errors of certain folk" (see Figure 1-2).[9] His few such

FIGURE 1-2. Giovanni Boccaccio, as painted by Andrea del Castagno.

8. The quotations and much of the substance of this paragraph were taken from Panofsky, *Renaissance and Renascences in Western Art*, 10–11.

9. See Ferguson, *Renaissance in Historical Thought*, 19. Boccaccio's conception of a literary revival is succinctly stated in a letter to his friend Jacopo Pizzinghe; see James Ross and Mary McLaughlin, eds., *The Portable Renaissance Reader* (New York: Viking Press, 1953), 123–26.

statements are seminal, and no explicit mention is made of classical models, but the derivation of the fundamental idea is clear, as are its implications.

By the end of the fourteenth century this new concept of history had acquired considerable currency. It was elaborated in some detail by Filippo Villani in his *Book Concerning the Famous Citizens of the City of Florence* (1380s or later). For him the noteworthy are primarily the artistic and literary luminaries of the Tuscan capital. He begins with the biographies of poets, perhaps because letters stood so high in the humanist scheme of things. Surprisingly, however, the first of these is Claudian (d. 404?), the last important Latin poet of Roman antiquity, who lived much earlier than any of the other people in the book and was in no wise a Florentine. Because Villani accepts the Petrarchan interpretation of cultural history, he must have wanted a point of comparison in classical times by which the achievements of his own age could be judged.

From Claudian Villani leaps ten centuries to Dante Alighieri (see Figure 1-3) and in passing dismisses the entire intervening period as one of decay and decline, which left poetry "lying prostrate without honor or dignity." Echoing Boccaccio, Villani declares in Petrarch's hieratic terms that it was Dante who then restored it "as from an abyss of shadows into the light," by reconciling poetic fiction with moral and natural philosophy, that is by drawing the various fields of humanistic study into harmony with Christian literature. And Villani sees that accomplishment as opening the way to the subsequent contributions of Petrarch and Boccaccio, whose biographies follow.

When Villani comes to the visual arts, he asserts similarly that Greek and Latin painting had been extinct for hundreds of years before being recalled to life by Florentine masters toward the beginning of the fourteenth century. He credits Cimabue with initiating the process of renewal and praises the artist not for consciously imitating the ancients but for his skill in depicting his subjects in a natural and lifelike manner. Cimabue's achievement in that regard then opens the way for Giotto,

FIGURE 1-3. Dante Alighieri, as painted by Luca Signorelli.

"who not only can be compared with the illustrious painters of Antiquity," in Villani's words, "but surpassed them in skill and genius [and] restored painting to its ancient dignity and greatest fame" (see Figure 1-4).[10]

Unlike the renewal of poetry and literature, where specific classical models were consciously followed, the rebirth of the visual arts was aimed at recovering the natural realism attributed to ancient art, which, in contrast to the stylized Byzantine imagery cultivated during the intervening age, was being ever more skillfully achieved by the painters named. Some of the most celebrated masterpieces of classical antiquity were yet to be discovered—the Apollo of Belvedere or the Laocoon, for example—and the careful study of well-known works that would lead to direct stylistic imitation still lay ahead. But because the ancient world was so much admired, the "return to nature" and the "return to the Antique" came to be seen as but two aspects of the same process of renewal.[11]

FIGURE 1-4.   *Madonna Enthroned*, by Giotto (Florence, Uffizi).

In the first half of the fifteenth century, literature received the most extensive and systematic discussion, in part because it was the professional domain of the humanists who wrote of such matters, in part because both the poets of the rebirth and their classical models were by then generally recognized, at least in Florence. Both Bruni and Biondo, for example, devoted considerable attention to literary developments. Not surprisingly, they retained their perception of history—borrowed from earlier authors as the basis for their periodization of political events—all the more naturally in their interpretation of cultural change. In 1436 Leonardo Bruni penned an extensive biography of Dante and Petrarch that included a brief history of both Latin and Italian letters. He opens that account with Cicero, in whom he sees the epitome of Roman literary accomplishment. The subsequent decline in the cultivation of good Latin style he attributes, like the decay of the Roman polity, to the ills that accompanied the end of the republic in the fifth century: the loss of civic freedom and the

10. See Ferguson, *Renaissance in Historical Thought*, 20–21.
11. The coalescence of these two concepts in the course of the fifteenth and sixteenth centuries in Italy has been lucidly exposed by Panofsky, *Renaissance and Renascences in Western Art*, 29–35.

increased influence of the invading barbarians, the Goths and the Lombards.

Bruni saw the revival of good letters, like the political rebirth of Italy, as coming only with the rise of the Italian communes and the consequent recovery of republican liberties. He believed Dante had led the way back out of the darkness, but while he admired Dante's vernacular poetry, he found his Latin rough and coarse. And since the humanists of Bruni's generation strove to restore a Latin style that was both correct and eloquent by classical standards, it was not Dante but Petrarch whom he viewed as the first to possess "such grace and genius that he could recognize and recall to the light the ancient elegance of style, which had been lost and extinguished."[12] However, in Bruni's judgment, even Petrarch had not entirely recaptured the Ciceronian ideal, and it was left to the humanist scholars of his own day to continue in its pursuit.

Bruni betrays his passion for classical literary models in an enthusiastic commentary on the revival of Hellenistic studies in Italy. Emmanuel Chrysoloras was brought to Florence in 1396 to fill a chair in Greek that had been newly created at the university. Both the professorship and Bruni's glowing observations testify to the growing interest in Greek letters and culture that would characterize the fifteenth and sixteenth centuries. This fascination with classical Greece may have been prompted in good measure by tenacious pride in the achievements of ancient Rome. Since Cicero, who was so widely admired and emulated, held Greek literature to be the true fountainhead of a proper Latin style, those who took him as a paragon might naturally follow suit.[13] In any case, as Hellenistic studies spread, so did their influence in all the areas of intellectual and artistic activity that had been important to ancient Greece, especially literature and moral philosophy. As we shall see, music, too, was to be affected significantly by the retrieval of Hellenistic culture.

Flavio Biondo interpolated an account of the rebirth of classical letters into his *Italia Illustrata* (written between 1448 and 1458), a learned amalgam of contemporary geography and his own painstaking antiquarian research. Following the pattern adopted for his *History by Decades*, he links the erosion of good literary style to the decline of the Roman Empire, dating its beginnings from the early fifth century, as Bruni had done. However, unlike the majority of Italian humanists, whose models were predominantly pagan, Biondo numbers Ambrose, Jerome, and Augustine, the doctors of the early Christian church, among the last writers of the classical period to use Latin with some degree of skill and elegance. He also gives honorable mention to Gregory the Great, the Venerable Bede, and St. Bernard, even though he had to transgress his own limits of literary decay by as much as seven centuries in order to do so. It was undoubtedly Biondo's affiliation with the papal court that led him

12. As quoted by Ferguson, *Renaissance in Historical Thought*, 22. Bruni's view of history is succinctly expressed in the excerpt from his life of Petrarch published in Ross and McLaughlin, eds., *Portable Renaissance Reader*, 127–30.

13. See Ferguson, *Renaissance in Historical Thought*, 24. The account of the restoration of Greek to the curricula of fifteenth-century Italian schools given by John Addington Symonds in his *Renaissance in Italy* (New York: Henry Holt and Co., 1888), 108–13, still makes lively and informative reading.

to include churchmen among the worthy stylists of Latin. But by doing so he provides an early example—by an Italian author—of a Christian interpretation of history within a humanist framework. That approach would be much more typical of northern scholars of subsequent generations, most of whom were more concerned with sacred than with secular matters.

From St. Bernard Biondo skips directly to Petrarch, whom he saw as initiating the return to Ciceronian eloquence but as incapable of completing it. The final touches he credits to the scholars of the following generations, beginning with John of Ravenna, Petrarch's secretary and student, whose itinerant teaching awakened enthusiasm for Cicero and the Latin poets in numerous Italian centers. Like Bruni, Biondo attributes the restoration of Greek letters to Chrysoloras and to those who became his disciples. He also recounts in detail the search for neglected ancient classics, both Roman and Greek. Under the impetus of humanistic scholarship, libraries all over the Western world were scoured for unknown sources, and the classic authors were taught in the newly established secular schools such as those of Vittorino da Feltre and Guarino da Verona.[14]

In the course of the fifteenth and sixteenth centuries, Petrarch's threefold division of history as exemplified in the writings of Bruni and Biondo was disseminated ever more widely across the face of Europe, together with its underlying assumptions. Since these writers were concerned with regional or even local personalities and developments, it is remarkable that their view of history spread so widely and quickly. However, the basic formula was sufficiently flexible that it could be adapted to virtually any geographical area and applied to most any aspect of intellectual or cultural history. The Italians were, themselves, the first to discover and explore its elasticity. While Boccaccio claimed only a revival of Latin poetry and of painting, Bruni and Biondo added to these the recovery of the literature of Greek and Roman antiquity and of classical Latin style. In the course of the fifteenth century, other facets of humanistic study and interest were included one by one among those that had been recalled from darkness to light in the recent past. By 1492 Marsilio Ficino (1433–99), who had translated Plato's dialogues from the original Greek into Latin, was able to extend the notion of a renaissance to a much wider spectrum of intellectual and artistic activity with no real fear of contradiction. As he wrote to a friend, "this century, like a golden age, has restored to light the liberal arts, which were almost extinct: grammar, poetry, rhetoric, painting, sculpture, architecture, music, the ancient singing of songs to the Orphic lyre, and all of this in Florence."[15]

For all of these, and more, classical antiquity provided models from the distant past that shone all the more brightly across the intervening centuries because of the darkness and decay that were seen to have followed the barbarian invasions. The

14. See Ferguson, *Renaissance in Historical Thought*, 23, and Symonds, *Renaissance in Italy*, 98–101.
15. See Ficino's letter to Paul of Middelburg in Ross and McLaughlin, eds., *Portable Renaissance Reader*, 79. Note Ficino's rather unconventional definition of the "liberal arts"; see Kristeller, *Renaissance Thought II*, 174–89. The distinction between "music" and "ancient singing . . . to the Orphic lyre" is discussed below, pp. 404–15.

theological terminology used early on to describe the period of decline—abyss, ignorance, darkness, for example—reflects a contempt for all it had produced. Even the more neutral terms adopted somewhat later—Latin equivalents of "Middle Ages" such as *media aetas* or *medium aevum*—implied an uneventful intermission between epochs of more noteworthy achievement.[16] The new beginning was also identified by terms with religious connotations, Latin words such as *fons, origo, initium*. And, as we have seen, subsequent developments were usually regarded as steady improvement, culminating in the admirable attainments of the writer's own generation.[17]

THE IDEA OF A RENAISSANCE SPREADS TO NORTHERN EUROPE

The fact that Italian humanists, most notably in Florence, claimed a decisive role for their own cities and for native-born writers and artists in bringing about this renaissance did not deter writers in other localities from adopting their scheme of history. The idea that their age could be distinguished from the relatively recent past and compared to a glorious antiquity by the excellence of its intellectual and artistic endeavors appealed to the pride of historians everywhere, and those north of the Alps were quick to serve their own regional and professional interests by espousing it. Thus French historians, who accepted—along with Italian models for the writing of state history—the priority claimed by Italian authors for the revival of arts and letters, could attribute the advances made in France to scholars of the late fifteenth century and date the rebirth of arts and letters there from the reign of Francis I (1515–47). German authors, by contrast, generally took patriotic pride in the notion that the Roman *Imperium* had been transferred to the Teutonic peoples through Charlemagne and, as a result, in their own medieval traditions. Understandably, they resented being cast in the role of barbarians and were reluctant to accept Italian claims of cultural superiority.

Nevertheless, northern humanists, particularly in Germanic regions, came to be more and more preoccupied in the late fifteenth century with reforming the Christian church and its educational systems. One of the leading spirits of this movement was Erasmus (ca. 1466–1536; see Figure 1-5), whose interpretation of cultural history was widely accepted because of his extraordinary influence among the educated classes.[18] Following a line of reasoning that was already implicit in Biondo's writings, Erasmus

16. See Ferguson, *Renaissance in Historical Thought*, 73–77, concerning the terminology and its implications.

17. The concepts underlying this tripartite division of history, the terms used to designate both the historical process and its principal parts, and the manner in which these were adapted to the locality and the time of the writer have been succinctly summarized—with a special focus on the treatment of music within this scheme—by Leo Schrade, "Renaissance: The Historical Conception of an Epoch," in *Twentieth-Century Views of Music History*, ed. William Hays (New York: Charles Scribner's Sons, 1972), 114–25, and in Schrade's collected writings.

18. For a study of Erasmus, see Cornelis Augustijn, *Erasmus: His Life, Works, and Influence*, trans. J. C. Grayson (Toronto: University of Toronto Press, 1991).

adapts the concept of rebirth to the purposes of religious renewal. He argues that the high literary achievements of classical antiquity included the works of the early Church Fathers and that the decline in good letters attendant upon the barbarian destruction of the Roman Empire had corrupted good religion as well.

He believed, moreover, that restoring the ancient Greek and Latin literary texts to their original state, without the barbaric glosses and ignorant commentaries of medieval scholasticism, would in turn help return Christianity to its ancient purity. This conviction led Erasmus and his followers to search out the writings of the Church Fathers—just as Italian humanists were doing for the authors of pagan antiquity— and to edit them with critical methods that were being systematically formulated and rigorously applied for the first time.

FIGURE 1-5. Desiderius Erasmus, by Hans Holbein.

Once the impetus toward religious renewal began, it was not to be deterred until it culminated in both the Protestant Reformation and the Counter-Reformation mounted by reactionary elements within the Catholic church. Unfortunately, instead of seeking compromise and reconciliation, both sides adopted positions so extreme that reform could not be contained within the framework of the established church. The fabric of Western Christendom was consequently torn asunder for all time. The ensuing fragmentation of its administrative structures not only carried the gravest of theological implications but in many instances also brought social and political turmoil. These sometimes violent events were in a very real sense rooted in the burgeoning Renaissance of humane letters, which was both its source and, for many, its justification. Proponents of the Reformation then helped to spread the new historical viewpoint and to maintain its currency into modern times.[19]

THE NOTION OF FONS ET ORIGO EVOLVES

As we have seen, the flexibility inherent in defining the Renaissance historically allowed contemporary writers to shift its origins with respect to their own generation's perspectives, geographical location, and interests in Western culture. Indeed, some northern humanists gloss over the contributions made by Italians in the early

---

19. The reactions of northern humanists to the idea of a rebirth of arts and letters have been summarized by Ferguson, *Renaissance in Historical Thought*, 29–46.

fifteenth century by identifying Erasmus as "the first to raise up good letters at the time when they were being reborn."[20]

Similarly, the Italians revise their earlier views when their first models slip further into the past and appear increasingly deficient compared with more recent ones. As early as 1436 Leonardo Bruni was himself credited with having brought about the revival of Latin letters. That view persisted in the writings of Florentine historians and biographers throughout the fifteenth century. By 1490 Dante and Petrarch were simply dismissed by one Ciceronian purist as unworthy of contemporary standards of Latin style and eloquence.[21] Moreover, as humanist scholarship evolves, the organic metaphor becomes ever clearer. Developments are seen more and more in terms of rebirth, growth, maturity, and—inevitably—old age and decay.

Such an organic interpretation of the historical process is already clearly articulated in the work of Giorgio Vasari (1511–74).[22] Painter, architect, and historian, Vasari was educated in Florence in the humanist mold and had ample opportunity to assimilate the viewpoint that informed local history from Bruni on. His artistic activity put him in touch with many contemporary Italian masters and took him to the major centers of the peninsula, where he became acquainted with much of the artwork that could be seen in sixteenth-century Italy. Drawing upon both sides of his experience, Vasari wrote—in the Italian vernacular rather than the Latin preferred by earlier humanist scholars—*The Lives of the Most Excellent Architects, Painters, and Sculptors of Italy from Cimabue until the Present* (first published in 1551 and again in 1568 with revisions and additions).

His use of the biographical format undoubtedly reflects a well-established Florentine tradition. But by the time he wrote, he could have modeled his work directly on the distinguished authors of antiquity such as Plutarch and Suetonius, who were dear to the heart of the humanist. The period covered by Vasari's title clearly derives from the new tripartite periodization of history. Like other humanist writers of the age, he focuses on figures of the relatively recent past and follows the conventional chronological order for biographical history. But Vasari also attempts to group his artists according to their style (*maniera*). And, in the introduction to each of his book's three sections, he presents a coherent picture of the stylistic development of his times.

As expected, Vasari begins with a brief history of the classical arts. Even here he uses organic terms, tracing the progress of the visual arts from their origins to mature perfection and on into subsequent decline. The rapid downward swing, which he sees as well under way by the reign of Constantine, he attributes largely to the bar-

20. From the introduction to Erasmus's *Adagia* published in 1571 as quoted by Ferguson, *Renaissance in Historical Thought*, 32.

21. Paola Cortese in his *Dialogue of Learned Men*, dedicated to Lorenzo de' Medici, as summarized by Ferguson, *Renaissance in Historical Thought*, 24–26.

22. Concerning Vasari, see the studies by Leon G. Satowski, *Giorgio Vasari: Architect and Courtier* (Princeton: Princeton University Press, 1993), and Patricia Lee Rubin, *Giorgio Vasari: Art and History* (New Haven: Yale University Press, 1994).

barian invasions, on the one hand, and to Christian iconoclasm, on the other. Beyond an occasional example of noteworthy architecture, he finds little to praise from the early fourth century until the middle of the thirteenth. A rebirth (*rinascità*)—to use Vasari's very term—comes with a new generation of Tuscan artists who abandon the old style and begin to imitate the ancients. Sketching subsequent developments, Vasari compares them specifically to maturity and aging in the human body. He divides his history into three ages (*età*), groupings that are implicit in his metaphor and also used for classical mythology by poets, such as Ovid, whom the humanists favored.

Vasari values the first age for its new beginnings rather than for the works it brought forth, which, in his view, are not without imperfections. He therefore adjusts the historical view of earlier Florentine humanists to the perspective of his own generation. While still regarding Giovanni Cimabue and Giotto as the source of renewal, he reinterprets the significance of their achievements in light of contemporary standards.

During the second age—essentially the fifteenth century—the arts grow from childhood to early maturity. Painters and sculptors improve their ability to depict nature in the most lifelike manner possible. (Emulating the ancients is now done indirectly rather than according to specific models.) Vasari sees the best examples of competence in the brushwork of Masaccio (1401–28?) and the statuary of Donatello (ca. 1386–1466). In architecture Filippo Brunelleschi (1377–1446) rediscovered the numerical ratios the ancients used and verified them by accurately measuring the buildings of classical Rome. His careful study of those monuments, from both archaeological and artistic points of view, enabled him to restore the ancient orders in his own buildings. He thus prepares the way for more direct reliance on classical models in painting and sculpture as well. Although Vasari does not say so explicitly, Brunelleschi contributed significantly to the sense of order and proportion that was beginning to shape painting. He devised a systematic and mathematical technique of applying linear perspective to painting that enhanced both proportionality and realism.[23]

The third age—essentially the sixteenth century—begins with Leonardo da Vinci (1452–1519) and brings with it the manner that Vasari considered modern. This style is characterized by an increasing interest in the examples of sculpture and painting that had survived from antiquity, some of which had only recently come to light. In such works it was the formal perfection, the idealization of beauty, that Vasari admired. In his judgment it was by "improving upon nature"—depicting the ideal that was intended without the flaws of reality—that the artists of his generation had achieved full perfection. His enthusiasm for the excellence attained is such that he

23. Brunelleschi's role in developing the use of perspective and the integration of classical motifs, figures, and models into the visual arts of the fifteenth century, beginning with architecture and architectural settings depicted in paintings, have both been discussed in detail by Panofsky, *Renaissance and Renascences in Western Art*, 123–27 and 162–210.

can see little hope of future improvement. Indeed he observes, "I may safely say that art has done everything that is permitted to an imitator of nature, and that it has risen so high that its decline must now be feared rather than any further progress expected."

Clearly, Vasari recognizes the fullest implications of his organic interpretation of history: after youth and maturity come senescence, decline, and death. If he does not elaborate further, it is probably because he sees himself at the crest of the wave, as each successive generation would do from the fourteenth century until late in the sixteenth. The blush of youth had faded enough, however, to let the inevitable conclusion of such cycles be acknowledged. The specter of death, having been raised by an author so widely read, would cast its shadow over the pages of historians for the remainder of the age as a harbinger of transition and change.[24]

Vasari's adaptation of the humanist historical view to the fine arts has been exposed here at considerable length, in part because his interpretation is so typical of the age, in part because his influence has been so profound and enduring. Interestingly, his work offers striking parallels to a similar treatment of music by Pietro Gaetano, written only slightly later, in which many of the same elements are present (see pp. 50–53). Moreover, as suggested by comparisons made by Vasari's friend, Cosimo Bartoli, between sculpture, painting, and music, the organic metaphors he adopted in tracing the development of art became generally accepted as a way of accounting for stylistic change in the music of the fifteenth and sixteenth centuries, by musicians and nonmusicians alike. Let us see, then, how the idea of a renaissance came to be applied to historical views of music.

"RENAISSANCE" MUSIC: THE HUMANIST VIEW

Remarkably, the idea of the Renaissance with its division of history into three periods also became a frame of reference for writings about music during the fifteenth and sixteenth centuries, giving some measure of the vitality and adaptability of the concept. For at the time, the state of the musical arts in Italy was radically different from that of the literature and visual arts about which Bruni and Biondo had written. The fourteenth century saw a noteworthy, if brief, flowering of notated polyphonic music—most of it secular—in northern Italy, where Florentine musicians were in many ways central to its development. Francesco Landini (d. 1397), Andrea da Firenze (d. 1415), and Paolo Tenorista (fl. 1406), all natives of the Tuscan capital, figure prominently in the major sources of the period, representing fairly as a

---

24. Vasari's threefold division of the Renaissance, as he perceived it, has been summarized in some detail by both Ferguson, *Renaissance in Historical Thought*, 60–67 (including the direct quotation given above), and Panofsky, *Renaissance and Renascences in Western Art*, 30–35. Vasari's *Lives* is available in several English translations.

group the finest musical achievement of trecento Italy (see Figure 1-6). However, a steady stylistic encroachment from the north is already apparent in their works. The notational conventions that were characteristically Italian began to be modified or replaced by French usage (see Appendix, pp. 1022–27). At the same time, the peninsula's indigenous verse forms gave way to the sacred genres then being cultivated north of the Alps—motets and Mass settings—and even to the use of French poetry in the secular repertory.[25]

With the end in 1417 of the Great Schism, which had divided the Catholic church and much of Europe into opposing political camps, and the subsequent return of the papal curia to Italy came an influx of northern musicians into the penninsula that continued unabated until the late sixteenth century. Their arrival coincided with the waning of the written musical tradition indigenous to northern Italy and must have worked powerfully to speed it along. Following the example of the papacy, Italy's brilliant secular courts began to import northern musicians and to establish chapel choirs on the French model. During the second half of the century in particular such centers as Milan, Ferrara, Naples, Venice, and Florence vied with one another for the most skilled singers and composers from the cathedral schools and courtly establishments to the north. They competed as well for the repertory of French music, both sacred and secular, that these musicians carried with them. Although Italians were not entirely excluded from the musical scene in their homeland, they did figure ever more rarely as composers, and identifiably Italian works came to be largely replaced in the sources by those of French origin or inspiration (see pp. 399–402).

By 1436, when the cathedral in Florence had been crowned with Brunelleschi's

FIGURE 1-6.   Florence, Brunelleschi's Duomo, Santa Maria del Fiore.

25. See Richard H. Hoppin, *Medieval Music* (New York: Norton, 1978), chap. 18, especially pp. 454–69.

dome and was ready for dedication, the papal choir was already dominated by north-ern musicians. One of their number, Guillaume Du Fay, composed the ceremonial motet to mark the occasion.[26] This was because when Bruni began to write about rebirth in the visual arts, beginning in the fourteenth century and coinciding with the renewal in Latin letters, Florentine music had not produced a comparably vigorous offspring. The native polyphonic tradition was by then moribund and about to be supplanted by an adoptive French one, more or less fully formed. It is no surprise, then, that Bruni said nothing of music and that the earliest writers to consider its his-tory in light of the humanist viewpoint were not Italians. They were instead north-erners who had received their musical training in the French tradition. Having crossed the Alps to the south in search of lucrative appointments and ecclesiastical benefices of papal provision, they were there exposed to the learning of the Italian humanists.

One of the first whose writings reflect the converging influences of north and south was a Carthusian monk named Legrense who was known in Italy as Johannes Gallicus.[27] Born in Namur about 1415, Legrense went to Mantua sometime prior to 1446. There, as he tells us, he had occasion to profit from the teaching of one of the era's great schoolmasters, Vittorino da Feltre. In the following years he set himself to writing a series of three treatises on music, which he must have completed by 1464 at the latest. The very title of the first, *The Most Ancient and the New Manner of Singing* (*Ritus canendi vestustissimus et novus*), was surely inspired by the historical vision of his Italian contemporaries (see Figure 1-7).[28] The preface refers even more explicitly to the notion of renewal with respect to the glories of antiquity. Legrense claims that his desire is "not so much to introduce something new as to renew in the Church of God, under Pope Pius II [1458–64], bright and shining, the pure, brief, and easy practice of sounds and notes of the antique fathers."[29]

MUSICAL TRADITIONS OF CLASSICAL ANTIQUITY

This declaration points up the dilemma of the humanist scholar regarding music. There *were* no models from classical antiquity to provide either a basis for the claims

26. For details, see Gustave Reese, *Music in the Renaissance* (New York: Norton, 1959), 79, and, for a reinterpretation of the symbolic significance of Du Fay's composition, the study by Craig Wright, "Dufay's *Nuper rosarum flores*, King Solomon's Temple, and the Veneration of the Virgin," *Journal of the American Musicological Society* 47 (1994): 395–441.

27. Like many northerners who established themselves south of the Alps during the fifteenth and six-teenth centuries, Johannes Legrense came to be identified by a variety of names: Johannes Gallicus, Carthusensis, and Mantuanus in the south; Jean de Chartreaux and de Namur in the north. See Cecil Adkins, "Legrense," *The New Grove Dictionary of Music and Musicians*, 10:614–15.

28. For an edition of the treatise in English translation, see Legrense (Johannes Gallicus), *The Manner of Singing* (*Ritus canendi*), ed. Albert Seay (Colorado Springs: Critical Texts, USA, 1981).

29. The adaptation of the concept of the Renaissance to a musical context by Legrense was first recog-nized by Schrade, "Renaissance: The Historical Conception of an Epoch," 119–20. Legrense's three trea-tises were published as a continuous series in the original Latin by Charles E. H. de Coussemaker, *Scriptorum de musica medii aevi*, 4 vols. (Paris, 1864–67), 4:298–421. The statement quoted appears on the first leaf of the manuscript, given in facsimile as fig. 1-7.

of a rebirth or a standard of style to which composers of the time might compare their own. Curiously, nothing survived of the music that was actually heard in ancient Greece and Rome. The nature of the art—sound unfolding through time—is such that it could not easily have been otherwise. Architecture, sculpture, and even painting can be conserved for centuries under the proper conditions, and the written word can be transmitted virtually intact across the ages (even when imperfectly understood). Music, by contrast, owes its existence to a process of continual transformation in which each successive sonorous event necessarily obliterates the preceding one. It produces only a certain effect upon the hearer and leaves no visible physical trace. As Augustine observed, "what the intellect perceives . . . is always of the present and deemed immortal, while sound, since it is an impression upon the sense, flows by into the past and is imprinted upon the memory."[30]

FIGURE 1-7. Legrense (Johannes Gallicus), beginning of his *Ritus canendi vetustissimus et novus* (*The Manner of Singing, the Most Ancient and the New*). (British Library, MS Harl. 6525, f. 1.)

Musical repertories of classical antiquity were in fact fixed *only* in the memory, and their transmission consequently depended upon rote learning of an oral tradition. Notation was not entirely unknown at the time, but its use seems to have been an exception to the usual musical practice; an invention of theorists, it was designed primarily for didactic ends. Even so, the few surviving examples of music from the Hellenist tradition use notation primarily as a mnemonic aid. It is sufficient to recall a composition to the mind of one already familiar with it, or to convey its substance to one acquainted with the musical practice from which it comes, but it can hardly fix the details of performance for later generations. Furthermore, there is no reason to believe that any trace of the ancient oral traditions survived into the fifteenth century. In any case, it was not until late in the sixteenth that some fragments of Greek music were first discovered. Because humanist scholars were only then beginning to

---

30. Augustine, *De ordine*, II, xiv, as quoted by Oliver Strunk, ed., *Source Readings in Music History*, rev. ed., ed. Leo Treitler (New York: Norton, 1998), 149, n. 1.

search for literary and musical sources, Legrense's own conception of Greek music could only have come from his reading of theoretical treatises.

What had survived the Middle Ages was a tradition of writing about music in a technical or philosophical vein, or both, the origins of which reached back as far as Pythagoras in the sixth century B.C. The Greek sources themselves had not been preserved in their original language and transmitted intact to the fifteenth century, at least not in the Western world. Rather, they had come down in fragmentary form with the thinking of the Greek theorists finely filtered through the Latin *compendia* that were compiled by such early medieval encyclopedists as Cassiodorus (ca. 485–585) and Isidore of Seville (ca. 560–636). The one notable exception to this general pattern was a substantial work by Anicius Manlius Severinus Boethius (ca. 475–525). The author, who had occasion to master Greek and, presumably, to read extensively in it during a stay in Alexandria, wrote in Latin a comprehensive distillation of Hellenistic learning in the four mathematical disciplines: arithmetic, geometry, astronomy, and music. (These he termed the *quadrivium*, and they were so known all through the Middle Ages.)[31]

The branch of mathematics concerning music was known to the ancient Greeks as "harmonics," definable as the study of the numerical proportions demonstrably inherent in sonorous phenomena. These are fundamental to the structure of their scalar systems and were thought to underlie as well the relationship of the soul to the body and of the spheres of the firmament to one another and to the earth. *De institutione musica*, the treatise in which Boethius presents the traditional views on these matters, was drawn primarily from the works of the clearheaded Greek harmonist, Ptolemy of Alexandria (fl. 2d century A.D.). The inclusion of the term "music" in Boethius's title might suggest a concern for the practical side of the musical arts, including poetry and dance, but because he was working within his own definitions, he had little to say of such matters.[32] In fact, he follows Ptolemy rather closely and deals essentially with harmonics, setting out the mathematical principles and rational procedures governing the combination of tones to form intervals, scales, and systems. A lengthy segment is also given over to abstract philosophical speculation on the numerical relationships themselves, an approach that takes the reader much closer to arithmetic than to any of the artistic activities associated with the Muses (Urania aside).

---

31. Of the four treatises by Boethius, only those on arithmetic and music are complete; the one on astronomy has been lost and that on geometry is fragmentary and of doubtful authenticity. Concerning the studies of the *quadrivium* (and of the preliminary *trivium*), see Hoppin, *Medieval Music*, 20–21, and the relevant essays in David L. Wagner, ed., *The Seven Liberal Arts* (Bloomington: Indiana University Press, 1983).

32. It was Boethius who formulated the threefold division used in the definition of *musica* all through the Middle Ages: *musica mundana*, relating to the harmonies of the spheres; *musica humana*, relating to harmonies of the soul; and *musica instrumentalis*, relating to the harmonies arising from sounding bodies. (See his discussion of these three categories in the excerpt from the *De institutione musica* translated by Strunk, ed., *Source Readings in Music History*, rev. ed., 140f.) He makes a further distinction in the last of these between the practical and the rational, and his interest is centered on the operations of reason (ibid., 85f.; also Hoppin, *Medieval Music*, 20–21).

Underlying this emphasis on mathematical proportions are the Pythagorean notions that numbers constitute the true nature of things and that all relationships can be expressed in numerical terms. However mystical such an idea may appear from our present vantage point, it was a central element in the cosmology of Greek antiquity, most notably in that of Plato. In the *Timaeus*, for example, he describes the creation of the universe, in which the separate spheres were formed and ordered according to the ratios embodied in the basic musical scale.[33] To the extent that Plato was known and accepted during the Middle Ages, then, the concept found a place in Christian philosophy as well. With the revival of Platonic teachings in the fifteenth century, starting—once again in Florence—with Marsilio Ficino, the importance of numerical proportions in determining the "harmonies" of both the ideal and the sensible worlds was reaffirmed. The consequences of that development were particularly significant for music and architecture, as we shall see, and they made themselves felt in the other arts as well.

That Boethius's treatise on music had such solid underpinnings in philosophy may help to explain its ever wider dissemination from the sixth century on. The persistent if undocumented tradition that he died a Christian martyr may also have contributed to the acceptance of his writings. In any case, no other book on music was so frequently copied, so much read, or so copiously cited by medieval theorists as was that of Boethius. It was not always clearly understood by those who used it, but even the misunderstandings to which it gave rise often proved fruitful. All through the Middle Ages it served as the standard teaching manual in the schools and universities so that by the fifteenth century it had acquired enormous authority as a didactic text. It represented, in and of itself, a tradition many centuries old and then as yet unchallenged.

For humanist scholars such as Vittorino and Legrense, Boethius had the added appeal of transmitting the musical learning of antiquity more directly and comprehensively than any other author known at the time. Vittorino apparently regarded his work as the one indispensable text for those concerned with music. And Legrense, who had studied Boethius under Vittorino's tutelage, used the *De institutione musica* as his principal and only reliable source. When he did cite a more recent theorist, Marchetto da Padova—who had written during the second and third decades of the fourteenth century and was well known and respected in northern Italy—it was generally only to hold him up for blame. In theoretical matters the "most ancient" was supplied by Boethius and the "new" by Legrense himself. All that lay in between was held to be of little worth.

MEDIEVAL TRADITIONS: CHANT AND POLYPHONY

Despite the lack of musical repertory handed down from ancient Greece or Rome, then, something tangible remained of the theoretical tradition, thanks to Boethius.

---

33. Plato's account of those events has been summarized in Beekman Cannon, Alvin Johnson, and William Waite, *The Art of Music* (New York: Thomas Y. Crowell, 1960), 10–12.

As an educated cleric, Legrense was also heir to a vast body of music that was of venerable origins: the liturgical plainchant of the Roman church. Its sources were nonclassical, of course, as Legrense recognized. The melodies had been shaped by a Judeo-Christian tradition that had very little to do with ancient Greek or Roman culture. Many of them were in fact codified and fixed by notation only during the Middle Ages—from the ninth to the eleventh centuries—when literature and the other arts were judged by the early humanists to have been in decline. Nevertheless, the chant continued to be viewed in the fifteenth century as a divinely inspired adjunct to worship; the legend of St. Gregory was not easily dispelled.[34] Moreover, the considerable uniformity and virtual universality of the religious experience in Christian Europe at the time made the music of the liturgy familiar to all. For the learned, in particular, it bore profound meanings and pregnant associations.

The chant could thus be considered an acceptable substitute for a repertory of classical pagan origins that had not survived, representing the music of ancient times. This was especially true for northerners such as Legrense who were firmly attached to the musical traditions of the Middle Ages. Ironically, their social and intellectual orientation, even for nonclerics, was determined to a greater degree by the church than was that of the urban laity of Italy. Not surprisingly, then, when Legrense turns in the initial chapter of his treatise to the rhetorical question, "Who was the first man to sing?" the brief account of music's genesis offered in reply is drawn from the Bible (casting Adam in the leading role) and supplemented by Josephus's *Antiquities of the Jews* rather than from classical literature. In this regard Legrense's approach is more typical of the northern humanist than of his Italian models. But, as we have seen, Biondo—and after him others, including Vittorino himself—was perfectly willing to receive early Christian as well as pagan authors into the literary pantheon. In any case the weight of liturgical usage was such, and the didactic authority of Boethius so pervasive, that Legrense's viewpoint came to be independently adopted for works on music by writers all over Europe.

Still, the recognition of liturgical chant as the only surviving musical tradition that could be traced to classical antiquity did not entirely resolve the dilemma for the writer attempting to apply the historical idea of a cultural rebirth to music. There was no real difficulty in assimilating the chant to other artistic achievements of ancient times, in much the same way as the writings of the Church Fathers had been included with those of classical Latinity. However, by the fifteenth century liturgical plainchant was becoming a closed repertory. Traditional melodies had become largely fixed in the course of the Middle Ages, and the conservative force of ecclesiastical regulation discouraged the composition of new ones except in very exceptional cir-

---

34. Concerning the medieval tradition that Pope Gregory I (590–604) composed a substantial number of the liturgical melodies used in the Roman rite with the Holy Ghost perched as a dove on his shoulder, see Hoppin, *Medieval Music*, 42–44.

cumstances.[35] The creative impulse was directed instead toward mensural polyphony—the harmonious combination of two or more melodic lines whose independent rhythms were coordinated by the systematic use of regular metrical patterns. For such music there was no demonstrable antecedent in the ancient world, either in classical Greece or in the early Christian church. For both ancient musics the compositional style was monophonic—as we now know—consisting essentially of a single melodic line; and their rhythmic organization, as far as we are able to tell, followed rather different principles.

Moreover, mensural polyphony, like the shaping and codification of the plainchant repertory for liturgical use, was a medieval creation. It was, moreover, one of the most ingenious and fruitful of that age. Its cultivation brought into existence compositional styles of such a distinctive nature that the musical culture of the Western world has been sharply differentiated from that of all other parts of the globe ever since. Because the polyphony of the fourteenth and fifteenth centuries differed no less radically both from the chant, which was well known at the time, and from the musical practice of ancient times, which was not, humanist authors had no easy task in drawing it into the tripartite scheme culminating in a renaissance "inspired by classical models."

THE IDEA OF REBIRTH AND MUSIC

In the fifteenth century the treatment accorded music was not unlike that given to painting. The very novelty of the compositional style then coming into use was taken as a general indication of the cultural rebirth believed to be under way. Musicians, like painters, seem to have been aware that the technical procedures being developed were both relatively recent and decidedly innovative—especially where polyphony was concerned—and to take pride in that fact. In the words of Ramos de Pareia, a theorist writing in Bologna in the 1470s, "If those highly esteemed musicians [of antiquity] whom we mentioned could be recalled to life, they would deny that the music of our time is the same as they had invented."[36]

Further, painting had sculpture and architecture as its companions in the process of stylistic renewal. These allied arts were even more deeply indebted to ancient models, both physical (surviving statues and buildings) and theoretical (the architectural theory such as Vitruvius transmitted). Similarly, musical practice responded to the theoretical tradition that had come down from ancient Greece. In the same man-

35. The only verifiable instance known to me of plainchant composition during the fifteenth century is Guillaume Du Fay's compilation of the melodies—many of them of his own creation—for the *Recollectio festorum Beatae Mariae Virginis* for the Cambrai Cathedral; see Barbara Haggh, "The Celebration of the *Recollectio festorum Beatae Mariae Virginis, 1457–1987*," in *Atti del XIV Congresso della Società Internazionale di Musicología (Bologna, 1987)*, ed. Angelo Pampilio, 3 vols. (Turin: Edizioni di Torino, 1990), 3:559–71.
36. Ramos de Pareia, *Musica practica*, ed. Johannes Wolf (Leipzig: Breitkopf und Härtel, 1901), "Prologus," p. 3, as translated by Schrade, "Renaissance: The Historical Conception of an Epoch," 121.

ner that statuary and construction drew their sister art gradually closer to classical models and principles, so did music theory exert a subtle but unremitting pressure on composition to bring it into conformity with the music of the past as it was understood at the time. In either case there was a considerable lag between the point at which "classicizing" tendencies first affected that branch of the arts most open to them and the moment at which they finally made themselves felt at the end of the chain.

It has been said, concerning painting, that, "With all the reservations appropriate to general statements of this kind . . . prior to the middle of the 1400s, classical motifs entered Italian painting chiefly through the intermediary of either sculpture or architecture or both."[37] One might also say, by analogy, that until very late in the fifteenth century the influence of classical thought on the music of the period is clearly traceable only in works of a theoretical nature. Moreover, when it did begin to affect musical practice more or less directly, it was primarily through the theorists that discernible change came about. As the basic Greek texts on harmonics were located, translated, and studied, factual discovery and critical reflection ensued. In that process, ways were found of relating the mensural polyphony that constituted the predominant style of the fifteenth and sixteenth centuries to some aspect of classical Greece's musical culture, now in one way, now in another.[38]

We shall later examine a number of connections that were made in this regard, together with the resulting impact on the development of musical style. Returning to Legrense, however, it is clear he had not yet raised the problem of associating current musical styles with models or pertinent concepts from antiquity. As we have seen, the music with which he chooses to deal is the liturgical chant of the Christian church, which he proposes to restore to its ancient glory, and the theoretical framework in which he places it is derived mainly from Boethius. He does not completely ignore the existence of polyphony. A sizable section of his treatise is devoted to counterpoint, but it mainly discusses consonant and dissonant intervals, defined in Boethian mathematical terms, as used between simultaneously sounding pitches. Neither the intricacies of mensuration nor the practicalities of contrapuntal writing are explored sufficiently to make the treatise truly useful to someone wishing to learn the rudiments of polyphonic composition. Symptomatic is the author's assertion, at the conclusion of a detailed discussion of the modes, that secular pieces need not be governed by the rules he has given—an opinion not generally shared by either the theorists or the composers of the next generation. And his essentially philosophical

37. Panofsky, *Renaissance and Renascences in Western Art*, 168, discusses extensively the degree to which classicizing trends were evident in literature and the visual arts from the fourteenth through the sixteenth centuries; see, especially, pp. 18ff. and his chap. 4, pp. 162ff.

38. The extent to which the writings of Greek and Roman antiquity influenced both theorists and musicians of the Renaissance has been explored in detail by Claude V. Palisca, "The Impact of the Revival of Learning on Music Theory," *Report of the Twelfth Congress of the International Musicological Society, Berkeley, 1977* (Kassel: Barenreiter Verlag, 1981), 870–78, and, more recently and comprehensively, *Humanism in Italian Renaissance Musical Thought* (New Haven: Yale University Press, 1985).

orientation becomes clearly evident in the treatise's final section, where he turns to numerical speculation in the purest Boethian vein.

TINCTORIS AND THE ASSIMILATION OF HUMANIST VIEWS

Greater prominence goes to practical matters in the writings of Johannes Tinctoris (ca. 1435–1511), apparently one of the most widely read and certainly the most justly renowned theorist of the fifteenth century (see Figure 1-8). Of the twelve known treatises attributed to him, nine deal in an orderly and systematic fashion with the technical knowledge needed to become first a competent performer and then a skillful composer. His emphasis is plainly on polyphony rather than liturgical plainsong. This is evident not only from the detailed treatment he affords mensuration (comprising six short treatises in all) and counterpoint (forming the longest of the nine) but also from his approach to certain topics traditionally related to the chant. These include the Guidonian hexachord system and, more particularly, the modes, where the author's overriding concern is obviously the fruitful application of the principles involved to the problems of polyphonic composition.

Tinctoris most likely acquired his own solid musical instruction in the north of Europe, probably in one of the cathedral schools in or near his native Brabant. This would explain the composers he takes as his models—Du Fay, Busnoys, Okeghem, and their likes—all of whom were trained in northern regions and spent at least part of their career there. In addition, the competencies he claims for himself in his writings presumably reflect the years spent in study at a university, perhaps in Orleans, where he is known to have been matriculated in the early 1460s. Before he reached Naples in the early 1470s, he had studied canon and civil law, the

FIGURE 1-8.   Portrait of Johannes Tinctoris: anonymous miniature (Valencia, Universidad, Biblioteca General y Històrica, MS 835 [olim 844], f. 2ʳ).

"arts" (probably those of the *trivium*), and mathematics (meaning, presumably, the *quadrivium*, which included music as harmonics).[39] He was, in short, already exceptionally learned for a man of his day when he entered the service of the Aragonese court as a tutor in music to the royal household and, subsequently, as a singer in the royal chapel.

Once there, Tinctoris must have had access to the rich library that was being accumulated during the reign of Alfonso the Magnanimous. He also had contact with the group of humanists that had gathered initially around that king and continued to flourish under the long rule of his son Ferrante (1458–94). The leading figure at court was undoubtedly Giovanni Pontano (1426–1503), who, in accordance with the pattern typical of the age, distinguished himself in the *studia humanitatis*—scholarship, poetry, history, and moral philosophy—while engaged with the duties of statesmanship. In 1487, as chancellor of the royal court, he signed on behalf of his sovereign a letter instructing Tinctoris to go to France and the Low Countries to recruit singers for the Neapolitan chapel.[40] Although that document is the only direct evidence of contact between the two men, the enthusiasm they shared for the works of classical Latin authors must have prompted frequent association over the twenty years or so that both were in Naples.

A more revealing glimpse of Tinctoris's involvement with the humanist circles nurtured by the patronage of the Neapolitan court is provided by a letter that he addressed to one of the most accomplished calligraphers of his day, Giovanni Marco "Cinico." The latter's graceful, flowing script in the new humanist style is seen repeatedly in the sumptuous manuscripts of the Latin classics compiled for the king's library. Tinctoris's epistle, which is clearly modeled on Cicero in both form and style, is concerned with the moral philosophy of the Cynics, from whom Cinico derived his pseudonym and his personal code of conduct. Our theorist dwells at length on a notion central to that system of thought: that wealth, glory, power, and the pleasures dependent upon them are transitory and vain. He sustains his argument with citations and examples drawn from the works of writers such as Varro, Sallust, Juvenal, Horace, Ovid, and Virgil.[41]

Tinctoris also cited frequently and knowingly, in his treatises on music, these same classical authors—especially Ovid and Virgil—together with others such as Cicero himself, Quintilian, and even Plato and Aristotle. Since he wrote the majority of

39. On Tinctoris see especially Ronald Woodley, "Johannes Tinctoris: A Review of the Documentary Biographical Evidence," *Journal of the American Musicological Society* 34 (1981): 217–48, and "Tinctoris's Translations of the Golden Fleece Statutes: A Text and a (Possible) Context," *Early Music History* 8 (1988): 173–244. Concerning the *trivium*, the *quadrivium*, their place in the traditional education of the Middle Ages, and their relationship to music, see Hoppin, *Medieval Music*, 20–21.

40. See Reese, *Music in the Renaissance*, 139, and the references to the published letter in n. 200.

41. The letter was first published in Latin by Tammaro de Marinis, *La Biblioteca Napoletana dei Re d'Aragona*, 4 vols. (Milan: Ulrico Hoepli, 1947–52), 1:80–81, which is still a valuable source of information concerning Cinico (see 1:42–46 and *passim*). For a recent edition, with English translation and a careful commentary, see Woodley, "Tinctoris's Italian Translation of the Golden Fleece Statutes," 194–202 and 236–44.

these works within a decade after settling in Naples, it is not possible to tell if he had made an extensive study of the Latin literature of antiquity prior to his arrival there. His learned allusions, though, obviously reflect first of all the intellectual interests and fashions of the royal Neapolitan court. Whether or not he acquired his classical learning primarily in French or in Italian territory remains to be seen. More importantly, however, his theoretical treatises show that when he wrote them, he had assimilated not only the major Latin works of humanist preference but also the characteristic view of history that had been formulated in Florence early in the century.

Already in the *Proportionale musices*, which he may have completed as early as 1473–74, these elements find clear and succinct expression. Tinctoris uses the dedication to his royal patron, Ferrante, to briefly outline the history of music from its origins until his own day. Giving precedence to the biblical account of musical genesis, as behooves a humanist of the northern tradition, he nonetheless puts greater emphasis on what he knows about the music of the ancient Greeks. He cites a number of names—some of them legendary (such as Amphion and Orpheus), others historical (such as Pythagoras, Plato, and Aristotle)—although he knew virtually nothing about the compositional procedures or the modes of performance to which those ancient authors might have been accustomed. But in Plato he had read of the importance ascribed to music in the Hellenistic educational system, and from Cicero, Boethius, and others he learned that music was believed to possess miraculous power to move not only human emotions but also beasts and inanimate objects.

During the fifteenth and sixteenth centuries the oft-repeated reports of marvels wrought anciently by skillful performers through an artful application of music's affective powers proved to be an endless source of fascination to humanists and musicians alike. To those who gave them even limited credence, as did Tinctoris, they provided—like the Hellenistic tradition of music theory—a means of comparing the music of their times with that of classical Greece, however little was known of the latter in practical terms. As a result, the aesthetic ideal of a music capable of powerfully affecting the listener, emotionally and even ethically—the ideal embodied in Pythagorean cosmology and Platonic philosophy and vividly illustrated in the tales that had been handed down—became a second source of "classical influence" in the stylistic development of the music of the period. These legends worked in a variety of ways to shape different aspects of the compositional process. Their influence persisted, moreover, growing ever more significant as time passed. Eventually such tales helped to bring about the radical shift in musical concepts and practical procedures that marked the end of the age we know as the Renaissance and inaugurated a new phase in the history of Western music.

For Tinctoris, of course, much of that was far in the future. After only passing mention of music's power to stir the emotions, he adds to the traditions of ancient Greece the somewhat later ones of Christian antiquity. This constitutes what appears to be for him the first great age in the history of musical art. In this context he cites Augustine and Boethius, who were among those instrumental in the transmission of classical learning to the Middle Ages, and Gregory and Ambrose, who were linked to the formation of liturgical plainchant. Lumped with them without comment are two distinctly medieval authors: Guido of Arezzo, who achieved lasting fame with his invention of the solmization system; and Jehan des Murs, the fourteenth-century French theorist who helped lay the groundwork for the system of mensural notation that was such an integral part of the polyphonic style in Tinctoris's time.[42] Tinctoris says nothing about the music of the relatively recent past. To the contrary, he asserts in the dedication to his treatise on counterpoint—also addressed to Ferrante and dated October 11, 1477—that music written more than forty years earlier is not worth hearing. He turns instead to the music of his own time, the possibilities of which he finds "so marvelously increased" that it appears to him as a "new art." The concept underlying his preference is clearly that of an artistic rebirth, adapted here to music. He asserts the renewal to be factual not in relation to specific models from antiquity but by analogy to the general cultural awakening that humanist historians were assuming as self-evident.

Following a well-established pattern, Tinctoris identifies for his reader the "fount and origin" of the innovations he so much admires. In so doing he gives a most unusual twist to the familiar interpretation of history upon which his brief survey is based. Finding no direct models for polyphony, either in the cultural legacy of classical antiquity or in the liturgical music of the church, he instead invokes stylistic and esthetic criteria. Significantly, this was precisely what had happened earlier with respect to painting when the close resemblance to nature achieved by Giotto and others was taken as an indication of artistic rebirth. Although such natural realism had meaning only for the visual arts at the time, Tinctoris does single out an aspect of style that was considered to be dependent upon physical reality.

For him sweetness of sound (*suavitas*) is the most notable feature to distinguish the music of his contemporaries from that of previous generations. Those pleasant sonorities derived, to his way of thinking, from the consonances arising in music, as in all of nature, from the harmonious numerical proportions that were believed to regulate the entire universe. It was not in his use of critical criteria, then, that Tinctoris departed so strikingly from the historical model provided by earlier writers but rather in his identification of the source of renewal. He credits the changes in compositional procedure that had brought about the newfound euphony not to anyone even vaguely associated with a classical tradition in the arts but to the English, specifically to John Dunstable, a composer of the preceding generation.

Somewhat less surprisingly, perhaps, but no less anomalously, he also sees his own compatriots as the first to recognize the increased beauty inherent in the "new" style and to cultivate it with even greater skill. In this manner he cheerfully subverted to

42. Concerning Ambrose and Gregory and their somewhat equivocal role in the creation of a musical repertory for the Christian church, see Hoppin, *Medieval Music*, 35–36 and 42–44; regarding Guido and des Murs, see pp. 60 and 353–54. (For a discussion of solmization and mensuration, see the Appendix.)

his own ends—as was done earlier for painting—the notion of emulating "classical" models that had originally been linked with the idea
of rebirth for literature and architecture. That
he did so consciously is revealed in his formulation of the concept: "As Virgil took Homer
for his model in that divine work the Aeneid,"
he declared, "so I, by Hercules, have used these
composers as models for my modest works,
and, especially in the arrangement of the concords, I have plainly imitated their admirable
style of composing."[43]

Although a theorist, Tinctoris contributed
nothing significant to the revival of Greek harmonics through a study of original sources,
perhaps because his approach to the topic was
practical rather than humanistic. In the dedication to his book on counterpoint he does name
a number of authors whose works are now recognized as among the most important still

FIGURE 1-9. Portrait of Franchinus
Gaffurius: anonymous artist (Lodì,
Civico Museo).

extant: Nicomachos, Aristoxenos, Philolaos, Archytas, and Ptolemy, for example.[44]
He had most likely read none of them, however. Since these authors had yet to be
translated into Latin, their study would have required an understanding of Greek,
which he did not have. He was probably familiar with them only through his study
of Latin authors, Boethius first of all, or Latin translations of such authors as Plato
and Aristotle, whose works had begun to circulate in that more accessible form. The
actual process of "reviving" theoretical thought for music on the basis of the original Hellenistic tradition could not begin without translations of the most important
Greek works into Latin, the common language of scholarship.

This process was apparently initiated by one of Tinctoris's younger contemporaries, Franchinus Gaffurius (1451–1522; see Figure 1-9). Interestingly, Gaffurius
was one of the first important theorists of the period to be of Italian origin. He may
have become acquainted with Tinctoris during the nearly two years he spent in
Naples, beginning in 1478, while Tinctoris was serving at the court of Ferrante of
Aragon. At the time, Gaffurius was no less dependent upon Boethius than was
Tinctoris for his knowledge of ancient Greek music theory, as is evident from the one
work he published during his stay. By the turn of the century, however, as he himself tells us, he possessed translations, made at his request, of a number of major trea-

---

43. The quotations from the two dedications cited have been taken from the English translation by
Strunk, ed., *Source Readings in Music History*, rev. ed., 191–93.
44. A brief summary of the primary sources for our knowledge of Greek harmonics is given by Gustave
Reese, *Music in the Middle Ages* (New York: Norton, 1940), 17–19.

tises on harmonics, including those by Aristides Quintilianus and Ptolemy.[45] From then on interest in the writings of Hellenistic authors on music increased unabated until the end of the sixteenth century, and well beyond.

As these works became more readily accessible in translation, the humanistically trained theorists began to assimilate the substance of Greek harmonic theory more fully than had been possible on the basis of Boethius alone. Naturally, they then attempted ever more conscientiously to integrate Greek concepts into their own systems of musical thought and to reconcile more completely the classical tradition with that of Western Christianity. As a result, for a century and more after Gaffurius the history of our music theory—like that of the visual arts—is concerned primarily with the manner in which the integration was tried and the extent to which it succeeded. Because of his seminal role in retrieving the ancient texts, Gaffurius himself was credited by his admirers with leading music (theory?) out of darkness and restoring it to its ancient excellence.[46]

Although Tinctoris brought little substance to these later developments, he was one of the first to make a significant historical contribution of a different kind; from the literature he knew he collected passages that refer in some manner to the music and the music making of classical antiquity. A fair number of them were incorporated into his incomplete treatise on *The Invention and Practice of Music*, probably the last that he wrote.[47] In the absence of more extensive sources it was short excerpts of this kind, in both prose and verse, that provided what little information there was concerning the musical practice of ancient Greece and Rome. Since that time, moreover, even with the development of modern historiography, fragments of this sort have continued to provide an indispensable fund of information upon which to build.

It is unfortunate, then, that the greater part of Tinctoris's late work has been lost; of the five books into which the complete treatise was divided there remain only a few chapters from the second, third, and fourth. Tinctoris had these printed shortly before 1487 for his friend Johannes Stokem, who was apparently in the service of Ferrante's daughter Beatrice at the Hungarian court at the time. Judging from the

---

45. This disclosure is found in Gaffurius's *De harmonia musicorum instrumentorum opus*, which was printed in 1518 but written around 1500; see Reese, *Music in the Renaissance*, 178–80. The author also had in his library—which was sufficiently rich to attract a user such as Leonardo da Vinci—at least some portion of the Latin translation of Plato prepared by Marsilio Ficino; see the discussion of "Gaffurio as a Humanist" by Palisca, *Humanism in Italian Renaissance Musical Thought*, 191–225, and Walter K. Kreyszig, "Franchino Gaffurio als Vermittler der Musiklehre des Altertums und des Mittelalters: Zur Identifizierung griechischer und lateinischer Quellen in der *Theorica Musice* (1492)," *Acta musicologica* 65 (1993): 134–50.
46. Several statements to this general effect are cited by Schrade, "Renaissance: The Historical Conception of an Epoch," 122.
47. The Latin text has been published with a useful introduction in German by Karl Weinmann, *Johannes Tinctoris und sein unbekannter Traktat "De inventione et usu musicae"* (Tutzing: Schneider, 1961); see also Ronald Woodley, "The Printing and Scope of Tinctoris' Fragmentary Treatise *De inventione et usu musicae*," *Early Music History* 5 (1985): 239–68.

title, the first book very likely included a synoptic history of music more comprehensive and more systematic in nature than the brief excerpts included in his two dedications to King Ferrante. If such an account did exist, however, it is clear from the surviving segments of the published treatise that it did not differ materially from Tinctoris's other writings in its outline and its interpretation of history.

If his view of such matters has been examined in greater detail than the slender evidence of his treatises would seem to warrant, it is precisely because his approach was not only typical of his generation but also clearly indicative of what was to follow. By the end of the fifteenth century the basic historical concepts that he assimilated from his humanistic milieu had become rather common coin. They can be traced in one form or another in the works of virtually every author on music from Tinctoris's time until well after the period with which we shall be concerned, and although the details vary considerably, the pattern is always the same.

THE EVOLVING CONCEPT OF A MUSICAL RENAISSANCE

The first flowering of musical culture is associated by analogy to literature and the other arts with classical Greece. This connection is justified both by the enduring tradition of theoretical harmonics and by the many indications in Hellenistic literature of the important role music played in Greek life and culture. By contrast, little is said of musical practice in ancient Rome, evidently because little was known. The Roman tradition is represented, nonetheless: by Boethius, on the one hand, for musical theory and, on the other, by the early Church Fathers. The latter not only helped to transmit classical learning concerning music but also, and perhaps more importantly, contributed to the formation of the Christian liturgy, which incorporated the only substantial repertory of music from antiquity known to the fifteenth century.

The period following the invasion of the Italian peninsula by the barbarian hordes from the north, which marked the beginning of what was already then becoming known as the Middle Ages, is seen as a time of decline into darkness for music as it is for poetry and the visual arts. But the return to light, the beginnings of which were commonly identified for the latter disciplines as early as the fourteenth century, is deemed to have affected music no earlier than about 1420 or so. In addition, as we have seen, two related notions are associated with the concept of a rebirth by the northern humanists who first applied it to music, ideas that are peculiar to its interpretation in that context. The first is that the musical Renaissance is inextricably linked to, or at least best exemplified by, the cultivation of mensural polyphony. This notion persisted even after the discovery that Greek music had been monodic—a realization that brought the contrapuntal style of the sixteenth century under critical fire. The second is that the renewal had originated for music with the northern composers who were most skillful at its cultivation.

For Tinctoris, then, the *fons et origo* for this rebirth of the musical arts lies neither with the theorists of antiquity nor with the distant fathers of the church who had been responsible for the codification of liturgical chant. Rather, it is due to the musicians of the preceding generation who had been trained in polyphonic composition and performance in the musical institutions of northern France and the Low Countries, many of whom were still alive or had died within the writer's own lifetime. A most curious twist, of course, is the inclusion of English masters whose works had first become known on the Continent only during the Hundred Years' War, and particularly in its final stages under the regency of the duke of Bedford (1422–35). The reasons for the English influence are discussed below in greater detail (pp. 216–20), but, clearly, they have to do with the fresh sonorities and the distinctive euphony characteristic of English music at the time, which Tinctoris heard as something decisively new.

With music, as for the visual arts, each successive generation of writers tended to shift the moment of reawakening closer to its own day. But the humanistic models that first prompted a tripartite historical perspective for music became increasingly significant as the fifteenth and sixteenth centuries unfolded. The basic concept of a renaissance persists, particularly in later treatises on music. Their authors were clearly influenced by scholarly trends in other branches of humanistic study, the visual arts in particular.

The Swiss humanist Heinrich Glarean (1488–1563), for example, who was both an admirer of Gaffurius and a friend of Erasmus, divides the music of his time into three ages, the first of which he places only some seventy years earlier. Glarean's periods correspond approximately to a generation of composers, making them considerably shorter than the century-long ages Giorgio Vasari formulated for his *Lives*.[48] There are, however, three periods in either case, and the organic concept of historical development remains the same. Like Vasari, Glarean equates the first age with infancy, the second with full maturity, and the last—that of his own day—with perfection. And since he too believed that nothing could be added to a perfect art, he sees no possibility for improvement in the musical style that had then been current for some twenty-five years.[49]

PIETRO GAETANO AS HUMANIST HISTORIAN OF MUSIC

Glarean's observations are made somewhat casually, as a means of introducing music that illustrates the modal usage that was central to his treatise. A much more extensive and systematic history of music, and one that offers a closer analogy to Vasari's work, is found in the work of Pietro Gaetano, a relatively obscure singer at St. Mark's Basilica in Venice (see Figure 1-10). Sometime around 1570 he composed an oration, in the Ciceronian manner, concerning music's origins and worth.[50] His treatise

48. See pp. 32–34.
49. This view is presented toward the end of Glarean's best-known musical treatise, *Dodecachordon* (Basel, 1547), book 3, 239–41; cf. the English translation by Clement A. Miller, 2 vols. ([Rome]: American Institute of Musicology, 1965), 2:247–48.
50. Gaetano's title is *Oratio de origine et dignitate musices*; the work has been preserved in a single copy (MS Ciconia 906) at the Museo Correr of the Italian National Library in Venice and has been neither published nor translated into English.

was not widely circulated in its time; neither was Gaetano a great intellect nor, apparently, an original thinker. Significantly, however, this would suggest that his little treatise was largely derivative and therefore sufficiently representative of his milieu and period to be of interest to us here.

Humanist concerns are evident throughout Gaetano's treatise, from its oratorical form and elevated Latin prose style to the classicizing nature of its ideas. Gaetano is interested in the topics and the authors cited earlier by Tinctoris, whose writings Gaetano knew and found praiseworthy nearly a century after their compilation. A good deal of space is given to music in ancient Greece. Gaetano writes about the most respected theorists and the most celebrated performers (whether historical or legendary), the significant role of the musical arts in Hellenistic culture, and the marvelous power they were thought to have to move men, beasts, and inanimate objects. He cites only a few authors specifically, but these include both Plato and Aristotle, the harmonists Arixtoxenos and Ptolemy, Donatus and Quintilian (for grammar and rhetoric), Augustine, Livy, and even Terence.

Like Legrense, Gaetano begins his historical narrative with an account of music's genesis drawn from the Bible and supplemented from Josephus. Only then does he attend to the music of the ancient Greeks. To this he adds what little he could

FIGURE 1-10.   Venice, a view of St. Mark's Basilica, by Jacopo de' Barbari, ca. 1500.

extract from Livy about music in Rome. Following the established pattern, he considers as well the musical traditions of Christian antiquity, the creation of the plain-chant repertory associated with Pope Gregory I, and the subsequent invention of the solmization system by Guido of Arezzo. Now practically finished with the Middle Ages, he is ready to discuss polyphonic music, for which, as he says, previous developments provide the foundation. He traces its beginnings back to an earlier time, "lost to the memory of man"—obviously the period of darkness and decline that was to be called medieval. This he designates as the first of five ages in music's history. The term he uses (*aetas*) is the Latin equivalent of Vasari's Italian (*età*), with all of its organic implications. And although he divides time into five segments rather than three, it is clear from what follows that his second, third, and fourth ages correspond to the three phases of stylistic development posited by Vasari for the visual arts.

Gaetano apparently accepted as the *fons et origo* for the polyphonic style those same northern composers that Tinctoris had cited in his treatises, but from Gaetano's more distant perspective the only merit of those remote figures is that they made a beginning and showed the way for the more skillful masters who followed. He judges their compositions—as Vasari does the painting of his first age—as far from perfect. He characterizes them in a jocular fashion as no less "hard and harsh to sing" than are their names "horrible to hear. Who is the soul so bold," he asks rhetorically, "as not to be frightened by these names: Duffai, Demomarto, Busnoys, Heloi, Barburgan, Binthois, etc.? [*sic*]"

The third age, however, produces a generation of musicians Gaetano deems worthy of lasting fame. Those whom he cites by name—northerners all, including Josquin Desprez, Brumel, Févin, Mouton, and Pierre de La Rue—had emerged around the turn of the century as the most accomplished composers of their time, and their works were still known and appreciated in Gaetano's day. He recognizes that the contrapuntal polyphonic style of the period came of age with their music. Moreover, the improvement in compositional skill that characterizes their mature works leads to a high point in its development.

In his view the musicians of his fourth age reached a level of excellence that could not be surpassed. He links its beginnings to the generation just preceding his own and sees its representative figures in composers such as Gombert, Carpentras, Janequin, C. Festa, Morales, Jacquet, Verdelot, and Adrian Willaert. Even here the northern composers predominate. The only exceptions are Festa, an Italian, and Morales, a Spaniard. First and foremost among them, in Gaetano's eyes, is Willaert, who "did so excel in this art that there came to him from all over eager musicians. . . . Through his teaching, as much by the judgment of his ears as by reason, he so purged music of certain ancient imperfections that many erudite persons desired to be taught by him music brought to such purity and elegance." Among the many disciples who flocked to Willaert were the celebrated composer Cipriano de Rore and the distinguished theorist Gioseffo Zarlino (again an Italian). In Gaetano's view, the particular achievements of those masters were such that the music of his own lifetime had come to be "perfect in all its numbers and parts," lacking nothing essential either in theory or in practice.

Since one cannot improve upon perfection, philosophically speaking, it is not surprising—especially considering the organic nature of Gaetano's historical scheme—that he views any alteration in established practice as a sign of imminent decay. Already in the 1570s, however, indications were that a fundamental and far-reaching change in musical style was in the making, one that was to be truly and literally dramatic in its consequences. It was evidently to account for such developments that Gaetano posits as under way a fifth age of music. He observes that it was producing an astonishing proliferation of composers, whose sudden appearance he compares in rather unflattering terms to a horde pouring forth from some Trojan horse. Because the quality of their numerous compositions is questionable, he concludes that many of them either intentionally altered or stupidly neglected the compositional manner of the superior masters of his fourth age. The end of the cycle of growth begun early in the fifteenth century was by then ever more apparent.[51]

CONCLUSIONS

Clearly, then, the period of history between the middle of the fourteenth century and the end of the sixteenth came to be regarded as a time of rebirth by the historians of that age. The concept seems to have originated very early on in Florence with men of letters such as Petrarch and Boccaccio and to have become increasingly current and ever more broadly applied with the passing of time. Conceived initially as a model for the development of Latin literature, the idea of a renaissance was subsequently used to account for artistic and even political history. Finally, as we have seen, it was adopted for music as well.

Thus, by the end of the sixteenth century it had become customary for educated men all over the Western world, and especially for those trained in the humanist mold, to view their age as characterized by a renewal of culture so general as to impinge upon all significant aspects of their history. They compared their achievements in art and literature with those of classical antiquity. At the same time, the very notion of a reawakening inevitably implied an intervening age of darkness and ignorance. This interpretation of cultural history became so deeply anchored in the thinking of the period that it has survived to the present day. In fact, successive generations of historians have strengthened and broadened its hold in a way that eventually enabled Burckhardt and Symonds to make their classic formulation of traditional views.

Undeniably, then, the music of the fifteenth and sixteenth centuries has been regarded since at least the time of Tinctoris as an integral part of the historical Renaissance. Conversely—perhaps in part as a result of this view—many twentieth-century histo-

---

51. The citations from Gaetano were taken from ff. 19–22 of his treatise *Oratio de inventione et usu musices.*

rians have traditionally accepted the Renaissance as a separate, identifiable historical period. Renaissance musical style is therefore also seen as clearly and convincingly distinguishable from that which precedes and follows, as much so as any other facet of its political or cultural history, including the literature and the visual arts with which the concept of rebirth originated.[52] But if, as Erwin Panofsky has observed, "the historian cannot help dividing his materials into 'periods,' nicely defined in the *Oxford Dictionary* as distinguishable, each of these spans of time has to have a certain unity; and if the historian wishes to verify this unity instead of merely presupposing it, he must needs try to discover intrinsic analogies between such overtly disparate phenomena as the arts, literature, philosophy, social and political currents, and religious movements."[53]

In our discussion of the music of this period, we shall attempt to show how the genres and styles of the fifteenth and sixteenth centuries can be distinguished by meaningful criteria from those of the Middle Ages; whether the development of musical style offers meaningful analogies to that of the visual arts and the literature of the period, particularly with respect to the emulation of models from classical antiquity; and, most significantly, whether there is in fact sufficient stylistic coherence and consistency over a span of nearly two centuries to justify their designation as a period in the history of Western music. We shall return to these questions at the conclusion of our study. But let us first acquaint ourselves with the social milieux in which music was then heard, with the intellectual matrix in which it was created, and, of course, with the definable elements of style within the music itself.

52. See, for example, Edward E. Lowinsky, "Music in the Culture of the Renaissance," in *Renaissance Essays*, ed. Paul O. Kristeller and Philip P. Wiener, 2 vols., Library of the History of Ideas, vol. 9 (Rochester: University of Rochester Press, 1992), 337ff.
53. Erwin Panofsky, *Gothic Architecture and Scholasticism* (New York: Meridian Books, 1957), 1.

CHAPTER 2

*The Christian Church
as Patron of Music*

INTRODUCTION

Music making is necessarily a social activity. Scholars of any age may take refuge in the silence of a library to explore the theory of music as written down in earlier times. Or they may in turn retire to a quiet study to set down, also in writing, their own views and opinions. Similarly, a composer of any period may seek peaceful solitude to notate the musical ideas of a creative imagination. These are mental exercises, whatever their ultimate effect on musical practice, and can take place entirely within the mind. But to bring those ideas to life in sound, whether they begin with words or notes or in some more intuitive form, requires a performance. Most performances entail interaction among musicians and between them and their audience, regardless of the circumstances and the function of the music heard.

It has often been said that music is inescapably transitory for the listener. It unfolds at its own pace, and its sounds can neither be made to linger nor later recalled at will. They dissipate into the ether as quickly as they are made. What is more, a performance leaves no trace of the social ambience in which it took place, the attitudes of the musicians, or the response of the listeners. Only with the modern marvels of an electronic technology that can record not only sound but also the movements and expressions of those involved—performers and audience alike—has it become possible to capture for history the complex social dynamics of musical performances. Unfortunately, videotapes and sound recordings simply do not exist for the many centuries preceding the twentieth.

To complicate matters even further, large parts of the musical repertories of the fifteenth and sixteenth centuries have not survived in written form. This is so for a number of reasons. Many notated sources of the period, both manuscripts and prints, have been destroyed with the passing of time. The notation of music that survives usually fails to specify such details of performance as the actual number of participants, the types of instruments employed (if any), the nature and extent of improvised melodic ornamentation, and the placement of most commonly used accidentals. Most significant, many musical works were seldom if ever reduced to a notated form: they were either taught to other musicians entirely by rote or were themselves improvisatory in nature. Music of this sort generally falls into one of three specific categories: secular solo song, with or without instrumental accompaniment; dance tunes, whether played by one or by several performers; and calls or fanfares sounded by trumpeters on the battlefield, at tourneys, and for public ceremonies.

There is good evidence that such pieces existed in considerable numbers. To begin, there are pictures showing groups of dancers accompanied by players with instruments but with no written music before them (see Figure 2-1). This is in clear contrast to the singing clerics sometimes seen in chapel scenes, usually huddled around a book (see Figure 2-2). There are also accounts of events in which secular music with no known written tradition figures repeatedly. Further, archival records reveal the existence of an entire class of professional musicians who sang and played on such occasions, but relatively little is known about their ability to use musical notation. Finally, there are notated sources for music that must have originated in unwritten musical practice. These include, on the one hand, songs that were written down because they became popular in circles where notation was current or were incorporated into polyphonic compositions (see pp. 298–304) and, on the other, dance tunes intended for the growing numbers of city dwellers who had the means and leisure to learn notation and take up music for their own pleasure (see pp. 829–38).[1]

FIGURE 2-1. Instrumental musicians playing (without written music) for dancers. *Basse danse* from the *Chronique d'Angleterre* by Jean de Waurin, 15th c. (Vienna, Österreichische Nationalbibliothek, MS. 2534, f. 17).

1. For some illuminating observations concerning the unwritten musical traditions of the period under discussion here, see Nino Pirrotta, *Music and Culture in Italy from the Middle Ages to the Baroque* (Cambridge, Mass.: Harvard University Press, 1984), 27, and for some instructive examples, see the essays nos. 3, 4, 5, 6, and 12.

It is not only useful, then, but essential that we distinguish for that period—as for our own—between the musical traditions that were written and those that were not, even though this is not always clearly and easily done. It is now clear that the sacred music of the period, which tends to be rather complex, was written down more consistently than secular pieces, in part because the written tradition originated within the Christian church. During the Middle Ages the church maintained the only system of schools in which the skills of reading and writing were regularly taught for both words and music, and its institutions continued to serve as the primary custodian of written traditions through the fifteenth and sixteenth centuries as well.

In addition, most sacred music—apart from plainchant, which began to be notated in the ninth century—was both polyphonic and mensural. For such works the multiple performers involved in complex musical relationships with one another usually made notation a necessity. Still, it is important to

FIGURE 2-2. Christmas Mass at the ducal court of John of Berry (*The 'Très riches heures' of Jean, Duke of Berry*, no. 120, f. 158ʳ, from the Musée Condé, Chantilly, published New York: George Braziller, 1969).

remember that improvised polyphony was frequently used in performance to embellish sacred chant—a practice that clearly left its mark on the written tradition of the fifteenth century, as we shall see. Conversely, certain genres of secular polyphony were included in notated sources as early as the twelfth century.

Unfortunately, some of the terms that have been adopted to help define the distinctions between written and unwritten repertories of music—"learned" as opposed to "naive" or "rustic," for example, or "art music" in contrast to "popular"—today have troublesome connotations. "Learned" and "naive" suggest value judgments as do, perhaps even more strongly, "art music" and "popular music." In a literate society a clear advantage is usually given to the written tradition, although its superiority can often be questioned. An unwritten musical practice can achieve a degree of complexity and sophistication that is comparable in every way to that found in notated music.

The improvisatory genres developed by the lutanists, vihuelists, and keyboard players of the fifteenth and sixteenth centuries are a case in point; they eventually gave rise to written repertories that clearly reflect the consummate skill of the virtuoso player-composer. It is to avoid such prejudicial notions that the more neutral terms "written" and "oral" or "unwritten" will be preferred in this book. Similarly, the word "popular" will be used here only to indicate broad acceptance of a specific element of musical culture by a cross-section of society, including groups that do not possess notational skills.

At the same time, meaningful distinctions between written and oral traditions of music reflect unmistakable and important differences in social class that concern both the musicians themselves and their patrons. In a very real sense the clergy of the Christian church constituted a closed and autonomous social system of its own, one that was supposed to be largely independent of the social hierarchies of medieval feudalism. But in reality noble birth brought there, as elsewhere, preferments that were not always deserved. A fair number of churches drew their administrative officers almost exclusively from aristocratic families.

Nevertheless, it was also possible within the church for the lowborn, the illegitimate, and the impoverished to enter the well-structured hierarchy of the priesthood and to rise as high as their abilities and energies would take them. In such cases their ecclesiastical status apparently brought them the respect (however grudging) of those who belonged by birth to higher social classes—landed aristocracy and wealthy burghers alike. If one may judge from the careers of men such as Guillaume Du Fay, Johannes Okeghem, and Josquin Desprez, this was particularly true of those cleric-musicians who distinguished themselves as composers.[2] (Women, by contrast, had such opportunities only within the convent.) For these reasons alone it is important to understand the organization of the Christian church in the fifteenth and sixteenth centuries. It will also be helpful to have some notion of the role that music played in the educational, liturgical, and social activities of the clergy.

The administrative structures used by the Western church in the fifteenth and sixteenth centuries were developed mostly during the Carolingian era.[3] The ancient provinces of the Holy Roman Empire provided the geographical framework within which the ecclesiastical organization took shape. In the provincial capital the chief prelate of the metropolitan church was designated an archbishop and given authori-

2. For instructive examples, see below the biographical sketches of the masters cited.

3. For a detailed study of the institutional organization and administrative functions of the Christian church as they developed through the Middle Ages—to which the following discussion is much indebted—see Jean-François Lemarignier, "Les institutions ecclésiastiques en France de la fin du Xe au milieu du XIIe siècle," and Jean Gaudemet, "Les institutions ecclésiastiques en France du milieu du XIIe au début du XIVe siècle," in *Histoire des institutions françaises au moyen age*, vol. 3, *Institutions ecclésiastiques* (Paris: 1962), ed. Ferdinand Lot and Robert Fawtier. Although directed specifically toward the church in France, many of the generalities concerning its hierarchical and social organization are valid for ecclesiastical institutions all over western Europe.

ty not only over his own episcopal see (the archbishopric) but also over the churches in the lesser cities of the province. Each of the important urban centers was, in turn, the seat of a cathedral church whose ecclesiastical head was a bishop. His jurisdiction extended, similarly, to the churches of the surrounding area, termed a diocese, whose geographical limits were carefully defined.

The administrative structures of the Roman church were thus established early in the Middle Ages on two levels: the diocese and the archdiocese. Interestingly, these divisions proved to be considerably more stable than the political entities upon which they were based. The boundaries of temporal states shifted frequently with the fortunes of ruling magnates and the outcome of the frequent conflicts among them. By contrast, the geographical divisions of the church, which were much less subject to pressures of that nature, were adapted much more slowly to changing circumstances. As a result, political and ecclesiastical borders coincided only occasionally during the fifteenth and sixteenth centuries. Differences were especially marked in territories that were a matter of dispute, first between France and England or the empire, and then between France and Spain (see Figure 2-3). Because of such conflicts, control of certain dioceses became strategically important enough to prompt repeated attempts by secular rulers to intervene in the church's internal affairs.

⸰ THE CATHEDRAL CHURCH ⸰

As the chief prelate or officer of the diocese, the bishop was invested with the fullest powers of his priesthood. Within its borders he alone was authorized to confer sacred orders—to ordain the priests and clerics who were charged with the celebration of the liturgy and the instruction of the faithful under his direction—and to consecrate churches, altars, and holy oils. As a mark of his high station, he was anointed in a ceremony analogous to that adopted for the consecration of kings, and the emblems of his office—ring, miter, and crosier—evoked those borne by secular rulers. At the same time, those symbols indicated the power of his own political jurisdiction, which was due to the territorial domains and sources of revenue under his control.

The bishop supervised the clergy subject to his authority first of all through regular visits to the churches of his diocese. For matters having more than local interest, he could also call together those clerics concerned in a synod, a body that could legislate for the diocese in special circumstances. The bishop was assisted in his administration of the diocese by lesser officials. The diocese was subdivided into archdeaconates, each with an archdeacon to act in the bishop's stead when the need arose, and into deaneries, with an archpriest to oversee the ministry of the priests under his supervision. In reality, however, both archdeacons and archpriests were apt to challenge the authority of their bishop almost as often as they sustained it. Causes for dispute arose on matters of all kinds—theological, jurisdictional, and fiscal.

Also assisting the bishop in governing the diocese and, more particularly, the episcopal see, was a body of clerics known as canons. They were so called because they were supposed to live in a community similar to that of a monastic order and observe a "rule." In dealing with the affairs of the cathedral church, the canons met frequently in chapter (from the Latin word *capitulum,* a diminutive for "head") and were therefore designated as a group by the same term. Direction was provided not only by the bishop but also by canons chosen by the chapter to fill the various offices known as dignities. These carried jurisdiction in particular areas over the clerics who served in the church. The head of the chapter was a dean (*decanus*) or provost (*praepositus*)—the titles varied. He was usually elected by the canons and installed by the bishop, to whom he swore an oath of allegiance, but his first loyalty was to the chapter itself. Second in command was the cantor (or *primicerius*), so named

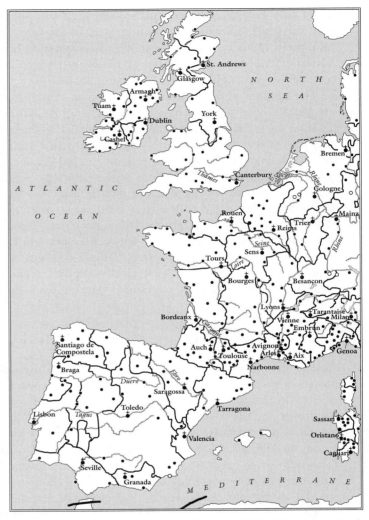

FIGURE 2-3. The ecclesiastical

because, originally, he supervised the choir in celebrating the liturgy. By the fifteenth century, however, his duties had become largely administrative, and the day-to-day direction of the clerics who chanted Mass and the Offices was left to a vicar who functioned in his stead.

In 1179 the Third Lateran Council decreed that every cathedral should provide a master to instruct the clergy of the church and, tuition-free, a number of young scholars. This edict, which was renewed in 1215, seems to have had relatively little effect in Italy, but it did encourage the development of cathedral schools elsewhere in Europe, particularly in France and England.[4] The canon charged with the direc-

4. For details, see Denys Hay, *The Church in Italy in the Fifteenth Century* (Cambridge: Cambridge University Press, 1977), 52.

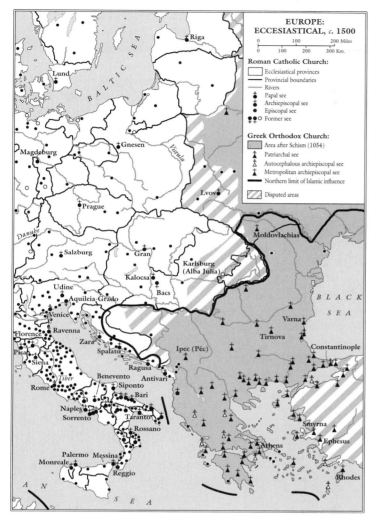

EUROPE:
ECCLESIASTICAL, *c.* 1500

| 0 | | 100 | | 200 Miles |
| 0 | 100 | 200 | 300 Km. | |

Roman Catholic Church:
- ☐ Ecclesiastical provinces
- Provincial boundaries
- Rivers
- ♦ Papal see
- ♦ Archiepiscopal see
- ● Episcopal see
- ♦●○ Former see

Greek Orthodox Church:
- ▨ Area after Schism (1054)
- ▲ Patriarchal see
- △ Autocephalous archiepiscopal see
- ▲ Metropolitan archiepiscopal see
- ━ Northern limit of Islamic influence
- ▨ Disputed areas

jurisdictions in Europe, ca. 1500.

tion of the school was the scholar or master (*scolasticus*). He appointed the teachers, looked after the library, and drafted the official acts of the chapter. During the fifteenth and sixteenth centuries, cathedral schools, and others modeled upon them, became primary centers for musical instruction. Their importance for the musical developments of the period is self-evident, and we shall return shortly to the curriculum offered there.

Another officer of the chapter, the chancellor (*cancelarius*), maintained the archives of the cathedral and supervised the notaries and scribes in producing the official documents needed for its administration. To these he affixed the chapter seal, of which he was the guardian. Cases of conscience and infractions of canon law were handled by the penitentiary, so named for his powers to impose penance and give absolution. Objects of value to the chapter—costly vessels and vestments for liturgical use and important privileges and charters, for example—were in the charge of the treasurer (also called the *camerarius*), who administered as well the finances of the church. The furnishings in daily use were the responsibility of the sacristan, who also directed the activities of the bell ringers (*pulsatores*) and the ushers (*ostiarii*). Local usage varied considerably, especially in the names designating the dignitaries mentioned thus far, and in some chapters yet other officers were named to assist with a variety of tasks.

A chapter of average size usually counted some thirty to forty canons. There could be more, of course, in the larger, wealthier dioceses and fewer in the smaller, poorer ones. In any case the number of clerics needed in a cathedral church to maintain the daily round of services, to care for the poor, and to teach in the school was considerably greater. The canons of the chapter were often helped by a number of vicars, who assumed some of the duties of those who were absent from the cathedral cloister. One of the regular roles of the vicars was primarily musical and therefore of particular interest here; they replaced the canons in choir to sing both the plainchant and the polyphony heard in celebrating the liturgy. At the Cambrai Cathedral, for example, the heart of the choir was constituted by the "minor" vicars—as few as sixteen in the fifteenth century but as many as twenty-five in the early sixteenth—who were joined when necessary by one or more of the "major" vicars and at least half a dozen choirboys.[5]

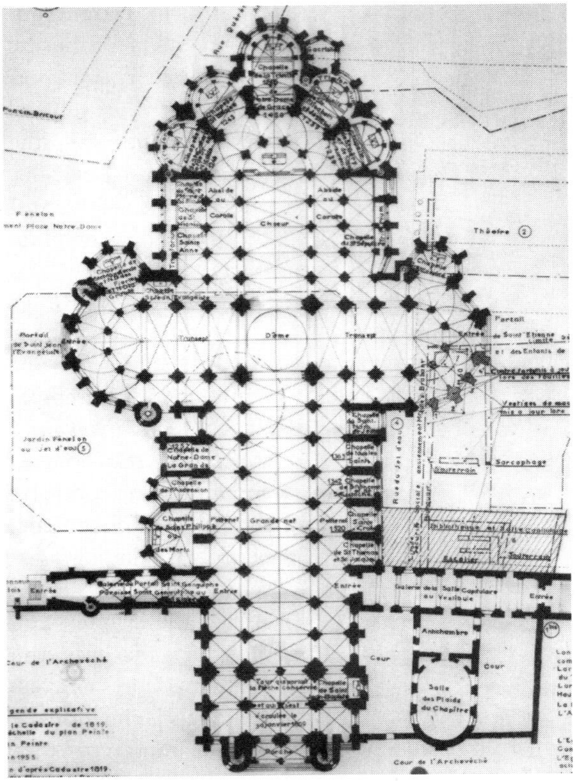

Yet other clerics were needed to minister to the lay members of the congregation, to hear confessions, and to provide the sacraments connected with birth, marriage, and death. The chancellery required notaries and scribes, and the treasury needed accountants. The sacristan also needed help in maintaining the furnishings of the church, especially when decorating the building and making other preparations for special occasions. And the cathedral school could function only if there were an adequate number of masters to teach the students.

In addition, the altars and chapels that lined the exterior walls of every cathedral (see, for example, Figure 2-4) were served by a sizable number of supplementary chaplains and priests. At the metropolitan

FIGURE 2-4. Floor plan of the cathedral of Cambrai: a nineteenth-century diagram based on a thirteenth-century drawing.

5. See Craig Wright's discussion of "Performance Practices at the Cathedral of Cambrai, 1475–1550," *Musical Quarterly* 64 (1978): 295–97. Despite regional differences and quirks of nomenclature, the role played by the vicars in the liturgical life of the cathedral church appears to have been much the same everywhere. For a more detailed discussion of the constitution and organization of ecclesiastical choirs generally, see below, pp. 128–35.

church of Rouen, for example, besides some ten dignitaries, fifty canons, and eight minor canons (whose duties must have been mainly musical), there were some seventy chaplains, or cleric-choristers, divided among five separate colleges. Since the canons (or their vicars) and the altar boys regularly celebrated the liturgy in the choir, such a large group of clerics with liturgical functions can only be explained by the seemingly endless round of commemorative services for the dead that were founded by wills and gifts to the chapter.[6] In view of these many tasks performed by the clergy of a cathedral, it is hardly surprising that a small diocese could have fifty or more canons in its chapter, in addition to the customary dignitaries and canons, and a larger one could count three times that many.[7]

⌁ THE COLLEGIATE CHURCH ⌁

Similar in most respects to a cathedral were those churches termed "collegiate" because they were served by a community of clerics—a "college"—similar in nature to the sort formed to assist with the government of a bishopric. Such a college consisted of a chapter of canons aided by a variable number of additional clerics. Nonetheless, there was a crucial distinction: a collegiate church was not usually involved with the affairs of a diocese but was subject instead to the authority of the local bishop. Exceptions were made only by a special charter (a papal bull) making the chapter answerable only to the pope. A diocese had only one cathedral, moreover, whereas collegiate churches were surprisingly numerous. Some of these were very ancient, having been founded at a shrine where the veneration of a saint attracted pilgrims and thus generated an ever greater number of privately endowed services. Others had evolved from the secularization of monasteries, some of which had long and venerable histories. Still others had been established—some anciently, others recently—by magnates or by wealthy prelates, including the pope himself.

These differences in age and origins were reflected in the variety among collegiate foundations in size, location, and function. Some were urban, others rural; some were exceptionally large and wealthy, others small and modestly endowed; some

6. According to Armand-Romain Colette, *Histoire de la maîtrise de Rouen* (Rouen, 1892; reprint, Geneva: Minkoff, 1972), 8–9, the five colleges were constituted as follows: Collège de la Commune, twenty-five chaplains; Collège de Darnétal, sixteen chaplains; Collège d'Albane, eight chaplains; Collège du Saint-Esprit, six chaplains; and Collège des Clémentines, sixteen chaplains. The nature of their duties is clearly indicated by the requirement that they know by heart not only the Psalter but also the hymns, antiphons, verses, and responds for all of the Offices, both common and proper. There is also a distinct possibility that such "colleges" had as well an educational role within the clerical community—hence our present use of the term; see below, pp. 77–80.

7. See the figures given for Brescia, Ferrara, and Milan by Hay, *Church in Italy in the Fifteenth Century*, 21–22. The situation was similar in the north as, for example, at the cathedral of Cambrai, which maintained in the early sixteenth century a chapter consisting of a provost, a cantor, a treasurer, a scholar, a deacon, four archdeacons, fifty other canons and, in addition, nine major vicars, eighteen minor vicars (the singers), six choirboys (who were also students in the choir school), and some fifty chaplains. See Craig Wright, "Musiciens à la cathédrale de Cambrai," *Revue de musicologie* 62 (1976): 205.

filled the functions of a parish church (see below), others did not. Those instituted by magnates were often placed and built with political and military ends in mind. They sometimes furnished clerics to assist with the administration of a secular court, in its council, its chancellery, or its chapel. As a result, even those collegiate churches that had their origins in a monastic order usually had more direct and frequent contact with secular society than other ecclesiastical institutions.

To illustrate, the chapter and colleges of most cathedrals remained "regular" until at least the eleventh century, sharing dormitories and refectories, holding their worldly goods in common, and ordering their daily activities to the rhythms of the liturgy in accordance with a quasi-monastic rule. "Secular" chapters became common at the cathedral only much later. By contrast, many collegiate churches were secularized before the year 900, allowing the clerics to live in private dwellings, own real property, and enjoy considerable personal freedom. The more liberal nature of collegiate life is also evident in the rules governing the appointment and the residence of its canons. To be named to a cathedral chapter, a cleric had either to be a priest or to be ordained within the ensuing year (and therefore to be at least twenty-five years of age). Once installed, he was allowed no more than four months' absence in the course of a year—at least in principle. Canons were admitted to secular chapters much younger, already at nine years of age in one instance at St. Martin's in Tours. Until they were ordained (if ever), they could hire a vicar to replace them in their religious duties. Moreover, those who were supposed to be in residence could be absent for as long as six months out of the year.

The worldly ways of certain collegiate churches are perhaps most strikingly revealed by their sponsoring trade fairs on special feast days in the very shadow of their walls. This led to renting market space to vendors, providing lodgings for visitors, and even lending working capital to participating merchants. Thus a collegiate church could help the local economy and stimulate urban development as well. In some instances the church and its dependencies formed a nucleus around which the city grew.[8]

Not surprisingly, collegiate churches became a haven for the younger sons of wealthy burghers and the nobility, those who stood little chance of inheriting either a family business or feudal lands. If, in addition, the collegiate church had a secular ruler as titular abbot, this facilitated access for the nobles to a well-paid appointment such as a dignity or a canonry. This was the case at St. Martin's of Tours, one of four collegiate chapters whose nominal head was the king of France.

Conversely, it was possible for the ruler to maintain a greater degree of control over a collegiate church whose canons were drawn in good part from members of his own clan or from related families who owed him fealty. This was desirable for a number of the reasons already cited. In addition to being situated in some cases along militarily strategic routes, and fortified at times like a castle, the collegiate church, like the episcopal see itself, often possessed extensive feudal domains, and these could

---

8. See Gaudemet, "Les institutions ecclésiastiques en France," 196.

make up an important part of the larger fief claimed by the ruling magnate. What is more, the revenues produced by such lands could provide a living for clerics attached to his court, thus easing the burden on his treasury.

A wealthy collegiate church could support a very large clerical community. At St. Martin's of Tours, which grew out of an ancient monastic house with venerable traditions and unusually large holdings, there were eleven dignitaries, fifteen provosts, fifty-six canons (and as many vicars), twenty-eight honorary canons (some of them laypersons), plus the dean of the chapter, and additional priests and chaplains to bring the total to 250 clerics (see Figure 2-5).[9] Where the college was large enough to rival or, as in the instance cited, to surpass the number of people attached to a cathedral, it was possible for the church to maintain both a school and a choir of some size. There is some evidence to suggest that magnates often called upon the clerics of such churches to provide music and to train musicians for their court.

The king of France drew chaplains and singers not only from St. Martin's but

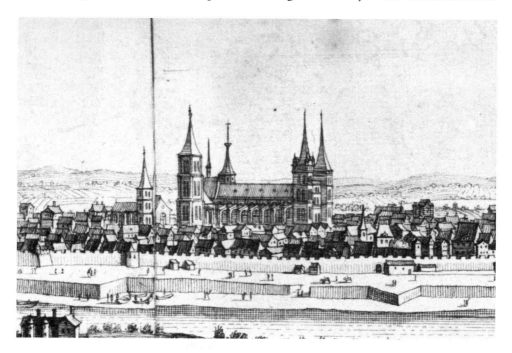

FIGURE 2-5. Church of Saint Martin in Tours with the city wall and the banks of the Loire river in the foreground. (Lithograph by Martens, 1657; Gaspar Merian, *Topographia galliae*, Tours, Bibliothèque Municipale.)

9. See Gaudemet, "Les institutions ecclésiastiques en France," 193. For a brief description of two northern collegiate churches with more modest means and a correspondingly smaller group of clerics, see Reinhard Strohm, *Music in Late Medieval Bruges* (Oxford: Clarendon Press, 1985), 12f. and 43f.

also—as the dukes of Berry had earlier—from the Sainte Chapelle in Bourges.[10] Duke Philip of Burgundy made similar use of the Sainte Chapelle in Dijon and the church of St. Peter in Lille; in 1425 he set up an endowment in each place for the maintenance and instruction of four choirboys.[11] Such clues concerning the role played by collegiate churches in training the musicians that served in church choirs and courtly chapels underline the importance of these churches for the musical culture of the period. Collectively, their contribution may well have rivaled that of the great cathedral churches.[12]

∽ THE MONASTIC HOUSES ↶

The monastic houses were among the most venerable of the medieval institutions that played an important role in the social and musical history of the Christian church during the fifteenth and sixteenth centuries. Like the collegiate churches, the convents and monasteries within a given diocese were usually subject to the authority of its bishop. But many of them also had a long and eventful history that in some cases included a dispensation making them accountable solely to the pope. Several of the many religious orders that came into existence during the Middle Ages were in fact founded with papal approval in response to specific social needs; theirs was a mission of service to the Christian laity at large. The Knights Templars were one such group. Like all of the fraternal associations whose chief mission was military, it was founded at the time of the Crusades to provide aid and protection for pilgrims to the Holy Land. Similarly, the Knights Hospitaller were established to furnish shelter and care for pilgrims who fell ill on the journey. Their role in caring for the sick and the needy on the pilgrim routes to Jerusalem was later extended to include routes to analogous sites in Europe.[13]

An equally active social function—in the spiritual rather than the temporal domain—was filled by the mendicant orders, in particular the Franciscans and Dominicans. Their earliest communities were founded in the thirteenth century to carry the message of the Christian gospel to the lay members of the church. The

---

10. Regarding connections between the court and St. Martin's of Tours, see Leeman L. Perkins, "Musical Patronage at the Royal Court of France under Charles VII and Louis XI (1422–83)," *Journal of the American Musicological Society* 37 (1984): 523–27 and 537–38. Evidence for an analogous relationship involving the Sainte Chapelle in Bourges has been cited by Paula Higgins, "Music and Musicians at the Sainte-Chapelle of the Bourges Palace, 1405–1500," in *Atti del XIV Congresso della Società Internazionale di Musicología (Bologna, 1987)*, ed. Angelo Pompilio, 3 vols. (Torino: EDT, 1990), 3:689–701.

11. See Jeanne Marix, *Histoire de la musique de la cour de Bourgogne* (Strasbourg: Heitz, 1939; reprint, Geneva: Minkoff, 1972), 162–63. It is noteworthy that shortly after the establishment of choir schools in these two churches, all references to choirboys attached to the court disappear from ducal registers.

12. For a general discussion of collegiate churches, see Gaudemet, "Les institutions ecclésiastiques en France," 192–97.

13. Concerning the Knights Hospitaller, see H. J. A. Sire, *The Knights of Malta* (New Haven: Yale University Press, 1994).

duties of these friars as preachers and teachers created a need for preparatory study that often involved them in the life of the medieval university. At the same time, they were in constant contact with the populace as well, drawing crowds eager to hear them wherever people were willing to listen. Famous religious shrines and even trade fairs gave them the widest possible audience for their message. With their daily conduct thus exposed to public scrutiny, the indiscretions of some mendicant monks earned them a reputation for moral laxity, especially with regard to the opposite sex. The most commonly held doubts about their probity are reflected in the literature of the period, including verses in a popular tone that were occasionally set to music.

Cloistered orders such as the Benedictines were the first to establish regular schools, however, and these provided models for both cathedral and collegiate churches. Typically, a monastic house was governed by an abbot (or, if small or dependent, a prior), who was assisted by a prior, a chamberlain, a treasurer, a cantor, a master for the novices, a cellarer, and others. In convents for women, which were in fact very numerous, the administrative offices were basically the same. The titles differ from those used in secular chapters, but they show clearly enough that the primary functions were essentially the same: besides looking after the lands and revenues of the order and seeing to the temporal needs of the community, they assured the regular celebration of the liturgy and the religious instruction of novices and young clerics.

As the organization of cathedral and collegiate chapters became increasingly set and the duties of its officers well defined, they were taken ever more frequently as a model by monasteries. By the fifteenth century the period of greatest importance for the monastic schools as centers of learning—with rich libraries and active *scriptoria* for the production and dissemination of books—was largely past. With the development of cities made wealthy by their manufacturing and trade, the educational functions of the Christian church were shifted to the urban institutions that shared in that affluence. In most instances this meant the cathedrals and collegiate churches, which gradually assumed the leading role as places of study and instruction.[14]

⚊◯ THE PARISH CHURCH ◯⚊

Collegiate churches and monasteries notwithstanding, the basic unit of the diocese on the local level was the parish. Centered around a church where services could be held, it covered a limited geographical area. The residents of the parish could come on foot to worship and were in fact bound under canon law to attend. The parish clergy celebrated the liturgy for the local faithful. They were also authorized to administer the sacraments of baptism and burial, at the least, and to collect tithes and

14. There is an extensive literature on monastic institutions of the Middle Ages and the Renaissance that touches on every facet of the multifarious activities in which the regular orders were involved. A relatively concise discussion of essential matters is given by Gaudemet, "Les institutions ecclésiastiques en France," 220–42.

offerings. The number of clerics was determined by the size of the congregation and the extent of their liturgical duties. The smallest parish required a single priest to carry out these basic functions.[15] However, chapels dedicated to a popular saint and foundations—endowed income for services on behalf of the dead—could increase the workload appreciably and thus require the aid of one or more vicars.

During the Middle Ages the obligation to worship in one's own parish was very real; every resident household was to be represented at Mass on Sundays and special feast days. This requirement ensured that the instructions and decrees read from the pulpit—some of which originated with the bishop or an episcopal synod—were adequately publicized. It also enabled the parish priest to maintain contact with the members of his flock. Those who failed to appear regularly were subject to punitive sanctions such as fines and, if unrepentant, could face the threat of excommunication, the ultimate penalty.

At the same time, strangers to the parish were excluded from services there, again by canon law, in part to encourage congregants to attend their own church and in part to prevent those who had been excommunicated elsewhere from slipping in to receive sacraments to which they were not entitled. Observance of these measures was strict enough to raise serious problems for itinerants such as musicians and singers. Because many of them had no fixed residence and thus no home parish, they were left in effect without status in the carefully regulated society of the Middle Ages. As a result, they organized into guilds in order to obtain a measure of acceptance and protection under both civil and canon law. By the fifteenth century a good many such guilds were already well established, and others were subsequently formed. Their existence had a distinct impact on the social uses of music, as will be seen, if not necessarily on the development of musical style.[16]

◡◠ THE BENEFICIAL SYSTEM ◠◡

To provide housing, food, clothing, and other basic necessities for the clerical communities, large and small, that served the various churches and monastic houses of a typical diocese required considerable sources of income. Financial support came from the material wealth of the individual institutions, which took three different forms. There were, first of all, the buildings themselves, together with their furnishings, both those used in the daily celebration of the liturgy and those intended simply to deco-

15. The rector or pastor of a parish church was supposed to be at least twenty-five years of age, of legitimate birth, of good morals, having been ordained a priest when appointed or within the first year of his tenure, and able to demonstrate under episcopal examination an adequate knowledge of his duties. In addition, for reasons that will become apparent presently, he was not to hold more than one such appointment. See Jean Gaudemet, "Les institutions ecclésiastiques en France," 206.

16. See Jean Gaudemet, "Les institutions ecclésiastiques en France," 204, and Walter Salmen, "The Social Status of the Musician in the Middle Ages," in *The Social Status of the Professional Musician from the Middle Ages to the Nineteenth Century* (New York: Pendragon Press, 1983), 25–29; also the discussion below, pp. 149–64.

rate and beautify the church. In the wealthier communities, some of these objects—vessels of silver and gold set with precious stones and richly woven vestments—were valuable enough to warrant being kept in the treasury. Whatever their worth, however (and it could be very great),[17] such items were not used to meet daily expenses.

More important in that respect was the real property of the church: buildings of various types (including the houses in which the clergy themselves were lodged), arable lands, and various commercial ventures. These produced income, both in kind, where agriculture and trade were involved, and in cash, from goods sold, rentals, and fees. Other major sources of funds for the church were the various offerings and taxes that could be collected regularly, the most basic of which were the tithes. There were, in addition, occasional bequests and gifts, most of them as endowment to provide for regular services on behalf of the souls of the donors after their death. These revenues, like the lands and buildings of a given church, were administered by the dean or provost and the canons of the chapter much in the manner of a feudal fief. They were divided into prebends or benefices, each of which was to supply a living for one or more members of the clerical community.[18]

Because the holdings of a diocese—and, to a lesser extent, of a collegiate church or a monastery—could be both extensive and strategically placed, the bishop or the head of the chapter was often an important feudal lord who could not escape from mundane political reality even if he were so inclined. Thus, the election of an important bishop, dean, provost, or abbot was subject to pressures of various kinds. On the one hand were the secular rulers, both local magnates and their liege lords, and on the other, the clerical hierarchy of the church, from the pope on down. The resulting conflicts could be especially violent where the church's holdings overlapped with two or more opposing polities, as they often did in the fifteenth century.

In principle the chief prelate of a diocese, a collegiate church, or a monastic house was chosen by the clerics of the community from among their number. A bishop, for example, was to be elected by the chapter of the cathedral and installed by the archbishop after an examination had established that he was qualified for the position.[19]

17. As an example, in 1479 King Louis XI gave to the church of St. Martin in Tours a magnificent grill-work of silver, which required nearly 3,389 pounds of the precious metal, as a decorative barrier around the saint's tomb. See Pierre Mesnard, "La Collégiale Saint-Martin à l'époque des Valois," *Mémorial de l'année martinienne M.DCCCC.LX–M.DCCCC.LXI* (Paris: Librairie J. Vrin, 1962), 96.

18. Some prebends in France actually included fiefs for which oaths of fealty had to be sworn to the king or one of his officers; sixteen of the canons at St. Martin's of Tours were feudal titularies in that specific sense. See Jean Gaudemet, "Les institutions ecclésiastiques en France," 192. For a description of the income produced by the fiefs held by the treasurer of the church, see Perkins, "Musical Patronage at the Royal Court of France," 525–26 and appendix III, 558–66.

19. Canon law prescribed that a bishop was to be at least thirty years of age, of legitimate birth, and of good morals; however, a papal dispensation could serve as a substitute for any of the three basic qualifications, age being the one for which exceptions were most frequently made. In addition, he was not to have gained his office by simony (i.e., he was not allowed to buy it). See Jean Gaudemet, "Les institutions ecclésiastiques en France," 164–72. He was to have received, in addition, sufficient instruction in matters liturgical, theological, and canonical to enable him to fulfill his functions, but it is far from certain that this was always the case.

In reality, however, the election often required the prior permission not only of the archbishop but also of the secular powers concerned, and the election results had to be approved by them as well. In some instances the king claimed the right to name the candidate to the position, and the election was then to be ratified by a submissive clergy. In others it was the pope himself who asserted that right. As with bishops, so also with deans, provosts, abbots, and priors; in each case the interested parties—from chapter to pope and from baron to king—tried to have the candidate of their choice elected.

Nor was this contest of wills limited to the chief offices of a given church or monastery. Dignities, canonries, chaplaincies, vicariates—in sum, any position with a prebend or benefice—became subject to the opposing claims of two or more aspirants. These conflicts had to be settled by the courts, civil as well as ecclesiastical, and they came to be so frequent and widespread that it was most unusual for an important benefice to be awarded without litigation.

The reasons for such vehement struggles for the control of prebends were of course financial as well as political. Every magnate wanted the power to name the clerics who assisted him with the administration of his court to a good living within the church. By so doing he could diminish the cash demands on his own treasury and provide a comfortable retirement for those in his service with no additional expense. Much the same was true for the pope; it was clearly in his interest to reward the numerous clerics who staffed the enormous bureaucracy of the papal court with generous benefices paid out by institutions in their homelands rather than having to draw upon his own treasury.

Yet it was not easy for the pope to impose his will in the bestowal of benefices in distant churches; a new incumbent could be elected and installed long before news of the vacancy reached the papal court. As a result, from the fourteenth century on popes increasingly made nominations *in commendam*. This meant issuing a papal bull that reserved the next prebend to fall vacant in a given institution for a candidate of the pope's choice.[20] Such tactics naturally prompted a good deal of resistance at the local level, both from the clerics who were thus deprived of coveted benefices in their own region and from chapters whose ranks were weakened and whose wealth was siphoned away by appointees who were not present to assist them with their liturgical and administrative duties.

In principle a prebend was not to be held in absentia, nor were benefices to be cumulated. In practice, however, a papal dispensation could make either allowable, and it was easy for a papal official or—to a lesser degree—a cleric in the service of an influential ruler to obtain one. The cleric so favored could thus collect the income of several rich prebends, providing where necessary the meager salary of a vicar, and continue in the service of the pontiff or of his lord.

20. Concerning the complex bureaucratic procedures involved in obtaining a benefice through the papal curia in general and the use of appointments *in commendam* in particular, see Pamela Starr, "Rome as the Center of the Universe: Papal Grace and Music Patronage," *Early Music History* 11 (1992): 223–62.

BENEFICIAL PATRONAGE AND THE MUSICIAN

That the beneficial system thus offered very appreciable material advantages to the rich and powerful is clear enough. That the abuses it caused were all too frequent and universally harmful—not only to smaller priories and to parish churches without the protection of a powerful patron but also to great cathedrals and large collegiate churches—is a matter of historical record. Of interest to us here, however, even more than its impact on the institutions and clergy of the church generally, is the manner in which it affected the lives of most composers and a good many singers in the course of the fifteenth and sixteenth centuries. The literate musical culture of this period continued to be dominated, like that of the Middle Ages, by clerics. They alone were trained in church schools to assume the priestly and musical functions required by the liturgy and the sacraments, and they were, as a rule, ordained to holy orders.

Moved by the same ambitions and needs as other clerics of the period, they actively sought to obtain prebends or benefices capable of bringing them prestige and power, thus providing themselves with a handsome living during their active years, security for their old age, and—if they were truly successful—a tidy fortune. Any wealth so accumulated could then be left either to assist younger relatives, or to endow a memorial service to help soften the pains of purgatory, or preferably both. For such men the acquisition of musical skills was but one facet of their education. Their first instruction was in language, as they learned to read and write both the Latin that was the universal language of the Western church and, by extension, their native vernacular. It is likely, in fact, that most skilled calligraphers and copyists of the times, including those who produced musical codices, received their initial training in clerical schools. Most of them also had at least a basic knowledge of mathematics—enough, in any case, to manage the complexities of the liturgical calendar. And some, like Du Fay and Tinctoris, acquired university degrees, usually in law.[21]

Many musicians, then, were prepared by their training to assume one of the major administrative functions required of the dignitaries and canons of a cathedral or a collegiate church. Since those posts were both the most prestigious and the most generously paid, it is only natural that musicians, too, aspired to them and tried to win appointments to the upper levels of the church's hierarchy. At a time when nobility of birth and influential family connections were still the surest and easiest means of access to such important positions, unusual musical gifts

---

21. Du Fay is identified on his funeral monument as "magister" and "baccalarius in decretis," both of which are titles bestowed by the universities of the period; see David Fallows, *Dufay* (London: J. M. Dent, 1982), figure 1 and p. 31. Tinctoris styled himself in a variety of ways that refer to his university studies (in Orléans), including "in legibus licentiatus," "jurisconsultus," and "legum artiumque professor"; see Heinrich Hüschen, "Tinctoris," *The New Grove Dictionary of Music*, 18:837f.

FIGURE 2-6. Guillaume Du Fay's funeral monument (Lille, Musée des Beaux Arts).

could be a crucial factor in the pursuit of a rich prebend, even when abilities in other areas were an important part of the overall picture.[22]

That Du Fay was made a canon of Cambrai Cathedral, where he had begun his clerical career as a choirboy, was due in large part to his reputation as a composer, which had gained him favor both at the papal court and at the ducal courts of Savoy and Burgundy (see Figure 2-6). Nevertheless, besides his direct involvement with the singers of the church, he was responsible for the "Office du four et du vin" and the "Office de l'aumosne"—purchasing bread and wine for the entire clerical community and distributing charitable gifts to the poor—as well as a variety of lesser nonmusical tasks.[23] What is more, he was part of the delegation representing the chapter of Cambrai Cathedral at the Council of Basel in 1438.[24]

Similarly, Johannes Okeghem, who served three successive kings of France as head of the royal chapel choir, undoubtedly owed the exceptional generosity shown him by his noble patrons primarily to his skills and reputation as a musician. In addition, he acquired a series of important prebends that would surely have been out of his reach without their powerful support even though he was trained to exercise at least some of the functions called for by the offices he held. The most noteworthy and lucrative of these was the dignity of treasurer at the church of St. Martin's in Tours, which made him the baron of Châteauneuf—that quarter of the city surrounding the collegiate church. As such, he oversaw police and justice, weights and measures for grains, wines, and other such goods sold in the city, and the collection of taxes from local merchants.[25]

It may also have been nonmusical skills that account for his part in diplomatic

22. For an informative discussion of the difficulties faced by a cleric of the period in the pursuit of his beneficial career, and the role that his musical skills could play in the process, see Christopher Reynolds, "Musical Careers, Ecclesiastical Benefices, and the Example of Johannes Brunet," *Journal of the American Musicological Society* 37 (1984): 49–97.

23. See the discussion by Craig Wright, "Dufay at Cambrai: Discoveries and Revisions," *Journal of the American Musicological Society* 28 (1975): 194–99.

24. See Fallows, *Dufay*, 48–51.

25. For details, see Perkins, "Musical Patronage at the Royal Court of France," 524–26 and 558ff.

missions for the crown and his inclusion among the members of the king's council.[26] Furthermore, a poem written some three decades after his death, and taking its principal argument from his music, describes Okeghem as "most learned in the mathematical arts, arithmetic, geometry, astrology, and likewise music."[27]

Josquin Desprez, finally, spent years in Italy in the service of the Sforza family and the papal chapel and also established his reputation as a composer with Louis XII of France, Philip the Handsome of the Netherlands, and Duke Ercole of Ferrara. Still, he was content to retire to the collegiate church of Condé-sur-l'Escaut in 1504 when he finally succeeded in having himself named provost of the chapter. It is likely, moreover, in view of the nature of that dignity, that his duties there were more administrative than musical.[28]

Josquin and Du Fay were but two representatives—albeit among the most famous—of a veritable army of northern singers and composers who descended on Italy in the fifteenth century with the express intention of capitalizing on their musical gifts and training. These musicians sought first to win a place in the papal choir, or in the service of a wealthy prelate, or at one of the brilliant secular courts established in the city-states of Italy. They then hoped to use the influence of their patron, whether ecclesiastical or secular, to obtain a desirable benefice, preferably in their home diocese. This pattern was repeated many times over by singers and composers trained in the church schools of northern Europe and had a profound effect upon the development of musical styles and genres in the fifteenth and sixteenth centuries.

The aspiring musicians who streamed across the Alps to the south—often with some of their own music and that of respected acquaintances and compatriots in their saddle bags—were exposed there to the works of composers from other regions, as well as to local musical culture. Upon returning to their home institutions, they brought with them new repertory and new musical ideas to be assimilated by the rising generation. This constant circulation of music and musicians from all parts of Europe through Italian centers contributed significantly to the remarkable stylistic stability that is observable in the written tradition of this period. And because the church and monastery schools where music was taught played such an important role in repertorial exchange and stylistic normalization, they clearly warrant our attention.

---

26. See Leeman L. Perkins, "Ockeghem," *The New Grove Dictionary of Music*, 13:490. The composer is identified as "conseillier et premier chappellain du Roy" in a legal document of 1477 relating to his role as the treasurer of St. Martin's in Tours (Tours: Archives Départementales d'Indre-et-Loire, G 418).

27. Paris, Bibliothèque Nationale, MS fonds français 1537, f. 59:

> Okhem tresdocte en art mathematique,
> Aritmeticque, aussy geometrie,
> Astrologie et mesmement musique.

28. Concerning Josquin, see the biographical note below, p. 430, and the further references given there.

⟳ THE CHURCH SCHOOLS ↺

From early medieval times, most churches of any size maintained a school for the boys who served in the choir and at the altar. (Girls were prohibited from serving, as these were functions of the priesthood from which, then as now, women were excluded.) While small rural parishes could offer only the practical necessities, cathedral churches were charged by conciliar decree with teaching a number of young clerics and poor scholars (see pp. 60–61). Most collegiate and cathedral churches must have found compliance with that mandate not only possible but, in fact, indispensable to the success of their daily functions and even to their very survival. For it was generally from among the choirboys that the clergy were recruited and in the choir schools that they acquired the liturgical, curatorial, and administrative background that they would need if they chose to make their life in the church. A boy very literally made his first entry into the priesthood with his acceptance as a chorister in a clerical community. He was supposed to be of legitimate birth—like any aspiring cleric wishing to be ordained—and within about a year on either side of the age of seven at which, according to canon law, he could be admitted to minor orders.[29] His commitment upon entry was for some ten years of unbroken service, and his parents had to agree beforehand not to withdraw him from the community until that term had been completed.[30]

He received his first tonsure (a symbolic shaving of the crown of the head) upon being installed and was usually ordained to minor orders soon thereafter. From the outset he was expected to participate regularly in the liturgical observances of his church. On Sundays and feast days—at the very least—he was to be present in the choir[31] at all of the canonical hours from Matins through Compline and at the various Masses said in the course of the liturgical day (see Figure 2-7).[32] Some chants and readings were reserved for the boys alone, such as the first lesson at Matins and the martyrology at Prime. Choirboys invariably took part in the processions for special feasts or events and often, as well, in the commemorative Offices founded by wills and individual bequests. The older boys, who were more familiar with the ceremo-

29. The minor clerical orders were four: doorkeeper, lector, exorcist, and acolyte. (There is evidence in the published studies that choirboys filled at least three of the functions indicated, but little is said of exorcism.) Concerning the requirements for ordination, see Hay, *Church in Italy in the Fifteenth Century*, 50.

30. For a detailed description of the selection and installation of choirboys in a typical setting, see J.-A. Clerval, *L'ancienne maîtrise de Notre-Dame de Chartres* (Paris, 1899; reprint, Geneva: Minkoff, 1972), 37–51.

31. "Choir" means here the section of the church between the transept and the altar where the singers were gathered for liturgical services.

32. A succinct outline of the Christian liturgy is given by Richard H. Hoppin, *Medieval Music* (New York: Norton, 1978), 92–142.

nial of the church, also served as acolytes, carrying the censer and assisting at the altar during Mass.[33]

The voices of these young singers were heard not only in the sanctuary but also on occasion in the houses of the dignitaries and canons of the chapter. Since prelates of that distinction were often members of the aristocracy and inclined in any case toward the entertainments of the noble courts, the pieces sung for them frequently included secular as well as sacred works. By the fifteenth century, moreover,

FIGURE 2-7.   Choirboy singing among adult singers, detail from the *Volto Santo*, fresco by Amico Aspertini, 1506 (church of San Frediano, Lucca).

most of the music heard in social gatherings of the sort was probably polyphonic.[34]

If the choirboys were to perform all of these tasks successfully, they needed a good deal of training. They had to know enough Latin to pronounce the texts they were to read and sing. They were in fact expected to become as fluent with Latin as possible—speaking and understanding it with some ease—and they were forbidden from using the vernacular in their schoolroom. Grounding in the basics of Latin grammar usually came early on, either from Donatus's *Ars minor* or from Villedieu's *Doctrinale puerorum*.[35] At the same time, they were taught to write, and the more apt among them were introduced to the scribal skills of the professional copyist.

As for music, the choirboys had to sing from memory all the chants for which

33. The duties of the choirboys have been described in detail for Chartres by Clerval, *L'ancienne maîtrise de Notre-Dame de Chartres*, 131–62 and 176–83, and for Rouen by A.-R. Colette, *Histoire de la maîtrise de Rouen*, 11–27. The similarities in usage between those two institutions suggest that there was some consistency from church to church despite the many small differences due to local custom.

34. Concerning the use of choirboys to provide musical amusements in the houses of the secular clergy, see Clerval, *L'ancienne maîtrise de Notre-Dame de Chartres*, 106–9; Colette, *Histoire de la maîtrise de Rouen*, 27–31 and 46–49; and Craig Wright, who cites evidence for such practices at the ducal court of Burgundy and at the Sainte Chapelle in Paris, *Music at the Court of Burgundy, 1364–1419: A Documentary History* (Henryville, Pa.: Institute of Mediaeval Music, 1979), 93 and n. 50.

35. See Otto F. Becker, "The Maîtrise in Northern France and Burgundy during the Fifteenth Century" (Ph.D. diss., George Peabody College for Teachers, 1967), 81–85.

they were specifically responsible and a good many more besides. To begin, if they were planning to make a career in the clergy, they would be expected to sing the entire Psalter by heart.[36] They also had to learn to read notation—not only the plainchant in square neumes, as it was written out in the missals and antiphonaries of the period, but also mensural polyphony, which became more and more a part of the festive celebration of the liturgy from the late fourteenth century on. As in their study of Latin, some bright young choristers familiar with both types of notation were taught the arts of the music copyist together with those of the literary scribe. The most gifted were probably initiated fairly soon into the complexities of poly-phonic composition.[37] Students in the choir schools might also learn to play upon a variety of instruments. Such study usually began with the organ, since it could have a place in the celebration of the liturgy, but secular keyboards were included and in some cases various string and wind instruments.[38] The training given choirboys in the fifteenth century was mainly practical and neither formalized nor in any way standardized. While there is little specific information about the teaching materials and methods then in use, documents of the time reveal which basic subjects were usually covered.

In 1424, in providing funds for the upkeep of four "enfants de choeur" at the Sainte Chapelle in Dijon, Duke Philip the Good of Burgundy decreed that they were to be instructed in "chant, counterpoint, and descant"—meaning both written and impro-vised polyphony in addition to plainchant—and "in the art of grammar so well that they will be able . . . to understand and speak their Latin congruently."[39] These stipu-lations correspond in most details with those of the *Doctrina pro pueris* (*Concerning the Education of Boys*), promulgated in 1408 by Jean Gerson, chancellor of the University of Paris. The author affirms that one master is to give instruction in gram-mar and logic while the "music master will teach the boys . . . principally plainchant, and also counterpoint and other virtuous compositions, but not licentious and lewd songs. Neither shall he occupy them so much with such matters that they fail to make progress in grammar."[40] The inclusion of counterpoint among the subjects for study—revealing, here, since polyphony was barred by statute from Notre Dame in Paris—may

36. Clerval, *L'ancienne maîtrise de Notre-Dame de Chartres*, 105, observes that in the early fourteenth century the "heuriers matiniers" at Chartres (the clerics who actually sang the Mass and the Office on a regular basis) were subject to a fine if unable to sing the Psalter from memory and also had to be able to sing Matins in the dark.

37. See Clerval, *L'ancienne maîtrise de Notre-Dame de Chartres*, 107–9.

38. Evidence for the teaching of instrumental skills in the choir schools is considerable and widespread, if often indirect; see, for example, Clerval, *L'ancienne maîtrise de Notre-Dame de Chartres*, 56–58, and David G. T. Harris, "Musical Education in Tudor Times," *Proceedings of the Musical Association* 65 (1938–39): 109–36.

39. The document of foundation is given by Marix, *Histoire de la musique de la cour de Bourgogne*, 162–63.

40. Gerson's *Doctrina pro pueris Ecclesiae Parisiensis* is cited at length in the original Latin by F.-L. Chartier, *L'ancien chapitre de Notre-Dame de Paris et sa maîtrise* (Paris, 1897; reprint, Geneva: Minkoff, 1971), 66–70.

suggest the frequency with which the boys were expected to sing in a secular setting. Ironically, the terse injunction against teaching the choirboys songs of profane and courtly love is perhaps the surest evidence we have that it was frequently done.

Since the choirboys were never very numerous—four to six, often, in the fifteenth century, eight to ten in the sixteenth—one or two teachers sufficed for their instruction. The usual arrangement was to divide the didactic duties between two masters, one for grammar and another for music, as Gerson suggests. Such a plan had the advantage of keeping the boys under constant supervision—as that author most emphatically recommended—without wearying unduly a single master. There were instances, however, in which one cleric carried the entire load. A single master could probably manage fairly easily half a dozen or so choirboys, but they were usually not the only ones to be taught. According to the Lateran decree of 1179 mentioned earlier, some of the children from the town were to join them in their studies, and others were apparently taken on by the masters for a fee.[41] Although these lay pupils did not participate with the choirboys in the liturgical observances of the church—and therefore had little need to learn plainchant—they probably learned Latin grammar along with the young clerics as well as the fundamentals of music.

In any case, a certain level of musical accomplishment became more and more desirable for the wealthy burgher of the fifteenth century, just as it had been for the nobility for literally hundreds of years. Moreover, the rapid expansion and evident success of commercial music publishing, following the invention of movable metal type in the late fifteenth century, clearly reflects the spread of musical literacy through the middle classes of European society. The teaching of music to nonclerics in the choir schools must have been a major factor in that evolution. It was not until well into the sixteenth century, when urban schools for lay children took up some of the essential functions, that choir schools began to lose their importance for the teaching of music in western Europe.

SECONDARY SCHOOLS AND THE CHURCH

When a choirboy finished his initial term of service, he was usually between sixteen and eighteen years of age. At that point he could return to secular life, or he could apply for holy orders and be ordained—at about eighteen—as a subdeacon. This was a serious step, requiring vows of chastity, and signaled his intention to make a career as a cleric.[42] He could then remain, as many did, with his cathedral or collegiate

---

41. The number of masters usually involved is discussed by Chartier, *L'ancien chapitre de Notre-Dame de Paris*, 65; Colette, *Histoire de la maîtrise de Rouen*, 106 (1425); Clerval, *L'ancienne maîtrise de Notre-Dame de Chartres*, 56–58; and Harris, "Music Education in Tudor Times," 111ff. Harris also mentions the inclusion of scholars from the neighborhood parish in the choir school (ibid.), as do Clerval (65–67) and Colette (106).

42. Concerning the requirements for ordination to the major orders of the Roman Catholic priesthood in this period, see Hay, *Church in Italy in the Fifteenth Century*, 51. He indicates that ordination as a deacon could follow at twenty years, as a priest at twenty-five (except for friars, who could become priests at twenty-two), and as a bishop at thirty.

church, taking his place in the choir as one of the adult singers (usually designated vicars). Or he could become a novice in a monastic order, where his musical duties would have been much the same. In either case, as a younger member of a college of clerics, perhaps aspiring to become a priest and to rise in the church's hierarchy, he would probably have continued with his schooling.

During the fifteenth and sixteenth centuries junior clerics just recently ordained to holy orders still received the instruction they needed in a kind of secondary school. A course of study at that level was offered virtually everywhere by the colleges of clerics attached to cathedrals, collegiate churches, and monastic houses. Historians have yet to explore in detail the educational scope of such schools, in part because of the growth in importance, from the twelfth century on, of the medieval universities. As the luster of these international centers of learning increased over the centuries, the lesser schools have been overshadowed.

Very little is known about them: how numerous they were, where they were located, or how they were related to the choir schools, on the one hand, and the universities, on the other.[43] Not surprisingly, then, the collegiate organization for such a program of studies is ill defined, and it is difficult in some cases to distinguish between a secondary *studium* (as they are sometimes called) and the choir school proper. There is little relevant information, as well, about the subject matter regularly taught there, especially with respect to music.

Since medieval universities grew up mainly around cathedral schools, the basic curriculum for the first years of university study probably reflected the educational practices of the collegial schools in which the universities originated. And since the course of study at the university was centered on the seven liberal arts, this was more than likely so in collegial schools as well.[44] Building on basic skills in reading and writing and whatever groundwork had been laid in the choir school, the students at the collegial school went on to study the subjects of the *trivium*: grammar, logic, and rhetoric. To these were then added the four topics of the *quadrivium*: arithmetic, geometry, astronomy, and music.

The first three of these traditional mathematical studies were a pragmatic necessity; they prepared the clerics to calculate the correct date for Easter, which determined the movable feasts for the entire liturgical year. By contrast, when it came to music, the usefulness of study in the quadrivial tradition—where it is treated in theoretical terms as a branch of mathematics with cosmological meaning—was not so evident. While some of the venerable texts on *musica speculativa*, such as the *De insti-*

43. Like many authors dealing with the educational institutions of the Renaissance, Gaudemet, "Les institutions ecclésiastiques en France," 299ff., seems to assume the existence of schools of the type posited here but does not include them in his discussion.

44. Gaudemet, "Les institutions ecclésiastiques en France," 299ff., asserts that the course of study in monastic and cathedral schools was based upon the *trivium* and the *quadrivium*, and although his comments concern an earlier period, they are presumably no less valid for the fifteenth and sixteenth centuries. (The term "collegial school" will be used here to designate whatever institutional structures were devised by the clerical community of a cathedral, collegiate church, or monastery for the secondary instruction of its members.)

tutione musica of Boethius, may actually have been read, practical theory dealing with plainchant—the scales, notation, and modal categories that were helpful in learning and performing it—was undoubtedly a more urgent need. And, in those churches and monasteries where mensural polyphony had become an important part of the ritual, mensuration and counterpoint must have been studied as well.

Since most of the treatises concerned with such topics were written in Latin until well into the sixteenth century, they would have been accessible only to readers with a knowledge of the language. A number of such books on music may have been intended from the outset for students in the collegial schools. So it is, for example, with a series of short tracts written by the English composer and theorist John Hothby, a graduate of Oxford University who was choirmaster (*precentor*) at the cathedral of St. Martin in Lucca from 1467 until 1486. Hothby also taught in the cathedral school, not only music but also grammar and arithmetic. Significantly, his writings deal with both the speculative and the practical branches of musical study. They include, on the one hand, brief explanations of musical intervals and of the monochord used to measure them and, on the other, concise essays on plainchant, mensuration, and counterpoint.[45]

Similarly, the books on music by Johannes Tinctoris, although written for the most part in the 1470s while he served at the royal court of Naples and had no known connection with a church school, may have been conceived with collegial students and even choirboys in mind. Practical matters relating to both chant and polyphony are at the heart of his work, as the titles alone suggest. And the division of the subjects into separate tracts, each of which deals concisely with a single subject in clear and simple language, points to a didactic purpose of that kind.[46]

At the same time, all members of a clerical community had day-to-day experience with the music of the liturgy, both chant and polyphony. For those involved with the choir, this could mean composition and the copying of music in addition to the routine rehearsal of works to be sung in the sanctuary. At Cambrai Cathedral—where Du Fay supervised for a time the minor vicars who were the heart of the church choir—church records and a surviving repertory of sacred music reveal that mensural polyphony played a major role in the observance of important feasts.[47] Such

---

45. The majority of Hothby's short treatises must have been written for his students in the cathedral school; see Nan Cooke Carpenter, *Music in the Medieval and Renaissance Universities* (Norman: University of Oklahoma Press, 1958), 177–78, and Albert Seay, "Hothby," *The New Grove Dictionary of Music*, 8:729–30. A number of his writings are found in both a Latin and an Italian version, and his longest work in the speculative vein, the *Calliopea legale*, is entirely in the vernacular.

46. Before going to Italy, Tinctoris had instructed the choirboys at the cathedrals of both Orléans (while a student at the university) and Chartres. However, his duties at court also included private instruction for Princess Beatrice of Aragon. See Heinrich Hüschen, "Tinctoris," *The New Grove Dictionary of Music*, 18:837–40, where Tinctoris's treatises are listed in a hypothetical chronological order, each with a brief discussion of its contents. Concerning the dates of their composition, however, see the studies by Ronald Woodley, "Tinctoris's Italian Translations of the Golden Fleece Statutes: A Text and a (Possible) Context," *Early Music History* 8 (1988): 173–244.

47. See Wright, "Dufay at Cambrai," 194–99.

intense use of both chant and polyphony in the ritual of the church reflects a highly sophisticated musical culture. It also implies a serious—if perhaps informal—program of practical and theoretical studies to help the young vicars quickly master the works they would perform and acquire their own compositional skills.

Clerical institutions and courtly chapels of the fifteenth and sixteenth centuries frequently staffed their choirs with singers and composers who had been trained in the schools of cathedrals and collegiate churches of northern France and the Low Countries. Du Fay is himself a case in point. Following his musical apprenticeship at Cambrai, he served in the papal choir and at the court of Duke Amadeus VIII of Savoy. He then returned to Cambrai, law degree in hand, to assume a canonry in the chapter of the church where he had sung as a boy. Many of the most famous composers of the period followed a similar pattern: Busnoys, Okeghem, Josquin, Obrecht, and Mouton, to name just a few. Doubtless many more also owed their musical training to collegial schools. In northern Europe, then, with the notable exception of England, it was the collegial schools and church choirs, rather than the universities, that provided the best training for a career as a singer and composer of mensural polyphony.[48]

⟶◯ THE UNIVERSITIES ◯⟵

Whatever the advantages of the collegial school, a choirboy who had completed his term of service could also go on directly to the university.[49] Once there, he would spend up to six years in the faculty of the arts—studying the seven subjects of the *trivium* and the *quadrivium*—before taking the examination for a bachelor's degree. If he succeeded at that level, he could apply some two years later for a *licentia docendi*, which made of him a master of the arts.[50] Only then could he gain admission to one of the professional faculties, which were traditionally medicine, law (either canon or civil), and theology.[51] Formal instruction in music naturally found a place in the arts faculty, but it was usually restricted to the speculative theory of the *quadrivium* with its emphasis on mathematical proportions and their cosmological implications. The universities of France and England were most conservative in this regard. In

---

48. Of the composers cited here, only Du Fay is known to have had a university degree, and he acquired it after his reputation as a musician was already well established. See Fallows, *Dufay*, 31–35.

49. See, for example, Clerval, *L'ancienne maîtrise de Notre Dame de Chartres*, 67–68.

50. See Gaudemet, "Les institutions ecclésiastiques en France," 299–310, for a description of the consecutive stages through which the student could pass in the course of his university career. It should be noted, however, that the length of time actually spent in acquiring a degree varied widely in accordance with local usage and the previous preparation of the individual student.

51. According to Hastings Rashdall, *The Universities of Europe in the Middle Ages*, ed. F. M. Powicke and A. B. Emden, 3 vols. (Oxford: Oxford University Press, 1936), 1:9, the right to grant degrees in at least one of the higher disciplines named was one of three characteristics that distinguished the universities from lesser schools. The other two were the international—or at least supraregional—composition of its student population and the multiplicity of masters constituting its teaching faculties.

Paris, for example, professors of mathematics continued to give whatever public lectures were offered on music right through the sixteenth century.[52] At Oxford and Cambridge, similarly, the *De musica* of Boethius was the single required text during the entire period.[53]

In Italy and Germany, by contrast, those who lectured in the universities on music were often composers and practical theorists in addition to being well versed in the *quadrivium*. Given their perspective, they were much more inclined than professors of mathematics to go beyond the time-honored texts on *musica speculativa* and to confront the actual problems connected with the performance and composition of plainsong and mensural polyphony. This appears to have happened at the University of Bologna, for example, even though no professorship in music can be documented for its faculties in either the fifteenth or the sixteenth century.[54] The Spaniard Bartolomeo Ramos de Pareia, who had lectured on Boethius at the University of Salamanca before going to Italy, taught publicly at Bologna as well, probably through some sort of informal connection with the university. The practical nature of his teachings is clear from the title of his treatise, *Musica practica*, which was published in Bologna in 1482. His off-center views on a variety of topics—from scales and solmization to the definition of consonant intervals and the use of accidentals (see pp. 990–92)—sparked a spirited public debate, suggesting that in Italy, interest at the time in questions of music theory was surprisingly keen.

Ramos attacked both Boethius and Guido, the twin pillars of medieval theory, impugning by the same token those who defended traditional views. His assault aroused the ire of Hothby and of Nicolaus Burtius, who entered the University of Bologna in 1472 as a student of canon law. Both upheld the writings of the two venerable authorities. Burtius sprang to their defense in his *Musices opusculum* of 1487, which also dealt with counterpoint and mensuration. The debate swirled on through a spate of publications by Giovanni Spataro and Franchinus Gaffurius that continued into the 1520s. Spataro, a composer and theorist who was choirmaster at Bologna's basilica from 1505, took up his pen on behalf of his teacher, Ramos. Gaffurius, who wrote his most important treatises after 1484, while choirmaster and composer at the Milan Cathedral, argued for the more conventional positions (see Figure 2-8).[55]

Music teaching in German universities also had its conservative side. The treatise most often read in studies of the *quadrivium* was the *Musica speculativa* (a summary based on Boethius) by the fourteenth-century mathematician and theorist, Jehan

52. See Carpenter, *Music in the Medieval and Renaissance Universities*, 140–53.
53. See Harris, "Musical Education in Tudor Times," 123–25.
54. See Carpenter, *Music in the Medieval and Renaissance Universities*, 139–40.
55. Concerning the connection of the protagonists in the debate with Italian universities, see Carpenter, *Music in the Medieval and Renaissance Universities*, 128–33 and *passim*. As evidence of the passion questions of music theory could arouse, see Bonnie Blackburn, Edward Lowinsky, and Clement Miller, eds., *A Correspondence of Renaissance Musicians* (Oxford: Oxford University Press, 1991), which follows Spataro's exchanges with Pietro Aron and Giovanni del Lago.

FIGURE 2-8. Franchinus Gaffurius with his students, woodcut from his *Angelicum opus musicae*, Milan, 1508, also used in his *De harmonia musicorum instrumentorum*, Milan, 1518.

des Murs, who had been trained at the University of Paris.[56] Practical theory also received serious scrutiny, however, judging from the books written by a number of fifteenth- and sixteenth-century authors who were connected with German universities. Most of these theorists also directed a church choir and taught in a preparatory school, either during their university study or later, and they were often competent composers as well. Adapting speculative theory to the practical needs of mensuration and counterpoint may sometimes have come about through close ties between a university and the choirs and schools of the local cathedral. Such a link existed in Leipzig and Vienna.

In Vienna there was, in addition, a tie to the musicians at the court of the Holy Roman Emperor, particularly during the rule of Maximilian I (1493–1519). From 1497 onward Conrad Celtis, a humanist scholar and poet, was active with the *Collegium poëtarum et mathematicorum*, established by Maximilian in 1501 within the faculty of the arts. Celtis's presence made the connection between the university and the court unusually direct and fruitful. Students of the university joined with the musicians of the court in presenting his dramas where, in emulation of classical models, both solo and choral song was an integral part of the action. In Heidelberg, similarly, the students of the university were able to serve, either simultaneously or subsequently, in the private chapel of the resident elector of the palatinate.[57]

The University of Cologne, because it was so widely emulated, played a particularly important role in adding practical theory to the musical training of German university students. Among its well-known graduates who wrote didactic treatises on music was Nicolaus Wollick, who studied with Melchior Schanppecher while preparing to become a master of arts. In 1501, the year his degree was awarded, he pub-

---

56. Des Murs is frequently identified by the Latin form of his name, Johannes de Muris. Concerning the use made of his writings in German universities, see Carpenter, *Music in the Medieval and Renaissance Universities*, 224–83. A careful account of the theorist's life and work is given by Lawrence Gushee, "Jehan des Murs," *The New Grove Dictionary of Music*, 9:587–90.

57. Connections between the university and cathedral or court choirs have been tentatively explored for these cities by Carpenter, *Music in the Medieval and Renaissance Universities*, 226–40 and 256–58.

lished his *Opus aureum musicae*, which contains, in addition to a section on plain-chant, a lengthy discussion of polyphonic composition written by Schanppecher, the first to appear in a book of that nature in Germany. After finishing his theological studies in 1507, Wollick spent a year as master of the boys at Metz Cathedral before going on to Paris, where he published an expanded revision of his work in 1509.

Johannes Cochlaeus, similarly, became a master of arts at Cologne in 1507. While still a student he published three editions of his *Musica*, which deals in a practical manner with the elements of music: plainsong, solmization, and the modes. He was then engaged as rector of the school of St. Lorenz in Nuremberg, where he reworked his treatise for the boys in the school, adding to it a section on mensuration and counterpoint. In 1511 he published the revised version under the title *Tetrachordum musices*.[58]

While a student at Cologne from 1506 to 1510 the Swiss poet and humanist Heinrich Glarean studied music with Cochlaeus. After settling in Basel in 1514 Glarean directed a boarding school based on the new humanistic model, with a course of study centered on Latin literature and Greek grammar. Music was also included, however, and Glarean may have written his *Isagoge in musicen* of 1516—which deals with the elements of music, solmization, and the eight modes—to meet the needs of his students. In 1529 he left Basel, where he had also lectured at the university, to become professor of poetry and later of theology at the university in Freiburg im Briesgau. Not only did he teach the humanistic disciplines throughout his career, he also knew some of the most important humanist scholars of his day. Shortly after arriving in Basel, he met Erasmus, who was to become a powerful influence in both his intellectual development and his religious life, and during a visit to Paris in 1517, he became acquainted with Guillaume Budé and others.

Glarean was one of many who were attracted to the new humanistic learning that was then being introduced in northern Europe by scholars who had studied in Italy. Rudolph Agricola, for example, had preceded him at Cologne already in the 1460s, and Conrad Celtis (who later followed Agricola to Heidelberg) in the 1470s. Glarean's interest in music drew him to a study of ancient texts, many of which were just then being brought to light. These writings deal with music either as a mathematical science or more directly as a significant element in the affective and ethical life of man. They led Glarean to the original formulation of the modes in six pairs (instead of the usual four) that formed the basis for his *Dodecachordon* of 1547. That his system is based upon the writings of the ancients reveals the extent to which classical scholarship was influencing the musical thought of his age. At the same time, the practical approach of the German universities is evident in the lengthy discussion, at the end of his treatise, that applies modal concepts to the mensural polyphony of his time (see pp. 1005–6).[59]

---

58. On music at the University of Cologne in the late fifteenth and early sixteenth centuries, see Carpenter, *Music in the Medieval and Renaissance Universities*, 240–49.
59. See Carpenter, *Music in the Medieval and Renaissance Universities*, 244–47, and cf. Clement A. Miller, "Glarean," *The New Grove Dictionary of Music*, 7:422–24.

In 1502 Frederick the Wise, the elector of Saxony, founded a new university in Wittenberg, his electoral seat, and invited Martin Luther to teach there. He thus laid the foundations for what was to become the intellectual center of the Protestant Reformation. Significantly, Luther saw music not merely as an acceptable form of recreation but even more as a powerful and positive force in communal worship. It is hardly surprising, therefore, that the combination of speculative theory and practical training that was typical of German universities generally was particularly marked in Wittenberg. There was no known professorship in music, but the *Musica* of Jehan des Murs was required reading for the master's degree—a sure indication that formal instruction in the discipline was highly conservative and squarely in the tradition of the *quadrivium*. However, there were close ties between the court chapel and the university, like those that obtained in Vienna and Heidelberg. And the extent to which practical instruction in music was pursued on an informal basis is evident from the number of university alumni who wrote treatises on music for use in the schools of the Reformation.

The pattern was set by Adam of Fulda, Frederick's chapelmaster. As early as 1490 he wrote a treatise dealing with both chant and polyphony—in addition to the traditional *musica speculativa*—and later apparently became the first to teach music at the newly founded university. He was followed in that role by the itinerant scholar Andreas Ornithoparchus, who attended the University of Wittenberg briefly in 1516 and published his *Musicae activae micrologus* in Leipzig the following year. His book was essentially practical in its approach, including sections on plainsong, mensuration, and counterpoint, as was by then becoming customary. Nikolaus Listenius was named a master of arts in 1531, and Heinrich Faber earned the same degree in 1545. Both of them wrote popular texts on music for students in secondary schools like those in which they taught. The colorful Adrianus Petit Coclico also offered private instruction in music at the university for some seven years and then published his own didactic manual, *Compendium musices*, in 1552.[60]

The treatises published by these authors serve as an important means for gauging the kind of practical music teaching that took place generally in German universities. In addition, they clearly indicate the emphasis given to music in the humanistically oriented secondary schools founded by the Reformers, and they help explain the flourishing, if conservative, musical culture of Germany in the sixteenth century. The printing presses in centers such as Mainz, Nuremberg, and of course Wittenberg itself turned out a steady stream of books on music as well as compositions with a specific didactic purpose. They also published sophisticated mensural polyphony by Josquin Desprez and other masters of the same generation and region, especially those who were most admired by Luther and his associates at Wittenberg.

Italy and Germany were the only countries in which the study of music at the university as both art and science gave rise to a sizable body of theoretical writings, but the teaching was everywhere much the same. Students could gain practical instruc-

---

60. See Carpenter, *Music in the Medieval and Renaissance Universities*, 260–71.

tion by singing in the choir of a church linked with a university or could learn from a musician who served a local ruler. Or they could arrange for private coaching, especially in instrumental skills. The social structure of the schools themselves made it easy to acquire musical competencies in that way even though—or perhaps precisely because—a conservative curriculum generally limited formal lectures to the traditional authors of the *quadrivium.*

The cosmopolitan community of the *studium generale* was divided first of all into nations. These owed their existence at the outset to the natural tendency of students who had come from many different areas—some of them far distant—to band together by region for mutual protection and support. In time, however, the nations became a means of organizing the large numbers of students for purposes of representation and governance within the corporate structure of the medieval university.[61] A student was assigned to an appropriate nation upon matriculation and stayed with it until he was ready to begin study with one of the professional faculties. In addition, most students were affiliated with a college, then as now a community of scholars (often, once again, from a single region) who shared a residence funded by a wealthy benefactor and were governed, as a rule, by a principal or master. Although originally created simply as places of residence, by the fifteenth century many colleges had taken on important teaching functions as well. In France and England in particular the college offered informal tutoring and, eventually, formal lectures for its residents and associates.[62]

Within each nation and college, as in the university generally, the important events that punctuated the academic year and the student's career were marked by celebrations in which music played a role. At solemn convocations of students and faculty, lengthy processions were held (as they still are), usually to the sound of trumpets and drums or woodwind bands. The awarding of degrees occasioned special Masses and Offices, and some festive celebrations were even accompanied by dancing. There was also a good deal of informal music making on a daily basis—students singing secular songs and playing instruments—bringing on many complaints and attempts to restrict it to hours and places that would not interfere seriously with studies and sleep.[63]

---

61. For example, by 1432 there were three Italian and sixteen non-Italian nations at the University of Bologna, each of which was a distinct corporation with its own statutes, officers, and meetings. In Paris, by contrast, the faculty of the arts was divided, somewhat arbitrarily, into four nations: the French (which included Italians, Spaniards, and Asians), the Normans, the Picards, and the English (renamed the German nation during the Hundred Years' War and comprising also the Scotch, Irish, Scandinavians, Hungarians, Poles, and Bohemians). See Rashdall, *Universities of Europe in the Middle Ages,* 1:184–85 and 312–21.

62. Concerning the role of the colleges, see Rashdall, *Universities of Europe in the Middle Ages,* 1:199–205 and 478–517.

63. Carpenter, *Music in Medieval and Renaissance Universities,* gives examples of the academic occasions and the didactic, social, and recreational activities involving music in connection with each of the universities examined in her study.

THE ENGLISH UNIVERSITIES

The dichotomy within the university between formal lectures on *musica speculativa*, on the one hand, and noncurricular and private instruction in practical theory and performance skills, on the other, is especially striking in the English universities, Oxford and Cambridge. There the corporate structure of the college was closer to the model of the cathedral or collegiate church than it was on the Continent. It included a group of choirboys (called choristers in England) who sang the daily liturgy in the college chapel in both plainsong and polyphony together with some of the younger scholars. The statutes drawn up for the foundation of Magdalen College in 1479, for example, called for four priests, eight chaplains, and sixteen choristers to celebrate divine services, and the articles specify that both priests and clerics must be competently taught to read and to sing. One of them was in fact to be expert enough to instruct the choir in both chant and "other" types of song.

At King's College, Cambridge, similarly, there was a *precentor* who was to instruct and direct the choir and, in addition, an organist and a teacher for the choristers. By the fifteenth century a regularly appointed organist for the college chapel was clearly the rule rather than the exception; he was expected to teach the singers to play keyboard instruments and to play himself as needed in the celebration of the liturgy.[64] The chapel choir thus created an immediate need for practical instruction and furnished, at the same time, a context in which it could be offered. For students not admitted to the choir there were, of course, the usual opportunities to acquire musical skills with private teachers.

The English universities were unique not only for including in their collegiate structures a full-fledged choir for liturgical celebration but also in granting degrees in music at both the baccalaureate and the doctoral levels. In doing so they considered both the book learning of the *quadrivium* and the practical knowledge and experience of performers and composers. At Oxford those who earned a bachelor's degree in music were entitled to lecture on "any of the Musical Books of Boethius." But when Richard Ede applied for the baccalaureate in 1507, it was specified that he had spent ten years in the study of music outside the university. His petition was granted on the condition that he compose a (polyphonic) Mass and antiphon to be sung on the day of his admission. At Cambridge the earliest record of a bachelor's in music dates from 1463–64. There, too, both speculative theory and practical experience were cited in the awarding of degrees, and in some cases the composition of a polyphonic work was likewise required.[65]

64. Regarding these and other colleges at both Oxford and Cambridge that maintained a choir comprising clerks and choristers with a *precentor*, an organist to direct and instruct the choir, and sometimes a master for the choristers, see Carpenter, *Music in the Medieval and Renaissance Universities*, 166–70 and 190–93.

65. With regard to the degrees in music granted by the two English universities, see Carpenter, *Music in the Medieval and Renaissance Universities*, 159–66, 200–208, and 315–16; she also cites the names of those who received them and the dates of admission.

In England, because practical musical skills were needed to obtain a university degree, many of the best composers and keyboard players of the fifteenth and sixteenth centuries were affiliated at some point with Oxford or Cambridge. At the same time, the ties between the collegiate chapels at the universities and the performing groups dependent upon the patronage of the royal court—the king's private chapel in particular—naturally grew closer. These developments are noteworthy, especially since they contrast so clearly with the general pattern in France and Italy, where collegial schools and choirs played a much greater part.

CONCLUSIONS

It is clear, then, that the universities of western Europe, like the choir and collegial schools, played a major role in fostering the study of practical music theory and in teaching performing skills and the techniques of musical composition. Surprisingly, this came about even though formal lectures were limited nearly everywhere to *musica speculativa* in the tradition of the *quadrivium*. That kind of training proved significant in the long run, however, because the study of music as a mathematical science kept alive an important intellectual tradition that sustained and stimulated those who were drawn to the problems of practical theory in the fifteenth and sixteenth centuries. During most of that period, virtually every important theorist had a university connection, and it is clear—despite the rigid curriculum and our lack of specific information on informal music making and private teaching—that the study of music within the university nourished the theoretical writing of the period, providing both formal models and a source for many of the age's most seminal ideas.

Moreover, as humanistic scholarship awoke renewed interest in the texts of Greek and Roman antiquity, a vital new impetus was given to studying the theoretical basis for the musical culture of the period. And, as we shall see, a growing understanding of the ancient precepts and esthetic views, together with new interpretations of those ideas, was to have a powerful effect upon the development of musical style.[66]

---

66. The impact of the universities upon the musical culture of the Renaissance has been briefly but effectively characterized by Carpenter, *Music in the Medieval and Renaissance Universities*, 329–71.

CHAPTER 3

Music at the Secular Courts

INTRODUCTION

The courts of Renaissance Europe contained within themselves a microcosm of the musical activity of the times, both sacred and secular. There was, almost always, a small chapter or college of clerics to care for the spiritual life of the courtly community and to celebrate the liturgy. In addition, a small group of instrumentalists and singers provided music for private recreation and for public events of all kinds from the ostentatious display intended to impress important visitors to preparations for battle. The musicians attached to a court were relatively few in number, and because they were specially privileged and handsomely remunerated, their positions were highly coveted. Conversely, magnates competed among themselves for the most skilled performers and gifted composers, making the secular courts a crucial source of musical patronage in the fifteenth and sixteenth centuries.

As musicians of all kinds vied for the wealth and protection that service with a powerful ruler could bring, they strove for the highest standards and attempted to master the compositional styles and techniques most in favor. Moreover, because the best of them moved from court to court and country to country, they helped break down the regional insularity of the late Middle Ages. Composers of exceptional ability and experience thus came to be known over a wide geographical area. They shaped the genres and styles that predominated throughout western Europe by the end of the fifteenth century, and the extraordinary dissemination of their works gave certain musical styles an international character not previously seen. In this manner, courtly fashions in music exercised a seminal influence on the stylistic development of music throughout the Renaissance.

Courtly society's part in defining taste and setting standards is most evident initially for mensural polyphony (in the written tradition). However, as instrumental skills grew and virtuoso players assumed greater importance as performers and teachers, their repertories were written down with increasing frequency, first for the use of their patrons and pupils and then for the wider audience served by the first commercial music publishers. Consequently, as the instrumental tradition of the period emerges as part of the historical record, it too gives evidence of the crucial role played by courtly patronage in its stylistic evolution.

As a result, secular musicians who lived from their artistry as performers emulated the cleric-singers trained in the church, acquiring the musical literacy needed to write down their compositions—with all that implied for the marketing of their creative work and the permanence of their reputations. Before the end of the sixteenth century, instrumental musicians of the court were organized in most places, in imitation of the clerics of the court chapel, in a hierarchy determined by the type of instrument played and the function filled. Let us examine, therefore, the administrative structure of that model.

THE CHAPEL

European society remained essentially and almost monolithically Christian through the Renaissance and well beyond. As we have seen, moreover, the church's administrative structures and those of secular governments were linked in a variety of ways. Ever since Charlemagne, magnates had been attempting to establish their right to rule as divinely ordained while prelates reigned as feudal lords over large territories and important cities. Virtually every secular court included officers recruited from the clerical ranks to perform a variety of administrative tasks from advising the ruler as a member of his council to drafting and copying decrees, letters, and other official documents. More importantly, in the view of the church, they also provided religious instruction and the Christian sacraments for the magnate and his household.

Clerics with religious duties are of primary interest in the present context, some of whom had primarily executive responsibilities while others were occupied mainly with the never-ending round of liturgical observances. The almoner and the confessor had important administrative functions in courtly governance, some of which went well beyond what their titles would imply. At the court of France, the confessor, in addition to his ministerial tasks, was expected to prevent clerics in the king's service from cumulating ecclesiastical benefices with wages from the royal treasury. He also saw to the speedy provision of prebends for such clerics in order to ease as much as possible the burden on the resources of the state. The almoner distributed noble largess, providing food and clothing for the needy and supervising the charitable institutions within his lord's jurisdiction. This could be a considerable burden, requiring the assistance of numerous chaplains, servants, and even a procurator for legal problems.[1] Such men had to be highly placed in the hierarchy of the church to be truly effective and

1. For a discussion of the functions of the confessor and the almoner at the royal court of France, see Jean Gaudemet, "Les institutions ecclésiastiques en France du milieu du XIIe au début du XIVe siècle," in *Histoire des institutions françaises au moyen age*, vol. 3, *Institutions ecclésiastiques*, ed. Ferdinand Lot and Robert Fawtier (Paris: Presses universitaires de France, 1962), 427f.; the evidence indicates that a similar pattern was followed elsewhere.

so were frequently given a bishopric or some similarly powerful position.

The clerics who held liturgical services for the magnate and his household formed a largely independent and self-contained entity. Their functions were like those of the specially designated clerics who were affiliated with a chapel in a cathedral or a collegiate church and celebrated the commemorative Masses and Offices established by its founders and by private endowments; they served in the same way in the private chapel of their ruler. Because the courts of the period were often itinerant, moving from one residence to another within their own territories and visiting on occasion the domains of neighboring lords as well, the term "chapel" signified not so much the room or building in which services could be held (even though that was a current meaning) as the choir of clerics who officiated for the church, regardless of where the liturgy was celebrated.[2]

Heading the group was the chapelmaster (*magister capellae*), or first chaplain, who was most often selected for his organizational abilities and had usually been ordained a priest at the time of his appointment.[3] In a few rare instances musical competencies may have taken precedence over other qualifications, but even then the exception was possible only because the musician was also a reasonably capable administrator. At the royal court of France, Johannes Okeghem—who was only a subdeacon when appointed but by far the most distinguished composer associated with the chapel in the fifteenth century—served three successive monarchs over a period of some forty years as first chaplain. Shortly after he entered royal service, the king named him to the lucrative and prestigious dignity of treasurer of the church of St. Martin in Tours, perhaps because of his learning and his personal qualities as much as his musical gifts, and by the end of his career he was referred to in official documents as a member of the king's council.[4]

During the sixteenth century, when most court chapels continued to grow in size and in importance as vehicles of cultural display, the chapelmaster was most often still a high-ranking prelate who left the day-to-day supervision of the chapel to a musician of lesser rank. In 1532, at the court of Francis I, the *maître de chapelle* was the cardinal of Tournon and archbishop of Bourges, whereas the liturgical and musical functions of the chapel were the direct responsibility of the *sous-maître*, the composer Claudin de Sermisy.[5] Similarly, at the Austrian court of Maximilian I, the humanist scholar (and

2. Concerning the various meanings attached to the word "chapel" from the seventh through the sixteenth centuries and the emergence of the concept of a chapel as a body of clerics and musicians with responsibility for the liturgy, see Adele Poindexter, "Chapel," *The New Grove Dictionary of Music,* 4:148–51.

3. Such was the case, for example, at the ducal court of Burgundy; see Craig Wright, *Music at the Court of Burgundy, 1364–1419: A Documentary History* (Henryville, Pa.: Institute of Mediaeval Music, 1979), 75–76.

4. Regarding Okeghem's role as first chaplain, see Leeman L. Perkins, "Musical Patronage at the Royal Court of France under Charles VII and Louis XI (1422–83)," *Journal of the American Musicological Society* 37 (1984): 522.

5. See Hans M. Schletterer, *Geschichte der Hofcappelle der französischen Könige* (Berlin: R. Damköhler, 1884), 224; for a more recent assessment of the French royal chapel under Francis I, see John T. Brobeck, "Musical Patronage in the Royal Chapel of France under Francis I (r. 1515–1547)," *Journal of the American Musicological Society* 48 (1995): 187–239.

later bishop of Vienna) Georg Slatkonia became chapelmaster in 1498.[6] Numerous other such instances could be cited, including that of the papal chapel in Rome.

The clerics of the court chapel are often identified in pay registers either by their ecclesiastical status or their particular functions, or both. At the courts of both France and Burgundy, a distinction was made in the fifteenth century based on clerical rank. The personnel of the Burgundian chapel was consistently divided between chaplains and clerks with a lower rate of pay for the latter, who had not been ordained as priests.[7] In the accounts of the French royal chapel, similarly, the chaplains identified as priests were entered before those who were merely *chapelains*, although there was generally no difference in salary. In the 1450s, however, the French royal chapel also maintained a pair of chaplains with a smaller salary who were listed separately, suggesting that they are not to be counted with the singers. They may have celebrated instead "low" Masses, those simply spoken rather than sung. By the 1460s there was usually, in addition, a pair of "clercs" who were likewise paid at a lower rate.[8]

In addition to their chaplains—as many as fifteen and rarely fewer than ten—and as many as five or six clerks, both of these chapels also had one or more "butlers" (*sommeliers*). The latter functioned as sacristans or vergers, looking after the books, vessels, vestments, and decorative hangings used in the celebration of the liturgy, and their remuneration was even more modest still. At the court of Burgundy there were also payments in the 1460s for a "quartermaster" (*fourrier*), who looked after the horses that transported the chapel's furnishings and provided for lodgings where required.[9]

The total personnel of the Burgundian ducal chapel varied between about twenty-one or twenty-two and twenty-five or twenty-six under Philip the Good (from 1436 until 1470), while at the French royal court the numbers were slightly smaller during the same period, usually between fifteen and eighteen.[10] Despite the distinctions

6. See Martin Picker, "Habsburg," *The New Grove Dictionary of Music*, 8:12; cf. above, p. 82.

7. See Wright, *Music at the Court of Burgundy*, 57–61.

8. It is often difficult to determine from payment records, which are virtually the sole source of information about the personnel of princely chapels, the different functions filled by the persons listed. There is some evidence, nonetheless, that the chapel of the royal French court traditionally included both singers (*chapelains et chantres*) and "other chaplains," who said Masses and Offices when circumstances did not require—or allow—them to be sung. See Perkins, "Musical Patronage at the Royal Court of France," 546–57.

9. A detailed description of the duties of the various functionaries at the Burgundian chapel was drawn up by Duke Charles in 1469; see the study by David Fallows, "Specific Information on the Ensembles for Composed Polyphony," in *Studies in the Performance of Late Medieval Music*, ed. Stanley Boorman (Cambridge: Cambridge University Press, 1983), 145–59, and cf. Jeanne Marix, *Histoire de la musique de la cour de Bourgogne* (Strasbourg: Heitz, 1939; reprint, Geneva: Minkoff, 1972) 128–31 and *passim*, where the notation and illumination of musical manuscripts are specifically mentioned among the tasks accomplished by the clerics of the chapel.

10. Lists of the chapel personnel employed at the Burgundian court during the reign of Philip the Good have been published by Marix, *Histoire de la musique de la cour de Bourgogne*, 242–63; a year-by-year summary for the royal French court between 1451 and 1475 is found in Perkins, "Musical Patronage at the Royal Court of France," 553–57.

of status and salary, all of those named were probably able to sing liturgical plain-chant, and most of them must have been schooled in polyphony as well. Both clerks and butlers were at times ordained priests, and they could advance from either position to a place among the chaplain-singers. Moreover, a number of fifteenth-century sources carry polyphonic compositions under names that appear on the Burgundian chapel rolls either as clerks or as butlers.[11]

In the fifteenth century, choirboys do not appear as regular members of the court chapel in either Burgundy or France. There is neither trace nor mention of them in the archives of the royal court for that period, although choirboys had figured among the personnel of the chapel earlier. The first Valois dukes of Burgundy did provide for the training of a small group of boys, most of whom subsequently took a place among the clerks and chaplains of the chapel, but these choristers led a separate existence and sang with the adults only on rare occasions. Under John the Fearless the choirboys being trained for service at the Burgundian court usually resided in Paris.

In 1406 three boys were entrusted to the care of Johannes Tapissier, a composer and pedagogue who maintained a school for music in that city. By 1409 their numbers had grown to five and their teacher was a certain Pierre Chorrot, a priest "residing in Paris." He was replaced in 1412 by Nicolas Grenon, a competent singer and composer, who was often in the company of his ducal patron in Flanders over the next six years and eventually joined the chaplains of the Burgundian court. At the death of Duke John in 1419 the three choirboys were once again "students in Paris."[12]

The instruction they received there was undoubtedly much like that given in the choir schools of cathedrals and collegiate churches. It is possible that one or more of their instructors—including Tapissier—were selected because they were already teaching the boys at a church that would allow them to take on the choirboys of the ducal chapel as private pupils. These pedagogues were obviously familiar with the kind of training provided for young choristers within the framework of the church; all three of them had been so schooled themselves, and Grenon was master of the boys at both Laon and Cambrai before he entered ducal service.[13]

Under the rule of Philip the Good the choirboys of the ducal chapel may have been more frequently in residence at the court, but references to the master charged with their tutelage cease in 1428. It would appear that the duke had by then decided to leave the education of young clerics who might one day serve in his chapel choir to the ecclesiastical institutions within his domains. In 1425 he endowed both

11. Both Petit Jehan Charvet and Guillaume Ruby were among the *clercs* of the chapel in the 1430s and 1440s. Ruby later joined the ranks of the chaplains, while Jehan Charvet became the first *sommelier*, and by 1461 Robert Morton was one of five clerks; see Marix, *Histoire de la musique de la cour de Bourgogne*, 242–63. All three are credited with chansons in the "Mellon Chansonnier," and Morton was one of the better-known composers of his generation.

12. See Wright, *Music at the Court of Burgundy*, 92–96, and Marix, *Histoire de la musique de la cour de Bourgogne*, 135–43.

13. See Craig Wright, "Grenon," *The New Grove Dictionary of Music*, 7:702.

the Sainte Chapelle in Dijon and the church of Saint Peter in Lille with a foundation to provide for the maintenance and instruction of four choirboys, who were to be taught—as we have seen—grammar, plainchant, counterpoint, and discant.[14]

If choirboys were not a regular part of the chapel during the fifteenth century at courts like those of France and Burgundy, who, then, usually sang the treble part or parts, whether for sacred or for secular works? It has been suggested that the clerks of the Burgundian chapel were in fact choirboys, at least from 1415 to 1419.[15] This is certainly conceivable, as the *clercs* were clearly the junior members of that body, and some of them may have joined it before their voices had changed. But even if

this were so during the years in question—which does not seem highly likely—it was clearly not so later on. Robert Morton was listed as a clerk for some fifteen years, starting in 1457, and a certain Claude le Petit, also a clerk, is identified as a *tenoriste*—not a singer in the treble range.[16] What is more, no choirboys are included in the miniature dating from the 1460s in which Duke Philip is depicted in his private chapel hearing a Mass sung by clerics in his service (see Figure 3-1).

Miniaturists usually compressed and simplified scenes such as this in order to fit them into a small space; in this case the numerous courtiers of the ducal household were reduced to the four at the edge of the picture. Within the limits of that artistic convention, the representation of the clerics of the ducal chapel— two priests serving at the altar, seven chaplains and clerks singing from an apparently polyphonic choirbook, and two others (the

FIGURE 3-1. Philip the Good at Mass, by a student of Jean le Tavernier (?), in *Traité sur l'oraison dominicale* (Brussels, Bibliothèque Royale de Belgique, Cabinet des MSS, No. 9092, f. 9).

---

14. See Marix, *Histoire de la musique de la cour de Bourgogne*, 160–64; cf. above, pp. 74–76.

15. The possibility has been raised by Wright, *Music at the Court of Burgundy*, 101 and 212–34.

16. Concerning Morton, see Allan Atlas, ed., *Robert Morton: The Collected Works* (New York: Broude Brothers, 1981), xvii–xxii, and cf. Marix, *Histoire de la musique de la cour de Bourgogne*, 254–62.

butlers?) seated nearby—is undoubtedly accurate in its essentials. The actual numbers shown are fewer than were supposed to be present when polyphony was sung, however; the ordinance of 1469 cited earlier called for at least fourteen singers (six high voices, three tenors, three basses, and two altos) for the performance of part-music.[17] Similarly, the painting showing Christmas Mass at the court of John, duke of Berry—a celebration at which polyphony was most likely heard—includes no choirboys and may reflect the usual practice there, even though four young choristers were attached to John's service early in the fifteenth century.[18]

There is likewise no evidence for the presence of choirboys in the royal chapel of France during the entire course of the fifteenth century. As late as 1532, when Francis I is depicted listening to Mass in an engraving published by the Parisian music publisher Pierre Attaingnant, the chapel choir is without youthful choristers (see Figure 3-2). Curiously, however, the assistant chapelmaster was paid a substantial sum in that same year for the care and education of eight to ten boys.[19] The choir-

Figure 3-2. Francis I at Mass (woodcut from Attaingnant, *Primus liber viginti missarum musicalium*, 1532).

17. See Fallows, "Specific Information on the Ensembles for Composed Polyphony," 110–17, who concludes that the high voices of the Burgundian court chapel were all adult singers.
18. The choirboys of Duke John are cited by Wright, *Music at the Court of Burgundy*, 92.
19. See Schletterer, *Geschichte der Hofcappelle*, who lists the personnel of the royal chapel for the year 1532–33 (Beilage A, pp. 224–25); included are eight adult altos (*hautes-contres*) and only one soprano (*dessus*), but a number of the singers are not identified as to voice range.

boys may have spent most of their time with their schooling, as was earlier the case at the ducal court of Burgundy, and only rarely joined the chapel choir in performance. One can conclude in any case—however tentatively—that adult sopranos and altos usually sang the treble parts in chapel choirs like those at the courts of France and Burgundy (just as male countertenors often do in present-day performances) during much of the fifteenth century and on into the sixteenth as well.

Even in the fifteenth century, however, courtly chapels were not limited everywhere to adult clerics. The English chapel royal maintained a group of choirboys as part of its regular organization more or less from its formal inception early in the fourteenth century. In this respect, as in others, it adhered more closely than on the Continent to the practice of the cathedral and collegiate churches upon which courtly chapels were modeled. The choristers (as the choirboys are called in England) in the chapel royal were as many as sixteen at the close of the reign of Henry V (1421–22), but the average during most of the fifteenth century was about ten. The boys were instructed by one of the adult musicians of the chapel, and a number of those who so served—men such as John Plummer, Gilbert Banester, and William Cornysh—were also distinguished composers.

In other respects the English chapel royal was similar to its Continental counterparts in France and Burgundy although usually somewhat larger. Under Henry V it counted as many as thirty-two adult singers, and during the remainder of the fifteenth century it numbered at times as many as thirty-six and seldom fewer than twenty-six. These clerics were divided between the chaplains—presumably those who had been ordained priests, about a third of the total—and the clerks or "gentleman clerks," who were selected primarily for the quality of their voices (see Figure 3-3). As in princely chapels elsewhere, not all of the men were expected to attend every service celebrated for the royal household, but the choristers were apparently continuously at court and participated regularly in the performance of both chant and polyphony.[20]

The tendency from the late fifteenth century into the sixteenth was toward somewhat larger choirs, both in churches and in courtly chapels, and more and more of the singers were routinely trained to perform polyphony. A modest increase in the size of the royal French chapel during the rule of Francis I is indicative of the general trend. Instead of the fewer than twenty chaplains on the roles in the fifteenth century, or the twenty-two at his accession in 1515, by 1532 the king had twenty-four adult singers in his service—all capable of singing polyphony since they are frequently identified by voice part—without counting the acting chapelmaster, the butler, the quartermaster, and some eight to ten choirboys. There were, in addition, two

---

20. Regarding the English chapel royal, see the discussion by Frank L. Harrison, *Music in Medieval Britain*, 2d ed. (London: Routledge and Kegan Paul, 1963), 21–24, and the more recent survey by Roger Bowers, "London," *The New Grove Dictionary of Music*, 11:151–52 (sec. 2, "Music at Court"). (Minor discrepancies in the numbers given by these two authors are presumably to be explained by the more recent research reflected in the later article.)

FIGURE 3-3.   Members of the Chapel Royal in procession for the death of Elizabeth I (London, British Library, MS Add. 35324, f. 31ᵛ).

chaplains to officiate at high (sung) Mass and a newly constituted choir of twelve clerics who sang only plainchant.[21]

At the English chapel royal, by contrast, the extraordinary number of singers enlisted in the choir in the late fifteenth century was never surpassed. After the glory days under Henry VI (1422–61) and Edward IV (1461–83), when the chapel musicians counted sporadically as many as thirty-six adults and ten choristers, the numbers stabilized at an average of thirty-two men and twelve children and so remained until virtually the end of the sixteenth century.[22] Even then its size represented an ideal to be emulated; a large courtly chapel rarely exceeded thirty to thirty-five adult singers (as compared to some twenty to twenty-five for most church choirs).[23]

DUTIES AND PERQUISITES OF CHAPEL MUSICIANS

A princely chapel had an unremittingly busy schedule of liturgical and musical duties. At the court of Burgundy ducal decree established that not only Mass but also Vespers and the Lesser Hours were to be celebrated on a daily basis,[24] and a similar practice was undoubtedly followed at the royal court of France and elsewhere. Most rulers of the period routinely heard Mass daily and usually attended Vespers and Matins as well on important feast days. Present or not, they would have wanted those Offices observed on their behalf as frequently as possible. A good deal of the liturgical activity at court may have been fairly perfunctory; on ferial days (when no special celebration was called for) the prescribed texts—even those of the Mass—could be sung in plainchant or, in some instances, simply read. In such circumstances services would not have required the participation of the entire chapel, and the clerics must have divided the indispensable responsibilities among themselves, as was usually done

21. See Schletterer, *Geschichte der Hofcappelle*, 224–26; cf. Brobeck, "Musical Patronage in the Royal Chapel," 208–18.
22. See Bowers, "London," *The New Grove Dictionary of Music*, 11:151–53.
23. See Adele Poindexter, "Chapel," *The New Grove Dictionary of Music*, 4:149–50.
24. For particulars, see Wright, *Music at the Court of Burgundy*, 70.

in any cathedral or collegiate church. It is important to remember that even when the magnate and his court were present for a solemn celebration of the liturgy, plain-chant would have had a greater part in the service than polyphony.

From mid-fifteenth century on, however, part-music was an increasingly important part of the liturgical services, especially Mass and Vespers. It was undoubtedly sung at courts like those of France and Burgundy on Sundays and all important feast days. But even on those occasions, all the singers of the chapel did not necessarily join forces for the performance. Mensural polyphony remained a soloistic art through much of the fifteenth century. Many works were undoubtedly sung with several singers to a part, especially during its final decades, as was the case at the ducal court of Burgundy (see pp. 93–94). Still, it must not have been unusual in the smaller chapels—or for that matter in some of the larger ones—to hear polyphonic works sung with no more than one or two voices for each part.

Regardless of how the clerics of the chapel divided up their liturgical duties, their involvement with the music made at court clearly did not end with the daily round of services. The composers among them set polyphonically secular poetry as well as the sacred texts of Mass and motet. As we have seen, their training in the choir and collegiate schools generally included learning to play instruments, not only the organ, which had its place in the chapel, but also strings and winds with pronounced secular connotations. The miniaturist who painted the double portrait of Guillaume Du Fay and Gilles Binchoys depicted each of them with what he judged to be an appropriate instrument, relying on associations that were commonly understood. Du Fay, priest, canon, and master of laws, stands next to a portative organ, while Binchoys, soldier and chapel musician at the Burgundian court, leans lightly on a harp, apparently a favorite instrument of the nobles for moments of private recreation (see Figure 3-4).[25]

FIGURE 3-4.   Guillaume Du Fay and Gilles Binchoys, anonymous miniature in *Le champion des dames* by Martin le Franc (Paris, Bibliothèque Nationale, MS f. fr. 12476, f. 98).

---

25. Ironically, there is no evidence with regard to Du Fay's abilities as an organist, although he undoubtedly learned to play, whereas the earliest documents relating to Binchoys's life record his activity as organist at the church of Ste. Waudru in Mons from 1419 to 1423; see David Fallows, "Binchois," *The New Grove Dictionary of Music*, 2:709.

An account of a visit made by the composers Robert Morton and Hayne van Ghizeghem to the city of Cambrai, perhaps in 1468, shows clearly the role chapel singers could play in the performance of secular works at court. It has survived, significantly, as the text of a polyphonic *rondeau*, and it links as companions in the musical events described two composers whose respective duties at the Burgundian court represent the opposing polarities of sacred and secular: Morton was a clerk in the ducal chapel, whereas Hayne was a singer and chamber valet who was never listed with the chaplains on court rosters. Yet the pair of them "played on soft instruments in great number and sang so heartily they were heard as far as Metz."[26] Similarly, but even more clearly and dramatically, the celebrated Banquet of the Oath of the Pheasant, which has been described in minute detail by Burgundian court chroniclers, shows that on ostentatious occasions of state, the chapel musicians—including choirboys from a church with links to the court—worked with court minstrels in preparing and presenting the spectacles that were intended to entertain and dazzle visiting dignitaries.[27]

However demanding and extensive the duties of the chapel singers, the rewards they enjoyed were nonetheless proportionately great. As a rule they were lodged and fed at the expense of their lord. Each year they received new livery, robes, and vestments, some of them lined with fur to protect them against the cold during the long hours of service in poorly heated stone buildings. Servants were provided them when needed, and when the court moved from place to place, horses and travel expenses. They received a regular salary, usually on a monthly basis, and were frequently given supplementary gifts for participating in the observance of special occasions at the court. In addition, every effort was made to obtain for each cleric of the chapel a number of ecclesiastical benefices, if possible in the locality of his choice, the revenues of which could be enjoyed in absentia while in court service and counted upon to furnish a comfortable living when the time came to retire.[28]

COURTLY CHAPELS IN SAVOY AND THE ITALIAN CITY-STATES

Particulars regarding the various functions of courtly chapels have been illustrated here mainly by examples taken from the ducal court of Burgundy and the royal courts of France and England because of their historical primacy. The musical institutions of the latter two are among the most venerable whose history can be traced,

---

26. See Atlas, ed., *Robert Morton: The Collected Works*, xx–xxi, where the complete text of the chanson is given.

27. An account in English of the musical *entremets* is given by Gustave Reese, *Music in the Renaissance* (New York: Norton, 1959), 57–59; it may be assumed that it was the chapel musicians singing motets and playing organs in the model of a church placed on one of the tables, and they may also have been among the twenty-eight musicians hidden in a huge pastry sitting on another table or involved with yet other performances described in the written accounts.

28. Concerning the various kinds of rewards usually enjoyed by chapel musicians at a secular court, see Wright, *Music at the Court of Burgundy*, 66–70 and 77–81, and Perkins, "Musical Patronage at the Royal Court of France," 522–34 and *passim*.

and all three were so admired in the fifteenth century that they were often taken as a model for courtly chapels more recently established, especially in Renaissance Italy. In the cisalpine city-states, where the *signori* of newly created dynasties were attempting to establish their power in emulation of the hereditary houses to the north, the structure and administration of their chapel were often imitated. Noteworthy examples include the ducal court of Savoy, Burgundy's neighbor to the south on the principal trade route to Italy, those of Milan and Ferrara, which vied with one another for a while in the 1470s—and with other courts at home and abroad—for the most competent singers and composers, and, a bit later on, Mantua.[29]

The duchy of Savoy was the first to found a chapel capable of emulation with those of its northern neighbors. Amadeus VIII (d. 1451), who was duke from 1416 on, had assembled an exceptional choir of clerics as early as the 1430s. In 1434, when the composer Guillaume Du Fay began his long, intermittent association with the court as master of the ducal chapel, the musicians who served under his direction included an organist, four boys, and an undetermined number of adult singers, one of whom worked as a copyist. By 1452, when Du Fay returned to Savoy at the request of Amadeus's son, Louis I, whom he served for some seven consecutive years, the chapel numbered upwards of fifteen adult musicians, including the master and the organist.

During the latter period choirboys were evidently no longer an integral part of the courtly establishment, but as in the neighboring duchy of Burgundy, young choristers were trained for ducal service by churches associated with the ruling house. Over the next decade the chapel continued to flourish; by the early 1460s there were regularly more than twenty singers on the rolls. Thereafter its fortunes rose and fell with those of the duchy, but its existence was maintained without significant interruption through the sixteenth century, even after the ducal court moved to Turin in 1563.[30]

In Milan Duke Galeazzo Maria Sforza began recruiting singers for his private chapel in 1473, and by the following year, when his musical establishment reached a transitory zenith, it included thirty-four chapel singers, all of them adults: twenty-one in the ducal chapel and another thirteen in a *cappella di camera*.[31] Among them

---

29. For a lucid overview of musical patronage at the courts of northern Italy in these years that includes brief histories of the chapels in Milan, Ferrara, and Mantua, see William F. Prizer, "North Italian Courts, 1460–1540," in *The Renaissance: From the 1470s to the End of the Sixteenth Century*, ed. Iain Fenlon, Man and Music, vol. 2 (Englewood Cliffs, N.J.: Prentice Hall, 1989), 133–55.
30. Concerning the musical establishment of the ducal court of Savoy in general, see David Crawford, "Savoy," *The New Grove Dictionary of Music*, 16:528; for additional information about the chapel, cf. Fallows, *Dufay*, 40–41 and 69, and Marie-Thérèse Bouquet, "La Cappella Musicale dei Duchi di Savoia," *Rivista Italiana di Musicologia* 3 (1968): 233–85, who lists all of the singers who appear in the surviving payment registers for the fifteenth and early sixteenth centuries (the last entry is for 1515).
31. For a thorough-going study of music at the Milanese court, see William F. Prizer, "Music at the Court of the Sforza: The Birth and Death of a Musical Center," *Musica disciplina* 43 (1989): 141–93; concerning the chapels organized in the early 1470s, see especially pp. 155–60.

were some well-known composers: Gaspar van Weerbeke, Johannes Martini, Loyset Compère, and perhaps Josquin Desprez.[32]

At the Este court in Ferrara the chapel, which flourished briefly under Leonello in the 1440s, was reorganized and expanded under Ercole I (1471–1505). Ercole experimented for a time with a double choir—the model for which has yet to be identified—which included a contingent of boys from Germanic regions, but later adopted the Franco-Burgundian model, making provision for some twenty adult singers capable of singing both polyphony and chant. Ercole was assisted, and perhaps guided, in the formation of his chapel by a series of capable musicians trained in the church schools of northern France and the Netherlands, some of whom also served the court of Milan at about the same time. These included the composer Johannes Martini, who entered the employ of the Este in 1473, and Josquin Desprez, who was with the chapel for a year beginning in 1503. When Josquin left, he was replaced by Jacob Obrecht, who served until he died of the plague in 1505.[33]

Following Ercole's death in the same year, the chapel was reduced somewhat in size, and subsequent dukes of Ferrara turned more to the secular side. During the second half of the sixteenth century their secular musical establishment was one of the most remarkable in all Italy. In the meantime the chapel maintained an accomplished corps of musicians as well, including such northern-trained composers as Antoine Brumel, Maistre Jhan, and eventually Cipriano de Rore. Later it included members of the Dalla Viola family, who were among the first Italians to attain prominence as professional musicians in the sixteenth century. Under Duke Alfonso I (1505–34) the court chapel also contributed significantly to a marked vogue on the peninsula for repertory originating with the French royal chapel. That trend gained considerable impetus from the French-Italian wars, peaking initially in the 1520s, when the house of Este, through its friendly relations with the French court, helped bring to Italy a substantial number of compositions by composers of the royal chapel.[34]

THE PAPAL CHAPEL

Despite its long and continuous musical tradition, during the fifteenth century even the papal chapel was influenced to a degree by French and Burgundian models. Pope Sixtus IV (1471–84) increased its numbers first to twenty and then to twenty-four

32. At the same time, the duke appears to have had in his employ an additional eighteen chamber singers for the secular music of the court; see Mariangela Donà, "Milan," *The New Grove Dictionary of Music*, 12:291.

33. The definitive study of the musical establishment at the Este court is Lewis Lockwood's *Music in Renaissance Ferrara, 1400–1505: The Creation of a Musical Center in the Fifteenth Century* (Cambridge, Mass.: Harvard University Press, 1984); concerning the chapel, see especially pp. 41–45 and 135–72.

34. See Lewis Lockwood, "Ferrara," *The New Grove Dictionary of Music*, 6:486–87. (For a more detailed treatment of these questions, see also his "Jean Mouton and Jean Michel: New Evidence on French Music and Musicians in Italy, 1505–1520," *Journal of the American Musicological Society* 32 [1979]: 191–246.)

singers, all adults. Because their voices covered all four of the ranges that were by then conventional, they could perform both chant and polyphony without the assistance of the choirboys, who had figured earlier in the chapel's history but whose presence at the papal court can be documented only sporadically in the later fifteenth and sixteenth centuries.[35] Sixtus also had a chapel built in the Vatican palace (the Cappella Sistina) in which liturgical services were regularly celebrated for the entire court. As a result, the singers of the papal chapel became an important influence in the musical life of sixteenth-century Rome and provided a model that was to be emulated in turn by a good many of the city's important churches.[36]

According to Sixtus's plan, the educational functions previously filled by the papal chapel were to be assumed by a separate choir attached to St. Peter's Basilica and consisting of twelve singers, twelve scholars, and two masters, one each for grammar and music. When that design was finally realized under Pope Julius II in 1513, the resulting choir took his name (the Cappella Giulia) and had a thriving existence through the remainder of the century and beyond. That the papal chapel continued to prefer adult singers nonetheless is suggested by its increasing dependence (beginning in the mid-1560s) on the voices of *castrati* for the treble parts of polyphonic compositions.[37]

THE ROYAL ARAGONESE CHAPEL IN NAPLES

In the kingdom of Naples the royal chapel flourished from the 1440s on under the Aragonese monarchs Alfonso V and Ferrante I. However, the model followed initially—particularly by Alfonso—was neither French nor English but rather that of the Aragonese court in Spain. As early as 1347 King Pedro IV was inspired by the example of his royal French cousins. He recruited northern singers in Avignon from among those drawn by the presence of the papal court, doubling the size of his chapel (from two singers to four), and included mensural polyphony in both the celebration of the liturgy and in the entertainments of his court. That tradition was maintained without interruption until the time of Alfonso V, who drew on it in forming a chapel for his Neapolitan kingdom.[38] However, the growing reputation of important courtly chapels on the Continent—about which Alfonso learned through diplomatic and artistic contacts with those polities with which he was com-

35. Concerning the role of boy singers in the papal choir, see Christopher Reynolds, "Rome: A City of Rich Contrast," in *The Renaissance: From the 1470s to the End of the Sixteenth Century*, ed. Iain Fenlon, Man and Music, vol. 2 (Englewood Cliffs, N.J.: Prentice Hall, 1989), 77–80.

36. For an overview of the papal chapel in the sixteenth century, its relationship to the pontifical court generally and to the city of Rome in particular, see Nino Pirrotta and Raoul Meloncelli, "Rome," *The New Grove Dictionary of Music*, 16:155–56 ("Renaissance and Baroque").

37. Concerning the use of *castrati*, see Thomas Walker, "Castrato," *The New Grove Dictionary of Music*, 3:875.

38. Concerning the development of a polyphonic tradition in the Spanish kingdom of the house of Aragon, see Maria del Carmen Gómez Muntané, *La Música en la Casa Real Catalano-Aragonesa, 1336–1442*, 2 vols. (Barcelona: Antoni Bosch, 1979), especially 1:1–24 and 83–112.

peting in the political arena—apparently prompted him to expand and reorganize his choir.

In 1422, the first year for which pay records have survived for Alfonso's chapel, he had only eight singers in his employ, but by 1444, when he was at last firmly settled in Naples, the chapel counted fifteen adult singers. That figure includes the acting first chaplain and a master for the boys (of which there were five) but no organist. The court chapel grew steadily, if not dramatically, over the next few years; by 1451 there were some twenty-two singers in addition to the two chapelmasters and two organists. The chapel choir stabilized at about that level for the remainder of Alfonso's reign and seems not to have changed significantly after his son Ferrante inherited the throne of Naples in 1458. By then, however, the choir was taking on a more international cast.

Judging from their names, a number of Alfonso's singers may have been northerners; still, only three of those serving in his chapel at his death had not come to Naples from Spain. By contrast, in 1480, the last year for which a roster of Ferrante's chapel survives, Spanish-named clerics constitute less than half of the some twenty-two singers cited. The majority are either Italians or northerners, including the influential theorist-composer Johannes Tinctoris. By then, references to the choirboys and their master had also disappeared, the latest one coming prior to 1465. This suggests that the Aragonese model for the royal chapel, which included choirboys in training to sing the treble parts in polyphonic performance, had been abandoned and that boys had been replaced with adult singers, as at the courts of Burgundy and France.[39]

ORGANS AND ORGANISTS IN COURTLY CHAPELS

Another particularity of the Neapolitan chapel—one that it shared more or less from its inception with that of the Savoyard court and with the English chapel royal—was the inclusion of two organists among its personnel. As noted, no organist is listed on the regular payment registers of the Burgundian and French courts in the fifteenth century, and no instrument is shown in the depiction of their respective chapels singing Mass (see Figures 3-1 and 3-2). That lack may be more apparent than real, however. Since the instruction of choirboys routinely involved learning to play instruments, it is likely that a number of the singers at either court were competent organists, as for example the Burgundian chaplain Gilles Binchoys (see p. 97). In the ducal chapel regular use of the organ is in fact implied by the payments made for the repair and maintenance of the instruments themselves and for their transportation when the household was on the move.[40] By contrast, there are no such indications for the French chapel, suggesting that the organ was heard more rarely there, and

39. The history of the Neapolitan court chapel has been carefully traced through the fifteenth century by Allan Atlas, *Music at the Aragonese Court of Naples* (Cambridge: Cambridge University Press, 1985); see especially 23–57.
40. See Marix, *Histoire de la musique de la cour de Bourgogne*, 130–31 and 62–63.

perhaps not at all, but no hard and fast conclusions are possible in light of the fragmentary state of court records.[41]

In fact, only two institutions systematically excluded the organ from their liturgical services, and these were important church communities rather than the chapels of secular courts. The papal choir, first of all, sang without instruments from the time of its foundation, establishing a performing tradition still known as "a cappella." In addition, the cathedral of Cambrai, which maintained an exceptionally skillful choir all through the fifteenth and sixteenth centuries, had no organ still as late as 1714, and its canons proscribed all other instruments from the sanctuary as well.[42] During the sixteenth century, however, the general exclusion of instruments from liturgical ceremonies became more and more the exception as instruments were given an ever larger role in the music—both sacred and secular—of church and court alike.

In the territories of the empire it is often difficult to determine the number of musicians serving in a courtly chapel where there is a close connection between the ruling magnate's choir and that of the churches associated with his court. Still, there is ample evidence of the important part organists played not only in liturgical services but in the composition and performance of secular music as well. At the ducal court of Bavaria the earliest record of a chapel choir dates from the reign of Albrecht IV (1467–1508), but when Albrecht came to power, the celebrated blind musician Conrad Paumann had already served as court organist under two previous rulers, starting in 1450, and continued in that role until his death in 1473.[43] At the imperial court of the Habsburgs, similarly, one of the central figures was the organist Paul Hofhaimer, who had been trained there as a boy under Frederick III. He subsequently returned to Habsburg service in 1489 under Maximilian I, whose patronage he retained until the emperor's death in 1519 (see Figure 3-5).[44]

---

41. The payments made to the members of the royal chapel at the death of Charles VI in 1422 include a certain Pierre Malelyme, "organ player"; however, there is no sign that the organ was used in the celebration of the liturgy during the rule of subsequent monarchs; see Perkins, "Musical Patronage at the Royal Court of France," 521 and 545.

42. Concerning Cambrai, see Craig Wright, "Performance Practices at the Cathedral of Cambrai, 1475–1550," *Musical Quarterly* 64 (1978): 322–27; as for Rome, see the comment of Nino Pirrotta, "Novelty and Renewal in Italy," in *Music and Culture in Italy from the Middle Ages to the Baroque* (Cambridge, Mass.: Harvard University Press, 1984), 168–69.

43. Paumann learned his art in Nuremberg, where he functioned as the organist at the church of St. Sebald before entering the service of the Bavarian court; see Chistoph Wolff, "Paumann," *The New Grove Dictionary of Music*, 14:308–9, and Horst Lechtmann and Robert Münster, "Munich," *The New Grove Dictionary of Music*, 12:781.

44. Note the prominence given to the organ and its player in the woodcut in contrast to the absence of any instrument in the chapel of Philip the Good or Francis I as shown in Figures 3-1 and 3-2. Concerning Hofhaimer's connections with the imperial court, see Manfred Schuler, "Hofhaimer," *The New Grove Dictionary of Music*, 8:631–32, and Martin Picker, "Habsburg," *The New Grove Dictionary of Music*, 8:11–13.

FIGURE 3-5. Emperor Maximilian I attends Mass at Augsburg, ca. 1418 (woodcut ca. 1518 by Hans Weiditz at the Graphische Sammlung Albertina in Vienna).

COURTLY CHAPELS IN GERMANIC REGIONS

These two courts were among the most important centers of musical patronage in German territories during the fifteenth and sixteenth centuries. In both instances, consequently, comparing the contribution made by their organists with that of the composers of sacred vocal polyphony is highly instructive. The Netherlander Heinrich Isaac was the chief ornament of the Habsburg court around the turn of the century. He learned music somewhere in the north and established his reputation in Florence before entering the employ of Maximilian I (1459–1519) in 1496. As one of the leading composers of his day, Isaac was undoubtedly expected to exemplify the contemporary "international" style at his new patron's court in order to put the Austrian chapel on a more equal footing with those of France and Burgundy, and the concessions the composer made to local traditions in musical genres such as the *Tenorlied* did not alter the essential nature of his compositional technique.[45] Following Maximilian's death in 1519 and the dissolution of his chapel in the following year, Isaac's pupil Ludwig Senfl became the leading figure in the ducal chapel of Bavaria. Although of German origin, Senfl strove—like many others—to emulate

45. Concerning music at Maximilian's Austrian court, see Martin Picker, "The Habsburg Courts, 1477–1530," in *The Renaissance: From the 1470s to the End of the Sixteenth Century*, ed. Iain Fenlon, Man and Music, vol. 2 (Englewood Cliffs, N.J.: Prentice Hall, 1989), 231–40.

the musical style of his master. In this manner courtly patronage of sacred vocal music in Germany hastened the dissemination of northern models and the acceptance of their compositional style as normative.[46]

By contrast, when it comes to organ music, the results were quite different. Encouraged by the patronage of generous princes, Paumann and Hofhaimer became key figures in establishing an important "German" school of organ playing and composition. Whatever the influence of French and Netherlandish masters on their own development as composers, their frequent travels as itinerant artists and their extensive teaching at home carried not only their fame but also their individual styles of performance and composition abroad, to Italy first of all but to the north and west as well. The special favor shown the chapel organists at the courts of the imperial Habsburgs and of the dukes of Bavaria recalls the situation in England but is a marked departure from the practice as known at the Burgundian and French courts. More importantly, it gave rise to a small independent stream of stylistic influence that ran bravely for a time against the strong current from France and the Low Countries.

Generally speaking, however, instrumental music at courts everywhere was the province of the various minstrels and chamber musicians rather than the chapel singers or even the organists. Let us see, then, how the secular musicians were organized and what functions they filled.

THE COURT MINSTRELS

Although historical focus tends to favor the chapel singers, who composed and performed the written repertory, secular musicians were at least as important at most courts as were those of the choir. In fact, minstrels were often employed in considerable numbers in places where no chapel choir can be traced. Their role is more difficult to define and their activities harder to reconstruct than those of cleric singers, not only at court but also in the urban society of the fifteenth and sixteenth centuries generally. There are two reasons for this: first, we know a good deal less about how and by whom minstrels were trained than we do about church musicians; and second, we are rather poorly informed about the nature and scope of their repertory.

Clerics who learned their music in one of the church schools were bound to be acquainted with the principles of mensural notation. By contrast, it is not always clear which, if any, of the lay musicians would have needed to understand its uses as well. We are rarely able to determine the extent to which minstrels drew on compositions from the written tradition and, even less, what part of their repertory they learned by rote—whether notated or not—and what they simply improvised. Unlike the clerics, all of whom were trained to sing the plainchant and the polyphony connected with the liturgy, secular musicians were divided into at least three separate categories

---

46. Concerning Isaac's influence on the development of musical styles and tastes in the empire, see Martin Staehelin, "Isaac," *The New Grove Dictionary of Music*, 9:329–32.

or classes, further complicating the problem. Each group had its own distinctive functions in the musical life of the courts and cities of the period and thus may have required its own level of preparation.

INSTRUMENT TYPES: HAUT AND BAS

A basic distinction was made at the time between instruments capable of producing a loud sound (described as *haut* in French) and those that were limited by their acoustical nature to a soft one (referred to as *bas*).[47] The sonority that an instrument could project dictated in large measure the uses to which it was put, and the resulting differences in function naturally had an effect on the social status of those who played.

The gentle vibrations of harp or lute are easily heard in relatively small chambers but dissipate quickly in the open air, however sharply the strings may be plucked, and are completely inaudible at any considerable distance. By contrast, trumpets and instruments with double reeds such as shawms and bombards usually speak loudly or not at all. Thus, while they are useful outdoors where they can be heard over a considerable distance, their effect can be overpowering in smaller, enclosed spaces. Consequently, soft instruments bespeak intimate surroundings and musical compositions to match—with or without text—the details of which encourage attentive listening from a small audience and may even invite their participation in the music making. Loud instruments, to the contrary, imply more strongly a secondary role for the music, as an accompaniment to dancing, for example, or a means of heightening the magnificence and splendor of processions, tournaments, and even war.

TRUMPETERS: DUTIES AND SPECIAL STATUS

Trumpets were the dominant sound source on the battlefield and in the lists during the fifteenth and sixteenth centuries. Their calls and fanfares announced the arrival of the nobility, called and rallied troops engaged in the field, and lent a festive martial air to tourneys. An instrument specifically designed for those purposes was called a "war trumpet." If its depiction in fifteenth-century art is accurate, it was usually fashioned of a straight pipe that flared at the end into a small bell, and it was played with a cuplike mouthpiece similar to those still in use.[48] A miniature from around 1460, showing King Charles V at the gates of Paris for a "royal entry," places instruments of this type in the hands of his four heralds (see Figure 3-6). In some instances, however, when the pipe was considerably lengthened to extend its range,

47. See Edmund A. Bowles, "*Haut* and *bas*: The Grouping of Musical Instruments in the Middle Ages," *Musica disciplina* 8 (1954): 115ff.
48. For a helpful discussion of the development of the trumpet through the fifteenth and sixteenth centuries, including some informative pictures, see Edward H. Tarr, "Trumpet," *The New Grove Dictionary of Music*, 19:214–17 ("History to 1500"); cf. idem, "Trumpet," *The New Grove Dictionary of Musical Instruments*, 3:641–43.

FIGURE 3-6. Charles V of France entering Paris, miniature by Jean Fouquet, ca. 1460 (*Grandes chroniques de France*, Bibliothèque Nationale, MS f. fr. 6465, f. 417).

FIGURE 3-7. Philip the Good of Burgundy being welcomed at Dijon by the clergy and townspeople of the city (Hôpital de Dijon, *Manuscrit du Saint-Esprit*, f. 18).

it was bent into a flattened S so that it would not be too unwieldy for the player to manage, as is illustrated in another miniature of about the same period by the instrument carried by one of the trumpeters accompanying Duke Philip the Good of Burgundy at his entry into Dijon (see Figure 3-7). Common to both is a banner with the arms of the noble patron draped from the instrument, thus identifying, like the livery worn by the player, the royal person thus announced.

As the trumpet became an unmistakable symbol of the privileged social status of the lord whose escutcheon it carried, every noble of any appreciable rank found it increasingly indispensable to have at least one or two players in his employ. Moreover, the trumpeters often became important figures at court; they were given armor to protect them when they went into battle and were occasionally assigned delicate missions as messengers and even as spies in addition to their regular duties.[49] Early in the 1400s a single player sufficed at many of the smaller courts, but the more prominent households often had a considerably larger contingent. Henry V of

49. Concerning the functions and the privileged status of trumpeters in the household of an important magnate, see Wright, *Music at the Court of Burgundy*, 34–38.

England arrived in Calais in 1416 with six trumpeters in his suite,[50] and Philip the Good of Burgundy also had six or seven players in his service through most of the 1430s.

By contrast, the French court usually had only two or three trumpets in the 1450s and no more than four or five in the 1460s. By then, surprisingly, the duke of Burgundy had reduced his players to about the same number. When circumstances called for a greater show of pomp or of force, however, yet others were hired, either from sympathizing neighbors or from nearby towns. Thus Philip the Bold of Burgundy, while on his way to Calais in 1396 to confer with the English, hired seven trumpeters in the towns of Ghent, Bruges, and Ypres.[51]

The number of players could fluctuate, then, from year to year and from court to court, in a manner that defies easy generalization. Nonetheless, the general tendency in the fifteenth and sixteenth centuries at European courts everywhere was toward larger musical establishments, and in many places it affected as well the number of regularly employed trumpeters. In France there were usually from six to eight on the royal roles in the 1490s and early 1500s, as compared to the four to five maintained earlier, and to these were added in 1494–95 three to four *tabourins suisses*, presumably drummers capable of piping on a fife at the same time.[52] Charles the Bold of Burgundy maintained twelve trumpets, nearly twice as many as his father, Philip the Good.[53]

In the 1430s Alfonso of Aragon had only three trumpeters in his service, but by 1441, just before he began residing regularly in his Neapolitan kingdom, there were six, and in 1491, under his son Ferrante, there were seven on a more or less regular basis.[54] During the reign of Henry VII of England nine trumpeters were provided with livery in 1503 and again in 1509, at the end of his life, but when Henry VIII was crowned in that same year, the number was increased to fifteen, and a total of eighteen were paid in 1547–48, the final year of the latter's rule.[55] At the Bavarian court in Munich there were twelve trumpeters in 1514, but their numbers had shrunk to seven by the end of the century when Orlande de Lassus was chapelmaster there. In the meantime, by contrast, instrumentalists of other kinds had increased

50. This is one or two more than are carried by the household accounts for his reign generally; see Richard Rastall, "The Minstrels of the English Royal Households, 25 Edward I–1 Henry VIII: An Inventory," *Royal Musical Association Research Chronicle* 4 (1964): 28.

51. The trumpet players at the Burgundian court are listed year by year from 1420 to 1468 by Marix, *Histoire de la musique de la cour de Bourgogne*, 264–75; for information on the trumpeters at the French court, see Perkins, "Musical Patronage at the Royal Court of France," 520 and 530–31.

52. See Stephen Bonime, "Anne de Bretagne (1477–1514) and Music: An Archival Study" (Ph.D. diss., Bryn Mawr College, 1975), 51–65.

53. See Marix, *Histoire de la musique de la cour de Bourgogne*, 60.

54. See Atlas, *Music at the Aragonese Court of Naples*, 99–100.

55. See Henry Cart de Lafontaine, *The King's Musick* (London, 1909; reprint, New York: Da Capo Books, 1973), 2–7; cf. Rastall, "Minstrels of the English Royal Households," 36–40. Since the payment records transcribed by Lafontaine were for occasions of state—funerals and coronations—it is possible that some of the trumpeters listed were extras hired for special ceremonies rather than regular members of the royal household; still, the general trend is clear enough.

from two to sixteen, some of whom may have been perfectly able to play the trumpet as well.[56]

TRUMPETERS AND MUSICAL REPERTORIES

Although it is possible to document the presence of trumpeters in some detail at a number of major European courts and to establish their participation in important historical events and civil ceremonies from contemporary paintings and chronicles, relatively little is known about the training they received and the music they played. Their repertory may have consisted in some cases only of formulaic calls and fanfares of the sort still used in traditional military encampments. Since music of that kind is not polyphonic or even mensural in the usual sense, trumpeters of the fifteenth and sixteenth centuries would not have needed to know the notational systems then in use. Consequently, those whose playing was limited to pieces of that sort could have prepared themselves for their musical functions in a fairly simple sort of apprenticeship.

An aspiring player had first to learn to handle the instrument, in any case, and to acquire the skills needed simply to make it sound. At the same time he could begin committing to memory the calls or tunes locally in current use. If these short pieces were played in unison by several players at once, as seems likely from the pictorial evidence, they would all have known the music well enough to avoid the clash of discordant pitches and to maintain the proper tempos and rhythms. Nonetheless, the fact that trumpeters are to be found more and more consistently in groups of three or four (and more) in the course of the fifteenth century would suggest that some sort of simple polyphony may have been practiced on occasion. The effect of part-music could have been achieved without resorting to notated composition simply by adding one or two low drones as a sonorous backdrop for stock melodic patterns moving by thirds, fourths, and fifths among the consonant pitches in the higher registers. Whatever the performing tradition, the instruction it required was apparently rudimentary enough that it has left no substantial trace in the documents of the period, either archival or didactic.

The possibility of polyphonic performance raises the further difficulty of determining the practical working relationship between the trumpeters and the minstrels who played other types of "loud" instruments. An administrative separation, reflected in pay records and similar official documents, is usually clear enough. At the courts of England, France, and Burgundy, for example, the trumpeters and the *ménestrels* are listed consistently as two distinct entities, generally at different rates of pay,[57] and similar practices were followed elsewhere. Despite these distinctions,

---

56. See Christoph Wolff, "Germany," *The New Grove Dictionary of Music*, 7:268–69 ("Art Music, Sixteenth Century").

57. On the separation between trumpeters and minstrels in the surviving Burgundian records, see Wright, *Music at the Court of Burgundy*, 41, and for England, Rastall, "Minstrels of the English Royal Households," 1–41.

toward the end of the fifteenth century trumpeters and minstrels were listed togeth-er in France as the musicians of the "stable" (*écurie*) and generally included a *trompette de ménestrel*. Taken together, those circumstances suggest a somewhat clos-er connection between the two groups, the possibility of mutual assistance, and per-haps even interchangeability in some instances.[58]

As far as one can tell, the "minstrel trumpet" differed from the "war trumpet" in that it was equipped with a slide—like the later sackbuts and trombones to which it gave rise. This was a crucial development because it allowed the player to change at will the length of the tube and consequently to play diatonically in any normal range; the pitches available to him were no longer limited to the partials of the harmonic series produced by a tube of invariable length. Since the player's technique was oth-erwise unchanged, it thus became possible for a trained musician to play either instrument and to function simultaneously both as a "war" trumpeter and as a min-strel. There are several instances where this is known to have occurred, and doubt-less yet others will come to light in the future.[59]

INSTRUMENTAL ENSEMBLES AT COURT

A minstrel trumpeter was invariably part of an ensemble that consisted primarily of shawms, perhaps with a bombard—woodwind instruments of the double-reed fami-ly that preceded the development of the present-day oboe and bassoon.[60] Such groups are depicted in fifteenth-century miniatures with remarkable consistency in threes: usually two shawms with either a bombard or a slide trumpet. Other combi-nations of instruments are also seen, however, and in the sixteenth century the bands tend to be slightly larger. Greater numbers are also found in the registers of those courts known to have employed minstrels on a regular basis.

In the 1440s the ducal court of Burgundy never had fewer than four, including the *trompette des ménestrels*, and there were usually five from the 1430s through the 1450s.[61] At the Este court in Ferrara, from the 1440s through the rule of Borso d'Este (1450–71), the wind ensemble consisted most of the time of the convention-al trio: initially two shawms and a bombard (*piffari*), later with the slide trumpet (*trombone*) as the third instrument. But under Ercole I (1471–1505) the band was increased to an average of four or five.[62] No record of the *hauts ménestrels* has been

---

58. Concerning the musicians of the king's stable at the court of France in the late fifteenth century, see Bonime, "Anne de Bretagne and Music," 51–65 and *passim*.

59. Marix, *Histoire de la musique de la cour de Bourgogne*, 104–5, cites two trumpeters in the employ of Philip the Good who served both as "war trumpets" and as "minstrel trumpets" and a trumpeter of the city of St. Omer who also played both instruments.

60. Regarding the instruments of the shawm family, see Anthony C. Baines, "Shawm," *The New Grove Dictionary of Music*, 17:237–43; cf. idem, "Shawm," *The New Grove Dictionary of Musical Instruments*, 3:364–70.

61. See Marix, *Histoire de la musique de Bourgogne*, 264–75; curiously, in the late 1460s the number of minstrels regularly paid drops off sharply until only the "minstrel trumpet" is left.

62. See Lockwood, *Music in Renaissance Ferrara*, 68–69, 96–97, and 142.

preserved for the royal court of France during most of the fifteenth century. However, early in the 1500s Louis XII engaged a band of six shawm and sackbut players, which he maintained until the end of his reign in 1515, and under Francis I the ensemble grew to a total of eight musicians.[63]

"LOUD" ENSEMBLES AND MUSIC FOR DANCING

In the paintings of the period, bands of three or four *ménestrels* are sometimes perched on a balcony or a raised platform from which they accompany dancers at a courtly entertainment (see Figure 3-8). They are included as well in other scenes, both indoors and out, in which a variety of festive occasions are represented—coronations, marriages, banquets, processions, and even the hunt (as in Figure 3-9). Written accounts of such events reveal that for those present the music added immeasurably to the brilliance and magnificence of the celebration.[64] In the paintings, significantly, the players invariably appear without written music, suggesting that the instrumental repertory for such festivities was either improvised (presumably in accordance with well-established practices), or drawn from memory, or some combination of the two. What is known about dance music points, in fact, to a fusion of memorization and improvisation.

The stately *basse danse*—one of the most assiduously cultivated court dances of the fifteenth and early sixteenth centuries—was included in dance manuals of the period with both steps and music indicated in an abbreviated form (see Figure 3-10). The music written into such collections was restricted to a single line of a secular part song (the tenor, usually), notated in even breves.

FIGURE 3-8. Musicians playing for a dance at the court of Yon of Gascony, miniature from the *Histoire de Renaud de Montauban*, executed for the duke of Burgundy ca. 1468–70 (Paris, Bibliothèque de l'Arsenal, MS f. fr. 5073, f. 117ᵛ).

63. See Bonime, "Anne de Bretagne and Music," 61–65.
64. See the illustrations gathered by Edmund Bowles, *Musikleben im 15. Jahrhundert*, Musikgeschichte in Bildern, vol. 3, part 8 (Leipzig: VEB Deutscher Verlag für Musik, 1977), 52ff. (dancing); 20ff. (coronations); 26ff. (marriages); 44ff. (banquets); and 122ff. and 138ff. (processions).

FIGURE 3-9. Hunt scene at the court of Philip the Good, ca. 1430–31, 16th-century copy of a painting (destroyed in 1608) by a follower of Jan van Eyck (Musée de Versailles).

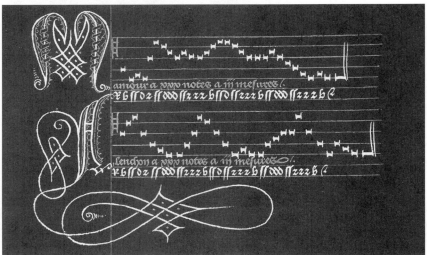

FIGURE 3-10. Two *basses danses*, "*M'amour* a xxx notes a iii mesures," and "*Alenchon* a xxx notes a iii mesures," from the Collection of Margaret of Austria, late fifteenth century, showing the sequence of steps to be danced: R = reverence (bow); b = branle (a rocking motion); ss = two single steps; d = double step; r = reprise (Brussels, Bibliothèque Royale de Belgique, MS 9085, f. 12). The original was inscribed with silver and gold inks on a black surface.

The corresponding choreographic movements are shown by letters next to each of the notes. To the best of present knowledge, the preexistent melody was played in extended rhythmic values (as suggested by the notation) by at least one of the musicians of the group—perhaps, in some instances, the trumpeter—while the others improvised a counterpoint of more rapid embellishing figures emphasizing the rhythms of the dance.[65]

Eventually, polyphonic dance music began to be fully written out in mensural notation. One of the earliest collections of music of this kind was brought out by the Italian publisher Ottaviano Petrucci, the first to print mensural music from movable metal type. In 1508 he published a book of dance music intabulated for lute that had been compiled by Joan Ambrosio Dalza. It contains a series of pavanes, each with a *saltarello* and a *piva* that together constitute a small suite.[66] Similar anthologies were printed in Paris, starting in 1530, by Pierre Attaingnant, who offered *basses danses*, galliards, pavanes, and other assorted dances. These were published not only in specially notated arrangements for lute or keyboard but also in regular mensural notation in separate parts for the use of various unspecified instrumental ensembles.[67] As other music printers established themselves later in the century, they published similar collections for instruments.

It seems likely that such prints were intended primarily for amateur players with some knowledge of notation rather than for professional minstrels; the latter probably had no great need for such material and could have found it expensive in the bargain. It is also possible to wonder whether or not most instrumental musicians of that time were trained to read mensural notation in any of its forms well enough to find such publications useful. There is no unequivocal answer to that question, but one can be inferred from the large place held in the instrumental repertory by vocal music from the written tradition, sacred as well as secular. In every part of western Europe where bands of minstrels were on the scene, the bulk of their known repertory derived from chansons, motets, and even sections of polyphonic Masses. This is especially true for the fifteenth century—at least until its final decades—before notated sources of instrumental music for ensemble became relatively common.

MINSTRELS AND MUSICAL LITERACY

Compositions created without texts in mind offer additional evidence for the musical literacy of instrumental musicians. Such pieces are scattered through the song

65. See Daniel Heartz, "Basse danse," *The New Grove Dictionary of Music*, 2:257–59; Lockwood, *Music in Renaissance Ferrara*, 69, is of the opinion that the tenors for the dance were normally played by the slide trumpet (*trombone*).

66. A facsimile edition of Dalza's tablature, *Intabulatura de Lauto Libro Quarto*, has been published by Minkoff Reprints (Geneva, 1980). Concerning the composer-arranger, see Joan Wess, "Dalza," *The New Grove Dictionary of Music*, 5:169; for a discussion of the primary genres of Renaissance dance music, see below, pp. 829–38.

67. See Daniel Heartz, *Pierre Attaingnant, Royal Printer of Music* (Berkeley: University of California Press, 1969); nos. 16 and 28 of his catalogue are representative collections of dance music for lute and keyboard; nos. 17 and 20 are for instrumental ensembles.

books of the late fifteenth and early sixteenth centuries, primarily in the company of chansons in the fixed forms, to which they usually bear a formal resemblance. A number of them also recall the *basse danse* in their use of a part lifted from a polyphonic piece combined with decorative, figural counterpoint. The gradual emergence of an important repertory of composed works of this kind indicates that, whatever the performance conventions, many minstrels, both at court and in the cities, were able to read mensural notation.[68]

In addition there is the occasional written source intended specifically for the use of instrumental musicians. These include, most notably, the "Casanatense Chansonnier" but more modest collections as well. A small notebook containing songs by Binchoys, Dunstable, and others was written and used by a ship's trumpeter on the trade route from Venice to Flanders in the late 1470s, and a hastily penned part book with songs in French and Dutch copied next to sacred polyphony and bits of chant may have been used by the city minstrels in Maastricht.[69] The probability that many minstrels were notationally literate finds further support in their proven collaboration with cleric-musicians of church or chapel in the performance of sacred polyphony, a practice that can be documented in a fair number of instances.[70]

Still, it is possible to argue to the contrary, that the minstrels were not *necessarily* musically literate; that the instrumental repertory was generally learned by rote and played from memory, whatever its source; that wind players had to learn by heart (and by rote) even those compositions they performed with the singers of the chapel; and that the written sources of secular music without text were made to preserve the repertory for the use of noble amateurs familiar with notation rather than for the wind players in their employ. There is, in addition, the occasional report of blind musicians, whose use for notation is questionable at best.[71] However, the growing body of instrumental compositions in the printed collections of the sixteenth centu-

---

68. For a systematic discussion of a number of such pieces, see Helen Hewitt and Isabel Pope, eds., *Harmonice musices odhecaton A* (Cambridge, Mass.: Mediaeval Academy of America, 1942), 74–83; for more recent views, see Warwick Edwards, "Songs without Words by Josquin and His Contemporaries," and Louise Litterick, "On Italian Instrumental Ensemble Music in the Late Fifteenth Century," in *Music in Medieval and Early Modern Europe: Patronage, Sources, and Texts*, ed. Iain Fenlon (Cambridge: Cambridge University Press, 1981), 79–92 and 117–30, respectively.

69. For evidence that the music of the "Casanatense Chansonnier" (Rome, Biblioteca Casanatense, MS 2856) included repertory used by wind players (*pifferi*) of the Este court, see Lockwood, *Music in Renaissance Ferrara*, 266–77; concerning the trumpeter's notebook, see Daniel Leech-Wilkinson, "Il libro di appunti di un suonatore di tromba del quindicesimo secolo," *Rivista Italiana di Musicologia* 16 (1981): 16–39; and for the fragmentary partbook, see Joseph Smits van Waesberghe, "Een 15e Eeuws Muziekboek van de Stadsminstrelen van Maastricht?" in *Renaissance-Muziek, 1400–1600: Donum natalicium René Bernard Lenaerts*, ed. Jozef Robijns (Louvain: Katholieke Universiteit Seminarie voor Muziekwetenschap, 1969), 247–73.

70. See David Fallows, "The Performing Ensembles in Josquin's Sacred Music," *Tijdschrift van de Vereniging voor Nederlandse Muziek Geschiedenis* 35 (1985): 32–35, for a thoughtful survey of the evidence concerning instrumental participation in the performance of vocal polyphony.

71. See Edmond vander Straeten, *La musique aux Pays-bas*, 4 vols. (Brussels, 1878–88; reprint, New York: Dover, 1969), 4:87, for an archival note citing a "poor blind" musician who played the *bombarde* for Marguerite of Austria in early October 1526, and cf. p. 118 below.

ry, especially when seen in the light of evidence like that presented here, points decidedly in the opposite direction toward an increasing reliance on notation by instrumental musicians of all kinds.[72]

A very convincing case can be made, in fact, for an unbroken tradition of instrumental participation in the composed polyphony of the late Middle Ages and the Renaissance, beginning with the motet of the thirteenth century and involving such central musical genres as the isorhythmic motet, the chanson, and—as we shall see—the cyclic Mass of the fifteenth century. Such an extended period of currency for a performance practice requiring the collaboration of minstrels and chapel singers strongly implies that instrumentalists were generally expected to learn the essentials of mensural notation as a matter of course.[73]

Remaining doubts as to the notational literacy of wind players in the loud ensembles during the fifteenth century can be resolved only if more is learned about their training. The so-called minstrel schools did not offer systematic instruction to aspiring young players. Rather, they were annual gatherings held during the Lenten season (when most music making was proscribed anyway) and frequented by as many musicians as were able to obtain the necessary leave from their duties and the funds to travel. The term *escolle* may have been justified by the exchange of repertory such as songs and dance music and the sharing of technical pointers concerning instruments and performance practices. Those who attended, however, were already skilled musicians, most of them with a well-established reputation and a secure position at some court or municipality.[74]

An apprenticeship appears to have been the most common means among wind players of acquiring the necessary technical and musical skills. There is no compelling evidence that court musicians commonly had apprentices in training as part of their duties (although it is perfectly possible that some did). However, town musicians, who filled similar functions for the municipalities they served, did so routinely. In fact, the right to train (and exploit) apprentices was one of the important prerogatives carefully protected by musicians' guilds all over Europe.[75] However, it is possi-

72. See the survey of surviving sources by Warwick Edwards, "Sources of Instrumental Ensemble Music to 1630," *The New Grove Dictionary of Music*, 17:702ff.

73. The evidence for instrumental participation in the performance of composed polyphony during the Middle Ages is examined briefly by Richard H. Hoppin, *Medieval Music* (New York: Norton, 1978), 347–49; the possible use of written music by wind bands in the Low Countries is raised by Keith Polk, "Municipal Wind Music in Flanders in the Late Middle Ages," *Brass and Woodwind Quarterly* 2 (1969): 1–15; indications that wind players were conversant with mensural notation have also been discussed by Lockwood, *Music in Renaissance Ferrara*, 142.

74. See the informative series of relevant documents published by Justin de Pas, *Ménestrels et écoles de ménestrels à Saint-Omer* (Saint-Ouen, 1903; reprint, Geneva: Minkoff, 1972), and cf. the observations of Wright, *Music at the Court of Burgundy*, 32–33.

75. See, for example, Walter L. Woodfill, *Musicians in English Society from Elizabeth to Charles I* (Princeton: Princeton University Press, 1953), 11–14 and *passim*, who reviews the practices of the London guild regarding apprentices, and Straeten, *La musique aux Pays-bas*, who cites a specific apprenticeship in Bruges in 1482 (2:17) and summarizes the statutes for the guilds in Antwerp (4:161ff.) and Brussels (4:207ff.); cf. also the discussion of guilds below, pp. 152–58.

ble—though never yet documented—that before beginning such an apprenticeship, some of the instrumental musicians of the period received at least the initial phases of their musical instruction in one of the many choir schools, either as a choirboy or as a paying student. If so, that would certainly account for their familiarity with mensural notation and, to a degree, with the polyphonic repertory of the period, both sacred and secular.

"*SOFT*" *INSTRUMENTS AND MUSIC AT COURT*

If some uncertainty remains as to whether or not the *haut ménestrels*—the players of loud wind instruments—of the fifteenth and sixteenth centuries could read notation, there can be little question as to the musical literacy of a third category of highly trained musicians, those who played and sang in the relatively intimate surroundings of the chambers of the nobility. Their instruments are described as "soft" (*bas*) and include harps, lutes, and other types of string instruments (whether played from a keyboard or with a bow); soft winds such as flutes and recorders; and of course the human voice. The best evidence—even though indirect—that musicians of this type were conversant with mensural notation is the repertory they performed on a regular basis: secular polyphonic songs.

Not surprisingly, the "chamber musicians" often appear to have been on a rather intimate footing with their noble patrons, more so in most instances, it would seem, than those of the stable or even of the chapel. They are charged with the musical instruction of the children of the noble households in which they serve. They attend the lords and ladies of the court in their private recreations, and, as is well known, the nobles themselves often join with them, making music informally in the relative privacy of the chamber. Louis, duke of Guyenne and dauphin of France until his death in 1415, played the harp and the organ, and he spent so much time with his minstrels that he was roundly criticized by a contemporary chronicler for wasting his energies on such frivolities while neglecting weightier matters.[76] Henry V of England was also "much given to instruments of music," and may have dabbled in polyphonic composition.[77] Charles of Burgundy, similarly, learned to play the harp in his childhood, enjoyed singing (despite a rather poor voice), and composed a number of polyphonic pieces, including several chansons and at least one motet.[78] Henry VIII of England followed in the same tradition and is but one of the many sixteenth-century nobles whose musical expertise is well established.[79]

One consequence of the familiarity between these musicians and their noble patrons is that chamber players and singers are not always immediately identifiable in the payment records of the court; they were sometimes given more prestigious posi-

76. For details, see Wright, *Music at the Court of Burgundy*, 48.
77. See Margaret Bent, "Roy Henry," *The New Grove Dictionary of Music*, 16:285.
78. See Sylvia Kenney, *Walter Frye and the Contenance Angloise* (New Haven: Yale University Press, 1964), 14–15.
79. See David Greer, "Henry VIII," *The New Grove Dictionary of Music*, 8:485–86.

tions in the household and might therefore be listed, for example, among the chamber valets or the ladies in waiting with no mention of their musical functions.[80] We also know from frequent if scattered reports that even chapel singers—who were often trained to play one or more of the soft instruments and could thus be called upon to instruct members of the noble household—participated on occasion in performing secular music. Already in the late fourteenth century Count Gaston Phoebus of Foix "took great pleasure in his minstrels . . . and willingly heard his clerks sing and descant songs, rondeaux, and virelais."[81] Typically, as when Duke John the Fearless of Burgundy entertained King Charles VI at dinner on Christmas Day of 1409, the playing of both loud and soft instruments accompanied the meal. Afterwards clerics of the royal chapel also sang, most probably secular songs.[82] Because they were routinely paid only for their service in the chapel, however, the participation of the clerics in courtly musical entertainments is not well documented; one can only speculate as to its extent and frequency.

There is also a real possibility, finally, that some of the players of "loud" instruments were equally skillful with some of the "soft" ones and therefore able to function in either group, even though the household accounts list them only with one. In other words, the neat administrative divisions among the three classes of musicians at court, which is reflected nearly everywhere in the pay roles, was probably not so carefully observed when a patron's musical tastes were to be satisfied, whether in public ceremony or private recreation. There may have been a good deal more give and take among the various groups than the bare archival record is able to convey.

In the fifteenth century the chamber musician most commonly found at court was the harper.[83] Traditionally, he was a more or less constant companion to his lord or lady, in some instances from the latter's very tender age. He accompanied his patron everywhere, even into battle, and was therefore the only player of soft instruments fitted with armor. Other minstrels were given considerable freedom to travel to visit neighboring cities and the courts of nearby magnates—where they might earn a generous gift in addition to their regular income—or to attend the yearly school, but the harper was usually required to be continuously in attendance on his master or mistress. He was to be available in any circumstances to sing or play at his patron's command, and he probably provided musical instruction as well in matters ranging from the practical skills of performance to the theoretical principles of composition.

That the harper was musically literate therefore seems most probable; in at least one case he appears in fact to have been a composer himself. Baude Fresnel, who

80. See Perkins, "Musical Patronage at the Royal Court of France," 518 and n. 22; also Rastall, "Minstrels of the English Royal Households," 1–6.

81. According to the *Chronicles* of Froissart (XI:88), as quoted by Wright, *Music at the Court of Burgundy*, 31.

82. See Wright, *Music at the Court of Burgundy*, 49.

83. Concerning the nature of the instrument in the fifteenth and sixteenth centuries, see Ann Griffiths and Joan Rimmer, "Harp," *The New Grove Dictionary of Music*, 8:194–97; cf. idem, "Harp," *The New Grove Dictionary of Musical Instruments*, 2:134–38.

played both the harp and the organ and served the Burgundian court from 1384 until his death in 1398, has been identified with the composer Baude Cordier ,whose compositions (all but one of which were secular) were copied into several important sources of the early fifteenth century.[84] And, as we have seen, the court composer Binchoys was evocatively depicted by a contemporary artist with harp in hand (see Figure 3-4).

Aside from the harper, the instrumentalists most frequently mentioned in the accounts for the chamber musicians are the lutanists. Indeed, judging both from the paintings of the period and from the relevant pay records, it seems clear that from the late fifteenth century on, the lute gradually replaced the harp as the preferred instrument for informal music making at court. In the earliest documents the lutanists are often named in pairs, indicating that the lute was still viewed as a melodic instrument and that two of them were needed for polyphony.

At the ducal court of Burgundy two Portuguese musicians who served Duchess Isabel from 1433 until at least 1456 are identified in the court registers as lutanists. They are also described as playing the *vielle* (a kind of fiddle) and other "soft" instruments, however, and many chamber musicians were probably similarly skilled. It is also reported that both of them were blind (like a surprising number of musicians over the ages); they must therefore have worked from memory, and whatever knowledge they had of mensural notation would have been useful only as a guide to performance.[85]

Two chamber players were also carried on the pay roles of the Ferrarese court, the virtuoso lutanist Pietrobono del Chitarino, who served the Este household from 1441 with few interruptions until his death in 1497, and—in the earlier phases of his career—his *tenorista*. The latter was probably also a lutanist, although it has been suggested that he played a viol. Whatever his instrument—or instruments—his role in performance can be construed only from his title, which implies the same sort of musical practice as has been suggested for wind bands that accompanied dancing: the combination of a tenor line taken from a polyphonic composition with figural embellishment improvised by a second lutanist using the treble range. In addition, Pietrobono, who was also famed as a singer, may have accompanied himself in that role, with or without the assistance of a *tenorista*.[86]

His song repertory may have been taken in part from written sources. However, most of it probably consisted of poems in the local vernacular set in an improvisatory style that relied upon short melodic formulas of the sort that became characteristic of the *frottola* (see pp. 406–15). It is certainly no coincidence that the Gonzaga court in Mantua, which played such a central role in the development of Italian secular music in the time of Isabella d'Este (1474–1539), was also a source of patron-

---

84. The evidence that Fresnel and Cordier are one and the same has been presented by Wright, *Music at the Court of Burgundy*, 132–33; he also underscores the special status of the harper at the ducal court, pp. 124–25.
85. See Marix, *Histoire de la musique de la cour de Bourgogne*, 30, 95, 117–18, and 267–73.
86. An extended discussion of Pietrobono's career is to be found in Lockwood's *Music in Renaissance Ferrara*, 98–108.

age for some of the most skilled lutanists of the age, most notably the celebrated Alberto da Ripa. And many of the lute players in Gonzaga service are also among the most prolific composers of *frottole*, including Marchetto Cara, Bartolomeo Tromboncino, and Michele Pesenti.[87]

LUTANISTS AND POLYPHONY

During the second half of the fifteenth century an important change in lute technique made it easier to play not only chords but even contrapuntal textures, thus facilitating the adoption of the instrument for the performance of mensural polyphony from the written tradition. The plectrum, which limited the player to a single melodic line, was abandoned, leaving the fingers of the right hand free to pluck several strings simultaneously. Significantly, lute tablature—a special form of notation that represents visually the strings of the instrument, the fingers to be used to stop them, and the rhythms to be observed (see Figures 3-11a and 3-11b)—was invent-

FIGURE 3-11a. Lute tablatures: the *Capirola Lute-Book*, f. 51ᵛ, Johannes Urreda's *Nunquam fue pena major* (Chicago, Newberry Library).

87. See Willam Prizer, "Lutenists at the Court of Mantua in the Late Fifteenth and Early Sixteenth Centuries," *Journal of the Lute Society of America* 13 (1980): 5–34.

FIGURE 3-11b. Attaingnant's *Dixhuit basses dances . . .* (1529-1530 new style), ff. 36ᵛ and 37, the *Pavane PB* and *Pavane Blondeau* (Berlin, Staatsbibliothek, Mus. ant. pract. A 680).

ed at about the same time. As a result, the instrument could be used to perform polyphonically any of the compositional genres then current.

Commercial printers, beginning with Petrucci, commissioned the arrangement and intabulation of pieces for lute, and the works published included not only dances and adaptations of vocal music, as might have been expected, but also solo works for virtuosic display and for teaching.[88] Consequently, an increasing reliance on musical notation, such as has been observed in connection with the developing repertory of music for "loud" instrumental consorts, also marked the spread of music intended for the lute. And this trend suggests, once again, that most players of "soft" instruments were taught the principles of mensural notation as a matter of course all through the period.

88. It is widely assumed that such pieces were usually improvised by skilled professionals, then occasionally written out to provide models for students and—when later published—interested amateurs. Concerning the development of the lute, its technique, and its repertory in the fifteenth and sixteenth centuries, see Ian Harwood and Diane Poulton, "Lute," *The New Grove Dictionary of Music*, 11:344–63; cf. idem, "Lute," *The New Grove Dictionary of Musical Instruments*, 2:553–74.

Aside from harp and lute, the social uses of other soft instruments played by the minstrels at court—and by the nobles themselves—follow no clear pattern. Keyboards, including portative or positive organs and a variety of instruments of the harpsichord and clavichord families, are perhaps those most frequently mentioned. From the fifteenth century there are references to bowed instruments of the fiddle family, such as the rebec and the *vielle*, and of other plucked strings, such as the gittern, which had many of the essential features later found in the guitar.[89] In the sixteenth century, together with greater numbers of minstrels in the employ of virtually every important city and court, came a wider variety of instruments. Those mentioned in the accounts of the royal court of England in the 1540s and 1550s included flutes, fifes, and drums (a combination recalling the *tabourins suisses* mentioned earlier, whose classification as "soft" may be disputed), "vialls" and "vyolls" (which were evidently not the same thing), violins, and the plebeian bagpipe.[90]

Records from the royal court of France also cite a pair of *cornetti*, wind instruments made of wood and played with a cupped mouthpiece like that of a trumpet but with a relatively soft sound.[91] Violins made their appearance there during the rule of Francis I (1516–47), but because their primary function was to accompany dancing, they were grouped—like the loud winds, the *haulxboys* (or shawms) and the *sacquebutes*—with the musicians of the king's stable.[92]

CONCLUSIONS

The foregoing list of "soft" instruments known to have been in use at those two courts in the sixteenth century is certainly far from exhaustive, but it appears to have been entirely representative. A depiction of Maximilian of Austria in his music room, seen in a woodcut prepared to illustrate his *Weisskunig* (1505–16), includes most of the instruments mentioned thus far as well as a few from the "loud" category (see Figure 3-12). Similarly, the chamber musicians of the ducal court of Bavaria under Lassus are shown with a combination of instruments from both the "soft" and the "loud" categories: viols, a lute, a flute, a recorder, and two cornetts from the former group, and a shawm, a bombard, and a sackbut from the latter (see Figure 3-13). The seemingly indiscriminate mingling of the two contrasting types of instruments in the Munich miniature may be nothing more than artistic license. Still, in light of other evidence of a similar nature, some of which has already been cited, the paint-

89. See Wright, *Music at the Court of Burgundy*, 29, who mentions players of the *vielle* and of the gittern in the employ of Charles V of France. As noted (p. 118), the two blind Portuguese who served Duchess Isabella at the Burgundian court also played the *vielle*. Concerning the instruments cited, see the articles by Mary Remnant, "Fiddle" and "Gittern," *The New Grove Dictionary of Music*, 6:527–33 and 7:409–12, respectively.

90. See Lafontaine, *The King's Musick*, 7–14.

91. Concerning the instrument, see Anthony C. Baines, "Cornett," *The New Grove Dictionary of Music*, 4:788–93.

92. For details, see Henry Prunières, "La musique de chambre et de l'écurie sous le règne de François 1er (1516–47)," *L'année musicale* 1 (1911): 215–51.

FIGURE 3-12. Maximilian I in his music room, surrounded by musicians and instruments (woodcut by Hans Burgkmair from Maximilian's autobiographical *Weisskunig*, 1505–16 [London, the British Library]).

ing is perhaps better understood as showing that the rather rigid distinction between *haut* and *bas* instruments seen in court registers either reflected rather imperfectly the musical realities of the age or was breaking down significantly in the second half of the sixteenth century. Most likely it was doing both.

To the instruments fashioned by human hands must be added, of course, the voices of the singers, who were identified at times in the fifteenth century as *ménestrels de bouche*. It is interesting to note, moreover, that although the professional musicians of the late Middle Ages and early Renaissance were almost exclusively male, a number of the singers are known to have been women.[93]

93. See Wright, *Music at the Court of Burgundy*, 27–29, who first suggested that "mouth minstrels" were singers rather than wind players. He also cites the existence of female minstrels, as does Atlas, *Music at the Aragonese Court of Naples*, 104–6.

FIGURE 3-13. Musicians of the ducal chamber in concert under Orlande de Lassus at the Court of Bavaria, ca. 1570, miniature by Hans Müelich (Munich, Bavarian State Library, Mus. MS A II S. 186).

As important servants of the court, some of whom had daily contact with their noble patrons, minstrels of both classes were well treated and generously remunerated. Like the trumpeters, who enjoyed a special status, they were given food and shelter, a handsome livery bearing the emblems and the colors of their lord, personal servants, horses when needed, and a daily wage. Since they were often allowed, or even commissioned, to travel to neighboring cities and courts, they could hope for the largess of those entertained along the way, and it seems they were rarely disappointed.[94] If their talents were highly prized by their lord, they could also expect his assistance with major expenses such as the purchase of a house, the care of aging parents, and medical treatment when ill.

In addition there were special gifts on important occasions, as when a minstrel was to be married or had a child to be christened. In many instances a secular musician of the court could expect a pension when age forced retirement or, in the event of an untimely death, for his surviving widow.[95] In sum, minstrels were perhaps not always as highly regarded as the singers of the private chapel, whose status as musicians was enhanced by their rank in the clerical hierarchy of the Christian church. Nor were they eligible for the wealthy prebends to which cleric singers could aspire. For that very reason, however, their daily wage was often higher, and the most gifted were eagerly sought out by officials of court and city alike, treated with considerable deference, and obviously much admired.

94. The generous reception usually accorded visiting minstrels at the princely courts of the period, even when they were in the service of other magnates—or perhaps precisely because that was so—is documented in some detail by Wright, *Music at the Court of Burgundy*, 26–32, and by the authors cited in the following note.

95. Concerning the social status of the minstrels at court and the material rewards they could expect for their services, see Wright, *Music at the Court of Burgundy*, 25; Marix, *Histoire de la musique de la cour de Bourgogne*, 88–93; Atlas, *Music at the Aragonese Court of Naples*, 98–110; and Lockwood, *Music in Renaissance Ferrara*, 95–104 (who traces, in particular, the instructive career of Pietrobono).

CHAPTER 4

Music in the Urban Context

INTRODUCTION

The cities of fifteenth- and sixteenth-century Europe, like the noble courts with which they were often so closely connected, were home to a number of social entities in which the musical arts were cultivated and encouraged in a variety of ways. Cathedrals and collegiate churches generally gave city residents the best opportunity to hear music of the written tradition, both the traditional chant of the liturgy and the mensural polyphony current at the time. If the city also had a university—as was ever more frequently the case in the fifteenth and sixteenth centuries—academic ceremonies offered yet other occasions when both chant and polyphony could be heard, during either solemn processions or special religious observances involving, as a rule, Masses and Vespers or Matins services, or both.

The scholarly community undoubtedly included, as in every age, a considerable number, among faculty and students alike, who were knowledgeable in musical matters of one sort or another. Some had been trained in the choir schools, as we have seen, and could both sing and, in many cases, play upon a variety of instruments. Others were familiar with the theoretical thought current at the time, from the Boethian traditions of the medieval curriculum to the most recent treatises on counterpoint and mensuration. In either case their presence in the city enriched its musical resources with performers and teachers who would not otherwise have been available.

There were probably also students who had as yet received little or no practical instruction in music but who wished to learn to sing or play for their own recreation. If so, they could have applied to a musician of the city—either a cleric or a layperson—who was willing to take on pupils. Teaching of that sort obviously created a market as well for those who made instruments and notated music for sale. In addition the secular entertainments of student societies must have offered opportunities for employment to the minstrels who made the music for their banqueting, dancing, and general revelry.

Professional guilds of merchants and artisans, on the secular side of urban life, and lay confraternities, among the more religiously oriented, both maintained a close association with some local church and sponsored not only devotional services, featuring the performance of sacred music, but also processions, banquets, and similar celebrations, all of which were traditionally accompanied by music (see pp. 158–64). Likewise, families and individual urban residents, especially the more prosperous, clearly thought of music as an indispensable ornament for a wide variety of social occasions. As a result, the demand for secular musicians—to teach as well as to play—became substantial enough in most towns and cities to sustain a fair number of professional minstrels who depended solely, or at least primarily, on their musical skills for a living.

The nucleus of any such group was usually the town waits or tower musicians, who came to be employed as watchmen in city after city during the fourteenth and fifteenth centuries. Posted on a high tower (usually that of the principal church or the town hall) from which they could easily see such dangers as hostile forces

approaching the walls from without or signs of fire or disturbance within them, their duty was to inform the town's inhabitants of the conditions observed from their special vantage point, whether threatening or peaceful, with flags, lanterns, cries, bells, and—as a rule in the absence of crisis—instruments of music (see Figure 4-1).[1]

Since genuine perils were, fortunately, relatively infrequent, these tower musicians customarily marked certain hours of the day with fanfares, tunes (including hymns), and—eventually—

FIGURE 4-1. Town waits with instruments on the battlements of the city, miniature from Diebold Schilling's pictorial *Chronicle of Luzern*, fifteenth century (Vienna, Österreichische Nationalbibliothek, MS 2761, f. 109ᵛ).

---

1. For a discussion of the role of such groups in towns of the Low Countries, see Keith Polk, "Municipal Wind Music in Flanders in the Late Middle Ages," *Brass and Woodwind Quarterly* 2 (1969): 1–15.

polyphonic compositions. When not engaged on the tower, they could also lend their art to the multifarious celebrations that punctuated urban life: civic processions, the "entries" of regional nobles, banquets, baptisms, betrothals, weddings, and funerals— to name but a few (see Figure 4-2). They could even join with the musicians of the city's churches for the devotional services of lay confraternities and, on occasion, to add greater luster to the celebration of the liturgy. In addition, they too provided some of the musical instruction needed or sought by town residents, lessons for the leisured on a variety of instruments and, more importantly, the training of apprentices to assure a pool of competent musicians for service with the municipality.[2]

Figure 4-2. The town waits of Nuremberg (*Stadtpfeiferei*), greeting the New Year, book painting by an unknown sixteenth-century artist (Berlin, Staatsbibliothek, MS Germ. fol., ff. 91ᵛ–92).

2. For a lively description of the role the municipal wind band played in the daily life of Antwerp, see Kristine K. Forney, "Sixteenth-Century Antwerp," in *The Renaissance: From the 1470s to the End of the Sixteenth Century*, ed. Iain Fenlon, Man and Music, vol. 2 (Englewood Cliffs, N.J.: Prentice Hall, 1989), 361–64; for a more general discussion, cf. Heinrich W. Schwab, "Stadtpfeifer," *The New Grove Dictionary of Music*, 18:50–52.

As regular employees of the municipality, the waits were among the first secular musicians to acquire a permanent urban residence and the legal status to which it entitled them. Not surprisingly, then, they also became key figures in the organization of guilds and confraternities for musicians. In that context, as in others, they concerned themselves primarily with the quality of performances by minstrels who were members of the guild, the regulation of their working conditions, their relationships with colleagues and patrons, and the training of apprentices. Well-regulated systems of apprenticeship resulted, and because an urban setting offered many opportunities for employment, the cities became the principal training ground and professional arena for secular musicians just as they were for church musicians (see pp. 74–87).

Regrettably, the further one strays from church and court in searching out the role of music in the European cities of the late Middle Ages and the Renaissance, the fainter is the trace of the written tradition in the historical record. There are fewer documents describing the musical practices of urban minstrels, as compared to their courtly counterparts, and fewer notated sources containing material derived from unwritten repertories of song and dance in a form allowing reconstruction of an earlier, presumably unnotated version. Nevertheless, the growing number of musical manuscripts copied in scribal ateliers of the late fifteenth century and the rapid growth of music printing as a viable international commerce in the sixteenth would suggest that musical literacy was increasing rather rapidly in urban centers throughout the period. This presumably signals a growing reliance on musical notation by the professional performer, as well as by the amateur, and an increasing use of it in the teaching process. That development is most evident in the secular domain. We shall begin, however, with the relatively firm historical evidence relating to the ecclesiastical institutions of the age—where the use of notated sources was the rule from the outset— with a discussion of the choirs responsible for the celebration of the liturgy.

THE CHURCH CHOIRS

Ironic though it may seem, it is often more difficult to determine the normal size and constitution of a church choir, even where archival documents are numerous and well preserved, than it is for a princely chapel. This is in part because the musical organization of the chapter in a typical cathedral or collegiate church was inherently more flexible. It originated early in the Middle Ages with the need for singers capable of executing properly liturgical chant and gave rise to the choir schools where young clerics could learn both the liturgy and its music firsthand. One important result of such a system was that many churchmen were trained in music and could add their voices to the choir when circumstances demanded, even if they were not usually expected to do so.

As polyphony became increasingly common in the celebration of the liturgy and, even more so, in paraliturgical devotions, the need for specialized musical instruction grew. As a result, the numbers of those able to perform complex mensural polyphony may have been smaller than was the case generally for plainchant. However, the schools and choirs where musical personnel were trained for church service underwent no significant organizational change in the process. Consequently, it is not always easy to determine which of the musicians were competent only for chant and which could be called upon to sing polyphony as well.[3] Nor is it always possible to discover which of the various groups within the church community—choirboys, vicars, canons, and the like—participated in services and whether or not they usually sang together or performed as separate entities.

As has been explained, the music of a church, whether chant or polyphony, was generally the domain of its vicars (see pp. 61–62). At the cathedral of Cambrai the minor vicars—*les petits vicaires*—regularly sang for liturgical services. They were divided into two more or less equal groups, each gathered around its own large lectern, facing one another from either side of the choir of the church (see Figure 4-3).[4] In the late fifteenth century their numbers varied from twelve to fifteen, but in the sixteenth—in keeping with the general tendency to increase the size of performing ensembles everywhere—there were never fewer than sixteen, and the average seems to have settled at about twenty.[5] Not all of

FIGURE 4-3. Singers with music, facing one another from opposite sides of the choir, miniature from the *Book of Hours* of Maréchal de Boucicaut, early fifteenth century (Paris, Musée Jacquemart-André, MS 2, f. 142v).

3. The point has been made by David Fallows, "The Performing Ensembles in Josquin's Sacred Music," *Tijdschrift van de Vereniging voor Nederlandse Muziek Geschiedenis* 35 (1985): 38–43.

4. Note that the word "choir" can refer either to that part of the church in which the clerics gathered to celebrate the liturgy or to the vocal forces responsible for the singing.

5. The names of those serving between 1474 and 1547 are given for approximately every tenth year by Craig Wright, "Musiciens à la cathédrale de Cambrai," *Revue de musicologie* 62 (1976): 212.

the vicars were present for every service, however, even though they could be fined when truant. This is clear from a regulation of the fifteenth century prescribing punishment—as well as the customary fine—for those absent whenever the number singing for services fell below a minimum of eight with at least four on each side of the choir. In 1504, with a larger contingent of minor vicars available, the minimum was raised to a total of ten with five on each side of the choir.[6]

It is therefore conceivable that the routine celebration of the liturgy—where plainchant must surely have been the rule and little or no polyphony ever sung—may have seen as few as eight or ten minor vicars in the choir stalls of the cathedral (roughly half of the total number). By contrast, on festal occasions it was possible not only to have most of them present but also to virtually double their ranks with reinforcements from one or both of the two other groups associated with the chapter that included trained musicians. There were, on the one hand, nine major vicars—*les grands vicaires*—any of whom could be called upon to sing in choir when necessary or desirable. (Payments made to reward them for this special service prove that this occurred from time to time.) When circumstances warranted, some half a dozen choir boys could participate as well in the performance of a polyphonic work. On at least one occasion, the visit of Emperor Charles V in January 1540, all three groups joined together—a total of thirty-four voices—to sing a motet in honor of the Virgin.[7]

In Cambrai it was not necessarily customary for the choirboys to sing with the adults of the choir for daily services, however, at least not from about 1500 on. During the sixteenth century the minor vicars counted both soprano and alto voices in sufficient numbers so that the boys were not required for a polyphonic performance, and, although precise information is spotty, the vicars appear to have sung rather often by themselves. More is known about performances for the votive services and the special commemorations established by endowment than for the daily liturgy because the acts of foundation often specified the singers responsible for the observance. Such documents call for a considerable and noteworthy variety of combinations. Some of them specify the minor vicars alone. Others mention a dozen of the most skilled singers selected from among the vicars, whether major or minor. Still others specify the choirboys, either by themselves or with their master, and, at times, a few other adult males to provide the lower parts. Or, when the endowment was particularly generous, the minor vicars, the choirboys and their master, and a number of assisting celebrants were to attend.[8]

It is admittedly difficult to compare the size of the choir in such a fluid and complex situation with that of a princely chapel where the liturgical requirements must

---

6. For a more detailed discussion of the organization of the choir, see Craig Wright, "Performance Practices at the Cathedral of Cambrai, 1475–1550," *Musical Quarterly* 64 (1978): 296–97.

7. Details are given by Wright, "Performance Practices at Cambrai," 296.

8. Regarding the use of the minor vicars and the choirboys both as separate choirs and as an integrated ensemble, see Wright, "Performance Practices at Cambrai," especially pp. 300–311.

have been much more straightforward. Turning, however, to a courtly musical establishment with which Cambrai Cathedral usually had close ties, the ducal court of Burgundy, we discover that the personnel of the chapel—which varied but little from between twenty-two and twenty-eight from the 1440s to the 1470s[9]—exceeded in number the minor vicars at the cathedral through most of the fifteenth century. Conversely, if one adds to the cathedral choir the major vicars and the boys, the total number of trained musicians available for a special occasion was clearly larger than at the court. At the same time the singers' duties at the cathedral were obviously much more demanding and time-consuming, given the staggering number of endowed Masses and special commemorations.

In either place a number of singers could apparently be absent from services at virtually any time, and they were probably all present only on rare occasions. One can thus surmise that the polyphonic ensemble of the cathedral could—and evidently did—vary in size from as few as eight to ten singers to as many as thirty or more, depending upon the circumstances and the resources available at the moment. By contrast, the singers of the courtly chapel were probably rarely as few as on lean days at the cathedral; as a rule they had no other religious duties to cut into their attendance at services. However, because their total numbers were smaller, they could not achieve by themselves the massive effect possible for their ecclesiastical counterparts at Cambrai Cathedral.

Whatever the size of the choir, some sort of balance had to be struck among the separate parts. That this was a serious consideration is evident from numerous indications, one of the most informative being the ordinances so carefully formulated in 1469 by Charles of Burgundy for the singers of the ducal chapel (see pp. 91–94). These prescribed a minimum of fourteen singers, including at least three basses, three tenors, two altos, and six sopranos. The preponderance of soprano voices—of which there were to be roughly twice as many as on any other part—was still pretty much the norm nearly a century later at the cathedral of Cambrai, judging from some mid-century accounts in which the singers are exceptionally identified by parts. Those paid for the first week of June 1547 included seven basses, five tenors, four altos, and seven sopranos, not counting the six choirboys. A year later there were still seven basses and six sopranos—in addition to the boys—but only three tenors and three altos. Although the highest voices were matched numerically by the lowest by this time, at least on the payment registers, the inner parts continued to be carried by fewer singers.[10]

There is no compelling *stylistic* reason for assigning a larger number of singers to the soprano than to the other parts in performing the polyphonic sacred repertory of the period. In the fifteenth century the tenor was frequently the most important structural element in such music, and in the sixteenth the trend was

9. See Jeanne Marix, *Histoire de la musique de la cour de Bourgogne* (Strasbourg: Heitz, 1939; reprint, Geneva: Minkoff, 1972), 242–63.
10. For details, see Wright, "Performance Practices at Cambrai," 310–11.

toward increasing melodic and contrapuntal independence of the parts. Nevertheless, the uppermost line was often the most interesting melodically, and the voices singing it were usually among the weakest of the choir. Either they belonged to choirboys, whose vocal powers were relatively undeveloped, or to adult males singing "falsetto," thus using the part of their overall range that was naturally the weakest. The picture drawn from archival evidence might be more informative if it were more complete. Unfortunately, the relative proportions among the voices in church choirs of northern Europe are difficult to determine for the period in general because, as has been noted, the singers are so rarely identified as to range or part.

In one other case for which there are specific indications, Brumel's *Missa Et ecce terrae motus* for twelve voices, they are characteristically ambiguous. The only surviving source for the work carries the names of the singers who performed it at the Bavarian court under Lassus in 1568–70; four are given for each of the alto and bass parts, three for each of the tenors, but none is written on the three soprano parts. If, as Fallows has suggested, the latter were sung by boys, perhaps a dozen strong, there would have been just four to a part as well—no more than for the altos and basses. Since the sopranos are not named, however, and because some of the parts may have been doubled by instruments as well, this example leads to no firm conclusions.[11]

It seems likely, nonetheless, that where adequate vocal resources were available, questions of balance would have drawn attention to the number of singers to a part and that a greater number was often assigned to the soprano for it to be clearly heard. Moreover, judging from the evidence of Italian cathedral choirs, to be examined presently, that convention may have been adopted virtually everywhere sacred polyphony was performed.

There were few churches anywhere on the Continent with as many trained singers among their clergy as at Cambrai Cathedral, at least during the fifteenth century. Just as the Burgundian chapel under Philip the Good and Charles the Bold surpassed in numbers and distinction that of every known rival—with the possible exception of the English royal house—so too that cathedral's choir appears to have been preeminent in the sacred realm during the same period of time. Unfortunately, the number of clerics assigned important musical functions cannot be determined for many northern churches, but where such information is available, it supports generally the conclusions outlined here.

At the church of Notre Dame in Condé, where the composer Josquin Desprez finished his career, there were sixteen vicars and six choirboys in 1523, just a couple of years after his death.[12] The cathedral of Our Lady in Antwerp,

11. Even though evidence in this case is inconclusive, David Fallows, who cites it in his discussion of "The Performing Ensembles in Josquin's Sacred Music," 43, believes that the kind of balance among the parts that can be demonstrated for the choirs at the Burgundian court and Cambrai Cathedral was also generally observed elsewhere (cf. pp. 43–55).

12. This is according to Herbert Kellman; see Fallows, "Performing Ensembles in Josquin's Sacred Music," table 1, p. 40.

which took steps to establish a polyphonic choir shortly after 1400 and had at some point among its vicars such well-known composers as Okeghem, Barbireau, and Obrecht, was still not able to boast more than eight choirboys and twelve adult singers at century's end.[13] Similarly, the church of St. James in Bruges usually had ten to twelve adults and four boys through the same general period.[14] These numbers may appear modest, but they would have allowed in every case two or three singers to a part in the lower voices, as called for by Charles of Burgundy's ordinance, and several more on the soprano line to maintain the balance. It appears likely, then, that other northern churches where polyphony was cultivated had choirs of like size in the fifteenth century: between four and eight choirboys, for example, and anywhere from a dozen to some sixteen or eighteen vicars.

In Italy the church choirs were smaller still early in the fifteenth century. When a certain "Jodocho de Frantia biscantore" took his place among the singers of the Milan Cathedral in 1459, there were only six adults and an unspecified number of boys to perform polyphony during the services. Between 1478 and 1481 at the cathedral in Florence there were never more than five or six adults—roughly two to a part for the lower voices—and four boys. Over the next three years, moreover, the adults were reduced to a total of four—just one to a part with a master for the boys—whereas the boys numbered between four and eight. In other northern Italian cities such as Modena, Padua, Treviso, and Bologna, the principal churches counted only between three and six adult singers, and in many cases there is no evidence that choirboys were

part of the establishment (see Figure 4-4, and cf. Figure 4-3). Even at the basilica of St. Peter in Rome there were only seven singers

FIGURE 4-4. Singers facing one another across a two-sided stand, miniature from the *Liber precum cum Calendario*, Book of Hours of Queen Giovanna I of Naples, late fourteenth century (Vienna, Österreichische Nationalbibliothek, MS 1921, f. 113).

13. See J. Van den Nieuwenhuizen, "De koralen, de zangers en de zangmeesters van de Antwerpse O.-L.-Vrouwekerk tijdens de 15e eeuw," *Antwerps Katedraalkoor, Gouden Jubileum Gedenkboek* (Antwerp: Choraelhuys, 1978), 29–72 (especially pp. 31 and 51), who explodes the myth that the church had a choir with thirty to forty singers to a side.
14. According to the figures given by Fallows, "Performing Ensembles in Josquin's Sacred Music," table 1, p. 40.

in 1478, four sopranos, one tenor, and two "contratenors" (either alto or bass).[15]

In the 1470s and 1480s Italian magnates such as the Sforza in Milan and the Este in Ferrara began to emulate northern nobles by establishing at their courts polyphonic choirs they hoped would rival those of France and Burgundy. Major Italian churches then followed suit, increasing in particular the complement of singers trained to execute mensural polyphony. The papal court led the way, even though the pontiff's private chapel functioned in virtually every sense more like that of a secular ruler than the choir of a cathedral or collegiate church; the number of singers in its ranks increased from as few as fourteen in the 1470s to as many as twenty-four in 1483.

More significantly, the number of singers in the major churches grew steadily and in some cases even dramatically. At the cathedral of Milan the adult singers increased from nine to fifteen between 1483 and 1489, and in the early years of the sixteenth century there were usually about a dozen (with a high of fourteen in 1516) who were usually assisted by some half a dozen boys. In Florence the number of singers at the cathedral fluctuated with the political fortunes of the city. The ten adults of 1485 increased to eighteen in 1493—a level reached by the church of the Santa Annunziata already in 1484—before dropping back to four adults and eight boys between 1498 and 1501. Total strength rose again in 1502 to sixteen: two sopranos, two altos, four tenors, two basses, five boys, and the latter's master. These numbers dropped to twelve in 1507 and to eight in 1512 and averaged only six adults and four to six boys during the troubled years between 1513 and 1526. When prosperous times returned, the cathedral choir was combined with that of the baptistry of St. John and numbered altogether twenty-four: the chapelmaster, seven sopranos (including four boys), seven altos, four tenors, and five basses.

In Bologna the choir of the basilica of San Petronio followed a more regular pattern, growing from seven to nine adults at the beginning of the century to thirteen by 1525 and fifteen in 1540 with an unspecified number of boys. Modena had six adults in 1494, between nine and eleven through the opening decades of the sixteenth century, and an undetermined number of boys. At the cathedral of Treviso, which maintained on average only four adult singers and a few boys in the 1470s, there were eight adults and up to five boys from 1488 to 1491. From 1509 to 1513 there was retrenchment (to five adults and five boys), but by 1527–28 the total had risen again to thirteen singers: two masters (whose participation in the singing is not specified), three altos, two tenors, two basses, and four boy sopranos. Subsequently, a dozen singers, with two adults on each of the lower parts and half a dozen sopranos, appear to have been considered sufficient. In Siena the increase was more striking, from six adults in 1508 to fourteen in 1517 and seventeen only three years later, but no choirboys are mentioned.[16]

15. See Frank A. D'Accone, "The Performance of Sacred Music in Italy during Josquin's Time, c. 1475–1525," in *Josquin des Prez*, ed. Edward E. Lowinsky and Bonnie J. Blackburn (London: Oxford University Press, 1976), 603.
16. The numbers have been taken from D'Accone, "Performance of Sacred Music in Italy during Josquin's Time," 606–8.

Compared with the impressive group of singers that could be assembled at a northern cathedral like that at Cambrai or, for that matter, the vocal resources available to some princely chapels in France, Burgundy, or—by the end of the fifteenth century—even Italy, many of the numbers cited for Italian churches are decidedly modest. They are nonetheless most informative regarding the performance of sacred polyphony at the time, indicating that many still considered it a soloistic art at the beginning of the sixteenth century. For the church, a performance with only one voice to a part—with perhaps two or three for the soprano—was deemed entirely acceptable. At the same time the gradual increase in the size of the average choir reflects a clear trend toward truly "choral" polyphony,[17] even though that term must be understood in a relatively limited sense. The ideal articulated by Duke Charles for the Burgundian chapel in 1469 called for only two or three singers to a part, at least in the lower voices. Even for the opulent chapel formed in the 1560s under Lassus at the ducal court of Bavaria, there is evidence, as has been seen, that three or four voices to a part were deemed sufficient.

Few churches were able or willing to devote to the training and maintenance of their choir the resources that would have been required to rival the largest of the princely chapels. Still, the number of cathedrals and collegiate churches that could enhance liturgical observances with a competent polyphonic ensemble seems to have grown steadily from mid-fifteenth century on. Moreover, many of those choirs—however modest by present standards—either equaled or surpassed in total numbers the minimum of fourteen prescribed by Charles of Burgundy for what was in 1469 one of the most prestigious princely chapels in all of western Europe. As a consequence, townspeople had ever more frequent opportunities to hear the kind of sacred polyphony that had long been routinely performed by the chapel singers of secular courts.

The extent and the effect of that public exposure to the music of the elite is difficult to assess. Nevertheless, the rising demand for private instruction in music through the sixteenth century and the concomitant success of commercial music publishers suggest that it may have contributed to a steadily growing interest in music of the written tradition, at least among those classes that were beginning to enjoy some measure of affluence and leisure. The developing taste for the subtle charms of the chanson and for the sonorous delights of the emerging instrumental genres, together with the time and money spent in acquiring the performance skills needed for music making as a private recreation in urban society, would otherwise be considerably more difficult to explain.

SECULAR SCHOOLS AND ACADEMIES

That choir schools and universities played a central role in the musical life of the cities of the fifteenth and sixteenth centuries is very clear. They impinged directly upon the

---

17. Manfred Bukofzer's substantive discussion of the question, "The Beginnings of Choral Polyphony," in *Studies in Medieval and Renaissance Music* (New York: Norton, 1950), 176–89, is still informative. He sees signs of such a tendency as early as the middle decades of the fifteenth century.

repertory and the quality of performances heard in local churches—whether plain-chant or polyphony—and they provided opportunities for musical instruction for at least part of the lay population. However, the church schools, including even the universities, were intended to meet first of all the needs of the mother institution—liturgical, didactic, charitable, and administrative—and the curricula that were established during the Middle Ages usually reflected those primary concerns.

Moreover, as has been seen, musical studies were shaped to a considerable degree, especially at the universities, by the venerable intellectual tradition passed down from antiquity. The theoretical concepts thus transmitted did suggest to imaginative minds solutions to some of the practical problems of composition and performance current at the time. Still, the ancient texts had a fascination all their own—stemming in part, no doubt, from their strong cosmological orientation—that often led instead to more speculative results. Happily, that did not inhibit music making in the church where the emphasis, naturally enough, was mainly upon the sacred compositional genres and, for both chant and polyphony (whether sacred or secular), upon pieces that had been notated.

In the course of the fifteenth century, as the progressive secularization of society already evident at least a hundred years earlier proceeded inexorably, lay schools were established in ever greater numbers at the courts and in the cities of western Europe. In some instances the schoolmasters were hired by the municipality (though they might also charge their pupils fees). In others the teacher took the initiative, opening an independent school and accepting students whose parents were able to pay the costs. For the nobility and the wealthy, finally, private tutors were usually brought into the home. Even the earliest of such schools, those established in Italy during the late Middle Ages, had seemingly ambitious objectives; the fundamentals of Latin grammar were usually the starting point for all instruction given, and Latin was often the only subject studied systematically, even in communal schools. Basic literacy (first in Latin and only much later in the vernacular), including reading and writing, was at that point always the first goal to be attained. The practical requirements of commerce soon prompted the teaching of mathematics as well, however, especially the use of the abacus and double-entry bookkeeping.[18]

The relatively systematic development of lay schools in a civic rather than an ecclesiastical setting came about first of all in the Italian communes. The cause was twofold: a notable decline in church schools during the twelfth century went hand in hand, ironically, with the growth of an economy based on manufacture, trade, and banking. The artisans and merchants, who were the leading citizens of the commune, saw in education both a practical necessity and a moral imperative for the "common good."[19] In the city-states of the peninsula, consequently, relatively large

---

18. Concerning the late medieval antecedents to government-sponsored schools in Italian communes and the three types of schooling adopted by urban laity, see Paul F. Grendler, *Schooling in Renaissance Italy: Literacy and Learning, 1300–1600* (Baltimore: Johns Hopkins University Press, 1989), 3–41.

19. Regarding the decline of church schools in Italy during the twelfth and thirteenth centuries, and the motives cited by communes for providing a school for their youth, see Grendler, *Schooling in Renaissance Italy*, 6–22.

numbers of boys—and girls—were given instruction in basic literacy, predominantly in Latin. A smaller number were also taught grammar, logic, and rhetoric and were introduced to Latin literature as preparation for the more advanced studies that were to supply notaries, lawyers, and copyists for Italy's flourishing commercial establishments.[20]

It was in this context that the humanist scholar began to assume an increasingly important role as a secular schoolmaster. Earlier, teaching in the lay schools had been most often done by clerics (who, despite the changes brought by the new age, continued to teach in secular schools through the sixteenth century and beyond). In the fifteenth and sixteenth centuries, however, it was ever more frequently the man educated in the *studia humanitatis* to whom magnates, city officials, and individual parents entrusted the education of their youth. This may well have been because humanists were thought better prepared than simple clerics, or even those trained at the university in one of the traditional professions (whether law, medicine, or theology), to offer what has been aptly termed "a program of education for life and citizenship."[21]

The disciplines that were the humanist's course of study—especially rhetoric, history, and moral philosophy—offered teaching materials that were virtually ideal for his purpose. They had already been used to good advantage by classical authors in developing in their students not only a sense of civic duty but also the rhetorical skills needed to function effectively in the commercial and political arenas. Humanist schoolmasters were therefore inclined to draw, from the ancient texts so familiar to them, useful and authoritative models for lay education in an urban setting. As a result, the educational ideals of the nascent Renaissance were shaped to an ever greater degree by their intellectual perceptions and cultural priorities.[22]

Two such men, Vittorino da Feltre (1378–1446) and Guarino da Verona (1374–1460), were particularly influential in the development of a humanist-inspired curriculum for both courtly and urban schools. They were not only exact contemporaries but also intimate friends and, for a considerable time, close neighbors. In fact, intermittently between 1414 and 1418 Vittorino studied Greek with Guarino. The latter had acquired a thorough grounding in the ancient language from Manuel Chrysoloras—one of the few scholars of the period truly competent to teach it—during a five-year sojourn in Constantinople, starting in 1403. By 1420 Vittorino's own

---

20. According to Wallace K. Ferguson, *Europe in Transition* (Boston: Houghton Mifflin Co., 1962), 278, the historian Giovanni Villani reported early in the fourteenth century that as many as 8–10,000 boys and girls were then being taught to read in Florence and that 550–600 boys were being instructed in grammar and logic as well.

21. The phrase quoted is from Ferguson, *Europe in Transition*, 303, and the discussion of which it is a part is pertinent and informative.

22. The transition from the educational practices adopted in urban areas during the late Middle Ages to those that came to currency under the influence of Renaissance humanism (and the religious conflicts of the Reformation) has been traced by Denys Hay, "Schools and Universities," in *The Reformation, 1520–1559*, vol. 2 of *The New Cambridge Modern History*, ed. G. R. Elton (Cambridge: Cambridge University Press, 1975).

experience as a teacher was well begun; he had established a boarding house in Padua, where he tutored students in Latin and mathematics (a very common pattern for an independent school). He also had a connection with the university—presumably a rather informal one at first[23]—that was steadily strengthened by his reputation for Latin scholarship and, no less importantly, for moral probity. As a result, he was appointed in 1422 to the vacant chair of rhetoric. This was a distinction rarely achieved by humanist scholars, for although many of them maintained loose ties with a nearby university, very few of them were actually named to a faculty.

It was not at the University of Padua that Vittorino was to make his most significant mark, however. He was engaged in the following year, on the recommendation of his friend Guarino, by the Marquis of Mantua, Gianfrancesco Gonzaga, who was seeking a tutor for his children. Vittorino set up his school in the park of the Gonzaga residence in an elegant garden house, which he decorated with frescoes of children at play and christened "La Casa Giocosa" (The Happy House) as an indication of the atmosphere in which his charges were to learn. There he lived and worked with the children of his patrons, the marquis and his consort Paola. To this nucleus of students, male and female, were soon added yet others.

First, naturally enough, came the sons of the leading families of the region, whose lineage or wealth opened to them the doors of the court school. Later, the gifted children of the poor were also admitted, boarded, and taught, in part at Vittorino's own expense but mainly by the charity of the ruling couple. The numbers of those being educated, in addition to the Gonzaga children, apparently reached as many as forty, at one point, or even seventy, at another.[24] More importantly, the notion that instructional opportunities ought to be available to those most apt to profit by them—regardless of the accidents of birth or wealth—was widely adopted thereafter by schools in the humanist mold.[25]

In his curriculum Vittorino attempted to reconcile "the moral and religious teaching of the Church with classical instruction on lines approved by Quintilian and the knightly disciplines of the Italian Castello, all being suffused with something of the Greek feeling for grace and harmony."[26] In addition to Quintilian, whose *Institutio* set an acceptable moral tone and offered didactic methods worthy of emulation, the texts studied were exclusively classical or patristic in nature. Cicero, under-

---

23. It was not uncommon for communal schoolmasters to appear on university payment rolls since they, like the faculty itself, were paid by local government (see Grendler, *Schooling in Renaissance Italy*, 23–29), but Vittorino's association with the University of Padua was clearly on academic rather than administrative grounds.

24. According to the data presented by Grendler, *Schooling in Renaissance Italy*, 17–22 and 51–56, a total of twenty-five to thirty students was about average for both communal and independent schools; those that counted forty or more were exceptionally large and usually required the assistance of a teacher's aide (*ripetitore*).

25. Concerning Vittorino and the court school at Mantua, see William Harrison Woodward, *Studies in Education during the Age of the Renaissance, 1400–1600* (New York: Teachers College Press, 1976), 10–25; the following discussion is much indebted to Woodward's scholarship.

26. The quotation is from Woodward, *Studies in Education*, 12.

standably, figured prominently as a model of Latin style in both writing and speaking. His letters, his treatise on rhetoric (*De oratore*), and a good many of his orations were considered suitable for the instruction of the more advanced students.

Among the poets, Virgil, a Mantuan, held pride of place, followed by Lucan, whereas Vittorino saw Ovid, Juvenal, and Horace as requiring more cautious use in the classroom. The plays of Plautus and Terence were also read, those of Terence in particular as a useful guide to Latin conversation. For history Livy was a favorite, but Sallust, Caesar, and Plutarch were studied as well. Greek, too, was studied by serious students who spent some years in the school, not surprisingly in view of Vittorino's knowledge of and zeal for the ancient tongue. The histories of Xenophon, the orations of Isocrates and Demosthenes, Homer's heroic epics, and the plays of Aeschylus and Aristophanes were among the works perused in the original.

Rigorous intellectual training was matched by a vigorous regimen of physical conditioning not unlike that traditionally associated with British schools. Classrooms and dormitories were unheated, diet was given careful attention, and no one was excused from the exertions of the playing fields. For those whose adult life was likely to require it, the handling of weapons was included as well. The immediate and obvious goal of such activity was robust health and physical strength, but developing the confidence, grace, and dignity indispensable for an effective role in public life were clearly seen as no less important.

Music, too, had a relatively significant place in Vittorino's educational program. As a mathematician he was probably familiar with the most widely circulated texts on music theory, including the *De musica* of Boethius. Evidence that Vittorino had read this well-known work may be seen in the fact that one of his pupils was Johannes Legrense (Gallicus), whose didactic treatises were well grounded in Boethius's writings. As has been observed, Legrense's works were among the first of their kind to evince a distinctly humanistic point of view (see pp. 36–37). It would seem, moreover, that Legrense himself went on to become an influential teacher of music and music theory. He counted among his pupils Nicolaus Burtius, who was indebted to his mentor for both the substance of his tracts and for their humanistic orientation.[27]

Vittorino was interested in more than just the intellectual tradition associated with music, however. He also espoused the Greek notion that music possesses a potent ethical force capable of shaping the character of the young; consequently, he prescribed its use as a daily accompaniment to meals. In addition, students were expected to sing regularly themselves, and, in some cases, they were also encouraged to develop instrumental skills. Vittorino must have given considerable attention to the choice of works performed since—like Plato—he had little use for trivial or wanton compositions. His preference was for music with wholesome texts, sober or martial in tone, that would help to inculcate in his students those qualities of temper-

---

27. The claim of Cecil Adkins, "Legrense," *The New Grove Dictionary of Music*, 10:614–15, that Legrense was also the teacher of Ramos de Pareia, Gaffurius, Spataro, and even Tinctoris does not seem well founded.

ance, courage, and high-mindedness deemed most desirable for men involved in civic affairs.[28]

The moral impact attributed to music by Vittorino and others was undoubtedly largely a function of the texts that were sung. Nonetheless, the aesthetic experience was valued as well, thanks to the Platonic notion that "rhythm and harmonia find their way to the inmost soul . . . imparting grace." According to the Platonic view, a person properly trained in music should recognize the harmonious and the beautiful, take pleasure in their contemplation, and thus "receive them into his soul to foster its growth and become himself beautiful and good." So formed, he (or she) would therefore also be inclined to reject that which is evil and badly shapen.[29]

Guarino's activity as a schoolmaster actually began somewhat earlier than Vittorino's, but initially he was connected with communal rather than courtly or independent schools.[30] In 1410, shortly after returning from Constantinople, he was invited to Florence, where, with the backing of a small group of prominent citizens, he opened a school that quickly acquired a considerable reputation. When, two years later, a public *studium* (a secondary school on the university model) was reopened in the city, his reputation as a Greek scholar earned him a nomination to that chair. Growing friction with his Florentine patrons led to his departure in 1414 for Venice, where he established an independent school for young patricians that also attracted older scholars, like Vittorino, who wished to learn Greek. Four years later he returned to his native Verona, where he was named Civic Professor of Rhetoric. While there, and later in Ferrara, he adopted a well-established practice that humanist schoolmasters continued to follow for generations to come, taking students into his home as boarders who paid both for their keep and for the instruction they received.

He went to Ferrara in 1429, having received an invitation from the Marquis Niccoló d'Este to become tutor to the latter's son Leonello. Like Vittorino in Mantua, Guarino was allowed—and in fact probably encouraged—to offer his schooling to other youths of the city, thus establishing an independent school like that of Vittorino in Padua. He continued to instruct other students even after his noble pupil married in 1435 (having, perhaps, by then completed his studies). In that same year Guarino acquired a house, as he had in Verona, in which his younger students could live and study as boarders. His ties with the city government, and therefore the communal character of his school, were strengthened in the following year with the establishment of a public *studium* and his appointment there as professor of rhetoric.

Leonello, by then Marquis of Ferrara, continued with the organization and expansion of the *studium* until he was able, in 1442, to obtain from the Habsburg

28. For details see Woodward, *Studies in Education*, 19–20.
29. The quotations are from Plato's *Republic*, in Oliver Strunk, ed., *Source Readings in Music History*, rev. ed., ed. Leo Treitter (New York: Norton, 1998), 14.
30. Concerning Guarino da Verona's career and didactic methods, see Woodward, *Studies in Education*, 26–47, to which the following paragraphs are much indebted.

emperor its recognition as a full-fledged university. It was for the times an exceptional institution, for even though it could then begin to grant degrees in the disciplines that had become traditional for the medieval university (law, medicine, and theology), it had been founded under the influence of one of the foremost humanist scholar-educators of the fifteenth century. As a result, Ferrara quickly assumed a leading role in integrating the fields of humanist study into the curriculum of Italian universities. As for Guarino, he divided his time between his public lectures (in the morning) and his private students (in the afternoon).

His instructional program was apparently very similar to that of his friend Vittorino. As in Mantua, physical activity and training in the use of arms had their place in the school at Ferrara, at least as long as Leonello d'Este was the principal student. Guarino's aims differed little from those of his friend and colleague, but his treatment of the humanistic curriculum was significantly more systematic. This may have been prompted, at least in part, by his closer and longer association with a university. One of Vittorino's chief strengths as a teacher was his ability to recognize the special predilections and abilities of each student and his willingness to devise—within limits—a program of study that would facilitate their fullest development. Guarino, by contrast, took a less flexible approach, dividing his instruction into three stages: the elementary, the grammatical, and the rhetorical.

His instruction began with reading and writing—Latin, to be sure—to which were added little by little the rudiments of Latin grammar, starting with regular declensions and conjugations. The second phase dealt with the niceties of accidence and syntax, picking up the study of grammar where it had been left at the elementary level. At the same time, attention was focused increasingly on the sense of the passages read, which were construed not only for their meaning but also, and more significantly, for their moral import. Grammar and syntax were learned through repeated attempts at composition. Moral lessons were mastered with the help of a notebook in which excerpts could be set down, organized under appropriate headings, and glossed with the pupil's own commentaries. These same passages, which students often committed to memory, would later serve as the starting point for further essays in composition in which they were to emulate the model, elaborating the same themes and imitating the Latin style. At this stage the study of Greek was begun as well, but primarily as an aid to the understanding of Latin rather than as an in-depth study of the language as with Vittorino.

Once the student had demonstrated his competence in Latin, both spoken and written, he could enter the third level of Guarino's educational program, referred to as *rhetorica*. Here the treatises on oratory ascribed to Cicero and Quintilian provided the point of departure. Also studied was the anonymous *Rhetorica ad Herennium*, thought at the time to represent Ciceronian teachings on the topic in their quintessential form. These were perused not only for their content but also, and more particularly, as examples of the classical genres of prose composition. As in Vittorino's school, the other authors read at each of these three stages were without exception classical or patristic: Virgil, Ovid, Seneca, Lucan, Juvenal, Terence, and Pliny, for instance, among the Latin writers; Homer, Plutarch, Aristotle, and Theocritus among the Greeks. However, Guarino also brought to the classroom his interest in the works of the Church Fathers, Augustine, Basil, and Jerome in particular.

In fact, the religious preoccupations and personal piety of both Guarino and Vittorino tend to belie the prevalent notion that the Renaissance was an era of unbelief marked by the growing influence of pagan myths and lax morality. Such a view is highly simplistic at best, and in most circumstances it is more than likely a serious distortion of historical reality. Except in the rarest cases, humanist scholars hardly questioned the basic tenets of the Christian church. Quite to the contrary, many of them were passionately engaged by their studies in the religious controversies of the age, either with the issues that led to the Reformation or, later, those taken up by the Catholic Counter-Reformation. It is no surprise, therefore, that in most secular schools of western Europe, the doctrines and morality of Christianity were routinely taught, or that the principal liturgical observances continued to play a role in the daily round of student activities throughout the fifteenth and sixteenth centuries. Moreover, with the spread of the Protestant Reformation and the corresponding reaction from the Roman side, the curricula of communal schools came to reflect ever more clearly the prevailing theological stance of the area in which they were located. It was not long, in fact, until such institutions were used systematically to instill partisan views in the minds of the young and thus to disseminate them more widely and quickly.

The schools of Vittorino and Guarino have been examined in some detail not only because they are in many respects typical but also, as the foregoing discussion implies, because they helped establish curricular patterns and didactic methods that spread with the new humanistic scholarship to every part of western Europe. And although music seems to have received less emphasis from Guarino than was given it by Vittorino, it became nonetheless an integral, if modest, part of the basic curriculum of many communal and independent schools in the humanist mold. Music was not held to be indispensable everywhere—as Baldassare Castiglione's discussion of the ideal courtier clearly shows[31]—and its overall importance in the humanistic scheme of things was perhaps less generally recognized in Italy than in the countries of northern Europe.[32]

Still, the dissemination of humanist scholarship from Italy outward—into France, Germany, England, and eventually Spain as well—together with the establishment of schools like those of Vittorino and Guarino in a growing number of localities often carried with it some instruction in music. Details as to the curriculum of such institutions are known in only a few instances, but the general pattern was apparently

31. For that author's views on the role of music in the courtly society, see the end of the first book of *Il cortegiano*, completed in 1514 and first published in 1528, in Strunk, ed., *Source Readings in Music History*, rev. ed., 326–28.

32. In his survey of *Schooling in Renaissance Italy*, Grendler mentions music only in connection with the schools run by religious orders (see pp. 392–95), and the emphasis given it probably depended, as in the case of Vittorino and Guarino, on the interests and competencies of the individual schoolmaster.

always much the same. Where music was taught, it was not in order to develop professional musicians—future singers, instrumentalists, or composers—as in the choir schools. Rather, the purpose was to embellish the humanistic learning of the students with the understanding and skills of the informed amateur, just enough so that music making could be a pleasant means of personal and social recreation. Excessive enthusiasm for such pleasures was frowned upon at the time in aristocratic and urban circles, but when held properly in check, musical abilities were generally viewed as an enviable social asset.

One of the earliest indications that humanist teaching was having an effect on the educators of northern Europe is to be seen in the Latin or "trivial" schools founded by the Brethren of the Common Life, beginning in the late fourteenth century. One of the best known, and one of the first to adopt a humanistically oriented curriculum, was the school at Deventer, where the rector from 1465 on was Alexander Hegius. Starting in 1474, after a period of contact with Rudolph Agricola—who was exposed to the new learning while at the Studium in Ferrara (and serving simultaneously as organist of the court chapel)—Hegius reorganized the school along humanistic lines. His reforms included improving the materials and methods used for teaching Latin and introducing Greek into the course of study. Their effectiveness may be judged from the frequency with which they were adopted by other schools and by the erudition acquired by some of those who were students there, men such as Erasmus and the future pope, Adrian VI.[33]

In France Guillaume Budé was clearly inspired by the humanist ideal of education when he sought the support of King Francis I to establish what was to become the Collège de France. Founded in 1530 as the Collegium Trilingue with chairs in Greek and Hebrew, the school added foundations for Latin and mathematics in 1534. Budé's passion for these ancient languages is evident from his treatise on the education of a prince, written for his royal patron upon Francis's accession in 1515. By his emphasis in that work on the importance of eloquence as a means of acquiring knowledge and an indispensable tool for an effective ruler of state, and by the large place he gave to the lessons of history in the schooling of a future magnate, he reveals his affinity for the type of curriculum developed in the humanist schools of Italy. He also points, of course, to the methods he adopted in his own teaching. Under his direction, the number of lectureships at the newly founded school was increased in 1545 from four to seven, despite predictable resistance from the University of Paris—thanks, no doubt, to the king's protection. Thereafter, the college flourished continuously, thus giving a clear indication of the extent to which the humanist spirit had penetrated French culture by mid-sixteenth century.[34]

Budé's initiative in Paris was matched in Bordeaux by the corporation of the city.

33. For a discussion of the school at Deventer, and others similar to it, see Woodward, *Studies in Education*, 82–86.
34. Concerning the founding of the school, see Ilan Rachum, ed., *The Renaissance: An Illustrated Encyclopedia*, (London: Octopus Books, 1979), 116; for a detailed discussion of Budé's views, see Woodward, *Studies in Education*, 130–38.

In 1534 that body undertook the reorganization in the new humanist mold of their venerable communal school, the Collège de Guyenne, in the hope that it would become one of the finest of its kind in all of France. To bring this about, the city fathers turned to André Gouvéa, who had been the director of a well-established college in Paris and whom Montaigne describes as "the greatest principal of France." Gouvéa assembled a distinguished faculty of humanist scholars, and together they set about reshaping the instructional program of the college. A detailed description from later in the century of the curriculum and methods they adopted shows them to have been similar in all essentials to those followed by Guarino in Ferrara.[35]

Gouvéa was able to bring to the school in Bordeaux, among others, Mathurin Cordier, whose sympathy for the Reformation also earned him an invitation from his former student, John Calvin, to go to Geneva and there assist with the founding of a Protestant school. Unfortunately, by 1536 the first signs of the developing conflict between the Catholic church in France, which enjoyed the support of Francis I, and the reformers, who would experience a long period of bitter persecution, had begun to appear. Yielding to growing pressure, perhaps to avoid embarrassing the city fathers and officials of the school, which remained steadfastly Catholic despite its relatively tolerant atmosphere, Cordier accepted Calvin's invitation.

He spent the remainder of his days in Switzerland, where he helped to reshape to humanist ideals the curriculum of the schools established by the reformers. During his final years he lived in Geneva, teaching in the city's public school, the Collège de la Rive, which was being administered by Calvin himself. His career was largely shaped, therefore, by the growing social and political rift produced by the Reformation (a lot he shared with a number of important composers of the same period whose works are considered below). Having left the college in Bordeaux because of his religious convictions, Cordier associated himself with communal schools in Switzerland that were used ever more openly and effectively to propagate the views and doctrines of the Reformation.[36]

The profound impact of the humanist movement on schools directed by Protestant reformers is nowhere more evident than in Germany. There Philip Melanchthon deployed his organizational genius in bringing both the spirit and the substance of classical education—as it had been newly fashioned in Italy—to all three tiers of an evolving school system (primary, secondary, and university). Shortly after his arrival in Wittenberg in 1518, he tried his own hand at teaching Latin at the primary level in an independent school (*schola privata*) held in his own house, and that experiment furnished the model for the founding or reorganization of other "trivial" schools in the region. His most notable effort at the secondary level was undoubtedly his part in planning for a new school established in Nuremberg in 1526. Although he declined an invitation to be its director, Melanchthon did consent to

35. The educational program, as outlined by Elie Vinet, a younger colleague of Gouvéa who later succeeded him as principal, has been summarized by Woodward, *Studies in Education*, 143–54.
36. Cordier's career and his methods as an educator have been traced succinctly by Woodward, *Studies in Education*, 154–66.

help with the formulation of the curriculum and the appointment of competent faculty.

Despite his enthusiasm and assistance, the school was not ultimately successful. The wealthy burghers of the city, for whose children the institution was intended, were more inclined to put their sons to work already at fourteen years of age in the commerce that was Nuremberg's economic life blood rather than send them to school. They apparently viewed as excessive in both time and means spent the ten years of arduous study required to learn Latin and Greek well, and they were not persuaded of the utility of such a course. Instead, they sent their offspring abroad to learn the living languages that would be most useful in their trade. The same pragmatic spirit seems to have dominated in France and Switzerland with similar results. Only in Italy, apparently, were the humanist schools regarded as something more than a luxury for the children of average townspeople.

Melanchthon's influence proved to be a good deal more far-reaching and enduring in the German universities than it was in the primary and secondary schools. During the fifteen years following his appointment in Wittenberg he contributed to the reorganization of several of the most venerable of these northern institutions, including the universities of Tübingen, Heidelberg, and Wittenberg itself. He also helped draw up plans for the founding of others, including those in Marburg, Königsberg, and Jena. In each instance he attempted to reconcile the educational ideals of the humanists with the theology and moral views of the Protestant Reformation and to achieve, at the same time, their assimilation to the traditions of the medieval university.

His choice of classical literature for the curriculum was thus governed not only by the customary humanist criteria of erudition and elegance but also by the subject matter and its capacity to edify. In addition to Greek, Hebrew was among the ancient languages to be studied, reflecting once again the religious interests of humanist scholars. In theology the scholastic authors were set aside in favor of Augustine and the Old and New Testaments. Even the study of medicine was affected, as the texts of the ancient Greek authorities Galen and Hippocrates were taken as a basis for formal instruction. Mathematics—apparently including that branch dealing with musical "harmonics" (see pp. 36–39)—and the natural sciences were likewise given systematic treatment for the first time, the latter in particular from the pertinent treatises by Aristotle.[37]

None of these innovations had a serious impact on the formal teaching of music at the university, however. Even though humanist scholarship brought to light an increasing number of the theoretical texts from Greek antiquity and favored an intellectual climate in which they were ever more completely understood, medieval traditions were often retained in the universities with little modification, as has already been shown (see pp. 80–82). Unfortunately, we are less well informed regarding the

---

37. Concerning Melanchthon and his role in bringing the materials and methods of humanist education to the schools of Protestant Germany, see Woodward, *Studies in Education*, 211–43.

role of music in primary and secondary schools of a humanist stamp in northern Europe. Some instruction—mainly of a practical nature—was apparently given in the northern schools under discussion here just as it was in the Italian schools upon which they were modeled, but, once again, more as an adjunct to the basic curriculum than as an integral part of it.

The evidence is perhaps most indirect for the Collège de France in Paris, where virtually the only indication that music was cultivated as both a science and an art is the presence of Oronce Finé from 1530 to 1555 as the first professor of mathematics. Finé's two extant Latin treatises on mathematics included sections on music in the traditional manner. He is also the author of one of the earliest technical manuals on playing the lute, a slight work that was eventually published in both Latin and the vernacular, and he is reputed to have been highly skilled with the instrument himself.[38] It may be, therefore, that instrumental skills were cultivated by some of the students as well.

At the Collège de Guyenne in Bordeaux music was also taught as a branch of mathematics, but only during the final two years of instruction. By contrast, the detailed description of the curriculum cited earlier makes no mention of practical exercises in music.[39] It seems likely, nonetheless, that singing was a part of the daily activities in which the students were engaged. Attendance at Mass was a routine part of the school day, and the liturgy was undoubtedly sung at times, at least for special feasts. It is also possible that students were taught to sing, as they were in other schools organized along similar lines, and made to participate in practical exercises of that sort for an hour or so nearly every day.

Such was the case, for example, at the Collège de la Rive in Geneva, where Psalms were sung daily from eleven to twelve o'clock by the entire school.[40] Music and singing were part of the regular routine in the schools of Protestant Germany as well, at both the primary and the secondary levels. At the Latin school of Eisleben, founded in 1525 in accordance with the pedagogical principles espoused by Melanchthon, an hour of each day was set aside for singing and the study of music (see Figure 4-5). In the third (and final) year basic mathematics were also introduced into the curriculum, and this may have included some fundamentals of music theory. Similarly, at the secondary school in Nuremberg, whose organization was directly supervised by Melanchthon, music was to be taught on a daily basis. The place given to musical exercises in the schools under the influence of the Wittenberg humanists may of course reflect in part Martin Luther's own affection for it. As Luther declared in 1524, "if I had children of my own, I would have them learn not only languages

38. On Finé, see Jane I. Pierce, "Finé," *The New Grove Dictionary of Music*, 6:564, and cf. Nan Cooke Carpenter, *Music in the Medieval and Renaissance Universities* (Norman: University of Oklahoma Press, 1958), 141.

39. On the instructional program at the Collège de Guyenne, see Woodward, *Studies in Education*, 139–54.

40. This is according to the *Colloquia* of Mathurin Cordier, who, as we have seen, spent his final years there. See Woodward, *Studies in Education*, 157–66.

and history, but singing and instrumental music, and a full course of mathematics as well."[41]

Similar examples, drawn from among the increasing number of schools founded or reformed under the influence of humanist ideals, could be multiplied at length, not only in France and the Protestant areas of northern Europe but eventually in Spain and England as well.[42] Since the same pattern was followed over and over again, however, there is little point in doing so. The study of Latin and Greek was always the primary preoccupation, with Hebrew being added at the upper levels, and classical authors were used almost exclusively for the instruction of the young.

FIGURE 4-5. A group of children being instructed in music by two masters (Nuremberg, Stadtbibliothek, woodcut, ca. 1500).

As will by now be evident, details as to the role of music in the educational programs of Renaissance schools are unfortunately rather sketchy at best and may even be entirely wanting. Nonetheless, exposure to music was often an accompaniment to other activities, such as eating or dancing, and the rudimentary instruction in singing, theory, or even composition offered by schools in the humanist mold was certainly not aimed at professional competence.

Professional training of any kind was in fact usually looked upon askance by humanist scholars. It was entirely eschewed in Vittorino's school, and his attitude appears to have been the prevailing one. Although his students usually remained with him until the age of twenty-one and emerged with a more thorough knowledge of the classics than virtually any university could then provide, he saw the kind of education he offered either as a foundation for further studies or, even more directly, preparation for an honorable career in government or commerce. Because this attitude spread with the adoption of humanist curricula and teaching methods, professional musicians continued to be trained as they had been in the past. Throughout the period (and well beyond) singers, organists, and composers for the church were trained in its schools. By contrast, secular musicians acquired their skills with ever

41. See Woodward, *Studies in Education*, 219–25 and 240.
42. For indications concerning conditions in the latter two countries, see Woodward's discussion of "Juan Luis Vives" and of "The Renaissance and Education in England," *Studies in Education*; these chapters deal primarily with pedagogical manuals, however, and only marginally with the curricula offered in Spanish and English schools of the period.

greater frequency through a system of apprenticeships and of course through practical experience (see Figure 4-6).

Nevertheless, the influence of humanist scholarship contributed to a fundamental shift in society's attitudes toward music. With the emphasis on *utilitas* rather than metaphysics, the affective power believed to be inherent in a musical composition assumed greater significance than possible cosmological implications. Attention was focused primarily on the emotional impact that a skillfully wrought work—especially one based on a powerful text aptly set—could have on the mind and the heart of the listener. The manner in which the mathematical proportions of its consonant intervals and mensural organization reflected the harmony and order of the universe was consequently pushed to the background. Such a basic change in esthetic orientation was undoubtedly encouraged by Plato's and Aristotle's views concerning music's influence on the development of character and, perhaps even more so, by the many tales from classical antiquity about music's miraculous ability to alter human behavior for good or ill.

It is ironic, of course, that at about the same time humanist scholars were restoring, and beginning to understand more fully, the Greek texts in which the ancient cosmology was most clearly and completely exposed. In the end, however, it was the rhetorical bias characteristic of humanism that acquired greater currency and greater historical significance for the sixteenth century. Music was seen more as a

FIGURE 4-6. Woodcut showing what appears to be instruction in music from the *Orgel oder Instrument Tabulatur* by Elias Nicolaus Ammerbach, printed in Leipzig, 1571.

means to enhance verbal expression, particularly when affectively laden, and as an ornament to social intercourse—albeit with a moral force to be valued—than as a key to the structure of the cosmos. Such notions permeate Castiglione's dialogue, for example, in which music, while clearly not a profession that would be acceptable for a nobleman, is held to be both a social embellishment and, in a very real sense, an esthetic necessity.[43] More's Utopians, similarly, found music useful for its power to "wonderfully move, stir, pierce, and inflame the hearers' minds."[44] Thus the emphasis on rhetorical skills that characterized education in the humanist schools came to affect, as profoundly as it did any other aspect of the culture of the Renaissance, the perspective in which music was viewed and the esteem in which it was held.

GUILDS AND CONFRATERNITIES

The commercial and fraternal associations that played such an important role in European city life in the fifteenth and sixteenth centuries had originated in most instances at least a century or two earlier. The guilds, whose actions were guided primarily by economic self-interest, were of two basic types, artisanal or mercantile, depending on whether the livelihood of their members derived from the exercise of a specific craft or from the handling of goods produced by others. Sometimes that distinction is not immediately self-evident; a number of guilds comprised artisans who were also merchants. It becomes meaningful even in such cases, however, when the principal activity of the craftsman or merchant (whatever the latter's artisanal skills) reaches beyond local markets and involves trade with other regions and countries.

For confraternities, by contrast, the primary purposes were religious, either devotional or charitable or both. Many of them were closely tied to one of the guilds, which usually included the protection of the health and economic welfare of individual members among their objectives. Others were attached instead to a church or a monastic order and were thus more directly (and obviously) oriented toward developing personal piety and giving charitable service.[45] Despite the differences among them, however, guilds and confraternities alike often sponsored or engaged in activities traditionally linked with music and thus contributed to the local musical environment.

Both craft and trade guilds had as their essential aim controlling local markets and providing protection against competing "foreign" interests. As means to that end the

---

43. See the relevant passages of *Il cortegiano*, from the 1561 translation of Thomas Hoby, in Strunk, ed., *Source Readings in Music History*, rev. ed., 326–29.
44. Sir Thomas More, *Utopia*, book 2, ed. Burton A. Milligan in *Three Renaissance Classics* (New York: Charles Scribner's Sons, 1953), 233.
45. Concerning the general nature and social structure of religious confraternities, see Ferguson, *Europe in Transition*, 64 and 358–59.

craft guilds found it useful to establish standards of workmanship, to monitor the training of apprentices, and to restrict the number of artisans given license to work. The primary reason for such measures was, understandably, to keep prices from collapsing and thus to guarantee a reasonable margin of profit to the artisan or tradesman, but the resulting "quality control" also offered a measure of protection to the buyer. There was another important consequence, however: the establishment of a well-defined, self-regulating social structure that reflected the medieval predilection for hierarchical order.[46]

As a rule the social stratification of the guilds resulted in three distinct and more or less separate layers. Leading and governing other members in all important matters were the masters, artisans who had earned through their reputation—aided on occasion by an advantageous marriage into a family of well-established craftsmen—both the capital needed to set up their own workshop and the right to take on apprentices. Although usually protected by a contract, an apprentice was fully subject to the supervision of the master and received little more than room, board, and other essentials regardless of the amount of productive work he was able to do. Once the apprentice had completed his training—a process that could require as many as five to seven years—he was recognized as a journeyman. He could then work in the shop of a master for wages but usually could not enter the latter's ranks until he was able to acquire the capital needed to set himself up in business—and the guild authorized him to do so.[47]

Even more importantly, besides establishing a stable social order for its members in which roles were clearly defined and some upward movement was possible, the guilds gave their members legal and social status within the urban community. This came about, undoubtedly, not only because craftsmen and tradesmen constituted a clear majority in every important city but also because the local economy was usually inextricably tied to their success. Not surprisingly, then, the relationship between guilds and city governments was generally both intimate and symbiotic. In fact, in major centers of industry and trade all over Europe, the privileges of citizenship were restricted to the members of the guilds and crafts.[48] Since most of the freemen were therefore also members of one of the guilds, it was also they—to the extent that democratic processes were followed—who elected their city government. Such was the case in London, for instance, where the masters of the twelve leading guilds also chose all important local officials.

Naturally, the more powerful a guild became, the greater its role in governmental affairs and the greater the influence it was able to wield in matters that concerned it. In that regard the economic circumstances of the fifteenth and sixteenth centuries favored as a rule the merchant guilds, who always had the potential of acquir-

---

46. For a brief description of the objectives of the guilds and of their impact on the life in the cities of the period, see "Guilds," *The New Columbia Encyclopedia* (New York: Columbia University Press, 1975), 1161.

47. Concerning the division of guilds into masters, journeymen, and apprentices, and some of the social consequences engendered by those distinctions, see Ferguson, *Europe in Transition*, 12–13.

48. See Ferguson, *Europe in Transition*, 111–12 and 128–29.

ing exceptional wealth that could be used to gain the upper hand with municipal officials and promote their own interests. It is true that those who engaged in trade, whether regional or international, were usually exposed to greater risks than the craftsmen whose market was largely restricted to the local area. There was always a danger that valuable goods could be lost in shipment, either to destructive storms at sea, to pirates, to thieves, or to marauding soldiers. Moreover, in cities where the domestic workforce came to be in conflict with the wealthy merchants, there was also the risk of plebeian rebellion and a consequent disruption in production. Such was the case in Florence, where circumstances of this sort led in 1378 to the bloody revolt of the *ciompi* (the wool carders).[49] However, the financial rewards, when such daring commercial ventures were successful, were commensurate with the hazards faced.

In sixteenth-century London the leading guilds, whose special status was visibly manifest in the distinctive livery their members were allowed to wear,[50] included the mercers (textile merchants), the grocers, the drapers, the fishmongers, the goldsmiths, the skinners, the merchant tailors, the haberdashers, the salters, the ironmongers, the vintners, and the cloth workers, only some of whom were craftsmen. All of them, however, were engaged in trade and dealt either in luxury items or in materials that involved international commerce or both.

A similar situation held in Florence, where the guilds were divided between the seven major arts, including the bankers and the mercantile guilds, and the fourteen minor arts, which were primarily those of the craftsmen and merchants who served mostly local markets.[51] By the fifteenth century the major guilds had gained control of the city, whereas the minor guilds had only minimal representation, and the workers who labored to produce the wool, silk, and furs that made for the city's wealth were paid a subsistence wage and given no voice at all in its government. Because it was the wool industry that had come by then to dominate Florence's economy, it was the *arte della lana* and the *calimala* (the wool manufacturers and finishers) who effectively controlled its elective offices. The *arte della lana*, in particular, achieved remarkable political power and autonomy in the course of the fourteenth century, having acquired the right to establish its own laws and police officers together with courts and prisons to see to their enforcement.[52]

49. See Harry A. Miskimin, *The Economy of Early Renaissance Europe, 1300–1460* (Cambridge: Cambridge University Press, 1975), 102–6.
50. Hence the name "livery companies"; see the relevant article in *The New Columbia Encyclopedia*, 1595.
51. As enumerated by Benedetto Varchi (1503–65) in his *Storia Fiorentina*, book 3, chaps. 20–22, those matriculated in one of the seven major guilds were as follows: (1) judges and notaries; (2) wool finishers (*calimala*); (3) bankers and money changers; (4) wool manufacturers; (5) silk manufacturers; (6) physicians and apothecaries; and (7) furriers. The fourteen lesser guilds included (1) the butchers; (2) the shoemakers; (3) the blacksmiths; (4) the linen-drapers; (5) the masons and stonecutters; (6) the vintners; (7) the innkeepers; (8) the oil sellers (who included the pork butchers and the rope makers); (9) the hosiers; (10) the armorers; (11) the locksmiths; (12) the saddlers; (13) the carpenters; and (14) the bakers.
52. See Ferguson, *Europe in Transition*, 111–12 and 271–72.

Although the degree of independence achieved by the wool merchants in Florence was unusual, it was not uncommon for the guilds of the period to be charged by their city government with regulating the affairs of their own members, legislating the rules and standards by which they were to work, judging disputes brought before their officers, and levying fines and other punishments where necessary. Even the musicians' guild of London, one of the weakest and least significant in the city, had such responsibilities.[53] For that to be possible, however, it was essential that the individual guild have recourse to a higher, more powerful authority. If the rights and privileges to be enjoyed by its members were to have any real value or its rules and regulations any force to govern their conduct, they had to be established by charter by the rulers of the area in which the guild functioned.

In a republic like pre-Medici Florence, where nobility were banned by law from holding public office unless a member of one of the major guilds, this meant recognition by the city government first of all. In towns where a local magnate exercised control, as was usually the case in the kingdoms of France and England, it was necessary in addition—or instead—to obtain the support of the reigning noble. Because such rulers soon recognized in the guilds a potential source of both political support and tax revenue, many of them acted quickly and systematically to bring organizations of that kind under their control. In France it was from the crown, from the late Middle Ages on, that the guilds derived their ultimate authority. In England the first charters were granted as early as the fourteenth century by Edward III, and it was Henry VIII who first fixed the order of precedence for the livery companies of London (as given above). In Germany and Italy, where governmental rule was much less centralized, it was usually the local ruler to whom the guilds turned for recognition and support.[54]

As an important microcosm of urban society the guilds of the period had their own carefully regulated internal structures, and their charters provided fairly comprehensive statutes to govern the conduct of their members. Details differed, clearly, from region to region and from trade to trade, reflecting local circumstances and usage, but common objectives and shared traditions tended to produce recurring patterns in organizational structures and administrative procedures among guilds of all kinds.

One of the earliest such corporations for musicians was established in Paris in 1321, when the provost of the city ratified statutes that had been proposed by thirty-seven minstrels, male and female, who were residing and working there.[55] Formulated in the

---

53. See Walter L. Woodfill, *Musicians in English Society from Elizabeth to Charles I* (Princeton: Princeton University Press, 1953), 8–11.

54. See Ferguson, *Europe in Transition*, 463; cf. *The New Columbia Encyclopedia*, 1161 and 1595, and the discussion below, pp. 154–56.

55. The details that follow were gleaned from Abram Loft, "Musicians' Guild and Union: A Consideration of the Evolution of Protective Organization among Musicians" (Ph.D. diss., Columbia University, 1950), 118–31. As was customary at the time for craft guilds of all kinds, the minstrels of Paris were clustered in a single quarter of the city; theirs was along the rue des Jongleurs, now the rue Rambuteau.

usual protectionist vein, these regulations prescribed that all musicians playing and singing for hire in the city must be members of the guild (or swear, at least, to obey its statutes), and violators were to be banished for a year and a day. Similarly, brokers or agents were forbidden from engaging minstrels on behalf of their clients. Other provisions, by contrast, were intended to ensure fair practices among the members of the corporation. For instance, a guild musician was not allowed to accept work for anyone except him- or herself (and customary partners), to send a replacement unless prevented from keeping an engagement because of a serious impediment such as illness or imprisonment, or to leave a job before the hour agreed upon for its completion. Apprentices worked under even tighter strictures, as they were allowed to take on employment only for themselves and members of their immediate family.

Such rules were clearly designed to prevent the most skilled of the minstrels from gaining control of the market by contracting on behalf of the less competent for a fee and from depriving competitors of work by cumulating overlapping engagements that could only be met by cutting corners. Their effect was beneficial for the patron as well, however, since he was assured of receiving the services for which he had bargained, and therefore helpful in maintaining a good professional reputation for musicians of the corporation. To these prescriptions were later added others, with an apparently similar intent, prohibiting minstrels from flocking unbidden to every celebration of which they had knowledge and from canvassing the city for jobs. Nor were members of the guild allowed to accost prospective customers who came to their quarter of the city in search of musicians for hire or to break in on negotiations already engaged between colleagues and their clients.[56]

Some seven years after the founding of the corporation, two of its members, recognizing the plight of the ill and the indigent among them, determined to set up a church and a hospital to provide for their care. In 1330 they purchased a site for the hospital on the rue St. Martin des Champs, together with a nearby house. That initiative was taken up in the following year by the entire corporation with the founding of a confraternity, which assumed the cost of the property that had been purchased and contracted for the construction of a chapel. Saints Julien and Genesius were chosen as the patrons of their fraternal order, and from that time forward the guild began to be identified with the confraternity to which it had given rise and known simply as the Confraternity of St. Julien.

The guild was governed by a provost (usually referred to as the *roy des menestrels*) who was chosen more and more frequently from among the musicians of the king's court. Thanks to the protection of the crown, its members were soon able to extend their jurisdiction beyond the city of Paris to other parts of the realm. In 1407 a new charter for the guild was promulgated by King Charles VI, who decreed that its provisions applied to all minstrels and players of instruments, both loud and soft, and was to be observed throughout his domains. Only the king himself could grant to

---

56. A summary of the statutes is given by Loft, "Musicians' Guild and Union," 118–21.

musicians who were not enrolled with the confraternity permission to play for hire, and even they were obliged to collect alms for its charitable purposes.

Among the most noteworthy of the charter's statutes were those regulating musical instruction. A term of six years was set for apprenticeships, the longest of any among the French *corps des arts et métiers*, and a satisfactory examination before the minstrel king or his deputy was required for admission to the ranks of the journeymen. In addition those wishing to offer public instruction in music (presumably only to nobles and wealthy merchants, who would not then compete with guildsmen for work) required a special license from the provost of the corporation.[57]

As was noted earlier, in cities less populous than Paris the first musicians to establish residency, and thus gain the advantages of citizenship, were invariably those engaged as waits or watchmen. In many localities, consequently, they invariably formed the core of the musicians' guilds and confraternities as they came into existence (see pp. 126–28). Unfortunately, associations of the sort that hardly reached beyond town walls to the surrounding countryside have attracted relatively little historical attention. More is known about some exceptional initiatives in Germany, where efforts were made in the late fourteenth and early fifteenth centuries to extend the protection and authority of a few local corporations of minstrels to a substantially wider geographical area.

One of the most successful was the Alsatian Brotherhood of Musicians, which will serve here as an illustration.[58] With the help and support of the noble Rappolstein family, residents of the area who patronized music, this confraternity succeeded in establishing its jurisdiction over an entire region in the course of the fifteenth century. By 1480 the guild had grown so large that it was necessary to divide it into three sections by geographical area in order to improve control and supervision of its membership. Even then it was governed by a single minstrel-king, like its French counterpart. Its statutes, as they were formulated in 1606 (no doubt reflecting the usage of the previous two centuries), contain most of the customary provisions. Predictably, the very first article decrees that no musician, regardless of his place of residence (including the wholly itinerant), was to perform or teach for hire under any circumstances unless first admitted to the brotherhood. Violators were to be punished and have their instruments confiscated.

The statutes also stipulated fees to be paid upon acceptance into the brotherhood and upon appointment to any of its administrative offices. Once admitted, members were required to pay annual dues and were also charged for the license that attested to their right to receive payment for playing or singing in the territories subject to the control of the corporation. (From these articles it would appear that officers of the guild were paid for the time and trouble devoted to the general welfare of the

---

57. See Loft, "Musicians' Guild and Union," 121–30.

58. Concerning the development of the Alsatian Brotherhood, see Loft, "Musicians' Guild and Union," 74–83, from which the following discussion is largely drawn. Loft also describes in some detail an impressive federation of the town and church musicians of Bohemia, Moravia, Silesia, and lower Austria, founded in 1497.

brotherhood.) The preparation specified for a license was much less rigorous than in France, however, involving only two years of study for those who wished to work in a town and only one year for those who planned to work in the countryside.

A number of provisions were intended to regulate the relationships among guild members and with those who would employ them. Minstrels of the guild were to respect the established work areas of their colleagues and to refrain from attempting to win away their pupils. As in Paris, they were not to appear unbidden at an event for which music was usually contracted nor come between a patron and the musicians he had hired by undercutting unfairly the prices already agreed to. In accordance with the pattern followed generally by guilds everywhere, disputes among members were to be resolved by the duly established court of the brotherhood, and only if such adjudication failed were the persons involved allowed recourse to the civil courts or the right of appeal to Count Rappolstein directly.

The business of the brotherhood was transacted during its yearly meeting at Rappoltsweiler in the hereditary domains of the guild's noble patrons, and every musician subject to its jurisdiction was expected to attend. Those absent were fined and—to protect the employment of those in attendance—were not allowed to work outside of their own territories while it was being held. Like all events of its kind, this annual gathering was marked by conventional forms of public ceremony and celebration. It began with a procession to the chapel, where Mass was said, and everyone then went to the castle, where the musicians swore allegiance to their noble patron in return for his promises of protection and support. A banquet followed, with wines provided from the Rappolstein cellar, and the participants then retired to the gardens of the castle for dancing and general merrymaking.

Several of the statutes of the Alsatian Brotherhood reflect the difficulties encountered by musicians as they struggled to gain both a degree of social acceptance and the legal status that would entitle them to some protection under the law. Minstrels, especially those who were itinerant, had been traditionally linked with the most unsavory elements of the social order—prostitutes, thieves, murderers, and other malefactors—and could consequently be beaten or otherwise mistreated with virtual impunity. The low esteem in which they were generally held is evident from the fact that a papal bull, issued in the early fifteenth century, authorized the clergy to administer the sacraments of the church to these secular musicians. Significantly, moreover, it required the communicant to abstain from work for two weeks before and after (see Figure 4-7).

To counteract the negative perceptions lying behind such an extraordinary measure, the brotherhood asked for a certificate of honorable birth (a requirement for entry into many guilds) in support of any application for admission. Further, the statutes of the confraternity declared that it "had been established . . . to [foster] the highest praise of God and especially of the most holy Virgin," and those purposes were advertised by a silver medallion bearing Mary's image that was worn by every guildsman. The annual convention was generally held on the Marian Feast of the Assumption (August 15), and each member was expected to attend confessional

FIGURE 4-7. Secular musicians gathered on the steps of a church; instruments depicted include fife and drum, triangle, various shawms, straight trumpet, harp, a pair of lutes, psaltery, and portative organ (the *Isabella Book*, ca. 1497, a Spanish Dominican breviary, London, British Library, MS Add. 18851, f. 184ᵛ).

Mass on all other Marian feasts as well, give alms, and pay for at least one additional Mass during the year.[59]

Among the few essentially local musicians' guilds that flourished during the fifteenth and sixteenth centuries about which a fair amount is known, the Company of Musicians of London is an interesting and instructive example, in part because its statutory organization took shape relatively late. Its origins undoubtedly go back at least to the fifteenth century, but the first known charter from the city apparently came only in 1500. As a result, its administrative procedures and its by-laws—which remained unchanged through the remainder of the century—reflect those of the older, wealthier (and more prestigious) guilds of the city, which the minstrel freemen took as a model.[60]

Following a common pattern, the Company of Musicians was administered by a master and two wardens who could be seconded in their functions by a number of assistants. The officers were elected by the entire membership (annually until 1518 and biennially until the end of the century) and handled virtually all of the company's important business with little further consultation. As with the other London guilds these officials had the right under the city's charter to protect themselves and their fellow guildsmen against competition from those who had not been admitted to their ranks. They could—at least in principle—prevent musicians who were not freemen of London from singing or playing for hire on those occasions that offered professional minstrels the greatest opportunities for gainful employment. Their authority in that respect was more limited than that enjoyed by most other guilds, however, as it did not extend to their most serious competitors: musicians in the service of the king and other powerful lords of the realm.

59. The questions of legal and social status for minstrels are touched upon briefly by Loft, "Musicians' Guild and Union," 74–83, who cites the bull issued by Pope Eugene IV that gave them access to the sacraments of the Catholic church (pp. 70–72). (The period of abstention from work, before and after taking communion, was reduced in 1508 to five days.)

60. Concerning the circumstances that prompted the minstrels' petition to the city government and the resulting charter (as described in the following paragraphs), see Woodfill, *Musicians in English Society*, 3–9.

These officers also had to contend occasionally with musicians who had somehow associated themselves with one of the other companies. They could thus enjoy the privileges of guild membership while escaping the more stringent regulations of the Company of Musicians concerning the number of apprentices a master could take and the time required for their training. The matter was of particular importance for the working musicians of the city because restricting the number of apprentices (to one per master, as a rule) was one of the few effective means of averting unfair competition. Unlike most other crafts, which usually required substantial capital to set up shop, a journeyman musician could take on an apprentice and go in search of clients almost as soon as his training had been completed. It was therefore important to limit the number of true journeymen, because the use of apprentices in performance, together with collaboration among family members, was virtually indispensable if musicians were to make a living wage.[61]

In return for the powers and privileges granted them the officials of the Company of Musicians, like those of the companies upon which it was modeled, were charged with maintaining order among its members. Specifically, they were to keep London's minstrels from rebuking or reviling one another "with unfitting language" and especially from coming to blows. They were to mediate—and to resolve if at all possible—disputes arising among members, thus making it unnecessary to take their differences into the public courts. And they were responsible for monitoring the activities of all minstrels so as to prevent anything that could provoke public disorder or encourage immoral behavior.

In this respect close attention by officers of the guild to the training and supervision of apprentices was particularly important. Such instruction usually began in the early to mid-teens,[62] and since the apprentice traditionally lived and worked with his master for at least seven years, the latter stood in a very real sense (at least initially) *in loco parentis* to his pupil. He was expected, first of all, to provide the technical training needed to become proficient in the "science or art of music." Since apprentices were not allowed to play publicly for hire until heard by officers of the guild and found sufficiently competent as to do credit to the profession, that was usually motivation enough for masters to be assiduous in their teaching. They were also responsible, however, for instruction in religion and common virtue that would lead to sound morals and good citizenship. And when apprentices were skilled enough to begin working for wages, their masters were not to send them out to play without adequate supervision but only in the presence of experienced freemen who could "offer and present the music" while monitoring the conduct of their younger colleagues.[63]

To help the officers of the Company of Musicians to successfully discharge their

---

61. See Woodfill, *Musicians in English Society*, 11–13.

62. Woodfill, *Musicians in English Society*, 25, suggests seventeen as the maximum age for the beginning of an apprenticeship.

63. The quotations are from Woodfill, *Musicians in English Society*, 17, who discusses extensively the apprenticeship system adopted by the London Company of Musicians (pp. 17–25).

duties toward their members and fulfill their obligations to the civil government, they were empowered to levy fines for infractions of the rules and regulations of the guild. When necessary (with the consent of the mayor and the chamberlain), they could even commit members to prison for appropriate punishment. Fines for misconduct were apparently an important part of the modest revenues available to the guild for administrative and charitable purposes. They could be imposed not only for disorderly conduct but also for failure to adhere to the requirements of the company, including the payment of dues and fees, the acceptance of elective office, and attendance at regular quarterly meetings or at special convocations for the burial of a member or other special business. Yet other funds came from quarterly dues and from fees paid upon the presentation of apprentices.

The monies collected were to be devoted, first of all, to accomplishing the fraternal purposes of the company—relief to poor and injured musicians unable to provide for their own needs and burial for those whose means were not sufficient to see them decently out of the world. They could also be used to defray general expenses such as were incurred for the procession and banquet that invariably accompanied the election of new officers and to provide for the special religious services—Masses and night offices such as Vespers and Matins, for example—usually celebrated in that connection in a church with which the guild had some sort of special relationship. Although there is no record of such matters for the London Company of Musicians, it seems probable that, like other similar associations, they were linked to one of the churches in the city where the patron saint of their guild—in this case St. Anthony— was held in special honor, having a chapel or an altar of his own.[64]

That most guilds had an affiliation with a particular church or monastery is clearly indicated by the pattern documented for Bruges, which was one of the most important commercial cities on the coast of western Flanders during the fifteenth century. Although such links have yet to be systematically explored for other centers of similar magnitude, those documented for Bruges give a fascinating glimpse into what must have been common practice, and they reflect the close relationship between the secular and religious spheres of urban life at the time. They also show that the religious confraternities established by the guilds became significant sources of patronage, the agencies through which they contributed to the artistic and musical activities of the communities in which they were located.[65]

One of the most important of the monastic houses in Bruges in the late Middle Ages was the Augustinian abbey of St. Bartholomew (the Eeckhout), whose abbot, as the highest ecclesiastical dignitary in the city, often presided over processions and other public ceremonies of a religious nature. A more immediate link between the monastery and the town's lay residents derived from its adoption by the confraternity of the guild of booksellers and illuminators as the center for their religious devo-

---

64. Cf. Woodfill, *Musicians in English Society*, p. 9.
65. See Reinhard Strohm, *Music in Late Medieval Bruges* (Oxford: Clarendon Press, 1985), who explores the musical life of Bruges from the social perspective; the following examples are drawn from his discussion of the guilds and their confraternities, pp. 60–73.

tions. These craftsmen, whose careful work still survives in hundreds of beautifully decorated manuscripts, had chosen as their patron saints the evangelists Luke and John (not surprisingly, since both men are depicted as writers in medieval art, and Luke was thought to be a painter as well). They celebrated the major feasts of their heavenly benefactors (October 18 for St. Luke and May 6 and December 27 for St. John) in the chapel of the confraternity at the abbey.

Because its members were prospering, the guild was able to rebuild the chapel altar in 1474 and have it decorated with panels newly painted by Hans Memling (see Figure 4-8). Services held there—both those for the patron saints and anniversary Masses commissioned by members of the confraternity—were usually sung and further embellished by the use of the organ. From at least 1457 on, singers from local churches were hired to provide the music, and there is every indication that they sang polyphony as well as plainchant in celebrating important liturgical occasions.[66]

FIGURE 4-8. The Najera Triptych, right panel, showing angel musicians playing trumpets (one straight, one s-shaped), portative organ, harp, and fiddle. Though this panel was not painted for any of the guild chapels in Bruges, those that were could have included a similar scene. (Antwerp, Koninklijk Museum voor Schone Kunsten.)

66. See Strohm, *Music in Late Medieval Bruges*, 60–62.

The monastery of the "Black" Augustinian friars, which was situated in the heart of the trading quarter of Bruges, sheltered the confraternities of a number of wealthy guilds, in particular those of various foreign mercantile associations and of their sailors. As at the abbey of St. Bartholomew, Masses and related services for the patron saints were celebrated in the chapels set aside for these associations within the church of the order, and endowments were established to mark the anniversaries of its wealthy members. Here, too, music (including, in some instances, polyphony as well as chant) is specified by the founding charters as an integral part of the liturgical exercises for which provision was made.[67]

Yet other merchant guilds active in Bruges found a home for their devotional activities with the mendicant friars of the Order of Our Lady of Mount Carmel. One of the most important of these was the Confraternity of St. Thomas Becket, established in the city in 1344 by the Fellowship of the Merchant Adventurers, which had its beginnings in 1296 as a branch of the London Company of Mercers. A private chapel was set aside for their use in the monastic church where, in addition to the usual ceremonies (including christenings and burials), a Mass was celebrated in honor of the patron saint every Tuesday (St. Thomas's special day). As a rule, the liturgy was sung by the friars of the order and, once again, must have included polyphony as well as plainchant on special occasions.[68]

When in 1347 the merchants of the Hanseatic League from Lübeck, Hamburg, and Danzig established themselves in Bruges, they too made their headquarters in the Carmelite house, where they shared the chapel of St. Thomas with their English counterparts (to whom, incidentally, they traded their leathers, fur, amber, and metalware for the wool and cloth produced in the British Isles). The Scottish merchants also associated themselves with the Carmelites, who granted them the use of a chapel dedicated to the Virgin Mary and to St. Ninian, as did the Aragonese, who were apparently active in the city's trade as early as 1400.

Like the wealthy associations of foreign merchants who traded in Bruges, some of the local craft guilds also had an altar or a chapel in one of the churches or monastic houses of the city. The sailors, brewers, rosary makers, lacemakers, candlemakers, and dyers were with the Carmelites, while the carpenters and the archers of St. Sebastian were with the Franciscan Friars Minor.

All of this of course added to the daily round of liturgical observances for which the friars of these orders were responsible, and it contributed at the same time to the frequency and richness of musical performances in their churches. This circumstance cannot have been without significance for the Carmelites, in particular, who nour-

---

67. Strohm, *Music in Late Medieval Bruges*, 62–64.

68. The relations between the English merchants and the Carmelite convent illustrate nicely the reciprocal advantages to be derived from the association of a church or convent with the guilds whose confraternities they housed. In this instance the merchants, who resided in the town only part of the year, rented houses and rooms from the order, which also provided lodgings for important visitors, and kept their charters and other valuable documents in the chapel or the refectory of the convent. See Strohm, *Music in Late Medieval Bruges*, 63–64.

ished an important tradition of their own for learning, including the study of music, and counted among their ranks a number of important theorists and composers.[69]

Naturally, religious confraternities—as opposed to those organized by and for the members of a guild—had their home in one of the ecclesiastical institutions of the city as well. Three of the larger ones also made use of the Carmelite church: the Confraternity of the Immaculate Conception, founded in 1429 (at a time when the dogma was still at issue); the Confraternity of Our Lady of Roosebeke, apparently established primarily to commemorate those who fell in the battle fought there in 1382; and the Confraternity of the Holy Ghost, which dated from 1428 and brought together the late heirs of the poetic tradition of the trouvères. Yet another, and one of the most important in the fifteenth century—the Confraternity of Our Lady of the Dry Tree, formed in 1396—forged a link with the Franciscans.

Each of these associations either sponsored or directly originated devotional activities with an important musical component. The rhetoricians of the Holy Ghost organized miracle and passion plays for important civic occasions, thus contributing to the devotional exercises of all the city's residents. The Confraternity of the Dry Tree, which brought foreign merchants together with local nobles and tradesmen, engaged the Friars Minor to celebrate Mass daily in their chapel, to sing Mass on Sunday in discant (which necessitated the hiring of singers from other churches in the city), and to mark the Marian feasts with special observances.[70] And in the Carmelite church, where the Confraternity of the Immaculate Conception had an altar with a panel depicting that very theme, a Lady Mass was sung every Saturday.

The battle at Roosebeke was marked by an annual pilgrimage, organized by the members of the confraternity, to a chapel standing near the field of combat that had been dedicated to the Virgin. The trip, which was punctuated with music virtually every step of the way, began at the Carmelite church of Bruges, where a *Salve regina* was sung. The participants then paused for a banquet, accompanied by music, before continuing to a hostel in a town nearby, where the trumpeters of Bruges played during supper. They concluded their journey on Sunday with a solemn procession through the streets of Roosebeke to the sounds of the trumpeters and minstrels of Bruges and two neighboring towns. Back in the city, meanwhile, the Carmelite friars sang special Masses on Sunday, Monday, and Thursday of the week of the pilgrimage.

As is suggested by the pattern briefly sketched for Bruges, devotions to the Virgin played a singularly important role in fostering musical activity in northern Europe from the late thirteenth century on. Marian confraternities sprang up in major cities all through the region, and one of their principal purposes was to increase and enhance observances in her honor, both liturgical and devotional. Clearly, the establishment of special services and the engagement of the finest singers available for their celebration encouraged schooling in music and provided a stimulus for the cul-

---

69. See Strohm, *Music in Late Medieval Bruges*, 64–66.
70. See Strohm, *Music in Late Medieval Bruges*, 67–73.

tivation of polyphony that contributed significantly to the international preeminence enjoyed by singers and composers from this region during the fifteenth and sixteenth centuries.

In the Netherlands, for example, the large place given to music in the public manifestations of the Marian confraternities has been documented for city after city and included, as a rule, a significant polyphonic component. During this period, one of the most important of these fraternal orders was the Confraternity of Our Lady, founded in 1469 at the church of Our Lady, the largest of the five parish churches of Antwerp (made a cathedral in 1559). The round of observances established in that connection is typical of what was being done everywhere.[71] Votive Masses to the Virgin Mary were undoubtedly celebrated in the cathedral at one or more of its Marian altars on a daily basis, as they had been in other churches of the city since the thirteenth century. In addition, a chaplaincy for the *Salve regina* was founded at a specific altar of the cathedral already in 1415, presumably to assure the continued celebration of a weekly devotional service in honor of the Virgin that had been performed each Saturday from Christmas to the Feast of the Purification (February 2) since 1404.

The Marian devotion for which the confraternity appears to have been most directly responsible, however, was the establishment of a daily *Salve* service, or *lof*—following a pattern that had already been adopted in at least one other of the city's churches—the first of which was held on February 12, 1479. It began with the ringing of the church bells, and its celebration was enhanced by the playing of the organ and the singing of the choirmaster, the choirboys, and four adults.[72] The centerpiece of the *lof* service was the Marian antiphon *Salve regina* (except during Eastertide, when it was replaced by *Regina celi*). The evidence suggests that the antiphon was usually sung in discant and accompanied by the organ, which played alone, both before and after, a keyboard arrangement of a motet or some similar work of a religious nature.[73] Hymns were also sung with some regularity, and prayers to the Virgin were recited as well. If, strictly speaking, the service was devotional rather than liturgical, still all of its components—at least those involving a text—were nevertheless drawn from the liturgy.[74]

71. The principal Marian confraternity established in the cathedral church and the liturgical and devotional practices for which its members made provision are described in some detail by Kristine K. Forney, "Music, Ritual, and Patronage at the Church of Our Lady, Antwerp," *Early Music History* 7 (1987): 1–57; most of what follows has been drawn from her study.

72. See Forney, "Music, Ritual, and Patronage at the Church of Our Lady," 9–11.

73. Concerning the liturgical chant featured in these services and the devotional uses to which they were put during the Renaissance, see Jeannine S. Ingram, "Salve regina," *The New Grove Dictionary of Music*, 16:435f. According to Forney, "Music, Ritual, and Patronage at the Church of Our Lady, Antwerp," 10, following the Tridentine reform, the Marian antiphon sung corresponded to that designated for Compline for a particular season of the liturgical year: *Alma redemptoris mater* from Advent to Christmas; *Ave regina celorum* from the feast of the Purification until Good Friday; *Regina celi* at Eastertide; and *Salve regina* from Trinity Sunday to Advent.

74. Among the guilds in Antwerp with musical connections were the Guild of St. Luke, which included the printers, bookbinders, and booksellers (and, after 1557, musical instrument makers), and the minstrels' Guild of St. Job and St. Mary Magdalene; see Forney, "Sixteenth-Century Antwerp," 370–72.

A prosperous and active Marian confraternity like that found at the church of our Lady is surely no surprise in a thriving commercial city such as Antwerp.[75] Similar groups of astonishing size and vigor were often established in much smaller towns as well, however. A case in point is the town of Bergen op Zoom, which counted only about 8,000 inhabitants toward the end of the fifteenth century. However, it enjoyed considerable prosperity at the time, thanks to its location near important commercial routes and the international trade fairs that were held there from at least the fourteenth century on, both spring (at Easter) and fall (at the Feast of St. Martin on November 11). As a result, the local ruler, John II of Glymes, who favored the collegiate church of St. Gertrude with his patronage, was able to embark in 1444 upon an ambitious program for its rebuilding. As the project neared completion in the early 1470s, he also commissioned the construction of a large organ to add luster to the services held in the new building.[76]

A chapel on the north side of the choir was furnished with an ornately decorated statue of the Virgin and dedicated to her special veneration. That chapel became, in turn, the home for the Guild of Our Lady, a Marian confraternity that was founded by John of Glymes and the town council around 1470 and numbered between 750 and 1,100 lay townspeople in the course of its existence. Toward the end of that same year the guild made provision for a daily devotional *lof*, to be sung by the choirmaster, the boys, and as many as six adult singers—a fair indication that polyphony was an essential part of the service. The singers who sang the *lof* were also obligated to participate in the celebration of all Masses in honor of the Virgin, and they were presumably involved as well in the three processions held each year in which the statue from the chapel was carried through the streets of the town. There was no mention of the organ in the documents of foundation, but that changed after the completion of the new instrument. From 1470 on the church bells were also rung at the conclusion of the service.[77]

One of the most celebrated, and most venerable, of the Marian brotherhoods established in the Netherlands was the association of clerics and scholars at the church of St. John the Evangelist in 's-Hertogenbosch known as the Illustrious Confraternity of Our Lady. Founded in 1318 under the authority of the bishop of Liège, it had a continuous existence into the mid-seventeenth century and counted among its members in the fifteenth and sixteenth centuries some of the most distinguished musicians of the region. A nightly *lof* apparently never became a regular part of observances there, perhaps because the organization was essentially a clerical

---

75. Antwerp grew from some 30,000 inhabitants in the late fifteenth century to more than 100,000 by 1560.

76. Concerning the parish church of St. Gertrude (which was elevated to the rank of a collegiate church in 1428), its musical establishment, and the Marian confraternity established there, see Rob C. Wegman, "Music and Musicians at the Guild of Our Lady in Bergen op Zoom, c. 1470–1510," *Early Music History* 9 (1989): 175–249. I am grateful to Mr. Wegman for making his study available to me before publication.

77. See Wegman, "Music and Musicians in Bergen op Zoom," 75–85.

rather than a lay order. But Vespers were sung in honor of the Virgin every Tuesday and Mass every Wednesday, and her special feasts were observed with particular solemnity, as is evident from the inclusion of motets and polyphonic settings for selected items of the liturgy. Music was also featured at the banquets of the confraternity, where secular and sacred pieces were sung and the instrumentalists of the area were heard as well.[78]

One consequence of the musical patronage of these northern confraternities was a more intense cultivation of polyphonic composition, producing a growing repertory of Masses and motets, many of them with Marian themes and references. These were copied for the use of the choir by the singers, who also served as scribes, and gathered systematically into large collections, a number of which have survived.[79] Of particular interest in this connection is mounting evidence of relatively frequent contacts and occasional collaboration among the major Marian confraternities of the region. These involved not only exchanges of repertory but also collaboration among choirs for celebrations of special significance, all which contributed to a wider, more rapid dissemination of the polyphony intended for these festive Marian commemorations than would otherwise have occurred.[80]

In light of the frequent use made of polyphony in the devotional observances of the confraternities, and of the quasi-liturgical nature of their services, there was likely more than occasional involvement of instrumentalists in their celebration. The players most frequently mentioned, where records of such activities exist, are the municipal musicians, and they participated not only in the processions that wound through city streets before entering the church but also in the services themselves.[81]

ITALIAN CONFRATERNITIES: THE LAUDESI COMPANIES

Lay confraternities similar to those just described also flourished in cities of the Italian peninsula from the mid-thirteenth century on. They, too, were constituted by townsmen drawn together, generally under the sponsorship of one of the churches or religious houses of the municipality, for pious purposes. These included, as usual, charitable works and religious observances, both liturgical and devotional. In some of these cisalpine towns, devotional services came to include a novel element: the

78. A brief survey of the musical life of the confraternity is given by Albert Smijers, "Music of the Illustrious Confraternity of Our Lady at 's-Hertogenbosch from 1330–1600," *Papers Read by Members of the American Musicological Society* (1939), 184–92.

79. See, for example, the surviving collections of music listed by Albert Smijers for the confraternity in 's-Hertogenbosch, "Meerstemmige muziek van de Illustre Lieve Vrouwe Broederschap te 's-Hertogenbosch," *Tijdschrift der Vereeniging voor Nederlandische Musiekgeschiedenis* 16 (1946): 1–30 and 63–106, and cf. the observations by Forney, "Music, Ritual, and Patronage at the Church of Our Lady," 32–40 and *passim*.

80. Instructive observations in this regard are given by both Smijers, "Music of the Illustrious Confraternity," 186, and Wegman, "Music and Musicians at Bergen op Zoom," 175ff. and *passim*.

81. See, for example, Forney, "Music, Ritual, and Patronage at the Church of Our Lady," 14–16. There is, of course, an ancient tradition concerning the veneration of the Virgin by secular musicians, to which allusion has already been made above, pp. 155–56.

communal recitation of prayers and singing of hymns or songs in the vernacular. The pieces sung in this context came to be called *laude*, literally praises, which were written in verse and addressed to the Virgin Mary, to Christ, and to the most popular of the saints.

The mendicant orders[82]—in particular the Franciscans, whose founder was one of the first to write hymns of praise of the kind favored for lay devotions—worked assiduously to foster piety by such means. As a consequence, they played a key role in the organization of fraternal associations, not only early on, when the first lay confraternities were established, but throughout the entire history of their development. A number of such companies must have flourished already during the first half of the thirteenth century. This would suggest that they became a factor in the lay devotions of northern Italian cities even before 1258, when an exceptional accumulation of catastrophic events—internecine warfare, corruption, and pestilence in particular—gave rise in Umbria to a popular religious movement of unusual intensity and duration. Inspired by the sermons of hermits and itinerant mendicant preachers, lay Christians in that area became persuaded that the wickedness and the suffering they saw on every side could only mean that the end of the world was imminent.

That perception gave renewed impetus to the people of the cities so affected to band together in fraternal associations, in keeping with the customs of the age, specifically in this instance to perform public acts of penance. Pilgrimages were organized to carry to other towns and regions the message of doom and to warn of the consequent need for repentance. In city after city processions of penitents streamed through the streets, wearing the garments (if, indeed, anything at all) and performing the acts of contrition that had become traditional for the Christian church. Their public manifestations were often (though not always) accompanied by the singing of well-known hymns and songs, including *laude* in the Italian vernacular. The most fervent of these groups (usually called *disciplinati*, but also *battuti*, or *flagellanti*) vigorously whipped their naked bodies as they moved in procession to indicate their renunciation of the evils and vanities of the world. Nourished by such dramatic scenes, the penitential movement swept northward on a wave of popular piety from its point of origins on the Italian peninsula into southern France and Germany and even beyond.[83]

Although the fervor of the early thirteenth century had largely spent itself by the dawn of the fifteenth, the religious sentiments that had surfaced so strikingly in these popular demonstrations of penitential zeal continued to find an outlet in fraternal associations all through the intervening period. Some of these companies continued

---

82. The four principal mendicant orders are the Augustinians (the Austin Friars), the Carmelites, the Dominicans, and the Franciscans. Concerning the role of the friars in the development of lay confraternities in thirteenth-century Italy, see Blake Wilson, *Music and Merchants: The Laudesi Companies of Republican Florence* (Oxford: Clarendon Press, 1992), 13–36.

83. For background on the fraternal companies of penitents, see Walter Salmen, "Geisslerlieder" (*Geissler* being the German equivalent of "flagellant"), *The New Grove Dictionary of Music*, 7:220; cf. also John Stevens, "Lauda," *The New Grove Dictionary of Music*, 10:538–40.

to gather their members for regular devotional services on a daily basis, as well as on special occasions of religious significance, and to organize or participate in public processions. Moreover, even though the wild enthusiasm of the initial movement waned fairly quickly, such confraternities grew steadily in number all through the fifteenth century. There were perhaps as many as forty in Perugia by the end of the thirteenth century and some seventy-three in Florence by the beginning of the sixteenth.[84]

Surviving documents in other cities have yet to be so systematically explored, but similar companies were also found in considerable numbers in other major Italian cities such as Bologna, Cortona, Rome, Venice, and Udine. Of course not all of these associations had as their primary focus lay worship featuring the singing of *laude*. In Florence, for example, only a dozen of the many lay confraternities whose archival records have been examined seem to have been constituted primarily for that purpose.[85]

Of particular interest here, of course, are those confraternities that took on a distinctive character due to the large role given to the singing of *laude* in their communal services, making it possible to designate them as *laudesi* companies.[86] From our present vantage point the early history of lay associations of this type appears to be largely bound up with the city of Florence. This may be a historical accident, due in large part to the fortuitous conservation of pertinent documents in the archives of the city and the interest of recent scholarship in delving into them; however, there is evidence for Florence's leading role.

The single largest notated source of monophonic *laude*, an illuminated collection from the early fourteenth century, once belonged to the Florentine Company of Santo Spirito.[87] And in the fifteenth century, when the traditional repertory began to give way to new poems sung as *contrafacta* to existing polyphonic pieces, a number of the best-known authors of *lauda* verse were closely, or even exclusively, associated with the city. These included personages such as the poet Feo Belcari (1410–84), Lorenzo de' Medici, and, later on, Girolamo Savonarola (1452–98), the Dominican friar who gave a special impetus to the cultivation of the genre by his condemnation of the secular poetry and music of his time.

Other indications point in another direction, however. Among the earliest authors of *laude* were not only St. Francis of Assisi (1182–1226), the founder of the Franciscan order, but also Jacopone da Todi (1230?–1306), a Franciscan as well, suggesting that the custom of singing praises to the Virgin in the vernacular—and

84. See John Stevens, "Lauda spirituale," *The New Grove Dictionary of Music,* 10:539.
85. See Wilson, *Music and Merchants,* 75–140.
86. Some form of the word often appears in the various titles by which such companies identified themselves. Note that it was the vernacular, nonliturgical components of these exercises, as well as the communal participation they entailed, that set them apart from analogous devotional services in other parts of Europe—those of the Low Countries, for example, that were discussed earlier.
87. MS Magliabecchiana II.I.122 of the National Library at Florence; it is one of five Florentine *laudarii* of the fourteenth century, but the only one with music. See Wilson, *Music and Merchants,* 154–64 (also n. 36), and 258.

hence the lay confraternities formed for that purpose—may be tied more closely to the history of the mendicant orders than to the destiny of a particular city. Nevertheless, the Florentine companies of *laudesi* were among the few that continued to cultivate communal singing regularly from the thirteenth century well into the sixteenth, and because their activities can be rather thoroughly documented, they offer insight as to the nature of such organizations elsewhere.

The first Tuscan confraternity to become a *laudesi* company—and therefore a model of sorts for all that followed—was the Society of the Holy Virgin Mary of the church of Santa Maria Novella (also known as the Company of the Laude of Santa Maria Novella), organized by San Piero the Martyr (whose name the company also bore) in 1244.[88] Its members were drawn primarily from the ranks of the city's merchants and artisans, who every six months elected four captains, six counselors, and three treasurers from among their number to administer their affairs. Spiritual direction was provided by a Dominican friar associated with the church.[89]

Initially the primary purpose of the organization was probably didactic, to combat a Cathar heresy and foster Marian devotion. Considerably later, perhaps between 1267 and 1288—the period during which the majority of the *laudesi* companies, strictly defined, came into existence—a significant portion of its membership transformed itself into a *compagnia delle laude*.[90] From its inception the brothers of the company met on the second Sunday of each month to sing *laude*, to walk with lighted candles in procession, and to hear sermons. By the late 1320s they had begun to hire trumpets and/or *pifferi* (wind players) to give greater brilliance to their devotional exercises on important occasions such as Christmas, Easter, the Assumption, and the feast days of Sts. Dominic and Thomas Aquinus.[91]

By 1288 the company had begun to gather daily for an evening service held before a painting of the Virgin in the chapel dedicated to San Piero the Martyr in the church of Santa Maria Novella. This ferial observance consisted primarily of monophonic hymns and songs sung in the vernacular by the members of the fraternity as they knelt before the image of the Virgin. (On the vigil of every feast they sang with a lighted candle in hand.) To conclude they intoned the antiphon *Ave Maria*, and if certain brothers of the company had special needs—because they were in ill health,

88. See Wilson, *Music and Merchants*, 37 and 109; the much earlier date of 1233, given by John Stevens, "Lauda," *The New Grove Dictionary of Music*, 10:538, apparently does not take into account the important distinction to be made between those confraternities that merely made some use of the *laude* and those that adopted the specialized forms of musical devotion that distinguish the *laudesi* companies.

89. See Frank A. D'Accone, "Le Compagnie dei Laudesi in Firenze durante l'Ars Nova," in *L'Ars Nova Italiana del Trecento*, ed. F. Alberto Gallo (Certaldo: Commune di Certaldo, 1969), 254–55; the number of counselors was initially twelve, then reduced.

90. Wilson, *Merchants and Music*, 109–18, traces the history of this company in some detail.

91. Other companies followed analogous but different calendars for their festal celebrations. For example, the *laudesi* of San Zanobi, founded in 1281 and associated with the Duomo, Florence's cathedral church, specified special observances for Easter, for the principal feasts of the Virgin "celebrated four times per year," for those of the four Evangelists, and for Sts. John, Philip, Stephen, Lawrence, Zanobi, Reparata, etc., encompassing in all some twenty-eight festal days. See D'Accone, "Le Compagnie dei Laudesi in Firenze," 264–65.

for example, or away from the city—another was sung on their behalf. The *laude* to be sung on any given evening were written on a chalkboard affixed to the chapel wall, and a book containing text and music for the items to be performed, large enough for all to see, was placed on a lectern visible to the members of the company.[92]

Among the charitable works that a *laudesi* company such as San Piero's was expected to provide for its members was a funeral and proper burial. It was just a short step, therefore, however surprising the development, from the obsequies of deceased members to commemorative services on behalf of the departed souls of those able to commission them. This usually took the form either of a *lauda* vigil, an anniversary meal, or even an anniversary Mass. The result was a kind of popular, secular substitute for the commemorative Masses that so occupied the chaplains and choirs of northern churches (see pp. 352–70). In place of the indulgences to be acquired from the liturgical service were those that had been decreed for both singing and listening to *laude*. And, like the Masses celebrated by clerics, the *laudesi* commemorations were sustained by endowments set up by the benefactors who paid for them.[93]

Like other Florentine companies, that of San Piero Martire maintained a school in which *laude* could be taught to children, who then not only participated regularly in the services but also grew up as members of the confraternity.[94] Very early on, however, musicians (both singers and instrumentalists) were hired to assist in performing the communal hymns and songs. In 1312 the first payments were made to young singers (*fanciulli che cantano*) who assisted with the service. Beginning in the 1390s, two and then three singers received regular salaries; by 1405 the number had increased to four; and from 1419 until early in the sixteenth century at least six and as many as nine singers were on the payroll. Usually between three and five were hired for the daily (ferial) services and between two and four for the festal occasions. As early as 1393 there were also special payments for the singing of the Passion (in a vernacular translation) and the Lament of the Virgin.[95]

The role of the paid singers in the services is specified only to a degree by the contracts drawn up by the company. Those engaged in 1406 were to come early to make preparations. This probably included laying out the altar cloth, setting up the benches, placing the music on the lectern, marking in the *laudario* the proper order of the items to be sung, and distributing (and collecting for) the candles to be burned during the singing.[96] During the actual service they would have led the others with their own voices and probably sang the stanzas of the *laude* while the members respond-

---

92. See D'Accone, "Le Compagnie dei Laudesi in Firenze," 255–56.
93. See Wilson, *Music and Merchants*, 49–54.
94. Wilson, *Music and Merchants*, 109; cf. D'Accone, "Le Compagnie dei Laudesi in Firenze," 256, n. 17, who cites payments made by the Company of Santa Maria Novella in 1395 to a certain Niccoló, who sings the *laude* and "teaches the boys to read."
95. See Wilson, *Music and Merchants*, 111–13, including tables 7 and 8, and p. 117.
96. See Wilson, *Music and Merchants*, 111, and, for analogous practices in other companies, 60–66.

ed antiphonally with the refrains. They may also have directed rehearsals, helping the members, especially the novices, to learn the *laude* most frequently sung. Later, especially in the fifteenth century, as polyphonic pieces were included in the evening services with increasing frequency, there must have been even greater reliance on the trained singers paid by the companies, both as performers and as instructors.[97]

Details concerning other companies of *laudesi* in Florence can add to the picture already drawn, illuminating both common practices and the different devotional practices that distinguished one confraternity from another. The Company of San Zanobi of the Laudesi, which was associated with the cathedral, met before Mass each Sunday morning for a procession through the church two by two, singing *laude* as they went. The brothers, carrying lighted candles, were led by two boys, each carrying a very large candle as well, to the choir of the church where the candles were offered at the altar. That ritual completed, the brothers were to stay and listen devoutly to the entire celebration of the Mass. It was also on Sunday that the members of this company gathered in the evening to practice their repertory of *laude*, with those who were new receiving instruction from the more experienced singers.[98]

The only confraternity of *laudesi* in Florence to deviate from the patterns described thus far in at least one noteworthy respect was the Company of the Madonna of Orsanmichele, founded in 1291. It was unique in not owing its existence to the initiative of friars; consequently, it had neither a home in nor clerical direction from one of the city's churches. It grew instead out of the popular veneration of two pictures, the one of the *Madonna delle grazie*, which was credited with working miracles, and the other of St. Michael, hung from pilasters in the loge of the grain market, and it was there that its members gathered for their devotional services.[99]

In most other regards, however, the company was very much like any other. It was administered by captains (six, at first, then eight) elected from among its members every four months and assisted by two groups of counselors, three treasurers, and a number of accountants, supervisors, and agents. (The more elaborate organizational structure apparently reflected the greater numbers and wealth of the confraternity as well as its secular origins and its consequent political importance.) Those admitted to its ranks were expected to pay monthly dues; to recite the Pater noster and the Ave Maria five times daily, and at the death of any brother the Ave Maria twelve times, concluding with a Requiem; to attend the sermon every Sunday and every day during Lent; and, in particular, to sing *laude* before the images in the loge at every feast of the Virgin Mary. Later in the four-

---

97. See Frank A. D'Accone, "Alcune Note sulle Compagnie Fiorentine dei Laudesi durante il Quattrocento," *Rivista Italiana di Musicología* 10 (1975): 98–99, whose documented description of the duties of the *laudesi* of San Zanobi around 1470 undoubtedly casts light on the practices in other companies as well.
98. See D'Accone, "Le Compagnie dei Laudesi in Firenze," 262–63.
99. For a more detailed history of these developments, see Wilson, *Music and Merchants*, 74–77.

teenth century, the singing of *laude* became a daily ritual, following the usual pattern, and a school was held on Sunday to teach the songs to those who needed instruction.[100]

Perhaps the most extraordinary consequence of the devotional activities of confraternities of *laudesi* like those in Florence was the development of a type of musical composition adapted to the requirements and limitations of untrained singers and the subsequent creation of a substantial repertory of such works. As one might expect, pieces of this type were originally monophonic, but polyphonic examples began to appear as early as the fourteenth century.[101] It seems likely that simple melodies such as those used by the earliest companies (and included in the manuscript collections that have survived) continued to dominate the devotional exercises of the *laudesi* well after polyphonic settings had become relatively numerous, and that the latter were sung mostly by the trained singers. Still, it is not unreasonable to suppose that, as polyphonic music became increasingly common, the brothers were themselves taught to sing in parts, at least for special occasions.

In any case, the net result was to extend considerably the musical culture of the age into the social fabric of the urban centers in northern Italy, both by providing a direct experience with musical performance and by increasing the frequency with which such music could be heard. In a number of these cities, as in Florence, *laude* were presumably heard on a daily basis in at least a dozen places from the thirteenth century into the sixteenth, thus enriching immeasurably the musical experience of those who participated and those who listened.

VENICE AND THE SCUOLE

In Venice, for example, although the confraternities established there appear to have been more similar to those found in the Low Countries than to the *laudesi* of Florence, the cultivation of the *lauda* must have been fairly intense. The associations of the Serene Republic, which brought together as many as 500 of the city's merchants, tradesmen, and craftsmen, were known as *scuole* (schools): the larger, wealthier ones were called *scuole grandi* (big schools), the smaller, poorer ones *scuole piccole* (small schools). As elsewhere, the earliest of these confraternities dates back to the 1260s, while the last of the six *scuole grandi* was founded as late as 1552.

Governing each company was a *guardiano grande*, elected by the entire membership from among the "original Venetian citizens"—an essential qualification for all such officers—to serve for a year. He was assisted in his duties by a legislative body (or *banca*) of twelve men (later with another group of twelve in reserve), similarly elected to serve six months or a year, one of whom (the *guardiano di matin*) became

---

100. See D'Accone, "Le Compagnie dei Laudesi in Firenze," 269–70.
101. For a discussion of the polyphonic *lauda* of the fifteenth century, see below, pp. 443–56.

the second in command.[102] Like all organizations involving citizens of the republic, the *scuole* were soon brought under the watchful eye of the municipal government, whose powerful Council of Ten approved their statutes and supervised their activities.

As with the Florentine companies, the purposes of the *scuole* were both charitable and devotional. They established hospitals to care for the ill and the infirm, assisted the poor among their own members, paid funeral expenses for impoverished families, and offered dowries for young ladies who otherwise would have had no prospect of marriage. Each company also erected a hall (or *oratorio*) in which services could be held to glorify God and to honor Christ, the Virgin Mary, and the saints important to the residents of the city. These buildings were designed by leading architects of the day and elaborately decorated with religious paintings by the most gifted artists available. They were to provide a meeting place that would not only enhance the effectiveness of the ceremonies held there but also redound to the reputation of the *scuola*. In more practical terms it cast these companies in a role of artistic patronage that resulted in commissions for important works to figures such as Sansovino, Giovanni and Gentile Bellini, Carpaccio, Titian, and Tintoretto.[103]

It seems likely that Venetian companies, like other groups of similar origin, gathered in the initial stages of their existence to sing *laude*. By the fifteenth century, however, communal singing had apparently given way to a choir of trained singers, including both clerics and laymen, albeit drawn still from among the members of the *scuola*, and the repertory may have been primarily polyphonic. Among the composers who wrote settings for *lauda* verse in the late fifteenth century (when, finally, the creators of the music come to be regularly identified) are Marchetto Cara, Innocentius Dammonis, Filippo de Luprano, and Bartolomeo Tromboncino, several of whom have Venetian connections.[104]

As part of their duties these member-musicians were expected to provide music for the funerals of paupers (of which there could be four or five per week). In addition, they sang Mass, either in the company's hall or in the parent church next door, on all Sundays of the month except the first and on minor feast days. The first Sunday of the month was marked by a more elaborate celebration that included a Mass in the *scuola*, a procession to the sponsoring church for a second Mass, and another procession back to the hall.

---

102. Concerning the organization of the Venetian *scuole*, see Jonathan Glixon, "Music at the Venetian *scuole grandi*, 1440–1540," in *Music in Medieval and Modern Europe*, ed. Iain Fenlon (Cambridge: Cambridge University Press, 1981), 193–94. As the author explains, the "original citizens" (*citadini originari veneziani*) were those whose families, although not noble, were among the most ancient and respected in the city.

103. Concerning the patronage of the *scuole grandi* in the visual arts, see Denis Arnold, "Music at a Venetian Confraternity in the Renaissance," *Acta musicologica* 37 (1965): 62–63, and cf. Glixon, "Music at the Venetian *scuole grandi*," 193–95.

104. See John Stevens and William F. Prizer, "Lauda," *The New Grove Dictionary of Music*, 10:539–41.

The feast day of the saint for whom the *scuola* was named[105] was the occasion for a "visit" from other companies in the city, who joined, together with their musicians, in both the religious observances and the public processions that were held to mark the event (in much the same manner as on the first Sunday of the month). These same musicians also represented their *scuola* in the spectacular celebrations mounted by the municipal government on the days that had civic significance in the Serene Republic: the feasts of St. Mark, Corpus Christi, St. Isidore, and St. Vido (see Figure 4-9). It was in these public ceremonies, when each company was attempting to distinguish itself by the brilliance of its contribution to the occasion, that the competitive spirit inevitably born of such circumstances emerged most clearly. And that rivalry clearly played a role in shaping the changes that took place in the musical practices of the *scuole grandi* in the course of the fifteenth and sixteenth centuries.[106]

As long as the music performed was monophonic—liturgical plainchant or devotional *laude*—a choir drawn from the membership of the confraternity was apparently sufficient. Toward the middle of the fifteenth century, however, as the use of polyphony became ever more common, a group so constituted was no longer capable of meeting the expectations of magnificence harbored by the officers of certain *scuole*. First an attempt was made to augment the number of competent singers available to these confraternities by recruiting them as members, and in 1448 the Council of Ten granted permission to the four *scuole grandi* then in existence to add six additional singers to their ranks. That measure must have failed to achieve the desired result, for the companies then turned with increasing frequency to a more overt form of musical patronage, hiring professional musicians to assist them with the most important public ceremonies. By the 1470s, when the council no longer required the *scuole* to seek permission before employing musicians for that purpose, this practice had obviously become the norm.[107]

For lesser occasions, like funerals for the impoverished, at which only monophony was sung, a choir consisting of four to six members of the company—now referred to as the "old singers"—was deemed sufficient, and they were paid for the services sung. For Sunday services and public processions, by contrast, four or five professionals—designated as the "new singers"—were engaged with an annual salary to assure their participation even in the face of tempting offers from rival companies. Toward the end of the fifteenth century some of the *scuole* also began to hire instrumentalists for the more important public observances, invariably including a procession. These players accompanied the singers and provided support for their voices in

---

105. The six *scuole grandi* that were active in Venice by the sixth decade of the sixteenth century (and the churches with which they were affiliated) were designated as follows: di Santa Maria della Carità; di San Giovanni Evangelista; di San Marco; di Santa Maria della Misericordia; di San Rocco; and di San Teodoro; cf. Glixon, "Music at the Venetian *scuole grandi*," 194.

106. Concerning the activities of the *scuole grandi* in which music played an indispensable role, see Glixon, "Music at the Venetian *scuole grandi*," 200; for a discussion of the rivalries that ensued, cf. Arnold, "Music at the Venetian Confraternity in the Renaissance," 63–64.

107. See Glixon, "Music at the Venetian *scuole grandi*," 196–97.

FIGURE 4-9. Gentile Bellini's famous painting showing a festive celebration on the Piazza of San Marco with the celebrated basilica in the background. The city's *scuole* regularly participated in these ritualistic events. (Venice, Accademia, no. 567.)

the open air. Initially this function was filled by a consort of three "soft" instruments—lute, harp, and viol—but these tended to be replaced later by a consort of four to six viols or *lironi*, assisted at times by "loud" instruments such as trumpets and shawms.[108]

Associations formed in other northern Italian cities had origins similar to those of the Venetian *scuole*, but none seems to have turned so quickly or so emphatically to musical patronage in order to enhance its public ceremonies. A more comprehensive picture will have to wait until more is known about such groups in other Italian centers. There is good reason to believe, however, based on what is known about cities as widely separated as Florence and Venice, that lay confraternities generally played an important role in bringing music into the lives of their members frequently and systematically. And, as a result, the modest genre of the *lauda* became an important staple in what can truly be seen as a popular musical culture in Italy.

108. See Glixon, "Music at the Venetian *scuole grandi*," 196–98.

CHAPTER 5

✓

The Musical Sources

INTRODUCTION

The two uniquely characteristic features of Western music—its contrapuntal textures and its elaborate notational systems—are closely related. One can in fact argue that the growing complexity of music during the Middle Ages prompted the development of music notation: written signs that can indicate concisely and precisely not only melodic motion (means for which had been found earlier in order to fix the ever expanding repertory of liturgical plainchant) but also metrical patterns and rhythmical relationships. As the number of voices grew and their independence increased, both melodically and rhythmically, notation of that kind became ever more indispensable, and the systematic cultivation of an intricate contrapuntal style—such as that of the fifteenth and sixteenth centuries—appears from our present vantage point to depend directly upon the rhythmic possibilities inherent in the mensural notation available for that purpose.[1]

Moreover, from the historical point of view, notated documents have made possible the reconstruction of medieval and Renaissance musical culture in a way that would not have been possible without them. The symbols used by musicians of ages past to represent their musical conceptions offer the scholar keys to the mental processes involved in composition and enable the performer to transform mere notes on a page into a sonorous reality. However uncertain either may be as to the extent to which the present-day result actually duplicates what may have been imagined and heard centuries ago, the musical work thus brought back to life can powerfully evoke both the intellectual achievement and the esthetic experience of that earlier time. Those advantages are not without certain inherent pitfalls, however. As with written records of any kind—archival or literary, for example—the musical sources of the past have been only partially and imperfectly preserved.

1. Concerning the notational systems in use during the fifteenth and sixteenth centuries, see Appendix, pp. 1027–35.

Some of them have been lost to the random excesses of warfare and civil disorders, and in this respect certain regions have suffered much more than others. The violence that accompanied the French Revolution led to the destruction of literally tons of documents, and books of music were among those that vanished forever. Similarly, the Savonarola-inspired "Burning of the Vanities" in Florence in the mid-1490s also saw the destruction of much music.[2] Fire in all its forms—whether started by the hot lead used to repair roofs and rain gutters, the burning candles that were so much a part of religious ceremonial, or the incendiary bombs of World War II— is an ever-present danger to books and music and was even less easily controlled in earlier times than it is now; once flames had taken hold, the means for bringing them under control were meager indeed. And in buildings made largely of stone, like churches, municipal buildings, and the residences of the nobility, it was usually the books and furnishings that fueled the conflagration.

In other cases, as books of music became outmoded and were therefore no longer of practical use, they were simply discarded. Regrettably, such volumes were usually not retired to a dusty corner to await rediscovery some centuries later. Parchment and paper had their uses even when written over; numerous fragments of music recovered from the bindings of nonmusical books show that cast-off music books were often used by publishers and binders as flyleaves or to strengthen the spine and pad the covers of other, newer volumes.[3]

Manuscripts written on vellum and richly illuminated were sometimes spared that fate because of their visual appeal, whatever their musical content. Nonetheless, because hand-written collections of this type were usually one of a kind, in purely statistical terms they were still at much greater risk than prints, which were usually produced in a press run of several hundred copies. Conversely, because prints were both less costly and more easily replaced, they tended to be more readily discarded than were the more valuable manuscripts. Despite the quantities produced, a substantial number of prints have disappeared without leaving a single surviving copy.

Whatever the reasons for haphazard patterns of preservation and loss, it is perhaps even more difficult to know what part of the repertories that originated during the fifteenth and sixteenth centuries has been saved in the surviving sources. Unless one bears in mind the very substantial gaps in our musical documentation that can be shown to exist, one may be tempted to believe that what has been transmitted includes everything of significance. It has been suggested that because recently discovered sources have brought few additions to the known works of the best-known

---

2. See Thomas G. Bergin and Jennifer Speake, eds., "Savonarola," *Encyclopedia of the Renaissance* (New York: Market House Books, 1987), 359–60; cf. Gustave Reese, *Music in the Renaissance* (New York: Norton, 1959), 170.

3. Perhaps the most dramatic example of notated compositions recovered from flyleaves and bindings of later, nonmusical books are the so-called "Worcester Fragments"; for an overview and the pertinent bibliography, see Ernest Sanders, "Sources, MS, VI: English Polyphony 1270–1400," *The New Grove Dictionary of Music*, 17:657–61.

composers of the fifteenth and sixteenth centuries, most of what they wrote has now been recovered.[4]

Such a view may be excessively optimistic. It is sobering to recall that a single manuscript—the "Chigi Codex" (a late fifteenth-century collection of Masses and motets from the Low Countries)—is the only known source for four of the fifteen Masses attributed to Johannes Okeghem, one of the most distinguished figures of his age, and that six others have been transmitted in but one additional collection. What is more, at least four other Masses, mentioned in theoretical treatises as the work of that composer, have not been transmitted by any known source.[5] Similarly, of the seventy-one chansons usually attributed to Antoine Busnoys, Okeghem's celebrated colleague and contemporary, nearly thirty are transmitted by only one or—at most— two musical sources. In most instances the loss of a single manuscript would deprive us either of a composition or of the ascription linking it to a composer.[6]

In fact, the large number of works of all kinds that have survived from this age in but one or two sources suggests that the greatest caution is necessary in estimating what part of its musical repertories has actually survived. Existing manuscripts and prints clearly represent only a small—and mostly indefinable—portion of the music given written form during the fifteenth and sixteenth centuries. Moreover, as we shall see, even though music was being "composed" and notated with ever increasing frequency through this period of time, certain forms of polyphony continued to rely a great deal on the memory and the improvisational skills of the performer.

In some regards the notation of the period was itself less than entirely explicit. Relative duration could be indicated with considerable precision and tempos were supposedly tied to the normal heart beat—at least in theory—although what was done in practice can often only be surmised. Relative pitch was also shown with sufficient clarity as a rule (except for certain kinds of "accidental" semitone inflections), but there was no "international" standard for tuning, as at present, to fix the frequency of notes on the scale. Actual ranges must have been determined by the acoustic properties and capabilities of the voices and/or instruments at hand.[7]

Volume or intensity of sound is rarely indicated until very late in the sixteenth century and seems to have been regarded as the inevitable (and perhaps invariable) consequence of the source of sound used in performance. Even the latter—whether voices or instruments and the number of each to a part—were often designated only

4. The opinion is expressed by Charles Hamm and Jerry Call, "Sources, MS, XI: Renaissance Polyphony," *The New Grove Dictionary of Music*, 17:668.

5. The source(s) for each of Okeghem's Masses are listed in the *Collected Works*, ed. Dragan Plamenac, 2d. ed., 2 vols. (New York: American Musicological Society, 1966), in the Editorial Notes; for those that have been lost, see Leeman L. Perkins, "Ockeghem," *The New Grove Dictionary of Music*, 13:495.

6. The sources for the chansons of Busnoys are listed by Leeman L. Perkins, "Conflicting Attributions and Anonymous Chansons in the 'Busnoys' Sources of the Fifteenth Century," in *Continuities and Transformations in Musical Culture, 1450–1500: Assessing the Legacy of Antoine Busnoys* (London: Cambridge University Press, 1998).

7. A more detailed discussion of the manner in which pitch, duration, and related matters were indicated in the notation of the period will be found in the Appendix.

in the most general way or left entirely unspecified. Such questions must have been settled in accordance with current practice in a given institution or locality or determined even more simply by whatever resources were available at the time. The loss of local traditions of performance to the passage of time therefore deprives us of an aspect of the musical culture of the period that can only be partially recovered from the written documents.

In sum, although one cannot expect from the sources of the fifteenth and sixteenth centuries the kind of detail that characterizes a modern orchestral score, they still provide the only solid basis we have for a history of the musical styles and genres of the period. And they often reveal as well, under close, thoughtful scrutiny, a good deal about the social contexts in which the music was conceived, circulated, and performed.

MANUSCRIPTS

From the moment a musical composition is written down, it takes on a life of its own; it can then pass as a notated abstraction from hand to hand and place to place independently of either composer or performer. Having become a musical artifact, it can be copied and collected by either individuals or institutions for their own purposes, including, of course, but not limited to study and performance. The visual appearance of such a collection of music reflects in any age both the use for which it was intended and the means of the patron who commissioned it or the resources of the institution for which it was prepared, just as its present condition evinces the treatment it has received over the intervening centuries. Thus the choice of writing material (whether vellum or paper), the training and experience of the scribe, and the nature and extent of the decoration added to the page of music suggest the esthetic impact—if any—intended at its inception and, therefore, the social context in which it originated. Consequently, the hand-copied books of music that have survived from the fifteenth and sixteenth centuries differ markedly in aspect from the decidedly homely and utilitarian to the most elaborate and luxurious.

Among the most modest and common type of repertorial compilation of music made at the time (but unfortunately the most infrequently preserved) was the so-called fascicle manuscript: one or more sheets folded together at the center to form a small cahier (not unlike an examination booklet). The leaves were usually ruled beforehand with staves to accommodate the music to be copied—whether a single relatively lengthy work, such as a cyclic Mass, or a small collection of shorter pieces—and were at first almost certainly left unbound. Such a cahier was of use to the composer who wished to make a fair copy of a newly finished work and to performers who wished to learn new repertory. In that unadorned but convenient format music could easily be carried in the saddle bags of singers (many of whom were remarkably mobile) or other, nonmusical couriers to a patron or fellow musician. It was likely in this manner that music was most frequently transmitted from one place to another and from fascicle manuscripts that the rehearsal of new works was begun.[8]

Many manuscripts of this kind must have been either worn out by regular use or simply discarded when they outlived the repertory they contained. In several instances, however, they were accumulated by a musical establishment, such as a cathedral choir or a court chapel, and later bound together to constitute a larger collection. Such a volume is necessarily composite in nature and betrays its origins by the variety of paper types and/or scribal hands included within it.[9] In other instances, conversely, fascicles were undoubtedly used as source materials from which works were copied systematically into books of music that were compiled to serve the needs of a chapel choir or some other group of musicians.

Chapel repertories—whether for church or for court—were constituted to provide, first of all, appropriate music for the celebration of the liturgy and for special occasions of a more or less foreseeable nature (ordinations, coronations, burials, visits from neighboring dignitaries, and other events of the sort). As a matter of practical utility the music books of these establishments were usually organized according to genre; cyclical settings of the Mass (both Ordinaries and Propers), motets, hymns, Magnificats, and the like were either copied into separate volumes or into separate fascicles of a larger collection. Since individual pages had to be readable for a sizable group of singers gathered around a single lectern (see Figure 4-3), they were generally rather large—in some instances as much as 26 × 19 inches to the page.[10] Because of the manner in which it was used, the format adopted for collections of this kind is known as "choirbook"; in it the same segment of each of the individual parts of a polyphonic work is copied separately onto the facing pages of an opening (usually with the higher voices, superius and tenor parts, on the left and the lower ones, altus and bassus parts, on the right) so that the pages could be read by and turned for all the singers at the same time (see Figure 5-1).

Every musical chapel also had some use for secular music. At court it was an indispensable component of the entertainment offered to visiting nobles and other similar dignitaries. Moreover, as was observed earlier (pp. 75–77), it was often used in the same way by the high-ranking prelates who presided over large churches (cathedrals and collegiate churches) and monasteries and was therefore sometimes included among the materials adopted for the training of choirboys (and that consequently found a place in the private recreations of clerics).

Collections of such pieces, called *chansonniers* after the predominant secular

8. Concerning the fascicle manuscript, see Charles Hamm, "Manuscript Structure in the Dufay Era," *Acta musicologica* 34 (1962): 166–84.

9. An instructive example is the collection of Mass sections, Magnificats, hymns, and motets now in the seminary library in Aosta; see the *Census-Catalogue of Manuscript Sources of Polyphonic Music, 1400–1550*, ed. Charles Hamm and Herbert Kellman, 5 vols. (Neuhausen-Stuttgart: Hänssler Verlag, 1979–88), 1:6–7, and the further references to the research of Marian Cobin Green upon which the entry is based.

10. These are the dimensions of a typical manuscript prepared for the Julian Chapel at the Vatican (Cappella Giulia XII 4), which is comparable in size to those compiled for the pope's private chapel (the Cappella Sistina), most of which measure at least 21 or 22 × 16 or 17 inches to the page; see the *Census-Catalogue of Manuscript Sources*, 4:16 and 27–62.

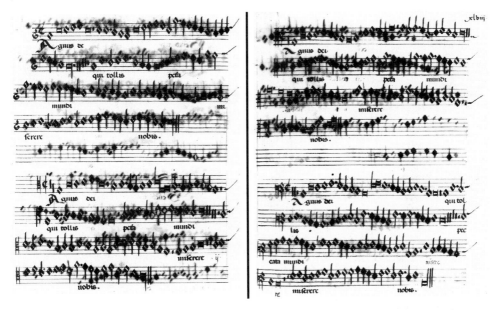

FIGURE 5-1.   Agnus Dei of the *Missa Ave Maria* attributed to Antoine de Févin (Rome, Biblioteca Apostolica Vaticana, MS Cappella Giulia XII 2, fols. 47ᵛ–48).

genre of the fifteenth century, were also copied using choirbook format, but since the number of parts rarely exceeded three or four, the pages were much smaller—measuring at times as little as 7 × 5 inches or less.[11] When there were only three voices, the two principal parts—cantus and tenor—were placed at the top of facing pages of an opening with the contratenor and additional strophes of text written in below (see Figure 5-2). The more costly of such manuscripts—those written on vellum and handsomely illuminated—were probably not subjected to the wear and tear of rehearsal and performance but served instead as sources from which individual pieces could be copied for practical use.

In the sixteenth century a new format came to be adopted with increasing frequency, especially for the secular repertory, with an individual book for each—or at least most—of the parts for which the music in the collection was written. These "partbooks" were undoubtedly more convenient for the individual musicians, particularly in those genres that were usually performed with one person to a voice or part (see Figure 5-3). This arrangement was easier for the printer, as well, and more economical of paper, which would explain why it was so frequently adopted for print-

11. These are the approximate dimensions of the "Dijon Chansonnier" (MS 517 at the Municipal Library, Dijon); see the facsimile edited by Dragan Plamenac, *Dijon Bibliothèque Publique manuscrit 517* (Brooklyn: Institute of Medieval Music, n.d.), 3. Measurements for other fifteenth-century chansonniers—most of them of similar size—are given by Leeman L. Perkins and Howard Garey, eds., *The Mellon Chansonnier*, 2 vols. (New Haven: Yale University Press, 1979), 2:150–85.

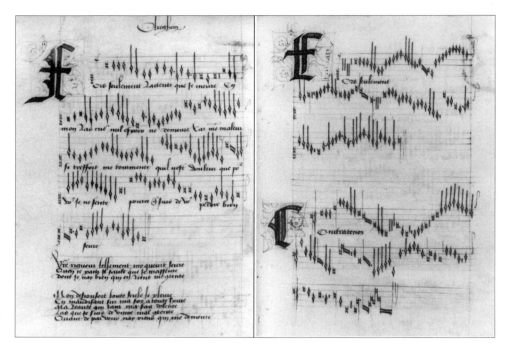

FIGURE 5-2. *Fors seulement l'attente* attributed to Johannes Okeghem (Dijon, Bibliothèque Municipale, MS 517, ff. xxvᵛ–xxvi).

ed collections. However, the division of a single composition among three or four partbooks, or more, also increased the likelihood of partial loss; if one or more of the

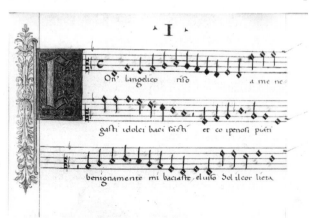

books in a set goes astray, the pieces in the collection can be completely recovered only when there are concordant sources.[12]

The use of score as a format for notating completed

FIGURE 5-3. Tenor part for Verdelot's *Con l'angelico riso* (Chicago, Newberry Library, Case MS VM 1578.M91, the "Newberry Partbooks," f. 77).

12. The "Newberry Partbooks" (a page of which is seen in Figure 5-3) are a case in point. At some time the altus part was separated from the original set of five and found its way into the library of Oscott College in England, while the other four—cantus, tenor, bassus, and quintus and VI (the latter two

works—whether on parchment or paper, by hand or in print—was surprisingly rare until very late in the sixteenth century, and even then it seems to have been adopted primarily for study purposes. There is some evidence that musical works may have been scored at times onto a slate or wax tablet during composition in order to facilitate the mental processes.[13] But once a piece was finished, it was written out in separate voices or parts, either in choirbook or in partbooks, depending on the purpose to be served by the copy and the preferences of patron, scribe, or printer.

In addition, specialized types of score notation—known as tablature[14]—were devised for players of keyboards and plucked string instruments such as lute and vihuela (a sixteenth-century antecedent of the guitar). The earliest surviving repertories so notated date from the fourteenth century, and the first fairly substantial collection of instrumental music from the period is that of the "Faenza Codex," which includes both polyphonic settings based on liturgical cantus firmi and arrangements of secular part songs.[15] It was written in a form of staff notation, not unlike a modern keyboard score, with barlines drawn through the staff to mark off the mensural units (see Figure 5-4). Although it antedates by some years the period under study, it is of interest here

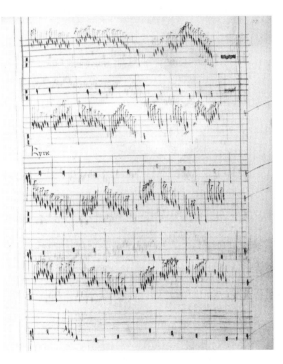

FIGURE 5-4. Anonymous *Kyrie* based on the *Kyrie cunctipotens genitor* (Faenza, Biblioteca Comunale, MS 117, f. 88 [=79]).

voices in a single book)—were acquired by the Newberry Library in Chicago. Fortunately, the errant part was not destroyed, and its connection with the four other partbooks was eventually discovered. See H. Colin Slim, ed., *A Gift of Madrigals and Motets*, 2 vols. (Chicago: University of Chicago Press, 1972), 1:xi, and idem, *Ten Altus Parts at Oscott College, Sutton Coldfield* (n.p., [1978]), 3.

13. A survey of surviving scores from the sixteenth century and some discussion of the uses to which they were put is to be found in Edward E. Lowinsky's "Early Scores in Manuscript," *Journal of the American Musicological Society* 12 (1960): 126–73.

14. Concerning these forms of notation, see Thurston Dart and John Morehen, "Tablature," *The New Grove Dictionary of Music*, 18:506–15.

15. See John Caldwell, "Sources of Keyboard Music to 1660," *The New Grove Dictionary of Music*, 17:718.

because both the notational format and the mix of repertory contained in the source were used time and again in the two centuries that followed.

Similar in content but more typical of true tablature in its notation is the collection of pieces for keyboard known as the "Buxheim Organ Book." Compiled, it seems, in Munich, mostly in the 1460s, it reflects the activity of the celebrated blind organist, lutenist, and composer Conrad Paumann. The repertory it transmits includes, in addition to preludial pieces and some of Paumann's didactic exercises from the *Fundamentum organisandi*, settings of various cantus firmi—secular as well as sacred—and intabulations of both chansons and Lieder.[16] Its tablature uses staff

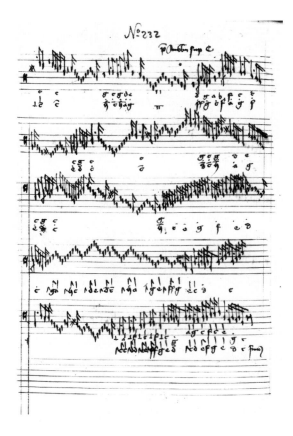

notation for the upper part, as in the "Faenza Codex," but the lower voice or voices are written as letter names over which mensural indications have been inscribed to clarify the intended rhythms. Here, too, barlines mark off, more or less regularly, the mensural units (see Figure 5-5). Other, later forms of German organ tablature differ as to detail but continue to rely on letter names with overlying rhythmic signs to notate at least some of the parts.

Score notation for the lute, vihuela, and related instruments makes its appearance relatively late with the earliest known sources dating from the second half of the fifteenth century.[17] This is undoubtedly because its develop-

FIGURE 5-5. *Praeambulum super C* (Munich, Bayerische Staatsbibliothek, Mus. MS 3725, the "Buxheim Organ Book," f. 128ᵛ, [no. 232]).

---

16. A brief description of the collection, which gets its name from the monastery library where it was held until 1883, is given by Eileen Southern, "Foreign Music in German Manuscripts of the Fifteenth Century," *Journal of the American Musicological Society* 21 (1968): 258; concerning Paumann, cf. Christoph Wolff, "Conrad Paumann," *The New Grove Dictionary of Music*, 14:308–9.

17. For the earliest examples, with illustrative photographs, see Walter H. Rubsamen, "The Earliest French Lute Tablature," *Journal of the American Musicological Society* 21 (1968): 286–99, and David Fallows, "Fifteenth-Century Tablatures for Plucked Instruments: A Summary, a Revision, and a Suggestion," *Lute Society Journal* 19 (1977): 7–33.

ment followed that of the technique used in playing the instrument and the emergence of uniquely instrumental genres. As long as plucked string instruments were used primarily to play melodic lines, striking the successive pitches with a plectrum of some sort, the existing staff notation was entirely adequate. Only when players put down the plectrum and began to use the fingers of the right hand to pluck several strings at once was a notational system needed that could show several notes sounding simultaneously on different strings. And only when that kind of polyphonic independence had been attained could a single lutanist or vihuelist play unassisted not only the preludial pieces in a style idiomatic for instruments of that kind but also arrangements ("intabulations") of vocal and dance music originally written in parts. As a consequence of the relatively tardy evolution of this type of score notation, printed collections—for which the publishers of the period obviously found a ready market—tend to be more numerous than manuscripts and historically at least as significant.

The tablatures variously favored in Italian, French, and Spanish regions, although differing from one another in detail, were all based on an ingenious adaptation of the conventional five- or six-line staff. In appearance it is not unlike the vocal music of the period, but the meaning of the notation is radically different. Instead of the steps of the gamut, the staff lines actually represent the strings of the instrument, which is to say pitches a third or a fourth apart depending upon the way it has been tuned.[18] French and Spanish sources follow a sort of sonorous logic in the arrangement of the lines, with the lowest-sounding string shown at the bottom, whereas in Italy the strings are depicted in their physical relation to the player, with the highest sounding string at the bottom of the tablature. The frets (or finger stops), which are placed just a semitone apart on the instrument, are identified on the notational "string" either by numbers, starting with 0 for the open strings (in Italian and Spanish sources), or by letters, starting from a (in French ones, see Figure 3-11). As in some keyboard tablatures, the rhythmic values are represented by conventional symbols placed above the individual notes.

Typical in its notation as well as in content is the "Capirola Lute Book" (as it is called), which includes intabulations of both sacred and secular polyphonic pieces—*frottole*, chansons, and even a few motets and Mass sections—together with the dances and preludial *ricercari* that make up the bulk of the collection. Exceptional, by contrast, for a collection of this kind is the rich decoration of the pages. As expressly stated in the opening leaves, the illuminations were added to ensure the book's survival even after the music it contained was no longer of interest to its owner (see Figure 5-6).[19]

18. Except for the highest-sounding string, plucked instruments were usually strung in courses—that is, with two closely lying strings tuned to the same pitch. On an instrument with six courses they were tuned with a fourth between each of the two outer pairs and a third between the inner pair, thus spanning a double octave from the highest open string to the lowest; G and A were the two pitches most used as a starting point for this sequence of intervals.

19. For an edition of the manuscript with a detailed discussion of the repertory it contains, see Otto Gombosi, ed., *Compositione di Meser Vincenzo Capirola: Lute-book (circa 1517)* (Neuilly-sur-Seine: La Société de Musique d'Autrefois, 1955).

FIGURE 5-6. *Gintil princep* (Chicago, Newberry Library, Case MS VM C.25, the *Capirola Lute-Book*, f. 50ᵛ).

The lute tablature adopted in Germanic regions, while based on a similar principle—that of indicating the frets to be stopped—was a bit more complicated. The open strings were designated by numbers, but the sequence of letters crossed from string to string. No staff was used to show visually the movement from one string to the next, but each melodic line was given its own space on a vertical plane. Here, too, rhythms were indicated by signs placed above the notes to which they applied. A representative example is the collection of dances and intabulated polyphonic Lieder copied by Jacob Thuerner of Vienna for his own use during his student days in the early 1520s (see Figure 5-7).[20]

Clearly, the identity of the copyist and the intended purpose of the collection of music loom as crucial questions in assessing both the sociohistorical and the musical significance of the manuscript sources that have come down to us from the fifteenth and sixteenth centuries, and they are often not easily answered. In some instances we know the music to have been copied by the first owner of the book for personal study or private performance. The lute book just cited originated in that manner, as did the manuscript compiled in the 1460s by the physician and humanist Hartmann Schedel of Nuremberg (1440–1514), mostly during his student years in Leipzig, a collection

20. For an edition and a complete facsimile, see Rudolf Flotzinger, ed., *Das Lautenbüchlein des Jakob Thürner* (Graz: Akademische Druck- und Verlaganstalt, 1971).

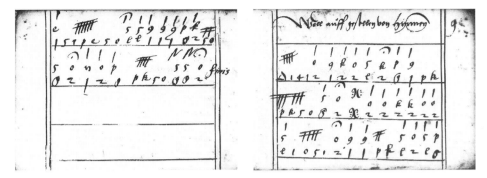

FIGURE 5-7. *Woll auf, Gesellen, von Hinnen* (Vienna, Österreichische Nationalbibliothek, Mus. MS 9704, the *Little Lute Book of Jacob Thuerner*, ff. 9–9ᵛ [no. 7]).

of 108 secular pieces, primarily on French and German texts, to which he added a Magnificat and eighteen Latin motets.[21]

One sign of musical miscellanies such as these—which were copied by an individual for personal use, generally over a relatively extended period of time—is the mixing of genres, whether vocal or instrumental, that were usually kept systematically separate in institutional manuscripts. Melding of this kind does occur, as noted, in the instrumental collections cited above, as it does in the "Schedel Songbook." An example in partbook format—unfortunately only partially preserved—is the collection compiled in Glarus, Switzerland, around 1540, by the soldier, statesman, and chronicler Aegidius Tschudi (1505–72), and there is a fair number of additional codices of similar character.[22] Many of them share yet another rather striking feature: the relatively awkward hand of a nonprofessional copyist (see Figure 5-8).

A considerably greater degree of training and skill is displayed by the scribes who prepared manuscripts for church choirs, court chapels, and wealthy patrons. The majority of them probably developed their notational and calligraphic abilities in the church schools where they acquired their musical competencies, and they belonged in most instances to the musical establishment for which they did their copying. In a few cases—usually involving large, wealthy institutions whose archives have been exceptionally well preserved—the names of the copyists have reached us either through payment records or in the manuscripts themselves.

A number of the scribes who worked at the papal court in Rome, copying music for the Sistine Chapel in the papal residence and the Julian Chapel in St. Peter's Basilica, have been identified by name.[23] One of the most prolific was Johannes

21. See the *Census-Catalogue of Manuscript Sources*, 2:236.
22. See the *Census-Catalogue of Manuscript Sources*, 3:146–47. Collections of this kind include the songbook compiled by Johannes Heer, one of Tschudi's friends (ibid., 3:145–46); a series of manuscripts connected with the Amerbach family in Basel (ibid., 1:28–33); and perhaps even the early fifteenth-century collection at Oxford, Bodleian Library, MS Canonici misc. 213 (ibid., 2:275–76).
23. The copyists who are known to have been employed at the papal court are identified in the *Census-Catalogue of Manuscript Sources*, 4:14–71.

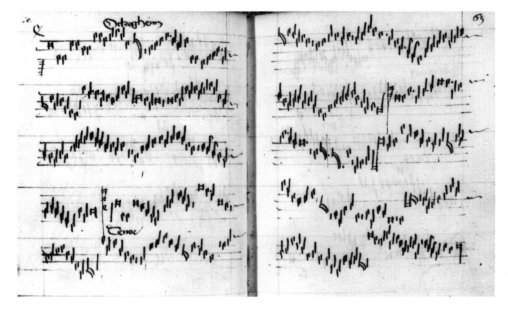

FIGURE 5-8. *Ma bouche rit*, attributed to "Ockegheim" (Munich, Bayerische Staatsbibliothek, MS Germ 810, the *Schedel Songbook*, ff. 62ᵛ–63).

Parvus, who was a singer and composer as well. He contributed to the preparation of some twenty-seven manuscripts still in existence (all but one currently in the Vatican Library), entering both music and text unaided for the greater number and collaborating with colleagues on yet others.[24] Similarly, at the cathedral of Cambrai, Symon Mellet—who was first a minor, then a major vicar of the church and therefore a singer in the choir—received numerous payments between 1446 and 1475 for copying music.[25] From the entries in the accounts it is clear that he too wrote not only the notes (for chant as well as for polyphony) but also the texts.

Further evidence from these and other institutions suggests that—like Parvus and Mellet—most musician-scribes were trained to copy both notes and letters. Exceptionally, Mellet was also paid on at least one occasion for illuminating the cahiers of music he had written, and there is a further reference to his artistry in yet another connection.[26] This is surprising, as scribes can rarely be credited directly with

24. The codices copied by Parvus are listed in the general index to the *Census-Catalogue of Manuscript Sources*, 5:330.
25. See Jules Houdoy, *Histoire artistique de la cathédrale de Cambrai* (Lille, 1880; reprint, Geneva: Minkoff, 1972), 188–201.
26. In 1462 he was given 25 sous for having "written, notated, and illuminated in 5 processionals the responsories sung for the feast of St. Fursy"; in the following year he was paid 43 sous for having repainted a marker in front of the chapel of the Trinity, illuminating and adding vignettes to the arms it bore, those of the defunct cardinal Pierre D'Ailly; cf. Houdoy, *Histoire artistique de la cathédrale de Cambrai*, 194.

the decoration of the books they copied. A musical manuscript was prepared in several stages; staves had to be ruled onto parchment or paper and the leaves folded and gathered into cahiers (as they might eventually be bound) before the copyist could plan the layout and begin work. Notes and texts were usually entered—in that order—by a single scribe, although on larger projects, two or more sometimes collaborated. Decorative capitals could then be drawn at the beginning of each part, often on every page, and only then would any further illumination have been added.

In many cases the musician-scribe who did the copying also drew the capitals and at times supplied some modest decoration. Collections of liturgical polyphony compiled for use in the choir of institutions like the papal court were most often produced in that way. Even in more elegant codices, like the repertory of motets known as the "Medici Codex"[27] and the sumptuous manuscripts prepared at the Netherlands Court of the Habsburgs, many of which were intended as princely gifts, the capital letters—excepting those that were painted by artists—were most often the work of the skillful scribes who copied music and text.[28] Even in collections of sacred polyphony such as these, however, the decoration done separately in an illuminator's atelier is usually limited to a few leaves at the beginning of the manuscript or, if a more splendid effect was desired, the opening at the beginning of each new composition.

In every case professional illumination is a sign that the book was intended for some extraordinary purpose such as a gift for some important and powerful person. It was at least as common in books of secular music as in those containing only sacred works, moreover, and was at times even more consistently applied there. In some instances, however, it is difficult to tell if there has in fact been a division of labor between scribe and artist. In the "Dijon Chansonnier," an exquisite collection of part songs copied onto vellum in an elegant professional hand—to take a conspicuous example—there is as yet no reason to believe that the capital letters were drawn by anyone other than the principal copyist, even though he failed to complete the task. Less certain is the possible identity of the artist who began to fill in the letter forms with pen drawings of fauna, flora, and human faces, some of which were then colored.[29] If the music scribe was artistically gifted, like Symon Mellet, he may have decorated the manuscript himself, but that he did so is far from incontrovertible. By contrast, it is quite clear in other instances that the text scribe expected capitals and

27. Regarding the copyists who entered the music, texts, and most decorative capitals in this manuscript, see the edition (with facsimile) prepared by Edward E. Lowinsky, *The Medici Codex of 1518: A Choirbook of Motets Dedicated to Lorenzo de'Medici, Duke of Urbino*, 3 vols. (Chicago: University of Chicago Press, 1968), and cf. the introduction, 1:5–16.

28. Concerning the complex of manuscripts that can be linked with the Netherlands court, see Herbert Kellman, "Josquin and the Courts of the Netherlands and France: The Evidence of the Sources," in *Josquin des Prez, Proceedings of the International Josquin Festival-Conference*, ed. Edward E. Lowinsky and Bonnie Blackburn (London: Oxford University Press, 1977), 181–216.

29. See Plamenac, ed., *Dijon Bibliothèque Publique manuscrit 517*. The initials with colored drawings reach to f. xvii and are seen again between ff. xlviii and lvii and between ff. lxxiii and lxxxi; the pen drawings otherwise go only as far as f. xli, and from f. lxxxiii on even the capital letters are missing.

illuminations to be added later, and probably elsewhere, because he wrote in the space left for the decoration a small catch letter as a guide to the specialized artisans who would complete and embellish his work.[30]

In sum, while the work of illuminating—and of course binding—a finished manuscript was hired out to artisans who specialized in those crafts, most copying (of notation and text) was done either by the individual musician, when for his own use, or "in house," when the needs of an institution were to be served. There may also have been public or commercial scriveners such as plied their trade in every sizable city—especially one with a university or an important secondary school—whose skills included those required for the copying of polyphonic music. If so, their task would have been rather different from the customary duplication of the standard texts used in school curricula or even service books for liturgical and devotional purposes from reliable exemplars. For music such exemplars apparently did not exist. Although there are examples from the sixteenth century of music copied largely from printed books (which thus served as exemplars of a sort), most manuscript collections of polyphony are *unica* in the truest sense of the term. There is not a single example of a book of compositions having been copied directly from another in a commercial establishment for public sale.[31]

When the copying of polyphonic repertory was done on contract or on commission—as happened on occasion—it was probably managed in much the same manner as can be documented for the exceptionally gifted musician-scribe known as Pierre Alamire. His earliest known work as a professional copyist came in 1496 in 's-Hertogenbosch, where he copied motets and Masses for the Marian confraternity, filling two books and part of a third. He is next traceable in 1503 in Antwerp, where he must have made his first contact with the ducal court of Philip the Fair, to whom he sold a large collection of liturgical polyphony, including several Masses. In 1509 he was attached to the chapel of Archduke Charles (later Charles V) as "scribe and keeper of the books," a position he held until he was pensioned off in 1534.

Some forty surviving manuscripts give evidence of his personal activity during those twenty-five years of service, and another eleven of his collaboration with two other copyists who also served the court. Many of these codices were prepared for his patron and other members of the Habsburg dynasty, such as Marguerite of Austria and Emperor Maximilian, or their highly placed functionaries. Yet others were intended as gifts from the ducal court to curry favor with powerful figures known to have a strong predilection for music: Pope Leo X, Henry VIII of England, Frederick the Wise of Saxony, and the wealthy traders from Augsburg, the Fuggers. At the same time, Alamire continued to work on commission, in particular for the Marian confraternities in Antwerp and 's-Hertogenbosch. This he was presumably able to do (at least in part) because he had ready access to the repertory of the ducal chapel—Masses and motets by the leading

---

30. Such letters may be seen, for example, in the facsimile of the "Mellon Chansonnier," ff. 16ᵛ, 19, 21ᵛ–22, 34, and *passim* as well as in a number of other chansonniers of the period that were similarly decorated.

31. For an example of a manuscript copied from prints, see the *Census-Catalogue of Manuscript Sources*, 3:177.

FIGURE 5-9. *Absalon, fili mi*, attributed to Josquin (London, British Library, MS Royal 8.G.VII, ff. 56ᵛ–57).

masters of the age such as Josquin (see Figure 5-9), Pierre de La Rue, Mouton, Févin, Obrecht, Isaac, and others now less well known, as well as a fair number of secular works—and permission to copy them for certain other musical establishments.[32]

A few other scribes may have been similarly favored and thus able to work in a similar manner, even though there are none whose production can be documented in the same way. In any case the rapid rise of printing firms in response to an ever widening commercial market, beginning early in the sixteenth century, suggests that the demand for polyphonic music, both secular and sacred, existed well before the new technology was adapted to the special requirements for printing mensural music. It is therefore also possible that this demand was being met to a degree by professional scriveners before printed music entered the marketplace.

PRINTS

Music printing had its origins in the same social and economic forces that contributed to Gutenberg's invention of moveable metal type for the printing of written

32. Concerning the remarkable career of Pierre Alamire (obviously a musicanly *nom de plume* deemed preferable to Peter van den Hove), see Herbert Kellman, "Alamire," *The New Grove Dictionary of Music*, 1:192–93.

texts: increasing literacy (musical, in this instance) and a growing urban population with the means to purchase books and the leisure not only to read but also to make music one of its diversions.[33] Not surprisingly, then, music printing first appeared, and continued to flourish, in important religious and commercial centers, in particular Rome, Venice, Lyons, Paris, and the port cities along the Rhine. There the enterprising craftsman had both a good potential market immediately to hand and access to trade routes and fairs capable of opening a much wider field to his activity. The adaptation of the newly developed technology to the publication of music, making it possible to print mensural notation from moveable metal type, was in fact first realized and exploited for profit in Venice, the most quintessential of the commercial cities of the Renaissance and home of the celebrated press of Aldus Manutius.[34]

This considerable achievement is credited to the imagination and exceptional skill of Ottaviano dei Petrucci of Fossombrone, the scion of an impoverished noble family from Fano who received a humanistic education at the court of Guidobaldo I, duke of Urbino.[35] When he arrived in Venice in about 1490, printers in Germany and Italy had already devised means for printing in two impressions the simpler note forms required for plainchant. By contrast, polyphonic music in parts was only occasionally included in printed books—as examples in texts on music theory, for instance—and was there brought to press from wood engravings rather than from metal type.

In 1498 Petrucci petitioned the doge and Great Council of the city for an exclusive privilege to print mensural polyphony and tablatures for keyboard and lute in Venetian territories. He supported his request with the claim that he had succeeded, at rather considerable expense, in doing "what many, not only in Italy but elsewhere had long attempted in vain"—that is, in developing a process for printing polyphonic music from moveable type. The privilege, which was to eliminate any competition in the Venetian states for a period of twenty years, was therefore defended as an economic necessity. Only if so protected could he hope to recover his initial outlay and make some return on his investment of time and means before others imitated his procedures and encroached on his potential market.

The requested monopoly was granted on May 25, 1498, but it took Petrucci another three years to cast his type, refine his methods, and begin collecting and editing the repertory he intended to publish. The first volume to issue from his press was, properly speaking, a chansonnier (the first of a series of three), even though the texts are generally incomplete and identifiable only from an *incipit* (or tag beginning). Entitled *Harmonice musices odhecaton A* (meaning, roughly, "100 polyphonic songs"), the collection consisted of some 103 leaves in oblong quarto laid out as a choirbook and containing 96 compositions: secular pieces primarily by northern

33. Concerning the printing of music, beginning in the early sixteenth century, see Edmund Poole, "Printing and Publishing of Music," *The New Grove Dictionary of Music*, 15:232ff.
34. Manutius (1450–1515) was a student of the humanist scholar Guarino da Verona and established his printing shop in order to publish the classic authors of Greek—and later Latin—antiquity; see Ilan Rachum, ed., *The Renaissance: An Illustrated Encyclopedia* (London: Octopus Books, 1979), 325.
35. See Martin Picker, "Petrucci," *The New Grove Dictionary of Music*, 14:595–97.

composers such as Alexander Agricola, Busnoys, Compère, Hayne, Isaac, Japart, and Josquin, together with a smattering of works originally written for texts in Latin (8), Flemish (5), Italian (2), German (1), and Spanish (1), or perhaps even for instrumental performance.

Striking, first of all, is the repertory selected for this inaugural publication. Since a number of the composers represented never worked on the Italian peninsula, the music included can be seen as reflecting predominant musical tastes—not only in northern Italy, where Petrucci was working, but also in the neighboring regions, where he hoped to sell his wares. Surprising, consequently, is the absence of complete texts (except for a few of the Latin pieces), a circumstance that has been variously explained. It has been suggested that Petrucci's editor could not handle the foreign tongues, or that the problems were technical—that the inclusion of the verse was either so difficult or so costly that the printer was not prepared at that point to tackle it. It seems more likely, however, that the words to which the music was originally composed were omitted simply because, as we shall see, the clear preference for performing chansons in Italy was an instrumental ensemble.

Subsequent publications included all of the principal genres of the period, from polyphonic Masses (for which Petrucci first adopted partbooks in 1502), motets, hymns, and Magnificats to the burgeoning repertory of *frottole*—secular part songs on Italian verse—(of which he printed eleven books between 1504 and 1514) and polyphonic *laude*. He even brought out two volumes of polyphonic settings for the Lamentations of Jeremiah, a relative rarity at the time. The first printed tablature appeared in 1507, two volumes of secular and sacred works, mostly from the vocal repertory of northern composers. Francesco Spinacino, who intabulated and edited this group of pieces, also contributed a group of twenty-seven preludial *ricercari* that were intended to set off in performance his arrangements of the music of others. Later collections for lute included a series of dances, some of them grouped in modest "suites," intabulated by Joan Ambrosio Dalza, who also supplied a series of introductory ricercars. These were followed by two books of *frottole*, edited by Franciscus Bossinensis, with the soprano printed in mensural notation and the lower parts intabulated to provide a lute accompaniment.

Despite this attention to Italian repertory, composers from France and the Netherlands continued to predominate in Petrucci's publications, especially in the sacred repertory. Masters of the generation of Brumel, Josquin, La Rue, and Obrecht are well represented in the earliest of his prints, and there is a distinct focus on the musicians of the French royal court, especially Févin and Mouton, in the collections that he printed in his birthplace, Fossombrone, after returning there in 1511. In this regard it seems likely that he was responding, once again, to musical tastes in the regions where his collections were marketed. In any case it is surely fair to say that, on balance, his "editions constitute the most representative and important body of music issued by any printer during the first two decades of the 16th century."[36]

---

36. The judgment is Martin Picker's, "Petrucci," *The New Grove Dictionary of Music*, 14:597.

Technically, too, Petrucci's work is noteworthy. His typography is characterized by the slender elegance of note heads and stems, the accuracy of his registrations, the careful spacing of the characters (both musical and textual), and the graceful design of capitals and other decorative elements (see Figure 5-10). The beauty of the finished page suggests that, like the first printers to deal only with texts, he was emulating the visual effects achieved by the most skillful copyists of his time, and the standard he set was rarely equaled by his successors. His accomplishment is all the more remarkable since the printing process he developed initially entailed three separate impressions—the first for staves, the second for notational symbols, and the third for texts—and even with later simplifications never fewer than two.

Ironically, even though the printing of polyphonic music with moveable metal type was presumably designed to supplant the more laborious process of engraving wood blocks for the purpose, the latter procedure continued to be used in competition with Petrucci's until at least 1540. The first serious proponent and major practitioner of printing polyphony from wood engravings was Andrea Antico, a cleric from the town of Montona on the Istrian peninsula.[37] He began his career as

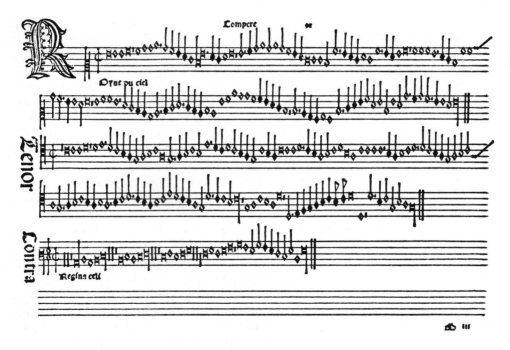

FIGURE 5-10. *Royne du ciel*, attributed to Loyset Compère (Petrucci, *Harmonice musices odhecaton A*, f. 91).

37. See Martin Picker, "Antico," *The New Grove Dictionary of Music*, 1:467–69.

engraver and publisher of mensural polyphony in Rome, where Petrucci's Venetian privilege did not apply. His inaugural publication, which appeared in 1510, was a volume of *frottole*, about half of which were drawn from Petrucci's collections. On the strength of that achievement, Pope Leo X granted him a ten-year privilege in early October 1513 to print music in the papal states. Antico then brought out in rapid succession three further volumes of *frottole*, relying much less on Petrucci's publications than he did initially.

Later in the same month, notwithstanding, the pope accorded the same privilege to Petrucci, who also won an exclusive license to publish keyboard tablature. The Venetian printer must have found difficulties in adapting his new methods to the format customary for that type of score, however, because he produced no music for keyboard in the three following years. In late December 1516 Leo X consequently revoked Petrucci's privilege and transferred it to Antico. The latter, whose wood blocks posed none of Petrucci's technical problems, was able to publish less than a month later the first collection of keyboard music printed in Italy. It consisted primarily of arrangements of *frottole* that had been included in Antico's earlier volumes of vocal music. Another noteworthy achievement of Antico's Roman years was the publication in 1516 of a handsome folio edition of fifteen polyphonic Masses (*Liber quindecim missarum*), which was actually printed by Antonio Giunta, with another printer, Ottaviano Scotto, providing part of the capital. The repertory, which included works by Brumel, Févin, Josquin, Mouton, and others, reflected once again the Italian penchant for music by the masters of the French royal chapel (see Figure 5-11).

Antico's subsequent involvement with the publication of mensural music shifted from Rome to Venice, where he was associated with other printers. These included Luca Giunta, Antonio's nephew, for whom he engraved collections of *frottole*, chansons, and motets in 1520–21, and Ottaviano Scotto, with whom he worked between 1533 and 1540. (His whereabouts during the intervening decade are unknown.) He engraved for Scotto and for Anthoine dell'Abbate yet more chansons, but by the 1530s the *frottola* was quickly being replaced by the newly minted secular genre known as the madrigal, of which he prepared several collections, including one in tablature for lute. The crowning achievement of his Venetian period was a beautifully engraved collection of motets (*Mottetti . . . libro secondo a quattro voci*, 1539) by the city's leading composer, Adrian Willaert, master of the chapel at the basilica of San Marco, which Antico published with the Scotto firm.

The most decisive technological improvement of the age for printing mensural polyphony from moveable metal type—one that put earlier methods, including the use of wood blocks, at a distinct economic disadvantage—was the achievement of the Parisian engraver, type founder, and printer Pierre Attaingnant.[38] He seems to have received his musical training as a choirboy in the diocese of Arras and came to Paris as a scholarship student at the College of Dainville, which served the needs of the

---

38. See Daniel Heartz, "Attaingnant," *The New Grove Dictionary of Music* 1:673–76.

FIGURE 5-11. *Kyrie, Missa Ave Maria*, attributed to Antoine de Févin (Antico, *Liber quindecim missarum*, ff. 94ᵛ–95).

cathedral chapters of Arras and Noyon. As it happened, the college leased that part of its buildings looking onto the rue de la Harpe to Philippe Pigouchet (fl. 1490–1514), a printer-engraver celebrated for his books of hours. Attaingnant later married one of Pigouchet's daughters and thus became his heir, suggesting not only that he was apprenticed to the master printer following his studies at the college but also that he showed exceptional promise in his chosen craft.

The earliest evidence of Attaingnant's career as a publisher dates from 1525, when he collaborated on the production of a breviary for the diocese of Noyon with Poncet le Preux (1481–1559). The latter had married another of Pigouchet's daughters and was to become one of the four official booksellers of the University of Paris, master of the printers' guild, and a prolific publisher of scholarly texts. Since printed liturgical books of the period have rarely survived the heavy wear to which they were subjected and the changes in usage that came toward the end of the sixteenth century, it seems likely that Attaingnant continued to publish such volumes throughout his life, even though copies of only three others have survived, all of them for Noyon. Another presumed staple of his shop, doubtless prompted by the proximity of the college and connections with the Sorbonne, were instructional compendia for young scholars, but only two of them are still known.[39] Competition in these areas was extremely keen, however, and may have prompted Attaingnant to experiment with the printing of mensural notation, which was not then being done successfully by any Parisian shop.

To avoid the necessity of printing staves and notes separately, as Petrucci had done, he divided the type into short segments of musical staff, most of which also carried one of the notes, rests, or other symbols that might be required at any point in a mensural composition. This was a technical innovation of revolutionary importance for the industry at the time, the advantages of which, both musical and economic, were considerable. A single impression could produce a page of music, and the problem of matching precisely the registration of successive printings—so that notes and staves would be accurately aligned—was entirely avoided; the labor, time, and expense of producing a collection of music were thus roughly halved. Not that the new procedure was altogether devoid of problems. To rival esthetically the work of a skillful scribe, the individual pieces of type had to match perfectly in the thickness and the spacing of the lines of the staff, and any failure to align them perfectly produced wavy or ragged horizontal lines. In fact, even a master printer, such as Attaingnant clearly was, found it impossible to eliminate entirely minute gaps and irregularities in the staff lines, which consequently betray the method used (see Figure 5-12).

Judging from the rapidity with which Attaingnant's technology was adopted by printers of music all over the Western world, the problems they posed must have been much easier to cope with than those connected with earlier methods—either Petrucci's multiple impressions or Antico's wood engravings—especially in light of the enhanced speed and economy of production that it made possible. These advantages are reflected in and probably account in good measure for the extraordinarily abundant output of Attaingnant's atelier. His first collection of polyphonic music, entitled *Chansons nouvelles en musique, a quatre parties*, was published as four partbooks in early April 1528, and within the year he brought out no fewer than seven other chanson anthologies.

On the strength of his achievement Attaingnant was able to apply for a royal privilege to prohibit the copying of his books of music by other printers for a period of three years. A further privilege, granted in 1531, provided the same sort of copyright for an additional six-year term. His fertile activity earned for him the support of the cardinal of Tournon, the nominal master of the royal French chapel and a powerful figure at the court of Francis I, and in 1537 he succeeded not only in having his privilege renewed but also in having himself named "royal printer and bookseller in music to the King," a title that had not previously existed. Ongoing contact with the humanistically oriented court of Francis I may also have prompted him to begin replacing the gothic typefaces he had used earlier for texts with italic and roman fonts more in keeping with the tastes of his patrons.

39. A complete catalogue of the items published by Attaingnant's shop is included in the extensive study by Daniel Heartz, *Pierre Attaingnant, Royal Printer of Music* (Berkeley: University of California Press, 1969). (The liturgical books are nos. 1, 98, 138, and 139; the didactic broadsides are nos. 58 and 59.)

FIGURE 5-12. *Doulce memoire*, attributed to Pierre Sandrin (Attaingnant, *Second livre contenant xxvii Chansons nouvelles* . . . 1538, no. 7).

The prolific musical production of Attaingnant's shop in the rue de la Harpe continued more or less unbroken from his earliest publications in 1528 until the printer's death in 1551 or 1552, and a few scattered items were brought out subsequently by his widowed second wife until 1558. Over that period of time the sheer number of volumes printed—many of them in press runs of up to 1,000 copies—is simply astounding. There were some 80 collections of chansons and another 22 reprints or revisions for a total of more than 1,750 individual pieces. The printing of polyphonic Masses began in 1532 with a series of 7 folio choirbooks and went to a total of 14 volumes, one of which was reprinted, containing all told some 32 Mass Ordinaries and 3 Requiem Masses. Motets, which he began publishing in partbooks as early as 1529, went to some 28 individual items and 2 further reprints with more than 415 separate works, a total that does not include the 25 settings of the Magnificat or the 2 Passions that were part of the series of 14 books of motets published between 1534 and 1539.

There were, in addition, two sets of polyphonic settings of the Psalms and other liturgical texts in French translation for a total of 56 compositions (suggesting, perhaps, that Attaingnant was not entirely out of sympathy with the religious reformers then active in France). No less impressive is his contribution to the instrumental repertory of the period: a total of 20 publications, 2 of them containing chansons and dances intabulated for lute, a series of 7 volumes for keyboard including both secular and liturgical music, and another 11 collections of dance music for consorts of instruments of various kinds, largely unspecified.

Following Attaingnant's demise, the tradition he had established in Paris was taken up first by Nicolas Du Chemin (c. 1515–76)[40] and then by the firm of Le Roy and Ballard, established by Robert Ballard and his cousin Adrian Le Roy in 1551.[41] The latter, in particular, who enjoyed the favor of the royal court and were granted Attaingnant's title as music printers to the king, flourished until the end of the century and beyond, playing the predominant role in the publication of music in France. In Venice, where Petrucci had inaugurated his pathbreaking work, the printing of music was subsequently taken up by the Scotto family,[42] mentioned earlier, and by a number of others, including Antoine Gardane.[43] The latter, who was born in southern France and began his career as a printer in Venice in 1538 with a volume of chansons by Janequin, adopted Attaingnant's methods of production, and the business he established was carried on by his sons after his death in 1569.

Two members of the Giunta family, a dynasty of printers originating in Florence, were active as publishers of the polyphonic music engraved by Antico, as we have seen.[44] In Venice Luca Antonio's involvement with mensural music ended with the eight books of polyphony printed from Antico woodcuts in 1520–21. After Antico's departure from Rome, however, Antonio collaborated with others, including Giovanni Giacomo Pasoti of Parma and Valerio Dorico, with whom he published a series of eight books of polyphony in 1526. Dorico, who was established as an independent printer and bookseller by 1531, used Petrucci's double impression method in the 1530s and 1540s but then adopted the procedure developed by Attaingnant, beginning with a collection of Masses by Morales in 1544. With his brother Luigi he brought out some twenty-six musical collections and a pair of treatises before his death in 1565, and his heirs continued printing music until 1572.[45]

Because of its role as the seat of the papacy, Rome was able to sustain a modest level of music printing throughout the sixteenth century—with something of a hiatus in 1527 following the sack of the city by the forces of Charles V. Its importance was more political than commercial, however, and it never saw the kind of ongoing competitive production, both qualitatively and quantitatively, that characterized cities such as Venice, Paris, and Nuremberg. Even the great late sixteenth-century

40. See Samuel F. Pogue, "Du Chemin," *The New Grove Dictionary of Music,* 5:670f.
41. See Samuel F. Pogue, "Ballard," *The New Grove Dictionary of Music,* 2:83–86.
42. See Thomas W. Bridges, "Scotto," *The New Grove Dictionary of Music,* 17:85–87.
43. See Thomas W. Bridges, "Gardane," *The New Grove Dictionary of Music,* 7:158–59.
44. See Thomas W. Bridges, "Giunta," *The New Grove Dictionary of Music,* 7:415–17.
45. Regarding Antonio and Luigi, see Suzanne G. Cusick, "Dorico," *The New Grove Dictionary of Music,* 5:576–77.

master Pierluigi Palestrina, whose career was spent almost entirely in the papal states, and mostly at the papal court, had more of his music published in Venice than in his home city.

Other urban centers where the printing of mensural music flourished included Lyons, whose location at the confluence of the Rhône and Saône Rivers and four yearly trade fairs made it one of the most important commercial cities of western Europe. There the Istrian-born printer Jacques Moderne published some fifty collections of music between 1532 and his death in the early 1560s, using the single-impression method developed by Attaingnant. The more than 800 compositions that he brought to press included a series of eight books of motets, eleven or more of chansons, books of polyphonic Masses, collections of music for instrumental ensemble, and intabulations for the lute. Like his Parisian competitor, Moderne also brought out a number of collections devoted entirely to the works of a single composer, most notably books of Italian *canzoni* by Francesco de Layolle and Mattio Rampollini.[46]

Single-impression printing was introduced to Antwerp, another of Europe's most important industrial and commercial centers, by Tylman Susato, composer, calligrapher, and town minstrel. Two years after the dissolution of an abortive partnership formed with two of Antwerp's book printers in 1541, Susato launched a career as a music printer that was to last until his death in the early 1560s, when his son took over the firm. During that time he published, like his competitors, in all of the major genres: twenty-five books of chansons, three of Masses, and nineteen of motets. Perhaps the most arresting side of his activity, however, is the series of eleven *Musyck boexken*, collections of secular music, the first two containing Flemish songs, another a group of dances based on popular tunes as arranged by Susato himself (undoubtedly reflecting his long-time role as a town minstrel), and eight books of *Souterliedekens*, polyphonic settings of Psalms that had been translated into the Flemish vernacular.[47]

When Susato's son died in 1564, his widow sold his type fonts to Christopher Plantin, who is best known as a publisher of scholarly books on a variety of subjects. In the 1570s, having acquired as official printer to King Philip II of Spain a monopoly for the printing of missals and breviaries in the royal dominions, Plantin published more than 50,000 service books, most of which were sent to Spain. He began to publish polyphonic music only in 1578 with a collection of Masses by the Antwerp-born composer George de la Hèle, who had spent ten years as a choirboy in the chapel of King Philip and returned to Spain as his chapelmaster two years later. In the eleven years that followed, Plantin published another ten collections of music,

46. See Samuel F. Pogue, *Jacques Moderne, Lyons Music Printer of the Sixteenth Century* (Geneva: Librairie Droz, 1969), which includes a comprehensive catalogue of the items that bear the mark of Moderne's press; cf. also Pogue's brief article, "Moderne," in *The New Grove Dictionary of Music*, 12:452–53.

47. For additional details regarding his production as a printer, see Susan Bain, "Susato," *The New Grove Dictionary of Music*, 18:378–79.

primarily Masses, motets, and chansons by composers of good reputation such as Philippe de Monte, de Kerle, Le Jeune, and Pevernage.[48]

Despite his considerable stature and historical importance as a printer, Plantin had less of an impact on the publication of music in Antwerp than did Pierre Phalèse in the nearby city of Louvain, who became bookseller to the University of Louvain in 1542. Before the end of the decade he had published (but did not print)—together with a number of scholarly and scientific books—five volumes of chansons intabulated for lute. Success in that venture, or perhaps that enjoyed by Susato in Antwerp, may have prompted him in 1551 to apply for a license to print polyphonic music from moveable type. With that privilege in hand Phalèse began to print motets and chansons by composers of his native region such as Clemens (non Papa) and Crecquillon, more French lute tablature, and, gradually, composers of a more international stature such as Lassus and de Rore—the latter often in reprints of collections originally brought out by Le Roy and Ballard.

In 1570 he formed with the Antwerp printer Jean Bellère a partnership that was maintained after Phalèse's death in the mid-1570s by his sons, first Corneille and then Pierre junior. The latter moved to Antwerp, where he can be traced as early as 1581. There he took up his father's activity as a printer of music where the elder Phalèse (and his eldest son) had left off—in the middle of a multivolume collection of motets by Lassus—and maintained it until he died in 1629, leaving the firm at that point in the hands of his two daughters.[49]

In Germany the music publishing industry had its most significant and productive representatives in the commercial city of Nuremberg. Single-impression printing of mensural music was apparently first introduced there by Hieronymus Formschneider. Formschneider is famous for his collaboration with Albrecht Dürer, for whom he printed a substantial number of woodcuts, and for his publication of Luther's German Psalter and Prayer Book. His first musical publication, brought out in 1532, was a volume of largely vocal works—Psalm settings and Lieder by composers of German culture such as Thomas Stoltzer, Ludwig Senfl, Paul Hofhaimer, and Johann Walter—but arranged for bowed string instruments in consort or intabulated for lute by Hans Gerle. Two further books of lute music edited by Gerle were to follow, the first (1533) containing mostly intabulations of preexistent vocal works, sacred as well as secular, together with a number of preludial pieces, and the second (1552) fantasias and dances from older publications.

Formschneider also printed collections of chansons (*carmina*), motets, Magnificats, and Lieder—including entire books given over to the works of Senfl and Heinrich Finck—some of which appeared under his own name and others under that of his colleague and friend, the publisher and bookseller Hans Ott. Perhaps his most significant contribution to the musical repertory of the period was his

48. See Susan Bain, "Plantin," *The New Grove Dictionary of Music*, 14:851.
49. Concerning this dynasty of music printers, see Susan Bain, "Phalèse," *The New Grove Dictionary of Music*, 14:617–20.

publication of the three-volume set of polyphonic settings of Mass Propers for the entire liturgical year, the celebrated *Choralis Constantinus* composed by Heinrich Isaac.[50]

Also publishing music in Nuremberg in the sixteenth century were Johann Petreius, who had received his education and early training in the printing trade in Basel, and the firm of Montanus and Neuber. Petreius, for whom music was but a small fraction of his output overall, published a substantial number of didactic treatises on music as well as collections of Psalm settings and other motets, Masses, and polyphonic Lieder.[51] The partnership of Johann van den Berg (Montanus) and Ulrich Neuber was established in 1542. Berg had come to Nuremberg from Paris, where he had been a student, leaving for religious reasons. His colleague, Neuber, was a craftsman without specifically musical training about whom relatively little is known. Together they published a considerable quantity of music—none of it particularly distinguished in technical or typographical terms—including (as with Petreius) a number of theoretical treatises, an extensive series of Psalm settings and motets of various other kinds, and the usual smattering of polyphonic songs on German texts.[52]

There were yet other cities where music printing took place, albeit on a much more modest scale—Frankfurt, London, Madrid, Naples, and Strasbourg, to name a few.[53] But to examine the activity there would add nothing of substance to the picture already drawn. Printers everywhere tended to respond first of all to local demand, publishing familiar genres and composers known and loved in the immediate area. Most of them then attempted to reach a wider, more international market with works in all of the current genres by composers whose stature could be counted upon to generate interest and sales. Unfortunately, some of them were apparently willing to resort to authorial attributions of questionable authenticity in the process, causing endless problems for the present-day historian.

Seen from the present perspective, the development of music publishing in the sixteenth century seems almost explosive in nature. If initially the industry was supported by the needs of court chapels and church choirs and a relatively small group of city dwellers who were musically literate, it appears to have generated with surprising rapidity a much broader base of commercial support. Printers provided repertories of the finest sacred music then written for small establishments that could not afford the luxury of a resident composer; they offered professional and amateur musicians alike a wide variety of secular compositions for small combinations of voices and/or instruments; and they fostered a dramatic increase in musical literacy with a modest flood of instrumental tutors and didactic treatises on music. By making the works of the most highly gifted and widely celebrated composers of the age available

50. Formschneider's publications in music have been listed by Hans Albrect, "Formschneider," *Die Musik in Geschichte und Gegenwart*, 4:651.
51. See Marie Louise Göllner, "Petreius," *The New Grove Dictionary of Music*, 14:586.
52. See Marie Louise Göllner, "Berg," *The New Grove Dictionary of Music*, 2:539–40.
53. Some additional details are given by Heartz, *Pierre Attaingnant, Royal Printer of Music*, 139–68.

in multiple copies all over the Western world, the publishers of music changed forever the nature of musical patronage and put the pleasures of musical performance within reach of ever widening segments of the urban population. The far-reaching effects of their achievements are with us still and continue to shape, over the centuries, our musical culture.

PART TWO

The Fifteenth Century

THE CONSOLIDATION OF

GENRES AND STYLES

A WORD ABOUT ESTHETICS

Before proceeding to a discussion of the musical styles and genres of the Renaissance, let us pause to consider what can be surmised concerning the impact that music had on the intellect and the senses of those who heard it at the time. Unfortunately, such insight is not easily acquired. Esthetics, as a field of systematic philosophical inquiry, was then still several centuries from its inception, and there was no well-established place in the traditional modes of discourse about music (as there was, by contrast, in the nineteenth century) for personal appreciations of music's sensual qualities or reasoned examination of the subjective and affective reactions it was capable of provoking.

True, there are two important strains of Greek thought, reaching back as far as Plato and Aristotle, that relate to the effects of music on those who performed or heard it. One of these was concerned with the *ethos* of the art, its presumed power to move the human soul and to influence both the behavior and therefore, eventually, the moral character of the those who were exposed to it, especially the young.[1] The other arose from the notion, elaborated in Plato's *Timaeus*, that the order of the universe, as well as that of the soul, was essentially mathematical in nature and that its proportional relationships are the same as those embodied in musical consonance (see Appendix, pp. 1037–41).

These ideas had been transmitted directly and continuously from the writers of antiquity to those of the Renaissance. However, discussion of them was constrained by the long tradition of which they were a part and the authority of the figures with which they were associated. As a consequence, speculative writings on music dating from the late Middle Ages simply reworked for the most part the formulations of ear-

---

1. Pertinent passages from Plato's *Republic* and Aristotle's *Politics* are included in Oliver Strunk, ed., *Source Readings in Music History*, rev. ed., Leo Treitler, gen. ed. (New York: Norton, 1998), 9–19 and 23–34. Unless noted otherwise, all citations to Strunk's work are to this edition.

lier authors, and the technical treatises, which were concerned with practical matters pertaining to composition and execution, rarely raised esthetic questions except in passing.

The more significant of these two conceptual threads for the esthetic orientation of composers of the late Middle Ages and early Renaissance was the notion that the simple proportions used to regulate both musical consonance and mensuration were those that had been adopted by the creator of the universe to achieve a harmonious balance among its constituent elements. This idea had been codified in the traditional tripartite division of music into *musica mundana* (the "music of the spheres"), *musica humana* (relating to the harmony of the soul), and *musica instrumentalis* (the actual sounds produced by voices and instruments) and had become a traditional part of the *quadrivium* (see pp. 38–39).

In the sacred music of the period these small multiple and superparticular ratios were sometimes used to govern the mathematical relationships among major sections of the structure. A case in point is the *Missa Se la face ay pale*, a cyclical Ordinary attributed to Guillaume Du Fay (ca. 1400–74) and one of the first to be based on a secular cantus firmus.[2] A verbal canon for the Gloria and the Credo instructs the performer(s) of the tenor to sound it three times, first augmented by three, then by two, and finally as it is written, thus creating the simple proportions of 3:2, 3:1, and 2:1 among the relative durations of the cantus firmus. Similarly, the Kyrie, Sanctus, and Agnus have the canon, or rule, "Tenor crescit in duplo," indicating that its duration would be augmented by two in performance.

Even more striking, if the significance of its structure has been correctly construed, is Du Fay's isorhythmic motet *Nuper rosarum flores/Terribilis est locus iste*, written for the dedication of the dome of the cathedral in Florence, Santa Maria dei Fiori, on March 25, 1436 (see pp. 35–36).[3] The tenor cantus firmus, which was appropriately drawn from the beginning of the Introit for the Dedication of a Church, is written out in mensural notation but once. Its execution, as in the *Missa Se la face ay pale*, is regulated by a verbal canon, specifying that the tenor part is to be sounded four times in succession but with each statement under a different mensuration, these being indicated by the symbols O C ¢ ◓.

If the relationships suggested by these signs are literally construed, the isorhythmic sections (*taleae*) of the motet are related in duration to one another by the proportional sequence 6:4:2:3. This includes the ratios for all of the "perfect" consonances as they were then reckoned in the Western world: octave (2:1), fifth (3:2), and fourth (4:3). Significantly, these were also the proportions of Solomon's temple—60, 40, 20, and 30 cubits being dimensions either mentioned specifically or resulting by extrapolation from the description of its construction—and it has been suggested that the symbolic allusion was intentional and would

2. See the edition of the Mass in Du Fay's *Opera omnia*, ed. Heinrich Besseler, 6 vols. (Rome: American Institute of Musicology, 1947–66), 3:1ff.

3. See the motet as edited by Besseler in Du Fay's *Opera omnia*, 1:70ff.

have been readily understood by the educated prelates (and others) gathered for the occasion.[4]

In fact, during the fifteenth century proportional relationships such as these occur between the principal sections of large-scale musical works rather frequently, enough to suggest that they were usually intentionally devised by their authors.[5] Viewed in conjunction with the adoption of consonance as the norm for vertical intervals in counterpoint and of basic binary and ternary proportions for the common patterns in mensuration, they indicate that composers of this period still conceived the numerically definable characteristics of their compositions as a possible reflection of the harmony deemed to be present in the universal creation. They apparently believed that the proportions built into the structure of a musical composition, even those that were not consciously perceived by an experienced musician, could convey to their creator—if not always to their listeners—a pleasing sense of harmonious order.

It may have been this notion that Johannes Tinctoris had in mind when he praised the music of the composers he believed worthy of emulation as "exhaling sweetness" (*suavitudinem redolent*). For while he specifically rejected the traditional doctrine that the revolution of celestial bodies produced audible consonant sounds, he asserted (citing as his authority the Church Father Lucius Lactantius) that the pleasure (*voluptas*) of the ear is derived from the "sweetness" of concords in sounds and melodies "produced by earthly instruments with the cooperation of nature."[6]

Interestingly, the esthetic appreciation of less erudite listeners reflects a similar sensitivity to the quality of musical sound and to its sheer sensual impact. It is not unusual for chroniclers such as Olivier de la Marche, Mathieu d'Escouchy, or Georges Chastellain—men who served as official chroniclers at the courts of Burgundy and France in the mid- to late-fifteenth century—either to speak of the sweetness of voices and melodies or to mention the effect of loud instruments and massed sounds.

In their detailed descriptions of the fabulous Banquet of the Pheasant, offered by Duke Philip of Burgundy for the knights of the Order of the Golden Fleece in 1454, de la Marche and d'Escouchy speak of "a very sweet song" (*une tres doulce chanson*), of organs playing "most sweetly" (*moult doucement*), and of instruments that were

4. Concerning the significance of the reference, see Craig Wright, "Dufay's *Nuper rosarum flores*, King Solomon's Temple, and the Veneration of the Virgin," *Journal of the American Musicological Society* 47 (1994): 395–441.

5. There is considerable disagreement still among scholars as to the manner in which numerical relationships were used by composers of the period in designing musical structures. In an extreme example, Marcus Van Crevel attributed cabalistic significance to structural relationships in the Masses of Johannes Obrecht; see his editions of the *Missa Maria Zart* and the *Missa Sub tuum presidium* in volumes 7 and 6, respectively, of the *Opera omnia editio altera*, ed. Albert Smijers and Marcus Van Crevel, 9 vols. (Amsterdam: Vereniging voor Nederlandse Muziekgeschiedenis, 1953–59); note that his arguments in that connection have not been universally accepted.

6. See the dedication to his treatise on counterpoint as translated by Strunk, ed., *Source Readings in Music History*, (New York: Norton, 1950), 197–99.

"pleasant to hear" (*bon a oyr*). They also refer, by contrast, to the fanfare played by four trumpets "very loudly" (*moult hautement*), and Chastellain says of the din raised by the trumpeters and minstrels that invariably attended tourneys and jousts that it would be impossible to hear the thunder of God above their playing.[7] Certainly, to ears accustomed to much less ambient noise than is the rule in our own mechanized age (and unjaded by continuous exposure to electronically recorded and amplified sound), the impression made by live musical performance must have been very vivid indeed.

The understanding that the effects of music were due in some significant sense to the "harmony" that could be numerically expressed was a persistent one. In the second half of the sixteenth century still, no less a theorist than Gioseffo Zarlino was explaining *armonia* in terms of mathematical proportions, which he extended to include both the major third (5:4) and the minor third (6:5) as well as their combination within the compass of a fifth (see Appendix, pp. 1039–43). Meanwhile, authors less skeptical than Tinctoris continued to affirm the idea of the harmony of the spheres. As the composer Giovanni Francesco Alcarotto (Algarotti) declared in the preface to his first book of madrigals in 1567, "All the wise of the world . . . commonly assert, that of all the activities of the human intellect, none is more similar than music to that most consonant order with which the Supreme Creator produces and governs this universe."[8]

In the course of the sixteenth century the esthetic focus began to shift from ultimate causes to more immediate and sensible effects, from the mysteries of cosmic and animistic harmonies to the observable power of music to move the emotions and its putative ability to influence character and morals. As a rule such questions were not addressed in the technical treatises on music but rather in historical essays clearly indebted to humanistic models. The distinction is nowhere clearer than in the writings of Johannes Tinctoris. In addition to his comprehensive series of treatises dealing with specialized theoretical topics, he authored circa 1473–74 a book of a very different kind entitled *Complexus effectuum musices* (*The Embrace of the Effects of Music*).

Transmitted, unfortunately, only fragmentarily as a series of excerpts selected for and dedicated to Johannes Stockem, a friend and colleague who was at the time in the service of Beatrice of Aragon at the Hungarian Court, the *Complexus* is a kind of social history of musical instruments—including the human voice—from antiquity to his own time. Tinctoris takes much of his material from pertinent passages found either in the Bible or in the classical literature of Greece and Rome. He passes on many of the legendary accounts concerning quasi-miraculous effects achieved by

---

7. For pertinent citations from these chroniclers, see Jeanne Marix, *Histoire de la musique et des musiciens de la cour de Bourgogne* (Strasbourg: Heitz, 1939; reprint, Geneva: Minkoff, 1972), 35–47.

8. Quoted by Alfred Einstein, *The Italian Madrigal*, 3 vols. (Princeton: Princeton University Press, 1949), 1:217, in his discussion of "Cosmos and Music." (Einstein identifies the source of the citation as Alcarotto's second book of madrigals but gives the date of 1567, which is that of the composer's first book.)

music through the agency of particularly skilled performers, but he relies on personal experience for the music of his day.

In the process he touches frequently, if somewhat indirectly, on the ethical questions raised by the philosophers of Greek antiquity: music's power to alter human conduct and to shape character; its role in the education of the young; its therapeutic uses; and—as might be expected from a cleric and chapel musician— its place in religious worship. That this treatise was a humanistically inspired departure from the traditions of medieval theory is evident from the fact that, unlike Tinctoris's technical writings, it had few counterparts among writers of subsequent generations. Only Pietro Gaetano's disquisition of the 1560s on the *Origins and Worth of Music* follows a comparable pattern and deals with similar concerns (see pp. 50–53).

If music theorists usually omitted discussion of such matters in their technical works, composers were nonetheless increasingly conscious of the expressive potential of their art and of the consequent expectations of performers and listeners. Their views are often left unexpressed, even when their music clearly reflects their expressive concerns.[9] However, prefaces to printed collections of music did provide a context in which the subject could be taken up, and some of the statements found there clearly reveal that the composers' aim was to move the emotions of their audience. In dedicating the motets and madrigals of Adrian Willaert's *Musica nova* of 1559 to Alfonso d'Este, for example, Francesca della Viola declared of his former mentor that, "whenever called upon, he arouses in the soul all of the affections that he wishes to move."[10]

In the course of the sixteenth century, making music capable of exciting the emotions became much more than just an aim for skilled composers and performers; it was an ideal adopted by humanists as well, and the notion that it could in fact achieve the desired effect attained wide currency. Similar sentiments are expressed as early as 1507 by Carlo Valgulio, who served as secretary to Cardinal Cesare Borgia. Although not a trained musician, he declares (in his preface to a Latin translation of Plutarch's *De musica*) that, "the essence of music is the movement of the soul, driving away the evils and troubles that have invaded it . . . to draw the soul where it wants."[11] Some few years later (1517) and far from Rome, Thomas More says of the music of Utopia: "in one thing doubtless they go exceeding far beyond us. For all their music both that they play upon instruments, and that they sing with man's voice doth so resemble and express natural affections, the sound and tune is so applied and made agreeable to the thing, that whether it be a prayer, or else a ditty: of gladness, of patience, of trouble, of

9. See below, for example, the discussion of the Italian madrigal, chap. 18.
10. See the Willaert *Opera omnia*, ed. Hermann Zenck, Walter Gerstenberg, et al., 15 vols., Corpus mensurabilis musicae 3 ([Rome]: American Institute of Musicology, 1950–77), 5:x: "ad ogni sua richiesta fa sentir nell'animo tutti gli affetti, che si propone di muovere."
11. Quoted by Claude V. Palisca, *Humanism in Italian Renaissance Musical Thought* (New Haven: Yale University Press, 1985), 16.

mourning, or of anger, the fashion of the melody doth so represent the meaning of the thing, that it doth wonderfully move, stir, pierce, and enflame the hearers' minds."[12]

As is evident from More's own formulation, the tendency for one espousing such a point of view was to see the expressive powers of music as somehow inextricably linked with a text, as requiring in most circumstances a verbal specification of the affections to be given musical expression. Such a perspective proved to be intrinsically inimical to the Platonic idea that what polyphony expressed most aptly and essentially, in all of its complexity, was the proportional harmony of the universe and of the human soul. As a result, the intelligibility of the word became paramount, and the marvelous, mystical beauty of intricate contrapuntal structures was no longer universally seen as an apt reflection of the divine nature but—at least by some—more as an obstacle to verbal comprehension. In the oft-quoted formulation of Giulio Cesare Monteverdi, writing in 1607 in defense of the expressive innovations in polyphonic composition termed *seconda pratica* by his brother Claudio, "true art . . . the one that turns on the perfection of the melody, . . . considers harmony not commanding, but commanded, and makes the words mistress of the harmony."[13]

During the second half of the sixteenth century, as this altered view of the art of music gained currency, a new theme began to be woven into formal discourse on music, one that was more explicitly descriptive of musical style than theoretical writing had traditionally been, and it appears both in the writings of nonmusicians and of the theorists themselves. A well-known example comes from Cosimo Bartoli (1503–72), a Florentine humanist who embedded comments on music into his *Ragionamenti accademici* (first published in Venice in 1567). Although he gives lengthier attention to performers, in whose skills he seems to have greater interest, he takes up composers first. A friend and admirer of Giorgio Vasari, with whose approach to art history he was obviously familiar (see pp. 32–34), he begins with Johannes Okeghem, whose accomplishment in bringing music back from the abyss he compares to Donatello's with sculpture, and Josquin Desprez, whose inventive genius he compares to Michelangelo's.[14]

His critical comments concerning most composers are not very informative, limited as they are to general expressions of praise. However, he does describe rather cogently the dense imitative counterpoint of Nicolas Gombert (ca. 1495–ca. 1560) as a distinctive musical style, echoing in fact rather closely observations made by the

---

12. *Utopia*, Book 2, "Of the Religions in Utopia," in Oliver Strunk, ed., *Source Readings in Music History*, (New York: Norton, 1998), 535–44.

13. For the entire essay, a lengthy gloss on a declaration by the composer printed with his *Fifth Book of Madrigals* of 1605, see Strunk, ed., *Source Readings in Music History*, 535–44. For a concise discussion of Monteverdi's esthetic viewpoint in this connection, see Gary Tomlinson, *Monteverdi and the End of the Renaissance* (Oxford: Clarendon Press, 1987), 21–30.

14. For a careful, illuminating discussion of Bartoli's dialogues on music (including the original Italian text), see James Haar, "Cosimo Bartoli on Music," *Early Music History* 8 (1988): 37–79.

theorist-composer Hermann Finck in his *Practica musica* of 1556.[15] He also notes a certain stylistic affinity between the compositions of Adrian Willaert (ca. 1490–1562), the distinguished composer who finished his career as the chapelmaster at the basilica of San Marco in Venice, and those of Jacquet of Mantua (1483–1559), who spent the final decades of his life in Mantua as chapelmaster at the cathedral under the patronage of Ercole Gonzaga, cardinal and bishop of the diocese. Significantly, though, Bartoli's greatest praise is reserved for Philippe Verdelot (after 1470–before 1552), not only because of the composer's association with the author's native city in the 1520s but also, and more importantly, because his music could be "light, grave, noble, compassionate, fleeting, plodding, mild, angry, or imitative, according to the sense of the words to be set to music.[16]

Closer still to the descriptive language of modern analysis are the seven terms of stylistic characterization introduced by the amateur musician and theorist Lodovico Zacconi (1555–1627) in the second part of his *Prattica di musica*, published in Venice in 1622. He asserts that the various modes and manners of mensural polyphony can be distinguished by their artfulness (*arte*), their melodic writing (*modulatione*), their capacity for giving pleasure (*diletto*), their compositional texture (*tessitura*), their counterpoint (*contrapunto*)—specifically that written to a cantus firmus—their inventiveness (*inventione*), and the order and disposition of the separate voices (*buona dispositione*).[17] With the exception of *diletto*, none of these criteria is concerned either with cosmically significant proportional structures or with music's ability to move the emotions and refresh the human soul. Their connotations are instead specifically compositional and stylistic, and they suggest approaches for analytical study of the works to be considered.

In examining the music of the fifteenth and sixteenth centuries, we shall consider it from whichever of these three points of view seems most appropriate. In some instances, as we shall see, proportional structures are very much a part of the compositional concept, in others, clearly, not at all. Expressive tendencies, especially as they relate to the treatment given a text, are particularly significant for the secular genres of vocal music and warrant our attention. And the definition of musical style—with respect to melodic writing, the use of consonance and dissonance, and the contrapuntal textures of the polyphonic web—will help us to discern important new developments as they appear.

15. Regarding Gombert, Bartoli observes that the texture is continuous, with few rests, and that the parts are imitative, tightly interwoven with one another, producing a kind of grandeur and a delightful harmony (see Haar, "Cosimo Bartoli on Music," 55, for the original Italian); similarly, Finck notes the lack of rests, the imitative counterpoint, and the rich, full harmonies (see George Nugent, "Gombert," *The New Grove Dictionary of Music*, 7:512, for any English translation of the pertinent passage).

16. Bartoli's terms are "del facile, del grave, del gentile, del compassionevole, del presto, del tardo, del benigno, dello adirato, del fugato"; for the original text, see Haar, "Cosimo Bartoli on Music," 54.

17. For a probing discussion of the intended meaning of these terms (upon which the present summary is largely based) within the context of Zacconi's treatise, see James Haar, "A Sixteenth-Century Attempt at Music Criticism," *Journal of the American Musicological Society* 36 (1983): 191–209; cf., however, the cautionary comments regarding Zacconi's competence as a theorist by Gerhard Singer, "Zacconi," *The New Grove Dictionary of Music*, 20:611–12.

CHAPTER 6

The Contenance Angloise:
English Music at Home and Abroad

INTRODUCTION

The political events that had a significant impact on the development of music in the British Isles and on the interplay of musical genres and styles between England and the Continent during the fifteenth century go back to the long reign of Edward III (1327–77). His decision in 1337 to open hostilities against the French—thus initiating what is now known as the Hundred Years' War—marked the beginning of an English presence in territories of French language and culture that would last for more than a century. Despite the hostile nature of the English enterprise, it made possible comparisons between the respective achievements of the two peoples in literature and the arts and brought about contacts that facilitated exchange and mutual influence.

To wage war across the channel, Edward was obliged to turn to Parliament again and again for financial support, thus giving it (and especially the Commons) a greater role in regulating the affairs of the kingdom. He prepared himself for a protracted campaign by contracting with his barons and knights to form companies of men-at-arms and paying them to maintain and direct their troops. Although costly, this practice raised the armies of trained mercenaries that defeated superior French forces at Crécy (1346), at Poitiers (1356), and later at Agincourt (1415). Unfortunately, it also resulted in the companies of freebooters that devastated the French countryside repeatedly for nearly a century and eventually wreaked havoc in England as well.

Also crucial for fifteenth-century English life were the internal struggles concerning the right of succession to the English throne. During the minority of Richard II (1377–99), who came to the throne at the age of ten, Parliament asserted its authority, putting the real powers of government into the hands of five nobles, the so-called lords appellant. When, at last, Richard was able to take full control of his kingdom, he did so with a vengeance, levying heavy taxes and adopting despotic measures that aroused the animosity of his subjects. Among those with ample cause for dissatisfaction was the duke of Hereford, one of the lords appellant, whom

Richard had banished. When the king confiscated the Lancastrian estates to which he was heir, Hereford was provoked to armed rebellion. Profiting from Richard's absence on an expedition to Ireland, Hereford returned to England and quickly garnered broad support. Having defeated the forces loyal to Richard, he obtained the consent of Parliament to force his cousin to abdicate and have him imprisoned.

Crowned to rule as Henry IV (1399–1413), Hereford became the first of the Lancastrian monarchs. Since his claim to the throne—as a descendant of Edward III through his fourth son, John of Gaunt—was less than direct, (see Genealogies, p. 1058) he reigned, in a sense, at the pleasure of Parliament. His son, Henry V (1413–22), had a more secure grasp on the crown. However, when he decided, with considerable popular support, to press his claims to the throne of France by renewing the armed struggle on the Continent, he, too, had to seek parliamentary support in levying the taxes needed to finance his military ventures (see Figure 6-1).

Henry V's premature death left the crown to his infant son, who was proclaimed king as Henry VI before his first birthday. The long minority of the new monarch, followed by the bouts of insanity (from 1453 on) that limited his ability to rule, once again allowed Parliament to affirm its increasing ascendancy, consolidating the gains it had previously made, turning precedents into fixed custom, and establishing its prerogatives under the law. It was also during the rule of Henry VI that the political and domestic legacy of Edward III—the Hundred Years' War, on the one hand, and seven living sons, on the other—bore its last bitter fruits. By mid-century it was increasingly apparent that the French territories to which the English had laid claim—and had, in fact, briefly held—had been irretrievably lost. The English people laid much of the blame on their ineffectual monarch and on his French queen, Margaret of Anjou, to whom he had been wed

FIGURE 6-1. Musicians in the English army that had laid siege to the city of Belle-Perche, during the Hundred Years' War: on the left four trumpets (three straight and one s-shaped) and on the right three shawms. Their playing greets the arrival of the duchess of Bourbon flanked by the counts of Cambridge and Pembroke.

in 1445. His weakness as a ruler also encouraged dissension among the greater magnates of the faction-ridden royal council, many of whom were descended from one of Edward III's numerous sons.

Moreover, many of the nobles who had fought in France had discovered a means to recapture a measure of the power and independence that their antecedents had enjoyed earlier under the feudal system. The English armies had been recalled from the Continent, but a good number of the soldiers were either unwilling or unable to return to peaceful pursuits. They hired out instead to nobles who were thus able to reconstitute companies of armed mercenaries like those they had commanded in France. England was then quickly plunged into anarchy as the lawless barons turned the barbarous skills they had honed at war with a foreign enemy against their own countrymen, terrorizing the unprotected and intimidating the courts of justice and the officers of the crown.

It was against this background of what has aptly been termed "bastard feudalism"[1] that the factional rivalries within the royal council developed into full-fledged civil war. The complicated train of events that followed eventually resolved itself to a power struggle among competing branches of the royal family, in particular the house of Lancaster (to which Henry VI himself belonged), led primarily by the Beaufort family, and the house of York, whose early champion was Richard, duke of York. Because he was descended from Edward III through both his paternal and maternal lines, York was in fact heir presumptive to the crown until a son was born unexpectedly to Henry VI and Margaret of Anjou after nearly a decade of childless marriage. Richard had assumed the regency during the king's first bout of insanity in 1453, but when Henry recovered briefly in the following year, the queen, mistrusting York's ambition, persuaded the king to ban him from the royal council.

In 1455, deprived of all access to power by Margaret's suspicions and the implacable enmity of the Lancastrians, Richard took up arms against them at St. Albans in what was to be the first battle of the Wars of the Roses (so named because a red rose was the emblem of the Lancastrian dynasty whereas a white rose stood for that of York). He was defeated and killed in 1460, but his son Edward was victorious over the Lancastrian armies in the following year, forcing Margaret into exile in Scotland together with her infant son and the aging king. The young duke of York was then able to march into London and have himself crowned king as Edward IV.

The latter was in turn forced into exile in 1470 when his cousin, the earl of Warwick, who had assisted his rise to power, espoused the Lancastrian cause—with the encouragement of Louis XI of France (see p. 269)—and helped restore Henry VI to the throne. The Yorkist pretender found an ally in Duke Charles of Burgundy, who provided not only refuge in his territories but also the military assistance Edward required to return to England a year later and recapture the crown. In the

---

1. The expression is taken from Wallace K. Ferguson, *Europe in Transition* (Boston: Houghton Mifflin Co., 1962), 205, to whose penetrating analysis of the political and social situation in England during the fifteenth and early sixteenth centuries the present discussion is much indebted.

course of that conflict Warwick was killed, Queen Margaret was captured, and both King Henry VI and the infant prince were murdered. This left Edward IV with a firm grasp on the royal scepter, and during the remaining years of his short rule, he began the difficult task of restoring order to the kingdom.

Unfortunately, his premature death in 1483 left the throne of England once again to a minor, his son Edward V, who was but twelve years of age at the time. A struggle for the regency ensued, pitting Richard, duke of Gloucester, Edward IV's brother, against the queen, Elizabeth Woodville, and members of her family, thus bringing the country back to the brink of civil war. Richard dealt with the opposition of the Woodvilles by having a number of them peremptorily executed and succeeded in gaining control. He appeared at first content to rule as regent, but he soon had his nephews declared illegitimate and was himself crowned king as Richard III before the year was out. An abortive rebellion led by the duke of Buckingham was soon crushed, and it was darkly rumored that Richard had his two young nephews murdered as the surest means of eliminating any further challenge to his right to rule.

The Lancastrians had not abandoned their efforts to wrest control of the government from the house of York, however. Henry Tudor, the son of a Welsh nobleman who could trace his lineage to the royal family through his mother, Margaret Beaufort, was promoted by the Lancastrians on the strength of that slender tie as a pretender to the throne. The older members of the dynasty had him brought up in Brittany, to keep him out of harm's way during the reign of Edward IV, and waited for an opportunity to assert his dubious claim. Ironically, Richard III's violent seizure of the monarchy and his ruthless use of its power aroused the opposition of his subjects, opening the way for Henry to land in England at the head of a French army and to challenge the increasingly unpopular Yorkist ruler. At the first major battle between them in August 1485, Richard was killed and his forces defeated. The young Tudor was proclaimed king soon thereafter as Henry VII.

Like Henry IV—the first of the Lancastrian monarchs, as we have seen—Henry VII had thus mounted the throne, despite the weakness of his hereditary claims, by a combination of conquest and the confirmation of Parliament. He found it politic, consequently, to respect the role that had by then become traditional for that body in the government of the kingdom. Three decades of civil strife had left the English weary of the turmoil, however, and commensurately desirous to see the reestablishment of a strong, stable central authority. By pursuing policies that were favorable to gentry and burghers alike, Henry was able not only to begin recovering the power of the monarchy but also to use the Parliament as a tool in achieving that end. At the same time, he exercised the prerogatives that were clearly within his royal right with efficient vigor to restore order to the realm and replenish a much-depleted treasury.

A crucial step in restoring peace to the kingdom was his marriage in 1486 to Elizabeth of York, which united the remnants of the two warring factions and laid to rest the troublesome questions of succession. There remained the difficult task of suppressing the private armies of mutinous barons. This he managed by creating within the royal council a special court known as the Star Chamber, which was not subject to intimidation or coercion. And once the illegal bands of marauding soldiers had been cleared from the countryside, it was possible to entrust the policing of the shires once more to the sheriffs and justices of the peace, who were appointed from among the local gentry.

At the same time, Henry VII achieved solvency for the crown by reintegrating into the royal domain lands that had earlier been ceded to others and by confiscating the possessions of the rebellious and the lawless. So successful was he with this strategy that his revenues were soon sufficient for the requirements of his court, and since he avoided the costly entanglements of war, he had little need to depend upon taxation that could only have been imposed with parliamentary approval. These are remarkable feats of statesmanship, but it is only fair to observe that they were undoubtedly facilitated considerably by the unfortunate circumstance that the civil wars had decimated the English nobility, weakening or entirely destroying many of the older dynasties and, as a result, the forces of possible opposition to the monarchy.

Despite the internecine conflicts within the kingdom during the Wars of the Roses, English commerce continued to develop unabated all through the period— wool and other exports actually increased, for example—and the status of the growing merchant class improved as well. Henry Tudor acted to protect this source of English prosperity by bettering relations with his Continental neighbors. He signed a peace treaty with the French, negotiated with Philip the Handsome an agreement protecting English wool markets in the Netherlands, and forged an alliance with Spain by marrying his eldest son, Arthur, to Catherine of Aragon, the daughter of Isabel and Ferdinand. That union proved to be fraught with consequences that Henry VII could not foresee, but he regarded it as sufficiently important that when Arthur died in 1502, the king arranged to replace him with his younger brother, the future Henry VIII. When the first Tudor monarch died in 1509, then, he could bequeath to his dynastic successors a kingdom at peace with itself and with others, a royal treasury well filled, and a strong central government in which a representative Parliament continued, nonetheless, to play a significant role.

Music flourished in fifteenth-century England, despite the political turmoil of the period, in part because it was rooted in a long and vigorous tradition. The polyphonic genres and styles that originated on the Continent in the eleventh and twelfth centuries as a means of embellishing the Christian liturgy (and that were soon adapted to the pleasures of courtly entertainment) were quickly adopted by English institutions, where they found a congenial home. At the same time, English clerics who studied at a Continental university, such as the Sorbonne, mastered the theoretical tradition as well and often committed to writing what they had learned abroad. This provided a basis for the cultivation of notated polyphony that was maintained continuously from the twelfth century through the sixteenth with no apparent interruption in the development of an essentially indigenous tradition.

One finds evidence of its use not only in the major cathedrals and important collegiate churches, as on the Continent, but also in a significant number of monastic houses, especially those of the Benedictine order, nine of which also had a cathedral under their rule, and in the colleges of Oxford and Cambridge universities. Statutory provision for the regular maintenance of a group of singers for polyphonic performance in monastic houses and university communities seems to have been characteristically English and without parallel in Continental Europe. Such a tradition is perhaps not surprising in the cathedral churches under monastic rule, especially in those cases where liturgical services were intended for lay members of the church, and the training of the boys in their school choirs to read mensural notation must have followed as a matter of course. Similarly, where there is record in other types of monastic communities of a customary use of polyphony, it is almost invariably in connection with the Lady Chapel, which stood outside the confines of the cloister and had as its principal purpose to foster lay devotions in honor of the Virgin Mary.

In the universities it was the very nature of the collegiate community, which was very closely modeled on that of secular cathedrals, that led to a regular celebration of the liturgy, the training of scholars in music, and the adoption of polyphony as a regular component in most of the important religious services. In most such institutions where the use and teaching of polyphony can be documented, the earliest pertinent records rarely reach back beyond the mid-fifteenth century. There is every indication that the polyphonic tradition in England was continuous, however, from as early as the eleventh century on. Whatever its origins, the systematic cultivation of polyphonic composition in universities and monastic houses, in addition to the cathedrals and collegiate churches as was customary in France and the Low Countries, resulted in an exceptionally broad foundation for the didactic and practical musical traditions that developed in English institutions.[2]

In England, as elsewhere, the nobles, beginning with the monarch himself, looked to such schools to provide clerics skilled in music for their private chapels whose functions included, as we have seen, the celebration of occasions of state and the illustration of courtly entertainments. The king's chapel was already fully organized by the end of the fourteenth century with some eleven chaplains and clerks, including at least one composer of polyphony.[3] It was a bit smaller than the French royal chapel of some thirty years later, but it was constituted in much the same fashion and must have served very similar purposes.

In view of Edward III's involvement in Continental politics—his marriage to Philippa of Hainaut, his claim to the throne of France, and the time he spent campaigning there (accompanied, undoubtedly, by at least some of the clerics of his chapel)—it is hardly surprising that his musicians were familiar with musical practice across the channel. In fact they may not have needed to leave the British Isles to

2. Concerning those institutions in which the musical arts were taught and polyphony adopted early on as a part of important liturgical observances, see Frank L. Harrison, *Music in Medieval Britain*, 2d. ed. (London: Routledge and Kegan Paul, 1963), 1–45 and 156–201. For a discussion of the teaching of music in church schools generally, see above, pp. 74–80.

3. Those are the figures given for 1393 by Harrison, *Music in Medieval Britain*, 21. For a discussion of the organization of the clerical and musical personnel in princely chapels generally, and the chapel royal in particular, see above, pp. 89–96.

come into contact with it. King John the Good of France, who was captured at the battle of Poitiers in 1356 together with his son Philip the Bold, the future duke of Burgundy, was held in England for ransom until the signing of the Treaty of Brétigny in 1360, and members of his personal household—including a number of his musicians—were allowed to join him there. Obviously, then, King Edward and the members of his household had ample opportunity to become acquainted with the kind of chapel music that usually graced the wealthier courts on the Continent, and he appears to have taken them as a model in the reorganization of his own private chapel.[4]

By contrast, Continental composers seem not to have been significantly influenced by English music at that time, perhaps because the English presence in France at the beginning of the Hundred Years' War was both short-lived and relatively superficial in nature. The primary tactic adopted by English armies fighting in France was the *chevauchée*, a sort of prolonged guerrilla raid. As a result, their campaigns were enormously destructive but rarely ended in the capture of lands and cities. Once terms had been settled at Brétigny, ceding considerable territories to the English

FIGURE 6-2. King Henry V of England (London, National Portrait Gallery).

crown in exchange for a promised ransom and the release of John the Good, a few castellanies were placed under the authority of a resident English lord, but there were few changes in the structure of local government in general. Edward's French subjects were left more or less to govern themselves, and exposure to English music was apparently minimal or entirely nonexistent for most of the next half-century.

When hostilities were resumed under Henry V, the situation changed dramatically. After the critical engagement at Agincourt in 1415, the English monarch spent most of his remaining years on the Continent, probably with the musicians of his chapel in his retinue (see Figure 6-2).[5] Following Henry's death in 1422, the English crown was represented in France until 1435 by John, duke of Bedford, who acted as regent, and he also maintained in

---

4. As Harrison observes (*Music in Medieval Britain*, 222–24), "It seems certain that the development of the music of the Royal Household Chapel under the early Lancastrian kings owed much to the French idea of the manner in which a great Christian ruler should order his daily and festal observances."

5. According to Harrison, *Music in Medieval Britain*, 22, the personnel of Henry V's chapel—numbering about twenty-seven chaplains and clerks, including a number of composers of polyphony, and as many as sixteen choristers—joined him in Normandy as early as 1417.

his retinue singers and composers of polyphony, including the celebrated John Dunstable (see Figure 6-3). During that same period of time another important French hostage was being held in England; Duke Charles d'Orléans, one of the century's most accomplished poets, was captured at Agincourt and not released until 1440. Since French lyrical art was closely associated with the polyphonic chanson, it is possible to suggest that his English residence became a locus for cultural exchange, making it possible for his captors to become acquainted not only with the French poetic tradition that he represented so brilliantly but also with some of the music it had inspired.

FIGURE 6-3. The duke of Bedford, English regent in France after the death of Henry V. (London, British Library, MS Add. 18850, f. 256ᵛ, detail.)

Furthermore, the repeated incursions of English armies into French territories, especially during the final phase of the Hundred Years' War in the first half of the fifteenth century, coincided with the growth of a flourishing English wool trade. The most important markets, clearly, were those closest by, the commercial and manufacturing cities of northern France and the Low Countries, and access to them was facilitated by the political alliances that brought successive dukes of Burgundy into an enduring, if sometimes stormy, relationship with the kings of England.[6] In addition, the English were active on the Continent in ecclesiastical politics, as English prelates participated in the attempts being made to bring to an end the Great Schism, in particular at the Council of Constance in 1415–18.

One result of these various contacts was to make English music and musicians known in the regions of western Europe to an extent that has never been seen either before or since. English names appear on the roles of a number of nobles' chapels, most notably at the ducal court of Burgundy, and in some church choirs as well. Their works, both sacred and secular, were copied in increasing numbers into the

---

6. See the study by Reinhard Strohm, *Music in Late Medieval Bruges* (Oxford: Clarendon Press, 1985), which touches on the role played by English music and musicians in one of the major trading centers of northern Europe during the fifteenth century through the establishment of a community of English tradesmen in the city.

musical manuscripts of the period. Particularly striking, in light of the scarcity of fifteenth-century musical sources of English origin, is the large number of compositions by English composers in collections that were compiled in northern Italy, most notably those now found in Aosta, Modena, and Trent.[7] More importantly, as we shall see, the distinctive sound of the English style struck the ear of the uninitiated listener as novel and appealing by virtue of its characteristic use of consonance. This led Continental composers to pay their insular counterparts the sincerest of compliments, imitating their compositional procedures.

Although English music never again commanded the leading role it assumed in the early decades of the fifteenth century in the development of the polyphony of the European Renaissance, it continued to develop within the context of a strong indigenous tradition. It remained nonetheless open to the stimulating influence of musical practice on the Continent, and access to the works of composers who were active across the channel was undoubtedly facilitated by the repeated contacts occasioned by the political circumstances summarized here. As was mentioned, the consort of Henry VI was the French princess, Margaret of Anjou. All through the troubled events of the Wars of the Roses, the Lancastrians sought and received assistance from the French while the Yorkists relied upon the support of the duke of Burgundy.

When Henry Tudor, the Lancastrian claimant who was brought up in France, came to power, his alliances with Continental rulers kept open the channels of communication by which the English could stay abreast of musical developments in the countries of western Europe. His son, Henry VIII, through his own involvement in Continental politics, continued to provide English musicians with opportunities to become familiar with the works of their counterparts in France and the Low Countries, as when Henry and Francis I met in 1520 near Calais at the Field of the Cloth of Gold and the chapel musicians of the two monarchs competed with one another.

THE *CONTENANCE ANGLOISE*

In his attempt to apply the historical notion of a "renaissance" to music (see pp. 43–47), Johannes Tinctoris identified the new beginnings, curiously enough, with English composers of the preceding generation. As he declared to his patron, King Ferdinand I of Naples, in the dedication to his treatise on proportions of circa 1476,

> At this time, consequently, the possibilities of our music have been so marvelously increased that there appears to be a new art, if I may so call it, whose fount and origin is held to be among the English, of whom Dunstable stood forth as chief. Contemporary with him in France were Du Fay and Binchoys, to whom directly suc-

---

7. For a summary description of these manuscripts and their contents, see Charles Hamm and Jerry Call, "Sources, MS, XI, 3, Renaissance Polyphony," *The New Grove Dictionary of Music*, 17:675–77; cf. below, pp. 222–24.

ceeded the moderns Okeghem, Busnoys, Regis, and Caron, who are the most excellent of all the composers I have ever heard.

Tinctoris even went so far as to affirm that the music written prior to that time was hardly worth hearing.[8] Since we have accepted for the purposes of this study the chronological boundaries for the Renaissance suggested by writers of the period, this assertion would suggest that an examination of the music should begin with Dunstable and his English contemporaries.

It is conceivable, of course, that Tinctoris's historical vision was little more than a humanistically inspired fiction. However, there is at least one independent witness to confirm that there was a significant shift in musical style at about the time the theorist indicated and that it was inspired by the music of English composers. Martin le Franc, a poet of considerable talent, who was also a cleric serving at the time as secretary to the antipope Felix V (Duke Amadeus VIII of Savoy), penned in 1440–42 a long didactic poem, *Le champion des dames*, that he dedicated to Duke Philip the Good of Burgundy.[9] In it he touches upon the music of his age, declaring:

> Tapissier, Carmen, Cesaris
> Not long ago did sing so well
> That they astonished all Paris
> And all those who came to hear;
> But never did they make discant
> With such choice melody,
> So I'm told by those who were there,
> As G. Du Fay and Binchoys.
>
> For they have a new way of composing
> With lively consonances
> In both loud and soft music,
> With accidentals, rests, and hexachordal changes
> And have adopted the guise
> Of the English and follow Dunstable,
> Whereby marvelous delight
> Makes their song joyful and memorable.[10]

8. See the translation of the dedication to the *Proportionale musices* by Oliver Strunk, ed., *Source Readings in Music History* (New York: Norton, 1998), 291–92, and Tinctoris's dedication to his *Liber de arte contrapuncti* (New York: Norton, 1950), 199.

9. See the *Encyclopédie illustrée du Pays de Vaud*, vol. 6, *Les arts: Architecture, peinture, littérature, musique* (Lausanne: Imprimeries Réunies, 1976), 75.

10. The French verse, as given by Gustave Reese, *Music in the Renaissance* (New York: Norton, 1959), 12–13, is as follows: "Tapissier, Carmen, Cesaris/N'a pas longtemps si bien chanterrent/Qu'ilz esbahirent tout Paris/Et tous ceulx qui les frequenterrent;/Mais oncques jour ne deschanterrent/En melodie de tel chois,/Ce m'ont dit qui les hanterrent,/Que G. Du Fay et Binchois. Car ilz ont nouvelle pratique/De faire frisque concordance/En haulte et en basse musique,/En fainte, en pause, et en muance,/Et ont prins de la contenance/Angloise et ensuy Dunstable,/Pour quoy merveilleuse plaisance/Rend leur chant joyeux et notable." Reese offers a translation in verse; I have preferred a more literal interpretation.

Modern observers have also noted a definable change in musical style on the Continent that begins with Dunstable and his contemporaries, thus confirming pragmatically the observations of those who experienced it firsthand. Moreover, as we shall see, the two major sacred genres of the period, the motet and the polyphonic Mass Ordinary, underwent significant transformations due to the influence of English composers.

However, as we turn to English polyphony of the fifteenth century, we face a striking anomaly; very little music by English composers has been transmitted in sources of English provenance. There is but one such collection of any size dating from the beginning of the period to have survived more or less intact, the manuscript mentioned earlier known as "Old Hall" from the library of St. Edmund's College where it was formerly held.[11] Completed toward the end of the second decade of the century, the repertory it has transmitted—settings for the Mass Ordinary arranged by liturgical type (forty Glorias, thirty-five Credos, twenty-seven Sanctus, and nineteen Agnus Dei) with twenty-six motets later copied into the leaves between the Mass fascicles—is somewhat retrospective in character; the earliest pieces may in fact date back to the 1370s.

For the remainder of the fifteenth century only two other sources of any size are known: a collection of eighty motets, twenty-five Mass Propers, eleven hymns, and a Lamentation, now at Magdalene College in Cambridge (MS Pepys 1236), dating from the early 1460s; and a manuscript from the 1430s and early 1440s now in the British Library (MS Egerton 3307) that is divided between liturgical items (one Mass, six processional hymns, two Passions) together with nine motets, and a group of some thirty-two carols.[12]

Fortunately, the lack of English sources is offset to some extent by the inclusion of a substantial quantity of music by English composers in Continental manuscripts, most of them of Italian origin. One of the most important of these is a collection currently in Modena at the Biblioteca Estense e Universitaria (MS α.X.1.11), compiled in Ferrara circa 1448 for the court chapel of Leonello d'Este (ruled 1441–50) with later additions during the reigns of his successors, Borso (1450–71) and Ercole I (1471–1505).[13] Best represented among the English composers in the collection is Dunstable, who is credited with at least 25 of the 131 compositions included in the repertory, while another 26 may be either by him or by lesser-known masters such as Benet, Forest, Plummer, Power, Standley, and Stone.[14] Other composers with a sig-

11. It is now in the British Library, MS Additional 57950; see the *Census-Catalogue of Manuscript Sources of Polyphonic Music, 1400–1550*, ed. Charles Hamm and Herbert Kellman, 5 vols. (Neuhausen-Stuttgart: Hänssler-Verlag, 1979–88), 1:82–83.
12. See Charles Hamm and Jerry Call, "Sources, MS, IX, 3, 4: Renaissance Polyphony," *The New Grove Dictionary of Music*, 17:677–78.
13. See the *Census-Catalogue of Manuscript Sources*, 2:172.
14. An accurate count of attributions is not easily made because of the numerous instances of conflicting indications in the sources, on the one hand, and the possibility, on the other, that yet others, where no conflict exists, may nonetheless be inaccurate. In addition, some names that appear to be English may in fact not be, and vice versa, and there is the further difficulty posed by the large number of pieces that were entered in the sources anonymously. For the problems with this collection in that respect, see the *Census-Catalogue of Manuscript Sources*, 2:172–73.

nificant share of the collection are Dunstable's celebrated Continental contemporaries, Gilles Binchoys with 13 attributions (and another 4 possible), and Guillaume Du Fay with 47 (and 2 more possible).

Two other manuscripts from northern Italy bring much smaller numbers of compositions attributed to English composers. One of these is now in the Biblioteca Universitaria in Bologna, MS 2216, the first forty leaves of which were probably inscribed before 1440 in Venice, the remaining seventeen somewhat later in Brescia. Of the eighty-five compositions, mostly sacred, included in the collection, more than a third are anonymous, and of the fifty-three with ascriptions, only four are credited to English musicians: two to Dunstable, one to Power, and one to an otherwise unidentified Anglia, whereas their Continental colleague, Du Fay, has eleven works.[15]

A much larger repertory of pieces, sacred and secular (Bologna, Civico Museo Bibliografico Musicale, MS Q15), was also compiled prior to 1440, possibly in Piacenza. Of its 308 compositions only 14 (plus another possible) can be attributed to known English composers—about the same proportion as in the smaller codex just cited. These works include 3 ascribed to the mysterious Anglia, 2 to Benet, 4 to Dunstable (with another in dispute), 1 to Gervays de Anglia, and 3 to Power. The Continental composers best represented in the same source are Du Fay, with 69, and Johannes de Lymburgia—the link with Piacenza—with 42.[16]

A composite collection from approximately the same period, only part of which was copied in Italy, contains a much larger proportion of English compositions than either of these wholly Italian sources. Housed at present in the Biblioteca del Seminario Maggiore in Aosta (MS A¹D19), it consists of four principal sections, the first inscribed in Bologna circa 1430–35, the second and third in the region between Basel and Strasbourg, circa 1435–43, and the last at Innsbruck, circa 1443–46, and includes a total of 197 compositions (of which 17 are duplications within the collection). Of this number 35 (with 2 more in dispute) can be credited to English masters: 3 to Anglia, 3 to Benet (or Dunstable), 1 to Byttering, 14 to Dunstable, 4 to Dunstable or Power, 9 to Power, and 1 to Sovesby. Binchoys, with 24 attributions (and 3 more possible) and Du Fay, with 25 (and 2 more in dispute), are once again the Continental composers best represented in this manuscript.[17]

The circulation of English music on the Continent later in the fifteenth century can be documented to a degree by the large repertory of polyphonic music (the greater part of it sacred) that was collected and copied between circa 1430 and 1480 in Trent, which was then an important city on a much-used trade route connecting regions of Italian and German linguistic culture. Of the six manuscripts currently known, all of which are held either by the Museo Provinciale d'Arte (MSS 87, 88, 89, 90, 91, and 92) or the Museo Diocesano (MS 93), four were actually inscribed in Trent by cleric musicians of the cathedral, while the other two—which are also the earliest, dating from the 1430s—were copied elsewhere and subsequently brought to

15. See the *Census-Catalogue of Manuscript Sources*, 1:88.
16. See the *Census-Catalogue of Manuscript Sources*, 1:69.
17. See the *Census-Catalogue of Manuscript Sources*, 1:6–8.

their present home. These two collections (MSS 87 and 92) are both composites, the different sections of which were probably copied in part in the regional axis between Basel and Strasbourg, in part, perhaps, in the area around Venice, and in one instance (MS 87, Part III) as far away as the province of Namur in present-day Belgium.

The earliest manuscripts are also those that have the greatest proportion of works ascribable to English composers. Trent MSS 87 and 92, both of which were completed before about 1440, have 12 (of a total of 187) and 41 (of 217), respectively, although some of these have conflicting attributions to Continental composers such as Binchoys and Du Fay. Manuscripts 90 and 93, which have a large initial section in common and were both completed by 1460, contain, respectively, 32 (of a total of 333) and 19 (of 272) pieces that can be credited—conflicts of ascription notwithstanding—to English masters. By contrast, MS 88, which was compiled between 1460 and 1465, has only 7 possibly English works (of a total of 219), and in MS 89, which dates from the 1460s and 1470s, there are but 3. Manuscript 91, finally, which was copied over the same period of time, has no English attributions for any of its 158 compositions.[18]

In the earlier layers of this repertory, the Continental composers with the most attributions are again Binchoys and Du Fay, as is to be expected. In the later segments, as the English influence begins to fade, their works yield in turn to those of Tinctoris's generation, including a few by Busnoys, Okeghem, and even the theorist himself. Let us attempt to discover, then, from sources such as these in what sense English models contributed to the emergence of a "new art" (to cite Tinctoris's expression) and what effect they had upon the development of two significant polyphonic genres that were already well established when the fifteenth century began: the motet and settings for the Ordinary of the Mass.

THE ENGLISH MOTET IN THE FIFTEENTH CENTURY

THE ISORHYTHMIC TRADITION

As the fourteenth century came to a close the motet had already seen more than 100 years of cultivation and use as a musical genre. Over that period of time it had acquired on the Continent, where it originated, a number of distinguishing characteristics, and its social uses were rather well defined. The motet had been polytextual from its very inception. Of its three or four parts, duplum and triplum (in ranges that would soon be known as superius and contratenor altus) each carried its own words, usually written in verse, and although the two texts often dealt with related topics, they differed, as a rule, in versification and even length.

In most instances the preferred language was Latin, but Guillaume de Machaut

---

18. Concerning dates and provenance for the "Trent Codices," see the *Census-Catalogue of Manuscript Sources*, 3:222–34.

(and a few others as well) kept alive the practice of the preceding century by setting French verse. The choice of idiom appears to have been primarily a function of a composition's intended purpose. During the 1300s the motet was conceived ever more consistently as an occasional piece prepared specifically to celebrate a particular event and, no less importantly, to become part of the written record concerning it. When this was its intended role, Latin was obviously preferable to the vernacular because of its well-established ceremonial (and even liturgical) associations. When the subject was amatory, however, as in the thirteenth-century tradition, French was apparently deemed more appropriate.

The tenor part also bore a text, if only symbolically, because although it was almost always performed instrumentally,[19] it was generally derived from a preexistent melody, usually a liturgical chant. As the foundation of the compositional structure, this cantus firmus was almost invariably selected to resonate in some significant way with the words that were to be sung, whether Latin or French. It thus provided for them, implicitly at least, a hieratic commentary of sorts that has been appropriately described as a reverse trope. (A fourth part, if present, usually shared the range of the tenor, hence its customary designation as contratenor bassus, and in most instances it was likewise taken by instruments.)

The single most arresting feature of the tenor, however (and usually of the low contratenor as well, when present), is its isorhythmic organization. The borrowed melody, referred to by some theorists of the time as a *color*, was limited for the most part to a rather modest number of notes and repeated one or more times to accommodate the complete declamation of the text in the other parts. Its total length was then divided by a recurring rhythmic pattern (or patterns) into segments known as *taleae* (literally cuttings). Once the pattern was established, the durational values of the *talea* were frequently subjected to proportional diminution, thus accelerating in a systematic way the movement of the tenor and shortening the isorhythmic sections of the composition.

To underscore this rhythmic structure, the *taleae* of the tenor were frequently separated by rests and the joints between them made more readily audible by the use of animated figures (most characteristically hockets) in the upper parts. Perhaps as an extension of this process, the fully texted voices were eventually drawn into the isorhythmic plan as well, first in part and then in their entirety, assuming their own individual *taleae* and changing their patterns each time diminution was applied.[20] But if the rhythmic order of the composition thus became sensibly audible to a greater degree, its real significance for the composer undoubtedly lay in its affinities with the numerical relationships that were thought to regulate the cosmos.

19. Even if, as some argue, performance by voices alone was more frequent in some places than the sources would suggest, the human voice, in presenting the extended note values characteristic of a tenor cantus firmus, whether with the original (e.g., liturgical) text, solmization syllables, or even nonsense syllables, is treated very much like a mechanical instrument; the singer would have been concerned solely with pitch and duration and not with the declamation that is the primary role of the cantus and altus parts.
20. For a more detailed discussion of isorhythm, see Richard H. Hoppin, *Medieval Music* (New York: Norton, 1978), 362–67; cf. Ernest Sanders, "Isorhythm," *The New Grove Dictionary of Music*, 9:351–54.

These compositional conventions were apparently also well known to English composers of the late fourteenth and early fifteenth centuries. Some fairly typical examples of the isorhythmic motet were included among the relatively few representatives of the genre entered in the "Old Hall Manuscript," works showing all of the complex stylistic features associated at the time with occasional and ceremonial compositions on the Continent. One such piece is the *Alma proles regia/Christi miles/Ab inimicis nostris*, attributed to John Cooke (d. by July 1419), a member of the chapel royal who was probably a student or an associate of Leonel Power (see p. 230). The tenor is derived from a Rogation litany, "Defend us from our enemies, O Christ," and the sentiments implicit in the liturgical text—even if it was not sung—provide the thematic context for the verse in duplum (labeled contratenor) and triplex, which combine prayers to St. George, the Virgin Mary, and Christ on behalf of the (English) king and his armies. In both tone and content these supplications suggest that the motet could have been prepared in connection with the unsuccessful negotiations with the French that preceded the battle of Agincourt in 1415 and that it would have been found most appropriate for the celebration that accompanied the return of the victorious monarch, Henry V.[21]

Characteristic of the genre generally are the recondite procedures used to generate the isorhythmic structure based upon the liturgical cantus firmus. The tenor is stated three times in proportional diminution, and each statement is divided into a pair of equal *taleae* that are fully isorhythmic in all three parts. For the initial *color* each breve in the tenor is perfect, equal to three ternary semibreves or nine minims in the other two voices. In the first repetition each breve is ternary still, but the semibreves are binary, thus reducing the total duration of the tenor breve to six minims (eighth notes in the modern transcription). And in the final statement the breves are binary as well, further diminishing the length of the tenor breve to four minims (see Example 6-1). Consequently, the proportions linking the three major structural segments of the work—and its constituent *taleae*—are 9:6:4—that is, two consecutive sesquialteral ratios.[22] It is possible to conclude from the notational and numerical complexity of this design that the learned compositional procedures were seen as an appropriate musical counterpart to the solemn prayers for peace and protection being declaimed by the upper voices.[23]

Less typical of the Continental motet was the decided English proclivity for texts having a primarily liturgical rather than a more generally ceremonial orientation. Although the motet owed much of its origins to thirteenth-century tropes written for the discant clausulae of liturgical organum,[24] that connection was utterly aban-

21. See Margaret Bent, "Cooke, J[ohn]," *The New Grove Dictionary of Music*, 4:712.

22. Concerning the proportions of Boethian arithmetic that were believed to regulate the harmony of the spheres, the human soul, and sounding music, see Appendix, pp. 972–74.

23. For further discussion of three-part isorhythmic motets ascribed to English composers, see J. Michael Allsen, "Style and Intertextuality in the Isorhythmic Motet, 1400–1440" (Ph.D. diss., University of Wisconsin, Madison, 1992), 144–86.

24. See Hoppin, *Medieval Music*, 252–55; cf. Ernest Sanders, "Motet," *The New Grove Dictionary of Music*, 12:617–25.

EXAMPLE 6-1. John Cooke, *Alma proles/Christi miles* (mm. 1–6, 37–39, 55–57)

TRIPLEX: Kindly daughter, royal ruler of heaven, grace-filled mistress of all the world . . . Your compassion knows not how to refuse help. . . . Jesus, guard the servants of thy holy Mother.

COUNTERTENOR: Glorious soldier of Christ, most holy George, who art the ornament of armies, now dwellest in heaven . . . protect thy country and defend the king. . . . O golden pillars [George and the Virgin], plead for peace in our time.

TENOR: Defend us against our enemies, O Christ. (Rogation litany)

doned on the Continent, whereas the English seem to have clung to it tenaciously throughout the history of the genre. As a result, one finds in the insular motet repertory of the early fifteenth century a kind of isorhythmic motet that had no counterpart cross-channel.

A striking example is the remarkably sophisticated isorhythmic setting of texts relating to the feast of Pentecost, the *Veni Sancte Spiritus et emitte/Veni Sancte Spiritus et infunde/Veni Creator Spiritus/Mentes tuorum* (see Figure 6-4).[25] This is one of eleven such works (counting only those that have survived complete) attributed to John Dunstable (ca. 1390–1453), the most celebrated English composer of the age, who may have served in the household of John, duke of Bedford, while the latter was regent for the English crown in France, 1422–35. The tenor consists of

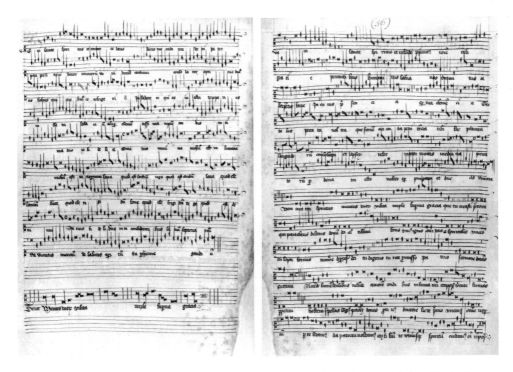

FIGURE 6-4.   Dunstable's motet *Veni Sancte Spriritus/Veni Sancte Spiritus/Veni Creator Spiritus/Mentes tuorum* ("Old Hall Manuscript," British Library, Additional MS 57950, ff. 55ᵛ–56).

25. See Dunstable's *Complete Works*, ed. Manfred Bukofzer, Musica Britannica 8 (1953), with revisions and additions by Margaret Bent, Ian Bent, and Brian Trowell (London: Stainer and Bell, 1970), 88–91, no. 32, and Andrew Hughes and Margaret Bent, eds., *The Old Hall Manuscript*, 3 vols. ([Rome]: American Institute of Musicology, 1969–73), 2:66ff. This composition was also widely circulated on the Continent, having been inscribed in the Modena and Aosta manuscripts described above (pp. 222–23) and in Trent MS 92.

the second and third phrases of a hymn for Pentecost, *Veni Creator Spiritus*, the complete melody of which (in the Sarum version) is quoted a phrase at a time in the top part (triplex 1) of the duos preceding the entry of the tenor in the first four *taleae*. The text for that part is not taken from the hymn, however, but from a sequence in honor of the Holy Ghost, the melody of which plays no role in the polyphony. It is the duplum (contratenor) that carries the words to the hymn, all six strophes, but without making reference to its melodic material. Meanwhile, the second triplex comments, tropelike, on the text of the voice above. The result is a congeries of texts, all related to the descent of the Holy Ghost upon the Apostles of Christ, linked by both the words and the music of the hymn specified for the liturgical celebration of that event.

Structurally and formally the relationships are no less complex. The *color* derived from the hymn is stated three times and divided in each instance into an equal pair of fully isorhythmic *taleae*, as in Cooke's *Alma proles*. Here, too, the repetitions of the *color* are successively diminished, the proportions in this case being reducible to the sequence 3:2:1, thus combining the ratios for the fifth and the octave. Clearly, the primary concern of the composer was the multiplicity of texts in praise of the Holy Ghost, presented in a structure harmoniously organized by numbers that reflect in musical sonorities the order of the cosmos. Whether or not the Latin texts or the carefully crafted proportional relationships were discernible to human ears was obviously not an essential consideration; they were intended first of all for the Divine Intelligence, who was sure to grasp them all.

IMPROVISED POLYPHONY AND MOTET STYLE

The unbroken association of the motet with liturgical and devotional functions in England, in addition and perhaps even in preference to the ceremonial role that had become traditional on the Continent, may have led to a radical transformation of the genre. Elaborate isorhythmic structures such as those described above undoubtedly required lengthy rehearsal, even for performers of exceptional skill, and their preparation was probably undertaken only for occasions of particular solemnity. However, the evident taste for polyphony in religious celebration could be satisfied in a much simpler manner, and consequently on a more routine basis, merely by improvising discant note-against-note in two or even three parts for those chants that were best loved and most often heard, in particular the processional and devotional antiphons.

Among the compositions grouped with the more traditional motet types in the "Old Hall Manuscript" is a significant number conceived stylistically in a manner suggesting that they reflect such an improvisatory practice and that it was just then being codified as part of the written repertory. Like all the music in a straightforward discant style included in that collection, of whatever genre, these pieces were written in score and were presumably sung with the liturgical text declaimed simultaneously by each of the voices. They consist, as a rule, of a chant whose melody has been cast in mensural notation with parts added both above and below for a total of three. Typical is the setting of the antiphon *Ave regina celorum* attributed to Leonel Power (d. 1445), who served in the household of Henry V's younger brother, Thomas, duke of Clarence (d. 1421), and was later master of the choir at Christ Church, Canterbury.[26] The chant is quoted faithfully by the tenor—not a single pitch has been either added or omitted—but with its rhythmic values fixed by mensural notation.

Midway through the piece there is a shift from imperfect tempus with major prolation (i.e., 2 × 3) to perfect tempus with minor prolation (i.e., 3 × 2) with the minim (the eighth note) remaining constant. This division provides just a hint of the sectional organization characteristic of the isorhythmic motet and thus suggests a generic affinity between two pieces that are otherwise very different in style. Declamation is regulated in the first section either by the semibreve (quarter note) or the breve (half note) with melismatic extensions and in the second section by breves (dotted half notes) or semibreves (quarters), also with melismas. Some melodic embellishment of the texture is achieved by dividing the longer values in one voice or another. However, the relationship among the parts remains fundamentally homophonic, and the simplicity of the underlying discant is emphasized by the simultaneous delivery of the text. Even the well-known and widely traveled *Quam pulchra es*, attributed both to Dunstable and a certain Egidius (Binchoys?), although not based on any recognized chant melody, is similarly homophonic in texture and declamatory in style, and it may reflect the same unwritten tradition.[27]

Despite their relative rhythmic sophistication, neither of these antiphon settings is far removed technically from a contrapuntal practice that could be improvised with no great difficulty, not only in two parts but also in three. Adding a single part to a notated chant, above or below in any range practical for the discanting voice, was accomplished by English singers using a process called "sighting." This involved merely imagining on the staff near the chant a pitch that, either sung where placed or transposed up or down by an appropriate interval (a fifth, octave, or twelfth) produced tones consonant with those actually notated.[28] Adding a pair of voices could be more difficult if they were to be consonant with one another as well as with the chant, but a special type of sighting termed *faburden* provided an easy method for doing so. One voice was placed above the chant, following in strict parallel motion at the perfect fourth, and the second below, either at the fifth—especially at the beginnings and ends of phrases (but not twice in a row)—or at the third.[29]

26. For a modern score, see Power's *Complete Works*, ed. Charles Hamm, 2 vols. ([Rome]: American Institute of Musicology, 1969–76), 2–3, no. 2; also Hughes and Bent, eds., *Old Hall Manuscript*, 1 (pt. 1): 127–28, no. 43, and Sarah Fuller, ed., *The European Musical Heritage, 800–1750* (New York: Alfred A. Knopf, 1987), 138–41.

27. For a modern score, see Dunstable's *Complete Works*, 112–13, no. 44; also Claude V. Palisca, ed., *Norton Anthology of Western Music*, 3d ed., 2 vols. (New York: Norton, 1996), 1:99–101.

28. See Brian Trowell, "Sight, Sighting," *The New Grove Dictionary of Music*, 17:307.

29. See Brian Trowell, "Faburden," *The New Grove Dictionary of Music*, 6:350–54; two fifths in a row would produce parallel fifths, which by then were to be avoided in polyphonic composition.

THE CHANSON AND MOTET STYLE

Yet another innovative motet type, one less dependent on the tradition of improvised discant than on the notated repertory of secular song, combines the treble-dominated texture of the chanson of the period with the kind of structural articulation typical of the native English carol (see pp. 250–56). These features mark a three-part setting of the processional Marian antiphon *Alma redemptoris mater*, attributed in the sources to both Dunstable and to Power. The chant is quoted briefly (at the upper fifth) in the opening duo by the superius, which is the only part fully texted throughout and clearly intended to be sung (see Figure 6-5). Subsequently there are only brief allusions to the liturgical melody: for the words "Mater, que per-via" (mm. 15–18) and at the beginning of the two sections to follow (mm. 59–61 and 89–92; see Example 6-2). Otherwise neither the treble line nor the lower two parts makes any significant use of it, and even the polyphonic final fails to coincide with the modal orientation of the chant quotations.[30]

The motet is divided into three sections, corresponding to principal incises of the chant, both textually and musically. The structural articulation is made clear not only by the unmistakable cadences at the close of the first two

FIGURE 6-5.   The antiphon *Alma redemptoris mater*, from the *Antiphonale Sarisburiense* (Cambridge University, University Library, MS Mm2.9, the "Barnwell Antiphoner").

---

30. The liturgical antiphon is notated with a final on F and classified as mode 5. Consequently, if transposed up a fifth, as in the opening of the motet, the final should be on C, but the polyphonic setting is clearly oriented to a final on G.

EXAMPLE 6-2. John Dunstable or Leonel Power, *Alma redemptoris mater* (mm. 89–128)

Virgin first and last, receiving from the mouth of Gabriel that "Ave," be merciful
to sinners. (NOTE: In this and in all following examples pitches clearly derived
from liturgical chant are marked with a small +.)

segments but also by a shift in texture, juxtaposing the treble-dominated solo song
of the first and the last with the vocal duo at the center. In the final section there is
a distinctive mensural shift as well (from ternary to binary). It is in its sectional organization and the concomitant contrast between two- and three-part writing that this
setting of the popular Marian text resembles to a degree the polyphonic carol, even
though the principal melodic line of the latter was generally borne by the tenor
rather than the treble voice. (The differences in texture could have been emphasized
by alternating a choral solo—two or more voices carrying the texted line—accompanied by instruments with a soloistic duo.)

Whatever its ultimate origins, this organizational principle was both compositionally useful and, it would seem, esthetically appealing in performance.
Understandably, then, formal segmentation came to be a common feature in motets

of the fifteenth century, especially those written by English masters. Motets that cir-culated on the Continent also display this formal feature, as may be seen from the *Beata mater* ascribed both to Dunstable and to Binchoys.[31] However, in the latter work there is no trace of the chant melody corresponding to the liturgical text set to music, and the contrast between the active treble line and the slower moving sup-porting parts points once again to the influence of the contemporary chanson.

THE ORDINARY OF THE MASS IN ENGLAND

Written polyphonic settings for the Ordinary of the Mass cannot be documented before the fourteenth century. Until then the traditional texts that were a daily part of the eucharistic liturgy—and therefore at the very heart of formalized Christian worship—were undoubtedly sung to one of the several chant melodies that had become associated with them over the ages. However, by the eleventh century the practice of embellishing the chants of the Ordinary with tropes on feast days and other special occasions was becoming increasingly common. These additions, which were textual, musical, or both, could take the form of an introduction to the liturgi-cal text (or one or more of its individual sections) or of new material interpolated in various ways into the traditional elements. They functioned, in a very real sense, as a gloss on the texts and melodies that had by then become relatively fixed, explaining and amplifying their significance, generally in relation to a particular feast or liturgi-cal season. And they were intended to add to the celebration of the Mass not only deeper meaning but also brilliance and luster.[32]

Polyphonic "troping" may have been conceived as a means of further enhancing the solemnity of important liturgical occasions and probably began with simple, improvisatory discant. When at last notated settings of the Mass Ordinary begin to appear in the sources, the widely divergent musical styles and compositional proce-dures they display suggest that, whether taken as five individual liturgical units or—as was eventually to happen—as an interconnected series, a distinctive musical genre had not yet been developed in that connection. Lacking any previous tradition upon which to build, composers, when setting the texts (and chants) of the Ordinary, used procedures and styles characteristic of those genres that were well established in the practice of the period: the treble-dominated chanson, the tenor motet (particularly of the isorhythmic variety), and the strictly imitative *caccia*—citing only those that appear to have had the most immediate impact. Improvisatory discant in two or three parts of the kind traceable in the development of the English motet seems also to have played a role, especially early on.

31. For a modern score, see Dunstable's *Complete Works*, 160; also Fuller, ed., *European Musical Heritage*, 141–43.
32. Concerning tropes, see Hoppin, *Medieval Music*, 143–54; cf. Ruth Steiner, "Trope," *The New Grove Dictionary of Music*, 19:172–87.

IMPROVISED POLYPHONY AND MASS COMPOSITION

The earliest layer of the "Old Hall Manuscript"—comprising mainly compositions written in score—consists primarily of plainsong settings, usually with the chant for the Ordinary given to the middle voice.[33] Typical of such pieces in most respects is one of four settings of the Sanctus attributed to W. Typp (fl. ca. 1410) (see Example 6-3). Its polyphonic texture resembles that of Power's *Ave regina celorum* discussed earlier (p. 230); the counterpoint is essentially a strict discant, note against note, with steady rhythms that are only lightly animated in one voice or another by modest divisions of the longer note values. As has been noted, these are characteristics that point to possible origins in an unwritten tradition of extemporized polyphony.

Also similar to the *Ave regina* is the literal quotation, pitch by pitch, of the chant prescribed for the Sanctus on all major duplex feasts[34] (in the Sarum rite), which is announced by the monophonic incipit sung by the celebrant both at the beginning and at the opening of the "Benedictus." Typp has not restricted the liturgical melody to the tenor voice (and the middle range), however, but has caused it to migrate, first to the contra below (mm. 10–13) and then to the triplex above (mm. 17–21). In the process he has transposed the original notes both to the upper fourth (chant incipits and mm. 1–5, 10–14, and 29–36) and to the upper octave (mm. 6–9, 15–28, and 37–38). It is noteworthy that this pattern introduces the chant each time with an implied transposition of the final to G (with b-flat signed), thus reflecting the modal orientation of the polyphonic composition overall. Nonetheless, the chant cantus firmus ends on the original final (D, at the upper octave) at the end of both principal sections (mm. 28, 38), even though the polyphonic cadence at that point is to G.[35]

THE CHANSON AND MASS COMPOSITION

Later additions to the "Old Hall" repertory of Mass Ordinaries—including the music of four composers known to have served with the chapel royal during the reign of Henry V: Thomas(?) Damett (ca. 1389–1436–37), N(?icholas) Sturgeon (d. 1454), J(ohn) Cooke (d. by 1419), and John Burell (fl. 1413–37)—show more

33. The "Old Hall Manuscript" has separate fascicles for the Gloria, the Credo, the Sanctus, and the Agnus Dei but no compositions for the Kyrie. That lack has been seen as evidence that a plainsong Kyrie was preferred at the time to a polyphonic setting, but it is possible that a fascicle containing Kyries originally opened the collection and has since been lost; see the *Census-Catalogue of Manuscript Sources*, 2:82.
34. In the Roman rite, liturgical celebrations are classified according to degrees of solemnity. There are three major categories: solemn feasts, duplex feasts, and simplex feasts, with further distinctions among the duplex feasts (e.g., major, first class, second class, and semiduplex). Their purpose is to establish priority when two feasts fall on the same day (e.g., one from the Temporale and one from the Sanctorale).
35. A similar work, but in four parts instead of three, is a setting of the Sanctus for Sundays in Advent and Lent attributed to Power (Hughes and Bent, eds., *Old Hall Manuscript*, 1 [part 2]: 353–56, no. 117; also included in Archibald T. Davison and Willi Apel, eds., *Historical Anthology of Music*, 2 vols. [Cambridge, Mass.: Harvard University Press, 1962], 1:67), except that the chant there remains with the tenor throughout and the texture is at times slightly more treble dominated.

EXAMPLE 6-3. W. Typp, Sanctus (mm. 1–14)

Holy, holy, holy, Lord God of the heavenly hosts.

clearly the growing influence of the Continental chanson. These works display a narrow spectrum of related compositional styles that range from a kind of modified discant, in which the rhythmic divisions are largely confined to the upper voice (thus giving it greater prominence in the polyphonic texture), to the full-blown treble domination associated at the time with French song forms.

Such a piece is a Gloria ascribed to Sturgeon, all of whose Mass settings fall within these stylistic parameters (see Example 6-4). Following the first incise of the

EXAMPLE 6-4. N(?icholas) Sturgeon, Gloria (mm. 1–12)

Glory to God in the highest and on earth peace to men of good will. We praise thee, we bless thee, we adore thee, we glorify thee.

plainsong, sung by the celebrant, the polyphony begins with a duo for triplex and tenor, neither of which makes any melodic reference to the liturgical chant announced by the chant intonation, even though both of them have been given the same final (G) and are cast in the same ambitus (an octave apart).[36] They appear instead to have been freely composed, but they are hardly equal partners; the higher of the two—the only voice provided with text in the source—is considerably more active and melodically more interesting than the tenor. And when the contratenor joins in, twelve breves (i.e., six mm.) later, it shares the tenor's range, its relatively sedate rhythmic motion, and its tendency to proceed by leap rather than by step. The resulting texture, as we shall see, is very much like that of the chanson of the period.

Also in evidence in this work is the formal articulation by means of contrasting sonorities that was adopted for the English carol (as we shall see presently), and—perhaps in imitation of that native genre—for many antiphon motets as well. It is equally useful for dividing into syntactically coherent segments the setting of a long text from the Ordinary such as the Gloria. Following a perfect cadence (to D) to close the first segment of the text (m. 35), the texture thins to the triplex-tenor duo for "Qui tollis peccata mundi, miserere nobis." Another clear cadence (this time to the final, G) marks the end of the second section (m. 45), and the contratenor returns to restore a three-part sonority for the remainder of the composition, beginning with the second "Qui tollis."

THE ISORHYTHMIC TRADITION AND MASS COMPOSITION

English settings of the Mass Ordinary modeled on the isorhythmic motet are much fewer in number than either those showing rhythmically animated discant on a plainchant cantus firmus or those freely composed in a treble-dominated style. There are such compositions, however, and by two of the most important masters of the age, John Dunstable and Leonel Power, as well as by others whose works are less well known. Representative of the type is a Gloria in four parts found in the "Old Hall" repertory, one of a half-dozen settings attributed to Power (see Example 6-5). If the composer adhered to the isorhythmic motet tradition, he should have derived his tenor part from a preexistent melody, whether sacred or secular, but in this case no source for the borrowing has been discovered. Nevertheless, with its F final (signed with a b-flat), it matches reasonably well the introductory incise of the mode 6 chant to be intoned by the celebrant—even though its ambitus is authentic rather than plagal.[37]

As in the isorhythmic motets, the tenor *color* is stated twice, the second time with

36. The chant quoted is similar to the Gloria for duplex feasts included in the *Liber usualis Missae et Officii pro Dominicis et Festis* (Paris: Desclée et Socii, 1960), 28, which is classified as mode 8 on G.
37. The chant implied by the intonation is similar to a Gloria prescribed in Roman usage for duple feasts; see *Liber usualis*, 34.

EXAMPLE 6-5. Leonel Power, isorhythmic Gloria (mm. 1–16)

For English translation of text, see Example 6-4.

all note values reduced by half. It is divided each time into two equal *taleae*, which are fifty-six imperfect breves long in the first *color* (twenty-eight in major prolation and another twenty-eight in minor prolation) and the equivalent of twenty-eight in the second (fourteen in major prolation and twenty-eight in minor prolation with diminution by two). The result is to establish a 3:2 proportion between durations of the ternary and binary segments within each *talea* and of 2:1 between the two full statements of the tenor melody. Characteristically, isorhythmic organization of the tenor is extended to the other parts; each of them has two individual *taleae*, one for each statement of the *color*, and each of these *taleae* is repeated with that of the tenor.

Both triplex parts are given words in the source, but after the first two phrases, which they both sing (mm. 1–10), the declamation alternates for the most part between them. Words having particular liturgical significance are carried by both voices, but most of the time one part provides sustaining counterpoint, presumably with the melismatic extension of an appropriate vowel, while the other presents the next segment of text. In this manner the polytextuality traditional for the isorhythmic motet is in a sense simulated even though it is not actually present. By contrast, the contratenor, like the tenor in whose range it lies, is entirely without text in the manuscript. However, its rhythmic and melodic activity matches now that of its contrapuntal companion, now that of the pair of texted voices above, though it moves more frequently with the latter.[38] Given its essential structural and stylistic characteristics, then, a composition such as this can be distinguished from an isorhythmic motet only by its place in the liturgy of the Mass.

STRICT IMITATION IN MASS COMPOSITION

Even rarer than isorhythmic settings of Mass Ordinaries are those that rely on strict imitative procedures, regulated as a rule by a more or less abstruse verbal canon. Such works may have been inspired by the French *chace*, whose two or (more often) three voices are derived in strict imitation from a single written part; or—perhaps even more probably—by the Italian *caccia*, which combined canonic imitation in two parts with a sustaining tenor. (Both genres were extensively cultivated in the fourteenth century.) However, strict imitation was known in England even earlier, if one can judge from the popular canon *Sumer is icumen in*.[39] There are in all seven Mass Ordinaries composed in this manner, two of them anonymous and the others

38. It has been suggested that this Gloria and the *Credo Opem nobis* (Hughes and Bent, eds., *Old Hall Manuscript*, 1 [part 2]: 264–69, no. 84), also attributed to Power, were conceived as a pair. This hypothesis is not very compelling, however, despite the common modal orientation of the two works (an F final and b-flat signature). The Credo has but three parts, instead of four, only one statement of the tenor *color*, and three equal *taleae* with no internal mensural shift and no diminution of any kind. (Concerning Mass pairs and cycles, see pp. 241–49.) Margaret Bent, "Power, Leonel," *The New Grove Dictionary of Music*, 15:178, links this Credo instead with Gloria no. 24.

39. Concerning the *chace* and the *caccia*, see Hoppin, *Medieval Music*, 370–74 and 443–46; also 346 regarding the "summer canon"; cf. Alfred Mann and J. Kenneth Wilson, "Canon," *The New Grove Dictionary of Music*, 3:689.

ascribed to little-known English composers of the period: one to Byttering (fl. 1410), the remaining four to Pycard (fl. 1410).

Perhaps the most arresting composition of this kind is an anonymous Credo in the "Old Hall Manuscript" that deploys three voices with text in canonic imitation above a sonorous but untexted foundation of tenor and contratenor (see Example 6-6). Remarkably, although the three canonic voices are all generated from a single written part, each is read under a different mensuration, anticipating by more than half a century the procedures used by Johannes Okeghem in his celebrated *Missa Prolationum*. As a result, the longer values assume different durations in each of the parts whenever they appear, thus changing the time interval separating their successive entries from phrase to phrase. The consequent difficulties for the performers have been described as a "proportional exercise of truly doctoral complexity."[40]

In addition to presenting the challenge of reading the mensural notation correctly, the piece, as copied in the unique source, raises practical problems for performance by its idiosyncratic use of specified accidentals. Those entered in the manuscript all too often introduce awkward melodic intervals and dissonant cross-relations, all of which presumably prompted the performers to make adjustments by a judicious application of *musica ficta*. Still, however sophisticated its underlying conception, and whatever the skills required for its execution, this composition, like the other settings for the Ordinary of the Mass discussed above, clearly demonstrates the lack of the kind of clearly defined compositional tradition that was usually characteristic of well-established musical genres at that point in the history of Western music.

ENGLISH MASS ORDINARIES IN GROUPS AND CYCLES

In the "Old Hall Manuscript," not only were polyphonic settings for the chants of the Mass Ordinary gathered in a separate fascicle, as noted earlier, they were also arranged in a descending order of liturgical solemnity. This was to be expected, moreover, since the missals of the Middle Ages were usually organized in the same manner with all the chants of the same category grouped together. However, as early as the fourteenth century there was a clear trend toward arranging plainsong Ordinaries in cycles by matching chants of comparable musical complexity and style in accordance with the liturgical rank of the feasts on which they were customarily sung.[41] There were good reasons for doing so, practical as well as esthetic, and this development may reflect the same artistic impulse that led to the embellishment of Ordinary chants with tropes in order to relate them more directly to a particular feast

40. Margaret Bent, "Pycart," *The New Grove Dictionary of Music*, 14:720.
41. Concerning this development, see Leo Schrade, "News on the Chant Cycles of the *Ordinarium missae*," *Journal of the American Musicological Society* 8 (1955): 66.

EXAMPLE 6-6. Anonymous, Credo (mm. 1–11)

I believe in one God, all powerful Father, creator of heaven and earth, of all
things visible and invisible.

or liturgical season while heightening the overall impact of the ritual. (A similar procedure was followed by the Benedictine monks of Solesmes in their attempt to restore the liturgy to a more pristine state, as may be seen from the organization of Ordinary "cycles" by liturgical rank and function in "modern" service books such as the *Liber usualis*.)

It is hardly surprising, therefore, that a similar grouping of polyphonic Ordinaries for the Mass followed not long after. The earliest of such cycles, which are found in Continental sources of the fourteenth century, were for the most part arbitrary, an assemblage in liturgical order of compositions by different composers and in various compositional styles. By contrast, the "Old Hall" Mass repertory includes some of the earliest examples of polyphonic Ordinaries that, although separated in the source, appear to be intentionally connected, structurally and stylistically. The linking began with settings for those chants that are similar to one another textually and musically and that come one after the other in the celebration of the liturgy: the Gloria was paired compositionally with the Credo and the Sanctus with the Agnus Dei. A half-dozen such pairs have been proposed by scholars from among the works in this collection.[42]

Significantly, four such pairs—two of Gloria and Credo and two of Sanctus and Agnus—can be attributed to Leonel Power, and these are among those for which the most convincing case for intentional linking can be made. The connection is noteworthy since Power, together with John Dunstable, clearly played a central role in developing the compositional procedures that were used to unify settings of two or more texts of the Ordinary and, consequently, in establishing the cyclic Mass as a distinct and historically important musical genre. These Mass pairs warrant our attention because they illustrate clearly the various musical means that later composers used quite deliberately, relating settings of these heterogeneous texts to one another both musically and liturgically.

The Gloria and the Credo in the pair ascribed to Power ("Old Hall Manuscript," nos. 21 and 77) share the following features: the same set of clefs for their constituent parts; identical signed flats (all the more noteworthy since they are unusual); a shared (and uncommon) final on B-flat; identical patterns of mensuration; and a sectional structure with comparable alternating textures (à 2, à 4, and à 5). Similarly, a Sanctus–Agnus pair ("Old Hall Manuscript," nos. 118 and 141) share like clefs; a common final; an identical sequence of mensurations (C, C, O, C); and the same unusual number of parts (four). In addition, both members of the pair make use of the liturgical chants prescribed in the Roman rite for Sundays in Advent and Quadragesima.[43] There can be little doubt in either case that the two Ordinaries were conceived and written as a pair.

About the same time or a bit later, all of the procedures just cited were also used

---

42. See, for example, Andrew Hughes, "Mass Pairs in the Old Hall and Other English Manuscripts," *Revue belge de musicologie* 19 (1965): 15ff.

43. Although not identical to Sarum usage, closely related chants are found in the *Liber usualis*, 61, Mass 17.

by composers on the Continent to link polyphonic Ordinaries of the Mass, and priority for their adoption to that purpose would be difficult to establish. To the contrary, however, the English were clearly responsible for a striking innovation in Mass composition, one that was fraught with consequences for the subsequent development of the genre. This was to use the tenor cantus firmus characteristic of the motet, and many of the compositional procedures associated with it, to tie together either two or three individual sections of the Ordinary or, should there be reason to do so, a complete cycle of polyphonic settings.

One of the earliest such works is the *Missa Rex seculorum*, which carries attributions to both Leonel Power and to John Dunstable in the sources. Curiously, the Kyrie, which was set with the trope "Deus creator omnium," is found only in an English manuscript, Emmanuel College, Cambridge, MS 300, unfortunately incomplete, whereas the remainder of the Mass has been transmitted only in Continental sources: the "Aosta Choirbook" and the "Trent Codices" 90, 92, and 93 (see the discussion of these manuscripts, pp. 223–24). The inclusion of a troped Kyrie in a polyphonic Mass, for which the English seem to have had a particular predilection, was not customary on the Continent. Consequently, English Masses, which were otherwise frequently sung and widely copied, were often separated from their troped Kyries by Continental scribes.

The tenor of the *Missa Rex seculorum* is based on an antiphon in honor of St. Benedict (see Figure 6-6), that recurs from section to section much like the *color* of a vast isorhythmic motet (see Example 6-7). The presence of the liturgical melody inevitably invokes its text, which—although not usually written into the sources and in most cases probably not sung—brings to the work the same sort of implicit polytextuality that earlier characterized the isorhythmic motet.[44] And just as the liturgical melody, repeated with each of the five compositions of the Mass, binds them together with a recurring element of musical unification, so the repeated references to the text of the borrowed chant provide a liturgical unity of sorts for the otherwise autonomous entities of the Ordinary, relating them not only to one another but also to a Proper feast or a specific occasion.

However, the mensural rhythms imposed on the pitches of the antiphon in shaping it as a tenor cantus firmus differ in each major section of the Mass cycle rather than repeat from one segment to the next as in the *taleae* of an isorhythmic motet, and the notes themselves are not always exactly quoted from one time to the next. As a comparison of the successive statements of the *Rex seculorum* tenor will show,

44. It has in fact been suggested that in some localities, beginning with the earliest English Mass cycles, the words of the plainchants from which the tenor was derived were sung in preference to the text of the Ordinary; see Alejandro E. Planchart, "Fifteenth-Century Masses: Notes on Performance and Chronology," *Studi Musicali* 10 (1981): 19–29, and "Parts with Words and without Words: The Evidence for Multiple Texts in Fifteenth-Century Masses," in *Studies in the Performance of Late Mediaeval Music*, ed. Stanley Boorman (Cambridge: Cambridge University Press, 1983), 242–51; also Gareth R. K. Curtis, "Brussels, Bibliothèque Royale MS 5557, and the Texting of Dufay's 'Ecce ancilla domini' and 'Ave regina celorum' Masses," *Acta Musicologica* 51 (1979): 73–86.

FIGURE 6-6. The antiphon *Rex seculorum* in honor of St. Benedict (Worcester Cathedral Library, MS F.160, f. 22ᵛ).

auxiliary pitches and passing tones are now added, now eliminated; repeated pitches are often ignored; relatively substantial passages of freely composed material have been either interpolated here and there (or, if derived from the chant, highly ornamented), especially at the ends of subsections; and in the Agnus Dei, whose text is markedly shorter than that of the preceding sections, a considerable segment of the borrowed melody (beginning with the words "Quos erutos") has simply been eliminated.

Still, there is a regularity to the articulation of the structure from one section to the next that is reminiscent of the *taleae* of an isorhythmic motet. In addition, recurring patterns of mensural change of the sort found in isorhythmic constructs—which, as we have seen, were used as a unifying device in paired Ordinaries—contribute to the perception that the individual settings are parts of a greater whole. The

NOTE: The pitches taken from the chant have been marked with a small cross in order to show at a glance the notes added, changed, or eliminated by the composer in these two brief segments. (Repeated tones are indicated by the number of crosses over a given note and the words of the chant added below to facilitate the identification of portions not used in those sections of the Mass.)

SANCTUS: Holy, holy, holy, Lord God of hosts.
AGNUS DEI: Lamb of God, who takest away the sins of the world.

structural organization of the Mass overall (excluding the fragmentary Kyrie) is summarized in the following table:

Gloria
O – Et in terra, à 3, (Rex seculorum, m. 33): 68 ternary breves[45]
C – Qui tollis, à 3 (Exaudi te, m. 70): 68 binary breves
O – Quoniam tu solus, à 2 (Quos erutos, m. 104): 19 ternary breves
O – Cum Sancto Spiritu, à 3 (Christe salus, m. 124): 22 ternary breves

45. The length of the various sections in breves must be seen as approximate. The final *longa* of each section has not been counted, as its duration is apparently indefinite, and it is not clear that the sections having the sign for integral imperfect tempus (C) should not in fact be sung as if the stroke of diminution were present (as in the "Et resurrexit").

Credo:

O – Patrem omnipotentem, à 3 (Rex seculorum, m. 33): 79 ternary breves

₵ – Et resurrexit, à 3 (Exaudi te, m. 99): 98 binary breves (dim.)

O – Et unam sanctam, à 2 (Quos erutos, m. 104): 29 ternary breves

O – Et expecto, à 3 (Christe salus, m. 175): 26 ternary breves

Sanctus:

O – Sanctus, à 3 (Rex seculorum, m. 1): 34 ternary breves

O – Pleni sunt, à 2 (Exaudi te, m. 36): 32 ternary breves

C – Osanna, à 3 (Tui benedicti, m. 69): 43 binary breves

C – Benedictus, à 2 (Quos erutos, m. 91): 62 binary breves

O – Osanna, à 3 (Christe salus, m. 122): 27 ternary breves

Agnus Dei:

O – Agnus Dei I, à 3 (Rex seculorum, m. 1): 46 ternary breves

O – Agnus Dei II, à 2 (Exaudi te, m. 49): 45 ternary breves

C – Agnus Dei III, à 3 (Christe salus, m. 95): 40 binary breves

O – Dona nobis pacem, à 3 (?): 10 ternary breves

Significantly, the tenor cantus firmus has been divided into four principal segments, which correspond in a sense—even though they are neither equal nor proportional in length—to the *taleae* of an isorhythmic structure. Further, the individual compositions that constitute the cycle have been divided in turn into four subsections, each of which is based on one of the four segments of the borrowed chant.[46] The only exceptions are the Sanctus, where the repetition of the "Osanna" adds a fifth division, and the Agnus Dei, where, as noted, the segment of the chant beginning "Quos erutos" was not used. Three of these subsections are each time in perfect tempus (O), whereas only one is in imperfect tempus (C) (if one construes the first "Osanna" and the "Benedictus" as a mensural continuum within the Sanctus, which may or may not have been performed in diminution). However, the pattern of mensural organization established in the Gloria and Credo (O, C, O, O) has been altered in the Sanctus and Agnus Dei (O, O, C, O), suggesting that, although they are all linked by the same tenor, both the Gloria and Credo and the Sanctus and Agnus continued to be treated in important ways as pairs.

The impression of pairing within the cycle is strengthened by the articulation of the successive subsections by means of the contrapuntal texture. In the Gloria and Credo it is with the third segment, that based on "Quos erutos," that the three-part writing gives way to a duo, whereas in the Sanctus and Agnus Dei, it is with the second, that based on "Exaudi te." Similarly, both Gloria and Credo open with an introductory duo of exactly thirty-three ternary breves before the entry of the tenor

46. It is perhaps noteworthy in this connection that chant has been treated as essentially musical material; its original incises have otherwise been generally ignored, and internal articulations within the sections of the Mass often break the melody arbitrarily, not only within the phrase but also in the middle of a word.

cantus firmus—another hint of *talea*-like regularity—while the tenor is heard in the Sanctus and Agnus Dei from the outset.

Melodically, it is the cantus firmus—a mode 6 chant with F as the final and a signed b-flat—that imposes upon the cycle, as upon its individual sections, its "tonal" unity.[47] Each of the major sections of the Mass carries (with reasonable consistency) the signed flat that was customary for the mode, and each closes on its regular final. The same is true of all of the subsections save one (the first in "Agnus Dei III," which makes its cadence to A) and many of the internal articulations as well. Other cadences are, for the most part, to the scale degrees deemed appropriate for closure in the Lydian modes in both chant and polyphony—the final, the confinal, and the third between them—but there are important cadences to G and to D as well, implying commixture with modes of the Dorian pair.

From our present perspective the tenor cantus firmus looms large as an agent of musical unification, hence as a remarkably fruitful and versatile artistic conception, in linking settings of the Ordinary of the Mass into pairs, groups, and complete cycles. Still, it may have been primarily for its symbolic value and potential liturgical significance that it was borrowed from motet composition and adapted for use in the polyphonic Mass. It could function there, as it had in the motet, as a kind of reverse trope. The original text, even when only implied by sounding the melody traditionally associated with it, could impart to the unchanging words of the Ordinary a context of meaning derived from a Proper feast or related to an important occasion of state. It was surely this festal, liturgical function that caused its use to be so quickly and widely disseminated and, as a consequence, that established the cyclic Mass so firmly as a new musical genre. And, as we shall see, having assumed one of the primary functions of the isorhythmic motet, together with the compositional procedures most characteristic of its facture, it would soon replace the older motet type in the musical repertory as well.

However, as important as these questions of musical structure and emblematic meaning are for the history of the polyphonic Mass in the fifteenth century, let us not forget that it is not they but the novel English sonorities that elicited comment from writers of the period. An emphasis on imperfect consonances (both thirds and sixths), in contrast to the perfect ones given pride of place in Continental repertories of the previous generation, a more carefully controlled use of dissonance, and a contrapuntal texture that is somehow more transparent, more homophonic in its basic conception, all contributed to the impression of "sweet" harmony that authors as diversely occupied as Martin le Franc and Johannes Tinctoris so admired. And it may well be that euphony—the characteristic of the repertory in question to which even listeners of our own time are often most sensitive—that was primarily responsible for the wide dissemination of English music in Continental sources of the period, even more so than other, less audible, innovations of English composers.

---

47. "Tonal" is to be understood here, as elsewhere in discussions of musical style, as referring to the criteria by which the medieval tones, or modes, were defined: final, range, and intervallic species; see Appendix, pp. 996–97.

⟶ CAROLS: THE POPULAR VOICE ⟵

The polyphonic carol was for England the one truly indigenous musical genre of the late Middle Ages. Moreover, the surviving repertory is a rather substantial one, numbering nearly 120 compositions. And although the direct influence of the carol on Continental masters seems to have been slight, its impact on the development of the Latin genres, first at home—as has been seen—and then, indirectly, abroad, was considerable and significant.

Sources for the carol, both text and music, are exclusively English. Of the collections to include music, the earliest and most extensive date from the early fifteenth century. A parchment roll currently in the Trinity College Library, Cambridge (MS 0.3.58), which was probably copied early in the first half of the fifteenth century, contains thirteen English carols, all without attribution. A manuscript now in the Bodleian Library at Oxford (MS Selden B.26), which can be dated to approximately 1425–40, brings together carols on texts in English, Latin, and a combination of the two, thirty-two in all, with a hymn and a small group of motets, some of which can be attributed to Dunstable and Power. A third compilation, currently in the British Library (MS Egerton 3307) and dating from about 1430–44, has music for the Mass, both Proper and Ordinary, processional hymns, motets, and a pair of Passions in an initial section and in a second fascicle a group of thirty-two carols, once again on texts in English, Latin, and the two combined. A somewhat later collection, datable to the period 1460–1510, also held by the British Library (MS Additional 5665, the "Ritson"), includes forty-four Latin and English carols in addition to a repertory of Mass Ordinaries, hymns, and motets.[48]

In its early history the development of the English carol is probably related to that of the French *carole*, a song form characterized by strophic verses and a recurring refrain that was used in courtly society as an accompaniment for dancing. The genre was already well developed by the 1100s and was widely cultivated and disseminated in the West over the following centuries. Courtly carols on English texts made their appearance as French began to fade as the spoken language of insular aristocratic circles, and they persisted in the English tradition well into the sixteenth century. Late examples, such as the setting of *Green groweth the holly* attributed to King Henry VIII and other like pieces, were copied into a manuscript given over entirely to secular music prepared for use at Henry's court, and they reflect the erotic diction of the courtly carol and its social functions in lay festivals, processions, and amorous games.[49]

48. Concerning the most important of the relevant musical sources, see John Stevens, "Carol," *The New Grove Dictionary of Music*, 3:806 (including two others dating from the sixteenth century), and for detailed information on the manuscripts cited here, see the *Census-Catalogue of Manuscript Sources*, 1:130, and 2:298, 89, and 43.

49. The social uses of the carol in England during the period in question have been summarized by John Stevens, "Carol," *The New Grove Dictionary of Music*, 3:803–11, to which much of the following discussion is indebted. Regarding the codex cited, which is known as "Henry VIII's Songbook" (MS Additional 31922 in the British Library), see below, pp. 703–7.

Literary references suggest that by late in the thirteenth century the carol had found favor in more plebeian circles as well. There, although it continued to be used as accompaniment to the dance, it also saw other uses. The most enduring of these were evidently in the realm of popular piety and religious devotion. As a consequence (as Stevens has observed), the vast majority of the texts that have survived from the fourteenth and fifteenth centuries (roughly five out of six) deal with religious or moral themes, many of them with a clearly didactic slant. Most also relate in some way to the Christmas season and—like many Latin conductus of the twelfth century—honor the Virgin Mary in connection with the mystery of the Incarnation.[50]

Further evidence of the broader audience for which they were intended may be seen in the language of the texts, which is simple and straightforward and makes frequent use of stock phrases. Even the Latin locutions with which many of them are laced are an indication of the carol's deliberately popular character; they are usually taken from the best-known elements of the liturgy, especially hymns and Marian antiphons, and artfully interpolated into the English verse so as to illuminate and enhance its meaning. Imagery, too—such as references to the effect of the sun shining through the historiated windows of colored glass that commonly graced the churches of the period—was selected for its familiarity and easy comprehensibility. A didactic slant is often unmistakable, even in the Latin carols, which may have been intended for the young choristers and other students in the schools of cathedrals and collegiate churches (and in some instances, perhaps, also written by them).

As was often the case during the Middle Ages with devotional music of a popular cast, the cultivation and dissemination of the carol can be linked with the activities of Franciscan friars—even though there is no obvious English equivalent to the lay confraternities of urban Italy for whose devotions the analogous *laude* were written and performed (see pp. 443–56). Carols were likely adopted as processional music for lay worship, perhaps in place of Latin hymns and antiphons—like the conductus, once again—and at the celebration of popular feasts such as Christmas and New Year's Day.

The singing of carols was clearly not limited to festivities of a public nature, however; they also served as "household" music in devotions at court and in the homes of the noble and wealthy, and they were used as substitutes for votive antiphons in the schools and before the altars of private chapels. Judging from the political overtones of some of their texts, they may also have been heard at ceremonies of state. In addition, their inclusion in collections of music for Mass and the Office, together with particular rubrics in some of those sources, suggest that they may even have found a place on occasion in the traditional liturgy.

Like the *lauda*—and the courtly *carole* before it—the devotional English carol of the Middle Ages may have originated as monophonic song. Only ten melodies can be identified as coming from this early phase of its development, but others may have

---

50. Concerning the Latin conductus and the topics addressed by its verse, see Hoppin, *Medieval Music*, 242–44.

survived, unrecognized, in one of the voices of a later polyphonic setting. It is possible, too, that many carols were once sung to the melodies of secular songs or even well-known Latin hymns. Because the most common verse form consists of a refrain, called a "burden," of two lines and a strophe of four (rhymed either aaaa or aaab with roughly four stressed syllables to the line), it could be readily adapted to the music for one of the many liturgical hymns that—though without the burden—are constructed in much the same way.

The anonymous setting of *Deo gracias, Anglia,* the so-called Agincourt carol, although representative of the fifteenth-century repertory of polyphonic carols in most respects, is unusual for the occasional character of its subject (see Example 6-8). Since it refers specifically to Henry V's decisive victory over the French toward the end of the Hundred Years' War, it was likely written for the celebrations that

EXAMPLE 6-8. Anonymous, *Deo Gracias, Anglia* (the Agincourt carol)

Thanks be to God, England, pray for victory.

greeted him upon his triumphal return to England. The use of familiar Latin words or phrases in the burden—here two rhyming lines of unequal length (eight and seven syllables, respectively)—is frequently seen, even where the stanzas are entirely in English. In this instance, however, the acclamation "Deo gracias" returns, refrainlike, at the close of each strophe as well, appended for effect without apparent regard for the versification (four lines of fairly regular iambic tetrameter with a single rhyming syllable). The declamation generally follows the rhythm of the verse, and the relationship of notes to syllables is direct enough as to make clear that the stress should always fall at the beginning of the ternary semibreve.

Of the two voices, and then three, for which the piece is written, it is the lowest one that maintains the declamatory rhythm most soberly, suggesting that it was the first to be composed (and could therefore be considered the tenor). In addition, that part fills exactly the regular ambitus of the first mode (an octave above and a step below the D final), and it approaches the cadential pitch at the conclusion of each phrase from above—further evidence of its melodic priority within the contrapuntal fabric. (The internal cadences, incidentally—to D, A, F, and G—are also consistent with traditional melodic patterns in mode 1.)

The upper part in the first burden and the verse ornaments, more freely than its companion, the longer values to which the declamation is tied, and its approach to the pitches upon which cadential figures come to rest is invariably from below. When a third part is added for the second burden, the two upper lines are similar in their rhythmic activity and their cadential functions, indicating that both of them were added to the primary melody to which the text was sung in order to embellish it with animated melodic figures and consonant sonorities. Contrasts in texture, resulting from the separate sections in two and then three parts, may have been intended to help achieve a climactic effect. The opening burden opens with a passage in unison before the second voice goes its own way, and if the three-part burden were held back until the last verse had been sung, it would conclude the work with music that was both more extended and fuller in sound than the two-part version.

More traditional as to topic is the anonymous carol *Nowell, nowell: In Bethlem,* which was undoubtedly intended for the Christmas season since it refers, as was customary, to Mary and the virgin birth (see Example 6-9). At first blush the poetry strikes one as more sophisticated than that of the Agincourt carol; the strophes consist of six lines, counting the interpolation of the acclamation "nowell" from the burden as the fourth in each of them, with the rhyme scheme aaabab. However, the verse is neither so regular nor so polished: the iambic pattern of its rhythm does not always begin with an anacrusis (e.g., strophe 2/verse 2, "And be nailëd on a rood," also 3/1; or 3/6); the stressed syllable is followed at times by two unaccented ones (as in 1/1, "In Bethlem that child of life is born," also 1/2; or 2/3), or by none at all (as in 3/3, "And save mankind in this wise"), and is sometimes awkwardly placed (as in 2/6, "To slay so gentle a jewel"). And the line, although carrying four stressed syllables most of the time, appears at the opening of the verse to have only three (1/1, "In Bethlem that child of life").

These irregularities require some adjustments by performers in adapting syllables to notes. This was presumably achieved by matching as closely as possible the declamation of the verse to the rhythmic patterns of the music, placing whenever possible the stressed syllable at the beginning of the ternary semibreve (i.e., the measure). Once again the lowest voice is the least ornamented, presenting the text in the most directly syllabic manner possible, and it approaches cadential finals from above. Its melodic ambitus is that of mode 8 on G for burden 1 and the verse; however, the introduction of b-fa (mm. 24–29) and an internal cadence to F imply a commixture with mode 5. The implications of that modal shift become apparent in burden 2, which is written in three parts in this carol as well. There the range of the "tenor" shifts to the fifth above C, the pitch on which the final cadence comes to rest. Consequently, if the three-part burden were held in abeyance until the end of the piece, as has been suggested, the modal shift at the conclusion would add a dramatic touch.

CAROLS, SONGS, AND CHANSONS

It is easy to see why the carol was such a popular musical genre in England. The texts, which were frequently in the native vernacular and declaimed homophonically, were

EXAMPLE 6-9. Anonymous, *Nowell, nowell: In Bethlem* (mm. 1–29)

more readily accessible to their intended audience than Mass settings, motets, or chansons. The music, too, is more accessible and may therefore have had a more immediate impact. Every carol is divided into discrete phrases, corresponding to the lines of verse, each of which is clearly articulated with a cadence. The alternation of a recurring refrain with a single setting for all strophes limits dramatically the amount of music to be assimilated by the listener, and there is rarely anything intentionally abstruse in the compositional facture (such as isorhythm), either conceptually or practically. Although more challenging than plainchant or monophonic song, the difficulties posed performers by polyphonic carols are considerably less than for the more complex genres cited. Finally, they are exceptionally versatile and can be adapted to a variety of contexts, from the liturgical to the devotional to the festal.

This flexibility, together with the popularity of the genre, may help to explain why—aside from the carol—there is so little evidence of a native tradition for polyphonic secular song in England during the early years of the fifteenth century. With a compositional type so easily adapted to a variety of circumstances and, evidently, so esthetically satisfying to audiences, the need to create an English counterpart to the Continental chanson may have been felt less keenly. Unlike the carol, moreover, the polyphonic chanson was at the time primarily courtly in character, both in its diction and its social uses. And since French continued to be the language of courtly society in England in the early decades of the fifteenth century, the chanson must have been sung there as readily as it was on the Continent.

Whatever the reasons, polyphonic English songs are very rare in this period, showing up in limited numbers in sources mostly from the second half of the century, and the few English masters who put their hand to song composition—beginning with Dunstable—appear to have set French (and even Italian) texts more often than poems in their own vernacular. In structure and style as well the few English songs known to have originated during this transitional phase in the development of Western polyphony are virtually indistinguishable from the chansons with which they are usually gathered. Symptomatic of the situation at the time are two manuscript collections from the first half of the fifteenth century in which songs and chansons are the predominant genres: Cambridge University Library MS Additional 5943, compiled in Somersetshire about 1415, and Oxford, Bodleian Library MS Douce 381, from about the same time but of unknown provenance.

The aggregate repertory transmitted in these two codices is surprisingly small. Manuscript Additional 5943 has but nine English pieces (together with four chansons, a Gloria, a Credo, a Latin hymn, and a motet),[51] while MS Douce 381 has five English songs (in addition to two chansons and an instrumental work).[52] Moreover, there are some pieces common to both. In view of the small number of compositions that have survived to the present and their close formal and stylistic affinities with the French secular music of the period, it is simply not possible from our present perspective to define English song adequately as a separate and distinctive musical genre.

---

51. See the *Census-Catalogue of Manuscript Sources*, 1:131f; a facsimile edition made by Leslie Hewitt with an introduction by Richard Rastall has been published under the title *A Fifteenth-Century Song Book*, Early Music in Facsimile, vol. 1 (Leeds: Boethius Press, 1973).
52. See the *Census-Catalogue of Manuscript Sources*, 2:279.

CHAPTER 7

✓

French Secular Music of the Fifteenth Century

INTRODUCTION

For the French-speaking regions of Europe, as for England, many of the most crucial historical events of the fifteenth century were linked in some manner to the Hundred Years' War.[1] This was true not only for political events and for the strains that the resulting circumstances put on the social fabric of the areas concerned; it was so for music as well. As armies prepared themselves to go into battle, the liturgy was celebrated with particular fervor. As we have seen, John Cooke's motet *Alma proles regiae/Christi miles/Ab inimicis nostris* combines prayers to the Virgin, Christ, and St. George on behalf of the English king and his armies and was undoubtedly inspired by one of the periodic campaigns that marked the long struggle (see p. 226).

Encounters between opposing forces, whether in treaty negotions or on the battlefield, were punctated by the sounds of trumpets, identifying the nobles with whose armies they served and signaling back and forth as the battle unfolded. Chapel singers often accompanied their patrons to the very battlefield, where they continued to celebrate Mass and other important services. They also joined with the court musicians to entertain the noble combatants and their companions in moments of relative leisure, performing both sacred motets and the songs that charmed the recreations in castle halls and chambers in times of peace. When victorious warriors returned, their success was often celebrated with a festive *entrée*; as was observed, the Agincourt carol, *Deo gracias, Anglia*, was probably written to mark the triumphant return of Henry V and his armies after their rout of superior French forces on that famous field.

A long and spasmodic war of attrition began soon after the accession to the

---

1. The principal events in the conflict have been recounted by Desmond Seward, *The Hundred Years War: The English in France, 1337–1453* (New York: Atheneum, 1978), and analyzed by Christopher Allmand, *The Hundred Years War: England and France at War c. 1300–c. 1450* (Cambridge: Cambridge University Press, 1988).

French throne of Philip VI (ruled 1328–50), the first French monarch from the Valois dynasty. Philip had himself crowned successor to his cousin, Charles IV, who left no male heir, by forcibly setting aside the claims of Charles's infant daughter. This encouraged Philip's even more distant cousin, Edward III of England—who was also duke of Guyenne (Aquitaine) and count of Ponthieu and therefore in principle a vassal of the king of France—to assert in turn, in 1337, his own indirect claim to the French crown through his mother, Isabel, Charles's sister (see Genealogies, p. 1059). He acted in part out of anger at Philip's failure to restore to him, as promised, lands taken by Charles IV that Edward claimed as part of his duchy. But a more important objective was to maintain control of wool markets in Flanders that were such an essential element of the English economy of the late Middle Ages.

Hostilities were opened in the small enclave held by the English around Ponthieu (see Figure 7-1). The outcome of the conflict, initially at least, was a series of disastrous defeats inflicted on the French by smaller English forces, most notably those at the naval battle of Sluys in 1340, at Crécy in 1346, and at Poitiers in 1356. As a result, Edward III was able to expand considerably his holdings on the Continent around his two French fiefdoms, particularly in Aquitaine, and to capture the key port of Calais, which the English held until 1558 (cf. the maps in Figure 7-1 and Figure 7-2).

The French debacle at Poitiers was for the English a signal military victory, but it also provided them an opportunity to observe firsthand the musical practices of the French court, for King John the Good was taken prisoner by the English in the course of the battle and spent the next three years in London awaiting the negotiation of a ransom that would allow him to return home. As a royal prisoner of admirable courage, he was comfortably lodged and allowed to summon from his court some of the personnel of his household, including both minstrels and singers of his private chapel, and there is good evidence that his religious devotions included the polyphonic music that he would have heard in France just as his recreation included the performances of secular musicians.[2] It may also have given the musicians in John's service a chance to become better acquainted with the music of the English, more so than was probably possible in France, for in the early phases of the conflict the English had only a minimal presence on the Continent, leaving the administration of their domains there mostly to local officials.

THE VALOIS DUKES OF BURGUNDY

The events at Poitiers also sowed the seeds of other political developments that were to threaten the autonomy of the French monarchy. Taken captive with King John

---

2. Some of the details concerning musical activities in the entourage of John the Good during his years of captivity in England have been summarized by Craig Wright, *Music at the Court of Burgundy, 1364–1419: A Documentary History* (Brooklyn: Institute of Mediaeval Music, 1979), 11–17; cf. also below, pp. 270–71.

FIGURE 7-1. France in 1337. (From Desmond Seward, *The Hundred Years War*, p. 265.)

was his youngest son, Philip of Valois. Although a lad of fourteen at the time, he stood by his father's side as the battle raged and attempted to defend him. His courage won for him not only the epithet "the Bold" but also his father's admiration and gratitude. As soon as the young prince came of age, the king rewarded his valor with the duchy of Burgundy, a gift that was confirmed by his elder brother, Charles V, when he succeeded to the royal throne in 1364. Philip added adroitly to his newly acquired lands by contracting a promising marriage with Margaret of Flanders, the only surviving child of Count Louis of Male and Margaret of Artois and hence heir

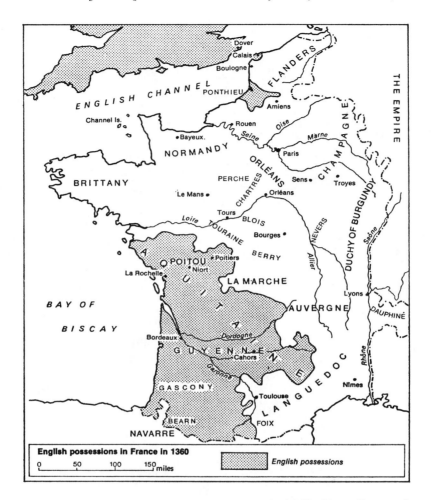

FIGURE 7-2.   English possessions in France in 1360. (From Desmond
Seward, *The Hundred Years War*, p. 266.)

to all their domains. The pair were wed in 1369, and when Louis died in 1384, Philip
added to his holdings the counties of Flanders, Artois, Rethel, Nevers, and the
Franche-Comté; later he purchased the adjacent county of Charolais as well.

Nevers and Rethel were partitioned off following Philip's death in 1404, during
the reign of John the Fearless, but the territorial expansion of the Valois dukes continued during the long reign of Philip the Good (1419–67), who extended his hegemony to Holland, Zeeland, Brabant, Hainaut, Luxembourg, Boulogne, Picardy,
Vermandois, and Macon. The resulting dominions were extensive enough by fifteenth-
century standards to form a rather formidable kingdom, but they were awkwardly
divided geographically into two separate enclaves. It was while attempting to weld

them together by extending his rule to the duchies of Bar and Lorraine that Charles the Bold (1467–77) met his death, bringing to a close the relatively brief Valois dynasty of Burgundy.[3] (For an overview of the territorial expansion achieved by the Valois dukes of Burgundy in just a little more than a century, see Figure 7-3). The French monarchy had thus brought unwittingly into existence on its northern and eastern frontiers a rival state made powerful both by the extent of its territories and by the wealth generated by the industry and commerce of its cities.

As vassals of the king and members of the royal family, the Valois dukes should have been loyal allies of the French crown, but this was not often the case. As their wealth and power increased, so did their potential for political independence and their inclination to use it. When Charles V came to the throne in 1364, the ducal dynasty had only just come into being, and as there was no serious conflict between the king and his younger brother, Charles could devote much of his energies to recovering the lands ceded to Edward III under duress by a treaty of 1360. New ships were built to strengthen the French fleet, and a standing army was raised, thus diminishing the need to rely upon the assistance of the companies of freebooters— aptly termed *écorcheurs* by the French because of their lawless depredations in the countryside.

ENGLAND ON THE CONTINENT: THE LAST SUBSTANTIAL SUCCESSES

The newly constituted French forces, under the leadership of Charles's wily general, Bertrand Duguesclin, proved their worth by wearing down three successive English armies in a prolonged if intermittent war of attrition and by recapturing nearly all the territories that had previously been lost. But when Charles V died in 1380, the authority of the crown was challenged once again. The future Charles VI was but twelve years of age at the time, and during his minority France suffered under the joint regency of three of his uncles, the dukes of Anjou, Berry, and Burgundy. More intent upon exploiting the resources of the kingdom for their own ends than affirming royal sovereignty, this ducal trio—with Philip the Bold of Burgundy taking the lead—depleted the royal treasury with ostentatious fêtes and tourneys and provoked popular uprisings by the oppressive taxes levied to finance their pleasures. When, in 1388, Charles VI was finally able to take matters into his own hands, he dismissed his uncles, recalled the able ministers who had served his father, and appointed his brother Louis, duke of Orléans, as his counselor. Unfortunately, his efforts to restore order to the government of the kingdom were short-lived; only four years later he suffered the first bouts of the insanity that was to compromise his ability to rule for the remainder of his life.

3. For a concise account of the territorial acquisitions of the Valois dukes of Burgundy in the course of the fourteenth and fifteenth centuries, see Richard Vaughan, *Valois Burgundy* (Hamden, Conn.: Archon Books, 1975), 14–31. Also informative on political matters is the brief article by Craig Wright, "Burgundy," *The New Grove Dictionary of Music*, 3:464–68.

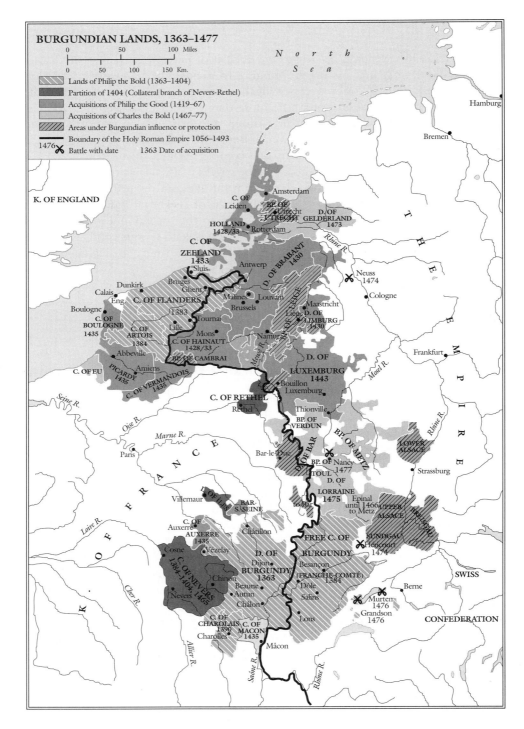

Figure 7-3. Burgundian lands, 1363–1477.

Philip the Bold was quick to renew his hold on the powers of the monarchy, and that course of action soon brought him into direct confrontation with the duke of Orléans. In the ensuing struggle, France divided itself into two warring factions: on the one hand were the Burgundians—the duke and his partisans—and on the other the Armagnacs—those who sided with the duke of Orléans under the banner of his future father-in-law, the count of Armagnac. Philip's death in 1404 did nothing to attenuate the conflict; it was carried on with renewed vehemence by his son, John the Fearless, who had his rival murdered in the streets of Paris only three years later. That assassination plunged the country into a full-fledged civil war, during which both sides resorted to the dangerous expediency of seeking the support of the English with offers of territorial concessions.

In 1413, while France was thus torn by internal strife, Henry V acceded to the throne of England and promptly began to press his claims to that of France as well. He reopened hostilities on the Continent in 1415, waging a relatively sustained and largely successful campaign. Having captured the strategic port city of Harfleur, he inflicted a humiliating defeat on the more numerous French armies that had assembled near Agincourt to check his advance. Two years later he set about a systematic invasion of Normandy that was concluded in January 1420 with the fall of Rouen, the chief city of the region, and the territories taken in the course of that operation were to remain under English rule for some thirty years (see Figure 7-4).

In the meantime John the Fearless of Burgundy had in turn fallen a victim to murder; he was cut down by the Armagnacs in September 1419 as he was negotiating with them an agreement to join forces against the English, whose encroachments he had begun to

FIGURE 7-4. John Plantagenet, duke of Bedford, battling the French at Vernueil. Miniature from *Abrégé de la chronique* by Enguerrand de Monstrelet. (Paris, Bibliothèque Nationale, MS f. fr. 2680, f. 35.)

fear. John's son, Philip the Good, was incensed by the assassination, and his anger was directed in particular against the dauphin of France, the future Charles VII, who had the support of the Armagnacs and appeared to have been personally implicated in the plot to take his cousin's life. In his rage Duke Philip joined forces with Henry V. Together they negotiated with Isabeau of Bavaria (acting on behalf of her demented consort, Charles VI) the treaty signed in Troyes on May 20, 1420. By its provisions the dauphin Charles was disinherited, and Henry V of England was recognized as the legal heir to the French throne. Henry also agreed to marry Catherine of France, the daughter of Charles VI and Isabeau, and to conquer the territories that remained in the hands of the dauphin and his allies.

Unfortunately for Henry, he did not live to win the crown or rule the lands to which that agreement entitled him. He died in late August 1422, at the age of thirty-five, and six weeks later Charles VI also expired. With both monarchs dead, the dauphin, with the support of the Armagnac faction, repudiated the Treaty of Troyes and declared himself king as Charles VII of France. The struggle between English and French then resumed with Henry V's younger brother John, the duke of Bedford, acting as regent in France for Henry VI, the infant offspring of Henry V and Catherine of France. The uneasy alliance between the English and the Burgundians was also cemented to a degree in 1423 by the marriage of Bedford with the sister of Philip the Good, and their combined armies continued to gain ground against the dauphin's forces.

English fortunes on the Continent reached their apex soon thereafter. By 1429 they controlled not only their traditional enclave in Guienne but also virtually all French territories between the Loire River to the south and the domains of the empire and the duchy of Burgundy to the east and north (see Figure 7-5). This time the consequences of their success were not merely military or political in nature; the quasi-continuous presence of English magnates on French soil for nearly fifteen years, accompanied as they were by their chapel singers and secular musicians, exercised a significant influence on the developing polyphonic style of the fifteenth century (see pp. 219–20).

ENGLAND AND FRANCE: THE TIDE BEGINS TO TURN

The turning point for the French came in May 1429, when Joan of Arc appeared before the walls of Orléans at the head of the armies loyal to Charles VII and raised the siege the English had laid the previous October. That victory, and the few subsequently won by the Maid of Orléans, had a psychological impact that transcended by far her modest military success. Joan's assertion, that she had been instructed by heavenly voices to come to the aid of her sovereign and see him consecrated in the cathedral at Rheims, was the most potent moral weapon she could have wielded in his defense. When that consecration actually took place just a few weeks later, it was finally possible for those fighting on Charles's side to believe in the legitimacy of his birth—which his own mother had called into question—and consequently in the validity of his claim to the royal throne of France.

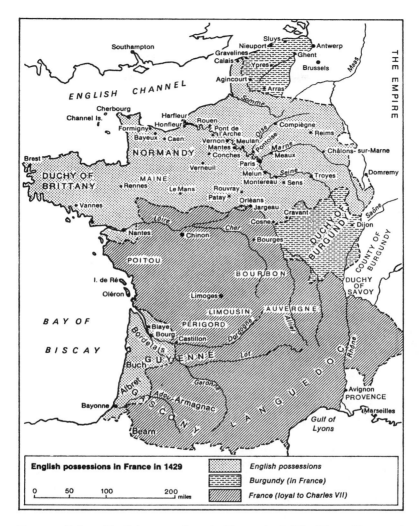

FIGURE 7-5.   English possessions in France in 1429. (From Desmond Seward, *The Hundred Years War*, p. 267.)

Over the next few months the royal armies, heartened by Joan's conviction and inspired by her example, went on the offensive and made some modest gains. Their momentum was dissipated rather abruptly, however, when Joan was captured by Burgundian troops and sold to the English in May 1430. For the latter, in particular, the Maid's contention that Charles's right to rule had been divinely sanctioned was an acute moral and political embarrassment. They attempted to discredit her testimony as quickly and convincingly as possible by trying her for heresy and, when she would not recant, burning her at the stake. Meanwhile the ever capable duke of

Bedford recovered most of the ground the English had lost. Nearly two decades of almost incessant warfare had taken their toll, however, both on the resources required for sustained warfare by the English armies and on the energies of the regent who led them on behalf of their infant king. The Norman countryside, ravaged by war, produced less and less as the conflict continued, and the home islands found it increasingly burdensome to supply funds and provisions to maintain their forces in the field.

In the fall of 1435 the English suffered two crippling blows almost simultaneously; the duke of Bedford died in mid-September, and less than a week later Philip the Good and Charles VII signed a treaty of peace in the city of Arras. Under the terms of that agreement the duke of Burgundy was exempted from paying homage to his traditional liege lord and given possession of the lands he held at the time, including royal domains north of the river Somme and the fortified towns that served to defend them. In exchange for these concessions Philip was to recognize Charles as the legitimate heir to the throne of France and to withdraw from his alliance with the English.

Although he appeared somewhat weak and indecisive as a young man, Charles VII ultimately proved to be a competent military strategist and an effective ruler (see Figure 7-6). The manner in which he began exploiting the more advantageous position he had won by the Treaty of Arras would suggest that he was just then beginning to come into his own. Freed from the threat of Burgundian aggression on his flanks, he began to dislodge the English systematically from the territories they had occupied. Paris fell to his armies in 1436, and by 1441 he had driven the enemy from their last bastion in central France. The English were finally sufficiently hard pressed to seek a truce, signed in Tours in 1444, which lasted five years.

Charles took advantage of this break in hostilities by reorganizing his finances and rebuilding his armies. To provide regular and adequate revenues to the crown, the king and his council devised a permanent tax structure based on the three types of levies that

FIGURE 7-6. Portrait of King Charles VII of France by Jean Fouquet (Musée du Louvre).

had been used with increasing frequency during the Middle Ages: a type of sales tax, a duty paid on salt, and a head and property tax.[4] A dependable fiscal organization made possible in turn the maintenance of a standing army of the sort raised earlier by Charles V. By a decree of 1445 the king called for the formation of fifteen *compagnies d'ordonnance*, each consisting of 100 "garnished lances," and by 1446 France had twenty such companies.[5]

A further edict of 1448 provided for a veritable national infantry of 8,000 bowmen, more or less on the English model. Each parish (about fifty families) was to furnish and equip one such soldier, who was to be paid only in time of war but enjoyed in addition exemption from the usual head tax (hence the designation *franc-archer*).[6] To round out his military forces, Charles VII also invested considerable sums on artillery, which had by then been developed into a genuinely effective siege weapon. In sharp contrast to the typical soldiers of the fifteenth century, the French forces were well armed, well disciplined, and regularly paid; moreover, they owed allegiance only to the authority of the crown. In short, they had become in every sense an essentially modern army.

With his armies reconstituted as a quasi-permanent fighting force and the royal treasury somewhat replenished, Charles VII turned his efforts to bringing under the authority of the French crown all of the lands then occupied by the English. In July 1449 he launched a well-coordinated campaign to recapture Normandy and in little more than a year succeeded in doing so. He then set about the conquest of Guienne, the ancient fief of the Plantagenet kings of England. The first incursions into the region were made in the fall of 1450, and Bordeaux and Bayonne fell toward the end of the following summer. Although Bordeaux, and much of the territory around the city, rose in revolt one last time with the assistance of an English army that disembarked in October 1452, the English were decisively defeated at the battle of Castillon the following July, and within a few months French rule had been reestablished in the entire region. Contemporary observers could hardly see it at the time from either side of the channel, but the Hundred Years' War was winding to its end. The English hold on the Continent had been broken for all time, and they were left with Calais as their only remaining outpost.[7]

FRANCE AND BURGUNDY: DOMESTIC POLITICS

In the course of an exceptionally long reign, Charles VII had to contend not only with the English and with his own rebellious magnates; he had to face as well the

---

4. In France these taxes were known, respectively, as the *aides*, the *gabelle*, and the *taille*. As a rule the nobles and other privileged classes were exempt from such levies.

5. The "garnished lance" was apparently a unit of five to six mounted soldiers, a man-at-arms with two archers, and two or three additional armed men in support.

6. The (questionable?) effectiveness of these common soldiers has been linked with the song about the armed man (*l'homme armé*) that played such a colorful role in the polyphonic composition of the fifteenth and early sixteenth centuries; see Lewis Lockwood, "Aspects of the L'homme armé tradition," *Proceedings of the Royal Musical Association* 100 (1973–74): 97–122.

7. For additional information concerning this crucial period in the history of France, Burgundy, and England, see Edouard Perroy, *The Hundred Years War* (Bloomington: University of Indiana Press, 1962).

usual challenge to secular authority stemming from the temporal powers of the papacy. In 1438, in an attempt to limit papal prerogatives within his domains, he issued from Bourges, with the support of both his nobles and the ranking French clergy, the first Pragmatic Sanction, which asserted the divine right of the crown to act in the secular sphere without papal direction or interference and affirmed the independence of the Gallican church in the administration of its own internal affairs.

As a gesture of conciliation toward the reigning pope, the Pragmatic Sanction of Bourges was revoked by Charles's son Louis at the very beginning of his reign in 1461, but it continued to define the limits of papal power within the kingdom informally and practically long after it had been ostensibly abandoned. As in other European nations of the period, the result was to give the king considerable control over the appointments made to high ecclesiastical office and to positions carrying income in the form of a prebend or benefice. Quite naturally, these were most frequently used by successive monarchs for political purposes, but they were also used to provide a good living for the cleric-singers who served in the royal chapel.[8]

During the final years of his father's rule, the future Louis XI appears to have sided repeatedly with the magnates of the realm against him. He joined them in the revolt of 1440 known as the Praguerie, for example, and as a result of further conspiracies of which he was a part, he was first exiled to his appanage in the Dauphiné and then, in 1456, obliged to take refuge from his father's troops with Philip the Good of Burgundy. Despite the nominal peace of the Treaty of Arras, the latter was clearly only too happy to defy his old enemy by giving asylum to his mutinous son and to ignore as long as Charles lived his requests to have Louis returned to the court of France. Once Louis acceded to the throne in 1461, however, he proved to be as determined as his predecessors to extend the authority of the crown and, consequently, to limit the real power of the greater nobles. Like Charles V, he took as his ministers capable men of low birth upon whose loyalty he could rely and worked to win the support of the cities that were at once fortified bastions for his troops and the source of his most important tax revenues (see Figure 7-7).

FIGURE 7-7.   Portrait of King Louis XI of France struck on a medal (Paris, Bibliothèque Nationale).

8. For a detailed study of the reign of Charles VII, see Malcolm G. A. Vale, *Charles VII* (Berkeley: University of California Press, 1974).

These policies brought him inevitably into conflict with the powerful princes of the blood, and opposition to the crown continued to be led by the Valois dukes of Burgundy. Although Louis had been received with an exaggerated show of deference at the court of Philip the Good when he sought protection from his father, as king of France his relations with the duke and his son Charles of Burgundy soon became strained. It was the ducal Valois who called together the leading magnates of the realm in the so-called League of Public Weal in 1465 in an attempt to replace Louis XI as king of France with his own younger brother. Similarly, it was with the encouragement of Charles of Burgundy, who inherited his father's domains in 1467, that Duke Francis II of Brittany invaded Normandy, as the English had done earlier, and at Charles's request that Edward IV of England landed on the Continent in 1475 with an army that was to have joined with Burgundian forces against the king of France. As a result, he found himself in a situation not unlike that faced by his father, obliged to struggle for the territories of his realm and the autonomy of the monarchy against an alliance of the king of England and the duke of Burgundy.

Little by little, Louis's sound domestic policies and astute statesmanship turned the tide in his favor. After a period of truce with the duke of Brittany, the royal armies were able to move back into Normandy and reestablish the king's rule there. Louis dealt with the alliance between Charles of Burgundy and Edward IV of England by lending his support to the Lancastrian king, Henry VI, whom Edward had deposed, helping him to recover his throne. And when Edward, who had once again risen to power, came with his armies to the aid of the Burgundians, Louis simply bought him off. In order to undo, finally, the dynastic designs of Charles of Burgundy, Louis united against him the enemies that Charles had made in the empire by pursuing his dream of reconstituting the ancient kingdom of Lotharingia. It was the ablest of these foes, the Swiss, who in 1476 decisively defeated the ducal armies, first at Grandson and then at Morat. And it was in combat against a coalition of the Swiss and the armies of Lorraine that Charles was killed, bringing an end to the Valois dynasty of Burgundy (see Figure 7-8).[9]

Louis reacted to the death of the duke of Burgundy by seizing his duchy and the fortified towns along the river Somme in Picardy. By 1483 he had gained control of Artois and the Franche-Comté as well, although he was later forced to give them up (see Figure 7-3). His intention, clearly, was to extend his hegemony to all the territories that had come under the sway of his Valois cousins. He was frustrated in this design, however, by Mary of Burgundy, Charles's only surviving heir, who was obviously little inclined to cede her rights and lands to the king of France.

Mary rejected Louis's offer of marriage to the young dauphin, who was to rule as Charles VIII, and the political solution such a match implied. She then won the support of the cities of Holland, Brabant, Flanders, and Hainaut by granting the Great Privilege, which restored to them the liberties that had been abrogated during

9. For a concise account of the final phases of the conflict between Louis XI and Duke Charles of Burgundy, see Vaughan, *Valois Burgundy*, 194–227.

FIGURE 7-8.   Portrait of Duke Charles of Burgundy (*dit le téméraire*) by Roger van der Weyden (Berlin, Staatliche Museen, Preussischer Kulturbesitz, Gemäldegalerie).

the reigns of Dukes Philip and Charles. And to defend her dominions against the threat of a French invasion, she called to her aid Maximilian of Austria, the young Habsburg prince to whom she had been offered in marriage in 1473. He arrived in haste at the head of an imperial army, and the two were wed shortly after. As Mary's consort Maximilian succeeded in defeating the French at Guinegate in 1479, but he was unable to effectively impose his rule on the Netherlands, especially after Mary was killed in a hunting accident in 1482.

Nonetheless, when Mary gave birth in 1478 to Philip the Handsome, a new dynastic line was founded, one that could lay legitimate claim to all the dominions that successive dukes of Burgundy had brought under their sway in more than a century of uninterrupted rule. Once Philip came of age, he made in turn a promising marriage with Joanna of Castile and Aragon, the daughter of Ferdinand and Isabella. He thus fell heir to both Spanish kingdoms in addition to his domains in the Netherlands, and it was the eldest son born of that union, the future Charles V, who eventually gathered under his rule not only those territories but the far-flung dominions of the Holy Roman Empire as well. Although Louis XI had put an end to the threat to his kingdom due to the regal ambitions of the Valois dukes of Burgundy, his failure to gain control of their holdings in the Netherlands undoubtedly contributed in large measure to the growing power of the Habsburg dynasty, which was to become France's greatest enemy in the course of the sixteenth century.

MUSIC IN HISTORY

Despite these difficulties, Louis left the French monarchy much strengthened at his death in 1483. He also left the royal court with a flourishing musical establishment, having built in that regard, as in his politics, on the traditions of his fathers. There is every indication that the Valois kings of France held music in high esteem, both as a prestigious enhancement of courtly ritual and as an essential element in the distractions and entertainments of the nobility. Already by the reign of John the Good (1350–64), it was customary for the monarch to be served by chaplain-singers (including an organist), who celebrated the liturgy of the Christian church regularly in his private chapel, and to maintain trumpeters and minstrels in his entourage.[10]

The resident musicians of the royal court were clearly among the best available anywhere and were certainly capable of performing mensural polyphony from both sacred and secular repertories of the period. A choir of chapel singers, as many as twenty strong with polyphonic and instrumental skills, can be documented, together with the usual assortment of trumpeters and minstrels, from the mid-fourteenth century on, with little interruption (even during John's three-year captivity in England), at least until the death of Charles VI in 1422. During the latter's reign, Charles's son, the dauphin Louis (who died prematurely in 1415), had his own chapel singers, about fifteen in number, and trumpet players and minstrels as well. Accumulating evidence suggests in addition that other princes of the blood were similarly, if not so elaborately, served.[11]

The fortunes of the musicians at the royal court of France are more difficult to trace during the early years of the reign of Charles VII, but in view of the troubled circumstances under which he assumed the crown, it is likely that they were a good deal less certain than they had been previously. Nevertheless, by 1451 at the latest the chapel choir had been reestablished on a firm footing with seventeen or eighteen clerics, and it flourished thereafter continuously throughout the fifteenth and sixteenth centuries. Among those who served there were not only singers skilled in the mensural polyphony that was regarded as the highest achievement of the musical culture of the times but also musicians capable of composing it. The latter provided liturgical music for use in the king's chapel, as was to be expected, but they also set texts for special occasions of state, which were invariably marked by the participation of the musicians of the court, clerical and secular alike, either in the course of the customary ritual or during the accompanying entertainments.[12]

At the rival court of the Valois dukes of Burgundy music was given an equally important place, and the musical establishment there can be considered representative—if on a grander scale—of what was done at the court of many fifteenth-century nobles whose musical activities have left fewer traces in the historical record. Philip the Bold, who evidently followed his father's example in the organization of his own musical forces, presumably had some trumpeters and minstrels in his service already when he came into possession of the duchy, and by 1384 at the latest he had pro-

---

10. For details concerning the roles played by each of the three primary categories of musicians cited here in the rituals and social life of the times, see pp. 89–116.

11. For a summary description of the musical personnel who attended John the Good and also a few indications concerning music at the court of the dauphin Louis, see Wright, *Music at the Court of Burgundy*, 11–18 and 48–49.

12. Concerning the musical personnel of the French royal chapel through much of the fifteenth century, see Leeman L. Perkins, "Musical Patronage at the Royal Court of France under Charles VII and Louis XI (1422–83)," *Journal of the American Musicological Society* 37 (1984): 507–66.

vided for a choir of clerics in his private chapel as well. At his death in 1404 his chaplains numbered twenty-eight, apparently more than either the king of France or the pontiff of the Roman church could boast at the time.

Subsequently, until the death of Charles of Burgundy in 1477, the growing power and wealth of the Valois dukes found a reflection in the musical patronage of the court. The Burgundian chapel choir continued to be the envy of all Europe, rivaling or surpassing in size and quality—and in the number of distinguished composers on its roles—that of every other ruler. Even after the male line of the dynasty was extinguished, the maintenance of an exceptional troop of musicians, sacred and secular, had become such a firmly established tradition that it was carried on without serious interruption by the Habsburg princes who fell heir to the Valois domains in the Netherlands—and by their female regents.[13]

Because there was such an important musical component to virtually every facet of day-to-day life at these two courtly establishments, both became important centers of musical patronage, offering composers, singers, and players of various instruments an opportunity to earn rich rewards for their skills, both directly in the form of generous salaries and indirectly through the granting of special privileges and appointments to positions providing yet other sources of income, such as ecclesiastical prebends. Neither court could be considered a significant training ground for young cleric-singers, however, nor indeed could any other of the period whose musical institutions have been studied, including even the papal court.

The composers and singers brought together by a ruler to serve in his chapel choir were trained, as a rule, in the *maîtrises* of cathedrals and collegiate churches (see pp. 74–77). It was the large urban churches, in particular those flourishing in the wealthy industrial and commercial cities of France and Burgundy, that had the means and the personnel to embellish their liturgical celebrations with polyphony. Consequently, it was primarily in those centers—on the Continent, at any rate—that the skills needed to compose, write, and perform it were taught. A great deal has yet to be learned about many of these important churches, but it is already clear that cities such as Cambrai, Bruges, St. Quentin, and Amsterdam—to cite only a few of those about which the most is known—played a leading role during the fifteenth century in providing musicians trained in mensural polyphony for courtly chapels in much of western Europe, and undoubtedly contributed significantly to the musical distinction of the chapel choirs at the French and Burgundian courts.

---

13. For a detailed study of the musicians of the Burgundian court in the late fourteenth and early fifteenth centuries, see Wright, *Music at the Court of Burgundy*; the reign of Philip the Good has likewise been thoroughly covered by the French scholar Jeanne Marix, *Histoire de la musique de la cour de Bourgogne* (Strasbourg: Heitz, 1939; reprint, Geneva: Minkoff, 1972). For a succinct account, see Wright, "Burgundy," *The New Grove Dictionary of Music*, 3:465–66.

THE CHANSON AT THE TURN OF THE FIFTEENTH CENTURY

Of all the musical genres associated with courtly life in the late Middle Ages, perhaps none is so prototypical as the polyphonic chanson, and by the second decade of the fifteenth century, it was solidly rooted in tradition with well-established social and stylistic conventions for both the verse and the music. Those conventions must have been forged in large measure by Guillaume de Machaut (ca. 1300–77), if one can judge from the large number of manuscripts containing his music, both those given over entirely to his works and anthologies in which his pieces were included.[14] The point of departure for such a composition was a poetic text dealing, for the most part, with the traditional themes of courtly eros, cast almost without exception in one of the—by then—equally traditional fixed forms. Both the topics and the formal principles embodied in the verse had their origins in the vernacular poetry of the troubadours and trouvères, cultivated in courtly society from the twelfth century on. Not surprisingly, then, the polyphonic chanson had its beginnings as a courtly genre with verse written by lettered aristocrats (or members of their household with literary training) and set to music by composers in their employ.

Those musicians were not necessarily of aristocratic stock—quite to the contrary—and, as has been noted, were usually trained in the schools of cathedrals and collegiate churches rather than at court. Although such institutions often had close affiliations with local lords, they were invariably located in the larger centers of population whose inhabitants were increasingly educated and inexorably drawn, in the fifteenth and sixteenth centuries, to the literary and musical recreations of the aristocracy. As the age of the Renaissance began to unfold, urban culture became an ever more significant force in the development of the arts generally, and it had a decided impact on the polyphonic chanson as well. It prompted, for example, the treatment of topics that reflect in a more realistic manner the circumstances of the city dweller and the adoption for their expression of a more appropriately popular diction.

THE FORMES FIXES

Formal structures for the polyphonic chanson were regulated from the outset, for both text and music, by the fixed poetic forms, usually as codified during the fourteenth century (in good measure by Machaut himself), in particular the ballade, the rondeau, and the virelai. Each of these formal types had its own historical development, and there was some differentiation as well within the individual categories—

---

14. Concerning Machaut and the polyphonic chanson of the fourteenth century, see Richard Hoppin, *Medieval Music* (New York: Norton, 1978), 421–32, and Gilbert Reaney, "Machaut," *The New Grove Dictionary of Music*, 11:428–36.

for example, in the length of the lines, the number of verses to the refrain, the number of stanzas written, and other such details. However, departures from the fixed forms themselves continued to be rare until late in the fifteenth century, when a number of subgenres emerge and other—nonetheless related—types of formal order begin to be employed.

Of the three fixed forms, the first to be seriously cultivated in polyphonic composition (and also the first to be abandoned) was the ballade. A venerable poetic tradition lay behind it, and it gained considerable prestige during the fourteenth century through substitution for the isorhythmic motet as an occasional, celebratory composition. Even after the ballade begins to disappear from the polyphonic sources in the 1420s and 1430s, its versification is usually in accordance with long-established conventions. The decasyllabic line with a caesura after the fourth syllable prevails, although not exclusively; octosyllables and heptasyllables are also found. The rhymes of the first pair of lines, which often alternate between feminine and masculine, are repeated by the second pair: comparing the anonymous late fourteenth-century *Medée fu*[15] with Du Fay's *Resvelliés vous et faites chiere lye* (see Example 7-1), line length (decasyllables with a heptasyllable after the opening quatrain) and rhyme scheme are identical (e.g., a'b, a'b).[16] The second pair of lines is sung to a repetition of the initial section of music, and the remainder of the strophe is set to the second. It is usually linked to the opening quatrain by repeating its final rhyme and concludes, as a rule, with another four lines that introduce a new pair of rhymes (e.g., c'c'd D in *Medeé fu* where the linking rhyme is missing, and bc'd'c'D' in the Du Fay). When there are at least two strophes—as is most often the case—the concluding verse recurs, serving as a refrain.

Another of the fixed forms, the virelai, was still primarily a monophonic genre in the time of Machaut, who was one of the first to begin setting it polyphonically, and it was still relatively rare among the chansons of Binchoys and Du Fay. Only with the next generation did the polyphonic virelai regain relative currency, thanks especially to Busnoys and Okeghem, and in the sources of the second half of the century it came to constitute about a sixth of the known chanson repertory. In Machaut's codification of the poetic form, the virelai always had three complete stanzas, but that pattern was rarely used by others even in his own time. In the fifteenth century the form virtually never included more than a single set of strophes—a format sometimes identified with the *bergerette*, as described (rather vaguely) by Pierre Fabri and other fifteenth-century theorists of the "second rhetoric."[17]

Like the rondeau, to which it is clearly related in its versification (see below), the

---

15. For a transcription, see Richard Hoppin, ed., *Anthology of Medieval Music* (New York: Norton, 1978), 165–68, no. 68.

16. Following common convention, the letters used to represent rhyme schemes are capitalized for refrains and marked with an apostrophe when the rhymes are feminine; clearly, the opposite combination of masculine and feminine rhymes is also possible (e.g., ab', ab'), as are rhymes either uniformly feminine or masculine.

17. See Robert W. Linker and Gwynn S. McPeek, "The Bergerette Form in the Laborde Chansonnier: A Musico-Literary Study," *Journal of the American Musicological Society* 7 (1954): 113–20.

EXAMPLE 7-1. Guillaume Du Fay, *Resvelliés vous et faites chiere lye*

Awake and rejoice, every lover who loves nobleness; Take your pleasure, flee melancholy, and be not weary of serving well, For today will be the wedding with great
honor and noble sovereignty. Thus is it fitting for each one to celebrate to swell
the fair throng: Noble Charles, known as Malatesta. (One additional strophe.)

virelai opens with a refrain, usually of four or five lines linked by a pair of rhymes,
either feminine, masculine, or alternating between the two. Two of those possibilities are seen in another pair of works that bridge the turn of the century, Jacob
Senleches's *La harpe de melodie*[18] and Busnoys's *A une damme j'ay fait veu* (see
Example 7-2). The latter has a straightforward four-line refrain in octosyllables—the
most common line length for the virelai—all of them masculine (rhyming ABBA),
whereas the verses set by Senleche alternate feminine and masculine rhymes and
interpolate lines of three and four syllables among the prevailing heptasyllables (e.g.,
A'A'B[3] B A'[4] B). A poem treated in this manner is described in contemporaneous treatises on versification as *layé*, presumably because verses of unequal length
recalled the medieval *lai*. Its use in this instance suggests a certain freedom with the
facture of the verse, which is more frequent among virelais than among the other
fixed forms.

The virelai differs significantly from the rondeau, however, in its second structural element, a pair of short stanzas, often designated *ouvert* and *clos*, usually consisting of two (as in *A une damme*) or three lines each (as in *La harpe de melodie*) and
introducing new rhymes (i.e., c'd-c'd and c c d[4] respectively, with the *layé* interpolation also used in these short strophes of the latter piece). The formal distinction
is musical as well as poetic; the paired stanzas are sung to a second section of music
that is repeated with the rhymes of the verse, frequently with different endings that
correspond to the syntactically "open" and "closed" segments of the poem. This is

18. For a transcription, see Hoppin, *Anthology of Medieval Music*, 169–71, no. 69.

EXAMPLE 7-2. Antoine Busnoys, *A une damme j'ay fait veu*

1, 5. A   u - ne dam - me j'ay ___ fait ___
4. Car   au fort quant ___ il se - ra

Tenor: A une damme j'ay fair veu

Contra-tenor: A une damme j'ay fair veu

veu   Pour ___ le grant bruit ___ de ___ sa va - -
sceu   Que ___ d'el - le soy - - - e ser - vi - -

leur   Que je ne por - te - ray cou - - - - - leur ___
teur   Onc - ques ne m'a - vint ___ tel hon - - - - neur ___

___   Se   ce n'est le jau - - - - - - ne et le ___ bleu.
___   Sans   sail - lir l'es - cu ___ tant soit ___ peu.

To a lady I've made a vow, because of the great acclaim of her reputation, that I'll wear no color except yellow or blue. These two together, without change, I shall maintain for her beauty; one as a sign of discretion, the other to show my loyalty. For in fact, when it shall be known that I am her servant, never shall I have received so great an honor without sullying the escutcheon the slightest bit. To a lady I've made a vow, etc.

followed by a return to the refrain section of music, first for a long strophe having the same line lengths and rhyme scheme as the refrain itself, then (as a rule) for a full repetition of the refrain, both text and music.

By the 1420s the rondeau was already well on its way to becoming the most widely cultivated fixed form for polyphonic composition, and its formal design is also the most regular. It consists of a refrain, generally either of four lines (the *rondeau quatrain*) or of five (the *rondeau cinquain*), and both of these formats represent an amplification of the form by comparison with the three-line refrains of Machaut's *rondeau double*.[19] The verses of the refrain are always linked by a pair of rhymes, at times all feminine (as in Busnoys's *A qui vens tu tes coquilles*, A'B'B'A') or masculine (as in Caron's *Accueilly m'a la belle*, AABBA), but more commonly in a combination of the two (e.g., A'BBA', as in Hayne's *De tous biens plaine* (see Example 7-3).[20] A

19. See, for example, his *Se vous n'estes pour mon guerredon nee* in Hoppin, *Anthology of Medieval Music*, 143–45, no. 63.
20. Transcriptions of all three are found in Leeman L. Perkins and Howard Garey, eds., *The Mellon Chansonnier*, 2 vols. (New Haven: Yale University Press, 1979), 1:58–59 (no. 10), 1:42–43 (no. 3), 1:120–21 (no. 32) respectively; Examples 7-2 and 7-3 are taken from this edition.

short stanza based on the rhymes of the first two lines (in a *rondeau quatrain*) or three lines (in a *rondeau cinquain*) is then sung to the initial section of the musical setting, followed by a repetition of the corresponding lines of the refrain. A long

EXAMPLE 7-3. Hayne van Ghizeghem, *De tous biens plaine*

que ja - mais fu dé - es - - - - - - - - - - - se.
mot por - te - ray sans ces - - - - - - - - - - se:

> With every good is my mistress filled; everyone owes her honorable tribute for she is as accomplished in virtue as was ever any goddess. Seeing her I have such pleasure that it is paradise in my heart. With every good . . . I care not for another reward except to be her servant, and because there is nothing better, I will always have as my motto: With every good . . .

stanza modeled on the complete refrain is then sung to the complete musical setting, and the formal design is completed, presumably, by a full repetition of the refrain itself.[21] It has been suggested that the refrain repetitions were at times only partial, mirroring the *rentrement* (an abbreviated refrain) found in the literary sources from the second half of the century,[22] but in the majority of cases such a truncation cannot be achieved without considerable adjustment to the musical setting given for the poem.

There were some departures from the constraints of these fixed poetic—and musical—forms in the course of the fifteenth century, but most of them can be explained by the development of particular subgenres and a degree of hybridization involving other important compositional types (see pp. 298–308). Nonetheless, they held for the vast majority of polyphonic chansons written in the fifteenth century.

PERFORMING TRADITIONS

The chanson was meant to be heard in relatively intimate circumstances, in the chambers of the noble (and with increasing frequency the wealthy as well) where music making also included playing upon the "bas instruments"—those of soft sound, such as harps, lutes, flutes, and keyboards. It was an essential part of the recreation and entertainment of aristocratic society and accompanied their dancing as well.[23] In the

21. The full pattern, if realized in this manner, would be—taking Hayne's *De tous biens plaine* as an example—A'BBA'; a'b; A'B; a'bba'; A'BBA'.

22. The suggestion was first put forward by Howard Garey, "The Variable Structure of the Fifteenth-Century Rondeau," in *The Sixth Lacus Forum* (Columbia, S.C.: Hornbeam Press, 1979), 494–501, and "Can a Rondeau with a One-line Refrain Be Sung?" *Ars lyrica* 2 (1983): 9–21; see also Howard M. Brown, "A Rondeau with a One-line Refrain Can Be Sung," *Ars lyrica* 3 (1986): 23–35.

23. See Christopher Page, "The Performance of Songs in Late Medieval France: A New Source," *Early Music* 10 (1982): 441–50, who cites numerous passages in the fifteenth-century French romance *Cleriadus et Meliadice*, in which the assembled company "danserent aux chanchons" (447).

FIGURE 7-9. *Garden of Love,* miniature illustrating the *Roman de la Rose,* ca. 1490; note the three people singing a song to the accompaniment of a lute in the center of the picture. (London, British Library, MS Harley 4425, f. 12ᵛ.)

course of the fourteenth century polyphonic compositions apparently came to replace with ever greater frequency the monophonic songs that had similarly served for centuries. That such was the course of events is suggested by the history of the virelai, which had a long, traditional association with courtly dancing. It continued to be written for a single voice until very late in the 1300s, even by Machaut himself; only with the composers of the next generation was the virelai routinely set as a polyphonic piece.

Judging both from the layout of polyphonic chansons in the manuscripts of the period and from the contrapuntal relationships among the parts, the genre appears to have been conceived from the outset as accompanied solo song (see Figure 7-9). The dominant part is nearly always the highest voice, often called the cantus. It is the only one, in most cases, with the text copied directly under the music in the sources and clearly intended to be sung, even when the declamation of syllables was set off by considerable melismatic embellishment (as it very often was). One or more additional parts accompany the cantus, usually identified in the sources as tenor and, when a third part is present, contratenor. These are usually less graceful than the cantus melodically, less active rhythmically, and were apparently meant for instrumental performance. Not until the closing decades of the fifteenth century, when the fixed poetic forms were at last beginning to give way to more varied and flexible structures, did the genre evolve decidedly toward a wholly vocal compositional conception.

That stylistic trend, and the performance conventions that accompanied it, may have been encouraged to a degree by polyphonic chansons that were also polytextual. Pieces of the kind, which are found already among the works of Machaut, clearly reflect the compositional procedures associated with the motet. Not surprisingly, the earliest examples occur among the polyphonic ballades, whose perceived affinity with the more venerable genre is also evident from its adaptation now and again in the fourteenth and fifteenth centuries as a substitute for an isorhythmic motet with festal or occasional functions. That the motet continued to provide a compositional model for composers working through the turn of the century is suggested by the polytextual chansons attributable to them. Three of the seven chansons ascribed to Johannes Cesaris (fl. ca. 1385–1420)—one of the three masters mentioned by Martin le Franc as having astounded all Paris with their music (see p. 221)—were also bitextual: *Pour la douleur/Qui dolente*, à 2, and *Se par plour/Se par plour* and *Mon seul voloir/Certes m'amour*, both à 3.[24]

In fact, the cultivation of the polytextual chanson persisted continuously in one form or another throughout the fifteenth century and beyond. With the composers of the next generation one of the best known and most widely traveled, Guillaume Du Fay (ca. 1400–74), contributed to this specialized repertory with his triple chanson à 3: *Je vous pri/Ma tres douce amie/Tant que mon argent dura*.[25] This work, with its bits of dialogue, is one tantalizing indication among many that the chanson also found a place in some of the dramatic literary genres being developed at the time. (Unfortunately, such hints have for the most part proven difficult to trace and to document.)[26]

Another factor contributing to a more wholly vocal (that is, declamatory) conception of the chanson—and further evidence still of a tenacious link between the Latin and secular genres of the fourteenth century—is the emergence of the motet-chanson, a hybrid subgenre in which a secular text sung by the cantus in a treble register was combined with a tenor carrying its own Latin text and one or two contratenors, perhaps meant for instruments. Two parts fairly equally matched in an upper register—perhaps even in strict imitation one with another—may also point to the motet as a model, even when they carry the same text.

When the imitative writing is sustained, however, the determining influence may have been instead the secular polyphony of trecento Italy, either the *caccia* (having two texted voices in strict imitation over a slow-moving tenor) or an imitative madrigal, which may also owe its contrapuntal style to the *caccia*.[27] Northern musicians who worked in Italy were especially inclined to adopt the format, as may be seen from a number of chansons in the MS Canonici Misc. 213, which was compiled in or near Venice. Some of these are attributed to Guillaume Du Fay, who also set several Italian texts in this manner, as for example his *Quel fronte signorille*.[28] Familiarity

24. For transcriptions, see Gilbert Reaney, ed., *Polyphonic Music of the Early Fifteenth Century*, 7 vols., Corpus mensurabilis musicae 11 (Rome: American Institute of Musicology, 1955), 1:19–20, 22–26, nos. 1, 4, and 5.

25. For a transcription, see Du Fay, *Opera omnia*, ed. Besseler, 6:45.

26. A noteworthy exception to this generalization is the informative study by Howard M. Brown, *Music in the French Secular Theater of the Fifteenth Century* (Cambridge, Mass.: Harvard University Press, 1963).

27. See Hoppin, *Medieval Music*, 443–44, 450, and 457–58.

28. For a transcription, see Du Fay, *Opera omnia*, ed. Besseler, 6:11. Essentially the same music was also used for a French text, *Craindre vous vueil*, and a pair of Latin contrafacts, *Bone pastor, panis vere* and *Regina celi letare*; see Charles Hamm, "Dufay," *The New Grove Dictionary of Music*, 5:682–84.

with Italian models may therefore help to account as well for chansons such as *Entre vous, gentils amoureux*[29] in which cantus and tenor are both fully texted and in strict imitation at the fifth.

Despite the patterns described, suggesting that voices and instruments were frequently mingled in the performance of the chanson repertory, there are those who claim—and not without supporting grounds—that instrumental and vocal music were most often kept separate and that all (two or three) parts of the chanson were usually performed by voices alone.[30] This view has not gone unchallenged; one scholar has in fact gone so far as to refer to it as the "new secular *a cappella* heresy."[31] The pertinent evidence is multifarious and sometimes conflicting. It includes the art and literature of the period, in which music making is often depicted, as well as archival notices, the disposition of the sources, and matters of musical style. It seems likely that performing practices were often tied to local usage and were dependent to a degree on the availability of competent performers. It is possible, as well, that a firm distinction between voices and instruments was not so clearly maintained in the medieval mind as it tends to be at present. Voices may have been treated as instruments—used in performance with solmization or nonsense syllables rather than a declaimed text—and instruments substituted for voices much more freely than has been imagined. It is already clear, in any case, that the debate will be a lengthy one.[32]

THE CHANSON IN THE TIME OF THE VALOIS KINGS AND DUKES

From the 1420s on the composers who contributed most significantly to the growing repertory of secular music on French texts were in the service of one of the Valois lords who reigned at the time either in the kingdom of France or in the duchy of Burgundy, suggesting that the patronage of their respective courts played a crucial role in the ongoing cultivation of the chanson and its codification as a musical genre throughout this important period in its history. This seems to have been the case, in particular, during the relatively long reigns of Charles VII (1422–61) and Louis XI (1461–83) as king of France and those of Philip the Good (1419–67) and Charles the Bold (1467–77) as duke of Burgundy.

It is surprising in fact how many of the musicians named in the chanson sources

29. For a transcription, see Du Fay, *Opera omnia*, ed. Besseler, 6:49.

30. The main proponent of this view, in both his performing and his scholarship, has been Christopher Page; see, for example, his study "Performance of Songs in Late Medieval France," 441–50.

31. See Howard M. Brown's review of *The Castle of Fair Welcome*, a recording of late fifteenth-century vocal music by Page and his Gothic Voices, in *Early Music* 15 (1987): 277–79; see also his more extended (but earlier) study, "Instruments and Voices in the Fifteenth-Century Chanson," in *Current Thought in Musicology*, ed. John W. Grubbs (Austin: University of Texas Press, 1976), 89–137.

32. For example, Dennis Slavin has come to the defense of proponents of all-vocal performance of chansons on the basis of his study of the sources, "In Support of 'Heresy': Manuscript Evidence for the *a cappella* Performance of Early Fifteenth-Century Songs," *Early Music* 19 (1991):179–190.

of the period were at some time on the payrolls of one or another of these rulers or linked with them in some significant way.[33] In the French kingdom the dominant figure was undoubtedly Johannes Okeghem (ca. 1410–97), who served three French monarchs as the musical director of the royal chapel (see Figure 7-10). At the court of Burgundy the major masters of the genre included Gilles Binchoys (ca. 1400–60), Antoine Busnoys (ca. 1430–92), and Hayne van Ghizeghem (ca. 1445–97), whose *De tous biens plaine* became one of the most widely circulated chansons of the age.[34]

The more peripatetic Guillaume Du Fay (ca. 1400–74) also seems to have had relations with the Burgundian court, due primarily to his long residence in Cambrai as a canon of the cathedral. Aside from his years with the papal chapel in the late 1420s and 1430s, his only documented courtly service was with Malatesta of Pesaro early in the 1420s and in the duchy of Savoy in the 1450s. It is undoubtedly significant that the poetry of a number of his chansons reflects the urban culture of a city such as Cambrai, with which he had a life-long association, more than princely patronage.[35]

FIGURE 7-10. Jean de Okeghem (presumably the distinguished older man with glasses) in the midst of a choir singing a plainchant Gloria, a miniature illustrating a *chant royal* in the composer's honor (1523), part of a collection from the Puy de la Conception de Rouen (Paris, Bibliothèque Nationale, MS f. fr. 1537, f. 58ᵛ).

THE SOURCES: FIFTEENTH-CENTURY CHANSONNIERS

Given that the chanson was essentially a manifestation of French culture, it is again astonishing—as with the transmission of the English music of the early decades of the fifteenth century—that so many of the manuscript sources (and later the printed ones) for the fifteenth-century repertory are of Italian provenance. These include,

33. See Frank Dobbins, "Valois," *The New Grove Dictionary of Music*, 19:508–9.

34. It was included in at least twenty-three separate manuscript sources from both sides of the Alps; see Figure 5-10.

35. For relevant details regarding Du Fay's life and work, see David Fallows, *Dufay* (London: J. M. Dent, 1982), especially 18–85 and 86–102.

interestingly enough, some of the same codices that contain the works of English composers in significant numbers: collections such as MS 2216 of the Biblioteca Universitaria and MS Q15 of the Civico Museo Bibliografico Musicale, both in Bologna, and the six "Trent Codices." In addition, the earliest collection in which the chansons of Binchoys, Du Fay, and the composers of their generation are found in considerable quantity, MS Canonici Miscellany 213 of the Bodleian Library in Oxford, is also of Italian origin. It was probably compiled in Venice (or nearby in the Veneto), mainly between 1422 and 1428, but its primary contents are some 235 settings of French verse (as compared to 24 Italian pieces, 38 Latin motets, 6 *laude*, and a smattering of settings for the Ordinary of the Mass).[36]

The earliest northern chanson collection containing a substantial number of works attributable to Binchoys and Du Fay (among sixty-two pieces overall), MS V.III.24 of the Escorial Library, is somewhat later, having been inscribed circa 1430–45. It is, significantly, the only important source from the first half of the century whose origins are traceable directly to the region between Dijon and Bruges that was ruled at the time by the dukes of Burgundy.[37] Ironically, it is in fact possible—as a brief survey of some of the most representative manuscripts will show—that this manuscript is the only sizable chansonnier that can be confidently described as geographically Burgundian. The central chanson sources of northern origins from the second half of the century, all of which are related in both appearance and content, were probably compiled without exception in regions ruled by the Valois kings of France rather than by their cousins, the dukes of Burgundy.

The crucial evidence regarding the provenance of this family of manuscripts is a collection of fifty-four chansons (together with an incomplete motet and one Italian piece), MS 287 of the ducal library in Wolfenbüttel, which was copied in the 1460s and decorated somewhere in the Loire Valley—Nantes, Angers, or Bourges being the most likely localities.[38] Moreover, the codex can be linked directly to the French court by means of a dedication, in the form of an acrostic, to Estienne Petit, probably the younger of two royal officers of that name (father and son), who was named in 1467 to replace his father as "secretaire et notaire du roy."[39]

Three other manuscripts, once thought to have come from territories under

---

36. For a discussion of the manuscript in English, see Gilbert Reaney, "The Manuscript Oxford, Bodleian Library, Canonici Misc. 213," *Musica disciplina* 9 (1955): 73–104.

37. See the *Census-Catalogue of Manuscript Sources of Polyphonic Music, 1400–1550*, ed. Charles Hamm and Herbert Kellman, 5 vols. (Neuhausen-Stuttgart: American Institute of Musicology, 1979–88), 1:212.

38. There is a complete edition of the manuscript prepared by Martella Gutiérrez-Denhoff, ed., *Der Wolfenbütteler Chansonnier, Wolfenbüttel, Herzog August Bibliothek, Codex Guelf. 287 Extrav.*, Musikalische Denkmäler, vol. 10 (Mainz: B. Schotts Söhne, 1988); cf. also her earlier study, *Der Wolfenbütteler Chansonnier, Wolfenbüttel, Herzog August Bibliothek, Codex Guelf. 287 Extrav.: Untersuchungen zu Repertoire und Ueberlieferung einer Musikhandschrift des 15. Jahrhunderts und ihres Umkreises*, Wolfenbütteler Forschungen, vol. 29 (Wiesbaden: Otto Harrassowitz, 1958).

39. The connection was discovered by David Fallows, who has discussed its implications in a reassessment of Busnoys's career, "'Trained and Immersed in All Musical Delights': Towards a New Picture of Busnoys," in *Continuities and Transformations in Musical Culture, 1450–1500: Assessing the Legacy of Antoine Busnoys* (Oxford: Oxford University Press, 1998.

Burgundian sway, are interrelated, not only by concordances among their respective repertories but also by the presence in all of them of a single distinctive notational hand. The smallest of the group, MS Thott 291 of the Royal Library in Copenhagen, numbers only thirty-four songs.[40] Although dating from the 1480s, about a decade later than the "Wolfenbüttel Chansonnier," its decoration is strikingly similar, suggesting that it, too, was copied and illuminated in one of the urban centers of the Loire Valley.

Since the same scribal hand is found in all three codices, this implies in turn the same provenance for the other two members of the family.[41] Compilation of the earlier of the remaining two, the "Laborde Chansonnier," MS M2.1.L25 at the Library of Congress, was likely begun early in the 1460s, but a number of its 102 chansons (to which were added a pair of motets and two Italian pieces) were copied considerably later, some apparently during the decades just before and after the turn of the fifteenth century.[42] The largest collection of the group, MS 517 of the Municipal Library in Dijon, containing 160 compositions, was apparently inscribed and decorated in the same general region as Wolfenbüttel and Laborde early in the 1470s.[43]

One other collection, the "Chansonnier Nivelle de la Chaussée" (MS Rés. Vmc 57 of the Department of Music at the National Library in Paris), dating from the late 1460s and early 1470s, is related to the four of the manuscript family just described only through concordances, but it, too, was decorated by artisans working in the Loire Valley.[44] Its repertory consisted originally of sixty-three chansons, some of which have been partially erased, and was probably copied in the late 1460s and early 1470s.[45]

Although the repertory of polyphonic French song carried by these northern manuscripts is very substantial and comprehensive of all the subgenres cultivated during the fifteenth century, manuscripts of Italian provenance are at least as important to the history of the chanson of the period as the French chansonniers. The surprising number of Italian manuscripts given over almost entirely to French song forms is in fact perhaps the best indication of the extent to which northern musicians dominated the chapels of major Italian courts from the 1460s on.

---

40. See the *Census-Catalogue of Manuscript Sources*, 1:162–63. For an edition in modern score, see Knud Jeppesen, ed., *Der Kopenhagener Chansonnier* (Copenhagen, 1927; reprint, New York: Da Capo Press, 1965).

41. These are the conclusions drawn by Jeppesen, ed., *Der Kopenhagener Chansonnier*, xxv–xxvi, who believed, however, that all four manuscripts were Burgundian in origin.

42. See the *Census-Catalogue of Manuscript Sources*, 4:125–26.

43. See the *Census-Catalogue of Manuscript Sources*, 1:168–69; for a facsimile reproduction, see Dragan Plamenac, ed., *Dijon Bibliothèque Publique Manuscrit 517*, Publications of Mediaeval Musical Manuscripts, no. 12 (Brooklyn: Institute of Medieval Music, n.d.).

44. Concerning the limitations inherent in statistical methods of relating manuscripts to one another solely on the basis of shared repertory, see Leeman L. Perkins, "Modern Methods, Received Opinion, and the Chansonnier: Review of *Der Wolfenbütteler Chansonnier, Wolfenbüttel, Herzog August Bibliothek, Codex Guelf. 287 Extrav.*, by Martella Guttiérez-Denhoff," *Music and Letters* 69 (1988): 356–64.

45. See the *Census-Catalogue of Manuscript Sources*, 3:12; for an edition in facsimile, see Paula Higgins, ed., *Chansonnier Nivelle de la Chaussée*, Bibliothèque Nationale, Paris, Res. Vmc. ms. 57, ca. 1460 (Geneva: Minkoff, 1984).

The general trend is well illustrated by a trio of important chansonniers, all of which were copied on the peninsula during this time. The earliest of the three, MS 91 in Yale's Beinecke Library, was compiled in the kingdom of Naples, probably in the mid 1470s and perhaps under the supervision of the famed theorist (and sometime composer) Johannes Tinctoris (ca. 1435–1511?). Its repertory comprises forty-seven chansons (together with two devotional motets in Latin, four pieces with Italian texts, three on English poems, and one in Spanish).[46]

Early in the 1480s another large collection was compiled, this time in Florence, the "Pixérécourt Chansonnier" (MS français 15123 at the National Library in Paris), with 143 chansons (and again 2 devotional motets, 20 pieces on poems in Italian, 3 in Spanish, and 1 in Dutch).[47] Soon after, in the first years of the 1490s, work was begun in Florence on a second manuscript, now MS *Banco rari* 229 of the National Library in Florence—perhaps initially on commission for King Mathias Corvin of Hungary (who died before the manuscript was completed). It is an exceptionally extensive collection, bringing together 163 chansons (accompanied here, too, by a pair of devotional motets and by 15 pieces based on Italian verse, 1 on Flemish, and 86 with no text at all).[48]

A third Florentine collection, also dating from the early 1490s, MS Cappella Giulia XIII 27 of the Vatican Library, reflects the musical patronage and the francophile tastes of the Medici, who played a considerable role in the introduction of repertories (both secular and sacred) of northern musicians into courtly circles of the Italian peninsula. It comprises eighty-three chansons (together with a section of the Mass Ordinary, two motets, as many motet-chansons, and secular pieces on other vernacular texts: Italian [ten]; Spanish [nine]; and Dutch [two]).[49]

The popularity of the chanson in Italy culminated at the turn of the century in the largely retrospective publication by the Venetian printer, Ottaviano de' Petrucci, of the great three-volume collection of French secular music, the *Odhecaton A*, *Canti B*, and *Canti C*, comprising a total of some 300 compositions.[50] By then,

---

46. For an edition in facsimile with modern score, see Perkins and Garey, eds., *Mellon Chansonnier*; concerning Tinctoris, cf. ibid., 1:17–26, and Ronald Woodley, "Johannes Tinctoris: A Review of the Documentary Biographical Evidence," *Journal of the American Musicological Society* 34 (1981): 217–48.

47. See the *Census-Catalogue of Manuscript Sources*, 3:23–24.

48. See Howard Mayer Brown, ed., *A Florentine Chansonnier from the Time of Lorenzo the Magnificent*, 2 vols., Monuments of Renaissance Music, vol. 7 (Chicago: University of Chicago Press, 1983); concerning the possibility that the manuscript was originally destined for the Hungarian monarch, cf. ibid., 1:12–13.

49. See the edition of this manuscript by Allan Atlas, ed., *The Cappella Giulia Chansonnier*, 2 vols., Musicological Studies, vol. 27 (Brooklyn: Institute of Medieval Music, 1975–76). Concerning other sources for the French secular music of the time, from both sides of the Alps, see Atlas's classification of the relevant manuscripts by regional family, 1:233–58, and the lists of concordant sources in the editions previously noted.

50. For modern editions of the first two, see Helen Hewitt and Isabel Pope, eds., *Harmonice musices Odhecaton A* (Cambridge, Mass.: Medieval Academy of America, 1942; reprint, New York: Da Capo Press, 1978); and Helen Hewitt, ed., *Ottaviano Petrucci, Canti B numero cinquanta*, Monuments of Renaissance Music, vol. 2 (Chicago: University of Chicago Press, 1967).

however, the chanson was undergoing a stylistic revision of considerable significance that was transforming irreversibly the genre as it had been known at the courts of the Valois, bringing to it new compositional procedures and modes of performance.

POETIC THEMES

All through the fifteenth century the predominant themes for the lyrical verse in the fixed forms cultivated at court were drawn from the erotic traditions of *fin'amors*, much as they had been celebrated centuries earlier by the *trouvères*. Poetry of this kind, with or without a musical setting, had a long and vigorous development in aristocratic society. It was particularly appropriate for the relatively intimate circumstances of the courtly chamber, where the finely regulated subtleties of the complicated sexual relationships among the high-born—matters with which the authors deal in formalized literary fashion—were often debated. They were less likely to be heard in the great halls, where ceremonial encounters took place and matters of state were handled, but were performed on occasion there as well.

Perhaps the most notorious example is the celebrated Banquet of the Pheasant, staged by Philip the Good of Burgundy in 1454 for the knights of the Order of the Golden Fleece as part of the festivities marking their oath to undertake a new crusade to free the Holy Land. The detailed written accounts of those events, commissioned by the duke himself, mention repeatedly the music heard in the course of the evening. The pieces cited cover the entire spectrum from the sacred to the instrumental and include a number of chansons, some of which are specifically identified.[51]

Moreover, as the famous painting *The Hunt of Philip the Good* shows, the singing of chansons could also accompany activities out-of-doors. Not only did the artist depict a trio of "loud" instruments (a sackbut and two shawms in the left background), whose presence was to be expected, but also a singer (to the right), open-mouthed and holding a sheet of mensural notation that can only be a (monophonic?) song (see Figure 3-9).

Perhaps the most common of all the topics to be treated repeatedly by poets of the courtly tradition is what might be called the *complainte amoureuse*, which usually expresses the anguish felt by the male lover whose passion for his chosen lady is unrequited or the sorrow caused by a forced separation from the object of his affection. Closely related to the *complainte* are the *louange*, in which the poet praises extravagantly his lady love, detailing her qualities, both moral and physical, and the *serment*, in which he declares himself to be her loyal vassal, regardless of how he is or ever will be treated.

References to the classical thirteenth-century idealization of "courtly love," as found in the *Roman de la Rose* (by Guillaume de Lorris and Jean de Meung), often

---

51. The references to music in the various chronicles that describe the events of the banquet in considerable detail have been summarized by Marix, *Histoire de la musique de la cour de Bourgogne*, 37–43.

figure in these poems, either in the form of such personifications as Bel Acueil, Bien Amer, Esperance, Ennuy, Pitié, Mercie, Courtoysie, and, of course, Dame Fortune, or in the military imagery used to describe the campaign of the lover as he attempts to overcome all defenses raised against his suit. In such contexts the voice of the poet is usually masculine, either overtly or implicitly, but the feminine voice is heard as well. Busnoys's *Ung plus que tous* can be understood as the lady's reply to her lover's *serment*, in which she promises her "servant" the best "terms" possible, and Binchoys's unusual *rondeau sixain*, *Comme femme desconfortee*, is simply a *complainte amoureuse* from a woman's point of view.[52]

Characteristic of such works in most respects, at least for the first half of the century, is *Dueil angoisseus*, one of the many chansons attributable to Binchoys that was inscribed in the MS V.III.24 at the Escorial Library (see Example 7-4). The text by Christine de Pizan may actually be a personal expression of grief, prompted by the premature death of her husband at 34, followed soon after by the death of the youngest of her three children.[53] Still, it takes the form of a conventional plaint, albeit one of unusual intensity, and gives eloquent voice to a passion perceived as both unrequited and hopeless. It is cast in the most traditional of the fixed forms, that of the ballade (of which only one strophe is now known).[54] By the time the work was entered in this important source, however, the ballade was near the end of its history as a lyric form for polyphonic composition. Although it reigned supreme in the fourteenth century—even assuming, as noted, ceremonial functions of the sort earlier reserved to the Latin motet—it began to give way in the early decades of the fifteenth to the rondeau, which became in turn the fixed form most commonly adopted for compositional elaboration.

Musically, too, the piece is fairly typical for the time. The texture is dominated by the treble voice (the only one, as well, to bear the text in the manuscript) while the tenor and—to a lesser extent—the contratenor move at a more deliberate pace. The melodic style, then, is that of accompanied solo song of the sort that had already come to the fore in the secular music of the previous century, and it may have been performed by a single voice supported by a pair of "soft" instruments such as harp, lute, fiddle, or flute (see the discussion of performance practices on pp. 281–84).

The verse is declaimed for the most part syllabically, line by line, each time with an articulation (by rest or cadential formula) to mark its close and often a lesser one as well for the caesura in the line. The formal structure of the poetry, and its syntax too, are further thrown into relief by the melismatic extension of the first phrase—

---

52. Transcriptions of both pieces are found in Perkins and Garey, eds., *Mellon Chansonnier*, 1:54–55 (no. 8) and 1:100–101 (no. 27), respectively.

53. See Françoise Du Chatel, *Damoiselle Christine de Pizan, veuve de Me. Etienne de Castel, 1364–1431* (Paris: Picard, 1972), 35–38.

54. The poem is in decasyllables with the conventional caesura after the fourth syllable, rhyming a′b, a′b, b c b c; the first four lines are sung to the first section of music, repeated with *ouvert* and *clos* endings, the last four to the second section, and an extensive "musical rhyme," sung melismatically, links the end of the piece to the *clos* ending (mm. 13–21 = 45–53).

EXAMPLE 7-4. Gilles Binchoys, *Dueil angoisseus* (mm. 1–22)

Sorrowful anguish, immeasurable rage, grievous despair full of harsh constraint, endless languor and unhappy life full of tears, anguish, and torment. [Dolorous heart, living in darkness, shadowy body about to disappear are my lot unceasingly, continually, and thus I can neither be cured nor yet die.] (Two further stanzas.)

perhaps with pictorial intent to stress the excessive nature of the pain felt—the fourth line (the *clos* ending of the first section), and the final line of the poem with its musical repetition of the phrase for line 4.

A similar theme is treated by *M'a vostre cueur mis en oubli*, known at present from a setting ascribed to Busnoys that was included in all three manuscripts of the French family cited earlier—the Laborde, Dijon, and Wolfenbüttel chansonniers—as well as the large Florentine collection, MS *Banco rari* 229, and other Italian sources. This time the grieving lover, whose sex is left indefinite as she or he addresses not the person of the beloved but only her (his?) heart, appears to have had some encouragement before the apparent rejection that is the subject of the plaint. The fixed form, however, is now the virelai (sometimes referred to as a *bergerette* when there is only one complete stanza) rather than the ballade.[55] Although well developed already in the works of Machaut, the virelai fell into relative neglect during the opening decades of the fifteenth century. Busnoys, who is thought to have written the verse as well as the music for many of his chansons, appears to have played a role in restoring it to honor, with the result that he was even credited with its invention.

Busnoys's setting of the poem reflects (like his choice of fixed form) the changes in compositional style that marked the treatment of the genre beginning with the older masters of his own generation. The most striking of these is the introduction of "syntactic imitation" as a prominent element in the polyphonic fabric (see Example 7-5). The text continues to be declaimed—in this instance less rigorously syllabically than in *Dueil angoisseus*—line by line, each one articulated in what had become the customary manner with a rest and/or a cadential figure. In addition, important syntactic units are now presented with a point of musical imitation, starting with the opening strain and recurring with the third and fourth lines of the refrain as well as both verses of the short strophe (mm. 1, 24, 49, and 62). Most of the time the imitation involves only the two structural parts, cantus and tenor—first with the former and then the latter leading the way—but at the opening of each major section the contratenor is drawn in as well, anticipating the entries of the other two parts.

An important consequence of linking the voices imitatively is to make them more similar to one another melodically and rhythmically—if not necessarily more independent contrapuntally. The hierarchical relationship among the parts adopted earlier for accompanied solo song of this sort has given way in this composition to greater equality, and the treble voice now dominates only by its range.[56] Noteworthy, in addition, is the exuberance of the melodic writing as each verse of the poem in turn is given a considerable melismatic extension—a stylistic trait that appears most characteristically with texts in the courtly tradition.

Stylistically similar in every essential respect is *Fors seulement l'attente* in a setting

---

55. The refrain of the poem, which is in octosyllables, consists of four lines, rhyming A B B A; the *ouvert* and *clos* (the short strophes), sung to the second section of music repeated (but with only one ending), have two lines each, rhyming c'd, c'd; and the long strophe matches the rhymes of the refrain and is sung to the same music.

56. The thoroughgoing integration of cantus and tenor in particular prompted Brown to provide text for both in his edition of it, even though none of the sources for the piece gives the complete text for any part except the cantus; see Brown, ed., *Florentine Chansonnier*, 298 and 536–39.

EXAMPLE 7-5. Antoine Busnoys, *M'a vostre cueur mis en oubli* (mm. 1–7, 49–53)

Has your heart forgotten me? . . . If your tender heart rejects me . . . I shall die, and I warn you of my death. . . . From him was I accustomed to receive hope.

attributed to Okeghem that was also inscribed in all three of the directly related northern French sources cited earlier (see pp. 286–87), as well as in a Swiss-German and two Italian collections.[57] The text is once again a plaint, unconventional only in that it is in the feminine voice, but the poetic form is now the most popular and current of all, the rondeau, in this instance a *rondeau cinquain* (i.e., with a refrain of 5 lines).[58] Imitative interplay is limited here to the two upper parts, cantus and tenor, which are so similar in range and melodic ductus that there has been confusion in the sources as to which is supposed to be which. And in a later manuscript, MS

57. For a transcription, see (inter alia) Johannes Ockeghem, *Collected Works*, vol. 3, *Motets and Chansons*, ed. Richard Wexler and Dragan Plamenac (Philadelphia: American Musicological Society, 1992), 3:62–63, no. 4.

58. As was noted above (p. 279), rondeaux are distinguished by the number of lines in their refrain. *Fors seulement* is written throughout in decasyllables with a regular caesura after the fourth syllable. The refrain, rhyming A'A'B'B'A', is sung to the entire composition with its lines divided between the two sections of music three and two; the short strophe, of three lines, matches rhymes with the first three lines of the refrain and is sung to the same music (followed by a repeat of the shortened refrain), whereas the long strophe (of five lines) matches those of the complete refrain and is followed by a (complete?) repetition of it.

français 1597 in the National Library, Paris (ff. 36ᵛ–37)—a collection compiled in Paris around the turn of the sixteenth century[59]—both parts are provided with text despite the long tradition in France of writing the words only under the cantus.

Among the chansons heard in 1454 during the celebrated Banquet of the Pheasant at the court of Philip the Good are two mentioned by name: *La saulvegarde de ma vie* and *Je ne vis onques la pareille.* The former is not found in any of the sources currently known, but the latter, a *rondeau quatrain* attributed to both Binchoys and Du Fay, circulated widely and was inscribed in more than ten different collections. Its text is a traditional *louange* for a lady, whom the masculine voice of the poem declares himself ready to serve, but like many such songs, this one does not make entirely clear whether the *dame* in question is a real acquaintance of flesh and blood or a courtly idealization of the Virgin Mary.[60] It was perhaps that very ambiguity that led to the selection of the chanson for the occasion in question.

In analogous circumstances chansons figured frequently somewhat later among the entertainments prepared to welcome rulers to the cities of their realm. On the occasion of an initial visit or an important state event they often chose to make a formal entry through the principal gate and then parade through the streets, where they were greeted on every hand by banners, specially erected statues and monuments, and groups of musicians, singing and playing to honor the visiting dignitaries.

DEPARTURES FROM COURTLY DICTION

Although chansons in the courtly tradition are decidedly in the majority in the sources of the fifteenth century, the same manuscripts also contain—albeit in much smaller numbers—pieces on texts whose implications point in quite different directions. In some of these the poetry has a satirical twist, either humorously ironic or cynically caustic in its implications. In either case the effect is achieved by a kind of parody of the traditional themes, mocking both the assumptions underlying courtly eros and the stylized diction that had come to characterize its treatment.

Such a piece is *Plaindre m'estuet de ma damme jolie,* a *rondeau cinquain* ascribed in the MS Canonici Misc. 213 to Hugo de Lantins (fl. 1420–30). On the surface the poem appears to be simply an amorous plaint in the courtly tradition in which a male voice accuses his lady of faithlessness. Rather than yield to melancholy, however, suffering in adoring and hopeless silence, he vows that he will abandon her company for that of another who has caught his eye. Such a course of action is a patent betrayal of well-established literary conventions, which required the lover to serve faithfully the lady to whom he had sworn allegiance (in the feudal manner, as it were) regardless of the tests to which she might put his loyalty. A much more biting and person-

---

59. See the *Census-Catalogue of Manuscript Sources,* 3:21f; there is also a photographic facsimile of the MS that bears neither the date nor the place of publication.
60. The chanson has been edited several times; see Du Fay, *Opera omnia,* ed. Besseler, 6:109; and Wolfgang Rehm, ed., *Die Chansons von Gilles Binchois (1400–1460),* Musikalische Denkmäler, vol. 2 (Mainz: Schotts Söhne, 1957), 54, no. 57.

al comment on the failed relationship is hidden in an acrostic formed by the first letter of each verse of the poem that rudely describes the lady in question as a *putain
de merde.*

The musical setting gives no hint of these textual ironies, however. The declamation follows the gentle ternary rhythms, syllabically at first, then with a melismatic
extension of the framing phrases (the first, third, and fifth). Cantus and tenor make
their first two entries imitatively, thus making use of the compositional procedure
that, beginning with Du Fay and a few of his immediate contemporaries, transformed
the contrapuntal style of the genre during the fifteenth century. All three parts move
at essentially the same pace, leaving hardly a trace of the hierarchical relationships in
the polyphony that is still discernible in the early songs of Binchoys. The individual
lines have in fact enough melodic interest that the copyist of MS Canonici Misc. 213
did not hesitate to enter the complete refrain under the corresponding line of notation in each of them.

This unusual disposition of the text may reflect the experience of the scribe, who
had doubtless become familiar with the Italian tradition of performing secular song
as a vocal duo (usually with an instrumental tenor, however). Or the copyist may
have been following the intentions of the composer, who was himself familiar with
Italian performance practices, having spent some time along the northern Adriatic
coast in the area where the Canonici manuscript was copied, as is attested by a motet
honoring the doge of Venice and a ballata in praise of Cleofe Malatesta.[61]

Similar to *Plaindre m'estuet* in its use of a theme and diction traditional for courtly love to slyly mock its conventions is a *rondeau cinquain, Non pas que je veuille
penser,* found in the "Laborde Chansonnier" and in three Italian sources in a setting
attributed to Gilles Joye (1424 or 1425–83), who served in the Burgundian chapel
before becoming a canon at the church of St. Donatian in Bruges.[62] Although ostensibly a *serment,* in which the lover proclaims his intention to give loyal service to the
lady of his heart, each stanza concludes with a subtly ambiguous verse that reveals
the cynical self-interest lying behind the declaration.[63]

More explicitly satirical, and perhaps reflecting a slightly sardonic urban reaction to the exaggerated romanticism of the courtly conventions, is a *rondeau quatrain, A qui vens tu tes coquilles,* which was included in both the Mellon and the
Dijon chansonniers in a setting attributed to Busnoys. The poem parodies another of ironic intent, a rondeau by Charles d'Orléans in which the poet compares
false lovers to counterfeit pilgrims, those who wore shells on their hat to make
others believe that they had piously made the trek to the tomb of St. James in
Compostella, hoping to hide thereby a multitude of sins. The later author takes
the satire a step further, replacing the hypocritical lovers with an old lecher sent

61. See Hans Schoop, "Lantins, de (Hugo)," *The New Grove Dictionary of Music,* 10:457–58.
62. See David Fallows, "Joye," *The New Grove Dictionary of Music,* 9:742.
63. The short strophe, for example, declares, "To her service and honor I would dedicate myself completely, As long as I gain something by it"; for a transcription with commentary, see Perkins and Garey,
eds., *Mellon Chansonnier,* 2:234–39, no. 13.

on his way from a bawdy house because he was no longer able to perform satisfactorily.[64]

Verse of the kind just sampled, although set polyphonically in much the same style as chansons in the courtly tradition, moved further and further from conventional themes and forms of expression. It reflects instead, with increasing clarity, the practical preoccupations and earthy realism of a more plebeian urban society. Other songs in a similarly humorous vein and a decidedly more popular flavor make sport of matters that were presumably of greater concern and more immediate interest to the typical city dweller than parodies of courtly love songs. An example is a *rondeau cinquain, Ce qu'on fait a quatimini*, which was entered in the "Laborde Chansonnier" (from which it was subsequently lost) and in four manuscripts of Italian provenance, in one of which it is ascribed to Joye. It brings an amusing commentary on current religious attitudes—symbolized in a sense by the poet's macaronic mixture of French and Latin—by slyly sanctioning the use of the confessional for women inclined to take lusty advantage of opportunities for clandestine (and presumably extramarital) sexual activity without unduly burdening their conscience.[65]

Also showing, perhaps, even more urban than courtly influence are the polyphonic chansons whose texts reveal that they were intended for the celebration of commonly observed holidays and festivals. Characteristic of such pieces are those written specifically to be sung at New Year's and for May Day. A number of works of this type were included in the MS Canonici Misc. 213, several of them with an ascription to Du Fay, whose ongoing contacts with urban society were particularly important for his secular music.[66]

The text of the *rondeau cinquain Entre vous, gentils amoureux* is a formula for passing the first day of the New Year in carefree pleasure.[67] Its musical setting combines syllabic declamation of the unpretentious text, embellished by a relatively modest melismatic extension of the successive musical phrases (all except the second), with rather sophisticated contrapuntal procedures (see Example 7-6). In this instance, surprisingly, the text is presented by a vocal duo in the Italian manner rather than as accompanied solo song, possibly in emulation of the secular music of trecento Italy with which Du Fay became acquainted during his first sojourn on the peninsula; both cantus and tenor carry the words while the contratenor provides (presumably instrumental) sonorous support. More striking still is the strict imitation at the lower

64. For a transcription and commentary by Howard Garey, see Perkins and Garey, eds., *Mellon Chansonnier*, 2:223–27, no. 10.
65. For a transcription and commentary, see Perkins and Garey, eds., *Mellon Chansonnier*, 2:218–23, no. 9.
66. See Du Fay, *Opera omnia*, ed. Besseler, 6:49, 51, 57, 58, 59, and 76; for transcriptions of these same pieces using the original notation in parts, see Guillaume Du Fay, *Chansons: Forty-five Settings in Original Notation from Oxford, Bodelian Library MS Canonici 213*, ed. Ross W. Duffin, SR4 (Miami: Ogni Sorte Editions, 1983), nos. 2, 3, 8, 10, 13, and 15.
67. The poem is in octosyllables; the rhyme scheme of the refrain, A A B'B'A, is carried over in the usual way into the long and short strophes.

EXAMPLE 7-6. Guillaume Du Fay, *Entre vous, gentils amoureux*

Among yourselves, noble lovers, on this New Year's day, let each one take care to
serve well his lady love and to flee melancholy if you wish to be joyful. Be desirous
of nothing except amusements and games and to live the good life. Among yourselves, noble lovers . . . Have no care for the envious, who are vile and contemp-
tuous. Sing, dance, whatever others say, and he who cannot sing, let him laugh; I
cannot give you better advice. Among yourselves, noble lovers . . .

fifth between cantus and tenor; having no notation of its own, the latter derives its
part from that written for its *dux* by means of a learned verbal canon.[68]

Similar in every significant respect is *Je veuil chanter de cuer joyeux*, also a *rondeau
cinquain*, this one in honor of May Day.[69] (An acrostic, Jehan de Dinant, suggests that
it was composed for a patron or a friend, probably the singer Johannes de Lotinus
Dinantius, to whom Tinctoris dedicated the treatise *Expositio manus*.)[70] Again cantus
and tenor are treated as a vocal duo and begin imitatively, this time with the tenor
leading the way (see Example 7-7). The imitation does not dominate, being used only
for the first and third lines of the poem, but alternates instead with phrases in simultaneous declamation. In addition, the text has been set in a severely syllabic style that
yields to modest melismatic extension only for the final pair of verses. All in all the
effect is one of considerable melodic simplicity, and the ductus of the text-bearing
parts—with their repeated pitches and short melodic cells of limited range—suggests
the incorporation into the polyphony of a preexistent tune from the oral tradition.

⌒⊃ THE COMBINATIVE CHANSON ⊂⌒

Distinctly plebeian elements, often exploited for their humorous potential, also mark
the fifteenth-century codification of the polytextual chanson. An intentional juxta-

68. "Iste rondellus de se facit tenorem fugando duo tempora et accipiendo in tridiezeugmenois," meaning, "this rondeau makes its own tenor, following [the cantus] two breves later and starting at the lower
fifth." (Note the use of Greek tetrachordal terminology to designate the interval of imitation.)
69. The poem is in octosyllables with the refrain rhyming A A B'B'A and the other strophes following suit.
70. See Allan Atlas, *Music at the Aragonese Court of Naples* (Cambridge: Cambridge University Press,
1985), 47 and 94.

EXAMPLE 7-7. Du Fay, *Je veuil chanter de cuer joyeux*

I want to sing with joyful heart in this lovely month of May, sing loud and clear no matter what others may say. Love wishes it, and let no one contradict who is a true lover. With all my heart shall I take care, in spite of the envious, to serve well my sweetheart. I want to sing. . . . Her have I chosen for, so help me God, she has no equal under heaven, to my mind, nor is any other as fine. Nor could anyone ever be found as much to my taste. I want to sing . . .

position of stylistically disparate elements—courtly and popular, textual and musical—which are nonetheless related by a discernible commonality of subject matter, was introduced ever more frequently into pieces of this type during the fifteenth century. In fact, this manner of treating songs with multiple texts was used with enough frequency and consistency that it has been recognized as a separate subgenre of the chanson, characterized as "combinative."[71]

The first of several levels of more or less comic contrast made possible by the compositional integration of such heterogeneous components comes with the coupling of texts: a poem in a fixed form that draws upon the diction—if not always the themes—of the courtly literary tradition (usually carried by the cantus) opposed to a song or songs from the popular, presumably oral repertory (sung by one or more of the lower voices, tenor and/or contratenor[s]). In a few instances the melodic material taken for the lower part(s) was constituted by combining snippets from a number of songs to create a centonization or quodlibet suited to the purpose. There is but one work with an identifiable quodlibet in the "Dijon Chansonnier," which contains the largest single collection of combinative chansons of any source of the period, the anonymous *Souviegne vous/A bien amer*, whose tenor is composed of a half-dozen melodic fragments from as many different songs.[72] Generally, melodies borrowed from the monophonic repertory for polyphonic composition were taken over in their entirety.

Whether or not the poem in fixed form dealt with a topic appropriate to the courtly context, it was usually set to a melody in the style associated with such verse: lyrical and flowing, gently syncopated, making full use of the modally normative range, and going well beyond the number of notes needed to declaim the words in melismatic flourishes and extensions of the musical phrase. The tunes borrowed from the unwritten monophonic repertories, by comparison, were mostly confined in range to small melodic cells and characterized by a syllabic declamatory style that made much use of repeated pitches, often taken in pairs.

Such unmistakable differences in style apparently had their own potential for

71. The term was coined by Maria Maniates, to whose study of this particular subgenre of the chanson the following paragraphs are much indebted. See her "Combinative Chansons in the Dijon Chansonnier," *Journal of the American Musicological Society* 23 (1970): 228–81, and her edition of representative pieces from the surviving repertory, *The Combinative Chanson: An Anthology*, Recent Researches in the Music of the Renaissance, vol. 77 (Madison: A-R Editions, 1989).
72. See Maniates, "Combinative Chansons," 229–30 and 260.

humor with the informed audiences of the period, and the musical contrasts were undoubtedly heightened by the sometimes marked disparities in point of view and diction between the elegant locutions of courtly verse and the direct, earthy language that was typical of the more plebeian oral tradition. The possible effect of such a juxtaposition is illustrated by the anonymous *Se je mue la couleur/Adieu pour mesouen*, also included in the repertory of the "Dijon Chansonnier"; a traditional plaint of unrequited love, a *rondeau cinquain* (sung by the cantus), is combined with a song, *Adieu pour mesouen*, belonging to the monophonic repertory that gives a woeful account of the equally unsuccessful attempts of a clearly noncourtly suitor to win his lady's love.[73] The borrowed tune is divided, together with its text, between a pair of voices in the tenor range that sing in alternation with one another until they join in the final phrase. A fourth part without text (presumably intended for instrumental performance) was added to the texture in order to maintain a sonority of at least three parts while the two tenors are exchanging lines.

When the poem in fixed form also adopts noncourtly vocabulary and means of expression, there is the added potential for humor in an incongruous combination of sophisticated melody with a text that was purposefully common, perhaps even coarse. Such is clearly the case with the anonymous *Puisque a chascun ris et quaquettes/ Pardonnez moy/L'autrier m'aloie esbanoyant*, also included in the "Dijon Chansonnier," in which the *rondeau quatrain* of the cantus warns a young woman that loose sexual behavior could lead to the loss of her figure and beauty (to say nothing of her reputation).[74] The voice newly composed for the rondeau is combined in this case with a pair of apparently preexistent monophonic songs, one of which (*Pardonnez moy*) is distinctly courtly in its diction, while the other (*L'autrier m'aloie esbanoyant*) is considerably more popular in tone. To these has been added a textless contratenor (probably meant here as well for an instrument).

Borrowed melodies such as these, when quoted completely (as, it would seem, in the examples cited), had their own formal structure—most often the ternary pattern aba, to be seen in *Adieu pour mesouen*[75]—and this had to be accommodated somehow with the fixed form upon which the cantus was based. At the same time, the preexistent tune was frequently divided between a pair of voices, as in the song just cited, either in alternation or in an imitative texture with overlap between the parts.

The latter solution was adopted for *Il sera pour vous conbatu/L'homme armé*, a

---

73. The piece has been edited in modern score by Maniates, "Combinative Chansons," 270–72, and in *Combinative Chanson: An Anthology*, 57, no. 22.

74. For a transcription, see Maniates, "Combinative Chansons," 279–81, and *Combinative Chanson: An Anthology*, 86, no. 32.

75. The form in which this chanson was cast is in fact that of the virelai, which was often adopted for popular lyrics of the kind. Consequently, the overall ternary design is further articulated by internal repetition, producing the pattern A/bb/aAA'. (The letters here indicate sections; A is the one-line refrain, a the matching strophe, and bb the *ouvert* and the *clos*, each consisting of two lines, while A' indicates a repeat of the refrain with a variant in its melody.) Cf. Maniates, "Combinative Chansons," 234, 261–62, and 270–71.

combinative chanson based on one of the most celebrated and widely known monophonic chansons of the age. There are two sources for the work, both of Italian provenance, and two versions of it, one with text for all three voices, the other without words and with a fourth part added.[76] Neither has a dependable attribution; the "Borton" of the "Casanatense Chansonnier" (MS 2856 of the Biblioteca Casanatense in Rome) has been construed as an Italian scribe's misreading of Morton—presumably Robert, an English composer active on the Continent (1457–75)—but a claim has been made for Busnoys's authorship as well.[77] In either case the piece is clearly a product of French-Burgundian musical culture and is particularly worthy of note because it provided the starting point for the long series of polyphonic Masses that took the *L'homme armé* tune as cantus firmus.

That melody, which is cast in the clearest of aba forms, is carried primarily by the tenor (see Example 7-8). Only for the second phrase of the second section (mm. 9–11) does the contratenor take a brief turn; elsewhere it provides for the other two voices a counterpoint punctuated by fanfare figures on the words "l'homme armé" and "a l'assaut" that are tossed imitatively back and forth between contratenor and tenor (mm. 3–4, 5–6, 7–9, and 14–15). The newly composed cantus, meanwhile, presents a *rondeau quatrain* concerning the valor—most likely mock-imaginary—in fighting against the Turks of a certain Maistre Symonet le Breton, a singer who served at the Burgundian chapel from 1436 until 1465, when he retired to a living at Cambrai Cathedral. (There is reason to suspect that little Symon's best strokes were at table rather than at war, however, since the "crocq de ache" of the poem could be a celery stalk rather than an axe.)[78]

A more evenhandedly imitative treatment of tenor and contratenor is to be seen in one of the most widely circulated of the combinative chansons, a setting of *Petite camusette* attributed to Okeghem that was included in nine manuscripts—four of them northern, three Italian, one Spanish, and one German—as well as Petrucci's *Canti C* of 1504.[79] In this composition the fourth part, a low contratenor, also participates in the imitation—which is anticipated by the opening figure of the cantus—and is provided with text (at least in those sources where the poetry is included), suggesting the expectation of a totally vocal performance. This may be an indication that combinative chansons—as bi- or polytextual duos, trios, and even quartets—contributed significantly to the shift in performance style in regions of French culture from the accompanied solo song of the fifteenth century to the wholly vocal conception of the sixteenth.

76. For transcriptions of these pieces, see Perkins and Garey, eds., *Mellon Chansonnier*, 1:124–25, no. 34 (à 3 only), and *Robert Morton: The Collected Works*, ed. Allan Atlas, Masters and Monuments of the Renaissance 2 (New York: Broude Brothers, 1981), 7–10, nos. 3 and 3a (both versions).

77. See Antoine Busnoys, *Collected Works*, ed. Richard Taruskin, Masters and Monuments of the Renaissance 5 (New York: Broude Trust, 1990–), pt. 3, Latin-texted works, pp. 35–37; regarding Morton, see Atlas, *Robert Morton: The Collected Works*, xvii–xxii.

78. See Howard Garey's commentary in Perkins and Garey, eds., *Mellon Chansonnier*, 2:331–35, no. 34.

79. For a facsimile and a transcription with commentary, see Perkins and Garey, eds., *Mellon Chansonnier*, 1:44–45, 2:198–203, no. 4.

EXAMPLE 7-8. Antoine Busnoys?/Robert Morton?, *Il sera pour vous con-batu/L'homme armé*

CANTUS: He will be confronted by you, the dreaded Turk, Master Symon—there can
be no doubt—and with an axe spur [a stalk of celery?] struck down. We hold that
his pride will be beaten down if he falls into your hands, the wicked one. He will
be confronted. . . . In no time you will have beaten him, God willing, then will
they say: "Long live little Symon the Breton! For he has battled the Turk." He will
be confronted . . .

TENOR AND CONTRATENOR: The man of arms is to be feared. The cry has been
raised everywhere bidding everyone to arm himself with an iron hauberk: "To the
assault!" The man of arms is to be feared.

∽ "MOTET-CHANSON" AND "SONG-MOTET" ᄃ

Another subgenre of the period, the so-called motet-chanson, can be considered a
special species of the combinative chanson since it combines a setting of a secular
poem with a Latin cantus firmus (or at least a melody conceived and labeled to give
the appearance of one). Compositions so conceived should be clearly distinguished
from what have come to be known as "song-motets," pieces having the format and
style of a chanson but a text in Latin.[80] In some song-motets the music appears to
have been written expressly for the Latin words, and the choice of compositional
style seems to have been dictated by their intended use as devotional music for intimate circumstances or private observances that could be performed with the same
modest forces that were needed for a chanson.

One frequently finds compositions of this kind included in manuscript collections
of chansons, where they seem to invoke the indulgence of an understanding saint for
a genre concerned primarily with human eros and similar or related follies. Two such
works figure in the repertory of the "Mellon Chansonnier," both of them attributed
to Johannes Tinctoris, the putative compiler of the codex. In both the texts are formulated as a prayer to the Virgin, the one beginning "O Virgo, miserere mei," the

80. There has been some uncertainty as to the proper use of these terms, which represent modern coinage
rather than fifteenth-century usage. The definition for motet-chanson as given by Gustave Reese, *Music
in the Renaissance* (New York: Norton, 1959) 55, is that adopted here, whereas Fallows, "Motet-
chanson," *The New Grove Dictionary of Music*, 12:647—despite Reese's warning—has in fact confused the
motet-chanson with the song-motet. Concerning the latter, see below, pp. 318–21.

other "Virgo Dei throno digna."[81] However, an inscription entered over the first of these, "Beatissime virgini domine Beatrici de Aragonia," indicates that the composer was probably thinking in both cases of his earthly patron rather than the heavenly queen.[82] The two works are very similar in style; all three parts are woven fairly equally into an animated but nonimitative contrapuntal fabric.

In the majority of cases chanson-motets were simply contrafacts, chansons whose vernacular texts had been replaced by Latin ones in order to make them suitable for devotional or even liturgical use.[83] Such was the case for Du Fay's *Craindre vous vueil*, cited above (p. 283), and also, apparently, for the three-part *Ave regina celorum* attributed to Walter Frye (fl. ca. 1450–75), an English composer whose music is known primarily from Continental sources. Frye's work was apparently originally a ballade with musical rhyme, to which the Latin text was fitted as a formally compatible responsory.[84]

By contrast, in the motet-chanson the combination of vernacular lyrics and Latin text is essential to the conception of the work, and the effect sought by that juxtaposition could be either humorous or serious. Clear comic intent may be seen in *Je ne puis plus ce que j'ai peu/Unde veniet auxilium mihi*, an early example of the type included in the MS Canonici Misc. 213, where it is credited to Du Fay.[85] The text of the cantus, apparently the refrain strophe of a *rondeau quatrain* in which the male voice complains of his waning sexual powers, is in ironic contrast with a phrase from an antiphon sung at Terce on Thursday, the Latin text of which asks "Whence cometh my help?" A kinship with the motet, from which the use of a tenor cantus firmus is certainly derived, is underlined by the quasi-isorhythmic treatment of the borrowed chant; it is sung three times in successive diminution (as prescribed by a verbal canon), first in duple proportion, then in triple, and finally in sextuple.

On the serious side is the *naenia*, or lament, prompted by the death of a near friend or important patron, a compositional type that occurs often enough to constitute a small subgenre of its own. Such a work is the *déploration* on the death of Binchoys (1460), *Mort, tu as navre/Miserere*, found among the combinative chansons in the "Dijon Chansonnier" and attributed to Okeghem in the Montecassino MS 871.[86] The fixed form used for the vernacular verse in this case (and hence for

81. For transcriptions, see Perkins and Garey, eds., *Mellon Chansonnier*, 1:84–85 (no. 19) and 1:194–95 (no. 57).

82. See the discussion by Perkins, in Perkins and Garey, eds., *Mellon Chansonnier*, 1:17–20; the Latin inscription can be translated as, "To the most blessed virgin, lady Beatrice of Aragon."

83. See Reese, *Music in the Renaissance*, 94. Chansons with Latin *contrafacta* were particularly characteristic of the manuscript collections compiled in German territories, where the knowledge of French was undoubtedly limited; see Reinhard Strohm, *The Rise of European Music: 1380–1500* (Cambridge: Cambridge University Press, 1993), 501–2, 513–14, and *passim*.

84. See Brian Trowell, "Frye," *The New Grove Dictionary of Music*, 6:876–79; and cf. Reese, *Music in the Renaissance*, 93–94.

85. For a transcription, see Du Fay, *Opera omnia*, ed. Besseler, 6:51.

86. For a transcription, see Isabel Pope and Masakata Kanazawa, eds., *The Musical Manuscript Montecassino 871: A Neapolitan Repertory of Sacred and Secular Music of the Late Fifteenth Century* (Oxford: Clarendon Press, 1978), 427–30, no. 107.

the music) was the ballade of three strophes, perhaps in recognition of the distinction it had acquired during the previous century as a vehicle for important texts of an occasional nature.[87]

The tenor was pieced together from liturgical chants familiar to Binchoys and his circle, primarily those associated in some manner with the services for the dead. However, the melody for the first section appears to have been incompletely texted, and in the second section only the final phrase has thus far been traced to its source (see Example 7-9); it is the last line (words and music) of the great medieval sequence for the dead, *Dies irae*.[88] That segment of the liturgical melody is heard not only in the tenor but also in two other parts: in anticipation at the upper fifth in the contratenor altus and in imitation at the lower fifth in the contratenor basis. Since both of these were left without text, it is possible that they were intended for instruments, and in view of the performing tradition associated with the Latin motet at the time and the textual anomalies in the tenor, that part may also have been played rather than sung.

Despite its relatively limited dissemination in the sources of the period, Okeghem's lament appears to have had a considerable impact on the masters of the next generation, for whom it served as a model. One of the most important of these was undoubtedly Josquin Desprez (ca. 1440–1521), who wrote in turn a *déploration* on the death of Okeghem (1497): *Nymphes des bois/Requiem*.[89] He adopted for his work the same basic concept, even though he treated it compositionally in a much different manner.

87. The poem is in octosyllables, rhyming a b a b (sung to the first section of music, repeated), b c'b C' (sung to the second); the same rhymes are used for all three strophes of the poem.

88. See the *Liber usualis*, 1813.

89. For a transcription, see Albert Smijers, ed., *Josquin Desprez, Wereldlijke Werken*, 2 vols. (Amsterdam: Vereniging voor Nederlandse Musiekgeschiedenis, 1921–56), 1:5, and Edward E. Lowinsky, ed., *The Medici Codex of 1518: A Choirbook of Motets Dedicated to Lorenzo de' Medici, Duke of Urbino*, 3 vols., Monuments of Renaissance Music, vols. 3–5 (Chicago: University of Chicago Press, 1968), 4:338, no. 46.

EXAMPLE 7-9. Jean de Okeghem, *Mort, tu as navré/Miserere* (mm. 42-60)

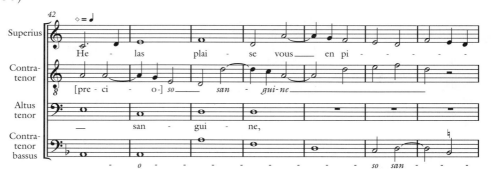

CANTUS: Alas! I beg of you have pity; pray for the soul.
TENOR: Whom thou hast redeemed upon the cross with thy precious blood, holy
     Lord Jesus, grant him peace.

Josquin's tenor is based solely and clearly upon the Introit to the Mass for the dead, and a canon indicates that it is to be sung a semitone lower than written, a transposition that changes the mode of the melody from the sixth (with an F final) to the fourth (usually with an E final, hence with a semitone as the first melodic interval of its scale).[90] Leaving aside the void notation current at the time, Josquin used only filled black notes, undoubtedly to symbolize mourning. He wrote in no clef signs either, but only fa's (flats), to indicate the scalar structures to be observed, obviously as homage to the dead composer who was celebrated for his clefless pieces (see Figure 7-11).

In striking contrast to Okeghem's lament for Binchoys are the declamation and the texture of Josquin's composition. The four voices woven around the tenor cantus firmus are all conceived, as in the motets of the late fifteenth century, to carry the text, which is written out in full in the manuscript for each of the parts. Together the

90. See the facsimile in Lowinsky, ed., *Medici Codex of 1518*, 5: ff. 125ᵛ–126, and cf. the *Liber usualis*, 1807.

FIGURE 7-11. *Nymphes des bois/Requiem* by Josquin (Florence, Biblioteca Medicea-Laurenziana, MS Acq. Doni 666, the "Medici Codex," ff. 125ᵛ–126).

five voices result in a gently moving, nonimitative counterpoint that is virtually homophonic in its effect. Despite these stylistic differences, both works give evidence of the persistent conceptual and structural affinities that linked secular and sacred composition all through the fifteenth century, even when developments within distinctive genres appear to be taking different directions.

CHAPTER 8

✓

The Motet in the Fifteenth Century

⟶ SOURCES ⟵

With few exceptions the sources in which the known repertory of motets by Continental composers of the fifteenth century have been transmitted are those cited earlier in connection with the dissemination of music by English musicians and, to some extent, of the chanson. These include the large collections given over primarily to sacred music, such as the two Bologna manuscripts, Civico Museo Q15 and Biblioteca Universitaria 2216, the "Aosta Choirbook," and of course the "Trent Codices." A few motets, especially devotional works and song-motets, were also inscribed in secular sources such as MS Canonici Misc. 213, which includes thirty-eight pieces of the sort. Given the importance of Italian manuscripts to our knowledge of both the English and French repertories already surveyed, it is perhaps not surprising that most of the sources for the motet in this period are also Italian—for the first half of the century in particular—even though the vast majority of the works they contain are by northern composers.

There is in addition a substantial collection of Germanic origin, the so-called "St. Emmeram Codex" (Latin MS 14274 of the Bavarian State Library). It was compiled in the 1430s and early 1440s, apparently for the choirboys and students at the collegiate school of St. Stephen's in Vienna, mostly by Hermann Pötzlinger, a priest come from Bayreuth to study at the university, and some of his students. It was later carried by its owner to the Benedictine monastery of St. Emmeram in Regensburg, where Pötzlinger served as schoolmaster.[1] In this source as well the composers identified by its scribes—besides Englishmen such as Dunstable and Power, who are modestly represented—are in good measure those trained in urban centers of the

---

1. Concerning the origins and history of the manuscript, see Ian Rumbold, "The Compilation and Ownership of Munich, Clm 14274," *Early Music History* 2 (1982): 161–235; additional studies are listed in the *Census-Catalogue of Manuscript Sources of Polyphonic Music, 1400–1550*, ed. Charles Hamm and Herbert Kellman, 5 vols. (Neuhausen-Stuttgart: Hänssler-Verlag, 1979–88), 2:239–40.

French-speaking north. There are some 36 possible attributions to Du Fay, for example, and another 13 or so to Binchoys. However, 149 of the 276 pieces inscribed in the manuscript are without attribution, and their authors remain unknown. Like a small number of the pieces whose composers are named in the source but are little known outside of the circle in which the manuscript was compiled, many of them may be by local musicians.

Sources for the motet from areas of French culture are relatively rare until somewhat later. Compilation of one of the earliest, MS 5557 of the Royal Library in Brussels, apparently did not begin before about 1461. Judging from its substantial English component, the opening section (ff. 2–49ᵛ), which is the central nucleus of the collection, was probably prepared at the Burgundian court in connection with the marriage in 1468 of Duke Charles the Bold with Margaret of York. Later additions may date from the 1470s.[2] The collection includes a relatively small group of motets—only seven in all—together with eleven Masses, three Magnificats, and a hymn.

The only other manuscript from the same general area that is of real importance for the sacred repertory under discussion is Chigi C VIII 234 of the Vatican Library (generally referred to as the "Chigi Codex"). Copied and illuminated about 1498–1503 in the ateliers that served the Netherlands court of the Habsburgs for one of its officers, Philippe Bouton (1418–1515), it, too, contains a relatively modest number of motets, only nineteen in all, in the company of an equal number of Masses, a Requiem, and a Credo. Although a surprisingly rich source for the music of Okeghem (with some fifteen attributions), it contains relatively few works by his immediate contemporaries—such as Busnoys (one) and Regis (four or five)—and was rounded out with music by composers of the next generation, including Josquin, Compère, and Isaac.[3]

Also dating from the second half of the fifteenth century are the first of the important music manuscripts that began to be generated in increasing numbers by the musical institutions associated with the papal court in Rome. Of exceptional interest is San Pietro B 80, most of which was compiled for use in the great basilica of St. Peter by Nicholas Ausquier, who sang "contra" (the altus part) in the choir. His work is cited in payment registers for 1475–76, but the repertory he copied came in large part from two earlier collections, the one completed in 1458, the other in 1462.[4] Included in this manuscript are some twenty-eight motets, a significant

2. In this connection see Flynn Warmington, "A Very Fine Troop of Bastards?: Provenance, Date, and Busnois's Role in Brussels 5557," *Abstracts of Papers, American Musicological Society, Annual Meeting Philadelphia, 1984*, p. 11, and Rob C. Wegman, "New Data concerning the Origins and Chronology of Brussels, Koninklijke Bibliotheek, Manuscript 5557," *Tijdschrift van de Vereniging voor Nederlandse Muziek Geschiedenis*, 36 (1986): 5–25. For earlier studies, see the *Census-Catalogue of Manuscript Sources*, 1:92.

3. Concerning the "Chigi Codex," see Herbert Kellman, "The Origins of the Chigi Codex: The Date, Provenance, and Original Ownership of Rome, Biblioteca Vaticana, Chigiana, C.VIII.234," *Journal of the American Musicological Society* 11 (1958): 6–19; for further studies, see the *Census-Catalogue of Manuscript Sources*, 4:12–13.

4. Concerning this collection, see Christopher A. Reynolds, "The Origins of San Pietro B 80 and the Development of a Roman Sacred Repertory," *Early Music History* 1 (1981): 257–304; for further studies, see the *Census-Catalogue of Manuscript Sources*, 4:66–67.

component in a large repertory comprising in addition sixteen Masses, fourteen Magnificats, a Te Deum, and twenty-seven hymns. Not surprisingly, in view of the date at which many of these pieces were first copied, the composers best represented are Du Fay (with some twelve attributions) and Binchoys (three or four). Attributions are virtually lacking in the choirbook itself, however, and composers are as yet unknown for much of the music it contains.

The next significant source for the motet to originate with the papal establishment is the Cappella Sistina MS 15, which was drawn up during the final years of the century. As one of the earliest compiled and/or collected to serve the needs of the pontiff's private choir in celebrating the liturgy in the Sistine Chapel, it is of particular interest. Not surprisingly, it consists entirely of sacred music appropriate in some sense for that purpose: motets (a total of forty-one) and related genres (fourteen Magnificats and twenty-eight hymns). Oddly, in view of its date of origin, Du Fay is once again the best represented in the source with nineteen or twenty possible attributions, giving the repertory a somewhat retrospective cast. It, too, may have been compiled in part from earlier collections, and Du Fay's compositions are accompanied in much more modest numbers by those of a later generation, in particular Josquin, Compère, Martini, and Weerbeke.[5]

Experimentation with the stylistic conventions of the motet, as they had been codified in the course of the fourteenth century, is to be seen in these sources not only in the works of the English composers discussed earlier but also in those of their Continental contemporaries. Significantly, as the repertories they contain clearly show, English works circulated across the channel in ever greater numbers in the 1420s and 1430s. Some were undoubtedly brought by chapel musicians who accompanied the English armies during the final episodes of the Hundred Years' War, others by those who attended the English prelates who participated in the Councils of Constance (1414–17) and Basle (intermittently from 1431 to 1449). As a result, Continental composers of the period did not lack for English models, and many of them began to emulate the works of their cross-channel counterparts. They adopted, on the one hand, the contrapuntal procedures responsible for the perceived "sweetness" of English sonorities, which garnered the praise of the theorist Tinctoris and others, and, on the other, the stylistic idiosyncrasies and structural innovations that marked English treatment of established genres.

As a consequence of these developments, at least in part, the Latin motet underwent considerable change in the course of the fifteenth century at the hands of the musicians trained in the urban centers of northern Europe. The elaborate isorhythmic structures that had been deemed appropriate for impressive occasional works began to yield to simpler compositional procedures. At the same time, verse specifically written to celebrate an important event gave way to words suitable for use in a

---

5. Concerning the holdings of the Sistine Chapel generally, and MS 15 in particular, see Richard Sherr, *Papal Music and Papal Manuscripts in the Late Fifteenth and Early Sixteenth Centuries*, American Institute of Musicology, Renaissance Manuscript Studies 5 (Neuhausen: Hänssler-Verlag, 1996); for further studies, see the *Census-Catalogue of Manuscript Sources*, 4:29.

wider variety of contexts. More and more these texts were drawn from scripture, from the vast devotional literature that had accumulated in Christendom over the centuries, and of course from the liturgy as well.

This transition may have reflected to some degree changes in individual or even communal tastes, but no less important were evolving patterns of public and private worship, both within the framework of the prescribed liturgy and in the more informal atmosphere of a wide variety of devotional exercises. (Moreover, a meaningful distinction between the two is not always easily made.) Whatever the causes, the end result was to restore the polyphonic motet to much closer ties with the liturgy from which it had originally emerged, especially that for Mass and for Vespers.

A shift in textual preference was accompanied by a dramatic change in musical style. The melodic and rhythmic hierarchies characteristic of the medieval genre, with its solo voices (for the texted parts) accompanied by instruments (for tenor and contratenor), began to give way (as in the chanson) to a greater contrapuntal equality, the most obvious symptom of which was an increasing use of imitation. As we shall see, this changing relationship among the constituent parts would lead first to a primarily, then to a wholly vocal conception of the genre, with text provided for each of the voices. At the same time, the performance practice of the period gradually shifted away from small ensembles of specialized soloists to the first polyphonic choirs with more than a single performer to a part.[6]

ISORHYTHMIC MOTETS

The isorhythmic motet did not disappear from Continental repertories overnight, nor was its use as a type of occasional composition immediately abandoned. Its continued cultivation into the fifteenth century by composers of northern Europe such as Binchoys, Du Fay, and Brassart reflects nonetheless the shift to more consistently sacred functions for the genre and the tendency toward a more essentially vocal conception overall. The wider role given to works of this type is discernible already in the texts of motets by composers active earlier in the century, including, among others, the trio mentioned by Martin le Franc as having "amazed all of Paris," Carmen (with three motets), Cesaris (one), and Tapissier (one). At the same time, these works illustrate well the compositional procedures that had become traditional for isorhythmic structures in the course of the fourteenth century.

A representative example is Tapissier's *Eya dulcis/Vale placens*, one of the motets

---

6. A detailed study of the transition from the medieval conception of the motet to that associated with the Renaissance has been undertaken by Julie Cummings; see, for example, "The Emergence of the Renaissance Motet," paper read at the annual meeting of the American Musicological Society, Pittsburgh, 1992.

included in the primarily secular repertory of MS Canonici Misc. 213.[7] As it is a lament upon the internal divisions within the Catholic church during the Great Schism, it must thus date from before the end of the Council of Constance (1414–17). In fact, judging from the sentiments of its text, it may have been written in that connection. Given that genesis, one could assume that the tenor was derived from a plainchant with appropriate liturgical and/or textual connotations. It is not labeled in any way in the manuscript, however, and its source has yet to be identified.

Two separate but related poems—one for each of the two texted voices—have been cast in rhyming Latin verse in stanzas of four lines each, presumably expressly for a musical setting. Their rhyme schemes differ, nevertheless, as do their line lengths (see Example 8-1).[8] Significantly, poetic forms and musical structure do not

---

7. For an edition, see Gilbert Reaney, ed., *Polyphonic Music of the Early Fifteenth Century*, Corpus mensurabilis musicae 11 ([Rome]: American Institute of Musicology, 1955), 1:72–78; also included there are Carmen's *Pontifici decori speculi*, *Salve Pater/Felix et Beata*, and *Venite adoremus dominum/Salve sancta* and Cesaris's *A virtutis ignicio/Ergo beata nascio/Benedicata filia tua*.

8. The strophes for the higher of the two voices (triplum) have lines of ten syllables and a single rhyming combination per stanza (AAAA); those for the lower of the two (duplum) have eight syllables for the first three lines (rhymed AAA) and seven for the fourth (with a different rhyme), except for the final stanza, which is in uniform octosyllables.

EXAMPLE 8–1   Jean Tapissier, *Eya dulcis/Vale placens*, first two stanzas of text from the triplum and the first stanza from the duplum

TRIPLUM

Eya dulcis adque vernans rosa,	Come, o sweet and blooming rose,
Virgo placens, puella formosa,	Pleasing virgin, beautiful maid,
Dei mater valde gloriosa,	Mother of God most glorious,
Spira preces voce clamorosa.	Exhale prayers with clamorous voice.

O spes nostra, multum indigemus,	O thou, our hope, we are in great need,
Plorat Roma omnis, nos rigemus;	All Rome weeps; we are wet [with tears];
"Tolle scisma!" ad te dirigimus,	"Remove the schism!" we cry unto thee,
Corde laudes tibi porrigimus.	We lift our heart in praises unto thee.

(Two additional strophes of identical prosody.)

DUPLUM

Vale placens peroratrix,	Hail, pleasing advocate,
Salve decens impetratrix,	Hail, comely protectress,
Gaude potens imperatrix	Rejoice, powerful queen
Virtutis et glorie.	Of virtue and glory.

(Three additional strophes of identical prosody.)

coincide: the four stanzas are spread over three *taleae* of thirty-eight measures (breves) each, which are fully isorhythmic in all four parts. What is more, the second and third stanzas are broken internally by the melismatic passage at the beginning of each *talea* (see below).

Cadential articulation does not necessarily correspond to the conclusion of a textual strophe either, except for the first pair (m. 31), although it does fall as a rule at the end of a verse in at least one of the two texted voices. If such structural correlation does not occur more regularly, it is in part because the text (judging from its placement in the manuscript) is to be declaimed at different rates in the two upper voices. Although they begin their initial strophes together, by the end of the third stanza the parts have gone their separate ways. Rather than articulate the verses cadentially, the composer has marked their ends with longer note values and/or rests, as was so often done in the isorhythmic motets of the fourteenth century (see Example 8-2).

As a consequence, the isorhythmic structure is largely autonomous; it is defined primarily by the syncopated, melismatic passage with which each *talea* begins (see Example 8-3) and by the proportional contrasts and shifts in mensural organization within. In the opening melisma, for example, triplum and duplum move against one another in a hocketlike manipulation of imperfect tempus and major prolation (com-

EXAMPLE 8-2 Jean Tapissier, *Eya dulcis/Vale placens* (mm. 18-35)

TRIPLUM: Mother of God most glorious, exhale prayers with clamorous voice. O thou,
    our hope, we are in great need; all Rome weeps . . .
DUPLUM: Rejoice, powerful queen of virtue and glory. Ever, do you now reach your
    ends, seeing that you ever offer prayers . . .

parable to a $^{6}_{8}$ compound meter) that emphasizes the division of the breve into two
groups of three minims, whereas the contratenor moves in perfect tempus (comparable to a simple $^{3}_{4}$), dividing the breve into three semibreves of two minims each.

    Midway through each *talea* (mm. 22–30; 60–68; 98–106) there is a rather dra-
matic change to an entirely binary division of the breve in the upper three parts with
triplum and duplum in a syncopated pattern that again simulates the effect of a hock-
et. Intense rhythmic and melodic activity then yields briefly to rest as they come
together on a breve before reverting to the compound mensuration of the opening
section (see again Example 8–2). The rhythmic complexity is thus considerable,
though certainly not extreme, reflecting only to a degree the abstruse style cultivated in the late fourteenth century. Moreover, it is largely limited to the upper pair of
texted voices, which are clearly distinguished from the tenor and (to a lesser degree)
the contratenor not only by vocal rather than instrumental performance but also by
markedly more animated rhythms. It is noteworthy, and instructive, that in all such
details the work harks back to the kind of hierarchical relationship among the voices

EXAMPLE 8-3. Jean Tapissier, *Eya dulcis/Vale placens* (mm. 1–4; 39–42;
77–80)

that was characteristic of the development of the isorhythmic motet in the fourteenth century.

Whether despite or because of its venerable traditions, the genre continued to be cultivated by composers of the next generation as well, including leading figures of the day such as Binchoys and Du Fay. It is perhaps significant, however, that many pieces of this type were written for non-French patrons, such as those ascribed to Johannes Brassart (fl. 1420–45), who served at the imperial Habsburg court of King Sigismund. Binchoys, for example, who served first English patrons and then at the ducal court of Burgundy, is credited with only one surviving work of this type, *Nove cantum melodie/Tanti gaude* (found, however, only in the Italian source Modena, Biblioteca Estense e Universitaria, MS α.X.1.11), which was written in 1431 to celebrate the baptism of Anthoine, the firstborn son of Duke Philip the Good of Burgundy.

Unfortunately, the opening section is incomplete in the sole surviving source for the upper pair of voices, but from what has survived it seems clear that only the tenor was isorhythmically conceived. It is stated three times with the *color* corresponding to the *talea*, but for each repetition there is a typical change in the mensuration, in this instance from ternary to binary and back with the upper parts written in diminution (𝄵 and 𝇍, respectively) above the final two statements.[9] Unusual for a piece of this kind is the provision of text for all three of the upper parts, including the con-

9. See the transcription of the motet by Jeanne Marix, ed., *Les musiciens de la cour de Bourgogne au XVe siècle* (Paris: Droz, 1937), 212–17.

tratenor, instead of the customary vocal duo with an instrumental pair below. Each part has its own poem, moreover, and that given to the superius is of unusual historical interest; it mentions by name some seventeen singers of the ducal chapel, who are called upon to celebrate in song the birth of the noble scion.[10]

The largest repertory of isorhythmic motets attributable to a single master of this generation is that credited to Du Fay. Thirteen such works have survived in the sources under his name and are datable, because of their topical allusions, to the period between 1420 and 1442. Among the best known are *Supremum est* (à 3), written to celebrate a treaty of peace between Pope Eugene IV and Sigismund of Austria in 1433,[11] and *Nuper rosarum flores*, cited earlier (see pp. 35–36), written for the dedication of the Florence cathedral in 1436.[12] Characteristic for the genre in the latter instance is the adoption of a chant from the liturgy intended for the dedication of a church, the Introit *Terribilis est locus iste*, and its disposition in extended values, apparently for instrumental performance. Also typical is the fourfold statement of the borrowed melody, generated from a single notated line. Here, too, each *color* corresponds to a complete *talea*, and the proportional differences in the duration of individual notes from one statement to the next is indicated "canonically" by means of prescribed changes in mensuration (in the sequence O, C, ₵, ₡).

Unusual, by contrast, is the dual statement of the borrowed chant (in tenors I and II) in two different rhythmicizations notated a fifth apart (starting from G and d respectively). As has been suggested, the intervallic relationship between these two parts and the mensural manipulations of the two tenors may have been derived from the proportions implicit in the biblical description of the dimensions of the temple of Solomon in Jerusalem, seen as a spiritual prototype for the cathedral (see pp. 206–7). In a further departure from tradition the customary vocal duo erected over this liturgical foundation was provided with but a single text, declaimed nonetheless independently in each of the two voices.

However, when compared with a work such as Tapissier's *Eya dulcis/Vale placens*, for example, perhaps the most striking of the stylistic innovations embodied in this composition—as well as others of the same decade—lies with its sonorities rather than its rhythmic structure or its mensural usage. The richly consonant sound of the *contenance angloise* is evident in the harmonic combinations from first to last, and the four parts have been woven together contrapuntally with such skill that every interval in every vertical combination of sounds is carefully controlled in accordance with the rules given by theorists of the period.

Still, despite the adoption of more "modern" characteristics for the composition

10. See Reinhard Strohm, *The Rise of European Music, 1380–1500* (Cambridge: Cambridge University Press, 1993), 195–96.

11. All these works are included in Guillaume Du Fay, *Opera omnia*, ed. Heinrich Besseler, 6 vols. (Rome: American Institute of Musicology, 1947–66), vol. 1; *Supremum est* is also included in Noah Greenberg and Paul Maynard, eds., *An Anthology of Early Renaissance Music* (New York: Norton, 1975), 251.

12. Also accessible in Claude V. Palisca, ed., *Norton Anthology of Western Music*, 2 vols. (New York: Norton, 1980), 1:101.

of isorhythmic motets by a master such as Du Fay, the genre was on the verge of disappearing from the musical landscape already in the 1430s. It would be replaced, as we shall see, by works of a different stylistic stamp, whether dependent to a degree on the isorhythmic tradition like the tenor motets of succeeding decades (see pp. 321–327), or modeled on different compositional genres, as was the song-motet mentioned earlier.

Whatever the format and the compositional procedures selected, from mid-fifteenth century on motets were based in ever greater numbers on texts drawn either from the liturgy or from the devotional literature associated with it, most notably writings of Marian inspiration of the sort so frequently included in books of hours for private worship. When a text associated with a specific chant was set, the melody was often incorporated into the counterpoint as well. In works deriving from the isorhythmic tradition, the plainsong was often laid out as a tenor foundation. In those more akin in style to the chanson the melodic substance of the superius was usually based upon it. And in yet other works the two procedures were combined in various ways. Thus, the increasing mastery of polyphonic composition, and of the musical skills needed for its performance, led increasingly to compositional treatment of chants for liturgical use, both text and tune.

The result was a widening repertory of motets in the newly developing styles and a fundamental redefinition of the compositional parameters of the genre. These changes were accompanied by the emergence of a series of polyphonic subgenres written specifically to be sung within a liturgical context. Among the motets of the period, consequently, are groups of compositions that are very similar in scope and conception—and not infrequently in musical style as well—because of their specific place and function in the celebration of Christian ritual. Settings for the Office include antiphons, Psalms, hymns, Magnificats, the Te Deum, and the Lamentations of Jeremiah; those for the Mass include the Propers (which had not been so treated in a systematic way since the twelfth century), the Passion, and even substitute texts for both Proper and Ordinary in combinations that came to be designated *motetti missales*. These works are often designated generally as "motets," but, as we shall see, their liturgical characteristics lend themselves in some instances to distinct and recognizable compositional types that warrant separate scrutiny.

⟶ MOTETS BASED ON ANTIPHONS ⟵

SONG-MOTETS

The liturgical chants most often selected for polyphonic treatment in the fifteenth and sixteenth centuries appear to have been the antiphons, especially those that had processional or votive functions in the liturgy. The majority of those selected for composition honor the Virgin Mary, and the texts set most frequently were undoubtedly those sung at Compline, the four great antiphons, beloved of the

Middle Ages and frequently used in a variety of religious observances: *Alma redemptoris mater*, *Ave regina celorum*, *Regina celi*, and *Salve regina*.[13] These are independent of the Psalms and canticles to which antiphons were usually linked in the liturgy and were sung in a variety of processional, votive, and devotional contexts. All were set time and again during the fifteenth century (and in the sixteenth), especially the latter two. The *Salve regina* was particularly popular, perhaps because it was prescribed for use on Saturday in connection with a votive Mass dedicated to the Virgin.[14]

Like their cross-channel counterparts, a number of Continental composers—apparently those with the strongest ties to English institutions and/or the greatest exposure to the music of English masters—treated the antiphon as a song-motet. Still relatively close in conception to an improvisatory tradition are two settings à 3 of the antiphon *Alma redemptoris mater* attributed to Du Fay, both of them based on the plainsong (and both early works). One of these carries the liturgical melody in the tenor, in the English manner, with the pitches of the chant laid out entirely in even (ternary) semibreves, interrupted only occasionally by a longer breve.[15] In the other the composer has shifted the borrowed plainsong to the superius, where it is rhythmicized and embellished in a lively and varied melodic style that recalls for much of the piece his approach to the chanson.[16] At the close of this work, for the text "sumens illud Ave, peccatorum miserere" ("[Mother] . . . having heard that Hail, have mercy on sinners"), he adopted a strictly syllabic homophonic style (possibly intending simultaneous declamation of the words in all three parts) with durations made indefinite by the placement of a corona above each successive chordal combination.

Despite the differences between the two works in placing and handling the liturgical melody, both reflect the vital influence of the chanson tradition for a northern master of Du Fay's generation in their use of a treble-dominated style in which melodic and rhythmic interest lie primarily in the upper voice—which is also the primary bearer of the text. The extent to which such procedures were found effective (and deemed appropriate) in setting antiphons polyphonically may be judged from the collection of some twenty-one Magnificat-antiphons divided between San Pietro B 80 and Trent 89, ten of which are common to both. All are for three parts and are very much alike stylistically; the mensuration calls uniformly for perfect tempus, the polyphony is preceded by a brief intonation of the chant, and the liturgical melody

---

13. For the Latin texts and traditional melodies (in at least one version that circulated widely at the time), see, for example, the *Liber usualis*, 273–76.

14. See Michel Huglo, "Antiphon," *The New Grove Dictionary of Music*, 1:480. For a thoughtful examination of a fifteenth-century repertory of Marian antiphon-motets and the uses for which they were possibly intended, see Howard M. Brown, "The Mirror of Man's Salvation: Music in Devotional Life about 1500," *Renaissance Quarterly* 43 (1990): 744–73.

15. See Du Fay, *Opera omnia*, ed. Besseler, 5:115.

16. Also included in the Besseler edition of Du Fay's *Opera omnia*, the piece is well known because of its inclusion in Archibald T. Davison and Willi Apel, eds., *The Historical Anthology of Music*, 2 vols. (Cambridge, Mass.: Harvard University Press, 1962), 1:70.

is carried thereafter in the superius with little change beyond a fairly straightforward rhythmicization.[17]

A further example reflecting the impact of the chanson tradition on motet composition is the setting of *Ave regina celorum, Mater regis*, a chant with strong English connections, the text of which begins with the same acclamation as the antiphon for Compline. The polyphony, which is ascribed to Binchoys, is found, once again, only in an Italian source, the mid-century Ferrarese collection in Modena, Biblioteca Estense e Universitaria, MS α.X.1.11.[18] In compositional style it is not unlike Powers's treatment of the more traditional liturgical text, discussed earlier, but it appears to be somewhat further removed from improvised discant than similar works by Du Fay. Significantly, aside from the opening phrase, where the plainchant is quoted briefly in both cantus and tenor, the liturgical melody is not directly traceable in any of the contrapuntal parts. (However, that quotation does at least prove that the music was originally intended for the antiphon and not simply adapted to its text by the rather common practice of textual substitution.)

Further distinguishing this composition from a plainsong setting is its apparent conception as a vocal duo with a presumably instrumental contratenor as accompaniment (see Example 8-4). The upper pair of voices, both of which were provided with text by the fifteenth-century scribe, are linked to one another by imitation in the two opening phrases and through a long melismatic passage in the heart of the work (mm. 25–36). The considerable melodic extension of the latter phrase, as well as of those written for the final two verses of the antiphon text, offers additional evidence that the work is more closely related to the traditions of secular song than to the improvisation of polyphony over a given chant, and in this respect Binchoys's composition invites comparison with other, presumably English, works (see pp. 231–34), such as the much loved and widely circulated *Quam pulchra es*, usually credited to Dunstable.[19]

The affinity between the secular works of this period and motets in chanson style is perhaps most clearly revealed by the numerous instances in which the latter are simply derived from the former by the substitution of a Latin text, liturgical or devotional—a contrafact—for the original verse in the vernacular. Typical of the many examples that illustrate this practice are Binchoys's *Ave dulce tu frumentum*, origi-

17. See Reynolds, "Origins of San Pietro B 80," 290–94.

18. For a modern transcription, see Marix, ed., *Les musiciens de la cour de Bourgogne*, 189–90, or the more recent edition by Philip Kaye, *The Sacred Music of Gilles Binchois* (London: Oxford University Press, 1992), 183–85, no. 32.

19. However, as Margaret Bent has noted (*The New Grove Dictionary of Music*, 5:724), the ascription to "Dunstapell" in the "Aosta Choirbook" was erased and "Egidius" written in its place (presumably pointing to Binchoys); more recently, David Fallows has also questioned Dunstable's authorship, "Dunstable, Bedyngham, and *O rosa bella*," *Journal of Musicology* 12 (1994): 288. For a transcription, see Palisca, ed., *Norton Anthology of Western Music*, 3d ed., 2 vols. (New York: Norton, 1996), as well as John Dunstable, *Complete Works*, ed. Manfred Bukofzer, Musica Brittanica, 8 (1953), with revisions and additions by Margaret Bent, Ian Bent, and Brian Trowell (London: Stainer and Bell, 1970), 112–13, no. 44.

EXAMPLE 8-4. Gilles Binchoys, *Ave Regina celorum* (mm. 1-10)

Hail, Queen of the heavens, Mother of the King of angels . . .

nally a setting for the ballade *Je loe amors* (included in the MS Canonici Misc. 213),[20] and the even more widely circulated *Ave regina celorum* attributed to Walter Frye.[21]

Although the latter piece was copied into at least seventeen manuscripts, included in recognizable form in three paintings, and intabulated for keyboard in three different arrangements, all of which are identified only with the liturgical Latin,[22] it may have been originally conceived as a ballade. Its musical form corresponds to the pattern traditionally adopted for poems in that fixed form and points to secular origins. Coincidentally, that is also the formal structure of the liturgical responsory, and that circumstance may have contributed to its selection for contrafaction with those particular Latin words.[23]

TENOR MOTETS

With the composers of the next generation the antiphon came to be treated more and more frequently as a type of cantus firmus composition that recalls in its con-

20. See David Fallows, *The New Grove Dictionary of Music*, 2:717.

21. For an edition in modern score, see Walter Frye, *Opera omnia*, ed. Sylvia Kenney, Corpus mensurabilis musicae 19 ([Rome]: American Institute of Musicology, 1960), 8–9, no. 5a, or Greenberg and Maynard, eds., *Anthology of Early Renaissance Music*, 71.

22. The text is essentially the same as that set by Binchoys but with the third and fourth verses repeated at the end in the manner of a responsory; see Gustav Reese, *Music in the Renaissance* (New York: Norton, 1959), 93f.

23. This interpretation has been questioned by Strohm, *Rise of European Music*, 397, who suggests that Frye's *Ave regina* "might have been written as a votive antiphon (in the form of a liturgical responsory)."

ception, facture, and function the isorhythmic motet of earlier in the century. In fact, it may be precisely because of the festal and votive connotations of the more significant stylistic features of this venerable genre that they were adopted by later composers for certain of the texts selected for polyphonic elaboration. Indicative of this kinship is the setting à 4 of the *Ave regina* written by Du Fay late in his life and left with instructions that it was to be sung at his bedside as death was approaching.[24]

The composition is constructed around the chant melody, which serves as a structural cantus firmus carried in its entirety by the tenor. In addition, anticipatory citations—however brief—are heard in the uppermost part of the counterpoint each time a new phrase of the antiphon text is introduced in the other three voices, most noticeably in the introductory duos that precede the tenor entry in each of the work's two principal *partes*. Once these voices (superius, altus, and bassus) have declaimed the words for one of the four clearly articulated sections into which the liturgical text is thus divided, they continue with an interpolated trope, a prayer for assistance and mercy that makes specific mention of the composer by name and must surely be of his own invention.

It seems fairly certain that the work was conceived for vocal performance in all four parts, even though a number of the musical phrases have very substantial melismatic extensions where text placement poses practical problems for the performers. In his disposition of the tenor, moreover, the composer has assimilated it rhythmically (as well as melodically) to the other parts; although he has generally given the pitches derived directly from the plainsong the longer values, he has not hesitated to embellish, fill in, and extend the borrowed melody with material of his own in order to match the Tenor line stylistically to the surrounding voices.

Important structural and conceptual parallels with earlier isorhythmic motets are thus fairly self-evident: the occasional character of Du Fay's conception, in particular; his selection of a liturgical melody as the structural cantus firmus because of its relevance to his purpose (and its obvious personal resonance); his placement of it in the tenor of a four-part contrapuntal structure; and the bitextuality that results from the personalized trope he provided for the other voices.[25] Also reminiscent of earlier procedures is the division of the motet into two *partes*, distinguished from one another rhythmically by a shift from ternary to binary mensuration. In other respects, by contrast, this is a very different work, one—as we shall see—that is much indebted to the compositional experience that Du Fay and his contemporaries had gained in adapting

24. For a facsimile of the sole surviving source, see Christopher A. Reynolds, ed., *Vatican City, Biblioteca Apostolica Vaticana, San Pietro B 80*, Renaissance Music in Facsimile 23 (New York: Garland, 1986), ff. 25ᵛ–27; for a modern edition, see Du Fay, *Opera omnia*, ed. Besseler, 5:124, or Susan Fuller, ed., *The European Musical Heritage, 800–1750* (New York: Alfred A. Knopf, 1987), 153.

25. Interestingly, Du Fay's personal self-reference is not unique; further examples may be seen among the motets attributed to Busnoys: *Anthoni usque limina* and *In hydraulis* (with further reference to Okeghem, whose *Ut heremita solus* may have been written in response to the latter work), both of which are constructed over a tenor devised for the purpose by the composer. See the modern edition in Antoine Busnoys, *Collected Works, The Latin-texted Works*, ed. Richard Taruskin, 2 vols., Masters and Monuments of the Renaissance 5, pt. 2 (New York: Broude Trust, 1990), 2:138 and 151.

cantus firmus composition and many of the features of isorhythmic construction to the setting of the Mass Ordinary as interrelated cycles (see pp. 355–59).[26]

The relationship between such pieces and the earlier isorhythmic motet is even clearer when both the polytextuality of the generic model and the tropelike relationship between the text of the tenor and that (or those) of the other voices have been maintained. Significantly, typical (and relatively early) examples of works of this kind are found among the motets attributed to Johannes Regis, who may have served as Du Fay's "clerc" and could have been his student in composition as well.[27] Five of his seven surviving motets are so constructed, and the importance they assumed toward the end of the century as compositional models of the genre is suggested by their relatively wide circulation and the inclusion of several of them in the motet collections printed by Octaviano Petrucci early in the sixteenth century.

Representative of these works in all essential respects is the setting of *Clangat plebs flores*, which is found not only in one of the Petrucci prints in question but also in the "Chigi Codex" and in two of the manuscripts from the repertory of the Sistine Chapel (see Figure 8-1).[28] The tenor is derived from the chant "Sicut lilium inter spinas" that served as both a Gradual and as a Second-Vespers antiphon for the feast of the Purification of the Virgin Mary. Around it are woven contrapuntally four additional parts, all of them apparently intended to carry the second text, a poem in praise of the Virgin Mother written in somewhat irregular Latin distiches of self-consciously erudite diction.

Reminiscent of the older isorhythmic tradition is the bitextuality resulting from this combination and, structurally, the threefold statement of the liturgical chant. Also analogous to structural principles associated with isorhythm is the division of the piece into a pair of clearly articulated *partes*, the first measured in perfect tempus (O), the second in diminished imperfect tempus (₵).[29] The initial statement of the borrowed melody begins in extended note values with such lengthy rests between its separate segments that only half of it is presented in the *prima pars*. In the *secunda pars*, by contrast, the tenor rhythms are assimilated to those of the other parts, as if some sort of irregular diminution derived from isorhythmic practice were being applied to the opening values. Both the second half of the first statement and two

26. In a perceptive discussion of this motet, Alejandro E. Planchart, "Notes on Guillaume Du Fay's Last Works," *Journal of Musicology* 13 (1995): 56–58, suggests that it may have been inspired in some respects by the famous English *Missa Caput.*

27. See David Fallows, "The Life of Johannes Regis, ca. 1425 to 1496," *Revue belge de musicologie* 43 (1989): 159f. It is not certain, however, that the Regis in question was the composer; concerning another Johannes Regis in Okeghem's circle at the church of St. Martin in Tours, see Pamela Starr, "Roman Light on Johannes Regis," *Revue belge de musicologie* 49 (1995): 27–38.

28. For a transcription, see Johannes Regis, *Opera omnia*, ed. C. Lindenburg, Corpus mensurabilis musicae 9 ([Rome]: American Institute of Musicology, 1956), 2:21–29.

29. The mensuration signs are O and ₵, respectively, and although the first section is only 36 (ternary) breves in length while the second is 106 (binary) breves long, they would actually be roughly equal in duration if the mensural proportion is construed literally as 2:1 with respect to the semibreve, for each would then be measured by a total of 105 *tactus* (not counting the final long in either case), assuming of course that the tactus would be about the same for both sections.

FIGURE 8-1. Johannes Regis, *Clangat plebs flora* (Rome, Vatican Library, MS Chigi C VIII 234, the "Chigi Codex," ff. 281ᵛ–282).

repetitions of the entire chant are then heard, the latter two statements still with relatively little ornamentation of the liturgical melody. The effect, then, is not unlike that produced by a series of isorhythmic *taleae* but with a nonproportional diminution of the written note values from one to the next.

In none of the major sections is the structure articulated by successive isorhythmic *taleae*, as in the motets of the fourteenth century. Rather frequent contrapuntal cadences and kaleidoscopic changes in texture from phrase to phrase set each one apart, as in Du Fay's *Ave regina celorum*. To illustrate (see Example 8-5), the first entry of the cantus firmus is preceded by an opening trio consisting of the superius and the two contratenors (mm. 1–5), an imitative duo between superius and the high contratenor (mm. 6–8), a nonimitative duo between the low contratenor and the bassus (mm. 8–12), and yet another, pairing once again superius and contratenor altus (mm. 12–15). Thus the rich sonorities made possible by the five voices—one more than was to be customary for much of the motet repertory of the early sixteenth century—are actually used very sparingly and primarily at points of particular structural significance. The prevailing textures through most of the piece consist of only two or three of the five parts, alternating in the manner observed among the

EXAMPLE 8-5. Johannes Regis, *Clangat plebs/Sicut lilium* (mm. 1–16)

Let the people ring out garlands [of praise] to the Mother of God with sonorous voice,
that she consider the conduct of [her] servants without delay, to whom, with a clear
throat, let songs be raised . . .

various registers. Significantly, of all the compositional techniques adopted for the
motet in the late fifteenth century, perhaps none was to find greater currency with
the composers of the next generation than these successive contrasts in ambitus and
texture.

That the motet type based on a tenor cantus firms was widely cultivated in the fifteenth century is evident from statistical evidence alone. Of the 167 motets included by Wolfgang Stephan in the list of works for his pathbreaking study of 1937,[30]
nearly a third (some 52 compositions) have a separate tenor cantus firmus. Its
melody was borrowed either from a preexistent chant or from some polyphonic

30. See Wolfgang Stephan, *Die burgundisch-niederländische Motette zur Zeit Ockeghems* (Kassel: Bärenreiter, 1973), 104–15.

work—whether sacred or secular—(very often the tenor part of the original), or constructed in some ingenious fashion to serve the same purpose. (As we shall discover, one of the devices most frequently employed to that end was the manipulation of hexachordal syllables to extract a melody from the vowels of a verbal phrase, creating what the Italians called a *soggetti cavati dalle parole*.)

All the major figures, not only of Regis's own time but also of the generation that followed, adopted a tenor cantus firmus for certain of their motets: Compère, Isaac (one of several who drew upon secular works such as Binchoys's *Comme femme desconfortee*), Josquin (known, among others, for *soggetti cavati* and hexachordal manipulation), Weerbeke, de Orto, Obrecht, and Pipelare—to name but a few.

Since the tenor motet could be composed to newly written texts of a topical nature and based upon a cantus firmus melody capable of conveying appropriate symbolic connotations, it came to be the preferred compositional type when, during the fifteenth and sixteenth centuries, the musical function was occasional rather than liturgical. In that sense it may be seen as a replacement for the earlier isorhythmic motet as the latter faded from use. An examination of the compositions that have been designated "state motets" because of their clear topical references to the events of historical significance for which they were prepared—births, deaths, marriages, coronations, official visits, and the like[31]—quickly demonstrates that the vast majority are constructed over a tenor cantus firmus. Clearly, it is in works of this type that the structural concepts that lay behind the isorhythmic motet continued to make themselves manifest long after strictly isorhythmic procedures had been abandoned and forgotten.

---

31. See Albert Dunning, *Die Staatsmotette, 1480–1555* (Utrecht: A. Oosthoek, 1970), for which a recorded anthology of selected examples was produced under the same title.

CHAPTER 9

Liturgical Polyphony for Office and Mass

⌐◯ EMERGING TRADITIONS ◯⌐

A polyphonic setting of any Latin text, whether liturgical, devotional, or occasional, could be referred to as a motet, at least in very general terms. Johannes Tinctoris defined the genre as a "composition of moderate length to which a [Latin] text on any topic, though most often a sacred one, may be sung."[1] Such a formulation applies not only to the compositional types discussed in the previous chapter but also to those to be considered here. During the fifteenth century a distinctive tradition emerged for a number of liturgical chants, especially those prominently featured in services attended on festal occasions by the laity. The initial development of these relatively new compositional types was undoubtedly fostered by the musical capacities and religious purposes of urban churches—cathedrals, basilicas, and collegiate institutions—with their well-developed choirs and their large (and often affluent) lay congregations.

The Office Hours most frequently attended by lay members were Vespers and Compline, in particular, but also Matins and Lauds and of course the Mass. Not surprisingly, then, the chants for which separate motetlike genres took shape were the Psalms, hymns, and Magnificats ordinarily prescribed for the evening Hours and the Lamentations of Jeremiah sung during Passion week. Also treated as a distinguishable type were the Te Deum, which had its regular place at the end of Lauds but was often sung as a hymn of praise in other circumstances as well; the "Benedicamus Domino," which was used (together with "Deo gratias") to conclude each of the canonical Hours; and the Propers of the Mass, either in conjunction with a poly-

---

1. "Motetum est cantus mediocris, cui verba cuiusvis materiae sed frequentius divinae supponuntur"; see his *Terminorum musicae diffinitorium* (1495), ed. Carl Parrish (London, Free Press of Glencoe, Collier-Macmillan, 1963), 42. Tinctoris does not mention that motets were by this time almost exclusively on Latin texts, but the linguistic distinction had become an important criterion of the genre.

phonic Ordinary cycle or by themselves. In every instance the compositional procedures that came to be characteristic of the polyphonic setting reflect either the peculiar structure of the text or the stylistic characteristics of its chant melody, and very often both at once. It is informative, therefore, to examine these liturgical genres separately.

✧⟶⟳ HYMN SETTINGS ⟲⟵✧

One of the first categories of chant for which a distinguishable polyphonic tradition arose was the hymn. Especially beloved of the laity, its popularity was undoubtedly due in no small measure to its strophic regularity in both music and verse, the straightforward syllabic relationship between syllables and notes, and the accessible but artfully tuneful character of the melodies. Already in the fourteenth century polyphonic hymns came into the written repertory, first as simple discant settings that may have been modeled on improvisatory contrapuntal elaborations of the chant.

The earliest known repertory of such pieces is a modest series of ten hymns that were copied, together with settings for the Ordinary chants of the Mass (ten Kyries, ten Glorias, ten Credos, four Sanctus, and one Agnus Dei) and four motets, in a manuscript currently found in the Chapter Library of the cathedral of St. Anne in the southern French city of Apt.[2] It appears likely that these ten pieces are a mere remnant of a much larger collection that originally included hymns for all the major feasts of the liturgical year; a repertory of that sort may well have been prepared for use at the papal court in nearby Avignon in the final quarter of the fourteenth century. In any case the surviving settings already exemplify procedures that will be used in hymn composition all through the fifteenth century: the chant melody is carried in a lightly ornamented form by one of the three parts (the superius in every case but one), the text is treated syllabically, and the parts declaim the text together in a relatively simple discant style (see Example 9-1 and cf. Example 9-3 below).[3]

Like the Apt manuscript, the sources of the early fifteenth century that include polyphonic hymns in substantial numbers—in particular the Bologna MS Q15 and the Modena MS α.X.1.11 (see pp. 222–23)—have them grouped in a separate section. In Bologna Q15 the hymns were copied at the end of the collection with the Magnificats, which were also sung at Vespers, and the sequences, which usually were

2. See the entry for MS 16bis in the *Census-Catalogue of Manuscript Sources of Polyphonic Music, 1400–1550*, ed. Charles Hamm and Herbert Kellman, 5 vols. (Neuhausen-Stuttgart: American Institute of Musicology, 1979–88), 1:8; for transcriptions see A Gastoné, ed., *Le manuscrit de musique du Trésor d'Apt*, Publications de la Société Française de Musicologie, ser. 1, vol. 10 (Paris: E. Droz, 1936), or Guilio Cattin, Francesco Facchin, and Maricarmen Gómez, eds., *French Sacred Music*, 2 vols., Polyphonic Music of the Fourteenth Century, vols. 23a–b (Monaco: Editions de l'Oiseau-Lyre, 1989–91), 23b: 356–65, nos. 76–85.

3. See Tom Ward, "Hymn:III," *The New Grove Dictionary of Music*, 8:841–45.

EXAMPLE 9-1 Anonymous, *Conditor alme siderum* (mm. 1–17)

Kindly creator of the stars, eternal light of the believers, Christ, redeemer of all, hear the prayers of the supplicants.

not; in Modena α.X.1.11 they were entered at the beginning of the collection in liturgical order and are followed by the Te Deum, a Psalm setting (by Binchoys), a pair of "Benedicamus Domino" (by Du Fay), and a series of nine Magnificats—all suitable for use in the celebration of the Canonical Hours—followed by the motet fascicles. Both codices contain essentially the same repertory of polyphonic hymns, however: a complete cycle, attributed to Du Fay, for all of the major feasts of the liturgical year (those that are classified as "semi-duplex" or higher).[4]

4. See Ward's table 1, *The New Grove Dictionary of Music*, 8:842. Concerning the ranking of liturgical feasts, see p. 235, n. 34.

The evidence would suggest that these works were written during the composer's first extensive stay at the ducal court of Savoy in 1433–35. The choice of hymns for polyphonic elaboration includes not only a core of chants sung nearly everywhere on major feast days but, in addition, a fair number that reflect practices and preferences specific to the region.[5] With few exceptions Du Fay's treatment of the genre follows a consistent pattern. All his settings are in three parts (not until the end of the century did four parts become more common for liturgical hymns), and they are intended for what came to be known as *alternatim* performance, meaning the alternation of chant and polyphony. As a rule, odd-numbered strophes were sung monophonically to the liturgical melody, whereas even-numbered stanzas were sung in parts. Initially, the polyphonic composition was also treated strophically with successive even-numbered stanzas sung to the same music (only much later did a more through-composed pattern come into use). In addition, the chant was invariably incorporated into the part-writing (in the topmost part in every case but one) with only slight melodic embellishment, applied principally in cadential patterns.

Typical of this approach to the genre is Du Fay's setting of *Pange lingua*, a hymn prescribed for use at the feast of Corpus Christi (see Example 9-2 and Figure 9-1).[6] As usual the liturgical melody is rhythmicized and lightly embellished (primarily, as is to be expected, in precadential figures), but it remains the most prominent of the composition's musical elements. Its placement at the top of the contrapuntal texture assures its preeminence, which is enhanced by the use of the superius to declaim the text. (The other parts may also have been sung, but they were given only incipits in

5. See David Fallows, *Dufay* (London: J. M. Dent, 1982), 135–46.

6. A complete transcription is found in Guillaume Du Fay, *Opera omnia*, ed. Heinrich Besseler, 6 vols. (Rome: American Institute of Musicology, 1947–66), 5:53–54, no. 21.

EXAMPLE 9-2. Guillaume Du Fay, *Pange lingua gloriosi corporis mysterium*

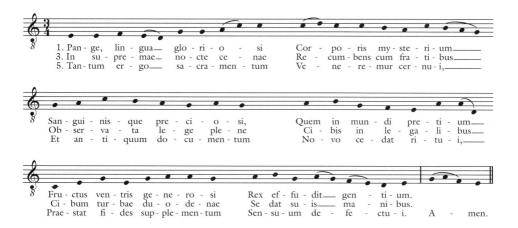

Contra-
tenor

2. Nobis datus
4. Verbum caro
6. Genitori

Tenor

2. Nobis datus
4. Verbum caro
6. Genitori

2. No - bis da - tus, no - bis na - tus Ex - in
4. Ver - bum ca - ro, pa - nem ve - rum Ver - bo
6. Ge - ni - to - ri, ge - ni - to - que Laus et

ta - cta vir - gi - ne, Et in mun - do con -
car - nem ef - fi - cit, Fit - que san - guis Chri -
ju - bi - la - ti - o, Sa - lus, ho - nor, Vir -

ver - sa - tus Spar - so ver - bi se - mi - ne,
sti me - um, Et si sen - sus de - fi - cit,
tus quo - que Sit et be - ne - di - cti - o,

Su - i mo - ras in co - la - tus Mi - ro clau -
Ad fir - man - dum cor sin - ce - rum So - la fi -
Pro - ce - den - ti ab u - tro - que Com - par - sit

sit____or_____di__ne.
des____suf_____fi__cit.
lau__da_____ti__o.

1. Relate, O Tongue, the mystery of the glorious body and of the precious blood, that, as a ransom for the world, fruit of a generous womb, the King of the people shed. 2. Given to us, born to us of a virgin undefiled, and brought into the world by the scattered seed of the Word, lived out his time [and] closed the wondrous order. 3. At the supper on the final night, seated with the brethren, the law fully observed by means of food prescribed by the law, food was given to the group of twelve by his own hands. 4. The Word, by the precious Word, makes the true bread flesh and makes wine of the blood of Christ, and, if understanding fails, for the strengthening of a sincere heart faith alone suffices. 5. As much, therefore, as we venerate the Sacrament in prone adoration, and [as much as] the Old Testament yields to the new ritual, so faith stands supreme as a supplement to defective reason. 6. To the Father and the Son, praise and jubilation; greeting, honor, and power also, and may a blessing proceeding from each of them be equal to the praise. Amen.

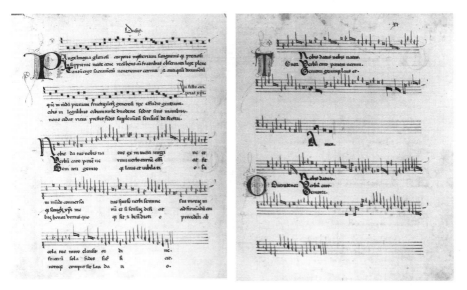

FIGURE 9-1.   Guillaume Du Fay, *Pange lingua gloriosi* (Modena, Biblioteca Estense, MS α. X.1.11, ff. 13ᵛ–14).

EXAMPLE 9-3. Guillaume Du Fay, *Conditor alme siderum*

1. Con - di - tor al - me si - de-rum,   E - ter - na lux cre - den - ti - um,
3. Ver - gen - te mun - di ves - pe - re   U - ti spon - sus de tha - la mo
5. Te   de - pre - ca - mur a - gi - e   Ven - tu - re iu - dex se - cu - li

Chri - ste,   re - dem - ptor o - mni - um   Ex - au - di pre - ces sup - pli-cum.
E - gres - sus ho - ne - stis - si - ma   Vir - gi - nis ma - tris clau - su - la:
Con - ser - va nos in - tem - po - re   Ho - stis a te - lo per - ti - di.

2. Qui___ con - do - lens in te - ri - tu Mor - tis pe -
4. Cu - jus for - ti po - ten - ti - e Ge - nu cur -
6. Laus,___ ho - nor, vir - tus, glo - ri - a De - o pa -

Faulx bourdon

2. Qui___ con - do - lens in te - ri - tu Mor - tis pe -
4. Cu - jus for - ti po - ten - ti - e Ge - nu cur -
6. Laus,___ ho - nor, vir - tus, glo - ri - a De - o pa -

Tenor

Qui condolens

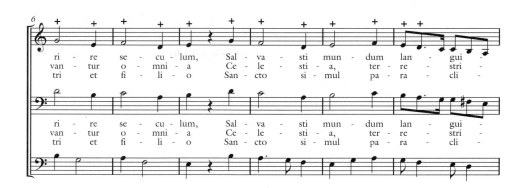

ri - re se - cu - lum, Sal - va - sti mun - dum lan - gui -
van - tur o - mni - a Ce - le - sti - a, ter - re - stri -
tri et fi - li - o San - cto si - mul pa - ra - cli -

ri - re se - cu - lum, Sal - va - sti mun - dum lan - gui -
van - tur o - mni - a Ce - le - sti - a, ter - re - stri -
tri et fi - li - o San - cto si - mul pa - ra - cli -

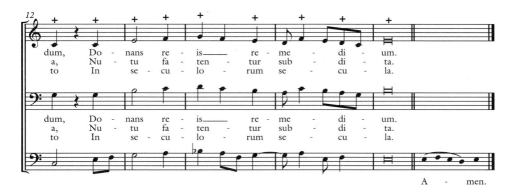

1. Kindly creator of the stars, eternal light of the believers, Christ, redeemer of all, hear the prayers of the supplicants, 2. Thou who, suffering the destruction of death, the demise of the people, freed the languishing world, providing a remedy for sin. 3. To experience the turning of the world toward evening, the Bridegroom is come forth from his chamber, from the most chaste womb of the virgin Mother. 4. [Thou], before whose mighty power all will bend the knee in heaven and in earth and will confess subjection to thy command. 5. We beseech thee, holy judge of the days to come, save us in time from the weapon of the perfidious enemy. 6. Praise, honor, power, and glory to God the Father and the Son, and to the Holy Ghost the same, throughout all eternity. Amen.

the sources, suggesting that the hymn melody may have been further set off by the contrasting sonorities of an instrumental accompaniment.) Also reflected in the polyphonic setting is the structure of the hymn, both text and music; within the strophe each of the verses is clearly punctuated by a contrapuntal cadence and/or a rest.

An examination of other hymns in the repertory of some twenty-four attributed to Du Fay—three of which appear in the sources with two different texts[7]—confirms his consistency in the compositional procedures adopted for the genre. However, in a considerable number of his settings Du Fay made use of *fauxbourdon*, writing out only the superius and the tenor and leaving the contratenor to be added between them in performance in strict parallel fourths with the upper part. The result, as seen, for example, in his well-known setting of the Advent hymn *Conditor alme siderum* (see Example 9-3),[8] is not far removed from what might have been obtained had the polyphony been improvised in three parts directly from the chant, whether in

7. Like the monophonic melodies to which the hymns were sung, the polyphonic settings could be adapted to any text having verses of the same length with the same number of verses per strophe, making textual substitutions relatively easy and common.

8. See Du Fay, *Opera omnia*, ed. Besseler, 5:39; also Claude V. Palisca, ed., *Norton Anthology of Western Music*, 3d. ed., 2 vols. (New York: Norton, 1996), 1:107.

fauxbourdon itself or an analogous English use of "sights" known as *faburden*.[9] The adoption of such a simple contrapuntal procedure for the written repertory is perhaps the best evidence available that well-loved liturgical chants were embellished for important feasts with improvised discant of some such sort long before the written repertory came into existence and that such practices may have continued in use for a good while after written polyphony had become the rule.

The compositional procedures used by Du Fay apparently established a pattern that came to be followed in most respects by the majority of his contemporaries. However, Johannes de Lymburgia provided for the Easter hymn *Ad cenam agni providi* a polyphonic setting for each of the odd-numbered strophes, and for the Christmas hymn *Criste redemptor omnium* he provided three separate settings, one for each consecutive pair of stanzas (1,2; 3,4; 5,6), the outer sections à 3 and the inner one à 2.[10] Different polyphonic settings for alternate strophes, whether the odd- or the even-numbered, indicate a more elaborate treatment of the genre, and the pattern adumbrated in hymn settings such as those attributed to Lymburgia was followed with increasing frequency by composers of subsequent generations, especially those affiliated with the papal court, as we shall see.

MAGNIFICAT SETTINGS

Except for the Ordinary of the Mass, no other liturgical text was so frequently treated polyphonically in the course of the fifteenth and sixteenth centuries as the Magnificat, and no other is so well represented in the sources of that time. As with the hymns the earliest written examples go back to the second half of the fourteenth century; a fragment has been preserved from that period in a manuscript now in the Cambridge University Library (MS Kk.1.6). However, the embellishment of the chant with improvised discant, at least on Sundays and feast days, may have begun much earlier. Not until the early 1400s do sources for the polyphonic Magnificat begin to be fairly numerous, but by the end of the century some 300 had been entered in the manuscripts still extant. Surprisingly, perhaps, given what appears to be a rather slow start in Magnificat composition, another 1500 works were inscribed in the known collections of liturgical music during the first half of the sixteenth cen-

9. Continental *fauxbourdon* in three parts could be improvised directly from a written chant simply by singing it at the upper octave, placing a second part in parallel fourths below, and adding a third part that begins and ends each phrase at the octave (and sounds it for variety at any point in between) and otherwise moves only in parallel sixths. *Faburden* was essentially the same except that the chant was taken (at pitch) as the middle voice with a second part added above it in parallel fourths and a third part below in parallel thirds (i.e., a sixth below the upper part) but with a fifth below (i.e., an octave below the upper part) to begin and end the phrase. See Brian Trowell, "Faburden" and "Fauxbourdon," *The New Grove Dictionary of Music*, 6:350–54 and 433–38.
10. See Keith Mixter, "Johannes de Lymburgia," *The New Grove Dictionary of Music*, 9:666–67.

tury (counting just the scribal entries and not the total number of pieces, some of which were copied in many different sources).[11]

The attention devoted to setting the Magnificat in the fifteenth and sixteenth centuries is nevertheless readily understood since, like the hymn, it was a very important element of the Vespers service—its culmination in fact. Moreover, its cultivation was linked to the universal popularity of the cult of the Virgin, which was so tenacious that it survived the Protestant Reformation, even in those regions where reform was most fervently embraced. Musically, however, the two categories of chant are fundamentally different. For while each hymn was provided with an individual plainsong melody (even if some tunes served for more than one text), the Magnificat was sung to one of the recitation tones that, although a bit more elaborate than the Psalm tones, correspond in their formulaic simplicity to the latter's general design.

It was the use of those tones, coupled with the structure of the biblical canticle itself—which, like the Psalms, consists of paired, parallel verses—that governed the polyphonic treatment of the Magnificat. The antiphonal style of performance that was traditional for psalmody was generally applied as well to settings of the canticle of the Virgin. Chant and polyphony followed one another in *alternatim*, usually with the even-numbered verses set polyphonically (beginning with "Et exultavit") but also with the odd-numbered verses in parts (beginning with "Anima mea") and the others sung monophonically to the liturgical tone.

Most works in the genre incorporate the chant into the polyphony, usually in the superius, where (at least in the earliest examples) it tends to be only lightly decorated, and—as in the hymns, once again—mostly at cadences. Representative of this phase in its development is a *Magnificat primi toni* that is somewhat unusual in that it is found in two of its five sources—all of them Italian—with polyphony for the entire text, save only the opening intonation.[12] Its authorship is contested in the sources; the work is ascribed to both Binchoys and Du Fay in the Modena MS α.X.1.11 and to Binchoys alone in the Bologna University Library MS 2216.[13] Interestingly, this setting of the canticle is one of six that have been attributed to Binchoys, one in each of the first four tones (a circumstance that may vouch for his paternity for the first of the group) and one each in the sixth and the eighth.[14] Absent from this piece, in any case, are the repetition schemes characteristic of compositions more securely attributed to Du Fay. For example, the latter's *Magnificat quinti toni* has much the same music from verse to verse, and his *Magnificat sexti toni*—which, exceptionally once again,

---

11. See Winfried Kirsch, *Die Quellen der mehrstimmigen Magnificat- und Te Deum-Vertonungen bis zur Mitte des 16. Jahrhunderts* (Tutzing: Schneider, 1966), 29ff.

12. It was also inscribed in two other manuscripts with only even verses and in yet another with only the odd ones, clear indications that *alternatim* performance was customary under most circumstances.

13. See the list of works as compiled by David Fallows, "Binchois," *The New Grove Dictionary of Music,* 2:717.

14. See Philip Kaye, ed., *The Sacred Music of Gilles Binchois* (London: Oxford University Press, 1992), 139–72, nos. 22–27. Number 26, a *Magnificat sexti toni* (of which there is only one verse), may be a *contrafactum* of Binchoys's chanson *Mort en merchy,* the attribution in the unique source, the "St. Emmeram Codex," is to "Egidius Prachoys."

makes provision for polyphonic performance of all twelve verses—has only five sections in all. If the entire text is to be sung to this music, the individual segments must be repeated, possibly in the sequence ABCDEBCDEBCD.[15]

Like most Magnificat settings from about this time—presumably the 1430s or thereabouts—Binchoys's (?) *Magnificat primi toni* is in three parts with the chant formula quoted with relatively little embellishment in the superius, most of it once again in cadential passages (see Example 9-4).[16] Retained as well, consequently, is the syllabic declamation characteristic of the liturgical tones, which is broken significantly only at cadences. The counterpoint is in a relatively straightforward homophonic style that lends itself to a simultaneous delivery of the text from all three parts. (Since words are provided for all three in some of the sources, moreover, there is reason to believe not only that all-vocal performance was adopted in certain localities of northern Italy but also that the composer may have written for it.) Noteworthy in this connection is the composer's reliance upon a lightly decorated *fauxbourdon* as the primary compositional procedure. The resulting style is very similar to that used by Du Fay for his *fauxbourdon* hymn settings, and it suggests, as it does in that context, that the Magnificat, like the hymn, may

15. See the discussion by Fallows, *Dufay*, 149–50, and the formal diagrams, 234–35.
16. For a complete transcription, see Jeanne Marix, ed., *Les musiciens de la cour de Bourgogne au XVe siècle*, (Paris: Droz, 1937), 131–37, or Kaye, ed., *Sacred Music of Gilles Binchois*, 139–46, no. 22.

EXAMPLE 9-4. Gilles Binchoys/Guillaume Du Fay(?), *Magnificat* [*primi toni*], verses 1–2 (mm. 1–23)

My soul doth magnify the Lord, and my spirit hath rejoiced in God my Savior.

have been enhanced on special occasions by polyphonic improvisation long before written versions were first entered in the sources, and perhaps long afterward as well.

An apparently later—and clearly more sophisticated—setting of the canticle, a *Magnificat "tertii et quarti" toni* also ascribed to Du Fay, gives an indication of the compositional procedures that were to be adopted with increasing frequency by the masters of subsequent generations. It was included in a large collection of sacred polyphony compiled in the kingdom of Naples during the final decade of the fifteenth century, MS 871 of the library of the Benedictine monastery at Montecassino. Given the date of its earliest source, this work may have been among the last of the sort to have come from Du Fay's pen.[17] Although exhibiting the economy of means

17. For a complete transcription, see the edition by Isabel Pope and Masakata Kanazawa, eds., *The Musical Manuscript Montecassino 871* (Oxford: Clarendon Press, 1978), 287–94 and 602–3; also Du Fay, *Opera omnia*, ed. Besseler, 5:91–94.

that the composer often achieved in his usual manner by repeating serially a limited number of sections of music—in this case again following the sequence ABCDE-BCDEBCD—this particular setting was also apparently intended to provide polyphony for all twelve verses of the canticle.

More significant than the composer's adherence to established patterns, however, are his stylistic innovations, the freedom with which he treated the liturgical tone, on the one hand, and the variety he imparted to the sonorities and the textures, on the other (see Example 9-5).[18] The first of the five sections is written in three parts (only one of which may have been intended for vocal performance), the second in two, the third in four, the fourth again in two, and the fifth once more in three. In addition, the mensuration changes after the first two sections, which are written in perfect tempus (O), to diminished imperfect tempus (₵), and then back to perfect tempus for the fifth and last. These changes in voicing and meter are accompanied, and also underscored, by stylistic distinctions between the sections in three and four parts and the two duos, both of which are noticeably more active rhythmically than the other three and the only ones (except the last) to make fairly systematic use of melodic imitation. As we shall see, by the end of the century these compositional features were commonly associated with polyphonic cycles based on the Mass Ordinary,

18. It was undoubtedly this stylistic variety that allowed the work to be identified as "tertii et quarti toni" in two of its five manuscript sources; however, allusions to the liturgical tone in all five sections, and especially in those written for three and four parts, point unambiguously to the third tone.

EXAMPLE 9-5. Guillaume Du Fay, *Magnificat "tertii et quarti" toni* (mm. 20-37)

. . . and my spirit hath rejoiced in God my Savior, for he hath regarded the low estate of his handmaiden . . .

and because of the growing importance of that genre, they were often adapted to settings of other lengthy texts with similarly clear structural divisions.

～◯ PSALM SETTINGS ◯～

As in the case of the hymns and Magnificats—the two categories of chant for the Office whose polyphonic treatment has already been considered—the singing of Psalms was apparently also embellished on festal occasions by improvised discant of some sort. Judging from the character of the earliest Psalm settings included in the written repertory, it seems probable that *fauxbourdon* (or some similarly simple procedure) was most often adopted for that purpose from the early fifteenth century on. That polyphonic improvisation was in fact common practice for the recitation of the Psalms in a liturgical context is clearly implied by the tenacious persistence of *falsobordone*—an adaptation of *fauxbourdon* with an added fourth voice—throughout the sixteenth century and well into the seventeenth. Such a development is easily explained only if *fauxbour-*

don was favored for polyphonic psalmody at the beginning of the period in question and that the later practice grew directly and naturally out of the earlier one.

Also pointing to a vigorous and ongoing tradition of improvisatory polyphony as an embellishment for the Office Psalms is the paucity of notated pieces for liturgical use in the sources containing fifteenth-century repertory. Significantly, once written compositions do begin to appear, they are confined in every instance to the Psalms prescribed for Vespers, in particular those for Sundays throughout the year, providing a precious clue as to when the Psalms were most often dressed up polyphonically. Equally instructive is the circumstance that the earliest written examples rely very heavily—in fact almost exclusively—on contrapuntal procedures derived directly from improvised *fauxbourdon*.

Such a work is the setting attributed to Binchoys of *In exitu Israel* (Psalm 113), the fifth and last of the Psalms sung at Sunday Vespers, which includes not only all of its verses but also the antiphon *Nos qui vivimus* and a lengthy melismatic "Amen" to close.[19] Like so much of the sacred music attributed to northern masters of this period, this work has been transmitted only in manuscripts of Italian provenance: the Ferrarese collection Modena, Biblioteca Estense e Universitaria, MS α.X.1.11, and Florence, National Library, MS Magl. 112bis, which apparently originated in Genoa in the 1460s.[20]

The polyphony, which is remarkably simple in its adherence to the formulaic counterpoint of *fauxbourdon*, is based entirely on the liturgical formula, in this instance the *tonus peregrinus*, which was traditionally associated with this, the "pilgrim's Psalm" (see the *Liber usualis*, 160).[21] The chant-derived melodic material is carried by the superius throughout, and the lower parts follow mostly in parallel fourths and sixths with the tenor moving in contrary motion to make an octave with the topmost part only, as a rule, at the cadences with which the verses conclude. Relief from the uniformity of the homophonic declamation is offered solely by changes in rhythm and tempo, some of which arise from the proportional shifts in mensuration—from ternary (Ȼ) to binary (C, m. 115) and back to ternary (Ȼ, m. 261, and C3, m. 365)—that occur in the course of the piece.

The Montecassino MS 871 contains an uninterrupted series of anonymous three-part settings for all five of the Psalms sung at Vespers on Sundays throughout the year: *Dixit Dominus* (Psalm 109), *Confitebor tibi Domine* (Psalm 110), *Beatus vir* (Psalm 111), *Laudate pueri* (Psalm 112), and *Laudate Dominum omnes gentes* (Psalm 116).[22] Only two parts have been written out, superius and tenor, with the higher of the two apparently derived in every instance from an elegant version of the Psalm tone, rhythmicized in mensural notation and lightly embellished at the

---

19. For a transcription see Marix, ed., *Les musiciens de la cour de Bourgogne au XVe siècle*, 196–208, or Kaye, ed., *Sacred Music of Gilles Binchois*, 203–17, no. 40.

20. Concerning the Modena manuscript, see p. 222; for the Florence manuscript, see the *Census-Catalogue of Manuscript Sources*, 1:225.

21. See "Tonus peregrinus," *The New Grove Dictionary of Music*, 19:67.

22. See the edition by Pope and Kanazawa, eds., *Musical Manuscript Montecassino 871*, 192–218, nos. 30–34.

cadences.[23] As may be seen from the briefest of excerpts, the third section of *Dixit Dominus* (see Example 9-6), these pieces are not without a certain rhythmic interest, deriving primarily from an alternation of binary and ternary groupings (all under ¢)—apparently to facilitate a more correct declamation of the text. By contrast, they are contrapuntally simple in the extreme due to their unremitting adherence to the formulae of *fauxbourdon*.[24]

Less typical, surely, but more interesting both musically and historically, is another setting of *In exitu Israel*, this one in four parts, with an attribution to Pietro Oriola

23. The Psalm tones used apparently fall into the following sequence: *Dixit Dominus* (tone 6); *Confitebor* (tone 2); *Beatus vir* (tone 4); *Laudati pueri* (*tonus peregrinus*) *Laudate Dominum* (tone 8). There is no indication of the reasons for those choices, but the tone of the Psalm usually coincides with the mode of the antiphon with which it is paired.
24. Curiously, the manuscript has no rubric indicating the mode of performance, but the steadily formulaic character of the part-writing can leave no doubt that three-part *fauxbourdon* was intended.

EXAMPLE 9-6. Anonymous, *Dixit Dominus domino meo*, verse 3 (mm. 19-33)

The rod of thy strength shall the Lord send out of Zion; rule thou in the midst of thine enemies.

(fl. ca. 1440–80), a composer of Aragonese origins who served at the royal court of Naples (see Example 9-7).[25] Once again the recitation formula is that of the *tonus peregrinus*, carried by the superius, the declamation is syllabic, and the texture is homorhythmic throughout. Only the first pair of verses has been set, however, the implication being that subsequent verses were to be adapted in performance to the same music—not an impossible task for singers who knew the Psalm texts by heart and were accustomed to making a similar adaptation monophonically with the liturgical Psalm tones. If such was in fact the intention of the composer—or of the scribe—this treatment of the Vesper Psalms is surely yet further evidence for a long-standing tradition of improvised polyphony in their performance.

25. For a complete transcription, see Pope and Kanazawa, eds., *Musical Manuscript Montecassino 871,* 123–24; concerning Oriola, see Isabel Pope, *The New Grove Dictionary of Music,* 13:822; regarding the historical significance of this composition as an early example of *falsobordone,* see pp. 560–63.

EXAMPLE 9-7. Pietro Oriola, *In exitu Israel*

When Israel went out of Egypt, the house of Jacob from a people of strange language, Judah was his sanctuary, and Israel his dominion.

A bit later on, as we shall see, when Psalm settings began to be written for divided choir, they were given a somewhat more elaborate treatment, first, it would seem, in the 1470s at the Este court in Ferrara by Johannes Martini and Johannes Brebis. Psalm texts also came to be set, either whole or in part, as motets more narrowly defined rather than for strictly liturgical use, as at Vespers, but that, too, came later in the century. Josquin Desprez, who represents the next generation of composers after Martini and Brebis, was the first to have as many as twenty such works ascribed to him, suggesting that he may have been instrumental in establishing the subtype. Not surprisingly, the plainchant formulae are rarely heard in such settings. Of greater interest to the composer, clearly, were the texts themselves with their ecstatic declarations and subjective cast, and the focus turned to an effective expression of their affective content by means of a newly developing musical rhetoric. The purposes for which such pieces were composed remain something of a mystery, but it appears likely that they were intended primarily for votive, processional, or devotional use, either in the ecclesiastical community or in the household of the noble and the wealthy.

~~~◯ LAMENTATIONS ◯~~~

At this point it should be abundantly clear that polyphonic elaboration of liturgical chants for the Office was largely confined, at least in the written repertory, to the Vespers services, perhaps because they were so often attended by lay members of the church. Exceptional, then, in this respect were the Lamentations of Jeremiah, which were used as Lessons at the first Nocturne of Matins on Maundy Thursday, Good Friday, and Holy Saturday—the *triduum sacrum* (the three holy days preceding Easter)—which are also known as the *Tenebrae* Services (cf. the *Liber usualis*, 626–761). Polyphonic treatment of chants from Matins, a service generally observed regularly only in monastic communities, must be due in this instance to the importance of the liturgical season and to the fact that the services in question were also celebrated in collegiate and cathedral churches that served the needs of urban centers.

Inasmuch as these lessons were sung to formulaic tones very similar to those used for the Psalms, they too may have been sung in parts using improvisatory procedures long before the added voices began to be written down. In any case the earliest settings included in known polyphonic repertories of the period were not entered in the surviving sources before mid-fifteenth century. One of the first has an attribution to the English composer John Tuder (fl. 1466–96), whose activity can be traced to New Romney, Kent, but is otherwise very little known. His Lamentations were included—together with hymns, motets, and polyphonic Propers for the Mass—in MS Pepys 1236 of the library of Magdalen College, Cambridge, which was copied in the County of Kent circa 1460–65.[26]

Although only the superius of the Lamentations has survived, that is enough to see that the composer based his polyphony on a liturgical tone used to recite the lessons in the celebration of the liturgy, one not unlike that found in present-day service books (cf. *Liber usualis*, 631). He also set to a melisma the Hebrew letter at the head of each section (a curious vestige of the acrostics upon which the original texts were based), thus matching the procedure adopted for the chant but with a considerably greater melodic extension.

Systematic cultivation of polyphonic settings for the Lamentations of Jeremiah seems to have been slow in developing, however, even in the final decades of the fifteenth century. The first substantial collection of such works known to us at present comes considerably later, and since it was printed—a two-volume set published by Petrucci in 1506—it may be an attempt to exploit commercially a paucity of compositions in the genre. The composers selected for inclusion by the Venetian publisher represented a variety of regions and linguistic and musical cultures: Alexander Agricola, Marbrianus de Orto, Johannes de Quadris, Gaspar van Weerbeke, Erasmus

---

26. See the edition by Sidney R. Charles, ed., *The Music of the Pepys MS 1236*, Corpus mensurabilis musicae 40 ([Rome]: American Institute of Musicology, 1967), 53–59.

Lapicida, Johannes Tinctoris, Bartolomeo Tromboncino, and Johannes Ycart.[27] But since all of them were at one time active in Italy, it would appear that a new impetus for polyphonic settings of the *Tenebrae* texts, whatever its ultimate origins, was most strongly felt there.

One of the earliest to have been written in Italy, and apparently by an Italian composer, was undoubtedly the two-part setting attributed to Johannes de Quadris.[28] It consists of a complete sequence appropriate for liturgical use with three readings for each day of the *triduum sacrum*. Neither part follows uninterruptedly one of the appropriate liturgical tones, as in the Tuder setting, but the superius is clearly derived—at least in part—from a tone similar to that prescribed for the Roman liturgy by the Council of Trent (see Example 9-8, mm. 20–38, and cf. the *Liber usualis*, 631). Also derived from the liturgical model, if less clearly, is the slightly more tuneful, syllabic treatment adopted for the initial declaration, "Incipit lamentatio Ieremie prophete," and the melismatic flourish for the Hebrew letters of the original acrostic. Moreover, since these letters are sung each time to the same imitative phrase, and the melodic formulae of the liturgical tone tend to appear always at the beginning of a section, the quasi-strophic effect of the chanted readings is maintained in the polyphony (as it is in the settings of several of the composers represented in the Petrucci print).[29]

Perhaps the most surprising aspect of the de Quadris Lamentations is the adoption of a two-voice texture for the entire setting at a time when most polyphony was being written for at least three parts and many works called for four and more. One cannot posit here, as in similar instances, the addition of a third part in accordance with some simple improvisatory practice such as *fauxbourdon*; the contrapuntal independence of the tenor does not lend itself to any such procedure currently known. It may be that the reasons for such restraint were either practical or esthetic. The two-part counterpoint may reflect very limited resources for polyphonic performance at the church for which these Lamentations were written. Or it may be that greater sonorous opulence was not deemed entirely fitting for such a solemn liturgical observance.

Whatever the cause, de Quadris was quite alone in showing such reticence, and as polyphonic Lamentations established themselves as a significant subgenre of the motet in the course of the sixteenth century, the composers who added to the growing repertory—including nearly every major figure of the age—adopted not only the

27. For an edition of the settings by de Orto, de Quadris, Lapicida, Tromboncino, Ycart, and the composer anonymously included in the Petrucci print, see Günther Massenkeil, ed., *Mehrstimmige Lamentationen aus der ersten Hälfte des 16. Jahrhunderts,* Musikalischer Denkmäler der Akademie der Wissenschaft und der Literatur 5 (Mainz: Schott, 1965); those attributed to Agricola, Weerbeke, and Tinctoris have been or will be included in the complete works of these composers. (Cf. Günther Massenkeil, "Lamentations," *The New Grove Dictionary of Music,* 10:410–12.)

28. For an edition, see Johannes de Quadris, *Opera,* ed., Giulio Cattin, Antiquae musicae italicae: Monumenta veneta sacra 2 (Bologna: Bardolino, 1972), 10–63.

29. See Massenkeil, ed., *Mehrstimmige Lamentationen,* 9ff., for a discussion of the use of the liturgical tone as a cantus firmus and the repetitions and strophic structures engendered thereby in the polyphonic settings of the early sixteenth century.

EXAMPLE 9-8. Johannes de Quadris, *Lamentationes Jeremiae Prophetae*, Feria V. Ad Matutinum, Lectio prima (mm. 20-48)

> How doth the city sit solitary, that was full of people! How is she become as a widow! She that was great among the nations, and princess among the provinces, how is she become tributary!

cantus firmus techniques already seen in connection with the pieces under discussion and in the polyphonic elaboration of chants for the Office generally but also the freer contrapuntal procedures used for the motet, properly speaking.

THE TE DEUM

The Te Deum is a solemn and venerable chant of praise, the text of which may date back to the fourth century, at least in good part. The chant to which it was sung is formulaic in character, in fact not far removed in its degree of elaboration from the tones for the Magnificat. Surprisingly, however, there is but one basic melody associated with it in the liturgical books of the Middle Ages and the Renaissance (albeit with the usual variants in melodic detail from source to source). The Te Deum had its regular liturgical place at the end of Matins on Sundays and feast days, but it was perhaps used even more frequently as a processional chant, as a conclusion to liturgical drama, and as a song of thanksgiving to mark special events: the consecration of a high-ranking prelate, for example, the dedication of a church, the coronation of a secular ruler, the signing of a peace treaty, and similarly joyous occasions. According to contemporary reports, moreover, when so employed it was frequently sung to the accompaniment of instruments—notably bells—and also, presumably, with improvisatory polyphonic elaboration.[30]

Such sonorous embellishment may help to explain why polyphonic settings of the Te Deum entered the written repertory very gradually at first and why it took so long to establish a distinctive compositional tradition for the genre. Very few of the sources for sacred and liturgical polyphony dating from mid- to late-fifteenth century include an example; even the extensive collection of polyphonic music gathered in the six "Trent Codices" included only two, and no other manuscript collection of the period had them in any greater numbers. Further, only one musician of the period—Gilles Binchoys—has been credited directly with a work of this type,[31] that inscribed in the Vatican manuscript San Pietro B 80 in the mid-1470s.

Binchoys's treatment of the traditional melody is what we have come to expect from his settings of other chants for the Office—hymns, Psalms, and Magnificats—and evokes the sort of improvised discant that was presumably often used on festal occasions for all of them until notated composition began to be preferred. The chant is quoted, rather literally, in the upper voice of the two that are written out—superius and tenor—and a third part is to be added in parallel fourths below the chant-bearing voice in accordance with the rubric *fauxbourdon* (see Example 9-9).[32]

In the course of the sixteenth century the Te Deum began to be set more frequently. As we shall see, however, the compositional procedures adopted for the polyphonic Te Deum seem never to have been codified as they were for some of the other motetlike subgenres. Some masters treated it much like the Magnificat, with

30. See Ruth Steiner, "Te Deum," *The New Grove Dictionary of Music,* 18:641–43, and cf. the *Liber usualis,* 1832–36; note that the "tonus simplex" is simply an abbreviated version of the solemn tone.

31. There were, of course, some anonymous settings in the manuscripts of this time; concerning the sources for the Te Deum, see Winfried Kirsch, *Die Quellen der mehrstimmigen Magnificat- und Te Deum-Vertonungen bis zur Mitte des 16. Jahrhunderts* (Tutzing: Schneider, 1966), 57ff.

32. For a complete transcription, see Marix, ed., *Les musiciens de la cour de Bourgogne au XVe siècle,* 219, or Kaye, ed., *Sacred Music of Gilles Binchois,* 243–53, no. 48. One of the sources for this work, the Segovia MS (Archivo Capitular de la Catedral, MS ss., ff. 101ᵛ–102), transmits only the first six strophes but in a version for four voices—the original superius and tenor with two new contratenor parts, one above and one below the tenor—but the revision may not be by Binchoys himself.

EXAMPLE 9-9. Gilles Binchoys, Te Deum (mm. 1-15)

God, we praise thee, eternal Father, all the earth doth honor thee.

chant and polyphony in *alternatim* and the liturgical melody figuring prominently in the counterpoint in one or more of the parts. Others approached it as they would any other motet text, producing a type of composition that was stylistically indistinguishable from works in that genre as most narrowly defined. Perhaps this variety reflects the many different contexts in which the Te Deum was performed, both sacred and secular.

"BENEDICAMUS DOMINO"

The traditional conclusion for each of the Canonical Hours was the versicle "Benedicamus Domino" with the response "Deo gratias." This was also sung at Mass, in place of the *Ite, missa est* on those occasions when the Gloria was excluded from the liturgy (during Lent and on fast days throughout the year). Monophonic tropes and *versus* including these liturgical phrases began to be written for festal celebrations from the tenth century on, and polyphonic elaboration of such texts can be traced back as far as the eleventh century.[33] If such a tradition was maintained through the fifteenth century as well, it did not stimulate the development of a distinct polyphonic genre in the written tradition. There is a pair of settings for three voices in the sources of the period, both ascribed to Du Fay, and at least one of them suggests once again a context of improvised polyphony.[34] At the time notated settings of this much-used versicle appear to have been rare in most areas of Europe, however, and polyphonic repertories of the early fifteenth century include very few of them. The Bologna MS Q15 has only one of those ascribed to Du Fay, for example, and Montecassino MS 871 has only one short anonymous setting in four parts. Despite the significance of its liturgical placement, the unadorned versicle and response seem not to have provided Renaissance composers of polyphony with an enduring source of musical inspiration.

33. See Steiner, "Benedicamus Domino," *The New Grove Dictionary of Music*, 2:471.
34. See Du Fay, *Opera omnia*, ed. Besseler, 5:87–94, nos. 35 and 36.

CHAPTER 10

Liturgical Polyphony for the Mass

THE POLYPHONIC ORDINARY: FROM PAIRS TO CYCLES

As was observed in the discussion of music in England at the beginning of the fifteenth century, a written repertory of compositions to the texts of the Ordinary of the Mass had its beginnings in the fourteenth century. However, in the early stages of what can now be seen as a nascent tradition most such works appear to have been conceived as individual compositions rather than as part of a larger group of pieces. The adventurous notions that led to unified pairs of settings for Ordinary texts that were juxtaposed in the liturgy and, even more remarkably, a complete cycle for the Mass conceived as a single, multipartite composition took shape only gradually. This is evident, first of all, from the polyphonic sources of the fourteenth century containing works of this kind, collections such as those now found in the libraries at Apt and Ivrea. Like the "Old Hall Manuscript," they are ordered by liturgical category, with separate sections for each of the Ordinary texts, and not as complete Masses, whether arbitrarily formed compilations or works actually so planned.[1]

Nevertheless, the factors that led to the constitution of plainsong Ordinaries in the fourteenth century apparently had much the same effect for polyphonic settings as well.[2] Fundamental, it would seem, was the desire to put together a group of compositions that were comparably appropriate liturgically, first of all, and perhaps even esthetically. The practical result was the combination, for a given celebration or order of feasts, of pieces that reflected in their musical elaboration a similar degree of solemnity or religious significance. Such a tendency is perhaps best demonstrated in the present connection by the polyphonic Ordinary "cycles" of the fourteenth cen-

1. See Theodor Göllner, "Mass," *The New Grove Dictionary of Music*, 11:783.
2. See Leo Schrade, "News on the Chant Cycles of the *Ordinarium missae*," *Journal of the American Musicological Society* 8 (1955): 66–69.

tury (which are currently identified by the cities in which their sources are preserved): the Masses (so-called) of Tournai, Barcelona, and even Besançon.

To judge from the striking stylistic diversity of their separate sections, however, all of them (with the possible exception of the Besançon Mass) appear to be composites, more or less arbitrary groupings of pieces that were probably written by different masters at different times and places. Even the sole polyphonic Ordinary of the period attributable to a single composer, the *Messe de Nostre Dame* by Guillaume de Machaut, has the character of such a compilation. The declamatory discant of the Gloria and the Credo stand in sharp contrast to the motetlike isorhythmic facture of the other sections. There is little evidence from the compositional perspective of a comprehensive plan to impart structural or even liturgical coherence, much less musical unity, to the whole.[3]

In the course of the fifteenth century the scribes who compiled the surviving Continental collections of polyphonic music for liturgical use placed compositions for the Mass Ordinary in pairs, groups, and cyclical arrays with ever increasing regularity. In the earliest of these sources—manuscripts such as MS Canonici Misc. 213 (ca. 1420–36) and Bologna, MS 2216 (before 1440)—settings for the Ordinary continue to be relatively few in number, and the copying of those compositions in pairs, small groups, and especially complete cycles is still relatively infrequent. By contrast, in manuscripts that were inscribed only slightly later—such as Bologna Q15 (ca. 1440) and the "Aosta Choirbook" (before 1446)—Mass Ordinaries predominate, forming far and away the most substantial component of those collections, and groups and cycles are ever more numerous.

Initially such groupings—like the compilations of plainchant Ordinaries—were apparently largely arbitrary still. Moreover, they were presumably determined not so much by musical considerations as by questions of practical utility. It was clearly a convenience to find side by side in compilations of liturgical polyphony settings for those texts that follow one another directly in the service. More useful still, perhaps, were complete cycles for the Ordinary that were judged appropriate for a given occasion or a particular category of liturgical feast. Eventually, however, such combinations apparently inspired the creative imagination of composers, suggesting to them that the individual pieces in such a group could be connected not only liturgically but also musically. They then began to develop the means that were to be used for such a purpose, going beyond general stylistic and structural affinities to specific compositional procedures. These included not only techniques and devices that could impart the desired musical coherence from section to section but especially those that could be laden at the same time with symbolic meanings and intertextual references.

As a consequence, arbitrary pairings and groupings gave way ever more frequently in the sources to others that are clearly intentional and compositional in

---

3. See Richard Hoppin, *Medieval Music* (New York: Norton, 1978), 385–95, and cf. Göllner, "Mass," *The New Grove Dictionary of Music*, 11:783.

nature. The evidence of the manuscripts indicates, in fact, that composers must have begun linking settings of the Ordinary texts by musical means even before the 1420s, starting as intimated with those that followed one another closely in the liturgy. Thus, the temporal juxtaposition of Gloria and Credo during the Preparation and of Sanctus and Agnus Dei during the Sacrifice may have suggested setting them in recognizably similar ways.

Obvious structural and/or stylistic resemblances may have played a role as well; formulaic chants and syllabic declamation contribute to the perceptible affinity between plainchants for the Gloria and Credo, for example, whereas those for the Kyrie, Sanctus, and Agnus Dei share clear structural divisions and melismatic text-setting. Even subsequently, when the five texts of the Ordinary were set as a cycle, the pairings and groupings arising from such similarities, and from liturgical proximity, continue to be in evidence. Apparently, such affinities were significant enough for composers of the period that they continued to be observed even after procedures had been developed for the musical unification of complete polyphonic Ordinaries.

The musical elements in the earliest layers of the repertory that give evidence of an authorial intention to connect the separate settings of a Mass Ordinary can be summarized as follows:[4]

1. identical or very similar combinations of clefs for the three or four voices for which the piece is written;[5]
2. common mensural usage, in particular where a series of several different signs is adopted (and the chance of coincidence thus diminished);
3. a common final, hence, usually, a similar pattern of internal cadences, pointing toward a common modal orientation;[6]
4. similarities in format, such as alternating patterns of texture generated by contrasts in voicing (high range versus low, for example, or three- and four-part passages juxtaposed with duos);
5. general commonalities of style—that is, the use of arresting compositional techniques such as imitative counterpoint or homophonic declamation; and, finally,
6. a common opening motto or "head motive," always a sure indication of artistic intent.

4. The formulation given here follows that of Charles Hamm, "The Reson Mass," *Journal of the American Musicological Society* 18 (1965): 5ff.; cf. the discussion of English Mass pairs, above, pp. 241–49.

5. It should be noted, however, that this may be a largely practical matter arising from the ranges of the individual voices available to sing polyphony in a given institution.

6. The significance of such consistency is quickly evident if one recalls that in a plainsong setting for a given feast, each of the chants is likely to be in a different mode.

From pairings and groupings based on liturgical proximity and/or affinity, Continental composers went on to the composition of complete cycles in which all five sections of the Ordinary are linked by the compositional devices just enumerated. Examples showing their application to polyphonic Mass composition are relatively numerous in collections such as Bologna Q15. Included there are two tripartite "sets" ascribed to Du Fay, both of them for three voices. However, one of them, an unbroken sequence of Kyrie, Gloria, Credo, is probably the result of a scribal rather than a compositional decision. Except for the declamation of the text (in Gloria and Credo) in alternation between the upper pair of voices (without telescoping), there is nothing to connect the sections in a way that would suggest intentional use of unifying compositional factors.[7] In the other group, by contrast, a series comprising Kyrie, Sanctus, and Agnus Dei—in this case, ironically, not contiguous in the manuscript—the latter two sections are connected by both a common opening "head motive" and a tenor cantus firmus identified with the tag "Vineux."[8]

Of even greater interest in the present context are the three complete cycles included in Bologna Q15, works attributed to Du Fay himself and to his lesser-known contemporaries, Johannes de Lymburgia[9] and Arnold de Lantins. There is also a complete set of related Ordinaries attributable to Johannes Reson that is scattered through the other collection in Bologna, MS 2216.[10] All four works display, to a greater or lesser degree, the features listed above as evidence of an authorial intent to link the separate sections by means of common musical elements.

The five sections of Du Fay's *Missa Sine nomine*, for example, share a common final (G) and identical clefs and signatures (b-fa for tenor and contratenor only). As a consequence they have similar ranges and a single modal orientation as well (a commixture of mode 1 in tenor and contratenor and mode 2 in the cantus).[11] There is also a recurring mensural pattern (from imperfect tempus with major prolation to perfect tempus with minor prolation: C, O) that occurs in every section except the Credo. The latter, exceptionally, takes its mensural cue from the beginning of the Gloria (which is in imperfect tempus with minor prolation: C), thus pairing these liturgical neighbors within the cycle by means of a link that is not shared by the other sections.

In addition, as David Fallows has shown, the Mass derives some of its most memorable gestures, both melodic and harmonic, from Du Fay's nuptial ballade of 1423, *Resvellies vous*, including a direct quotation of the opening phrase for the words "Qui

---

7. The compositions in question are nos. 187, 187b, and 188 in the manuscript; see Guillaume Du Fay, *Opera omnia*, ed. Heinrich Besseler, 6 vols. (Rome: American Institute of Musicology, 1947–66), 4:3–7, no. 1. The style of text placement in question has been termed "cursiva"; cf. David Fallows, *Dufay* (London: J. M. Dent, 1982), 177 and 229.

8. These pieces are nos. 17, 21, and 32 in the codex; see Du Fay, *Opera omnia*, ed. Besseler, 4:8–16, no. 2, and cf. Fallows, *Dufay*, 173–75 and 229.

9. Concerning Mass composition by Lymburgia, see Philip Gossett, "Techniques of Unification in Early Cyclic Masses and Mass Pairs," *Journal of the American Musicological Society* 19 (1966): 205–31.

10. Concerning the latter see Hamm, "Reson Mass," 5ff.

11. See Du Fay, *Opera omnia*, ed. Besseler, 2:1–14, no. 1.

sedes" in the Gloria (see Example 10-1). Also derived from the beginning of the chanson is a related melodic figure used with only slight variation as a head motive for the Kyrie and the Sanctus and, in a somewhat more compressed form, the Agnus Dei.[12]

Perhaps even more representative of this stage in the development of the cyclic Ordinary on the Continent is the *Missa Verbum incarnatum* attributed to Arnold de Lantins.[13] Written for three voices throughout, the same clefs (hence ranges) and signatures (b-fa for tenor and contratenor) are consistently maintained. In addition, a single cadential final (F) is used to close each of the five main sections, thus implying a uniform modal orientation for the entire cycle. Since the Sanctus and the Agnus Dei both make clear reference to the chants of the liturgical cycle prescribed in Roman usage for Sundays during Advent and Lent—the only two of that particular group to be classed as mode 5[14]—the circumstance is of particular interest for the question of musical coherence. It is possible to assume that the mode for the remaining sections was set to match that of the two chants that provide a seasonal frame of reference for the work as a whole. Still, the most incontrovertible indication of an intention to tie the five sections together musically is the melodic head motive in the superius, two breves in length, with which each of them begins. In the Sanctus and Agnus Dei, moreover, the accompanying tenor and contratenor are identical as well (see Example 10-2).

Grouping and pairing of sections within the cycle is also evident, first of all from the quotation of plainsong melodies and the fully identical head motives in the Sanctus and the Agnus Dei just mentioned. Also contributing to such internal distinctions are the two different sequences of mensurations that help to articulate subdivisions within the five primary sections. In the Kyrie, Gloria, and Credo the succession is from imperfect tempus with major prolation to perfect tempus with minor prolation and back, with a final segment in imperfect tempus with minor prolation in the Kyrie and the Credo (i.e., C, O, C, C). In the Sanctus and the Agnus Dei, by contrast, the mensuration shifts from perfect tempus in diminution to integral perfect tempus with the former then returning with the "Osanna" in the Sanctus while "Agnus III" finishes, like the Kyrie and the Credo, with imperfect tempus and minor prolation (i.e., ₵, O, ₵ and ₵, O, C, respectively).[15]

Also of interest here are the settings for the Ordinary texts included with the Propers in the cyclical Masses by Du Fay and Reginaldus Libert. The Ordinary set-

---

12. See Fallows, *Dufay*, 165–68; for further comment on the relationship between the ballade and the Mass, see also Allan Atlas, "Gematria, Marriage Numbers, and Golden Sections in Dufay's 'Revellies vous,'" *Acta musicologica* 59 (1987): 126.

13. This composition, which was inscribed sequentially in the Bologna MS Q15 as nos. 172–76, has been edited by Charles Van den Borren, in *Polyphonia sacra* (Burnham, Buckshire: The Plainsong and Medieval Music Society, 1932; reprint, University Park: Pennsylvania State University Press, 1962), 1–36.

14. See Roman Mass XVII, "In Dominicis Adventus et Quadragesimae," *Liber usualis*, 61–62.

15. Concerning the unifying features in the polyphonic Ordinaries ascribed to Johannes de Lymburgia and Johannes Reson, respectively, see Keith E. Mixter, *The New Grove Dictionary of Music*, 9:666; Hamm, "Reson Mass," 5ff.; and Gossett, "Techniques of Unification," 205–31.

EXAMPLE 10-1. Guillaume Du Fay, *Resvelliés vous et faites chiere lye* (mm. 1–3) and *Missa Sine nomine*, "Qui sedes" (mm. 63–65)

EXAMPLE 10-2. Arnold de Lantins, *Missa Verbum incarnatum*, Kyrie (mm. 1–9), Sanctus (mm. 1–12), and Agnus Dei (mm. 1–10)

KYRIE: Lord, Word incarnate announced by the prophets for the salvation of mankind, Lord, have mercy.

SANCTUS: Holy, holy, holy . . .

AGNUS DEI: Lamb of God, who takest away the sins of the world . . .

tings included in Du Fay's *Missa Sancti Jacobi* may represent a compilation of sorts in the sense that the sections from the Preparation (Kyrie, Gloria, and Credo) follow one structural plan whereas those for the Sacrifice (Sanctus and Agnus Dei) use another. In the first instance the texture alternates between segments in three parts, often designated "chorus" in the source, and others in two parts marked "duo" (presumably to indicate a pair of solo voices).

These divisions are grouped in turn by threes through a mensural pattern that shifts from imperfect tempus with major prolation (à 3) to perfect tempus with minor prolation (à 2) to a completely binary division (again à 3), producing the sequence ℂ, O, C. In the Sanctus and Agnus Dei, by contrast, the "chorus" sections are in four parts. And although these alternate with contrasting duos, the mensural pattern adopted in setting the other texts is nowhere in evidence. In addition, the liturgical plainsong, although embellished and extended, has been used as a kind of structural cantus firmus in the tenor of both concluding sections, whereas the compositional procedures in the Kyrie, Gloria, and Credo show no such dependence on preexistent melodies.[16]

The Ordinary segments of Libert's complete Mass in honor of the Virgin Mary follow a similar pattern. Here, however, liturgical chant provides the basis for the Kyrie as well as for the Sanctus and Agnus Dei. Moreover, like the Propers with which they have been combined, these three Ordinary chants were traditionally associated with the feasts of the Virgin. Each of them has been set in the same way; the liturgical melody—extended, even paraphrased, and elaborated mensurally—is carried by the superius in a three-part texture constantly maintained, where it functions as a melodic (rather than as a structural) cantus firmus. In addition, the work displays considerable stylistic consistency throughout. This is achieved by means of an unvarying use of three parts in similar ranges, relatively uncomplicated contrapuntal procedures (typified by an alternate version of the Sanctus in *fauxbourdon*), and even a certain modal coherence. All of the finals are either on D or G, usually in the latter instance with a b-fa signature for the tenor and contratenor, pointing toward the first (Dorian) pair.

Still, the most essential unity can be seen as liturgical rather than musical, deriving more from the adoption of chants associated with the feast of the Virgin than from any particularly striking compositional procedure. The esthetic impetus behind such a work must have been much the same as that which led to the compilation of plainsong Masses. Setting such chant Ordinaries as a polyphonic cycle with the liturgical melody paraphrased in the superius was to become a traditional practice, moreover, in particular for those Masses that were intended for Marian devotion. Examples by composers no less celebrated in their time than Josquin Desprez and Antoine Brumel have survived from later in the fifteenth century.[17]

---

16. See Fallows, *Dufay*, 170–71.

17. Polyphonic cycles based on chant melodies adapted to mensural notation and elaborated for use as melodic cantus firmi have been described as "paraphrase" Masses; see Gustave Reese, *Music in the Renaissance* (New York: Norton, 1959), 68.

Interestingly, the same fundamental compositional procedure was also adopted for yet another variety of polyphonic cycle that came into existence in the course of the fifteenth century, the Requiem Mass. Since in this instance Proper and Ordinary elements were so closely related liturgically and so highly specific in their ceremonial use, it was perhaps only natural that the polyphonic settings of the period also include both. One of the earliest works of the kind to survive is that ascribed to Johannes Okeghem,[18] but other masters were to follow suit later in the century, including major figures such as Johannes Prioris and Pierre de La Rue.

None of the Mass cycles by Continental composers discussed thus far make use of the compositional device adopted by English composers to give the texts of the Ordinary a Proper liturgical frame of reference: a plainchant cantus firmus. At some point, however, still early in the century, they did in fact adopt the English model, apparently in emulation of an English *Missa Caput* that was for many years attributed to Du Fay. A fully cyclic polyphonic Ordinary, the latter is based on the concluding melisma for the antiphon *Venit ad petrum*, which was prescribed for use in the Sarum rite for the ritual washing of feet that commemorates Christ's symbolic gesture of service to his apostles (the *pedilavium*), following Vespers on Maundy Thursday.[19] And like the earliest of the English cycles, this *Missa Caput* also reflects clearly the adaptation of structural features derived from the isorhythmic motet.[20]

Each section begins—like a typical isorhythmic motet—with a lengthy duo between superius and altus preceding the entry of the borrowed liturgical melody. The latter, disposed as a cantus firmus in rhythmic values generally longer than those of the upper parts, is carried exclusively by the tenor. In each major section of the Mass it is given two full statements that are identical with respect to pitch and the rhythmic values notated; they differ only in that the first is executed in perfect tempus (O), the second in imperfect tempus (C), resulting in the kind of proportional reduction that was so characteristic of late isorhythmic structures.[21] In addition the overall sonorities of the Mass have been enriched by a fourth part, a contratenor bassus in the range below that of the tenor (apparently intended, like the cantus firmus itself, for instrumental performance).[22]

With the exception of the Kyrie, which is in a peculiarly English format that orig-

18. See the edition in Johannes Ockeghem, *Collected Works*, ed. Dragan Plamenac, 2d ed., 2 vols. (New York: American Musicological Society, 1959–66), 2:83–97.

19. See Manfred Bukofzer, "*Caput*: A Liturgico-Musical Study," in *Studies in Medieval and Renaissance Music* (New York: Norton, 1950), 230–41.

20. See the edition of the three surviving Caput Masses in Alejandro E. Planchart, ed., *Missae Caput*, Collegium musicum 5 (New Haven: Yale University, 1964), 1–52; the composition now thought to be by an anonymous English master is there ascribed to Du Fay.

21. For a penetrating discussion of the compositional features carried over from the isorhythmic motet to the cantus firmus cyclic Mass, see Thomas Brothers, "Vestiges of the Isorhythmic Tradition in Mass and Motet, ca. 1450–1475," *Journal of the American Musicological Society* 44 (1991): 1–56. The author sees these procedures more fully exemplified in a series of Masses beginning with Du Fay's *Missa Se la face ay pale* and Busnoys's *Missa L'homme armé*.

22. See Bukofzer, "*Caput*," 259–66.

inally included extensive tropes in addition to the liturgical text, this work appears to have served as a model for the *Missa Caput* first of Okeghem and then of Obrecht. In both instances the composer took over the tenor cantus firmus from the earlier polyphonic setting, retaining the pitches, note values, and segmentation of the original. Each also provided (as in the model) for two full statements of the borrowed melody in each of the principal sections, the first in tempus perfectum (O), the second in tempus imperfectum (now, however, with the vertical stroke that signals diminution, ¢).[23]

Okeghem departed from his model structurally only by shifting the cantus firmus to the bassus from its traditional locus in the tenor. Since it is rather more difficult to place a borrowed melody at the base of the polyphonic fabric than to use it in the conventional manner as an internal part, this was perhaps an emulatory gesture intended by the composer to draw attention to his remarkable contrapuntal facility.[24] Obrecht retained the tenor cantus firmus of the English prototype in nearly every detail, but in other respects he betrays his familiarity with Okeghem's Mass as well.[25] Whatever the differences in stylistic detail between them, however, their appropriation of cantus firmus composition in the new English manner for the increasingly important genre of the polyphonic Mass Ordinary obviously helped to establish those compositional procedures in current usage on the Continent as well.

In adopting for the cyclic Ordinary the structural matrix and the contrapuntal techniques of cantus firmus composition—such as are to be observed in the *Missa Caput*—Continental musicians clearly indicate their continuing understanding of the powerful liturgical and symbolic associations that could be evoked by basing a work of that kind on a well-known melody, whether sacred or secular in its origins. It must surely have been this aspect of cantus firmus composition that initially motivated the liturgically conservative English composers to appropriate for Mass composition the procedures that had become traditional with the isorhythmic motet. Far from being a bold, artistic step, "the result of the weakening of liturgical ties at the oncoming of the Renaissance" and "startling" from a liturgical point of view, as was once suggested,[26] it was surely inspired instead by the familiar medieval tradition of troping.

The recurrence from one section to the next of a musical element that was immediately recognizable, if borrowed, or of discernibly appropriate significance, if invented, was capable of relating the Ordinary texts of the Mass to a readily identifiable Proper feast or a particular celebratory or devotional frame of reference. For the *Missa Caput* the most obvious proper liturgical connection would be with the feasts in

23. See Planchart, ed., *Missae Caput*, 53–97 and 98–153, and cf. Bukofzer, "*Caput*," 263–71. (The Agnus Dei of the Masses of both Okeghem and Obrecht are found in Claude V. Palisca, ed., *Norton Anthology of Western Music*, 1st ed., 2 vols. [New York: Norton, 1980], 171 and 177, respectively.)
24. Concerning the compositional problems engendered by that transposition, see the introduction to the edition in Johannes Ockeghem, *Masses and Mass Sections*, ed. Jaap van Benthem, 3 vols. (Utrecht: Koninklijke Vereniging voor Nederlandse Muziekgeschiedenis, 1994), 1:x.
25. Concerning Obrecht's *Missa Caput*, see Rob C. Wegman, *Born for the Muses: The Life and Masses of Jacob Obrecht* (Oxford: Clarendon Press, 1994), 265–67.
26. See again Bukofzer, "*Caput*," 225f.

honor of St. Peter, most probably for a church of which he was the patron saint. Or it may have been intended as a symbolic claim to divine authority for the anointing and crowning of a pope, a bishop, or even of a lesser prelate.

Whether or not Du Fay himself was familiar with the *Missa Caput* that has been linked with his name, he adopted early on the combination of English and Continental devices that were used to impart musical unity to the Mass Ordinary. More importantly, he eventually made exclusive use of a borrowed cantus firmus to provide a liturgical and/or topical context for the polyphonic cycle. That he understood perfectly the associative and symbolic possibilities of the device, whatever the genre in which it appears, seems clear enough not only from his own isorhythmic motets but also from his mature cantus firmus Masses. Typical and especially instructive are those with obvious Marian significance, such as the *Missa Ecce ancilla Domini* and the *Missa Ave regina celorum.*[27]

The latter in particular can be seen in a very real sense as the composer's personal homage to the Queen of Heaven. This is evident from the strikingly personalized troping of the liturgical text in a late motet based on the same Marian antiphon, a work that Du Fay had prepared to be sung during his final agony and upon which he drew in the composition of his Mass. It has been suggested that the work was intended for the dedication on July 5, 1472, of the Cambrai Cathedral, which was itself consecrated to "Notre Dame." It is also possible, and perhaps more plausible in light of recent research, that it was prepared for Du Fay's own Mass/obit foundation.[28] In either case, the composition would have evoked in a way entirely typical of medieval piety Du Fay's personal devotion to the Virgin through a characteristic celebration of appropriate Marian liturgy, whether for public purposes or on behalf of his own salvation.

CYCLIC MASSES ON SECULAR CANTUS FIRMI

Du Fay was also among the first to make use of a secular composition as the source for the tenor cantus firmus of a cyclic Ordinary. His *Missa Se la face ay pale*—which was also among his earliest full-blown cantus firmus Masses—is based on a ballade of his own composition. The chanson probably dates from his first sojourn at the ducal court of Savoy in the mid-1430s and may have been written to celebrate the beauty of Duchess Anne de Lusignan. A Mass based on such a work may seem at first blush

---

27. See the modern edition of these works in Du Fay, *Opera omnia*, ed. Besseler, 3:66ff. and 91ff., respectively; there is some discussion of both Masses by Edgar H. Sparks, *Cantus Firmus in Mass and Motet, 1420–1520* (Berkeley: University of California Press, 1963), 124–29.

28. See Fallows, *Dufay*, 79 and 209–12, but cf. Reinhard Strohm, *The Rise of European Music, 1380–1500* (Cambridge: Cambridge University Press, 1983), 284–86. For a detailed and comprehensive discussion of the problem, see Alejandro E. Planchart, "Notes on Guillaume Du Fay's Last Works," *Journal of Musicology* 13 (1995): 63–72.

rather difficult to explain from a liturgical point of view, but in this instance once again the ease with which the sacred and the secular were mingled at the time offers a clue as to its possible destination. It was most likely conceived as a nuptial Mass, perhaps specifically intended to celebrate the consummation of the marriage of the eldest son of Duke Louis of Savoy, Amadeus, with Yolande of France in October 1452.[29] It is not inconceivable, however, that despite the unmistakable allusion to physical love adduced by the cantus firmus, the Mass was intended instead as an homage to the Virgin Mary in a typically medieval transfer of the most elevated sentiments of courtly eros to the cult of the Mother of God.

A similar, and perhaps even more persuasive, explanation can be made regarding the use of the *L'homme armé* tune as a Mass cantus firmus. The song would have provided an appropriate reference to any of the most popular soldier-saints of the age— George, Martin, or Michael, for example—and may also have been connected in the minds of those who knew it with the Crusades. In the combinative setting of the popular melody the *rondeau* sung by the cantus speaks of a rather unlikely armed encounter of an improbable hero, Symonet le Breton, with the "dreaded Turk."[30] Symonet was for years a member of the Burgundian court chapel, and a polyphonic Mass Ordinary based on the well-known tune would have been particularly appropriate for the religious ceremonies of the Order of the Golden Fleece, founded by Philip the Good on the occasion of his marriage with Isabel of Portugal in 1430. As the ostensible purpose of the knightly association was to organize a new Crusade to wrest the territories around Nicopolis (the site of the great debacle of the ill-fated Crusade of the fourteenth century) from the hands of the Turks, Saint Andrew, who was traditionally associated with the region, was chosen as its patron.[31]

If a connection was in fact commonly made between the song about the armed man and the Crusades, it would help to explain the proliferation of Masses on that particular cantus firmus in the late fifteenth and early sixteenth centuries. These include the gift of a grand cycle of six such Masses from the duke of Burgundy to the royal court of Naples,[32] and the group of five *L'homme armé* Masses copied into the "Chigi Codex."[33] One of the earliest such works is that ascribed to Busnoys, who

29. See Fallows, *Dufay*, 70 and 194–96; also the brief discussion by Sparks, *Cantus Firmus in Mass and Motet*, 80–81, 120–22.

30. See Leeman L. Perkins and Howard Garey, eds., *The Mellon Chansonnier*, 2 vols. (New Haven: Yale University Press, 1979), 2:331–35.

31. See William Prizer, "Music and Ceremonial in the Low Countries," *Early Music History* 5 (1985): 128f.

32. See the study by Judith Cohen, *The Six Anonymous L'homme armé Masses in Naples, Biblioteca Nazionale, MS VI E 40*, Musicological Studies and Documents 21 ([Rome]: American Institute of Musicology, 1968), and her modern edition of the entire manuscript under the same title (Corpus mensurabilis musicae 85 [Neuhausen: Hänssler-Verlag, 1981]).

33. The settings in question are those attributed to Okeghem, Busnoys, Compère, Brumel, and Josquin; see Herbert Kellman, "The Origins of the Chigi Codex: The Date, Provenance, and Original Ownership of Rome, Biblioteca Vaticana, Chigiana, C.VIII.234," *Journal of the American Musicological Society* 11 (1958): 6–19, and the edition of the manuscript in facsimile, *Vatican City, Biblioteca Apostolica Vaticana, MS Chigiana C VIII 234* (New York: Garland Publishing, 1987).

enjoyed the patronage of the ducal court of Burgundy at the time of its composition (apparently in the late 1450s). And he may have embodied in its structure the number 31, which can be related to the knightly order established there.

As has been observed by the editor of Busnoys's Latin-texted works, the popular melody as notated mensurally—in both Busnoys's Mass and in the combinative chanson *Il sera pour vous conbatu*—contains exactly 31 semibreves. Similarly, the "Et incarnatus est" section of the Credo, which falls, structurally, very much in the center of the cycle overall, also contains precisely 31 *tempora*. Moreover, because 31 is a prime number, its notational representation at that point in the Mass stands in sharp contrast to the simple superparticular ratios reflected in the mensurations and durations of the surrounding sections. As it happens, however, from the time of its inception until 1517, the Order of the Golden Fleece numbered just 31 chevaliers. Consequently, it is tempting to believe that Busnoys conceived these subtle numerical arrangements as symbolic references to the members of the order for whose liturgical observances the Mass may well have been written.[34]

In other respects as well Busnoys's *Missa L'homme armé* is a classic example of the tenor cantus firmus Mass cycle of the fifteenth century.[35] The historical and stylistic links with the isorhythmic motet are still very much in evidence in a variety of features: the retention of the original notation of the preexistent melody for each of the five major sections; its proportional manipulation by means of a series of changing mensurations; and (except for the Kyrie) the extended soloistic duos and trios that precede each time the entry of the cantus firmus.[36] The borrowed melody is divided into two segments, approximately at the center (between mm. 16 and 17 in the Kyrie, Gloria, and Agnus Dei, in m. 19 in the Gloria, and between mm. 20 and 21 in the Sanctus) with a complete statement in each principal section of the Mass. In addition, there is a second statement—in the original rather than in mensurally extended values—in the "Qui tollis" section of the Gloria and a partial one in the "Confiteor" of the Credo—a structural parallel that links this pair of sections within the cycle.[37]

The five sections of the cycle are tied to one another not only by the shared cantus firmus, however, but also by the Continental device of a common head motive. In a duo of three breves' duration between superius and altus the latter quotes the opening phrase of the *L'homme armé* tune (see Example 10-3). Also reflective of the Continental tradition is the alternation between four parts where the cantus firmus is present and three when it is not (as in the "Christe," the "Pleni sunt" and

---

34. See Antoine Busnoys, *Collected Works*, ed. Richard Taruskin, Masters and Monuments of the Renaissance 5 (New York: Bronde Trust, 1990), pt. 3, pp. 17–21. Thomas Brothers offers another possible explanation for the length of this section, however, in its putative relationship to the *Missa Se la face ay pale*; see his "Vestiges of the Isorhyhmic Tradition in Mass and Motet, ca. 1450–1475," *Journal of the American Musicological Society* 44 (1991): 10–11, 18–24.

35. See the edition in Busnoys, *Collected Works*, ed. Taruskin, pt. 2, pp. 1–48.

36. Concerning the structural traits of the isorhythmic motet embodied in this Mass cycle, see Brothers, "Vestiges of the Isorhyhmic Tradition," 1, 18–24.

37. See Busnoys, *Collected Works*, ed. Taruskin, pt. 3, p. 2.

EXAMPLE 10-3. Antoine Busnoys, *Missa L'homme armé*, Gloria (mm. 1–7)

. . . and on earth, peace to men of good will.

"Benedictus" of the Sanctus, and the "Agnus Dei II"). Interestingly, this structural parallel, which is not shared by the two central sections of the Mass, serves to link these three within the cycle. Musical integration is further assured by the clear modal orientation of the borrowed melody and the maintenance of its G final from one section to the next. In this respect, however, there is an interesting difference between the polyphonic setting of the combinative chanson and Busnoys's Mass cycle. In the song the melody is sung in the hard hexachord with b-mi—that is, with the species of fourth and fifth characteristic of mode 7 (the Mixolydian). By contrast, the Mass uses a b-fa signature for all voices throughout, thus casting the popular tune very clearly in the species of mode 1 (the Dorian) in its most common transposition.

Yet another feature of Busnoys's Mass may be seen as an early harbinger of the contrapuntal artifices with which the northern composers of his own and subsequent generations sometimes embellished their polyphonic cycles. A verbal canon for the Agnus Dei instructs the performer(s) of the cantus firmus to invert the notation, thus reading every ascending interval, as notated, in descent and every descending interval in ascent (see Example 10-4).[38] One of the practical consequences of this procedure was to place the tenor in a range below that of the bassus. This Busnoys had already done in the Credo by means of a canonic transposition of the cantus firmus downward by a fourth. It is interesting that Okeghem, who (unlike Busnoys) retained the Mixolydian orientation of the borrowed tune for his *Missa L'homme armé*, transposed it to the lower fifth for his Credo and to the lower octave for his Agnus Dei, thus placing the cantus firmus in the bassus range in both instances. For the Credo, then, both composers employed a downward transposition to the first pitch that would conserve the species of fifth of the original range. Because the cantus firmus melody begins at the bottom of its ambitus, however, Busnoys was able to achieve an effect similar to that of Okeghem's octave transposition simply by inverting the intervals specified by its notation.

If Busnoys was familiar with Okeghem's Mass and wished to surpass the work of the older master in some significant regard, he found a most effective way of doing so. Assuming that he did in fact take Okeghem's general plan as his model, he added an ingenious contrapuntal manipulation of the recurring cantus firmus in order to shift it into the bassus register for the closing section of the Mass. If his intention in doing so was to display even greater skill than was required for Okeghem's simple transposition, Busnoys's *Missa L'homme armé* may be an early example of the artistic emulation that came to be associated with Masses based on the popular tune. Such artifice was deployed ever more frequently—and elaborately—by musicians who adopted the song as the cantus firmus for a cyclic Ordinary and were obviously familiar with the earlier compositions of rivals and/or predecessors. Busnoys's possible contribution to that tradition presupposes the chronological priority of Okeghem's Mass, however, and the sequence in which the earliest Masses based on the well-traveled tune were written has yet to be firmly established.[39]

From the earliest examples, which appear to date from the 1430s and 1440s, through the remainder of the century, polyphonic cycles of the Ordinary of the Mass came to be constructed ever more consistently on borrowed material of one sort or another, both secular and sacred. As the structural model shaped by the composers discussed in the previous pages was disseminated across Europe together with their works, it began very soon to be emulated by composers in other localities as well.[40] Thus it was that the tenor cantus firmus–based format—derived in several essential respects, as we have seen, from the isorhythmic motet, to which the cyclic Masses

---

38. The canon reads, in translation, "Wherever the scepters descend, there make an ascent, and vice versa"; see the edition of the Mass, in Busnoys, *Collected Works*, ed. Taruskin, pt. 2, pp. 41–48, and pt. 3, p. 34.

39. See Leeman L. Perkins, "The L'homme armé Masses of Busnoys and Okeghem: A Comparison," *Journal of Musicology* 3 (1984): 363–96.

40. For a discussion of polyphonic cycles of the Ordinary dating from the 1450s to the 1470s and based exclusively on German Lieder, for example, see Adelyn Peck Leverett, "Song Masses in the Trent Codices: The Austrian Connection," *Early Music History* 14 (1995): 205–56.

EXAMPLE 10-4. Antoine Busnoys, *Missa L'homme armé*, "Agnus I"

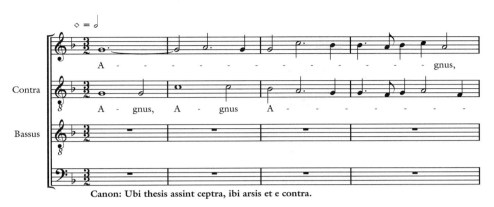

Canon: Ubi thesis assint ceptra, ibi arsis et e contra.

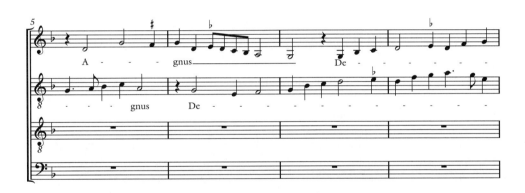

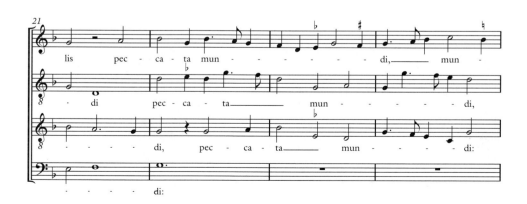

Lamb of God, who takest away the sins of the world, have mercy upon us.
CANON: Where the scepters ascend, there ascend, and vice versa.

owe so many of their structural and stylistic features—came to be the most common of the compositional procedures used in such works.

∽ THE MASS-MOTET CYCLE ∾

Perhaps nothing illuminates the close historical and stylistic affinities between polyphonic Mass Ordinaries and tenor cantus firmus motets more clearly than what has been called the Mass-motet cycle.[41] Consisting of settings for the texts of the Ordinary to which a motet has been added, all of which are based on the same preexistent melody, it is perhaps best seen as a logical extension of the tenor Mass cycle. The implication, of course, is that singing a motet during the celebration of the Mass, very often at its close, had become a fairly common practice in the course of the fifteenth century. However, only half a dozen such cycles have been uncovered thus far, suggesting that the linking of the motet to the sections of the Ordinary was an experiment of sorts and rather short-lived. The relevant sources indicate as well that the practice was geographically localized. Even so it is of unquestionable historical significance, and there may be other such cycles that have yet to be pieced together and identified for what they once were.

The first inkling that these compositions were extended cycles including a motet, rather than Mass cycles based on a motet tenor, came from the discovery that two of them had been included in a manuscript now in Prague (Museum of Czech Literature, Strahov Library, MS D.G.IV.47). Primarily a repertory of liturgical polyphony, it contains music for both the Mass (ten cyclic Ordinaries, five pairs, and thirty-two individual settings—twenty-one Kyries, one Gloria, eight Sanctus, and two Agnus—together with fifty-eight Propers, mostly Introits) and the Office (fourteen Magnificats and sixty-nine hymns) together with seventy-three motets and twenty-one secular pieces. It was probably compiled over a couple of decades, reaching completion around 1480, and must have originated somewhere in the region: perhaps at the Olomouc Cathedral in Moravia (although Bohemia and Silesia have also been suggested).[42]

One of the Mass-motet cycles inscribed in its leaves is based primarily on the tenor of the famous polyphonic song once claimed for Dunstable but now generally credited to Bedyngham, *O rosa bella*.[43] The anonymous composer, writing for four

41. The term was coined by Robert J. Snow, who first drew attention to the existence of a small repertory of compositions that can be so designated; see his study, "The Mass-Motet Cycle: A Mid-Fifteenth-Century Experiment," in *Essays in Musicology in Honor of Dragon Plamenac*, ed. Gustave Reese and Robert J. Snow (Pittsburgh: University of Pittsburgh Press, 1969), 301–20.

42. See the *Census-Catalogue of Manuscript Sources of Polyphonic Music, 1400–1550*, ed. Charles Hamm and Herbert Kellman, 5 vols. (Neuhausen-Stuttgart: Hänssler-Verlag, 3:60–61; but cf. Strohm, *Rise of European Music*, 513.

43. There is an attribution to each composer in one of the sources, but for a convincing marshaling of the evidence in favor of Bedyngham's authorship, see David Fallows, "Dunstable, Bedyngham, and *O rosa bella*," *Journal of Musicology* 12 (1994): 287–305.

voices, has built each of the five sections of the Ordinary and the motet, *O pater eterne*, on a tenor derived from the borrowed melody. In addition, he has taken his head motive from the cantus of the song, making explicit the connection of all sections of the cycle, including the motet, with the polyphonic setting of the well-traveled *giustiniana*. The motet is unique to the "Strahov Codex," but the settings for the texts of the Ordinary are also found in the Trent MS 89 and in a choirbook copied in Ferrara in 1481 for use in the chapel of Ercole I d'Este.[44]

For the other Mass-motet cycle in the Strahov manuscript, conversely, the four settings for the Ordinary are apparently unique to the collection (the Kyrie is wanting), whereas the motet, *O gloriosa mater Cristi Maria*, is also found in Trent MS 89, albeit with a choice of two different texts. The composer, a certain Philipus Francis (who has yet to be identified more fully), has based both the Ordinary items (written for four parts) and the motet (with an optional fifth voice) on a preexistent tenor that is identified in the sources for the motet with the phrase, "Hilf und gib rat" ("help and give counsel"), perhaps the incipit for a German song that is not otherwise known. He has further tied the segments of the cycle together with a head motive in two parts (three in the motet with the added fifth voice), the superius of which is clearly related to the cantus firmus.[45]

A third Mass-motet cycle, found in Trent MS 88, includes all five texts of the Ordinary, set for three parts, and a motet, *Gaude Maria virgo*, for four. The composer (again anonymous) drew the cantus firmus from the tenor of a chanson ascribed to Binchoys, *Esclave puist yl*, and emphasized the connections among the segments with a head motive clearly derived from the cantus of the model but transposed to the upper fourth.

The three remaining Mass-motet cycles are incomplete in their respective sources, their separate elements being divided among two or more manuscript collections. Settings of the Ordinary texts for three voices based on the tenor of the ballade by Walter Frye, *So ys emprentid*, found in Trent MS 90 with an ascription to W. le Rouge (Guillaume Rouge), are matched by an anonymous motet for four, *Stella celi extirpavit*, inscribed in Trent MS 88. The Ordinary is also found (with the tenor incipit "Soyez aprantiz") without attribution in the Vatican manuscript, San Pietro B 80, a collection of liturgical polyphony copied for use by the choir of St. Peter's Basilica in Rome in 1474–75.[46] As in the other cycles, the tenor cantus firmus is common to all six sections, but there is no head motive.

Another set of anonymous polyphonic Ordinaries in the Strahov manuscript (lacking again the Kyrie) can be tied by a common cantus firmus, the Introit chant *Meditatio cordis*, to a motet in the Trent MS 88, *Gaude Maria virgo*. Again,

---

44. See Snow, "The Mass-Motet Cycle," 303–5, including his examples 1 and 2; concerning the "Trent Codices," see above, pp. 223–24; for the Ferrarese collection, now in Modena at the Biblioteca Estense, MS α.M.1.13 (Lat. 456, *olim* V.H.10), see the *Census Catalogue of Manuscript Sources*, 2:167–68.
45. See Snow, "Mass-Motet Cycle," 305–6.
46. Concerning this choirbook, see Christopher A. Reynolds, *Papal Patronage and the Music of St. Peter's, 1380–1513* (Berkeley: University of California Press, 1995), 80, 98.

there is no head motive, but all five segments of the cycle are for four voices. Finally, the *Missa Summe trinitati*, ascribed to Walter Frye in the Brussels MS 5557, shares with the anonymous motet *Salve virgo mater pia* not only the same tenor cantus firmus borrowed from a plainchant responsory but also a common head motive.[47]

It is striking that all of the composers who can be identified in connection with the known Mass-motet cycles are English or, in the case of Binchoys and Rouge, believed to have had English connections. Equally noteworthy is the provenance of the sources. Although the Mass Ordinaries were disseminated more widely, all of the motets belonging to one of these cycles are found only in collections that reflect repertory in the Austrian and southern German areas that were under the sway of the Habsburgs in the fifteenth century.[48] It is possible, as Snow suggests, that they were the creation of English composers who found patronage with one of the courts or cathedral choirs established in that region. In any case the intended effect is crystal clear: to connect the texts of the Ordinary with specific feasts, segments, and/or seasons of the Christian liturgy, thus making them more "proper" for the occasions in question. Particularly prominent in these six cycles is the emphasis on the Virgin Mary, who was in so many ways the mainstay of popular religion in the fifteenth century.

MASS ORDINARIES BASED ON CANONIC PROCEDURES

There are a few exceptions to the general prevalence of the tenor cantus firmus Mass. A number of polyphonic Masses make use (like earlier English settings of individual sections) of canonic procedures involving strict imitation. One of the most striking of such works is Okeghem's *Missa Prolationum*, a technical *tour de force* that was probably intended to serve didactic as well as liturgical purposes. It embodies, first of all, a compendium of mensural practice, both traditional and current, combining simultaneously in each section of the Mass the four prolations of Vitry's formulation (see Appendix, pp. 1017–20) and making use as well of the diminished forms of both tempus perfectum and imperfectum (Ⓞ, ₵). At the same time it provides in systematic fashion examples of strict imitation at every interval from the prime to the octave.

Only two of the four voices needed in performance are written; the other two are derived from them following the indications of the notation (see Figure 10-1). Either the two parts derived from a single written line begin together and then separate themselves temporally because one is read in perfect tempus and the other in

FIGURE 10-1. Jean de Okeghem, *Missa prolationum*, Kyrie (Rome, Biblioteca Vaticana, MS Chigi C VIII 234, the "Chigi Codex," ff. 106ᵛ–107ʳ).

imperfect tempus—a procedure referred to as a "mensuration canon"[49]—or the second voice enters after a period of silence specified by written rests. The true mensuration canon results of course in a full four-part texture, whereas the use of rests reduces the texture to two or three voices.

The pitch interval separating the two parts to be derived from a single line of notation is indicated in one of two ways. Either there are written instructions—a canon—(as in the "Christe"), or the two mensuration signs under which the notation is to be construed define the vertical distance between the resulting parts. In the course of the Mass that interval is expanded methodically from a prime ("Kyrie I") to a second ("Christe"), a third ("Kyrie II"), a fourth ("Gloria"), a fifth ("Credo"), a sixth ("Sanctus"), a seventh ("Pleni sunt"), and an octave ("Osanna"), before reverting to a fourth ("Benedictus") and concluding with a fifth (Agnus Dei).[50] A

49. Because the ternary breves each contain three semibreves, whereas the binary ones count only two, their simultaneous use at the beginning of a section causes the part in imperfect tempus to move ahead of that in perfect tempus. When the desired interval of temporal separation has been achieved, it can be maintained by using smaller values—such as semibreves and minims—which have the same duration in both of the mensurations specified for a given line.

50. For the first "Kyrie," for example, both mensuration signs are written in the same space, whereas for the second "Kyrie" they are a third apart, for the Gloria a fourth apart, for the Credo a fifth, and so forth (see Figure 10-1).

more comprehensive contrapuntal exercise would be difficult to imagine.

The compositional elaboration of such an elaborate design may have provided a model, or at least a source of inspiration, for composers of the next generation who occasionally (if not quite so methodically) relied upon canonic imitation as the fundamental compositional procedure for the cyclic Ordinary. There are two such Masses ascribed to Josquin Desprez, for instance: the *Missa Ad fugam*, the title of which aptly describes the strict imitation that permeates the structure, and the *Missa Sine nomine*, so called because of the absence of borrowed material in its compositional fabric.[51] As a rule, however, Masses that were entirely free of identifiable borrowed material were rare indeed. More characteristic of general trends, perhaps, is the *Missa Ave sanctissima Maria* à 6 ascribed to Pierre de La Rue, which derives its head motive from a devotional motet in honor of the Virgin, also in six parts. Like the motet, the Mass has but three lines of notation from which another three are to be derived in strict imitation. However, aside from the brief quotation from the earlier work at the beginning of each section, the Mass borrows from its model only the canonic derivation of half of its voices.[52]

MULTIPLE BORROWINGS IN THE CYCLIC ORDINARIES

At this point in the development of Mass cycles based on a polyphonic work—surprisingly enough, in the majority of cases, a secular composition—the cantus firmus was usually taken from the tenor of the model. Nevertheless, there was always the possibility of drawing upon more than one part of the preexistent piece, whether simultaneously from two or more parts at once or serially, quoting first from one voice, then from another. For composers of the period who had mastered the use of a tenor cantus firmus as the structural armature for a cyclic Mass, it must have been an easy step indeed to lift not only the principal voice from its original context but to quote as well from the surrounding parts, combining and recombining them in a variety of possible configurations, old and new.

Ancillary borrowings of this sort were once thought to be relatively rare—and late—in cyclic settings of the Ordinary, and their use was seen primarily as an intermediary phase in the development of the so-called parody Masses of the sixteenth century. Surprisingly, a comprehensive survey of fifteenth- and early sixteenth-century Mass repertory identified more than ninety such works and revealed that multiple

51. See the *Werken*, ed., Albert Smijers, (Amsterdam: Vereniging voor Nederlandse Musikgeschiedenis, 1921–56), *Missen*, 3:61–91 (no. 28) and 167–91 (no. 32), respectively.

52. The Marian motet was selected to open the collection of chansons compiled expressly for Marguerite of Austria, MS 228 of the Royal Library in Brussels; see Martin Picker, ed., *The Chanson Albums of Marguerite of Austria* (Berkeley: University of California Press, 1965), frontispiece and 172–79. The Mass, as edited in Pierre de La Rue, *Liber missarum: Première transcription moderne*, ed. A. Tirabassi (Malines: Dessain, 1941), 135ff.

borrowings can be traced back to the beginnings of Mass composition on secular models with cycles such as Du Fay's *Missa Se la face ay pale*.[53] According to Steib, the material borrowed for any given Mass—both the cantus firmus and the surrounding parts—could be quoted quite literally, paraphrased (at times rather extensively), or presented in some combination of the two techniques. Moreover, most composers of the period were very consistent in their use of one of these three techniques, to the extent that it can be seen as an important and characteristic trait of a given master's individual style.[54]

One of the earliest examples of such compositional procedures is to be seen in the *Missa Dueil angoisseux* ascribed to Bedyngham, which is based on a ballade by Binchoys. There are some significant differences among the four surviving sections of the Mass. They were inscribed in one of the two known sources as two separate pairs, and the Credo is written for four parts instead of the three provided for the Gloria, the Sanctus, and the Agnus Dei, but all are linked nevertheless by a similar relationship with the secular model.[55] Not only is the beginning of each major section derived from the opening of the chanson, but the internal articulations within them are based on subsections of the model as well. This is clearest at the "Qui tollis" of the Gloria and the "Et incarnatus" of the Credo, both of which draw their opening material from the beginning of the second section of the chanson. The governing principle in this case appears to be the concept of the head motive, here derived from a polyphonic chanson and extended to internal divisions of the liturgical texts, rather than the more usual tenor cantus firmus.

More common was the adoption of one part of the model as the underlying cantus firmus of the Mass with ancillary use of other parts as well, more or less incidentally, either as separate melodic entities or in the contrapuntal relationships already implicit in the model. Examples include Faugues's *Missa Le serviteur*, which uses the tenor of Du Fay's chanson as its cantus firmus.[56] The composer subjected the part so derived to successive (if irregular) mensural augmentation in a manner reminiscent of isorhythmic structures but quotes extensively from the cantus of the model as well.

Illustrative of this type of melodic borrowing—which is found in every section of

53. See Murray Steib, "Imitation and Elaboration: The Use of Borrowed Material in Masses from the Late Fifteenth Century" (Ph.D. diss., University of Chicago, 1992), 267–328, where all of these compositions are listed, together with their sources and (when available) modern editions.

54. See Steib's "Imitation and Elaboration," 221–42, and his "A Composer Looks at His Model: Polyphonic Borrowing in Masses from the Late Fifteenth Century," *Tijdschrift van de koninklijke Vereniging voor Nederlandse Muziekgeschiedenis* 46 (1996): 5–41.

55. The Gloria is paired with the Credo and the Sanctus with the Agnus Dei in separate sections of Trent 88 (ff. 27–31 and 17–21, respectively). All four have been published from the "Trent Codices" 88 and 90 by Guido Adler et al., eds., *Sechs Trienter Codices: Geistliche und weltliche Kompositionen des XV. Jahrhunderts*, Denkmäler der Tonkunst in Oesterreich, Jahrgang XXXI (vol. 61), 127ff. (R. Graz: Akademische Druck- und Verlaganstalt, 1959). A setting for the Kyrie is wanting.

56. The Mass, as edited by George C. Schuetze Jr., has been published in the *Collected Works of Faugues*, Gesamtausgaben 1 (Brooklyn: Institute of Mediaeval Music, 1960), and facsimiles of the sources are included in the *Opera omnia Faugues*, ed. George C. Schuetze Jr. (Brooklyn: Institute of Mediaeval Music, 1959). Du Fay's chanson is found in Du Fay, *Opera omnia*, ed. Besseler, vol. 5, no. 92.

the Mass—is the superius of "Kyrie II," where the cantus of the chanson is taken over at some length, though not in its original relationship with the tenor. Perhaps even more interesting, in light of the subsequent development of the genre, is Faugues's use of the imitative passages of the chanson, especially those that involve all three of its parts (as in mm. 10f., 15ff., and 24ff.). These occur in every section of the Mass, even where the texture includes all four of its voices, but most notably once again in "Kyrie II" (e.g., mm. 14–16 and 20–25; see Example 10-5).[57]

Also noteworthy in this connection is Okeghem's *Missa Fors seulement* in five parts, based upon his three-voice *rondeau*, a cycle for which only the Kyrie, Gloria, and Credo are found in surviving sources.[58] One of five cyclic Ordinaries attributed to Okeghem in which at least some ancillary borrowing is found,[59] this Mass is essentially a cantus firmus structure using in alternation both the tenor and the cantus of the chanson. The composer also extensively quotes ancillary material

---

57. See George C. Schuetze Jr., *An Introduction to Faugues* (Brooklyn: Institute of Mediaeval Music, 1960), 18ff. and table 4, p. 38.
58. The Mass is found in Ockeghem, *Collected Works*, ed. Plamenac, 2:65–76.
59. See Steib, "Imitation and Elaboration," 185–201.

EXAMPLE 10-5. Guillaume Du Fay, *Le serviteur hault guerdonné* (mm. 10–25), Guillaume Faugues, *Missa Le serviteur*, "Kyrie II" (mm. 14–16, 20–25)

RONDEAU (REFRAIN ONLY): [The servant, highly rewarded, satisfied, and most fortunate,] the elite of the blessed of all France, I find myself through the provision [of a single, well-ordered word.]

KYRIE: Lord, have mercy.

from all parts of the model but not, as a rule, in their original relationship with the cantus firmi, which in this instance migrate rather frequently from part to part in the Mass.

In addition, the opening point of imitation in the chanson has been recast, each time in a different way, to provide a unifying head motive of sorts for the three major sections of the Mass. The Kyrie, for example, begins with the cantus of the rondeau presented in imitation between the contratenor (beginning at the lower fifth) and the superius of the Mass simultaneously with the contratenor of the model in bassus [1], also at the fifth below (see Example 10-6). Then, once the beginning statement has

EXAMPLE 10-6. Jean de Okeghem, *Fors seulement l'attente* (mm. 1–18), and *Missa Fors seulement*, "Kyrie I" (mm. 1–29)

RONDEAU (REFRAIN ONLY): Excepting only the expectation of death, no hope remains in my weary heart . . .
KYRIE: Lord, have mercy.

been made, the contrapuntal fabric is woven around the melody taken from the chanson for use as a cantus firmus.[60]

Equally instructive examples of tenor cantus firmus Masses with ancillary borrowings from their polyphonic models could be adduced for most of the major masters of the second half of the fifteenth century, and many of the lesser ones as well. These include Obrecht, Isaac, and Josquin, on the one hand, Agricola, Brumel, Caron, Compère, Gaffurius, Gaspar van Weerbeke, Ghiselin, Cornelius Heyns, La Rue, Martini, de Orto, Vincenet, and of course a fair number of anonymi on the other,[61] and their works carried this compositional tradition well into the sixteenth century.

However, the next decisive steps in the development of the cyclic Ordinary of the Mass was to come only with the composers of the following generation, most specifically figures such as Antoine de Févin and Jean Mouton who were associated with the royal French chapel. They would take as a model ever more frequently a Latin motet, rather than a French chanson, and treat it as an integral polyphonic entity instead of simply a source for a usable—and presumably evocative—cantus firmus. Their innovative compositional procedures were undoubtedly rooted to a degree in the multiple borrowings used to embellish the cantus firmus Masses of the late fifteenth century, but they reflected even more significantly changes in compositional

60. For further discussion of this Mass, see Reese, *Music of the Renaissance*, 127ff., and Sparks, *Cantus Firmus in Mass and Motet*, 155–65.
61. See the inventory drawn up by Steib, "Imitation and Elaboration," 281ff.; the author has chosen, for very good reasons, to focus his study on Martini, Compère, Obrecht, Isaac, and Josquin in particular.

style that came about primarily through the redefinition and transformation of the motet. It was the latter genre that began to replace the polyphonic Mass in the final decades of the fifteenth century as a focal point for elegantly skillful contrapuntal display and, apparently, for artistic patronage as well.

MASS PROPERS

One might easily conclude from the fifteenth-century sources that have reached the present age that the composition of polyphony for the proper chants of the Mass was an intermittent and geographically spotty activity. For example, the largest surviving collection is contained in the "Trent Codices," which transmit more than 260 such settings (including duplications from one collection to the next). The majority of these—some 227 compositions in all—were inscribed in the manuscripts that were apparently copied in the city itself: Trent 88, 89, 90, and 91. However, another 24 pieces (mostly Introits appended to cycles of settings for the Ordinary) were included in the section of Trent 92 that seems to have originated in a southerly German-speaking region along the axis between Strasbourg and Basel, perhaps in part in connection with the Council of Basel.[62] A third, more distant, locus for the composition of polyphonic Propers is suggested by the English repertory of the Cambridge MS Pepys 1236, which includes twenty-five settings for the Propers of the Mass.

The wide geographical compass covered by these sources, and the contacts among musicians of the widely separated regions represented in them, may at first surprise the reader. They can perhaps be explained, however, by the inclusion of large contingents of singers and composers among the many delegates who flocked time and again to Basel from all over Europe and England for the sessions convened successively in the 1430s and 1440s and their consequent exposure to one another's music for better than a decade. This circumstance would suggest in turn that polyphonic Mass Propers were disseminated more widely than the surviving repertories would indicate, and rather quickly. Particularly significant in this connection are the indications that in 1449–50 some 168 folios of polyphonic music for the Propers of the Mass were copied for use at the cathedral at Cambrai. This represents the equivalent of some 21 complete cycles—unfortunately, all of them now apparently lost—only about a third less than the 228 folios inscribed during the same period with music for the Mass Ordinary.[63]

Also noteworthy is the systematic attention given to the composition of such works by Cambrai's most distinguished cleric-musician of the age, Guillaume Du Fay. He appears to have contributed more substantially than any of his contempo-

62. Concerning the contents and provenance of the first section of Trent MS 92, see Tom R. Ward, "The Structure of the Manuscript Trent 92-I," *Musica disciplina* 29 (1975): 127–47.
63. See David Fallows, "The Life of Johannes Regis, ca. 1425 to 1496," *Revue belge de musicologie* 43 (1989): 161.

raries to the definition (or redefinition) of the polyphonic Proper as a compositional genre. It is consequently possible to conclude that the evidence of the sources is incomplete—in this case perhaps even more than in others—and that while the fifteenth-century tradition may have originated in one of the regions from which the earliest repertories stem, the picture as seen at present reflects primarily the accidents of manuscript preservation.

Some of the Proper texts received more attention than others, in particular the Sequences and, to a lesser degree perhaps, the Introits. As with the other motet-related genres that have been under discussion, a useful distinction can be made here between settings based directly upon the chant melody, hence apparently intended for liturgical use, and those that are in "motet style," which may have been prepared for other purposes: processional, votive, or more generally devotional. Of the liturgical type, clearly, is the series of eight sequences ascribed to Du Fay—perhaps part of a group originally conceived as a liturgical cycle.[64] Seven of these works were written for three voices and designed for *alternatim* performance; the chant is presented as a melodic cantus firmus in the superius (or superius and tenor), a clear indication that liturgical use was planned.

Representative of this group of works—and fairly typical of the plainsong settings of Du Fay's generation in general—is the Christmas sequence *Letabundus exultet*, attributed to the master himself.[65] Because the initial member of the paired repetitions that characterize the sequence is to be sung each time in plainchant, only the alternate segments have been set in parts. The liturgical melody is also quoted in the polyphonic sections. It is in the superius for every verse except the fifth, where it is carried instead by the tenor. The chant thus provides the essential melodic substance of the polyphonic verses and dictates, at the same time, a quasi-syllabic declamation of the poetic text (see Example 10-7).

Although there is no *fauxbourdon*, the contrapuntal texture is fairly simple. Individual lines have relatively little melodic elaboration. Rhythmic animation is likewise limited, consisting largely of passing and neighbor-note figures around the chant pitches themselves with an occasional displacement by minim syncopation of the basic motion in semibreves. The melodic material is new for each successive pair of strophes, but the effect for the listener is not unlike that produced by Du Fay's polyphonic hymn settings (see pp. 331–36).

That the Introit, like the Sequence, was at times singled out for polyphonic treatment when the other Proper texts of the Mass were sung in plainsong is suggested by an unusual series of composite Mass cycles in the opening section of MS Trent 92. These consist of an Introit followed, usually, by a series of settings for the Ordinary of the Mass. Other Propers are included in the collection as well, however, as are motets and—surprisingly—music apparently intended for the Office: hymns

---

64. See Fallows, *Dufay*, 146–50.
65. For a transcription, see Du Fay, *Opera omnia*, ed. Besseler, 5:5–8.

EXAMPLE 10-7. Guillaume Du Fay, *Letabundus*, In Nativitate Domini, verses 1a and 1b (mm. 1–10)

Greatly rejoicing, let the chorus of the faithful exult, Alleluia; The womb of the virgin
has brought forth the King of kings, an astonishing occurrence.

and Magnificats.[66] In addition, Introits account for the majority of the fifty-eight
Mass Propers included in the MS D.G.IV.47 of the Strahov Library in Prague, which
was probably copied in the 1460s and 1470s in Bohemia or Silesia (possibly even in
Moravia).[67]

　　Complete cycles of Mass Propers for a given liturgical occasion are much rarer
than individual settings. Nonetheless, a series of polyphonic settings in three parts,
intended for Masses in honor of the Virgin, was also copied into Trent 92 (ff. 51ᵛff.),
where it is attributed to Reginaldus Libert.[68] It includes, in addition to the five texts
of the Ordinary, all of the Propers requisite for any season of the liturgical year:

66. See Ward, "Structure of the Manuscript Trent 92-I," 127–47.
67. See the *Census-Catalogue of Manuscript Sources*, 3:60–61.
68. See Ward, "Structure of the Manuscript Trent 92-I," 129–33, and idem, "Libert," *The New Grove Dictionary of Music*, 10:718.

Introit, Gradual, Alleluia, Sequence, Tract, Offertory, and Communion.[69] All but the Gloria and the Credo (whose formulaic chants perhaps offered too little of interest to the composer) are based upon an appropriate liturgical plainsong, carried in the superius with only the modest melodic embellishments that generally result from the rhythmicization of chant for mensural polyphony.

A similar pattern was followed for a cycle in honor of St. James that was apparently completed somewhat earlier and is attributed to Du Fay. This group of works was inscribed under the suggestive rubric *Missa Sancti Jacobi* in the Bologna MS Q15, which carries all five texts for the Ordinary and four for the Propers: Introit, Alleluia, Offertory, and Communion.[70] Here, too, the plainsong melodies are present, but the various ways in which they have been treated would suggest that a compositional tradition for Mass Propers as a genre had yet to be established. In the opening section of the Introit, "Mihi autem nimis," for example, the chant has been laid out as a tenor cantus firmus in longer values as the foundation for a motetlike structure in four parts (see Example 10-8). Adjusted to this foundation are a (presumably instrumental) contratenor, sharing the range and motion of the tenor, and a texted vocal duo in the upper registers, where the rhythmic activity is considerably more animated. The verse is to be sung to the liturgical psalm tone, thus introducing the *alternatim* principle. For the *repetitio* of the antiphon the composer reverted to

69. Concerning one strand of the subsequent history of Mass cycles that includes both Ordinary and Proper sections for a given feast, see Thomas Noblitt, "The Earliest Plenary Mass for Easter," in *From Ciconia to Sweelinck, Donum Natalicium Willem Elders*, ed. Albert Clement and Eric Jas, Chloe Beihefte zum Daphnis, 21 (Amsterdam: Editions Rodopi B.V., 1995), 31–47, who traces the tradition for Easter Masses in German-speaking regions from the 1470s until well into the sixteenth century.
70. The settings for the Ordinary were also included—without the Propers—in the Aosta Choirbook under the more general rubric *De apostolis*; see Fallows, *Dufay*, 168ff. For an edition, see Du Fay, *Opera omnia*, ed. Besseler, 2:17–44.

EXAMPLE 10-8. Guillaume Du Fay, *Mihi autem nimis*, Introit (mm. 1–5) and *repetitio* (mm. 1–5)

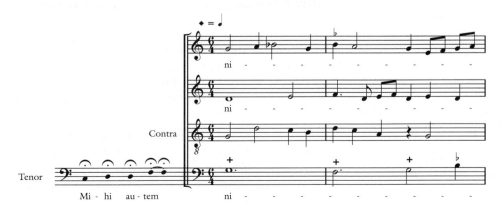

To me, moreover, greatly honored are thy friends, O God . . .

three-part writing and shifted the chant to the treble voice, recalling the style then customary for the polyphonic hymn.

The Alleluia, "Hispanorum clarens stella," appears to have been handled throughout in the same manner as the opening segment of the Introit with the sole exception of a short duo section in the Verse (mm. 49–62). But because the original chant for this particular text—which makes specific reference to St. James[71]—has yet to be identified, details of the cantus firmus treatment cannot be determined with absolute certainty. By contrast, for the Offertory, "In omnem terram," a slightly different structural plan has been adopted. Here the general facture of the work recalls a characteristic aspect of the isorhythmic motet: the entry of the tenor cantus firmus is preceded by a lengthy introduction in three parts—a vocal duo once again, this time with a sustaining (instrumental) contratenor (see Example 10-9). While the tenor is silent, the chant is carried by an inner voice, the lower of the two texted parts. Once the tenor makes its entry (m. 21), it proceeds with the liturgical melody

71. This specificity is found only in the Alleluia; the other three Propers included in the Mass were all used in the celebration of the feasts of other Apostles as well.

EXAMPLE 10-9. Guillaume Du Fay, *In omnem terram*, Offertory (mm. 1–26)

Into all the earth their sound went out . . .

in regular extended values (exclusively breves and longs). But when it drops out briefly just before the final section (mm. 59–81), the lower member of the duo takes over once again as the bearer of the liturgical melody.

For the Communion, "Vos qui secuti estis," the composer reverts once again to the three-part texture of the polyphonic hymn. The chant is borne by the cantus here as well, and the stylistic similarity with much of the liturgical polyphony intended for the Office is further emphasized by the use of a *fauxbourdon* to generate the inner voice at the fourth below the plainsong-derived upper part. (Incidentally, this is one of the earliest appearances of that particular compositional procedure in the sources of the period.)[72] In this series of Propers, then, not only did the composer use the

72. Concerning the origins of *fauxbourdon* and its possibly symbolic significance in this polyphonic Communion, see Willem Elders, "G. Dufay's Concept of Fauxbourdon," *Revue belge de musicologie* 43 (1989): 173–95; the author credits Du Fay with the invention of this peculiar compositional method and suggests that the term, originally the French name for the male bee (drone), was chosen to invoke not only the buzzing sound produced by the "bridal" flight of the queen bee accompanied by the drones of the hive but also an image of the faithful followers of Christ. As Elders observes, in the Christian tradition of the Middle Ages Jesus's Apostles were compared to bees following their "king" and the church was itself described as a society of bees.

plainchant in three different positions (as melody, inner voice, and tenor foundation), he also introduced three contrasting polyphonic textures (in two, three, and four parts) and borrowed compositional procedures in turn from the hymn, the antiphon motet, and the isorhythmic motet.

The stylistic uncertainty implicit in this variety of textures and contrapuntal procedures appears never to have been fully resolved for the genre by the masters of Du Fay's generation. Still, as we shall see, when composers of the early sixteenth century returned to the composition of Mass Propers, they seem to have understood—if nothing else—that the inclusion of the chant melody in the polyphony as a substantial element of the compositional fabric, whether melodic or structural or both, had become a tradition that was to be honored (see pp. 591–96).

THE LITURGICAL PASSIONS

The commemoration of the Passion of Jesus of Nazareth, as recorded in the four Gospels of the New Testament, found its place in the liturgy of the fifteenth and sixteenth centuries as the Gospel reading at Mass during the final week before Easter. The account according to Matthew was heard on Palm Sunday; that given by Mark on the following Tuesday; Luke's on Wednesday; and John's as part of the special liturgical observance that replaced Mass on Good Friday (the *Actio liturgica post-meridiana*).[73] Because of the extraordinary significance of these texts for Christian theology and liturgy, special lesson tones were devised for them very early on so that they could be intoned rather than simply read. Virtually from the outset the dramatic nature of the story—poignant exchanges in dialogue alternating with the narrative of the Evangelist—was reflected in differing pitch levels for the reciting notes of the chant formulae and distinctive styles of delivery for the various protagonists. By the thirteenth century these contrasts had been reinforced by a modest measure of personification. Separate singers represent the narrator, Christ, and the *turba* or crowd (the various groups whose spoken words are recorded: disciples, soldiers, and the chief priests and scribes of the Jews).

It was apparently not until the fifteenth century, however, that attempts were made at setting in polyphony the texts of the Passion, and even then but rarely. Only four of the manuscript sources of sacred polyphony that originated before 1500— three of them English and one Italian—contain music for this particular part of the liturgy. The earliest of these, MS Egerton 3307 of the British Library, was probably copied either for the chapel of St. George at Windsor or at Meaux Abbey between 1430 and 1444.[74] It includes a fragment of the Passion according to Matthew and a

---

73. See the *Liber usualis*, 599, 611, 621, and 729. See also Kurt von Fischer, "Passion," *The New Grove Dictionary of Music*, 14:277, to whom the following paragraphs are much indebted.

74. For an edition of the manuscript, excepting only the carols, which have been published separately, see Gwynn S. McPeek, ed., *The British Museum Manuscript Egerton 3307* (London: Oxford University Press, 1963).

complete setting for the Passion according to Luke. (There is, in addition, a collection of carols, four hymns, three antiphons, a Mass ordinary, and some miscellaneous items.)

The *Passio Domini Nostri Jhesu Christi secundum Lucam*, which opens with a setting of the opening rubric, thereafter combines chant and polyphony in alternation in a manner that has been termed "responsorial." The narrative of the Evangelist and the utterances of Christ are to be chanted to the traditional lesson tone, but polyphony was provided for the words of the other protagonists: the disciples; the questioners who provoked the denials of Peter; the soldiers who made Jesus prisoner; the chief priests and scribes who were his accusers; and other participants in the unfolding drama, whether represented as individuals or as members of the *turba*.

Still evident in the superius of a uniform three-part fabric, in addition to the largely syllabic delivery of the text characteristic of liturgical recitation, are the repeated pitches and the cadential formulae of the lesson tone (see Example 10-10). In keeping with the fundamental simplicity of this approach, both the rhythmic organization and the part-writing were kept relatively simple. The counterpoint is in a note-against-note discant style that is rather strictly maintained, and the resultant texture, like the declamation, is essentially homophonic. Only the occasional melismatic extension of the precadential figures adds a modestly decorative touch to the otherwise restrained polyphonic elaboration of the liturgical tone.

Two other Passions, one according to Matthew and the other according to John, were inscribed in yet another English collection of polyphony from about the same period, a set of partbooks of which but a single one survives.[75] Unfortunately, both works are woefully incomplete as a result, but they appear to be similar in style to the setting of the Passion according to Luke in Egerton 3307. A fifth English Passion, this one based on the Gospel according to Matthew and carrying an attribution to

EXAMPLE 10-10. Anonymous, *Passio secundum Lucam* (mm. 312–20)

Si tu es rex Ju - de - o - rum, sal - vum te____ fac____

If thou be the king of the Jews, save thyself.

---

75. The manuscript is Shrewsbury School VI; see Fischer, "Passion," *The New Grove Dictionary of Music,* 14:278.

Richard Davy, was included in the repertory copied into the "Eton Choirbook" about 1490. It, too, is responsorial, providing—like the Egerton Passion discussed above—settings for all of the spoken dialogue except the words of Christ. Sadly, it is also incomplete due to gaps in the source. Still, the surviving segments indicate that it was written in four parts throughout rather than the three of the earlier English Passions. And the counterpoint appears to be generally much less dependent upon the liturgical lesson tones for its melodic substance than was the case in earlier works.[76]

In contrast with England there is but a single Continental source for the polyphonic Passion from the fifteenth century, a choirbook prepared for use at the ducal court of Ferrara, completed in 1481, and now in the Biblioteca Estense e Universitaria in Modena, MS α.M.1.12. It contains a pair of compositions on the traditional texts, the one from Matthew and the other from John. Both settings are again responsorial in character, but the latter is unfortunately incomplete. Although there are a few sections in the Matthew Passion written for six to eight voices, the greater part of both works consists of *fauxbourdon*-derived counterpoint based on the liturgical lesson tone, which is carried by the uppermost part. No composer is given for either setting, but similar compositional procedures were used by two masters in residence at the Ferrarese court at the time, Johannes Brebis and Johannes Martini; they are credited with the polyphonic hymns and psalm settings for double choir that form the bulk of the manuscript and its companion collection, MS α.M.1.11.[77]

As we shall see, polyphonic treatment of the four Passions, as liturgically defined, gradually became both more common and more widespread in the course of the sixteenth century. Still, the repertory always remained relatively limited, perhaps because its use was restricted to just the one week prior to Easter. Perhaps, as in the case of other liturgical chants of a simple, syllabic nature (such as the hymns and the tones for Psalms and Magnificats), the skillful use of such improvisatory polyphonic practices as *faburden* and *fauxbourdon* made written composition in a similar style more or less superfluous.

76. See John Caldwell, "Davy, Richard," *The New Grove Dictionary of Music*, 5:285–86; for an edition, see Frank L. Harrison, ed., *The Eton Choirbooks*, Musica Britannica, vol. 12 (London: Stainer and Bell, 1961).
77. See Lewis Lockwood, *Music in Renaissance Ferrara, 1400-1505: The Creation of a Musical Center in the Fifteenth Century* (Cambridge, Mass.: Harvard University Press, 1984), 250–57.

CHAPTER 11

Secular Polyphony on the Italian Peninsula

INTRODUCTION

In the early fifteenth century the Italian peninsula was divided into three separate regions, and in each of them a fundamentally different political and economic situation obtained (see Figure 11-1). In the south was the feudal kingdom of Naples, which had few cities and little significant trade. It had come under the sway of Charles of Anjou, the founder of the Angevin dynasty, in 1266, together with the island of Sicily. But Charles lost Sicily to the Aragonese in 1282, and the ensuing conflict between those two ruling houses, one French and the other Spanish, lasted well into the sixteenth century.

The Aragonese, who had retained control of Sicily, wrested the kingdom of Naples from the Angevins in 1443 under Alfonso V "The Magnanimous." He left it, when he died in 1458, to his illegitimate son Ferdinand or "Ferrante" I. The latter managed to retain until his death in 1494 a throne made precarious by revolt from within and the threat of foreign intervention from without (see Figure 11-2). His success in doing so was clearly due in large part to diplomatic negotiations with possible allies as widely scattered as Milan, Burgundy, and Hungary. He arranged, or attempted to arrange, interdynastic marriages with the rulers of all three areas in the hope of consolidating the rule of his own house. The Angevin claims to the throne of Naples persisted, however, like a heavy cloud on the horizon to the northwest. When they passed by inheritance to the French royal line in 1486, they provided a pretext for the first of the French invasions of Italy, which began under Charles VIII in the very year of Ferrante's death.[1]

Although the most immediate and obvious result of the rivalry between the dynasties with pretenders to the royal crown of Naples was the unease of political

---

1. Concerning the kingdom of Naples, see Wallace K. Ferguson, *Europe in Transition* (Boston: Houghton Mifflin Co., 1962), 169–70.

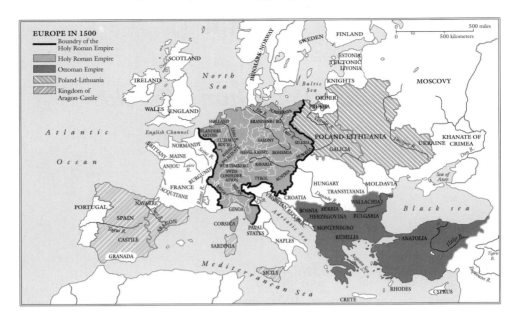

FIGURE 11-1. Europe, ca. 1500.

conflict and the violence and destruction of all-out warfare, the impact of the actual events upon musical developments of the period is fairly typical. The Aragonese connections allowed the kings of Naples to bring musicians from Spain for service at their court; their contacts with Burgundy gave them access to music and musicians from areas of French and Flemish culture to the north; and their presence on the Italian peninsula allowed exchanges with neighbors such as Rome, Florence, and Milan. As a result, music heard at the Neapolitan court included not only that from Spanish- and French-speaking regions—much of it carried in by the composers and performers hired abroad to serve in the Aragonese musical establishment—but also works that originated with "native" Italians. Even the invasion of Naples by the French armies in 1495 brought to the Italian peninsula (in addition to the horrors of warfare and the *mal francese*) an influx of northern musicians and their compositions, as later French campaigns were wont to do as well.

In the north of Italy, after the collapse of the Hohenstaufen dynasty in the late thirteenth century, the gradual disintegration of the feudal domains of the Holy Roman Empire resulted in the rise of numerous communes, many of them quite tiny. During the fourteenth century, by contrast, the larger urban centers, sustained economically by their industrial and commercial activities, began to develop through a process of expansion and annexation into a smaller number of relatively powerful city-states. The most important of these for the fifteenth century were controlled by Milan, Venice, and Florence, but less powerful states such as Genoa, Mantua, Modena, and Siena also played a role in the political and cultural events of the period.

Although as communes these polities were governed initially by the relatively democratic institutions of a republic, territorial expansion was generally accompanied by a tendency toward absolutism. Florence, Genoa, and Siena retained at least some semblance of republican rule into the sixteenth century, but the only northern Italian state to maintain both its traditional form of government and its political autonomy into the seventeenth century was Venice. Sooner or later all the other territories came under the control of a ruling family of magnates—*signori*—who transformed or subverted the republican institutions in order to establish a hereditary dynasty.

In some instances the *podestà*, the head of the medieval commune who ruled generally at the pleasure of its citizens for a limited period of time in accordance with established custom, was given ever larger powers and allowed to govern for ever longer periods of time. This opened the way for a *signore* to establish his authority in more absolute terms and, ultimately, his family as hereditary rulers. The Este, for example, came to dominate Ferrara in just this manner. More frequently, it was the *capitano del popolo*, the political leader of the guilds representing the city's artisans and tradesmen, who was allowed to assume increasingly unrestricted control of the government over ever longer periods of time. In this way as well the groundwork was laid for the presumption of a hereditary right to rule. Through just such a train of events the Gonzaga came to power in Mantua and the Visconti in Milan.

In an effort to invest their newly founded family dynasty with the familiar hall-

FIGURE 11-2. King Ferrante returning to Naples after the Battle of Ischia, 1465 (Tavola Strozzi), detail, anonymous painting (Naples, Museo Nazionale di San Martino).

marks of legitimacy and permanence, many of the *signori* turned to the Holy Roman Emperor, the nominal feudal lord of the territories that these local despots had come to control, to obtain formal recognition of the status they had but recently acquired. Even though they were effectively powerless by then in the Italian regions to which the empire had long laid claim, the successive emperors were usually willing to sell the title of imperial "vicar" to these political upstarts. By so doing they freed the *signori* from any remaining limits to their authority stemming from the democratic procedures customarily observed in republican communes and provided them with a new pretext for territorial expansion. Thus it was that Giangaleazzo Visconti was able to acquire the title of duke of Milan in 1395 from Emperor Wenceslas (in exchange for a hundred thousand florins) and that Francesco Gonzaga succeeded in having himself named marquis of Mantua in 1432 by Emperor Sigismund.[2]

Republican governments of the communes were thus gradually subverted into autocratic city-states controlled by members of a ruling family with some sort of hereditary or imperial justification for their new status. Abandoned along with republican forms of government was the use of citizen armies to defend—or capture—the territories to which these rulers laid claim. Disenfranchised citizens were understandably reluctant to go into battle against neighboring cities on behalf of a grasping despot, and the newly established autocrats were just as understandably hesitant to arm a potentially rebellious citizenry. As a result, the waging of war was turned over to bands of mercenaries whose leadership was assumed by a professional soldier of fortune known to the Italians as a *condottiere*.

The evils engendered by this system, from the depredations of the hired soldiers against a defenseless populace, in peace as in war, to the weakening of Italian defenses against foreign invasion, are too numerous to chronicle here. An indication of the possible abuses may be seen in the fact that some of the *condottieri* managed to gain control of the territories they were hired to defend, displacing the ruling family that had been in power. Such was the case, for example, for Francesco Sforza. He had prudently required for his services the hand of the natural daughter of Filippo Maria Visconti, and when the latter died without leaving a male heir, Sforza was able to wrest the dukedom of Milan from the Visconti family. In other, more numerous instances it was the lesser *signori* who took up the business of war as *condottieri*, thus providing for themselves both a means of defending their territories and a source of potential revenue.[3]

Between the kingdom of Naples to the south and the city-states that had taken shape to the north lay the Papal States, a considerable territory that was viewed by the papacy as its temporal domain. It extended from Rome's Mediterranean coast to

---

2. Concerning the political transformation of the Italian communes in the fourteenth and early fifteenth centuries, see Ferguson, *Europe in Transition*, 145–55.

3. The tendency toward despotism with its attendant changes in social, governmental, and military organization has often been discussed by historians of the Renaissance, beginning with the classic study by Jacob Burckhardt, *The Civilization of the Renaissance in Italy*, 2 vols. (New York: Harper and Brothers, 1958), 1:21–142. For a more recent and concise treatment of the matter, see Ferguson, *Europe in Transition*, 145–71.

the north and west in a relatively wide but irregular band to the Adriatic Sea (see the map, Fig. 11-1). In the late Middle Ages, however, the process of political fragmentation that characterized events in the Italian domains claimed by the Holy Roman Empire was at work in the Papal States as well. This was especially true during the fourteenth century, when the authority of the popes was much diminished there.

First came the long absence of the papal seat from the Italian peninsula during the Babylonian Captivity, as it is called, when French popes ruled from Avignon (1309–78). This was followed by the Great Schism (1378–1417), when all of Christendom was locked in the struggle between rival popes and their supporting factions. Profiting from the resulting confusion, enterprising despots took over a number of the city-states lying within traditionally papal dominions, most notably Perugia, Urbino, Bologna, and Ferrara. Perugia, although nominally under papal jurisdiction, came to be ruled in fact by tyrants whose grip on the commune was broken only in 1540. Bologna, too, ostensibly a papal possession governed by an appointed legate, came under the sway of Giovanni Bentivoglio in 1401, and he and his descendants were able to maintain their hold on the city-state for more than a century. Not until 1512 was the papacy finally able to reaffirm its authority there.

Urbino came to be ruled by the Montefeltro family as early as 1234, and these *signori* became first the counts and then—thanks in part to the prowess of Federico da Montefeltro (1422–82) as a *condottiere*—the dukes of Urbino. The last Montefeltro to bear the title was supplanted in 1508 by a nephew of the pope, Francesco Maria della Rovere, but the new dynasty did not return the diminutive duchy to direct papal hegemony until 1626. Ferrara, similarly, even though traditionally part of the papal domains, came to be dominated by the Este family. In 1452 Borso d'Este (1450–71) succeeded in having himself named duke of Modena and Reggio by Emperor Frederick III, and in 1471 he was made duke of Ferrara by the pope himself. His successors managed to retain the ducal title until the last male heir of the house of Este died in 1598; only then was the papacy able to reestablish its claim to the territory.[4]

In the papal states as elsewhere, then, the newly established hereditary dynasties attempted to legitimate their hold on the governmental powers they had in fact usurped from legitimate rulers and traditional institutions. There, too, they based their claims on titles and appointments ostensibly deriving from the feudal system. However, their right to rule was clearly much less well grounded than that of the kings of France and England, whose feudal domains had been established for centuries, whose hereditary lordships had been recognized for generations, and who were thought to rule by divine right.

It would seem, in fact, that self-made *signori* all over Italy were acutely aware of

---

4. The factual material for the preceding paragraph has been drawn primarily from appropriate entries in Ilan Rachum, ed., *The Renaissance: An Illustrated Encyclopedia* (London: Octopus Books, 1979), and *The New Columbia Encyclopedia* (New York: Columbia University Press, 1975). There are articles on all four of the localities mentioned in *The New Grove Dictionary of Music*, but only those on Ferrara (6:486–89) and Urbino (19:463–64) include discussion of the political context.

the questionable nature of their claims to hereditary dominion. For in every aspect of their personal comportment and political activity they attempted to convey an impression of the magnificence expected of rulers with their dynastic pretensions. By emulating the customs and manners of those magnates whose legitimacy was beyond question, they apparently hoped to demonstrate that their own right to rule was no less defensible.

The king of France, in particular, as one of the most powerful and visible feudal sovereigns of the fifteenth century, was frequently taken as a model. When their power and influence were at their peak, the successive dukes of Burgundy also provided an impressive example. Consequently, the ceremonial display at northern courts such as theirs and the pomp that was considered to be the rightful panoply of a feudal lord were assiduously emulated by the emerging Italian dynasties. Jousts, tourneys, pageants, and spectacles of every kind were offered as evidence that they were entitled to the princely prerogatives they had assumed.

This courtly ostentation had some very important musical components. All through the Middle Ages the nobility had traditionally played host to poets and musicians—to *trouvères* and minstrels, amongst others. In addition, trumpeters had become a permanent part of the household of every important magnate; they wore their patron's livery, suspended his coat of arms from the long shaft of their instrument, and called attention to his presence and movements not only with this visual display but with sonorous fanfares as well. Most importantly, at least for the history of Western polyphony, the aristocratic rulers with sufficient power and wealth usually staffed their private chapels at court with a fair number of singers and, where possible, composers. Musicians capable of creating and performing complex contrapuntal compositions clearly had a role to play in adding beauty and luster not only to the celebration of the liturgy but also to a good many of the secular entertainments intended to dazzle visitors and impress neighboring states.

Consequently, *signori* attempting to establish their courts in emulation of northern models often imputed considerable importance to a wide variety of cultural activities and seriously fostered the cultivation of music in all of its forms. In the early fifteenth century a number of them began competing among themselves and with their neighbors to the north for the best-trained musicians available. These included composers, singers, and instrumentalists of many kinds, from the humble purveyors of music for dancing to the celebrated virtuosi whose services were disputed by the wealthiest and most ostentatious courts of all Europe. So intense was the rivalry and so considerable the resources deployed by magnates such as the dukes of Milan and Ferrara that they can be regarded as pursuing a conscious policy of cultural one-upmanship with respect to the arts in general and music in particular. Conscious of their inability to compete successfully with older and better-established dynasties in the arena of international politics, the Italian despots apparently believed, and not without some justification, that they could at least show themselves to advantage in the traditional role of the noble Maecenas.

The one ruler on the Italian peninsula about whose legitimacy there could be no

FIGURE 11-3.   Pietro Perugino, the delivery of the keys to Peter, showing two Roman triumphal arches (modeled on the Arch of Constantine) and the ideal church of Alberti's *Treatise on Architecture* (fresco, 1482, Sistine Chapel, the Vatican).

serious question was of course the pope; his claims to primacy in the government of the Christian church was traditionally traced back to its very origins (see Figure 11-3). In the exercise of that authority his primary concerns were to have been essentially religious and spiritual in nature. In the course of the Middle Ages, however, the church had become an increasingly integral part of the political fabric of Europe. Under Carolingian rule the bishops and archbishops who had come to represent ecclesiastical authority in the urban centers were given a share in secular administration. When the empire collapsed, they assumed even more fully the functions of government. And as the feudal system developed, the pious gifts and legacies that constituted the accumulating wealth of the church came increasingly in the form of large grants of land deeded to its monasteries and cathedral churches. This made of the abbots and bishops who were their chief ecclesiastical officers feudal lords in a very real sense.

In the light of these circumstances it was undoubtedly inevitable that the church, and the papacy in particular, became increasingly involved in secular politics. Not surprisingly, then, the papal curia came to resemble more and more the courts of the temporal rulers with whom it had to deal in matters of secular dominion. During the fourteenth century especially a series of pontiffs with organizational acumen worked to establish a strong central administration. A highly structured bureaucracy and an efficient system of taxation were devised to provide support for a proliferating officialdom of officers, clerks, and servants. Soldiers, too, were needed to help govern effectively the temporal domains claimed by the papacy and to wage war in defense of its temporal interests. In addition, like any secular head of state, the pope sent his emissaries abroad, received the embassies of others, engaged in negotiations with other European powers, and forged alliances in support of his political objectives.

There was, nonetheless, an important difference between the papacy and the government of any other polity of fifteenth-century Europe. Whereas the dominion of the secular rulers was defined entirely by territorial holdings and claims, that of the Roman pontiff reached well beyond the Papal States. He expected not only spiritual obedience but also material support from the clergy of the church regardless of the region in which they exercised their ecclesiastical functions. In fact, the conflicts that arose between the pope and one or another of the ruling magnates were most often due to the overlapping of their respective jurisdictions and interests, especially in fiscal matters. Competing demands were thus made on the loyalties of highly placed ecclesiastics, for many of whom their duty toward Rome was tempered by family ties with local rulers.

At the same time, the church provided for the disparate regions and cultures in which it was established a unifying force, the basis for a generally acceptable morality, a significant body of shared religious beliefs and practices, and a common language. Latin served not only the needs of the communal liturgy but also—and perhaps more importantly in the present context—as a means of communication among the educated, whatever their social class or their scholarly interests.

If the papacy's involvement in temporal affairs and the abuses spawned by the increasing secularization of the papal court contributed to the dissatisfaction of reform-minded clerics and eventually to the bitter conflicts, both doctrinal and political, of the Reformation itself, its impact on the development of music was much more fortunate. Like the secular rulers of the Italian peninsula, the popes often went to considerable pains to staff their private chapel with the finest singers and composers available in all of Europe. In this sense the papacy may be seen as simply competing with its political rivals for unusual talent to ornament its court. But in a larger perspective it may instead be viewed as an ancient and venerable institution that, by maintaining a long-established musical tradition, provided a model for the celebration of the liturgy. And since this was usually done in a manner capable of exciting the admiration of visiting dignitaries, both ecclesiastical and secular, papal ceremonies could also inspire the latters' emulation in a showy observance of the rites of the church.

The temporal lords who wished to engage a brilliant corps of musicians, whether to enhance the liturgical celebrations of their chapel or to lend luster to the secular entertainments of their court, generally had recourse to substantial salaries as a means of attracting to their employ the most skillful and renowned of the available players, singers, and composers. The pope, who required first of all chapel musicians of clerical rank, trained by the church to officiate in its services, had at his disposal an even more powerful inducement to draw musicians into his employ; he held jurisdiction over a large number of prebends and benefices, the essential source of income for the professional clergy of the period.

Many of those skilled in music were more than willing to sing with the papal choir while they sought through papal intervention to obtain a benefice in the region in which they had been brought up and trained. So important was the possession of ecclesiastical prebends to these church musicians—even those who pursued their religious functions almost exclusively within the confines of the secular courts—that rulers in the temporal domain also attempted to gain control of a certain number of benefices that could be offered to those whom they wished to enlist in their service.

The consequent combination of papal and secular patronage made of the numerous small but brilliant Italian courts a veritable magnet for musicians of every kind. No less than their secular counterparts, the singers who had been taught the complexities of mensural polyphony in the schools of cathedrals and collegiate churches in regions of French and Flemish culture sought appointments south of the Alps. The more or less continuous movement of musicians from one place of employment to another that ensued made it possible for those so engaged to compare theoretical traditions, compositional procedures, and performance practices much more freely and frequently than ever before. As we shall see, the result was a degree of stylistic consistency in the polyphonic music of western Europe, beginning toward the end of the fifteenth century, that had never been achieved before, nor has been since.

THE IMPORTATION OF MUSICIANS AND REPERTORY

Discussion thus far of the major sources for the music of the fifteenth century has pointed to some rather startling anomalies in the relationship between musical repertory and geographical origins. As has been observed, the English music of the period is found primarily in collections of Italian provenance.[5] The same is true as well for northern European composers, especially those from the early part of the century, masters such as Binchoys, Du Fay, and their immediate contemporaries.[6] At the same time, strangely enough, those same Italian sources contain relatively little music by Italian composers.

In fact, in view of the thriving musical culture that established itself on the peninsula in the course of the fourteenth century, known Italian composers from this period are astonishingly rare. However curious it may appear, the musical repertories that have survived from the early fifteenth century with attributions to composers identifiably Italian are small and relatively undistinguished, and the careers of those whose names are known are difficult to trace. The last major figure to represent Italian musical culture of the late fourteenth and early fifteenth centuries appears to have

5. There are, of course, some notable exceptions, such as the "Old Hall Manuscript," MS Egerton 3307 at the British Library in London, and MS Pepys 1236 at the Magdalen College Library in Cambridge.

6. Here again there are exceptions, but, while noteworthy, they are surprisingly few and far between: collections such as MS V.III.24 at the Escorial Library and MSS 6 and 11 of the Municipal Library in Cambrai.

been the blind Florentine Francesco Landini.[7] It is symptomatic that only one master of the following generation native to the peninsula, a certain Antonio Zachara da Teramo, is represented in the Italian sources of the period. Typically, moreover, the compositions attributed to him are rather few in number: nine Mass pairs and as many secular works, all of the latter being settings of Italian texts.[8]

A brief survey of the manuscript collections to which reference has most frequently been made in the foregoing chapters will quickly demonstrate how truly small is their Italian component. Manuscript Canonici Misc. 213 of the Bodleian Library at Oxford, a large mixed repertory of secular and sacred works (some 325 in all) that was compiled in the Venetian area circa 1420–36 with repertory dating back to the 1380s, names 56 different composers. Of those cited, only 10 were probably native Italian, whereas the lion's share of the music is ascribed to Du Fay (51 pieces) with a substantial number as well by the northerners Arnold de Lantins and Hugo de Lantins (with 19 or 20 apiece). In addition, the vast majority of the compositions were written either to French or Latin texts; only 6 are *laude* and 24 others are settings of secular Italian verse.

Similarly, of the some 46 known composers represented in MS Q15 of the Civico Museo Bibliografico Musicale in Bologna, also a large mixed repertory that was possibly copied in Piacenza in the 1430s, only 5 or so have Italian names. And of the 308 pieces included overall, there are but 11 *laude* and a single secular Italian piece. Du Fay is again the best represented, with 69 works, followed closely with 42 by the northerner Johannes de Lymburgia, who served for a time in Vincenza "instructing young clerics."[9]

Attributions are considerably more sparse in the MS 2216 of the Biblioteca Universitaria in Bologna, which was copied in the late 1430s and early 1440s between Venice and Brescia; only thirty-two of the eighty-five compositions carry a name. Nonetheless, of the twenty-one known composers represented, there are but five of possible Italian origin, and all are represented by a single piece except for a certain Vala, who is credited with five. Du Fay is again the clear leader with a total of eleven pieces. As the repertory is primarily sacred, Latin predominates, but eleven pieces are Italian *laude* while nine others set secular Italian texts.[10]

Even more striking is the repertory in MS α.X.1.11 of the Biblioteca Estense in Modena, which was prepared for use by the court chapel of Leonello d'Este circa 1448 (with later additions). Of the 131 sacred works that compose it, the greatest number are by Du Fay, with 47, the English master Dunstable, with 25, and Binchoys, with 13; furthermore, the other 12 composers named are all either of English or French origin.

---

7. See Richard H. Hoppin, *Medieval Music* (New York: Norton, 1978), 454ff.

8. See Gilbert Reaney, "Zacar," *The New Grove Dictionary of Music*, 20:609–10, who observes that "nothing is known" of Antonio's life but succeeds nevertheless in distinguishing between his works and those that were more probably composed by an immediate contemporary named Nicola Zacharie.

9. See Keith E. Mixter, "Johannes de Lymburgia," *The New Grove Dictionary of Music*, 9:666–67.

10. Concerning these two codices, see pp. 223–286.

Also apparently devoted almost entirely to works by English and French masters is MS A¹D19 of the Library of the Seminario Maggiore in Aosta, the initial section of which was compiled in Bologna circa 1430–34. Of the 197 sacred compositions entered in its 3 major sections only 2 carry names suggesting Italian roots. English and Continental musicians again predominate; Du Fay is credited with at least 25 pieces, Binchoys with 24, and Dunstable with 14, while the other 25 identifiable figures are represented by fewer compositions.

Even the musical institutions associated with the papal court in Rome adopted a repertory that was imported, for the most part, from north of the Alps. Illustrative of the general trend, in addition to the earliest manuscripts copied for the Sistine Chapel choir, is the principal source for the polyphony sung at St. Peter's Basilica in Rome, MS San Pietro B80. A collection for liturgical use that includes Mass Ordinaries, a cycle of hymns for major feasts of the entire year, Magnificats, antiphon settings, and motets, the attributions made thus far show once again the privileged status of Du Fay (with at least thirteen works) and his contemporaries, Binchoys (four?), Barbingant (two?), Caron (two?), Compère (one), Dunstable (one), Guillaume Rouge (one), and probably Busnoys, Faugues, and Martini. Of these, Barbingant, Compère, Faugues, and Rouge may have served briefly with the choir.[11]

Clearly, the evidence of the sources suggests that at the very moment when Italy began to be recognized as the birthplace of a cultural renewal that encompassed not only the humanistic fields of study (poetry, literature, and history) but also the visual arts (painting, sculpture, and architecture), the situation with respect to music was strangely anomalous. Instead of leading the way under the direction of musicians who were native born and trained, the musical institutions of the Italian peninsula were importing singers and composers from north of the Alps. They were also relying to an increasing degree on the repertory these immigrants brought with them.[12] This included not only sacred works on Latin texts for use in liturgical and devotional services, an adoption that may be comprehensible to a degree, but also, much more surprising, secular pieces written to texts in French.

As will be evident from the discussion that follows, the pattern seen in the sources of Italian origin that are composed primarily of works by musicians born and trained in other geographical areas—hence within very different linguistic and cultural contexts—is reflected in the individual musical genres found in the repertories they contain. This is true even of those secular pieces ostensibly based on poetic texts in the vernacular. Particularly striking in this regard is the clear indication in each of the

11. See Christopher A. Reynolds, *Papal Patronage and the Music of St. Peter's, 1380–1513* (Berkeley: University of California Press, 1995), 340–46 (for an inventory of MS SPB 80) and 302–9 (for the evidence upon which the hypothetical association of these composers with the basilica is based).
12. In his comprehensive study of *Papal Patronage and the Music of St. Peter's,* Reynolds illuminates the ascendant role of northern musicians as singers and composers—and of their musical works—in the choir of the papal basilica during the fifteenth century. Reynolds traces in great detail the various factors—geographical, economic, cultural, ecclesiastical, and political—that contributed to their predominance in Italian courts and chapels at the time.

manuscript sources cited (and a number of others as well) that the indigenous secular song forms that flourished in Italy in the fourteenth century were replaced with surprising rapidity in the opening decades of the fifteenth by their counterparts from the French tradition.

BARZELLETTA AND FROTTOLA

Signs of the submersion and ultimate disappearance of the indigenous tradition for secular Italian polyphony that culminated in the trecento with the compositions of Francesco Landini are to be seen already in the works he wrote late in his life. These indications of the encroaching influence of the French secular tradition include his adoption of a three-part texture (in lieu of the vocal duo that had been customary earlier) and of some conventions of the notational system credited to the French composer-theorist Philippe de Vitry.

Nonetheless, Italian texts did not cease entirely to be set after Landini. Virtually all of the songbooks of the fifteenth century that were inscribed in a region where Italian was spoken—chansonniers such as Escorial IV.a.24, Mellon, Pixérécourt, and *Banco rari* 229, cited earlier in this connection—contain at least a few secular pieces on Italian texts. The largest group of such works, however, was included in the "Chansonnier Cordiforme," a collection that originated in the duchy of Savoy on the borders between French and Italian linguistic cultures (see Figure 11-4). Fourteen of its forty-four pieces, approximately a third of the total repertory, are on Italian texts.[13]

Ironically, if typically for the period, many of these compositions carry attributions to northern and even English composers. Included, for example, are Du Fay's *Dona gentile*, Vincenet's *Triste qui spero morendo*, the famous and ubiquitous *O rosa bella*, attributed to both Dunstable and Bedyngham,[14] and the latter's *Gentil madona*. What is more, although the twenty-three anonymous works leave a good deal of room for uncertainty, not a single Italian composer has thus far been identified as having contributed to this repertory. Some of the Italian songs may be simply *contrafacta*—compositions with Italian verse substituted for the original French (or English). This may well be the case for *Gentil madona*, for instance, which is found in other sources with the incipit "Fortune elas." In any case all but a very few of the Italian-texted songs are virtually indistinguishable stylistically from the chansons with which they are found.

---

13. The manuscript was so named because its leaves were cut in the shape of a heart; when opened, therefore, it presented the romantic image of two hearts joined (see Figure 11-4). Concerning its provenance and contents see the *Census-Catalogue of Manuscript Sources of Polyphonic Music*, ed. Charles Hamm and Herbert Kellman, 5 vols. (Neuhausen-Stuttgart: Hänssler-Verlag, 1979–88), 3:35f.

14. For a judicious review of the evidence concerning the authorship of this well-traveled piece, see David Fallows, "Dunstable, Bedyngham, and *O rosa bella*," *Journal of Musicology* 12 (1994): 287–305, who makes a convincing case for Bedyngham.

FIGURE 11-4.   *Zentil madona*, attributed elsewhere to Bedyngham, in the "Cordiforme Chansonnier" (Paris, Bibliothèque Nationale, fonds Rothschild 2973, ff.3ᵛ–4).

Not until the closing decades of the fifteenth century did clearly indigenous genres of secular music begin once again to find notated form in Italy. In this instance the qualification "notated," with its implied distinction between written and oral traditions, appears highly advisable. The evidence—both historical and musical—would suggest that the secular Italian works transmitted in the sources (in this case both manuscript and printed) originated in an earlier, unwritten repertory, one that had arisen from the practice of declaiming lyric poetry to an instrumental accompaniment. More, perhaps, than any other body of music of the fifteenth and sixteenth centuries, this one shows signs of having begun as a quasi-improvisatory mode of composition.

It is clear in any case that the authors of pieces conceived in this particular cultural matrix relied upon musical phrases that were formulaic in nature, both melodically and harmonically. These could be fashioned to fit a given poem—or simply (as we shall see) a common type of verse—and stored in the memory until needed for performance. Consequently, many pieces may have taken shape over a period of time and reached a more or less final state long before a composer or a scribe had reason to fix them in ink upon the page.[15]

15. Pertinent in this connection are the comments of Baldassare Castiglione, *The Courtier*, bk. 2, chap. 13: "pricksong [i.e., notated music] is a fair music, if it be done upon the book surely and after a good sort. But to sing to the lute is much better" (in the 1561 translation of Sir Thomas Hoby).

The stylistic and formal characteristics of the written repertory that point to such a course of compositional development are the following: syllabic declamation with considerable use of repeated pitches; clearly defined musical phrases corresponding unequivocally to the number of verses to be accommodated; and schematic repetitions of those phrases especially in accordance with recurring rhyme schemes. All of these features helped to assure maximum economy of means and assisted the memory in recalling text and music together in performance. In addition, the lowest part often leaps about by fourth and fifth, intervals that are easily played upon a lute, for example, and the inner voices reflect the kind of passagework that was typical for that instrument at the time.

Perhaps the most dramatic manifestation of the schematic character of such pieces may be seen in the musical formulae capable of adaptation to any number of poems having the same verse structure and/or rhyme scheme. These were actually labeled simply as an *aria* (melody) for the singing of a given formal type. A number of such works are found in the collections of *frottole* published in Venice early in the sixteenth century, to be discussed presently. Also revealing in this connection is the use of a single musical composition for two or more texts, as occurs for example among the works ascribed to Marchetto Cara.[16]

Prior to 1500 compositions of this sort rarely occur in manuscript collections of secular music, and they are not usually identified as to genre. Early in the sixteenth century, by contrast, Ottaviano Petrucci, the first to print music from moveable metal type, began to publish entire collections given over exclusively to pieces of the kind described.[17] It may well be, in fact, that Petrucci's creation of a commercial outlet for the newly developing repertory of Italian song led directly to the notation of a good many pieces whose only source previously had been the memory of those who performed them. Whatever the case, between 1504 and 1514 Petrucci brought out eleven such collections, some of which must have gone through several impressions, and other printers followed suit soon thereafter.

In these circumstances, significantly, publication apparently meant a certain transformation of the original compositional conception. Pieces that presumably began their existence as melodies sung to a lute or keyboard were first printed as consort songs with the sustaining sonorities of the accompanying instrument written out as (four) separate parts. Ironically, the technical procedures adopted for this improvisatory repertory of accompanied solo song were those that had been invented initially to accommodate the linear counterpoint of northern composers, their chansons, motets, and Mass settings. As a result, when Petrucci later decided to publish some of the *frottola* repertory in what was presumably its original form—for lute and voice—he was obliged to have lute intabulations made of the altus, tenor, and bassus of the four-part version.

16. See William Prizer, *Courtly Pastimes: The Frottole of Marchetto Cara*, Studies in Musicology 33 (Ann Arbor: UMI Research Press, 1980), 199f., and nn. 4, 14.
17. See the summary list of Petrucci's prints and the bibliography given by Martin Picker, "Petrucci, Ottaviano," *The New Grove Dictionary of Music*, 14:597.

Petrucci thus provided, through his commercial exploitation of a popular indigenous genre, both a reason for notating oral repertory and, at the same time, new technological means for its rapid dissemination. However, it was the patronage of the Este and the Gonzaga families at the courts of Mantua and Ferrara that apparently gave the primary impetus for the cultivation of this improvisatory musical practice and the codification of its characteristic forms and styles. More than any other, Isabella d'Este (1474–1539), who was married in 1490 to the marquis of Mantua, Francesco II Gonzaga, played a central role in the development of the secular Italian repertory (see Figure 11-5). Tied by family relationships or by marriage to the courts of Ferrara, Milan, Naples, and Urbino, and through her sister-in-law, Lucrezia Borgia, to the papal court in Rome, she became the friend of painters—from Correggio to Mantegna, Bellini, and Titian—and the correspondent of poets and other important literary figures such as Serafino dall' Aquila, Vincenzo Calmeta, Galeotto del Carretto, Pietro Bembo, Castiglione, Ariosto, and Tasso.[18] She was also a skilled musician, trained during her childhood in Ferrara by the chapelmaster there, Johannes Martini, to sing and to play the lute and keyboard instruments.[19]

Isabella had at one time in her employ both Marchetto Cara and Bartolomeo Tromboncino, two of the composers who contributed most to the definition of the new genres and, it would seem, to their increasing popularity. Cara—lutenist and singer as well as composer—figured at the court of Mantua from the time of his arrival in 1494 until his death some thirty years later toward the end of 1525.[20] Tromboncino, the son of a *piffero* (a wind player) who also

FIGURE 11-5.   Portrait of Isabella d'Este by Leonardo da Vinci (Musée du Louvre).

18. See the preface to the detailed study by Julia Cartwright, *Isabella d'Este, Marchioness of Mantua, 1474–1539: A Study of the Renaissance*, 2 vols. (New York: E. P. Dutton, 1903), 1:v–xii; also the concise appreciation by Alfred Einstein, *The Italian Madrigal*, 3 vols. (Princeton: Princeton University Press, 1949), 1:38ff.
19. See the brief sketch of Isabella by Prizer in *Courtly Pastimes*, 2ff.
20. See Prizer, *Courtly Pastimes*, 35ff.

played, sang, and acted, was in Mantua only sporadically after an initial period of more or less continuous service from 1494 to 1501. Subsequently he seems to have been attached for a time to the Este court at Ferrara (1502–13?) before finishing his career in Venice, where he died circa 1535.[21] To these two is attributed the greatest number of the pieces included in Petrucci's prints of Italian secular music.[22]

In these published collections the compositions are identified in a general sense by the term *frottola* (plural *frottole*)—etymologically defined, perhaps a bit fancifully, by the writers of the period as deriving from *frocta*, meaning a congeries of random or unrelated thoughts—and more specifically by the poetic genres or types comprehended under the broader designation.[23] These include a rather bewildering variety of different formal schemes designated by terms such as *barzelletta, strambotto, oda, canzonetta, capitolo, sonetto, ballata, canzone,* and *villotta,* to name only those most frequently encountered. By the end of the fifteenth century rhyme schemes, verse lengths, and lines per stanza had been fixed for all of these, at least within general parameters. They had also been described by those theorists of language and poetry who were the direct Italian successors to the earlier literary tradition of the *seconde réhtorique.*[24]

Among the subgenres of the *frottola* identifiable by poetic type the clearest distinction to be made is perhaps that between the verse forms with a *ripresa* (or refrain) and those without. The most characteristic and most widely circulated of all the refrain forms was the *barzelletta,* a descendent of the *ballata* of the fourteenth century. Its name may in fact derive from the French term *bergerette,* which designates the same general form. It is clearly indicative of the popularity of this particular poetic genre that, when used without further qualification, the term *frottola* usually referred to the *barzelletta.*

Typical of this subtype in all respects, both poetically and musically, is Tromboncino's *Se ben hor non scopro el foco,* which was printed by Petrucci in his book 1 of 1504 and included as well in five of the manuscript sources of the period (see Example 11-1). Like the great majority of the *barzellete* in the written repertory, this one is in octosyllables with a refrain of four verses, rhyming ABBA. (There are poems in which the rhyme scheme for the refrain is ABAB, others where it consists of only two lines, AB, but they are relatively rare.) The strophes that follow the first full statement of the refrain are composed of three additional elements: two pairs of lines rhyming cd, cd, called, in Italian poetic theory of the period, *piedi* (literally "feet") or *mutazioni* ("changes," perhaps with reference to the new rhyming syllables), and another pair of lines, dA, termed the *volta* ("turn"), which bridges the

21. See William Prizer, "Tromboncino, Bartolomeo," *The New Grove Dictionary of Music,* 19:161–63.
22. See the list of composer attributions published by Knud Jeppesen, *La Frottola: Bermerkungen zur Bibliographie der ältesten weltlichen Notendrucke in Italien,* 3 vols., Acta Jutlandica, vols. 41–43 (Copenhagen: Munksgaard, 1968–69), 2:263ff.
23. See Don Harrán, "Frottola," *The New Grove Dictionary of Music,* 6:867–73.
24. Regarding the poetic forms in question and the musical structures to which they gave rise, see the examples described below, and cf. Prizer, *Courtly Pastimes,* 64ff.

EXAMPLE 11-1. Bartolomeo Tromboncino, *Se ben hor non scopro el foco*

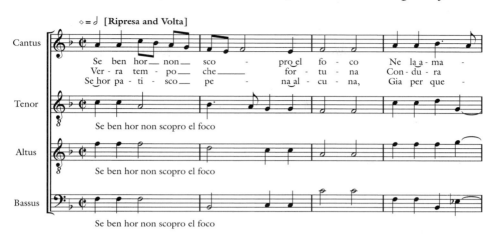

RIPRESA: If I now reveal fully neither the fire nor my bitter life, this wicked, biting pain, let it be known in due time and place.

STROPHE: The time will come when Fortune will bring my ship home. If now I suffer some pain, it hasn't killed me yet; let the torment that I wrongly suffer be known in due time and place. (Three additional strophes.)

rhymes from the *piedi* to the *ripresa*.[25] (Exceptionally, the return to the opening rhyme of the refrain brings with it here a literal repetition of its fourth line; usually it would be a newly composed verse.) Each stanza is followed in turn by a repetition of the refrain, usually abbreviated. As a rule the music written for the shortened *ripresa* provided for the declamation of at least the first pair of lines, but in this setting only one verse has been accommodated.

Formally the music conforms to the patterns of the verse. There are four short phrases, one for each line of the refrain, with cadences only to the modal final (the first and last) and to the confinal (the second and third). The first phrase of music is then restated at the end to provide for the truncated repetition of the refrain between the stanzas. In addition, the third is identical to the second, thus mirroring the juxtaposition of the two lines of the refrain with the same rhyming syllables. Similarly, the paired lines of the *piedi* are sung to the two opening phrases of music, which are repeated like the rhymes themselves. This is followed by the *volta*, which is sung to the second pair of phrases, once again with the iteration of the rhyme scheme from the last line of the *piedi* to the first of the *volta* reflected in the musical repetition. The text is declaimed in an essentially syllabic style, mostly in minims and semibreves, using only the briefest of melismatic ornaments in the melodic line. Characteristic in particular are the repeated pitches at phrase ends, matching the feminine rhymes that predominate in the Italian verse of the period.

There is a single departure from the strictest compositional economy: the sequen-

25. In this discussion of versification, the convention of distinguishing between refrain lines, which use capitals, and those of the strophes, which use lower-case letters, will be observed when possible.

tial repetition of the first two words of the final line of the refrain, "Fia scoperta," which—together with the imitative figure with which it is introduced—extends the length of the phrase from the three breves provided for the preceding three verses to a total of six. The setting for the abridged refrain is spun out in like manner, after the voice has made its final cadence, in this instance by a sequential figure in altus and tenor that has the flavor of a short instrumental postlude. This closing tag may be a surviving trace of the presumably original conception of the piece as accompanied solo song. Although not all *frottole* have such a passage, in some instances the presumably instrumental extension of the closing phrase is even more elaborate.

All in all, then, the composer has made the most of a minimum of musical materials, crafting in the process a highly concentrated yet easily perceptible structure that can be diagrammed as follows:

$$\text{Text:} \quad \text{A B B A (A?): c d, c d, d A, A : etc. (four strophes)}$$
$$\text{Music:} \quad \alpha \ \beta \ \beta \ \gamma \ \alpha' : \alpha \ \beta, \alpha \ \beta, \beta \ \gamma, \alpha' : \text{etc.}$$

Among the poetic forms without a refrain, the one most commonly set to music was the *strambotto*. Moreover, the *barzelletta* aside, it was the type most frequently included in the written repertory. Also known as *ottava rima* because it consists of a single strophe of eight lines, its verses are uniformly hendecasyllabic, as a rule, and are rhymed abababab or ababbcc. With its prosodic regularity and limited rhyme scheme the *strambotto* thus lends itself perhaps even more readily than the *barzelletta* to the formulaic approach that characterizes this repertory. A representative example is *Ameni colli*, attributed to a certain Ludovico Milanese, a priest who served as singer and organist in one of the churches in Lucca.[26] Petrucci first published it in his *Frottole libro VIII* of 1507 (ff. 29ᵛ–30), then later included it in the second of two volumes of *frottole* intabulated for lute and voice by Franciscus Bossinensis, which he brought out in 1509 and 1511.

The musical substance of Ludovico's setting is slight indeed (see Example 11-2). Only two phrases have been provided for the eight verses, and this schematic formal solution, which requires three repetitions of the music to declaim the complete poem, is entirely typical of settings for *ottava rima*. The musical material added at the end, allowing for a repetition of the last part of even-numbered verses, gives the appearance of a less formulaic, more sophisticated approach. However, nearly all of its melodic material consists either of repeated pitches or of conventional cadential patterns.

For the lute accompaniment Bossinensis has reduced the four parts of the vocal version to three, generally by simply eliminating the altus, as indicated by the title page of the print.[27] Characteristic of this intabulation, once again, is the frequent

---

26. See William Prizer, "Ludovico Milanese," *The New Grove Dictionary of Music*, 11:306.
27. It states, "Tenor and bass intabulated with the soprano in mensural notation to sing and play with the lute."

EXAMPLE 11-2. Ludovico Milanese, *Ameni colli*, as arranged by Franciscus Bossinensis

Pleasant hills, sunlit slopes, fresh fountains, and delightful shores, green meadows adorned with flowers, which give the heart, thinking of you, delight and life, thickets sheltering singing birds that make martyrs of lonely souls, how gladly would I be among you if only my nymph were there as well.

motion in the bass line by fourths and fifths, usually involving one or more of the three open strings at the bottom of the instrument's register (here A, D, and G). Noteworthy as well is the sequential coda that spins itself out following the closing cadence of the voice, recalling a similar figure, also intended for instrumental performance, at the end of the *barzelletta Se ben hor non scopro el foco.*[28]

Of the lesser-used verse types the *oda* and the *canzonetta* are similar to one another in the sense that both consist of quatrains and are strophic in structure. They differ, however, in that the *canzonetta* repeats the initial line of the first stanza as a refrain at the end of every strophe, including the first, whereas the *oda* has no such repetition of verbal material. Dissimilar, too, is the versification: the *canzonetta* has lines of equal length and a single rhyme for all the verses within a strophe except the refrain (e.g., AbbA, cccA, dddA, etc.), whereas the length of the fourth line of the *oda*'s stanza is usually different from that of the first three—either longer or shorter—and the rhyme scheme is generally interlocking (e.g., abbc, cdde, effg, etc.).

A typical *canzonetta*, in most respects, is *Cara's Aiutami, ch'io moro*, which has lines of seven syllables and the rhyme scheme shown above (see Example 11-3). The musical setting is characteristically formulaic, using four wholly syllabic phrases of extreme concision (two breves apiece). The second and the third are identical, corresponding to the recurring rhyme, and the last is a variation of the first, from which it also derives the textual refrain. By way of comparison, the *oda Signora, anzi mia dea*, which is credited to Tromboncino, has strophes composed of three heptasyllables followed by a tetrasyllable with the interlocking rhyme scheme as indicated (see Figure 11-6). Its compositional setting is equally terse, consisting of three phrases articulated only by rests in the soprano (rather than the cadences utilized by Cara) with the last subdivided to provide for the brief closing verse. There are no literal repetitions, but the second phrase restates the first sequentially a third lower, and the last is a varied extension of the second. The only exceptional characteristic is the untexted phrase at the end of the piece, presumably intended, once again, for instrumental performance.

Curiously, of all the verse forms found in the *frottola* repertory of the early sixteenth century, the three associated with the literary traditions most honored in sixteenth-century Italy—the *capitolo*, the *sonetto*, and the *canzone*—were perhaps the most rarely found, at least in the earliest collections published by Petrucci. The *capitolo*, venerated as the versification adopted by Dante for the *Divina commedia*, is also known as *terza rima* because it consists of successive stanzas of three hendecasyllabic lines with an interlocking rhyme scheme (e.g., aba, bcb, cdc, etc.). The sonnet, whose structural patterns are relatively familiar due to their appropriation by English poets of the sixteenth century, consists of fourteen hendecasyllabic lines divided into

---

28. For further discussion of the relationship of a published part song with the instrumental arrangements based upon it, see pp. 812–13 and 823, the observations concerning Tromboncino's setting of the Petrarchan canzona *Si e debile il filo*, which was published by Petrucci in his book 7 of 1507 and in the Bossinensis intabulations (book 1) of 1509, then by Antico in his *Canzoni novi* of 1510 and in the keyboard intabulations of 1517.

EXAMPLE 11-3. Marchetto Cara, *Aiutami, ch'io moro*

1. Help me, I am dying; I pray thee delay not, o singular lady: help me, I am dying.
   2. Thou canst give me life and make me happy again that I no longer consume myself: Help me . . . 3. No longer can the heart burn with great torment; have pity on the unhappy heart: Help me . . . 4. I can no longer bear such pain nor such cruel chains; sweet goddess and all my happiness: Help me . . . 5. I am so weary and worn and so sorely wounded in the flank that I feel myself always in decline: Help me . . . 6. Let my lament move you, if not my torment; leave me no longer in grief: Help me . . .

a pair of quatrains and a pair of tercets with a repeating rhyme scheme such as abba, abba, cdc, cdc.

As for the *canzone,* which combines lines of seven and eleven syllables in changing patterns with a variety of different rhyme schemes, its use in polyphonic composition is connected with the origins of the madrigal rather than, in any significant way, with the development of the *frottola* and will be discussed below (pp. 652–60). The sonnet and the *canzone* undoubtedly owed their distinction at least in part to their culti-

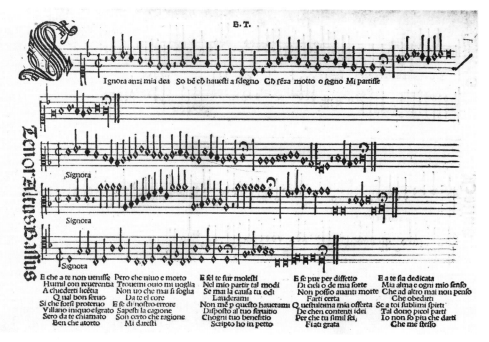

FIGURE 11-6. Tromboncino's oda *Signora, anzi mia dea*, from Petrucci's *frottola* collection, *Libro III*, no. 62 (Venice, 1504).

vation by Petrarch, whose poetry was being viewed more and more at the time as a stylistic paradigm. For it was Petrarch's Tuscan dialect that was taken as a model by those who, like the historian, theorist, and poet Pietro Bembo (1470–1547), were attempting to establish Italian as a respectable literary language.[29]

But if the *capitolo* and the *sonetto* had a more noble ancestry than the *oda* and the *canzonetta*, they lent themselves no less well to the schematic compositional procedures that characterize the *frottola* repertory generally. For the Petrarchan sonnet *Sonno, che qli animali* . . . , for example, Cara composed only three short, syllabic phrases of music, and the second is to be repeated for the two quatrains, thus reflecting the duplication of rhyming syllables in a musical iteration.[30] Otherwise, there is nothing exceptional about the setting, save perhaps the composer's slightly archaic use of a ternary mensuration and of a gently rocking rhythm, which may have been suggested by the reference in the opening verses to "sleep."

Tromboncino's treatment of the *capitolo Amor! Che vuoi?* is considerably more

---

29. Bembo's signal contribution to that movement was of course his treatise *Prose della volgar lingua* (1525).

30. First published by Andrea Antico in his *Libro tertio* of 1517, the piece is available in modern transcription in Andrea Antico, *Canzoni, sonetti, strambotti et frottole: Libro tertio*, ed. Alfred Einstein, Smith College Music Archives, no. 4 (Northampton, Mass.: Smith College, 1941), no. 3.

generous, for he set to music two complete tercets. Moreover, he limited melodic repetition largely to cadential formulae at the ends of lines and wrote a lengthy instrumental interlude to be played between the successive pairs of stanzas.[31] This may have been because the poem represents a dialogue between an unidentified lady and Amor, both of which are systematically personified, textually and musically, throughout the piece, resulting in a miniature theatrical scene. Its presence in this repertory inevitably raises questions as to possible connections between songs in the vernacular, such as this, sung to instrumental accompaniment, and the increasingly numerous dramatic productions of the period, many of which called specifically for musical interludes.

Ferrara, in particular, became an important center for theatrical activity under the reign of Ercole I d'Este (1431–1505), Isabella's father. In view of the central role played by members of his family in encouraging the cultivation of the *frottola*, it is not surprising that the two easily related forms of expression were brought together there. Compositions that can be linked more or less directly with dramatic spectacles of the period include both those performed as accompanied solo song (apparently in the tradition out of which the *frottola* emerged) and others conceived instead in a rather different style for vocal ensemble in four parts.[32]

On the one hand are pieces specifically intended for a single character in a drama. Such a song is the *strambotto* attributed to Baccio Ugolino, *La morte tu mi dai*, which he is reported to have sung to the lyre in the title role of Angelo Poliziano's play *Orpheus*. Similarly, Tromboncino's *Crudel fugi se sai* was written to be sung by Pan in Carretto's *Le nozze di Psiche e Cupidine*.[33] The evidence suggests that songs such as these were frequently introduced into a play as an integral—if not entirely indispensable—part of the dramatic action.

On the other hand are compositions for an ensemble of voices and (perhaps) instruments that serve a rather different theatrical function. These made a festive conclusion for an act or an entire play in the manner of the "chorus" of ancient Greek theater. Such presentations evolved little by little into *intermedii*, the entertainments presented between the acts of the spoken drama. Mimed by costumed actors, danced, and sung, they could perhaps be justified by invoking classical precedent. However, they appear to have had as a rule only a general relationship—if any at all—to the thread of the plot and are consequently rather more difficult to identify.

Some spectacles of this kind may have been inspired by the medieval tradition of the *moresca*, but the majority of them resembled instead, both in style and in content, the Carnival songs, to be discussed presently. Typical of the *canti* and the *balli* of the mummers of the Carnival season in its wholly vocal conception and its declamatory, homophonic style, for example, is the masquerade *Forestieri a la ventura*. It

---

31. The piece has been edited from the print in question by Alfred Einstein, "Andrea Antico's *Canzoni novi* of 1510," *Musical Quarterly* 37 (1954).
32. See Nino Pirrotta, *Music and Theater from Poliziano to Monteverdi* (Cambridge, Mass.: Harvard University Press, 1981), chap. 3, "Classical Theater, *intermedi* and *frottola* Music."
33. See Pirrotta, *Music and Theater*, 35 and 74, respectively.

expresses, in the first person plural, the sentiments of musical pilgrims come to Rome and may well have been conceived originally as a Carnival song.[34] Equally characteristic in its depiction of a scene from daily life is the hunting piece *A la chaza*, which recalls with its general animation and narrative—including calls to the dogs and the successful conclusion of the hunt—the *caccia* of the fourteenth century. Both pieces were included in the sources that transmit the more lyrical *frottole* typical of the secular Italian repertory of the period generally—the former in Petrucci's *Libro sesto* of 1506 and the latter in a manuscript compiled in Ferrara or Mantua and dated 1502, MS Res. Vm7 676 of the National Library in Paris.[35] But their special theatrical character suggests that they may have had their origins, or at least their place, in one of the dramatic productions of the age.

THE *CANTI CARNASCIALESCHI*

By the fifteenth century a long-standing tradition had been established in Florence for celebrating with song the festivals associated with particular seasons of the year—most notably the pre-Lenten Carnival and the *calendimaggio*. The latter, which marked the return of spring (beginning on May 1 and culminating on June 24 with the feast day of the patron saint of the city, St. John the Baptist), was observed in Florence with particular enthusiasm.[36]

The most typical manifestation of the *joie de vivre* inspired by these occasions—and probably the first to be regularly seen (and heard)—were the *mascherati*, men and boys in disguise (not infrequently "in drag"). They went through the streets of the city on foot (and usually by torchlight), stopping on the squares and in the courtyards to sing salacious songs filled with double entendres and the playful humor of thinly veiled obscenities. In the latter half of the fifteenth century these popular celebrations apparently took on somewhat more elevated artistic aims, especially during the rule of Lorenzo the Magnificent (1469–92). He involved artists and musicians of his patronage in devising decorations, costumes, poetry, and music to enhance the customary expressions of Florentine exuberance, writing verse for a number of the songs himself.

It may have been due to his wealth and influence that the performers began to make more frequent use of *carri*, horse-drawn carts elaborately decorated (in the manner of the present-day parade float) and carrying costumed figures who represented the various quarters of the city, the guilds of artisans and merchants, and personages and scenes of daily life, all treated in a more or less satirical and humorous manner. From their mobile stages the figurants of *tableaux-vivants* explained the significance of their representation in songs written for the purpose. In addition to

---

34. See Pirrotta, *Music and Theater*, 57; the text begins, "Foreigners in search of fortune, we have come to holy Rome; each one of us can sing various modes with good measure."
35. Concerning the latter, see the *Census-Catalogue of Manuscript Sources*, 3:14f.
36. See Frank D'Accone, "Canti carnascialeschi," *The New Grove Dictionary of Music*, 3:721.

FIGURE 11-7. Design for a triumphal *carro* by Baldassare Peruzzi, possibly depicting the goddess Cybele (London British Museum, Department of Prints and Drawings, no. 1880-5-8-82).

carri of the sort indicated there were other presentations of a more moralistic orientation called *trionfi* ("triumphs"), which illustrated themes or topics drawn from humanistic disciplines such as history, philosophy, mythology, and science (see Figure 11-7).[37]

The poetic forms, strophic and nonstrophic alike, adopted for the Carnival songs were those described in the preceding discussion, with the *barzelletta* taking once again pride of place. As has been suggested, however, the musical style for the Carnival songs is different both conceptually and practically from that found in the notated *frottola* repertory. Characteristic are an entirely vocal conception in three or four parts, a homophonic texture maintained with great consistency, and regularly syllabic declamation, executed simultaneously in all the voices—all of which helped the intended audience to hear and understand the texts in a performance "al fresco."

A characteristic example is the anonymous *Ben venga maggio*, a three-voice setting of a *ballata* by Angelo Poliziano (1454–94), the humanist scholar and poet who served in the household of Lorenzo the Magnificent in the 1470s (see Example 11-4). The verse, which undoubtedly conveys something of the atmosphere that must have accompanied such popular celebrations, refers directly to the *calendimaggio*, welcoming the season and urging the young, particularly those of the

37. According to Federico Ghisi, "Carnival Songs and the Origins of the Intermezzo Giocoso," *Musical Quarterly* 25 (1939): 325–33, the *carri* and *trionfi* were not of Lorenzo's invention, but the brilliance achieved by their use during the time of his unofficial control of the Tuscan capital caused them to be ascribed to him by popular tradition.

EXAMPLE 11-4. Anonymous, *Ben venga maggio*

RIPRESA: Be welcome, May, the wild banner.

STROPHES: 1. Be welcome, springtime, that urges man to love, and you, bands of maidens with your admirers, who with roses and flowers make May beautiful. 2. Come out to the fresh air of green trees. Every fair one can be sure among so many noble maidens that the animals and birds ignite May with love. (Six additional strophes.)

fair sex, to profit from the pleasures it offers—love first of all. Formally it consists of a *ripresa* of two lines, rhyming AA, and eight strophes comprising two *piedi* and a *volta* of two lines each, rhyming bc, bc, da, all in heptasyllables.

These are, of course, the structural elements of the traditional medieval verse form of the *ballata*, as represented here, which were retained for the *barzelletta* of the fifteenth century when it was derived from its parent. And, as is to be expected, the musical setting mirrors the poetic structure in this piece no less faithfully than in the *frottole* examined earlier. There are two concise phrases for the refrain, two more for the *piedi* (repeated, of course, like the corresponding rhymes), and a final pair for the *volta*. In the Carnival song, however, the articulation of the phrases is somewhat archaic in flavor, as it is accomplished primarily by means of linear rather than contrapuntal cadences. This melodic punctuation is reinforced by an interruption of the rhythmic flow, in the refrain by a corona over the concluding note of the phrase and in the final two sections by intervening rests.

Curiously, the most regular, coherent melody of the piece is that carried by the tenor, and it is possible to wonder if an older, monophonic Carnival song—or even a melody from some other source—was taken as a secular cantus firmus for that part in the polyphonic setting.[38] If so, the compositional process must be seen as essentially different from that of the accompanied solo song of the *frottola* repertory. Equally striking is the contrast in contrapuntal textures, for the text of *Ben venga maggio* is declaimed simultaneously by all three voices in a strictly syllabic and homophonic style.

That it was the intention generally of the authors who prepared texts for these festivities to make humorous sport of familiar aspects of daily life in the streets of Florence—usually by giving a slyly erotic interpretation to the most common of objects and situations—will be readily seen from the briefest sampling of the repertory. Such was obviously the aim in the case of the *Canto de' profumieri* ("Song of the Perfumers"), the text of which may be from the pen of Lorenzo himself. In this respect it is typical of the songs relating to the various guildsmen and merchants active in the city (see Example 11-5). As in the verses declaimed by the "Forestieri a la ventura," discussed earlier (pp. 414–15), the discourse here is in the first person plural. Those represented are identified as "galanti di Valenza," traveling merchants

38. Of interest in this connection is the study by Bonnie Blackburn, "Two 'Carnival Songs' Unmasked," *Musica disciplina* 35 (1981): 121–78, who has shown that one such *canto* is based on a French tune, *Tambur, tambur,* and another on the melody that serves as a tenor cantus firmus in Obrecht's *Meskin es hu,* published by Petrucci in the *Odhecaton.*

EXAMPLE 11-5. Anonymous, *Canto de' profumieri*

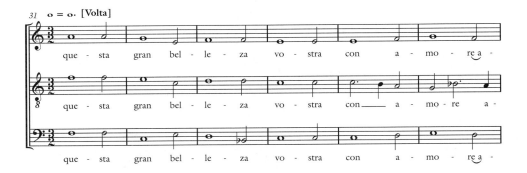

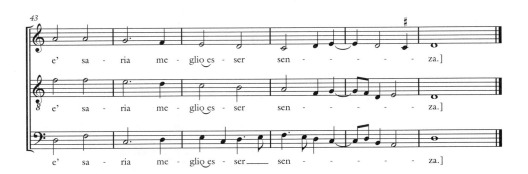

RIPRESA: We are gallant men of Valencia come here by chance, already caught and bound in love by the women of Florence.

STROPHES: 1. Most noble and beautiful are the ladies in our land, but you surpass them by far, as can be seen from your face, your great beauty accompanied by love; if you are not in love, it would be better to be without. 2. Following our custom, we still use naked the little instruments; oils and perfumes we carry with us. They have a sweet odor and give nature a real boost; if there is a lady with hardness toward love, it will soften her. (Five additional strophes.)

from the city mentioned,[39] who vaunt their wares—perfumes, oils, soaps, and "uselletti" (perhaps a small container in human form?)—in terms replete with suggestive images and sexual innuendo.[40] The poem is a *ballata* in octosyllables consisting of a *ripresa* of four lines, rhyming ABBA, and seven stanzas, each with two *piedi* of two lines, rhyming cd, cd, and a volta of four lines, rhyming deea.

Turning to the music, the anonymous setting is in essential ways very much like that for *Ben venga maggio*, despite significant differences of detail. For both the refrain and the *volta* there are two compact phrases of music, each carrying two verses, thus corresponding to the two syntactic entities of the poetry rather than merely to the number of lines, and these are articulated with a contrapuntal cadence as well as a rest or a held note.

By contrast, each of the two lines of the individual *piede* is given a separate phrase, articulated in the same way and then repeated to accommodate the second pair of lines with the same rhyming syllables. In this composition the smoothest, most tuneful melodic motion is in the cantus rather than the tenor. In the latter part much of the counterpoint consists of parallel thirds and, to a lesser extent (primarily in cadential passages), parallel sixths. The texture, then, in the manner typical of *canti carnascialeschi* generally, remains consistently homophonic overall, broken only, like the strictly syllabic declamation, by a modest precadential melisma.

As is suggested by the possible presence of a preexistent tune in the tenor of *Ben venga maggio*, it is entirely conceivable that Carnival songs were not polyphonically set before Lorenzo began to take an interest in the celebration of the festivities. It is not unlikely either that the northern-trained musicians in his employ—composers such as Alexander Agricola and Isaac—helped to set the pattern for the polyphonic style. Whoever these polyphonists were, they adopted for their flagrantly secular purpose the homophonic, declamatory texture that was often used at the time to give rhetorical emphasis to words of particular import in the sacred repertories of Mass and motet.

A more impressive demonstration of contrapuntal skill is Heinrich Isaac's well-known contribution to this repertory, *Donna di dentro*, which has few of the common features of a Carnival song. Its witticisms, in fact, are as much musical as verbal. It combines simultaneously in various overlapping configurations three different songs that must have been thoroughly familiar to Florentines of that day, thus juxtaposing a flowery sentiment addressed to a lady with a ditty about "mazacroca" (presumably a sweet of some sort) and a reference to dame Fortune.[41]

---

39. Presumably Valence, a town on the Rhone in southern France; however, Valencia, in the ancient kingdom of Aragon, is also a possibility.

40. In a similar vein is the anonymous *Orsu, car' signori* (in Claude V. Palisca, ed., *Norton Anthology of Western Music*, 1st ed., 2 vols. [New York: Norton, 1980], 1:228), which ostensibly deals with the preparation of "bulls" by the professional scribes of the city, exploits the potential ambiguity of the term *bolle* (which can be either official documents or syphilitic sores) and imparts a sexual connotation to the gesture of dipping the pen in the inkwell and squeezing out the excess ink.

41. See Noah Greenberg and Paul Maynard, eds., *An Anthology of Early Renaissance Music* (New York: Norton, 1975), 277–83.

The influence of northern-trained contrapuntists is perhaps clearer in the more serious Carnival songs whose purpose was to explain the visual imagery of the "triumphs." A representative example is the *Trionfo delle quattro complessioni* ("Triumph of the Four Temperaments") attributed to a certain Giovanni Serragli, a local composer (see Example 11-6). Its text comments upon the four basic temperaments as they had been posited centuries before by the celebrated Greek physician Galen: the sanguine (here typified by the lover), the choleric, the phlegmatic, and the melancholic. These are linked, "in harmony and in discord," with the four traditional elements: air, fire, water, and earth, respectively. Formally, the poem consists of six identical strophes, but these fail to conform to any of the established patterns. Instead, they consist of seven lines, rhyming ababacc and alternating between seven and eleven syllables.

If Serragli's setting remains formulaic in the sense that each successive stanza is to be sung to the same music, the extreme economy achieved in the *frottola* repertory by internal repetitions of segments corresponding to the recurrence of rhyming syllables has now been abandoned. The strophe has been entirely through-composed with a new phrase for each line of the poem, articulated again here by cadential patterns, both melodic and contrapuntal, and by longer notes extended by a corona or (in one instance) a rest. Declamation, using primarily breves and semibreves, continues to be strictly syllabic, and the texture is predominantly homophonic, except, as in the *Canto de' profumieri*, for brief precadential melismas.

However, as might be thought appropriate for a more solemn text with didactic overtones, a fourth voice has been added to enrich the sonority. In addition, the uniform texture of constantly sounding voices has been varied by a reduction first to two parts (tenor and bass, mm. 21–26), then to three (cantus, altus, and tenor, mm. 27–32), and enlivened by a brief point of imitation (mm. 45–47). The result is quite unlike anything to be found among the *frottole*; it is more similar to the style of the *motetti ducales* (see pp. 429–39) than either the accompanied solo song that was favored by musicians in the service of the Este and the Gonzaga or even the more modest Carnival songs in three voices.

After the demise of Lorenzo in 1492 and the subsequent rise to power of Savonarola (1494–98), the Medici were driven from Florence, and the relatively licentious festivals were replaced by religious processions and the singing of *laude*. Secular music of doubtful moral intent was censured. At one point the licentious pre-Lenten revelry was even replaced by the "bonfire of the vanities," which illuminated the Piazza della Signoria by the burning not only of numerous books and paintings deemed in some sense wanton or depraved but also a large quantity of secular music and numerous instruments of the sort most frequently used in its performance.

In 1498, when the Medici were restored to power, the secular festivals were reinstituted as well. The preparation of *carri* and *trionfi* was resumed, and the verse and music needed in that connection were cultivated anew. (Serragli's piece may in fact date from this second period.) But with the Medici installed as titulary dukes of Tuscany instead of merely the de facto rulers, the popular festivals gradually gave way

EXAMPLE 11-6. Giovanni Serragli, *Trionfo delle quattro complessioni* (mm. 1–6, 21–32, 45–52)

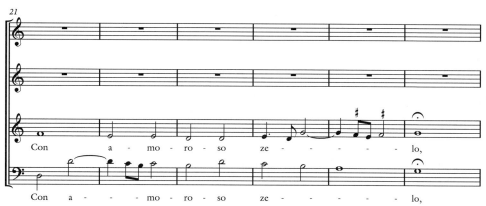

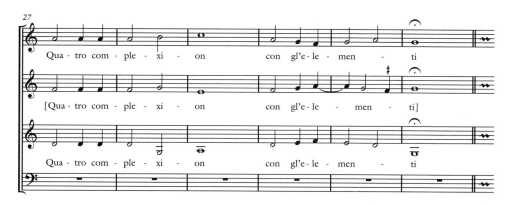

That prince who rules in high heaven [to conserve the life of the living] with loving zeal four temperaments [anger, love, phlegme, and melancholy] with the elements [fire, air, water, and earth] [under the covering cloud mixed and combined in diverse forms] in part discordant with themselves, in part concordant.

to manifestations "infused with courtly ceremonial and princely pomp."[42] In the meantime, as we shall see, the madrigal had emerged from the various strands of secular music that were being woven into the cultural tapestry of northern Italy in the late fifteenth century, largely replacing in the process the earlier repertories and less sophisticated musical genres.

THE *VILLOTTA*

Somewhere between the *frottola* and the *canto carnascialesco* in both function and style are those pieces on secular Italian texts that have been identified as *villotte*.

42. See D'Accone, "Canti carnascialeschi," *The New Grove Dictionary of Music*, 3:723.

Reflecting as it does in some sense significant features of both of its indigenous cousins, the genre does not lend itself in its earliest manifestations to unambiguous definition. No poetic form is consistently connected with the *villotta*, and the term itself does not appear in musical sources until 1530.[43] In fact, the sole textual quality seen as generally characteristic of the type is the "popular" nature of its topics and diction.

As suggested by the word itself, the associations are with country life and folk. In this sense it can be viewed as the Italian counterpart to polyphonic settings of the *chansons rustiques* that began to appear in French sources in the second half of the fifteenth century. There are some indications as well that the *villotta* either had its origins in, or soon came to be connected with, a kind of rustic theater that achieved its comic effect with the courtly and urban audiences toward which it was directed by treating peasant costumes, dialects, and pleasantries with ironic mockery.

A well-documented example of the possible connection is the troupe called La Compagnia degli Ortolani (market gardeners—the fifteenth-century equivalent of truck farmers). It was led by "il Ruzzante" ("the clown"), an actor-playwright who had been born into a prominent merchant family under the name of Angelo Beolco (1502–42).[44] The Venetian diarist Marino Sanuto described an appearance of this group—some twenty-two strong—during the Carnival season of 1524 (February 4) in which the performers carried rustic instruments of music and accompanied their movements with the singing of *villote*.[45]

There is also a report of a performance in Ferrara by a smaller troupe—five men and two women—led by Ruzzante, again during Carnival (January 24, 1529); the occasion was a banquet offered by Ercole d'Este to his father, Duke Alfonso, his sister Isabella, the archbishop of Milan, and others. In this instance the players appeared between the sixth and seventh courses, singing "canzoni e madrigali alla pavana" (in the Paduan manner) "while going around the table vying in the recital of peasant jokes in the Paduan dialect, most amusing, dressed as Paduan peasants" (*contadini*).[46]

As the genre began to take on a more consistent identity, perhaps the two clearest identifying features for the verse—when one or both are in fact present—are the *nio* (*nido* or "nest"), "a dancelike refrain," often introducing a ternary measure, and the *lilolela*, a term for a series of nonsense syllables.[47] Characteristic of the music in the most representative pieces of this type is the adoption of a preexistent melody. In fact, a kind of *villotta* emerged that has been referred to as an *incatenatura*, literally a chain of melodies that is essentially a quodlibet.[48] The borrowed melodic mate-

43. This is according to Walter Rubsamen, "Villotta," *Die Musik in Geschichte und Gegenwart*, 13:1647.

44. See Rachum, ed., *The Renaissance: An Illustrated Encyclopedia*, 474.

45. See Denis Arnold, "Villotta," *The New Grove Dictionary of Music*, 19:779; and cf. Einstein, *Italian Madrigal*, 1:344.

46. As quoted by Einstein, *Italian Madrigal*, 1:344.

47. See Prizer, *Courtly Pastimes*, 82.

48. The term was apparently coined by Fausto Torrefranca, *Il segreto del Quattrocento: Musiche ariose e poesia popolaresca* (Milan: Hoepli, 1939), 219ff. and 303ff.

rial is most often introduced and carried by the tenor. This suggests a vocal conception and points to the probable influence of the northern musicians working in Italy at the time who made similar use of such tunes in compositions of several other genres, both sacred and secular. A case in point is Isaac's *Donna, di dentro*, the Carnival song cited earlier, in which at least three different songs are woven together contrapuntally.

A connection between the *villotta* and the *frottola* repertory is suggested by the inclusion in Petrucci's printed collections of compositions such as Tromboncino's *Poi che volse la mia stella*, which was published not only in the *Libro tertio* of 1504 but also in the intabulations for lute and voice of 1509 by Bossinensis and those for lute alone of 1508 by Joan Ambrosio Dalza. Although Tromboncino's composition does not include a *lilolela*—unlike a *villotta* on much the same text published some fifty years later—it does conclude with a quotation (in the cantus) from the refrain of the song *Che fa la ramacina*.[49]

The latter is also found in a Petrucci print, the *Libro quarto* of 1505, in an arrangement ascribed to Compère, together with his setting of another "popular" Italian song, *Scaramella fa la galla*. In both instances the northerner has adopted for his treatment of the preexistent melody compositional procedures that were clearly derived from the contemporaneous chanson, placing the borrowed material in the tenor and making use of brief points of imitation and independent counterpoint as well as the homophony that was more customary for the *frottola*.[50]

The *villotta* appears to have come into its own no later than the 1520s, judging from the number of clear examples of the genre included in the *Libro primo de la croce*, which was published in Rome by Pasoti and Dorico in 1526; seven of the twenty-two pieces included in the collection are of that type.[51] Reasonably representative of this relatively early assortment of *villotte* is the setting of *Le son tre fantinelle*, attributed in the print to "MC" (Marchetto Cara). All of the characteristic features, both textual and musical, appear to be present, including the irregularity of a versification that defies conventional classification (see Example 11–7).

Given the regularly profiled arch of the tenor melody and its consistent use of repeated pitches and syllabic declamation, the polyphonic composition could very well be based upon a preexistent tune. Whatever the case, the opening phrase, which is introduced by the tenor singing solo, is then taken to constitute the characteristic *nio* with its dancelike movement (although not, here, in ternary meter). Separating this initial statement of the refrain from its return as the concluding strain is the *lilolela*, in this case a series of syllables ("tan daridundella") meant, it would seem, to

49. For the sources see Jeppesen, *La Frottola*, 2:247; a transcription of the piece in score is found in Einstein, *Italian Madrigal*, 3:75–76, no. 35, together with the later setting, 3:77, no. 36, which is attributed to Filippo Azzaiolo.

50. Compère's villottistic essays have been noted both by Einstein, *Italian Madrigal*, 1:340ff., and by Walter H. Rubsamen, "From Frottola to Madrigal," in *Chanson and Madrigal, 1480–1530*, ed. James Haar (Cambridge, Mass.: Harvard University Press, 1964), 63ff.

51. For a complete edition of this print in modern score see William Prizer, ed., *Libro primo de la croce: (Rome: Pasoti and Dorico, 1526) Canzoni, frottole, and capitoli* (Madison: A-R Editions, 1978).

EXAMPLE 11-7. Marchetto Cara, *Le son tre fantinelle*

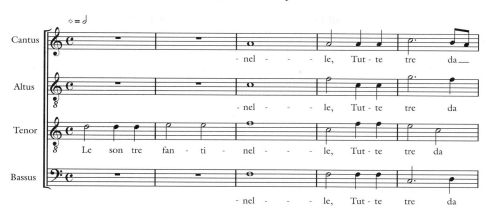

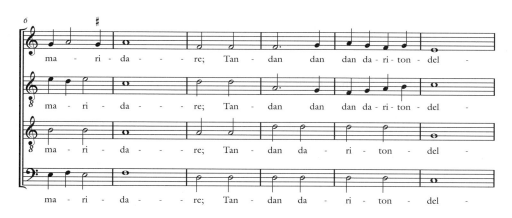

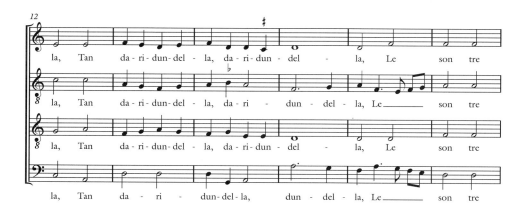

They are three little soldiers, all three to be married; Tandan dan dan daritondella, Tan daridundella, daridundella. They are three little soldiers, all three to be wed.

suggest onomatopoetically the beating of a drum. All in all the text is very slight and wanting the narrative and/or explication characteristic of the Carnival songs; perhaps there were at some point additional strophes that were not included in the publication of the music.

Cara is remembered most particularly, to be sure, for his elegant contribution to the *frottola* repertory. This composition, by contrast, with its four-voice, homophonic texture, its syllabic declamation consistently coordinated in all the voices, and its potential for mimetic dramatization, is clearly much more closely related to the (by then) well-established traditions of the *canti carnascialeschi*, both by the social context to which it refers and by its musical style.

CHAPTER 12

1

Sacred Polyphony in Italy

◯ *M O T E T T I   M I S S A L E S   O R   D U C A L E S* ◯

A novel compositional conception appears to have originated in the 1470s in the chapel of the duke of Milan, Galeazzo Maria Sforza (1444–76), but its formulation was carried out primarily by the northern composers in his service. A number of them have been credited with cycles of what were termed *motetti missales* or *ducales*: groups of related motets to be sung in lieu of the liturgical plainchant for the Mass, including both the Ordinary and (less consistently) the Propers. The reasons behind this extraordinary practice have yet to be fully explored, but there are four such cycles that give special emphasis to the words of a verset addressed to the Virgin Mary as the Madonna of Grace and Mercy:[1] "Maria mater gratiae,/mater misericordiae." Significantly, Galeazzo ordered the daily recitation of that particular verset at Mass shortly before his assassination, and his veneration of the Virgin reflects a tradition that can be traced back through the lineage of his Visconti forebears for several generations. Giangaleazzo Visconti (d. 1378), who had the Certosa of Pavia dedicated to the Madonna of Grace, also vowed, as a votive offering to the Madonna of Mercy, that all his descendants would have Maria as their second name. On the basis of those connections it has been suggested that the duke may have concerned himself directly with the liturgy of the ducal chapel and explicitly commissioned the four works in question from the musicians in his employ.[2]

As has been observed, the forging of an essentially new musico-liturgical concept at the hands of northern musicians resident in Italy is symptomatic of the situation on the peninsula at the time. Foreigners dominated as both composers and singers,

---

1. This astute observation was made by Patrick Macey, "Galeazzo Maria Sforza and Musical Patronage in Milan: Compère, Weerbeke, and Josquin," *Early Music History* 15 (1969): 149–214.

2. Macey, "Galeazzo Maria Sforza and Musical Patronage in Milan," 149ff. The cycles in question are by Compère (two), Weerbeke, and Josquin; concerning the problematic nature of Josquin's relationship to the Milanese court, see below, p. 430.

even at the most celebrated of Italian chapels, whether courtly or ecclesiastical, until well into the sixteenth century. The prevailing musical genres and the styles associated with them were therefore those that had become in a very real sense "international." These included not only the polyphonic Mass Ordinary and the Latin motet, as might be expected, but also the chanson, as is evident from the triptych with which Petrucci inaugurated his newly invented process for the printing of polyphonic music. Unfortunately, the arrival of these foreigners in such considerable numbers must also have contributed significantly to the increasing neglect of local traditions.

It was the recruiting of the northern-trained musicians that brought the composers believed responsible for the origination and cultivation of the so-called substitution Mass[3] into the service of the duke of Milan. Starting early in the 1470s, Galeazzo Maria sought to establish a brilliant court on the French model. This included necessarily a chapel of singer-composers who were expert with the polyphonic repertory that was considered to be the most prestigious ornament of such a choir.[4] His munificence attracted to his court, for periods of varying duration, three of the most skilled masters of the age (among others): Alexander Agricola, who was at Galeazzo's court from 1471 to 1474;[5] Gaspar van Weerbeke, who served in the ducal chapel for nearly a decade beginning in the winter of 1471–72;[6] and Loyset Compère, who was at the Milanese court for an indeterminable period in the mid-1470s.[7]

Also at the court was a certain Josquin, commonly believed until recently to have been the young Josquin Desprez. He entered Sforza service in January 1473, apparently from the choir of the nearby cathedral, where he had been since at least 1459.[8] It seems increasingly likely, however, that the Milanese Josquin was not the famous composer. The latter was probably not born until the late 1450s—rather too late to have been in service at the cathedral by 1459—and cannot be traced in archival records until 1477, when he was in the service of René d'Anjou.[9]

Although due primarily to these northerners, the repertory of the court (and, simultaneously or subsequently, that of the cathedral) is now known primarily through the editorial activity of an Italian musician, Franchinus Gaffurius (1451–1522), who was cleric, singer, theorist, composer, and, from 1484, the *maestro di cappella* at the cathedral of Milan. While there he supervised the compilation of sacred polyphony for use by the choir in four large volumes now in the archives of the Fabbrica del Duomo

3. The term was adopted by Gustave Reese, *Music in the Renaissance* (New York: Norton, 1959), 227.

4. See above, chap. 3, "Music at the Secular Courts," and "The Chapel."

5. See Edward R. Lerner, "Agricola," *The New Grove Dictionary of Music*, 1:162.

6. See Gerhard Croll, "Weerbeke, Gaspar van," *The New Grove Dictionary of Music*, 20:290–92.

7. See Joshua Rifkin, "Compère, Loyset," *The New Grove Dictionary of Music*, 4:596.

8. For one assessment of the evidence concerning Josquin's affiliation with the Milanese court that includes recent discoveries, see Lora Matthews and Paul A. Merkley, "Josquin Desprez and His Milanese Patrons," *Journal of Musicology* 12 (1994): 434–63.

9. See the convincing interpretation of the pertinent evidence by David Fallows, "Josquin and Milan," *Plainsong and Medieval Music* 5 (1996): 69–80. For the archival discovery that proves incontrovertibly that the older Josquinus de Picardia was not Josquin des Prez, the composer, see Lora Matthews and Paul Merkley, "Iudochus de Picardia and Jossequin Lebloitte dit Desprez: The Names of the Singer(s)," *Journal of Musicology* 16 (1998): 223–26.

and generally known as the "Gaffurius Codices": *librone* 1 (1484–90), *librone* 2 (ca. 1490–1500), *librone* 3 (ca. 1500), and *librone* 4 (early sixteenth century), adding pieces here and there (especially across gatherings) in his own hand.[10]

A broad sampling of the polyphonic repertory of the period is found in these large choirbooks: individual motets and settings for the Ordinary of the Mass (treated both as separate items and cyclically), Magnificats, hymns, the Te Deum, and the Lamentations of Jeremiah. They also contain the *motetti missales* referred to earlier, motets in cycles to be sung either in combination with polyphonic settings of the Ordinary or, as indicated, as polyphonic substitutions for some or all of the chants usually sung at Mass.[11] And although the cycles have been transmitted with the repertory of the cathedral, it seems very likely indeed that they were initially prepared for use at the ducal court; Gaffurius himself referred to them as *motetti ducales.*[12]

The most obvious examples of the substitution Mass are those compositions with rubrics that specify the manner in which they were meant to be used. Cycles of this sort included (in whole or in part) in the "Gaffurius Codices" have attributions to Weerbeke, Compère, Josquin, and Gaffurius himself. They can comprise as many as eight separate motets, which may be identified—as in the case of Compère's cycle *Ave virgo gloriosa* for five voices—by explanatory rubrics: "loco [i.e., 'in place of' the] Introitus," "loco Gloria," "loco Credo," "loco Offertorii," "loco Sanctus," "ad Elevationem," "loco Agnus," and "loco Deo gratias."[13] This work, which is also known as the *Missa Galeazescha*, honors not only the Madonna of Mercy, as intended, but, as has been suggested, Galeazzo Maria as well.[14] Other cycles found in the Milan choirbooks have fewer sections, either because they were only partially constituted or because they simply provided for different combinations of texts to replace the traditional items of the Ordinary and/or the Proper.

Interestingly, elements from these cycles, both greater and smaller, were included in yet other collections of music, manuscript and printed (especially the early motet prints by Petrucci), sometimes as complete cycles but also in smaller groups and as individual works. There are, for example, two additional cycles that can be attributed to Martini, who was in Milan briefly in 1474;[15] both were entered into a manuscript copied in or near Innsbruck.[16] In addition, the seven-part motet cycle by

10. See the *Census-Catalogue of Manuscript Sources of Polyphonic Music*, ed. Charles Hamm and Herbert Kellman, 5 vols. (Neuhausen-Stuttgart: Hänssler-Verlag, 1979–88), 2:151–54.

11. See Lynn Halpern Ward, "The *Motetti Missales* Repertory Reconsidered," *Journal of the American Musicological Society* 39 (1986): 491–523.

12. See Clement A. Miller, "Early Gaffuriana: New Answers," *Musical Quarterly* 56 (1970): 380–82.

13. See Loyset Compère, *Opera omnia*, ed. Ludwig Finscher, 5 vols., Corpus mensurabilis musicae 15 ([Rome]: American Institute of Musicology, 1958–72), 2:1–25. As the Kyrie was not part of the Ambrosian Mass, whose traditions were still followed in Milan in the fifteenth century, it is usually missing from the motet cycles.

14. Concerning this cycle in particular, see Macey, "Galeazzo Maria Sforza and Musical Patronage in Milan," 149ff.

15. See Ward, "*Motetti Missales* Repertory Reconsidered," 491–92, who cites the research of Thomas Noblitt.

16. Munich, Bavarian State Library, MS 3154; see the *Census-Catalogue of Manuscript Sources*, 2:225–26.

Josquin, *Vultum tuum*, which is given only partially in Gaffurius's *librone* 4 but as a complete cycle in Petrucci's *Motetti libro quarto* of 1505, is one of the four to make use of Galeazzo's verset.[17]

Even granting that these motet cycles were commissioned by Galeazzo Maria, as has been argued, evidence such as this raises questions concerning the use of polyphonic motets at the celebration of the Mass. Was the custom of substituting a motet for one or more of the chants of the Mass already well established in the area around Milan in the early 1470s, when the duke was constituting his court chapel, and simply observed more systematically there? If not, how were such motet cycles used in other urban centers in Italy and German-speaking regions nearby? Is there any direct historical connection between them and the Mass-motet cycles discussed earlier (see pp. 370–72)? All of these problems need further elucidation if we are to have a clearer view of the uses, both social and liturgical, for which motets such as these were written.

In the compositions of this type that can be traced directly to composers who served in Galeazzo's chapel, liturgical coherence (when demonstrable) is achieved primarily by means of the texts selected. Most have been stitched together from a variety of liturgical and biblical sources through a process of selective centonization. Even Propers for feasts other than the one for which the substitution Mass was actually intended are included; in one instance an Introit was taken from its Proper place to become the text for a motet that was to be substituted for another Introit in a newly constituted cycle.

The impetus toward musical coherence is evident as well, as may be seen from a number of characteristics, most of which have already been noted in connection with the earliest Continental cycles of the Ordinary. These include common clefs from motet to motet for all the voices of the polyphonic setting (usually four or, at most, five); a common final (and hence modal orientation) for each of the pieces; consistent mensural usage (including a given sequence of mensural signs) from one motet to the next; and motivic connections that link individual compositions. Stylistic affinity with the cyclic Mass Ordinary of the period is particularly striking in Compère's motet cycle *Ave Domine Jesu Christe*, which also has a cantus firmus—as yet unidentified—in six of its eight constituent sections.[18]

Equally typical of the *motetti missales* in significant ways is the five-part cycle for four voices, beginning "Quam pulchra es," that is attributed to Weerbeke. It was inscribed in the second of the four *libroni* compiled by Gaffurius (ff. 48ᵛ–53). There it follows immediately a *Missa Primi toni brevis* in five sections for four voices—Kyrie,

17. The motets have been edited in Josquin's *Werken*, ed. Albert Smijers et al., *Motetten*, 5 vols. (Amsterdam: Vereniging voor Nederlandse Muziekgeschiedenis, 1921–56), 1:7ff.; concerning this cycle in particular, cf. Ward, "*Motetti Missales* Repertory Reconsidered," 505, and Patrick Macey, "Josquin's 'Little' Ave Maria: A Misplaced Motet from the Vultum tuum Cycle?" *Tijdschrift van de Vereniging voor Nederlandse Muziekgeschiedenis* 39 (1989): 38–53.
18. Published in Compère, *Opera omnia*, ed. Ludwig Finscher, 2:26–40; concerning the characteristic features of the genre generally, see Thomas Noblitt, "The Ambrosian *Motetti Missales* Repertory," *Musica disciplina* 22 (1968): 77ff.

Et in terra, Patrem, Crucifixus, and Sanctus—by Gaffurius himself. There are no rubrics in the manuscript for the individual pieces to indicate which of the traditional chants of the Mass they were to replace. However, the index to the volume clearly affirms that this is a "Messa di Gaspar, sostituita da 5 motetti" (a Mass by Gaspar [van Weerbeke], substituted by five motets).

As the celebrated text drawn from the Song of Songs was commonly associated with the Virgin Mary, it suggests that the cycle was intended for one of her feasts or for one of the votive Masses frequently sung in her honor. That surmise is confirmed by the texts selected for the four remaining motets—*Ave, regina celorum* (not the liturgical antiphon that begins in the same manner); *O Maria, clausus hortus*; *Ave, domina angelorum*; and *Quem terra pontus aethera . . . claustrum Mariae*, all of which address praise and supplication to the "Queen of heaven."[19] Excepted only are the two relatively brief passages in which reference is made directly to the Host ("Ave, corpus Domini" and "O salutaris hostia")[20] that may, therefore, have been intended for the Elevation.

The unity of this particular cycle is less pronounced musically than it is textually. The first three motets have the same clefs for all four voices and a b-fa signature, but the last two have a different set of clefs, which points to slightly lower ranges for the individual parts. Similarly, the mensuration for the first three pieces is integral imperfect tempus, whereas the concluding pair have the sign for diminished imperfect tempus, even though the range of note values is essentially the same. Conversely, both the first and the last of the five pieces conclude with a shift to ternary movement under a sesquialteral proportion that is not found in the three other motets of the cycle. All five share the same Dorian modal orientation with a final on G, however, except for the first of the passages that relate to the Host. There the final is shifted to F, and the melodic writing makes a brief but fairly strong allusion to the Lydian species of fourth and fifth (still with b-fa as the signature).

As to the contrapuntal textures and techniques displayed in the motets of this cycle, the only real consistency is in the full deployment across the total work of the various procedures that had by then become fairly current. *Quam pulchra es* opens with homophonic declamation only lightly ornamented with independent rhythmic figures and modest melismas, but the chordal texture soon yields (mm. 16ff.) to dense syntactic imitation involving all four voices (see Example 12-1). With the shift to a ternary meter comes the pairing of voices—superius and tenor on the one hand, altus and bassus on the other—first in simultaneous homophonic declamation (mm. 38–46), then, after a brief passage engaging all four parts, in imitation at the octave (mm. 50–56).

---

19. Although this is not one of the four cycles connected with Galeazzo by Macey ("Galeazza Maria Sforza and Musical Patronage in Milan"), the Marian topoi and the use of the Virgin's name suggest intentional homage to Galeazzo Maria.

20. See the transcription in Gaspar van Werbeke [sic], *Messe e mottetti*, ed. Giampiero Tintori (Milan: Veneranda Fabbrica del Duomi de Milano, 1963), *Ave, regina celorum*, p. 83, and *Ave, Domina angelorum*, p. 91, respectively.

EXAMPLE 12-1. Gaspar van Weerbeke, *Quam pulchra es* (mm. 13–26, 38–50)

[How fair and how pleasant art thou, O love, for delights!] This thy stature is like to a palm tree, and thy breasts to clusters of grapes. [Thine head upon thee is like Carmel, thy neck is as a tower of ivory.] Come, my beloved, let us go forth into the field. . . . Let us see . . . whether the tender grape appear [and the pomegranates bud forth: there will I give thee my breasts]. (Song of Solomon 7:6–7; 5, 4, 11–12)

These same contrapuntal procedures shape the remaining four motets as well, although each time with a different sequence and mixture of events. *Quem terra pontus*, for example, the final piece of the cycle (see Example 12-2), opens with homophonic declamation first in two voices, then in three, and finally in all four (mm. 1–15). It then begins anew with the pairing of parts—this time with systematic changes in the ranges of the voices coupled, however—and never introduces the rhythmic independence of truly imitative writing. By contrast, the two sections where reference is made to the Host make use of a singular type of homophonic declamation using all four parts in even breves, each surmounted by a corona (presumably to indicate that each note is to be held more or less at will without being subjected to the steady tactus of the mensural system). In the first instance this unusual style of performance was applied only to the opening acclamation, but for

EXAMPLE 12-2. Gaspar van Weerbeke, *Quem terra pontus* (mm. 23–43)

Blessed bountiful Mother, whose celestial creator, holding the world in his hand, was closed up in the ark of the belly. Blessed by heavenly annunciation, made fecund through the Holy Spirit, by whose womb the one desired of the people is brought forth.

the second it was used for the entire text (see Example 12-3),[21] as it was, in fact, for the majority of the motets that were to be sung during the Elevation.

Despite the general uniformity of style in this particular cycle, then, details such as the slight discrepancies in notational detail and, even more importantly, the presence of two sections relating to the Host would perhaps suggest that it is a composite, bringing together compositions that may have been written earlier, either as individual works or as separate sequences. If so, they provide some interesting insight into the composer's reactions to the exigencies of producing a large repertory of

21. See the edition in Werbeke, *Messe e mottetti,* ed. Tintori, 83 and 91.

EXAMPLE 12-3. Gaspar van Weerbeke, *Ave domina angelorum,* "O salutaris hostia," (mm. 53–68)

O saving sacrifice, that openeth the door of heaven . . .

polyphony in a relatively short period of time—pressure such as could be generated by the aggressive musical patronage practiced by Duke Galeazzo Sforza.

THE VESPER PSALMS: EARLY POLYCHORAL POLYPHONY

Matins and Vespers continued to be important services for the laity of the Christian church, who were expected to be in regular attendance on all important feast days. This may be seen in the ever increasing numbers of polyphonic settings written for the principal chants prescribed for their observance: processional antiphons, hymns, canticles, the Magnificat, the Te Deum, the Benedicamus Domino, and, already in the closing decades of the fifteenth century, the Psalms.[22] If polyphonic elaboration was more or less to be expected for most of these categories of liturgical chant, given the arresting role that each of them tends to play within the Office of which it is a part, the same cannot easily be said of the Psalms.

Since the texts of the Psalter provide much of the substance of each of the services in question, and because the psalmody takes up a good deal of their total duration, there was every reason to avoid any embellishment, however attractive, that might leave the words themselves less readily understood or unduly prolong their delivery. Moreover, there appears to have been a tradition for improvising a simple sort of homophonic polyphony in two or even three parts directly upon the declamatory formulae of the Psalm tone. That practice made written composition redundant, in a sense, especially when—as was usually the case—the notated composition was in the same simple discant style as that resulting from singing *super librum*.[23]

These observations are of course based on the assumption that the polyphonic setting of a text from the Psalter was actually intended for use during the liturgical Office in the traditional manner rather than merely as a motet for some other purpose, whether liturgical or devotional—an important distinction to which attention has already been drawn. Of particular interest in this regard is one of the earliest collections of liturgical polyphony written specifically for the celebration of Matins and Vespers and consisting principally of Psalms set systematically in accordance with the requirements of the liturgy. The repertory in question, MSS α.M.1.11–12 of the Estense Library in Modena, was undoubtedly compiled for the court chapel of Duke Ercole I d'Este (1431–1505) early in the 1470s, soon after Ercole came to power and began to compete with Galeazzo Maria Sforza of Milan for the best of the northern-trained singers and composers then arriving in Italy.[24]

---

22. See chap. 8, "The Motet," and chap. 9, "Liturgical Polyphony for the Office."
23. See chap. 9, "Psalm Settings."
24. Concerning the contents and significance of this collection, see Lewis Lockwood, *Music in Renaissance Ferrara, 1400–1505: The Creation of a Musical Center in the Fifteenth Century* (Cambridge, Mass.: Harvard University Press, 1984), 250–57.

Among those who came to Ferrara to help constitute (and further train) the chapel choir were Johannes Martini, who served the Este court from about 1473 until his death in 1498 (excepting the few months in 1474 spent in Milan), and Johannes Brebis, whose presence at the court can be documented from 1471 until 1478.[25] Brebis and Martini were apparently largely responsible for the contents of these manuscripts, which contain—in addition to four Magnificats, eight hymns, a tract, and two Passions—sixty-eight Psalms. Of the latter, thirty-five were the ferial Psalms for Vespers and thirty-three were for Matins on Maundy Thursday, Good Friday, and Holy Saturday. They provide, in other words, all the Psalms required for Vespers of Quadragesima and Matins of Holy Week.

An unusual, in fact unique, feature of this liturgical repertory is its organization, as may be seen, for example, by turning first to its hymns, a familiar genre that was cultivated rather assiduously in the course of the fifteenth century. Unlike the settings by earlier composers, who followed the pattern of Du Fay in contrasting chant with polyphony, providing for performance in *alternatim*, those by Brebis and Martini have settings in parts for all strophes. They are divided, however, between the two choirbooks of the collection, with all the odd-numbered stanzas in one (MS α.M.1.11) and the even-numbered ones in the other (MS α.M.1.12).

The same holds true not only for the Magnificats but also for all of the Psalms; odd-numbered verses are in the first of the two complementary volumes, even-numbered ones in the latter. Intended, clearly, was performance by a double chorus that preserves polyphonically the antiphonal exchange between sides of the choir that was traditional for liturgical psalmody. This corresponds, moreover, to what is known of the organization of the Este court chapel from the early 1470s until about 1482; the archival evidence indicates that through that period Ercole maintained a double choir with one group "of twenty-four adolescents and the other of adult singers, to the same number, of the highest quality, who taught the younger ones."[26]

Polyphonic performance by a divided choir may not appear in this context to be a significant innovation since it merely perpetuated an age-old liturgical practice. Nonetheless, it appears to have transformed what was undoubtedly a custom designed initially with an eminently practical end in view—to rest in alternation the singers on opposite sides of the choir during the celebration of the lengthy nocturnal Offices. In the settings presumed to be by Martini and Brebis, that venerable practice assumes a new status, becoming a kind of esthetic principle. These simple compositions may thus have laid a foundation for the kind of polychoral composition that was to be developed in northern Italy in the course of the sixteenth century by Italian composers, becoming at last one of the glories of the Basilica of San Marco in Venice.

In other aspects, by contrast, the musical style of the Psalms of the Ferrarese repertory is not particularly prepossessing. The polyphony adheres not only to the strictly syllabic declamation of the liturgical Psalm tones but also to their melodic formulae; the

---

25. Concerning the affiliation of Martini and Brebis with the musical establishment at the Este court, see Lockwood, *Music in Renaissance Ferrara*, 167–72 and 160–61, respectively.
26. See Lockwood, *Music in Renaissance Ferrara*, 157–59 and 250f.

melodic material of the superius is slavishly derived from the chant, including even the long sequences of repeated pitches that are its most characteristic element. The counterpoint, moreover, relies relentlessly, and with only slight embellishment at cadences, upon parallel imperfect consonances, usually sixths between superius and tenor.

In the setting of Psalm 131, *Memento Domine David*, prescribed by the manuscript for *feria quinta* (Thursday) in the weekly cycle, only two parts are written out; a third must be supplied as a *fauxbourdon*, running in parallel fourths below the superius (see Example 12-4a and Figure 12-1). The polyphony for Psalm 58:1, *Eripe me de inimicis meis*, is only slightly more elaborate, perhaps because it was intended for Matins during Holy Week (see Example 12-4b);[27] all three voices have been composed and notated, but parallel sixths continue to predominate. Bassus and tenor are in essentially the same range, moreover, and although this allows them to trade pitches in a lengthy passage of single-note recitation (verse 6, m. 5), no actual change of sonority results.

Of greatest interest, perhaps, in both compositions is the relatively free rhythm of the declamatory setting. No mensuration sign is given, and the semibreves and minims used almost exclusively to bear individual syllables of the text cannot be grouped systematically by either twos or threes. The composer's intention appears

FIGURE 12-1.   Psalm 131, feria quinta (Modena, Biblioteca Estense, MS α.M.1.12, ff. 17ᵛ–18ʳ).

27. See the *Liber usualis*, 706, *Feria VI in Passione et Morte Domini (in tertio nocturno)*.

EXAMPLE 12-4. Anonymous (Johannes Brebis and/or Johannes Martini?), (a) *Memento Domine David*, verses 2 and 4; (b) *Eripe me de inimicis meis*, verses 2 and 4

(a)

(a): 1. Lord, remember David and all his afflictions; 2. How he sware unto the Lord and vowed unto the mighty God of Jacob. 3. Surely I will not come into the tabernacle of my house, nor go up unto my bed; 4. I will not give sleep to mine eyes, or slumber to mine eyelids. (b): 1. Deliver me from mine enemies, O my God: defend me from them that rise up against me. 2. Deliver me from the workers of iniquity, and save me from bloody men. 3. For, lo, they lie in wait for my soul; the mighty are gathered against me; 4. Not for my transgression, nor for my sin, O Lord; they run and prepare themselves without my fault.

to have been to follow the natural rhythms of the Latin, as he understood them, rather than to conform to a predetermined pattern of musical meter.[28]

All of this suggests that, although notated, these Psalm settings may well reflect an earlier tradition of enhancing the psalmody on special occasions with extemporized polyphony. Still, despite the relative severity of their musical facture, their historical importance as the core of an early and very substantial repertory of polychoral polyphony warrants our attention. In that perspective they foreshadow yet another of the important creative achievements realized in the course of the fifteenth century by northern musicians in the service of Italian churches and, in particular, the wealthy patrons of its city-states.

⤳ THE POLYPHONIC *LAUDA* ⤶

The religious and social circumstances that gave rise to the performance of *laude*— sacred "songs of praise"—in Italian as well as in Latin, by groups of singers from lay

28. There is no evidence, however, of an attempt to recapture the quantities of classical Latin by means of musical rhythms such as is to be found in the works of composers more profoundly influenced by humanistic scholarship.

confraternities has already been considered.[29] Noted as well was the encouragement undoubtedly given such devotional exercises by certain monastic orders—especially the Franciscans, given their particular zeal for inspiring popular piety—whose members very likely joined in during these observances on many occasions. As for the texts to be sung as the central gesture in these devotional manifestations, they were addressed primarily to the Virgin Mary and Christ, touching in the latter case such matters as his passion and resurrection. Also included, however, were topics inspired by the veneration of the Holy Spirit and popular saints (especially those with local significance), and the ever-present threat of death (undoubtedly a question made pertinent by the mortal plagues and other cataclysms of the *trecento*).[30]

In the course of the thirteenth and fourteenth centuries the singing of *laude* as the essential part of devotional services for certain lay confraternities in Italy gave rise to a very large repertory of devotional music. Like the plainchant hymns on which they were modeled, these vernacular songs were primarily monophonic. The number of texts prepared for use in this connection was enormous; over 200 manuscript collections of this type of religious verse have survived. Surprisingly, the number of musical sources for the genre is dramatically fewer; only 2 reasonably substantial collections are now known, one with 46 melodies, the other with 89, 10 of which are found in both manuscripts.[31]

The modest quantity of music still available for the large body of *laude* poetry from the earlier period is to be explained by a variety of circumstances. It seems clear, for example, that the adaptation of several texts with similar poetic structures to a single preexistent melody must have been a fairly common practice in this repertory. As with hymns and other similar pieces, the regular strophic structure of the poems lent itself admirably to a process of contrafaction. Consequently, the total number of musical settings used in the performance of *laude* may never have been anywhere near as great as the individual items of devotional verse, which continued to be written all through the long history of the genre. In Florence, in particular, new *lauda* texts were still being assiduously written in the final decades of the fifteenth century and at the beginning of the sixteenth. Lucrezia de' Medici, mother of Lorenzo the Magnificent, wrote a fair number of such poems, as did Lorenzo himself.[32] Other authors cultivated the genre as well, including the poet Feo Belcari (1410–84), who has been credited with a fair number of the texts, and even the pious Savonarola (1452–98), who had little use for the complex polyphonic textures of northern-trained composers.[33]

---

29. See chap. 4, "Guilds and Confraternities," pp. 149–64.

30. For an instructive overview of the cultural and intellectual currents that helped bring the *laudesi* companies into existence, see Blake Wilson, *Music and Merchants: The Laudesi Companies of Republican Florence* (Oxford: Clarendon Press, 1992).

31. See John Stevens, "Lauda spirituale," *The New Grove Dictionary of Music*, 10:539.

32. Concerning the cultivation of the *lauda* in Lorenzo's Florence, see Patrick Macey, "Some New Contrafacta for *Canti Carnascialeschi* and *Laude* in Late Quattrocento Florence," in *La musica a Firenze al tempo di Lorenzo il Magnifico*, ed. Piero Gargiulo (Florence: Olschki, 1993), 143–66.

33. See William Prizer, "Lauda spirituale," *The New Grove Dictionary of Music*, 10:541; concerning the important influence of Savonarola in particular, cf. Patrick Macey, "The Lauda and the Cult of Savonarola," *Renaissance Quarterly* 45 (1992): 439–83.

Toward the end of the fourteenth century simple polyphonic *laude* began to be used for the traditional devotional exercises as well, apparently both as spiritual contrafacta of preexistent secular pieces and as newly composed pieces in the same style. Among the composers who can be identified with such works are some of the better-known names of the period, including Jacopo da Bologna, Niccolà da Perugia, and Francesco Landini himself.[34] Clearly, however, the monophonic repertory must have continued in use long after polyphony began to be adopted for the genre, and its existence may even have significantly inhibited the composition of polyphonic settings. Moreover, the polyphonic *laude* of the late fourteenth century show that the complexities of *trecento* notational practice and its concomitant musical style were intentionally ignored; the known musical settings are mostly for two or three voices and are largely syllabic, homophonic, and declamatory in nature.[35]

Such compositions were included in small numbers in several of the manuscripts compiled around the middle of the fifteenth century that were mentioned earlier as containing polyphony intended for liturgical and/or devotional use. Among the most noteworthy are MS 2216 of the University Library in Bologna, with 11 *laude* among its 85 compositions, and MS Q 15 of the Civico Museo Bibliografico Musicale, with 11 of 308.[36] To these may be added MS 7554 (*olim* Italiani IX, 145) of the Marciana Library in Venice (dating from mid-fifteenth century) with 29 *laude* in two parts out of a total of 49 pieces, and MS Aldini 361 of the University Library in Pavia (from about the same time), which, although mostly taken up by fourteenth-century treatises, includes 12 *laude*—8 in Latin, 4 in Italian—among its 18 compositions. Significantly, the majority of such musical sources originated in Venetian territories.[37]

After mid-century the development of the polyphonic *lauda* appears to have run in tandem with that of the secular repertory of Italian song, resembling at first the French chansons on which some of them appear to have been modeled and then *canti carnascialeschi* and *frottole*. The same composers provided music for secular and sacred texts alike, whether intentionally or unwittingly; pieces from both song repertories were in fact converted to devotional use in fair numbers by the familiar process of textual substitution. Evidence for the practice is abundant in the textual sources where the music to which new *laude* were to be sung was identified with the phrase "cantasi come . . ." ("sung to the tune of . . ."). The compositions so designated ran the gamut from well-known and widely circulated chansons to some of the more obscure melodies used to sing devotional vernacular verse.[38]

In Florence the homophonic style of the *canti carnascialeschi* seems to have been

34. Concerning the music of these composers, see Richard H. Hoppin, *Medieval Music* (New York: Norton, 1978), 448–69.

35. Cf. William Prizer, "Lauda," *The New Grove Dictionary of Music*, 10:540–41.

36. Concerning these manuscripts, see p. 223.

37. Regarding the latter two collections, see the *Census-Catalogue of Manuscript Sources*, 4:72f., and 3:41f., respectively. For a more detailed discussion of the musical sources of the fifteenth century, see Wilson, *Music and Merchants*, 167–76.

38. Concerning the *cantasi come* tradition, see Wilson, *Music and Merchants*, 164–67 and *passim*.

preferred for polyphonic settings, due perhaps in part to Savonarola's negative view of complex counterpoint.[39] Elsewhere, however, particularly in the Veneto, it seems to have been the *frottole*, and most notably the works of Cara and Tromboncino, that were taken as stylistic paradigms for the *lauda* to an ever greater degree as the fifteenth century drew to a close. Still, the overall repertory—to the extent that it was notated and can still be identified as such—remained relatively modest in size.

Consequently, the number of manuscripts in which polyphonic *laude* have been transmitted was really very small compared with those given over to other sacred genres such as Mass and motet, and the "songs of praise" continued to form a rather modest component in most of the collections in which they figure. For example, in MS Panciatichi 27 of the National Library in Florence, which was copied early in the sixteenth century in northern Italy (both Mantua and Tuscany have been suggested), there are only 5 laude among its 187 pieces. Similarly, in MS 871 of the Monastery Library of Montecassino, which probably originated in a Benedictine cloister in Naples during the final decades of the *quattrocento*, only 4 or 5 of some 141 sacred and secular works are *laude*. And in MS 431 of the Communal Library in Perugia, which was inscribed at about the same time and, perhaps, in the same place, 11 of the 129 compositions can be so classified.[40]

At about the same time the innovative printer of music, Ottaviano Petrucci, apparently found enough of a demand for *laude* to bring out two printed collections of them, a *Libro primo* in 1508, and a *Libro secondo* in 1507.[41] Still, his comparatively limited output in this particular genre may well reflect the small size of the available repertory. The first book, with fifty-one pieces on Italian texts and fifteen for Latin verse, was exclusively the work of Innocentius Dammonis, a cleric of the Congregazione Salvatori in Venice, whose *Piangete Christiani* (discussed below) figured in the print.[42] Such a collection must represent either a repertory prepared for local use and/or, perhaps, a commission from the printer.

The second book, which gives evidence of having been hastily and carelessly assembled, has twenty-three works on Italian verse, thirty-one on Latin, and another pair combining the two tongues; most of these compositions can be attributed to composers known from the *frottola* collections. Compared with the eleven books of secular Italian repertory that Petrucci published in the same period, however, or even the three volumes of French secular music with which he began publication—the *Odhecaton A*, *Canti B*, and *Canti C*, which together contain nearly 300 pieces—this appears to be a very slender harvest.

The largest surviving manuscript repertory of *laude* is a collection of sacred music

39. See Macey, "Some New Contrafacta for *Canti Carnascialeschi* and *Laude* in Late Quattrocento Florence," 143–66, including a number of music examples.
40. See the *Census-Catalogue of Manuscript Sources*, 1:232, 2:173f., and 3:43, respectively.
41. The surviving copy of *Libro primo* is undoubtedly a second printing; the first edition must have come out early in 1507 or even late 1506.
42. Concerning the Dammonis collection, see Jonathan Glixon, "The Polyphonic Laude of Innocentius Dammonis," *Journal of Musicology* 8 (1990): 19–53.

currently at the Public Library in Capetown, South Africa, MS Grey 3.b.12, which probably originated in northern Italy (somewhere between Florence and Mantua) shortly after the turn of the century, perhaps, like the Montecassino codex, in a Benedictine monastery. Of its eighty-four compositions—canticles, Psalms, hymns, Lamentations, motets, and the like—twenty-four are *laude*, some of which apparently date from the early part of the fifteenth century while others are in the frottolistic style that predominated later, especially outside of Florence.[43]

Among the earlier compositions included in this repertory is one of two known settings of the text *Piangete christiani*, an anonymous work for three voices (see Example 12-5). Stylistically it is not unlike a chanson of the mid-fifteenth century, or even a treble-dominated song-motet, and presumably reflects the musical influences that were prevalent in Italy at the time of its writing. For although text was copied into the manuscript for each of the voices and the musical phrases are clearly marked by a corona or a contrapuntal cadential formula or both, the individual parts are relatively independent of one another, melodically and rhythmically. Homophonic declamation, where clearly intended, is limited to the first few syllables at the beginning of a line of verse. What is

43. See the edition of this manuscript by Giulio Cattin, *Italian Laude and Latin Unica in MS Capetown, Grey 3.b.12* (Neuhausen-Stuttgart: American Institute of Musicology, 1977).

EXAMPLE 12-5. Anonymous, *Piangeti christiani*

Bewail, O Christians, the sorrow of Mary; bewail the great afflictions and the bitter, cruel death of Jesus Christ, our hope and life. Bewail, every one, the cruel passion.

more, the melismatic extension of the musical phrase that follows matches in most cases the decorative melodic writing associated with the chanson of the period, and in the concluding measures it even rivals the exuberance of the secular repertory of the *trecento*.

A later setting of the same text, that attributed to Innocentius Dammonis in Petrucci's first book, obviously mirrors the shift in musical style that took place in the final decades of the fifteenth century as Italian composers of the *lauda* abandoned the paradigms of the chanson (and related genres) for that offered by secular music written to texts in the Italian vernacular. This version of *Piangete christiani* is in a frottolistic style for four voices with text supplied only for the cantus (see Example 12-6). Even though the text is declaimed to breves and semibreves in a texture that is essentially homophonic—even more so than in many *frottole*—the lower three parts make use to a limited extent of the kinds of passing figures in relatively rapid rhythms that characterize the presumably instrumental accompaniment of Italian solo song.[44]

By contrast, *laude* that originated in Florence usually show much more clearly the

44. For an edition of the entire piece, see Knud Jeppesen and V. Brøndal, eds., *Die mehrstimmige italienische Laude um 1500* (Leipzig: Breitkopf und Härtel, 1935), 143–44, no. 83.

EXAMPLE 12-6. Innocentius Dammonis, *Pianzeti christiani* (mm. 1–14)

For English translation of text, see Example 12-5.

influence of the Carnival songs, some of which were simply appropriated to more pious uses by textual substitution. These pieces are strictly homophonic and declamatory, suggesting that all the voices joined in the delivery of the text. Curiously, although they date to the closing decades of the fifteenth century, a number of such pieces were published in Venice as late as 1563, by Fra Giovanni (Serafino) Razzi (1531–1611) in his *Libro primo delle laudi spirituali*.[45] Typical of the musical style is the setting of one of several *lauda* texts attributable to Savonarola himself, *Iesù sommo conforto* (see Example 12-7). With the melody in the middle of the texture, the three voices proceed simultaneously in virtually identical rhythms, declaiming the text syllabically phrase by phrase.

The inclusion in Razzi's collection of texts and tunes for *laude* sung by Savonarola and his followers in the 1480s and 1490s is the key to understanding historical developments that are doubly ironic. Razzi, a Dominican who had been trained at Savonarola's monastery of San Marco in Florence, was among those who attempted, in the face of considerable opposition from both church and state, to maintain the cult of the martyred friar as prophet and saint. His purpose in assembling the pieces of his *Libro primo* appears to have been religious, perhaps even political in nature; it was clearly an attempt to preserve a body of quasi-popular song that had figured prominently in the devotions of the Savonarolan movement in the Florence of the 1490s and that was beginning to be lost. This helps to explain the retrospective character of the repertory and the inclusion of as many pieces as possible with Savonarolan allusions, however carefully veiled.[46]

The irony, on the one hand, is that Savonarola and his followers made extensive

45. For a facsimile reprint of the collection see Serafino Razzi, ed., *Libro primo delle laudi spirituali* (Bologna: Arnaldo Forni, 1969); concerning Razzi, see Iain Fenlon, *The New Grove Dictionary of Music*, 15:630–31.

46. See, in this connection, Macey, "Some New Contrafacta for *Canti Carnascialeschi* and *Laude* in Late Quattrocento Florence," 143–48, and idem, "*Infiamma il mio cor*: Savonarolan *Laude* by and for Dominican Nuns in Tuscany," in *The Crannied Wall: Women, Religion, and the Arts in Early Modern Europe*, ed. Craig A. Monson (Ann Arbor: University of Michigan Press, 1992), 161–89.

EXAMPLE 12-7. Anonymous, *Iesù sommo conforto*

Jesus, supreme comfort, thou art all my love, my blessed portal and holy redeemer. O great goodness, sweet piety, blessed is he who is united with thee.

use of the *lauda* to motivate and to move the citizens of Florence at a time when the *laudesi* companies themselves had abandoned their weekday evening services and left the singing that was done entirely to hired singers. When the friar was executed, these confraternities were already in what proved to be an inexorable decline that was surely accelerated by the political instability of the next half-century.[47] On the other

47. See Wilson, *Music and Merchants*, 212–30.

it is that the singing of *laude*, which began as a popular expression of pious devotion, fostered and encouraged by the mendicant order, was driven into hiding behind the walls of Dominican cloisters—at least in Florentine territories—where it served only the friars and nuns as evening recreation and/or as an accompaniment to informal processions.[48]

It is interesting to consider in this connection whether or not some of the polyphonic *lauda* settings of the fifteenth century were actually based upon melodies that were originally part of the repertory of the thirteenth and fourteenth centuries.[49] Such a link has been demonstrated in only a few instances (and a systematic study of such relationships has apparently yet to be undertaken), but there are some intriguing indications. For example, Savonarola's *Iesù sommo conforto* was given a four-voice setting by Giovanni Animuccia (ca. 1500–71), who, like Razzi, was born and received his early schooling in Florence.[50] Also published in 1563, Animuccia's composition makes use of a melody very similar to the one found in Razzi's collection, raising the possibility that the tune itself belongs to an older tradition.

An even stronger case can be made for the melody associated with the Latin text *Cum autem venissem*. It is found in various versions in twelve different sources whose dates span more than a century. These include two settings for two voices of which one was copied into MS Aldini 361, mentioned earlier as one of the earliest polyphonic sources in which *laude* were inscribed.[51] Another—attributable to Johannes de Quadris, a composer active in the Veneto in mid-fifteenth century—was published by Petrucci as an item in his *Lamentationum Jeremiae prophete liber primus* of 1506.[52] In addition, the same melody was taken as the cantus part for at least two other settings in four parts, one of which was copied into the MS Montecassino 871[53] and the other printed by Petrucci in his second book of *laude*.[54]

A comparison of several of these different polyphonic settings of *Cum autem venissem* shows few differences in the notation of the traditional melody; it is set out mainly in semibreves and breves, with the division between the phrases that correspond to the successive lines of text clearly indicated by a corona (see Figure 12-2). That credited by Petrucci to Johannes de Quadris (see Example 12-8) is, in addition, very similar in style to the arrangement printed by Razzi; in both pieces the two-part counterpoint is strictly note against note, except for some modest cadential orna-

48. See Macey, "*Lauda* and the Cult of Savonarola," 439–41.

49. See William Prizer, "Lauda," *The New Grove Dictionary of Music,* 10:541.

50. See Macey, "*Lauda* and the Cult of Savonarola," 451; the print, *Il primo libro delle laudi,* was brought out by Animuccia in Rome.

51. For a transcription, see Giulio Cattin, "Le composizioni musicali del Ms. Pavia Aldini 361," in *L'Ars nova italiana del trecento,* 2 vols. (Certaldo: Commune di Certaldo, 1968), 2:14f.

52. For a complete edition of this setting, see Johannes de Quadris, *Opera,* ed. Giulio Cattin, Antiquae musicae italicae: Monumenta veneta sacra (Bologna: Bardolino, 1972), 71.

53. See the edition of the manuscript by Isabel Pope and Masakata Kanazawa, eds., *The Musical Manuscript Montecassino 871: A Neapolitan Repertory of Sacred and Secular Music of the Late Fifteenth Century* (Oxford: Clarendon Press, 1978), 479, no. 120.

54. Cf. Prizer, "Lauda," *The New Grove Dictionary of Music,* 10:541.

ments, and the declamation is severely syllabic. Although for four voices rather than two, even the version of the Montecassino manuscript is also very much the same, its only real gain over its more modest cousins being its richer chordal sonorities.

Paradoxically, then, just as a single polyphonic composition could serve for the singing of more than one text, so the best known and most beloved of the devotional poems were provided with more than one setting, perhaps either to provide for local needs or in response to changes in musical styles and tastes.[55] The different versions of *Cum autem venissem* could have arisen from either cause. The earlier ones, of which the Razzi and de Quadris settings are typical, are so rudimentary that they could easily have been improvised "upon the book" by a skilled singer, where-

FIGURE 12-2. Anonymous, *Cum autem venissem* (Serafino Razzi's *Libro primo delle laudi spirituali*, 1563, pp. 115–16).

as the later ones, including most examples of the genre datable to the closing decades of the fifteenth century, show clearly the stylistic influence of the secular repertory of *frottole* that was being created at the same time.

A case in point is the anonymous setting included in Petrucci's *Libro secondo* (see Example 12-9).[56] The ancient melody is divided as usual into its constituent phrases by a brevis with a corona, the articulation being underscored in four places (mm. 16–17, 23–24, 31–32, and 41–42) by a more or less conventional contrapuntal cadence. In the majority of cases, however (mm. 6, 12, 20, 28, and 36), the points of internal closure are reached in a rather unusual way; missing is the prototypical two-part formula of a dissonant suspended seventh resolving to a major sixth and then expanding to an octave. This melodic cantus firmus—the only voice provided with text—lies in the cantus, which is generally at the top of the four-part structure. The other parts are coordinated with it rhythmically a good deal of the time, but as

55. See, in this connection, Glixon's inventory of the Dammonis collection, "The Polyphonic Laude of Innocentius Dammonis," *Journal of Musicology* 8 (1990): 46ff.

56. For a transcription of the complete piece, see Jeppesen and Brøndal, eds., *Die mehrstimmige italienische Laude um 1500*, 8–9, no. 5.

EXAMPLE 12-8. Johannes de Quadris, *Cum autem venissem* (mm. 1–28)

When therefore I came to the place where my son was to be crucified, they placed him in the middle of all the people and, stripped of all clothing, they delivered up naked the most holy body.

in Dammonis's *Piangeti Christiani,* they do move on occasion in the short, independent scalewise figures of the sort judged typical of a lute or keyboard accompaniment. All in all, then, despite the absence of the schematic repetitions characteristic of much of the *frottola* repertory, the texture of this *lauda* is very like that of its more secular cousins.

In functional terms the Italian *lauda* can be viewed as a kind of counterpart to the English carol that was discussed earlier (pp. 250–56), and it is likewise similar to the French *noël* considered below (pp. 646–48). Like them, it is religious music

EXAMPLE 12-9. Anonymous, *Cum autem venissem* (mm. 1–25)

e - - um in me - di - o o - mnis po - pu - li,

For English translation of text, see Example 12-8.

spawned by and intended for manifestations of popular piety in a devotional context, and its regular strophic verse, like that written for carols and *noëls*—whether in Latin, in the vernacular, or, as happened at times, a mixture of the two—was decidedly non-liturgical.

Of the two repertories, however, the English is less variable in its fundamental features and its musical style. The settings provided for the Italian *lauda* reflect not only the long period during which the verse was in constant use and continuous cultivation but also the utilitarian nature of the music. As a consequence, the examples found in the surviving musical sources are often ill defined as to genre and inconsistent as to style. As one scholar has observed, the *lauda* was a derivative type of musical composition that never attracted the interest of skilled masters working in courtly circles.[57] Consequently, as will be shown presently, it shows perhaps greater affinity to the French *noël* than to the English carol.

57. See Glixon, "Polyphonic Laude of Innocentius Dammonis," 40–41.

CHAPTER 13

✓

Polyphony in Germany: Indigenous Traditions

INTRODUCTION

Perhaps the most striking example of the political fragmentation brought about in the late Middle Ages by feudal practices is to be seen in the vast realm brought together toward the beginning of the ninth century by Charlemagne. Already in 843 with the death of Louis, his sole surviving son and heir, the far-flung lands over which he had gained suzerainty were divided among three of his grandsons, and no one ruler was ever again able to bring the entire domain under his authority. The western portion, which was governed initially by the French Carolingian dynasty, began its slow evolution into the independent kingdom of the late fifteenth and early sixteenth centuries. The middle kingdom, which included a narrow strip of land from the mouth of the Rhine River southward into the Italian peninsula, was divided in turn into three parts at the death of its first sovereign in 855 and quickly disappeared as a political entity.

The German lands to the east continued to maintain at least a nominal identity for centuries, perhaps in part because of the effective rule of Otto I, "the Great" (936–73) and in part because of the theory of the Roman Imperium by which Charlemagne had rationalized his dominion. According to this concept, the Roman Empire had not come to an end with the abdication of the last of the Roman rulers in 476 but had merely been interrupted until Charlemagne appeared on the scene to claim the imperial scepter. Some credence was given this idea when Charlemagne, who had given unremitting support to the papacy in its conflicts with secular authority, was given the imperial crown by Pope Leo III on Christmas Day in the year 800.

When Otto came to power, he revived the imperial traditions, laid claim to the territories of the adjacent middle kingdom—including Italy—and succeeded in having himself crowned by Pope John XII in 962, thus laying the foundations for what was to become the Holy Roman Empire. He may have intended as well to establish a ruling family dynasty; however, the hereditary principle of the feudal system was limited to some extent in the imperial domains by an electoral process. Beginning in Otto's time, the emperor-designate, known (after 1045) as "king of the Romans," was elected by the German princes from among their number. He was then obliged to seek both ratification of his election and coronation as emperor at the hands of the pope. Although initially the German electors often did little more than approve dynastic succession, the elective principle was considerably strengthened during the thirteenth and fourteenth centuries, primarily as a result of the controversy over lay investiture of ecclesiastical offices that were also feudal fiefs of some importance.

The emperors, who tended to regard themselves as the vicars of Christ in the temporal domain, just as the popes were his vicars in spiritual matters, claimed the right to appoint those abbots and bishops whose administrative control of significant land holdings also made them nominal vassals within their realms. Since the imperial choice in such cases was usually dictated by what was perceived as politically advantageous rather than what was spiritually desirable, this practice led to abuses that the papacy could not easily tolerate. The resulting conflict came to a head during the rule of the Hohenstaufen dynasty, especially that of Frederick II (1194–1250).

Having inherited from his mother Constance the kingdom of Sicily, where he was raised and lived most of his life, Frederick became much more interested in the Italian domains to which the empire could lay claim than in his German territories, which he held in check largely by making concessions to both cities and principalities in return for peace and nominal fealty. In Italy, by contrast, he was almost incessantly at war as the imperial Ghibellines struggled for temporal dominion against the Guelph factions loyal to the papacy. Death overtook him, however, before he was able to impose his authority in Italy or to reaffirm it in his German states. As a consequence, the empire was left in a state of chaos, considerably weakened in Germany and with no further hope of reestablishing its dominion in Italy.

During the prolonged interregnum that ensued (1254–72), none of the foreign potentates who were elected emperor actually succeeded in ruling the imperial domains. This allowed the principalities to assume even greater independence at the expense of the customary prerogatives of the empire, and the process of political and territorial fragmentation continued. Among those who profited from these chaotic conditions to carve out for themselves small, independent fiefs were the members of the Ritterschaft, the knightly class that had come into existence in Germany only in the late Middle Ages. Because they were inclined to rule with little regard for the fealty they owed by custom to their nominal liege lord and to pursue their own interests in armed combat, they contributed a good deal to the tumult and lawlessness that characterized the period.

The election of a minor Swabian count, Rudolf of Habsburg, as king of the Romans ended the interregnum in 1273, and although it did not lead directly to the establishment of a new imperial dynasty, the groundwork was laid during his rule for the rise of the Habsburgs as powerful pretenders with hereditary rights to the imperial throne. Having crushed a rebellious vassal, Ottokar of Bohemia, Rudolf was able to add to his modest Swabian holdings the extensive fiefs that he had taken from his enemy in Austria and Styria. Since, by then, the emperor had very little power to impose taxes or to require military service outside of his own domains, this provided the Habsburgs with the territorial base that was indispensable to the reestablishment of a stronger central government.

Rudolf's success was such, in fact, that the very princes who had elected him, jealous of their own rights and fearful of the newly acquired power that made the Habsburgs much more dangerous rivals, reasserted the elective principle and chose their next king from another ruling house. They went on to strengthen their hand even further in 1338 at the diets of Rhense and Frankfurt by declaring their right to choose the emperor without papal approval, presumably in response to the troubles caused in a number of instances by the pope's refusal to bestow the imperial crown on the candidate of their choice.

The empire reached the nadir of its power and authority under Charles IV of Luxembourg (1346–78), who made damaging concessions both in Italy and in Germany in order to have a freer hand with the affairs of his Bohemian kingdom. In exchange for papal recognition of his title and the ritual coronation in Rome in 1355, Charles renounced all imperial claims to authority in the papal states and agreed not to enter them without the pope's permission. The privileges that the electors had wrested little by little from imperial control were then sanctioned by the Golden Bull of 1356, which fixed the number of electors at seven: the archbishops of Mainz, Cologne, and Trier, the king of Bohemia, the count palatine of the Rhine, the duke of Saxony, and the margrave of Brandenburg. By protecting their respective fiefs, which were declared indivisible, and making those ruled by magnates subject to inheritance by members of a dynastic family, the papal decree assured the primacy of the prince electors in the affairs of the empire.

Further erosion of imperial authority resulted when the Golden Bull was taken as a legislative model by yet other major principalities. They, too, moved to protect their territories against further division and to establish their right to dynastic inheritance by primogeniture. This made it possible for the principalities to counteract to some extent on a local level the forces tending toward political fragmentation. With the cooperation of the towns, which needed their protection, the ruling magnates developed systems of taxation to make them independent of their troublesome vassals of the Ritterschaft. They could then hire mercenaries answerable only to themselves to consolidate their rule and to extend their territories at the expense of lesser and weaker nobles. As a consequence, the number of separate fiefs diminished somewhat, and the size of those that were already large enough to be viable tended to increase.

All this was accomplished at the expense of imperial authority, however, and led not to a centralized government but to what has been called "the triumph of particularism."[1] Not until the election of Albert II in 1438, the first in what proved to be

1. The expression comes from Wallace K. Ferguson, *Europe in Transition, 1300–1520* (Boston: Houghton Mifflin Co., 1962), 106–16, to whose discussion of conditions in the empire during the late Middle Ages the preceding pages are much indebted. Also informative for the matters at hand is the *New Columbia Encyclopedia*, ed. William H. Harris and Judith S. Levy (New York: Columbia University Press, 1975); see the entry on the Holy Roman Empire and those dealing with the specific historical personages concerned.

the dynastic succession of the Habsburg house on the imperial throne, did a measure of continuity allow the successive emperors to begin to recover some of the powers that had been lost. Their dominion was restored to its widest reach and greatest power under Charles V (1519–56), who united his possessions in the Netherlands and Spain with the German lands of the imperial Habsburgs. Even then, however, the empire remained a loosely knit agglomeration of territorial states. The authority of the crowned head in any of these could vary enormously from that of a traditional but remote and essentially powerless liege lord to that of a ruler who was physically present and exercising real control (see Figure 13-1).

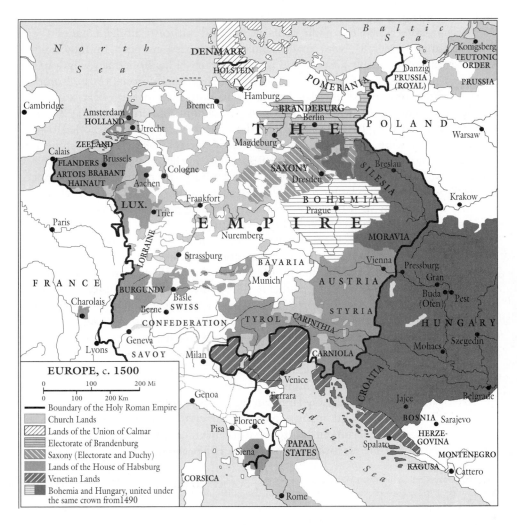

FIGURE 13-1. Central Europe, ca. 1500.

The relative independence of the individual states was to have important consequences for the cultural history of the empire during the fifteenth and sixteenth centuries. When the Reformation began to take root as a separate religious movement, severing traditional ties with the papacy, its leaders had little hope of finding protection in a more or less unified kingdom like that of France, in which the monarch was in fact a political ally of the pope. Only in England, where the king himself imposed on his subjects a break with Rome, were the reformers able to flourish under a strong central government. By contrast, the welter of small but relatively autonomous states scattered through northern Germany offered a greater possibility of protection from some lesser magnate who could be persuaded to lend his support to the Reformation, whether for religious or political reasons.

The variety and diversity of these principalities were also factors in the development of music in the territories of the empire. In those in which the musical traditions of western Europe had come to be seriously cultivated—and financial penury was not a chronic condition—vigorous musical institutions were established and important performers and composers were active. Such was the case at the imperial court of the Habsburgs, for example, not infrequently in the capital cities of the seven electors, and later on, of course, at the Habsburg courts in the Netherlands. In addition, some of the larger free cities such as Nuremberg, Strasbourg, and Ulm, which enjoyed considerable prosperity thanks to their industry and trade, also achieved some prominence in the musical developments of the sixteenth century.

In general, however, the petty states of the empire tended to remain something of a cultural backwater throughout the fifteenth and sixteenth centuries. Although there seems to have been some awareness there of what was being done elsewhere and even some modest levels of patronage, there is no indication of a serious contribution to what was noteworthy and new. One must conclude that the frequent disorders to which some of those areas were subject, combined with a lack of substantial monetary means, tended to discourage significant achievement in literature and in the arts. Even the large and relatively independent kingdoms of Bohemia, Hungary, and Poland figure prominently in the musical history of the age only on occasion, and then—like the smaller states—more as sources of patronage for musicians trained abroad than as indigenous centers of creative activity.

THE INDIGENOUS POLYPHONIC TRADITIONS

As has been demonstrated in the discussion of musical developments in Italy during the fifteenth century, the musical culture of French-speaking Europe—especially that based on Latin texts and associated in some manner with the liturgy—was carried well beyond the linguistic and geographical borders to the south, and much the same was true over most of the rest of the Continent as well. The presence of musicians trained in the choir schools of northern France and the Low Countries, or at least the adoption of their compositions, had a profound effect on the musical culture of court and cathedral choirs in neighboring regions. The genres in which these musicians were most accomplished—polyphonic Mass Ordinaries and motets in particular—were generally taken as models by their native-born colleagues, and the latter tended to emulate in other genres as well the compositional styles to which they were thus exposed. As has been seen, even the chanson achieved an international currency that had its impact upon secular works based on other vernaculars.

In some areas an indigenous musical tradition had been well grounded before musicians trained in the musical establishments of northern French-speaking regions began to arrive in such considerable numbers as were seen in the fifteenth and sixteenth centuries. There, some local genres usually survived, or were in fact fostered and developed, thanks to the stimulating influx of teachers and composers brought up in the most prestigious of the musical traditions then current. This was apparently the situation in the German-speaking regions stretching toward eastern Europe as it was in the areas of Hispanic culture on the Iberian peninsula. In either instance the written sources from the fifteenth and sixteenth centuries clearly reflect the extent to which the sacred genres and styles originating in northwestern Europe penetrated local usage nearly everywhere. At the same time, however, an important indigenous repertory came into existence, not only in emulation of the imported repertories of liturgical and devotional polyphony but also in genres both sacred and secular that were based on the local vernacular.

RUFEN AND LEISEN

Germany in particular appears to have had a strong and durable indigenous musical tradition that reached well back into the Middle Ages. On the sacred side the fourteenth century saw a brief flowering of songs that originated with the groups of penitents—constituted primarily, it would seem, by the urban poor—who went from town to town in an attempt to escape somehow, whether through their travels or their religious exercises, the devastation of the Black Death. Known as *Geissler*, because of the ceremonial flagellation with which they humbled themselves in the fervor of their penitence, these groups appear to have been formed in emulation of the lay confraternities in Italy, and like the *laudisti*, they accompanied their processions and their public worship with singing. The small written repertory of simple monophonic songs that has survived, the *Geisslerlieder*, seems to have had no direct impact on the development of the polyphonic genres of the fifteenth century, but it is conceivable that some of them continued to be sung in public acts of popular devotion.[2]

Perhaps more venerable, and certainly with greater significance over a broader area for the development of polyphonic music based on the vernacular, were certain

---

2. See the discussion of them, with examples, in Richard H. Hoppin, *Medieval Music* (New York: Norton, 1978), 315–18.

types of popular acclamations known as *Rufe*, of which there are examples in Dutch and in Czech as well as in German. These were sung at major feasts by lay members of a worshiping congregation (at Mass or Vespers, for example) as a response to the names of saints, an "Alleluia," or the repetition of a line sung by celebrant or choir.[3] Because these were short (usually just a pair of lines or even less) and undoubtedly formulaic in nature, most of them did not find their way, as such, into the written repertory. An example (cited by Lipphardt) is the rhymed couplet, "Sant Mari, muoter unde meit,/All unser not si dir gekleit" ("Holy Mary, mother and maid,/May all our needs be covered in thee").[4] Such a congregational response could easily have found a place in a variety of Marian contexts. More significant, however, some *Rufe* apparently supplied a point of departure for the hymns of the Protestant Reformation—the chorales—some of which have been in use to the present day.

Exceptionally, one type of *Ruf*, that known as the *Leise*, did emerge from the oral tradition and find its way into the polyphonic repertory of the fifteenth century. More elaborate than a simple *Ruf* of two lines, it usually consists instead of four verses and terminates with the acclamation "Kyrie eleison" (or a varied or abbreviated form thereof), from which the *Leisen* derive their name. At least twelve known melodies have been identified with the genre. The earliest of these, *Christ ist erstanden*, a *Ruf* for the Easter season, can be traced back to the middle of the fourteenth century.[5] Polyphonic settings begin to appear already at the end of that century, beginning, undoubtedly, with those associated with the most important of the major feasts such as Easter and Christmas.

Settings of *Christ ist erstanden* occur in the sources of the fifteenth and sixteenth centuries more frequently than any other polyphonic *Leise*. An early example in three parts was one of several such pieces included in the Trent MS 90 (see Example 13-1). The anonymous composer gave the preexistent melody to the highest voice and departed from syllabic delivery and the original tune only for modest precadential melismatic extensions at the ends of phrases. In its treatment of the (preexistent) melodic material, and in its musical style generally, the piece is not unlike a chanson of the period.

Essentially similar are several other settings of *Christ ist erstanden* included in the "Glogauer Partbooks." In one of these the traditional melody, lightly embellished with precadential melismas, is once again carried by the highest of the three parts (see Example 13-2). However, the first entry of that part is anticipated imitatively in

3. See David Fallows, "Ruf," *The New Grove Dictionary of Music*, 16:318, and Walther Lipphardt, "Leisen und Rufe," *Die Musik in Geschichte und Gegenwart*, Supplement, 16:1108.

4. This *Ruf* is one of those cited by Lipphardt, *Die Musik in Geschichte und Gegenwart*, 16:1108; it may be a reference to the visual representation of the Virgin as the protectress of mankind with her cloak spread to give shelter to all who seek it.

5. See Johannes Riedel, ed., *Leise Settings of the Renaissance and Reformation*, Recent Researches in the Music of the Renaissance, vol. 35 (Madison: A-R Editions, 1980), vii, where the twelve tunes are given in unembellished form.

EXAMPLE 13-1. Anonymous, *Christ ist erstanden*

Christ has risen from all his torment; therefore should we all rejoice. Christ should be our solace: Lord, have mercy.

EXAMPLE 13-2. Anonymous, *Christ ist erstanden*

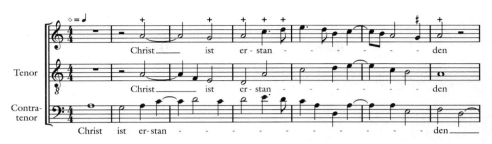

For English translation of text, see Example 13-1.

the low contratenor. In addition, the piece is divided into two sections by a shift in mensuration from duple to triple for the final acclamation. Striking as well, and not entirely characteristic, is the substitution of a joyfully repeated "Alleluia" for the more usual "Kyrie eleison."[6]

Other *Leisen* melodies given polyphonic treatment already in the fifteenth century include *Sei willekommen, Herre Christ*, which is linked textually with the Nativity. One setting of this tune (from MS 332 of the Municipal Library in Erfurt) has the traditional melody in the tenor (in this instance the lowest part) mostly in longer note values.[7] Interestingly, this approach to the borrowed material is typical of a compositional style that came to be much more favored in the region than the treble-dominated facture of *Christ ist erstanden*. Combining the treble placement of the traditional melody typical of the chanson and its presentation in longer values characteristic of cantus firmus composition in Germanic regions is a setting of *Nun bitten wir den heiligen Geist*, a *Leise* for Whitsuntide also found in the "Glogauer Partbooks." For the strophe the traditional melody is laid out exclusively in breves and semibreves in the topmost of the three parts, but the "Kyrie" section, which is marked by a shift to a ternary mensuration, is somewhat freer in its rhythmic usage.[8]

6. For other examples in modern notation, see Heribert Ringman, ed., *Das Glogauer Liederbuch*, Das Erbe Deutscher Musik, series 1, vol. 4, *Erster Teil: Deutsche Lieder und Spielstücke* (Kassel: Barenreiter, 1936), 4, nos. 2 and 3.

7. For an edition of this piece, see Heinz Funck, ed., *Deutsche Lieder des 15. Jahrhunderts*, Das Chorwerk, vol. 45 (Wolfenbüttel: Kallmeyer, 1937), 5, no. 1.

8. For an edition, see Ringman, ed., *Das Glogauer Liederbuch*, vol. 1, *Deutsche Lieder und Spielstücke*, 5.

Other melodies cited by Riedel include *In Gottes Namen fahren wir*, a processional *Ruf* for pilgrimage; *Mitten wir im Leben sind*, a later example whose purpose is clearly didactic; *Also heilig ist der Tag*, again for Easter; *Dys sind die heylgen zehn gebot*, also didactic in nature; *Gelobet seist du Jesu Christ*, for the Nativity; *Gott sei gelobet und gebendeiet*, for Corpus Christi; *Jesus Christus, unser Heiland, der den Tod ueberwand*, for Easter; *Mensch willst du leben seliglich*, also didactic; and *O du armer Judas*. *Christ der ist erstanden*, a melody not cited by Riedel, appears to be a variant of the venerable Easter *Leise*.[9]

As we shall see, composers who continued to cultivate *Leisen* into the sixteenth century contributed to a clearer sense of the stylistic traits to be associated with the genre. Four (or more) voices become the norm, all of them text-bearing as a rule (in contrast to the solo song of the earlier versions à 3), and the traditional melody is usually carried by an inner voice such as the tenor. It is as if the borrowed element was at that point more clearly recognized as a cantus firmus in the traditional sense and somehow cast into sharper relief in the overall polyphonic structure. But already in the course of the fifteenth century polyphonic *Leisen* came to constitute a relatively substantial repertory of music suitable for liturgical services and devotional exercises in a considerable variety of contexts. And their ongoing use for the enhancement of lay worship by both Protestants and Catholics alike constitutes a compelling claim for their historical importance.

◁◦ THE *TENORLIED* ◦▷

Related to the development of the polyphonic *Leise* as a well-defined sacred genre, and similar to it stylistically in significant ways, was the first notable flowering in Germanic regions of part songs based on secular poetry in the vernacular. This newly burgeoning compositional type was rooted, obviously, in the tradition of courtly lyric verse—known as *Minnesang*—that can be traced back to the twelfth century. Interestingly, the emergence of the polyphonic *Lied* in the fifteenth century shows striking parallels with the earlier development of the monophonic repertory in its reliance on French models. For if indeed there existed a truly independent body of courtly love songs in German prior to the twelfth century, its evolution from that time forward was clearly shaped by the themes and formal structures of the songs of the *troubadours* and *trouvères*.

There is no need to trace here in detail all of the means—including the intercultural exchange that resulted from the experience of the Crusades as shared by the armies of a variety of European polities—by which these courtly songs found their way into territories of German language and culture. Nonetheless, the circumstances at the court of Frederick Barbarossa (Holy Roman Emperor 1155–90) are perhaps

9. Yet other *Leisen* cited by Gustave Reese (*Music in the Renaissance* [New York: Norton, 1958], 633, 674, and 679)—including *Jesus ist ein süsser Nam'*—and by Lipphardt, *Die Musik in Geschichte und Gegenwart*, 16:1105f., appear not to have been transmitted with their melodies.

paradigmatic in this connection since his marriage to Beatrix of Burgundy in 1156 brought into his entourage the *trouvère* Guiot de Provins and opened his realms to ongoing exposure to the love lyric of northern France.

The cultural consequences of his union to a lady of that region may be gauged to a degree by the extent to which French songs were subsequently taken as a model for imitation and emulation in the realms over which Frederick held sway. In a number of instances the German songs that have reached us in the written repertory are clearly little more than a paraphrase of *trouvère* lyrics transmitted in earlier sources from French-speaking regions. And with the adoption of the theme and diction of a specific poem came, it would seem, the appropriation of the melody that had been fashioned for its performance.[10] Similarly, just as the cultivation of courtly lyrics in areas of French culture was emulated by educated townsmen, who organized themselves into guilds to further their art and held regular *puits* (contests in which the best poems submitted were given some mark of distinction), so did the *Minnesinger*

of Germany give rise in urban centers to *Meistersinger*, who likewise formed guilds, formalized the rules of composition, and vied with one another for artistic distinction.[11]

In much the same way, although the polyphonic *Lied* of the fifteenth century had its origins with the *Minnesang* of the late Middle Ages, the initial stages of its development were marked by the influence of French models. This is amply evident in the work of Oswald von Wolkenstein (ca. 1377–1445), a poet-composer of minor nobility from the southern Tirol who apparently played a central role in bringing about the transition from medieval monophony to a new polyphonic genre (see Figure 13-2). Of the settings for some 123 poems that have been transmitted under his name, the monophonic songs outnumber the polyphonic compositions by two to one (83 to 40). Moreover, a fair number of the latter can be shown to be contrafacta, mostly of secular works on French texts from the late fourteenth and early fifteenth centuries, but also of *trecento* Italian pieces. Yet other adaptations of this

FIGURE 13-2. Portrait of Oswald von Wolkenstein, perhaps by Pisanello (Innsbruck, University Library, MS B, 1432).

---

10. See Hoppin, *Medieval Music*, 304–12.
11. See Horst Brunner, "Meistergesang," *The New Grove Dictionary of Music*, 12:73–79, who points out that the *Meistersinger* tended to give a larger place in their output than the earlier *trouvère* poets to religious themes, as did the poets of the northern French *puits* in the last stages of that tradition.

kind may lie hidden among his compositions, moreover, because their models are no longer known.[12]

As an example, Vaillant's bird-call *virelai Par maintes foys* served Wolkenstein as a model for his *Der may mit lieber zal*.[13] More typical, presumably, of the works for which he himself composed the music—and more indicative of his own contrapuntal skills—is his *Wach auff, myn hort* for two parts (see Example 13-3), a piece that came to be sung all over German-speaking Europe in the course of the fifteenth century. In a lightly embellished homophonic style, it makes use primarily of conso-

12. See Ivana Pelnar and Christoph Petzsch, "Oswald von Wolkenstein," *The New Grove Dictionary of Music*, 14:15–19, in particular the list of works.
13. See Reese, *Music in the Renaissance*, 12.

EXAMPLE 13-3. Oswald von Wolkenstein, *Wach auff, myn hort*

Awake my treasure, there shines forth from the East the bright day. Look through the mist, behold the gleam, how the purest blue of the heaven's crown gathers itself amid the gray of the horizon's bulwark. I fear the day will dawn soon.

nances in parallel motion, including not only sixths and tenths but also parallel fifths and octaves (assuming the piece to have been correctly copied). If considerably less sophisticated than compositions of this type that would be written by subsequent generations, it is at least typical of the genre-to-be in one significant respect: the melody of the song is carried by the tenor in the two-part version and may well have been independently conceived as a monophonic setting for the poem.

That the tenor part could be perceived at the time as an independent song melody is indicated by the fact that it was copied by itself in one of the three important sources for the polyphonic *Lied* from the second half of the fifteenth century, the "Lochamer Liederbuch," MS 40613 of the State Library of Prussian Culture in Berlin, a compilation of urban origin copied in Nuremberg circa 1452–60.[14] This collection, like Oswald's repertory of secular song, is divided between monophonic and polyphonic pieces (all of them, unfortunately, without attribution in the source), but with an even larger proportion of the former. Only nine part songs on German texts were entered among the thirty-two melodies (including the tenor of Wolkenstein's *Wach auff, myn hort*) and three Latin *contrafacta* of secular pieces.[15] Also contained in the manuscript, incidentally, is a copy of the *Fundamentum organisandi*, a series of instructional studies attributed to Conrad Paumann, the blind keyboard player, whose contribution to the instrumental music of the period is discussed below (see pp. 790–95).

The other two sources alluded to above—the "Schedel Songbook," MS Germanicus monacensis 810 of the Bavarian State Library in Munich, and the "Glogauer Partbooks," MS 40098 of the former Prussian State Library in Berlin—show more clearly than the "Lochamer Liederbuch" the ongoing influence of polyphonic songs in the French manner on Germanic musical culture. The former was compiled, as we have seen, by Hartmann Schedel in the 1460s when, as a young medical student, his travels took him to Leipzig, Augsburg, and Nuremberg. A personal miscellany, his collection juxtaposes a Magnificat and eighteen Latin motets with nineteen secular pieces composed to French verse, two with Italian incipits, seventeen without text, and seventy German songs, all but two of which are polyphonic.

Texts are given, in whole or in part, for the majority of the *Lieder*, but their placement gives no real indication as to the type of performance that was intended: they are not adjusted to the music but simply written in wherever there was room—even apart on separate pages. As in the Lochamer songbook, the music was copied without attribution, but among the composers who can be identified by means of concordant manuscripts are Barbingant, Bedyngham, Du Fay, Frye, Morton, Okeghem,

---

14. Concerning the manuscript, see the *Census-Catalogue of Manuscript Sources of Polyphonic Music*, ed. Charles Hamm and Herbert Kellman, 5 vols. (Neuhausen-Stuttgart: Hänssler-Verlag, 1979–88), 1:58f.
15. For an edition of this repertory, with all concordant sources listed, see Walter Salmen and Christoph Petzsch, eds., *Das Lochamer Liederbuch*, Denkmäler der Tonkunst in Bayern, new ser., special vol. 2 (Wiesbaden: Breitkopf und Härtel, 1972); the "tenor" of *Wach auff* (p. 7) includes a presumably instrumental prelude eight breves in length not included in the two-part version.

Pullois, and Touront—the most celebrated masters of the French tradition active in the second half of the fifteenth century.[16]

The "Glogauer Partbooks," by contrast, were obviously prepared for use in an ecclesiastical institution, most likely the cathedral in Glogau, and date from the decade 1475–85. Their contents reflect that social context and their intended use; the bulk of the repertory consists of liturgical and devotional compositions: 18 Mass Propers, 19 hymn settings, 120 motets—some of which, however, are Latin *contrafacta* of secular music—and 4 sacred works on German texts. On the secular side are pieces that were presumably included for the entertainment as well as the instruction of the young clerics. Fifty-nine of them are without text, but unidentified chansons are mixed in with dances and pieces with German titles, while one work has an Italian incipit.[17]

The remaining sixty-three compositions can be identified as polyphonic *Lieder*, although none of them has a complete text; the secular verse was perhaps thought inappropriate in a collection prepared for use in an ecclesiastical institution. Its absence raises important questions concerning the performance conventions of the period, however, and suggests that the music may have been either solfaed (for didactic purposes) or—more likely—played on instruments by the young clerics being trained in the choir. It is also possible, of course, that the verse was widely known, perhaps even in written form, and that the texts were therefore not held to be indispensable. As in the "Schedel Songbook," there are no attributions, but the composers that can be identified by means of concordances are once again those associated with the French tradition, including (in addition to those represented in the earlier collection, listed above) Busnoys, Caron, Hayne, and Martini (or Isaac).

The German songs transmitted by these sources are mostly in three parts, and they continue to be essentially polyphonic arrangements of the melodies fashioned for a monophonic presentation of the verse.[18] The implication for polyphonic performance, clearly, is that they were originally intended as solo song with instrumental accompaniment—a mode of performance that may have had its origins in an unwritten practice and that resulted in written form in a stylistic counterpart to the chanson. The similarity between the two genres is all the more evident in those *Lieder* that carry the melody in the topmost part, a placement of it that can be demonstrated on occasion in the earlier layers of the repertory, as, for example, in Isaac's setting of *Innsbruck, ich muss dich lassen*. However, as in the case of the contemporaneous *Leisen*, the tune is carried in the majority of instances by the tenor, and as compositional procedures for the genre were codified, that became the consistent practice. As with the chanson, moreover, the accompanied solo song of the earliest examples gradually gave way to provision for wholly vocal performance in the print-

16. See the *Census-Catalogue of Manuscript Sources*, 2:236.
17. See the *Census-Catalogue of Manuscript Sources*, 1:43–44.
18. For a contrary opinion, however, see Norbert Böker-Heil, "Lied," *The New Grove Dictionary of Music*, 10:831, who asserts that "most melodies have obviously been modified to fit polyphonic settings, or were originally composed."

ed sources, and of course the use of instruments for some or all of the parts was always an option.[19]

Typical in most respects is the anonymous *O wie gern und doch entbern* in three parts from the "Lochamer Liederbuch" (see Example 13-4). The melody has been given to the tenor, as is evident from a different setting in the "Glogauer Partbooks," and the piece itself was also included in the latter source with a contrafact Latin text, *In preclare barbare virginis*, written in for the cantus and tenor parts.[20] Formally, however, this *Lied* does not conform to the usual pattern of two *Stollen* (strophes of identical versification) and an *Abgesang* (concluding verses). Consequently, the articulation into two parts, marked by a clear cadential formula and a repetition of the opening section, which is characteristic of many pieces in this repertory, is not present here.

19. For a careful discussion of the evidence bearing on performing practice, see Stephen Keyl, "*Tenorlied, Discantlied*, Polyphonic Lied: Voices and Instruments in German Secular Polyphony of the Renaissance," *Early Music* 20 (1992): 434–45.

20. See Robert Eitner, *Das deutsche Lied des XV. und XVI. Jahrhunderts*, 2 vols. (Berlin, 1876–80; reprint, New York: AMS Press, 1975, 2:139–42), nos. 53c and 53b, respectively.

EXAMPLE 13-4. Anonymous, *O wie gern und doch entbern*

O how gladly, and yet sadly [*entbern*] must I ever be concerning that for which I struggle. Daily rage rises in my heart, fully blossomed. Lord God, protect me that I will it
not. The guilt is mine and should well be; but I fear lest it be too much.

Taken collectively, the three sources under discussion suggest that the growing
repertory was appreciated not only in the courtly milieu, where, presumably, the
majority of the songs originated, but also among the urban populations where musical literacy was becoming ever more widespread and the interest in a repertory of
song in the vernacular would have been particularly keen. After a considerable hiatus as far as the sources are concerned, but with every indication that cultivation of
the new polyphonic genre had continued apace, come—one after the other—three
printed sources that originated in separate German cities: Augsburg, where Erhard
Oeglin brought out a collection in 1512; Mainz, where Peter Schoeffer produced a
second in the following year; and Cologne, which saw a third produced by Arnt von
Aich toward the end of the decade.

The compositions included in these anthologies reflect the evolution of the genre
through the end of the fifteenth century. The *Lieder* are now uniformly in four parts,
and the melody is carried almost invariably by the tenor. Since that voice is also the
only one provided with text, it is possible to conclude that the genre continued to

be viewed as accompanied solo song, with the cantus and altus above as well as the bassus below played in most instances instrumentally.

If the commercial viability of printed miscellanies of this sort is evidence for the popularity of the *Lied* with the musically literate segments of the urban population, the list of composers who contributed most significantly to the genre would suggest that the courts of ruling nobility (whether their titles were secular or ecclesiastic) continued to be a primary locus for its cultivation. Although no composers are named by the prints in question, those that can be identified by means of concordances in later sources include Paul Hofhaimer, Heinrich Finck, Heinrich Isaac, and Ludwig Senfl, all of whom served primarily in courtly establishments.

Hofhaimer (1459–1537), the celebrated organist, served first Duke Sigmund of Tirol in Innsbruck (from 1478) and then—amongst others—Maximilian I, with whom he was associated in some manner from 1486 until the emperor's death in 1519, whereupon Hofhaimer became organist for the archbishop of Salzburg, Matthaeus Lang.[21] Finck (1444–1527) enjoyed the patronage of Prince Alexander of Lithuania (later king of Poland), starting in 1498. From the latter's employ he went first to the ducal court in Stuttgart (from 1510) and from there—like Hofhaimer— to the service of the archbishop of Salzburg, presumably as a composer in the cathedral chapter, and finished his days in Vienna.[22] Isaac (ca. 1450–1517) entered the service of Maximilian I in 1497, and his relationship with the imperial court continued until his death.[23]

An essentially typical example of the courtly *Tenorlied* at this stage of its development is Hofhaimer's *Mein's traurens ist* (see Example 13-5).[24] The topos of unan-

---

21. See Manfred Schuler, *The New Grove Dictionary of Music*, 8:631–32.
22. See Lothar Hoffman-Erbrecht, *The New Grove Dictionary of Music*, 6:559–62.
23. Concerning Isaac, see Martin Staehelin, *The New Grove Dictionary of Music*, 9:329–37.
24. For a transcription in modern score, see Archibald T. Davison and Willi Apel, eds., *The Historical Anthology of Music*, 2 vols. (Cambridge, Mass.: Harvard University Press, 1962), 1:96.

Example 13-5. Paul Hofhaimer, *Mein's traurens ist*

My grief is, the cause to me is clear, that I can complain to no one, for you alone, my
shining sun, hold I responsible for my suffering. I would, believe me, rather embrace
death than to leave you thus.

swered devotion is conventional for the genre, and the "bar" form, consisting of two
Stollen for the *Aufgesang* (the opening verses) followed by the *Abgesang* (or epi-
logue), is equally traditional. As usual, the melody is given to the tenor part, which
is the only one provided with text in the Forster print of 1539. Surprising, by contrast, is the clear Phrygian orientation of the texted voice, the ductus of which results
in exposed melodic tritones at the end of both sections of music. The composer's
treatment of the tune includes an anticipatory imitation in the other three parts (raising the possibility for present-day editors and performers that all four parts could be
sung). Free counterpoint follows, however, and the relatively regular rhythms of the
tenor are set off in the other parts by fleeter motion, featuring dotted patterns and
syncopation (thus suggesting a more "instrumental" style).

Isaac is credited with two settings of the well-traveled melody for *Innsbruck, ich
muss dich lassen*, one of them found in manuscript sources now in Basel and Munich,
the other in Forster's printed collection of 1539.[25] Although the text is a conven-

25. See Noah Greenberg and Paul Maynard, eds., *An Anthology of Early Renaissance Music* (New York:
Norton, 1975), 178–84, and cf. Palisca, ed., *Norton Anthology of Western Music*, 3d. ed., 2 vols. (New
York: Norton, 1996), 142–44, no. 48.

tional lament of separation, it does not have the barform typical of the courtly *Lied* but consists instead of two parallel tercets linked by a common rhyme (aab, ccb). The symmetry of the verse is reflected in the melody, whose second half is essentially a lightly modified repetition of the first. In the version transmitted only in manuscript the preexistent melody is carried in fairly strict imitation by the middle pair of voices (altus and tenor) with presumably instrumental parts above and below. It is possible to speculate that the lower three voices of this setting—which make perfectly good sense contrapuntally by themselves—represent an earlier, three-part version of the *Lied* to which the topmost part was added later in conformity with sixteenth-century practice.

The version published in Forster's print departs from the usual style of the *Tenorlied* in that the preexistent melody is carried by the cantus, and the final line of text and music is repeated in the manner characteristic of the polyphonic chanson of the sixteenth century. This may be a reflection of Isaac's training in the French tradition, reinforced by his experience in Italy with the *frottola*. The piece is also unusual for its simplicity, being essentially syllabic in its declamation and homophonic in its texture.

Isaac's setting of *Zwischen berg und tiefem tal*,[26] which is likewise lacking the initial repetition of paired *stollens*, also departs from the pattern typical of the *Lied* in its treatment of the tenor melody. The initial entry of the tune is anticipated imitatively again by the three other parts, and it is then carried in imitative alternation between tenor and bassus, neither of which has an unembellished version of it all the way through. But whatever the apparent deviations from standard compositional paradigms in these three (of the many) polyphonic *Lieder* attributed to Isaac, and regardless of the differences in compositional detail among them, they clearly illustrate the influence of the sophisticated contrapuntal skills of composers trained in the French tradition on the development of the genre.

The same sort of compositional competence and a similar interest in the complexities of imitative counterpoint is to be seen in the setting of *Schön bin ich nicht* ascribed to Heinrich Finck, which was included in three different printed collections of the sixteenth century (see Example 13-6).[27] Based on a poem in regular barform—although not exactly courtly in its diction—it opens the initial motive of the *Lied* with a regular point of imitation that moves systematically in descent from the cantus through all four parts. Thereafter the tune is borne by the tenor alone, and the second section, after a beginning in homophonic declamation, settles into a lively contrapuntal texture. Interestingly, the sources for this work suggest that the traditional mode of performance—as solo song with instrumental accompaniment—may have begun to yield in the early sixteenth century to the wholly vocal presentation

---

26. For a transcription in modern score, see Davison and Apel, eds., *Historical Anthology of Music*, 1:91.
27. For a complete transcription in modern score, see Heinrich Finck, *Ausgewählte Werke*, ed. Lothar Hoffmann-Erbrecht and Helmut Lomnitzer, 2 vols., Das erbe deutscher Musik, vol. 70 (Frankfurt: C. F. Peters, 1962–81), 182–84, no. 38; sources are listed on pp. 208–9.

Example 13-6. Heinrich Finck, *Schön bin ich nicht* (mm. 1–15)

Handsome I am not, my greatest treasure; do not make me suffer for it! Love goes to
the fair in many places, but I'll not complain of that. Love overcomes many a friendly
youngster without making him seek beauty . . .

that was by then becoming typical of secular music in both France and Italy, for one of them has text provided for all of the voices.

Undoubtedly the most prolific composer of polyphonic *Lieder* in the sixteenth century was Ludwig Senfl (ca. 1486–1543), Isaac's scribe and most noteworthy pupil, who began his affiliation with the chapel of Maximilian I already as a choirboy in 1496. He then continued in imperial service without interruption until Maximilian's death in 1519, replacing his mentor as composer to the court chapel when Isaac died, and he spent his last years (from 1523 on) at the court of Bavaria's Duke Wilhelm IV. In addition to a very considerable body of sacred music, Senfl left 260 German songs, compositions in which Senfl set texts of all sorts and exploited to the fullest all of the stylistic possibilities opened for the genre by the composers of the previous generation.[28]

In setting *Da Jakob nu das Kleid ansah*, the biblical text apparently inspired him to adopt a style of motetlike complexity.[29] Imitation—in alternating pairs as well as in full textures—is contrasted with free counterpoint and with homophonic declamation in longer values, largely in accordance with the significance of the text. These compositional procedures—to be seen at the time in the polyphonic chanson as well as the motet—could not help but weaken the predominant place of the tenor in the contrapuntal fabric. The resulting equalization of the parts must have contributed to a trend toward full texting of all the voices, as noted earlier, either as a cause or as an effect.

Illustrative of Senfl's imaginative approach to the genre are his settings of the traditional melody and text *Ich stuend an einem Morgen*, five of which were included in Ott's printed collection of 1534.[30] The first of these (see Example 13-7), in four parts, carries the preexistent melody in the tenor, which is the only one provided with text in the sources. After an opening in chordal homophony, the style changes quickly to a freely contrapuntal texture that is subsequently maintained to the end of the work. Noteworthy is the dotted ascending figure encompassing a fifth that first appears in measure 28 of the bassus, to which it returns in an increasingly sequential series of repetitions on various pitches in measures 34–43. In two of the remaining four settings, all of which are for five parts, the composer has added another text with its associated melody and in another makes use of strict canonic imitation between bassus (the notated voice) and discantus (the one derived), something of a contrapuntal tour de force.

That the *Lied* melody given such elaborate treatment was a traditional one is indicated by its inclusion in two of the many *quodlibets* that were constituted by stitching together melodic phrases from the presumably monophonic repertory as the

28. Concerning Senfl, see the concise biography and the work list compiled by Martin Bente, *The New Grove Dictionary of Music*, 18:131–37.

29. For a transcription in modern score, see Davison and Apel, eds., *Historical Anthology of Music*, 1:114.

30. For a complete transcription in modern score of all five pieces, see Ludwig Senfl, *Sämtliche Werke*, vol. 4, *Deutsche Lieder*, ed. Arnold Geering and Wilhelm Altwegg (Wolfenbüttel: Möseler, 1962), pt. 2, pp. 5ff.

EXAMPLE 13-7. Ludwig Senfl, *Ich stuend an einem Morgen* (mm. 1–6, 28–44)

I stood one morning secretly in a corner, as if I had hidden myself there, and I heard words of complaint from a fair, fine maiden standing with her lover who was about to part. (Six additional strophes.)

basis for an entire polyphonic composition.[31] (Such pieces are useful, obviously, in attempting to discover which of the voices in a three- or four-part texture is the actual bearer of a preexistent melody.)

The spate of printed collections from publishers such as Ott, Egenolff, Schoeffer, Apiarius, Formschneider, and Forster, beginning in the 1530s, reflects the rising prominence of Nuremberg as a center for the printing of music in Germany, presumably as a consequence, at least in part, of its well-established importance as a center for trade. It is also indicative of the ongoing popularity of the genre, especially with the musically literate urban population to which the published repertories appear to be increasingly directed. Comments in these collections concerning the suitability for both voices and instruments of the compositions published are an additional clue to the essentially commercial objectives pursued by the printing houses. By the early 1550s, however, the heyday of the—more or less indigenous—polyphonic *Lied* had passed. Examples from later in the century show the fundamental traits that had been established in the course of the fifteenth century eclipsed to an ever greater degree by stylistic features borrowed from sixteenth-century genres, the motet, the chanson, and, to an ever greater extent, the Italian madrigal.

---

31. See Eitner, *Das deutsche Lied*, 1: *passim.*

CHAPTER 14

✝

Polyphony on the Iberian Peninsula

INTRODUCTION

Events on the Iberian peninsula following the invasion of Muslim Berbers in 711 were of a nature to produce the same kind of political fragmentation that characterized the development of the Holy Roman Empire in the late Middle Ages. Efforts to recapture the territories held by the Moors, as they were called, began almost immediately and brought about a progressive partitioning of the northern regions into relatively small Christian kingdoms. The Spanish March established by Charlemagne as a defensive buffer between his Frankish domains to the north and the Moorish emirate to the south became the independent principality of Catalonia. The Basques, whom the Moors were never able to vanquish, found protection in the Pyrenees Mountains to the north. The remnants of the Visigoths withdrew to the north-central corner of the peninsula, where the kingdom of Asturias was formed.

From there was launched the Christian reconquest of Moorish Spain, in the course of which large grants of land made to the victorious nobles gave rise in time to the independent kingdoms of Navarre, Leon, Castile, Aragon, Valencia, and Portugal. By the thirteenth century the Muslims had been reduced to the small southern kingdom of Granada, but at that point the reconquest was stalled for nearly two centuries as the powerful nobles and crusading orders quarreled among themselves (Figure 14-1).

Despite the turmoil that characterized this period generally, the enduring result of the predominant political process—which combined armed conflict with alliance by marriage—was, surprisingly enough, a gradual reintegration of the political fabric of the peninsula rather than the continued splintering that might have been expected. The kingdoms of Leon and the two Castiles were united under a single crown, absorbing Asturias and Galicia in the process. Similarly, the Crown of Aragon added to its own territories those of Catalonia and Valencia. When Isabella

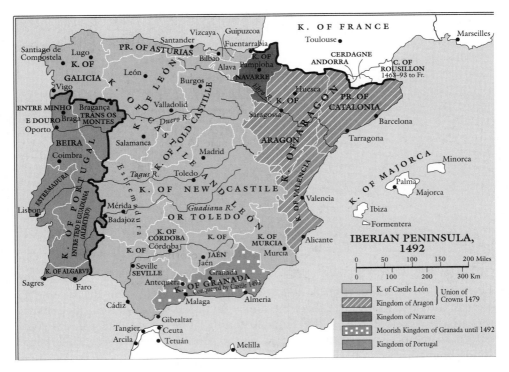

FIGURE 14-1. Iberian peninsula, 1492.

I of Castile and Ferdinand II of Aragon (who were married in 1469) began a long joint rule of their respective kingdoms in 1479, all that lay outside of their united dominions on the Iberian peninsula were Portugal and the tiny kingdoms of Granada and Navarre.

Although their separate realms were never formally united in their lifetime, they pursued in common a policy aimed at strengthening and centralizing the authority of the monarchy in every important respect. To that end they made use of all the social, political, and administrative tools at their disposal. In their efforts to diminish the power of fractious nobles they turned for support to the cities, many of which had earlier been fortified and granted considerable privileges by kings wishing, like themselves, to enlist the aid of the townsmen against rebellious vassals.

In the early years of their reign they also made use of the *cortes*, legislative bodies of long standing that represented the three primary social orders of late medieval society: the nobility, the clergy, and the burghers. They reorganized popular bands, which had originated in the Castilian towns as a defense against lawlessness, as the Santa Hermandad (Holy Brotherhood), a centralized militia that they used not only to combat brigandage but also to strengthen the monarchy against powerful local magnates. Once their authority had been securely established, moreover, they moved in turn against these same bodies in order to remove checks on their own absolute authority, limiting the autonomy of the cities, calling the *cortes* ever less frequently into session, and abolishing the Hermandad.

Both monarchs were outwardly deeply religious and devoutly Catholic, but they also took steps to make of the church an instrument of national unification. They objected to the right of papal provision to the major benefices of the Spanish church, which in effect allowed a foreign power to appoint its principal administrators within their borders, and in 1482 they obtained permission to nominate their own candidates for the most important ecclesiastical offices. By extending this privilege in practice to lesser benefices as well, they were able to exercise effective control over the governing hierarchy of the Spanish clergy.

When, in addition, the Inquisition was introduced into Spain in 1478—although ostensibly to deal with the *marranos*, Jews forcibly converted to Christianity who continued to practice secretly their hereditary faith—the resulting combination of ecclesiastical authority and secular arms created a political tool of enormous power. At the same time the Reyes Católicos, as they were called, reshaped the royal councils to create an efficient central administration, reformed the collection of taxes so as to greatly increase their revenues without resorting to onerous new levies, and—to free themselves from dependence on the proud grandees for military strength—proceeded to the creation of a national army.

With their newly acquired military might they brought to a conclusion the long-stalled reconquest of Moorish Spain, taking possession of the kingdom of Granada in 1492. In 1512 Ferdinand also added to his holdings in Castile that portion of the kingdom of Navarre located on the Spanish side of the Pyrenees. This completed the political unification of the entire peninsula with the sole exception of Portugal (see Figure 14-1). In 1503 he even managed to reclaim from the French the kingdom of Naples, which remained, under the rule of a viceroy, a Spanish possession until the late eighteenth century.

Not satisfied, apparently, with political union, the Catholic monarchs likewise attempted a forcible social integration of their realms. Under the Inquisition the considerable population of unconverted Jews remaining in the territories they governed—considerable both in their numbers and in their artisanal and commercial skills—had been subjected to mounting levels of intimidation and persecution. The surge of religious and nationalistic fervor that followed victory in Granada then provided an atmosphere in which it was possible to expel them from the kingdom entirely, and this was done rapidly and brutally.

The conquered Muslims, by contrast, were treated rather tolerantly at first, but in 1502 they, too, were forced to leave. In just a few years, then, even though the economic and political circumstances that facilitated governmental centralization had been slow to make themselves felt in Spain, the royal couple had prepared the way for a permanent fusion of their respective kingdoms and for the creation of a society unified not only by a sense of national identity but also by their adherence—forced though it may have been—to a common religious faith.

In the course of their reign the Catholic monarchs also laid the foundations for

FIGURE 14-2. Ferdinand and Isabel and their daughter Joanna as pictured in the *Livre d'heures de Jeanne la folle* (Chantilly, Musée Condé).

the political predominance among the nations of Europe and the financial prosperity that Spain was to enjoy during the sixteenth century, her "Golden Age" in both a literal and a figurative sense. Much of the actual gold was to come from Spain's colonies in the New World, which owed their existence to the voyage of discovery made by Christopher Columbus in 1492 under the patronage of Queen Isabella. Equally fortunate were the alliances through marriage by which the royal couple hoped to confirm their reign and extend their influence. In 1496 their daughter Joanna (later known as "the Mad") was wed to the archduke Philip the Handsome (1478–1506) (see Figure 14-2). The son of the Habsburg prince Maximilian of Austria and of Mary of Burgundy, Philip was heir both to the domains of the Habsburgs and to the extensive territorial holdings that the dukes of Burgundy had accumulated in the Netherlands over nearly two centuries of rule.

The political outcome of that union may not have appeared too promising when, in 1506, Philip suddenly died and Joanna became too deranged to rule. However, their surviving son and heir, although only six years of age at the time, was the future Charles V. He was raised in the Netherlands by his aunt, Margaret of Austria, who also acted in his stead as regent during his minority and, later, during his prolonged absences as he looked after other parts of his dominions. He took the reigns of government in those northern regions at the age of fifteen (see Figure 14-3). Ferdinand, who had been ruling both Aragon and Castile following the death of Isabella in 1504, died in the following year (1516), and Charles was proclaimed the successor to the Spanish thrones of both his royal grandparents. And when Maximilian I died in turn some three years later, Charles hied immediately to the eastern territories ruled by the Habsburgs. There he managed to buy (with funds borrowed from the Fuggers, the immensely wealthy merchant family from Augsburg) the votes of enough of the electors to have himself named to succeed his paternal grandfather as king of the Romans in June 1519.

At that point, as monarch not only of his Spanish kingdoms but as the nominal ruler of the Netherlands and the Holy Roman Empire as well, he began a struggle to reunify his far-flung dominions under the imperial crown. He attempted even to reassert the imperial right to rule in northern Italy, laying claim to the duchy of Milan. However, that effort brought him repeatedly into armed conflict with the king of France, the pope, and the magnates who supported the reform both in Germany and in the northern provinces of the Netherlands, and it ultimately proved unsuccessful. Although Charles did manage to have his election to the imperial throne consecrated by a papal coronation in Bologna in 1530—the last of his line to

FIGURE 14-3. Young Charles V depicted on a throne with a trio of musicians to his right playing wind instruments, cornets, and/or shawms, an illustration for Remi du Puis's *La tryumphante et solenelle entree faicte sur le joyeux advenement de Treshault et Trespuissant prince Monsieur Charles* (Vienna, Nationalbiblióthek, MS 2591, f. 44).

be so honored—by midcentury the forces of particularism had become too powerful to be overcome even by a personage as energetic and forceful as he. Weary and disillusioned with the struggle, he abdicated in 1555.[1]

---

1. For a concise account of developments on the Iberian peninsula during the period of interest for this study, see Wallace K. Ferguson, *Europe in Transition* (Boston: Houghton Mifflin Co., 1962), 463–70. Additional information may also be gleaned from pertinent articles in *The New Columbia Encyclopedia*, ed. William H. Harris and Judith S. Levy (New York: Columbia University Press, 1975), and Ilan Rachum, ed., *The Renaissance: An Illustrated Encyclopedia* (London: Octopus Books, 1978).

◠◡ NORTHERN MODELS AND COMPOSERS ◠◡

The fortunes of the arts in the Spanish kingdoms, and of music in particular, reflected in good measure the political events that have been briefly summarized here. As early as the thirteenth century a vigorous tradition of secular monody had been developed on the Iberian peninsula. The genres of sacred polyphony that had originated in French territories north of the Pyrenees were also known there, as is clear from the repertory of a manuscript from the monastery of Las Huelgas in Burgos dating from the early fourteenth century.[2] In addition, the royal court of Aragon served as a conduit that brought music and musicians of the French polyphonic tradition into Spain during much of the fourteenth and early fifteenth centuries.

The singers at the Aragonese chapel were occasionally recruited from among those of the papal court in Avignon, especially around the turn of the century, and they brought with them both their skills as performers of mensural polyphony and usable repertory, sacred and secular.[3] The musical traffic between Aragon and France may also have encouraged fairly early on the teaching of polyphonic music in the choir schools of Spanish churches, thus helping to lay a foundation for rapid and brilliant developments in sacred music on the peninsula in the course of the sixteenth century.

However, there is little direct evidence of a distinctively indigenous polyphonic tradition in Spain until the kingdoms of Isabella and Ferdinand were united in the final decades of the fifteenth century. Their union marked the dawn of an era of new luster and of important indigenous development in the musical culture of the Iberian peninsula, beginning with the musicians in their service. Both monarchs gave evidence of the importance they attached to music in the daily life of their courts by the generous stipends, tax exemptions, perquisites, and privileges with which they attracted musicians to their employ.

The number of singers in their respective chapels grew steadily during their joint reign from twelve in Ferdinand of Aragon's choir and nine at Isabella's Castilian court in 1469 to twenty-four for the former and thirty-four at the latter by the time of the queen's death in 1504. Similarly, the trumpeters in Ferdinand's service increased from four (with a single drummer) to eight (with four drummers) by 1515, while those at Isabella's court grew from six to ten or eleven in the last years of her life. And although the *ministriles altos* (the players of the loud wind instruments, sackbuts and shawms) were not augmented so dramatically, Ferdinand's band went

---

2. Concerning the musical repertories, both monophonic and polyphonic, that were cultivated in Spain during the Middle Ages, see Richard H. Hoppin, *Medieval Music* (New York: Norton, 1978), 318–22 and 325–52.

3. Some scattered indications, and further references, concerning the use of musicians and repertory that had originated in territories of French culture at the court of Aragon during the period in question may be found in Craig Wright, *Music at the Court of Burgundy, 1364–1419: A Documentary History* (Brooklyn: Institute of Mediaeval Music, 1979), 72–74, 116–19, and *passim*.

from five or six to as many as eleven during the same period of time.[4] More significantly, as we shall see, Spanish verse began at that point to be set polyphonically by Spanish composers who were in the employ of the royal and other secular courts. It appears to have been at that moment as well that sacred polyphony began to be more widely used in all regions of Spain, both at court and in the churches.

Later, when the Habsburg prince Philip the Handsome was wed to Joanna of Aragon and Castile, he made two extended visits to Spain. The newly joined couple came first in 1502 and stayed for nearly a year. Then in 1506, two years after the death of Queen Isabella, they came again, this time to lay claim to the throne of Castile. Philip was accompanied both times by the private chapel of the Netherlands court, which could boast a rich tradition for polyphonic music—both sacred and secular—cultivated for generations under the generous patronage of the dukes of Burgundy. And although he died inopportunely in Burgos within the year, many of Philip's musicians lingered in Spain for a number of months thereafter.

The presence of such a distinguished corps of singers and composers must have provided a powerful stimulus for the development of the musical arts in Spain, despite the relatively brief duration of their stay. That visit was followed, in any case, by an extraordinary burst of creative energy as music flowered in a variety of contexts and Spanish composers came to develop their own characteristic genres and styles. Their achievement was such that the sixteenth century has aptly been termed "the Golden Age of Spanish polyphony."[5]

During much of the fifteenth century, however, Spain, like Italy and Germany, depended to a considerable degree upon northern composers and their compositions to provide models for the written polyphonic repertory that was both sung and written by local musicians. Moreover, as was seen earlier, the flow of music and musicians came not only across the frontiers with French-speaking territories directly to the north—via Avignon, for example, during its years as a papal city—but also through the kingdom of Naples. After successfully asserting his claims to that realm in 1442, Alfonso V of Aragon (1396–1458), styled "the Magnanimous," spent a good deal of his time in his Italian possessions while his Iberian lands reflected in rather more modest measure the brilliance of the Neapolitan court.

In spite of an aggressive policy of military expansion, Alfonso was also an enthusiastic and generous patron of the arts. As a consequence, his ongoing activity in that role—whether in spite or because of his frequent absences—helped to open to his subjects in the kingdom of Aragon yet another window on musical practice in the rest of Europe. What is more, the cultural contacts between Naples and Aragon were maintained even after Alfonso's death when his realms were divided between his illegitimate son Ferrante I (1431–94), who ascended the throne of Naples, and his

4. Concerning the flourishing musical establishment at the courts of the Catholic monarchs, see Tess Knighton, "The Spanish Court of Ferdinand and Isabella," in *The Renaissance: From the 1470s to the End of the Sixteenth Century*, Man and Music, vol. 2 (Englewood Cliffs, N.J.: Prentice Hall, 1989), 341–60.
5. Hence the title chosen by Robert Stevenson for his very informative study, *Spanish Cathedral Music in the Golden Age* (Berkeley: University of California Press, 1961).

brother John II of Aragon (1397–1479), who rose to rule his Spanish territories.

The importance of foreign models for the growing musical culture in Spanish territories during the second half of the fifteenth century is suggested by the numbers of compositions by northern masters in the few surviving manuscripts that originated in the region during that period. The two largest collections to include sacred music dating from the late fifteenth or early sixteenth century are the unnumbered manuscript currently held by the cathedral in Segovia and MS M. 454 at the Biblioteca de Catalunya in Barcelona.

The Segovia manuscript was apparently compiled in Toledo for use at the Castilian court of Queen Isabella right around the turn of the century and may owe some of its repertory to the visit of Philip's Burgundian chapel in 1502. It contains an unusual mixture of sacred and secular works with a pronounced international flavor. In addition to polyphonic Mass settings and other pieces for liturgical and devotional use—including Magnificats, hymns, Lamentations, litanies, a Te Deum, forty-three motets, and two pieces on Spanish texts—there are secular works on texts in French (fifty-one), Flemish (thirty-three), Italian (six), and Spanish (thirty-five) and four with no text at all.[6] The Barcelona codex, which was copied around the turn of the century, has a similar sacred repertory—Masses, Magnificats, Psalms, hymns, a Lamentation, a Passion, and fifty-three motets—but the relatively few secular pieces copied into its leaves are either settings of Spanish verse (twenty-six) or are textless.[7]

Attributions that can be made to northern musicians in these two collections include some of the most celebrated figures of the age: Agricola, Brumel, Busnoys, Compère, Févin, Hayne, Isaac, Josquin, Martini, Mouton, Obrecht, Okeghem, the theorist Tinctoris (who had been active at the Aragonese court of Naples), and Johannes Urreda. The last named was the only one of the group to have spent a substantial period of time in the courtly chapels of the Iberian peninsula. By 1476, at the latest, he was a singer in the chapel of the first duke of Alba, Garcia Alvarez de Toledo, and from 1477 into the early 1480s he was listed with the household of King Ferdinand II of Aragon.[8]

Significantly, the works of these musicians of international reputation are found side by side with those of a rising generation of professionally trained Spanish composers. More than thirty who were active during the final quarter of the fifteenth century and the first quarter of the sixteenth have been identified, at least by name.[9] The majority of those about whose careers something is known came to be associated, like Urreda, with one of the courtly chapels that were founded in Spain in the closing decades of the fifteenth century.

Alonso de Alba, for example, served in Isabella's chapel from 1501 or earlier until

6. See the *Census-Catalogue of Manuscript Sources of Polyphonic Music*, ed. Charles Hamm and Herbert Kellman, 5 vols. (Neuhausen-Stuttgart: Hänssler-Verlag, 1979–88), 3:137f.

7. See Emilio Ros-Fabregas, "The Manuscript Barcelona, Biblioteca de Catalunya, M. 454: Study and Edition in the Context of the Iberian and Continental Manuscript Traditions," 2 vols. (Ph.D. diss., City University of New York, 1992); cf. the *Census-Catalogue of Manuscript Sources*, 1:17f.

8. See Isabel Pope, "Urreda," *The New Grove Dictionary of Music*, 19:467f.

9. See Robert Stevenson, *Spanish Music in the Age of Columbus* (The Hague: Nijhoff, 1960), 199.

her death in 1504 and then, probably, in Ferdinand's.[10] Juan de Anchieta sang, with Alba, first in Isabella's chapel from 1489 on and then in that of her daughter, Joanna, in whose entourage he visited Flanders and southern England while on the way back to Spain with Philip in 1506.[11] Juan del Encina was in the employ of Duke Fadrique II of Alba from 1492 until 1498.[12] Francisco de Peñalosa became a singer in 1498 in the chapel of Ferdinand of Aragon, in whose household he continued until its dissolution in 1516.[13] And Pedro de Escobar, whose origins were Portuguese, was, together with Anchieta, a singer in Isabella's chapel from 1489 to 1499.[14]

However, nearly all of these musicians also received appointments in one of the large ecclesiastical institutions that flourished in Spain at the time. Encina, who had found a niche at the papal court in Rome late in the 1490s, returned to his homeland upon the death of Leo X in 1521 to finish his days (ca. 1529) as prior of the Cathedral of Leon. With the passing of Queen Isabella in 1504, Peñalosa took up residence in Seville, where he held a canonry at the cathedral. And although he absented himself in 1517 to accept an invitation from Leo X to sing in the papal chapel, he returned, like Encina, when the pope died to finish his days in Seville. Escobar, who had returned to Portugal when he left Isabella's service, was called to become the master of the boys at the cathedral in Seville, perhaps at Peñalosa's suggestion, and so labored until 1514.

The importance of the patronage of the monarchs of Aragon and Castile—and of course that of a number of other courts where polyphony was part of the customary display of power and prestige—for the development of a native polyphonic tradition in Spain is evident from the few biographical details given above. It was instrumental in producing the first generation of Iberian composers known beyond the borders of their own region. At the same time, it is equally clear—once again just from the few indications given—that the clerics at ecclesiastical institutions in such widely scattered cities as Barcelona, Leon, Seville, and Toledo (and, if perhaps somewhat later, in other major centers as well) performed polyphony in choir and provided the instruction needed to do so to their choirboys. Not surprisingly, then, based as it was on the dual foundations of professional training and wealthy patronage, the cultivation of polyphonic music on the Iberian peninsula, once well grounded, flourished through the sixteenth century and beyond, producing a considerable repertory of compositions, both sacred and secular, and, as we shall see, some of the greatest masters of the age.

All of the composers just cited, together with some of their lesser-known countrymen, contributed to the sacred repertory represented by the manuscripts at Segovia and Barcelona, working in the sacred genres that have been discussed in preceding chapters. As has been observed, however, they took their compositional par-

10. See José Llorens, "Alba, Alonso," *The New Grove Dictionary of Music*, 1:195.

11. See Robert Stevenson, "Anchieta, Juan de," *The New Grove Dictionary of Music*, 1:394f.

12. See Isabel Pope, "Encina, Juan del," *The New Grove Dictionary of Music*, 6:159–61.

13. See Robert Stevenson, "Peñalosa, Franciso de," *The New Grove Dictionary of Music*, 14:347–48.

14. See Robert Stevenson, "Escobar, Pedro de," *The New Grove Dictionary of Music*, 6:243f.

adigms—like their counterparts in lands of Italian and German culture—from the repertory that was, by then, becoming an international standard. They worked within the parameters of structure and style that had been established by those musicians trained in the northern schools whose works were included in the manuscripts copied for local use. Moreover, despite a venerable medieval tradition for lyric verse in the Iberian vernaculars, which was sung monophonically,[15] there is no trace in the notated sources of a polyphonic repertory of secular song having its roots in fourteenth-century practice. One can assume, therefore, that courtly patronage provided the necessary impetus for the establishment of new indigenous genres of secular polyphony. And, as we shall see, this, too, was accomplished in emulation of genres known from the French and, to a lesser degree, the Italian tradition.

⌒ IBERIAN SOURCES AND COMPOSERS ⌒

The scope and vigor of the artistic activity in Spain resulting from the happy confluence of systematic musical instruction and the sympathetic interest of noble patrons is clear from two of the several sources of the period that are given over primarily to repertory of a secular nature. The more modest in scope is a collection that may have been copied in Seville late in the fifteenth century—one of many later acquired for the library of Ferdinand Columbus, son of the famous navigator, and left to the Capitular Library of the cathedral of that city (now MS 7-1-28). Sixty-one settings of Spanish verse can be numbered among its ninety-three compositions, together with two chansons, one piece mixing Spanish and Latin, and four more with no text.[16] The inclusion in this repertory of some twenty pieces attributed to Juan de Triana—a composer otherwise unknown in the musical sources of the period who held a prebend at the Seville Cathedral in 1478[17]—indicates that it originated in a circle where the composer was well known and appreciated, perhaps even that Triana himself may have played a role in its compilation.

By comparison with the Seville manuscript the other such collection, a *cancionero* copied during the opening decades of the sixteenth century for use at the court of Ferdinand II of Aragon (d. 1516), now MS 1335 in the library of the Royal Palace in Madrid, is gigantic in scope. Although some 90 compositions have been lost since its completion, it comprises at present 458 pieces (including duplicates and texts without music), 425 of them on Spanish texts. Here the sacred component is little more than a pious gesture of a kind not unusual in collections of secular music (a

15. See Richard H. Hoppin, *Medieval Music* (New York: Norton, 1978), 318–22.

16. See the *Census-Catalogue of Manuscript Sources*, 3:142f.; the sacred music in the collection is so disparate and so modest in quantity—two Mass segments, a Magnificat, a Psalm, nine motets, and twelve pieces with Spanish text—that the manuscript can hardly have been intended for liturgical use.

17. See Isabel Pope, "Triana, Juan de," *The New Grove Dictionary of Music*, 19:137; cf. Stevenson, *Spanish Music in the Age of Columbus*, 195–99, who discusses Triana's sacred music and one of his three song-motets.

Psalm and a motet), and the pieces using vernaculars other than Spanish are a very small part of the total (10 with Italian, 2 with Latin and Italian, another 2 with Latin and Spanish, 1 with Latin alone, 2 chansons, and 2 instrumental pieces).

The composers named were mostly Iberian, as well, but three settings of Spanish texts thought to be by the Fleming Urreda were included, as were Italian *frottole* by Josquin, Lurano, and Tromboncino and a chanson by Morton.[18] Significantly, given the large number of concordances between the Madrid *cancionero* and other, earlier sources of music on Spanish verse, the manuscript reflects rather effectively the development of secular composition on the Iberian peninsula during the late fifteenth and early sixteenth centuries.[19]

THE SECULAR SONG FORMS

The song types represented in this repertory are essentially three in number: the *romance*, the *canción*, and the *villancico*, even though formal and stylistic relationships between the latter two are occasionally sufficiently ambiguous as to make distinctions difficult. The verse forms—fixed to a greater or lesser degree—upon which these secular genres were generally based were of course well establised and widely cultivated. The type that had gained greatest currency on the Iberian peninsula by the end of the thirteenth century was similar in all essentials to the French *virelai*. In the fifteenth century it came to be designated a *canción*, and its direct descent from aristocratic medieval antecedents is suggested by the topoi and diction that characterize the poetry as well as the form itself. The stylized eros of courtly convention, cast in regularly octosyllabic verses, is couched in the customary expressions of emotional anguish from the point of view of the suffering unrequited suitor.

THE CANCIÓN

Such poems begin with an *estribillo*, a refrain usually of four lines, rhyming abba or abab, but occasionally of five, rhyming abaab or abbaa. This is followed by a section called the *mudanza*, apparently in reference to the change in the rhyme scheme; it consists of two pairs of verses, rhyming cd, cd or cd, dc, thus constituting two short strophes sung to the same musical material. The form is completed by a *vuelta*, a return to the verse structure and the rhyme scheme of the *estribillo*, often incorporating its concluding verse or verses and sung to the same music.[20]

18. See the *Census-Catalogue of Manuscript Sources*, 2:135f.
19. Concerning the remaining traces of an earlier repertory and some earlier sources for the secular music of Iberian origin of this period, see David Fallows, "A Glimpse of the Lost Years: Spanish Polyphonic Song, 1450–70," in *New Perspectives in Music: Essays in Honor of Eileen Southern*, ed. Samuel A. Floyd Jr. (Warren, Mich.: Harmonie Park Press, 1992), 19–36; and cf. Jack Sage, "Cancionero," and "Canción," *The New Grove Dictionary of Music*, 3:679–81 and 679, respectively.
20. Concerning the form of the *canción*, considered in its historical context, see Isabel Pope, "Musical and Metrical Form of the Villancico," *Annales musicologiques* 2 (1954): especially 198ff.

Representative of this type of composition at a fairly early stage in its development as a polyphonic genre is Urreda's *Nunca fue pena mayor* (see Example 14-1), a work that achieved remarkable currency in the late fifteenth century. Other composers were to draw upon it time and again as the starting point for new polyphonic works,

EXAMPLE 14-1. Johannes Urreda, *Nunca fue pena mayor*

ESTREBILLO: Never was there greater pain or torment so extreme that it can equal the suffering that I feel when deceived.

MUDANZA: And this knowledge makes my days sad, thinking the thought that for love you spoke to me.

VUELTA: And I would, at the most, deem death less hurtful than the torment and the pain that came from deceit.

ESTREBILLO: Never was there greater pain . . .

both vocal and instrumental.[21] Significantly, the poem upon which it is based was written by one of Urreda's patrons, the first duke of Alva, about 1470. The text follows the pattern outlined above; an *estribillo* of four regularly octosyllabic verses, rhyming abab, is sung to the four separate phrases of the first section of music with a combination of rests and cadential figures to mark internal caesuras and the ends of lines. The *mudanza*, rhyming cd, cd, is sung to the two phrases of the second section, both of which have an internal articulation, with a musical repetition to match that of the rhyme scheme. For the *vuelta*, which duplicates the rhyme scheme of the *estribillo* but incorporates only its last two words, the performer returns to the music of the opening section.

The musical style is clearly derived from that of the contemporaneous chanson—not surprisingly in view of Urreda's northern origins. The three-part texture, to which the composer has given considerable contrapuntal interest, lends itself easily to the kind of accompanied solo song associated with the French genre. Similarly, the melody, which conforms to a regular mode 3 ambitus from e to e', is not without its

21. See Isabel Pope, "Urreda," *The New Grove Dictionary of Music*, 19:467.

lyrical flights, particularly in the melismatic extensions into the cadences. The suggestion that it is based on a popular Spanish tune seems ill founded in light of the modal regularity of the cantus part and its similarity to that of so many chansons of the period. Moreover, its use by a younger contemporary, Belmonte, as the tenor for his *Pues mi dicha non consiente*, tends to confirm that it was original with Urreda.[22]

The affinity of the musical style of the *canción* to that of the chanson of the period, including the use of points of imitation, is equally marked in the compositions of Johannes Cornago, despite his rather more declamatory treatment of the text. This is perhaps to be explained by the circumstance that, although apparently of Catalan origin, Cornago appears to have spent the greater part of his career at the Aragonese court of Naples.[23] A number of his companions there were musicians trained in the northern traditions, composers of chansons as well as the sacred genres of Mass and motet. His long residence in Italy will also explain why most—but not all—of his compositions, including those on Spanish texts, are found in Continental rather than Spanish sources.

That the chansonlike character of his *canciones* was recognizable to a northern master is suggested by a reworking à 4 of Cornago's three-part *¿Qu'es mi vida preguntays?* by Johannes Okeghem, chapelmaster at the royal French court, presumably in connection with a diplomatic mission to the court of Castile in which Okeghem participated in 1470. As may be seen from a comparison of the opening phrase of the two versions (see Example 14-2), Okeghem has taken over Cornago's cantus and tenor parts in their original relationship to one another with only the most minor changes of pitch or rhythm. He also quoted the opening figure of Cornago's contratenor quite literally, but at the lower octave, and thereafter treated it very freely, using many of the same notes—now at pitch, now at the lower octave, and now at

22. The possibility of popular origins for the tune was raised by Higinio Anglès; see Pope, "Urreda," *The New Grove Dictionary of Music*, 19:467.
23. Concerning Cornago, see Johannes Cornago, *Complete Works*, ed. Rebecca L. Gerber, Recent Researches in the Music of the Middle Ages and Early Renaissance 15 (Madison: A-R Editions, 1984), vii; and cf. Isabel Pope, "Cornago," *The New Grove Dictionary of Music*, 4:779–80.

EXAMPLE 14-2. Johannes Cornago and Johannes Okeghem, *¿Qu'es mi vida preguntays?* compared (mm. 1–10)

What is my life, you ask? I don't wish to deny to you that it is to love and to lament . . .

the upper—but refashioning it as needed in order to add a second contratenor of his own at the bottom of the contrapuntal fabric.[24] The resulting composition is significant not only as an indication of Okeghem's exposure to the secular music of a Spanish court but also, and more importantly, as an early example of the recomposition of polyphonic chansons that was to play such an important role in the development of the instrumental *canzona* (see pp. 763–75).

24. See Isabel Pope, "The Secular Compositions of Johannes Cornago," in *Miscelánea en homenaje a Monseñor Higinio Anglés*, 2 vols. (Barcelona: Consejo Superior de Investigaciones Científicas, 1958–61), 2:689–705, for full transcriptions of both works and a discussion of the relationship between them.

VILLANCICO *AND ROMANCE*

The possibility that the melodies used in some of the polyphonic settings of Spanish texts derived from popular songs is perhaps a bit stronger when it comes to the *villancico*, the genre whose very name (like that of the *villotta*) suggests more plebeian origins. It is a diminutive derived from *villano*, a word used in all Romance languages (and English) to designate the servants, laborers, and artisans connected in some manner to the household of a person of rank.[25] And it is characterized by more modest formal structures and greater metrical irregularity than was tolerated in *canciones*. This, coupled with increased freedom in diction and the choice of themes, may justify to a degree the assumption that such songs did in fact have their origins with the urban classes rather than in courtly circles. However, the cultivation of polyphonic settings for them obviously presupposes trained composers and performers, and we have already observed in connection with the chanson the tendency of the nobility to appropriate for their own use popular themes and materials, poetic and musical.

The *villancico* also begins with an *estribillo*, but unlike that of the *canción* it can be of only two or three verses, possibly of variable length, including at times a truncated verse ("pie quebrado"), and may either constitute or conclude with a rhymed couplet. The *mudanza*, too, may have only two or three verses, in which case all have the same rhyme and are sung to the same music, but two pairs of verses, rhyming bc, bc or bc, cb, for example, are also found. The crucial formal distinction with the *canción*, even when both *estribillo* and *mudanza* consist of four octosyllables with the usual rhymes, lies with the rhymes of the *vuelta*, which begin with that of the *mudanza* and then turn to the one concluding the *estribillo*, with which it shares its verse structure, its musical setting, and usually a final segment—at least a few words and as much as a pair of verses.[26]

Typical in most respects is the setting in three parts of *Levanta, Pascual* attributed to Juan del Encina (see Example 14-3). The *estribillo* consists of only three verses, rhyming abb, but, as in a *canción*, the *mudanza* has four, rhyming cd, dc (and requiring the usual repetition of the second section of music). Moreover, the entire poem—which is found in Encina's printed collection of verse (a *Cancionero de las obras* printed in 1496) with twelve strophes—is written in regular octosyllables. At the *vuelta*, however, with a return to the verse structure (and the music) of the *estribillo*, comes the characteristic linking of the earlier rhymes, here cbb, and the incorporation of the final verse as a recurring refrain throughout the poem.

The subject matter, which is historical rather than erotic, is presented in the form of a dialogue between two men of the people, Pascual and his unnamed companion, as their reaction to the news that Granada, the last Muslim stronghold on the Iberian peninsula, had fallen to the forces of Ferdinand and Isabella (an event that took place in January 1492). The plebeian tone of the verse is established by the choice of vocabulary as Pascual (a "common" name) is urged to hie to Granada to see for himself what had transpired, taking with him his dog, his knapsack, and his cloak, crook,

25. See Pope, "Musical and Metrical Form of the Villancico," 191.
26. See Pope, "Musical and Metrical Form of the Villancico," 196–98.

EXAMPLE 14-3. Juan del Encina, *Levanta, Pascual*

ESTREBILLO: Get thee up, Pascual, get thee up, let us go to Granada, for they say that it has been taken.

MUDANZA: Get thee up now, I pray thee; take thy dog and thy pouch, thy jacket and thy great coat, thy pipes and thy staff.

VUELTA: Let us go see what has happened to the populous city, for they say that it has been taken. (Twelve additional strophes.)

and pipes, all of which identify him as a shepherd. (The analogy with the annunciation of the Nativity to the shepherds of the Gospel accounts is amusing and probably intentional.) The result is a miniature dramatic scene in a pastoral setting, and, as we shall see, it was apparently conceived as part of a larger structure.

Musically, too, the setting has characteristics of a popular nature, notwithstanding the point of imitation and the lightly melismatic phrase with which it opens. Thereafter syllabic declamation—in a relatively narrow melodic range and with a few repeated pitches at the beginning of the *mudanza*—not only conveys an impression of artless simplicity but also emphasizes the lilting ternary rhythms that reflect without complication the mensuration in which they are written. Even though this melody was probably carefully crafted by the composer rather than borrowed from an oral tradition, the overall impression—and the one that was undoubtedly sought—is that of a popular tune.

Encina's *Levanta, Pascual* is also an example of a *deshecha*, currently defined as a kind of courtly farewell, which is in practical terms a *villancico* that is paired with another song (of a type without refrain) as a conclusion or a comment upon it. In this instance the pastoral dialogue is linked to another poem by Encina, beginning "¿Qu'es de ti, desconsolado?" (see Example 14-4), the first in a series of rhetorical questions addressed to the defeated Moorish ruler of Granada. The poet's intention is ostensibly an attempt to persuade the "infidel" that he could save at least his soul, if not his kingdom, by turning to the Christian faith. Here the dialogue is implied even though the king does not answer, and the two poems, taken together, suggest a pair of related tableaux whose dramatic significance is explained in song.

¿Qu'es de ti, desconsolado? is thus representative of a narrative song type known as

EXAMPLE 14-4. Juan del Encina, *¿Qu'es de ti, desconsolado?*

¿Dón - de tie - nes tu mo - ra - da?

1. What has befallen thee, disconsolate? What has befallen thee, king of Granada? What of thy lands and thy Moors? Where now wilt thou dwell? 2. Abjure now Mohammed and his wicked sect, for to live in such madness is a mockery mocked. (Five additional strophes and an envoy.)

a *romance*, a kind of ballad whose text usually consists of a series of quatrains without refrain. In this instance the individual strophes are rhymed abcb with some assonance linking the "a" and "c" rhymes and the "b" rhyme running through all seven strophes and the closing envoy of two verses. As was customary, the verses of each stanza are to be sung to the four clearly articulated phrases of the polyphonic setting. The melodic style is characterized here, even more markedly than in the *deshecha* to follow, by repeated pitches—reflective of the syllabic treatment of the text—in a relatively narrow range, and this declamatory simplicity is stressed by the fundamentally homophonic texture of the counterpoint.

The cantus parts of the two related pieces are further linked by their modal orientation in a plagal ambitus with a final on G and a b-flat signature (indicating a transposition of mode 2). One is tempted to observe, even though direct connections by means of recognizable melodic formulae have yet to be made, that the melody of this *romance*—like that of many others in this genre—is evocative of an oral tradition for singing narrative verse that has been posited for the epics of the Middle Ages and presumably has very ancient roots.

It is conceivable, in any case, that some of the tunes used both for *romances* and *villancicos* (and, consequently, their texts as well) circulated unwritten in urban centers before being set to the cantus of a polyphonic composition.[27] Evidence for such a process of transmission may be seen in the two settings of the *villancico Nuevas te traigo, Carillo*, the first of which was entered without attribution in a version for three parts in the *cancionero* of the Colombina Library (MS 7-1-28), while the second, in four parts, is found under Encina's name in the somewhat later Madrid *cancionero* (MS 1335). The cantus parts in both pieces are essentially the same for the *estribillo* and are similar in the *mudanza* section as well (see Example 14-5).[28]

27. See, in this connection, Fallows, "A Glimpse of the Lost Years," 24–25.

28. See Stevenson, *Spanish Music in Age of Columbus*, 270; the two works have been edited, respectively, by Miguel Querol Gavaldá, *Cancionero musical de la Colombina*, Monumentos de la música española, vol. 33 (Barcelona: Consejo Superior de Investigaciones Científicas, Instituto Español de Musicología, 1971), 65, no. 59, and Higinio Anglès and José Romen Figueras, eds., *La música en la Corte des los Reyes Católicos: Cancionero musical de Palacio*, 3 vols. (Barcelona, 1947), 2:51–52, no. 281.

EXAMPLE 14-5. Anonymous, *Nuevas te traigo, Carillo*, melody and polyphonic setting by Juan del Encina

ESTREBILLO: I bring thee news, Carillo, of thy misfortune. Tell me then now, Pascual.

MUDANZA: Knowest thou that Bartolilla, the daughter of Marimingo, was wed Sunday with a fellow from the village?

VUELTA: It is great pain and shame to thy misfortune, because thou art such a good fellow. 2. Tell me if this is jest or idle talk, or if thou tellest the truth, for in so lamentable a case, thou hast no reason to deceive me. I spoke with her Tuesday at the gate, but never did she tell me such a thing.

It may be, of course, that Encina was simply attracted by the theatrical potential he perceived in the earlier polyphonic piece. A second strophe with Carillo's incredulous reply to the bearer of bad news—that his sweetheart was to marry another—is found with his version of the work (and an expansion into a pastoral dialogue of twelve strophes is given as well). But the dancelike rhythms, the narrow range of the syllabic melodic line, and the clear articulation of the musical phrases all suggest that a popular tune may be embodied in both polyphonic pieces. Nonetheless, a much more extensive study of pieces of this kind will have to be undertaken before firm conclusions, if any, can be drawn.

The reworking, with some elaboration, of an earlier piece recalls, of course, the compositional practices linked to the chanson, even though the borrowed melody there was usually placed in the tenor. Constructive devices of the kind found with the chanson—and the motet, as well, for that matter— can also be seen on occasion in the *villancico* repertory. An anonymous setting à 4 of *A los baños dell'amor*, for example, is built over a recurring hexachordal *soggetto cavato* in the tenor, *so, la, mi, re*, and these syllables, when construed as actual words, echo the refrain line of the *estribillo*, "sola m'iré" (see Example 14-6).[29] In a similar vein, Encina's *Mortal tristura me dieron* takes for its tenor a segment of a Kyrie sung in Spain for Masses of the dead, thus evoking a literal meaning for the otherwise conventional expression of the "fatal sorrow" of unrequited passion in a courtly context.[30]

Also found in this repertory are examples of the *quodlibet*, such as Alonso's three-

29. See Stevenson, *Spanish Music in the Age of Columbus*, 301.

30. See Stevenson, *Spanish Music in the Age of Columbus*, 269, for a discussion of the piece with a music example.

EXAMPLE 14-6. Anonymous, *A los baños dell amor*

To the baths of love I shall go alone and bathe myself in them . . .
CANON: I shall pause for two breves and then sing "sol, la, mi, re."

part *La tricotea Samartín la vea*, music stitched together from pieces that were current and reasonably well known, more with an eye for comic effect than for discernible sense.[31] Here, too, the Iberian song forms have their counterparts in the secular repertories of the Continent, from *chanson* to *Lied* to *frottola*.

Noteworthy, in particular, is Encina's dramatic use of the *villancico*, which he

31. Stevenson, *Spanish Music in the Age of Columbus*, 267.

integrated into the plays for which he is noted in literary circles, to introduce, conclude, or relieve the action on stage.[32] His use of them in this context may have been inspired by Italian models with which he became familiar during his years of association with the papal court in Rome. Some of his compositions are not unlike the Florentine *canti carnascialeschi* with their homophonic, four-part textures, their syllabic declamation, and their representational intent.

It may have been in emulation of such pieces that Encina began to transform the genre from the three-part accompanied solo song found in the earlier sources to a four-part homophonic style that lends itself readily to wholly vocal performance. Such a work is his *Triste España*,[33] which is thought to have been written in connection with the death of Prince Juan in 1496. Despite the simplicity of its compositional procedures, the work succeeds in capturing something of the somber drama of the political event. It also stands as a symbol of the fruitful interchange between Iberian and Continental musicians that will continue to enrich the styles and repertories of both regions throughout the sixteenth century.

32. See Isabel Pope, *The New Grove Dictionary of Music*, 6:160.
33. For a transcription of this work in modern score, see Noah Greenberg and Paul Maynard, eds., *An Anthology of Early Renaissance Music* (New York: Norton, 1975), 195.

PART THREE

The Sixteenth Century

THE ESTABLISHED GENRES

AND STYLISTIC CHANGE

CHAPTER 15

The Motet as Genre and Compositional Type

─────── GENERAL OBSERVATIONS ───────

From the final decades of the fifteenth century into the first two of the sixteenth, the motet emerged as the leading sacred polyphonic genre of the age. Literally thousands of compositions so designated were produced before the 1500s drew to a close. The manuscripts of the period are filled with them, and the printers, whose shops were to be found in an ever greater number of cities toward the end of this period, brought out collection after collection given over entirely to this one compositional type. From the bibliographical evidence alone it is clear that an increasing number of chapels and choirs were performing polyphonic compositions on a regular basis and making motets in particular part of their daily repertories.

When viewed in comparison with Mass Ordinaries, which were cultivated continuously throughout the same period, motets seem to have held the greater interest for many composers of the sixteenth century, especially during its early decades. The reasons for this preference are far from obvious. Certainly, polyphonic Masses were not being sung any less frequently than they had in the past, and the genre—because of its scope and the rich compositional traditions associated with it—would continue to challenge both the creative imagination of the author and the musical skills of the performer well beyond the period dealt with here.

It is possible, of course, that liturgical practice played a role. Since an increasing number of polyphonic Masses were genuine Ordinaries that could be used, in principle, on any given day and not just for the special feast or event for which earlier cycles had been written, a few such works could fill a multitude of needs. By contrast, the texts for motets had always to be proper to the occasion or the liturgical season in some sense of the word, and each required a separate musical composition. It may also be that some masters, precisely because the compositional procedures associated with the polyphonic Mass were so firmly tied to tradition, saw it as leaving less room for experimentation and innovation than the motet, particularly in the

507

area of rhetorical and mimetic text expression, which was then becoming an ever more significant aspect of motet composition.

Preference for one genre or the other seems to have reflected regional or personal taste as well and to have evolved from one generation to the next. Composers whose careers unfolded primarily in the Netherlands apparently directed more of their creative energies to Mass composition than to motets, if one can judge from the works that have been transmitted in the surviving sources. Such was certainly the case for Johannes Obrecht (ca. 1450–1505), who had appointments in the ecclesiastical establishments of Bruges, Antwerp, and Bergen op Zoom before entering the employ of Ercole I d'Este in Ferrara, and for Pierre de La Rue (ca. 1460–1518), who served for many years at the Burgundian court of the Habsburgs, especially under Maximilian I and Marguerite of Austria. It is noteworthy as well that a large proportion of their motets bear Marian texts, often liturgical in nature, suggesting that they were probably written primarily for use during the *Lof* or for similar devotional, votive, or processional purposes.

Some idea of the relative compositional emphases of these masters emerges from a rough comparison of the music in both genres that each has written. Obrecht is credited with twenty-eight complete Mass Ordinaries—in every case with five large sections—and only twenty-six motets (the rough equivalent of about five Masses), and eight of the motets are on Marian texts.[1] La Rue's name is linked to thirty-two Masses and only twenty-three motets (roughly equal to about four Masses), six of them on the antiphon *Salve regina*.[2]

By contrast, musicians who spent considerable time in Italian establishments, as did Heinrich Isaac (ca. 1450–1517) and Josquin Desprez (ca. 1440–1521), or with the royal French chapel, as did Jean Mouton (ca. 1459–1522) and Antoine de Févin (ca. 1470–1512), apparently gave greater attention (if not greater care) to motet composition. Thirty-six Masses have been included in Isaac's list of works as compared to 52 motets and nearly 100 motet-related cycles of Mass Propers.[3] Similarly, 18 Masses have been included thus far in the Josquin canon as compared to more than 80 motets (see Figure 15-1).[4] To Mouton are attributed some 16 Masses and over 100 motets;[5] and Févin is known to have authored 10 Masses and some 15 motets, a relatively small number when compared with Mouton.[6] Although English composers apparently had little direct contact with colleagues on the Continent, they

1. See Rob C. Wegman, *Born for the Muses: The Life and Masses of Jacob Obrecht* (Oxford: Clarendon Press, 1994), 79–85, 138–46, 156–60, 292–310, and *passim*.

2. For details and a list of La Rue's compositions, see Martin Staehelin, "La Rue, Pierre de," *The New Grove Dictionary of Music*, 10:473–76.

3. See Martin Staehelin, "Isaac," *The New Grove Dictionary of Music*, 9:332–37.

4. See Jeremy Noble, "Josquin Desprez," *The New Grove Dictionary of Music*, 9:728–36. In the case of Josquin, however, a significant number of the source attributions have been questioned, and the definitive canon, if one is ever achieved, could be even smaller.

5. For the list of works, see Howard Mayer Brown, "Mouton," *The New Grove Dictionary of Music*, 12:659–60.

6. For the list of works, see Howard Mayer Brown, "Févin," *The New Grove Dictionary of Music*, 6:516.

seem also to have had a particular, if not exclusive, affection for the motet, as well as one can judge from the few remaining musical sources.

The largest and earliest of these is the "Eton Choirbook," which was prepared in the 1490s and early 1500s for use by the college chapel. Of the ninety-three compositions listed in the original table of contents (twenty-nine of which have now been lost), sixty-eight were motets, twenty-four were polyphonic Magnificats, and one was a Passion for Palm Sunday from the Gospel according to Matthew.[7] The other two manuscripts from the period, the "Lambeth Choirbook" (which includes seven Masses, four Magnificats, and eight motets) and the "Caius Choirbook" (comprising ten Masses and five Magnificats) present a less monolithic picture but serve to emphasize the ongoing use of polyphony for both Mass and Office.[8]

IOSQVINVS PRATENSIS.

FIGURE 15-1. Josquin Desprez, woodcut included in Petrus Opmeer's *Opus chronographicum orbis universi*, p. 440 (Antwerp, 1611), supposedly modeled on a portrait once found on an altar in the church of Ste. Gudule in Brussels.

As in the case of the composers of Obrecht's generation active in Flemish territories, the vast majority of the motets included in the "Eton Choirbook" are based on texts with Marian associations—fifteen settings of the *Salve regina* were copied into the collection consecutively, for example. This is undoubtedly because the repertory of the "Eton Choirbook" was compiled to provide for the established custom of singing a polyphonic antiphon to the Virgin every evening as part of the common devotional exercises. And all but eleven of Eton's motets are for five or six voices or more, usually with a plainchant cantus firmus as an essential part of the texture.

With the next generation interest in the motet as a compositional genre is still more pronounced and apparently comes at the expense of the Mass Ordinary. Nicolas Gombert (ca. 1495–1560), who followed La Rue as a singer in the Burgundian chapel of the Habsburg Archduke Charles after the latter was elected Holy Roman Emperor in 1519, apparently served in the Netherlands during his entire career; however, he wrote but 12 Masses as compared to over 160 motets. Josquin, with whom he is reported to have studied, may have been the decisive influence in focusing his compositional efforts on this genre.[9] Clemens (non Papa) (ca. 1510–15 to

7. See the inventory by Frank L. Harrison, "The Eton Manuscript," *Annales musicologiques* 1 (1953): 168–75.

8. See Charles Hamm and Jerry Call, "Sources," *The New Grove Dictionary of Music*, 17:694–95.

9. See George Nugent, "Gombert, Nicolas," *The New Grove Dictionary of Music*, 7:512–16.

1555–56), who apparently spent his relatively short career entirely in the Low Countries, authored some 233 motets, compared to only 15 Masses.[10] Interestingly, his works were among the most widely circulated of his day as a result of an ongoing business arrangement with the prolific Antwerp publisher Tilman Susato.[11] The Italian Costanzo Festa (ca. 1490–1545) and the northerner Adrian Willaert (ca. 1490–1562), both students of Mouton who spent most of their professional life on the Italian peninsula, reflect in their compositional output the same trend. To Festa are ascribed only 4 Masses as compared to over 50 motets,[12] to Willaert 8 Masses and more than 170 motets,[13] and the majority of their immediate contemporaries followed a similar path.

In England the situation is a bit more complex and conclusions concerning the status of the motet consequently more difficult to draw. Sources are sparse for the music of the generation following the compilation of the "Eton Choirbook," even for the most significant of the composers active at the time, Robert Fayrfax (1464–1521), William Cornysh (d. 1523), and John Taverner (ca. 1490–1545). This may be due in part to the disruptions caused by England's rather brusque identification with the Protestant Reformation, starting in the 1530s (see pp. 745–49). However, even though Henry VIII brought about the separation of the English church from Roman Catholicism, he was apparently not an ardent champion of religious reform (at least not as it was understood by the followers of Luther, Zwingli, or Calvin).

Latin continued to be the language of the liturgy until the end of his reign in 1547, which meant that the motet continued to be cultivated in his kingdom without interruption until that time. Moreover, contacts with the Continent were certainly more frequent and—for musicians as for others—more significant than they had been just previously. They resulted not only from the increased diplomatic activity sparked by Henry's attempts to have his marriage to Catherine of Aragon annulled but also from his involvement in Continental politics, most notably his participation in the Holy League, beginning in 1511. The ensuing conflict with the French brought him to the plain between Ardre and Guine in 1520 for the famous encounter with Francis I at the Field of the Cloth of Gold. There his singers joined with those of the French royal chapel in a kind of emulatory celebration of the liturgy, and of the event.[14]

---

10. See Willem Elders, "Clemens (non Papa)," *The New Grove Dictionary of Music*, 4:476–80.

11. Concerning Clemens's place in the motet repertory of the sixteenth century, see Jennifer S. Thomas, "Modern Myopia and the Renaissance Motet," *Abstracts of Papers Read*, Sixtieth Annual Meeting of the American Musicological Society, Minneapolis, October 29, 1994, 34.

12. See Alexander Main, "Festa, Costanzo," *The New Grove Dictionary of Music*, 6:501–4.

13. See Lewis Lockwood and Jessie Ann Owens, "Willaert, Adrian," *The New Grove Dictionary of Music*, 20:421–28.

14. Concerning the meeting of the two kings and their chapels, see S. Anglo, "Le Camp du Drap d'Or et les entrevues d'Henri VIII et de Charles Quint," and P. Kast, "Remarques sur la musique et les musiciens de la chapelle de François I au Camp du Drap d'Or," in *Fêtes et cérémonies au temps de Charles Quint* (Paris: Editions du Centre National de la Recherche Scientifique, 1960), 113ff. and 135ff.

One consequence of such contacts—encouraged, it would appear, by Henry's own intense interest in music—was to expose the musicians of the chapel royal to the compositional techniques of their Continental counterparts. As an example, they may have seen, or perhaps even used for performance the "Newberry Part Books," a collection of music comprising thirty motets and thirty madrigals for four, five, and six voices by Verdelot and other Continental masters that was probably presented to Henry by a Florentine delegation in 1529.[15] In any case, the influence of foreign models was undeniably seminal for the motets of the composers who were then serving, or soon to serve, the English crown, in particular William Mundy (ca. 1529–91), John Sheppard (ca. 1515–59 or 1560), Thomas Tallis (ca. 1505–85), and Christopher Tye (ca. 1505–ca. 1572).

Compositional attention to the Latin motet was interrupted at the accession of Edward VI in 1547 by Protestant reform, which established English as the language for public worship. A brief reflowering of Latin-texted polyphony, which included renewed cultivation of the motet, followed during the relatively brief reign of Mary Tudor (1553–58), but it brought nothing strikingly new to the stylistic development of the genre. Finally, with the accession of Elizabeth I and a return to the liturgical practices of the Church of England, there was a definitive shift away from the motet back to the English-texted polyphonic genres that had been forged to serve the needs of the Anglican service.

The foregoing observations apply only to the motet as a genre narrowly defined. To be considered apart are the motetlike but generally rather less elaborate plainsong settings for liturgical use that had by then become established as individual compositional types. Hymns, Psalms, Magnificats, Lamentations, Passions, Te Deum settings, and Mass Propers, for example, continued to maintain an independent existence, if not in every case a distinctive stylistic profile. Among the other texts drawn from the liturgy the Marian antiphons, in particular, continued to be set in substantial numbers. As has been seen, the stylistic conventions for compositions of that type came to be defined with considerable clarity already in the final decades of the fifteenth century, and they were sung not only in strictly liturgical contexts but also in processions and for a wide variety of devotional and votive exercises.

Even thus defined as a distinct compositional genre, it appears that the motet was being integrated ever more regularly into liturgical services as an officially sanctioned component, with or without texts specified for use at a given service or even for a particular feast. This is suggested not only by the increasing numbers in which motets were produced in the course of the sixteenth century but also by such other circumstances as the organization of the musical sources. One of the earliest collections printed by Ottaviano Petrucci was titled *Motetti De passioni, De cruce, De sacramento, De beata virgine et huiusmodi B* (1503), thus indicating explicitly the liturgical purposes that it was designed to serve.

15. See H. Colin Slim, ed., *A Gift of Madrigals and Motets,* 2 vols. (Chicago: University of Chicago Press, 1972), 1:105–16; concerning the madrigals in this repertory, see below, pp. 659–64.

Similar concerns are evident in the practices of printers working later in the century. The Parisian Pierre Attaingnant (active 1528–50)—to cite but a single instance—published a numbered series of thirteen books of motets in which the tenth is given over to the music for Passiontide and the twelfth to antiphons for the Virgin Mary, thus following in a sense the pattern adopted earlier by Petrucci. In addition, many of the individual compositions in the other volumes have rubrics indicating their place in the liturgy.[16] Also typical—to take another illustration among many—is the first book of motets by the celebrated Roman master Palestrina that was published in 1563 under the title *Motecta festorum totius anni cum Communi Sanctorum* (*Motets for the Feast Days of the Entire Year, together with the Common of Saints*).

Equally instructive in this connection are the manuscript motet collections of certain churches, which were organized with reference to the local liturgical calendar. Such was the case, for example, at the cathedral in Treviso, where MSS 7 and 8 in the Capitular Library (which were copied over a period of years beginning in the 1550s) have carefully compiled tables of contents with the motets (including in this instance settings for the Propers of the Mass) listed according to the liturgical celebration for which they could be sung: Easter, Christmas, Corpus Christi, specific feasts of the Virgin Mary, and a variety of saints' days.[17]

Significantly, the works identified and classified as motets in sources like those described, whether manuscript or printed, include a noticeably broader spectrum of textual types than was to be found in motets of the fifteenth century, and many such texts have no specified place in the liturgy. Their diversity and the variety of sources from which they were drawn consequently raise questions as to how the motets based upon them would have functioned in the prescribed rituals of liturgical celebration. Although fully satisfactory answers may never be found due to the scarcity of relevant documentation, there is evidence that the Mass itself was frequently embellished on important occasions by the interpolation of one or more motets that were at best paraliturgical if not clearly nonliturgical.

The tradition of the *motetti missales*, although it may have been confined largely to Milan, suggests that the substitution of a motet for one of the chants of the Mass, Ordinary or Proper, was regarded as liturgically admissible.[18] The fact that one motet of such a series was usually designated for performance in place of the Offertory and/or during the Elevation of the Host at the Canon of the Mass gives yet another indication of an appropriate place for the insertion of material that was not specifically liturgical. Similarly, the Mass-motet cycles discussed earlier (pp. 370–72) give a clear indication that the motet that shared its cantus firmus with the settings of the

16. See Daniel Heartz, *Pierre Attaingnant, Royal Printer of Music* (Berkeley: University of California Press, 1969), "Bibliographical Catalogue," 255–80.
17. For a list of the composers represented in these codices, see the *Census-Catalogue of Manuscript Sources of Polyphonic Music*, ed. Charles Hamm and Herbert Kellman, 5 vols. (Neuhausen-Stuttgart: Hänssler-Verlag, 1979–88), 3:237–39.
18. See the discussion in chap. 12, pp. 429–36.

Ordinary was also sung at Mass. There is also mention of motets having been sung at the conclusion of Mass, following the "Ite, missa est," perhaps as a substitute of sorts for the "Deo gratias" or the "Benedicamus Domino" that was usually heard at that point. Antiphon motets were apparently often used as well in place of liturgically prescribed hymns in processions and votive ceremonies.[19]

Despite the dramatically greater numbers in which motets survive from the sixteenth century (compared with earlier periods) and the wider variety of textual material used in their composition, they can generally be classified according to a limited number of textual types. Those most commonly adopted for use during this period include the following: (1) liturgical texts (as has been indicated), in particular the great processional antiphons that were associated with a specific service or season of the year; (2) excerpts from the Bible, both the Old and the New Testament, whether or not they had a specified place in the liturgy; (3) liturgical and/or biblical centonizations, with and without connective interpolations; and (4) texts expressly written in response to particular events and/or circumstances.

Centonizations of the sort described were preferred for the *motetti missales* in Milan during the reign of the Sforzas. They also appear to have been in particular favor in France, as they are frequently found in the works of composers having some sort of connection with the French royal chapel. In addition, they often appear in the great occasional pieces—the so-called state motets[20]—composed expressly for the celebration of important events of a political character, the texts of which were usually written (or assembled) to order either by the humanist scholar-poets associated with the court in question or even by the composers themselves. Although relatively few in number, they were widely cultivated. This was perhaps because of their important extramusical role as an integral part of the pomp and public display that invariably accompanied occasions of state and political negotiations of every sort.

Within these general categories the fairly rapid expansion of textual possibilities found appropriate for the motet is generally associated with Josquin and, to a lesser extent, with other composers of his generation. It may be explained to a degree by an awakening interest in material with an affective, subjective content that would lend itself to the expression of individual words and phrases through musical gestures, both rhetorical and mimetic, inspired by the images and conceits of the text. The Psalms, in particular, set wholly or in part, were often selected for motet composition. Not surprisingly, then, the passages most frequently derived from the Psalter for polyphonic elaboration in the style characteristic of the genre were those

19. Concerning liturgical uses for the motet, defined as a separate compositional genre, see Anthony M. Cummings, "Toward an Interpretation of the Sixteenth-Century Motet," *Journal of the American Musicological Society* 34 (1981): 43–59; also Mitchell P. Brauner, "The Catalogue of Rafaele Panuzzi and the Repertory of the Papal Chapel in the Fifteenth and Sixteenth Centuries," *Journal of Musicology* 8 (1990): 434.
20. The term was introduced into current use by Albert Dunning in his study *Die Staatsmotette, 1480–1555* (Utrecht: A. Oosthoek, 1970).

marked by special emotional poignancy, including reflections of an introspective nature with which the listener could identify in a personal manner.

By the end of the fifteenth century the stylistic norms for the motet as a genre had come to be fairly well defined, and there was a clear tendency for some of the textual types—Marian antiphons and occasional, celebratory verse, for example—to be set with the most traditional of compositional procedures because of the associative significance they had acquired. In all cases, however, a wholly vocal conception (and mode of performance), with all of the parts provided with text, had become a matter of course—which did not preclude, obviously, the possibility of doubling the voices instrumentally. As a consequence, four parts, spread across the most common ranges of the human voice from soprano to bass, were the rule. Three-voice textures did not entirely disappear from the repertory, but they came to be written more and more infrequently (except for internal sections of large works in contrast to the greater overall sonorities) and usually for didactic purposes or in response to particular needs.

⌒⌒ DEFINING THE STYLISTIC PARAMETERS ⌒⌒

Regardless of the number of voice parts involved, all of the contrapuntal procedures that were to be characteristic of the motet as a genre through the end of the sixteenth century had already been established in compositions written by Josquin and his immediate contemporaries as early as the 1470s. Illustrative of these practices and the textures and structures produced by their means is Josquin's *Ave Maria . . . virgo serena* (see Example 15-1), which apparently dates from his Milanese period.[21] The text is a centonization not unlike the kind used in those years for the *motetti missales;* it

21. See Thomas Noblitt, "Die Datierung der Handschrift Mus. MS. 3154 der Staatsbibliothek München," *Die Musikforschung* 27 (1974): 36–56.

Example 15-1. Josquin Desprez, *Ave Maria . . . virgo serena* (mm. 78–119)

For English translation of text, see below.

combines the first two lines of a *prosa* in honor of the Virgin (quoted with its melody) with five strophes of a hymn often included in fifteenth-century books of hours. The Latin verse celebrates the various Marian feasts that had come to be included in the liturgical calendar: Mary's (immaculate) Conception, her Nativity, the Annunciation of the Virgin birth of her son, Jesus, her Purification, and her Assumption.

In Josquin's setting the strophes of the hymn, together with the verses borrowed from the prose, are clearly divided by cadential formulae into discrete sections. The beginnings and endings of individual verses are similarly articulated by cadential figures and by changes in voicing and contrapuntal texture. Continuity is achieved at the same time, however, by simply overlapping the parts contrapuntally. After the opening section, with its quotation of the liturgical melody—which is given as a regular point of imitation moving systematically from superius to bassus—the four voices are frequently combined in pairs that succeed one another either homophonically, imitatively, or in free counterpoint. The resulting duos and trios culminate in passages for full choir, giving further definition to the formal design. In addition, the contrapuntal writing alternates with homophonic declamation, which is used to underscore textual elements of particular significance, casting them into relief against the generally contrapuntal texture and making them more easily understood. The resulting structure may be as seen in the following summary analysis of compositional procedures.

Josquin Desprez: *Ave Maria . . . virgo serena*

1. Ave Maria,	*Hail Mary,*	point of imitation à 4
2. Gratia plena,	*Full of grace,*	point of imitation à 4
3. Dominus tecum	*The Lord is with thee*	point of imitation à 4
4. Virgo serena.	*Serene virgin.*	point of imitation à 4
5. Ave cujus conceptio	*Hail, whose conception*	homophonic bicinia: S & A, T & B
6. Solemni plena gaudio	*Full of great jubilation*	homophonic declamation à 4
Celestia, terrestria	*Fills heaven and earth*	free counterpoint
Nova replet letitia.	*With new joy.*	free counterpoint
7. Ave cujus nativitas	*Hail, whose birth*	point of imitation à 2: S & A
Nostra fuit solemnitas	*Brought us celebration*	point of imitation à 2: T & B
8. Ut lucifer lux oriens	*As Lucifer, the morning star,*	point of imitation à 4
9. Verum solem preveniens.	*Goes before the true sun.*	free counterpoint à 4
10. Ave pia humilitas	*Hail, pious humility,*	homophonic bicinia à 2: S & A
Sine viro fecunditas	*Fruitful without a man,*	homophonic bicinia à 2: T & B
11. Cujus annunciatio	*Whose annunciation*	free counterpoint à 2: S & A
Nostra fuit salvatio.	*Brought us salvation.*	point of imitation à 2: T & B
12. Ave vera virginitas,	*Hail, true virginity,*	homophonic declamation à 4 with shift to ternary meter
Immaculata castitas,	*Immaculate chastity,*	homophonic declamation à 4 in ternary meter
Cujus purificatio	*Whose purification*	homophonic with contrapuntal animation
Nostra fuit purgatio.	*Brought our cleansing.*	homophonic with contrapuntal animation

13. Ave preclara omnibus	*Hail, glorious above all others*	imitation à 4 with voices paired; shift back to binary meter
Angelicis virtutibus	*In all angelic virtues*	repeats music for preceding verse
14. Cujus fuit assumptio	*Whose assumption*	voices paired in free counterpoint
15. Nostra glorificatio.	*Brought our glorification.*	voices paired in free counterpoint
16. O mater Dei, Memento mei, Amen.	*O, Mother of God, Remember me, Amen.*[22]	declamatory homophony à 4

With an arsenal of compositional procedures of such variety and flexibility a composer could provide a musical setting for virtually any text. The point is aptly illustrated by the fact that Josquin himself undertook to dress polyphonically even such unlikely material as the genealogy of Christ—the *Liber generationis Jesu Christi* and *Factum est autem*[23]—in both cases essentially just a series of names linked by the verb "genuit." Even with such limiting material a composer could simply divide the words into manageable syntactic units, select for each of these an appropriate contrapuntal procedure, and articulate the musical sections by means of cadences, rests, and changes in texture. Excessive fragmentation could be avoided by overlapping phrases. Once these relatively simple procedures had been mastered, he could in addition strive for musical coherence by observing modal norms in the individual parts and, where desirable, by infusing the rhythmic and melodic motives introduced from phrase to phrase with aurally discernible motivic relationships.

Psalm Motets

The musical style described above—with reliance, first of all, on syntactically determined points of imitation—came to be used in the course of the sixteenth century for all kinds of motets (properly speaking), regardless of textual type. Moreover, as we shall see, it was adapted to a greater or lesser degree to most other genres of the period. It was especially favored, however, for motets based on texts taken from the Psalter. This style may be seen, for example, in a four-part setting of Psalm 145 (146 in the King James Bible), *Lauda anima mea Dominum*, attributed to Pierre de La

22. The numbers in the poem correspond to the phrases used by Févin in his cyclic Mass based on this motet; see pp. 583–91.
23. For a complete transcription in modern score, see the edition of these works in Josquin Desprez, *Werken*, ed. Albert Smijers et al. (Amsterdam: Vereniging voor Nederlandse Muziek-geschiedenis, 1921–56), *Motetten*, vol. 1, fasc. 6.

Rue (see Example 15-2),[24] which combines features of the traditional polyphonic elaboration of the liturgical Psalm tones with the various and contrasting compositional procedures that are exemplified by Josquin's *Ave Maria . . . virgo serena*.

The inclusion of the entire text of the Psalm together with continuous and unmistakable references to the traditional plainchant suggests that the piece may have been intended for liturgical use. However, the only commonly prescribed place for Psalm 145 (aside from the weekly repetition of the entire Psalter observed only in monastic communities) is in the Office for the Dead. Surprisingly, the plainchant citations refer to the relatively rare *tonus peregrinus* (the "wandering" or "frolicsome" tone), which usually had less somber connotations and is considerably more elaborate than the simple formula usually employed in that Office because of its alternation between

24. For a complete transcription of the motet in modern score, see Nigel Davison, ed., *Vier Motetten*, Das Chorwerk, vol. 91 (Wolfenbüttel: Möseler, 1964), 16–23, no. 91, no. 3.

EXAMPLE 15-2. Pierre de La Rue, *Lauda anima mea Dominum*, Psalm 145 (mm. 1–24)

Praise the Lord, O my soul. While I live will I praise the Lord; I will sing praises unto my
God while I have any being . . .

a and g as a reciting pitch and its relatively lengthy terminations.[25] In addition, neither the Doxology, which was always sung with a Psalm used liturgically, nor the "Requiem aeternam," appended to Psalm 145 in the Office for the Dead, was included in the polyphonic setting.

The composition opens, nonetheless, with the psalmodic formula intoned by the tenor alone (with c as the note of formulaic inflexion rather than the b-flat seen in the *Liber usualis*), followed immediately by homophonic declamation in all four parts for the remainder of the initial phrase. In fact, the composer continues to cite the liturgical Psalm tone throughout the work, albeit with increasing degrees of coloration and elaboration. He presents it primarily in the tenor but gives it to the superius toward the end of the *prima pars* (mm. 78–103)—the first of two independent sections—and involves other voices as well whenever he turns to the syntactic imitation that plays such a fundamental role in the contrapuntal facture of the motet.

The other parts, meanwhile, are woven around the cantus firmus material in ever varying contrapuntal textures. The contrasting melismatic figure in the superius (mm. 6ff.), cascading downward from d' through the entire octave, is taken up imitatively by altus and bassus and may be a mimetic gesture intended to illustrate the word "laudabo" (I shall praise). It is answered by an ascending figure (a rough inversion of the first, mm. 20ff.) associated with the word "psallam" (I shall sing) that may also have expressive significance. Both figures recur throughout the motet, however, contributing, like the Psalm tone itself, to the motivic coherence of the composition.

The second verse of the Psalm is presented as a point of imitation in three parts based on the Psalm tone (mm. 29ff.). Subsequently, the composer makes use of homophonic declamation—first in two voices (mm. 61ff.) then, briefly, in three (mm. 91–93)—further points of imitation based on the Psalm tone (e.g., mm. 53ff., 73ff., from bassus to superius, altus, and tenor), and passages in free counterpoint in three and four parts (e.g., mm. 36–52), one of which brings the *prima pars* to a close. In the *secunda pars* he features, in addition, two passages with two parts in close imitation, the first of which opens the section with a lengthy duo, while the second (starting in m. 148) leads to a short spurt of homophonic declamation (for "et vias peccatorum"). This he dissolves in turn (like the "ways of the wicked") with a shift to ternary meter (by means of a sequialtera proportion) into a freely contrapuntal conclusion that presents the triumphant final verse of the Psalm, "Regnabit . . . " ("thy Lord will reign forever, O Zion, and thy God through all generations") with an appropriately joyful dancelike swing and the fullest sonorities possible.

Increasingly, then, a syntactic approach to composition in which imitative writing played by far the most fundamental role came to predominate in the motets of the sixteenth century. However, it did not displace immediately—or ever, for that matter, entire-

25. See "Tonus peregrinus," *The New Grove Dictionary of Music,* 19:67, and compare, in the *Liber usualis,* the simple recitation tone given for the Office of the Dead, p. 1776, with the formula for the *tonus peregrinus,* p. 117.

ly—more venerable compositional strategies. There is a sharp contrast, for example, between La Rue's setting of Psalm 145, for which liturgical use is surely conceivable and was perhaps intended, and Josquin's massive setting of Psalm 50, *Miserere mei, Deus.*

One of the most widely circulated of the Psalm motets ascribed to him, it was included in eight prints and as many manuscripts, mostly from German and Italian centers—most notably, perhaps, a carefully copied and beautifully decorated collection of motets prepared in 1518 for Lorenzo de' Medici, duke of Urbino, apparently on the occasion of his marriage to the French noblewoman Madelaine de la Tour d'Auvergne.[26] With its intensely dramatic repetitions of the supplication with which it opens (and its full, five-voice texture), it surely cannot have been conceived for routine liturgical use, either at Lauds on Holy Saturday or during the Offices for the Dead;[27] the scale to which it was constructed appears much too massive for such a purpose.

The recurring formula "Miserere mei, Deus"—treated in this work, text and music, like a cantus firmus, even though only two pitches are involved—is moved stepwise from e at the top of its range down through an octave in the *prima pars*, back up through the octave to e in the *secunda pars*, and down again a fifth to a in the final section. The "cantus firmus" voice, with its considerable symbolic significance and expressive power, transforms the piece into a festal work on a grand scale, and that appears to have been Josquin's intention.[28] The exceptional compositional means and extraordinary rhetorical effect were undoubtedly the composer's response to a special request from a ducal patron, Ercole d'Este, probably made in 1503 or 1504.[29] At the same time, although not comparable in scope to Josquin's festal work, La Rue's *Lauda anima mea Dominum* is a considerably more complex and elaborate treatment of both text and chant formula than the sixteenth-century Psalm settings prepared specifically for liturgical use (see pp. 556–60).

⟋⟍ CANTUS FIRMUS MOTETS ⟋⟍

Large-scale celebratory motets in the manner of Busnoys, Okeghem, and Regis in particular were massive in conception and design with five-part textures, a borrowed liturgical cantus firmus, bitextual implications, and considerable mensural and struc-

26. The manuscript has been edited with a complete facsimile and an elaborate commentary by Edward E. Lowinsky, *The Medici Codex of 1518: A Choirbook of Motets Dedicated to Lorenzo de' Medici, Duke of Urbino*, 3 vols., Monuments of Renaissance Music, vols. 3–5 (Chicago: University of Chicago Press, 1968); Josquin's *Miserere mei* is no. 41 (4:270–95); it is also found in Josquin, *Werken*, ed. Smijers, *Motetten*, vol. 2, fasc. 21.
27. For the specific liturgical uses prescribed for this Psalm, see the *Liber usualis*, 652, 714, 774, 1763, and 1800.
28. See, however, in this connection, Lester D. Brothers, "On Music and Meditation in the Renaissance: Contemplative Prayer and Josquin's *Miserere*," *Journal of Musicological Research* 12 (1992): 157–87.
29. Concerning the origins of this motet, see Patrick P. Macey, "Josquin's *Miserere mei, Deus*: Context, Structure, and Influence" (Ph.D. diss., University of California, Berkeley, 1985), 15–26; the author explores as well in great detail the rhetorical and expressive features of the work.

tural intricacy, as we have seen. Such works never completely disappeared from the repertory, although they receded gradually into the background in the course of the sixteenth century. They continued to be written, naturally enough, for those special occasions with which they were linked by tradition. The use of cantus firmus and canonic imitation thus came to signal circumstances of exceptional social significance or liturgical solemnity by enhancing at once the aural brilliance and the symbolic and/or allegorical implications of the musical setting. Such devices are to be seen, first of all, in the elaborate polyphonic treatment given certain plainchants, especially those with Marian associations that were used for processional and votive purposes. They were also adopted with some frequency for occasional works with a celebratory and/or political purpose.

Typical in most respects of such pieces is Josquin's five-voice setting of the sequence in honor of the Virgin Mary, *Inviolata, integra et casta* (see Example 15-3).[30] Written, apparently, considerably later in his life than the *Ave Maria . . . virgo serena*, it also circulated even more widely, having been included in ten manuscripts and eight prints before the end of the century. The liturgical chant has been divided into three segments, each of which has been treated as a separate *pars* of the motet. To each of the first two *partes* have been allotted two pairs of lines from the sequence—the second with a different order for the verses than that found in the Roman liturgy—and to the third the supplicatory acclamations with which it concludes.[31] Typically, Josquin incorporated the traditional melody into his polyphony together with the

30. For a transcription in modern score, see the *Werken*, ed. Smijers, *Motetten*, vol. 2, fasc. 25; also Lowinsky, ed., *The Medici Codex*, 4:231–40.
31. The difference in the order of verses between the motet and the chant upon which it is based may be seen from a comparison of the polyphonic setting with the sequence as given by the *Liber usualis*, 1861.

EXAMPLE 15-3. Josquin Desprez, *Inviolata, integra et casta* (mm. 1–21)

Inviolate, pure, and chaste is Maria . . .

text of the chant. He also gave it weight and substance by presenting it not only in regular long values (semibreves and breves, mostly) but also in canonic duplication between tenor II (at pitch) and altus (at the fifth above).

The parallel repetitions that are the hallmark of a sequence melody are not reflected in the polyphonic form, even though the chant has been woven into the surrounding contrapuntal fabric by means of syntactic imitation. Rather, the starting point of the cantus firmus is continually shifting with respect to the binary tactus of the polyphony and is accompanied each time by a different series of contrapuntal figures. Some of these melodic and rhythmic patterns, like the descending passage moving stepwise through an entire tenth first heard in the superius (mm. 4–7), are used either sequentially or repetitively—as in the close imitation (dissolving into parallel tenths) between bassus and superius (mm. 7–14)—thus contributing to a sense of musical coherence.

Each of the first two *partes* opens with a point of imitation based on the phrase of the chant associated with its text at that point (involving all five voices in the first section and four of the five in the second), building the sonority from a solitary voice to the full complement with which each closes. The second *pars*, although it opens with a fairly lengthy duo (twelve breves), suggests acceleration with respect to the first by a more consistent use of smaller note values, a shorter time interval separating the entries of the imitative voices (two breves instead of three), and a more concise exposition of the four lines of text (forty-two breves instead of sixty-three).

By contrast—and undoubtedly for rhetorical effect—the reiterated supplications with which the third *pars* begin are solemnly presented in extended values in all five voices, and here the melodic repetitions of the chant are at last audibly mirrored in the polyphonic setting. The climax of the work as a whole comes with the final laudatory phrase, "inviolata permansisti." Here the composer maintains the full texture of the opening of the *pars* but sets the passage off by greater animation. The kinetic energy of its melodic and rhythmic figures is dissipated only gradually after the altus reaches its final c in measure 32, and that pitch and its lower fifth (or octave) are sustained like an organ point through the last eight breves of the composition.

Similar in many ways in both design and conception is a representative motet from the "Eton Choirbook," a five-voice setting of the Marian antiphon *Salve regina* (see Example 15-4) attributed to John Browne (fl. ca. 1490).[32] Even more than Josquin's *Inviolata*, Browne's motet looks back to the solemn polyphonic antiphons of the late fifteenth century in the manner of Regis. Unlike his Continental counterparts, however, Browne—who is typical in this regard of his English contemporaries—has made no use of the traditional liturgical melody beyond the initial salutation of the motet, "Salve," where it is heard an eleventh above pitch in the treble.[33]

---

32. Concerning the composer, see John Caldwell, "Browne, John," *The New Grove Dictionary of Music*, 3: 345; for a transcription of the motet in modern score, see Frank L. Harrison, ed., *The Eton Choirbook*, Musica Britannica, vols. 10–12 (London: Stainer and Bell, 1956–61), 10:124–30.

33. The relatively unusual transposition comes about because the final of the motet is F with b-fa in the signature for the four lower voices, whereas the antiphon, although classified as mode 5, has its final on C.

Instead, like most of the composers of the Eton repertory, he has added as a tenor cantus firmus the melody (but not the text) of a different antiphon. In this case it is *Maria ergo unxit*, a chant prescribed for use at the Mandatum, the ritual by which Jesus's washing of his disciples' feet is commemorated during the Vespers Mass on Maundy Thursday,[34] perhaps indicating that the motet was intended for use during that liturgically significant period of the year.

Stated twice in its entirety with very few changes—such as added passing tones and the deletion of repeated pitches—the borrowed melody (identified by crosses in the example) is recognizable as a cantus firmus only because it moves consistently in longer values than those found in the other parts. It drops out—independently, it would seem, of the tenor part—after its first incise as the texture is reduced to three voices (mm. 7–19 and 23–34) and again at the end of the first full statement (mm.

34. The ceremony is so named because of the beginning of the antiphon with which it begins, *Mandatum novum do vobis* ("I give unto you a new commandment").

EXAMPLE 15-4. John Browne, *Salve, Regina* (mm. 1–6, 23–41)

Hail O queen, mother of mercy. . . . We cry unto thee, exiled sons of Eve; unto thee do we sigh, groaning and weeping in this vale of tears . . .

76–104) for a three-voice setting of four verses troped into the antiphon text. In its second statement it is interrupted twice more by duos and trios (mm. 116–44 and 156–81), to which are set each time further tropes—rhymed quatrains inserted into the liturgical text. When the full textures and the cantus firmus return for the final phrases, the borrowed antiphon is treated a bit more freely than previously, especially in the approach to the final cadence.

Helping to articulate the structure of the music in accordance with that of the text are the usual devices: clear breaks produced by cadential patterns; sustained final sonorities with a suspension of normal rhythmic and melodic activity (in mm. 6, 21, 34, 75, 104, 115, 145, and 183, for example); changes in texture from four or five voices to two or three and vice versa; and the accompanying shifts in vocal orchestration from higher ranges (m. 7) to lower ones (mm. 23 and 76) and from outer parts (m. 116) to inner ones (m. 156). The troped sections in particular are clearly set off by the reduced scoring, and the antiphon text is similarly divided in the opening section of the motet, giving rise to a certain symmetry between the two main divisions of the composition. However, the contrasts achieved by Josquin in his *Ave Maria . . . virgo serena* by shifts in contrapuntal technique from imitation to free counterpoint to homophonic declamation are largely wanting here. Particularly striking is the sparse use made of imitative counterpoint, points of which occur only in sections for two or three voices, if at all, and are very brief in duration.

Browne's setting of the *Salve regina* is typical of the repertory of the "Eton Choirbook" for its length, its clear sectionalization, and its timbral articulation in contrasting full textures with segments for reduced forces. It is in rather sharp contrast, nonetheless, to a four-voice motet, *Ave Maria mater Dei*,[35] attributed in the same collection to William Cornysh (ca. 1465–1523).[36] The devotional text of supplication to the Virgin Mary apparently has no established place in the traditional liturgy, and the composer seems to have eschewed as well a plainchant cantus firmus that might have had symbolic or referential value. Instead, he has set the text rather simply phrase by phrase, articulating the musical structure lightly by changes in texture and voicing—moving initially, for example, from four voices to three and then two before coming back to four. Virtually absent from his counterpoint is any hint of imitative writing, and the relatively lengthy melismatic "amen" (for such an unusually compendious piece) brings the work to a close with full sonorities in free counterpoint.

Of Josquin's immediate Continental contemporaries, Johannes Mouton, who spent the last twelve years of his career in the service of the French court, was perhaps the composer most inclined to make use of borrowed cantus firmi and strictly imitative procedures to create works of the kind described. A skilled contrapuntist,

---

35. For a transcription of the motet, see *Eton Choirbook*, ed. Harrison, 12:57–58. Harrison's transcription has been reprinted in Claude V. Palisca, ed., *Norton Anthology of Western Music*, 1st ed., 2 vols. (New York: Norton, 1980), 1:108.
36. Concerning Cornysh, see David Greer, *The New Grove Dictionary of Music*, 4:795–96.

he apparently took pleasure in the construction of elaborate canons for solemn occasions, using the device to generate works in five, six, or even eight independent parts that are impressive both for their complex facture and for their rich sonorities.

Representative of his works in this style is his five-voice setting (in a single *pars*) of *Per lignum salvi facti sumus*, a processional antiphon prescribed by the liturgy for both Good Friday and Easter Sunday.[37] It was included, together with five very substantial motets by Josquin (his *Miserere mei* and *Inviolata, integra et casta* among them) and nine other motets by Mouton in the "Medici Codex" of 1518. One of those nine is a composition for eight voices; of the remainder one is for six, three are for five—all of them antiphon settings—and four are for four voices.

In *Per lignum servi*, typically, the liturgical melody is notated with minimal melodic embellishment for the altus at the upper fourth and—reversing Josquin's procedure in *Inviolata, integra et casta*—duplicated in strict imitation in the tenor at pitch only a semibreve later, thus providing both the contrapuntal complexity and the full sonorities thought appropriate for the venerable Easter liturgy (see Example 15-5). Like Josquin, once again, Mouton has opened the piece with a point of imitation (between cantus and the noncanonical tenor II), only gradually building to the full five-voice texture (mm. 1–10). The syntactic elements of the text are clearly articulated by means of contrapuntal cadences—either to the modal final (G-Mixolydian) or the confinal (m. 40)—despite the attenuating effect of the contrapuntal overlap between phrases. Rhythmic deceleration and homophonic declama-

---

37. For a transcription in modern score, see *Medici Codex*, ed. Lowinsky, 4:246–50, and cf. the *Liber usualis*, 746.

EXAMPLE 15-5. Johannes Mouton, *Per lignum salvi facti sumus* (mm. 43–65)

[By the wood are we saved . . . the fruit of the tree seduced us;] the Son of God redeemed us, alleluia.

tion (without, however, abandoning the canonic imitation!) combine to throw into rhetorical relief the words "Filius Dei" (mm. 43–53), the culminating reference to the Son of God who had brought redemption by means of the cross and whose Passion and Resurrection were being celebrated.

That this manner of treating important liturgical chants on festive liturgical occasions had considerable currency still through much of the sixteenth century—and that this composition was judged to be a particularly effective polyphonic elaboration of one such melody—is suggested by the fact that it has been transmitted in six manuscripts and three printed sources.[38]

CEREMONIAL MOTETS

More typical of Mouton's production generally, and that of his colleagues and successors in the royal French chapel, are the four-voice texture that had become the norm and the clearly articulated, nicely balanced musical structures that were facilitated by the more modest format (as was evident already in the discussion of Josquin's *Ave Maria . . . virgo serena*). Characteristic in this regard is his ceremonial motet *Non nobis, Domine*, written for a royal birth in 1510 (see Example 15-6).[39] Here the composer made use of a refrain-like acclamation to help shape the two *partes* of the conventional formal design. "Vivat rex!"—the traditional salutation for a newborn heir to the throne—occurs midway through the text as well as at the end of each of the two principal sections of the work. Similarly, the melodic material used for the first presentation of these words is repeated when they recur halfway through the second section (cf. mm. 31–48 and 108–24) and is recalled as well—though with the melodic material modified for presentation in homophonic declamation and a shift to ternary meter—at the close of both *partes* (cf. mm. 72–86 and 150–71). In this manner the composer has made of this slight but significant bit of text (taken with the phrase introducing the acclamation, "ergo clamemus in coelum") a means both of formal division and of climactic conclusion.

Greater attention to the intelligibility of the text such as that found in Mouton's *Non nobis, Domine* is rather typical of celebratory compositions. Exceptional in this regard, however, are those motets for which an appropriate cantus firmus was adopted for symbolic purposes as the structural foundation, giving rise to the expanded sonorities and contrapuntal devices that had become traditional for such works. In some instances this was perhaps because the verses expressly written to mark occasions of state were necessarily unfamiliar to the intended audience and yet depended to a degree for their effect upon a fundamental grasp of their meaning. Those pieces are often characterized, as in this instance, by clear declamation of individual words, careful observance and articulation of syntactic units, and, as has been seen, changes in rhythm and/or texture to give declamatory emphasis to key elements of the text. Also used are mimetic musical ges-

38. See the concordances in Lowinsky's commentary, *Medici Codex*, 3:184.
39. For a transcription in modern score, see Jean Mouton, *Fünf Motetten*, ed. Paul Kast, Das Chorwerk, no. 76 (Wolfenbüttel: Möseler, 1959), 1–8.

EXAMPLE 15-6. Johannes Mouton, *Non nobis, Domine* (mm. 112–24, 150–71)

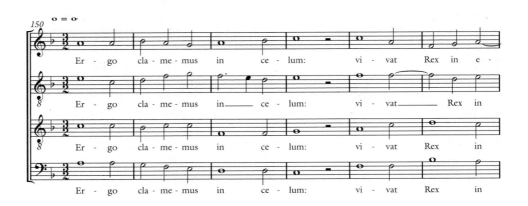

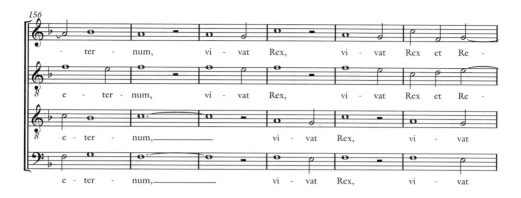

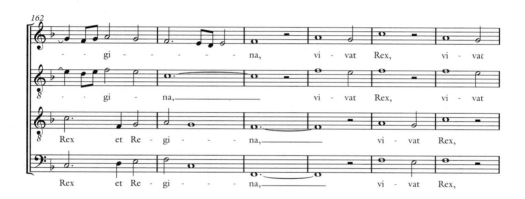

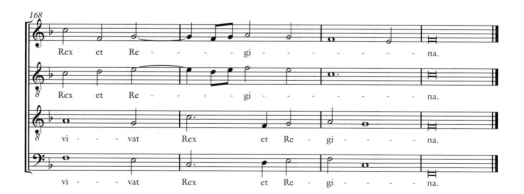

Therefore let us cry unto the heavens, may the king live forever!

tures capable of evoking some of its basic conceits. By contrast, the liturgical texts most frequently set were known to everyone. Since they were quickly recognized and their general meaning understood even by those who knew no Latin beyond what might be absorbed through regular exposure to the liturgy, they could be treated more freely.

The same is also true to a degree of compositions with possible liturgical connections when their texts are relatively unfamiliar or have been combined in a novel way. Intelligibility of the words sung may have been a concern for Mouton, for example, in the composition of his Christmas motet *Noe, noe, noe psallite*, the kind of piece that could well have been sung in a ceremonial context at the termination of a Mass or even to substitute for one of its liturgical chants.[40] The text is a centonization combining rather disparate elements from the liturgy: an antiphon for Lauds at the Nativity of the Lord ("Angelus ad pastores ait"),[41] which would not have been frequently heard, and verses 9–10 of Psalm 24.

This motet is strikingly similar in musical style to *Non nobis, Domine*, in large part because of the recurring homophonic refrain "noe, noe," (first heard in mm. 40ff. and differing melodically from the figure used with the same words for the point of imitation with which the motet begins). Clearly declaimed and easily recognizable, it punctuates the structure with a clear break and a change of texture while simultaneously furnishing an element of musical cohesion. Significantly, for this, the liturgical feast perhaps most frequented by Christian laity, the composer has achieved something of a popular touch by means of the yuletide acclamation "noe," which was apparently derived from the vernacular. It is clearly possible that the simple melodic figure to which it is repeatedly sung may have been familiar through its association with a monophonic tune, even to those who resided at the royal court.

By musical example, as well as by precept through his considerable didactic activity, Mouton apparently passed on to other composers with whom he had contact— relatively important figures such as Lhéritier, Verdelot, Willaert, and the Italian Constanzo Festa—a similar concern for carefully fashioned musical structures. Since most of these masters subsequently worked for long periods in one or more of the major musical establishments in Italy, these same compositional procedures were taught in turn to Italian musicians. Moreover, the ever greater accessibility of polyphonic music resulting from its relatively rapid dissemination in printed collections provided numerous models that could be used to illustrate in notated form the contrapuntal techniques being passed from one generation to the next.

The degree to which some of the younger composers relied upon models from composers of the French court is reflected in Costanzo Festa's setting of *Quis dabit oculis*, the lament upon the death of the queen of France, Anne of Brittany, in 1514. Although Festa entered the papal choir as early as 1517, he is believed to have been associated with the French chapel at the time. This would explain his access to the same text that had been adopted for motet composition earlier by Mouton, presumably in his role as a cler-

40. For a transcription in modern score, see Claude V. Palisca, ed., *Norton Anthology of Western Music*, 2d ed., 2 vols. (New York: Norton, 1988), 1:130.
41. See the *Liber usualis*, 397.

ic in the royal chapel. Correspondences between the two compositions are significant enough to raise the possibility of a direct personal relationship between the two men, perhaps that of student to teacher.[42] This suggests in turn that a budding young Italian composer of the period, such as Festa, would have found it both appropriate and useful to complete his instruction in composition with a master in the employ of the French court. Further dissemination of the compositional procedures embodied in such a work is demonstrated in this instance by the inclusion of Festa's motet, with changes in the text making it suitable for ceremonies ensuing upon the death of Maximilian I of Austria (d. 1519)—and an erroneous attribution to Ludwig Senfl—in a printed collection brought out by the Nuremberg publisher Johannes Ott in 1538.[43]

TEXTUAL RHETORIC AND MUSICAL EXPRESSION

Josquin's influence, although felt all over Europe, was apparently not as marked in Italy, where the composers of the royal French chapel held unusual sway, as it was, apparently, on the Iberian peninsula or in Germany, where his motets continued to be published through the sixteenth century. Nevertheless, he was clearly a key figure in the stylistic definition of the genre. One of his most signal contributions in this regard is believed to have been an approach to setting text that was informed increasingly not only by its syntactic order and its declamatory qualities but also by its literal meanings, its rhetorical emphases, and even its affective implications. His reputation in that connection is clearly warranted, certainly, in light of works such as his *Miserere mei, Deus.*

Perhaps one of the most striking examples of the compositional style that could result from orienting the compositional procedures then current to such expressive ends is *Absalon, fili mi,* the setting of David's lament for his beloved but rebellious son that is attributed to Josquin in two of the three known sources (see Example 15-7).[44] The brief text, chosen without doubt for its subjective and affective qualities, was drawn not from the liturgy but directly from the Old Testament, primarily the his-

---

42. Concerning Festa, see Alexander Main, *The New Grove Dictionary of Music,* 6:501–4.
43. Concerning the relationships among the three motets in question, see Alexander Main, "Maximilian's Second-hand Funeral Motet," *Musical Quarterly* 47 (1962): 172ff.
44. In spite of the attributions to Josquin in the surviving sources, his authorship has been questioned by both Joshua Rifkin, "Problems of Authorship in Josquin: Some Impolitic Observations, with a Postscript on *Absalon, fili mi,*" in *Proceedings of the International Josquin Symposium, Utrecht 1989,* ed. Willem Elders and Frits de Haen (Utrecht: Vereniging voor Nederlandse Muziekgeschiedenis, 1991), 45–52, and Jaap van Benthem, "Lazarus versus Absalom: About Fiction and Fact in the Netherlands Motet," *Tijdschrift van der Vereniging voor Nederlandse Muziekgeschiedenis* 37 (1989): 54–82. They have proposed Pierre de La Rue as the composer; however, Nigel Davison, "*Absalom fili mi* Reconsidered," *Tijdschrift van de Koninklijke Vereniging voor Nederlandse Musiekgeschiedenis* 46 (1996): 42–56, has carefully reviewed all the arguments and concludes that Josquin is at least as likely to have composed the motet as is La Rue.

EXAMPLE 15-7. Josquin Deprez or Pierre de La Rue(?), *Absalon, fili mi* (mm. 69–85)

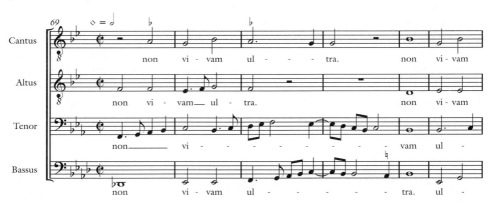

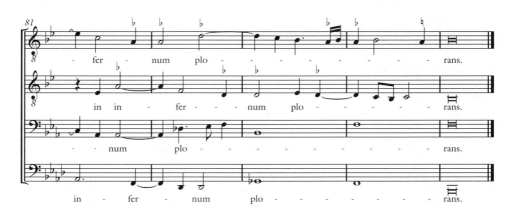

Let me live no longer but descend into hell, weeping.

torical account of 2 Kings 18:33 but with echoes of Psalm 37:35 and even Job 7:16.[45]

The exceptionally low range in which the motet has been notated,[46] together with the unusual key signatures—two fa's for the upper pair of voices, three for the tenor, and four for the bassus!—should be viewed as expressive in intent, signaling the depth of David's despair and the extreme alteration of his affective state. These generate in turn extraordinary points of cadential closure that include B-flat (treated, surprisingly, as the modal final), E-flat, and a Phrygian formula on G (mm. 8–9 between altus and bassus) with an A-flat. Similarly, the repeated syllabic exclamations "Absalom, my son" with which the motet begins gradually dissolve into running melismatic figures that are suggestive of a protracted wail of lamentation, taking up nearly half of the piece and overlapping with the next phrase of text, "Quis det ut moriar pro te" ("that I might die for thee").

The most graphic of the eloquent mimetic devices lavished upon this work come with the final phrase, "let me live no longer but descend into hell, weeping" (mm. 52–69). The descent is illustrated literally by a figure proceeding by consecutive falling thirds passed imitatively from voice to voice and culminating in a suggestive melismatic flourish for "plorans" (mm. 65–68). In the process the part-writing is so conceived as to generate, by means of downward semitone inflection, fictive hexachords on increasingly remote scale degrees, thus introducing into the written counterpoint both D-flat and G-flat. Finally, as if to emphasize the dramatic poignancy of this unusual passage, as extreme in its departure from conventional norms as the grief of David himself, it is repeated literally to conclude the composition.

A more skillful use of the compositional procedures of the period for expressive purposes would be difficult to imagine, and with Josquin being the putative author in the minds of his contemporaries, his impact upon the compositional style of the sixteenth century precisely in this respect should not be underestimated. Northern composers of the next generation tended to be more restrained in their use of rhetorical and affective expression, however. Fairly typical in this respect is Clemens (non Papa) (Jacob Clement, ca. 1510–15 to 1555 or 1556), whose some 233 motets are mostly based on liturgical and biblical texts, including Psalms, canticles, Old Testament prophets, and New Testament passages concerning Christ and his mother Mary.[47] Among the number, however, are at least four ceremonial pieces, all of them with specific textual references either to the household of the Emperor Charles V or to one of his greatest generals, Philippe de Croy, duke of Aerschot, whom Clemens apparently served as chapelmaster for a time.[48]

---

45. Similar in textual character and in musical style is Josquin's setting of King David's lament for Saul and Jonathan, *Planxit autem David*; see Jeremy Noble, *The New Grove Dictionary of Music*, 9:721.
46. This is assuming that the clefs and registers of the manuscript source, Royal 8.G.VII of the British Library in London, were original with Josquin rather than the higher ranges of the German prints; cf. Helmut Osthoff, *Josquin Desprez*, 2 vols. (Tutzing: Scheider, 1962–65), 2:108ff.
47. See Willem Elders, "Clemens," *The New Grove Dictionary of Music*, 4:476–80.
48. For a detailed discussion of Clemens's ceremonial motets, see Albert Dunning, *Die Staatsmotette, 1480–1555*, 190–203.

One of these "state" motets was occasioned by the duke's death in 1549, for which a lament in his honor, *O quam moesta dies*, was set by Clemens for five voices (see Example 15-8). In providing for a musical declamation of this humanistically inspired text, the composer follows fairly closely the conventional rhythms of the Latin. By contrast he makes a clear grasp of the verbal syntax relatively difficult by his use of numerous overlapping repetitions of short segments of text and a virtually continuous contrapuntal fabric; clearly articulated cadences are surprisingly rare and usually relatively weak. In a texture that is almost relentlessly contrapuntal (often in fact imitative), two exceptional passages stand out. A brief allusion to the archaic device of *fauxbourdon* for the words "qua morte Philippus" ("[the day] in which Philip died," mm. 125–26) may be meant to convey the egregious nature of the loss.[49] More striking still to the ear, at the final supplication for eternal peace for the dead man's soul, are the homophonic texture and rhythmic stasis introduced rather abruptly for "eterna statuat requiescere pace" ("decree rest in everlasting peace," mm. 164–69).

Aside from these two brief passages, rhetorical or symbolic devices meant to be expressive of the text are rather restrained. Breaking the verses into short fragments and giving some of them particular emphasis through repetition—for example, "O quam moesta dies" (mm. 1–18) or "adsunt tristia quaeque" (mm. 36–47)—may have been intended to suggest the power of grief to interrupt rational discourse, as in *Absalon, fili mi*. The key signature (with both B- and E-flat) is unusual for a work with a final on F. Although not as extreme as in the motet just cited, its very pres-

---

49. Concerning the possibly symbolic significance of *fauxbourdon* in the fifteenth and sixteenth centuries, see Willem Elders, "G. Dufay's Concept of Fauxbourdon," *Revue belge de musicologie* 43 (1989): 173–95.

EXAMPLE 15-8. Clemens (non Papa), *O quam moesta dies* (mm. 157–76)

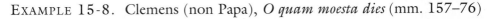

May the redeemer decree [that Philip] shall rest in the company of the saints in eternal peace.

ence may have been no less symbolic of the grief-altered emotional state described by the text.

In musical terms the practical result is to establish B-fa as an irregular confinal with the same species of fourth and fifth above it as are found above the final, and it functions very much in that way, both in shaping the ductus of the melodic lines and at cadences (including the one used to close the *prima pars*). If, as it seems, the intention was to give particular prominence to motivic figures characteristic of mode 6, the composer may have shared Zarlino's opinion as to its nature: that it is appropriate for "works that are grave and pious, that express commiseration, and adapt it to subjects of a tearful sort."[50]

There is some indication, as well, of a compositional concern for musical coherence. This is most evident in the similarity of the melodic materials used at the opening of each of the two *partes*, but it is more pervasively, if more subtly, felt in the many phrases cast within the fourth above either F or B-fa, especially in superius and tenor. Clemens's motet exemplifies, then, the marriage achieved in the course of the sixteenth century between compositional procedures that are motivically coherent, one might even say organic, in the way in which the melodic and rhythmic ideas appear to relate to one another, and those that are capable of interpreting the text, as it were, in declamatory, syntactic, rhetorical, mimetic, and even affective terms.[51] In this sense it reflects an important development of the first half of the sixteenth century. The motet, which clearly had come to dominate the sacred music of the period, became the genre in which these compositional techniques were first nurtured and then made to serve so effectively the exposition of the text.

50. See Gioseffo Zarlino, *Le Istitutioni harmoniche* (Venice, 1558, reprint, New York: Broude Brothers, 1965), Quarta Parte, Cap. 23, "Del Sesto Modo."
51. Concerning the various levels on which music and text were related to one another in the composition of the fifteenth and sixteenth centuries, see Perkins, "Toward a Theory of Text-Music Relations in the Music of the Renaissance," to be published in the Proceedings of the First International Conference on Gilles de Bins, dit Binchois, held at The Graduate School and University Center of the City University of New York, October 31–November 1, 1995.

CHAPTER 16

↗

Liturgical Polyphony for the Office

INTRODUCTION

There is perhaps no better evidence for the ever more common use of polyphony in the liturgy during the period of interest to us here than the multiplication of settings for Psalms, hymns, and Magnificats from the late fifteenth century on. Taken together, the large numbers of polyphonic compositions based on texts—and chants—in these three categories strongly suggest that polyphonic performance at Vesper services on major feast days had become a matter of course for virtually every musical chapel, ecclesiastical or secular, with the requisite number of trained singers. Such a development is not difficult to explain since Vespers, like Mass, was a service usually attended by the laity of the church on days of particular liturgical significance.

A broader scope for polyphony in the day-to-day celebration of the liturgy is further indicated by settings of yet other canonical texts, although for some of these the number of compositions remained relatively small. Compositional types that can be so described, but that had achieved nonetheless a distinct generic identity (even if only as a subgenre of the motet), included the Te Deum (traditionally sung at the end of Lauds but also as a hymn of thanksgiving on any special occasion), the Lamentations of Jeremiah (sung at Matins during Holy Week), and the Passions (also sung during Holy Week as Gospel lessons at Mass).

⌒⌐ HYMNS ⌐⌒

As we have seen, the earliest liturgically ordered cycle of polyphonic hymns for Vespers dates back to the late fourteenth century, and the musical sources of the fifteenth give ample evidence that cultivation of the genre was continuous from that point forward. That polyphonic hymns continued to be destined primarily for liturgical use is also clear simply from the order in which they were usually entered in the sources; most collections comprise the major feasts of the Temporale (semiduplex and higher) in calendaric order, beginning with Advent, to which were added the most important of the saints' days, including—especially in Germany—those of special local significance.[1] If, as is commonly believed, Du Fay, who was apparently the first to have written single-handedly a cycle of polyphonic hymns for major feasts of the entire year, actually completed that task as early as the 1430s, his immediate contemporaries were apparently not quick to follow his example. Not until the sixteenth century does one find in increasing numbers similar cycles attributable to a single composer.

Significantly, the great majority of all the musicians whose liturgical hymn cycles are known to us spent a major part of their career on the Italian peninsula, and it was undoubtedly for Italian institutions that most of their work in the genre was done. One of the first to follow Du Fay's lead appears to have been Johannes Martini, who, as we have seen, served the Este court in Ferrara from 1473 until his death in 1497–98 and whose *Liber primus hymnorum*—published posthumously in Venice by Petrucci in 1507 (and, unfortunately, now lost)—was the first such collection to have been printed. Some of Martini's hymn settings have survived in the manuscripts for double chorus prepared for the chapel of Duke Ercole I d'Este in 1481 that were cited earlier in connection with antiphonal psalmody for polyphonic performance. Divided between these two choirbooks, with even-numbered verses in the one, odd-numbered in the other, are eight hymns for Vespers written by Martini and Johannes Brebis, his colleague in the ducal chapel.[2]

Several decades then elapsed before Carpentras (Elzéar Genet), who served intermittently at the papal court in Rome between 1508 and 1526, published his collected polyphonic hymns in the mid-1530s.[3] Costanzo Festa, who was also associated with the papal chapel from 1517 until his death in 1545, had likewise completed by the mid- to late-1530s a polyphonic cycle that would remain in the repertory of Roman choirs until the end of the century.[4] In Florence Francesco Corteccia, who spent his entire career in the musical institutions, ecclesiastical and courtly, of his native city, composed a cycle of polyphonic hymns in the early 1540s.[5] In Venice, similarly, Adrian Willaert, chapelmaster at the Basilica of San Marco from 1527 until his demise in 1562, published a collection for liturgical use in 1542 under the title *Hymnorum musica*.[6] And Jacquet de Mantua (Jacques Colebault), who served in that

1. See Tom Ward, "Hymn," *The New Grove Dictionary of Music*, 8:843–44. For the meaning of the liturgical categories such as "semi-duplex," see above, p. 235, n. 34.

2. The codices in question are MSS α.M.1.11 and 12; see Lewis Lockwood, *Music in Renaissance Ferrara, 1400–1505: The Creation of a Musical Center in the Fifteenth Century* (Cambridge, Mass.: Harvard University Press, 1984), 251; cf. the *Census-Catalogue of Manuscript Sources of Polyphonic Music*, ed. Charles Hamm and Herbert Kellman, 5 vols. (Neuhausen-Stuttgart: Hänssler-Verlag, 1979–88), 2:166–67.

3. See Howard M. Brown, "Carpentras," *The New Grove Dictionary of Music*, 3:820.

4. See Alexander Main, "Festa, Costanzo," *The New Grove Dictionary of Music*, 6:501–3.

5. See Andrew C. Minor, "Corteccia," *The New Grove Dictionary of Music*, 4:807–8.

6. See Lockwood and Owens, "Willaert," *The New Grove Dictionary of Music*, 20:423–26.

city from 1526 until his death in 1559, also authored a polyphonic cycle, perhaps as early as the 1540s and surely no later than 1556, even though it was not printed until 1566.[7] As the century wore on, moreover, Italy appears to have remained the primary locus for the composition and publication of polyphonic hymns in liturgical cycles. They were produced there in ever increasing numbers, and most of the celebrated figures of the age—as well as many lesser-knowns—contributed to the genre.

By contrast, of the masters active in regions of Germanic culture around mid-century, only two are currently credited with a complete cycle of polyphonic hymns: Sixt Dietrich, whose compositions in the genre were published on the Protestant presses of Georg Rhau in Wittenberg in 1545,[8] and Benedictus Ducis (ca. 1490–1544), whose collection for the courtly chapel in Heidelberg has been lost.[9] (An earlier repertory of hymns, published by Rhau in 1542, was an anthology of works by various composers and was not strictly ordered according to the liturgical calendar.)

The tradition thus opened for Germany was later maintained, albeit on a relatively modest level, but in England and in French-speaking regions of the Continent there is hardly any evidence that the polyphonic hymn (here understood as a notated musical genre) was much cultivated—or perhaps even much performed—until very late in the sixteenth century.[10] None of the composers that can be linked with the royal French chapel in its heyday has a liturgical cycle to his credit, and neither Attaingnant (in Paris) nor Moderne (in Lyons), the two principal publishers of polyphonic music in France at the time, brought out a collection of hymns. It may be that the older practice of using improvised counterpoint in a liturgical context when polyphony was wanted persisted much longer there than in Italy or Germany and thus impeded the development of a written repertory.

There was considerable compositional consistency in all fifteenth-century cycles of hymns for Vespers. The liturgical melody was almost invariably retained in one of the voices as the fundamental compositional element in an essentially homophonic texture, and the syllabic character of the chant was generally respected in its polyphonic setting, not only in the voice bearing the cantus firmus but in the others as well. Polyphonic performance, as a rule, was in *alternatim* style, beginning usually with the second stanza, while the remainder were restricted to the liturgical plainsong.

In the simplest polyphonic elaboration of the strophic form characteristic of the hymn, a single stanza was set to music. All of the even- or—in a few exceptional instances—the odd-numbered strophes could be sung to this one short composition, just as the alternate stanzas were intoned to a single chant melody. As we have seen, this was the solution generally adopted by Du Fay and by the majority of his contemporaries. By the end of the century, however, a more elaborate procedure had

7. See George Nugent, "Jacquet of Mantua," *The New Grove Dictionary of Music*, 9:456–58.
8. See Manfred Schuler, "Dietrich," *The New Grove Dictionary of Music*, 5:469–70.
9. See Louise E. Cuyler, "Ducis," *The New Grove Dictionary of Music*, 5:671.
10. See Tom Ward, "Hymn," *The New Grove Dictionary of Music*, 8:841–45.

been devised in which different music was composed for each of the stanzas to be sung in parts, varying as a rule the number of voices from one polyphonic strophe to the next.

The earliest liturgical cycle of polyphonic hymns to make systematic use of individual settings for more than one of the stanzas not sung in plainchant is found in a manuscript prepared for use by the papal chapel in the closing years of the fifteenth century, MS Cappella Sistina 15 of the Vatican Library.[11] Starting in most instances with a version attributable to Du Fay, composers now unknown added one or two more, often in four parts, so that each strophe sung polyphonically would have its own music, and the tendency—if not the rule—was to increase the sonority for the concluding stanza. In this the Vatican hymns differ from those for double choir composed for the ducal court in Ferrara by Martini and Brebis. Although earlier, the latter do not constitute a comprehensive liturgical cycle, nor do they alternate between chant and polyphony in the traditional way; rather, as has been observed, they apply the *alternatim* principle to antiphonally opposed polyphonic choirs who sang an individual setting for each strophe of the hymn.

It is entirely possible, in light of the evidence offered by the sources, that the hymn repertory of MS 15 of the Sistine Chapel represents a musical tradition that originated with the papal court. It was, in any case, clearly with that collection as a point of reference that the papal musicians Carpentras and Festa each began work on a liturgical cycle of polyphonic hymns. Festa's settings in particular must have been much admired, if one is to judge from their broad dissemination. In this instance, as in so many others, the practice of the papal chapel was apparently taken as a model elsewhere, for his cycle was copied not only into luxurious manuscripts for the use of both the papal choir (MS Cappella Sistina 18) and the Julian Chapel in St. Peter's Basilica (MS Cappella Giulia XII.6 of the Vatican Library) but also, wholly or in part, in seven other Italian sources, most of them Roman but some reaching as far north as Lucca, Bologna, and Casale Monferrato. Its widespread adoption may also have been helped by its usefulness since it included all thirty items called for by the principal observances of the Roman calendar: Advent, Christmas, Epiphany, the beginning of Lent, Holy Week, Easter, Eastertide, Ascension Day, Pentecost, Trinity Sunday, Corpus Christi, the Dedication of a Church, those saints' days that were universally celebrated, and Sundays throughout the year.[12]

The compositional consistency characteristic of the polyphonic hymn as a genre—at least in Italy—is clearly reflected in Festa's cycle. *Alternatim* performance continued to be the rule, usually with odd-numbered strophes sung in plainchant and even-numbered ones to individually composed settings in parts. For hymns

11. See Tom Ward, "The Polyphonic Office Hymn and the Liturgy of Fifteenth-Century Italy," *Musica disciplina* 26 (1972): 166–69, table 2.
12. See the introduction to the edition by Glen Haydon in Costanza Festa, *Hymni per totum annum, 3, 4, 5, 6 vocibus*, Monumenta polyphoniae italicae, vol. 3 (Rome: Pontificio Instituto di Musica Sacra, 1958), including the listing of the hymns by feast, pp. v–ix. Concerning the two Vatican manuscripts, see the *Census-Catalogue of Manuscript Sources*, 4:32 and 17–18, respectively.

with an odd number of strophes overall Festa either set the last two for consecutive polyphonic performance (as in *Christe redemptor omnium,* for Christmas, which has seven strophes) or began in parts with the first stanza, composing then for only the odd-numbered ones to follow (as in *Aures ad nostras . . . preces,* for the first Sunday in Lent, which has nine stanzas). The first to be set, in any case, was invariably written for four voices, the penultimate usually for three and the last either for five or six, thus providing for a climactic conclusion by means, first of all, of enhanced sonorities.

Since the added voice was generally the result of a strict canonic imitation of the part bearing the chant, the sense of climax was further heightened by a duplication of the traditional melody and the venerable nature of the complex contrapuntal procedures. In such cases the plainchant was invariably imbedded in the polyphony in the manner of a structural cantus firmus, often in rhythmic values that were distinctly longer than those seen in the other parts, such as breves and semibreves. In strophes for four voices the chant was usually placed in the tenor (though not always), whereas it was given to the superius in settings for three voices and was generally carried by either tenor or superius when canonic imitation was present. Concern for "correct" Latin pronunciation is also discernible—as it had been occasionally in the earlier Vatican repertory—in that the declamation of the strophic text is adjusted from one stanza to the next to avoid putative medieval barbarisms. (Most of these generalizations are equally valid for the cycle by Carpentras even though he tended to give the chant melody more consistently to the tenor.)[13]

Festa's setting of the Vespers hymn for the first Sunday in Advent, *Conditor alme siderum,* is characteristic of his treatment of the genre in the entire cycle (see Example 16-1).[14] The second of its six strophes (the first to be given polyphonic dress) has been written for four voices, with the tenor bearing the liturgical plainsong. The traditional melody is cast primarily in alternating breves and semibreves, thus retaining, together with its syllabic declamation, the ternary meter that had become conventional for the monophonic performance of this hymn already by Du Fay's time.[15]

The other three voices reflect, much more so than was the case in Du Fay's time, the stylistic influence of motet composition. They open with a point of imitation (in which the tenor also joins for a measure) and weave themselves around the cantus firmus in lines that are considerably more florid and melismatic than the hymn, except when they actually imitate its melody. Such imitation happens with some regularity, however, each time in anticipation of the cantus firmus itself, as in the

13. See the *Opera omnia* of Elzéar Genet (Carpentras), ed. Albert Seay, 5 vols., Corpus mensurabilis musicae, 58 ([Rome]: The American Institute of Musicology, 1972–73), vol. 3.

14. For a complete edition of the hymn in modern score, see Festa, *Hymni per totum annum,* ed. Haydon, 1, no. 1, and cf. the *Liber usualis,* 324, *Creator alme siderum.*

15. See the edition of Du Fay's setting in the *Opera omnia,* ed. Heinrich Besseler, 6 vols. (Rome: American Institue of Musicology, 1947–66), 5:39, or Claude V. Palisca, ed., *Norton Anthology of Western Music,* 3d ed., 2 vols. (New York: Norton, 1996), 107–8.

EXAMPLE 16-1. Costanzo Festa, *Conditor alme siderum*, 1, 2 (mm. 1–8), 4 (mm. 14–20), 6 (mm. 28–38)

1. Kindly creator of the stars, eternal light of the believers, Christ, redeemer of all, hear the prayers of the supplicants. 2. Thou who, suffering the destruction of death . . . 4. . . . [all will bend the knee] in heaven and in earth . . . 6. [Praise . . . and to the] Holy Ghost the same, throughout all eternity.

superius (m. 4, the characteristic ascent by thirds), the bassus (mm. 5 and 13ff.), the altus (m. 8ff.), and the three together (mm. 18ff., again with the ascent by thirds).

For the fourth strophe ("Cuius forti potentiae") Festa reduced the texture to the three lower parts, which open (again imitatively) with the same melodic figure as the second. The bassus then presents the first phrase of the chant in anticipation of the altus, which thereafter bears the traditional melody to the end of the stanza. Against the slower-moving cantus firmus, the tenor and bassus repeat, imitatively, with short, syllabic figures, key words of the hymn text, making considerable use of the successive thirds characteristic of the hymn melody, in descent as well as in ascent. Hymn composition did not lend itself readily to essays in musical rhetoric expressive of textual meaning, limited as it was by its strophic form and the traditional procedures of cantus firmus elaboration. In this instance, however, the quickly declaimed repetitions of the terms "celestia, terrestria," are perhaps intentionally suggestive of the multitude of creatures in heaven and earth whose knee would bend to the power of the Lord.

Canonic imitation (at the upper fifth) between tenor and altus I in the sixth and final strophe swells the number of voices to five. The canon shares with the other three parts a point of imitation on the same chant-derived figure used to open the two previous polyphonic strophes. In addition, it doubles the presence of the liturgical melody in the contrapuntal fabric, but because the altus enters each time only after the tenor has completed its phrase, the five parts rarely sound simultaneously. As a result, the intended sense of a fitting climax may have been thought to derive as much from the use of a recondite contrapuntal technique as from the melodic replication of the plainchant that it engenders.

Nonetheless, it was surely the increasing pervasiveness of the liturgical melody in the course of the hymn that must have struck the sixteenth-century listener. Sung alternately alone and in parts, the chant was heard at pitch in the second (polyphonic) strophe, at the upper fifth in the fourth, and at both levels in consecutive succession in the sixth. Its permeation of the contrapuntal fabric is further intensified once again in the final strophe by the frequent imitative quotation of its motivic figures in the other voices. The effect overall is one of remarkable motivic integration, and the undeniable tonal coherence of the work as a whole is further solidified by Festa's adherence to the modal orientation of the traditional chant with its plagal range and Phrygian final on E.

The pattern established for the polyphonic treatment of the hymns in Italy apparently had no significant impact on the German tradition in the sixteenth century, perhaps in part because the Protestant Reformation intervened at a crucial moment, creating a barrier that insulated Lutheran communities in the north from the influence of liturgical practice in Catholic Italy. In any case the collection printed by the Lutheran printer Georg Rhau in Wittenberg in 1542, the *Sacrorum hymnorum liber primus*, which gathered works from a variety of German-speaking composers (the most important of whom were probably Thomas Stoltzer, Heinrich Finck, and Johann Walter), included many settings that must have been prepared for Catholic worship since they are found in manuscript sources going back to the beginning of the century.[16]

These works reflect the considerable variety typical of German hymn composition at the time in that alternate settings are given for a good number of the texts, often with differing melodies as the starting point. Provision is made as well for many more than the thirty feast days included in Festa's cycle. Differing in yet another way from the polyphonic hymns being written in Italy at about the same time, they follow the earlier practice of Du Fay in offering polyphony for only one strophe of verse, the music for which was undoubtedly to be repeated in *alternatim* for subsequent ones together with the monophonic melody with which it was associated.[17]

If Rhau's print of 1542 was largely a compilation—a repertory upon which Protestant communities could draw in observing the newly reformed Vespers services in accordance with Luther's outline of 1536[18]—the collection he brought out three years later was much more systematically ordered. It was prepared specifically for Protestant worship by Sixt Dietrich (ca. 1493–1548), who became associated with the Reformation in 1527 when it established itself in the city of Constance, where he was a prebendary musician at the cathedral. Included in the three volumes of this *Novum opus musicum* ("containing three volumes of sacred hymns") were 122 compositions (counting a setting of the Te Deum) arranged in a comprehensive liturgical cycle. In essential respects these polyphonic hymns reflect the well-established medieval tradition; they are all based on the appropriate chant melody laid out, as a rule, as a cantus firmus in longer values and carried, usually, by either superius or tenor.

Like Rhau's earlier collection, however, this publication reflects the greater variety that had come to characterize German liturgical practice, offering alternate settings for many of the texts and providing for many more liturgical occasions than contemporaneous Italian cycles. Once again there is, as a rule, but a single polyphonic setting for any given hymn. A striking exception, however, is the treatment given the chant prescribed for Saturday in Septuagesima, *Cantemus cuncti*, which was turned into an elaborate composition divided into eight separate *partes* in a motet-related style. In addition, a number of the hymns in Dietrich's third tome have polyphony for two separate stanzas. Also of note—and a significant departure from Italian practice—is the inclusion in his setting of the Passion hymn *Rex Christi, factor omnium* of a lively instrumental interlude entitled *Rumpel Metten*, presumably to be inserted between the strophes.[19]

Anything but typical, by contrast, is *Veni sancte spiritus/Veni creator spiritus*,

16. See Tom Ward, "Hymn," *The New Grove Dictionary of Music*, 8:845.

17. See the *Sacrorum hymnorum liber primus* of 1542 as edited in modern score by Rudolf Gerber for the ongoing series Das Erbe deutscher Musik, vols. 21 and 35 (Leipzig: Fr. Kistner and C. F. W. Siegel, 1942–43).

18. See chap. 21, pp. 730–35.

19. See the hymns of the *Novus opus musicum* in Hermann Zenck and Wilibald Gurlitt, eds., *S. Dietrich: Hymnen*, Das Erbe deutscher Musik, vol. 23, (1942–60), 42–44; *Rex Christi* is no. 27.

which was not one of the twenty-two polyphonic hymns ascribed to Heinrich Finck (1444–45 to 1527) in *Rhau's Sacrorum hymnorum liber primus.*[20] Curiously, it combines in *quodlibet* style the words and chants (laid out in even semibreves) of two separate hymns in honor of the Holy Ghost, with three additional melodic lines. After the opening entries the three untexted parts of the polyphonic fabric rarely give much more than a hint of imitative writing, relying more on relatively rapid passages in parallel (imperfect) consonances. Their greater animation and free contrapuntal character, together with the practical problems they pose for text placement, suggest instrumental performance. It is difficult to imagine that such a piece would have had liturgical use, even though the involvement of instruments in its performance may have been in much the same spirit as Dietrich's *Rumpel Metten*. More than anything, though, it seems to reflect the Germanic predilection for *quodlibets* of all kinds, in this instance a sort of intellectual play with a typically serious textual background.

MAGNIFICATS

As with the hymns for Vespers, so with the culminating chant of that service, the Magnificat, the earliest polyphonic settings date from the late fourteenth century. Once again it was the composers of the generation of Binchoys and Du Fay who first established durable compositional traditions for the genre. It was of course to be expected that once Vespers began to be celebrated polyphonically, the Magnificat would be seen as especially appropriate for polyphonic elaboration, even in areas such as France and England, where notated hymn settings were relatively rare.

Unlike the hymns, however, whose proper texts—and melodies—change with each feast, the Magnificat is always the same and, as was noted, was chanted to formulaic tones like those used for the Psalms, albeit somewhat more elaborate. In addition, the tone of the canticle had to correspond with that of the antiphon by which it was framed liturgically, and the antiphons for the Magnificat represent all eight of the modal categories then current. Consequently, there was a need for Magnificat settings based on all eight of the liturgical tones, and from mid-fifteenth century on most composers who cultivated the genre provided polyphony for several of them, if not systematically then at least for those most commonly used: the eighth, the sixth, and the first.[21]

With the sixteenth century came the first complete cycles of Magnificat settings,

20. The hymns printed by Rhau in the *Sacrorum hymorum libri princi* have been published in Das Erbe deutscher Musik, vols. 21 and 25, ed. Rudolf Gerber (Lippstadt: Kistner and Siegel, 1961). *Veni sancte/Veni creator* is found in *Der Mensuralkodex des Nikolaus Apel*, ed. Rudolf Gerber, Das Erbe deutscher Musik, vol. 32 (Kassel: Bärenreiter Verlag, 1956), 48–49, no. 42, and is easily accessible in Archibald T. Davison and Willi Apel, eds., *Historical Anthology of Music*, 2 vols. (Cambridge, Mass.: Harvard University Press, 1962), 84 (no. 80), and in *Das Chorwerk*, vol. 32, ed. Rudolf Gerber (Wolfenbüttel: Kallmeyer, 1935), 19–20, no. 10.
21. This is according to Winfried Kirsch, "Magnificat," *The New Grove Dictionary of Music*, 11:496.

one for each of the eight plainchant formulae used for liturgical recitation of the canticle. Conceptually, such collections correspond in a very real sense to the cycles of polyphonic hymns that were being written at about the same time, and often by the same composers. For example, a set of eight by Costanzo Festa—one for each of the liturgical tones—was copied, like his hymns, in the late 1530s into choirbooks prepared for use by the Sistine and Julian chapels at the Vatican, and another by Carpentras was also inscribed in the latter source.[22]

During that same decade two German composers also known for their polyphonic hymns, Sixt Dietrich, who was then associated with the Protestant reformers in Constance, and Ludwig Senfl, who was serving at the time in the ducal chapel of Catholic Bavaria, also completed a series of Magnificats on all eight tones. Through the remainder of the century virtually every major figure—and, again, many minor ones as well—contributed to the genre; its cultivation can be documented for every area of western Europe where sacred polyphony was being written, in England, France, and Spain no less than in Italy and Germany.[23]

The "Eton Choirbook," a major source for the elaborate antiphon settings being written in England around the turn of the century, originally contained a series of twenty-four polyphonic Magnificats (presumably three complete sets of eight), only ten of which have survived intact. In 1534 the Parisian printer Attaingnant published, as part of the thirteen-volume series of motets mentioned earlier, two books of Magnificat settings, and while these compositions are attributable to a variety of composers, they have been carefully arranged according to their tones: twelve in the *Liber quintus* in tones 1 through 3, and another twelve in the *Liber sextus*, in tones 4 through 8.[24] Two other French publishers also produced collections of Magnificat settings later in the century, Du Chemin in 1553 and Le Roy and Ballard in 1557.

The Spanish composers Cristóbal de Morales (ca. 1500–53), Francisco Guerrero (1528–99), and Tomás Luis de Victoria (ca. 1548–1611) all contributed substantially to this repertory as well, including complete sets in all eight tones among their compositions in the genre. And while both Morales and Victoria spent critical years in the papal chapel in Rome, the currency of polyphonic settings of the Magnificat in Spain is attested not only by the works of Guerrero but also by the substantial number of pieces that were intabulated for *vihuela* and published in Spain in the 1540s and 1550s.[25]

That interest in the polyphonic Magnificat and, one must assume, the frequency of its use continued unabated through the century and beyond is suggested by the large numbers in which settings were produced in the late 1500s. The celebrated

22. These are the MS Cappella Sistina 18 and the MS Cappella Giulia XII.5, respectively; see the *Census-Catalogue of Manuscript Sources*, 4:32 and 17.
23. See Winfried Kirsch, *Die Quellen der mehrstimmigen Magnificat- und Te Deum-Vertonungen bis zur Mitte des 16. Jahrhunderts* (Tutzing: Schneider, 1966), 29ff.
24. See Daniel Heartz, *Pierre Attaingnant, Royal Printer of Music* (Berkeley: University of California Press, 1969), 264–65.
25. See Kirsch, "Magnificat," *The New Grove Dictionary of Music*, 11:496.

Roman master Pierluigi Palestrina (1525–26 to 1594) published in 1591 a collection of 34 settings, four in each tone except the first and sixth (for which there were five each), and Orlande de Lassus (1532–94), while employed at the ducal court of Bavaria, turned out more than 100 polyphonic versions of the beloved Canticle of the Virgin.

However, no collection of settings on all eight tones achieved wider circulation, apparently, than that attributed to Morales, which was published in three separate editions already in the mid-1540s, the earliest by the Venetian printer Scotto in 1542, another by the Protestant Rhau in 1544, and a third in 1545 by Scotto's rival in Venice, Gardane.[26] Thirteen more printings were to follow, the latest in 1619, to say nothing of those that were copied into the manuscript collections of the period.[27]

In light of the tradition for *alternatim* performance of the Canticle, with verses in chant and polyphony succeeding one another—a convention that had been firmly established in the course of the fifteenth century—Morales's settings appear to be unusual in providing polyphony continuously for all twelve of its verses. This arrangement apparently reflects practice at the papal chapel, where *alternatim* performance was normally eschewed for this particular chant; Festa's polyphonic Magnificats are similarly arranged in the manuscripts inscribed for the Sistine and Julian chapels. However, for those musical institutions where chant and polyphony were sung as usual in alternation, Morales's compositions actually offered two complete sets in all eight tones, one with the odd-numbered verses sung in parts, the other with the even-numbered verses so performed.[28]

In other respects, however, the settings by Morales are typical of the genre as it was cultivated on the Continent, as may be seen from the *Magnificat octavi toni*, which has only the even-numbered verses set in parts (see Example 16-2).[29] In the first of these, "Et exultavit," the chant formula is heard in the superius, an octave above pitch, unembellished and in relatively long values (breves and semibreves) until the final cadential elaboration (mm. 18–20), where it finally dissolves into more rapid movement.[30] At the opening of verse four, "Quia fecit," the superius appears to follow the chant formula once again but leaves it after the intonation to pursue a freer course unrestricted by the repeated pitches of the chant. The literal quotation of the recitation formula is then left to the bassus, which enters only in the sixth measure and at the lower fourth (from D). In verse 6, "Fecit potentiam," the liturgical formula is given to the altus at the upper fifth (from d); thus enveloped by the other

26. See Kirsch, "Magnificat," *The New Grove Dictionary of Music*, 11:496.
27. See Robert Stevenson, "Morales," *The New Grove Dictionary of Music*, 12:556.
28. According to Kirsch, the Morales Magnificats were printed as a continuous series by Scotto and Rhau but as two separate groups by Gardane; *The New Grove Dictionary of Music*, 11:496.
29. For an edition of the entire piece in modern score, see Cristóbal de Morales, *Opera omnia*, 8 vols., ed. Higinio Anglès, Monumentos de la música Española (Barcelona: Consejo Superior de Investigaciones Científicas, Instituto Español de Musicología, 1952–71), 17:125–32.
30. Cf. the liturgical tone in the *Liber usualis*, 212.

Example 16-2. Cristóbal de Morales, *Magnificat octavi toni*, 4 (mm. 21–42)

For he that is mighty hath done to me great things; and holy is his name.

parts of the polyphonic fabric, it becomes still more difficult to perceive, particularly in the homophonic opening.

The tenor first assumes its traditional role as bearer of the cantus firmus only in verse 8, "Esurientes implevit," where it enters after five full breves of silence (m. 67), presenting the liturgical melody in extended values and without embellishment but at the upper fourth (from c). It then returns the tone to its original pitch (now with the reciting tone on c) for a repetition of the last phrase of the text, "et divites dimisit." The superius then takes up the chant once again, presenting verse 10, "Sicut locutus est"—like the second—in longer note values and without melodic coloration at the upper octave.

For the final doxology, "Sicut erat," there is a simultaneous heightening of sonorities and of contrapuntal complexity for climactic effect as the texture expands to six parts, including two in strict canonic imitation. Such an enhancement of the concluding section was typical not only of Magnificat composition but also, as we have seen, of the polyphonic hymn—as it was of other liturgical genres yet to be discussed. Altus II opens with the intonation formula at the upper fifth; tenor II follows three breves later with the same melody at pitch, and the chant-derived pitches are set off once again by their greater duration. In practical terms, though, they are not easily perceived as individual melodies because of the lively contrapuntal tapestry woven around them by the four surrounding voices.

For composers who held *varietas* to be an accepted esthetic principle, one of the primary difficulties in setting the Magnificat was to avoid the potential for monotony inherent in the repeated reciting pitch of the liturgical tone. In numerous instances other composers tended to resolve this problem simply by progressively diminishing in the course of a composition the reiteration of the reciting pitch, retaining at last from the chant little more than the opening and closing formulae. Morales, however, appears to have skillfully avoided that pitfall in a different way.

Although he adhered faithfully to the chant formula—even doubling it for the final verse of the Canticle—and to the regular G final of the eighth mode, he made the borrowed material increasingly difficult to discern in the contrapuntal fabric overall. He achieved this effect not only by shifting it from the outer to the inner parts but also by transposing it to other pitch levels (thus mitigating the inevitable emphasis on the repeated note), by extending its temporal durations to obscure its familiar melodic progressions, and by separating its phrases with rather lengthy rests. The result is a surprising degree of variety within the essentially organic unity of the composition—and a very successful exemplification of the esthetic ideal of the period.

Also to be noted here is the assimilation to Morales's Magnificat setting of motet-related compositional procedures, textures, and styles in a manner recalling the contemporaneous treatment of the polyphonic hymn, as observed in the previous discussion. Until the expansion of the final section, four voices are used throughout, all of them fully texted and so written as to facilitate the declamation of the words. Syntactic units are clearly articulated—following the formulaic structure of the chant itself—with a rest, a cadence, or both marking the division between the two halves of the verse with a degree of emphasis corresponding to the relationship between them. In measures 10–12 and measures 31–32, for instance, the cadential effect is mitigated by the use of imperfect consonance and the continuity of the part-writing, whereas in measure 50 and measures 94–95 the cadence is perfect and overlap is minimal.

In addition, imitative counterpoint has been adopted as the fundamental compositional procedure. Besides the strict canon of the final verse, three of the five remaining sections open with a point of imitation—all based, moreover, to some degree on the intonation of the chant. The imitation dissolves as usual, however, into free counterpoint as the phrase unfolds, and both contrapuntal types are relieved by passages of homophonic declamation (as in mm. 14f.). The latter style is also used for the opening of verse 6, perhaps to give special emphasis to the words of the text, "He hath showed strength with his arm," and, in a modified way, for the beginning of verse 10.

Exceptions to these stylistic generalities, although rarely seen in the Continental repertory, are to be expected in the works of English composers, who did not usually base their Magnificats on the plainsong formulae but rather upon some part of a preexistent polyphonic piece. Such is the case, for instance, in the Magnificat repertory of the "Eton Choirbook." As for composers of a later generation, such as Orlande de Lassus, the recitation tones of the chant are finally abandoned in favor of *imitatio* (so-called parody) of other polyphonic works, a compositional procedure borrowed from the cyclic Mass, where it first appeared and was, as we shall see, most assiduously cultivated.[31]

31. See Kirsch, "Magnificat," *The New Grove Dictionary of Music*, 11:497. For a study of the "parody" Magnificats by Lassus, see David Crook, *Orlando di Lasso's Imitation Magnificats for Counter-Reformation Munich* (Princeton: Princeton University Press, 1994).

⟶ PSALM SETTINGS ⟵

A significant distinction must be made—stylistical as well as liturgical—between settings of Psalm texts and even complete Psalms as motets, on the one hand, and Psalms simply arranged polyphonically for use at Vespers, on the other. For the latter liturgical use was unambiguously prescribed, whereas the functions in Christian ritual for which motets were intended are not always easily determined, although the Mass appears to be one context in which they were frequently performed. As to style, Psalm-motets are in most respects indistinguishable from other compositions in the genre, while Psalm settings for liturgical performance are closely tied to the formulaic tones of the chant and are restricted melodically and harmonically by the narrow range and the repetitive nature of the plainsong. They are therefore more nearly akin to the polyphonic Magnificats (and those few other genres, to be discussed presently, in which a recitation tone is an important structural element) than they are to motets, properly speaking.

In addition, Psalm settings generally retain the antiphonal manner of their liturgical recitation, with the two sides of the choir answering one another either in polyphony—as in the case of the Ferrarese repertory seen earlier (see pp. 440–43) —or in *alternatim* between polyphony and chant. The simplicity of the counterpoint in the earliest written repertories would seem to indicate that they emerged from an earlier oral tradition in which the Psalm verses sung polyphonically were so treated in performance by means of improvisatory procedures. Even the settings for double chorus by Brebis and Martini rarely go beyond a simple declamatory *fauxbourdon* with the Psalm tone in the uppermost part.[32]

Significantly, the polyphonic elaboration of Vespers Psalms for double chorus in the manner instituted at the ducal chapel in Ferrara was taken up again in the sixteenth century, first of all by composers who had been associated at some point with the Este court. One of the most important collections of such pieces—because most seminal for the period—was that published by Gardane in 1550, containing, as indicated by its title page, settings by Adrian Willaert and Jacquet of Mantua (and also, though unheralded, pieces by Dominique Phinot and an anonymous composer).

Here one sees, in lieu of the three voices required for the *fauxbourdon* that predominated in the settings by Brebis and Martini, the four-part texture that had become the norm for the sixteenth century generally. The shift probably reflects, in particular, the artistic authority of the developing motet repertory, but the fuller sonorities clearly helped to compensate, too, for the lack of melodic interest and harmonic variety inherent in the relatively simple contrapuntal procedures used to embellish the Psalm tones for liturgical purposes.

Eight of these compositions, all of them attributed to Willaert and written for divided choir, have been designated *salmi spezzati* ("split" or "divided" Psalms), so

---

32. See Examples 12-4a and 4b, and cf. Lockwood, *Music in Renaissance Ferrara*, 256ff.

called because the two halves of each verse overlap and thus require two ensembles of four parts each—presumably placed on opposite sides of the choir—for their performance.[33] In twelve others the Psalm verses are compositionally self-contained—usually with the odd-numbered verses set by one composer and the even-numbered by the other—thus allowing for an integral polyphonic performance by either single or divided choir (or, of course, polyphony and chant in alternation).[34]

A third group of eleven Psalms, having only the odd-numbered verses in polyphony, were obviously conceived from the outset for *alternatim* performance.[35] The most interesting of these works historically are undoubtedly those actually intended for divided choir since, as has been suggested, they helped to lay the groundwork for the massive polychoral motets that were to have their beginnings in the musical practice of Venice toward the end of the century.

Despite a potential for greater sonority and a somewhat higher level of sophistication, the *salmi spezzati* do not differ markedly in their characteristic features from the remaining compositions of this repertory. Stylistic traits that were common to all may be seen, together with those distinctive of the "divided Psalms," in Willaert's treatment of Psalm 129, *De profundis clamavi*, which is prescribed for use at Vespers on Wednesday and also for the Office of the Dead (see Example 16-3).[36] The beginning of the first verse is intoned monophonically, using the liturgical formula for the fifth Psalm tone, and as the first choir joins in, the syllabic delivery of the chant is maintained fairly strictly in all parts, with only the briefest of cadential melismas. As the first of the polyphonic voices to enter, the tenor appears initially to continue without interruption the reiterated notes of the recitation tone, but the superius takes over immediately at the upper octave, presenting the cadential formula used in the chant to mark the end of the verse.

The second choir chimes in with verse 2 as soon as the final sonority for the first has been fairly struck (m. 6), using a concise imitative figure based on the psalmodic intonation in paired duos with superius and bassus answering altus and tenor at the distance of a semibreve. The formulaic beginning in rising thirds is carried by both tenor and superius, but it is the latter that introduces the *mediatio*, the internal cadence used to articulate the two halves of the verse (mm. 10–12); the latter voice then continues with the reciting pitch to the end of the second half (mm. 15–18), but this time the full closing formula of the chant has been avoided. As the first choir returns with verse 3 (m. 18), the formulaic intonation and the *mediatio* are heard in the tenor, but the superius once again takes over for its second half (m. 24) with the reciting note and the closing formula.

33. See Adriano Willaert, *Opera omnia*, ed. Hermann Zenck and Walter Gerstenberg, 15 vols., Corpus mensurabilis musicae 3 ([Rome]: American Institute of Musicology, 1950–77), 8:102–64, nos. 24–31.
34. See Willaert, *Opera omnia*, ed. Zenck and Gerstenberg, 8:1–72, nos. 1–12; cf. Lockwood, "Willaert," *The New Grove Dictionary of Music*, 20:424.
35. See Willaert, *Opera omnia*, ed. Zenck and Gerstenberg, 8:72–101, nos. 13–23.
36. See Willaert, *Opera omnia*, ed. Zenck and Gerstenberg, 8:122–28, and cf. the *Liber usualis*, 291 and 1774; note that the Psalm in question is no. 130 in the King James Version of the English Bible.

EXAMPLE 16-3. Adrian Willaert, *De profundis clamavi*, 1 to 3 (mm. 1–28)

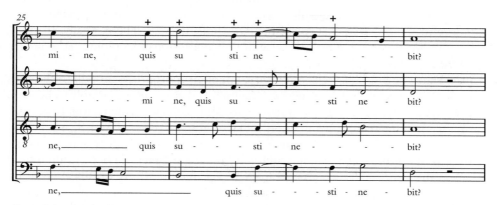

Out of the depths have I cried unto thee, O Lord. Lord, hear my voice; let thine ears be
attentive to the voice of my supplications. If thou, Lord, shouldest mark iniquities, O
Lord, who shall stand?

In a sense the insistence upon the opening formula of the liturgical tone in these initial verses is paradoxical since, as a rule, it was used in the monophonic recitation of the Psalm only once, at the beginning, while all subsequent verses began simply with the reciting tone. Its presence in Willaert's setting, therefore, like the polyphony itself, is an indication of liturgical solemnity, a feast or a season when a more elaborate tone might have been used. Once established in the manner described, however, the Psalm tone is treated with greater freedom. At the beginning of verse 4, for example, the rising thirds of the intonation are filled with passing tones (m. 28), and they are omitted entirely from verse 5 (m. 42), together with any obvious emphasis on a repeated reciting note. In the latter instance only the cadential pitches—c for the *mediatio* and a for the verse end—maintain the musical connection with the chant formula.

Unlike the polyphonic hymns, where longer notes in the cantus firmus can result in a modestly melismatic treatment of the text in the other parts, the Psalm settings usually retain with considerable consistency, as in this instance, the syllabic declamation characteristic of the psalmodic formulae. In this manner the sobriety appropriate to their liturgical function in the celebration of Vespers is maintained despite the relative opulence of the musical means.

Fairly typical of Psalm composition in the sixteenth century are the constantly changing textures deployed by the two choirs as they respond to one another antiphonally. Willaert alternates between the two mildly contrasting contrapuntal procedures illustrated by the opening verses, the one based on closely spaced imitative entries, the other on homophonic declamation. The point of imitation introduced at the beginning of verse 4 yields in its second half, for instance, to a compositional style that can be described as basically homophonic despite a light contrapuntal animation that increases at the approach to the cadence (as in mm. 40–42). The sonorities are then reduced to a pair of voices as the second choir takes up verse 6 (m. 59), with the altus imitating the intonation formula in the bassus at the upper fifth (from c), and again at verse 8 (m. 97), where the imitation is between bassus and superius. Until the very end, in fact, the full sonorities of the combined choirs are rarely heard for more than a breve or two where the two choirs overlap. There, finally, all eight voices join for the concluding half-verse of the conventional doxology, "et in secula seculorum, amen" (m. 129).

The climactic finish of the composition, although appropriate enough to the particular significance of the words being declaimed at that point, is probably to be seen as essentially musical and formal in nature and only coincidentally related to textual meaning. A more rhetorical intention is discernible in verses 6 and 8, where the paired imitation results in a repetition of verbal elements that are central to the sense of the Psalm: "From the morning watch until the night Israel will hope in the Lord. . . . And the same will redeem Israel from all her iniquities." As a result, two of its shortest verses carry the two lengthiest sections of music, apparently to give them special emphasis. Similarly, the repetition in verse 7 of "et copiosa" ("and copious is his redemption") in a medium such as this, where word repetition is generally carefully avoided, must surely have been expressive in its intent.

⌒⊃ Psalms in *Falsobordone*

Curiously, the writing out of Psalm settings based on, or even resembling, essentially improvisatory procedures never gained great currency in northern Europe.[37] Only in Italy and, to some extent, in Spain and Portugal was a written tradition for the polyphonic recitation of the Psalms in this manner maintained through the sixteenth century. Such compositions retained the declamatory, syllabic character and the repeated pitches of the liturgical tones, even after the plainsong formulae were themselves treated with considerable freedom—or even entirely ignored. The compositional procedure that came to be more or less universally adopted for the purpose was known as *falsobordone*, and although it employed unremittingly a four-part texture, it was clearly derived in both name and compositional concept from the three-part technique of northern *fauxbourdon*.

It is not clear how this new method of part-writing might have been derived from the earlier practice of improvisatory polyphony, but the resemblance is as unmistakable as are some of the differences.[38] The given melody, whether placed in the uppermost part, as was usually the case, or in the tenor (or some other voice), was harmonized in rather strict homophony using simultaneously all of the consonant intervals: thirds and fifths with their octave complements, sixths and fourths, and the octave itself (or the octave equivalents of these intervals: tenths, twelfths, thirteenths, elevenths, and, more rarely, fifteenths). Because of the equivocal nature of the fourth, which was perceived as a dissonance without another consonance below it, the interval between bassus and tenor was always either a third or a fifth. It may in fact have been to eliminate the fourth in the offending position at the bottom of the sonority that *falsobordone* was devised as a replacement for *fauxbourdon*.

As a consequence of this intervalic relationship between the two lower parts, the consonant possibilities for the remaining voices were relatively circumscribed: with a fifth between bassus and tenor, a fourth usually separated tenor and altus, a third altus and superius, a sixth tenor and superius, and an octave bassus and altus (see Example 16-4). When the interval between bassus and tenor was a third, however, the spacing between the other parts had to be adjusted accordingly.[39] The resulting sonority was simply repeated much like the reciting pitch of the liturgical tones in order to accommodate a phrase of any length, and it was altered only for the opening chords, where the third (or less frequently the fifth) was at times eliminated, and

---

37. See Paul Doe, "Psalm," *The New Grove Dictionary of Music*, 15:332.
38. See Murray C. Bradshaw, "Falsobordone," *The New Grove Dictionary of Music*, 6:375f., but cf. his earlier study, *The Falsobordone*, Musicological Studies and Documents, vol. 34 ([Rome]: The American Institute of Musicology, 1978), 21 and *passim*, in which he stresses the differences between the two related procedures.
39. See, for instance, Bradshaw's *Falsobordone*, 89, example 28, where a tenth between bassus and tenor is completed by a third from tenor to altus, a fourth from altus to superius, resulting in a sixth from tenor to superius and a double octave between the outer voices.

EXAMPLE 16-4. Pietro Oriola, *In exitu Israel* (mm. 1–13)

When Israel went out of Egypt, the house of Jacob from a people of strange language . . .

in cadential passages, where freer melodic movement could introduce dissonant passing tones, suspensions, and a sixth above the bassus (in place of the usual fifth or third).

The earliest examples of this sort of four-part formulaic Psalm settings are to be found in the sources of the late fifteenth century in both Italy and Spain. Of particular note in this regard is MS 871 of the monastic library in Montecassino, which originated in a Benedictine house in the kingdom of Naples in the last decade or so of the fifteenth century.[40] Also important is MS 454 of the Central Library in Barcelona, which was compiled somewhere on the Iberian peninsula over a consid-

40. See Isabel Pope and Masakata Kanazawa, eds., *The Musical Manuscript Montecassino 871: A Neapolitan Repertory of Sacred and Secular Music of the Late Fifteenth Century* (Oxford: Clarendon Press, 1978), 19–21.

erable period of time around the turn of the fifteenth century (with a number of additions from later in the sixteenth).[41]

Among the several polyphonic Psalms included in the Montecassino MS 871, as we have seen (see pp. 342–44), is a setting of Psalm 113, *In exitu Israel*, the last of the five Psalms prescribed for Sunday Vespers.[42] It is one of two pieces attributed in the collection to Pietro Oriola, a composer of either Spanish or Italian origins who served in the mid-1400s in the chapel of Alfonso V of Aragon, the king of Naples,[43] and it has the distinction of being the only such work in that entire repertory for which a written *falsobordone* is the basic compositional procedure. Based on the *tonus peregrinus*, with which this Psalm had a traditional association because of its subject (the flight of captive Israel from Egypt), it offers a texted setting of the first verse (see Example 16-4) and a second, untexted section that is sufficiently formulaic in character as to be adaptable to any of the subsequent verses.[44] Although brief, it shows clearly enough both the simple contrapuntal procedures adapted to the recitation tone and the somewhat more sophisticated writing employed at the approach to a cadence.

There is a steady, if modest, stream of such pieces through most of the sixteenth century and, a bit surprisingly, a notable increase in their numbers from the 1570s through the seventeenth and into the eighteenth century, reflecting what was apparently the durable popularity of this rather primitive compositional method. Some twenty-nine sources from the years prior to 1566 included one or more examples of this type of composition as compared to at least thirty-five during the last thirty years of the century, and the number of pieces in *falsobordone* in the later collections is substantially greater.[45] However, there is in the later repertory no significant departure in compositional process or style from the earliest examples known, as the examples compiled by Bradshaw clearly show.

If such a schematic compositional technique persisted for so long and was even adapted, as it appears, to instrumental repertories,[46] it was undoubtedly because it was mastered with relative ease and thus offered a useful didactic tool as well as a compositional method within reach of the most modest talent. In addition, it was apparently seen, by virtue of its contrapuntal simplicity and the consequent intelligibility of the sacred texts so treated, as an ideal way to satisfy the strictures on liturgical polyphony laid down by the Council of Trent. Whatever the reasons for its long-lived popularity, its ongoing association with Vesper Psalms in a liturgical context only serves to underline the distinction between such works and the compositions

41. Concerning the latter codex, see *Census-Catalogue of Manuscript Sources*, 1:17–18; for a comprehensive listing of the sources see Bradshaw, *Falsobordone*, appendix, pp. 159ff.

42. See the *Liber usualis*, 254.

43. See Isabel Pope, "Oriola, Pietro," *The New Grove Dictionary of Music*, 13:822.

44. For a complete transcription in modern score, see Pope and Kanazawa, eds., *The Musical Manuscript Montecassino 871*, 123–24, no. 7.

45. See Bradshaw, *Falsobordone*, 159–87, for a comprehensive list of the musical works in this category.

46. See Bradshaw, "Falsobordone," *The New Grove Dictionary of Music*, 6:375f., and *Falsobordone*, 73–88.

based on texts from the Psalms that were treated in the manner of the motet as a genre more narrowly defined.

LAMENTATIONS

It is noteworthy that the liturgical music for the night Offices, Matins and Lauds, was not generally given polyphonic treatment, at least none that has left any significant trace in the written repertory. The most conspicuous exceptions are connected with observances of particular solemnity, especially those prescribed for Holy Week. Aside from the Psalms, the texts from the Offices that were most frequently provided with a polyphonic setting in a manner that was to become distinctive and traditional were the Lamentations of Jeremiah, the readings formally intoned during the first Nocturne at Matins on Thursday, Friday, and Saturday of Holy Week—the *triduum sacrum*, as this three-day period is known in Latin. Still, it is undoubtedly symptomatic of the lateness of their establishment as a separate polyphonic genre that the earliest of the polyphonic Lamentations go back no further than the middle of the fifteenth century (see pp. 346–48).

With the Lamentations sung in parts, the Great Responsories with which the solemn readings from Jeremiah were answered in the liturgy eventually came to be set polyphonically as well. When, for example, the great Spanish master Tomás Luis de Victoria (1548–1611) published in 1575 (during his years of residence in Rome) a complete office for Holy Week—an *Officium hebdomadae sacrae*—he included, together with nine Lamentations and two of the Passions that were set forth by the liturgy for those somber celebrations, the eighteen Responsories traditionally sung at Matins.[47] However, because the Great Responsory was not generally handled in a manner to distinguish it clearly from the motet, except in England, we shall not give it further consideration here, even though a great many sets of polyphonic Responsories were published during the second half of the sixteenth century.[48]

Moreover, despite the liturgical importance of the Holy Week rituals, the number of polyphonic settings for the Lamentations was not especially significant. Attaingnant included in his selection of music for Passion Week—in the tenth of his series of thirteen books of motets published in 1534–35—three scattered sections for each of the three days of the *triduum sacrum*, compositions with attributions to Antoine de Févin and Claudin de Sermisy, both of whom served in the royal French chapel.[49] Yet other polyphonic Lamentations were published by the Protestant printer Georg Rhau in Wittenberg in 1538, by Montanus and Neuber in Nuremberg in 1549, and by Le Roy and Ballard in Paris in 1557. In each case, however, the col-

47. See Robert Stevenson, "Victoria," *The New Grove Dictionary of Music*, 19:704–9.
48. See the (unsigned) article, "Responsory," *The New Grove Dictionary of Music*, 15:764.
49. See Daniel Heartz, *Pierre Attaingnant, Royal Printer of Music*, 273–74.

lection was a compilation by several different composers, offering mensural settings of only some of the sections from the readings prescribed for each of the three Matins services.

The first full set of Lamentations by a single composer to have survived intact, following that of de Quadris discussed earlier, consists of nine *lectiones*, three for the first Nocturne of each of the three Matins services, and was published in Avignon in 1532 by the composer Carpentras (Elzéar Genet), known for his long period of service with the papal chapel. It would seem that they were written considerably earlier, however, perhaps even during his first sojourn in Rome between 1514 and 1521, for he heard them sung by the papal choir in 1524 when he returned to the Vatican city after an absence of three years. Finding the music used for that performance corrupt—as he expressly claims—he had the works copied for the Medici Pope Clement VII in an elegant dedicatory codex, now Cappella Sistina MS 163.[50] Remarkably, his Lamentations were then sung annually by the papal choir until 1587, when Pope Sixtus V—over the protests of his chapel singers—commissioned Pierluigi Palestrina to recompose Jeremiah's mournful texts.

Later in the century additional sets—not all of them complete, however—were published by yet other masters, most notably Cristóbal de Morales (Venice, 1564) and Tomás Luis Victoria (Rome, 1581), both of whom also had connections with the papal choir. Yet others were written by Giammateo Asola (Venice, 1584, 1588, and 1602), Orlande de Lassus (Munich, 1585), Jacob Handl (Prague, 1587), and of course Palestrina (Rome, after 1564). Thus polyphonic settings of the Lamentations came to be widely used in western Europe in the course of the sixteenth century, and the prestige of the papal choir, coupled with the compositional conventions observed by the composers who served there, may have worked once again to establish and shape the genre.

Turning again to the Lamentations by Carpentras, it is possible to see clearly the extent to which the developing stylistic parameters of this genre reflect the influence of the motet of the early sixteenth century (see Example 16-5).[51] This is evident both in the master's treatment of the liturgical melody and in the compositional procedures adopted for setting the biblical texts. In the first place, notwithstanding the chantlike "Incipit" with which the prophet's prayer begins on Holy Saturday, there is little evidence in this lengthy series of pieces of the close adherence to a recitation tone that generally characterized earlier settings of Jeremiah's plaints (see pp. 347–48, the discussion of the Lamentations attributed to Johannes de Quadris). Of the fourteen sets of Lamentations edited by Günther Massenkeil from sources of the early sixteenth century,[52] for example, eleven are based on one of the liturgical formulae,

50. See Howard M. Brown, "Carpentras," *The New Grove Dictionary of Music*, 3:819.
51. For a complete transcription in modern score, see Genet (Carpentras), *Opera omnia*, ed. Seay, 2:82–96.
52. See Günther Massenkeil, ed., *Mehrstimmige Lamentationen aus der ersten Hälfte des 16. Jahrhunderts*, Musikalischer Denkmäler der Akademie der Wissenschaft und der Literatur, vol. 6 (Mainz: Schott, 1965).

EXAMPLE 16-5. Elzéar Genet (Carpentras), *Oratio Jeremiae prophetae*, 1 (mm. 1–10), 5 (mm. 144–55)

Here begins the prayer of Jeremiah the prophet. . . . We have drunk our water for money; our wood is sold unto us. (Lamentations 5:1, 4)

the majority on that most frequently used for these readings in Italy, the so-called Roman tone.[53]

Had Carpentras elected to quote extensively and frequently from any of the liturgical melodies traditional for the Lamentations, one could expect it to have been the latter, the one most closely associated with the Roman church. However, there is seldom anything more in his setting than an occasional brief allusion to some element from the well-known formulae, such as the outline of the medial cadence of the tone in extended values in the superius about halfway through verse 5, "Aquam nostram . . . bibimus" (mm. 147–53). Quite to the contrary, the final for each of the major sections is G, rather than the F of the mode 5 recitation tone, and the melodic ductus of superius and tenor, together with an emphasis on C and G for internal cadences, suggests a mode 8 orientation not found in any of the more familiar tones.[54]

Gone, too, from Carpentras's Lamentations are the literal repetitions and strophic procedures—deriving, obviously, from a closer adherence to the liturgical model with its textual iterations and its recurring melodic formulae—that also marked earlier settings of the Jeremiah readings. De Quadris and other composers represented in the Petrucci print of 1506 had recourse almost exclusively to such utilitarian procedures. Carpentras did maintain, however, the clearly articulated sectionalization of the readings by verse—including a separate melismatic segment provided for each of the Hebrew letters retained from the acrostic of the original language—that remained a characteristic of the genre throughout the period under consideration. At the same time—unlike many other early sixteenth-century composers, who often adopted for an entire series of sections the same number of voices—Carpentras brought to his Lamentations the variety in textures and sonorities that had become by then characteristic for the motet.

He wrote the opening section for a tenor duo; for the second verse (m. 23) he added an altus to that pair of voices; for the third (m. 55) he introduced for the first time in this *lectio* the bassus, making a total of four voices. With the fourth verse (m. 93) he reverted to a lighter sound, writing for a pair of sopranos, and only in the fifth (m. 130) did he make use of a full five-voice choir. In verse 6 ("Cervicibus minabamur") he used again a five-voice texture, introducing the segment with a lengthy trio, however. And after a third brief duo for the seventh verse ("Patres nostri") he brought in voice by voice for verse 8 ("Servi dominati sunt") the six parts with which the composition concludes in the ninth ("Jerusalem").

Similarly, Carpentras has deployed in this series of discrete pieces all of the contrapuntal techniques that are so well exemplified in the motet repertory of the time. An introductory motif in homophonic declamation opens the initial duo but then

53. The tone in question is that given in the *Liber usualis*, 754–59 (and elsewhere). According to Bruno Stäblein, as many as 150 to 200 such melodies may have come into use during the Middle Ages, but all appear to have been largely formulaic in nature, and there are significant similarities among many of them; see his discussion and the accompanying examples in *Die Musik in Geschichte und Gegenwart*, 8:135–38.

54. Cf. the melodies excerpted by Stäblein for *Die Musik in Geschichte und Gegenwart*, 8:135–38.

yields rather soon to imitative (mm. 5ff.), then to free contrapuntal writing (mm. 17ff.). The second verse opens with its three parts in imitation and closes with a free contrapuntal flourish, which is followed in the fourth by an introductory phrase in solemn homophonic declamation (in breves and semibreves). This gives way in turn to a phrase that begins with paired imitation (mm. 64ff.) that dissolves into free, melismatic counterpoint in all four voices (mm. 72ff.) and is then repeated to bring the section to a close. Obviously, the straightforward compositional procedures and transparent contrapuntal textures that usually distinguish polyphony intended for strict liturgical use have been superseded in this group of compositions for one of the most solemn of Christian observances by a compositional style of considerable—and presumably appropriate—sophistication.

⟳ THE TE DEUM ⟲

The general paucity of polyphonic settings for the Te Deum throughout the sixteenth century would indicate that the use of part-music for Matins and Lauds—essentially monastic services except for the age-old observances of Holy Week—was very slow in coming and in fact never became widely established as routine. It seems likely that the relatively few compositions of this kind written at the time were prompted as a rule by its use on special occasions as a hymn of praise and thanksgiving (cf. the discussion pp. 348–50). Beginning, roughly, with the generation of Binchoys, whose Te Deum was examined earlier, only about sixty-five different settings of this text have been transmitted by the extant sources, some eighty manuscripts and ten prints. None of the earliest of the sixteenth-century printers—Petrucci, Attaingnant, Gardane, Scotto, or Moderne—published a single polyphonic Te Deum. It is undoubtedly symptomatic, as well, that there is but a single such work—attributed to the papal singer Costanzo Festa—in the entire collection of manuscripts held by the Sistine Chapel.[55]

Nor did even the best known of these compositions circulate very widely. Binchoys's, for example, one of the very few from his time, was copied into only five manuscripts. The most widely disseminated of all—a piece with attributions to Andreas de Silva, who sang in the papal choir in the time of Leo X,[56] has been transmitted in only ten sources. (The work is also credited to Josquin and Mouton, while in seven cases no author is named.) Significantly, nine of these collections are German, reflecting apparently a greater affection for the text in those regions than in Italy or France.[57]

55. This is Cappella Sistina MS 20; see José M. Llorens, *Capellae Sixtinae Codices*, Studi e testi, vol. 202 (Vatican City: Biblioteca Apostolica Vaticana, 1960), 43.
56. See Winfried Kirsch, "De Silva, Andreas," *The New Grove Dictionary of Music*, 5:389.
57. See the list of sources for composition in Andreas de Silva, *Opera omnia*, ed. Winfried Kirsch, 2 vols., Corpus mensurabilis musicae 49 ([Rome]: American Institute of Musicology, 1970–77), 1:xvii.

Of the remaining masters of the period who worked in the genre, only the most celebrated did more or less as well; Johann Walter's Te Deum was included in seven sources, Ludwig Senfl's in five, Cristóbal de Morales's in four, and Costanzo Festa's in three.[58] These numbers are in sharp contrast to the rapid expansion of the motet repertory generally during the same period and in particular to the proliferation of settings for the Magnificat, which are found by the dozens in literally hundreds of sources.

In light of these circumstances, it is perhaps not surprising that no consistent compositional tradition appears to have been forged for the Te Deum as it was for other well-defined liturgical genres. In the setting attributed to De Silva, for example, the plainsong has been incorporated into the polyphony, where it is passed back and forth between superius and tenor (see Example 16-6).[59] Those voices are virtu-

58. See Kirsch, *Die Quellen der mehrstimmigen Magnificat- und Te Deum-Vertonungen*, 57.
59. For a transcription of the complete work in modern score, see Silva, *Opera omnia*, ed. Kirsch, 1:71–79, and cf. the *Tonus simplex* as given in the *Liber usualis*, 1834.

EXAMPLE 16-6. Andreas de Silva, *Te Deum laudamus* (mm. 1–30)

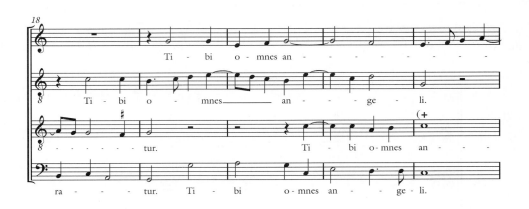

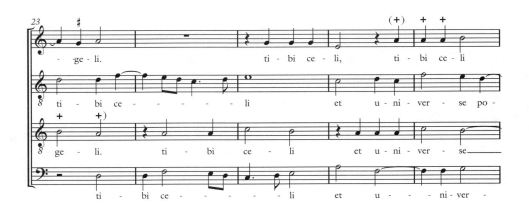

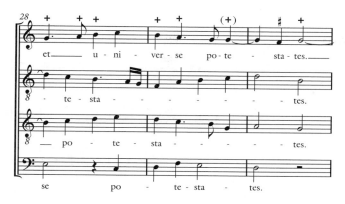

We praise thee, O God; we acknowledge thee, O Lord. Eternal Father of all the earth, we worship thee. Thou rulest over all the angels, the heavens, and the universe.

ally indistinguishable from the others, however, both rhythmically and melodically, and the facture of the work generally is in all respects that of a typical motet.

The text is divided into three *partes* (with new sections at "Patrem immense majestatis" and "Te ergo quesumus"), as might be expected in view of its length, but is otherwise set continuously. Passages in free counterpoint, homophonic declamation, and imitation alternate with one another as successive phrases of the hymn unfold, the sonorous textures shifting in the process from high voices to low and from duos to the full sound of the choir. At the same time, the relatively clear cadential articulation marking the completion of each syntactic unit is always mitigated to an appropriate degree by the overlapping of the parts.

The setting by Festa, by comparison, is much more closely tied to the liturgical chant, which is carried by the superius throughout (see Example 16-7).[60] Because the polyphony begins with the second verse, "Te Dominum confitemur," it must be preceded by the initial phrase of the text sung in plainsong. Thereafter the successive incises of the traditional melody are strongly articulated, each of them handled as a separate section ending with an unmistakable cadence and, usually, a pause. It is the kind of treatment that would lend itself easily to an *alternatim* performance, all the more so since the polyphony is based unremittingly on homophonic declamation of the words of the hymn, relieved only slightly by a brief melismatic flourish at the approach to the closely spaced points of cadential closure. But every verse of the hymn—except the first—has been set in parts for a fully polyphonic performance. This may be simply because the protocols of the papal choir prescribed that manner of presentation; in any case, alternation between chant and polyphony was clearly possible in an institution where it was the customary liturgical practice.

Inasmuch as Walter's setting of the Te Deum provides polyphony only for the

60. For a transcription of the entire piece in modern score, see Festa, *Opera omnia*, ed. Main, 4:81.

Example 16-7. Costanzo Festa, *Te Deum laudamus* (mm. 1–17)

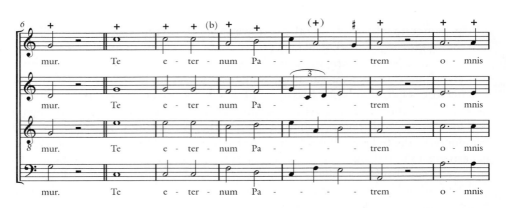

We praise thee, O God; we acknowledge thee, O Lord. Eternal Father of all the earth,
we worship thee.

even-numbered verses, beginning with "Te eternum Patrem," *alternatim* performance was clearly intended. It was written, moreover, in much the same style as the arrangement attributed to Festa. The chant is carried in this instance by the tenor, however, and because it is laid out in longer values than those used in the surrounding parts (even breves and semibreves), mildly melismatic figures and a loosely contrapuntal facture replace the strict homophony of Festa's composition.

Walter's Te Deum—one of the most widely circulated of the sixteenth century—was included in the first songbook compiled for use in Lutheran schools and communities, the *Geystliches gesangk Buchleyn* of 1524.[61] This reflects the great affection that Luther and his followers apparently had for this hymn of praise and thanksgiving, as does the large number of German sources for the Te Deum ascribed to De Silva.

Its association with the reformers may help to explain a rather curious parody of the liturgical text that transforms the ecstatic acclamations addressed to God into violent imprecations against Luther himself, beginning "Te Lutherum damnamus." However, the composer of the latter text—apparently Maistre Jhan, who was serving at the ducal court of Ferrara in the mid-1530s, when the piece must have been written—so ordered his music that it would accommodate the liturgical hymn as well as its anti-Reformation parody. It is in fact not clear for which set of verses the polyphony was originally prepared, the original chant or its polemical transformation.[62]

In any case, Maistre Jhan's compositional handling of the work is clearly oriented toward the contemporaneous motet, like that of the setting attributed to De Silva. He divided the text into the same three *partes* and set it continuously from beginning to end with the liturgical melody providing the substance for the superius. Consequently, just as his work in this form bears witness textually to the often violent conflicts that arose between Catholics and Reformers, it also reflects the significant impact of the motet of the sixteenth century upon some of the genres of polyphonic composition that were intended for liturgical use.

61. For a transcription of the work in modern score, see Johannes Walter, *Sämtliche Werke*, ed. O. Schröder, 6 vols. (Kassel: Barenreiter, 1953–73), 2:123–30.
62. See George Nugent, "Anti-Protestant Music for Sixteenth-Century Ferrara," *Journal of the American Musicological Society* 43 (1990): 228–91, especially 235–55.

CHAPTER 17

*Liturgical Polyphony
for the Mass*

As we have seen, the compositional types that emerged in the course of the fifteenth century as well suited for polyphonic settings of texts of the five Ordinary chants of the Mass included the following:[1]

1. A cyclic series built on a musical idea of the composer's invention that recurs in each of the major sections of the work (such as the head motives used early on by Continental composers). Pieces of this type—sometimes identified in the sources as "sine nomine"—are occasionally found in the fifteenth and sixteenth centuries as well but become increasingly rare as other types of Mass composition come to the fore, in particular that based on a cantus firmus.

2. Mass cycles based on some technical tour de force such as Okeghem's *Missa Prolationum* and Josquin's *Missa Ad fugam*. By the sixteenth century—following, perhaps, Josquin's example—the deployment of strictly canonic imitation appears to have become the favored technical procedure for Masses of this type. There is some overlap here, moreover, with compositions of the first category since the musical materials were usually of the composer's invention.

3. Cycles built upon the paraphrase and elaboration of the Ordinary chants appropriate for a specific purpose or occasion, such as feasts of the Virgin Mary or the Requiem Mass. Since these melodies take on something of a Proper character by virtue of their particular liturgical association, they were often so used whereas the ferial (everyday) Ordinaries were rarely given such a role. As has been noted, Mass Ordinaries of this type were written to

---

1. See the discussion in chap. 10.

honor the Virgin Mary by composers of the fifteenth century from Libert to Josquin, and the lengthy series of polyphonic Requiems was apparently opened by composers of the generation of Du Fay and Okeghem.

4. Masses based on a cantus firmus that is usually—but not always—carried by the tenor: a borrowed melody, for example, or, less frequently, a *soggetto cavato* or a hexachordal scale. This then provides the scaffolding for the counterpoint in each of its successive sections. (Here, too, canonic imitation is not uncommon, especially as a means of increasing the number of voices in culminating sections, but it does not serve as the fundamental principle of organization.) As has been noted, this was the compositional procedure adopted with increasing frequency as the cyclic polyphonic Ordinary was established as a distinctive musical genre.

The culmination in the development of cycles of the latter type came already with the composers of the late fifteenth century, especially in the works of such masters as Josquin Desprez, Jacob Obrecht, Heinrich Isaac, and Pierre de La Rue. There is some evidence as well, if one is to judge from the Mass repertory of a composer such as Obrecht, that cantus firmus Mass composition continued to be preferred in the Low Countries even after its dominance had begun to wane in other regions. It is clear, in any case, that some of the most elaborate contrapuntal structures to be grounded in the cantus firmus usage of the period are to be found in Obrecht's Masses (see Figure 17-1).

The lengths to which the procedure could be carried, both conceptually and compositionally, are perhaps best exemplified by his *Missa Sub tuum presidium.* Although the work begins with only three notated voices for the Kyrie, rather than the more usual four, another is added in each of the subsequent sections, reaching a total of seven for the "Agnus Dei III" (see Example 17-1). Added to the climactic effect of

FIGURE 17-1. Anonymous portrait of Jacob Obrecht, 1496 (17¼" × 11"; Fort Worth, Kimbell Art Museum).

EXAMPLE 17-1. Jacob Obrecht, *Missa Sub tuum presidium*, "Agnus III" (mm. 1–9)

DISCANTUS I: But deliver us always from all dangers, blessed Virgin.

DISCANTUS II AND TENOR I: Queen of heaven, rejoice . . .

ALTUS I: O merciful, O kind, O sweet Mary.

OTHER VOICES: Lamb of God, who takest away the sins of the world . . .

gradually swelling sonorities is an increasing number of chants borrowed from the liturgy for inclusion in the contrapuntal fabric.[2]

The cantus firmus proper is an antiphon of ancient origin in honor of the Virgin that apparently had its primary liturgical place at the time in the litany of Loreto—the series of solemn supplications associated in particular with the Santa Casa, a much-visited place of pilgrimage at the time.[3] The chant is quoted in full (primarily in longer values, breves and semibreves, like all of the borrowed melodies), together with its original text, by the first of two discantus parts in all five sections of the Mass.[4] The other six chants woven into the work all have Marian connections as well. Like the principal cantus firmus, they, too, are sung with their original texts, and as they are treated compositionally in much the same manner, they can be seen to have not only a similar musical function but also the same symbolic purpose.

The first of these, "Audi nos, nam te filius nichil negans honorat" ("Hear us, thou whom the Son honors, refusing nothing"), introduced as the fifth voice (a second discantus) in the Credo, is the seventh strophe of the sequence for the octave of the Assumption of the Virgin, *Ave preclara maris stella*. At the Sanctus Obrecht added the second of the supplemental chants, "Mediatrix nostra, que es post Deum spes sola" ("Our mediation, who is, after God, our only hope"), the second half of the ninth strophe of the sequence for the feast of the Assumption, *Aurea virga prime matris Eve*, weaving it into the compositional fabric in duplicate between discantus II and tenor I, who sing it in alternation an octave apart.

Running through the first two sections of the Agnus Dei are two more supplemental cantus firmi, the third and fourth. The first to enter, "Celsus nunciat Gabriel nova Gaudia" ("The mighty Gabriel announces a new joy"), is the second half of the third strophe of *Aurea virga*; it replaces "Mediatrix nostra" in duplication at the octave between discantus II and tenor I. At the same time the first altus sings "Supplicamus nos emenda" ("We beseech thee to make us better"), the final strophe of the sequence for Epiphany, *Verbum bonum et suave*. For the third and final Agnus Dei the supplemental chants, the fifth and the sixth to be combined with the ongoing cantus firmus, "Sub tuum presidium," are drawn from two of the great Marian antiphons sung at Compline, *Regina celi* and *Salve regina*. Obrecht took from the former the first incise and part of the second and gave them once again to discantus II and tenor I, singing still at the octave. From the latter he has cited only the final expressions of supplication and praise, "O clemens, O pia, O dulcis Maria" ("O mer-

2. Concerning this Mass, see Rob C. Wegman, *Born for the Muses: The Life and Masses of Jacob Obrecht* (Oxford: Clarendon Press, 1994), 337–40.

3. According to a tradition that became popular in the fifteenth century, the house of the Virgin Mary in Nazareth was miraculously transported to Loreto in the year 1294.

4. For the chants imbedded in the polyphony of the Mass, see the edition by Marcus Van Crevel in Jacob Obrecht, *Opera omnia editio altera*, ed. Albert Smijers and Marcus van Crevel, 9 vols. (Amsterdam: Vereniging voor Nederlandse Musiekgeschiedenis, 1954–64), 6:xlvi ff.; in addition, M. Jennifer Bloxam, "Plainsong and Polyphony for the Blessed Virgin: Notes on Two Masses by Jacob Obrecht," *Journal of Musicology* 12 (1994): 51–75, discusses the melodies adopted for the Mass with regard to the liturgical and chant traditions of the cities in which Obrecht was employed.

ciful, O pious, O sweet Mary"), which replaces "Supplicamus nos" in the first altus.

The Marian implications of this work are of course both multifarious and, to a degree, self-evident. Less obvious, but no less compelling, are the links that can be made between the chants introduced as cantus firmi and extraordinary devotional exercises prompted by outbreaks of the plague to invoke in particular the help and protection of the Virgin. For such a purpose the composer apparently thought it fitting to combine the contrapuntal artifices that progressively enhanced textural complexity and systematically expanded the sonorities heard with the polytextuality of the medieval motet. He thus reverted to the developmental matrix for the cantus firmus techniques used in the cyclic Mass and invoked the powerful verbal associations that made its use such an effective means of artistic expression, creating a musical monument of truly impressive dimensions. His intention must surely have been to present to the mild Mother of Christ a cluster of praise and pleas in a rich polyphonic sheave in the hope that she would intervene on behalf of those faced with the terrifying dangers of a deadly and uncontrollable pestilence.

If the essential character and purpose of cantus firmus composition is truly reflected in a cyclic Mass of this sort, then much of its earlier effect was undoubtedly altered when the differentiation of the individual parts upon which it was based began to give way to the assimilation of all the voices in a more homogeneous contrapuntal

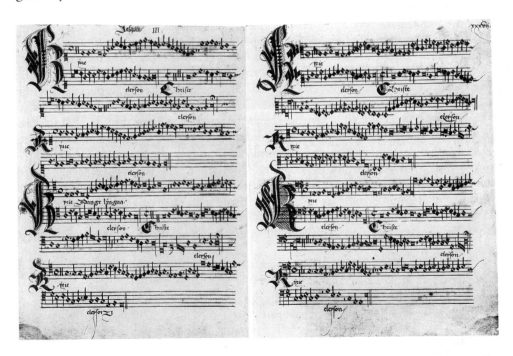

FIGURE 17-2. Kyrie of Josquin's *Missa Pange lingua* from the manuscript Rome, Cappella Sistina, Cod. 16.

fabric. And, as we have seen, polyphonic writing in such a style resulted from a mix of syntactic imitation, free counterpoint, and homophonic declamation, which had emerged in the motet repertory as the fundamental compositional techniques of the age. In such a context there was an unmistakable tendency either to assimilate a borrowed melody to the contrapuntal structure, causing it to penetrate the whole in successive points of imitation, or to mask its presence by embedding it in passages of equal-voiced free counterpoint or homophonic declamation.

Nowhere can the impact of this stylistic trend on cantus firmus composition be seen more clearly than in Josquin's *Missa Pange lingua,* (see Figure 17–2), which is based on the melody of the hymn for the feast of Corpus Christi. Although its essential features are those of a "tenor cantus firmus Mass," the structural functions of the borrowed plainsong have been radically altered, even though the symbolic function is unchanged. At the beginning of the Gloria, for example, the first phrase of the hymn is introduced by the tenor but immediately imitated, if in a somewhat truncated form, by the bassus at the lower fifth (see Example 17-2). That pair of voices

EXAMPLE 17-2. Josquin Desprez, *Missa Pange lingua,* Gloria (mm. 1–25)

. . . and on earth peace to men of good will. We praise thee; we bless thee; we glorify thee. We give thanks for thy great glory . . .

is echoed in turn at the upper octave by superius and altus in a classic example of paired imitation. As a consequence, the melodic material derived from the hymn is carried from voice to voice in notes of essentially comparable duration, permeating the contrapuntal fabric of the initial phrase, and there is little to distinguish the primary bearer of the cantus firmus from the other parts, either melodically or rhythmically.

The acclamations of praise that follow (mm. 11–21) are also presented in imitative pairs—with the altus responding to the superius and the bassus to the tenor—each duo having its own melodic material but with no evident trace of the chant. When Josquin reintroduces the hymn into the contrapuntal fabric with its second phrase (m. 21), he reverses the order of the first appearance. He quotes the borrowed melody first in the superius, then imitates it in the altus, and echoes that pair of voices at the lower octave in tenor and bassus. Subsequent references to the liturgical tune are so brief and so far from literal that one cannot be entirely certain that they are intentional. The point of imitation used to open the "Qui tollis" (mm. 45–55) was probably derived from the third phrase of the chant ("Quem in mundi"), and the rising fifth in the tenor (at m. 64) may be related, if somewhat distantly, to its fourth line ("Fructus ventris"), transposed up a fifth. However, the similarities may be due more to the general characteristics of the mode and the composer's intuitive response to his material than to an intentional purpose.

In any case, Josquin appears to have relied only on his own melodic invention for the remainder of the section. He shapes his motives to accommodate both the syntax and the accentual rhythms of the Latin text and presents them in a contrapuntal texture rooted in paired imitation, relieved only occasionally by homophonic declamation either for two (mm. 84–85) or for all four voices (mm. 67–73). In other sections of the Mass he quotes more consistently and systematically from the hymn melody. It is especially prominent, as one would expect, in the Kyrie, thus assuring from the outset that it will be recognized by all. But his use of it in the Mass generally is clearly more for its associative and symbolic value rather than for its structural possibilities. The cantus firmus is no longer, as with Obrecht, the foundation upon which the counterpoint has been based; it has instead been subjected to the newly developed compositional matrix of syntactic imitation and lost its distinctive identity in the process. Consequently, although the *Missa Sub tuum presidium* and the *Missa Pange lingua* could both be described, with considerable justification, in the same terms as "tenor cantus firmus" compositions, they are dramatically different in style.

Perhaps equally important in redefining the musical style of the cyclic Mass Ordinary in the early sixteenth century were the experiments of fifteenth-century composers with multiple borrowings from a single polyphonic model, even where the structure was still determined in its essentials by the presence of a borrowed cantus firmus, as in Okeghem's *Missa Fors seulement*. The increasing utilization of equal-voice counterpoint, whether in textures of independent linear activity (imitative or not) or homophonic identification, apparently encouraged the assimilation of the new compositional procedures to the concept of associative borrowing in the creative imagination of the period's composers.

Models began to be chosen from the motet repertory, in particular, where the newly popular styles of writing had been developed, thus offering perhaps yet another bit of evidence for a liturgical link between Mass and motet. More importantly, the materials borrowed for contrapuntal elaboration were the points of imitation and/or the passages of homophonic declamation that were fundamental to the musical syntax of the work taken as a model. Moreover, to the extent that the preexistent material continued to provide a "proper" reference to a liturgical event or a text appropriate to a specific occasion, the motet offered an acceptable substitute for the cantus firmus melody that had earlier been used for the purpose.

The rather dramatic change in the compositional procedures found appropriate for the cyclic Mass in the early sixteenth century appears to have been the achievement, first of all, of composers associated with the royal French chapel. Févin and Mouton, in particular, followed by their younger contemporaries, appear to have been among the first to take the decisive step, joining the notion of polyphonic borrowing with the essentially imitative style of the Latin motet.[5] This process is often referred to as "parody" in the scholarly literature, but it is more aptly identified in many sources of the period by the indication "ad imitationem" coupled with the title of the model. Given the dubious and often negative connotations of the modern term "parody," "imitation Mass" is probably a preferable designation.[6]

5. See Lewis Lockwood, "Mass," *The New Grove Dictionary of Music*, 11:786.

6. Arguments bearing on the terminological issues have generated at this point a considerable scholarly literature, but the essential groundbreaking studies are by Lewis Lockwood, "A View of the Early Sixteenth-Century Parody Mass," in *Queen's College 25th Anniversary Festschrift*, ed. Albert Mell (Flushing, N.Y.: Queen's College Press, 1964), 53–77; and idem, "On 'Parody' as Term and Concept in Sixteenth-Century Music," in *Aspects of Medieval and Renaissance Music: A Birthday Offering to Gustave Reese*, ed. Jan La Rue et al. (New York: Norton, 1966), 560–75. More recent articles have been more concerned with "imitation" in cantus firmus Masses with multiple borrowings.

Two of the fifteen or sixteen known cyclic Ordinaries attributed to Mouton, *Missa Quem dicunt homines* and *Missa Verbum bonum*, are based on motets by composers of the next generation, Jean Richafort and Pierrequin de Therache, respectively. Févin took similar models for three of his ten cycles; the *Missa Sancta Trinitas* is based on a motet of his own, while two more, *Missa Mente tota* and *Missa Ave Maria*, draw motivic substance from motets by Josquin. The latter may in fact be one of the earliest compositions to display the approach to Mass composition in which a preexistent polyphonic composition is reworked systematically, being expanded, contracted, and/or modified as necessary to accommodate the various texts of the Ordinary.

The *Missa Ave Maria* had to have been written prior to Févin's premature death in 1511–12, even though the earliest source for it is a collection published by Petrucci in 1515;[7] the Josquin motet upon which it is based had been in circulation in any case since the 1480s. Févin apparently viewed his model as a sequence of some sixteen separate polyphonic phrases,[8] and he drew from them, one by one, the musical materials that constitute key elements in the contrapuntal fabric of his Mass, as will be clear from Table 17-1.

The manner in which Févin adapts the materials of his model to the texts of the Mass may be seen in some detail from a brief examination of the Kyrie (see Example 17-3). He takes the point of imitation with which the motet begins as the opening motive of the Mass as well. However, instead of introducing the four voices at regular intervals from the top down as Josquin had done, Févin leads with the altus, pairing it imitatively at the upper octave with the superius (which enters in m. 3). He then answers those two voices with tenor and bassus similarly paired but with the latter a fifth below the former and much more closely spaced—a semibreve apart instead of five as in the first entry (mm. 9–10). As an extension of the opening melodic phrase in the superius, Févin interpolated a motive of his own, a descending, syncopated line that culminates in a cadence to c (mm. 7–10).

Investing that figure with a compositional life of its own, Févin uses it in a short point of imitation between altus and tenor at the unusual interval of a lower third (mm. 22–26). As a counterpoint to that tenor line, he introduces in the bassus a dotted figure that ascends first through a fourth (mm. 24–25) and then (in imitation in the altus) through a fifth (mm. 28–29), sounding the second time against the superius carrying the initial motive derived from the motet. That ascending line was adopted in turn as the opening motive for the Christe, heard first in the altus and then in imitation (either from c or from g) in the bassus (mm. 41 and

---

7. See Howard M. Brown, "Févin," *The New Grove Dictionary of Music*, 6:515–17; for a complete edition of the Mass, see J. A. Bank, ed., *A. Fevin, Missa Ave Maria ad modulum Josquini Pratensis, 4-vocum inaequalium* (Amsterdam: Annie Bank, n.d.), or Edward Clinkscale, ed., *Les oeuvres complètes d'Antoine de Févin*, 4 vols. (Henryville, Pa.: Institute of Mediaeval Music, 1980–96).

8. These segments are numbered in sequence in the compositional analysis of the Josquin motet discussed earlier; see chap. 15, pp. 517–18, and Example 15-1.

TABLE 17-1. ANTOINE DE FÉVIN: *Missa Ave Maria*
POLYPHONIC PHRASES OF JOSQUIN'S MOTET
AS THEY APPEAR IN THE MASS

Ordinary	Section	Phrases	Final
Kyrie	Kyrie I	1	C
	Christe	2	C
	Kyrie II	3, 4	C
Gloria	Et in terra	1, 5, 6a, 6b, 9	G
	Domine Deus (duo)	None	C
	Qui tollis	10, 8(?), 9(?), 11, 12	C
Credo	Patrem omnipotentum	1, 10, 6(?), 7, 6	G
	Crucifixus (duo)	9 (or 1?), 6b	G
	Et resurrexit (duo)	None	C
	Et iterum (trio)	8	C
	Et in spiritum Sanctum	9 (or 1), 6b (or 14), 10, 6, 12, 16	C
Sanctus	Sanctus	1 (or 9), 14	C
	Pleni sunt (duo)	11(?), 9 (or 1)	C
	Hosanna	12	C
	Benedictus (trio)	13	C
Agnus Dei	Agnus I	1, 7, 6b	C
	Agnus II (duo)	14(?), 1(?)	C
	Agnus III	= Agnus I	C

46), the superius (mm. 45 and 52), and the tenor (mm. 50 and 53). As a result, the second motive derived from the model (introduced by the superius in m. 38 and by the tenor in m. 42) seems to play a secondary role. That impression is strengthened by the appearance in the altus (m. 45) of a second descending figure, not unlike the first, as counterpoint to the principal melodic element of the section, and that descending figure was treated in turn as a full-blown point of imitation, moving from bassus to altus to tenor to superius (mm. 56ff.) to bring the section to a close.

The final Kyrie begins with a systematic point of imitation based on the third full phrase of Josquin's model. It passes from altus to bassus to superius to tenor (mm.

EXAMPLE 17-3. Antoine de Févin, *Missa Ave Maria*, Kyrie

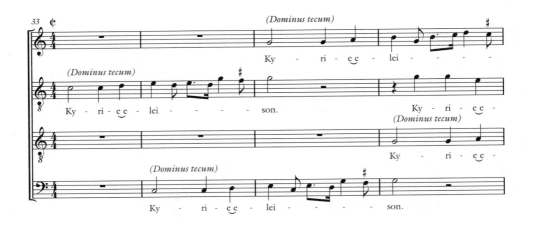

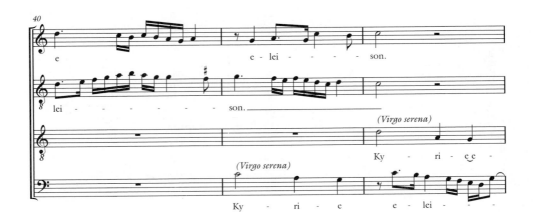

Lord, have mercy. Christ have mercy. Lord have mercy.

66–74) and overlaps with the fourth phrase derived from the motet, which begins in the same manner (mm. 72–78). The latter is then coupled in a pair of duos with running contrapuntal passage work before bringing the entire section to a close with a point of imitation based upon the same fourth phrase of the motet. It rises from the bassus to include each of the voices in turn and to generate full four-part sonorities for the closing cadence. The final upon which the concluding sonorities come to rest is of course the C of the model, just as internal points of articulation make use of the cadential finals most frequently employed by Josquin in his motet: C, E, and G.

For the four sections of the cycle that follow, even though they differ in some details, Févin adopts the same basic compositional procedures, crafting a work that makes unmistakable reference to its model, but presenting the borrowed materials in new guises and in combination with motives and figures of his own invention that come to constitute a significant part of its substance.

That Févin's Mass, and others of the period like it, established a compositional model that was followed in its essentials through the remainder of the century is clearly suggested by a comparison of his working procedures, as described in the preceding paragraphs, with the prescriptions given for the composition of a polyphonic Mass by Pietro Cerone. In his widely circulated treatise *El Melopeo y Maestro*, published in 1613, the theorist offers carefully detailed instructions that can be summarized as follows:[9]

1. In the motet the musical materials of the successive sections should differ from one another, but in the Mass it is obligatory that the same motive be used to open each of the major sections—Kyrie, Gloria, Credo, Sanctus, and Agnus Dei—yet each time in a different harmonic and contrapuntal configuration.

2. The Christe may be based upon a subsidiary motive taken from the model (whether motet or madrigal) or may use material of the composer's own invention, provided it conforms to the model in mode and style.

3. The beginning of "Kyrie II" and "Agnus II" and "Agnus III" may be of the composer's own invention, but he may also borrow a motive from his model.

4. The cadential material used to conclude each of the major sections—Kyrie, Gloria, Credo, Sanctus, Osanna (!), and Agnus III—should be in imitation of the model as to material and modal final.

5. Cadences at the end of subsections—for example, the "Christe," "Et in terra," "Patrem," "Pleni sunt," or "Benedictus"—can close on the confinal of the mode rather than the final, provided that no two subsections in succession conclude on that pitch (a stricture that does not apply to the final itself).

6. The more use the composer makes in the course of the Mass of motives derived from internal phrases of the model, the more praiseworthy it will be.

7. When the Mass is for an important feast, the Kyrie, Sanctus, and Agnus Dei should be more extended and solemn in nature than if it is for ferial (everyday) use.

8. The Gloria and Credo, with the exception of internal sections for two or three (soloistic?) voices, should be syllabic, with shorter, clearer phrases in the counterpoint.

9. It is appropriate, because of their significance, to treat the words "Jesu Christe," "Et incarnatus est," and "Crucifixus" in homophonic declamation with extended note values.

9. See the English translation given by Oliver Strunk, ed., *Source Readings in Music History* (New York: Norton, 1950), 265–68.

10. Some of the internal subsections—such as the "Christe," the "Crucifixus," the "Pleni sunt," and the second Agnus—may be written in reduced textures, usually as a duo or a trio, in which case they should be treated "with greater artifice and learning and in a more lofty and elegant style," that they may become "the flower of the whole work."

11. For a fuller effect at the conclusion, "greater harmony and sonority," a part or two can be added for the final Agnus Dei.

12. A Mass based upon a motet, madrigal, or chanson—the most common manner of proceeding—is usually identified by the incipit of the borrowed composition (e.g., *Missa Virtute magna*, etc.). The composer may also write a Mass using newly invented materials of his own, and he may either leave them unidentified, as in a *Missa Sine nomine*, or make reference to them, as when they are derived from a hexachordal sequence or a *soggetto cavato* (e.g., Josquin's *Missa La sol fa re mi*). Or he may base his composition on the formulas of the tones, as in a *Missa Primi toni*, or on the plainsong prescribed for a given feast, as in a *Missa De Beata Virgine*, or making an appropriate reference to the liturgical occasion, as in a *Missa Ecce sacerdos magnus*.[10]

There are obviously many differences of detail from one composer to the next, even one composition to the next. As is clear from Cerone's lengthy discussion, moreover, Masses making use of the older and perhaps therefore more venerable structural principles continued to be written, if only in limited numbers. Nonetheless, the great majority of cyclic Mass Ordinaries added to the sacred repertory in the course of the sixteenth century were *ad imitationem*. The first genre to be so adapted was the motet, but as chansons and madrigals took on many of the same stylistic characteristics, in particular the contrapuntal textures that had become characteristic for the motet, Masses were based on secular models as well. Interestingly, all of those so conceived conform to a greater or lesser degree to the pattern established early in the sixteenth century as exemplified in Févin's *Missa Ave Maria* and so carefully described by Cerone. We shall examine presently some of the many ways in which that paradigm was adapted by composers of the late sixteenth century to their needs and personal styles.

⟶⟋⟍⟋ MASS PROPERS

As was observed earlier, the Propers for the Mass continued to attract the attention of composers of polyphony from the time of Du Fay until the end of the sixteenth

10. It is instructive to compare Cerone's description of the compositional types associated with the cyclic Mass at the end of the sixteenth century with the summary given earlier (pp. 574–75) of those that had been established in the course of the fifteenth.

century. Most of the time, however, they were taken as individual texts and set in the manner of a motet with little indication as to whether they were actually intended for liturgical use or had been prepared for some more general purpose, either devotional or processional. This ambiguity of function is perhaps best illuminated by the so-called *motetti-missales*, motets that were written to substitute for the liturgically prescribed Propers (and Ordinaries) in the celebration of the Mass (see pp. 429–36). Given the existence of such works, it should not surprise us that the Proper texts were sometimes set as motets for liturgical use with no explicit indication as to their intended function.

Occasionally, too, a single category of Proper chant was singled out for polyphonic composition, as is evident from the series of polyphonic Introits that were linked with cyclic Ordinaries in Trent MS 92. Pierluigi Palestrina, whose career was defined by his service at a series of Roman institutions, including the papal choir, prepared a cycle of polyphonic Offertories for Sundays and major feast days throughout the year, according to Roman usage, some sixty-eight compositions in all.[11] The sequence, too, was held in particular affection and thus set polyphonically with some frequency. Tomás Luis de Victoria, who divided his career between Rome and his native Spain, composed in a grand antiphonal manner (for eight voices divided between two choirs) three of the five sequences that remained in the liturgy after the Council of Trent, those for Corpus Christi, Pentecost, and Easter.[12]

Considerably less common, however, was the systematic polyphonic treatment of all of the Proper chants for a given liturgical feast (or feasts) such as was attempted on a relatively modest level by Du Fay for the *Missa Sancti Jacobi* (see pp. 359 and 384). Only two composers active during the sixteenth century seem to have focused their attention on Mass Propers in that manner: the northerner Heinrich Isaac, who spent a substantial portion of his career in Florence (from 1485 on) before entering the service of the Habsburg emperor, Maximilian I, in 1496;[13] and the English master William Byrd, the recusant Catholic who served in the court chapel of Elizabeth I of England in the 1570s and 1580s before retiring to the country in Stondon Massey, Essex.[14] Both of them, however, have left an extraordinary body of compositions intended expressly for use in the Proper liturgy of the Mass.

The greater part of Isaac's settings for the Propers of the Mass were gathered by the Nuremberg printer Hieronymous Formschneider and published posthumously in three grand volumes (the first in 1550, the second and third in 1555) under the title *Choralis Constantinus*. That designation is a reference to a commission that Isaac

11. The Offertories were published in 1593 under the title *Offertoria totius anni secundum Sanctae Romanae Ecclesiae consuetudinem*; see Jessie Ann Owens, "Palestrina," *The New Grove Dictionary of Music*, 14:134–35.
12. These are *Lauda Sion, Veni Sancte Spiritus*, and *Victimae paschali laudes*, respectively; see Robert Stevenson, "Victoria," *The New Grove Dictionary of Music*, 19:708. The contribution of both Palestrina and Victoria to the polyphonic repertory of the late sixteenth century is discussed in greater detail below.
13. See Martin Staehelin, "Isaac," *The New Grove Dictionary of Music*, 9:329–30.
14. See Joseph Kerman, "Byrd," *The New Grove Dictionary of Music*, 3:537–44.

received in 1508 from the Cathedral Chapter in Constance (Switzerland) for cycles of Mass Propers for the liturgical feasts that were observed there with particular solemnity. It would appear, however, that only the second of the three volumes published by Formschneider contains music prepared in that connection, whereas the other two contain repertory intended for the Habsburg court chapel.[15] In all there are more than 100 Proper cycles, each of which usually included at least an Introit, a verse for the Alleluia, and a Communion. Not infrequently a Sequence and occasionally a Gradual or a Tract was added as well.[16]

Perhaps the most striking feature common to this entire body of music is Isaac's unswerving adherence to the liturgical melody as the starting point for his polyphony. In the process, as was to be expected, he employed all of the techniques and procedures familiar to northern-trained composers for cantus firmus-based composition. At times he provided mensural rhythms for the preexistent melody that make it indistinguishable from the other voices, weaving it into the texture in free counterpoint or even in syntactic imitation. For celebrations of particular significance he sometimes doubled or tripled the plainchant by means of canonic imitation. More frequently, however, he opted for what appears to have been a typically Germanic solution, laying out the liturgical melody in longer notes of equal value—often semibreves—as a foundation for the relatively florid counterpoint in the other voices.[17]

Such a work is his setting of the Introit designated for use at the Common of the Apostles, *Mihi autem nimis honorati sunt* (see Example 17-4),[18] the same chant that had been set earlier by Du Fay for the *Missa Sancti Jacobi* (see pp. 384–85 and Example 10-8). Proof that both of these works were intended for liturgical use is to be seen in the alternation between chant and polyphony that characterizes their structure. Each begins with the initial words in plainsong. However, Du Fay left the entire Versus (*Domine probasti me*) in plainsong while Isaac maintained the alternation, setting the second half of it.

Once the polyphony begins, Isaac's cantus firmus, like Du Fay's in his opening section, is at the bottom of the contrapuntal web and set apart from the other voices by its more deliberate pace. Du Fay cited the chant at pitch, however, and thus left it in an ambitus where it occasionally crosses with the contratenor, whereas Isaac treated it as a true bassus, transposing it down a fifth, where it is well below the ranges of the other parts. More strikingly, Isaac maintains the same style of cantus firmus treatment throughout, whereas Du Fay reverts, for the *Repetitio*, to a treble-dominated texture in three parts (like that of the chanson), with the chant providing the melodic substance for his superius.[19]

15. This is according to Staehelin, "Isaac," *The New Grove Dictionary of Music,* 9:331.
16. See the list of works drawn up by Staehelin in *The New Grove Dictionary of Music,* 9:333–34.
17. Cf. Staehelin's observations, *The New Grove Dictionary of Music,* 9:331.
18. For a complete transcription of the piece in modern score, see Heinrich Isaac, *Choralis Constantinus, Book III,* ed. Louise Cuyler (Ann Arbor: University of Michigan Press, 1950), 77–78.
19. Isaac does not provide new music for the repetition of the Introit's antiphon; if the return was called for liturgically, the opening text could have been sung either to the opening section or to the plainchant.

EXAMPLE 17-4. Heinrich Isaac, *Mihi autem nimis,* Introit for the Common of the Apostles (mm. 1–31)

To me, moreover, greatly honored are thy friends, O God, greatly comforted is the chief among them.

Isaac's counterpoint also differs from that of the earlier master in its frequent recourse to imitative writing. The altus enters with the rising fourth first heard in the bassus (at the lower octave). Tenor and discantus join in, each in turn, with an identical figure quickly passed from one to the other (again at the octave, mm. 5–6), and they continue to be thus linked imitatively throughout the work, rarely drawing into their orbit the altus as well (but see the versus, 32–34). Particularly striking in this connection are the rapid running figures used either in descent, like the falling fifth in the Introit that is passed from voice to voice, though not always in the same rhythmic configuration (mm. 10–11, altus, superius, and tenor; 13–14, altus; 17–21, altus, superius, and tenor; 25, tenor), or in ascent, like the rising fourth introduced in the versus (mm. 32–35, altus, superius, and tenor). Here one sees a trace not only of the imitative syntax typical of the motet but also of the rapid figuration that Isaac used so skillfully in his instrumental *canzone*.

As has been suggested, although Isaac used a variety of contrapuntal procedures in setting the liturgical plainchant, the entire body of works constituting this remarkable repertory of Mass Propers offers primarily a study in cantus firmus composition. And this may be an indication that, in the early sixteenth century at least, ongoing interest in compositions of this type was largely limited to regions of Germanic culture.[20] There appears to have been considerable reluctance there, even after the Reformation had set in, to make use of the kind of freewheeling substitution of motets for the Proper chants of the Mass that has been documented for the ducal court of Milan under the Sforza and was presumably adopted rather widely in Italian chapels and churches.

Regardless of the musical practice on the Continent at the time, William Byrd's systematic series of polyphonic settings for Mass Propers must be seen as exceptional, if only because public celebration of the Catholic liturgy was actually proscribed in England at the time that most of these pieces were written—and published. In view of the very real danger Byrd incurred by making such an open manifestation of his religious sentiments, he must have had compelling personal reasons for doing so. He gave some indication—necessarily veiled, no doubt—of his motivation in a dedicatory letter to his patron, friend, and fellow recusant, Sir John Petre, lord of Writtle. There he declared that he wished "to leave to posterity a public testimony, at least in some sort, of a heart grateful and referring all things . . . to [his] Creator."[21]

It would appear, then, that he determined in his last years to provide polyphonic music for the principal services and feasts of the Catholic liturgy in a relatively comprehensive manner. His intention was perhaps that recusant families, like his own,

20. The majority of the liturgical melodies used by Isaac appear to be drawn from the Germanic tradition; however, for a discussion of the difficulties involved in unequivocally identifying sources for the chants he set, see Theodore C. Karp, "Some Chant Models for Isaac's *Choralis Constantinus*," in *Beyond the Moon: Festschrift Luther Dittmer*, ed. Bryan Gillingham and Paul Merkley (Ottowa: Institute of Mediaeval Music, 1990), 322–49.
21. The dedication, published in Byrd's *Gradualia liber secundus* of 1607, is given in full by Strunk, *Source Readings in Music History*, p. 330.

should have appropriate music for their private celebrations of the liturgy wherever and whenever that became feasible. The works compiled and composed for this purpose were therefore made accessible to the largest audience possible in two printed volumes that carried the suggestive title of *Gradualia*, one of them published in 1605, the other in 1607.[22] That he was able to do so with relative impunity must have been due in part to his long-standing official involvement with the publication of music in England under royal patent. He was further sheltered, undoubtedly, because of his position with the chapel royal and by the support of powerful patrons—men such as Sir John Petre, to whom he inscribed the second volume, and Lord Henry Howard, earl of Northampton, to whom he dedicated the first.

He included in the first collection a number of motets, antiphon settings, and Marian hymns, some of which he may have written at an earlier period. Still, nearly half of its pages and virtually all of the second book were filled by a systematic series of settings for the Propers of the Mass, some 109 pieces in all.[23] These compositions constitute a complete cycle of polyphonic Propers for each of the major celebrations of the liturgical year. Included are All Saints, Corpus Christi, the Nativity, Epiphany, Easter, the Ascension, Pentecost, Sts. Peter and Paul, St. Peter's Chains, and the four principal feasts of the Virgin Mary—together with Saturday Lady Masses (votive Masses for the Virgin) for every liturgical season (five in all) and two votive Masses for the Blessed Sacrament. Byrd provided for each cycle the appropriate Introit, Gradual, Alleluia or Tract, Offertory, Communion, and where traditional, a Sequence.[24]

Surprisingly, there is no hint in this repertory of Isaac's concern for the melodies traditionally associated with the words to be set or of his preoccupation with cantus firmus procedures.[25] Quite to the contrary, Byrd's Propers reflect, more than anything else, the pervasive influence of motet composition on the musical style of the sixteenth century. They fall into two basic categories: settings for the relatively short texts of the Offertory and the Communion, which often display considerable concision and economy, and by contrast the longer chants—Introits, Graduals, Alleluias, and Sequences—which fall into clearly articulated sections.[26]

When there was no need to recombine individual segments to adjust to the changing liturgical requirements of seasons such as Lent and Pascal Time,[27] he sometimes

22. See Kerman, "Byrd," *The New Grove Dictionary of Music*, 3:545; there was a second edition of both volumes in 1610.

23. See the summary of contents in Joseph Kerman, *The Motets and Masses of William Byrd* (Berkeley: University of Califorina Press, 1981), 216–18.

24. See Kerman, *Masses and Motets of William Byrd*, 218–22; cf. *The New Grove Dictionary of Music*, 3:545–46.

25. See, in this connection, Peter Le Huray, "Some Thoughts about Cantus Firmus Composition," in *Byrd Studies*, ed. Alan Brown and Richard Tarbet (Cambridge: Cambridge University Press, 1992), 1–23.

26. The observation is Kerman's, *Masses and Motets of William Byrd*, 229.

27. The Alleluia was avoided during Lent, for example, as inappropriate jubilation in a time of self-mortification and denial and replaced by the Tract, whereas during Pascal Time two Alleluias were generally sung, one of them replacing the Gradual, in keeping with the joyous nature of liturgical celebration after Easter; cf. the *Liber usualis*, 496–684 and 804–92.

set the longer, sectional pieces as a single unbroken series. Such was the case, in particular, for the Propers to be sung after the Epistle—the Gradual, the Alleluia, and their respective verses—which he sometimes linked together in a continuous compositional chain in the following manner: Gradual, verse, Alleluia, verse, Alleluia. More frequently, however, he articulated clearly the various segments of the polyphonic structure through a reduction in voice parts for one or more of the internal sections. They were thus distinguished from the surrounding components by their contrasting sonorities, a form-building device frequently adopted at the time in the composition of multipartite motets and Mass Ordinaries. For example, he divided all the Introits in the following manner: Introit, verse, Doxology, Introit. The verse he set for three voices and the other sections for the full choir of four, five, or six voices.[28]

A relatively typical, if particularly brilliant, example of Byrd's treatment of the Mass Propers may be seen in his settings of the texts for Easter. The Introit is divided as usual into its four components, and the versus is set off from those that precede and follow by a reduction to three voices from the full complement of five used elsewhere. That segment is written, moreover, in the severely imitative style that characterizes so many of Byrd's trios in the *Gradualia*. Gradual and Alleluia, by contrast, are strung together as a single unit with no change of sonority or texture to articulate the traditional points of division. Such techniques are applied instead to the lengthy Sequence. Byrd divided it into seven segments, each with a different vocal scoring. For internal sections he adopted a pair of duos, a trio, and a quartet, but he deployed the full choir as sonorous pillars to anchor his structure at the beginning, the end, and the center.[29]

The Communion, *Pascha nostrum*, illustrates the highly developed contrapuntal style adopted by Byrd for the full-voiced sections (see Example 17-5). In the opening point of imitation he juxtaposes two related motives based on a fourth, the one being an inversion of the other; bassus and superius I (m. 1) respond to the trio of altus, tenor, and superius II (mm. 1–2). However, he breaks up the tightly woven imitative texture very quickly with homophonic declamation. Voices in pairs echo the ecstatic acclamation, "Alleluia" (m. 6); three parts declare together "Itaque" (the other two being displaced by only a minim on either side, m. 7). A further pairing of voices introduces the words "sinceritatis et veritatis" (mm. 10–11), which are then declaimed emphatically by all five voices together (m. 13). The homophony thus serves to throw into relief the most significant elements of the liturgical text, "therefore, let us join in the feast of integrity and truth." Bringing the piece to a close is a concise, densely imitative setting for the final "Alleluia" that stands in clear contrast to the preceding material (mm. 15–23).

Byrd's distinctive treatment of the word "Alleluia"—especially when, as here, it concludes the liturgical text (as it often does in the Propers of Byrd's composition)—has been seen as a stylistic innovation that helps to give this remarkable repertory of

---

28. See the discussion in Kerman, *Masses and Motets of William Byrd*, 234–37.
29. See Kerman, *Masses and Motets of William Byrd*, 271–75.

EXAMPLE 17-5. William Byrd, *Pascha nostrum immolatus est*,
Communion for Easter

Christ our paschal lamb has been sacrificed, alleluia. Therefore, let us feast on the unleavened bread of sincerity and truth, alleluia.

Mass Propers a characteristic stamp.[30] Be that as it may, it is but one of the many compositional procedures that Byrd derived—whether directly or indirectly—from the typical motet of the period. His reliance on that model helps to explain, as well, the sharp contrast in style between the Propers of the *Gradualia* and the more traditional cantus firmus–based works of Isaac's *Choralis Constantinus*. Seen in this light, Byrd's Mass Propers are yet one more indication of the extent to which the compositional procedures that gave the Latin motet its characteristic stylistic profile came to dominate as well those genres intended for liturgical use that had earlier been handled with considerably simpler means.

PASSIONS

As we saw earlier, polyphonic settings of the Passion texts that were traditionally intoned at Mass during the final days of Holy Week began to appear in notated form already in the fifteenth century. It is noteworthy, however, that all of the fifteenth-century Passion sources now known are either of English or of Italian provenance. In the sixteenth century Italy continued to produce polyphonic Passions, if in relatively modest numbers. England appears to have faded as an important locus for the genre, but its cultivation was taken up with some enthusiasm in German regions, especially those in which the Reformation held sway. In the French-speaking areas of northern Europe, by contrast, composers apparently had little reason to give serious attention to the polyphonic Passion. Only two are known to have originated there, both of which were printed by Attaingnant in the tenth book of his 1534 series of thirteen books of motets; one is by Claudin de Sermisy, the assistant chapelmaster of the royal court, while the other is without attribution. Later in the century musicians working on the Iberian peninsula would contribute to the repertory as well, modestly but significantly.[31]

The examples that have survived more or less complete from the fifteenth century are all of the type best described as "responsorial." This is because the lesson tones of the plainchant, used for the narrative portions of the Evangelist, are answered by settings in parts first for the cries of the *turba* (the "crowd"), then for the words of the various individual personages that figure in the dialogue (such as Pontius Pilate and the apostle Peter), and sometimes for the replies of Christ as well.

Early in the sixteenth century a new type of Passion composition made its appearance, different in that the entire text is set in a manner that reflects (once again) the motet composition of the period. The texts used for pieces of this kind were of two basic types. On the one hand were those that made use, like the responsorial Passions, of the complete account of Jesus's betrayal and suffering as given by a single Evangelist; on the other were those that combined segments from all four Gospels to give a summary—a *summa passionis*—of the events that led up to the crucifixion and death of Christ. In addition, abridgements of the Passion as recounted by a single

30. See Kerman, *Masses and Motets of William Byrd*, 232f.
31. See Kurt von Fischer, "Passion," *The New Grove Dictionary of Music*, 14:281.

FIGURE 17-3. Miniature from a plainchant *Passionale*, placed at the beginning of the Passion according to Matthew (Olomouc, Státni Archiv).

Gospel came into currency in the Protestant localities of Germany (see Figure 17-3).[32]

One of the earliest compositions of the motet type to be entered in the polyphonic manuscripts of the sixteenth century was a work with conflicting attributions that was to have a long and fruitful history. It was inscribed between 1503 and 1512 in one of the codices prepared for the papal choir, Sistine Chapel MS 42, under the name of Johannes a la Venture, who is otherwise unknown. It is also found with an ascription to Antoine de Longueval, a composer who appears to have been in the service of the French court chapel for at least a decade in the years around 1507–17.[33] The work is given to him in a collection at the National Library in Florence, MS II.I.232, which apparently originated in the city itself in about 1515.[34] In addition, it was included, under the name of Johannes Obrecht, in a volume printed by Georg Rhau in 1538, his *Selectae harmoniae quatuor vocum de passione Domini*, which was widely disseminated in Lutheran Germany.[35]

This work's formal affinity with the motet is immediately evident from its division into three clearly articulated *partes* (see the *secunda pars*, Example 17-6).[36] That it was intended for use in the celebration of the liturgy is equally clear, however, from the composer's systematic adherence to the recitation tones of the plainchant as the basis for the polyphony. The custom of distinguishing by vocal ambitus or range each of the three principal entities represented in the text—the narration of the Evangelist, the words of

32. See von Fischer, "Passion," *The New Grove Dictionary of Music*, 14:279.

33. See Stanley Boorman, "Longueval," *The New Grove Dictionary of Music*, 11:221.

34. Concerning the sources in question, see the *Census-Catalogue of Manuscript Sources of Polyphonic Music*, ed. Charles Hamm and Herbert Kellman, 5 vols. (Neuhausen-Stuttgart: Hänssler Verlag, 1979–88), 4:46f., and 1:216, respectively.

35. See Victor Mattfeld, "Rhau," *The New Grove Dictionary of Music*, 15:788.

36. For a transcription of the entire Passion in modern score, see Jacob Obrecht, *Werken*, ed. Johannes Wolf, 30 vols. Vereeniging voor Noord-Nederlands Muziekgeschiedenis (Amsterdam: G. Albach, 1908–21), 8:1–20, fasc. 28.

EXAMPLE 17-6. Antoine de Longueval/Johannes a la Ventura/Jacob Obrecht?, *Summa Passionis*, second part (mm. 1–20)

Pilate brought Jesus forth and scourged him, and the soldiers, having platted a crown of thorns . . .

Christ, and the reactions of the *turba*—is observed as well; the narrator is pitched on "middle" c, Jesus a fifth below on F, and the "crowd" on the f an octave higher.[37] Like the plainchant formulae themselves, the polyphonic style is essentially syllabic and declamatory, and the texture is largely homophonic. Contrapuntal interest is supplied by differences in rhythmic values that cause the individual voices to declaim the text independently, each at its own pace (as at the beginning of the *secunda pars*), and by modest points of closely spaced imitation (as at mm. 15–16). There is often, as well, a modest melismatic flourish at the approach to a cadence (e.g., mm. 11–15 or 32–34). When the Pharisees clamor to have Jesus crucified (mm. 75–79 and 98–100), the cadential extension takes on a more dramatic dimension, undoubtedly for expressive purposes. Despite the motetlike facture of the work, the recurrent use of repeated pitches and the frequently reiterated cadential articulations (most of them to F, the final of the composition overall) preserve a good deal of the flavor of the plainchant formulae.

This setting of the *summa passionis* apparently made its strongest mark in Germanic regions, especially those of Protestant persuasion, beginning, of course, with its publication by Rhau. It subsequently found its way into over twenty sources both in its original four-voice format and with two added parts. Its text was taken for composition by others as well, including Johannes Galliculus, whose four-voice version in motet style was included by Rhau in his 1538 publication. Late in the century Jacob Handl and Jacob Regnart wrote between them a total of four polyphonic Passions, presumably for the imperial court in Prague. More common, however, were Passion settings of the responsorial type. A model for Protestant worship in a simple homophonic style that was frequently emulated was provided early on by Luther's friend and musical advisor Johann Walther.[38]

In Italy responsorial Passions continued to be produced in small numbers by some of the most celebrated masters of the age as well as some lesser-knowns. Among the more distinguished to have contributed to the genre are the Florentine Francesco Corteccia, who set the Passion according to both John (1527) and Matthew (1532). Vincenzo Ruffo, known for his espousal of the musical ideals of the Council of Trent, composed the versions from Matthew and Luke (1574–79). However, Corteccia and Ruffo applied polyphony only to the introductory verses, beginning "Passio Domini nostri, Jesu Christi," the *turba* sections, and the closing words of the Evangelist's narrative.

Among those who also set the words of other individual speakers—with the important exception of Christ—were Jacquet of Mantua, who used John's account (ca. 1540), and Giaches de Wert, who chose Mark's (ca. 1580). One of the first to set the words of Jesus as well was Gasparo Alberti, who, during his years as organist and choirmaster in Bergamo, composed two settings for the Passion taken from the Gospel according to John and a third from Matthew (ca. 1540).[39]

37. These "protagonists" are identified in the transcription by the letters E[vangelista], C[hristus], and T[urba]; note that the basic pitch for the Evangelist is occasionally transposed to the upper octave, as at mm. 27ff. and 64ff. of Example 17-6.
38. See von Fischer, "Passion," *The New Grove Dictionary of Music*, 14:280–82.
39. See von Fischer, "Passion," *The New Grove Dictionary of Music*, 14:279.

On the Iberian peninsula an independent tradition seems to have developed as early as the late 1480s. Based uniquely upon the recitation tone used in Toledo, it differs from typically Italian usage in that the words set polyphonically, besides the opening and closing sections, are not those of the *turba* but rather selected verses from the Evangelist's narrative and certain of the declarations of Christ. By contrast, the Passions according to Matthew and John published by Tomás Luis de Victoria in Rome in 1585 follow the Italian tradition. This was perhaps to have been expected, given the Spanish master's long years of residence in the papal city between the mid-1560s and 1587. More surprising, perhaps, is that Francisco Guerrero followed a similar pattern in his five settings of the Passion texts, including one from each of the four Gospels, two of which were also printed in Rome in 1585.

Guerrero, however, also gave evidence of his familiarity with Spanish custom. In three of his compositions in the genre he set polyphonically not only the sections for the *turba* but also one of those particularly dramatic moments in the narrative accounts of the Evangelists that were usually so treated in the earlier Iberian Passions. In the compositions for five voices based on the Gospels according to Matthew and Luke as well as in the one for four voices taken from Mark's account, he set off the key phrases "Flevit amare" ("he cried bitterly," Matthew 26:75 and Luke 22:62) and "Et cepit flere" ("and he began to weep," Mark 14:72). This he did not only by setting them in parts but also by swelling the number of voices to six.[40]

In all of these responsorial Passions, then, the sober simplicity of the monophonic lection tones was set off against the relative opulence of the sections done in polyphony. Nonetheless, the latter tend toward the syllabic and the homophonic, in keeping with the character of the somber liturgy of Holy Week. Typically, the compositional procedures adopted in setting them show a greater affinity with the utilitarian polyphony written for the chants of the Office—the hymns, Psalms, and Magnificats—than with the more sophisticated contrapuntal facture of the motet. Only occasionally were the two compositional styles—the simple homophony that characterized the responsorial Passion, on the one hand, and the motetlike part-writing of the *summa passionis*, on the other—brought together in the same work.

That amalgamation was achieved by Orlande de Lassus in the four Passions that he wrote between 1575 and 1582 for the Bavarian court chapel by adopting a straightforward *falsobordone* for the *turba* scenes and duos and trios of a more essentially contrapuntal character for the individual protagonists.[41] But it appears to have been the juxtaposition of formulaic chant and choral polyphony that led most directly to the dramatic Passion settings of the seventeenth and eighteenth centuries and to the combination of narrative recitative with aria and chorus that were later to constitute their fundamental stylistic substance.

40. Both passages refer to Peter's great distress when he realized that he had just denied his Lord three times, as the latter had predicted.
41. See von Fischer, "Passion," *The New Grove Dictionary of Music*, 14:280.

CHAPTER 18

1

Secular Polyphony in France

～⌒ CHANSONS ⌒～

At the approach of the sixteenth century the chanson was clearly in a transitional period as a genre. Its traditional formulation as a type of accompanied solo song, usually for three parts, was giving way ever more frequently to a work for four voices, each of which was shaped to accommodate the natural rhythms and inflections of the poetic text. The transformation was a gradual one, of course, and proceeded with varying rates of progress and in slightly different directions according to the circumstances that obtained in a given locality. A number of different influences were at work to bring these changes about, and those that had the greatest impact appear to have varied as well from one region to another.

In the Low Countries the decisive factor may have been the development of the motet, which apparently began to be taken more and more as a compositional model for texts of a secular nature in the decades around the turn of the century. The extent of the resulting affinity between motet and chanson can be judged in some measure from a collection of chansons prepared at the Burgundian court for Marguerite of Austria during the years around 1520, MS 228 of the Royal Library in Brussels. An anthology of considerable sweep, the manuscript includes chansons by composers of the preceding generation such as Johannes Okeghem, Alexander Agricola, Loyset Compère, and Johannes Prioris, many of whom had been associated with the royal French court, and by Josquin, who ended his career nearby at Condé sur l'Escaut. Nonetheless, the most important component of this collection of fifty-eight compositions are the fifteen songs attributed to Marguerite's own court composer, Pierre de La Rue (ca. 1460–1518), who served at the Netherlands court of the Habsburgs more or less continuously from the early 1490s until his retirement in 1516.[1]

---

1. See the study by Martin Picker, ed., *The Chanson Albums of Marguerite of Austria* (Berkeley: University of California Press, 1965), 36–47. Concerning La Rue, whose Habsburg patrons included, in addition to Marguerite, Maximilian I, Philip the Fair, and the young Charles V, cf. Martin Staehelin, *The New Grove Dictionary of Music*, 20:473–76.

Representative of La Rue's contribution to this repertory—and a clear reflection of the growing influence of the motet on secular composition—is the four-part chanson *Autant en emporte le vent* (see Example 18-1).[2] Formally an octosyllabic *cinquain*, rhyming A A B'B'A, the poem upon which the chanson is based could be a rondeau refrain but probably was not. More importantly, it was treated much differently than was customary for a conventional fixed form. Far from typical for chansons of the fifteenth century, for example, is the considerable textual repetition resulting initially from paired imitation in homophonic pairs (such as is often seen in the motets of the period) with cantus and contra responding to tenor and bassus (mm. 1–9).

Reiteration emphasizes the central idea of the verse, that the heart must give its "proof" (*touche*) if a kiss is to have any lasting significance, even when given upon the mouth. Roughly a third of the piece's total duration—fourteen of the forty-one breves—is taken up by the musical elaboration of that pair of verses (mm. 20–33). Moreover, unlike composers of the preceding generation, whose prolongation of a phrase usually took the form of an ornamental melismatic passage, La Rue extends the poetic line without giving up the syllabic declamation—much of it on reiterated pitches—that characterizes the delivery of the text. Obviously, to highlight an isolated element of the text in this manner runs directly counter to the formal objectivity required by a setting of strophic design and indicates unequivocally that no fixed form was intended.

Most striking of the stylistic changes illustrated by this piece, however, and perhaps most significant, is La Rue's rejection of the treble-dominated texture of fifteenth-century solo song. Following the paired homophony adopted for the first couplet, he introduces the third verse with a kind of quasi-imitation. Two voices present the text simultaneously and the other two enter either after a short pause or in anticipation with melodic material similar to but not exactly the same as that of the homophonic pair (mm. 9–20). Not until the fourth verse, which reveals the poem's essential meaning, does the composer have recourse to a fairly systematic point of imitation, first between altus and bassus (mm. 20–23), and then involving each of the four voices in turn (mm. 23–33). To underscore the fifth and final verse, which clarifies and amplifies the essential conceit of the text, he presents it in a dual statement, reverting to the sort of quasi-imitation used earlier with two of the four parts declaiming the text together.

Clearly, La Rue's chanson does not have the duration, complexity, or contrapuntal weight of a typical motet of the period. It is a more intimate piece, written for and appropriate to the ambience of the courtly chambers in which it was likely to be performed. Nonetheless, it makes use of the same compositional procedures as its sacred counterpart: imitation, equal-voiced counterpoint, and declamatory homophony in a text-oriented, fully vocal melodic idiom. Although it falls short of the scope and

---

2. For a transcription of the entire piece in modern score, see Picker, ed., *Chanson Albums of Marguerite of Austria*, 204–5, no. 8.

EXAMPLE 18-1. Pierre de La Rue, *Autant en emporte le vent* (mm. 1–9, 20–41)

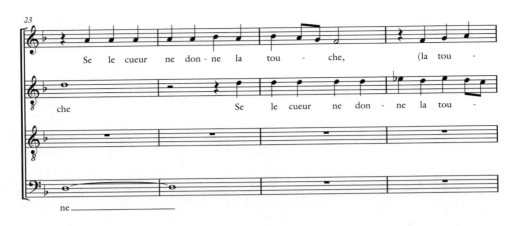

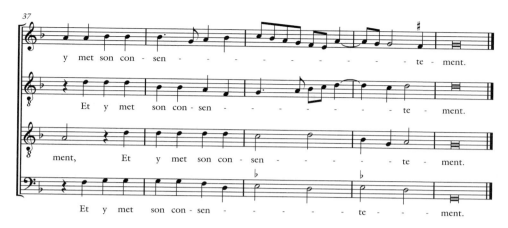

It's as if gone with the wind [that there is only a kiss, even when given with the mouth], unless the heart is in it and gives its consent.

substance of most contemporaneous motets, it is still very different in conception and style from the chanson of the fifteenth century—as are most of the pieces in the collection.

THREE- AND FOUR-PART ARRANGEMENTS

Another factor that may have contributed to the stylistic transformation of the chanson in the decades around the turn of the sixteenth century was the accumulation of a significant body of monophonic chansons—referred to in printed sources published later in the century as *chansons rustiques*—the texts and tunes of which were generally of a decidedly popular cast. It is therefore tempting to assume that the monophonic repertory had its origins in an oral tradition. Nevertheless, it circulated widely enough to become familiar to every layer of the social order, and a considerable part of it was eventually fixed in notated form. Two substantial manuscript collections survive from around the turn of the century. One of these, French MS 9346 of the National Library in Paris (known as the "Bayeux Manuscript"), includes 100 songs, mostly from the Ile-de-France and Normandy.[3] The other, French MS 12744 of the National Library in Paris, comprises 143 items, apparently drawn from a somewhat wider geographical area.[4] Significantly, 35 of the best-known pieces were inscribed in both songbooks.[5]

3. The collection has been edited with a transcription of the music by Théodore Gérold, *Le manuscrit de Bayeux, texte et musique d'un recueil de chansons du XVe siècle* (Strasbourg: University of Strasbourg, 1921).

4. The manuscript was published in an edition by Gaston Paris and Auguste Gevaert, eds., *Chansons du XVe siècle* (Paris: Société des Anciens Textes Français, 1875; reissued 1935).

5. Concerning these two monophonic chansonniers, see Gustave Reese, *Music in the Renaissance* (New York: Norton, 1959), 205–7.

The integration of such songs into the secular polyphony of the period brought about noteworthy innovations in its facture, both textual and musical. Contributing most significantly to the changes were composers active in the northern regions of French-speaking Europe, not the least of which were those associated with the royal chapel.[6] Not only did these masters draw upon the popular monophonic tradition for tunes that must have been known and loved by people of all classes; they also found there the inspiration to set in other contexts poems that broke away from the courtly tradition, making use of fresh themes and patterns of diction.

Some of the fifteenth-century polyphonic settings of melodies that appear to have originated as *chansons rustiques*—tunes such as *L'homme armé* and *Petite camusette*—were among the first to be unequivocally intended for fully vocal performance. As has been seen, however, the preexistent songs were most often used by the likes of Busnoys and Okeghem as a kind of cantus firmus imbedded in the setting of another, usually contrasting, poem (see pp. 298–304). With the next generation of composers, by contrast, tune and text were taken by themselves as the starting point for polyphonic elaboration. These have been designated by present-day scholars, appropriately enough, as "three-part" and "four-part arrangements," and newly composed chansons of this kind are found in surviving sources in much more substantial numbers than the earlier combinative chansons.[7]

Most characteristic of the three-part arrangements, perhaps, or at least among the most numerous in the sources, are those attributable to Antoine de Févin. His setting of *Faulte d'argent* is a representative example of more than fifteen such pieces included in MS 1760 of the Pepys Library at Magdalene College, Cambridge. Copied in France shortly before 1514, the collection comprises in the main twenty-four motets and twenty-six chansons, most by composers associated at one time with the royal French court. Although probably compiled by musicians in service there, and perhaps even intended initially for the king's household, it appears to have been designated at some point as a gift for one of the young Tudor princes—either Henry VII or Henry VIII—presumably because it was deemed to constitute a creditable sampling of courtly repertory.[8]

---

6. See Gustave Reese and Theodore Karp, "Monophony in a Group of Renaissance Chansonniers," *Journal of the American Musicological Society* 5 (1952): 8–12, for a list of some sixty-eight polyphonic chansons that incorporate in some way one of the songs included in the two monophonic collections. Composers represented there, in addition to Mouton and Févin, include, among others, Josquin, Compère, Weerbeke, Gascongne, Isaac, Agricola, and Ninot le Petit.

7. Concerning the polyphonic arrangement of the *chanson rustique*, see Howard M. Brown, "Chanson," *The New Grove Dictionary of Music*, 4:140, and his more detailed discussion, "The Genesis of a Style: The Parisian Chanson, 1500–1530," in *Chanson and Madrigal, 1480–1530*, ed. James Haar, Isham Library Papers, vol. 2 (Cambridge, Mass.: Harvard University Press, 1964), 21ff.

8. See the *Census-Catalogue of Manuscript Sources of Polyphonic Music*, ed. Charles Hamm and Herbert Kellman, 5 vols. (Neuhausen-Stuttgart: Hänssler Verlag, 1979–88), 1:128. Besides the motets and chansons the manuscript contains three hymns, three Lamentations, and an Italian piece; in addition to Févin the composers represented include, among others, Brumel, Festa, Gascongne, Josquin, Prioris, and Mouton.

The *chanson rustique* beginning "Faulte d'argent" is not among the songs found in the known monophonic chansonniers, but its prior existence as part of the "popular" repertory is well attested. A very different five-voice setting is attributed to Josquin, and an instrumental *canzona* by Girolamo Cavazzoni appears to be modeled on another polyphonic version that has yet to be identified. Moreover, Févin's handling of the tune follows the pattern he adopted for three-part arrangements generally (see Example 18-2).

EXAMPLE 18-2. Antoine de Févin, *Faulte d'argent* (á 3)

l'es - veil-le,   Ma - da - me dort__ pour ar - gent on   l'es - veil - le.

Want of money is a pain without equal. If I say so, alas, I know well the reason why.
Without means one has to lie low. My lady sleeps; for money one wakens her.

The preexistent melody is given to the tenor, which is placed between a pair of voices that are virtually in the same range—surprisingly, in view of the tendency at the time to separate parts into discrete registers. Only the tenor quotes the song literally and completely phrase by phrase, apparently with a minimum of decorative ornament, usually with a cadence and a rest to mark the divisions between verses. Since the tenor is also the only part in this manuscript provided with text, it is possible that it was meant to be alone in declaiming the verse and that as a rule the cantus and bassus were performed instrumentally.

Each phrase begins with a point of imitation based on the secular cantus firmus, generally with the cantus and bassus in anticipation of its principal bearer. Once the tenor has entered, however, the other two parts tend to go their own contrapuntal way rather quickly, leaving it to complete the presentation of the borrowed tune by itself. In this instance that compositional formula is so consistently applied that imitative counterpoint yields only once, and briefly, to a homophonic texture (mm. 7–10). In other chansons, by contrast, Févin has made significantly greater use of passagework in parallel imperfect consonances and treated the imitative writing more freely.[9] In several respects, then, the three-part arrangements were more like the traditional chansons of the fifteenth century than the motetlike compositions for four voices being cultivated at about the same time by La Rue and others at the Habsburg court in the Low Countries.

Much more similar to the latter repertory, in fact, are the polyphonic chansons that can best be described as four-part arrangements. This affinity becomes quickly evident in comparing La Rue's and Févin's pieces with a characteristic four-part arrangement such as Mouton's setting of *Jamés, jamés, jamés,* for which the earliest

---

9. For further discussion of the three-part arrangement, see Howard M. Brown, " Genesis of a Style," 21ff., including examples 5–7, and the representative pieces published earlier in Brown, ed., *Theatrical Chansons of the Fifteenth and Early Sixteenth Centuries* (Cambridge, Mass.: Harvard University Press, 1963).

datable source is Petrucci's *Harmonice musices odhecaton A* of 1501 (see Example 18-3).[10] There is nothing in the facture of this work to suggest that a single privileged part was intended to be the bearer of both the preexistent melody and of its text. All four parts are clearly meant to be sung, and the point of imitation with which the chanson begins illustrates a contrapuntal equalization of the voices that

10. For a complete transcription of the chanson in modern score, see Helen Hewitt and Isabel Pope, eds., *Harmonice musices odhecaton A* (Cambridge, Mass.: Mediaeval Academy of America, 1942), 296–98, no. 36.

EXAMPLE 18-3. Johannes Mouton, *Jamés, jamés, jamés* (mm. 26–55)

Jack-the-man has a woman; we shall steal her, by Our Lady; she said that she would come.
Never, never will Jack-the-man have the goods . . .

would make it virtually impossible to identify any one of them as adhering more closely to the borrowed material than the others.

Imitative counterpoint quickly yields to quasi-homophonic declamation in four voices (mm. 14–25) where the bearer of the original tune is no more easily discernible than in the preceding counterpoint, even to someone who knew it well. In fact, the variety of textures and sonorities that follows is more reflective of the Latin motet of the period than of either the fifteenth-century chanson or even the three-part arrangement. Declamatory duos respond to one another in quickly alternating pairs, contrasting altus and bassus first with cantus and tenor (mm. 26–37), then the higher two with the lower two (mm. 43–50). In the closing phrases the prevailing homophony is often tempered by the contrapuntal or declamatory independence of at least one of the parts (e.g., mm. 50–55, 58–74).

A sesquialteral proportion is introduced against the fundamentally binary mensuration at two points in the course of the piece, the first time to vary the presentation of what appears to be a kind of refrain (mm. 44–55), and the second (mm. 63–78) to introduce new material leading to what could be considered the punch line of the text: "If I had a good purse, I wouldn't care much [that I've lost my love]."[11]

Josquin's treatment of the *chanson rustique* also warrants our attention, even though it appears to have been virtually unique for the time. It differs markedly from both three- and four-part arrangements, first of all, because Josquin invariably relied for pieces of this type upon the learned compositional procedures of canonic imitation, even in setting the most frivolous of monophonic songs. Moreover, since the canonically generated parts were always added to the basic combination of a vocal quartet, the sonorous mass was inevitably increased to at least five or six voices. The result was invariably a richly contrapuntal texture in which all of the parts were conceived for the declamation of the text and made to participate in the polyphonic elaboration of the borrowed melody through a systematic series of points of imitation based upon it.

Characteristic in these respects is Josquin's setting of *Faulte d'argent* in which the contratenor carries the cantus firmus in the natural hexachord from c.[12] It is followed in strict imitation at the lower fifth by the quinta pars singing the borrowed melody in the soft hexachord from F.[13] Similar in basic design but delightfully different in

11. For further discussion of the four-part arrangement, see Brown, "Genesis of a Style," 24–26, and his example 8, Mouton's *Resjouissez vous bourgeoises*, p. 155.

12. Concerning the reliability of this attribution to Josquin (hence the likelihood that the composition is really his), see Lawrence F. Bernstein, "A Canonic Chanson in a German Manuscript: *Faulte d'argent* and Josquin's Approach to the Chanson for Five Voices," in *Von Isaac bis Bach: Studien zur älteren deutschen Musikgeschichte: Festschrift Martin Just zum 60. Geburtstag*, ed. Frank Heidlberger, Wolfgang Osthoff, and Reinhard Wiesend (Kassel: Bärenreiter, 1991), 53–71.

13. For an edition of the work in modern score, see Josquin, *Wereldlijke Werken*, ed. Albert Smijers, 2 vols. (Amsterdam: Vereniging voor Nederlandse Muziekgeschiedenis, 1921–56), 1:5; Sarah Fuller, ed., *The Heritage of European Music, 800–1750* (New York: Alfred A. Knopf, 1987), 195–99; or Archibald T. Davison and Willi Apel, eds., *Historical Anthology of Music*, 2 vols. (Cambridge, Mass.: Harvard University Press, 1962), 1:93.

detail is Josquin's setting of *Petite camusette*, a song that had earlier been taken for polyphonic composition in four parts by Johannes Okeghem. Josquin wrote instead for six voices, a pair in each of three separate registers, taking for the central core of the counterpoint the tenor and contratenor in canonic imitation at the unison just a breve apart. The other voices are also handled in pairs—cantus and quintus above and sextus and bassus below—each of them engaged in a distinctive series of imitative exchanges on motives derived largely from the monophonic model (see Example 18-4).[14]

Despite the trivial subject matter, Josquin displays in these pieces, as in all similar works, a serious sophistication of musical means that is much more akin in spirit to the chansons of fellow Netherlanders at the court of Marguerite of Austria than to the light-hearted three- and four-part arrangements of the musicians serving at the royal French court.

∽ CHANSON STYLES AND *VOIX DE VILLE* ⌒

It was in France, however, with the next generation of composers, that the truly decisive steps were taken in the stylistic transformation of the polyphonic chanson. Among those masters whose contributions appear to have been most crucial to the changes that took place are Claudin de Sermisy and Clément Janequin. Claudin, whose long service with the royal French chapel has already been noted, was a *clerc* from before 1515 to about 1524 and *sous-maître* from 1532 until at least 1554.[15] Janequin, by contrast, spent a good deal of his career in ecclesiastical appointments in Bordeaux and Angers before finally settling in Paris in 1549.[16]

An enormous role was undoubtedly played as well by the printers of music who began to be active in French territories just as these two composers were hitting their stride. As has been noted, it was in 1528 that Pierre Attaingnant published the first of the more than seventy books of chansons that were to come from his presses during the first half of the century.[17] And in 1538 Jacques Moderne initiated his series of eleven collections that were to appear over the next fifteen years under the general title *Le parangon des chansons*.[18]

At the same time, the poets of sixteenth-century France also had their part to play. By the 1520s the fixed forms and conventional diction of medieval tradition were beginning to give way once and for all to the freer formal structures and topical inno-

---

14. For a transcription of the entire piece in modern score, see Josquin, *Wereldlijke Werken*, ed. Smijers, 1:5, or Noah Greenberg and Paul Maynard, eds., *An Anthology of Early Renaissance Music* (New York: Norton, 1975), 172–77.

15. See Isabelle Cazeaux, "Sermisy," *The New Grove Dictionary of Music*, 17:171–72.

16. See Howard M. Brown, "Janequin," *The New Grove Dictionary of Music*, 9:491–92.

17. See Daniel Heartz, *Pierre Attaingnant, Royal Printer of Music* (Berkeley: University of California Press, 1969), for a comprehensive catalogue of Attaingnant's prints.

18. See Samuel F. Pogue, *Jacques Moderne, Lyons Music Printer of the Sixteenth Century* (Geneva: Librarie Droz, 1969), for a complete listing of the music books published by Moderne.

EXAMPLE 18-4. Josquin Desprez, *Petite camusette* (mm. 1–15)

Little pugnose, you have slain me.

vations of such gifted authors as Clément Marot (1496–1544), who served both Marguerite of Angoulême and her brother, King Francis I, before he was obliged to take refuge in Geneva for his Protestant sympathies and turned his talents to verse translations of the Psalms.[19]

Both representative and symptomatic of this stage in the development of the chanson is Claudin's *Tant que vivray*. It is one of more than 200 pieces composed in the course of the sixteenth century to verse ascribed to Marot, involving in all some 100 of his poems. The style of both text and music is typical of the secular polyphony being written by composers working in courtly circles from the late 1520s on (see Example 18-5).[20] No significant vestige of either the formal designs or the traditional themes typical of the fixed forms of the fifteenth century remains in Marot's verses, which were first published in 1528.

There is no refrain, and the individual strophes (of which there were four as published without the music) alternate between six and seven verses in lines of variable length, first ten syllables, then four and eight. Only the recurring rhyme scheme in

19. See Frank Dobbins, "Marot," *The New Grove Dictionary of Music*, 11:695f.

20. For a transcription of the entire chanson, see Claudin de Sermisy, *Opera omnia*, ed. Gaston Allaire and Isabelle Cazeux, 6 vols., Corpus mensurabilis musicae 52 ([Rome]: American Institute of Musicology, 1970–86), 4:99–100, no. 150; or Pierre Attaignant, *Transcriptions of Chansons for Keyboard (1531)*, ed. Albert Seay, Corpus mensurabilis musicae 20 ([Rome]: American Institute of Musicology, 1961), 99–104, no. 10 (with keyboard intabulation).

EXAMPLE 18-5. Claudin de Sermisy, *Tant que vivray*

As long as I am in the prime of life, I shall serve the powerful king of love in word and deed, in songs and harmonies. Several times he has kept me languishing, but after sorrow he left me rejoicing, for I have the love of the fair one of noble body. Her allegiance is my faith; her heart is mine, mine is hers. Let sadness be gone, let joy live, since there is so much good in love. (Three additional strophes.)

the odd-numbered stanzas harks back to earlier practice. However, that particular kind of structural symmetry is never entirely abandoned by the poets of the period; rather, it is used to replace to a degree the repetition schemes of the fixed forms. Also gone is any remaining trace of the plaintive tone of the unrequited lover, lamenting a fate that was seen as leading inevitably to the destruction not only of his (or her) happiness but also of health and even life itself. In its place is a cheery affirmation of shared affection and of its durable nature.

Claudin's setting follows closely both the speech rhythms of the individual verses and the formal structure of the two contrasting stanzas. Declamation is strictly syllabic except for a single ornamental flourish in cantus and tenor (m. 10) and a syncopated anticipation in the cantus at the final cadence, and the longer notes correspond in most cases either to the masculine rhyme at the end of a verse or, in the lines of ten syllables, to the caesura following the fourth. Formally, the sense of articulation conveyed by the longer notes terminating the first three verses is reinforced, for the first and third, by a cadential formula, and the recurring rhyme scheme of the first strophe is mirrored in a repetition of the first section of music.

Similarly, the couplets of the second stanza are accommodated each time by a repetition of the short phrase of music to which the rhyming lines are sung (mm. 13–22). There is also a repeat of the final phrase, text and music, which, although much more abbreviated here than was usually the case, came to be a regular feature of the chanson of the period. Moreover, as if to place these rhythmic features in the sharpest possible relief, Claudin has ruffled the limpid homophonic texture of the piece only once with the briefest touch of independent motion in altus and tenor (mm. 14–16).

What is most remarkable about this chanson, however—and wonderfully evocative of the various strands being woven into the genre during this period—is that its text and music are based on an earlier piece in the monophonic repertory, *Resjouissons nous, tous loyaulx amoureux*.[21] Marot obviously derived from his model not only the formal structure he adopted for this poem but also, if less directly, the topic and the diction. Claudin, for his part, has borrowed the preexistent melody with few modifications of any substance—although the changes he did make evince clearly his admirable skills as a composer.[22] Nothing could illuminate more clearly the stimulus for renewal and change provided for poets and composers at the time by the monophonic repertory of "popular" song than this arresting example of collaborative borrowing.

Still, not all poems inspired of the "rustic" tradition are as "courtly" in their choice of language as Marot's *Tant que vivray*. Nor are all chansons by Claudin and his French contemporaries as declamatory and homophonic in nature as his setting of it—however characteristic these traits are generally seen to be for this repertory.

---

21. See Paris and Gevaert, eds., *Chansons du XVe siècle*, 64–65 and 113–14, no. 115.
22. See the discussion of this piece by Leeman L. Perkins, "Toward a Typology of the 'Renaissance' Chanson," *Journal of Musicology* 6 (1988): 441–47.

Poems of a distinctly salacious character whose topoi and diction could readily be qualified as *grivois* also found their way into the literary traditions of the times; their authors often avoid the vulgar or obscene only by virtue of their considerable wit.

A rather surprising example is Marot's *Martin menoit son porceau*, for which the poet chose the usually elegant decasyllable to tell a tale of pastoral dalliance that risked being pulled off track by a pig (see Example 18-6). Claudin, perhaps similarly inspired, dressed this poem of unprepossessing content in a sophisticated contrapuntal setting. Combining patterlike declamation on repeated pitches with imitative counterpoint, he coordinated the parts, where necessary, by means of melismatic

EXAMPLE 18-6. Claudin de Sermisy, *Martin menoit son porceau* (mm. 1–17)

Martin was taking his pig to market with Alice, who, on the big plain, begged Martin to sin with her in superposition, and Martin asked her, and who will watch our pig, wicked girl?

extensions of the melodic line, generally eschewing homophonic textures of any kind.[23]

Other chansons from the repertory of this period, whether by Claudin or one of his Parisian colleagues, run the textual gamut from refined courtly eroticism to expressions of earthy realism reflecting urban and country life. They also vary in polyphonic style from unalloyed homophony to rigorously imitative counterpoint, at times within a single piece. There was, in addition, a distinct subspecies of the genre that appears to have been the unique contribution of Clément Janequin. It is to be identified by its one unmistakable feature: the use of onomatopoetic imitation, both verbal and musical, of natural sounds as a fundamental and substantial part of the compositional fabric.

The titles alone of pieces of this type suggest the kinds of sonorities taken as points of departure: *Le chant des oiseaux* (bird songs), *Les cris de Paris* (street cries in Paris), *Le caquet des femmes* (chattering women), *La chasse* (the hunt), and—perhaps the most celebrated of all—*La guerre* (war).[24] The first of these recalls in striking fashion the "bird call" or "realistic" *virelais* of the fourteenth century, both because of its subject matter and because of the manner in which the sounds embodied in the text are imitated musically. Despite that similarity, however—odd as it may seem— there is no evidence of an unbroken tradition to connect Janequin to the earlier

23. For a transcription of the complete piece in modern score, see Sermisy, *Opera omnia*, ed. Allaire and Cazeux, 4:19–22, no. 103.

24. For a comprehensive catalogue of Janequin's chansons, see Howard M. Brown, *The New Grove Dictionary of Music*, 9:493f.; for transcriptions, see the edition in Clement Janequin, *Chansons polyphoniques*, ed. A. Tillman Merritt and François Lesure, 6 vols. (Monaco: Editions de l'Oiseau Lyre, 1965–71).

repertory.[25] By contrast, in *La guerre*, which was probably written to celebrate the victory of the French armies at Marignano in 1515 under Francis I, Janequin extended the palette of stylized musical sonorities to include all those then associated with the battlefield (see Figure 18-1): trumpet fanfares, calls to arms, shouting soldiers, cannon fire, and even the contrapuntal clash of opposing armies (see Example 18-7).

Whatever their links with earlier repertory, Janequin's onomatopoetic chansons remained something of an isolated experiment and appear to have had little impact on the subsequent development of the genre. More important for the second half of

25. It would seem, however, that the place of bird-related imagery and diction underwent change and reinterpretation in late sixteenth-century France; see Kate van Orden, "Sexual Discourse in the Parisian Chanson: A Libidinous Aviary," *Journal of the American Musicological Society* 48 (1995): 1–41.

EXAMPLE 18-7. Clément Janequin, *La guerre*, second part (mm. 1–6, 93–101)

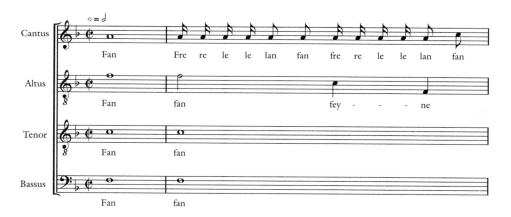

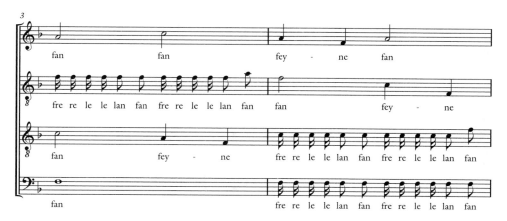

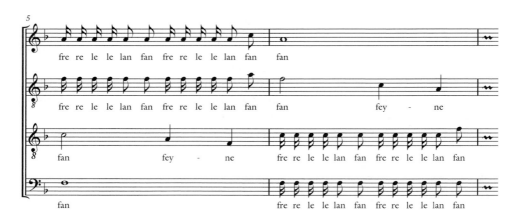

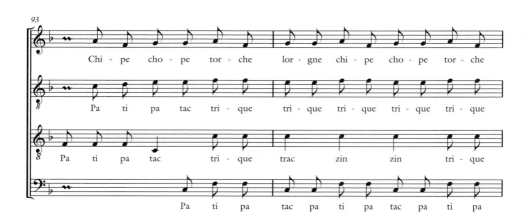

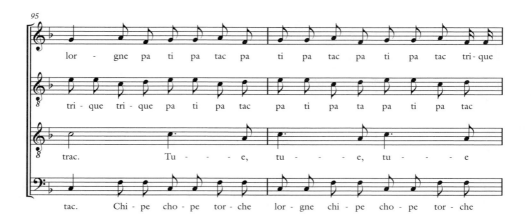

Fan, fan fre re le le lan. . . . Chipe chope torche lorgne . . . Pa ti pa tac trique
trac zin, zin . . . etc., kill, press; noble, gallant men, be valiant . . .

the sixteenth century, clearly, was the continuing and fructifying effect of the popular tradition, this time in the form of what by then was being called the *voix de ville*
(literally "city voices"). Like the term, the poetic tradition upon which this song type
was based can be traced through a process of transformation to a locality in
Normandy: the Vau de vire, a picturesque valley on the river and near the city of the
same name. As late as 1611 its place of origin was mentioned in connection with the
following definition of "vaudeville," an earlier form of the word: "a countrey ballade,
or song; a Roundelay or Virelay; so tearmed of *Vaudevire*, a Norman towne, wherin
Olivier Bassel, the first inventer of them, lived."[26]

26. See Randle Cotgrave, *A Dictionarie of the French and English Tongues* (London, 1611; reprint,
Columbia: University of South Carolina Press, 1968). Bassel (more commonly Basselin or Bachelin) was
a poet of the fifteenth century whose sixty-some songs were finally published early in the seventeenth by
a compatriot, Jean Le Houx.

FIGURE 18-1. King Francis I at Marignano (detail

Initially both the repertory of verse and its topoi were predominantly local in nature, dealing—as to be expected—with personages and events of the region, although including as well love songs and drinking songs of a more general nature. These compositions may reflect the activity of a guild of poets—perhaps on the order of the medieval *puys*—referred to as the "bons compaignons du Vau de Vire" in the song *Hélas, Olivier Basselin*, whose members reputedly sang their verse to melodies already in existence. Some of these may in fact have been included in the "Bayeux Manuscript," one of the monophonic collections mentioned earlier, in which Basselin's name is also mentioned.[27]

Toward the middle of the sixteenth century, poets working in courtly and urban milieux became interested in the genre, perhaps in part as a result of the humanist scholars' preoccupation with the forms of lyric expression thought to have been current in antiquity when the bard was pictured reciting his verses to the lyre. The poetry, as a result, tended to become more courtly in nature, but the melodies continued to be drawn from a preexistent pool.[28] Many of them may actually have originated as dance tunes. When, in 1576, Jehan Chardavoine published nearly 200 such pieces, text and tune, in *Le recueil des plus belles et excellentes chansons en forme de voix*

27. See Clifford Barnes, "Vaudeville," *The New Grove Dictionary of Music*, 19:564–65.
28. Van Orden, "Sexual Discourse in the Parisian Chanson," 31–41, associates the emergence of the *voix de ville* with the moral dilemma faced in France by the *nouveaux nobles*, a new aristocracy of wealthy merchants and professionals who were able to purchase seigneurial titles from the crown. She suggests that the hard-working bourgeois had difficulty reconciling their own fundamental values with the traditional recreational pursuits of the hereditary aristocracy, in particular the conventionally acceptable uses of music as a pastime with the seductive lure of its sensual powers.

from a bas-relief on Francis's tomb at St. Denis).

de ville, he identified the source of the melodies as pavanes, galliards, branles, tour-
dions, and "other songs that are commonly danced and sung in the cities." By then
the expression had taken on the denotation that became most current in the sixteenth century: it was understood to refer to "courtly lyrics, written upon or set to
simple melodies, sung monophonically or with homophonic accompaniment."[29]

Just as *chansons rustiques* had been taken for polyphonic composition around the
turn of the century by some of the leading figures of the day, the repertory of *voix de
ville* attracted in turn the attention of a number of the most skilled masters active during its middle decades. One of the first, apparently, to include polyphonic settings of
them among the chansons published under his name was Pierre Certon, who served
first as *clerc* (from 1532) and then as master of the choirboys at the Sainte-Chapelle
in Paris (from 1536 until his death in 1572). By virtue of that appointment he was,
for all intents and purposes, a member of the royal music establishment, acquainted,
for example, with both Claudin and Attaingnant's partner, Hubert Jullet.[30] It is noteworthy, therefore, that his *Premier livre de chansons*, brought out in 1552 by Le Roy
and Ballard (Attaingnant's successors as royal printers of music), contained sixteen
songs of this type: settings for four voices in a simple homophonic style of strophic
poems that had been sung (monophonically) to relatively catchy syllabic tunes.

29. "D'autres chansons que l'on dance et que l'on chante ordinairement par les villes"; this and the next
quotation are drawn from the illuminating study by Daniel Heartz, "*Voix de ville*: Between Humanist
Ideals and Musical Realities," in *Words and Music: The Scholar's View*, ed. Laurence Berman (Cambridge,
Mass.: Harvard University Press, 1972), 115–35.
30. See Aimé Agnel, "Certon, Pierre," *The New Grove Dictionary of Music*, 4:80–82.

Framing this group of pieces are arrangements of two odes by Mellin de Saint-Gelais (1491–1558), who served as almoner and librarian at the court of Francis I but gained fame as a poet, primarily by singing his verse to his own instrumental accompaniment in what was considered to be the "ancient" manner. He was praised by a contemporary as one "who writes, better indeed than all others, lyrical verses, sets them to music, sings them, plays and performs them on instruments . . . being poet [and] musician." Like Marot earlier in the century, then, Saint-Gelais appears to have made a signal contribution to the chanson repertory of the period; between 1529 and 1590 more than seventy of his poems were taken for polyphonic composition by fifty-four different masters.[31]

Among them, *Puisque vivre en servitude*, another of the odes set by Certon for his modest collection of 1552, will serve to illustrate both the essential traits of the song and of a characteristic arrangement in four parts (see Example 18-8).[32] Saint-Gelais's stanza consists of seven heptasyllables, rhyming a'b a'b b c c. The iterated rhymes of the second pair of lines is matched by a literal repeat in the musical setting, and the third pair of lines is set by two half-phrases in an antecedent–consequent relationship (mm. 13). With the final verse of the strophe comes a cadential formula, and the asymmetry that would otherwise result from the heptastych is avoided by repeating that final line, thus producing four phrases of four ternary breves, each beginning with an anacrusis of two minims and divided into two matching halves.

As Heartz observes, the rhythms here follow unremittingly a pattern found in the galliards and the saltarellos of the period, and the regularity of the phrase structure is likewise characteristic of the dance. It is possible even to wonder if Saint-Gelais did not fashion his poem to fit the rhythms and phrases of a well-known dance melody rather than to shape (or have shaped) a tune to match his verses.[33] Whatever the case, Certon did nothing in setting the song polyphonically to veil the regular rhythmic order of the piece; it is, instead, reinforced by his strict homophony and the orderly placement of the cadences.

CHANSON STYLE AND THE FLEMISH NETHERLANDS

Compositions of such facture and style were, of course, a far cry from many of the chansons being published during the second half of the sixteenth century by the

31. The citation is from Barthélemy Aneau's *Le Quintil Horatien* of 1550 in which he defends Saint-Gelais, responding to an attack from Joachim Du Bellay in *La deffence et illustration de la langue françoyse* of 1549; see Frank Dobbins, "Saint-Gelais, Mellin," *The New Grove Dictionary of Music*, 16:390, and cf. Heartz, "*Voix de ville*," 115–18.

32. An edition of this chanson is given as example 1 by Heartz in his study *Voix de ville*, 118, and has also been edited by Jane A. Bernstein, *The Sixteenth-Century Chanson*, vol. 6, *Pierre Certon* (New York: Garland, 1990), 20–21.

33. See Heartz, "*Voix de ville*," 119.

EXAMPLE 18-8. Pierre Certon, *Puisque vivre en servitude*

Since I must live in such sad and dolorous servitude, I see myself as fortunate to be in so
excellent a place. My pain is most extreme, but Love has so ordained; please have pity.
(Six additional strophes.)

printing houses in France and in the nearby urban centers of the Low Countries,
especially Louvain and Antwerp. It is in fact mildly astonishing how many collections
of polyphonic chansons were brought out during the sixteenth century by the two
principal music presses in the Flemish-speaking region of northern Europe, those of
Tylman Susato and Pierre Phalèse. A burgeoning European trade in printed books
and music can explain only to a degree the scope of their activity in an area that was
not for the most part linguistically French.

Susato (ca. 1500? to 1561–64) obtained a privilege for printing music in 1542, having spent the early years of his career as calligrapher and trumpeter at the cathedral in
Antwerp, then as a town minstrel. Over the next decade or two he issued—in addition
to three books of Masses, nineteen books of motets, eleven anthologies of Flemish
songs and instrumental dances, and eight books of *Souterliedekens* (settings of the
Psalms translated into Flemish)—twenty-five collections of polyphonic chansons.[34]

Phalèse (ca. 1510 to 1573–76), who began as a bookseller to the University of
Louvain in 1542, applied for a privilege to print music in 1551, having previously
prepared for publication five books of chansons arranged for lute that were printed
for him by licensed printers: Baethen, Sassen, and Velpen. Between 1552 and 1560
he also printed seven books of chansons for four voices and two more for five or six
voices. In 1570, following the death of Susato, Phalèse joined forces with the
Antwerp printer Jean Bellère. The partnership thus formed published only a small
handful of additional chanson anthologies; the firm brought out instead collections
of French secular music by composers such as Lassus, Jean de Castro, and Philippe
de Monte.[35]

34. See Susan Bain, "Susato," *The New Grove Dictionary of Music*, 18:378–79.
35. Concerning the printing ventures of the Phalèse family, see Susan Bain, *The New Grove Dictionary of Music*, 14:617–20.

Although commercial opportunity helps to explain the chanson collections put on the market by the printers of the Low Countries, the attention accorded the genre by composers working in the region is more difficult to account for, especially given the magnitude of their output. Engagement with the chanson was perhaps not too unusual for someone like Jean Richafort (ca. 1480–ca. 1547), for although he finished his career in Bruges, he had served earlier at the royal court of France. With a total of only eighteen songs (eight for three voices, seven for four, and three for five), his surviving repertory is not large, in any case.[36] Some of these pieces are arrangements based on preexistent *chansons rustiques*, others are freely composed, but none of them display the declamatory, homophonic style that was cultivated just a bit later by court-related composers such as Sermisy and Certon.[37]

Much more surprising is the prolific chanson production of masters such as Thomas Crecquillon and Clemens (non Papa), who spent their entire careers in Flemish-speaking areas of the Low Countries. Crecquillon (between ca. 1480 and 1500–57?), whose only known appointment was to the choir of Emperor Charles V, wrote nearly 200 chansons, most of which were included in one of the numerous printed anthologies of the period.[38] Many of them appear in the collections brought out by Susato, as is to be expected, but a small handful was published in Lyons in Moderne's tenth book of *Le parangon des chansons* of 1543.[39] So few of Crecquillon's chansons have been edited in modern score that it is difficult to generalize about his style, but it is clear just from the few examples readily available that imitative counterpoint is the prevailing compositional procedure and that the resultant textures are similar to those seen in his motets.

Clemens (between ca. 1510 and 1515 to 1555–56), who was associated in the course of his career with both the church of St. Donatian in Bruges and the Marian brotherhood of 's-Hertogenbosch, may also have served Philippe de Croy and had connections with Charles V. He is credited with only eighty-nine chansons (of which just seventy-seven are considered authentic and included in the complete edition of his works) and is much better known for his settings of the Psalms in the Flemish vernacular, the *Souterliedekens*.[40] One of the earliest of his chansons was printed by Attaingnant in 1536, and a fair number are in the homophonic, declamatory style characteristic of Claudin and other composers of the French royal court. In his *Misericorde au martir amoureulx*, in particular, the chordal texture is maintained with great consistency.

More characteristic, however, is his setting for five voices of *La belle Margaritte*

36. Concerning Richafort, see Howard Mayer Brown, *The New Grove Dictionary of Music*, 15:839–40.

37. As a chanson composer, Richafort has been linked with Clemens (non Papa) and Crecquillon by Reese, *Music in the Renaissance*, 300–3.

38. See Howard Mayer Brown and Barton Hudson, "Crecquillon," *The New Grove Dictionary of Music*, 5:26–29.

39. See Pogue, *Jacques Moderne*, 178–80 and 327.

40. See Willem Elders, "Clemens (non Papa)," *The New Grove Dictionary of Music*, 4:476–80.

(see Example 18-9).[41] Clemens's reliance on imitative counterpoint for chanson composition is typified by the canonic imitation at the octave between superius and tenor,

41. For examples of Clemens's chanson style, see Jacobus non Papa Clemens, *Opera omnia*, ed. K. Ph. Bernet Kempers, 21 vols., Corpus mensurabilis musicae 4 ([Rome]: American Institute of Musicology, 1951–76), vols. 10 and 11. For *Misericorde au martir amoureulx*, see 10:140–42 (no. 37), and for a complete transcription of *La belle Margaritte* in modern score, see 10:82–86 (no. 25).

EXAMPLE 18-9. Clemens (non Papa), *La belle Margaritte* (mm. 1–24)

The beautiful Daisy is a noble flower. Although she is small, she has great value. She is
   young and prudent and thus has no bitterness at all: [the most beautiful little flower
   that I can find in all the world].
CANON: At the lower octave.

but the use of that device—although reminiscent of Josquin—appears to be unique to this one example. Of particular interest, given the consistently contrapuntal texture of the piece, is the treatment accorded certain elements of the text: eight lines of hexasyllabic verse, rhyming A'B A'B C'D C'D. The second pair of lines, "Although she is small,/She is of great value," culminates in a repetitive extension that illustrates "grand valeur" not only by textual reiteration but also the long notes to which the last word is sung (mm. 10–15 in particular). Similarly, the final pair of lines, "The most beautiful little flower/That I can find in the world," which repeats the opening musical material, is spun out, surely for textual emphasis, for sixteen breves (mm. 33–49), fully a third of the total duration of the piece.

The elaborate contrapuntal procedures marshaled to present such a seemingly modest text and the emphasis given to those verses most flattering to the "belle Margaritte" suggest that there may be more to this chanson than would at first appear. It may have been meant as homage to one of the noble Marguerites who played important roles at the Netherlands court of the Habsburgs, conceivably Marguerite of Austria, regent of the Netherlands from 1507 until her death in 1530, or, more likely, Marguerite of Parma (1522–86), the daughter of Charles V by a Flemish woman. A second setting of the same text for six voices may be seen as supporting evidence for the hypothesis, especially since both duplicate settings and six-voice formats are rare in Clemens's chanson repertory.[42]

A number of composers of the period (in particular those such as Jacques Arcadelt and Orlande de Lassus who spent much of their careers in Italy and Germany and thus became as familiar with the Italian madrigal as they were with the chanson) tended to invest the latter with compositional procedures that had emerged with the development of Italian secular music. These included traits just seen in the chanson repertories that originated in the Low Countries: motetlike contrapuntal textures (imitative as well as free); homophony not only for emphatic declamation but also as an element of musical contrast; and changes in vocal registration to produce sonorities of varying volumes and qualities. In particular it meant applying to the polyphonic chanson the expressive techniques of a highly developed musical mimesis usually described as "madrigalistic" and consisting of the use of rhythmic, melodic, and harmonic ideas to illustrate the individual conceits of a text.

The adoption of expressive compositional procedures of the sort for settings of French verse was more than just an innovation, however; it was in a sense also an aberration. From the very inception of the genre its most essential and fundamental characteristics had been, instead, the intelligibility of its declamation, the limpid articulation of its textual and musical syntax, and the clarity of its formal structures. And this continued to be true of the most typical of the polyphonic chansons of the sixteenth century. This may help to explain, on the one hand, the enduring popularity of the *voix de ville* from the 1550s on and, on the other, the development of the closely related *air de cour.*

---

42. For the setting in six parts, see Clemens, *Opera omnia,* 10:119–23 (no. 32).

The preface to the first collection of pieces to be so designated, the *Livre d'air de cours miz sur le luth par Adrian Le Roy*, published by the royal printers Le Roy and Ballard in 1571, affirms that the simple strophic settings that it contains were of the kind previously known as "vaudevilles." As indicated by the title, all twenty-two pieces included in the print had been arranged by Le Roy for solo voice and lute, but thirteen of them had previously been published as *voix de villes* harmonized for four voices.[43] Through the remainder of the sixteenth century the prints that advertised "airs" in their titles were all written for vocal ensemble rather than accompanied solo voice. Judging, however, from the flood of songs for voice and lute that began early in the seventeenth, performers must have continued to reduce the part-writing of the ensemble pieces for performance by solo voice with accompaniment all through the intervening period.

As with the chanson repertories from earlier in the sixteenth century, those published during its second half reflected once again the influence of the prominent poets of that age, in particular those included in the brilliant literary constellation known as the Pléiade: Pierre de Ronsard, Joachim du Bellay, Jean Antoine de Baïf, Jean Dorat, Pontus de Tyard, Etienne Jodelle, and Rémy Belleau. Imbued with the historicizing humanism of the age, these authors espoused ancient models, encouraged the imitation of classical meters and forms, and strove for a lyricism of the sort they believed to have been achieved by ancient authors who were capable of singing their own verses to the lyre using music of their own invention.

They seem to have accepted as axiomatic that an intimate union of words and music was possible. None of them attempted to explain specifically how such an ideal was to be realized, but the few examples offered by Ronsard as an appendix to his *Amours* of 1552 would suggest that these poets believed an effective declamatory style to be more essential to their rhetorical objectives than musical gestures to illustrate individual words and conceits. Since Ronsard deemed it possible to sing any of the poems in the collection to one or another of the musical settings provided for that purpose, it is clear that the criteria for making such a match had to be fundamentally metrical and formal rather than expressive in nature.[44]

MUSIQUE MESURÉE À L'ANTIQUE

A similar esthetic orientation appears to have been adopted by the musicians and men of letters who affiliated themselves with the Académie de Poésie et de Musique, which was organized under royal patronage in 1571 by Antoine de Baïf (see Figure 18-2) with the assistance of Joachim Thibaut de Courville (who is elegantly styled as the "king's Lyre player"). Meeting regularly in the poet's home, members of the Académie prepared performances of what came to be called *musique mesurée*, com-

---

43. See John H. Baron, "Air de cour," *The New Grove Dictionary of Music*, 1:183.
44. See Howard M. Brown, "Chanson," *The New Grove Dictionary of Music*, 4:143.

positions written on verses in a poetic style newly conceived by Baïf himself as *vers mesurés à l'antique*. The "measure" in question was derived from the quantitative prosody of antiquity. In accordance with a fairly complex set of arbitrary rules, long and short values were assigned (in a strict ratio of 2:1) to the individual syllables of the French language, making it possible to adapt to poetry in the vernacular the meters of classical verse in Greek and Latin. The purpose of the "musiciens" of the Académie in doing so was to recapture music's fabled power to move deeply the listener, evoking virtually at will the intended emotional response.[45]

FIGURE 18-2. Jean Antoine de Baïf as depicted on a medal by Primavera.

Although the experiment was of relatively short duration—the meetings of the Académie had ceased by 1584, and Baïf himself reverted to rhymed, accentual verse for his latest works—it was not without lasting repercussions on the chanson of the late sixteenth century. For *musique mesurée* the quantities of the verse were to be made explicit in the rhythms of the music with long syllables set to notes twice as long as those used for short syllables. If adherence to such a rigid compositional procedure was potentially stultifying for the composer and monotonous for the listener, it changed nonetheless radically the rhythmic character of the secular French repertory of the period. Instead of conceiving of rhythm as arising from duple or triple divisions of larger values (such as semibreves and breves), composers treated it as an additive process in which binary and ternary groupings succeeded one another in accordance with the quantities of the syllables being set.

One of the most successful in overcoming the limitations inherent in this new manner of rhythmic organization by his exceptional melodic gifts and harmonic imagination was Claude Le Jeune (1528–30 to 1600). A Protestant composer who enjoyed the protection of Henry of Navarre (the future Henry IV of France), he became one of the leading lights of Baïf's Académie. His *Vien, belle, vien*, a representative example of the *air* as cultivated late in the sixteenth century, illustrates not only the genre but also the rhythmic character of *musique mesurée à l'antique* (see Example 18-10).[46]

45. See Frank Dobbins, "Baïf," *The New Grove Dictionary of Music*, 2:34.
46. For a transcription of the entire work in modern score, see Claude Le Jeune, *Airs a III. IIII. V. et VI Parties* (1607), ed. D. P. Walker, 4 vols. ([Rome]: American Institute of Musicology, 1951–59), 2:65–67.

EXAMPLE 18-10. Claude Le Jeune, *Vien, belle vien, rechant* (refrain) and *chant* (stanza) à 4

RECHANT: Come, fair one, come play in this beautiful day; come, I await thee, desiring love so much.

CHANT: Already that gleaming star whose day is far advanced has begun to show us the dawn lighting the heavens. (Four additional strophes.)

The poem, attributed to Baïf, combines a recurring refrain or *rechant* consisting of two dactylic lines (both of four feet, though the second is truncated), rhyming AA, with a series of identical strophes of four lines each, rhyming bccb. Judging from the musical setting, which duplicates homophonically the quantities of the verse, the meter of the *chant* or stanza is much less regular than that of the refrain, combining a dactyl with a trochee and a spondee in the first pair of lines with an anapest, a dactyl, and a spondee for the third and trochees and spondees in alternation (with the last truncated) for the fourth and last.

Le Jeune has provided two settings for the *rechant*, the first for four voices, the second for six, with the top part of the former retained as the *sixième* of the latter. Since the refrain was presumably sung to begin and then between each of the subsequent stanzas, the six-part version may have been held in reserve for the final reiteration. There is, by contrast, but one section of music for the *chant*, which must be repeated for each of the strophes. Overall the musical substance is relatively modest, then, the first section consisting of two phrases, the second of four, with a clear cadential articulation only at the end of each. Moreover, the regular rhythms of the *rechant* could easily be subsumed under a regular duple mensuration with four units to the phrase.

In the *chant*, to the contrary, the rhythm is additive, with the duple patterns interspersed with triple figures in a manner that a regular mensuration could not accommodate. The charm of this rhythmic irregularity, coupled with the skill of the melodic invention and the harmonizations, saves the song from the possible boredom of excessive and repetitive uniformity. More noteworthy in the present context, however, is the historical significance of such freely ordered rhythmic designs. Not only did they remain characteristic for the *airs de cour* for lute and solo voice in the seventeenth century, but they set the pattern as well for recitative in the French style as first codified in the *tragédies lyriques* of Jean-Baptiste Lully.

<hr />

◯ *CHANSONS SPIRITUELLES* AND *NOËLS* ◯

Given the licentious nature of certain of the texts set as polyphonic chansons in the course of the sixteenth century—particularly, as we have seen, those borrowed from or inspired by the monophonic repertory of a "popular" character—it should come as no surprise that the genre drew the censure of moralizing religionists. Those, in particular, who associated themselves with the Protestant Reformation inveighed against the songs they considered "dishonest, dissolute, and outrageous." In an attempt, therefore, to prevent the corruption of the young, who naturally had a particular affection for amorous lyrics, without depriving them entirely of their musical recreations, poets and musicians with Calvinistic views began to provide pieces that were well known and loved with alternate texts that were pious or moralizing rather than erotic in tone.[47]

Faulte d'argent, for instance, the plaint of the amorous man whose lack of funds prevents the fulfillment of his desire, became a declaration concerning the importance of faith, *Faulte de foy, c'est erreur non pareille*. And Marot's *Tant que vivray* was rewritten to shift the object of intended service from the "powerful god of love" to the "all powerful Lord . . . Jesus Christ."[48]

Such pieces, identified in the documents of the period as *chansons morales* or *spirituelles*, were seen by authors and/or composers with Protestant sympathies not only as a pleasantly sober tool for the instruction of their youth but also as a means of spreading the moral views and the doctrines of the Reformation. Songs were used as well for blunt attacks, often in harshly polemic tones, on what were judged to be the failings of the Roman clergy. If, however, despite its obvious importance for the religious and social history of the age, this segment of the secular French repertory of the sixteenth century has received relatively little attention from music historians, the reason is not difficult to determine.

Chansons spirituelles were more of a literary than a musical phenomenon; they were usually little more than pious parodies of existing texts that were to be sung to the melodies and/or the part-songs written for the original poetry. Not surprisingly, therefore, when they were published, it was generally without incurring the expense that would have been entailed by the inclusion of musical notation. Anthologies of verse created in the manner described began to appear as early as the 1530s, and the

<hr />

47. Dorothy S. Packer, "Collections of Chaste Chansons for the Devout Home (1613–1633)," *Acta musicologica* 61 (1989): 175–216, although concerned primarily with a later period, sketches some of the background for the *chanson spirituelle* and illuminates its lasting influence in France on music making at home and at school for Protestants and Catholics alike.

48. See Howard M. Brown, "The Chanson Spirituelle, Jacques Buus, and Parody Technique," *Journal of the American Musicological Society* 15 (1962): 145–46.

progressive accumulation of such texts culminated, in a sense, in the very large *Recueil de plusieurs chansons spirituelles & chrestiennes*, printed in 1555, probably in Geneva. Containing over 200 items, it became the central source of "spiritual" song texts for the French Reformation of the sixteenth century and went through at least five editions, the last of which dates from 1678.[49]

There were basically only two significant exceptions to the general pattern just described, instances in which a collection of *chansons spirituelles* was freshly invent-ed, both text and music. The first of these, the *Premier livre de chansons spirituelles*, printed in Lyons by the Beringen brothers in 1548, consisted primarily of settings in four parts by Didier Lupi Second of poems by Guillaume Guéroult. (It also includ-ed, however, five Psalm settings, a Te Deum, and a set of Lamentations in French translation.) Lupi's chansons reveal two distinct compositional styles, both of which had been widely established earlier as characteristic for works in the genre.

For the strophic texts, on the one hand, he adopted a simple facture, fundamen-tally homophonic in nature and with a relatively tuneful melody in the tenor. The effect is not unlike that cultivated by most Protestant composers of the period for their Psalm settings, which are, from a stylistic point of view, the sacred counterpart to the *voix de ville*. One of the pieces composed in this manner, Lupi's tripartite set-ting of *Susanne un jour*, was to have an extraordinary postcompositional destiny; it was reworked by some thirty different composers, Protestant and Catholic alike, in at least forty different arrangements, most of which were based on Lupi's tenor.[50] For the nonstrophic texts, on the other hand, he used a through-composed contrapun-tal style, alternating points of imitation with passages in homophonic declamation in accordance with the contrapuntal practice that had been in current use for the chan-son from the 1530s on.[51]

The other exceptional collection was Claude Le Jeune's crowning contribution to the repertory of *chansons spirituelles*, his *Octonaires de la vanité et inconstances du monde*, published posthumously in 1606. Based on moralizing poems by the Calvinist preacher Antoine Chandieu, the collection appears to reflect a certain pre-occupation with systematic number. Each poem is of exactly eight lines—hence the "octonaires" of the title—and there are in all thrity-six compositions. These are divided into twelve groups of three, each comprising one chanson for three voices and two for four, and ordered according to their modal orientation.

The system of classification adopted for the purpose, interestingly enough, was the "new" one propounded by Zarlino with twelve modes (instead of the tradition-al eight) and with C as the final for the first pair (instead of D). A further indication of growing Italian influence in French music of the late sixteenth century is Le

49. For a succinct survey of the pertinent sources, see Brown, "The Chanson Spirituelle," 147–49.
50. For a transcription of the original composition and a history of its treatment at the hands of later com-posers, see Kenneth Levy, "'Susanne un jour': The History of a Sixteenth-Century Chanson," *Annales musicologiques* 1 (1953): 375–408.
51. See Marc Honneger and Frank Dobbins, "Lupi, Second," *The New Grove Dictionary of Music*, 11:336.

Jeune's use of madrigalistic word painting in the chansons of this collection.[52]

If the *chanson spirituelle* can be viewed primarily as a product of the Protestant Reformation in French-speaking regions, its counterpart on the Catholic side is undoubtedly the *noël*. Like the "spiritual songs," *noëls* were modeled on preexistent texts that already had a musical setting, either monophonic or polyphonic, to which the new poem was to be sung. They differed in content only in their relatively narrow focus. The majority of the pieces so designated—though not all of them by any means—have to do with the Nativity, as is suggested by the term itself, and the acclamation, *noël*, was not infrequently included in the new text as a kind of refrain. Because the substitute texts usually consisted of several stanzas (forty or more in rare instances), their performance—if with music—necessarily entailed strophic repetition of the piece taken as a model. And since that music was already well known, as a rule, and hence circulating in some form, the *noëls*, like the *chansons spirituelles*, were usually copied or published without notation.[53]

The two earliest collections of texts explicitly identified as *noëls* date from the end of the fifteenth century. One of them, MS 3653 of the Bibliothèque de l'Arsenal in Paris, is an elegant parchment manuscript that may have been inscribed in the 1490s for King Charles VIII of France. The other, MS français 2368 of the National Library, also belonged to Charles VIII and, after him, to Louis XII; consequently, it too must date from the 1480s or 1490s.

However, the vast majority of the more than seventy surviving sources for the genre are of a much different character. *Noëls* circulated mainly in prints of modest format and size; most of them are in octavo and contain on average thirty or so poems, although the largest collections have many more and some considerably less. Often these verse anthologies appear to have been rather hastily put together, and because they were intended for a large urban market, they were relatively inexpensive. Since, as we have seen, music was not generally included, the text upon which the *noël* was modeled—and hence the music to which it could be sung—was in most cases identified by a sort of verbal tag consisting of the beginning of the original verse and known as a *timbre*.[54]

Where these terse indications can be followed to a notated source, they lead to musical works in three rather different categories: liturgical plainsong, secular monody, and polyphonic chansons. Among the most venerable of the *noëls* are those based on a well-known chant—hymns, tropes, and Sequences for Advent being among those most frequently taken as a model. The hymn *Conditor alma siderum*, sung to its original liturgical melody either in Latin or in a French parody, appears to have been a fairly traditional opener for such collections and, together with the Latin hymn *Puer nobis nascitur*, a great favorite.

52. See Reese, *Music in the Renaissance*, 384.
53. For a succinct description of the genre, see Adrienne F. Block, *The Early French Parody Noël*, 2 vols. (Ann Arbor: UMI Research Press, 1983), 1:5–6.
54. Concerning the sources for the *noël*, see the annotated catalogue of seven manuscripts and sixty-two prints included in Block, *Early French Parody Noël*, 1:119–48.

Much more numerous, however, are the melodies taken from the monophonic secular repertory of the fifteenth and early sixteenth centuries. Some of these tunes were probably borrowed from that part of the oral tradition that was never fixed in notation, including songs fashioned for theatrical performances or used to accompany dancing. Others, to the contrary, are among the tunes that have been transmitted in one of the monophonic chansonniers or in a polyphonic setting that is clearly based upon a preexistent song of the same sort.

However, a *timbre* is not necessarily an entirely unambiguous indication of the song upon which a given *noël* was modeled. Poets of the period were not averse to borrowing the opening line of a popular piece as the starting point for new verse. As a result, a given *timbre* could point to more than one preexistent chanson. Moreover, where a melody is found both in monophonic form and as the basis for a polyphonic composition, there is usually no way of knowing to which version the tag refers. In fact, the choice may have been left intentionally vague to the potential performer.[55]

The complexity of the problems posed by the presumed relationship between the *noël* and its putative model is illustrated rather well by a collection apparently published by Moderne in Lyons in the mid-1530s, *La fleur des noelz nouvellement notés,* one of only nine such anthologies in which monophonic melodies were included for some of the texts. This relatively opulent little volume contains twenty-one *noëls,* ten of them with tunes (including the two Latin hymns just mentioned) and eleven others with only *timbres.* Five of the notated melodies included in the collection are found in no other source of the period in monophonic form, although three of the texts in question are found in other prints with a *timbre.*

Of the remaining three, one is clearly related to the cantus of a polyphonic chanson by Claudin, *Vivray je tousjours en soulcy,* which may or may not have its origins in the monophonic repertory. The other two give every indication of having been lifted from an earlier *chanson rustique,* but they are otherwise known in the written repertory only in polyphonic arrangements. One is by Jean Richafort and the other by Adrien Willaert, both of whom had connections with the French royal chapel. In this small miscellany, then, are representatives of all the primary sources from which music was taken for the performance of *noëls*: liturgical chant, monophonic melodies, and possibly a voice part from a polyphonic chanson.[56]

Exceptionally, in two of the printed volumes with musical notation tunes apparently newly composed are given for some of the *noëls* included in the publication.

---

55. Concerning the difficulty of matching text and music from the printed anthologies, see the reflections of Block, *Early French Parody Noël,* 1:69ff.

56. See the discussion of this collection by Block, *Early French Parody Noël,* 1:74–77. The various types of musical compositions to which the *noëls* could be sung are amply illustrated by vol. 2 of her study, an annotated edition of Pierre Sergent's *Les Grans noelz nouveaulx composez nouvellement en plusieurs langaiges sur le chant de plusieurs chansons nouvelles* of about 1567. For each of the 150 items it contains she has traced the *timbre* to the possible musical sources and has provided transcriptions of compositions associated with a textual model for many of the poems in the collection.

The *Cantiques du premier advenement de Jesu Christ*, for one, brought out by Nicolas Denisot in 1553, contains nineteen poems, fourteen of which are provided with melodies not found elsewhere in the repertory. Similarly, the *Noelz et chansons nouvellement composés*, published by Nicolas Martin in Lyons in 1555, included sixteen items with notated tunes that have no counterpart in other such collections.[57]

More unusual still are the two books of *noëls* that included notated polyphony, in either case settings in two or more parts clearly intended for use in the schools. The earliest of these, entitled *Se ensuyvent les nouelz nouveaulx*, appeared as early as 1512. It included among its twenty items four poems with polyphonic settings for two voices by François Briand, who was at the time regent of the school of St. Benoit in Le Mans. The other, the *Genethliac noel musical et historial*, published in Lyons in 1559 by Barthélémy Aneau, consists, as is indicated by the title, of a play in the vernacular written for the students of Trinity College. Some seventeen *noëls* have been integrated into the drama, and for sixteen of them there are polyphonic settings that range in style from the homophonic to the imitative. Two voices survive, cantus and tenor, but the counterpoint appears to be incomplete, suggesting that there may have been originally another voice or two.[58]

As for the *noëls* in the many text anthologies without notation whose *timbres* apparently refer to polyphonic chansons, either for three voices or for four, the numbers seem to increase gradually in the course of the sixteenth century. In the earlier collections, dating from the final decades of the fifteenth century until the mid-1520s, the majority of such pieces can be identified as three- or four-part arrangements of songs from the monophonic repertory. Later, by comparison, the number of polyphonic chansons demonstrably based upon a *chanson rustique* that were adopted as models for *noëls* appears to diminish with each passing decade. The decline may be more apparent than real, however. Many of the pieces in question actually have some of the most significant earmarks of a polyphonic arrangement, even though no preexistent melody can be unequivocally identified.[59]

This was a genuinely popular repertory, then, and the uses to which it was put were clearly primarily domestic and didactic. As to modes of performance, the evidence that can be extrapolated from the surviving sources, as briefly summarized here, suggests that even though polyphonic performance of the *noël* was certainly possible, and undoubtedly occurred, the use of a single solo voice, with or without instrumental accompaniment, was probably more usual. Indications of this kind also tend to emphasize the manifold connections made between courtly and urban culture during this period of history and to bring to our attention once again the stimulating impetus for innovation and artistic renewal that the former drew from the latter.

---

57. See Block, *Early French Parody Noël*, 1:77–78.
58. See Block, *Early French Parody Noël*, 1:88–90.
59. See Block's discussion in *Early French Parody Noël*, 1:88–98.

CHAPTER 19

The Madrigal

INTRODUCTION

During the second decade of the sixteenth century there began to emerge in Italy, especially in Florentine circles, a genre of secular music that was distinguishable in essential ways from both the *frottola* and the *canto carnascialesco*. It partook, however, of important characteristics of both and may be viewed in a sense as the melding of those two distinctive but related musical traditions. Indispensable, from the frottolistic side, was the vital development of lyric verse in the Italian vernacular that accompanied—or perhaps even led to—the dramatic multiplication of musical settings to which it could be sung. The musical style, by contrast, apparently took its point of departure not from the accompanied solo song of the *frottola* but rather from the declamatory vocal homophony of the carnival songs. A crucial role in this process was played by musicians trained in the musical traditions of northern Europe, whose frame of contrapuntal reference included the polyphonic Mass, the motet, and the wholly vocal chanson of the early sixteenth century.

No less important, it would appear, was the part played by the rapidly developing industry of music publishing. At the same time that some of the most competent and admired of the composers working in Italy were developing an interest in setting verse in the local vernacular, print shops were springing up in most major cities of the peninsula. Alert, of necessity, to any exploitable commercial opportunity, these craftsmen saw in the newly emerging secular genre music with relatively broad appeal for both courtly and urban circles, and they eagerly assisted with its dissemination throughout Europe. It was these same printers, moreover—responding no doubt to the need for a title that advertised the contents of a collection for sale—who gave the newly coined genre a name. Taking for general use the term *madrigal*, which had been appropriated from trecento parlance for the most recent of the lyric poetic forms then being cultivated, they applied it without further distinction (as a rule) to all the musical compositions of the same type.[1]

Whatever the relationship around the turn of the century between the development of Italian poetry and the burgeoning repertory of *frottole*, the emergence of the madrigal as an independent musical genre would be difficult to imagine without the serious literary evolution involving the verse with which it was to be so intimately joined. If the texts found in the earliest printed collections of *frottole* were often light in tone and slight of substance, there was a clear shift as the repertory grew in size and currency—a tendency visible already in the later volumes published by Petrucci—toward material of deeper significance and greater literary prestige. Even as the *frottola* was beginning to come into its own as a poetic-musical type, there was earnest discussion among Italian humanists of the "questione della lingua," the question being whether or not Italian could take its place beside Greek and Latin as a serious and significant literary language.

If the answer, ultimately, was incontrovertibly in the affirmative, the outcome was due in large measure to the work and influence of Pietro Bembo (1470–1547). Born of the Venetian patriciate, he was educated in the—by then—traditional humanistic studies. During a period of residence in Florence while still in his youth, he developed an exceptional enthusiasm for the great poets of the Tuscan language: Dante, Boccaccio, and Petrarch. This led him to prepare for the press of Aldo Manuzio, the scholarly Venetian printer, an edition of Petrarch's *Canzioniere*, which appeared in 1501, making the poet's work widely available for the first time. This was followed in 1502 by his edition of Dante.[2]

However, it was in the works of Petrarch—and, to a lesser extent, those of Boccaccio—that Bembo found the models most worthy of emulation, linguistically and stylistically. He adopted Petrarchan themes for his own first work in the vernacular, *Gli Asolani* of 1505, a dialogue among courtly personages that "completely changed the fashionable concept of love in the sixteenth century" and had an enormous impact on the topoi and the diction of the verse written in subsequent decades.[3]

More importantly, Bembo provided a theoretical basis for his espousal of written Tuscan as a legitimate literary language with a serious treatise, *Della volgar lingua*, published in 1525. With its dissemination among a reading public where—thanks to his earlier activity—Petrarch's poetry was already well known and much admired, the die was cast; Tuscan was well on its way to becoming the preferred vernacular for literature in all of the Italian peninsula. Petrarch, similarly, was emerging as the paragon whose themes and images were to permeate to some degree much of the vernacular

---

1. The first publication—of many—to carry the term *madrigal* in its title was, apparently, *Madrigali de diversi musici: Libro primo de la Serena*, published in Rome in 1530.

2. For a succinct biographical sketch of Bembo, see James Haar, *The New Grove Dictionary of Music*, 2:459–60.

3. The quotation is from Alfred Einstein, *The Italian Madrigal*, 3 vols. (Princeton: Princeton University Press, 1949), 1:110.

lyric poetry written in Italy through the end of the sixteenth century and beyond. Imitation of Petrarch went so far, in fact, that it has been seen by some as choking the original voice of some of the younger poets—including Bembo himself—a danger from which only the most gifted and original among them were able to escape.[4]

Bembo's familiarity with the musical recitation of poetry of a lighter vein in the manner of the *frottola* may date—if it had not been acquired still earlier—from a lengthy stay at the Estense court of Ferrara from 1497 to 1499. By 1505 he had made the personal acquaintance of Isabella d'Este, whose singing to the lute he much admired. In the course of their subsequent correspondence he sent her poems of his own to be set by her court composers and performed by the marchioness herself.[5]

Bembo's close association with Florentine circles, where the crucial transition in musical style was to be realized, can be dated at the latest from 1513. In that year he became secretary to the newly elected Medici pope, Leo X, whom he served until the latter's death in 1521. In that connection, too, his influence may have been seminal. Bembo's preference not only for Petrarchan verse but also for the poetic qualities inherent in it—the variable alternation of lines of seven and eleven syllables (as exemplified in the *Canzoniere*); the use of word accent and rhyme for sonorous effect; the division of style into high, middle, and low; the Petrarchan contrast between *gravità* (seriousness, even severity) and *piacevolezza* (pleasantness); and the notion of decorum—may well have affected the choice of the Italian verse that was being set at the time by musicians living and working in Florence.[6]

⟶ THE EMERGING MADRIGAL ⟵

A conscious turn to serious texts is clearly evident in one of the earliest printed collections to be dedicated entirely to the works of a single Florentine composer. Bernardo Pagoli, called Pisano (1490–1548), had served in the foremost musical establishments of his native city, the cathedral and the baptistry, when in 1514 he was called to Rome by Leo X to sing with the papal choir. Although he settled there permanently only in 1520 and maintained his contacts with Florence and the Medici lifelong, he must have become well acquainted with Bembo, or at least with his work, while at the papal court.[7]

4. For an appraisal of Bembo's activity (and references for further study), see Martha Feldman's richly illuminating study, *City Culture and the Madrigal at Venice* (Berkeley: University of California Press, 1995), 10–13, 124–55, and *passim.*

5. Two *canzoni* from *Gli Asolani* were later included in Petrucci's printed collections: *Non si vedra giammai stanca* in book 7, and *Voi mi poneste in foco*, in book 11; see Einstein, *Italian Madrigal*, 1:112.

6. For a discussion of these concepts and their impact on the madrigal of the sixteenth century (but in a Venetian rather than a Florentine context), see Feldman, *City Culture and the Madrigal at Venice*, especially 124–26.

7. Concerning Pisano, see Frank D'Accone, *The New Grove Dictionary of Music*, 14:772.

FIGURE 19-1. Bernardo (Pagoli) Pisano, *Si è debile il filo*, tenor voice from the partbook (Florence, Biblioteca Nazionale Centrale, MS Magl. XIX 166, ff. 2ᵛ–4).

In 1520 Petrucci published his *Musica . . . sopra le canzone del Petrarcha*, whose very title points to Bembo's influence and the growing appreciation of Petrarch's poetry that was made possible by the publication of his verse. Of the seventeen compositions included in the collection only seven were based on *canzoni* by Petrarch (whose name was undoubtedly featured on the title page largely to attract potential purchasers), but the other ten poems set by Pisano—single-stanza *ballatas* and madrigals of the new type—were in the same elevated style.

That these compositions departed stylistically from the *frottole* published by Petrucci earlier is evident already from the format in which they were printed. Instead of the choirbook arrangement, in which the four parts were all placed on facing pages of a single opening, a separate part book, complete with a text fully laid out for the individual singer, was prepared for each voice (compare Figure 5-10 with Figure 19-1). The nature and extent of the stylistic difference that lay behind this change in disposition can perhaps best be demonstrated by a comparison of a setting by Tromboncino of Petrarch's *Si è debile il filo* and the composition that Pisano wrote to the same text (cf. Examples 19-1 and 19-2).

In Tromboncino's composition a declamatory melody dominates the texture.[8]

8. For a transcription of the complete piece in modern score, showing not only the parts as printed by Petrucci in his *Libro VII* of 1507 but also the intabulation for lute and voice by Franciscus Bossinensis of 1509 and the intabulation for keyboard by Andrea Antico of 1517 (as in Example 19-1), see Benvenuto Disertori, ed., *Le frottole per canto e liuto intabulate de Franciscus Bossinensis*, Istituzioni e monumente dell'arte musicale italiana, new ser., vol. 3 (Milan: Ricordi, 1964), 271–77, no. 39.

EXAMPLE 19-1. Bartolomeo Tromboncino, *Si è debile il filo* (mm. 1–27), showing the versions in four parts, for keyboard alone, and for lute and voice

So weak is the thread holding my unhappy life that, if others do not help me, it will soon
    come to an end. For after the painful departure that took me from my sweet treasure,
    one hope alone has been until now a reason for me to live, saying: ["Why, deprived as
    you are of seeing what you love, do you maintain your soul in sadness?" . . .] (Six
    additional strophes and an envoy.)

EXAMPLE 19-2. Bernardo (Pagoli) Pisano, *Si è debile il filo* (mm. 1–30)

For English translation of text, see Example 19-1.

There are many notes of equal duration, repeated pitches (e.g., mm. 13–16), and stereotypical cadential figures, deriving at least in part from the invariably feminine rhymes. Although the piece is through-composed rather than strophic, recitation formulae are frequently repeated, most noticeably for consecutive verses of the same length that also share a rhyme. This reduces the considerable musical substance of some fifty-four breves to a small number of related phrases. Not surprisingly, given the nature of the melodic writing, the counterpoint is essentially homophonic with the light rhythmic animation of running figures generally characteristic of an instrumental accompaniment.

In sharp distinction is Pisano's wholly vocal conception.[9] In his counterpoint the four voices are often individualized in points of imitation (as at the beginning) or free contrapuntal writing. What is more, despite the melodic independence of the separate lines, each of which must be devised to make an effective presentation of the text, the declamation is hardly less sensitive to the natural accents and rhythms of the verse than the solo song of the *frottola*. Stressed syllables usually fall at the beginning of the mensural unit or are extended in duration, while those not so emphasized, if

9. For a transcription of the complete work in modern score, see Bernardo Pisano, *Collected Works*, ed. Frank D'Accone, Corpus mensurabilis musicae 32, vol. 1 ([Rome]: American Institute of Musicology, 1966), 1:29–32, no. 11.

at the beginning of a verse, are frequently introduced after a short rest with a discreet anacrusis figure.

Where homophony is used as a contrasting texture, it is often for rhetorical rather than strictly declamatory effect. Such is the case, for example, in the final verse of the opening *piede*, where simultaneous declamation gives emphasis to the conclusion that the frail thread holding the poet's wearisome life is about to snap (mm. 15–21). The paired couplets in the poem are reflected in the music not in literal repetition, as in Tromboncino's piece, but by means of melodic sequence, the repeated figures being accompanied each time with new counterpoint (as in mm. 9–15, 25–30).

Although individual lines are cadentially articulated, the melodic and harmonic formulae used for the purpose effect varying degrees of closure, depending upon the voices in which they appear, the intervals of resolution (whether perfect or imperfect consonance), and the extent of the overlap from one phrase to the next. After the clear break at the end of the first line of the second *piede*, for example, cadential punctuation is either entirely avoided or significantly attenuated until the end of the quatrain (mm. 25–36), thus corresponding to the continuity of expression in those three lines. Here and there a verse is repeated for emphasis (as in mm. 30–35), and at the end, a repetition of text and music (with some variation in the latter) provides a formal as well as a rhetorical close to the work.

Only the first stanza of the *canzone* was included in the Petrucci part books, but the complete poem comprises six more plus a *commiato*, or envoy. Since the strophes are identical as to their prosody, it would be possible in principle to sing all of them to the same music (including the *commiato*, although it would require only the last segment of the piece), and Tromboncino may have given conscious consideration to that eventuality in composing his relatively formulaic piece. The text is declaimed simply and syllabically from start to finish with a repetition only for the final verse. Since the rhythmic patterns of the poetry change little from one strophe to the next, the music would lend itself about as well to any of them.

That Pisano's setting was to be considered adaptable in the same manner is, by comparison, highly unlikely. First of all, the internal repetitions of selected words and phrases link the music much more directly to the stanza given in the print. If retained mechanically in an unchanged musical setting, they would not have the same rhetorical logic in the remaining strophes. It is just possible, too, that some of the musical gestures are derived from the meaning of specific words. The modest melisma in the cantus with the word "s'attene" (mm. 6–9) may have been meant to illustrate the connecting thread of the text, for example, and the silence following "dipartita" (m. 25)—which interrupts the continuities of meaning and syntax—may have been intended to represent the separation of that leave taking.

Source evidence suggests that this new manner of setting Italian texts, which is so clearly indebted stylistically to both the motet and the fully texted chanson of the

FIGURE 19-2.   Portrait of Verdelot with a singer known as Ubretto by Sebastiano del Piombo, painted in Venice, ca. 1510 (Berlin, Staatliche Museen).

period, continued to be cultivated primarily in Florence, at least through the 1520s.[10] Another set of part books, MS Q21 in the Civico Museo Bibliografico Musicale in Bologna, which was copied toward the middle of the decade, contains some seventy-one compositions, most of which are similar in nature to the one just discussed, and two or three of them are by Pisano himself.[11] Unfortunately, none of these pieces is given an attribution in the source, but seven of them are identified elsewhere as the work of Philippe Verdelot (ca. 1470–80 to ca. 1530–40?), a key figure in the development of the new madrigal (see Figure 19-2). He is thought to have come to northern Italy—perhaps Venice—about 1510, and by 1522 he had settled in Florence, where he served as the chapelmaster at the baptistry and stayed until about 1530.[12]

As the 1520s drew to a close the newly reestablished Florentine Republic found itself struggling with famine and pestilence and under increasing pressure from Pope Clement VII and Emperor Charles V to return to the hegemony of the Medici. The

10. For a more detailed examination of the evidence that also gives Florence precedence in the development of the new genre, see James Haar, "The Early Madrigal: A Re-appraisal of Its Sources and Its Character," in *Music in Medieval and Early Modern Europe: Patronage, Sources, and Texts*, ed. Iain Fenlon (Cambridge, Mass.: Cambridge University Press, 1981), 163–92.

11. See the study and partial edition of this collection by Claudio Gallico, *Un canzoniere musicale italiano del cinquecento*, Biblioteca historiae musicae cultores, vol. 13 (Florence: Olschki, 1961).

12. See H. Colin Slim, "Verdelot," *The New Grove Dictionary of Music*, 19:631–34.

city's elected officials, desperate for external help in such precarious circumstances, decided to send an embassy to Henry VIII of England in order to seek his support. In accordance with customary protocol, they thought to dispose the king favorably to their pleas by offering him an appropriately luxurious gift. They apparently called upon Verdelot to compile for that purpose an exceptional collection of music, an art of which Henry was known to be particularly fond. The composer selected sixty compositions, thirty of them motets, another thirty Italian madrigals in the new style, at least half of them his own. These were copied into a set of five elegantly decorated part books in late 1527 or early 1528 to make a presentation suitable for a king.[13]

That the Italian-texted works were included in equal numbers with a repertory of motets for four, five, and six voices by the most distinguished composers of the day must be viewed as evidence not only of their relative novelty—which would have had its own charm for the music-loving king—but also of the seriousness with which they were regarded, both by the compiler of the collection and by the city fathers who presumably commissioned it. The choice of verse forms and authors represented in the Italian-texted repertory confirms that indication.

More than half of the poems are either *canzoni* (thirteen), a genre at the serious end of the stylistic spectrum, or derive from it their basic characteristics of form (three). The *ballate* (three) and *ballata*-like poems (three) are by sixteenth-century authors and—like the *canzone*—make use of a variable alternation between lines of seven and eleven syllables rather than the verses of equal length that were characteristic of the lighter verse set by frottolists. Five of the poems are of the (then) new, more freely formed type that came to be called madrigal. There is also a single sonnet, the dialogue *Quando nacesti, Amor*, which was to be set repeatedly in the course of the century.[14] The authors whose works are most numerous in the collection— Niccolò Machiavelli (1469–1527) (with five poems) and Ludovico di Lorenzo Martelli (ca. 1500–ca. 1530) (with three)—both have Florentine connections. So do some of the other poets, including Petrarch himself (one poem). Thirteen poems remain anonymous, but all of the writers who have been identified were among the most respected Italian men of letters of the period.[15]

This manuscript also offers evidence of the multifarious links between polyphonic settings of lyric verse and the theatrical productions of various kinds that were so much a part of Italian culture in the fifteenth and sixteenth centuries. Carnival songs, which were in a very real sense the stylistic prototypes of the pieces under discussion, were themselves conceived for quasi-dramatic performance. They were sung—usually, it seems, by costumed singers making appropriate gestures—from the movable

---

13. See H. Colin Slim, ed., *A Gift of Madrigals and Motets*, 2 vols. (Chicago: University of Chicago Press, 1972), 1:105–9.

14. Concerning the poetic forms that were current at the time—and that continued to be cultivated all through the sixteenth century—see Don Harrán, "Verse Types in the Early Madrigal," *Journal of the American Musicological Society* 22 (1969): 27–53; also above, pp. 402–15.

15. See Slim, ed., *Gift of Madrigals and Motets*, 1:81–92.

stages constructed on the *carri* that rolled through the city's streets in times of popular celebration. There is also early evidence for the integration of song into the theatrical works of the period. It is not surprising to discover, then, that three of Verdelot's compositions in the collection (nos. 6, 10, and 11) are on *canzoni* that were inserted into Machiavelli's comedy *Mandragola* for a performance that was planned for 1526 (but never given). Two of those, plus one other (nos. 9, 10, and 11), were also part of his text for *La Clizia*, completed in 1524 and presented in Florence in 1525.[16]

Of these four, the piece that can be most convincingly connected with a theatrical performance is *Quanto sia lieto il giorno* (no. 9), from the prologue to *La Clizia* (see Example 19-3).[17] The dramatic context for the verse is made explicit by personification as the singers identify themselves as a nymph and three shepherds, come to join in the celebration of "ancient things" (mm. 29–33). The regular structure of the *canzone* with its two prosodically identical *piedi* (abC, abC) is reflected in the music

16. See Slim, ed., *Gift of Madrigals and Motets*, 1:92–104.
17. For a transcription of the complete madrigal in modern score, see Slim, ed., *Gift of Madrigals and Motets*, 2:341–43.

EXAMPLE 19-3. Philippe Verdelot, *Quanto sia lieto il giorno* (mm. 1–11, 22–47)

One sees how joyful is the day in which the ancient things are now revealed and celebrated by you [because all the friendly people have gathered round from every side]. We,
who spend our days in the woods and forests, have also come here—I a nymph, and
we shepherds—already singing together of our loves. (One additional strophe.)

by a literal repetition, the only deviation being a semibreve displacement with respect
to the underlying mensuration. Syntactic continuity is respected by delaying clear
cadential articulation until the concluding third verse of each *piede* (mm. 1–11 =
12–22).

The piece opens with a modest point of imitation in short declamatory phrases
corresponding to the heptasyllables of the first two verses. Italian cannot have been
Verdelot's native tongue, but he respects the natural rhythms of its pronunciation no
less carefully than Pisano had done before him. The imitative beginning is followed
by contrapuntally overlapping pairs of voices (two high, two low) in homophony,
and the longer third verse (eleven syllables), now fully homophonic in all four parts,
culminates with a brief ornamental melisma to help mark the approach to the first
clear cadence (m. 11).

The *sirima* makes much more consistent use of fully voiced homophonic declamation. That texture is broken only when the nymph identifies herself in solo, followed by the three lower voices representing the shepherds. As the final phrase

unfolds toward cadential closure, the melodic material is once again extended melismatically, this time rather more expansively, and a repeat of the line (mm. 39–47) gives formal and rhetorical closure to the stanza.

Since there is a second strophe to the *canzone*, at the end of which the nymph and her shepherd companions take their leave to return to their "ancient loves," one must wonder if it, too, was sung to Verdelot's setting at the performance of the comedy. No definitive answer can be given; however, inasmuch as the patterns of verbal accentuation do not change significantly from one strophe to the next, it is clear that the music will accommodate either one more or less equally well.

The one gesture specific to the text, the solo voice of the nymph answered by the three shepherds (mm. 31–33), is matched by a repeat of that pair of lines in the second stanza. And if the concluding melisma is construed as musical mimesis—as indeed it might well be—it can be seen as no less fitting for the dancing steps of the departing singers ("torneremci") as it would have been for the singing ensemble of the first strophe ("cantando insieme"). Verdelot's compositional solution for this text is thus not unlike those being used at the time for the chanson (see pp. 618–23). Significantly, that similarity points up as well the affinities of Verdelot's compositions in the "Newberry Partbooks" with their carnivalesque Italian antecedents, and it reflects an early stage in the development of a secular genre that was to turn rather rapidly to an ever more word-specific approach to the treatment of the text.

If Florence was, as it would appear, the hearth in which this new song type first took shape and was initially nourished, other centers apparently lost little time in adopting it as their own. During the years of the Medici papacies (roughly 1513–34, critical years in the development of secular polyphony in Italy)—excepting only the brief period of tension and conflict following the establishment of the last Florentine republic, 1527–30—the connections between Florence and Rome were usually very close. In addition, the sympathetic patronage of two worldly, music-loving popes, Leo X and Clement VII, must have done much to encourage the assiduous cultivation of secular music in the ancient capital of Christendom.

Their affection for it must account in some measure for the sustained attention given the setting of Italian texts by the papal singer Constanzo Festa. One of the most admired composers of the sixteenth century, he spent all the years of his maturity in the service of the papal chapel and contributed substantially to its polyphonic repertory—not only Masses and motets but also, as we have seen, hymns, Magnificats, and Lamentations—many of which continued to be sung by the papal choir long after he was dead. His ecclesiastical obligations notwithstanding, Festa is identified in the secular sources of the period as the author of numerous compositions on vernacular texts.[18]

However important Medici tastes may have been in this connection, it is nonetheless important to recall that by the 1530s music printing was beginning to play a significant role in the dissemination of polyphonic music and, at the same time, in

18. See Alexander Main, *The New Grove Dictionary of Music*, 6:503, for a list of Festa's compositions.

spreading the reputation of those skilled in its composition. Consequently, by providing composers with both a commercial outlet and a means of dramatically extending their potential audience, the publishing houses were in fact themselves becoming a new source of patronage, both directly and indirectly. Festa's secular works, for instance, appeared in no less than twenty different printed collections between 1530 and 1549, and the advantages that could accrue from that sort of exposure must surely have encouraged him—as it did so many others—to continue working in the new secular genre even as he was producing the traditional sacred music called for by his duties in the papal choir.

More than eighty madrigals in the surviving sources can be attributed with some degree of confidence to Festa. Surprisingly, although all of them have been accessible in a modern edition for some time now, Festa's role in defining the genre stylistically during the early stages of its development has yet to be fully assessed. Still, it is quite clear that his contribution, like that of Verdelot, with whose works Festa's appear in the earliest printed collections, must have been seminal. He appears to have pioneered, in particular, settings for three voices, which he composed in fair numbers.[19]

Of more than usual interest in this category is his *Altro non è'l mio amor* (see Example 19-4), composed to a *canzone* by Luigi Cassola, whose lyrical verse enjoyed considerable currency with madrigal composers early on.[20] Of particular note in this instance are the echoes of Cassola's poem in the works of later authors who took his first hemistich as the starting point for parody. Like the poetry itself, Festa's music is related in varying degrees to seven other settings, including those for five voices by Verdelot and Maistre Jhan, and the musical affinities are pronounced enough to suggest emulation or at least conscious citation.[21] It is difficult to know which of these three masters stands at the head of the chain, but it is quite conceivable that it was Festa whose work was deemed a model worthy of imitation. In any case, the piece is representative in significant ways of Festa's three-voice madrigals generally, and it was his compositions in this modest format that apparently served as a paradigm for others who were to adopt it later on.

Because *Altro non è'l mio amor* is essentially syllabic in its declamation, its length is measured by that of the single stanza of verse that Festa elected to set. At least two of its three voices move together most of the time, pronouncing the text simultaneously. Only once (at mm. 19–20) do the voices enter one after the other as if begin-

19. See the madrigals by Festa in the *Opera omnia*, ed. Albert Seay, 8 vols., Corpus mensurabilis musicae 25 ([Rome]: American Institute of Musicology, 1962–78), vols. 7 and 8. Seay credits the composer with thirty-one settings of Italian verse for three voices (7:x), of which twenty-five are complete; cf. the comments by Einstein, *Italian Madrigal*, 1:158–59 and 257–58.

20. For a transcription of the entire piece in modern score, see Festa, *Opera omnia*, ed. Seay, 7:45–46, no. 25.

21. Festa has also left us a setting of an answer to Cassola's poem, beginning "Altro non è'l mio amor che canto et riso" (*Opera omnia*, ed. Seay, 7:53–54, no. 30), in which the images of love's torment are replaced by those of pleasure and joy; see James Haar, "*Altro non è'l mio amor*," in *Words and Music: The Scholar's View*, ed. Laurence Berman (Cambridge, Mass.: Harvard University Press, 1972), 93–114.

EXAMPLE 19-4. Costanzo Festa, *Altro non è'l mio amor* (mm. 1–19, 34–49)

My love is nothing but a veritable hell, for hell is simply to see one's self deprived of contemplating in the heavens a single living God, nor is there any other pain in eternal fire. [Therefore a virtual hell is my love because I am entirely deprived of seeing the one sweet treasure that I wish to see. Alas, love's power, how strong thou art] that thou canst make us feel hell or even death.

ning a point of imitation, but while cantus and tenor carry it through to the cadence, the altus quickly abandons its presentation of the melodic line to join the lower part in declaiming the words. The result is a characteristic texture, fundamentally homophonic but lightly animated here and there by the rhythmic and/or contrapuntal independence of at least one of the voices.

The formal design shows a clear affinity with the chanson of the period. The rhyme between the second and third verses is reflected in a literal repetition of the music (mm. 6–10 = 10–14), and final closure is achieved in a manner typical of the secular French genre by a repetition of the final verse, both text and music (mm. 34–40 = 40–46). At first blush it would seem that the modest use of melisma with the word "foco" ("fire," m. 17) is pictorial in intent, but the recurrence of similar precadential flourishes for more neutral words suggests that its purpose is instead primarily formal. Examples are "veder" ("to see," mm. 27f.) and "anzi" ("nay even," mm. 38f., 44f.), and the latter word overlaps when sung with "morte" ("death") in tenor and bassus.

The final gesture, however, a postcadential extension repeating the words "anzi la morte," with the cantus melodically static and in longer values, is perhaps meant to be construed mimetically as evocative of death, the final image of the poem. In addition, the composer's choice of a Phrygian modal orientation (with the final on

A so often adopted for modes 3 and 4 in the sixteenth century) may have been prompted by the melancholy tone of the verse.

Other three-voice madrigals by Festa, like most of those for four and five voices, display somewhat greater variety in their stylistic profiles than *Altro non è'l mio amor.* They also mark a clearer tendency toward the kind of textual illustration that was to become increasingly characteristic of the genre. At the other end of the stylistic spectrum, however, is his setting of *Quando ritrovo la mia pastorella*—assuming that it is in fact by Festa[22]—which is considerably more strictly homophonic and declamatory than any of the other pieces in three parts attributed to him. Although a madrigal of the new stamp, the text treats in narrative dialogue the venerable and conventional theme of the pastoral, an encounter between a man, usually of the upper classes, with a more or less pliant shepherd maid. The frivolous tone of the verse is not far removed in this instance from that of the carnival song. If it was in fact intended for the kind of quasi-dramatic performance usually given such pieces, that might account for the composer's simplicity of means.

Festa's madrigals for four and five voices show, as a rule, considerably greater compositional sophistication than that seen in *Quando ritrovo*, more so even than is characteristic of their three-voice counterparts, whose facture appears to be more directly indebted to carnival songs than those requiring four or more voices. A greater number of lines makes possible a more varied contrapuntal fabric, as may be observed in Festa's setting for the anonymous madrigal *Cosi suav' è'l foco et dolce il nodo* (see Example 19-5).[23] The opening deploys contrasting and combining vocal duos in a manner quite typical of the composer (see also mm. 26–30); cantus and altus in free counterpoint are echoed by tenor and bassus in a kind of paired imitation before all four parts join in full sonorities to conclude the verse. In contrast to the two pieces discussed above, homophonic declamation is largely eschewed here, the only clear instance of it being the passage for four voices in measures 14–17. By contrast, genuine points of imitation in three or four parts are relatively numerous (as in mm. 7–9, 30–32), and the contrapuntal independence of the voices is quite pronounced.

About midway, stylistically, between these two extremes of compositional facture—strict homophony, on the one hand, and imitative counterpoint, on the other—is Festa's setting for four voices of another madrigal, *Dur'è'l partito dove m'astringete.*[24] The lightly animated homophony of the opening section, which is varied in texture as well by the alternation between duos and full sonorities, finally yields to a modest amount of imitative writing (mm. 21–26, 38–43). Its text may be a witty reply, in the female voice, to the plea, "give me a yes or a no," as framed by

22. For an edition of this piece by Seay, who questions the attribution, see Festa, *Opera omnia*, 8:46–47, no. 21; it is also found in Archibald T. Davison and Willi Apel, eds., *Historical Anthology of Music*, 2 vols. (Cambridge, Mass.: Harvard University Press, 1962), 1:140.

23. For a transcription of the entire work in modern score, see Festa, *Opera omnia*, ed. Seay, 8:14–15, no. 6; or Einstein, *Italian Madrigal*, 3:36–38, no. 21.

24. For a transcription in modern score, see Festa, *Opera omnia*, ed. Seay, 8:9–14, no. 4; also Einstein, *Italian Madrigal*, 3:33–35, no. 20.

EXAMPLE 19-5. Costanzo Festa, *Cosi suav'è'l foco et dolce il nodo* (mm. 1–26)

So gentle is the fire and sweet the knot with which Love inflames and ties me that I burn
and, captured, take delight. Nor would I ever seek to extinguish or to untie the fire or
the bond. To the contrary . . .

the poem *Madonna, non so dir tante parole*, attributed to Bonifazio Dragonetto and
set by Verdelot.[25]

More significant still, perhaps, in this composition is the unmistakable use of
musical mimesis. The conceit of proceeding slowly ("Andat'adagio") is given rhetorical emphasis by declaiming the key words homophonically and illustrated by a shift
to longer durational values, first in two parts and then in four. The contrasting
notion of haste ("correte'in fretta") is then conveyed by rapid movement and a running melisma, again heard both in two and in four voices. It is as if the composer
wished to underscore the difference in character between the two phrases by the par-
allelism of the structure. (Note, however, that he has ignored—naively, in the eyes of
later critics—the negation of the acceleration in movement thus illustrated.)

However modest Festa's attempts to express verbal meaning with musical means,
as in this instance, they demonstrate nonetheless that the formal, schematic relationship between text and music to be found in compositional settings of strophic conception—like that of the *frottola* or even the carnival song—has been replaced in the
madrigal by a much more direct and intimate union of word and tone, one that effectively precludes most strophic repetition. It is no surprise, consequently, to discover
that Festa set, as an independent work wedded closely to its text, the third strophe
of Petrarch's *Si e debile il filo*, beginning "Ogni loco m'attrista."[26]

With the 1530s came wider dissemination of the madrigal as a genre and its cultivation by a younger generation of composers. These are primarily northerners still,
however, and the majority were apparently in some sense in Verdelot's orbit. The
precise nature of the relationships among them is difficult to determine, primarily

25. For an edition of this piece, see Philippe Verdelot, *Madrigals for Four and Five Voices*, ed. Jessie Ann
Owens, 3 vols., Sixteenth-Century Madrigal, vol. 28–30 (New York: Garland, 1989), 29:40–43, 7; for a
discussion of the music, see Einstein, *Italian Madrigal*, 1:177.
26. See Festa, *Opera omnia*, ed. Seay, 7:7–9, no. 4.

because there is no documentary trace of Verdelot after the siege of Florence began in 1527. As evidence that he lived on into the 1530s, and perhaps the 1540s, we have only the printed collections that included his madrigals; at least six of them appeared between 1535 and 1540 with his name on the title page.

Whether he was himself alive or dead at the time, his works evidently achieved wide currency during that period. A number of the publications in question went through several editions—in one instance as many as eleven![27] Verdelot's madrigals traveled, significantly, with those of Festa and Adrian Willaert, both of whom are also cited on occasion by those same title pages, and by the end of the decade they were included in smaller quantities in collections published in Venice under the names of Jacques Arcadelt (ca. 1508–68) and Maistre Jhan (ca. 1485–ca. 1545).

There is some indirect evidence, but no proof, that both Verdelot and Arcadelt had connections with Venice and with each other by the 1530s. It is certain, nonetheless, that the young Arcadelt had been in Italy for a number of years before his madrigals began to be printed in 1538–39. He can be traced to Florence in 1534–35 and might have been there already in the late 1520s, but he probably left Tuscany (for Venice? for Rome?) as early as 1537. Some two years later he may have been associated briefly with the Cappella Giulia in St. Peter's Basilica before earning an appointment with the papal choir in December 1540.[28]

Before the end of 1539 four books of madrigals were published by Gardane and Scotto in a numbered series under his name (all for four voices). The first of these, *Il primo libro di madrigali*, proved to be one of the most durable collections of the century. It went through at least 45 editions, the last of which appeared as late as 1654. Arcadelt must have been prolific as well; the sources of the period have transmitted more than 200 madrigals under his name, all of them written, surely, before he left Italy in 1551 to return to France.

His contribution to the development of the genre must have come after its primary characteristics had already been formulated in the compositions of Verdelot and Festa. Still, it was considerable if one is to judge not only from the enduring popularity of some of his settings but also from the subtle evolution of his compositional skills within the genre. In addition, the madrigals of his *Libro primo* seem to have provided models for younger men trying their hand with lyric Italian verse, as well as basic repertory for performers, court-employed professionals and urban amateurs alike.

No single composition by Arcadelt appears to have seen wider dissemination over a longer period of time than his *Il bianco e dolce cigno* (see Example 19-6).[29] Its wide

27. See the observations made by Jessie Ann Owens in the introduction to Verdelot, *Madrigals for Four and Five Voices*, 1:xi–xii.

28. Concerning Arcadelt, see Albert Seay, *The New Grove Dictionary of Music*, 1:546–48; for greater detail, and a sharper focus on his contribution to the development of the madrigal, see James Haar, "Towards a Chronology of the Madrigals of Arcadelt," *Journal of Musicology* 5 (1987): 28–54.

29. For a transcription of the complete work in modern score, see Jacques Arcadelt, *Opera omnia*, ed. Albert Seay, 10 vols., Corpus mensurabilis musicae 31 ([Rome]: American Institute of Musicology, 1965–71), 2:38–40; the piece is also available in Sarah Fuller, ed., *The European Musical Heritage, 800–1750* (New York: Alfred A. Knopf, 1987), 263.

EXAMPLE 19-6. Jacques Arcadelt, *Il dolce e bianco cigno* (mm. 1–15, 30–39)

The white and gentle swan dies singing, and I, weeping, reach the end of my life.
 [Strange and diverse fate, that he dies disconsolate and I die in bliss a death that,
 dying, fills me entirely with joy and desire.] If in dying I feel no other pain, I should
 be happy to die a thousand times over each day.

appeal must surely have stemmed as much from his characteristically sensitive
approach to the text as from the cryptically erotic verse itself.[30] The severely homophonic declamation of the initial lines throws into sharp relief Arcadelt's generation of
both rhythms and melodic inflections from the natural pronunciation of the words.
His attention to syntax can be seen in his treatment of the initial tercet of the poem.
The division of the three verses into two clauses with enjambment is mirrored in the
music, which is similarly divided with cadential articulation (after "more"). Musical
articulation thus separates the two members of the grammatical construct instead of
the rhyming lines of the poetic structure, as was so often the case. In addition, the
restrained use of musical figures as mimetic gestures to be found in most of his madrigals is achieved late in the piece by means of the first point of imitation (mm. 34ff.);
the repeated entries that follow in voice after voice were clearly meant to suggest the
thousand deaths (in an erotic sense) that the poet declares himself ready to suffer.[31]

VENICE AS A CENTER OF MADRIGAL PRODUCTION

If the part played by Verdelot and Arcadelt—if any—in making Venice an important
center for the cultivation of the Italian madrigal is still largely conjectural, that of

---

30. For an attempt to explain the lasting charm of this madrigal, as well as de Rore's equally ubiquitous
Anchor che col partire, see James Haar, "Popularity in the Sixteenth-Century Madrigal: A Study of Two
Instances," in *Studies in Musical Sources and Style*, ed. Eugene K. Wolf and Edward H. Roesner (Madison:
A-R Editions, 1990), 191–212.
31. Concerning the erotic imagery of this poem (and many similar ones set by the madrigal composers
of the period), see Laura Macy, "Speaking of Sex: Metaphor and Performance in the Italian Madrigal,"
Journal of Musicology 14 (1996): 1–34.

Adrian Willaert can be much better documented. From his appointment in 1527 as chapelmaster at the municipal basilica of San Marco until his death in 1562, he was in quasi-continuous residence in the city, quickly becoming its most illustrious musical figure (see Figure 19-3).[32] That he was in touch with Verdelot during the crucial period in the development of the genre, or at least took the older master's madrigals as a model for his earliest compositions on Italian texts, is suggested by two significant circumstances. On the one hand, Willaert's madrigals first began to circulate in the collections printed under Verdelot's name in the 1530s and 1540s. On the other, Willaert arranged for voice and lute a selection of Verdelot madrigals that was published in 1536.

FIGURE 19-3. Portrait of Adrian Willaert, woodcut published by Antoine Gardane in *Musica nova* (Venice, 1559).

To be noted in passing is what is implied by the preparation of such a collection. It clearly suggests that, despite the wholly vocal conception that underlay madrigal composition at the time, its performance as solo song must have been rather common. Such must have been the case, moreover, virtually from the moment of its inception as a musical genre, and perhaps especially in those areas where the frottolistic traditions had become well established.

The significance of Willaert's unique contribution to the stylistic development of the madrigal is perhaps best seen from the repertory published in 1559 under the attractive but puzzling title of *Musica nova*—puzzling because there is every reason to believe that the repertory it contained had been in existence for a rather long time

---

32. Concerning Willaert, see Lewis Lockwood, *The New Grove Dictionary of Music*, 20:422; for a more detailed assessment of Willaert as a composer of madrigals, see Feldman, *City Culture and the Madrigal at Venice*, 197–259 and *passim*.

before it was published. Interestingly, like the "Newberry Partbooks" apparently compiled by Verdelot for the Florentine Republic, this collection also brings together madrigals and motets in more or less equal numbers; included were twenty-seven motets for four, five, six, and seven voices and twenty-five madrigals in the same combinations.[33] This physical juxtaposition of works of both genres may be seen, in the *Musica nova* as in the earlier manuscript, as a way of emphasizing a new seriousness in the approach being taken to the composition of secular Italian texts.

An even clearer indication of Willaert's earnestness of purpose in this repertory is the mounting evidence that he drew melodic material for a fair number of these compositions, both motets and madrigals, from the opening phrases of well-known sacred melodies, many of them liturgical. These citations, although unidentified and without their original text in the sources, are always placed in a voice prominent in the counterpoint (cantus or tenor) and usually encompass a complete incise of the borrowed melody. They usually appear, moreover, in juxtaposition with an important segment of the text being set.

For the listener who recognized—or was made aware of—the quoted material imbedded in the counterpoint, the words to which allusion was thus made must have served as a kind of trope, illuminating or interpreting in a particular sense the words actually being sung. In a significant number of instances the borrowings evoke Savonarolan themes or associations, and it has been suggested that they are meant to refer in covert terms to the republican sentiments of exiled Florentines living in Venice: their nostalgia for their homeland, the frustrations borne of their unsuccessful attempts to unseat the Medici rulers, and their hopes for an eventual return.[34]

In musical terms the stylistic affinity between motet and madrigal is considerably more marked than it had been in the works of the previous generation. For example, the madrigals of this collection are generally divided into two *partes*, each of them a self-contained musical entity, as was by then common for settings of Latin motets. Similarly, particularly significant phrases of text are often repeated for rhetorical emphasis—a compositional procedure commonly seen in the motet but rarely in the earlier madrigals. In addition, the homophonic declamation so characteristic of Italian secular music in the 1520s and 1530s has largely given way here to a denser, darker texture in which the independence of the individual voices predominates, whether in points of imitation or freer contrapuntal writing. The result was described by a contemporary as a "carefully wrought invention . . . so coherent, so sweet, so

---

33. The entire collection has been published in Adriano Willaert, *Opera omnia*, ed. Hermann Zenck, Walter Gerstenberg, et al., 14 vols., Corpus mensurabilis musicae 3 ([Rome]: American Institute of Musicology, 1950–77), vol. 5 (motets) and vol. 13 (madrigals).

34. See Michèle Fromson, "Themes of Exile in Willaert's *Musica nova*," *Journal of the American Musicological Society* 47 (1994): 442–87, who asserts that "these melodic citations and the texts to which they allude constituted a powerful symbolic network that served to commemorate their native city, its fallen Republic, and the most prominent spokesman for that government, the [martyred] religious reformer, Girolamo Savonarola" (487).

correct, so admirably well suited to the words," that it surpassed everything he had previously experienced.[35]

It is increasingly clear that the motets and madrigals of the *Musica nova* were written over a period of years, most of them probably between the late 1530s and the mid-1540s, for one of the composer's most admiring patrons, the Florentine exile Nero Capponi. Antonfrancesco Doni (1513–74), musical amateur and author (who was also Florentine by birth), recounts hearing some of them at a private concert in Capponi's house. He commented in particular on the musical skills of one of the performers, Polisena Pecorina, who both played and sang on that occasion and whose reputation as an interpreter of Willaert's music was clearly unparalleled in Venice at the time. It was in fact she who eventually came into possession of this collection of pieces, which was popularly known by her name, "la Pecorina." It remained an essentially private repertory, then, until she sold it to Alfonso d'Este (1533–97), the last duke of Ferrara, who made arrangements to have the music published by the Venetian press of Antonio Gardane in 1559.[36]

The madrigals of the collection constitute an even more unified repertory than the Latin-texted works, however; all but one—Panfilo Sasso's dialogue *Quando nacesti, Amor*, set earlier by Verdelot and included in the "Newberry Partbooks"— are based on sonnets by Petrarch. Such uniformity suggests a preconceived design— one that is not without its Tuscan implications—realized methodically over a period of time. The end product is an extensive and stylistically consistent cycle of textually related works. It is all the more exceptional in this sense since the remainder of Willaert's production as a composer of madrigals is much more varied. In other cases the texts Willaert set are much less uniformly elevated as to themes and diction and his approach to them often more tuneful and easily accessible.[37] Nonetheless, they reflect evolving esthetic attitudes toward polyphonic composition for Italian verse. At the time they also provided a stylistic model whose lessons were not lost on the composers of the next generation, not only Willaert's students such as Girolamo Parabosco, Perissone Cambio, and Baldassare Donato but also—and more importantly—no less a master than Cipriano de Rore.[38]

Willaert's earnest and sensitive treatment of this exceptional body of serious poetry

35. Antonfrancesco Doni recorded these observations concerning Willaert's music in his *Dialago della musica* of 1544: "di quella sua diligente invenzione . . . sì unita, sì dolce, sì giusta, sì mirabilmente acconcie le parole" (as quoted by Feldman, *City Culture and the Madrigal in Venice*, 32–33 and n. 38, with a somewhat different English translation).

36. To sort out the tangled tale regarding the origins of the repertory of the *Musica nova* and its long-delayed publication has required the labors of a considerable number of scholars working over the years; for a summary of their findings, with most of the pertinent references, see Feldman, *City Culture and the Madrigal in Venice*, 31–37 and *passim*.

37. Concerning the contrasts between Willaert's madrigals generally and the exceptional repertory of the *Musica nova*, see Feldman, *City Culture and the Madrigal in Venice*, 197–259.

38. Willaert's impact on the madrigal composition of his students has been explored by Feldman, *City Culture and the Madrigal at Venice*, 311–406, as has the stylistic affinities and possible connections between Willaert and de Rore, 260–310.

may be seen in his setting of *Giunto m'ha Amor—Nulla posso levar* (see Example 19-7). He has divided the sonnet (as he does throughout the *Musica nova*) into its two structural components, setting the two quatrains as the *prima parte* and the two tercets as the *seconda*. The first cadential articulation falls not at the end of a verse, however, but at the caesura in the second line with the words "a torto" ("wrongfully"), and the next cadence comes only at the end of the quatrain. Because the initial phrase of music arises from a point of imitation, the voices do not conclude together with either text or melody. Rather, their successive cadences in pairs, together with the repetition of key elements of the poem, prolong both the musical closure and the overlap between verses (mm. 12–17). The end of the quatrain brings the only obvious musical depiction of a verbal conceit; with the last word of the line—"taccia" ("be silent")—all five voices do indeed become mute for the space of a semibreve before beginning to declaim the following verse (mm. 39–40).

EXAMPLE 19-7. Adrian Willaert, *Giunto m'ha Amor/Nulla posso levar* (mm. 1–23)

Love has reached me in beautiful and cruel arms that slay me wrongfully, and if I complain, the pain redoubles. Therefore, however, as I am wont to do, it is best that I die
loving and be silent . . .

Although the *seconda parte* begins more homophonically than any other section
of the piece, the two tercets are treated in much the same vein as the quatrains.
Cadential articulation follows syntax and meaning rather than the rhyming lines of
the poetry, and the more important conceits of the text are given prominence by repetition. Striking, in fact, in comparison with many earlier pieces in the genre, is
Willaert's studied avoidance of musical structures that follow routinely the regular
rhyme scheme and hendecasyllabic verses of the sonnet. Rather, the poem is taken as
a series of syntactic units, each of which is declaimed with the individual melodic
inflections and rhythmic patterns that the composer has deemed appropriate to the
text, its natural pronunciation and, perhaps even more importantly, its meaning.

More fascinating still, however, is Willaert's citation in the closing period of the
piece of the opening incise of a Credo that was printed by Giunta in Florence in 1535

and that circulated widely on the Italian peninsula during the sixteenth century. The borrowed melody is presented with very little elaboration in the tenor (mm. 119–23), where its implied text, "Credo in unum Deum, Patrem omnipotentem," is apposed implicitly with that actually being sung, "le mie speranze" ("my hopes"). The reference here to Savonarolan republicanism—if one is intended—is clearly not overt, but because the reform-minded monk conceived of the republican experiment in the Florence of the 1490s as centered in its faith in God, such an interpretation is certainly plausible.[39]

It is difficult to determine whether Venice became such an important center for the cultivation of the madrigal because of the actual presence there of some of the composers most directly responsible for its early development or as a result of the printers who made it a primary point of dissemination for the genre. For although Willaert can be securely placed in the city, Venetian connections remain speculative for both Verdelot and Arcadelt, as we have seen. By contrast, there can be no doubt as to the major role played by the publishing houses established there toward mid-century and specializing in mensural polyphony.

Antoine Gardane (d. 1569) came to Venice from southern France and began printing music in his adoptive city as early as 1538. From his presses came Arcadelt's popular *Libro primo* (1538) as well as Willaert's *Musica nova* (1559) and, in the course of his career, literally dozens of other collections of madrigals featuring the leading masters of the day.[40] Girolamo Scotto (d. 1572), the scion of a Venetian dynasty of booksellers and printers, began publishing music just a year after Gardane, and he too produced a continuous stream of madrigal prints.[41] The two houses frequently borrowed material from one another as well, with one press at times reprinting entire collections just recently brought out by the other in a manner suggesting rather intense competition (although it was conceivably in accordance with some sort of quasi-contractual agreement). Collectively they had no serious rival in all of Italy in the 1540s and 1550s.

Perhaps it was the printers as well, even more than the composers, who were largely responsible for a new notational style used with increasing frequency in the 1540s and known as *a note nere* or *cromatico*. It was so called because of the many notes of smaller value (those with "colored" or "blackened" heads) that characterized its appearance. To generate this "coloring" of the notational picture, it was necessary only to revert to the basic binary mensuration in undiminished form, specified by the sign C, rather than to use the more common diminished variety marked ₵. The practical effect of this simple change of sign was to shift the tactus from the

39. The citation of the Credo is one of the many uncovered by Fromson, "Themes of Exile in Willaert's *Musica nova*"; see especially 446–74.
40. Concerning Gardane, see Thomas W. Bridges, *The New Grove Dictionary of Music*, 7:158–59; for a detailed study and a catalogue of Gardane's production, see Mary Lewis, *Antonio Gardane, Venetian Music Printer, 1538–1569: A Descriptive Bibliographical and Historical Study*, Garland Reference Library of the Humanities, vol. 718 (New York: Garland, 1988).
41. Regarding Scotto, see Bridges, *The New Grove Dictionary of Music*, 17:86.

149

FIGURE 19-4. Portrait of Cipriano de Rore by Hans Müelich (Munich, Bayerische Staatsbibliothek, MS Mus B S., f. 304).

breve to the semibreve and hence to suggest an approximate doubling of the duration of every note written. As a consequence, the same rapidity of movement under the two mensurations demanded notes of about half the value—thus generating roughly twice as many with "colored" heads in the newly fashionable "black note" manner as in conventional usage.[42]

It may also have been in Venice, and under the aegis of Willaert, that Cipriano de Rore (ca. 1515–65), one of the most important composers of madrigals of the next generation, acquired his initial training and experience with the genre (see Figure 19-4). As in the case of Verdelot and Arcadelt, there is as yet no documentary proof that de Rore lived and worked in Venice in the 1540s. However, his first three books of madrigals, all for five voices, were published there between 1542 and 1548–49. The last of these, quickly reprinted under the suggestive title *Musica . . . sopra le stanze del Petrarca*, opens with a cycle of settings that de Rore composed for Petrarch's *canzone* in honor of the Virgin Mary, *Vergine bella* (*canzone* 366), consisting of ten stanzas of thirteen lines each and a closing *commiato* of seven set as eleven self-contained pieces.[43] Although published a decade before Willaert's *Musica nova*—the publication of which, as we have seen, was apparently long delayed—they point to Willaert's influence, as does the sophisticated contrapuntal style of de Rore's earliest madrigals generally.[44]

---

42. It is important to observe in this connection that this particular adoption of a novel notational style has all the earmarks of a clever commercial ploy; it had no direct effect on the musical style, and not a few madrigals of the period were actually circulated in both notational patterns. See James Haar, "The *Note Nere* Madrigal," *Journal of the American Musicological Society* 18 (1965): 22–41.

43. For a discussion of this cycle in the context of de Rore's development as a composer of madrigals, see Feldman, *City Culture and the Madrigal at Venice*, 407–26.

44. Concerning de Rore, see Alvin Johnson, *The New Grove Dictionary of Music*, 16:185–90; for reflections on the stylistic affinities (and differences) with Willaert, see Feldman, *City Culture and the Madrigal at Venice*, 260–310.

FERRARA AS A CENTER OF
STYLISTIC INNOVATION

By 1547 de Rore was serving Ercole II at the Este court of Ferrara, which was by then already becoming an increasingly important center for the cultivation of the new secular genre. The ruling family there, like the Gonzaga family in nearby Mantua with whom the Este were closely related by marriage, had maintained a lively interest in music from early in the fifteenth century (see pp. 405–6). Inasmuch as the cultural corridor between Ferrara and Mantua had provided crucial patronage and support for the flourishing repertory of *frottole* around the turn of the century, it is not surprising that these two courts encouraged in a similar manner the cultivation of the madrigal. The master of the ducal chapel in Ferrara in the 1520s, Maistre Jhan, had tried his hand at the setting of Italian texts in the new manner even before the "Newberry Partbooks" were completed in 1527–28, as is clear from the inclusion of his *Deh, quant'è dolc'amor* in that collection.

Following the death in 1505 of Ercole I, whose primary concern was the sacred music of his chapel, his successors to the ducal throne—Alfonso I (ruled 1505–34), Ercole II (1534–59), and in particular Alfonso II (1559–97) gave greater priority to secular music. With the appointment of Cipriano de Rore as master of the Ferrarese chapel in 1547, Ercole II had in his service one of the most gifted composers of the age, and one whose contribution to the development of the madrigal would prove to be central.

After his arrival at the Este court de Rore apparently turned his compositional energies both to contemporary texts and to a four-voice format; three collections of madrigals à 4 were to follow in 1550, 1557, and, posthumously, in 1565. His reasons for opting for fewer parts are not clear—they may have stemmed simply from the preferences of his new patron or the capacities of the singers then present at the court—but he did turn at the same time to a less rigorously contrapuntal texture and a clearer declamation of the text. More significantly still, he strove ever more consistently in his later works to give musical expression to the meaning of the words, thus carrying the compositional style associated with the madrigal decisively toward the affective rhetoric and pictorial mimesis that came to typify the genre.

Representative of these trends is de Rore's setting of a sonnet by Giovanni della Casa (1503–56), *O Sonno*, published in 1557 (see Example 19-8).[45] In accordance with Willaert's model, de Rore divided the quatrains and the tercets into two separate *partes*, but his texture in this work is much more homophonic and declamatory than anything to be seen in the madrigals attributed to the older master. Only occasionally is there a hint of more contrapuntal writing or a point of imitation (as in mm. 12, 39ff., 53, 69ff.).

---

45. For a transcription of the complete work in modern score, see Cipriano de Rore, *Opera omnia*, ed. Bernhard Meier, 8 vols., Corpus mensurabilis musicae 14 ([Rome]: American Institute of Musicology, 1959–77), 4:66–69.

EXAMPLE 19-8. Cipriano de Rore, *O sonno/Ov'è'l silentio* (mm. 1–20, 53–60)

O sleep, O placid son of the quiet, humid, shadowy night; O comfort of mortal ills,
  sweet forgetting of such grave evils, [which make life bitter and tedious. . . .] Where is
  the silence that flees from the day and the light . . .

The evocation of personified Sleep, with which the poem begins, is slowly and
calmly declaimed to falling melodic figures in all four voices, undoubtedly to suggest
the nature of the subject whose restorative benefits are extolled in the verses that follow. Silence marks the caesura that separates that initial salutation from the rest of
the line. Subsequently, the verses—which are consistently linked to one another by
enjambment except at the ends of quatrains and tercets—are divided for easier comprehension into their syntactic components by rests and, occasionally, cadences. As a
further reflection of the somnolence of which it speaks, the four voices present the
text throughout with great restraint both melodic and rhythmic.

Additional gestures of mimetic intent are scattered through virtually every phrase
of the music. Some of the most striking of these, because of their novelty, are
achieved by harmonic means. In the opening phrase, for example, c♯, g♯, and b-mi
maintain consistently a major (rather than a naturally minor) tenth between the bassus and cantus or altus, thus creating a series of unexpected sonorities. These were
apparently intended to envelop the clause describing Sleep as "the placid son of the
quiet . . . night" in a kind of peacefully atmospheric harmony. The word "dolce" (as

part of "sweet forgetting") is illustrated by a semitone inflection from e to eb in the tenor, generating in turn a semitone descent from b-mi to b-fa in the cantus (for "mali").

Such melodic progressions are truly extraordinary for the period. They have neither basis nor justification in either the linear motion or the contrapuntal facture of the piece. Consequently, they can be explained only as expressive gestures, making the composer's intent absolutely unmistakable. Equally clear is the image of rising motion conveyed by the raised b-mi for "solleva" ("raise up," m. 38) and the c♯ for "A me t'envola" ("fly to me," m. 40ff.)—which is also given rhetorical emphasis by a literal repetition. The notion of "light dreams" apparently suggested the use of b-mi, f♯, g♯, and even d♯, which was very rarely seen in the counterpoint of the period under any circumstances (mm. 60–63). Again at the beginning of the *seconda parte*, where Sleep is described as the "silence that flees from day and light" (mm. 53ff.), the expected sonorities are transformed by accidentals, b-mi, f♯, and, again, d♯.

The latter passage is also marked, quite literally, by a pictorial gesture, notational in nature this time, whose meaning is discernible only to the eye. A gentle sesquialteral proportion introduced into the mensuration with the query "Where is the silence?" (mm. 53–57) is indicated by means of blackening, thus suggesting the darkness sought by the silence "that flees from day and light" (mm. 57–60). Such means, referred to by the scholars who first described it as "eye music,"[46] may appear a bit naive from our present vantage point, but they offer insight nonetheless into the social uses of secular music in sixteenth-century Italy. As the madrigal was intended for performance "in chamber" by accomplished amateurs as well as by professionals, it was not unreasonable to present the musicians with a subtle reference to the meaning of the text through the notational patterns that lay under their eyes as well as by musical gestures intended for those listening.

In addition to the expressive effects largely dependent on accidental inflection and the resultant harmonies are melodic gestures such as the rapid melismatic flourish for the word "fugge" (mm. 58–59), the general musical stasis at the end of the *prima parte* for the conceit "spread and settle thy brown wings over me" (mm. 46–52), and the use of dissonant suspensions (involving ninths and elevenths) for words and ideas such as "aspra" ("bitter"), "noiosa" ("tedious," mm. 22–23), "piume d'asprezza" ("feathers of bitterness") and "notti acerbe" ("harsh nights," mm. 81–83 and 87–88). In fact, de Rore's composition contains a veritable catalogue of the types of musical devices by which verbal conceits could be suggested—the so-called madrigalisms—and illustrates nicely the mental process by which they were generated. Any word or expression for which one could devise a recognizable parallel in music—for example, those making reference to number, direction, space, velocity, stasis, harmony, dissonance, even silence—or that could be imitated or suggested by a sonorous equivalent such as singing, laughing, sighing, and the like, generated ever more frequently a mimetic ("madrigalistic") musical response.

---

46. See, for example, Einstein, *Italian Madrigal*, 1:234–45.

De Rore was also sensitive to the affective atmosphere conveyed by a poetic text overall (as was to be increasingly the case with composers of the second half of the century). It is more difficult, however, to identify in specific terms the musical means adopted by the masters of the period in their attempt to give expression to that aspect of the verse being set. This is perhaps in part because madrigalistic gestures tend to call the listener's attention—and apparently the composer's as well—to individual words and phrases rather than to the text as an integrated whole. Nevertheless, the rate and velocity of the rhythmic activity, together with the range and energy of the melodic movement, usually reflect by and large the underlying mood of the poem. In addition, the choice of modal orientation and specific harmonic combinations were undoubtedly determined in many instances by the composer's sense of what was appropriate generally for his verbal material.[47]

All of these elements—rhythmic, melodic, and modal—come together in de Rore's *O Sonno* to illuminate the psychological and emotional background of the text with their own expressive means. The manner in which rhythm and melody contribute to that end will be apparent to a degree from the foregoing discussion, but equally significant is his choice of modal orientation. The generally Phrygian framework established by a series of cadential formulae descending by semitone to the pitch of resolution (mm. 20, 28, 30, 34, 42, 46, 86, and 91) provides a context of melodic and harmonic expectations without which the unusual progressions and sonorities produced by the specified accidental inflections mentioned earlier could hardly have had their full effect.

The extreme use of accidental inflection and the departures from melodic and harmonic norms generated thereby appears to have been a contribution to musical expression in madrigal composition that was due primarily to musicians associated in some way with the ducal court of Ferrara. Following in de Rore's footsteps was his gifted student, Luzzasco Luzzaschi (ca. 1545–1607), whose mastery of a highly inflected chromatic style is evident from a small group of pieces that stand stylistically apart from the rest of his *oeuvre*. They take their significance, therefore, from the greater body of his works in the genre, which generally make use of much more conventional musical means. Particularly striking in this respect is his setting of two tercets drawn from Dante's description of the sighs, cries, groans, and laments of those cast into the darkness of infernal regions, beginning "Quivi sospiri" (see Example 19-9).[48]

In this composition the final, the range, and the pitches of cadential resolution all point clearly to mode 1 on D, but the presence of a signed b-fa in all five parts is a

---

47. See Leeman L. Perkins, "Toward a Theory of Text–Music Relations in the Music of the Renaissance," to be published by Oxford University Press in the Proceedings of the First International Conference on Binchois, The Graduate School and University Center of the City University of New York, October 31–November 1, 1995.

48. The text is from *L'Inferno*, canto 3, 22–27; the work in question, which was published with Luzzaschi's *Secondo libro* of 1576–77, has been edited by Alfred Einstein, ed., *The Golden Age of the Madrigal* (New York: G. Schirmer, 1942), 53–58.

EXAMPLE 19-9. Luzzasco Luzzaschi, *Quivi sospiri* (mm. 1–17)

There sighs, weeping, and loud groans resounded through the starless atmosphere . . .

departure from earlier conventions—an initial though modest hint of the extraordinary melodic inflections to follow. The first of these comes with the opening point of imitation where the word "sospiri" is set off by rests meant to suggest the audible effect of a sigh (by then already a cliché of madrigalistic composition) and made more expressive by semitone motion to e♭ in tenor I (m. 2). "Pianti" ("weeping") evokes in quick succession e♭ (m. 5), f♯, and b-mi (mm. 6–8), a wrenching shift from the (implied) soft hexachord transposed to B-fa to the hard on G with a semitone below, and the upward melodic movement (including the leap of a fourth) serves to illustrate at the same time "alti guai" ("loud cries"). A c♯ produces a major third (m. 10) for the declamation of "risonavan" ("resounding") and is followed again by an abrupt shift to the (presumably darker) flat side with e♭, a♭, and even d♭ to imply downward transpositions of the soft hexachord, thus suggesting the idea of starless heavens (mm. 11–12).

A rising progression through a fourth by semitone (in basso, alto, and canto) serves to illustrate musically (mm. 18–25) the phrase "al cominciar ne lagrimai" ("as [these sounds] began, I wept [to hear them]"). The musical material for "diverse lingue" ("diverse tongues") is presented as a symbolically significant point of imitation (mm. 26–30) and "orribili favelle" ("horrible pronouncements") as voices in an appropriately shrill range (mm. 31–32). Rising semitone inflections return (mm. 36–44) for "parole di dolore" ("words of sorrow") and are countered with harsh-sounding, old-fashioned *fauxbourdon* for "accenti d'ira" ("angry inflections"). Similarly, shrill voices ("voci alti") in full, five-part declamation are answered (mm. 49–52) by hollow ones ("fioche"), three parts in relatively low range again moving by semitone. Regular homophonic scansion of the voices brings the sound of clapping hands into the final cadence, finally, once again with close juxtaposition of e and e♭ (m. 57).

Without doubt, the extreme chromatic inflections that were to characterize the madrigals of the celebrated prince of Venosa, Carlo Gesualdo (ca. 1561–1613), are fully anticipated in a work such as this, and Gesualdo's repeated visits to Ferrara in 1594–95, in connection with his second marriage to Leonora d'Este, gave him ample opportunity to become acquainted with Luzzaschi and his music.[49]

At least as significant for the development of the madrigal in the second half of the sixteenth century as de Rore's and Luzzaschi's experiments with uncommon accidental inflections was the cultivation in Ferrara under Alfonso II of a new, brilliantly virtuosic style of singing. The primary impetus for a renewal of interest in secular music and an increased level of patronage for it at the Este court was apparently the marriage in 1580 of the forty-five-year-old duke to his third wife, Margherita Gonzaga, the fifteen-year-old daughter of the duke of Mantua.[50]

To keep his young bride entertained, while satisfying his own taste for music,

49. Concerning Gesualdo, see Lorenzo Bianconi, *The New Grove Dictionary of Music,* 7:313–24.
50. See the instructive study by Anthony Newcomb, *The Madrigal at Ferrara, 1579–1597,* 2 vols. (Princeton: Princeton University Press, 1980), 1:7–19 and *passim.*

Alfonso gave new luster to his musical establishment, attracting to Ferrara some of the most skilled performers and composers then available on the Italian peninsula. Among the brightest stars in this constellation of exceptional musicians were three singers—Laura Peverara, Anna Guarini, and Livia d'Arco (joined briefly by a fourth, Tarquinia Molza)—whose social status at court was defined by their appointment as ladies in waiting to the young duchess. Unlike female vocalists heard earlier at court, however, who could be described as "courtiers who happened to sing," these became courtiers "because of their musical ability."[51]

The polished skills of these musicians quickly attracted the attention of the music-loving elite not only in neighboring regions but also at those courts all over Europe with which the Este had dealings, and the ladies of Ferrara became widely famous as the *concerto delle donne* ("the ladies' consort").[52] As a consequence, in addition to the composers who were in the duke's service, such as Luzzaschi himself, a number of others set madrigals specifically for them, whether as a tribute to the beauty and flexibility of their voices or as a means of ingratiating themselves with their noble patron. Included among those who did so were some of the most prominent masters of the age. Giaches de Wert (1535–96), who entered the employ of the Gonzaga family of nearby Mantua around 1558, dedicated his *Ottavo libro de madrigali a cinque voci* of 1586 to the duke and duchess of Ferrara in these flattering terms:

> In what part of the world could these be better sung than in Your Highnesses' court, where it is impossible to say which is the greater, the mastery of those who sing or the judgment of those who listen? . . . Who does not know today of the marvels of art and of nature, the voice, grace, disposition, memory, and other similar and rare qualities of the most noble young ladies of Her Serene Highness, the Duchess of Ferrara? Such considerations alone are sufficient to induce every composer in the world to dedicate his work to Your Highnesses so that it might receive the true and natural spirit of music from such divine voices and such a noble consort.[53]

Even making allowance for the hyperbole customary in such dedications, the extraordinary reputation enjoyed by the musical establishment at the ducal court of Ferrara among composers of the period is patently clear.

A number of them, most notably Giaches de Wert and Luca Marenzio, were represented in two elegant anthologies published in Ferrara by the ducal printer Baldini. Compiled by Torquato Tasso, the celebrated poet of the Ferrarese court, and his colleagues of the Accademia dei Rinnovati, both collections, as their titles reveal, were intended to honor Laura Peverara, for whom Tasso had conceived a passionate admi-

51. See Newcomb, *Madrigal at Ferrara*, 1:7.
52. For a discussion of this famous ensemble from a feminist point of view, see Karin Pendle, "Women in Music, ca. 1450–1600," in *Women and Music: A History*, ed. Karin Pendle (Bloomington: Indiana University Press, 1991), 31–53.
53. The translation is from Carol MacClintock's foreword to Wert's *Ottavo libro* in Giaches de Wert, *Opera omnia*, ed. Carol MacClintock and Melvin Bernstein, 17 vols., Corpus mensurabilis musicae 24 ([Rome]: American Institute of Musicology, 1961–77), vol. 8.

ration. The first, designated *Il lauro secco* (the "dry laurel," an obvious play on the singer's name), was published in 1582, while the second, *Il lauro verde* (the "green laurel"), appeared in 1583 in connection with her marriage to Count Annibale Turco.[54]

Of the composers whose response to the singing ladies of Ferrara led to a change in the vocal style of the madrigal, one of the most important, besides Luzzaschi, was in fact Giaches de Wert, whose long association with the Gonzaga family has already been noted.[55] By 1565 he had become chapelmaster of the ducal chapel of Santa Barbara in Mantua—the principal figure, therefore, in the Gonzagan musical establishment. As a result of the ties between the ruling houses in Mantua and Ferrara, he was in relatively close touch as well with the musicians in the employ of the Este.

The contacts were especially frequent during the 1580s, as Alfonso II began to expand the music personnel of his court and to make capital of the reputation of the performances that could be heard there. It was in that connection, presumably, that Wert made repeated visits to Ferrara, where he must have collaborated with the musicians of the ducal court.[56] The impact of the virtuosic singing of the *concerto delle donne* can be traced in his musical works as early as his seventh book of madrigals, published in 1581. It is particularly evident in his eighth book of 1586, as might be expected from the dedication to the ducal couple quoted above.

Characteristic of the change is an increased use of extended melismatic flourishes and rapid passagework, not only ornamentally but also as basic thematic material in the compositional process. This led to a description of the new style as "luxuriant,"[57] and the reasons for adopting such a term are amply illustrated by Wert's *Vezzosi augelli*, a madrigal based on a text drawn from Torquato Tasso's *La Gerusalemme liberata* (16, 12) and included in the *Ottava libro* of 1586 (see Example 19-10).[58] Here the vocal sonorities called for are unusual for the period generally but entirely typical of works created with the voices of the ladies of Ferrara in mind. Of the five parts that had become the norm, three are in ranges natural to women's voices. This second soprano—or, as here, a third—was in clear contrast to the earlier practice of writing a fifth part as a second tenor.

There was also a tendency in this newly "luxuriant" style, especially later in the decade, to deploy the high parts in soloistic passages above one or more of the less animated lower voices. Such is the procedure, for example, in the opening phrase of

54. See Newcomb, *Madrigal at Ferrara*, 1:69, 84. Newcomb has also identified a third anthology in honor of Laura, this one in manuscript—MS 220 at the Accademia Filarmonica of Verona—the compilation of which he places in Mantua prior to the singer's departure for Ferrara; cf. ibid., 1:188–89.

55. Concerning Wert, see Carol MacClintock, *The New Grove Dictionary of Music*, 20:351.

56. See Newcomb, *Madrigal at Ferrara*, 1:23–24. Wert's association with the musicians of the Ferrarese court must have been relatively frequent and prolonged if one can judge from his ill-fated affair with the singer Tarquinia Molza. An intimate relationship apparently began in 1583 or 1584 and lasted until 1589, when Molza was banished to Modena and forbidden all further contact with Wert; cf. Einstein, *Italian Madrigal*, 2:513.

57. See Newcomb, *Madrigal at Ferrara*, 1:76–77.

58. For a transcription of the complete madrigal in modern score, see Wert, *Opera omnia*, ed. MacClintock and Bernstein, 8:11–14.

EXAMPLE 19-10. Giaches de Wert, *Vezzosi augelli* (mm. 1–17)

Graceful birds among the green branches tune, in trial, little lascivious notes. The
breeze murmurs and makes the leaves and the waves complain, as variously she strikes
them . . .

this composition. As the three women's voices represent the "graceful birds among the green branches," they are sustained by tenor and bassus with a light rhythmic pattern on a single pitch for the words "Mormora l'aura," suggesting onomatopoetically the murmuring of the breeze.

The vivid imagery of the stanza, capable of making such natural sounds as these to vibrate like music in the imagination, proved particularly attractive to composers of the period, several of whom attempted a setting of it. They were undoubtedly drawn by the challenge of evoking with appropriate musical gestures the sonorous realities to which the verses refer, in particular the singing of birds and the sound of the wind stirring branches and waves.

Wert suggests the murmuring breeze with a word-generated rhythmic pattern, sung always, as mentioned, to a single pitch, and singing birds with relatively rapid declamation contained within a narrow ambitus and ornamented with melismatic figures of an increasingly virtuosic character. The first of these, as nature's songsters tune their voices, are of modest dimension (in mm. 3–4, 7–8), but as the birds are pictured alternating song with silence, the voices break into luxuriant melismatic movement of considerable duration (in mm. 21, 23, 25). The same kind of writing returns at the end of the piece to illustrate the idea of "sweet music" (mm. 35–38, repeated and extended into the final cadence, mm. 40–43). It was rapid passagework such as this, which requires the carefully trained, flexible voices of exceptional singers like those in the employ of the Ferrarese court, that came to distinguish the music making of the *concerto delle donne.*

Also inspired by the sounds invoked in the course of the stanza—and demanding, often, no less vocal skill—are such musical conceits as the isolated two-note figures for "garrir" (mm. 11–13), the quick dotted rhythms used to suggest the wind variably striking leaves and waves (mm. 13–16), and the loud response of the wind ("alto risponde," mm. 18–22). In the last instance there is, as well, a marked contrast in volume as a single voice, the cantus in a low register, represents the birds falling silent (mm. 17–18), while the rising wind is introduced as a rapidly building and extended point of imitation (mm. 18–22). Even the notion of alternating verses is captured musically in a dialogue of paired voices, quintus and altus, cantus and tenor, and cantus and bassus (mm. 32–35).

The virtuosic nature of the vocal writing in *Vezzosi augelli* is clear from the *note nere* notation in which it was published. However, it is important to note in connection with madrigals that can be linked in some manner with the performers in Ferrara that a written source may not always make entirely explicit the refined, florid style of singing cultivated by the musicians of the Este court. Compositions having a much more ordinary appearance may have been subjected to a considerable amount of improvisatory embellishment. The practice is described in some detail by a contemporary observer, Vincenzo Giustiniani (b. 1564) in his *Discorso sopra la musica*, published in 1628:

> There was great competence among those ladies of Mantua and Ferrara, who vied with one another not only with respect to the timbre and training of their voices, but

also in the ornamentation of exquisite passagework, opportunely placed . . . and also in the moderation and augmentation of the voice, loud or soft, making it smaller or greater according to what was appropriate, now holding it out, now clipping it, interrupting at times with the accompaniment of a sweet sigh, now dividing the notes in extended passagework, well and clearly executed, now in turns (*gruppi*), now by leaps, now with long trills, now with short ones, and now with sweet passages sung softly . . . and principally with facial expressions, glances, and gestures that accompany appropriately the music and the conceits [of the text], and above all with no movement of the body, mouth, or hands that is not pertinent to the end for which the singing was intended, to make the words entirely distinct so that every last syllable of every word could be heard, without interruption or suppression of those words either by the passagework or other embellishments.[59]

As so often happens (and as we have just seen), some of the decorative passagework began to be written out, as were those techniques of vocal expression that could be captured by the notational conventions of the times. Composers thus attempted to integrate into their compositions the embellishments and expressive figures that had earlier been left to the judgment and skill of the performers. Printers, as well, would have wished to provide the amateurs for whom their prints were intended with some helps to more accomplished performance. In any case, the resulting emphasis on the solo performer eventually had yet other and more far-reaching consequences for the style of madrigal composition, as we shall see.

The performance practices fostered at the Este court in the 1580s and 1590s were apparently emulated in Mantua and supported with the engagement of musicians capable of its difficulties, particularly after the accession of Duke Vincenzo Gonzaga in 1587. And because second sons of both the Este and Gonzaga families found, in accordance with custom, careers in the church, it was to be expected that the fame of the remarkable musical establishment at the Ferrarese court would quickly spread to Rome.

FERRARESE INFLUENCE IN ROME

A key figure in making the glories of Ferrarese music known to both patrons and musicians in the papal city was apparently the young Luca Marenzio (1553–99). He had been resident in Rome for some years when in 1578 he entered the employ of Cardinal Luigi d'Este, whom he served until the latter's death in 1586.[60] In 1580–81 he made a lengthy visit to Ferrara with those members of his patron's household who

---

59. The original text, with explanation and commentary, is found in Newcomb's study, *Madrigal at Ferrara*, 1:46–52; the entire treatise is available in an English translation by Carol MacClintock, Vicenzo Giustiniani, *Il Desiderio*, Musicological Studies and Documents 9 ([Rome]: American Institute of Musicology, 1962), cf. pp. 67ff.

60. Concerning Marenzio, see Steven Ledbetter, *The New Grove Dictionary of Music*, 11:667.

attended the ducal wedding. This gave him ample opportunity to become familiar with the musical life of the court and to establish contact with the musicians who served there. The influence of the celebrated *concerto delle donne* on his madrigal composition is clearly reflected in his contribution to the two "laurel" collections mentioned earlier and, more generally, in the style of his vocal writing of the 1580s.[61]

This phase of Marenzio's development as a composer of madrigals is clearly reflected in his setting of *Scendi dal paradiso Venere*, published in his *Quarto libro de madrigali* of 1584 (see Example 19-11).[62] Its five-part texture is dominated, as one would expect, by the two soprano parts at the top of its vocal register. The text, a

61. See Newcomb's discussion of stylistic features in Marenzio's madrigals traceable to the influence of the Ferrarese *concerto* in *Madrigal at Ferrara*, 1:86ff.
62. For a transcription of the complete piece, see Luca Marenzio, *Sämtliche Werke*, ed. Alfred Einstein, 2 vols., Publikationen älterer Musik (Leipzig: Breitkopf und Härtel, 1929–31), 6:12–15.

EXAMPLE 19-11. Luca Marenzio, *Scendi dal paradiso Venere* (mm. 1–14, 49–59, 83–92)

Descend from Paradise, O Venus, and with thee let Amor guide the cupids, the graces, and laughter. . . . [Let our songs reach the heavens] because the fair souls of Amaryllis and Tirsis are joined in a sacred, holy knot, like the vine to the elm and the ivy or acanthus to the tree trunk.

serene celebration of a matrimonial union, is without attribution, but it is penetrated by the Acadian nostalgia that marked so strongly the *Pastor Fido* of Giambattista Guarini (1538–1612). Guarini was yet another of the sixteenth-century poets who served the Este court in Ferrara and whose verse, like that of Torquato Tasso, became increasingly popular with madrigal composers late in the period.[63]

The lines of the anonymous poem are also laced with verbal conceits of the kind that lent themselves particularly well to musical mimesis. The very first word, "descend," is declaimed in a falling fifth, and Venus's flight earthward from paradise is borne on a descending scalar figure given emphasis by its reiteration in a point of imitation. The marshaling of the accompanying cupids ("pargoletti"), by contrast, is conveyed by homophonic declamation in all five voices (mm. 12–14).

With the introduction (mm. 15–23) of the Graces and laughter, both as concept and as action ("riso" and "rida"), come the first examples of the melismatic turns and "divisions" (the ornamental breaking of longer notes into the rapid running passages that characterized the "luxuriant" style). They return at the conclusion of the phrase that suggests, with a rising melodic line, the wedding songs rising to the stars ("stelle," mm. 42–49) and for the word "vines" ("vite," mm. 77–80). Other, more conventional, mimetic gestures include the slow, quasi-homophonic declamation depicting the Tiber as it joins the Tyrrhenian Sea (mm. 29–39). The union of the fair souls of Amaryllis and Tirsis (mm. 49–55) in a sacred knot (mm. 68–75), like vine clinging to the elm and the ivy or the acanthus to the trunk, are suggested by the contrapuntal winding of three or four of the voices about the slowly descending line heard first in the bassus and then in the two soprano parts (mm. 75–92).[64]

63. Concerning Guarini, see Barbara Russano Hanning, *The New Grove Dictionary of Music*, 7:770–72.
64. Cf. Einstein's comments concerning this composition in *Italian Madrigal*, 2:639–40.

Clearly, such a work partakes abundantly of the mimetic vocabulary that had been developed in the course of the century as a means of textual expression in setting Italian vernacular verse. In addition, both the treble-dominated texture and the restrained virtuosity of the individual parts point to the influence of the Ferrarese tradition. The surface of the music remains unruffled, however. Wanting are the accidental inflections and abrupt hexachordal and harmonic shifts used by composers at the Este court to capture the tone and feeling of texts dealing with deep pathos and similar emotional extremes. Such experiments in musical expression did continue at the hands of composers working at the secular courts of the Continent. But Roman composers (of whom Palestrina is surely the most representative for the time), caught up in the preoccupations of the Counter-Reformation, tended to focus their energies on other genres and other problems.

ON THE THRESHOLD OF STYLISTIC CHANGE

By the mid-1580s, or so it would seem, all of the stylistic tendencies associated with the madrigal in the final decades of the sixteenth century had already been clearly sketched, if not always fully developed. The declamatory homophony of the earlier repertory had given way in the 1540s and 1550s to a more motetlike contrapuntal idiom, but it came back into more prominent use in the following decade in those works that incorporated to a degree the more popular tone and style of the *canzona villanesca* and the *canzonetta*—compositional types to which we shall return shortly. A preference for the rich textures made possible by a palette of five or six parts, and for the sophisticated part-writing such scoring allowed, is reflected in the overwhelming preponderance in the sources of compositions written for more than four voices, whereas the three-part combination so successfully used for madrigals by Festa came to be relegated to the strophic genres of *canzonetta* and *villanella*.

The expressive musical language that came to be the hallmark of the madrigal began with the suggestive pictorialism that recognized in certain types of melodic motion and rhythmic activity parallels or analogies to verbal conceits. With de Rore and Luzzaschi the development of such means was extended to unusual chromatic inflections and the dislocations of hexachords and harmonies such alterations could produce, and these departures from the sonorous norms were perceived as having particular potential for the expression of pathos. To these devices were added, particularly from the 1580s on, the effects to be derived from a virtuosic style of performance, which was deployed not only to lend brilliance to the sonorous design but also for rhetorical and mimetic purposes. As a result of the efforts thus made to expand the range of possibilities for musical expression within the context of madrigal composition, the genre came to be, in a very real sense, the primary focus for stylistic development and change in the closing decades of the sixteenth century, just as the polyphonic Mass and the motet had been previously.

It should come as no surprise, therefore, that the ecclesiastics who were leading the Catholic Counter-Reformation in Italy should have wished, in adopting a strategy so effectively employed by the leaders of the Protestant Reformation, to appropriate for their religious purposes the considerable sensual charms of the madrigal. Textual *contrafacta* were therefore prepared, as they had been earlier in generating repertories of *laude, chansons spirituelles*, and *noëls*, and encouragement was given to the setting of sacred and devotional Italian texts.

Madrigali spirituali, which were musically quite indistinguishable from their secular counterparts, were thus brought into existence. De Rore may have been one of the first to contribute substantially to the development of such a repertory with his cycle of eleven compositions based on Petrarch's *canzone* in honor of the Virgin Mary.[65] Later, it was in particular composers working in Rome—presumably in response to the proximity of the papal court—who gave the most serious attention to works of that type. Palestrina apparently provided pieces for two printed collections, although only the second, published in 1594, has survived.[66] Luca Marenzio contributed to another that first appeared in 1584 and was reprinted with additions in 1610.[67]

All through its history the madrigal was published in part books, implying through its notational tradition that it was wholly vocal in its compositional conception. As we have discovered, however, arrangements for lute and solo voice appeared as early as 1546, and evidence for that mode of performance continues to build as the century draws to a close. Clearly, although conceptually and compositionally the madrigal remained very much in the realm of contrapuntal polyphony, the performance practice of the period appears to have carried it inexorably back toward the conventions of accompanied solo song often associated with its beginnings. This is clear from the following description of a typical afternoon of music making in the Este household in 1581, which also provides—despite the observer's undisguised lack of enthusiasm—precious insight into its social uses in a courtly context:

> After lunch we played *primiera*. . . . In this game the Duke, the Duchess, Donna Marfisa . . . and I took part. . . . At the same time the music began, so that I had to play cards, listen to the music, and praise and admire the passages, the cadences, the *tirate*, and similar things, all of which, beginning with the card game, I know little about and enjoy still less. This festivity lasted no less than four hours [!] because, after some other ladies had sung, there appeared Signora Peverara. . . . Under pretext of having me listen to one thing or another, either as a solo or accompanied by one or more instruments, she prolonged the session as long as possible.[68]

65. See Rore, *Opera omnia*, ed. Meier, vol. 3, and the discussion above, pp. 649–52.

66. For the list of Palestrina's known compositions in this genre, see Jessie Ann Owens, *The New Grove Dictionary of Music*, 14:135.

67. See Steven Ledbetter, "Marenzio," *The New Grove Dictionary of Music*, 11:669–70.

68. The passage in question is from the ambassador Urbani as translated by Einstein, *Italian Madrigal*, 2:826–27.

By the time Alfonso II d'Este died in 1597, the musical preeminence once enjoyed by the musical establishment at the Ferrarese court had already been pre-empted by that of Duke Vincenzo Gonzaga in Mantua. It follows, therefore, that the young Mantuan composer Claudio Monteverdi (b. 1567), who entered ducal service in the early 1590s, was well situated to bring about the final transformation of the madrigal. Having thoroughly mastered all of the compositional procedures associated with the genre, he went on to formalize in the written tradition the changes in performance practice and musical taste that had been taking place in the final decades of the sixteenth century. In his hands the madrigal became a soloistic piece for virtuoso singers, usually only one or two, in *concertato* style—that is, supported by keyboard and/or bass instruments capable of providing a harmonic underpinning. Those developments, however, more rightly belong to a discussion of the music of the coming age and will not be pursued here.[69]

VILLANESCA, VILLANELLA, AND CANZONETTA

Madrigal composers turned in the 1540s ever more resolutely to texts with serious literary pretensions and to compositional procedures of a highly sophisticated nature. It was perhaps to be expected, as a consequence, that the taste for both verse and music in a lighter vein would call into existence genres of a more popular character and a repertory capable of replacing the fading *frottola*, both functionally and stylistically. The first printed collection of pieces of this kind to have a definable stylistic profile appeared in Naples in 1537 under the title *Canzone villanesche alla napolitana.*

The texts of this and of subsequent collections of a similar nature brought out in the early 1540s were primarily in the Neapolitan vernacular and were parodistic in nature. They targeted, understandably enough, the fashionable new madrigal with its Petrarchan texts in Tuscan Italian. The compositional procedures were appropriately simple: a three-voice texture was preferred, together with syllabic declamation in a predominantly homophonic texture. In addition, a certain rustic naiveté is suggested by the frequent occurrence of—presumably intentional—parallel fifths between the outer parts. Like the *frottola* that preceded it, the *canzona villanesca* was strophic in conception and made use of internal repetition as well, usually in the pattern AABCC.[70]

By the mid-1540s the Neapolitan genre had become known in northern Italy. There it was taken up by local composers, particularly in Venice and the nearby cities of the Veneto (such as Padua), where its similarity to the earlier *villotta* would have

69. The literature regarding Monteverdi and his music is vast; see, as an introduction, Denis Arnold and Elsie M. Arnold, *The New Grove Dictionary of Music*, 12:514–34.
70. See Denis Arnold, "Villanella," *The New Grove Dictionary of Music*, 19:771.

been recognized and undoubtedly appreciated. The use of verse in the local vernacular, which had also been a characteristic of the *villotta*, continued to be an identifying trait of the *canzona villanesca* outside of Naples as well as in its original home, but of course the dialects adopted varied with the locality. Their multiplicity led, in fact, to the coining of a number of related terms to designate the genre—*Giustiniana, Greghesca, Moresca, Todesca*—each of them reflecting in some way a distinctive linguistic orientation and suggesting, obviously, a familiar social context.

Thus the *Giustiniana*—with *canzona* in its general meaning of "song" understood as a prefix—evoked through the name of a well-known Venetian poet the dialect of that city and the amorous adventures of old men, a characteristic topic for his verse. Similarly, the *Greghesca* made use of an "artificial Venetian-Greek patois";[71] the *Moresca* referred, linguistically as well as topically, to Moorish (i.e., African) slaves; and the *Todesca* satirized the difficulties of German soldiers (and, by extension, other foreigners as well) with the Italian tongue. The vocable *villanella*—presumably with reference to the rustic matters so often dealt with by the texts—first appeared in the title of a printed collection in 1555 and became increasingly common thereafter.

As local dialectical usage and rustic contexts gradually yielded to the more general theme of erotic love in the 1570s and 1580s, the term *canzonetta* also made its appearance, often together with the more or less synonymous *villanella*, in the titles of printed collections. The designation *mascherata* apparently derived from the use of pieces of this sort, like the *canti carnascialeschi* and *frottole* earlier, as an integral part of carnival festivities and theatrical entertainments of various kinds.[72]

The variable vocabulary by which compositions of this type were known is clearly indicative of the differences among them, particularly with respect to the verse upon which they were based. Similarities in formal conception and musical style appear nonetheless to justify their being considered as a distinctive and definable genre. As has been observed, the musical settings were formulaic in that they were intended for strophic performance, while the treatment of the text was syllabic and declamatory, and the textures were generally homophonic and always uncomplicated. These characteristics of musical style, together with a text of popular cast having a number of the features to be expected generally, are to be seen in *Madonna mia, famme bon'offerta*, one of the ten pieces attributed to Willaert in a collection of 1545 published by Scotto in Venice and entitled *Canzone villanesche alla napolitana* (see Example 19-12).[73]

The poem, three stanzas of the slightest substance, is presented as if capturing the sales pitch of a peasant offering his rooster to a lady (probably, as usual, with erotic *double entendre*). It clearly has no literary pretensions, for all of its comic possibili-

71. See Arnold, "Villanella," *The New Grove Dictionary of Music*, 19:771.

72. For a specific but typical example involving Orlande de Lassus at the Bavarian court, see Arnold, "Villanella," *The New Grove Dictionary of Music*, 19:772.

73. For a transcription in modern score, see Willaert, *Opera omnia*, vol. 14, ed. Helga Meier, 106–61.

EXAMPLE 19-12. Adrian Willaert, *Madonna mia, famme bon'offerta* (mm. 23–40)

[My lady, make me a good offer since I am carrying at present this big cock, which always sings at daybreak] to the hens, and says, "chichirchi." And this impresses the hen so greatly that she produces an egg every morning. (One additional strophe.)

ties, and displays the diction of a low style together with typically dialectical forms of expression. Willaert set it for four voices, rather than the three preferred by the composers then working in Naples, and he avoided at the same time—meticulous craftsman that he was—the parallel fifths used by those masters to suggest ignorance of or willful disregard for the rules of counterpoint. Taking the poem line by line, he articulates each one by means of a cadential formula, a rest, or both. Declamation follows the natural accents of the language, unfolding homorhythmically within a generally rather narrow range (except for the bassus, which makes considerable use of wider melodic leaps) with frequent repetitions of pitch.

Only the treatment of the onomatopoetic crowing of the rooster recalls a certain kind of text illustration by means of its suggestive rhythms and melodic patterns (mm. 27–30), but the model could just as well have been a chanson by Janequin as an Italian madrigal. Willaert also repeats the second verse of the strophe and the last, both text and music, thus conserving in its basic outline the formal pattern (AABCC) generally found in the Neapolitan collections of the preceding decade. The result, obviously, is a far cry in every respect from the sophisticated contrapuntal style being forged by Willaert in those same years for madrigal texts of a serious complexion.

Later in the century, especially in the 1570s and beyond, there was considerable hybridization of styles between madrigal and *villanella* or *canzonetta*, as the genre was most frequently designated by then.[74] A modest reintegration of homophonic declamation into the madrigal in clear imitation of the compositional procedure most characteristic of the lighter genres was alluded to above. Conversely, *villanella* and *canzonetta* were allowed not infrequently to take on characteristics of the madrigal: the fuller textures of five- and six-voice combinations, modest use of imitative counterpoint, and even some of the pictorial musical rhetoric that was such a prominent feature of the more serious genre. Of all of these, however, only the latter tended to compromise the strophic conception that was always fundamental to the lighter secular genres, whatever the geographical areas in which they were cultivated and the names by which they were known.

The other aspects of the musical culture of sixteenth-century Italy that were undoubtedly shared by madrigal and *villanella* were in matters of performing practice. The homophonic textures of the lighter genres lent themselves to use as accompanied solo song much more easily than the contrapuntal complexities of the serious madrigal, and accounts from the period make it clear that they were often presented in that manner. The growing tendencies that would carry Italian secular music to a preference for dramatic monody and a consequently radical shift in musical style were deflected by the *villanella* even less than by its more serious cousin.[75]

74. For a discussion of the difficulties with terminology and the complex relationships among the poetic genres—*villanella*, *canzonetta*, and madrigal—toward the end of the century, see Ruth I. DeFord, "The Influence of the Madrigal on Canzonetta Texts of the Late Sixteenth Century," *Acta musicologica* 59 (1987): 127–51.
75. Particularly instructive in this connection is the incident involving Lassus referred to by Arnold, "Villanella," *The New Grove Dictionary of Music*, 19:771.

CHAPTER 20

Songs and Madrigals in England

The sources of English secular music that have survived from the late fifteenth and early sixteenth century are few in number and generally mixed in character. One of the earliest, for example, the "Fayrfax Manuscript" (MS 5465 at the British Library), which must have been compiled around 1500 in London or nearby Windsor for use at the court of King Henry VII, contains twelve sacred works together with thirty-seven secular pieces.[1] Even more heterogeneous in nature is the "Ritson Codex" (MS 5665 at the British Library), which was apparently assembled at about the same time but with some much earlier repertory. As it was intended for use at an ecclesiastical institution, it contains liturgical music for both Mass and Office in addition to twenty-two motets, forty-four carols, a chanson, and eighteen English songs.[2]

A slightly later collection, known as the Henry VIII Manuscript, was probably copied during the second decade of the sixteenth century. It did not in fact belong to the king but can be considered an anthology of compositions then current at the royal court. A number of these pieces clearly reflect the "disguisings" and other festivities that graced the early years of Henry's reign, and the king himself is credited with being the composer of 34 of the 109 mostly secular pieces copied into its leaves (see Figure 20–1).[3]

Significantly, both English and Continental masters are represented in this collection, which comprises, in addition to fifty-three settings of English verse, a motet

---

1. See the *Census-Catalogue of Manuscript Sources of Polyphonic Music*, ed. Charles Hamm and Herbert Kellman, 5 vols. (Neuhausen-Stuttgart: Hänssler-Verlag, 1979–88), 2:42.

2. See the *Census-Catalogue of Manuscript Sources*, 2:43f.

3. Note, however, that in some instances, King Henry's compositions are demonstrably reworkings of the music of others. In some instances, for example, he simply added a single part to an existing composition, and his compositional role in this repertory generally is not easily defined; cf. David Greer, "Henry VIII," *The New Grove Dictionary of Music*, 8:486.

FIGURE 20-1. Miniature showing King Henry VIII playing the harp with his court jester, William Sommers (London, British Library, MS Royal 2 A XVI [miniature], f. 63ᵛ).

and a motet-chanson, fifteen pieces on French and Dutch texts—including the most widely circulated chansons of the fifteenth century—and another thirty-five works having no words at all, music presumably intended for instrumental use.[4] The MS Royal Appendix 58 at the British Library was apparently compiled over roughly a quarter-century beginning about 1515, again from repertory of the royal court. Like the "Ritson Codex," its contents include a polyphonic Mass, Office and processional hymns, motets, a carol, and twelve chansons as well as twenty-eight English songs.[5]

Rounding out this secular English repertory for the opening decades of the sixteenth century is the first polyphonic music to be printed in England, *XX Songes, ix of iiii partes and xi of thre partes* [sic], a collection of secular music published in 1530 (of which, unfortunately, only the bass partbook and a few other scattered leaves have survived). Even if this print is taken into account, however, the harvest of polyphonic English songs from this period is rather slender, especially when compared to the literally hundreds of pieces found in French and Italian sources of similar date. There are 156 English pieces overall, including concordances and duplications of which there are a fair number.

Equally striking—if not entirely surprising in light of the circumstances attendant upon the Reformation in England after Henry VIII—is the paucity of secular song on English texts from the next half-century or so. The only printed collection to have been brought out by an English press during that time was Thomas Whythorne's *Songes for Three, Fower and Five Voyces* of 1571. The extended hiatus between these two publications is to be explained in large part by the repeated delays in the development of music printing in Britain, but the manuscript sources do little to fill the gap.

Some of the English songs in these sources, especially those few actually written by native-born musicians to French texts, would be difficult to distinguish stylistically from their Continental counterparts, in particular the French chansons of the late fifteenth and early sixteenth centuries with which they are found in the Henry VIII Manuscript. Only two types emerge as being typically, if not uniquely, English. On the one hand are those identified specifically in a biographical document of the period as "freemen's songs." And on the other are compositions for solo voice and accompanying ensemble that have come to be known as "consort songs."

An explanation of sorts concerning the former is found in *The Lyffe of Sir Peter Carewe* in connection with the subject's relationship with King Henry VIII: "For the King himself being much delighted to sing, and Sir Peter Carewe having a pleasant voice, the King would very often use him to sing with him certain songs they called *fremen* songs."[6]

The origins of the term—which has not been used in any musical source of the period—have yet to be satisfactorily elucidated. It can be assumed, however, that the anonymous biographer was referring to a type of strophic song represented in fair numbers in the "Henry VIII Manuscript."[7] These pieces are based on poetry in a popular vein and written for three voices, each of them fully texted, in a homophonic and predominantly syllabic style. Their characteristic compositional features can be seen at their most basic in the setting, attributed to Henry VIII, for *Whereto should I express*, in which four short phrases accommodate the equally brief verses (in iambic trimeter) of the strophic quatrains, five of which were copied into the manuscript (see Example 20-1).[8]

Such songs represent the combination of relatively artless vernacular verse with appropriately simple musical settings. They have their analogy in the Italian *villanelle* and the French *voix de ville*.[9] Other, somewhat more sophisticated pieces of the same type reveal, however, that the true antecedents of the genre are not to be found on the Continent at all but rather with the fifteenth-century English carol (see pp. 250–56). Based on poems whose stanzas are punctuated with a recurring refrain, these compositions provide for that particular element of the text a discrete section of music identifiable as a *burden*. In some instances only the refrain seems to have been set (e.g., nos. 31 and 35), and the verses were presumably to be sung by a solo voice to a well-known tune. In others a separate segment was provided for the strophes as well (e.g., nos. 103 and 104).

The most elaborate of such pieces—and very carol-like in its facture—is *Lusti yough shuld us ensue*, also attributed to Henry VIII.[10] It consists of three separate sections (for three, two, and finally four voices) with repetitions to provide for a total

6. The passage quoted has been taken from Gustave Reese, *Music in the Renaissance* (New York: Norton, 1959), 769, but with the spelling modernized.

7. See the edition by John Stevens, *Music at the Court of Henry VIII*, Musica Britannica, vol. 18 (London: Stainer and Bell, 1962).

8. For a transcription in modern score, see Stevens, ed., *Music at the Court of Henry VIII*, 37, no. 47.

9. See pp. 699–702 and 627–32 respectively, and cf. Geoffrey Chew, "Song," *The New Grove Dictionary of Music*, 17:516.

10. See Stevens, ed., *Music at the Court of Henry VIII*, 70–71, no. 92.

EXAMPLE 20-1. King Henry VIII, *Whereto should I express*

of seven stanzas. More typical, however, is the anonymous *Where be ye, my love?* (see Example 20-2).[11] Following a full statement of the *burden*, the four strophes are sung to a separate section of music that concludes, however, with a restatement of the closing section of the refrain, first the tune (m. 16), then the text (mm. 18–21). In performance it would be possible either to repeat the entire *burden* between each of the strophes or to go directly from the partial repeat of the refrain at the end of the stanza to the beginning of the next, perhaps with a complete restatement of the *burden* at the end. However, there is no clear indication, either in the musical sources or in literary documents of the period, as to how it was usually done.

The polyphonic texture is very much that of the English carol—essentially homophonic with just a touch of contrapuntal animation—and the modest use of melisma in a precadential passage (mm. 14–15) is also what one might expect in the earlier genre. Because the words of the poem are matched for the most part syllabically with the notes, their placement should pose few problems. However, the verses do not always carry the same number of syllables, either because they are slightly corrupt or because an exact count was not held to be indispensable, making some adjustment necessary in matching notes and syllables from one strophe to the next.[12]

11. For the complete transcription in modern score, see Stevens, ed., *Music at the Court of Henry VIII*, 80–81, no. 104.
12. The metrical discrepancies between stanzas in this piece are slight; the divergences are much more marked in some of the other pieces. See, for example, those examples included in easily accessible anthologies, such as Cooper's *I have been a foster* in Archibald T. Davison and Willi Apel, eds., *The Historical Anthology of Music*, 2 vols. (Cambridge, Mass.: Harvard University Press, 1962), 1:90; Cornyshe's *Blow thy horne* in Noah Greenberg and Paul Maynard, eds., *An Anthology of Early Renaissance Music* (New York: Norton, 1975), 199; and *Adew, adew* in Davison and Apel, eds., *Historical Anthology of Music*, 1:90.

EXAMPLE 20-2. Anonymous, *Where be ye my love?*

Also strophic, but becoming increasingly sophisticated in their compositional make-up as the century unfolded, were the so-called consort songs, settings of English verse for solo voice and instrumental ensemble. Because surviving sources for the secular English music of this period are so limited, the origins of this song type are difficult to trace. It is in fact possible that the late sixteenth-century development of the consort song owed more to performance practices than to an abstract compositional concept.

Only by assuming this to be the case can one see in Whythorne's *Songes for Three, Fower and Five Voices* of 1571 what may have been some of the earliest examples of this genre, given that each of the printed voice parts is fully texted. Providing words for all of the voices implies not only a performance unassisted by instruments but also a wholly vocal compositional design. Of course the texting may have been primarily for commercial reasons, to make the collection as widely useful, and thus as fully marketable, as possible. Moreover, since the songs are predominantly homophonic in texture, and largely syllabic in their treatment of the text, laying out the words for each of the voices poses no real difficulty.

In any case, there is nothing in the musical style of these pieces to prevent their performance by either voices or instruments or by some combination of the two. Conversely, it is perfectly possible that the preferred manner of performance was a solo voice with an accompanying instrumental ensemble. As may be seen from the opening phrase of *Give not thy mind to heaviness*, Whytehorne's counterpoint shows little differentiation among the parts (see Example 20-3).[13] Soprano I is tuneful enough as it declaims the text, two syllables to a ternary measure in a mostly trochaic pattern, but none of the lower parts is markedly less melodious or dominated by leaps awkward for the voice. And the texture is largely homophonic with only the lightest of contrapuntal animation. The same is true, moreover, of all the pieces from this collection currently available in published score.[14]

13. See Peter Warlock (alias Heseltine), ed., *The Oxford Choral Songs from the Old Masters* (London: Oxford University Press, 1927), no. 364, mm. 1–16.
14. The eleven compositions from Whythorne's print of 1571 included in *The Oxford Choral Songs from the Old Masters*, nos. 354–64, all edited by Peter Warlock, are very much of the same stylistic stamp, whether written in four parts or in five.

EXAMPLE 20-3. Thomas Whythorne, *Give not thy mind to heaviness* (mm. 1-16)

As was so often the case in this period, the mode of performance probably depended in any given instance upon the circumstances and the means available. For instance, if one can judge from the moralizing tone of their texts, Whythorne's compositions must have been intended to provide proper didactic material for the training of young choristers in ecclesiastical institutions. He may have used them for this purpose himself after he was appointed, shortly after their publication, master of music in the chapel of Archbishop Parker.[15] In such a context singers were undoubtedly available as a rule for each of the voices. Nonetheless, it may have been that even in a choral institution like that of the archbishop's chapel, only one or two of the written parts were sung and that instruments played the others.

That the combination of a solo voice with an instrumental ensemble did in fact develop in the final decades of the century as a performance tradition for songs of this type is suggested by comments from William Byrd (1543–1623), perhaps the most gifted composer of Elizabethan England. In the introductory epistle to his *Psalmes, Sonets and Songs of Sadnes and Pietie* of 1588, he says of the pieces in the collection that although they have been fitted with words "in all parts for voyces to sing the same," they were "originally made for instruments to expresse the harmonie, and one voyce to pronounce the dittie" (i.e., the text).[16] Byrd's reasons for texting all the parts were undoubtedly once again primarily those of practical utility and commercial success, but in his polyphonic songs there is some stylistic evidence for a performance-based distinction between the melodious solo part in a treble register and the contrapuntal instrumental accompaniment below.

It would appear as well that Byrd wanted to give this particular song type greater sobriety and significance. To that end, typically, he chose a more self-consciously contrapuntal fabric than had been previously employed in song writing. He relied in fact to a considerable degree upon syntactic imitation, the principal compositional procedure associated with the Latin motet. He adopted it not only for metrical Psalms and other devotional texts in the vernacular but also—if somewhat less rigorously—for verse of an entirely secular cast. His serious approach to the compositional process may be seen at its most uncompromising in a song such as the five part *Lullaby, my sweet little baby*, which became so widely known and loved that it gave its name to the entire collection.[17]

A lullaby for the infant Jesus that speaks of both the martyr of the innocents and the flight into Egypt, it is clearly one of the "songs of sadness and piety" mentioned in the title. The opening pair of lines, "Lulla la lulla lulla lullaby,/My sweet little Baby, what meanest thou to cry," sung repeatedly (in the manner of a lullaby), is the sole text for the initial section of the piece and stands apart from the six-line stanza. The stanza itself is set as the "second part" of the work, concluding with the line "O woe, and woeful heavy day, when wretches have their will," which is repeated liter-

---

15. Concerning Whythorne, see James M. Osborn, *The New Grove Dictionary of Music*, 20:393–94.
16. See William Byrd, *The Collected Vocal Works of William Byrd*, vol. 12, *Psalmes, Sonets, and Songs (1588)*, ed. Edmund H. Fellowes (London: Stainer and Bell, 1948), xxxvi.
17. See Joseph Kerman, "Byrd," *The New Grove Dictionary of Music*, 3:541.

ally, text and music. (A clear cadence and a shift from binary to ternary mensuration mark the division between the two principal sections of the work.) If the remaining three stanzas of the poem were sung to the same music as the first, then presumably the entire "first part," the lullaby, was also heard again before each of them. Because the final verse is the same for the first three stanzas, it could be perceived to function as a recurring *burden*, all the more prominent by virtue of its literal repetition. In the final stanza its sad sentiment is reversed, although the music is unchanged, as it affirms, "Oh joy, and joyful happy day, when wretches want their will!"

Byrd's deployment of sophisticated contrapuntal skill is evident throughout the composition but perhaps nowhere more strikingly than at the beginning of the second part (see Example 20-4).[18] There one point of imitation follows another. All five

18. For a transcription of the entire piece in modern score, see Byrd, *Psalmes, Sonets, and Songs (1588)*, ed. Fellowes, 172–82, no. 32.

EXAMPLE 20-4. William Byrd, *Lullaby, my sweet little baby,* second part (mm. 52–71)

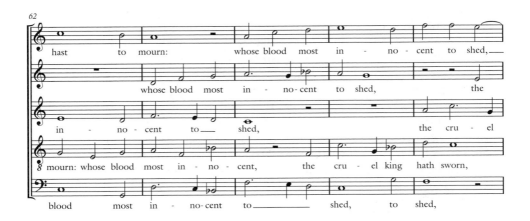

parts do not always repeat literally the principal motive, however; the bassus, in particular, has a tendency to go its own way. Still, the individual lines generally maintain a high degree of melodic integrity. Even where homophonic declamation is introduced as a contrasting texture for rhetorical effect (as at m. 88), it gives way rather quickly to imitative writing.

Given the strophic nature and the contrapuntal style of the piece, it is surprising to see with what skill and consistency Byrd has applied text to music. Strict imitation in all the parts allows one voice to follow another in the placement of the text as well, but freer linear writing poses rather more difficult problems. Despite that challenge, and the considerable repetition of words and phrases, the composer has succeeded in linking one musical segment smoothly to the next, thus maintaining a continuous, cohesive stream of polyphony. Still, there is no reason to doubt Byrd's assertion that even such a work as this was initially conceived as a consort song (intended, that is, for solo voice and accompanying instruments); it is in fact found in exactly that format in an earlier manuscript source.[19]

Byrd was considerably more flexible in his application of contrapuntal procedures to those texts designated as "sonets" (though that is not their poetic form), perhaps because he intended them, as he affirms in his introduction to the collection, for those "disposed . . . to be merrie." His treatment of lighter themes may be seen in his five-part setting of *Though Amaryllis Dance*, whose pastoral setting and Acadian characters clearly reflect the influence of Italian poetry on the tastes of Elizabethan England (see Example 20-5).[20] For the five strophes of seven brief lines each the composer has provided a single short section of music. As in Byrd's lullaby, the final verse, repeated, serves the successive stanzas as a kind of end refrain. He opens the piece with a concise homophonic phrase in the three lowest parts, then pits against this trio a higher one, which answers in (musically) imitative echo. Thereafter, however, the texture becomes richly contrapuntal, making considerable (if not entirely consistent) use of imitative writing.

In this instance, as in the one just discussed, the text is applied to all parts syllabically with such sensitivity that it appears to have been conceived from the outset for a wholly vocal performance. But here once again Byrd's assertion regarding its initial conception is confirmed by its inclusion in an earlier manuscript source prepared for performance by solo voice and instrumental consort.[21] It is consequently possible

19. See the list of works compiled by Kerman, "Byrd," *The New Grove Dictionary of Music*, 3:549.
20. For a transcription of the entire piece in modern score, see Byrd, *Psalmes, Sonets, and Songs (1588)*, ed. Fellowes, 60–63, no. 12.
21. See the list of works, compiled by Kerman, "Byrd," *The New Grove Dictionary of Music*, 3:550.

EXAMPLE 20-5. William Byrd, *Though Amaryllis dance* (mm. 1–16)

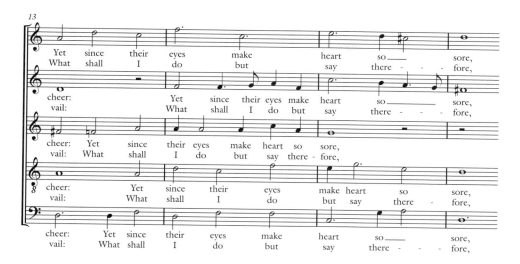

to conclude that the rich contrapuntal texture lavished upon a song of such slight substance was meant primarily to give satisfaction to an ensemble of accompanying instrumentalists and reflected a growing tradition of performance practice that was generating its own stylistic imperatives.

ITALIAN MADRIGALS ENGLISHED AND ENGLISH MADRIGALS

In the same year that Byrd published his first set of English songs (1588), another collection of music appeared that signaled a rapid and dramatic change in the musical landscape in England, one that was to have repercussions well into the seventeenth century. The print in question was a large anthology of Italian madrigals with their texts in English translation, edited by Nicholas Yonge and offered to the public under the title *Musica Transalpina*. Such a publication must be seen as a clear indication that the Italian madrigal had by then become well known and appreciated in England. The printer must have been persuaded that potential English buyers, who were charmed by the music but unable to understand the original Italian, would be willing to pay for singable translations in order to experience more directly the impact produced by text and music combined.

As we have seen, the introduction of Italian madrigals to musical circles in England went back to the genesis of the genre. One of the first substantial repertories of such pieces to have been compiled in a manuscript still extant, the "Newberry Partbooks," had probably reached the English court by 1528 at the latest (see pp. 659–64). Subsequently, a fairly steady stream of madrigal collections, particularly those being printed in such great numbers in Continental centers such as Venice and

Antwerp, must have been brought to England both by Italian musicians drawn to the court of Henry VIII and by music-loving English travelers. At the same time, as is well known, Italian poetry was ever more widely circulated and admired in English-speaking regions in the final decades of the sixteenth century and was being imitated there in significant ways.[22]

Not surprisingly, then, the first printed collection of Italian madrigals with English texts in translation was successful enough to be followed in 1590 by another, *Italian Madrigals Englished*, published by the poet Thomas Watson and dedicated primarily to the works of Luca Marenzio. After a lengthy hiatus, Yonge countered (in 1597) with a second volume of *Musica Transalpina*. This was followed in turn by two collections prepared by Thomas Morley (1557–78 to 1602), a gentleman of the royal chapel who was also a composer, music theorist, and successful publisher: *Canzonets, or Little Short Songs to Four Voices: Selected out of the best and approved Italian authors*, brought out in 1597, and *Madrigals to Five Voices: Selected out of the best approved Italian authors*, in 1598.

In the last three of these anthologies there was a clear trend away from the more serious compositions of the Italian repertory—madrigals that were sophisticated textually and, therefore, musically as well—toward the lighter madrigalistic styles and subgenres, as typified by the strophic canzonet. This was a shift for which Morley, who was a key figure in the Italianization of English secular music in the second half of the century, appears to have been largely responsible.[23]

Altogether these published anthologies made accessible to English musicians, both amateur and professional, more than 150 Italian madrigals and canzonets for four, five, and six voices, with their original Italian texts translated into English. The resultant repertory is modest indeed when seen against the background of Italian musical culture at the time and the hundreds of collections of madrigals that were then being published. Still, as we shall see, it was larger than any single Englishman was ever to produce. Its impact on English composers of the period had to have been considerable, moreover, since they adopted some 25 English texts directly from these anthologies for their own works in the genre, often taking at the same time the original Italian setting as a compositional model. In addition, another 50 or so Italian poems were similarly appropriated, translated for the use of an English master and made to serve—often together with their music, once again—as a basis for a new work on an English text.[24]

When, exactly, English composers began to write original madrigals in the Italian manner on English texts is far from clear. There may have been scattered essays in the genre as early as the 1580s, but there is no source for the English madrigal, either

22. See Joseph Kerman, *The Elizabethan Madrigal* (New York: American Musicological Society, 1962), 8–12; Kerman's is still the basic study of the English genres of madrigalian secular music in the late sixteenth and early seventeenth centuries.
23. For the contents of these anthologies and the sources from which the individual compositions were drawn, see Kerman, *Elizabethan Madrigal*, 48–69.
24. See Kerman, *Elizabethan Madrigal*, 70–72.

manuscript or printed, that precedes the anthologies of Italian madrigals Englished printed in 1588 and 1590. Among the first to try their hand at it, clearly, must have been those masters whose works constituted some of the earliest collections of English madrigals to be published by English presses, then newly liberated from the constraints of an inhibiting monopoly on music printing. By all accounts the most significant of these composers were Thomas Morley, whose influence on the definition and development of the newly adopted genre appears to have been the most central, and three of his younger contemporaries, George Kirbye, Thomas Weelkes, and John Wilbye.[25]

Morley was the first of the four to print collections of his own settings of secular English texts consciously derived from Italian models, and they reflect from the outset his propensity for inconsequential verse and uncomplicated musical textures. The earliest of these came already in 1593, his *Canzonets . . . to 3 Voyces*, comprising twenty compositions. Despite the title, ten of these are better described (in Morley's own terms) as madrigals, even though they are relatively light in character. In the following year he published *Madrigalls to Foure Voyces . . .*, again a set of twenty pieces to which four more were added when the collection was reprinted in 1606. Four of these display the features associated with the *ballett*, another four those of the *canzonet*, and of the remaining sixteen, madrigals all, only six are in a somewhat more serious vein.

Subsequently, with the exception of The *Triumphes of Orianna* of 1601 (to which we shall return presently), his published collections consisted primarily of subgenres of a popular nature: *balletts* for five voices (1595); *canzonets* for two voices (1595); *canzonets* for five and six voices (1597); and *canzonets* for four voices (1597), which included only a couple of his own pieces. Through these prints he scattered another seven pieces, all for five or six voices, that are easily recognized as madrigals, whatever the title pages may say.[26]

Following Morley's lead, if not his textual and stylistic preferences, came George Kirbye (d. 1634), a relatively minor figure employed as a musician in the household of Sir Robert Jermyn at Rushbrooke Hall near Bury St. Edmunds. In 1597 Kirbye saw into print a collection entitled The *First Set of English Madrigals to 4. 5. & 6. Voyces*—six à 4, twelve à 5, and six à 6, for a total of twenty-four pieces. Later in the same year Thomas Weelkes (1576?–1623), a church musician who served as organist both at Winchester College and at Chichester Cathedral, brought out the first of three sets of compositions. His *Madrigals to 3. 4. 5. & 6. Voyces* of 1597 included six pieces in each of the formats cited for a total of twenty-four. This was followed by two further publications of the same type: his *Ballets and Madrigals to Five Voyces*, printed in 1598, and his *Madrigals of Five and Six Parts*, in 1600. The former com-

---

25. See Kerman, *Elizabethan Madrigal*, 258–67.

26. See David Christopher Jacobson, "Thomas Morley and the Italian Madrigal Tradition: A New Perspective," *Journal of Musicology*, 14 (1996): 80–91, who classifies Morley's compositions according to the composer's own criteria (in the *Plaine and Easie Introduction to Practicall Musicke* of 1597) and explains satisfactorily the lack of precision in the titles of his published collections.

bined seven madrigals with fifteen *ballets* and the latter included ten madrigals in each of the two voicings. Finally, John Wilbye (1574–1638), a domestic musician in the service of the Kytson family at Hengrave Hall, also near Bury St. Edmunds, published a *First Set of Madrigals to 3, 4, 5, and 6 partes* in 1598 and a *Second Set . . .* in 1609.[27]

Morley's affinity for the lighter varieties of Italian secular music is perhaps nowhere more clearly seen than in his appropriation of the vocal *balletto* as a model for his own compositions. This new genre was apparently first published in notated form in a collection of pieces by Giovanni Giacomo Gastoldi (1550s–ca. 1622) that appeared in 1591: *Balletti a cinque voci con li suoi versi per cantare, sonare, e ballare.* The compositions so identified are syllabic, homophonic settings of strophic texts characterized by the interpolation of nonsense syllables at the ends of couplets or tercets (e.g., "fa-la," "na-na," etc.). They consist in most cases of two repeated sections of music (AABB). The relationship of such pieces to the earlier *villotta* and *villanella* is of course self-evident, and their well-defined rhythmic patterns suggest that they were in fact intended for dancing as well as singing, as indicated by the title page.[28]

Morley's affection for the lighter *canzonet* is everywhere evident as well, even in those pieces he included among the madrigals of 1594/1606. An example is his setting of *April is in my Mistress' face*, the text of which was translated from a *canzoneta* by Orazio Vecchi (see Example 20-6).[29] Here his musical means are nicely matched to the light wit of the poem, which consists of a series of calendaric analogies that move from the springlike softness of the mistress's face to the winter cold of her heart. Homophonic declamation in contrasting duos and trios introduces the first verse of the poem, which closes in full, four-part texture on a longer note, articulated by a rest. The second verse is also introduced in homophonic duo (m. 9) but continues with a point of (not too exact) imitation that rises from the bassus through the cantus.

Homophonic declamation returns, with relatively sedate rhythmic motion, to convey the cool September of the mistress's bosom, first in three and then in four voices (mm. 15ff.), while the wintry conclusion is given as a second point of imitation, textually repetitive and considerably expanded by means of an iteration of the final phrase to round out the form (mm. 23–31 = 31–38). There is obviously nothing profound in the "ditty" that would justify the kind of sophisticated musical rhetoric found in serious Italian madrigals like those of de Rore, Luzzaschi, and Marenzio. As noted, moreover, Morley was apparently not drawn to poetry of that nature in any case.

In marked contrast is Thomas Weelkes's *O Care, thou wilt despatch me*, for five

---

27. See Kerman, *Elizabethan Madrigal*, 221ff.
28. See Suzanne G. Cusick, "Balletto," *The New Grove Dictionary of Music*, 2:92f.
29. For a transcription of the entire piece in modern score, see Thomas Morley, *First Book of Madrigals to Four Voices (1594)*, vol. 2 of *The English Madrigal School*, ed. Edmund H. Fellowes (London: Stainer and Bell, 1921), 1–3, no. 1. For discussion of the work, see Kerman, *Elizabethan Madrigal*, 184; Jacobson, "Thomas Morley and the Italian Madrigal Tradition," 85, classifies the piece as a canzonet.

EXAMPLE 20-6. Thomas Morley, *April is in my mistress' face* (mm. 9–30)

voices (see Example 20-7).[30] Here the composer has divided the madrigal into two self-contained *partes*, the formal pattern so often chosen for the Latin motet upon whose contrapuntal language he draws. He opens each of them—as the text addresses its complaint to cruel "Care"—with a quasi-imitative contrapuntal passage in relatively protracted note values. This is characterized by an unremitting series of harmonic suspensions, mostly dissonant, and a plethora of expressive accidental inflections (cf. mm. 1–15 and 56–82). The deep sorrow implied by the verse is thus conveyed in the best tradition of the serious Italian madrigal by rhythmic, melodic, and harmonic elements, all adroitly combined.

30. The piece was included in his *Madrigals of 5 and 6 parts* of 1600, Nigel Davison, ed., *Neun englische Madrigale zu 5 und 6 Stimmen*, Das Chorwerk, vol. 132 (Wolfenbüttel: Moseler Verlag, 1983), 37–44; also Claude V. Palisca, ed., *Norton Anthology of Western Music*, 3d ed., 2 vols. (New York: Norton, 1996), 1:196–204.

EXAMPLE 20-7. Thomas Weelkes, *O Care, thou wilt despatch me* (mm. 1–12)

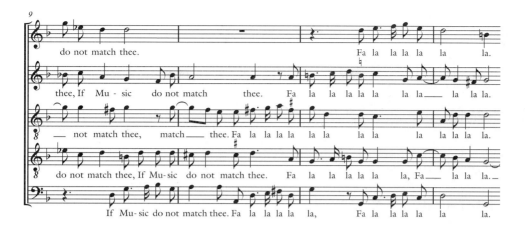

do not match thee. Fa la la la la la la.

thee, If Mu - sic do not match thee. Fa la la la la la la la la la la.

— not match thee, match — thee. Fa la la la la la la la la la la la la.

do not match thee, If Mu- sic do not match thee. Fa la la la la la la, Fa — la la la.

If Mu- sic do not match thee. Fa la la la la la, Fa la la la la la la.

Notwithstanding the weight and intensity generated by such compositional procedures, Morley's influence is to be detected in the "fa-la" passages that alternate with the slower-moving, chromatically inflected phrases. The nonsense syllables most certainly derived from the *ballett*, but Weelkes used them in this madrigal not only to generate form but also as an essential element of his expressive strategy. He achieved structural coherence in both *partes* by juxtaposing two slow sections (including those just described) with an animated strain of contrasting melodic and rhythmic motion, producing a kind of ABA'B' design in each half.

In addition, the passages of similar character are further related among themselves across the entire work by recurring motivic similarities in the melodic lines and the rhythmic patterns.[31] He used that same contrast in mood and musical material to serve his expressive purpose as well, emphasizing thereby the principal conceit of the poem: that only in music and mirth could the one speaking hope to find much-needed relief from the overwhelming grief he claims to feel.

Although much less adventuresome than Weelkes in his expressive use of accidental inflection, Wilbye, too, was more inclined than Morley to cultivate serious aspects of the Italian tradition in his settings of English verse. As may be seen in his *Stay, Corydon, thou swain*, for six voices, he maintains with some consistency a contrapuntal texture, frequently with syntactic imitation as an essential element of the structure (see Example 20-8).[32] For expressive purposes he makes use of a descending stepwise line in extended note values in the lowest-sounding voice (e.g., mm. 6–10), a device favored by Luca Marenzio. Wilbye is no stranger, either, to madri-

31. As Kerman has observed (*Elizabethan Madrigal*, 230), a formal pattern of contrasting sections in alternation—in this instance, specifically, A(slow)/B(fast)/A'(slow)/B'(fast), adopted for each of the *partes*—was used by Weelkes as a structural device in other madrigals as well.

32. The piece is from John Wilbye, *The Second Set of Madrigalists to 3, 4, 5, and 6 parts apt for Voyals and Voyces* (1609), vol. 7 of *The English Madrigalists*, ed. Edmund H. Fellowes, rev. Thurston Dart (London: Stainer and Bell, 1966), 214–23; it is also found in Claude V. Palisca, ed., *Norton Anthology of Western Music*, 2d. ed., 2 vols. (New York: Norton, 1980), 1:273–79.

EXAMPLE 20-8. John Wilbye, *Stay Corydon thou swain* (mm. 1–19)

galistic figures of a virtuosic nature. Instructive examples may be seen in the rapid melismatic passages used to illustrate such words as "flying" (mm. 34–36), "light" (mm. 47–55), "fly" (mm. 66–76), and "follow" (mm. 77–79). Morley's influence may be seen here too in the repeat of the final section, a formal device more regularly associated with the lighter secular genres than with the madrigal itself.

Representative in many ways of the English madrigal, its late flowering as a genre, its dependence on Italian models, its relatively small numbers, and its early eclipse by the indigenous lute song, was Morley's publication of 1601, *The Triumphes of Orianna*. It was based on one of the best-known and most widely circulated Italian anthologies, *Il Trionfo di Dori*, which was first published in 1592 and went through seven more editions. Commissioned by a Venetian patrician, Leonardo Sanudo, in honor of his bride, it consisted of twenty-nine settings, each by a different composer, of twenty-nine poems, each by a different author, all of which concluded with "Viva la bella Dori!" ("long live the beautiful Doris!"), the name having been chosen from mythology to represent the object of such extravagant adulation.[33]

The source of Morley's inspiration was apparently the madrigal written for this collection by Giovanni Croce, *Ove tra l'herbe e i fiori*, which had been included in the second set of Yonge's *Musica Transalpina* in 1597. There the recurring refrain had been translated "Then sang the shepherds and nymphs of Diana:/Long live fair Orianna!" Following the earlier model, Morley requested English poems—each of which was to conclude with this couplet—of some twenty-five different poets, many of whom modeled their verse on one of the original Italian madrigals. Individual composers were sought for the musical settings as well, with only Morley allowing himself the honor of two pieces in the collection, one for five voices and the other for six. The set was formally dedicated to Lord Howard of Effingham, who had commanded the fleet that had routed the Spanish Armada, but it was clearly intended to honor Queen Elizabeth, represented in the verse as the "fair Orianna," despite her apparent lack of enthusiasm for mythological word plays of that sort.[34]

Contributors to the music of the collection included some of the finest masters of the period—Weelkes and Wilbye, of course, among them—but others as well from whom no other example of the genre has survived. Although inevitably uneven in quality, given the limited number of competent composers experienced in madrigal composition upon whom Morley could call, it can be seen as a culmination for the entire development. Two years after *The Triumphs of Orianna* first appeared, Elizabeth I was dead, and the English madrigal was clearly in decline. It would be supplanted by the lute song, cultivated with consummate skill by composers like John Dowland, and the madrigal's traditional style would yield to that of a new era.

33. See Kerman, *Elizabethan Madrigal*, 194; Dori was the wife of the sea god Nereus, an appropriate figure for a Venetian celebration of the sort. For a study of the Italian collection and an edition of the music, see E. Harrison Powley, "Il trionfo di Dori: A Critical Edition," 3 vols. (Ph.D. diss., University of Rochester, Eastman School of Music, 1975) and *"Il trionfo di Dori": The 29 Madrigals of the 1592 Collection for Mixed Voices*, Renaissance Voices (New York: Gaudia Music and Arts, 1990).
34. Orianna was the beloved of the legendary knight errant, Amadis of Gaul—i.e., Wales.

CHAPTER 21

7

Music of the Protestant Reformation: Germany, Switzerland, France, Holland, and England

INTRODUCTION

As the history of the religious movements of the sixteenth century so clearly shows, the Protestant Reformation did not represent by any means a single unified movement. The focus of efforts to "correct" Catholic dogma or to reform religious practice differed from region to region in accordance with local circumstances. What is more, they were usually shaped by the particular views of one or more of the leading figures active there. The type and degree of changes sought depended as well on the political situation. Governments of church and state became inextricably intertwined in the course of the Middle Ages, and religious orthodoxy was often viewed by secular rulers—quite apart from their own religious convictions—as an important ingredient in maintaining the established social order.

Those magnates who dared to incur the wrath of Rome by sheltering dissidents and allowing them to promulgate their ideas had to have compelling reasons for doing so, whether personal or political. It was helpful as well to be far enough from spheres of temporal papal power and influence to be able to steer an independent course with relative impunity. Nowhere are the political dimensions of reform more evident than in the case of England's Henry VIII (1491–1547). But the approval and support of local rulers was no less indispensable in other areas where reformed communities began to flourish: the duchy of Saxe-Wittenberg, where Luther was able to freely profess his views; the Swiss canton of Zurich, where Zwingli made his influence felt; or the free canton of Geneva, where Calvin held sway.[1]

In matters of musical practice, as with questions of theological doctrine, the leaders of the reform movement did not necessarily agree on all points. Martin Luther

---

1. For a comprehensive treatment of the Protestant movements, see G. R. Elton, ed., *The Reformation, 1520–1559*, vol. 2 of *The New Cambridge Modern History* (Cambridge: Cambridge University Press, 1976).

(1483–1546), for example, who regarded music as "the excellent gift of God," did nothing to reduce its central role in the celebration of the liturgy. Instead, he stressed its importance in the training of the clergy and in the curricula of the Latin schools. He had a keen appreciation for polyphonic music, as well as plainchant and monophonic German hymns, and valued in particular the works of Josquin and of Ludwig Senfl.[2]

By contrast, Ulrich Zwingli (1484–1531), although apparently one of the most accomplished musically of all the major figures of the Reformation, concluded that the use of music for liturgical purposes could not be specifically justified by the scriptures. Ironically, then, because he found its powerful sensual effect a distraction to the worshiper—himself in particular—he banned music in the reformed churches under his direction and even had organs removed from buildings where they had been installed.[3]

John Calvin (1509–64) took a middle ground between the extremes of Luther and Zwingli, following the pattern established in Strasbourg by Martin Butzer (or Bucer, 1491–1551), with which he became familiar during a three-year sojourn in that city (1538–41). He found monophony acceptable for religious services, but only when sung in the current vernacular by the entire congregation.[4]

These divergent views produced predictably different results where the cultivation of music was concerned. In all three areas mentioned, and in Anglican England—where the reform was primarily a political matter at first—the musical practice followed its own course. Traditional compositional types—whether sacred or secular—were at first little affected by the Protestant movement. Most of them continued to enjoy at least some currency, even in areas significantly affected by the views of the reformers. Consequently, we shall not concern ourselves here with the impact of the Reformation on well-established musical genres. Instead, we shall give our attention to the birth and development of those that were due in large measure to the concepts of public worship and the attitudes toward music that were characteristic of Protestant communities.

POLYPHONIC *LEISEN*

In Lutheran Germany, where the underlying motivation for reform was essentially doctrinal, it is difficult in some respects to distinguish between musical styles and genres that were taken over by Protestant communities from earlier practice and those that were actually generated by the newly evolving patterns of worship. The

---

2. See Robin A. Weaver and Ann Bond, "Luther, Martin," *The New Grove Dictionary of Music*, 11:365–71.

3. See Robin A. Weaver, "Zwingli, Ulrich," *The New Grove Dictionary of Music*, 20:725–26; for a more detailed account, Charles Garside Jr., *Zwingli and the Arts* (New Haven: Yale University Press, 1966), chaps. 1–3.

4. See Albert Dunning, "Calvin [Cauvin], Jean," *The New Grove Dictionary of Music*, 3:630–32.

Latin Mass was at first only modified, with the elimination of the sacrifice and of saints' days (1523). However, a few years later (1526), Luther devised a *Deutsche Messe* especially for the use of congregations where neither the celebrant nor the members were well schooled in Latin.[5] Change was even slower in coming where polyphony was concerned. As we shall see, moreover, Lutheran tolerance for sacred polyphony, especially—but not exclusively—when written to texts in the German vernacular, made it possible for them to accept compositions deemed appropriate by musicians of any religious persuasion, whether Catholic or Reformed.

As has been observed, the *Leisen* had a long history behind them already in the fifteenth century (see pp. 462–67). However, perhaps because of the new emphasis given the use of vernacular for lay worship, new settings of the twelve traditional melodies continued to be written until late in the sixteenth century. Composers contributing to the repertory included not only those associated in some way with the Reformation but also masters whose activity unfolded primarily within the context of papal Catholicism as well.

Typical of the tolerant musical eclecticism of the period, for Lutheran communities at least, was the reception enjoyed by the music of Heinrich Finck (1444–45 to 1527) in the regions of northern Germany where that movement flourished. Although Finck spent most of his career in the service of Catholic courts, became a priest, and ended his life in a Viennese cloister, his hymns were published by the Protestant printer Georg Rhau in Wittenberg (in 1542), and his two *Leise* settings, *In Gottes Namen fahren wir* and *Christ ist erstanden*, were included in a collection of his German Lieder that was brought out by Formschneider in Nuremberg in 1536.[6]

Both of the latter compositions set the original text and rely upon the traditional melody as a structural cantus firmus. In his setting of *Christ ist erstanden*, in fact, both of the ancient tunes are an essential part of the five-voice texture (see Example 21-1).[7] The more common of the two makes its appearance in the tenor from the outset in even breves and semibreves and is echoed imitatively in the bassus, which is to become the second cantus firmus–bearing part. After a complete statement of the traditional melody, the customary *Kyrieleison* is extended in the other three voices by a repetition of the final two verses of the poem and the traditional acclamation.

The second melody (that associated with the textual variant "Christ, der ist erstanden") is introduced by tenor II, in an anticipatory imitation; it is presented in full, however, only by the bassus, once again in even breves and semibreves. The concluding *Kyrieleison* is extended in this instance as well by a repetition of the last two lines of the text, but this time the first melody returns with quotations alternating between tenor I and superius while the other three parts fill out the contrapuntal texture.

5. For details, see Lever and Bond, "Luther," *The New Grove Dictionary of Music*, 11:367.

6. The latter print was entitled *Schöne auserlesene Lieder des hochberühmten Heinrich Finckens*; see Lothar Hoffmann-Erbrecht, "Finck, Heinrich," *The New Grove Dictionary of Music*, 6:559–62.

7. For a transcription of the complete *Leise* in modern score, see Noah Greenberg and Paul Maynard, eds., *An Anthology of Early Renaissance Music* (New York: Norton, 1975), 140–46, and cf. the earlier anonymous settings above, Examples 13-1 and 2.

EXAMPLE 21-1. Heinrich Finck, *Christ ist erstanden* (mm. 27–62)

Christ has risen from all his torment, alleluia; therefore should we all rejoice, alleluia;
Christ should be our solace: Lord, have mercy.

Similar in many ways to the career of his older contemporary is that of Thomas Stoltzer (ca. 1480–85 to 1526). Like Finck, with whom he may have studied composition, Stoltzer became a priest and spent his mature years in the service of magnates who remained loyal to the Catholic cause, even though his sympathies apparently lay with the reformers.[8] Among his most sophisticated motets, significantly, are the four based on Luther's German translations of Psalms 12, 13, 37, and 86. His

8. See Lothar Hoffmann-Erbrecht, "Stolzer, Thomas," *The New Grove Dictionary of Music*, 18:170–72.

hymns were likewise appreciated in Lutheran circles. Rhau printed thirty-nine of them in a collection of 1542 and included, in addition, two *Leise* settings ascribed to Stoltzer in the collection of "spiritual songs" published in 1544 for use in the "common" schools.[9]

Interestingly, these two pieces are based on the same traditional melodies that were set by Finck, *In Gottes Namen fahren wir* and *Christ ist erstanden*. Unfortunately, the former was printed without its text, and the latter has a conflicting attribution to Heinrich Isaac.[10] They are similar enough in their use of the preexistent tune and in their musical style, however, that they could certainly have been the work of a single composer. Both begin with a point of imitation based on the ancient melody, after which the cantus firmus is carried primarily by an inner voice, the altus (a fifth above the original pitch) for *In Gottes Namen* and the tenor for *Christ ist erstanden*. There is in both, in addition, considerable imitation of the *Leise* tune—some of it anticipatory—in the other parts. The imitative writing is particularly pervasive for the final two verses of the latter work, where the borrowed melody is moved from voice to voice until all four have sung it, either at pitch or at the upper fifth.[11]

❧ HYMNS AND CHORALES ❧

When the Reformation began to take hold in German-speaking regions, there was already a long history of hymns sung in the vernacular. These included not only the *Leisen* (narrowly defined, as in the preceding discussion) but also Latin hymns in German translation and strophic Lieder of pious content and devotional intent. Understandably, these became increasingly important as the notion of congregational participation in the service gained wider currency and the vernacular hymns were actually given a place in the regular celebration of the liturgy. In addition, Luther and those associated with him saw congregational singing as a means of uniting the faithful in a meaningful response to the readings from the scriptures and the pastoral sermon (see Figure 21-1). As a result, they themselves actively contributed to the formation of an appropriate repertory, first with pieces fashioned specifically for a given place in the liturgy, later with those having a more loosely devotional function.

In either case the texts were often based, naturally enough, on the Psalms, and the melodies provided for their public recitation were drawn or adapted from a vari-

9. See Johannes Wolf, ed., *Newe deudsche geistliche Gesenge* (Wittenberg, 1544), Denkmäler deutscher Tonkunst, 1. Folge, vol. 34 (Leipzig: Breitkopf und Härtel, 1908); for the *Leisen*, see pp. 26 and 140.

10. Because it is given to Isaac in two manuscript sources, *Christ ist erstanden* is listed by Hoffmann-Erbrecht among the "doubtful works" in "Stolzer," *The New Grove Dictionary of Music*, 18:172.

11. *Christ ist erstanden* is readily accessible in Archibald T. Davison and Willi Apel, eds., *Historical Anthology of Music*, 2 vols. (Cambridge, Mass.: Harvard University Press, 1962), 1:112–13, no. 108 (where it is credited to Stoltzer).

ety of sources, sacred and secular. To have their full effect in communal worship, such compositions were to be sung in unison—*choraliter*—by the assembled faithful.[12] Consequently, pieces of this type are generally known as "chorales," but their strophic character both as verse and as music places them clearly in the traditional realm of hymn composition. Because of their intended function, they were monophonic at the start (like the Latin hymns upon which so many of them were modeled), but they lent themselves to the same kind of polyphonic elaboration as German Lieder and came to be similarly treated very early on.

Mention has already been made of the important contribution of Georg Rhau (b. 1488) in providing music for the Lutheran reform, including the several collections of hymns he published between 1538 and his death a decade later. Music was not, of course, the only material to come from Rhau's presses during his years as a printer in Wittenberg. Beginning in 1523, when he returned to the city where he had been

FIGURE 21-1. Portrait of Martin Luther by Lucas Cranach, 1520 (Uffizi, Florence).

a student at the university, he published books and treatises on theology, the biblical exegesis of the major figures of the German Reformation—Melanchthon, Bugenhagen, and of course Luther himself—as well as the Catechism and the sermons of the leader of the movement. By contrast, his publication of music reflected not only the growing needs of Lutheran congregations and schools at the time but also his own inclinations and competencies. He had been trained well enough in music to assume the post as cantor of the Thomaskirche and Thomasschule in Leipzig from 1518 to 1520—the same as was filled some two centuries later by J. S. Bach—and was himself author of treatises on both plainchant and mensural music.[13]

Surprisingly, perhaps, the majority of his publications in music retained the Latin texts of the medieval liturgy. Included were collections of polyphony for the Ordi-

---

12. See Leaver and Bond, "Luther," *The New Grove Dictionary of Music*, 11:365–68; cf. Robert L. Marshall, "Chorale," *The New Grove Dictionary of Music*, 4:312–16.
13. See Victor H. Mattfeld, "Rhau, Georg," *The New Grove Dictionary of Music*, 15:787–89.

nary of the Mass, the Ordinary and the Propers for the major feasts of the *temporale*, and motets for Lent and Passiontide. Other publications provided music for Vespers— complete settings for all of the texts to be sung by the choir for each day of the week, some 134 Vesper hymns, and 25 polyphonic Magnificats. For the Latin schools there were, in addition, anthologies of secular *bicinia* and *tricinia* intended for didactic as well as recreational purposes, and collections of devotional motets. It was only in the last volume of music to issue from his presses, the *Newe deudsche geistliche Gesenge* of 1544, that he gathered polyphonic settings of the strophic chorales appropriate for both congregational services and musical exercises in the schools.[14]

The latter was essentially an expanded edition of the *Geystliche Gesangk Buchleyn* published in 1524 under the name of Luther's friend and advisor for music, the composer Johann Walter (1496–1570). That first printing of Walter's compositions consisted of only forty-three works for three, four, and five voices, thirty-eight of them on texts in the vernacular and another five using Latin. Prior to Rhau's expansion of this collection some forty years later there were three further editions—in 1525, 1535, and 1537—each time with changes and new additions to the repertory. Such a substantial series of reprintings is perhaps evidence enough of the affection in which these compositions were held and the frequency with which they were to be heard both in the schools and in church services. Equally compelling, however, as an indication of their wide acceptance and popularity in Protestant communities is the frequency with which many of them were taken up in yet other collections of sacred polyphonic music based on the Lutheran chorale.[15]

With Rhau's *Newe deudsche geistliche Gesenge* of 1544 the repertory swelled to 123 compositions, 86 on German texts (63 of them chorale settings) and 37 using Latin. Added to the nucleus of works attributable to Walter are those of a dozen other composers, including several who were attached to Catholic courts and/or chapels.[16] Even the most cursory survey of this repertory immediately reveals how closely it is related to that of the secular *Tenorlied*. Common to virtually all of these chorale settings, including those of the younger masters, are characteristics already found for the most part in Walter's original collection of 1524.

In nearly every case the starting point was the melody (as well as the text) of the vernacular hymn, quoted usually in the tenor part (though occasionally in the superius as well) and most often in relatively extended and regular note values. Individual pieces differ from one another primarily in the extent to which the cantus firmus is set off in the polyphonic texture by the relatively greater activity of the added voices and by the extent to which they incorporate such compositional subtleties as the canonic doubling of the preexistent melody or syntactic imitation among the parts.

Typical in many respects of the polyphonic treatment given the chorale in collec-

14. Rhau's music prints, both theoretical and practical, have been listed (by year of publication) by Matt-feld, *The New Grove Dictionary of Music*, 15:788f.

15. Concerning Walter, see Werner Braun, *The New Grove Dictionary of Music*, 20:188–89.

16. Concerning these masters and their contributions to the collection, see Gustave Reese, *Music in the Renaissance* (New York: Norton, 1959), 678–82.

tions such as this is a four-part setting by Walter of *Ein feste Burg ist unser Gott.* It is one of two that he based on Luther's verse translation of Psalm 46,[17] sung to a melody that can perhaps be ascribed to the reformer as well (see Example 21-2).[18] As was customary, the chorale was given to the tenor, where it is laid out—cantus firmus style—in longer values (mostly in semibreves and minims). A brief melismatic ornament at the beginning of the second section is the only departure in that voice from regular rhythms and a steady syllabic declamation of the poetic text. In an opening gesture all

17. This Psalm, *Deus noster refugium* in the Latin Bible, has been Englished as "God is our refuge and strength" in the King James Version and the chorale as *A mighty fortress is our God* in the Lutheran hymnal.

18. For a transcription of Walter's chorale settings in modern score, see Johann Walter, *Sämtliche Werke,* ed. Otto Schröder, 6 vols. (Kassel: Bärenreiter, 1953–73), vol. 1; settings of *Ein feste Burg* are nos. 21 and 22, pp. 26–27.

EXAMPLE 21-2. Johann Walter, *Ein feste Burg ist unser Gott*

A mighty fortress is our God, a good defense and weapon. He helps us free from every difficulty that we now face. The old wicked enemy he now means to fight; great power and much cunning are his terrible preparation. On earth there is nothing like Him. (Additional strophes.)

four voices begin together and—for the first three syllables, at least—move homophonically. Otherwise, the parts above and below unfold more freely and quickly than the tenor melody (in minims and semiminims for the most part). In the process, obviously, they treat the text in a markedly more melismatic style.

In other chorale settings by Walter a homophonic texture is maintained with considerably greater consistency, his second version of *Ein feste Burg* being in fact a case in point.[19] Still, whatever the compositional and stylistic details, all of these compositions reveal to a greater or lesser degree the appealing combination of a familiar melody in a texture of substantial contrapuntal interest. At the same time, technical complications that would make them unduly difficult to perform by the student choirs (in both church and school) for which they were intended are largely avoided. It is not difficult to understand why these simple yet sophisticated compositions came to be so well loved and to circulate so widely within the German-speaking Protestant communities of the sixteenth century.

∽ Vernacular Psalm Settings ∾

John Calvin (1509–64) had neither Luther's musical sensibilities nor Zwingli's performing skills (see Figure 21-2). However, as a humanist scholar he was familiar with the belief of the ancient Greeks in music's powers to move human affections, and he accepted as well the notion that its origins were divine. He rejected instrumental music, however, because of its Old Testament connections. Nor would he countenance the use of polyphony in public worship because it made more difficult a clear perception of the text. He insisted that all elements of the service be drawn from Holy Writ, including the congregational singing, and that the texts be recited in the vernacular, once again for easy comprehension.[20] The practical result of these views was to restrict music for worship to the Psalms and a few canticles. All of them were translated into French for use in the reformed churches of French-speaking Geneva. And they were set syllabically to relatively simple melodies that could be sung in unison by the assembled faithful.

The Psalm texts were given verse translations, presumably to make them more memorable for the lay congregations. Calvin himself participated initially in the task, providing French poetry for the canticle of Simeon (*Nunc dimittis*), the Credo, and six Psalms. He subsequently had the assistance of the gifted poet Clément Marot (1497–1544), who published fifty Psalms in French verse in 1543, and of the scholar-theologian Théodore de Bèze (1519–1605), who completed the translation of the Psalter and first published all 150 poems in 1562.[21]

---

19. See Walter's *Sämtliche Werke*, ed. Schröder, 1:27, no. 22.
20. See Albert Dunning, "Calvin," *The New Grove Dictionary of Music*, 3:630–32.
21. Marot's contribution to the chanson verse of the sixteenth century was mentioned earlier (see pp. 618–23); concerning these two poets see, in addition, Frank Dobbins, "Marot, Clément," *The New Grove Dictionary of Music*, 11:695–96; and Paul-André Gaillard, "Bèze, Théodore," *New Grove Dictionary of Music*, 2:669.

FIGURE 21-2. Portrait of Jean Calvin (Paris, Bibliothèque Nationale).

The melodies used to sing the vernacular Psalms were adapted from a variety of sources. A number were borrowed from Latin hymns and sequences; some 13 were derived from German Psalm settings that were in use in the reformed churches of Strasbourg; and another 32 or so appear to have connections with secular song. For an intermediary edition of the Psalter, published in 1551, that brought together a total of 83 Psalms (in the translations of Marot and Bèze), the composer-theorist Loys Bourgeois (ca. 1510–15 to ca. 1560) compiled a collection of such melodies, of which there were in all 85. Bourgeois claims to have composed 34 of these (specifically for the Psalms translated by Bèze) and to have rewritten or revised another 36, leaving only 15 that he presumably took over more or less unchanged from earlier sources.[22]

When the completed Psalter was published in 1562, more than a decade later, another 40 tunes were added, making 125 in all (including, presumably, the 85 previously provided by Bourgeois), but some of these had to be used for more than one text in order to accommodate all 150 Psalms of the collection.[23]

Although polyphony was not used for public worship, it was acceptable for the training and edification of the students in Geneva's academy (see pp. 144–46) as well as for the honest recreation of musically literate burghers. Not surprisingly, then, the monophonic Psalm tunes began to be set in parts virtually as soon as they came into circulation. As early as 1546 Pierre Attaingnant brought out two collections of Psalms in the French vernacular in polyphonic settings for four voices.

The first of these included thirty-one compositions attributable to Pierre Certon (d. 1572), who was then master of the choirboys at the Sainte-Chapelle in Paris—interestingly enough a decidedly Catholic institution.[24] The second brought another seventeen Psalms and, in addition, a variety of other liturgical and devotional texts

22. Regarding Bourgeois, see Frank Dobbins, *The New Grove Dictionary of Music*, 3:111–13.
23. For a systematic catalogue of the Psalm melodies and their sources (where known), see Pierre Pidoux, *Le psautier huguenot du xvᵉ siècle: Mélodies et documents*, 2 vols. (Basel: Bärenreiter, 1962).
24. See Aimé Agnel, "Certon, Pierre," *The New Grove Dictionary of Music*, 4:80–82.

translated into French. In this collection the composer named is Antoine de Mornable (fl. 1530–53), who had himself been a choirboy at the Sainte-Chapelle before entering the service of Count Guy de Laval, a Protestant sympathizer.[25] (Unfortunately, both collections have apparently been lost, in whole or in part.)[26] The following year saw a collection of fifty Psalms by Bourgeois himself (*Pseaulmes cinquante de David*; Lyons, 1547), written in a strictly homophonic style with the given melody in the tenor, and of another twenty-four (*Le premier livre de pseaulmes . . . en diversité de musique*) that were mostly in the more contrapuntal manner of the motet.[27]

The most impressive musical monument to have been raised to the verse translations of the Psalms into French was the work of Claude Goudimel (ca. 1514–20 to 1572). A sympathizer of the reform associated with the Protestant community in Metz in the late 1550s, Goudimel died in Lyon, a victim of the St. Bartholomew Day's massacre.[28] Between 1551 (when the edition of eighty-three Psalms, with the eighty-five melodies compiled by Bourgeois, was first printed) and 1566 he published eight books of polyphonic settings of Psalms in the French vernacular as translated by Marot and Bèze. These comprise a total of sixty-seven compositions for from three to six voices, all of them in a contrapuntal motet style.[29]

Typical of these works in every respect is his setting of Psalm 46, *Des qu'adversité nous offense* (*Deus noster refugium*) from the *Second Livre de Psalmes. . . en forme de Motetz* of 1559 (see Example 21-3).[30] As comparison with Walter's modest strophic treatment of *Ein feste Burg*—the same Psalm in Luther's German translation—dramatically demonstrates, Goudimel's compositional conception was much more elaborate. Moreover, it derived directly from that of the polyphonic Latin motet rather than from any identifiable genre of secular song, as the title of his collection clearly indicates.

The eleven octosyllabic quatrains that constitute Marot's translation of the Psalm have been divided, as was customary for a lengthy motet text, into three *parties*: four strophes for the first, two for the second, and five for the third. Within this framework the French text has been through-composed (à 4 in the first and third *parties*, à 3 in the second) with new melodic material for each new stanza of the poem. As

25. See Frank Dobbins, "Mornable, Antoine," *The New Grove Dictionary of Music*, 12:585–86.
26. See Daniel Heartz, *Pierre Attaingnant, Royal Printer of Music* (Berkeley: University of California Press, 1969), 346–49.
27. Cf. Dobbins, "Bourgeois," *The New Grove Dictionary of Music*, 3:111–13.
28. See Paul-André Gaillard, "Goudimel, Claude," *The New Grove Dictionary of Music*, 7:578–79.
29. For a succinct survey of Goudimel's Psalm composition with pertinent comments as to the musical styles displayed in all ten of the collections published under his name (see below), see Eleanor Lawry, "Some Observations on Goudimel's Psalm Settings," in *Libraries, History, Diplomacy, and the Performing Arts: Essays in Honor of Carleton Sprague Smith*, ed. Israel J. Katz, Malena Kuss, and Richard J. Wolfe (Stuyvesant, N.Y.: Pendragon Press, 1991), 337–47.
30. The claim on the title page that the "second book" was "nouvellement reveu et corrige" suggests that there may have been an earlier printing; for a complete transcription in modern score, see Goudimel's *Oeuvres complètes*, ed. Henri Gagnebin, Rudolf Häusler, and Eleanor Lawry, 10 vols. Gesamtausgaben 3 (Brooklyn: Institute of Mediaeval Music, 1967–83), 2:44–59.

EXAMPLE 21-3. Claude Goudimel, *Des qu'adversité nous offense*, Psalm 46 (mm. 53–78)

Be still, and know of my great power. I am God and will be exalted in every land and nation. Conclusion: The Lord of hosts is with us in every danger . . .

expected, there is an internal cadence to signal the end of each strophe within the larger sections, but it does not interrupt noticeably the continuous texture of inter-locking contrapuntal phrases until the very last (mm. 69–70).

Individual verses within a quatrain are not usually separated from one another by similarly articulated cadential figures, yet each appears to generate its own melodic phrase. The introduction of a new line of text is often marked by a point of imitation, but homophonic passages are used as well, as for the second verse of the initial strophe and, more emphatically still, at the very end for the beginning of the eleventh. And even though the textual declamation is largely syllabic, as in the mono-phonic version, with only an occasional melismatic extension of a syllable or two within the line, there is no readily discernible reference to any of the melodies that appear to have been associated with Marot's text.[31]

31. For the tunes known to have been associated with this particular Psalm, see Pidoux, *Le psautier huguenot du xvi* siècle, 1:55–57; however, other settings, from the *Second livre* on, do make reference with increasing frequency to the monophonic melodies provided for communal singing of the vernacular Psalms; see Lawry, "Some Observations on Goudimel's Psalm Settings," 338.

Goudimel never completed the heroic task of setting the entire French Psalter in this elegant and sophisticated style; in fact he may never have had the intention of doing so. However, he subsequently composed two complete series of polyphonic settings for all 150 Psalms, perhaps as a consequence of his conversion to the doctrine of the reform around 1560. The first of these, published in 1564 (and reprinted in 1565) under the title *Les sent cinquante Pseaumes de David*, is in a strictly syllabic and severely homophonic style; even final cadences evoke only the slightest of rhythmic and harmonic embellishments.

Typical of the polyphonic compositions in this publication is the version it brings of Psalm 130, *Du fons de ma pensee* (see Example 21-4).[32] The polyphony is based upon an entirely literal quotation—soberly confined to semibreves and minims—of the monophonic melody of the Genevan Psalter. In this piece, as in all but 17 of the

32. In Latin the Psalm begins "De profundis clamavi"; in the King James translation, "Out of the depths have I cried unto thee, O Lord." For a complete transcription, see Goudimel's *Oeuvres complètes*, ed. Gagnebin, Häusler, and Lawry, 9:132.

EXAMPLE 21-4. Claude Goudimel, *Du fons de ma pensee*, Psalm 130

From the depths of my consciousness, in the depths of all difficulties, to thee have I
addressed my plea day and night. Hear my plaintive voice, Lord, it is time; let thine
ear be attentive to my prayer. (Three additional strophes.)

150 Psalms included in the collection, it is carried by the tenor. (In the remaining
cases it is given to the superius.) The eight verses that make up the initial strophe are
systematically separated by rests and, with only two possible exceptions (ll. 2 and 6)
are also articulated by contrapuntal cadences of varying degrees of finality. Implicit
in such a setting as well, obviously, is the repetition of the music for any additional
strophes that were to be sung.

Although much more severe in its syllabic homophony than Lutheran chorale settings such as Walter's *Ein feste Burg*, it is clearly in the same tradition. There is no
trace here of a "motet" style. Virtually as distant as well are the compositional procedures that were being adopted at the time for polyphonic settings of the Vesper
Psalms in Latin for the liturgy of the Roman church by composers such as Adrian
Willaert. (See above, for example, Willaert's treatment of the same Psalm, *De profundis clamavi*, for alternating choirs, pp. 556–60.)

Also strophic in conception, although markedly less ascetic in their musical means, are the settings of the Psalms included in Goudimel's collection of 1568 (reprinted in 1580), which comprised, once again, all 150 items included in the Psalter. The version of Psalm 130 from this publication, also entitled *Les sent cinquante Pseaumes de David*, will illustrate both the similarities and the striking differences with the more austere works of the earlier series (see Example 21-5).[33] The declamation is still essentially syllabic in all four parts, and the familiar melody is invariably present, often in the superius, as in the present instance. Here the Psalm tune is quoted exactly as it was in the earlier, strictly homophonic version, using not only the same pitches—transposed, of course, to the upper octave—but also identical rhythmic values. By contrast, the texture in the works of the later collection is, comparatively speaking, richly contrapuntal; the composer has made consistent use of imitative figures, and the cadential articulations between successive verses are

33. For a transcription of the complete Psalm in modern score, see Goudimel's *Oeuvres complètes*, ed. Gagnebin, Häusler, and Lawry, 10:132–33.

EXAMPLE 21-5. Claude Goudimel, *Du fons de ma pensee* (mm. 1–13)

For English translation of text, see Example 21-4.

attenuated, as in motetlike settings such as *Des qu'adversité*, by the continuous over-lapping of the phrases.

In the Netherlands the singing of Psalms in the vernacular cannot be so clearly linked with the Reformation as in Lutheran Germany or Calvinist Geneva. This is because the movement was largely suppressed in the region by the Spanish Habsburgs, who held sway there into the 1560s. Nonetheless, it was clearly under the influence of the popular religious currents emanating from nearby Wittenberg that a verse translation of the Psalter into Dutch was completed, presumably by a nobleman from Utrecht, Willem van Nievelt. These texts were published by Simon Cock of Antwerp already in 1540, and they quickly achieved and long maintained considerable currency—some thirty editions of the work were published overall. This may have been due in no small measure to the fact that the vernacular Psalms were meant from the outset to be sung. Provided with tunes adapted from well-known songs (most of them with texts in Flemish, but also in Latin, German, and French), they were quickly known as *souterliedekens*, literally "Psalter songs."[34]

The extraordinary popularity of these monophonic Psalm tunes may have prompted the composer and music printer Tylman Susato (ca. 1500 to 1561–64), who also worked in Antwerp,[35] to commission Clemens (non Papa) (ca. 1510–15 to 1555–56) to set them polyphonically in three parts. (Clemens, who was well known in the region, had been succentor at the cathedral in Bruges in 1544–45 and had served at the Marian confraternity in 's-Hertogenbosch for a few months in 1550.) The results of Clemens's—and Susato's—labors were included as volumes 4, 5, 6,

34. See the foreword to Jacobus Clemens (non Papa), *Opera omnia*, ed. K. Ph. Bernet Kempers, 21 vols., Corpus mensurabilis musicae 4 ([Rome]: American Institute of Musicology, 1951–76), 2:i–ii.
35. Concerning Susato, see Susan Bain, *The New Grove Dictionary of Music*, 18:378–79.

and 7 in a series of publications of secular music for household use that Susato began to publish in 1551 under the title *Musyck boexken* (music booklets).[36]

Typical of the pieces in these collections is the setting for Psalm 129, *Die Heer van hemel riep ick aen* (Psalm 130 in the Latin and French Psalters), the verse translation into Flemish of (once again) *De profundis clamavi* (see Example 21-6).[37] As in all the pieces of the collection, the part bearing the preexistent tune (here the middle voice) is labeled tenor, even when it is the highest of the three and in the cantus range. The borrowed melody—the original source of which was indicated, as here, in the Susato print whenever known—appears to have been derived from a vernacular song in praise of the Virgin, *Dy vrou van hemel roep ick aen*. In barform (that is, with the initial section repeated to accommodate the second pair of verses whose rhymes repeat those of the first), the melody maintains a verse-by-verse disposition of its successive phrases. Carried over to the new text as well is the presumably syllabic relationship to its original words, which is matched in the other two voices. The

36. Clemens's whereabouts in the final years of his life have not been documented; that he died in 1555 or 1556 is indicated by the fact that the last of the vernacular Psalm settings in the *Musyck Boexhen* in the latter year were actually composed by Susato himself. See Willem Elder, *The New Grove Dictionary of Music*, 4:476–80.
37. For a complete transcription in modern score, see Clemens (non Papa), *Opera omnia*, ed. K. Ph. Bernet Kempers, 2:104–5.

EXAMPLE 21-6. Clemens (non Papa), *Die Heer una hemel riep ick aen* (mm. 10–26)

Lord, hear my voice; let thine ears be attentive to the voice of my supplications. (Additional strophes.)

structure is thus clearly articulated, even though the fundamentally homophonic character of the compositional texture has been enlivened by a fair amount of independent contrapuntal movement.

Adding to the modest esthetic interest of the piece is the insertion of a ternary rhythm into the binary measure of diminished imperfect tempus at the end of three of the melodic phrases (mm. 5, 18, and 22). Clearly, however, the artistic aspirations of the composer were circumscribed in a repertory of this kind by the function for which it was intended: to provide polyphonic settings of unexceptionable texts—those of the Psalter—that could figure in the devotions and honest recreations of affluent townspeople whose musical skills also had their limits.

THE REFORM IN ENGLAND: ANTHEMS AND PSALM SETTINGS

As we have seen, the indigenous traditions that shaped the motet as a genre in England can be traced back to the early years of the fifteenth century. Moreover, if one is to judge from the selection of compositions included in the "Eton Choirbook," there is very little direct evidence of Continental influence in the English repertory from around the turn to the sixteenth century. It appears highly likely, therefore, that the cultivation of the genre was continuous cross-channel all through the period in question and that the direction of its stylistic development there was unbroken.

Unfortunately, however, our knowledge of the English sacred music of this period is unusually sketchy. Even the music of the best-known—and most skillful—composers of the period, Robert Fayrfax (1464–1521), William Cornysh (d. 1523), and John Taverner (ca. 1490–1545) has been preserved in surprisingly small quantities, suggesting that a great deal of it must have been lost. Fayrfax is represented in surviving sources by only six Masses, two Magnificats, and ten antiphon motets, while another six sacred works are known to have been lost.[38] Cornysh can be credited with only one Magnificat and five motets while four other sacred pieces and some Masses mentioned by inventories of lost sources are no longer to be found.[39] And Taverner, whose works appear to have been better preserved, is still known for only eight Masses, a few unrelated Ordinary settings, three Magnificats, a Te Deum, and some twenty-four motets.[40]

Not all of these compositions are complete, moreover, despite the fact that both Fayrfax and Cornysh were singers in the king's chapel, and that Taverner—perhaps the most respected composer of his generation—was associated for four years (from 1526 until 1530) with the magnificent musical establishment at Cardinal Thomas Wolsey's newly founded college at Christ Church, Oxford, and otherwise served in the most distinguished institutions of his native Lincolnshire.

The lack of musical sources from this period is of course to be explained in large part by the upheavals in the religious institutions that ensued upon Henry VIII's rejection of the ecclesiastical authority of the papacy, a course of action that brought about profound changes in the relationship between the state and the English church—and within the church itself. The difficulties began with his obsessive attempts to produce a male heir to the throne and thus assure the rule of the Tudor dynasty for at least one more generation. By the time he began to press the pope for a divorce from Catherine of Aragon in 1527, he had already learned from his able counselor, Thomas Wolsey—cardinal legate, archbishop of York, and royal chancellor—that the church could be subjected to the temporal power of the crown and its wealth confiscated, thus enriching the king's coffers in the process.

When the divorce proceedings were removed to the papal court in Rome, Henry gave vent to his personal irritation by moving first against Wolsey himself, whom he removed from office and had prosecuted under a statute that made it unlawful to appeal to Rome a case within the jurisdiction of the royal courts. He then fined the English clergy for having allowed Wolsey to act as he did, thus sharing in his offense. Further, in his attempt to pressure the papal curia into granting him the desired divorce, he stopped all payments to Rome from the ecclesiastical institutions in his realm.

The crucial consequences of such maneuvers for the English church followed shortly thereafter. First came the Submission of the Clergy in 1532, by which leading churchmen of the land were compelled to recognize the authority of the king and the necessity of his approval for any ecclesiastical legislation. This was followed in 1534 by the adoption of the Act of Supremacy, which declared the king to be "the only supreme head on earth of the Church of England"—and earned Henry a papal excommunication in the bargain. Two years later began the dissolution of the monastic houses, whose vast holdings were confiscated by the crown and whose control of eight cathedral churches was thus abolished.[41]

---

38. See Nicholas Sandon, "Fayrfax, Robert," *The New Grove Dictionary of Music*, 6:443–45.
39. See David Greer, "William Cornysh," *The New Grove Dictionary of Music*, 4:795–96.
40. See Roger Bowers and Paul Doe, "Taverner, John," *The New Grove Dictionary of Music*, 18:598–602.
41. See Jack Westrup, "England," *The New Grove Dictionary of Music*, 6:172.

Although the break with Rome was initially a matter of political expediency rather than of doctrine or religious practice, from that moment on the die was cast; England was on its way to becoming one of the major strongholds for the Reformation of the sixteenth century. Changes in doctrine and in the modes of communal worship came more slowly, most of them during the brief reign of Henry's minor son, Edward VI. Edward came to the throne in 1547 at the age of nine, and he died in 1553 before he came of age. As he was never able to take the reins of government in his own hands, however, the religious leaders of the reform found the circumstances unusually propitious for the enactment of more fundamental changes in the English church.

After Edward's death the throne was claimed by Mary I (Tudor), Henry's surviving daughter by Catherine of Aragon, who had followed her mother's example in remaining steadfastly Catholic. As expected, she attempted to undo the effects of the reform in England and to return the country fully to communion with the Roman church. If she failed ultimately in her purpose—despite a vigorous inquisition that saw as many as 300 Protestants burned for their beliefs—it was only in part because of the resentment caused by methods more severe than those to which the English were accustomed.

A related but more telling cause of dissatisfaction was her marriage to Philip II of Spain (Emperor Charles V's son and heir) and England's consequent political alignment with that country and with the empire. That led Mary to join her husband in 1557 in a war against France. The result was the loss of Calais, England's last remaining foothold on the Continent, with no discernible advantage. When Mary died in the following year, childless and disheartened, both her domestic and her foreign policy had been thoroughly discredited.

Mary was replaced on the throne by her half-sister Elizabeth, the daughter of Anne Boleyn, who was to rule England for nearly half a century. Elizabeth I inherited a realm that had weathered the conflicts between protagonists of the Protestant Reformation and the Catholic church. Confrontation in that arena had been painful, to be sure, but brought relatively little internal stress compared with the political and social upheavals it caused in France, the Netherlands, and some parts of the empire. This had been possible, at least in part, because of the strong centralized monarchy established by the first Tudor kings. Also positive in its effect was the continuous involvement in important matters of state by an increasingly powerful Parliament. By the time Elizabeth began to rule, however, the sympathies of the majority of her subjects had clearly been won for the reform. It was perhaps largely in response to popular preference, then, that she acted at the very outset of her reign to return the English church to the circumstances under which it had begun to function before Mary Tudor came to power.

Although her realm was relatively secure, there were problems and alarms as well. Catholic loyalists, fired in part by Elizabeth's papal excommunication in 1570, plotted to depose her in favor of Mary, Queen of Scots. Such conspiracies were hatched more or less continuously during the eighteen years that the Stuart monarch languished as an exile in royal custody. Only Mary's execution in 1587 in connection with one such attempt put an end to the threat she represented. English aid to rebellious Protestants in the Netherlands also led to deteriorating relations with Spain, culminating in 1588 with the decisive sea battle between the queen's fleet and the formidable Spanish Armada. Remarkably, Elizabeth emerged triumphant from all of those contests. Her kingdom prospered, acquiring wealth and power as a seafaring nation—through bold exploration, expanding trade, and even aggressive privateering—well beyond what might have been expected from a country of such modest size and human population. The way was thus opened for an unprecedented development in the arts, including that of music.[42]

Significant religious reform was begun during the minority of Edward VI under the leadership of Thomas Cranmer (1489–1556). English began to replace Latin for liturgical use in 1549, under the terms of the First Act of Uniformity,[43] and a new order for the services was prescribed in some detail by *The Booke of Common Prayer* (also of 1549). As with the Lutherans in Germany, the new liturgy was very close to the Catholic rite (and so it has remained). Polyphony continued to be employed, as it had been previously, for the Communion Service, as the Mass was to be known, and at the end of the two Offices in which the laity had always participated to some degree, Matins and Evensong, as Vespers came to be called.[44]

The new Communion Service was sufficiently similar to the Latin Mass that music originally written for the Ordinary could be adapted to the corresponding English texts, as in fact happened with two of Taverner's Masses.[45] It was equally possible to convert for use in the Anglican service compositions written for other purposes, either by translating and adjusting the texts of Latin motets into the vernacular or by replacing the original words with English *contrafacta*. This was done not only with motets but also with yet other types of pieces, and this process was also applied to several of Taverner's compositions. Two of his Latin motets were Englished in the manner described, and two different texts were set to the "In nomine" section of his *Missa Gloria tibi Trinitas*, which had begun to circulate in textless transcription as an instrumental piece.[46]

Similar adaptations were made with the music of other composers as well, including those of the next generation. By then, however, English texts appropriate for use at Communion or one of the Offices were being taken for polyphonic composition from sources of the kind most often used for such purposes by Protestant communities everywhere: the new English Bible, primers for reading, metrical translations

42. For additional detail concerning pertinent political and social developments in England during the fifteenth and sixteenth centuries, see Wallace K. Ferguson, *Europe in Transition* (Boston: Houghton Mifflin Co., 1962), 190–206 and 470–76.

43. See Peter Le Huray, "Anthem," *The New Grove Dictionary of Music*, 1:454.

44. For a detailed study of the impact of the Reformation upon musical practice in England, see Peter Le Huray, *Music and the Reformation in England, 1549–1660* (London: Oxford University Press, 1967).

45. See Roger Bowers, "Taverner," *The New Grove Dictionary of Music*, 18:602.

46. Concerning the instrumental "In nomine," see pp. 799–806.

of the Psalms, and the *Booke of Common Prayer*. In some instances music for liturgical use was conceived and organized directly as a "Service"—consisting, for example, of the Ordinary items for Communion or the canticles for Matins or Evensong.[47] Other compositions were written individually, especially as a substitute for the antiphon motet at the close of Compline.

Not surprisingly, in view of the significant liturgical and devotional role given to the Psalter translated into vernacular verse in Protestant communities everywhere, Psalms in metrical English verse began to circulate already during the reign of Henry VIII. It was not until 1562, however, that John Day published the first collection to include poetic versions of all 150 Psalms in the vernacular, the majority of them Englished by either Thomas Sternhold, a poet who had been in the service of the royal household in Henry's time, or a certain John Hopkins.

In that and subsequent editions of Day's complete English Psalter forty-eight melodies were also provided, making it possible to sing monophonically any of its 150 Psalms. Each tune was printed with the first strophe of a metrical Psalm laid beneath the notes, and for those texts for which no separate setting was given, there were references to melodies elsewhere in the collection to which they could be most readily adapted. Many of these melodies had been borrowed from the Geneva Psalter published by Bourgeois; others were taken from the Lutheran tradition; and a few were also of English origin.[48]

When the metrical Psalm texts began to be set polyphonically, a variety of compositional styles were used. Some of the earliest examples reverted to the Psalm tones of the Latin liturgy set in a simple homophonic style derived from the same sort of improvised *faburden* that had long been used to embellish the Psalmody of the Roman liturgy. Similar in compositional style but indebted instead to the strictly syllabic and homophonic manner adopted earlier by Continental musicians such as Bourgeois and Goudimel were four-part settings of the melodies associated in Day's Psalter with the metrical translations of Sternhold and Hopkins. As early as 1563 Day himself brought out a collection of some 141 such pieces, most of them with the pre-existent tune given to the tenor, as in Goudimel's severely homophonic settings, and the remainder, as expected, with the melody in the superius.

A substantial number of these pieces were attributed to William Parsons (fl. 1545–63), who was a vicar-choral and composer at Wells Cathedral,[49] indicating that they may have been intended for use in those few large English institutions that had not lost their choirs. However, the title page suggests that the accompaniments could be played by "all musical instruments" and that they were "for the increase of virtue and abolishing of other vain and trifling ballades," pointing rather to domestic use. Other, similar collections followed, notably *The Whole Booke of Psalms*, the first edition of which was published by music printer Thomas East in 1592. This was the first

47. See Peter Le Huray, "Service," *The New Grove Dictionary of Music*, 17:188–91, who cites examples by composers such as John Day, Thomas Tallis, and William Byrd, among others.

48. See Nicholas Temperley, "Psalms, metrical," *The New Grove Dictionary of Music*, 15:358–62.

49. See Philippe Oboussier, "Parsons, William," *The New Grove Dictionary of Music*, 14:249–50.

to include simple settings in four parts for all 150 texts of the English Psalter, as well as hymns that were in common use. East must have hoped that it, too, would find a place both in the private devotions and honest recreation of the musically literate and in the services of the Anglican church. It was possible, obviously, with this repertory as well, to perform the Psalm with a solo voice, leaving the other parts for an instrumental accompaniment.[50]

Together with other English texts having liturgical connections, the metrical Psalms were also set for use by a skilled polyphonic choir. It was of course only natural that for works of this kind a composer would draw to a considerable degree upon the well-established tradition of the polyphonic motet, making use of the more complex and sophisticated contrapuntal style that had become traditional for analogous Latin texts. In some instances the melodies that were associated with the verse of Sternhold and Hopkins in Day's English Psalter were taken as cantus firmi and presented in the usual manner, phrase by phrase, primarily in successive and interlocking points of imitation. In others, by contrast, no reference was made at all to earlier monophonic versions.

As the century wore on, pieces of the latter type in particular—whether based on English texts taken from the Psalter or some other source—were designated with increasing regularity by the term "anthem."[51] A word derived from the more ancient word "antiphon," it had been used more or less synonymously with it since at least the eleventh century.[52] Very soon, however, these works of motetlike facture with texts in the vernacular began to take on distinctive compositional features that were not common to the earlier Continental models and that would establish the English anthem as a recognizably separate genre. Unhappily, the initial phase of the transformation is shrouded once again to a degree by the small number and imperfect state of the surviving musical sources.

Only two manuscripts of uncertain provenance, both incomplete, contain service music from the period in some quantity. All that can be surmised regarding the stylistic traits that were beginning to characterize the newly emerging anthem is necessarily based on the repertories represented in these two collections: MSS Music School e.420–2 at Bodleian Library in Oxford, the "Wanley Partbooks," and MSS Royal Appendix 74–6 at the British Library in London, known as the "Lumley Partbooks." The Wanley manuscripts include ten Communion Services, another thirty-two Service sections, and forty-seven anthems; the Lumley volumes comprise eleven Service sections and seventeen anthems. Most of the music in these collections is without attribution, but of the contributing composers who can be identified, the

50. See Nicholas Temperley, "Psalms, metrical," *The New Grove Dictionary of Music*, 15:367–69.

51. For a survey of the various sources drawn upon for anthem texts during the genre's formative period (and a useful review of the pertinent literature), see John Morehen, "The Engish Anthem Text, 1549–1660," *Journal of the Royal Music Association* 117 (1992): 62–85.

52. See Le Huray, "Anthem," *The New Grove Dictionary of Music*, 1:454.

most important were all associated with the chapel royal: William Mundy (ca. 1529–91), John Sheppard (ca. 1515 to 1559–60), Thomas Tallis (ca. 1505–85), and Christopher Tye (ca. 1505–ca. 1572).[53]

As may be seen from Mundy's *O Lord, the maker of all things*, an anthem for Compline, four voices were the rule at that point, even though five-part writing was to become more common later on (see Example 21-7).[54] The work is divided into two sections, the last of which could be repeated if need be. Individual voice parts were clearly conceived for and provided with the text to be declaimed, and the predominant compositional texture is a kind of animated homophony with only short,

53. See the *Census-Catalogue of Manuscript Sources of Polyphonic Music*, ed. Charles Hamm and Herbert Kellman, 5 vols. (Neuhausen-Stuttgart: Hänssler Verlag, 1979–88), 2:294 and 111, respectively.
54. For a complete transcription of the piece in modern score, see Peter Le Huray, ed., *The Treasury of English Church Music* (London: Blandford, 1965), vol. 2.

EXAMPLE 21-7. William Mundy, *O Lord, the maker of all things*, second section (mm. 27–50)

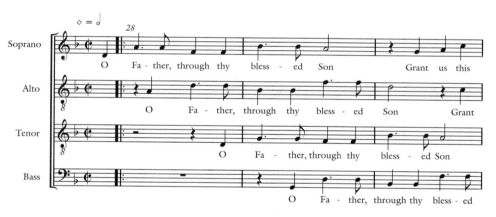

decorative patches of imitative counterpoint. At this juncture, then, the anthem was still not readily distinguished—except for the language of its text—from a Continental motet written in a fairly sober, syllabic style.

In other works of this type, however, especially those datable to a somewhat later period, there is a greater degree of internal sectionalization. The formal patterns adopted for these compositions recall, understandably enough, those seen in the antiphon motets of the "Eton Choirbook" (such as Browne's *Salve regina*, discussed earlier), which were maintained, by and large, in the antiphon motets of the generation of Mundy and Tallis. In those Latin-texted works shifts in texture are achieved by alternating between a section using relatively few voices (as in the three-part sections of Browne's motet) and the full choir (usually in five or six parts)—changes that may have been underscored by the contrast between solo and choral performance. This is matched in the developing anthem repertory by the succession of soloist and choir. Moreover, there is now a clearer textual basis for these contrasts in voicing, a distinction between verse (or strophe) and chorus (or refrain) that harks back to the carols of the fifteenth century.

Following a well-established tradition, the verses of anthems written in this new manner were sung by a solo voice (or voices), but to instrumental accompaniment—usually played on the organ. This mode of performance may have been inspired by that adopted for some of the early settings of the Psalms translated into metrical English verse when the simple homophonic settings were performed at church by a solo voice with organ. Or it may reflect instead the influence of the English consort song in the adoption of an ensemble of viols for the parts of the accompaniment. It is certainly likely, in any case, that the publishers of this music, like their predecessors, were aiming for a domestic market with compositions so conceived, without excluding in the process the possibility of ecclesiastical use.[55]

55. See Le Huray, "Anthem," *The New Grove Dictionary of Music*, 1:455–56.

A particularly fine example of the verse anthem in its fully developed state is the setting by William Byrd (1543–1623) of the Easter text *Christ rising again from the dead* (see Example 21-8).[56] The entry of the solo voices (here two sopranos) is pre-

56. For a complete transcription of the anthem in modern score, see *The Collected Works of William Byrd*, vol. 13, *Songs of Sundrie Natures (1589)*, ed. Edmund H. Fellowes, rev. Philip Brett (London: Stainer and Bell, 1940), 280; the piece is readily accessible in Davison and Apel, eds., *Historical Anthology of Music*, 165–67, no. 151; (the English text is based on 1 Corinthians 15:20–22 and Romans 6:9–11).

EXAMPLE 21-8. William Byrd, *Christ rising again from the dead*, first section (mm. 1–25)

ceded, as it often was in anthems by composers of Byrd's generation, by an instrumental introduction. In this case it is written for a consort of four viols, three of
which engage in an opening point of imitation. Rising melodic lines, in the voices as
in the instruments, are undoubtedly for mimetic effect, illustrating the literal meaning of the text. At the first entry of the chorus (in four parts, like the viol accompaniment) the richly contrapuntal texture of the initial verse gives way to a homophonic
texture and swings from the binary mensuration of the opening to a brief ternary
pattern—here, presumably, for a dramatic rhetorical effect. For the next two verse-
chorus pairs the textures continue to alternate similarly between complex contrapuntal patterns and homophonic declamation. Only at the fourth and last, where the

chorus replies with a repetition of the text of the preceding verse, does it take up not only the melodic material of the two soloists but also the imitative counterpoint that characterized their initial presentation of it.

It is undeniable that the reform in England had a devastating effect upon many of the musical institutions where choral polyphony had been most assiduously cultivated during the fifteenth and early sixteenth century—as it did, moreover, in Calvin's Geneva and Zwingli's Zurich. If one can judge from works such as this, however, the same period saw with the emergence of the English verse anthem the establishment of a significant new genre of polyphonic composition. It combined the alternating sonorities of solo and vocal performance with the complementary textures of contrapuntal and homophonic writing and the contrasting timbres of voices and instruments. And that was, unequivocally, an important artistic achievement.

CHAPTER 22

Performance Practice and Instrumental Music

INTRODUCTION

For the fifteenth century and, to a lesser degree, the sixteenth as well, music considered appropriate, or even intended, for instrumental performance is not always easily distinguished from the vocal repertory. The causes of confusion in this respect are not difficult to identify. There are good indications, both musical and historical, that instruments were routinely involved in the performance of the written repertories of secular polyphony from at least the thirteenth century on, but rarely are there clear cues as to exactly how they were used. It has seemed possible to conclude, for example, that instruments were heard to play the tenor parts in motets of the late Middle Ages. It has appeared likely, as well, that they provided accompaniment for the voice in the performance of polyphonic chansons, more or less from the inception of the genre in the fourteenth century. However, these interpretations have recently been challenged, and a vigorous argument is being made for the historicity of exclusively vocal performance of texted works.

Source evidence for the use of instruments is mostly negative. For example, the lack of a text for a given part of a polyphonic piece has been construed to mean that it was to be played rather than sung. However, only in the case of such instrumental types as keyboards and, subsequently, lutes—those for which a special type of score called tablature was devised—is doubt essentially removed by the notation itself as to whether or not instruments were meant to be involved in performance. Scattered sources of this type have survived from as early as the fourteenth century, two of which are particularly noteworthy.

The "Robertsbridge Codex" (MS Additional 28550, British Library, London), dating from circa 1325 to 1350, presents in tablature three *estampies* and instrumental adaptations of three motets.[1] Because the texted parts of the motets are

---

1. The *estampie* is an instrumental work in sections with paired repetitions featuring *ouvert* and *clos* endings; see Hendrik Vanderwerf, *The New Grove Dictionary of Music*, 6:254–58.

FIGURE 22-1. A page from the "Robertsbridge Codex" (London, British Library, MS Add. 28550, f. 43ᵛ).

imbedded in the instrumental arrangement, it seems clear that voices were not to be included in the performance of the music as written, but there is renewed discussion as to whether the tablature was intended solely for keyboard or for some other instrument or instruments (see Figure 22-1).[2]

This is even more pointedly the case for the "Faenza Codex" (MS 117, Biblioteca Communale, Faenza), which was probably copied circa 1410 to 1420 but contains repertory from around 1400. Included are not only arrangements of secular vocal pieces but also settings of liturgical chant. It is notated in what is usually identified as "keyboard" score (see Figure 5-4),[3] but the assumptions underlying that use of terms have also been questioned. Objections have been raised to the traditional interpretation primarily on the ground that performance at the keyboard would involve difficult hand crossing that would have been unlikely at the time. It has been suggested that, despite its familiar appearance and its liturgical content, the score was in fact prepared for performance by a pair of lutes, or by lute and harp—at least as far as the secular works are concerned.[4]

This interpretation has also been rejected, however, with the argument that

2. See John Caldwell, "Sources of Keyboard Music to 1660," *The New Grove Dictionary of Music*, 17:731; a complete facsimile of the source is available in *Early English Harmony*, i, plates 42–45.

3. See John Caldwell, "Sources of Keyboard Music to 1660," *The New Grove Dictionary of Music*, 17:718; this manuscript is also available in a complete facsimile edition.

4. See Timothy J. McGee, "Instruments and the Faenza Codex," *Early Music* 14 (1986): 480–90.

octave transposition of either the upper or the lower parts would obviate the supposed difficulty.[5] There are indications, nevertheless, that the relationship between repertories for lute and for keyboard may have been relatively close; the famed organist Conrad Paumann was also renowned as a lute virtuoso, and his was not an isolated case.[6] In light of such connections—and the proclaimed interchangeability of similar repertories in later Spanish sources—it is certainly possible that instrumental intabulation was adapted for use by players of more than one type of instrument, whatever the initial intentions of the intabulator.[7]

Aside from notation in tablature, evidence (whether notational, stylistic, or pictorial) for the use of instruments is largely indeterminate until well into the sixteenth century. Even when there is reason to believe that one or more players may have been involved in the performance of a given musical repertory, a specific instrument is almost never named in the source itself. It is in part because of the vague and often indirect nature of the clues for instrumental participation that a growing number of scholars are disinclined to construe what evidence there is as pointing clearly to instrumental performance, at least not in the most literal sense.

A consensus has begun to emerge among a number of scholars that, with the notable exception of the organ, instruments were rarely used in the performance of polyphony in a liturgical context. Only extraordinary events, such as the papal dedication of the cathedral in Florence in 1436, were apt to be commemorated with a written description, and those that have reached us focus on the unusual, the sumptuous, the magnificent, and the spectacular rather than modes of musical performance. In the case in question—as in many others—it is not clear whether voices and instruments were heard in concert with one another or simply shared the same space for separate performances.[8]

Archival documents have thus far yielded only the barest hint of instrumental participation in the daily round of liturgical celebration, even for special feast days, until rather late in the sixteenth century. Records from the cathedral in Cambrai, for example, suggest that even the organ usually found in fifteenth-century churches was wanting there and that all polyphony was performed by voices alone.[9] At the court of Burgundy, similarly, although skillful instrument-playing musicians were among those in the service of the ducal household, there is no reason to believe that instru-

---

5. See Roland Eberlain, "The Faenza Codex: Music for Organ or Lute?" *Early Music* 20 (1992): 461–66. Neither writer has considered the possibility that although the lines cross, the player need not have crossed hands but could have simply shifted the parts between the two hands.

6. On this point see David Fallows, "Fifteenth-Century Tablatures for Plucked Instruments: A Summary, a Revision, and a Suggestion," *Lute Society Journal* 19 (1977): 7–33.

7. Reference here is to Antonio de Cabezón's *Obras de música para tecla, arpa y vihuela* of 1578; see below, p. 788.

8. See, in this regard, the comments by David Fallows, *Dufay* (London: J. M. Dent, 1982), 45–49.

9. See, in this connection, the groundbreaking study by Craig Wright, "Performance Practices at the Cathedral of Cambrai, 1475–1550," *Musical Quarterly* 64 (1978): 295–328.

FIGURE 22-2. Solemn high Mass (a bishop is celebrating) performed by divided choirs with the participation of cornets and sackbuts, from the *Encomium musices quod ex sacris litteris concinnebat Philippus Gallaeus*, no. 17 in a series of engravings by Adrian Collaert based on drawings by Johannes Stradanus (Berlin, Staatliches Institut für Musikforschung).

mentalists and singers collaborated in the chapel to perform the polyphony that often accompanied both Mass and Office.[10]

The conclusions drawn concerning those two institutions seem to have been confirmed in more general terms by iconographical studies as well. Although images depicting liturgical services in the interiors of both urban churches and court chapels are fairly numerous for the fifteenth century, none of those currently known includes the presence of instrumental musicians.[11] By contrast, it has been observed that prominent reformers of the early sixteenth century—in particular Andreas Carlstadt (ca. 1480–1531), Erasmus Desiderius (ca. 1466–1536), John Calvin (1509–64), and even Martin Luther (1483–1546)—inveigh against the use of instruments at Mass in such energetic and closely reasoned terms that one can hardly believe that their concerns were not grounded in current practices (see Figure 22-2).[12]

Music in the secular realm is another matter. Here, too, the evidence is largely

10. In this regard see the detailed study by David Fallows, "Specific Information on the Ensembles for Composed Polyphony, 1400–1474," in *Studies in the Performance of Late Medieval Music*, ed. Stanley Boorman (Cambridge: Cambridge University Press, 1983), 109–59.

11. See in this connection the study by James W. McKinnon, "Fifteenth-Century Northern Book Painting and the *a cappella* Question: An Essay in Iconographic Method," in *Studies in the Performance of Late Medieval Music*, ed. Stanley Boorman (Cambridge: Cambridge University Press, 1983), 1–17.

12. See the arguments made in this respect by Leslie Korrick, "Instrumental Music in the Early Sixteenth-Century Mass: New Evidence," *Early Music* 18 (1990): 359–70.

negative, however. It has been suggested in this connection that instrumental musicians were probably not trained to read mensural notation with the result that they could not easily have assisted with the performance of written repertory. It has also been argued that the voice was itself considered an instrument of sorts and that where no text was given, rather than resorting to devices of human invention for producing pitched sounds, the notes would have been sung, perhaps to solmization syllables, or even nonsense syllables.[13]

Despite these arguments it seems quite likely that by the early fifteenth century even those instrumental musicians who played mostly for dancing (and probably largely from memory) were initiated at some point during their long apprenticeship to the mysteries of mensural notation. It is in fact certain that many of those who played at court (and taught their noble patrons to play as well) were well versed in its use. They often served as organists and/or singers in the chapel, where a knowledge of notation was indispensable, and some of them are also known as composers.

It was the *bas* instruments—those with a soft sound such as vielle, harp, and lute—that were deemed most appropriate for use "in chambers" where secular pieces were most often heard. They are therefore the instruments most likely to have been used to accompany the singing voice where that was in fact the practice. It is precisely instruments of this type that are most frequently depicted in the artworks of the period that show voices and instruments combined in musical performance in both courtly and urban contexts.[14] A famous example, though perhaps not the most instructive, is the Arras tapestry of circa 1420, showing a young woman in a castle garden playing a harp, apparently from a scroll of music held by an elegant gentleman who sits facing her (see Figure 22-3).[15]

Still, there is considerable evidence for wholly vocal performance of secular repertory and for a tendency to maintain both vocal and instrumental ensembles as separate entities in performance (see Figure 22-4).[16] This is true not only of the fifteenth-century chanson in French-speaking areas but also of secular music of the period in Italy and Spain.[17] However, in all three areas there is at least some evidence of a tra-

---

13. See Christopher Page, "Machaut's 'Pupil' Deschamps on the Performance of Music: Voices or Instruments in the Fourteenth-Century Chanson?" *Early Music* 5 (1977): 484–91.

14. The evidence in this connection, both iconographical and musical, has been rather thoroughly reviewed by Howard M. Brown, "Instruments and Voices in the Fifteenth-Century Chanson," in *Current Thought in Musicology*, ed. John W. Grubbs (Austin: University of Texas Press, 1976), 89–137.

15. For a discussion of this celebrated image, one among many, see Tilman Seebass, "The Visualisation of Music through Pictorial Imagery and Notation in Late Mediaeval France," in *Studies in the Performance of Late Mediaeval Music*, ed. Stanley Boorman (Cambridge: Cambridge University Press, 1983), 19–33.

16. For a discussion of the evidence to be derived in this connection from the French romance *Cleriadus et Meliadice*, see Christopher Page, "The Performance of Songs in Late-Medieval France: A New Source," *Early Music* 10 (1982): 441–50; for a more recent, and more reflective, consideration of the issues involved, see also Page's essay "The English *a cappella* Heresy," in *Companion to Medieval and Renaissance Music*, ed. Tess Knighton and David Fallows (London: J. M. Dent and Sons, 1992), 23–29.

17. Evidence that the vocal duo of the *trecento* madrigal carried over into the performance practice of fifteenth-century Italian musicians has already been mentioned (see pp. 281–84); for the Iberian repertory, see Tess Knighton, "The *a cappella* Heresy in Spain: An Inquisition into the Performance of the *Cancionero* Repertory," *Early Music* 20 (1992): 561–81.

FIGURE 22-3. *De ce que fol pense*, tapestry (Paris, Musée des Arts Décoratifs).

dition for instrumentally accompanied solo song, a mode of performance that seems not to have disappeared even after, in the sixteenth century, the secular genres were generally conceived for fully vocal performance and texted in all their parts.

If the indications for performance that are occasionally present are not more specific, it is probably at least in part because there was no need to make them so. Soft instruments seem to have been always readily at hand in courtly circles, together with players trained in their use, and their ranges coincided as a rule well enough with those of human voices in three or four parts to make their use entirely feasible. In any case the music of the repertories in question had not been imagined, as for a modern orchestral score, with specific timbres in mind, either instrumental or vocal. The sonorities chosen for the individual melodic lines undoubtedly depended in great measure on local customs and practices, which must have reflected in turn the means available in any given instance.

The elements of the contrapuntal fabric could be satisfactorily represented by any of the available sonorities, including that of the human voice itself. Consequently, instruments could have been used, when available, to play those parts of a composition left untexted, or perhaps to reinforce those for which words were given. Doubling of that sort may even have occurred on those particular occasions when voices and instruments were brought together in the churches or other places of public assembly for the performance of polyphonic Masses and motets. However, there is still much to be learned about these matters, especially with respect to specific times, places, and repertories.

From Chanson to *Canzona*

It is possible to argue, then, that combining voices and instruments for the performance of polyphonic secular music appears to have been a common practice more or less from its inception. It should therefore come as no surprise that the earliest pieces that were apparently actually intended for an ensemble or consort of melody instruments—those, that is, capable of playing only one pitch at a time (as opposed to those with some kind of potential for polyphonic performance)—were usually copied or printed with collections of music originally based upon a text. Nor is it remarkable that this shift to instrumental composition took its initial point of departure from the polyphonic songs of the late fifteenth century. Curiously, pieces of this sort first found currency primarily in Italy. However, the composers who contributed most substantially to this emerging repertory were in fact mostly the northerners who were for a time in residence there: most notably Alexander Agricola, Heinrich Isaac, Jacob Obrecht, and Josquin Desprez.

Perhaps the first indication

FIGURE 22-4. *The Garden of Delights* by Cristoforo de Predis (or his school) (Modena, Biblioteca Estense, MS α.X.2.14, la carta 10ʳ). At the right rear an ensemble of haut instruments, shawms and slide trumpet; in front a player of pipe and tabor and a lutenist; on the left three men singing, possibly in polyphony, from mensural notation.

of a tendency in Italian centers to regard chansons as primarily useful for instrumental performance may be seen in a change in attitude toward their texts. Surprisingly, and significantly, secular French pieces copied into the earliest Italian sources of the fifteenth century—those containing in substantial numbers the works of such northern composers as Du Fay, Binchoys, and their immediate contemporaries—appear with their French verse copied for the most part correctly and completely. This may have been primarily because the collections in question were compiled for institutions where the leading musicians (including those trained as scribes) were from French-speaking areas. Or it may have been that the patrons or intended users of the collections were francophile and fluent with the language. Vocal performance, at least of the cantus, was therefore possible, even if it was not specifically intended.

Around mid-century, by contrast, interest in French texts apparently began to wane rather rapidly, and the reasons for the change have yet to be fully explored.[18] Was it, for example, because the distribution of the repertory had widened well beyond the initial circle of patronage and interest? Had the chanson become a popular genre for recreational music making where instrumental performance predominated and where, in any case, one could not necessarily count on singers—or listeners—capable of understanding the French? Or was it, to the contrary, because polyphonic chansons, motets, and Mass sections had become the primary repertory for the wind bands fostered in Italy both at court and by urban municipalities, those instrumental ensembles in whose performances the words of a vocal piece had no place? Whatever the conclusions ultimately to be drawn in this regard, the sources give eloquent testimony of the shift.

In a center such as Naples, for instance, where musical activity, especially in the secular realm, was linked to the musicians of the royal court—including, ironically, the singers and composers of the king's chapel—a chansonnier (in the proper sense of the term) could still be copied well after mid-century with a fair degree of accuracy and completeness. This is clear from a collection of music such as MS IV.a.24 of the Royal Library of San Lorenzo at the Escorial, which was probably copied in Naples between 1460 and 1474, or the "Mellon Chansonnier," apparently prepared for Beatrice of Aragon in about 1475–76, even though an occasional stanza is omitted here and there in both codices.[19]

In sharp contrast is a songbook such as MS 15123 of the French National Library in Paris (the "Pixérécourt Chansonnier"), which was apparently copied in Florence

18. Concerning the apparent shift away from the use of French in Italian court circles of the period, see David Fallows, "French as a Courtly Language in Fifteenth-Century Italy," *Renaissance Studies* 3 (1989): 429–41.

19. Concerning the Escorial manuscript, see the *Census-Catalogue of Manuscript Sources of Polyphonic Music*, ed. Charles Hamm and Herbert Kellman, 5 vols. (Neuhausen-Stuttgart: Hänssler Verlag, 1979–88), 1:211–12; for a study and edition of the source, see Martha K. Hanen, ed., *The Chansonnier El Escorial IV.a.24*, 3 vols., Musicological Studies, vol. 36 (Henryville, Penn.: Institute of Mediaeval Music, 1983). The "Mellon Chansonnier" was discussed earlier, p. 288.

in the early 1480s.[20] There the text is usually limited to a refrain for each of the songs. Moreover, the French verse is often so corrupt that its inclusion appears to be primarily for cosmetic purposes, as if to create by means of a visual image the illusion of a genuine chansonnier. In fact, the words that were entered with the music can have had little practical value for the performer. The same is essentially true of MS *Banco rari* 229 of the National Library in Florence, an exceptionally large collection of chansons that was compiled there somewhat later (ca. 1491–92).[21] In that manuscript, too, the texts are so consistently incomplete and so rarely correct as to be virtually useless in performance.

One explanation for the lack of care taken with the French texts in secular collections such as these is that chansons were usually performed instrumentally in Italy and that the verse was consequently ultimately superfluous. Such a conclusion is certainly suggested by their appearance in some of the Italian sources where they are not only entirely stripped of their original text but also given a title that has nothing to do with the French verse to which they had been written. This was the case for two of the pieces included in the "Mellon Chansonnier": Okeghem's *L'autre d'antan*, which was copied into a somewhat later songbook (with a different contratenor) and identified only as *La trentana*; and Morton's *Paracheve ton entreprise*, which was subsequently entered in a generally textless collection with the tag *La perontina*.[22]

The sole opposing argument—that the French texts were not indispensable in the notated manuscripts of secular music because they were available separately in codices containing only the poetry—is not very compelling. Texts *were* included in the chansonniers copied during the same period in French-speaking regions, and, by the same token, there are no surviving Italian examples of the hypothetical books of French verse (although such collections of Italian verse are in fact to be found). What is more, some of the chansonniers that transmit their French poems in truncated and badly mutilated form (the Florence MS *Banco rari* 229 being a case in point) provide impeccable and complete texts for the relatively few Italian pieces that keep their French cousins company.

The clearest indication, however, that at least some musical manuscripts of this kind were actually intended for instrumental use is a "songbook" such as MS 2856 of the Biblioteca Casanatense in Rome, which was apparently prepared in Ferrara, perhaps as early as 1479–81, as a gift for Isabella d'Este at her betrothal and subsequent marriage to Francesco Gonzaga, marquis of Mantua. According to a payment record that probably refers to its compilation, it was "written and notated . . . *a la pifaresca*," an expression taken to mean that it was compiled for the use of the vir-

---

20. See the *Census-Catalogue of Manuscript Sources,* 3:23–24.
21. See Howard M. Brown, ed., *A Florentine Chansonnier from the Time of Lorenzo the Magnificent,* 2 vols., Monuments of Renaissance Music, vol. 7 (Chicago: University of Chicago Press, 1983).
22. The manuscripts are, respectively, Q16 of the Civico Museo in Bologna and 2856 of the Biblioteca Casanatense in Rome; cf. Leeman L. Perkins and Howard Garey, eds., *The Mellon Chansonnier,* 2 vols. (New Haven: Yale University Press, 1979), 2:265 and 357.

tuoso wind players employed at Italian courts such as those in Ferrara and Mantua.[23]

By the time Ottaviano Petrucci began printing music in Venice from moveable metal type at the beginning of the sixteenth century, instrumental performance of the chanson must have been more the rule than the exception. No other conclusion seems reasonable in light of the way the publisher chose to explore the commercial possibilities of his newly developed technology for producing mensural polyphony in multiple copies. He entered the market in 1501 with the *Odhecaton A*, a volume comprising ninety-six compositions in choirbook format, the majority of them chansons. Unlike the Masses and motets he began publishing in the following year, however, none of the pieces in that first anthology was provided with text. One can conclude, therefore, that the omission of the French verse was a conscious decision and not due simply to technical limitations in the new printing procedures.

Significantly, Petrucci followed that first volume of imported secular music in rapid order with two others of identical format—*Canti B*, with 51 pieces in 1502, and *Canti C*, with 139 in 1504—and there were at least three separate printings of the *Odhecaton* and two of *Canti B*.[24] His Venetian shop thus put into circulation within a three-year period some 180 chansons, none of them texted, apparently with considerable financial return. The very success of the venture points unequivocally to the well-established use of instrumental ensembles for their performance.

Whatever the process by which French texts were first truncated, then completely omitted, from Italian collections of polyphonic chansons, both manuscript and printed, it apparently points to the establishment of a new instrumental genre: the *canzona*. It is definable as a chanson arranged or recomposed expressly for instrumental performance. The term is of course simply the Italian equivalent for *chanson* and may have been applied initially to designate any piece from the French secular repertory, whether performed by voices or instruments or performed by a combination of the two. A significant distinction can be made, however, between those compositions that originally included a texted part for vocal performance (whether or not the texts were entered in an Italian source together with the music) and those that took as a point of departure a preexistent vocal model and reworked it with instrumental performance in mind.

Evidence for the emergence of a distinguishable compositional type arising from the latter process is to be seen first of all in the surprisingly large number of different compositions based on a relatively few pieces that were especially well known and loved: chansons such as Okeghem's *Fors seulement l'attente* and *D'ung aultre amer*, Busnoys's *Fortuna desperata*, and the anonymous *J'ay pris amours*. There are, for

23. See Lewis Lockwood, *Music in Renaissance Ferrara, 1400–1505: The Creation of a Musical Center in the Fifteenth Century* (Cambridge, Mass.: Harvard University Press, 1984), 224–26. (Other scholars have placed the copying of the codex closer to 1490; see the *Census-Catalogue of Manuscript Sources*, 3:112–14.)

24. See the introduction in Helen Hewitt and Isabel Pope, eds., *Harmonice musices odhecaton A* (Cambridge, Mass.: Medieval Academy of America, 1942), 3–10, and cf. Martin Picker, "Petrucci," *The New Grove Dictionary of Music*, 14:595–97.

example, some twenty-nine different compositions for three to five parts based upon the setting of *Fors seulement* attributable to what was presumably the "original" composer.[25] Similarly, the secular sources still extant transmit at least seventeen separate versions for two to five parts of *D'ung aultre amer*.[26] Busnoys's *Fortuna desperata* was reworked by both Isaac and Senfl, among others.[27] And *J'ay pris amours*—one of the most widely circulated chansons of the fifteenth century even though its author is nowhere identified—spawned at least twenty-seven other pieces for two to four parts.[28]

Naturally enough, the extent to which an arrangement or a reworking of one such piece differs from the model can vary a great deal. Most of the time the process of recomposition involved the retention of at least one of the parts from the original composition as a kind of secular cantus firmus. Typical in this regard are the various reworkings of the anonymous *J'ay pris amours*. Five of these versions (Taruskin's nos. 2–6) retain not only the tenor, the part that was most often kept when a new piece was based upon an earlier one, but also the cantus, perhaps in this instance because the two voices are so similar in style and so closely linked to one another by points of imitation (see Example 22-1). Each of them has a different contratenor, however.[29]

One of these pieces (Taruskin's no. 3) is found in a manuscript composed of repertory that has been connected with the court of England's King Henry VIII[30] and two more (Taruskin's nos. 4 and 6) in sources from German-speaking regions[31]—in every instance without text. This unusual circumstance of their dissemination would suggest that chansons were performed instrumentally not only in Italy but also in other regions close to France where a different vernacular was spoken.

More characteristic of the recompositional process that came to be associated with the *canzona* is the version of *J'ay pris amours* attributed in the Florentine manuscript *Banco rari* 229 to Johann Martini (born ca. 1440), who served in the ducal

25. For a modern edition including the original and all the pieces derived from it, see Martin Picker, ed., *Fors seulement: Thirty Compositions for Three and Five Voices or Instruments from the Fifteenth and Sixteenth Centuries*, Recent Researches in the Music of the Middle Ages and Early Renaissance, vol. 14 (Madison: A-R Editions, 1981).
26. For an edition, see Richard Taruskin, ed., *D'ung aultre mer*, RS 6 (Miami: Ogni Sorte Editions, 1983).
27. Cf. Martin Picker, "Busnois," *The New Grove Dictionary of Music*, 3:507.
28. For an edition, see Richard Taruskin, ed., *J'ai pris amours*, RS 5 (Miami: Ogni Sorte Editions, 1982).
29. The commentary to the edition of all twenty-eight compositions transmitted in the surviving sources (Taruskin, ed., *J'ai pris amours*, 2–5) traces the use of preexistent material from one reworking to the next, following the chronology of the sources.
30. London, British Library, MS Additional 31922; see the *Census-Catalogue of Manuscript Sources*, 2:64.
31. These are Trent MS 1947/4, which contains German secular music from the Tyrolian region in which it originated (see the *Census-Catalogue of Manuscript Sources*, 3:221); and the "Glogauer Partbooks," which originated in Silesia, formerly MS Mus. 40098 of the Preussische Staatsbibliothek in Berlin, now in the Jagiellonian Library in Krakow (see the *Census-Catalogue of Manuscript Sources*, 4:254 and 258). Interestingly, the latter source carries altogether four compositions derived in some sense from the anonymous *J'ay pris amours* (Taruskin, ed., *J'ai pris amours*, nos. 6, 21, 22, and 27).

Example 22-1. Anonymous, *J'ay pris amours* (mm. 1–16)

I have taken love as an emblem in order to win happiness. I shall be blissful this summer
if I can reach my goal. If there is anyone who belittles me for that, I must forgive
him; I have taken love. . . . It seems to me that such is the custom: who has nothing
is excluded and is honored by no one. Is it not quite right, then, that I seek it? I have
taken love . . .

chapel of the Este in Ferrara from 1473 until the end of his life in 1497–98 (except for a brief period in 1474 spent with the rival Sforza dynasty in Milan).[32] Although he, too, retained the well integrated cantus-tenor duo of the model as the basis for his own piece, he placed below it two additional parts of a much more active stamp, matching the breves and semibreves of the original declamation with running minims and semiminims (see Example 22-2). At the same time, he managed the rather remarkable technical feat of keeping the two parts that were newly composed in strict imitation at the unison just a minim apart.

That instrumental performance of this reworking of the texted original was intended from the outset is suggested—as it is with so many works of this type—by the rapid passagework, the wide leaps, the extensive range, and the contrapuntal complexity of the added parts. Noteworthy as well is the absence of any text (beyond a brief incipit of identification) in the manuscript source.

Northern composers of the following generation who spent at least part of their

32. See Lewis Lockwood, "Martini," *The New Grove Dictionary of Music*, 11:726.

EXAMPLE 22-2. Johannes Martini, *J'ay pris amours* (mm. 1–16)

active career in Italy continued to "arrange" well-known chansons in much the same manner. Perhaps even more typical of the newly emerging genre than Martini's reworking of *J'ay pris amours* (each in its own way) are three separate versions all attributed in the sources to Heinrich Isaac, who was in the service of the Medici in Florence from 1484–85 until the death of Lorenzo the Magnificent in 1492 (and perhaps later as well).[33] One of these, written in three parts and also included in the Florentine collection *Banco rari* 229,[34] uses the original cantus as the cantus firmus, adding to it a new tenor characterized by rapid rhythms and scalar passagework. Also new is a contratenor bassus, for which the opening motive of the borrowed voice is transformed into a sort of ostinato figure that begins from a variety of pitches: first from D and a, then, within the line, from E (mm. 3, 5, 10, and 12)—but with a leap up a fourth to a instead of a third to g—and finally from C (m. 20).

Of the other two pieces ascribed to Isaac, both of which were written in four parts, one (published in Petrucci's *Canti C* of 1504)[35] is a fairly straightforward can-

33. See Martin Staehelin, "Isaac," *The New Grove Dictionary of Music*, 9:329–30.
34. See Taruskin, ed., *J'ai pris amours*, 24–25, no. 11.
35. See Taruskin, ed., *J'ai pris amours*, 48–49, no. 19.

tus firmus setting based on the tenor of the original chanson. The remaining three parts are linked together by imitative figures, thus sharing as well the rapid rhythms, dotted figures, and scalar ornaments that stand in such clear contrast to the more tranquil pace of the preexistent part. Similar settings by Jean Japart (fl. ca. 1474–1507) and Johannes Ghiselin (fl. ca. 1490–1507)—taking, however, the cantus rather than the tenor as the cantus firmus (as in the Isaac version à 3)—were also published by Petrucci, the former in the *Odhecaton A* of 1501 and the latter again in *Canti C*. The third piece attributed to Isaac, which was inscribed in yet another Florentine collection,[36] appears at first blush to keep both the cantus and the tenor of the original composition (see Example 22-3). Both parts have been transposed down a whole tone, however, shifting the final from a to g (with a b-fa signature). And once the opening figures have been quoted, the preexistent melodic lines dis-

36. Florence, National Library, MS Magl. 178; see the *Census-Catalogue of Manuscript Sources*, 1:320; for an edition, see Taruskin, ed., *J'ai pris amours*, 18–19, no. 7.

EXAMPLE 22-3. Heinrich Isaac, *J'ay pris amours* (mm. 1–16)

solve into the same kind of rapid figuration that characterizes the parts that were composed entirely anew, leaving little trace of the borrowed material.

It seems likely that at least some of the various versions of widely circulated chansons like *J'ay pris amours* had their beginnings as an exercise in contrapuntal composition, in particular those pieces that simply provided a newly composed contratenor for the cantus-tenor duo of a skilled master. Similarly didactic in intent, it would seem, are the three settings included in MS 1013 of the Biblioteca Augusta in Perugia, a compendium of treatises on music (and calligraphy) with numerous notated examples included by way of illustration.[37] All add but a single part to the cantus firmus taken from the model. (The cantus was borrowed as the upper part for two of these arrangements, nos. 8 and 10 of Taruskin's edition; the other, no. 9, also has the cantus as the upper part for the first half but the tenor as the lower part for the second section.) The primary purpose of these pieces, however, was to exemplify a full range of the proportional notations that were deemed acceptable— at least theoretically—in the mensural practice that had developed during the fourteenth and fifteenth centuries. These included, in addition to the more common

37. See the *Census-Catalogue of Manuscript Sources*, 3:44; for the music, see Taruskin, ed., *J'ai pris amours*, 20–23, nos. 8, 9, and 10.

relationships—duple, triple, and sesquialteral—combinations rarely seen in the practical sources such as the 5:4 and 9:8 proportions seen in the second piece (Taruskin's no. 9).

Didactic duos aside, the essentially instrumental conception of the majority of the cantus firmus elaborations under discussion is reflected in their fleet, ornamental melodic lines, their active rhythms, and the recondite contrapuntal procedures embodied in the added parts. This is all the more evident when they are compared with a pair of pieces from the French tradition that also allude to the well-traveled *J'ay pris amours.*[38] Significantly, the primary interest in these compositions is clearly textual rather than musical. It derives from a rather free and humorous parody of the courtly poetry of the original, playing on phonic similarities with the original verse. The opening line, "J'ay pris amours à ma devise" ("I have taken Love unto my emblem") has become first "J'ay pris un pou à ma chemise" ("I have taken a louse into my shirt") and then "J'ay pris deux poux [two lice] à ma chemise." At the same time, however, the musical settings—in both instances for three parts—are much more similar to the model (to which they allude rather freely musically as well) than to the *canzone* of the composers who wrote for Italian instrumental ensembles.

Related generically to the recomposition of material borrowed from a courtly chanson are the polyphonic settings of "popular" tunes. The similarities are clear, even though such pieces draw upon a fundamentally different sort of preexistent melody, one that was probably monodic in its origins and often associated with a text of more or less plebeian stamp, whether erotic in nature or not. Some of these melodies apparently come from the French tradition, most notably the famous *L'homme armé* tune, but a number apparently originated in the Flemish-speaking Low Countries of northern Europe. Whatever their geographical provenance, those that were selected for polyphonic elaboration were often reworked repeatedly, like their courtly counterparts.

There are two instrumental versions of the *L'homme armé* tune, for example, one of them inscribed in a set of partbooks from German-speaking Switzerland,[39] the other (by Josquin Desprez) published by Petrucci in his *Canti B* of 1502. Two additional settings of this melody intended for instrumental ensemble—one inscribed in a manuscript of Florentine derivation,[40] the other included by Petrucci in his *Canti C* of 1504—combine it with another preexistent tune. In the first of these, ascribed to Philippe Basiron (d. ca. 1497), *L'homme armé* serves as a tenor cantus firmus while the cantus of Okeghem's *D'ung aultre amer*—which had its own series of derivative instrumental *canzone*—is quoted in the uppermost of the four parts. And in the other, attributed to Jean Japart—whose contribution to the development of

---

38. See Taruskin, ed., *J'ai pris amours*, 60–63, nos. 24 and 25.
39. Basel, University Library, MS F.X.1–4; see the *Census-Catalogue of Manuscript Sources*, 1:29.
40. Rome, Vatican Library, MS Cappella Giulia XIII.27; see the *Census-Catalogue of Manuscript Sources*, 1:18f.

the newly emerging genre has already been cited—it is heard together with the well-known monody *Il est de bone heure né*.[41]

The only other popular monody of French origin to have been similarly treated was *Comment peult avoir joye*, which is found in Italian and German sources in three separate *canzona* arrangements, two of them by Isaac and a third by Josquin. As it moved eastward into German-speaking regions this melody acquired a contrafact text in the local vernacular, beginning "Wohlauf gut Gesell von hinnen," which was then set at least three times in the manner of the polyphonic *Tenorlied*.[42]

Surprisingly enough, it would seem that popular Flemish songs were more frequently taken as the point of departure for instrumental *canzone* than monophonic chansons. Four such melodies, in particular, circulated widely in this guise. *Een vrolic wesen* spawned at least eleven apparently instrumental versions now found in sources of German and Italian provenance, two of them by Isaac.[43] *O Venus bant* gave rise to eight textless arrangements, all but one transmitted by Italian sources; one is by Isaac, one by Josquin, and two by Alexander Agricola (ca. 1446–1506)—another of the northern-born composers who spent considerable time in Italy.[44] *T'Andernaken* provided the starting point for ten different settings for instrumental ensemble, all but one in German and Italian sources; these include one by Agricola, two by Isaac's pupil Ludwig Senfl (for four and, exceptionally, for five parts), and one attributed to King Henry VIII, inscribed in an English collection.[45] Finally, *In mynen zin* prompted some eight settings that appear to have been intended for instruments—in two instances they have in fact been intabulated for keyboard—all found in German and Italian sources. Three of these are again by Isaac.[46]

To compositions such as these, identifiable as *canzone* because they belong to a family of compositions whose models are known, could be added a small group of works included in Petrucci's printed chanson anthologies. These have not been labeled with the usual textual incipits but rather with titles such as *La morra* or *La alfonsina*. There are four such compositions in the *Odhecaton* and another four in *Canti C*.[47] All eight display part-writing that could be described as markedly better for performance by instruments than by voices.

41. For a modern transcription of all the versions mentioned (together with selected sections extracted from polyphonic Masses based on the celebrated melody), see Richard Taruskin, ed., *L'homme armé*, RS 4 (Miami: Ogni Sorte Editions, 1980).

42. Modern transcriptions of all the various settings of this melody are included in the edition by Richard Taruskin, *Coment peult avoir joye / Wohlauf gut Gesellvon hinnen*, RS 1 (Miami: Ogni Sorte Editions, 1978).

43. See Richard Taruskin, ed., *Een vrolic wesen*, RS 2 (Miami: Ogni Sorte Editions, 1979).

44. See Richard Taruskin, ed., *O Venus bant*, RS 3 (Miami: Ogni Sorte Editions, 1979).

45. See Richard Taruskin, ed., *T'andernaken*, RS 7 (Miami: Ogni Sorte Editions, 1981).

46. See Richard Taruskin, ed., *In myen zin*, RS 8 (Miami: Ogni Sorte Editions, 1984).

47. The pieces in question are *Dit le burguygnon* à 4 (anon.), *La morra* à 3 (Isaac), *La stangetta* à 3 (Weerbeke/Obrecht), and *La alfonsina* à 3 (Ghiselin) in *Odhecaton*; *Vive le roy* à 4 (Josquin), *La spagna* à 3 (anon.), *Le hault d'alemaigne* à 3 (Mathurin), and *La bernardina* à 3 (Josquin) in *Canti C*; cf. the entries for these two collections in Howard M. Brown, *Instrumental Music Printed before 1600: A Bibliography* (Cambridge, Mass.: Harvard University Press, 1965).

As an examination of the repertory under discussion will quickly reveal, however, it can be difficult to distinguish with any degree of certainty between "vocal" and "instrumental" styles, whether on the basis of melodic lines, rhythmic activity, or contrapuntal complexity. Particularly striking in this connection are some of the Mass sections by composers such as Isaac, especially those presumably conceived for two or three solo voices that circulated as *bicinia* and *tricinia*, where the rhythms have the same nervous energy, the melodies the same ragged profiles, and the counterpoint the same contrapuntal sophistication as compositions that have been identified here as instrumental *canzone*.[48]

A stylistic link between the instrumental *canzone* based on secular material and the polyphonic Mass is perhaps clearest in those examples where the boundaries between the genres have been blurred. Although very different in function, the two genres share, of course, the use of cantus firmus techniques for which Mass composition provided a ready model. More importantly, equally fundamental stylistic similarities actually allowed some interchange between the repertories. Examples are the polyphonic pieces based on the tune found in the sources with texts in both French and German, *Comment peult avoir joye* and *Wohlauf, gut Gesell*. Surprisingly, three of the eight or so settings of this cantus firmus melody that were copied into collections of secular music were extracted from a Mass attributed to Heinrich Isaac. Two of them are for three parts and another, which features an elaborate threefold canon, is for five. In the context of Isaac's Mass one serves as the "Et incarnatus est" section from the Credo, a second as the "Qui tollis" from the Gloria, and the third—the big canonic piece—is the final "Agnus Dei."[49]

There is good reason, then, for seeing in the chanson "arrangements" that have been under discussion here the beginnings, at least in notated form, of a new instrumental genre. Their transmission without usable text is evidence that they were meant to be played rather than sung, and the geographical distribution of their sources through centers of Italian and Germanic linguistic cultures is equally suggestive of their intended use. More significant still is their clear relationship, conceptually and stylistically, with the instrumental *canzone* of the sixteenth century (for both ensemble and keyboard), a kinship that often extends to the dactylic rhythm that soon became a characteristic, even stereotypical opening gesture in the latter repertory. All of this strongly suggests that the new genre had its origins in the adaptation of French songs for instrumental performance in regions where other vernaculars were spoken.

48. See, in this connection, Martin Staehelin, *Die Messe Heinrich Isaacs*, 3 vols., Publikationen der Schweizerischen Musikforschenden Gesellschaft, ser. 2, vol. 28 (Bern: Verlag Paul Haupt, 1977), 1:25–34, Katalog der Messenkomposition Isaacs, and 3:192–93.
49. For transcriptions of these and the other five settings of this well-traveled melody discussed earlier, see Richard Taruskin, ed., *Coment peult avoir joye/Wohlauf gut Gesell von hinnen.*

CHAPTER 23

Instrumental Repertories: The Sources

INTRODUCTION

The difficulty of identifying the role of instruments in the music of the fifteenth and sixteenth centuries is much diminished—if not entirely obviated—when the primary sources are unequivocally designated as instrumental. This was done either indirectly, through the use of special notations devised specifically for the purpose (tablature or score), or directly, through the use of a title, as happened routinely with printed collections. Repertories of this sort are not numerous among the manuscripts and prints that have survived from the period during which the instrumental genres of the Renaissance were being defined and codified. Nonetheless, those that have come down to us are substantial and representative enough to provide instructive examples of all the basic types and general styles of instrumental music that were being cultivated at the time. The patterns established by the earliest sources prove to be those that were followed by and large through the end of the period.

THE MANUSCRIPT REPERTORIES

The largest and most varied of the manuscript repertories of this kind from the fifteenth century is the "Buxheim Organ Book," so named because it was once in the possession of the Carthusian Monastery located in that southern German town.[1] In view of the strict observances of the Carthusian order it would appear unlikely that this particular collection, with its mixture of sacred and secular compositions, was

---

1. For an English-language study of the codex, MS Cim. 352b in the Bavarian State Library in Munich, see Eileen Southern, *The Buxheim Organ Book* (Brooklyn: Institute of Mediaeval Music, 1963); for a survey of the relevant literature, see Martin Staehelin, "Buxheimer Orgelbuch," *Die Musik in Geschichte und Gegenwart*, Sachteil, ii (1995): 285–88.

actually compiled there, but it must have originated somewhere in the region, probably during the decade 1460–70.

The music is written in a type of organ tablature that is characteristic of the fifteenth-century keyboard sources from the region, few though they be.[2] The uppermost melodic line is given in regular mensural notation on a seven-line staff, while letters added in the space below indicate the notes of the remaining parts, of which there are usually no more than two. In addition, as an aid to the coordination of the simultaneously sounding pitches, vertical strokes through the staves mark off, irregularly at times, mensural or temporal units (see Figure 23-1).

While the sacred compositions of the repertory point clearly to the kind of liturgical use to be expected from a church organist at the time, the secular pieces are of the sort that were probably often used

FIGURE 23-1. *Wach uff myn hort* from the "Buxheim Organ Book" (Munich, Bayerische Staatsbibliothek, Mus. MS 3725, f. 57ᵛ).

for recreation in the clerical communities associated with cathedrals and collegiate churches. There is a significant didactic component as well.[3]

Of the some 250 compositions included in the collection, at least 142 appear to

---

2. See John Caldwell, "Sources of Keyboard Music to 1660," *The New Grove Dictionary of Music*, 17:724–29.

3. The entire repertory has been published in facsimile, Bertha A. Wallner, ed., *Das Buxheimer Orgelbuch*, Documenta musicologica, vol. 2 (Kassel: Bärenreiter, 1955), and in modern score, Bertha A. Wallner, ed., *Das Buxheimer Orgelbuch*, 3 vols., Das Erbe deutscher Musik, vols. 37–39 (Kassel: Bärenreiter, 1958).

be intabulations—that is to say keyboard arrangements of preexisting polyphonic pieces. Models have been identified thus far for about 100 of them: chansons (by composers such as Binchoys, Du Fay, Dunstable, Bedyngham, Morton, and Frye); Italian songs (including the well-traveled *O rosa bella*); Lieder; and Latin motets. Besides the occasional Lied and some 16 *basse danse* tunes, polyphonic settings of monophonic melodies include plainsongs for liturgical use. Particularly noteworthy is the music for the Ordinary of the Mass and for Vespers: several Kyries, a Gloria, a Credo, a Sanctus, Marian antiphons, and four Magnificats for Compline. All are designed for *alternatim* performance with the organ answering polyphonically the monody of the choir.

Also for use in a liturgical context, presumably, are the eighteen pieces that can be identified by the term *praeambulum*. The preludial function of these works is suggested not only by their title but also by the indication of the final—and hence, by implication, the mode—that each was intended to introduce. Such compositions are among the few apparently not based on some preexistent musical material, whether monophonic or in parts. Also original, but of more limited artistic significance, are the pieces intended for didactic purposes. Most of these are either clearly labeled or unequivocally recognizable as such. Pieces specifically identified in the manuscript as exercises are designed to teach the apprentice organist the techniques of polyphonic improvisation over certain characteristic melodic patterns (see below). They are largely derived from the *Fundamentum organisandi* attributed to the celebrated blind organist Conrad Paumann, whose place in the repertory is considerable.[4]

INSTRUMENTAL COLLECTIONS PRINTED IN ITALY

It was not until several decades later that instrumental repertories began to be printed. Some of the first came from the Venetian workshop of Ottaviano Petrucci early in his career. Already in 1507 he published two volumes of music that had been either arranged or composed by Francesco Spinacino and intabulated for the lute.[5] For this collection Spinacino adopted Italian lute tablature, which lent itself reasonably well to the printer's new technology. Using a six-line staff, each line of which represented one of the lute's six courses of strings, numbers (starting with 0 for the open string) are placed on the appropriate lines to indicate the sequence of strings to be struck and frets to be stopped. Flags above the notes indicate their temporal duration, and vertical strokes mark off (more or less regularly) mensural units (see Figure 23-2).

---

4. Concerning the nature of the Buxheim repertory, see Southern, *Buxheim Organ Book*, 16ff.

5. *Intabulatura de' lauto, Libro primo* and *Libro secondo*; see Howard M. Brown, *Instrumental Music Printed before 1600: A Bibliography* (Cambridge, Mass.: Harvard University Press, 1965), 12–14, 1507_1 and 1507_2.

The pieces selected for intabulation were of the same type as those brought out in the *Odhecaton* series (A, B, and C): chansons and *canzone* attributable primarily to northern masters, to which was added an occasional song motet. Compositions of this sort constitute twenty-one of the thirty-eight pieces in Spinacino's *Libro primo* and thirty-three of the forty-three in his *Libro secondo*. The remaining compositions in both collections are labeled *recercare*,

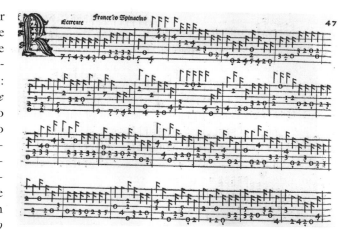

FIGURE 23-2. *Recercare* from Francesco Spinacino's *Intabulatura de' lauto, libro secondo*, f. 47 (printed in Venice by Petrucci, 1507).

a term that can be translated as "study" or "invention." That the latter were intended to serve primarily as introductions to the intabulated vocal pieces is indicated by the fact that a number of them are linked by their title to a specific chanson. Their function, then (like the *praeambula* of the "Buxheim Organ Book"), was to fix in each instance the appropriate final and modal orientation for the intabulation of a given polyphonic piece.[6]

Also included, as a preface to both volumes, were rules for reading the tablature ("Regula pro illis qui canere nesciunt") in both Latin and Italian. Instruction of this sort accompanied later Petrucci prints for lute as well, suggesting perhaps that even those musically literate otherwise were not necessarily expected to be familiar with the specialized notation of lute tablature. In order to assure the commercial success of collections of this kind, they were aimed at the widest possible audience. Amateurs and beginners must have constituted the largest number of potential buyers, so the didactic material was undoubtedly added to help draw their interest. It is not likely, after all, that a professionally trained musician who was also a skilled lutenist would have needed help in intabulating polyphonic pieces for his own use. Nor would he have had to rely upon notated sources for his preludial material, much of which appears to be improvisatory in character.

Following Spinacino's two books of intabulations of polyphonic chansons and *canzone* originally written for consort, Petrucci published in 1508 a collection of

---

6. Such pieces are the *Recercare de tous biens* and the *Recercare juli amours*; see the list of contents in Brown, *Instrumental Music Printed before 1600*, 12–13, 1507₁.

dances, edited and intabulated for lute by Joan Ambrosio Dalza.[7] At the heart of this repertory, forty-two pieces in all, is a series of nine pavanes ("padoane diverse"), each of which is accompanied by its *saltarello* and *piva* (or *springardo*). The result is an early example of a dance "suite," a sequence of dances, often based upon common musical materials, each moving more rapidly than the first, and usually involving a shift in meter from binary to ternary. In this instance the sedate pavane in duple meter (of which Dalza has provided some of the earliest examples) is followed by the leaping *saltarello* and the running *piva*. The latter pair are both in triple meter and are related motivically to one another and to the introductory pavane.[8]

It is conceivable, of course, that such suites were actually used at times for dancing in a domestic context. However, dance music has its own intrinsic and obvious charm. Its clear rhythms and repetitive patterns of meter and melody make it immediately and easily accessible to player and listener alike. It is consequently possible that this group of compositions may represent an early stage in the transformation of utilitarian suites for dancing into music intended primarily for playing and listening. Such a metamorphosis was often seen in subsequent centuries as the fundamental formal and stylistic features of the original dance were progressively stylized, removing it ever farther from the original purpose for which it was written.

Also included with Dalza's compilation of dance suites is a series of fourteen introductory pieces, some of which are designated "tastar de corde con li soi ricercar dietro," meaning, roughly, "a trying of the strings, followed by an invention." Here, too, although no specific connection is made in the print between the *recercari* and the dances, it can be assumed that their customary function was preludial. Closing the collection is a series of thirteen *calate*, which may have been intended for a similar purpose. They may have been used as *riprese*—that is, as instrumental interludes to precede, follow, or alternate with a dance or a song. A connection with settings of strophic verse is in fact suggested by one of Dalza's own titles, "Calata di strambotti."[9]

It was from the large repertory of pieces of the kind to which reference is thus made—the *frottole* that had begun to be published in such considerable numbers in 1504—that Petrucci drew the next repertory of music arranged specifically for instrumental performance. In 1509 he brought out the first of two books of secular Italian polyphony, arranged by Franciscus Bossinensis with the "tenor and bass intabulated" for lute and the "soprano [written] in mensural notation" and provided with text so that it could be sung in the usual manner, and a second collection of exactly

---

7. *Intabulatura de Lauto, Libro quarto*; see Brown, *Instrumental Music Printed before 1600*, 14–16, 1508₂. A third book, containing intabulations and *ricercari* by Joan Maria Allemani, was published in 1508, but no copy has survived.

8. Concerning the character of these dances and the music used to accompany them, see Alan Brown, "Pavan" and "Piva," and Meredith Ellis Little, "Saltarello," all in *The New Grove Dictionary of Music*, 14:311–13, 9:793–94, and 16:430–32, respectively.

9. See Daniel Heartz, "Calata," *The New Grove Dictionary of Music*, 3:612.

the same type followed in 1511.[10] In both of these anthologies a series of *frottole* (seventy in book 1 and fifty-six in book 2) was followed by a number of pieces designated *recercare* that were once again meant to fill a preludial function. That purpose, and the link with the specific pieces in the intabulated repertory with which each was modally compatible, was indicated in Petrucci's print by a system of letters.

FIGURE 23-3. Bartomoleo Tromboncino's *Si è debile il filo* as intabulated for keyboard in Andrea Antico's *Frottole intabulate da sonare organi, libro primo* (Rome, 1517).

To this succession of published collections of music for lute (and lute and voice) published by Petrucci may be added two other significant but slightly later sources of instrumental music, one printed and the other in manuscript. A book of *frottole* arranged for keyboard and intabulated in the kind of score notation that has since come into general use was brought out in Rome by Andrea Antico in 1517 (see Figure 23-3). The collection comprises twenty-six compositions from those layers of the repertory of strophic Italian song that preceded more or less immediately its eclipse by the emergence of the madrigal.[11]

At about the same time, a similar collection of music for lute was inscribed in a paper manuscript by a certain Vitale, an amateur lutenist living in Venice. It includes forty-two pieces that had been either intabulated or composed by Vitale's teacher, Vincenzo Capirola, a patrician of Brescian origin who was also living in the Serene Republic. Vitale took the sage precaution, as he explains in a short preface, of having his collection richly decorated and bound in order that it might have a better chance of escaping destruction. Fortunately, his strategy proved successful. He was less careful with the organization of the repertory, however. Capirola's compositions were copied at random with little regard for function or type, even though they include all of the genres being cultivated for the lute at the time: arrangements of vocal compositions (in this case chansons, *frottole*, Latin motets,

10. *Tenori e contrabassi intabulati col sopran in canto figurato . . . Libro primo* and *Libro secundo;* see Brown, *Instrumental Music Printed before 1600,* 16–20, 1509₁ and 1511₁. For a modern transcription of both volumes, see Benvenuto Disertori, ed., *Le frottole per canto e liuto intabulate de Franciscus Bossinensis,* Istituzioni e monumente dell'arte musicale italiana, new ser., vol. 3 (Milan: Ricordi, 1964).
11. Antico's *Frottole intabulate da sonare organi, Libro primo* (Rome, 1517) has been reprinted in facsimile (Bologna: Arnaldo Forni, 1970); for its contents see Brown, *Instrumental Music Printed before 1600,* 1517₁.

and even sections from polyphonic Mass Ordinaries); dances (pavanes and *basses danses*); and *ricercari*.[12]

~~~ INSTRUMENTAL COLLECTIONS ~~~
PRINTED IN FRANCE

</div>

A third substantial repertory of music prepared specifically for instruments was published in Paris by Pierre Attaingnant, beginning in October 1529. It is noteworthy that his production of books of this type began already in the second year of his career as a printer of polyphonic music and that a first phase in the printing of instrumental music was essentially completed within a two-year period. Such circumstances suggest a systematic effort to exploit quickly the market in all of the genres and types of instrumental music then current.

Attaingnant initiated this series with a collection of music for lute that combined an opening group of five preludes with intabulations of pieces from the (primarily secular) vocal repertory. Forty of these pieces are for lute alone; another twenty-four have been arranged for voice with lute accompaniment using the format adopted for the same purpose by Bossinensis.

The lute tablature in this case was French, which is very similar to the Italian notation described earlier. It differs only in that letters, instead of numbers, designate the fret to be stopped on the string, and these are placed in the spaces of a five-line staff (including those immediately above and below) rather than directly on the lines (see Figure 23-4). The inclusion of a brief tract explaining the specialized notation, like those found in the lute books printed by Petrucci, indicates once again that amateurs and beginners were among those to whom the publication was directed. If confirmation for that conclusion were needed, it is supplied by a declaration on the title page that the instructions were to help the reader "to understand and to learn by oneself to play all songs intabulated for the lute."[13]

A second tablature for lute appeared in early February of the following year, this one comprising a series of dances: eighteen *basses danses*, twenty-one *branles* or brawls (including the two advertised as *Haulberroys*); two *sauterelles*, fifteen galliards;

---

12. The manuscript, currently at the Newberry Library in Chicago, was edited in modern transcription with a detailed study of the repertory by Otto Gombosi, *Compositione di Meser Vicenzo Capirola, Lute-Book (circa 1517)* (Chicago: Société de Musique d'Autrefois, 1955).

13. All of the chansons were included in Attaingnant's *Tres breve et familiere introduction pour entendre & apprendre par soy mesmes a jouer toutes chansons reduictes en la tabulature du lutz* (Paris, 1529); see Daniel Heartz, *Pierre Attaingnant, Royal Printer of Music* (Berkeley: University of California Press, 1969), 225–26. The pieces for lute and voice have been published in modern score by Lionel de la Laurencie, Adrienne Mairy, and Geneviève Thibaut, eds., *Chansons au luth et airs de cour français du XVIe siècle* (Paris: Société Française de Musicologie, 1934); those for lute alone by Daniel Heartz, ed., *Preludes, Chansons, and Dances for Lute* (Neuilly-sur-Seine: La Société de Musique d'Autrefois, 1964).

and nine pavanes.[14] The heart of the collection is the group of *basses danses*, nine of which are ordered as a small suite with an accompanying *recoupe* and a *tordion*. Of courtly origins with a venerable history reaching well back into the fourteenth century, the *basse danse* reflects its status as the most aristocratic of steps in its stately striding movements and its rhythmic complexity.

Executed to a compound mensuration (with binary breves and ternary semibreves), the frequent use of hemiola in the musical settings must have made dif-

Figure 23-4. Claudin de Sermisy's *Tant que vivray* intabulated for lute for Pierre Attaingnant's *Tres breve et familiere introduction* (Paris, 1529).

ficulties for all but the most skillful dancers. The *recoupe*, or return, when present, was for a second sequence of steps, shorter than the first but in the same tempo, intended to bring the dancers back to the place from which they started. By contrast, the *tordion* was apparently done at twice the speed but without the leaps characteristic of the galliard or even the higher steps of the *sauterelle*.[15]

The pavane was modeled on the more courtly *basse danse*, albeit with some simplification reflecting its urban origins. It was performed at a similarly measured tempo—although in duple meter—with feet kept close to the ground. As in Italy, the pavane was usually followed in France by a rapid, leaping dance in triple meter, most commonly, it would seem, a galliard.[16] More often than not, a galliard follows a pavane in this collection, but whether or not they were originally meant to be played in sequence is difficult to say. By contrast, in two instances a *sauterelle* was obviously intended to form a short suite with the preceding pavane, from which it derives its musical material. The French term is obviously nothing more than a literal translation of the Italian *saltarello* (or vice versa), and in both compositional sets the musical material shared by the slow dance and its more energetic "after-dance" obviously mirrors the Italian fashion as seen earlier with Petrucci.[17]

14. Pierre Attaingnant, *Dixhuit basses dances garnies de Recoupes et Tordions, avec dixneuf Branles, quatre quant Sauterelles que Haulberroys, quinze Gaillardes et neuf Pavennes* (Paris, 1530); see Heartz, *Pierre Attaingnant, Royal Printer of Music*, 229–30. The dances have also been edited by Heartz, ed., *Preludes, Chansons, and Dances for Lute*, 53–117, nos. 41–102.

15. Concerning the *basse danse*, see Daniel Heartz, *The New Grove Dictionary of Music*, 2:257–59, and Heartz, ed., *Preludes, Chansons, and Dances for Lute*, xxxi–xxxviii.

16. See Alan Brown, "Galliard," *The New Grove Dictionary of Music*, 7:105–7.

17. See Heartz, ed., *Preludes, Chansons, and Dances for Lute*, 96–98 and 100–101, nos. 82 and 84.

This leaves the *branle* (or brawl), a dance (unlike its more courtly companions) of clearly popular origins with a surprisingly long history.[18] By the sixteenth century several different varieties had evolved, all of them characterized by movement from side to side but distinguishable by the meter (whether duple or triple) and the rapidity with which they are executed. They are identified in the print by name, as they are in the dance manuals of the period:[19] *branle gay* (in quick triple time), *branle simple* (more sedate in duple time), *branle de Poictou* (triple), and *branle du Haulberroys* (duple). In later publications other types appear as well, most notably the *branle de Champeigne.*

Because of their diversity of movement, it was clearly possible to string together a series of brawls of contrasting meters and tempos in a suite, but there is no indication in this collection that such combinations were established practice. Not until the Attaingnant firm's last collection of instrumental dances, the *Septieme livre de danceries* of 1557, were they so grouped in the source itself.[20] The question here is the same as for the lute dances of Petrucci. Were these pieces intended primarily to accompany dancing, or had they already come to be regarded more as music for playing and listening? Although loud consorts were required for practical reasons where dancers in fair numbers were gathered in large rooms, even a soft instrument such as a lute might have been used for a small group in intimate circumstances. It seems likely, however, that they were much more often performed simply for the entertainment and pleasure of the player—and whoever might have been present to listen.

A month or so after the publication of the second lute tablature, Attaingnant completed a set of four partbooks containing chansons (to be sung or played, apparently) with a dozen dances for instrumental consort, balanced equally between pavanes and galliards.[21] This was followed before the year was out with a second set of dances for instrumental ensemble. In this instance a significant number of pavanes and several galliards were rounded out by a pair of brawls and a series of *basses danses.*[22] Also included was a Latin translation of the brief tract on playing the lute, which opened the *Tres breve et familiere introduction* of 1529 and gave it its title, now ascribed to Oronce Finé.[23]

Attaingnant continued publishing instrumental music in the following year (1531) with an unbroken series of seven books of music for keyboard—of whatever

18. See Daniel Heartz, "Branle," *The New Grove Dictionary of Music*, 3:201–4, and Heartz, ed., *Preludes, Chansons, and Dances for Lute*, xxxix–xlviii.

19. See, for example, Thoinot Arbeau, *Orchésographie, Méthode et théorie en forme de discours et tablature pour apprendre a danser* (Langres, 1588; reprint, Geneva: Minkoff, 1972).

20. Concerning this collection, see Heartz, *Pierre Attaingnant, Royal Printer of Music*, 376, no. 173.

21. Pierre Attaingnant, *Six Gaillardes et six Pavanes avec Treze chansons musicales a quatre parties* (Paris, 1530); see Heartz, *Pierre Attaingnant, Royal Printer of Music*, 230–31.

22. Pierre Attaingnant, *Neuf basses dances, deux branles, vingt et cinq Pavennes avec quinze Gaillardes en musique a quatre parties* (Paris, 1530); see Heartz, *Pierre Attaingnant, Royal Printer of Music*, 234–36.

23. Oronce Finé, *Epithoma musice instrumentalis ad omnimodam Hemispherii seu Luthine a theoricam et practicam* (Paris, 1530); see Heartz, *Pierre Attaingnant, Royal Printer of Music*, 236. The entire tract has been published in facsimile in Heartz, ed., *Preludes, Chansons, and Dances for Lute*, plates 4 and 5.

type—printed in score. The first three collections were given over to intabulations of chansons, the great majority of them attributed to Claudin de Sermisy. All but two of these pieces (a reworking of *Fors seulement* by Pipelare and a dance tune) had been included earlier in one of Attaingnant's many anthologies of secular vocal music.[24]

These three volumes of secular repertory were balanced by three more that contained only sacred compositions. Featured were plainsong settings for Mass Ordinaries, the Magnificat, and the Te Deum—all entirely appropriate for liturgical use—together with three preludes. There was also an entire volume of motet arrangements.[25] This relatively brief flurry of publishing activity aimed primarily at instrumentalists ended with a book of dances (pavanes, galliards, brawls, and *basses danses*) intabulated once again for keyboard.[26]

In the following year he mentioned in the title of two books of chansons that included texts the possibility of performance on the recorder ("fleuste d'allemant") as well as voices, but he printed no more music prepared specifically for either lute or keyboard. Nor did he republish, as he did so often the vocal anthologies, any of those early collections of instrumental music. Only toward the end of his career did he turn again to the dance music repertory and publish once again collections explicitly intended for instrumental ensemble.

His Lyonnais competitor, Jacques Moderne, made only one attempt at the publication of music for instruments. About 1544 he brought out a mixed collection of pieces for consort entitled *Musicque de joye*. It comprised a series of *phantaisies*, all with attributions to composers active at the time in Italy followed by a varied assortment of dances.[27] This may have encouraged Attaingnant to return to what must

24. Pierre Attaingnant, *Dixneuf chansons musicales reduictes en la tabulature des Orgues, Espinettes, Manicordions, et telz semblables instrumentz musicaulx* (Paris, 1531); *Vingt et cinq chansons musicales reduictes en la tabulature . . .* (Paris, 1531); and *Vingt et six chansons musicales reduictes en la tabulature . . .* (Paris, 1531); see Heartz, *Pierre Attaingnant, Royal Printer of Music*, 236–39. All three have been published in a facsimile by Eduard Bernoulli, ed., *Chansons und Tänze* (Munich: C. Kuhn, 1914), and in modern score: Pierre Attaingnant, *Transcriptions of Chansons for Keyboard (1531)*, ed. Albert Seay, Corpus mensurabilis musicae 20 ([Rome]: American Institute of Musicology, 1961).

25. Pierre Attaingnant, *Tabulature pour le jeu D'orgues, Espinettes, et Manicordions sur le plain chant de Cunctipotens et Kyrie fons . . .* (Paris, 1531); *Magnificat sur les huit tons avec Te deum laudamus, et deux Preludes, le tout mys en la tabulature . . .* (Paris, 1531); and *Treze Motetz musicaulx avec ung Prelude, le tout reduict en la tabulature . . .* (Paris, 1531); see Heartz, *Pierre Attaingnant, Royal Printer of Music*, 239–41. All three have been published in modern score: Yvonne Rokseth, ed., *Deux livres d'orgues parus chez Pierre Attaingnant en 1531*, Publications de la Société Française de Musicologie, ser. 1, vol. 1 (Paris: Société Française de Musicologie, 1925), and idem, *Treize motets et un prélude pour orgue parus chez Pierre Attaingnant en 1531*, Publication de la Société Française de Musicologie, ser. 1, vol. 5 (Paris: Société Française de Musicologie, 1930).

26. Pierre Attaingnant, *Quatorze Gaillardes, neuf Pavennes, sept Branles, et deux Basses Dances, le tout reduict de musique en la tabulature du jeu D'orgues, Espinettes, Manicordions & telz semblables instrumentz musicaulx* (Paris, 1531); see Heartz, *Pierre Attaingnant, Royal Printer of Music*, 241–42. The dances have been published in modern score: Daniel Heartz, ed., *Keyboard Dances from the Earlier Sixteenth Century*, Corpus of Early Keyboard Music, vol. 8 ([Rome]: American Institute of Musicology, 1965).

27. Concerning this collection, see Samuel F. Pogue, *Jacques Moderne, Lyons Music Printer of the Sixteenth Century* (Geneva: Librairie Droz, 1969), 182–85, no. 41.

have been an increasingly profitable market. Between 1547 and his death in 1552 he brought out a series of four books for balanced consorts of four or five parts, the last of which was edited by Claude Gervaise.[28]

Attaingnant's widow continued the series, issuing two additional collections of dance music for instrumental ensemble between 1555 and 1557 and reprinting (also in 1557) the *Troisieme livre de danceries.* Two of these three collections were edited again by Gervaise and the last by Estienne du Tertre.[29] The dances in these anthologies were, for the most part, of the same types as those published earlier. However, the *basse danse*, which must by then have already gone out of style, disappeared after the *Second livre.* The (newly minted?) *allemand* made its first—and only—appearance in the *Troisieme Livre.* Interestingly, the brawls in the *Septieme Livre* have been grouped into "suyttes," thus realizing the potential for such organization inherent in the variety of meters and tempi associated with its basic steps.

INSTRUMENTAL COLLECTIONS PRINTED IN SPAIN

In Spain the publication of repertories of music for instruments appears to have been more the province of performer-composers than of the printers themselves. These Iberian virtuosi were surprisingly numerous in the sixteenth century, and the repertory they offered to the public is both extensive and diverse. The Spanish collections, like those produced elsewhere, were intended to serve a variety of needs, and the genres represented in them were similar in most essential ways to those found in Italian and French prints.

Among the earliest, and in important respects most typical, was the *Libro de música de vihuela de mano intitulado El maestro* of Luis de Milán (ca. 1500–ca. 1561), brought out in Valencia in 1536. Milán, who was both musician and writer, apparently spent most of his life at the ducal court of his native city. In *El maestro* he combined vocal music—*villancicos* and *romances* as well as settings by poems of Petrarch and Sannazaro—whose accompaniment was intabulated for vihuela (a direct ancestor of the modern guitar), with six pavanes, forty fantasias, and four *tientos* for vihuela alone.[30]

Perhaps even more indicative of then future trends were *Los seys libros del delphin*, compiled by Luys de Narváez (fl. 1530–50) and published in Valladolid in 1538. The composer, about whom relatively little is known, may have been for a time in the employ of Francisco de los Cobos, secretary to Emperor Charles V, and in the 1540s

28. These were numbered in sequence from the *second* through the *cinquiesme;* see Heartz, *Pierre Attaingnant, Royal Printer of Music*, 352ff., nos. 148 and 164–65. There is no surviving copy of the first edition of the Troisieme Livre.

29. See Heartz, *Pierre Attaingnant, Royal Printer of Music*, 372ff.: nos. 170 (*Sixieme livre*), 172 (*Troisieme livre*), and 173 (*Septieme livre*).

30. Concerning Luis de Milán, see Charles Jacobs, *The New Grove Dictionary of Music*, 12:300–301.

was master to the children in the chapel of the future king of Spain, Philip II. A virtuoso of the vihuela, Narváez presented his repertory in a tablature very similar to that in use in Italy (as did most of the masters cited here). Included were arrangements of vocal works by composers such as Josquin (six), Gombert (two), and Richafort, fantasias (one in each of the eight modes, indicating their preludial function), and variation sets identified as *diferencias.*[31]

Similar repertories were published by yet other performer-composers. Alonso Mudarra (ca. 1510–80), for example, a vihuelist and composer brought up in Guadalajara at the ducal court of the infantado who spent the last thirty-four years of his life as a canon of Seville Cathedral, published his *Tres libros de musica en cifras para vihuela* there in 1546. In addition to intabulations of Mass sections by Josquin and Févin, motets by Gombert and Willaert, and accompaniments for *villancicos, romances*, and songs in Latin and Italian, he offered to his public twenty-seven fantasias, eight *tientos*, a few dances, and several sets of variations.[32]

In the following year Enríquez de Valderrábano (fl. mid-1500s) published his *Libro de música de vihuela, intitulado Silva de serenas* in Valladolid. Also vihuelist and composer, who apparently served for a time the count of Miranda, he included among the seven "books" of this publication intabulations for vihuela and voice, vihuelas in pairs, and vihuela alone. The repertory comprises arrangements of vocal works, sacred and secular, by composers from northern Europe, Italy, and his native Spain: Josquin, Gombert, Layolle, Morales, Willaert, Ruggo, Sepúlveda, and others. His own works are limited to a set of pavanes and thirty-three fantasias, nineteen of which are based on musical materials borrowed from other composers: Gombert, Morales, Ripa (the well-known lutenist), Mouton, Lupus, and Josquin among the number.[33]

Intabulations of vocal models were an even more substantial part of the *Libro de música de vihuela agora nuevamente compuesta*, published in Salamanca in 1552 by Diego Pisador (1509–10 to after 1557). Unbounded admiration for the music of Josquin prompted him to intabulate eight of the northerner's Masses rather literally, most of them virtually in their entirety. Also included in the collection are arrangements of motets by Mouton, Morales, and Gombert; Spanish songs and *romances, villanesche* by Vincenzo Fontana, Giovanni da Nola, and Willaert; madrigals by Arcadelt and Sebastiano Festa; and, by Pisador himself, some fantasias and sets of variations.[34]

Miguel de Fuenllana (early 1500s to after 1568) was also an accomplished vihuelist and composer who was blind from birth. In 1553, when his only known works were published in Seville as the *Orphénica lyra*, he was at the court of Philip II. Later he served as chamber musician to the king's third wife, Elisabeth de Valois. The repertory included in this collection also comprises a good many intabulations of vocal repertory: motets, Mass sections, madrigals, *villancicos*, and the like, some by northern composers such as Josquin (again), Lhéritier, and Verdelot, others by

---

31. Concerning Narváez, see Hopkinson K. Smith, *The New Grove Dictionary of Music*, 13:39.
32. Concerning Mudarra, see Robert Stevenson, *The New Grove Dictionary of Music*, 12:757–58.
33. Concerning Valderrábano, see Charles Jacobs, *The New Grove Dictionary of Music*, 19:489–90.
34. Concerning Pisador, see Robert Stevenson, *The New Grove Dictionary of Music*, 14:771–72.

Spanish masters such as Morales and Guerrero. His own works included some fifty-two fantasias, many of them paired with an intabulated vocal piece in the same mode (indicating here again their preludial function), cantus firmus settings, and eight *tientos*.[35]

Compositions earlier published by a number of the composers mentioned thus far—Narváez, Mudarra, Valderábbano, and Pisador—were included in the *Libro de cifra nueva*, published in Alcalá de Henares near Madrid in 1557 by Luis Venegas de Henestrosa (ca. 1510–ca. 1557). More surprisingly, a *ricercar* attributed to Julio Segni in both the *Musica nova* of 1540 and the *Musicque de joye* of circa 1544 was also added to this repertory. Venegas, who served in the household of the cardinal of Toledo for about a decade (1534–35 to 1545), introduced a new type of intabulation for his collection, which includes, once again, intabulations of vocal compositions, plainsong settings, fantasias, *tientos*, and a set of variations.[36]

Among the works anthologized by Venegas were a number published for the first time under the name of the celebrated organist Antonio de Cabezón (1510–66). Born blind (like Fuenllana) but of noble lineage, Cabezón entered the service of the royal house in 1526 as chapel organist to Queen Isabella. Following her death in 1539, he continued to enjoy the patronage of the royal family, exclusively as organist to the chapel of Philip II from 1548 on. As a member of the king's household he traveled with him first to Italy, Germany, Luxembourg, and the Netherlands (from October 1548 to July 1551), then subsequently to the Netherlands and England (July 1554 to January 1556). The result was, for him, exposure to repertory that he might not otherwise have known, and for the areas visited a considerable impact on local keyboard repertory.

The majority of his works were published posthumously in Madrid (1578) by his son, Hernando, under the descriptive title, *Obras de música para tecla, arpa y vihuela de Antonio de Cabezón*. Included in the collection is a large and varied selection of music, comparable in every important respect to what has been seen thus far. There are plainsong settings, *glosas* (intabulations of polyphonic vocal works), strictly contrapuntal canons, *tientos* (corresponding to the fantasias and *ricercari* of Continental practice), and *diferencias*.[37]

Like the compositions of most of his fellow player-performers of sixteenth-century Spain, Cabezón's *obras* reveal both their strong indigenous roots—in the intabulation of pieces by native composers and the melodies upon which sets of variations were based—and the considerable influence of northern European masters, Josquin in particular. Even more importantly, the repertory represented by the printed collections cited here reflects the vigorous, increasingly cosmopolitan musical culture that flourished at the time on the Iberian peninsula and the very important place held within it by instrumental practice and composition.

---

35. Concerning Fuenllana, see John M. Ward, *The New Grove Dictionary of Music*, 7:6.
36. Concerning Venegas, see Charles Jacobs, *The New Grove Dictionary of Music*, 19:602–3.
37. Concerning Cabezón, see Macario Santiago Kastner, *The New Grove Dictionary of Music*, 3:572–74.

CHAPTER 24

✦

The Instrumental Genres

INTRODUCTION

The inventory of sources for instrumental music between the mid-fifteenth and the mid-sixteenth centuries surveyed in the previous chapter is necessarily highly selective. Nonetheless, despite differences in format and, as we shall see, in stylistic detail, the same basic compositional types were cultivated throughout the Renaissance. Patterns of instrumental usage represented in these collections remained basically unchanged until late in the sixteenth century. A few new instrumental genres emerged during the second half of the sixteenth century, but even they are based on structural types and compositional procedures already exemplified in the repertory surveyed above. Turning to individual cases, then, we shall begin to define the characteristics by which the genres in current use can be recognized and to discover the various terms by which they were identified to musicians of the time.

⟨⟩ DIDACTIC EXERCISES ⟨⟩

Perhaps the rarest kind of evidence relating to the history of instrumental music of the period is that offered by musical compositions specifically identified as didactic exercises. It is likely that many of the pieces included in the instrumental repertories still extant were in fact used for instruction, but in the fifteenth century only the *fundamenta* for keyboard were actually labeled so as to indicate that they were intended primarily, if not solely, for that purpose. Not until the publication of the first part of Girolamo Diruta's comprehensive treatise on organ playing, *Il Transilvano* of 1593, does one again find a repertory of pieces selected and written specifically for teaching.[1]

---

1. See Claude Palisca, "Diruta, Girolamo," *The New Grove Dictionary of Music*, 5:485–87; note, however, that the pieces selected by Diruta for his didactic purposes were not necessarily written with that end in view.

Of the pieces so marked in the sources of the period, some of the most substantial and earliest are those included in the *Fundamentum organisandi* attributable to the blind organist of Nuremberg, Conrad Paumann (ca. 1410–73), who traveled widely and finished his career in the service of the ducal court of Bavaria.[2] They are particularly relevant to the kinds of musical activity under discussion here because they reveal a systematic approach to the technical problems posed by the various performance situations in which keyed instruments were involved. Consequently, they offer precious insights into the kinds of skills, both digital and compositional, that the performer was expected to have mastered.

As we shall discover, two skills were commonly expected in those trained to play instruments with polyphonic potential—keyboards in particular and, to a lesser degree (once the plectrum was abandoned late in the fifteenth century), the lute and related plucked instruments. To be cultivated, on the one hand, was the ability to adapt more or less on sight a composition that had been written for consort (whether vocal, instrumental, or mixed) for a single pair of hands. On the other was the musicianship needed to dress polyphonically a single melodic line, whether for liturgical purposes or for secular recreation, again on sight if need be. In addition, a keyboard or lute player could be called upon to introduce the performance of a vocal composition by preludial improvisation that would establish the appropriate final and modal orientation.

Because the polyphonic elaboration of a given cantus firmus involved more or less extemporaneous composition as well as manual execution, it was the most difficult and appears to have driven the organization of the exercises in Paumann's *Fundamentum*.[3] Typical examples are two of the exercises copied into the "Buxheim Organ Book" (f. 124^V) with the labels "Ascensus simplex" and "Descensus simplex" (see Example 24-1). The nature of the problem for the performer is clear enough from the titles themselves.

In the first example an ascending line moves stepwise through a tenth in regular extended values—cantus firmus wise—a ternary breve at a time. The scalar pattern is broken only twice by modest ornamental diminution (the division of the breve into notes of shorter duration in mm. 4 and 7). The purpose of the exercise is to provide the novice with a stylistically acceptable model for the polyphonic presentation of such a series of pitches, thus helping him (or her) to develop the skills needed to improvise a polyphonic setting for any such passage. A second part was added in essentially the same range, moving homophonically in consonance with the given line. A third, placed in the treble ambitus, dances around and through pitches consonant with the other two in rapid divisions, making use in particular of scalewise passagework and turning figures.

---

2. Soncerning Paumann, see Christoph Wolff, *The New Grove Dictionary of Music*, 14:308–9.

3. See Christoph Wolff, "Paumann," *The New Grove Dictionary of Music*, 14:308–9. A complete modern edition of Paumann's *fundamenta*, prepared by Willi Apel, is found in Apel, ed., *Keyboard Music of the Fourteenth and Fifteenth Centuries*, Corpus of Early Keyboard Music, vol. 1 ([Rome]: American Institute of Musicology, 1963); other editions have been listed by Wolff.

EXAMPLE 24-1. Conrad Paumann, *Fundamentum organisandi*, "Ascensus simplex" and "Descensus simplex"

Descensus simplex

The same exercise is done in reverse for the descensus simplex, starting from the "e" reached in ascent and continuing again through a tenth to the "C" from which the first began. This time, however, the "cantus firmus" voice is more active. Diminution embellishes all but three of its nine ternary breves. That motion is matched by the part that shares its range, whereas the treble line begins with a pair of animated trills and then continues to weave about in rapid passagework, matching the rhythms of the other two parts only for one brief patch of syncopation (mm. 4–5).

<hr />

CANTUS FIRMUS COMPOSITION

Didactic exercises of the sort just seen were clearly meant to help prepare the keyboard player-in-training—by providing not only a compositional model but also some digital exercise—to devise a polyphonic accompaniment for any type of preexistent melody, whether for sacred or secular use, whatever the size or direction of the intervals from one pitch to the next. Consequently, other segments of the *fundamenta* were designed for systematic practice in dealing with each of the melodic sequences and intervals that the keyboard player was likely to encounter with any frequency. Once techniques of this sort had been mastered, the most obvious application for them was in the liturgical observances. By the fifteenth century it was customary in many places to present some of the plainchant in instrumental *alternatim* at virtually any important celebration, dividing discrete segments between monophonic choir and polyphonic organ. As will be clear from the foregoing survey of instrumental repertories, the chants most frequently treated in this way were those for the Ordinary of the Mass, the daily recitation of the Magnificat, and the festal Te Deum.

The manner in which the didactic exercise could be applied to any of the chants to be presented in *alternatim* is illustrated nicely by the *Kyrie angelicum*, found, like the *Fundamentum*, in the "Buxheim Organ Book" (see Example 24-2). The melody upon which it is based is essentially the same as that identified as "Cunctipotens Genitor Deus" in present-day service books, where it is prescribed for duplex feasts and much used on festal occasions. (The extent to which the two chants agree is indicated in the example by the small crosses in the lowest part over the pitches that correspond exactly with the chant as given there.)[4]

Some of the divergences between the cantus firmus and the chant used for comparison are certainly due to modest embellishment of the liturgical tune to facilitate its polyphonic composition, but the greater number undoubtedly reflect regional

<hr />

4. Compare the bottom line of the organ composition with the melody as given in the *Liber usualis*, 25, Mass Ordinary 4. The "Angelicum" of the Buxheim title refers to a trope text sung to the Kyrie melody during the Middle Ages in Germanic regions in place of the "Cunctipotens Genitor" trope that predominated in Italy and France. (Concerning troped Kyries, cf. Richard H. Hoppin, *Medieval Music* [New York: Norton, 1978], 150–51.)

EXAMPLE 24-2. Anonymous, *Kyrie angelicum*, "Kyrie 1" (mm. 1–11)

variants in the chant itself. Even without knowing note for note the version of the melody with which the organist-composer was working, however, the compositional procedure he adopted in setting it is self-evident. It is also strikingly similar to that used in the example from the *Fundamentum* discussed above.

The plainsong was first laid out in even semibreves; the regularity of that basic rhythm is broken briefly no more than once or twice in each section (see mm. 10, 16, 19, 30a, and 38), primarily to help with the counterpoint. A second part was written in the same range, moving in consonance against the liturgical cantus firmus and at the same rate of speed. Above this somewhat plodding foundation a more animated third part was added in the treble range, making continuous use of diminutions, short stepwise runs, melodic turns, and trills. These draw attention to the digital dexterity of the performer and generate the melodic and rhythmic interest that is otherwise largely lacking.

A single "Kyrie" section is followed by a "Christe" and then by two more for the "Kyrie." This sequence suggests that the alternation between choir and organ was regular, beginning and ending with the chant in the first "Kyrie" and the "Christe" but opening and closing with the organ for the final "Kyrie." However, the keyboard setting corresponds with the structure of the chant. The traditional threefold acclamations are generally based upon four sections of music; the first "Kyrie" and the "Christe" are each sung three times, the second "Kyrie" only twice, and the final "Kyrie" brings closure. Thus the four sections for organ made possible any pattern of alternation between choir and organ deemed appropriate for the circumstances.

Turning from the liturgical pieces in the "Buxheim Organ Book" to those published by Attaingnant in Paris nearly a century later, it is fascinating to see how similar these two small repertories are in structural concept and in musical style. The Attaingnant *Kyrie Cunctipotens* is also in a three-part texture with the chant cantus firmus disposed in even values (see Example 24-3). There are differences, however: (1) each of the three parts in the *Kyrie Cunctipotens* is kept for the most part in a separate range, whereas the two lower parts cross one another continuously in the *Kyrie angelicum*; (2) in the later work the two added parts tend to be matched fairly evenly in their melodic and rhythmic activity in contrast to the Buxheim piece, where only the two lower parts move together; (3) the treble domination of the earlier repertory thus gives way to a more balanced texture in the more recent one (this is emphasized in the second "Kyrie" section, where the cantus firmus is moved to the treble part, producing a polyphonic texture simply not seen in the earlier repertory); and (4) the Buxheim Kyrie moves to the regular final for mode 1 on D, whereas the Attaingnant piece concludes on A, the final of the chant in the Roman version (a difference that may reflect divergent traditions in the transmission of the liturgical melody but might also represent a compositional decision).

The pattern adopted for the "Kyrie" in the Attaingnant keyboard Mass is retained for the "Christe" as well; the cantus firmus is heard as the lowest part for the first section but as the treble for the second. For the third "Kyrie" the procedure is reversed; the chant is carried by the treble line in the first section and the texture

EXAMPLE 24-3. Anonymous, *Messe Cunctipotens*, "Kyrie 1": 1 and 3

reduced to two parts. A three-part texture is restored for the final "Kyrie," but the cantus firmus is placed there for the first time in the tenor range with the counter-point above and below in treble and bass. Only in the final "Kyrie," then, does the cantus firmus treatment conform to the most common usage for vocal composition from at least the fourteenth century on. As for the alternation between chant and organ, the four instrumental sections would suggest that plainsong was used for just a single acclamation in each of the three major divisions of the Kyrie. As was observed earlier, however, any pattern that might have been dictated by a given set of circumstances became possible with as few as four of the six keyboard sections offered by the Attaingnant print.

All through the period under consideration keyboard music for liturgical use—whether Mass Ordinary, Magnificat, Te Deum, or some other frequently performed chant—generally shared with the two examples just examined their fundamental characteristics. Such pieces were invariably designed for *alternatim* performance, and they always took the plainsong melody as a cantus firmus in the compositional process. Within those parameters there was some latitude, obviously. One clear tendency was to integrate into a work thus conceived stylistic features being cultivated at the time in the vocal repertory, in particular the systematic use of syntactic imitation, which would eventually be adopted for much instrumental music as well. Still, the evidence would suggest that church organists were of a conservative bent. They were inclined to adhere to the didactic and compositional traditions handed down from one generation to the next, hence the significant similarities between Mass sections composed nearly a century apart. More importantly, the paucity of sources for music of this kind, in manuscript or in print, is arresting. Attaingnant's failure to republish either of the volumes given over to sacred music for keyboard is surely symptomatic in this regard, suggesting perhaps that much of it was simply improvised and therefore rarely committed to written form.

⟳ SECULAR CANTUS FIRMI ↷

One might assume from the foregoing discussion that cantus firmus techniques were used only by church organists in setting plainsong melodies for liturgical celebration, but that was not by any means the case. Cantus firmus–based composition was much too fundamental to the Western polyphonic tradition, and much too useful in practical terms, to have been so restricted in its use. Cantus firmus procedures were adopted as well for a wide variety of secular instrumental genres. The link between the secular and the sacred for compositions of this kind—one easily made by performer-composers who worked in both domains—is perhaps most evident in instrumental genres that were based on chant even though they were apparently never intended for church use.

English musicians seem to have been particularly partial to compositions of this sort, many of which may have had their roots in liturgical practice that was later adapted to didactic purposes or simply appropriated for private music making.[5] The two families of pieces derived from the sacred realm that appear most clearly to have established themselves in the secular repertory are those designated by the Latin labels *Felix namque* and *In nomine*. Examples of both were included in the largest collection of music for keyboard instruments to have originated in sixteenth-century England, the *Fitzwilliam Virginal Book* (Cambridge, Fitzwilliam Museum, Mus.32.G.29). Copied by the determined Catholic, Francis Tregian, while he was being held for recusancy in the London Fleet Prison (between 1609 and his death some ten years later), it contains a representative repertory of the keyboard genres then current with some pieces dating back to the early 1560s.[6]

Among its nearly 300 compositions are a great many dances (more than 130), substantial numbers of intabulations (of songs and madrigals), sets of variations, and preludial pieces. Also included, however, are several secular cantus firmus settings. Two of these are based on the chant fragment *Felix namque*, which is derived from the Offertory *Salve sancte parens*. A plainsong peculiar to the Sarum rite, it was pre-

---

5. See Gustave Reese, *Music in the Renaissance* (New York: Norton, 1959), 853–58.

6. See the introduction to the edition in modern score by J. A. Fuller Maitland and W. Barclay Squire, eds., *The Fitzwilliam Virginal Book*, 2 vols. (London: Breitkopf und Härtel, 1894–99; reprint New York: Dover, 1963), v–ix; cf. Thurston Dart and Richard Marlow, "Tregian, Francis," *The New Grove Dictionary of Music*, 19:126–27.

scribed for use with certain votive Marian Masses, which were among those celebrated most frequently with polyphony. This may help to explain how the melisma for "felix namque" came to be isolated fairly early on as a cantus firmus for instrumental composition.[7] Both settings in Tregian's collection are attributed to Thomas Tallis (ca. 1505–85), who is known to have been a skilled keyboard player as well as a fine composer.[8] Both are also dated: the first from 1562, the second from 1564, years during which Tallis was a Gentleman of the Chapel Royal.[9]

The composer's approach is much the same in both settings. An opening section based upon the chant pitches sung with the word "felix" begins imitatively and is repeated to serve as an introduction. The next section also begins with an imitative figure, incorporating the pitches for the next incise of the chant (with the word "namque"), and then settles into a straightforward presentation of the cantus firmus melody in extended values. In the earlier of the two settings, the borrowed material is carried at the top of the compositional fabric as a treble line; in the later one it is placed instead in the tenor range, with added parts both above and below. There is considerable contrapuntal integrity to the individual lines, and the texture rarely exceeds three parts unless block chords are involved.

Comparable as well in these two works is the high level of technical proficiency required for a successful performance. Each of them displays a dazzling array of scalewise passagework, arpeggiation, sequential elaboration of motives, hocketlike alternation of parts, intricate embellishments, and similar feats of digital (and mental) dexterity in a changing kaleidoscope of meters and rhythms (see Example 24-4).[10]

Unlike the *Felix namque*, which appears to have been based throughout its history directly on the plainchant, the *In nomine* had its origins as a keyboard intabulation. The model was that section of the Benedictus sung to the words "In nomine" in the *Missa Gloria tibi Trinitas* attributed to John Taverner (ca. 1495 to 1545).[11] If the earliest examples are reasonably faithful transcriptions of Taverner's setting, however, those that came later were for the most part based primarily, or even solely, on the plainsong cantus firmus itself.[12]

There are three such pieces in the *Fitzwilliam Virginal Book*, two of them attributed to John Bull (ca. 1562–1628), another celebrated keyboard player who was also a Gentleman of the Chapel Royal.[13] Another is signed to John Parsons (ca. 1575–1623), who received an appointment as one of the organists at St. Margaret's,

7. See Frank L. Harrison, *Music in Medieval Britain*, 2d ed. (London: Routledge and Kegan Paul, 1963), 79 and 365; cf. Lewis Lockwood, "Felix namque," *The New Grove Dictionary of Music*, 6:458.

8. Concerning Tallis, see Paul Doe, *The New Grove Dictionary of Music*, 18:541–48.

9. For a transcription of these two pieces in modern score, see Maitland and Squire, eds., *Fitzwilliam Virginal Book*, 1:427–36 and 2:1–11.

10. See the discussion in Reese, *Music in the Renaissance*, 855–57.

11. Concerning Taverner, see Roger Bowers and Paul Doe, *The New Grove Dictionary of Music*, 18:598–602.

12. See Reese, *Music in the Renaissance*, 779 and 845; for the chant, see the *Liber usualis*, 914.

13. See Maitland and Squire, eds., *Fitzwilliam Virginal Book*, 1:135 and 160, the latter under the title *Gloria tibi Trinitas*. Concerning Bull, see Susi Jeans, *The New Grove Dictionary of Music*, 3:438–45.

EXAMPLE 24-4. Thomas Tallis, *Felix namque I* (mm. 107–53)

Westminster Abbey, in 1616.[14] Each composer has treated the cantus firmus some-what differently, but neither of them makes obvious reference to the Taverner Mass.

Parsons has placed the borrowed melody in the alto range, effectively burying it in the sonorous texture and disguising it rhythmically as well. Not until the final section does he show it briefly in long notes of regular length. Bull, by contrast, has made no secret of his use of the chant. In both settings he sets it at the top of the compositional fabric (in the *In nomine* at pitch and in the *Gloria tibi Trinitas* at the upper fifth) in an invariable ternary pattern (of semibreve plus minim). As may be seen from the *In nomine*, this evenly moving line is animated from below by means of a variety of compositional devices (see Example 24-5): chordal syncopation (beginning, nonetheless with an imitative figure); running passagework involving first one (mm. 19–31) and then two (mm. 36–38, 44–47, 53ff.) of the lines in the three-part texture; and short, imitative figures tossed from line to line in sequential elaboration (mm. 39–43 and 47–52). In view of Bull's compositional procedures in pieces of this type, it seems highly likely that cantus firmus techniques continued to have an important didactic function all through the sixteenth century, however else they might have been used.

That the *In nomine* established itself during that time as an independent instrumental genre completely independent of its earlier connections with the liturgy is convincingly demonstrated just by the numbers in which it has survived—nearly 100 have been identified thus far. Also significant is the fact that the *In nomine* came to be cultivated not only for keyboard but also for lute and for consort. Interestingly, the consort pieces are by far the best represented in the available sources.

A fairly spectacular example is the *In nomine "Crye"* attributed to Christopher Tye

14. See Maitland and Squire, eds., *Fitzwilliam Virginal Book*, 2:135. Concerning Parsons, see Philippe Oboussier, *The New Grove Dictionary of Music*, 14:248.

EXAMPLE 24-5. John Bull, *In nomine* (mm. 19–43)

(ca. 1505–ca. 1572), a graduate of Cambridge who spent considerable time at Ely Cathedral and also had connections at the royal court (see Example 24-6).[15] Around the traditional cantus firmus, laid out in even breves in the alto register, the composer has added four other parts (one above, three below). These enter imitatively with an arresting motive that begins with a rapidly repeating pattern (eight fusae and two semiminims) on a single note. The result is a series of fleeting repercussions on a variety of related pitches (A, D, E) sounding almost continuously throughout the initial section of the piece and continuing even after the shift to ternary meter and to modified motivic material that brings the piece to a close. Distinctive and striking, quite literally, the effect anticipates long before Claudio Monteverdi claimed to have invented it, the so-called agitated stye (*stile concitato*) that was to constitute a characteristic element in the musical rhetoric of the following age.[16]

It is important to remember, finally, that in addition to providing the foundation for the genres surveyed above, cantus firmus composition was more pervasive than would at first appear in many of the instrumental repertories of the fifteenth and sixteenth centuries. Even for those genres that were usually identified primarily by some other feature or function, including dances and variation forms, composers often

15. Concerning Tye, see Paul Doe, *The New Grove Dictionary of Music*, 19:297–300.
16. See Monteverdi's foreword to his *Madrigali guerrieri ed amorosi* of 1638 in Oliver Strunk, ed., *Source Readings in Music History*, revised edition, ed. Leo Treitler (New York: Norton, 1998), 665–67.

EXAMPLE 24-6. Christopher Tye, *In nomine "Crye"* (mm. 1–15)

made extensive use of preexistent melodic material. This was true, moreover, not only of the notated pieces for which we have the evidence; there is every reason to believe that such procedures were at least as fundamental to the improvisatory practices of the period as well. Consequently, we shall have occasion to note time and again the many techniques developed at the time for the elaboration of a cantus firmus, a number of which have been illustrated in the foregoing discussion.

KEYBOARD ARRANGEMENTS
AND INTABULATIONS

In the "Buxheim Organ Book" keyboard arrangements of preexistent nonliturgical music, both sacred and secular, seem in most instances to be also cantus firmus compositions. This is quite extraordinary inasmuch as many of these pieces, usually either strophic songs or hymns in the vernacular, are also found in polyphonic settings in sources of the period. In light of somewhat later practice in France and Italy, this is certainly not what one might have expected, but the evidence is virtually incontrovertible.

An instructive example is the Lied *Wach auff mein hort*, which has been transmitted in fifteenth-century sources both as a monophonic melody and in a polyphonic setting by Oswald von Wolkenstein (see pp. 469–70). There are two arrangements of the piece for keyboard from what might be called the Paumann school of organ playing: one in the *Fundamentum organisandi* included in a manuscript in Berlin (Staatsbibliothek, MS 40613) dated 1452, the other in the "Buxheim Organ Book" (see Example 24-7 and Example 24-8). Both carry the secular tune (beginning with the introductory melismatic phrase) in the lowest line of what is basically a two-part texture. It is treated in a cantus firmus style not unlike that seen in the liturgical settings, laid out for the most part in values long enough to stand in clear contrast to the treble line above.

In the arrangement from the *Fundamentum* (Example 24-7) the melody is quoted

EXAMPLE 24-7. Anonymous (Conrad Paumann?), *Wach auff mein hort*

kranz Gemenget schon . . .

Ich fürcht . . .]

For English translation of German text, see Example 13-3.

EXAMPLE 24-8. Anonymous, *Wach auff myn hort*

[Wach auf mein hort. . .

Plick durch die brau

Wie fein

Gemenget

Ich furcht . . .]

For English translation of German text, see Example 13-3.

quite literally (as shown by the small crosses above the notes corresponding to the Lied melody), while the upper line is animated by repeated pitches and modest use of the scales and turning figures featured in the didactic exercises discussed earlier. In the Buxheim tablature, by contrast, the borrowed melody is not treated with the same degree of respect as that usually accorded liturgical plainsong (Example 24-8); it is more frequently subjected to division and the interpolation of additional pitches. Where the greatest amount of freedom is taken, the rhythmic activity of the cantus firmus actually corresponds briefly to that of the added part (as in the syncopated counterpoint in dotted figures of mm. 5–6 or mm. 21–23). The figural decoration of the treble line dominates, nevertheless, most dramatically when it breaks into running scales (mm. 24–25). Surprisingly, however, there is no hint in either composition that the keyboard version could have been modeled on a previous polyphonic setting of the melody.

The *Leise, Crist ist erstanden*, the vocal setting of which was examined earlier (see pp. 462–66), has been treated in similar fashion by one of the anonymous player-composers of the "Buxheim Organ Book" (see Example 24-9). When compared with the polyphonic arrangement found in Trent MS 90, it is immediately obvious that the traditional melody, carried by the cantus in the vocal version, has been placed in the lowest part of the keyboard intabulation. As in the keyboard arrangements of *Wach auf myn hort*, the texture is once again two-part, a third pitch being added only for a few sonorities at the beginning and again at the end.

Curiously, even though the two versions of the basic melody associated with this

EXAMPLE 24-9. Anonymous, *Crist ist erstanden*

Christ soll . . .]

For English translation of German text, see Example 13-1.

text do not entirely coincide (as in the second phrase, "des soll'n wir alle froh sein," for example), much of the precadential ornamentation of the vocal setting is also present in the instrumental intabulation. It is instructive in this regard to compare the cantus of the vocal version with the cantus firmus of the Buxheim piece (where the extent to which pitches agree is indicated by small crosses) and both of those parts with the hypothetical syllabic reconstruction of the melody as given by Riedel (see pp. 463–67). Once again, however, there is no indication whatsoever that the keyboard arrangement was based on a preexistent polyphonic vocal model.

A much different pattern emerges from the keyboard intabulations found in the later sources, both the organ book published by Antico in 1517 and the chanson collections printed by Attaingnant in 1531. For both publishers the models for the instrumental arrangements were obviously compositions originally written in parts for a consort of individual performers and intended for vocal performance (for the cantus, in any case at the very least). Tromboncino's *Si è debile il filo*, for instance, first published in Petrucci's *Libro VII* of 1507 in choirbook format, was subsequently arranged for keyboard alone, and a comparison of the two versions (see Example 19-1) reveals that not only the treble and the bass lines but also—if to a lesser degree—the inner parts are derived from the preexistent vocal model.

This is clear, first of all, because it is possible to discern within the keyboard score the discrete contrapuntal lines of the piece as notated for consort and speak of them as such: cantus, altus, tenor, and bassus. Where the texture is reduced to three sounding pitches for keyboard performance, as happens now and again, the intabulator has usually chosen from the tenor and altus of the original the pitch deemed most necessary for the harmony (with a slight preference, consequently, for the tenor, especially at cadences). When tenor and bassus cross in the consort version (as in mm. 13 and 25), it is, of course, the lower of the two pitches that appears at the bottom of the keyboard score.

There is, in addition, a certain amount of decorative diminution in all parts of the intabulation. In the bassus, where the insertions are limited to an occasional passing tone, the resulting changes are minimal. The tenor, by contrast, has been animated to a considerable degree by turning figures and scalewise passagework, but the texture is dominated as a rule by the figural divisions of the treble line. This is most striking in those phrases where the original cantus drops to the bottom of its range (as in mm. 13–16, 28–35, and 49–52) and becomes an inner part. In the instrumental version, however, it is covered (in every sense of the word) by the lively melodic figures of the line sounding at that point above it.

A similar process, including the animation of the texture by means of figural diminution, is evident in the keyboard intabulations published by Attaingnant. If anything, the integrity of the individual lines of the vocal version is protected even more consistently in the keyboard arrangement of the chansons of the 1520s than it was in Antico's intabulations of *frottole* of the previous decade. The treatment given Claudin's *Tant que vivray* provides an instructive example (see Example 18-6). The four-part texture of the original consort is abandoned in the keyboard score only when one of the voices drops out temporarily, and even then four distinct lines are occasionally maintained in the intabulation (see, for example, mm. 13–18).

At the same time, however, there runs within the basic framework of the four original voice parts a steady stream of turning and stepwise figures derived by division from the longer note values of the chanson. Most of the time these embellishments are embroidered upon the treble line, but the tenor part takes an occasional turn as well (as in mm. 2, 10–11, and 21). In two instances even the bassus joins in (mm. 7 and 9), thus sustaining fairly constant rhythmic motion in eighth and sixteenth notes (the semiminims and fusae of the original) all the way through.

One could easily conclude that these systematic diminutions were embroidered upon the original contrapuntal fabric primarily to accommodate keyboards that produced sound by means of plucked or struck strings (the "espinettes" and "manicordions" of Attaingnant's titles or the "virginals" so popular in England). Because the tones produced by these instruments decayed so quickly, it was possible to maintain a fairly constant level of sonority only by repeating pitches or by dividing larger note values into smaller ones, as in the piece under consideration, hence the quasi-constant movement in short notes.

By contrast, organs posed no such problem, and it should be recalled that examples drawn from Paumann's *Fundamentum* and from the "Buxheim Organ Book" displayed the same kind of figural elaboration of the melodic line at the top of the polyphonic texture. It may be, therefore, that whatever the keyboard instrument chosen for performance, a display of digital dexterity, especially in the uppermost part (where it would be most easily heard and judged) was simply a traditional aspect of the performance style that was carried over into the written repertory.

That hypothesis appears to be borne out by the intabulations of motets included in Attaingnant's remaining print of 1531. As may be seen from the beginning of the keyboard arrangement made of Févin's motet *Sancta Trinitas*, the contrapuntal integrity of the vocal setting is in the main preserved (see Example 24-10). However, the homophonic declamation of the opening phrase of the motet has been trans-

EXAMPLE 24-10. Antoine de Fevin, *Sancta Trinitas* (mm. 1–25): motet and keyboard arrangement compared

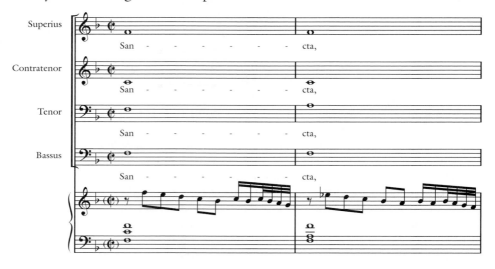

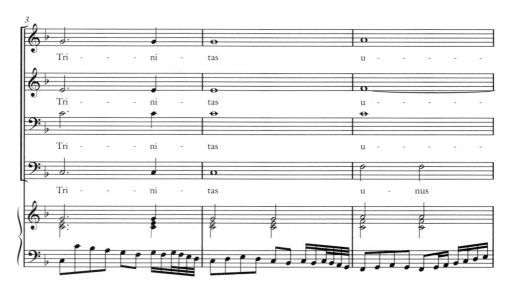

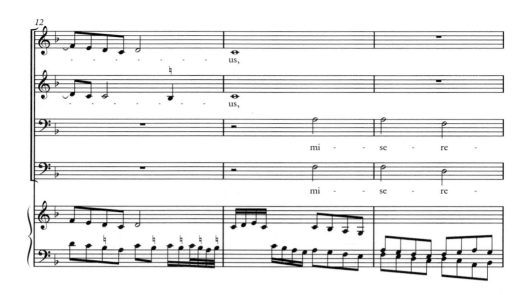

Holy Trinity, one God, have mercy upon us.

formed in the keyboard arrangement. Rhythmic stasis is energetically ruffled by scalar passages that cascade downward through the entire ambitus of the passage before settling into stepwise turning figures that both rise and fall. Similarly, wherever the texture of the motet thins to paired homophony, the organ maintains in those two parts the scalewise motion in diminution that will characterize the instrumental writing throughout.

LUTE ARRANGEMENTS AND INTABULATIONS

A similarly embellished texture with more or less constant movement in short rhythmic values is also characteristic of lute intabulations of preexistent polyphonic compositions. In this instance the sonorous capabilities of the instrument obviously played a key role in shaping the style of performance. No lute—or for that matter any of its contemporaneous cousins such as the vihuela—can sustain for long the gentle sound of its plucked strings; as soon as a note or even a chord is struck, the sound begins to decay and is quickly gone. Lutenists, consequently, must have had to learn from the very beginning the techniques for maintaining a fairly constant level of sonority through the use of scalewise divisions and ornamental figures. It is in fact possible, as we shall see presently, that the simpler compositions of the preludial type were intended, at least in part, as didactic exercises to help the tyro player begin to master those skills.

Surviving intabulations make clear, at any rate, that this embellished style of playing governed in large measure the treatment of vocal models when arranged for lute. Comparing Marchetto Cara's *frottola O mia cieca e dura sorte*, as arranged for voice and accompanying consort, with the intabulation of it in the Capirola lute book reveals that the changes made by the arranger are of two types (see Example 24-11). He has thinned the polyphonic fabric, first of all, generally reducing four parts to three (except where the slower strumming of full chords made fuller sonorities easier to manage and perhaps more necessary). He has also linked the primarily chordal sonorities of the vocal version with a continuous filigree of running passagework. Only occasionally, when the parts of the model move with relative rapidity, does he resort to simple plucked chords (as in mm. 5, 33, and 37), presenting the sonorities of the four-part version without ornament.

A similar sort of transformation, if somewhat less sweeping and dramatic, may be seen in the lute intabulation of Claudin's *Tant que vivray* as published in Attaingnant's *Tres breve et familiere introduction* of 1529 (see Example 24-12 and cf. Example 18-5). Here, too, while the melodic integrity of the individual lines has been

EXAMPLE 24-11. *Marchetto Cara, O mia cieca e dura sorte* (mm.1–20): vocal setting and lute intabulation compared

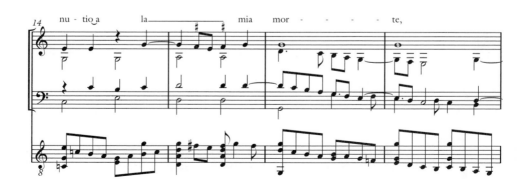

O my blind and cruel fate, ever nourished by pain; O misery of my life, doleful harbinger of my death . . .

EXAMPLE 24-12. Claudin de Sermisy, *Tant que vivray* (mm. 1–11): tablature and transcription for solo lute

For English translation of text, see Example 18-5.

carefully respected, the texture has been reduced to three parts—much more systematically than by Capirola—primarily by simply eliminating the altus of the four-part version. At the same time the rhythmic motion of the original has been filled in fairly consistently by running figures. After the initial chord no sonority longer than a quarter note (the minim of the tablature) is allowed to stand undivided (except in m. 8). The motion in half and quarter notes (semibreves and minims) that characterizes the vocal version is reduced to quarters and eighths (minims and semiminims) in the arrangement for lute with an occasional spurt of sixteenths (fusae) to further enliven and ornament the sonorous fabric. Only at the beginning of the second strain (mm. 9–12) are the catchy rhythms of Claudin's chanson left largely unaltered.

Even fewer changes were made in arranging secular pieces for voice with lute accompaniment. Whether one takes as an example Tromboncino's *Si è debile il filo* or Claudin's *Tant que vivray*, the procedure is much the same. Bossinensis, Petrucci's editor for the two volumes of *frottole* for voice and lute of 1509–11, simply intabulated the tenor and bassus parts, leaving the cantus in mensural notation for the voice and eliminating altogether the altus—as, in fact, he announced in his titles (see Example 19-1). In two places he transformed a short passing tone into an ornamental descending figure of four notes (mm. 24 and 51). Otherwise, the two lower lines of the consort version were left entirely unchanged as to rhythm or fundamental pitch.

This is not to say, of course, that a skilled lutenist would have missed the opportunity to animate the texture and enrich the sonorities with yet other turns and scale-wise passages (such as those seen in the arrangement for keyboard alone). However, the printed notation gives nothing but the barest skeleton, perhaps to make the pieces of the collection playable by amateur musicians of the most modest accomplishment. There is, nonetheless, one noteworthy addition. Because lute tablature specifies by fret every semitone of the gamut, Bossinensis was obliged to indicate in the accompanying parts every accidental inflection that he deemed appropriate for performance. Interestingly, his suggestions are largely corroborated by the keyboard score, which provides, in addition, evidence for accidentals that would have been applied by the singer.

The editor for Attaingnant's collection of 1529 was only slightly more adventuresome (see Example 24-13 and cf. Example 18-5). He, too, left the cantus part to the voice, printing it in mensural notation, but all three of the remaining parts of the consort version have been retained for the lute accompaniment. In addition, by dividing the original values he added a turning, stepwise passage in descent (mm. 3–6), thus animating the rather static texture of the first cadence and anticipating the short ornamental melisma of the voice (in m. 10). Here, too, semitone motion is specified. But because all the half steps needed for the lute accompaniment (including b-fa) were present in the Guidonian gamut, no accidentals had to be added. Arrangements such as this obviously did not require much imagination or even great compositional skill. They do reflect the patterns of performance that were current at the time, however. Thus they offer considerable insight into the uses made of instruments such as lute (and probably keyboard) in secular contexts and the kinds of skills that were expected of those who learned to play them.

INTABULATION AND THE *CANZONA* OF THE SIXTEENTH CENTURY

Obviously, any composition written for vocal ensemble—whether chanson, *frottola*, or madrigal—could easily be played by a consort of instruments of whatever kind. The fact that instrumental ranges generally duplicated by design those in which voice

EXAMPLE 24-13. Claudin de Sermisy, *Tant que vivray* (mm. 1–12): arranged for lute and voice

For English translation of text, see Example 18-5.

parts were written made such adaptations all the more readily feasible. Moreover, as printing made musical repertories ever more widely available, such adaptations must have been made with increasing frequency. For example, Italian musicians appear to have been surprisingly familiar with the newly forged stylistic features of the sixteenth-century chanson, and this must surely have been in good measure because instrumental performance of such pieces was a frequent occurrence, just as it had been earlier for fifteenth-century chanson repertory. Since there is no way of knowing whether a piece written for voices was actually sung or simply played, however, perhaps the best indication of a continuing interest in French secular music on the Italian peninsula lies with those pieces arranged for lute or keyboard.

Vincenzo Capirola must have been particularly partial to intabulations of sacred music, judging from the 1517 collection of his works. Still, he did adapt for lute several chansons that were well known in Italy at the time, including the two well-traveled favorites by Hayne, *De tous biens pleine* and *Allez regretz*. With later generations of Italian instrumentalists the interest shifted to more recent repertory. Marco Antonio Cavazzoni (ca. 1490–ca. 1560), a Bolognese organist and composer who spent most of his career in and around Venice, gave a substantial place to chanson intabulations in his published collection of 1523.[17] Entitled *Recerchari, motetii, canzoni . . . libro primo*, the collection balances two motet arrangements and a pair of *ricercari* with four chansons. Models have yet to be found in the vocal repertory for three of the songs, but the fourth has been identified as a reworking of Josquin's *Plusieurs regretz*.

Marco Antonio's son, Girolamo (ca. 1525 until after 1577), whose professional activities took him first to Urbino and then to the Gonzaga chapel at the church of Santa Barbara in Mantua, published a similar collection in 1543.[18] The first of two published volumes of his music for organ, its contents are summarized by its title, *Intavolatura cioe recercari canzoni himni magnificati . . . libro primo*. As indicated, it consists primarily of *alternatim* settings for the Mass, the Magnificat, and a number of hymns, to which have been added four *ricercari* and two chansons. The latter, identified as *canzoni* in Cavazzoni's title, appropriately enough, were not simply intabulations of the originals for vocal consort—the setting for five voices of Josquin's (?) *Faulte d'argent* and Passereau's *Il est bel e bon*—but rather thoroughgoing compositional reworkings of the material offered by the models.[19]

As a comparison of Cavazzoni's *Falt d' argens* with the earlier vocal version quickly reveals, no attempt has been made to carry the five-part texture of the vocal consort to the keyboard composition (see Example 24-14). The closely spaced imitation at the opening of the chanson between tenor and bassus, which begin at the unison just a minim apart, is replaced in the instrumental version by a second entry at the lower fifth a breve after the first. This is followed in the "intabulation" by a third

17. Concerning Marco Antonio Cavazzoni, see H. Colin Slim, *The New Grove Dictionary of Music*, 4:36–37.
18. Concerning Girolamo Cavazzoni, see H. Colin Slim, *The New Grove Dictionary of Music*, 4:35–36.
19. See John Caldwell, "Canzona," *The New Grove Dictionary of Music*, 3:743–45.

EXAMPLE 24-14. Girolamo Cavazzoni, *Falt d'argens* (mm. 1–15): compared with the vocal setting by Josquin Desprez (mm. 1–24)

For English translation of text, see Example 18-2.

entry and a fourth—each delayed by the unusual mensural lapse of three minims—transposed, respectively, up a fourth and an octave. In addition, the formal structure of the vocal setting, ABA'Coda (clearly articulated by cadences at mm. 24, 43, and 64) is replaced in Cavazzoni's recomposition by a binary organization (ABA'B'). The two halves differ from one another only by a displacement within the brevis unit (cf. mm. 2–5 and 31–34) and the final cadential closure. Surprisingly, the overall result is a considerable compression of the chanson material, whose seventy-two breves have been reduced to fifty-six in the keyboard setting.

With this composition one can observe already some of the characteristics generally associated with the instrumental *canzona* through the remainder of the sixteenth century, in particular the dactyllic rhythm of the opening figure, the contrapuntal texture, and the sectional structure. Yet to appear at this point are the contrasts between sections and the profuse ornamentation often seen in later repertory. It was not until the end of the century that these traits became common coin for *canzona* composition and only then, apparently, that the first examples of this stylistically modified genre were written without relying on a preexistent model. Claudio Merulo (1533–1604), one of the organists at the basilica of San Marco in Venice whose three collections of *canzone* were printed between 1592 and 1611, was among the first to publish keyboard works of this kind; only five of the twenty-three *canzone* brought out under his name can be linked directly to a vocal model.[20]

Some of the keyboard *canzone* published about this time may have been based on pieces in the genre written for instrumental consort rather than directly on a chanson, and works of this type were apparently among the first to be independently composed. As early as 1582 Florentio Maschera (ca. 1540–ca. 1584), a student of Merulo, brought out a *Libro primo de canzoni da sonare a quattro voci*, all of which are thought to have been original compositions. Other such collections followed, many of them by composers otherwise relatively little known, but the leading Venetian masters, including Merulo and his distinguished successor as organist at San Marco, Giovanni Gabrieli (ca. 1553–56 to 1612), made important contributions to the late flowering of the genre. However, since its evolution in their hands leads directly to the emergence of the sonata of the seventeenth century, a detailed discussion of those late developments lies outside the scope of the present discussion.

⌒⌒ Dance Music ⌒⌒

Turning from the arrangement and intabulation of vocal music for polyphonic instruments to music for the dance involves a shift from a tradition that was mostly notated to one that was largely unwritten—at least in its earlier stages—and from text-based repertories for vocal performance to those that were intended from the

---

20. Concerning Merulo, see Denis Arnold and Thomas W. Bridges, *The New Grove Dictionary of Music*, 12:193–94.

outset for instruments, whatever the ultimate source of the musical material adapted to the dance. This means entering the realm of an improvisatory practice much of which was undoubtedly never written down. Consequently, it can now be glimpsed only in part through those relatively few examples captured in some manner by a composer-performer of the period and given notated form.

In attempting to reconstruct something of the history of that practice, the polyphonic compositions that take us deepest into the fifteenth century are undoubtedly those associated with the most venerable of the courtly dances, the *basse danse* (see Figure 2-1 and Figure 3-8). Pieces of this type included in the written sources suggest that the music used to accompany it was based upon a stock of well-known melodies. Some of these may also have originated with vocal repertory; others may simply have had words added to them along the way, giving that impression. These tunes were treated by the instrumentalists essentially as cantus firmi, sounded in extended values of regular length by one of the participating instruments (or in one of the parts of a polyphonic instrument such as a keyboard or, eventually, a lute). The other part (or parts) embroidered upon it in divisions or diminutions, using the kind of idiomatic passagework that we have already seen in other types of cantus firmus composition.[21]

Some of these melodies have been notated and transmitted in treatises and dance manuals of the period, both manuscript and printed. One of the earliest and most spectacular collections of this kind (Brussels MS 9085, Royal Library) originated about 1470 in the county of Flanders, perhaps in Bruges, and was probably prepared for the ducal court of Burgundy. A large, retrospective repertory (consisting of some fifty-nine tunes), it is inscribed in silver on black with the melodies notated on a five-line staff in what had become a characteristic fashion: as even and "blackened" breves.[22] The tune is identified by a brief tag or incipit and described as to the number of notes and "mesures" (the planned sequences of steps). As to the dance itself, the movements to be executed are indicated underneath the notation by a series of letters: r = *révérence* or *desmarche*; b = *branle*; ss = *simples*; d = *doubles*; and r = *reprise* (see Figure 3-10).[23] Other, later collections follow similar conventions, but the blackened breves gave way to ternary semibreves in the sixteenth-century sources as integral mensurations yielded to diminished imperfect tempus.

Of the *basse danse* melodies included in collections of this kind, one of the most ancient and widely traveled is usually designated by a tag that includes or refers to the words *La Spagna*. It is also one of those first and most frequently set polyphon-

---

21. Concerning the *basse danse*, see Daniel Heartz, *The New Grove Dictionary of Music*, 2:257–59, and the bibliography given there. Although "soft" instruments were undoubtedly used to accompany dancing in relatively intimate circumstances, when it was intended for larger companies in the castle hall, "loud" instruments were the norm.

22. The coloration indicates a binary division of the breve; however, the mensuration was apparently ternary at the level of the semibreve.

23. There is a facsimile edition of the manuscript edited by Ernest Closson, *Le manuscrit dit des basses danses de la Bibliothèque de Bourgogne* (Brussels: Société des Bibliophiles et Iconophiles de Belgique, 1912).

ically.[24] There are three polyphonic arrangements of this melody in the Capirola lute book, one of them in the traditional meter of the *basse dance* and actually so labeled (no. 37, p. 109), the other two in the more modern meter of the *saltarello* (no. 6, p. 14, and no. 24, p. 73). Of the three the collection's no. 24 probably comes closest to an earlier mode of performance, one not dependent upon a notated version of the melody.

Whereas Capirola's *La Spagna I* and *Bassadanza La Spagna* both maintain quite consistently a three-part texture around the preexistent melody, *La Spagna II* is restricted to the two primary components of such a composition (see Example 24-15). The traditional melody is laid out cantus firmus style in regular ternary semibreves (and only occasionally broken into diminished note values). As counterpoint above it is rapidly running figuration, mostly in a higher register but making use of the full range of the instrument. Only for brief moments is a third voice added to the mix (as in mm. 20, 22–30, and again at the end); otherwise the juxtaposition of

24. For a discussion of a number of the polyphonic arrangements of this tune, and a comprehensive listing of all of those known to him at the time, see Otto Gombosi, ed., *Compositione di Meser Vincenzo Capirola: Lute-Book (circa 1517)* (Chicago: La Société de Musique d'Autrefois, 1955), xxxvi–lxiii.

EXAMPLE 24-15. Anonymous, *La Spagna II* (mm. 1-12): lute tablature and transcription

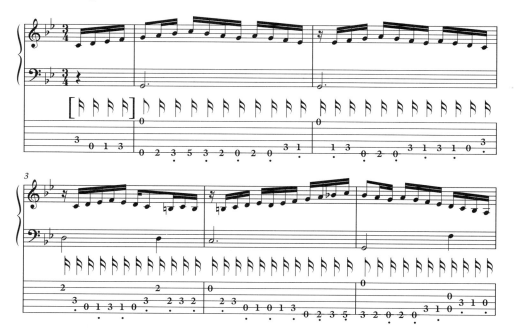

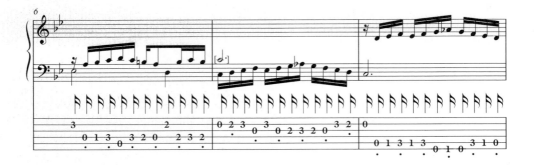

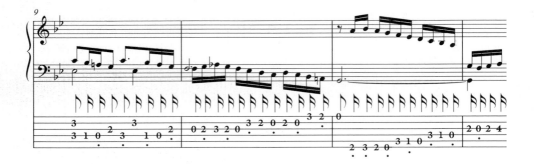

Note that the Dorian melody has been transposed in the transcription to a C final with
  flats on B and E, in accordance with the indications of the tablature and the tuning
  selected for the lute.

slow-moving preexistent melody and the accompanying passagework is clearly evident throughout the piece.

Even so, like the two related compositions in Capirola's collection (if to a lesser
degree), this setting of the well-known tune gives more the impression of a composition conceived for the pleasure of player (and eventual listener) than of one intended primarily to accompany dancing. That supposition is supported in some measure
not only by the absence of additional segments for a *recoupe* or a *tordion* but also by
the fact that the piece preceding *La Spagna II* is a *ricercar* on the same final. It is
possible, therefore, to view the two compositions as intentionally paired.

By the time Attaingnant's collections of dance music for lute and keyboard were
published in the early 1530s, the *basse danse* had been thoroughly popularized, and the
older melodies found in the manuals and treatises of the fifteenth century had been
abandoned for more current material. Several among the *Dixhuit basses dances garnies
de Recoupes et Tordions* for lute specified by the title of 1530 draw their musical mate-

rial from four-part chansons published earlier by Attaingnant himself.[25] Yet others are clearly based on preexistent melodies that have not been identified but that are obviously of relatively recent facture. Typical of the latter is the *Basse dance Saint Roch* (see Example 24-16). That it is based upon preexistent melodic material is evident from its listing in the dance manual published by Moderne in Lyons in the 1530s, *S'ensuyvent plusieurs basses dances*. In addition, several other arrangements of it found in the sources of the period, including another setting for lute in Attaingnant's *Dixhuit basses dances* as *La roque*, a version for keyboard in his *Quatorze gaillardes* of 1531, and an arrangement for consort published in Antwerp by Susato in 1551.[26]

From a comparison of the two lute settings it appears that the preexistent melody is not carried in this instance in extended values by the lower part, even though the slow pace of the "tenor" gives that appearance. Rather, it lies with the quickly moving treble line of the intabulation, where it is systematically divided and heavily dec-

---

25. In Attaingnant's collection these are no. 2 (*Puisqu'en deux cueurs*), no. 3 (*Le cueur est bon*), no. 6 (*L'espoir*), no. 9 (*Le corps s'en va*), and no. 10 (*Tous mes amyz*); cf. Daniel Heartz, *Pierre Attaingnant, Royal Printer of Music* (Berkeley: University of California Press, 1969), 229–30. All have been edited in modern score in Daniel Heartz, ed., *Preludes, Chansons, and Dances for Lute* (Neuilly-sur-Seine: La Société de Musique d'Autrefois, 1964), 54, 57, 58, 61, and 62 (nos. 42, 45, 46, 49, and 50, respectively).

26. See Heartz, ed., *Preludes, Chansons, and Dances for Lute*, lxxvi; the *basse danse La roque* is no. 48 (p. 60) in his edition.

EXAMPLE 24-16. Anonymous, *Basse dance Saint Roch*: lute tablature and transcription

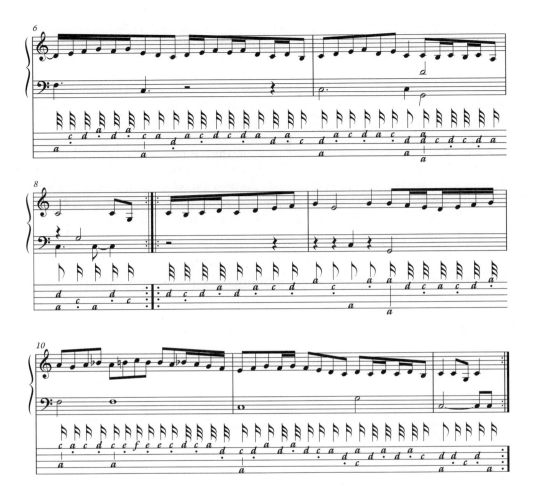

orated. The texture of the piece is nonetheless very similar to that of Capirola's *La Spagna II*. It is written essentially in two parts, with the lower line in longer values providing a sustaining sonority for the development of the melodic material above.

By contrast, the two pieces are very different structurally. The more or less continuous facture of Capirola's cantus firmus composition has been replaced in the *Basse danse Saint Roch* by three clearly marked strains, each of exactly the same length: eight ternary semibreves. That symmetry is further emphasized when the first two are repeated as a unit and then the third as well.[27] Moreover, the version of the

27. The melody for *Saint Roch*, which has no barring in the original tablature, has been barred in Heartz's transcription with an anacrusis of one semibreve, followed by three binary breves and another semibreve before the double bar and the repeat sign; *La roque*, to the contrary, is barred regularly in Attaingnant's tablature at every semibreve.

preexistent material given in *La roque* suggests that the first three phrases of the undecorated melody must have all begun in much the same way.

The clear articulation of phrases, underscored by the repetitions, lends to the structure of pieces so conceived a regular periodicity that is otherwise rarely present in the music of the fifteenth and sixteenth centuries, whether for instruments or for voices. As we have seen, not even the dance music of previous generations is characterized by such structural regularity. For the *Basse dance Saint Roch*, however, the periodicity of the initial segment is also maintained in the *recoupe* and *tordion* that follow; both consist of two phrases of eight ternary semibreves, each of which is repeated.

More significantly, every type of dance in the collection displays the same sort of formal regularity. Some of the *branles*, despite their plebeian origins, have an initial section in phrases of six semibreves (instead of four or eight), but cadential articulations and the regular repetition of relatively short segments make the underlying periodicity inescapably clear.

Similar patterns of phrase definition and repetition also characterize the dances for keyboard published in Attaingnant's *Quatorze gaillardes* of 1531, as may be seen in one of the anonymous paired sets of pavane and galliard included in that collection (see Example 24-17). The pavane consists of short phrases of four binary breves each (to be performed, of course, in a stately tempo), and that articulation is made clear by the characteristic trochaic rhythm with which each begins (mm. 1, 5, 9, and 13) and by the varied repetition of the first phrase by the second and the third by the fourth. (The last four breves provide a clear cadential close, the first of the piece, as a kind of coda.)

EXAMPLE 24-17. Anonymous, *Pavenne* (mm. 1–8) and *Gaillarde* (mm. 1–8): arranged for keyboard

[*Pavenne*]

[*Galliarde*]

Although the galliard is in a contrasting compound meter (with binary breves, still, but ternary semibreves), it is simply a reworking of the musical material of the preceding pavane, and the same pattern of repetition is discernible in this "movement" as well. Varied repetition also obtains, with the second phrase built upon the first and the fourth upon the third. However, in the latter two (mm. 9–15) the texture is altered. Juxtaposition of rapid figuration with chordal sonority, which was balanced fairly evenly between the two hands of the keyboard player in the pavane and the initial eight measures of the galliard, is used in this passage in a much more conventional manner. Chords are played by the left hand in the lower part of the instrument's range, and ornamental figuration is confined largely to the right hand in the treble. In addition, the cadential coda has been extended in the galliard, now occupying six full breves instead of the four seen in the preceding pavane.

Here again the variable irregularity of the closing phrases may be an indication that this pair of dances was composed first of all to be played and heard and not necessarily to accompany dancing. If so, the structural periodicity observed in this group of pieces is all the more historically significant. Having established itself in the dance repertory of the sixteenth century as a potentially powerful element of formal design, it continued to be so used in a variety of instrumental genres of the seventeenth century as well. And in the eighteenth century it became one of the most pervasive and important of compositional principles, permeating all of the formal types then in use in both instrumental and vocal genres.

In addition to the dance music for lute and for keyboard, Attaingnant published similar repertories for instrumental consort. The first of these, *Six Gaillardes et six Pavanes avec Treze chansons musicale a quatre parties* (1530), combined (as indicated by the title) a dozen dances—sedate pavanes and lively galliards in equal number—with thirteen texted chansons that could be sung as well as played. Another such collection, larger and more comprehensive, was published later that same year, *Neuf basses dances, deux branles, vingt et cinq Pavennes avec quinze Gaillardes en musique a quatre parties.* Of its nine *basses dances* three have Italianate titles and only one an accompanying "Tourdion." *Branles* are not well represented, and the pavanes and galliards are in separate series with nothing to link them, suggesting once again music for playing and listening more than for actual dancing.[28]

Additional collections of dance music for polyphonic ensemble were not published until 1547, when Attaingnant brought out his *Second livre*, containing fifty pieces arranged according to the eight traditional modes: *basses danses* (twelve), pavanes (three), galliards (three), *tordions* (nine), and *branles* (twenty-three), the latter classified as "gays," "simples," and "doubles."[29] Five of these—a *basse danse*, two *tordions*, and two *branles*—had already been published in Lyon some years earlier (ca. 1544) by Jacques Moderne. They were included in a collection entitled *Musicque de joye* that appended twenty-nine dances—pavanes (four) and galliards (two) in addition to the *basses danses* (five), *tordions* (five), and *branles* (thirteen) already mentioned—to a group of twenty compositions identified in the print as *phantaisies* (see pp. 785–86).[30]

In the final years of Attaingnant's life and beyond, however, his shop issued a veritable flood of polyphonic dances for instrumental ensemble. A *Troisieme livre de danceries* must have first been published prior to 1550. (What must have been a reprint appeared in 1557, after the fourth and fifth books.) It comprised an opening series of four pavanes, each paired with a galliard, four additional galliards, eight *almandes*, and seventeen *branles* (six labeled "simples," six "gays," and one "de Bourgogne"). This was followed in 1550 by a *Quart livre de danceries*, consisting solely of nineteen pavanes and thirty-two galliards with numbers 2–9 as pairs. The *Cinquiesme livre de danceries* was similarly specialized, including only *branles*, some of which were variously identified as "gays" (ten), "de Poictou" (eight), or "de Champaigne" (three).

The last two such collections followed Attaingnant's death in 1552. A *Sixieme livre de danceries* was printed in 1555, adding to the repertory three pavane–galliard

28. See Heartz, *Pierre Attaingnant, Royal Printer of Music*, 230–31 and 234–36, nos. 17 and 20; for transcriptions in modern score of the entire repertory, see F. J. Giesbert, ed., *Parizer Tanzbuch aus dem Jahre 1530* (Mainz: B. Schotts Söhne, n.d.).

29. See Heartz, *Pierre Attaingnant, Royal Printer of Music*, 352–54, no. 148.

30. The duplications have been identified by Samuel F. Pogue, *Jacques Moderne, Lyons Music Printer of the Sixteenth Century* (Geneva: Librarie Droz, 1969), 182–85. A facsimile, with an introduction by Pogue, has been published by the Editions Alamire (Peer, 1991); for a complete edition of the collection in modern score, see Jacques Barbier, ed., *Jacques Moderne, Musicque de Joye*, Collection Ricercar, vol. 1 (Tours: Centre d'Etudes Supérieures de la Renaissance, l'Université François Rebelais, 1993).

pairs, six additional galliards, and forty-one *branles*, most of them "de Champaigne" but others labeled "simples" (six), "courants" (two), and "gays" (nine). Finally, in 1557, as the penultimate publication issued by the workshop in the rue de la Harpe, appeared a *Septieme livre de danceries*, presenting a series of six pavane–galliard pairs and four "suites" of *branles*, each with four to six dances.[31]

This spate of publications suggests that by the 1550s dance music playable on a variety of individual instruments had become a favorite staple of recreational music making for the urban (and, undoubtedly, courtly) audiences for whom the repertory was intended. As their contents show, the *basse danse* with its paired *tordion* completely disappeared from the printed collections after mid-century, and the pavane–galliard pair, although still a modest compenent in the latest of them, was more and more eclipsed by the increasing popularity of the *branle*, despite (or because of?) the latter's more humble origins.

It is not difficult to understand what made this repertory so attractive, as a representative sample from the *Second livre* of 1547 will quickly show (see Example 24-18). Homophonic textures that harbor little in the way of rhythmic complexity make pieces such as these relatively easy to play. At the same time, the sprightly rhythms, evenly balanced phrases, and clear formal structures allow players and listeners alike to comprehend the compositional design and to follow the sonorous tapestry as it unfolds.

VARIATION AS GENRE

Variation has emerged as an important compositional procedure in several of the instrumental genres discussed thus far. Techniques of variation figure significantly in didactic exercises based on repetitive patterns, as in the stepwise figuration of Paumann's *Fundamentum*. It occurs, almost inevitably, in *alternatim* settings for organ when the plainsong returns unchanged from section to section, as in the Kyrie of the Mass discussed earlier, or in hymns, Psalms, Magnificats, or the Te Deum. It may be seen in the intabulations of vocal pieces in which melodic phrases are repeated several times, as in Tromboncino's *Si è debile il filo* or even Claudin's *Tant que vivray*. Variation is unavoidably present in those dances based upon a repeating pattern of some sort. It is also an integral part of the dance movements with recurring phrases and of dance suites in which the musical material of the first movement is drawn upon for those that follow, as in the pavane–galliard pair from Attaingnant's print. Finally, it is implicit in the preparation of multiple settings of a traditional melody like *La Spagna*.

One of several paradigms for variation technique was the *passamezzo*, which was used extensively in Italy as a structural framework for dances of various types. Its

---

31. For the contents of these collections, including references to modern editions, see Heartz, *Pierre Attaingnant, Royal Printer of Music*, 368–76, nos. 164, 165, 170, 172, and 173.

EXAMPLE 24-18. Anonymous, *Basse danse* (mm. 1–16) and *Branle gay* (mm. 1–12): for instrumental consort

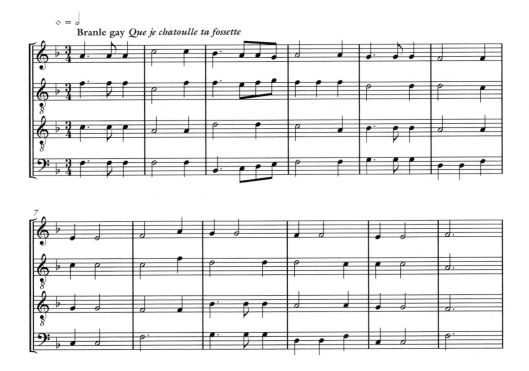

melody was apparently based upon a tetrachord descending in four equal breves from the third above the final, followed by another with the penultimate breve broken so as to conclude with the final, and this eight-breve sequence was accompanied by a bass-line counterpoint implying a fixed sequence of chordal sonorities.

An early example is the *Gaillarde* [*Passamezzo Antico*] from Attaingnant's *Dix-huit basses dances* of 1530 (see Example 24-19). The descending treble line (a♭, g, f, e; a♭, g-f, e, f) has been virtually hidden by ornamental divisions, but the underlying pitches are heard at the beginning of each brevis unit. The accompanying bass line (F, E♭, F, C; F, E♭-F, C, F) is considerably clearer, particularly since the texture of the piece is largely limited to two parts (excepting only mm. 2, 6, 8, and 10). Since the final four breves (mm. 9–12) are clearly a variation of the second half of the *pas-samezzo* pattern, which is in turn a variant of the first four breves, the result is a three-fold variation of the descending tetrachord and its accompanying bass, all of which is then repeated.[32]

Clearly, all of the basic compositional procedures generally associated with varia-

32. If the dance that has been edited by Heartz, ed., *Preludes, Chansons, and Dances for Lute*, 95, were transposed to a regular Dorian final (on D), the melodic sequence for the *passamezzo* would be as follows: f, e, d, c♯; f, e-d, c♯, d; and the corresponding bass-line counterpoint would be: D, C, D, A; D, C-D, A, D.

EXAMPLE 24-19. Anonymous, *Gaillarde* [*Passamezzo Antico*]: lute tablature and transcription

tion as a principle of formal organization—melodic transformation, cantus firmus elaboration, and harmonic grounding—were well developed and widely used by the early 1500s. Not until mid-sixteenth century, however, were new instrumental genres fashioned that relied primarily on those procedures to provide a structural foundation and an underlying compositional plan. It will come as no surprise that some of the earliest compositions to be constructed in this manner are in a very real sense cantus firmus based. There is also reason to believe, as we shall soon see, that the musical materials drawn upon for the purpose may have originated at some point with the improvisatory tradition of dance music that lies behind so much of the written instrumental repertory.

One of the first such musical components to be used with some frequency in the written repertory is identified in the sources by the tag *Guárdame las vacas* and consists of a patterned sequence of pitches in two parts (at least implicitly) eight mensural units in length. Significantly, this melodic-harmonic progression is strikingly similar to the Italian *passamezzo*. It, too, involves both a simple melodic line and an accompanying bass-line counterpoint. The "tune" is again a descending tetrachord in equal breves, repeated with a turn back to the final at the end, and the bassus, although different, uses many of the same melodic intervals. It is, in sum, the kind of periodic pattern that must have owed its existence at some point to the regularly repeated movements characteristic of the dance.

Iberian composers were the first to build upon these specific elements to construct sets of variations actually identified as such by the term *diferencias,* and this may help to explain the curious Spanish locution by which the underlying structural pattern was known. The earliest significant group of such compositions was that included by Luys de Narváez (fl. 1530–50), music master to the boys in the royal chapel of Philip II, in the large collection of music for the vihuela published in Valladolid in 1538 under the title *Los seys libros del Delphin.*[33] Significantly, in the variations of this repertory neither the descending melodic pattern nor the accompanying bass line of *Guárdame las vacas* is always the same. The implication is that the fundamental procedure was more important than the details of realization, which were naturally subject to the sort of variability that characterized the improvisatory practice from which it sprang.

In a set of four *diferencias* based on the well-known patterns Narváez has adopted for his structural framework a bipartite bass pattern that moves in ternary breves (each consisting in the score of three semibreves—see Example 24-20). The pitches are as follows: f, c, d, a; f, c, d-a, d. The progression differs, then, from that of the *passamezzo* only in that it begins from the third above the final rather than from the final itself. A descending tetrachord may not be self-evident in the melodic line of the treble part, but one is in fact implicit in the arpeggiated figuration. Starting from a"

---

33. Concerning Narváez, see Hopkinson K. Smith, *The New Grove Dictionary of Music,* 13:39. *Los seys libros del Delphin,* which were printed in a tablature derived from that used in Italy for the lute, has been edited in modern score by Emilio Pujol and published as vol. 3 of the Monumentos de música española (Barcelona: Consejo Superior de Investigaciones Científicas, Instituto Español de Musicología, 1945).

EXAMPLE 24-20. Luys de Narváez, *Cuatro diferencias sobre Guárdame las vacas, primera diferencia*: transcription of tablature for vihuela

(a third higher, again, than the point of departure for the *passamezzo* seen earlier), it moves stepwise through g" and f" to e", and continues down another step to the final, d", in its second statement. That same descending pattern is discernible in the melodic facture of the remaining three *diferencias* as well, but it is clearest in the fourth, where the skeletal pitches are sustained longer than in the previous variations. Unique to the fourth variation, by contrast, is a closing cadential coda of four breves' duration (mm. 25–34).

Directly after this set of *diferencias* in Narváez's collection comes another of three entitled *Otras tres diferencias (Hechas por otra parte)* (see Example 24-21). Despite the indication that "another part" has been used in its composition, the implication seems to be that this piece is also considered to be "sobre Guárdame las vacas." In this instance both of the constituent elements of the structural pattern are obvious from the outset. They provide in the first variation the outer parts of the counter-

EXAMPLE 24-21. Luys de Narváez, *Otras tres diferencias (Hechas por otra parte), primera diferencia*

point and move regularly a ternary breve at a time while a third part runs in shorter values between them.

The sequence of pitches is that seen in the Attaingnant *passamezzo*, however, with the bass line beginning from the modal final and the treble part a third above. Once again there is a cadential coda, this one only two breves in length but coming at the close of each of the three sections rather than only at the end. In the second *diferencia* only the bass foundation is clearly in evidence, whereas in the third a descending tetrachord is the primary armature for the compositional structure. This time there is an interesting twist, however; the melodic pattern now begins from a″ as it did in the first set, clearly profiled in longer values in the first strain and divided and embellished in the second. The bass pattern returns, finally, for the added cadential close, thus emphasizing once again its modal final.[34]

Variations on *Guárdame las vacas* for keyboard were being cultivated at the same time, as is clear from the works of Antonio de Cabezón (1510–66), the celebrated blind organist who served both Queen Isabella of Castile and Philip II.[35] Published posthumously in 1578 by his son, Hernando, under the title *Obras de música para tecla, arpa y vihuela*, they include several variation sets.[36] In the third of these the armature of treble and bass is reasonably clear in the opening *diferencia* (see Example 24-22). Movement from one sonority to the next is once again by ternary breves (i.e., every fourth semibreve as in Narváez) in each of the four variations. The treble begins its descending tetrachord from f, a third above the final (as in the Attaingnant *passamezzo*), but the bass part—through all of its divisions, scalar passagework, and added pitches—follows the outline of Narváez's *Cuatro diferencias*: F, C, D(-B♭), A; F, C, (D-G′)-A, D (mm. 1–12, 13–24).

Through the remaining three variations (starting at mm. 25, 49, and 73) the same structural relationship is generally maintained. The skeletal bass line is frequently obscured by the divisions and ornaments applied to and around it, whereas the descending tetrachord is more consistently present. However, the pattern is not always easily heard since it lies in the alto range and is often treated as an inner part.

The compositional procedures used by the two composers are fairly similar, then, in that while working within the established form-building patterns, each takes full advantage of the possibilities of his instrument for idiomatic passagework and melodic ornamentation. If the textures differ significantly, it is primarily because of the relatively greater technical difficulty in sustaining full-voiced contrapuntal activity on

34. For purposes of comparison, cf. the seven *diferencias* for lute by Enríquez de Valderrábano (fl. mid-sixteenth century), published in Archibald T. Davison and Willi Apel, eds., *Historical Anthology of Music*, 2 vols. (Cambridge, Mass.: Harvard University Press, 1962), 1:133; Valderrábano also uses a descending tetrachord from a′ and the bass sequence from F.

35. Concerning Cabezón, see Macario Santiago Kastner, *The New Grove Dictionary of Music*, 3:572–74.

36. Cabezón's keyboard music has been published in modern score: Antonio de Cabezón, *Obras de musica para tecla, arpa, y vihuela*, ed. Higinio Angles, 3 vols., Monumentos de música española, vols. 27–29 (Barcelona: Consejo Superior de Investigaciones Científicas, Instituto Español de Musicología, 1966), and in Cabezón, the *Collected Works*, ed. Charles G. Jacobs, 3 vols. (Brooklyn: Institute of Mediaeval Music, 1967–86), vol. 1.

EXAMPLE 24-22. Antonio de Cabezón, *Diferencias sobre las vacas*, first variation (mm. 1–25) for keyboard

the vihuela. (After all, the player of a plucked instrument has only half as many fingers available for that purpose as one with a keyboard.) Consequently, while Narváez's counterpoint is often restricted to two parts and rarely calls for more than three, Cabezón's is much more consistently in four parts, even where there is a considerable quantity of rapid finger work.

Still, what is perhaps most striking about the works of both composers is the fundamentally contrapuntal conception of the part-writing. Keyboards and, even more so, plucked instruments like the vihuela and the lute lend themselves technically much more readily to scalar passagework and chordal "strumming" than to linear counterpoint. Considerable musical skill and digital dexterity are required to maintain the integrity of the individual parts as is done in the compositions that have been under discussion. By mid-sixteenth century, obviously, the great importance attached to the vocal repertory and the respect commanded by the compositional procedures developed in the sacred genres of Mass and motet (in all of its various manifestations) had shaped instrumental composition in a decisive way. As we shall see, the historical consequences of that development were to be far-reaching.

⟝⟝⟝⟝⟝ SONG VARIATIONS ⟝⟝⟝⟝⟝

The other basic species of variation cultivated in the latter half of the sixteenth century appears to be rooted in vocal repertory rather than in music for the dance. Representative examples occur in fair numbers in the *Fitzwilliam Virginal Book*, as in other Elizabethan sources, and English composers, in particular, appear to have made the most significant contribution to the development of this generic type.

That those masters were well acquainted with variational techniques and of the use to which they were frequently put in the stylized dance movements being written at the time is clear enough from other pieces in the same source. These included pavanes and galliards with their several repeated strains, each dance of the pair being based on the same musical material and followed by its "variatio."[37] One might have expected something rather different from the variations based on preexistent songs, especially since the models appear to have been drawn from a popular, monophonic stock of tunes rather than relatively sophisticated polyphonic settings. The songs, too, however (perhaps precisely because of their unpretentious character), tend to be periodic in nature, consisting of short phrases with frequent repetitions.

Typical in most respects is William Byrd's setting of *The Carman's Whistle* (see Example 24-23). The melody that serves as a "cantus firmus" consists of just two strains—the first only a breve in length (i.e., the four ternary minims of the copyist's measure), the second two breves long—and each of them is repeated. Byrd has intro-

---

37. See, among the several suites of this kind included in the *Fitzwilliam Virginal Book*, the four consecutive movements ascribed to Ferdinand Richardson (in Maitland and Squire, eds., *Fitzwilliam Virginal Book*, 1:27–36, nos. 4–7) or the three attributed to John Bull (1:99–123, nos. 32–33).

duced the first statement of the borrowed material with an anticipatory imitation of the first phrase (from the octave and the twelfth below, mm. 1–2). This has the effect of balancing the two elements of the tune as a pair of clearly articulated segments of four breves apiece, but in the variations that follow he adhered to its original length (of six breves).

Through seven of the eight sections that ensue (each of which is to be repeated), melodic material derived from the song dominates the texture. The tune itself is stated repeatedly in a clearly recognizable form, especially the opening strain. Already with the second half of the second phrase, however, Byrd begins to divide the pitches of the borrowed melody, exploiting in his embellishment of the line the sequential structure of the model. Not until the final variation (no. 9), where the borrowed melody is treated as an inner part with a new treble line added above, does it lose its preeminent role.

Although the melody is easily discernible to the ear most of the way through, the texture changes constantly. The chordal accompaniment of the initial exposition gives way early in the second section (m. 13) to more lightly supported scalewise figures that move from one register to the next. A return in variation 3 to full chordal sonorities is followed in turn by quasi-imitative counterpoint in two parts below for variations 4 and 5. Variation 6 moves from an opening point of imitation in two parts (mm. 45–46) to a series of sequential figures traded back and forth in dialogue between upper and lower registers. By contrast, number 7 relies first on ornaments, systematically applied (for the tune), and contrapuntal syncopation. This then yields to a return of figural diminutions, which are spun out in a lower register most of the way through variation 8.

As the treatment of variations 4, 5, and 6 fairly demonstrates, the pervasive structural and stylistic influence of imitative counterpoint makes itself felt in the polyphonic variations on these simple song melodies, just as it does elsewhere. Nevertheless, the sense of linear integrity that was observed in the *diferencias* for both lute and keyboard is less pronounced in the song variations, and, at the same time, the texture is more fluid. Not that sharply profiled melodic lines are lacking in Byrd's variations; quite the contrary. However, the chordal accompaniments cannot easily be construed as the vertical combination of readily distinguishable contrapuntal lines. Conversely, the number of pitches sounding simultaneously at any given moment can go quickly from one or two to four, five, or even six with no attempt made to rationalize the voice leading from part to part. In that sense such pieces as the *Carman's Whistle* reflect perhaps more fully the idiomatic possibilities of the instrument for which they were written than many other instrumental genres of the period. This is particularly true for a special class of preludial compositions to be examined below.

PRELUDIAL GENRES AND INSTRUMENTAL STYLES

No discussion of the instrumental genres of the fifteenth and sixteenth centuries would be complete without careful consideration of original compositions with a preludial function. This is not an easy task, however, since these fall into several different categories with a confusing history of names and styles. The differences in terminology are unusual, in the first place, because they are clearly due in considerable measure to local linguistic preferences. This is in contrast to other genres of the period—such as the madrigal—that were generally known, when carried over linguistic borders, either by their name of origin or by a direct equivalent in translation.

To illustrate, not only are works that apparently share a preludial purpose often very different in style and scope, they are also identified in the sources by a wide variety of terms: *praeambulum* (or *priambel*) in Germany and, much later, in England; *prélude* in France; *ricercar* in Italy; *tiento* in Spain; and *fantasia* (in some form) in all of these countries.[38] That these terms were understood to be equivalent in some sense is clear from several different indications. For example, an *Intabolatura di liuto* published by Francesco Marcolini in Venice in 1536 contained nineteen pieces labeled *ricercari*. Of these seven were reprinted in Venice in 1546 as *fantasie*, seven

38. See Christopher D. S. Field, "Fantasia," *The New Grove Dictionary of Music*, 6:380–88.

in Louvain in 1568 as *fantaisies*, and one in Nuremberg as a *priambel*. Similarly, of thirteen pieces of a preludial type published by Antonio Castelioni in Milan in 1536 as *fantasie*, eleven were reedited in Nuremberg in 1552 as *preambels*.[39]

This terminological confusion is compounded by the use of some of these same names for pieces that are dramatically different in formal and stylistic conception. That compositions so unlike in scope, style, and structure were designated by the same term is an anomaly that would be difficult to account for in any way were it not for their similarity of function. The marked distinctions in style among pieces that were meant to serve much the same musical purposes are not so readily explained. It would seem, however, that they are rooted in growing friction between the older instrumental tradition with its roots in improvisatory practice, often of a virtuosic character, and the sophisticated new procedures and learned intellectual doctrines of written polyphony, especially that intended for voices. Compositions of the kinds under consideration here embody in a very real sense an enduring conflict in the instrumental music of the period between what was, on the one hand, idiomatically comfortable for the player—even potentially flashy—and what was regarded as skillful and admirable for a composer, on the other.

The earliest (and most conservative) examples usually exemplify most clearly the improvisatory virtuoso tradition, making use of chordal combinations and melodic patterns that lie easily under the fingers. Such materials also lend themselves to relatively simple means of compositional extension such as repetition, sequence, and melodic elaboration through diminutions and ornamental figuration. One of the several pieces of this type included in the "Buxheim Organ Book" is a *Praeambulum super Re*. It is relatively slight of substance—characteristically so for this repertory— and not unlike many of the didactic exercises of the Paumann *Fundamentum* in both texture and style (see Example 24-24).

The opening section makes use of pairs of repeated pitches in the upper two parts of a texture in three, while the lowest part moves at the same rate of speed (in even half notes or minims) but without doubling each note. Then, at the first cadence to D (the *re* of the title, in m. 7), the three-part fabric dissolves into a figurally decorated melodic line that winds its way down through an octave and a fifth, with just a few scattered notes of accompaniment, to end on the modal final.

Its companion piece (no. 242), although not labeled, is clearly of the same type. Initially a pair of parts, moving, again, in even half notes, provide support for a faster-moving melodic line in a higher register. But after a cadence is made to the confinal, a (m. 7), the middle voice drops out and the upper part, now moving even more consistently in rapid fusae (sixteenth notes), traverses in meandering scales and turning figures the octave and a fifth from a up to d' and back again before coming to rest on the *re* final. What both pieces accomplish with relative economy is to define the melodic patterns characteristic of the modal ambitus associated with the final and, at the same time, by means of some carefully specified semitone inflections, the

---

39. See Heartz, ed., *Preludes, Chansons, and Dances for Lute*, x–xi.

EXAMPLE 24-24. Anonymous, *Praeambulum super Re*

primary cadential pitches.[40] However, they do not engender in the process a sense of motivic or structural cohesion.

The earliest of the preludial pieces for lute to reach us in notated form, the *ricercari* of the collections edited for Petrucci by Francesco Spinacino and Joan Ambro-

40. The internal cadences are to D, a, and G; they come at mm. 4, 5, and 7 of no. 241 and mm. 1–2 and 5–7 of no. 242.

sio Dalza (see pp. 778–80), are very similar in conception to the earlier keyboard preludes of the "Buxheim Organ Book." Those by Spinacino are also diminutive in scope and limited in means, consisting of little more than running scale passages in alternation with short chordal sequences, some of which nevertheless involve simultaneously all six courses of the instrument.[41]

The bipartite *Tastar de corde con li soi recercar dietro* by Dalza are only slightly more sophisticated. The opening section, the *tastar de corde*, is usually much like a Spinacino *ricercar*, composed of short chordal sections connected by running passagework. Typical is one with an ending on G-sol (see Example 24-25). Here the last

41. For an example, see Davison and Apel, eds., *Historical Anthology of Music*, 1:101, no. 99b.

EXAMPLE 24-25. Joan Ambrosio Dalza, *Tastar de corde con li soi recercar dietro*: transcription of lute tablature

Finis seguita il recercar

of the scalar runs, which spans an octave and a fifth in rapid motion, leads directly into the section labeled *recercar*. It is slightly more regular in its structure than the *tastar de corde*. For example, the rhythmic motion is steadier, and contrast between chords (in quarter notes) and running passages (in eighths) is consequently less marked. There is even a suggestion of formal coherence; the melodic figures that open the first two phrases (mm. 40 and 43–44, respectively) are repeated in close juxtaposition (mm. 51–52) in the phrase that leads to the closing cadence, thus producing a structural design that could be sketched as ABCA'B'.[42]

For both pieces the practical function is clear: such works could be used, as indicated by the designation given them by Dalza, to test the strings of the instrument, thus making sure that they had been properly tuned. More importantly, they could be made to function, like the keyboard preludes discussed earlier, in establishing a final and defining the melodic patterns, the chordal sequences, and the cadential degrees that were generally associated with it.

Although relying as well primarily on compositional devices that derive idiomatically from the instrumentalist's repertory of improvisatory practices, the preludes published by Attaingnant early in the 1530s are both more extensive and more clearly structured than the pieces examined thus far. This may be seen from the *Prélude sur chacun ton*, which was published with the *alternatim* versions of the Magnificat in all eight of its plainsong tones (see Example 24-26 and cf. pp. 784–85). It is conceived so as to be playable from each of the four finals associated with the chant (by a judicious selection of clefs by which to construe the notes) and, consequently, could be used to introduce the liturgical Magnificat whatever the tone in which it was sung. From a stylistic standpoint the constituent elements are the same as those seen in earlier examples of the genre—chordal homophony and accompanied passagework—but their treatment evinces from the outset elements of structure and cohesion that lend themselves to a much more substantial and organic development of the compositional materials.

The chordal section used to open the piece leads to a quasi-cadence on the modal final (F, in the version given, in m. 6). Chords then give way to a descending melodic pattern that, after a brief hesitation, unfolds itself sequentially by successive fifths through the octave from g to G (mm. 8–12). A stereotypical melodic figure generally used for cadential purposes is introduced (without a clear cadential function), repeated sequentially in ascent, and replaced by an ascending version of the descend-

---

42. Another example by Dalza, similar in every way, has been published in Davison and Apel, eds., *Historical Anthology of Music*, 1:101, no. 99a.

EXAMPLE 24-26. Anonymous, *Prelude sur chacun ton* (mm. 1–26)

ing sequence (mm. 14–17). The ornamental figure is then used to articulate a partial cadence to d' (mm. 17–18) and to introduce again the descending melodic sequence, this time in the octave from d' to d. A return to the cadential ornament, leading again to d', introduces some parallel passagework in two parts, either a tenth (mm. 26, 31, 33–36) or a third apart (mm. 29–30).

These two elements—sequential elaboration of a recurring motive and scalar passages in parallel motion—constitute the motivic substance of the entire work. Sequential scalar figures return in a three-part texture in both ascent (mm. 39–40) and descent (mm. 69–73) and are linked with the earlier ones by a common rhythmic pattern (of a dotted quarter note and three eighths). That same figure, with the interpolation of four longer notes in between, provides the basis for yet another sequential development in descent (mm. 42–51) and, in an accelerated, diminished form (again descending), as preparation for the final cadence (mm. 79–82). Freer running passages, primarily in eighth notes and often in two parts with parallel thirds and tenths, are introduced by the melodic cadential ornament (as in mm. 52–62), which is also treated sequentially (mm. 67–68, 74–78), as it was earlier, together with the connecting material (as in mm. 57–68).

As will be evident from this example, reliance upon a limited number of motivic ideas developed consistently in sequential patterns leaves the listener with a much stronger sense of musical unity than can be derived from the pieces discussed previously. At the same time, such compositional procedures serve well the basic function of works of this kind: to define the melodic patterns and cadential pitches characteristically associated with a given modal final. And in most instances, apparently, the purpose of doing so was to introduce another piece with the same modal orientation.

Despite the relatively greater scope and more musically coherent facture of the *Prélude sur chacun ton* of 1531 by comparison with earlier examples of the genre considered above, its anonymous composer showed little tendency to give up the compositional procedures based on improvisatory practice for the imitative counterpoint that had by then become the staple of vocal composition. This may be a reflection of conservative predilections among church organists, as was suggested earlier. As has been observed, the keyboard player faces considerably less technical difficulty than the lutenist in executing music conceived as three or more contrapuntal lines rather than as a mixture of chords and running passagework. It seems ironic, therefore, that the stylistic norms of the written polyphonic tradition should already have made themselves clearly felt in the preludes for lute published with the *Tres breve et familiere* introduction two years earlier.

Taking as an example the second such piece in that collection, the ascending opening figure is introduced, strikingly enough, as a point of imitation in three parts (see Example 24-27). Starting in the treble range from f and continuing in bass and tenor ranges from the octave and the fourth below, respectively, the repetition of the motive from voice to voice is less than literal only because the first dotted figure is embellished with an ornamental turn. Thereafter, admittedly, imitation is hardly structurally significant or pervasive in the piece. There are short snatches of it here and there (as in mm. 6–7, 15, 19–20, and 24), but usually in the middle of a phrase where it is less important compositionally, and less noticeable than it would be in a position of syntactic prominence. Nor has it replaced to any significant degree the

EXAMPLE 24-27. Anonymous, *Prélude* (mm. 1–20; 33–49): lute tablature and transcription

compositional materials and procedures derived more from instrumental practice: the virtuosic finger work (as in m. 4), the chordal strumming (as in mm. 5 or 12–13), or the sequential development of simple motives (as in mm. 18 and 21–26). Nevertheless, there is a sense of linearity within the individual voice parts and of their integrity as contrapuntal entities that is entirely lacking in the lute *ricercari*.[43]

The incursion of imitative counterpoint into instrumental compositions with a preludial function, adumbrated in the lute preludes of 1529, led with the masters of the following generation to a fundamental conceptual transformation of the genre. Exploita-

43. This is not the case, however, with the analogous pieces attributed to Vincenzo Capirola; see Gombosi's discussion of the *ricercari* in Gombosi, ed., *Compositione di Meser Vincenzo Capirola: Lute-Book,* xxxi–xxxv.

tion of the idiomatic possibilities of a given instrument was largely abandoned in favor of the structures and contrapuntal procedures that had been developed for vocal polyphony—Mass and motet, chanson and madrigal. In sum, syntactic imitation became the fundamental compositional principle for the primary preludial genres.[44] The decisive steps were taken for the keyboard *ricercar* between the publication of Marco Antonio Cavazzoni's *Ricerchari, motetti, canzoni* of 1523 and his son Girolamo's *Intavolatura, cioe recercari, canzoni, himni, magnificati* of 1542. For whereas the father's two pieces in the genre are analogous in all important respects to the *Prélude sur chacun ton*—consisting primarily of chordal homophony in alternation with running passagework, developed sequentially for the most part to produce pieces of considerable length—those of his son are indubitably modeled stylistically on the Latin motet.

The younger Cavazzoni's novel approach to the genre is dramatically clear from the *Recercar quarto* of his publication of 1542 (see Example 24-28). The work opens with a point of imitation based on a relatively sedate figure—a falling fifth that is

44. For an intriguing attempt to explain the use of two radically antithetical styles in pieces uniformly identified as *ricercari* in light of classical texts on rhetoric, see Warren Kirkendale, "Ciceronians versus Aristotelians on the Ricercar as Exordium from Bembo to Bach," *Journal of the American Musicological Society* 32 (1979): 1–44.

EXAMPLE 24-28. Girolamo Cavazzoni, *Recercar quarto* (mm. 1–18, 83–99) for keyboard

filled in ascent by a third and two steps. Seemingly conceived so as to be readily usable for the declamation of text, the initial motive dissolves into more fluid part-writing with the entry of the alto part (m. 3), which follows a similar pattern even though the tenor entry comes only four and a half breves later (mid-m. 6). The bass comes in on the tenor's heels (m. 8), and a second entry is heard in the soprano before the first cadence to the final (F, in m. 14).

Without ever thinning appreciably the four-part texture, the composer follows that first point of imitation with a second. Overlapping with the resolution of the cadence, this one involves only soprano (from g half note, m. 13) and tenor (also g half note, m. 15). After a cadence to c' (m. 18), a third point of imitation is initiated by the tenor and, after cadences to C (m. 23) and F (m. 26), a fourth, starting again from the soprano (m. 26).

It is indicative of the nature of the counterpoint that one can discuss this composition in terms of its individual parts, the linear integrity of which is consistently maintained in the opening section up to the ornamental cadence to F (in m. 37). There follows a more episodic segment based on a dotted motive covering a sixth—a leap of a third combined with a stepwise fourth rising and a downward leap of a fifth—introduced by the alto immediately after the cadence (in m. 37) and imitated directly by the bass without the dotted rhythm. It then recurs repeatedly (mm. 41, 45, 48–49), the last time in imitation between alto and bass in a texture that is often in two or three parts, but rarely in four, leading to another cadence to F (m. 51).

The close imitation between soprano and bass that opens the next phrase (m. 52) yields to the sequential development of a short turning figure, first heard starting from f in the soprano (m. 55). The manner of its treatment also recalls imitative syntax, however, because successive statements of the figure come a fourth or a fifth apart, moving from f downward to c and F, upward again to c, f, and c', and then back down to g, d, and G before concluding on F (mm. 55–60).

Further on (mm. 71–82), episodic passagework, closing with a cadence to F, introduces a sesquialteral shift to a ternary mensuration (m. 83). This proportional section is also treated as a point of imitation based on a rising fifth with a leap of a third at the bottom. As the figure is very terse, the entries are closely spaced, either a ternary breve (mm. 83–85, 89–90) or at most two breves apart (mm. 85–88). Following a cadence to G (m. 91), the passage winds down episodically. Imitative ascending scale figures in the lower parts move against a slow descent in long values in the soprano. This culminates in a cadence to F and a shift back to the basic mensuration of the pieces for the final short phrase, largely a confirmation of the cadence.

If the structure and style of this work have been described in some detail, it is simply to illustrate to what extent the compositional procedures used in its facture are similar to those employed in the motet. Particularly noteworthy are the successive points of imitation in an essentially contrapuntal context; the occasional contrasts in texture by means of quasi-homophony (as in mm. 23–27) or a reduction in the number of parts (as in mm. 38–51); and, perhaps most striking, the proportional shift to a ternary mensuration just before the final cadential resolution, which had been an important compositional feature in the Latin motet since the time of Josquin's *Ave Maria, virgo serena.* Even the tendency to keep textures relatively full at the beginning of a new point of imitation by the overlapping of contrapuntal lines from the previous phrase can be seen as a reflection of motet style from the 1530s and 1540s on.

The adoption of the contrapuntal facture of the motet for the *ricercar*—however astonishing it may be in lute and even keyboard composition—is much more easily explained when the genre is intended for a polyphonic ensemble rather than a solo instrument. As we have seen, such consorts had been playing chansons, motets, and other vocal works from their individual parts since early in the fifteenth century at the latest. It is certainly no surprise, then, that a repertory of imitative *ricercari* for ensemble was taking shape already in the 1530s. A collection of twenty-one such pieces was published in Venice in 1540 by Andrea Arrivabene under the title *Musi-*

ca nova accomodata per cantar [!] et sonar sopra organi, et altri strumenti.[45] All of these were included in Jacques Moderne's *Musicque de joye* (ca. 1544), to which were added two more *ricercari* and the series of dances discussed earlier (see p. 837).

Unlike the dance music, which is nearly always anonymous, the *ricercari* carry attributions in the sources. One is ascribed in this collection to Girolamo Cavazzoni, the organist whose transformation of the keyboard *ricercar* led to the present discussion. Another five are by Adrian Willaert. But the majority of these compositions, eleven in all, are credited to Julio Segni (1498–1561). An organist, like Cavazzoni, he spent a little over two years at the basilica of San Marco in Venice (1530–33) during Willaert's tenure there and was thereafter primarily in Rome in the service of Cardinal Guido Ascanio Sforza.[46] Other, lesser-known composers round out Moderne's collection: a certain Guilielmo Colin; Girolamo Parabosco, a student of Willaert (two);[47] Nicolaus Benoist, and Gabriel Costa.

The individual compositions vary considerably in overall length and, therefore, in their musical substance. At his briefest, for example, Segni has crafted a piece in three parts of only 40 breves' (measures') duration, whereas Guilielmo Colin has extended his only work in the repertory to a total of 283 breves.[48] Characteristic of all of them, however, is the composers' unremitting reliance on contrapuntal procedures in which the individual lines spin out their melodic material independently. This is true even of the *ricercar* by Parabosco that is based on a cantus firmus, *Da pacem domine* (no. 14). Much of the time, moreover, the counterpoint is imitative, as may be seen from the opening of *Ricercar 17*, attributed to Julius de Modena [*sic*] (see Example 24-29). As in this instance, however, strict imitation often gives way rather quickly to freer treatment, and it is at times abandoned entirely, as in the opening of *Ricercar 13*, which is also ascribed to Segni.

CONCLUSIONS

The adoption of imitative counterpoint for the composition of musical genres with a preludial function, as seen in the *ricercari* for keyboard of Girolamo Cavazonni, was to become increasingly widespread in the course of the sixteenth century. The practice quickly crossed geographical borders and linguistic barriers and soon involved all of the instruments for which they were written. As we have seen, the *ricercar* for consort had become predominantly imitative and contrapuntal even before the publication of the younger Cavazzoni's collection, as may be seen from

45. For a study and complete edition of this collection, see H. Colin Slim, *Musica nova* (1540), Monuments of Renaissance Music, vol. 1 (Chicago: University of Chicago Press, 1964).
46. Concerning Segni, see H. Colin Slim, *The New Grove Dictionary of Music*, 17:105–6.
47. See H. Colin Slim, "Parabosco, Girolamo," *The New Grove Dictionary of Music*, 14:173–74.
48. These are nos. 10 and 11, respectively, in the complete edition prepared by Jacques Barbier, ed., *Jacques Moderne, Musicque de Joye*, 37–38 and 39–53.

EXAMPLE 24-29. Julius Segni [de Modena], *Ricercar 17* (mm. 1–8)

the twenty pieces of this type included in the *Musica nova* of 1540.[49] Indeed, the repertory for ensemble may have helped to determine the direction taken in the development of the *ricercar* for keyboard.[50]

The lutenists were slower to follow suit, perhaps in part because of the technical obstacles to be surmounted in playing counterpoint in three or four parts on a fretted fingerboard. Although the later works of both the "divine" Francesco da Milano (1497–1543) and his famous contemporary Alberto da Ripa (ca. 1500–51) are generally contrapuntal in concept and often imitative as well, there remains in them a great deal that is derived from the techniques of virtuoso improvisation.[51]

49. See the edition by Slim, ed., *Musica nova*.

50. See John Caldwell, "Ricercar," *The New Grove Dictionary of Music*, 15:836.

51. For the works of Francesco, see Francesco Canova da Milano, *The Lute Music of Francesco Canova da Milano (1497–1543)*, ed. Arthur J. Ness, 2 vols., Harvard Publications in Music, vols. 3–4 (Cambridge, Mass.: Harvard University Department of Music, 1970); for those of Alberto da Ripa, see *Oeuvres d'Albert de Rippe*, ed. Jean-Michel Vaccaro, 3 vols., Choeur des Muses, Corpus des luthistes français (Paris: Centre National de la Recherche Scientifique, 1972–75).

Spanish *tientos* and *fantasias*, whether for keyboard or for vihuela, followed much the same path of stylistic development. Luys de Narváez's *fantasias*, for example, are characterized by pervasive imitative counterpoint. They are marked as well by contrasts in register and texture, with paired voices giving variety from the fuller sonorities in four parts.[52] Likewise, Antonio de Cabezón's *tientos* for keyboard are contrapuntal in concept, adding augmentation and diminution of the motivic material to the techniques of part-writing borrowed from the vocal repertory for instrumental composition. Even the English fantasias for keyboard, at least as the genre is represented in the *Fitzwilliam Virginal Book*, rely heavily on imitative part-writing and related contrapuntal procedures for their facture. However, they also display a good deal of brilliant finger work and a fair amount of sequential development of motivic material. And of course those written for a consort of instruments, such as the increasingly popular viols, are even more rigorously and consistently imitative and contrapuntal in style.

By the end of the sixteenth century, moreover, it appears likely that for many pieces of this kind, especially those intended for use in the secular realm, the preludial function had gradually gone by the boards. Like the dance music of the period, they had become music intended primarily for playing and listening.

Interestingly, the quasi-universal adoption of imitative counterpoint for important preludial genres did not eliminate entirely from the musical scene those that were based instead in the techniques of improvisation and the virtuosic exploitation of the idiomatic capabilities of the instrument for which they were intended. Pieces making use of these compositional procedures continue to appear in novel and sometimes brilliant guises, often with new names as well. Among the works of the Venetian organists Andrea Gabrieli (ca. 1510–86) and Claudio Merulo (1533–1604), for example, are found not only sophisticated *ricercari*, some of which represent the contrapuntal elaboration of a single thematic idea, but also pieces called *intonazioni* and *toccate*.

The *intonazioni*, concise and chordal in character, continued to fulfill the practical function of establishing a specified modal orientation. The *toccate*, considerably more expansive and sectional in concept, combine contrapuntal passages with freer, more rhapsodic and virtuosic writing for keyboard.[53] In England, finally, the ancient term *praeludium* was retained to designate those compositions that consisted essentially of chordal strumming and fast finger work, as may be seen from the series of such pieces in the *Fitzwilliam Virginal Book*.[54]

If the adoption of imitative counterpoint for important preludial genres of the sixteenth century did not entirely displace improvisatory practices and idiomatic

---

52. See Hopkinson K. Smith, "Narváez," *The New Grove Dictionary of Music*, 13:39.
53. For a listing of the instrumental works of these two masters, see Elsie M. Arnold, "Gabrieli, Andrea," *The New Grove Dictionary of Music*, 7:59–60; and Denis Arnold, "Merulo, Claudio," *The New Grove Dictionary of Music*, 12:194.
54. See, for example, Maitland and Squire, eds., *Fitzwilliam Virginal Book*, 1:80–86, 180, 391–93, nos. 22–25, 49, 99, and *passim*.

styles, it was to have momentous historical implications nevertheless. When, in the early seventeenth century, a newly fashionable monodic, soloistic style of performance began to triumph in the vocal repertory, both sacred and secular, it was in these instrumental genres that the techniques of contrapuntal composition continued to be cultivated: cantus firmus elaboration, augmentation, diminution, canonic and syntactic imitation, and such like. Their continued use in the instrumental repertory thus provided aspiring composers with needed opportunities to develop and polish their part-writing skills. To begin to grasp just how important such a role was to be in the subsequent development of Western polyphony, one need only think ahead for a moment of the works of such eighteenth-century masters as J. S. Bach and G. F. Handel.

CHAPTER 25

✔

The Final Synthesis

INTRODUCTION

In defining the scope for the present study, the stated objective was to show how the genres and styles of the fifteenth and sixteenth centuries can be distinguished from those of the Middle Ages; to see if the development of musical style during the Renaissance offers meaningful analogies to that of the visual arts and literature, particularly with respect to the emulation of models from classical antiquity; and to determine whether or not there is enough stylistic coherence and consistency over a span of nearly two centuries to justify their designation as a period in the history of Western music.

We have seen in that connection the stylistic transformation of enduring medieval genres such as the chanson and the motet. We have observed the emergence of important new genres such as the cyclic Mass Ordinary, the madrigal, and instrumental compositions such as "inventions," preludes, and variations. We have also examined the use of models—from plainchant cantus firmi and popular melodies of the oral tradition to preexistent polyphonic works—and the emulatory tendencies generated by their adoption as the basis for a new composition. Composers of the period may have lacked models from classical antiquity such as those known to literature and the visual arts (with the exception of theoretical treatises). Nevertheless, the competitive revising of works of recognized excellence clearly played a crucial role in the compositional procedures of the period, as has been repeatedly demonstrated.

What, then, of the question of a Renaissance style, or, more appropriately, Renaissance styles? Is there sufficient coherence and consistency to warrant considering the fifteenth and sixteenth centuries as a separate, identifiable period in the history of Western music? In discussing the various genres cultivated during this time much has been made of the distinctions that can be convincingly made among them. Attention has been drawn to significant dissimilarities based not only on performance practices (combinations of voices and/or instruments), the language of the texts (when present), and the ritual or social function of the work but also on questions of musical style. As a result, the considerable diversity may have emerged more clearly than the common ground. There are, however, other perspectives from which to view the historical picture.

One mark of a stable musical culture with practices and compositional procedures that are well grounded in tradition is the clear definition of its musical genres. As we have seen, the fifteenth century did produce a measure of experimental ferment as the compositional types then current were codified, but the sixteenth century saw relatively little change in the basic conception of established categories until its final decades. New genres did continue to emerge, on the secular side especially; the madrigal is an exceptionally important case in point, and the instrumental repertories provide yet others. By contrast, however, sacred polyphony was characterized by relatively abiding traditions and well-founded musical genres.

The Latin motet was well defined as a compositional type during the second half of the fifteenth century and continued to be treated in much the same manner thereafter for at least another hundred years. The two primary approaches to the cyclic Ordinary—cantus firmus construction and *ad imitationem* reworking of a polyphonic model—were being adopted by composers everywhere by the second decade of the sixteenth century and continued in use more or less unchanged into its final years. Recognized practices were developed for the composition of hymns, Psalms, Magnificats, and the Te Deum, and similar conventions were also settled, albeit to a lesser extent, even for such relatively infrequently used liturgical texts as the Propers of the Mass, the Lamentations of Jeremiah, and the liturgical passions.

As for the secular song forms, the chanson provided an enduring model for composition based on the formal and syntactic structures of the texts set. To these were added, with the emergence of the madrigal as a freshly minted genre, a heightened emphasis on rhetorical and, especially, mimetic interpretations of the text for expressive purposes. Options for the performance of these repertories apparently always included solo voice and accompanying instruments, but for the text-based genres that were meant to be sung the prevailing style—as notated—tended consistently toward linear autonomy and a wholly vocal conception of the individual lines.

Given that compositional variety was viewed as esthetically desirable for music throughout the period, the diversity of texture that is such an important aspect of most of its compositional styles should come as no surprise. Contrast is achieved by an impressive arsenal of compositional devices. These include juxtaposing linearly independent parts with homophonic blocks of sound; points of imitation with free counterpoint; rapid rhythmic activity with slow movement, at times simultaneously; higher registers with lower ones; duos and trios with a full complement of voices (four, five, or more); and solo voices with the full choir.

Underlying this diversity, however, are concepts and practices that had remained astonishingly constant since at least the late fourteenth century. These concerned two very different areas of practical theory that were nonetheless very closely entwined: on the one hand, mensuration, and, on the other, the rules of counterpoint. The use of *modus*, *tempus*, and *prolatio* to divide systematically larger note values into groups of two or three smaller ones on several different levels was unchanged in its essentials from the early fifteenth century until the end of the sixteenth—despite some confusion as to the earlier mensural practice and some simplification of it.

Even more stable, and venerable, were the definitions of consonance and dissonance and the conventions by then current for handling them. Consonance continued to be classified as either perfect (unison, fourth, fifth, and octave with their octave duplications) or imperfect (minor and major thirds and sixths with their octave extensions). Perfect consonances of the same type were not to be used in parallel motion, and a sequence of imperfect parallels was to alternate as much as possible between major and minor varieties and be limited as to its length.

Distinctions were also made among the dissonances, though not so systematically, as to their relative asperity. Seconds and sevenths, minor or major (and their octave extensions), were considered less offensive than imperfect octaves and tritones, for example, and diminished fifths were less objectionable still, especially in a cadential context. All of these, if used, were to be introduced either by step, avoiding as a rule a position of excessive prominence such as the first note of a *tactus* (or measure), or by suspension from a previous consonance. They were also to be satisfactorily resolved, again by step whenever it could be managed.

The codification of these rules continued to be refined and clarified in the course of the sixteenth century, and their observance did not begin to break down until its final decades. By then they were so much taken for granted that their application could be treated rather freely. They could in fact be elided to the point that a composer could appear to have intentionally—or ignorantly—neglected them. Such was the case for the famous madrigals of Claudio Monteverdi's *Quinto libro* of 1605; it was the composer's compression of the canons of counterpoint—which he honored more in the breach than in literal fact—for purposes of textual interpretation that sparked the sometimes acrid debate between the late sixteenth-century theorist Giovanni Maria Artusi (ca. 1540–1613) and Claudio's brother, Giulio Cesare Monteverdi.[1] Significantly, however, the latter's justification of the composer's unorthodox treatment of dissonance was not a negation of the rules but rather an explanation of the procedures followed in terms of those very conventions.[2]

The extent to which the cultivation of the musical genres of the second half of the sixteenth century was bound by the conventions often established more than a

1. For a detailed study of the theoretical issues, see Claude V. Palisca, "The Artusi–Monteverdi Controversy," *The New Monteverdi Companion*, ed. Denis Arnold and Nigel Fortune (London: Faber and Faber, 1985), 133–66; for a feminist view of the matter, see Suzanne G. Cusick, "Gendering Modern Music: Thoughts on the Monteverdi–Artusi Controversy," *Journal of the American Musicological Society* 46 (1993): 1–25.

2. For excerpts from the actual exchange, *L'Artusi, ovvero Delle imperfezioni della modern musica* and Giulio's "Declaration" from *Il quinto libro de' madrigali*, see Oliver Strunk, ed., *Sources Readings in Music History* (New York: Norton, 1950), 393–412.

century earlier, and the degree to which the musical styles of its most celebrated composers are rooted in prevailing traditions and shaped by the works of preceding generations are evident in a variety of ways. There is, for example, what seems to have been a significant increase in the number of composers vying to get their works recognized and published. Pietro Gaetano describes those of his generation as legion, swarming about as if they had just emerged from some Trojan horse.

Without census figures of a kind not generally available for the time, his observations cannot be either confirmed or discredited. Still, they do appear to have had some basis in fact. Although less evidence has been lost for the musical activity of the late sixteenth century than for earlier eras, there does seem to have been a rather dramatic increase over its final decades in the number of composers whose names are known to history and whose works have reached our day. Some such proliferation of aspiring composers was certainly to have been expected. A growing industry of music printing enhanced the possibilities for economic rewards and patronage for composers, as did the continuing diffusion of musical culture as a preferred form of recreation among the urban classes.

At this point any conclusions drawn would be impressionistic at best, and it is likely to be some time before the demographic implications of these developments have been systematically explored as they ought to be. But whatever the results of such inquiries, it is difficult to believe that the flourishing musical life of the late sixteenth century would have been possible without a well-established didactic tradition that was grounded in a highly developed theoretical discipline and a relatively stable musical practice. That such a didactic tradition was in fact in place is demonstrated by the steady stream of treatises, both practical and speculative, produced by the presses of the period, promulgating far and wide the principles of mensuration and the rules of counterpoint on which all composition continued to be based.[3]

As for the musical practice, its stability is evident in the vast repertory that was disseminated through both manuscript and printed sources. It consisted, as has been seen, of works in genres that were well defined, that had been described by the writers of the period, and that were clearly well understood by composers, performers, and listeners alike.[4] A brief survey of trends in Europe and England, as seen through the works of a few leading figures of the age, will illuminate at least to a degree the continuities of tradition through more than a century and a half and the relative coherence of the stylistic developments associated with it.

---

3. Although not conceived as a survey of Renaissance theorists of music, Claude Palisca's *Humanism in Italian Renaissance Musical Thought* (New Haven: Yale University Press, 1985) gives ample evidence of the vigor of the theoretical tradition during the fifteenth and sixteenth centuries. Palisca draws into his discussion of humanism the works of Johannes Tinctoris, Franchinus Gaffurius, Ugolino of Orvieto, Ramos de Pareia, Giovanni Spataro, and Gioseffo Zarlino, among others. His focus on Italy leaves aside, of course, the proliferation of didactic treatises by German authors for the Latin schools.

4. A case in point is Pietro Cerone, whose lengthy treatise *El melopeo y maestro* gives clear directions for the composition of motets, Masses, Psalms, canticles (including the Magnificat), hymns, and the Lamentations of Holy Week; for an English translation of the relevant excerpts, see Strunk, ed., *Source Readings in Music History* (New York: Norton, 1950), 262–73 (and cf. above, pp. 590–91).

The composers selected for this survey—Pierluigi Palestrina, Tomás Luis de Victoria, William Byrd, and Orlande de Lassus—are both representative and exceptional. They are representative in that the musical practices and trends of the age and of the region, or regions, in which they worked are reflected in the works of each of them. Each is also exceptional, however, by virtue of his individual creative gifts and the recognition they earned for him, not only from contemporaries but also from subsequent generations. Striking, too, in every instance is their fecund creativity. The sheer quantity of music produced by these masters during their working years is nothing less than astonishing. It is also yet another testimony to the stability of the musical culture, to the then common understanding of musical genres and compositional practices. Historically, composers have generally been at their most prolific when the structural principles and compositional procedures of their art were most settled and well defined.

GIOVANNI PIERLUIGI DA PALESTRINA
(1525–26 TO 1594)

Although Palestrina is known by the name of the town in the Sabine hills near Rome where his family originated, his training and activity as a musician were associated virtually lifelong with Roman institutions, several of which were part of the papal establishment.[5] As a choirboy he was instructed at the ancient basilica of Santa Maria Maggiore, probably from the mid-1530s until the early 1540s. During those years at least two of the masters of the boys were from French-speaking regions: Robin Mallapert (1538–39) and Firmin Lebel (from 1540 on). Both men later served as the chapelmaster of the French national church in Rome, Saint Louis des Français—Mallapert only briefly, but Lebel for sixteen years—and both also went from there into papal service.

In 1561 Lebel entered the Sistine Chapel choir, where he spent another four years, and he finished his life and career in Rome.[6] Mallapert was appointed master of the choir of the Cappella Giulia in St. Peter's Basilica already in late 1539 and, except for a relatively brief hiatus (1545–50), he continued in that post until 1551.[7] Late in life Lebel held a benefice at Santa Maria Maggiore, to which Palestrina returned as chapelmaster from 1561 to 1566, and it was Mallapert that Palestrina replaced upon assuming leadership of the newly reorganized Cappella Giulia in 1551.[8] Palestrina's relationship to both men is in fact symptomatic of the extent to

---

5. For a concise, instructive biography of the composer, see Lewis Lockwood, "Palestrina," *The New Grove Dictionary of Music,* 14:118–37.
6. See Allan Atlas, "Lebel, Firmin," *The New Grove Dictionary of Music,* 10:578.
7. See Allan Atlas, "Mallapert, Robin," *The New Grove Dictionary of Music,* 11:586.
8. Concerning the Julian Chapel, founded by Pope Julius II in 1513, see Ariane Ducrot, "Histoire de la Cappella Giulia au XVIe siècle," *Mélanges d'archéologie et d'histoire* 75 (1963): 1:179–240 and 2:467–559.

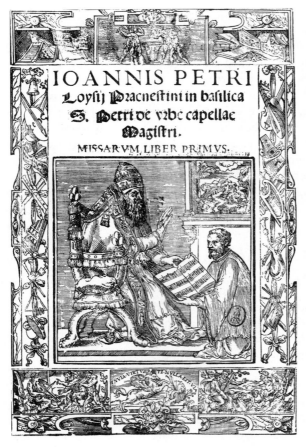

FIGURE 25-1.   Title page of Palestrina's *Missarum liber primus* (printed in Rome by Dorico in 1554), showing the composer presenting the publication to Pope Julius III.

which French-trained musicians—and their compositions—dominated the scene in Rome at the time and may help to explain the large part that French repertory played in the development of Palestrina's compositional style.

In 1544, his apprenticeship complete, Palestrina was appointed as organist and music teacher at the cathedral of San Agapito in his family's native town. There he remained until the bishop under whom he served in that diocese, Cardinal Giovanni Maria del Monte (1487–1555), was elected pope in 1550 as Julius III. Palestrina followed this powerful patron to Rome, where he served first in the Cappella Giulia (until mid-January 1555) and then, for three months, in the choir of the Cappella Sistina. It is a clear mark of papal favor that, although married, Palestrina was admitted to the papal chapel in flagrant violation of the choir's rules on celibacy. His appointment was made on the express orders of Julius III, to whom he had dedicated his first book of Masses in 1554 and, more significant still, without the customary examination and the consent of the other singers (see Figure 25-1).

Having lost his place in the Sistine Chapel choir when the rule of celibacy was reinstated shortly after the death of Julius III, Palestrina was named *maestro di cappella* at the great papal basilica of St. John Lateran—where Lassus had served earlier—on October 1, 1555. Frustrated by the poverty of its musical establishment, he stayed only until 1560. He then served, again briefly, at Santa Maria Maggiore (1561–66), and after a period under the patronage of Cardinal Ippolito II d'Este (1565–71), overlapping in part with his appointment at the church, he again assumed the position of chapelmaster at the Cappella Giulia, where he remained through the last years of his life.[9]

Palestrina must have been honing his skills as a composer for some time before his first Masses were published in 1554, but even so the number of compositions to come from his pen during the fifty or so years of his professional career is really prodigious. Taking into account only those works that can be securely attributed, his polyphonic repertory includes 104 Mass Ordinaries, more than 300 motets, 68 Offertories, 79 hymns, 35 Magnificats, enough settings of the Lamentations of Jeremiah to constitute five or six complete sets, a number of litanies, and 140 madrigals.[10]

PALESTRINA AND THE COUNTER-REFORMATION

It is noteworthy that, with the exception of the motets, which have no clearly fixed place in Catholic ritual, all of Palestrina's Latin-texted works were unequivocally intended for liturgical use. Even the titles of the publications in which they appeared leave little doubt in that respect. The hymns were brought out in 1589 in a volume headed *Hymni totius anni secundum Sanctae Romanae Ecclesiae consuetudinem*, indicating that settings have been supplied for all the major feasts of the liturgical year. Similarly, the Offertories appeared in 1593 in a print entitled *Offertoria totius anni . . .*, signaling the same comprehensive purpose and providing not only for the principal feasts from Advent to the ninth Sunday after Pentecost but also for Sundays throughout the remainder of the year. There was even a volume of motets (now lost) entitled *Motecta festorum totius anni cum Communi Sanctorum* (*Motets for Feasts throughout the Year with the Common for Saints*, 1563).

That his Magnificats were also intended for liturgical use is equally clear as they conform to the formulae of the eight plainchant tones with several settings for each of them. As a rule he set even-numbered verses for *alternatim* performance with the plainchant, but for every tone he composed at least one setting of the odd verses, perhaps because the Cappella Sistina, for which Palestrina regularly provided repertory, sang the entire canticle in polyphony.

Palestrina's Rome was, after all, the spiritual and intellectual center for the Catholic church's Counter-Reformation, and his career was touched in a variety of ways by the reforming and conservative tendencies associated with that movement. Following the pronouncements of the Council of Trent in 1562 and 1563 concerning sacred music, reform-minded prelates had two principal concerns. One was to eliminate the secular elements that had impinged upon Mass composition since the early fifteenth century; the other was to foster the intelligibility of the liturgical texts. A Commission of Cardinals was appointed in 1564–65 to see to the implementation

9. For a concise discussion of the musical institutions in Rome (and the musicians who served them) with which Palestrina had some connection, see Christopher Reynolds, "Rome: A City of Rich Contrast," in *The Renaissance: From the 1470s to the End of the Sixteenth Century*, ed. Iain Fenlon, Man and Music, vol. 2 (Englewood Cliffs, N.J.: Prentice Hall, 1989), 63–80.

10. See the work list compiled by Jessie Ann Owens, "Palestrina," *The New Grove Dictionary of Music*, 14:129–36.

of the conciliar decrees. In that connection the Sistine Chapel choir was summoned to the house of Cardinal Vitellozzi Vitelli, one of the commission's eight members, on April 28, 1565, "to sing some Masses and to test whether the words could be understood, as their Eminences desire."[11]

Palestrina's earliest biographer, Giuseppe Baini, claimed that the composer's *Pope Marcellus Mass* was commissioned for that occasion and that its clear, declamatory style persuaded the assembled cardinals not to ban polyphony from the celebration of the liturgy.[12] Although that assertion has become a veritable legend, disseminated far and wide in the Western world, it is not supported by existing documents and known facts.[13] Palestrina's music was known to members of the commission, however, in particular to one of its most distinguished and powerful prelates, Cardinal Carlo Borromeo, who was also archbishop of Milan.[14] And while it seems rather unlikely that the *Pope Marcellus Mass* was sung at the commission's "hearing" in 1565, the style of that work is just a part of the evidence suggesting that the composer was duly sensitive to the issues of intelligibility with which the cardinals concerned themselves.

Also significant, perhaps, in light of the Tridentine decrees, is the relative paucity of secular models for his Mass composition. With the exception of his two (more or less obligatory?) essays in the *L'homme armé* tradition and a few madrigals, the pre-existent materials upon which he drew were all sacred in character. The influence of the reformers may also help to explain Palestrina's turn in later years—with apologies for his earlier indiscretions—from secular to spiritual madrigals. His first book of madrigals for five voices, published in Venice in 1581, though not specifically titled as such, consisted in fact of settings of spiritual texts. A second book of *madrigali spirituali* was published in 1594, and his production in the subgenre came to a total of 49 pieces, more than a third of his madrigals overall. It was also in pursuit of Counter-Reformation goals that Palestrina and Annibale Zoilo were commissioned in 1577 by Pope Gregory XIII to revise the chants of the Roman Gradual and Antiphoner, in order to rid them of their "barbarisms, obscurities, contrarieties, and superfluities."[15]

MUSIC FOR VESPERS

Turning to Palestrina's compositional practice, there is ample evidence, whatever the genre, of the extent to which it is rooted in that of previous generations. His hymns,

11. See the relevant documents published in Pierluigi Palestrina, *Pope Marcellus Mass*, ed. Lewis Lockwood, Norton Critical Scores (New York: Norton, 1975), 10–36.
12. The pertinent passage from Baini's *Memorie storico-critiche della vita e delle opere di Giovanni Pierluigi da Palestrina*, published in Rome in 1828, is given in English translation by Lockwood, in Palestrina, *Pope Marcellus Mass*, 34–36.
13. See Lockwood's careful discussion of the historical issues, "Palestrina," *The New Grove Dictionary of Music*, 14:122–23.
14. Concerning Borromeo's involvement with the musical reforms decreed by the Council of Trent, see Lewis Lockwood, *The New Grove Dictionary of Music*, 3:67–68.
15. For an English translation of the papal brief authorizing the revision, see Strunk, ed., *Source Readings in Music History* revised edition, ed. Leo Treitler (New York: Norton), 1998, 375–76.

for example, reflect the traditions of the Sistine Chapel as established already in the time of Costanzo Festa. Palestrina's setting of the Advent hymn *Conditor alme siderum*, like Festa's, presupposes *alternatim* performance in accordance with established custom (see Example 25-1 and cf. Example 16-1).[16] Except for the initial line, which serves as a plainchant intonation, the odd-numbered strophes are set polyphonically, each with its own music, despite the strophic nature of the genre.

The mode 4 chant, which provides much of the melodic substance for the counterpoint, is elaborated by a variety of compositional strategies. For example, Palestrina makes of the hymn tune's second phrase (the first treated in parts) a point of imitation, starting with the altus and answering in cantus, bassus, and tenor in turn. He presents the third phrase mostly in uniform, longer values (semibreves), beginning with the tenor (which is echoed imitatively by the cantus), then shifting to the bassus. For the final phrase, which opens with free material in the upper three parts,

16. For a transcription in modern score of the complete work, see Giovanni Pierluigi da Palestrina, *Le opere complete di Giovanni Pierluigi da Palestrina*, ed. Raffaele Casimiri et al., 34 vols. (Rome: Edizione Fratelli Scalera 1939–52), 14:1–7.

EXAMPLE 25-1. Pierluigi Palestrina, *Conditor alme siderum*, 1 (mm. 1–9) and 3 (mm. 1–6)

Kindly creator of the stars, eternal light of the believers . . .

he gives the chant-derived melody first to the bassus, then to the tenor, which articulates with the cantus the cadence to the plainsong's final on E (over an A in the bassus).

Subsequent strophes display the same judicious mix of cantus firmus–like treatment of the chant with more freely invented material. At the opening of the third stanza the cantus presents the plainsong in longer values while the other three introduce an independent point of imitation. With the next Palestrina begins, in addition, the climax-producing process of adding voices and contrapuntal complexity, which had become customary for hymn settings in the papal tradition. Palestrina swells the sonority to five voices for the fifth strophe and to six voices for the seventh (and last). He gives the final stanza yet more compositional weight and liturgical significance by laying out the chant melody as an unembellished cantus firmus in canon between tenor II (at pitch) and altus II (at the upper fifth), anticipating their entry with an imitative statement of it divided between altus I and the cantus. He then brings the work to a close with all of the voices contributing to the contrapuntal fabric and to the fullness of the sonorous texture.

As has been observed, Palestrina's polyphonic Magnificats are also designed for the most part for *alternatim* performance. Most of them are written for the relatively modest format of four-voice choir with only four of the thirty-five settings for five voices and another four for six, a reflection perhaps of their recurring utilitarian role in the celebration of the liturgy.

An exception is his *Magnificat primi toni* for eight voices divided into two separate four-voice choirs (see Example 25-2).[17] Aside from the initial intonation in plainchant, all twelve strophes of the canticle are set without interruption. The formulaic tone, which figures prominently in the contrapuntal texture at the beginning, gives way rather quickly to freer melodic invention with only an occasional reminder

---

17. For a transcription of the complete work in modern score, see Palestrina, *Le opere complete*, ed. Casimiri et al., 16:323–34.

EXAMPLE 25-2. Pierluigi Palestrina, *Magnificat primi toni* (mm. 1–17)

My soul doth magnify the Lord, and my spirit hath rejoiced in God, my Savior . . .

through the rest of the piece of the intonation, the reiterated reciting pitch, and the cadential formula characteristic of the chant.

Of particular interest is Palestrina's handling of the polychoral style generally associated with late sixteenth-century Venetian masters (see pp. 556–60), with which he was clearly well acquainted. A substantial number of his motets are for eight voices in divided choirs,[18] and yet others are for twelve voices, disposed in three choirs of four voices each.[19] Here he makes use of similar compositional procedures, deploying the same sort of contrast between contrapuntal textures and blocks of declamatory homophony in alternation between the two choirs. He joins all the voices briefly at the end of the third strophe for the words "omnes generationes" ("all generations," mm. 28–32), perhaps in illustration of the text. Thereafter, however, the textures are relatively spare. In fact, beginning with the sixth strophe, "Fecit potentiam" (m. 56), the two choirs maintain their separate identities in strict alternation. They are heard separately even at the beginning of the Doxology (m. 102), which is marked nonetheless by a sesquialteral shift to a ternary mensuration for the words "Gloria Patri, et Filio, et Spiritui Sancto." Not until the very end are their sonorities finally massed again for the concluding words, "saeculorum, Amen."

The extraordinary means required for the performance of this Magnificat and its continuous setting of the complete text both suggest that it may have been intended for the Sistine Chapel choir. The tradition there, as we have seen, was to sing the canticle entirely in polyphony. Manuscript evidence points to the same conclusion as the work was copied into the chapel's MS 29, which is dated 1592. It is just one of many indications that, although Palestrina served in the papal choir only briefly, he had a more informal relationship with that august institution over most of his career.

MASS AND MOTET

Palestrina's Masses, of which thirteen books were published between 1554 and 1601, fall into the various categories that had been established for the most part already by the turn of the sixteenth century (see pp. 574–75). A considerable number—at least thirty-three—are based on chant. Sixteen of these draw upon plainsong Mass cycles: the Requiem Mass, two *Missa De beata virgine*, a *Missa De feria*, and a series of ten works commissioned around 1568 by Guglielmo Gonzaga, duke of Mantua, for the ducal chapel of Santa Barbara. The latter are based on chants peculiar to the Mantuan liturgy selected by the duke himself and are identified in accordance with their festal function: *De Beata Marie* (three); *Dominicalis* (for Sundays, one); *In festis Apostolorum* (for the Apostles, two); *In duplicibus minoribus* (for minor double feasts, two); and *In semiduplicibus majoribus* (for major semi-double

18. See, for example, Palestrina, *Le opere complete*, vols. 7 and 8, which contain thirteen motets; in all, sixty motets for eight voices are listed by Jessie Ann Owens, *The New Grove Dictionary of Music*, 14:131–33.
19. See Palestrina, *Le opere complete*, vol. 32, which contains five motets; a total of ten motets for twelve voices is listed by Jessie Ann Owens, *The New Grove Dictionary of Music*, 16:131–33.

feasts, two). The remainder make use primarily of liturgically significant antiphons and hymns. However, only seven of these works are in the venerable tradition of the tenor cantus firmus Mass, most notably the two that embody the long-celebrated *L'homme armé* tune, one for four voices, the other for five.[20]

Masses essentially free of borrowed material are rather rare in the Palestrina canon. Among them, however, is the famous *Pope Marcellus Mass*. There are, in addition, an example of the *Missa Ad fugam*, a canonic Mass in the tradition opened by Okeghem and consecrated by Josquin, a Mass structured by means of the hexachord *ut, re, mi, fa, sol, la*, and a number of others.[21]

The largest and perhaps historically most important component of Palestrina's Mass repertory is that constituted by the *missae ad imitationem*, those modeled on preexistent polyphonic works and often described as "parody" Masses (see pp. 582–91). His exemplars are mostly motets, but he also chose for that purpose four madrigals and a chanson—a genre in which (not surprisingly) he never worked. For twenty-two of the fifty-three Mass Ordinaries in this category Palestrina elaborated works of his own, but for the remaining thirty-one he adopted pieces by other composers. Because there are so many of the latter, his choice of models is highly instructive. These compositions are clearly representative of the repertory that was current in Rome at the time and of masters whose works were relatively well known there. In addition, and even more significantly, they are pieces with which Palestrina became intimately familiar and that he must have found worthy of emulation.

Significantly, the great majority of these motets stem from the French tradition, and many are attributable to composers of the previous generation. Of the twenty-three known works that Palestrina took as models, eleven were published in Lyons by Moderne in his *Motetti del fiore* of 1532 and 1538. Josquin, whose *Benedicta es* was his only motet borrowed by Palestrina for Mass composition, is one of the earliest among the composers represented. Others who, like Josquin, spent some part of their career on the Italian peninsula, include Jacquet of Mantua (1483–1559), from whom Palestrina took four models, Hilaire Penet (fl. 1515–19), Philippe Verdelot (ca. 1470–80 to before 1552), and Jean Lhéritier (ca. 1480 to after 1552). More surprising, perhaps, Palestrina also borrowed from five other northern composers for whom no Italian residence is known: Jean Maillard (fl. ca. 1538–70), Lupus Hellinck (ca. 1496–1541), Johannes Lupi (ca. 1506–39), Jean Richafort (ca. 1480–1547), and Mathieu Lasson (d. before 1595).[22]

Italian and Spanish composers from whom Palestrina derived models are much fewer in number. Cristóbal de Morales (ca. 1500–53), who was himself a singer in

---

20. See Lockwood and Owens, "Palestrina," *The New Grove Dictionary of Music*, 14:120–30; concerning the liturgical categories specified by these Mass cycles, see above, pp. 235, n. 34.
21. In this connection see Knud Jeppesen, "Problems of the *Pope Marcellus Mass*: Some Remarks on the *Missa Papae Marcelli* by Giovanni Pierluigi da Palestrina," in Palestrina, *Pope Marcellus Mass*, ed. Lockwood, 109–17.
22. Details concerning the lives of these composers can be found in any of the standard biographical dictionaries such as *The New Grove Dictionary of Music*.

the Sistine Chapel choir for a decade (1535–45), authored one, as did Andreas de Silva (b. ca. 1475–80), who may have been trained in the circles of the French court despite his Spanish origins.[23] As for Palestrina's countrymen, Domenico Maria Ferrabosco (1513–74), Giovan Leonardo Primavera (ca. 1540–45 to after 1585), and Cipriano de Rore (1515–16 to 1565) each penned a madrigal that he selected for Mass composition.

Characteristic of these composers generally, as seen in the motets Palestrina chose for polyphonic Mass composition, is their polished craftsmanship. Their works display a skillful use of counterpoint, both imitative and free, relieved by occasional passages in homophonic declamation; carefully balanced and articulated musical phrases; circumspect observance of the rules of counterpoint; and a clear sense of conventional modal parameters. Although declamatory values are respected, and rhetorical and even mimetic gestures are not entirely wanting, these composers generally treat the texts set with greater regard for their syntactic structures than for their potential for emotional expression.

These are, of course, among the traits that distinguish as well Palestrina's motet style. In addition, he is perhaps even more celebrated for his meticulous shaping of melodic lines. Whatever the voice part, from superius to bassus, smooth stepwise motion predominates; leaps, whether ascending or descending, are almost invariably balanced by a turn back in the opposite direction, and conventional ranges and modal parameters are respected. In his counterpoint dissonance is carefully prepared and just as carefully resolved. Phrases are clearly articulated and carefully balanced. Everything contributes, in sum, to the overall sense of structural equilibrium and clarity that epitomizes the *ars perfecta* of the late sixteenth century.[24]

Despite the difference in genre, these characteristics are also clearly exemplified in Palestrina's Mass composition. This is perhaps not so surprising when the model is a motet of his own composition. However, the same stylistic affinity between model and Mass is usually observable as well in those that Palestrina has based on the motets of other, earlier masters. An instructive example of this relationship, among the many that could be chosen more or less at random, is provided by his *Missa Nigra sum sed formosa* for five voices, first published in Rome in 1590 (see Example 25-3).[25] The motet upon which it is based, a setting for five voices by Jean Lhéritier of a text taken from the Song of Solomon that was used as an antiphon at Second Vespers for feasts of the Virgin Mary,[26] is among those published by Moderne in 1532 (see Example 25-4).[27]

23. See Winfried Kirsch, "De Silva," *The New Grove Dictionary of Music*, 5:389–90.

24. Palestrina's style has been analyzed in minute detail by Knud Jeppesen in his landmark study, *The Style of Palestrina and the Dissonance* (Oxford: Oxford University Press, 1927).

25. For an edition of Palestrina's Mass in modern score, see Palestrina, *Le opere complete*, ed. Casimiri et al., 15:89–129.

26. See the *Liber usualis*, 1259.

27. For an edition of the complete motet in modern score, see Johannes Lhéritier, *Opera omnia*, ed. Leeman L. Perkins, 2 vols., Corpus mensurabilis musicae 48 ([Rome]: American Institute of Musicology, 1969), 2:161–65; the remaining sources for the work are also of Italian provenance: manuscripts now in Florence, Rome, and Treviso and a reprint by Gardane in 1539.

EXAMPLE 25-3. Pierluigi Palestrina, *Missa Nigra sum*, "Kyrie I" (mm. 1–29), "Christe" (mm. 30–41), "Kyrie II" (mm. 62–69)

[Filia Jherusalem...]

Lord, have mercy; Christ, have mercy; Lord, have mercy.

EXAMPLE 25-4. Jean Lhéritier, *Nigra sum sed formosa* (mm. 1–41)

I am black but comely, O daughters of Jerusalem; therefore doth the Lord love me . . .
    (Song of Solomon 1:5)

Lhéritier, who is known to have been in the service of the Estense court in Ferrara as early as 1506, may also have spent a number of years in Rome. He is cited in a payment roll from the court of Pope Leo X dated May 1, 1514 (but with later entries) and served briefly as chapelmaster at the French national church of St. Louis des Français (1521–22) before joining the chapel of the cardinal of Auch, François de Clermont, papal legate of Avignon, about 1525.[28]

For *Nigra sum sed formosa* Lhéritier did not incorporate the liturgical melody into the motet, nor did he adopt its E final and mode 3 ambitus. He chose instead for his polyphonic elaboration of the text a D final with a b-fa signature and ranges and melodic species that point to mode 2. However, a melodic gesture (*fa, re, fa, mi*) at the beginning of the chant with the words "sed formosa" does figure prominently, and repeatedly, at the top of Lhéritier's counterpoint as well (e.g., mm. 8–15, 48–52, 68–72). In his approach to the text syntactic considerations were clearly paramount. Dividing it into five short phrases, he presents each in turn as a new point of imitation.

Lhéritier spins out the penultimate segment of the biblical text, "et introduxit me" ("and introduced me") at considerable length, presumably for rhetorical emphasis, with several repetitions in each of the voices (mm. 41–55) before completing the thought with "in cubiculum suum" ("into his chamber"). That resolution is emphasized in turn by the first unequivocal use (in the three inner voices) of homophonic declamation, even though the effect is mitigated by the sustained octave ds of superius and bassus (mm. 55–57). It is followed, however, by a literal repetition of the preceding section, text and music (mm. 41–55 = mm. 61–75). That repeat, combined with the reiteration of the "sed formosa" figure, contributes to a sense of motivic integration and formal coherence. It leads, finally, to a musical peroration, a new and extended setting in full sonority for the words "in cubiculum suum."

Palestrina's reworking of Lhéritier's material follows in its essentials the pattern established just after the turn of the century by the composers working at the royal French court, as exemplified in Antoine de Févin's *Missa Ave Maria*. Each of the five principal sections of the Mass begins with a point of imitation derived from the opening of the motet, and although it is treated somewhat differently in each occurrence, it is sufficiently recognizable to serve as a kind of head motive for the entire work. At the outset Palestrina's presentation of the material taken over from the model is fairly orderly and systematic, but as the Mass unfolds, section by section, his treatment of it is increasingly free.

For the first "Kyrie" the order in which the voices enter has been changed (from tenor 2, altus, superius, bassus, and tenor 1 to altus, superius, tenor 1, bassus, and tenor 2), as have the pitches on which it is based (from d and g to a and d), but the relationship between the Mass and its model is unmistakable nevertheless. Subse-

---

28. See Leeman L. Perkins, "Lhéritier, Jean," in the forthcoming revision of *The New Grove Dictionary of Music.*

quently (m. 14), Palestrina introduces the recurrent "sed formosa" motive (from m. 8), from b-fa as well as from f', and uses it, as does Lhéritier, as a kind of cadential preparation that brings the subsection to a close.

Palestrina initiates the "Christe" with the second point of imitation from the motet (mm. 15ff., 23ff.) but in a much sparer texture, this time with the same pitches (g and d') but following the order of the model's second statement of the idea (superius, altus) rather than the first (altus, superius). It may in fact be this reordering of materials in the motet that suggested to Palestrina a similar approach for the Mass. The model's third phrase (mm. 29ff.) is introduced only at the beginning of the second Kyrie, for which it furnishes most of the motivic material. At the approach to the cadence it gives way briefly to a scalewise descent through a sixth (mm. 87ff.) cleary derived from the end of that section in the motet (mm. 38ff.)

At the opening of the Gloria, Palestrina introduces again the opening point of imitation from the model, this time with the first three voices (tenor 2, altus, and cantus) taken directly from the model. The "sed formosa" motive makes its appearance early (m. 13) but leads this time—as it does in the fourth section of the motet—to a cadence to D, followed by homophonic declamation for "Gratias agimus tibi," recalling the only clearly homophonic passage in the model (mm. 55–57). A descending scale through a seventh for "propter gloriam tuam" (mm. 26–28) introduces again material from the third section of the motet to conclude this part of the Mass.

The "Qui tollis" (m. 72) goes on to quote from the fourth phrase of the model (mm. 45ff.), the beginning of the lengthy repeated section (mm. 65ff), with its ascending leaps of fourths, fifths, and octaves. The borrowing in this subsection is more subtle thereafter, hinting at the motivic material of the model rather than quoting it literally. At the conclusion, however (mm. 135ff.), Palestrina refers directly to the final cadence of Lhéritier's motet (mm. 83ff.).

In the remaining sections of the Mass Palestrina continues to draw in a similar manner upon the motivic material of his model, often rather freely and subtly, making his own compositional use of the preexistent contrapuntal substance. In the Credo, in keeping with tradition, the "Et incarnatus est" is preceded by a brief silence and then declaimed homophonically by all voices to a motive only vaguely related to the motet. The "Crucifixus," surprisingly, returns to the head motive drawn from the beginning of the motet, whereas the "Et iterum" follows the "Qui tollis" in quoting from the fourth phrase of the model (mm. 45ff.). For "Et in Spiritum Sanctum," by contrast, Palestrina indicates a sesquialteral shift to a ternary mensuration, for which there is no precedent in the model, and sets the words in strict homophonic declamation (mm. 166–89).

Similar procedures are found in the Sanctus and the Agnus Dei as well, with the clearest return to material borrowed from the model in the latter. For the head motive of "Agnus I" Palestrina recalls, nevertheless, the reworking of the initial point of imitation of the motet that he adopted for the Kyrie; the order in which the voices enter is changed yet again, and the intervals between them are defined here as well by A and D (rather than D and G). The second "Agnus" opens, like the "Qui tollis," with the ascending leaps of the fourth phrase of the model and refers anew to the "sed formosa" motive (of mm. 8–9).

In sum, as this lengthy description demonstrates, Palestrina's treatment of his model corresponds in every important respect to the prescriptions provided by Cerone for the composition of a Mass Ordinary of this type (see pp. 590–91).

THE PALESTRINA STYLE

Compositional procedures characteristic of the motet of the sixteenth century also predominate in the other genres of liturgical polyphony cultivated by Palestrina. His settings of the Offertories are both symptomatic and representative in that regard. For *Terra tremuit,* the Offertory for Easter Sunday, as for the settings of these texts from the Mass Propers generally, Palestrina has utterly ignored the chant melody with its E final and its sinuous melismas (see Example 25-5).[29] Rather, he has set each of its two syntactic units with a recurring point of imitation.

He has treated the words of the first ("Terra tremuit et quievit") entirely syllabically except for some modest cadential embellishment, but he spins out this small bit of prose by repeating twice (with variation) the initial point of imitation. By contrast, he introduces the second clause ("dum resurgeret in judicio Deus") with a rising

29. For a transcription of the entire composition in modern score, see Palestrina, *Le opere complete,* ed. Casimiri et al., 17:99–103.

EXAMPLE 25-5. Perluigi Palestrina, *Terra tremuit et quievit* (mm. 1–11, 20–27, 53–63)

The earth trembled and was still when God arose in judgment. Alleluia.

melisma for the interjectory "dum" in imitation among the upper three voices (mm. 20–21), perhaps as a mimetic gesture to suggest the idea of God rising again to judgment. Those words, however, are declaimed homophonically by the same three voices, and only as they move toward a cadence (on A) do tenor 2 and bassus take up the ascending melismatic figure.

That point of imitation is also repeated (again with variation), followed by a third statement of the text to new motivic material and a clear cadence to G (the final of this mode 7 composition). To conclude, the celebratory "alleluia" that is customary for the liturgical season is presented in a cascading series of imitative phrases, usually ending with a relatively extended melisma in rapid rhythms. This peroration begins modestly with cantus and altus, but the other three voices are quickly added to provide the full sonorities and animated counterpoint found appropriate for such expressions of joyous enthusiasm.

Palestrina has also adopted these same motet-related compositional procedures for his madrigals, both secular and spiritual. The points of imitation may be a bit less dense, the counterpoint less complex, and the use of homophony less sparing and discreet, but the differences with the Latin-texted works are more a matter of degree than of kind. In his setting of Petrarch's celebrated canzone *Vergine bella*, for example, Palestrina opens with consecutive points of imitation each of the first three verses of the poem (see Example 25-6).[30] And although there are hints of homophony from the very outset, as when altus and tenor 1 enter together, not until the very end (beginning with "soccorri alla mia guerra") does the texture become unmistakably chordal—and, at the same time, antiphonal—in nature.

30. For a complete transcription of this madrigal in modern score, see Palestrina, *Le opere complete*, ed. Casimiri et al., 9:1–8.

EXAMPLE 25-6. Pierluigi Palestrina, *Vergine bella* (mm. 1–22, 131–60)

Virgin most fair, clothed in sunlight, crowned with stars in the highest heaven . . . help
me in my struggle even though I am dust and thou art heaven's queen.

Palestrina's compositional style is remarkably consistent, then, whatever the
subtle distinctions from genre to genre. It has also been much admired, first of all
in his own day and time. Even more importantly, his reputation lived on after him
undiminished. It was, if anything, enhanced by the legend of his role in defining a
contrapuntal idiom that was acceptable to the reformers of the Catholic Counter-
Reformation. Long after the innovations of the *seconda practica* (to use Monteverdi's term) had taken western European polyphony in a much different direction,
Palestrina's music was viewed as the ideal realization of the so-called *stile antico*, and
it continued to be deemed uniquely appropriate for sacred music well into the
eighteenth century.

As a consequence, Palestrina's compositional procedures were gradually
enshrined as well in the didactic tradition of western Europe. Johann Joseph Fux
(1660–1741) took Palestrina as the model (in the most literal sense) for his *Gradus
ad Parnassum* (1725), the influential treatise on strict counterpoint that became the
principal source for textbooks on the subject until well into the present century.[31] He
described Palestrina as "the celebrated light of music," declaring that he owed the
Roman composer everything that he knew of his art and that he would never cease
to cherish his memory. As late as 1931 Knud Jeppesen, noted for his detailed studies of Palestrina's music, distilled from it the basic materials for his own teaching
manual, *Counterpoint: The Polyphonic Vocal Style of the Sixteenth Century.*[32] Surpris-

31. Concerning Fux, see Hellmut Federhofer, *The New Grove Dictionary of Music*, 7:43–46.
32. See Knud Jeppesen, *Counterpoint: The Polyphonic Vocal Style of the Sixteenth Century*, trans. Glen Haydon (New York: Prentice Hall, 1939), which had gone through four printings up until 1951.

ingly, perhaps, Jeppesen's text continued to be used for instruction in composition for generations thereafter.

In the nineteenth century veneration for Palestrina's music was given further encouragement through the efforts of the Cecilian Movement to reform the musical practices of the Catholic church. In addition to clearing the ground for an attempted restoration of the medieval chant tradition, its adherents attempted to keep alive the practice of choral singing *a cappella*, which had come to be associated with the papal choir and, not surprisingly, the music of Palestrina. Thus it is that his polyphonic style continues to be seen in a sense as a culminating achievement of the Renaissance, an art that embodies the esthetic ideals of the age in a quintessential way.[33]

TOMÁS LUIS DE VICTORIA
(1548–1611)

The vigor of the musical culture of sixteenth-century Spain is evident in the rich polyphonic tradition cultivated by the church choirs of the major ecclesiastical institutions in all of its important urban centers, from Málaga and Seville in the south to Valladolid and Burgos in the north, and from Madrid and Toledo in the heart of Castile outward to Spain's frontiers in all directions.[34] Similarly, the creative energy of its musical traditions can be judged from the exceptional achievements of its leading composers. Three stand out in particular, not only among their fellows on the Iberian peninsula but also as measured against the leading figures of their age in all of western Europe. These are Cristóbal de Morales (ca. 1500–53), about whom there has already been some discussion, his student Francisco Guerrero (1528–99), and Tomás Luis de Victoria. All three traveled and published abroad, including Guerrero—whose wandering took him as far as the Holy Land—even though he alone held no appointment with one of the choral institutions in Italy.[35]

Although Guerrero may have been, in a sense, a more popular composer, whose works were much recopied for use by cathedral choirs both in Spain and in the New World well into the eighteenth century, none, surely, was and is regarded with greater esteem than Victoria. He was trained as a choirboy at Avila Cathedral under the *maestros de capilla* Geronimo de Espinar (1550–58) and, more significantly, Bernardino de Ribera (1559–63), who was one of the leading composers of his day. Victoria also attended the school of San Gil, founded by the Jesuits in 1554. Conse-

---

33. Concerning the Cecilian Movement, see Karl Gustav Fellerer, *The New Grove Dictionary of Music*, 4:47–48.

34. For a succinct overview of Spain's musical traditions in the sixteenth century, see Robert Stevenson, "Spain," *The New Grove Dictionary of Music*, 17:785–88; for a more comprehensive study, see his *Spanish Cathedral Music in the Golden Age* (Berkeley: University of California Press, 1961).

35. Concerning Guerrero, see Robert Stevenson, *The New Grove Dictionary of Music*, 7:787–89.

quently, when his voice broke, some time between 1563 and 1565, he was sent to the Jesuit Collegio Germanico in Rome to pursue his studies.

After his schooling was essentially completed he held a series of apparently overlapping appointments: from 1568 to 1571 as director of the choir of the cardinal-bishop of Augsburg, Otto Truchsess, to whom he dedicated his first published volume of motets in 1572; from 1569 to 1574 as singer and organist at the Aragonese church in Rome, Santa Maria di Monserrato; and from 1571 to 1573 as a teacher of music to the students of the Collegio Germanico, where he subsequently served from 1573 to 1576 as *maestro di cappella*. Having been ordained a priest in 1575, he joined the Congregazione dei Preti dell'Oratorio, the then newly formed confraternity led by San Filippo Neri. In 1578 he obtained a chaplaincy at the church of San Girolamo della Caritá in Rome, which he held until 1585.

Wishing to return to Spain, in 1583 he dedicated his second book of Masses to King Philip II, expressing at the same time his desire to live quietly as a priest in his native land. He was gratified as a result with an appointment as chaplain to the monarch's sister, Dowager Empress Maria (daughter of Charles V and wife of Maximilian II), whom he served as chapelmaster at the Monasterio de las Descalzas de Santa Clara until her death in 1603. He then continued for another year as master of the choir—which counted twelve chaplains and four to six boys—and as organist for the convent until his death in 1611.[36]

Although not as prolific as Palestrina or as the extraordinary Orlande de Lassus, Victoria penned during his lifetime a very substantial repertory of polyphonic music, all of it, interestingly, sacred. He apparently took no interest in the Italian madrigal, as did Palestrina, despite his long residence in Rome, nor, for that matter, in the *canciones y villanescas espirituales* of which Guerrero published a collection in Venice in 1589. Victoria intended his music solely for liturgical and devotional use, and, like Palestrina, he worked systematically in the established genres of sacred polyphony, as the titles and sequence of his publications make clear.

During his Roman years he saw published in elegant folio editions, in addition to the volume of motets mentioned earlier, the following: a collection of Magnificats that included as well two settings of each of the four great Marian antiphons sung during the year, half of them for divided choir (1581); a set of thirty-two polyphonic hymns covering the principal feasts of the entire liturgical year (1581); two books given over primarily to Masses (1576 and 1583); a volume of polyphony for Holy Week, primarily settings of the Lamentations of Jeremiah and the Tenebrae responsories but with two Passions as well; and a second collection of motets that bore in its title (like an earlier print of Palestrina's motets) the claim that the music was for "feasts of the entire year together with the Common of the saints."[37]

---

36. Concerning Victoria, see Robert Stevenson, *The New Grove Dictionary of Music*, 19:703–9.
37. See the list of works given by Robert Stevenson, "Victoria," *The New Grove Dictionary of Music*, 19:707–8; as Stevenson observes, Victoria—apparently an inveterate reviser—included in many of these collections music from his earlier publications.

After his removal to Spain two further publications followed. In 1592 he was given permission to return to Rome to supervise the publication of *Missae, una cum antiphonis Asperges, et Vidi aquam totius anni, Liber secundus* of that same year. For reasons as yet unclear he remained in the papal city until 1595 and, while there, participated in the funeral procession for Palestrina (February 2, 1994). Back home in Madrid, he contracted with a local printer for the publication of a collection of polychoral polyphony, Masses, Magnificats, motets, Psalm settings, and other liturgical items, which appeared in 1600. These works demonstrate that, like Palestrina, Victoria was well acquainted with the traditions associated with music written for divided choir.

MUSIC FOR VESPERS

For his hymn settings Victoria adhered in every important respect to well-established *alternatim* tradition. By contrast with Palestrina, who generally set the odd-numbered verses and built to a climax by adding voices and contrapuntal complexity for the final strophe(s), Victoria set the even-numbered verses and simply reduced the texture of the penultimate polyphonic stanza (e.g., from four voices to three) to make the last seem more splendid. This is the case, for example, in his music for the Advent hymn *Conditor alme siderum*, where the second and sixth strophes are written for four voices and the fourth for only three (see Example 25-7).[38]

Victoria also observed the well-established custom of imbedding the chant into the polyphony and deriving from it a substantial part of the melodic material used. In the first strophe set (the second of the hymn), for example, he gave the tenor—

38. For a transcription of the complete composition in modern score, see Tomás Luis de Victoria, *Opera omnia*, ed. Felipe Pedrell, 8 vols. (Leipzig: Breitkopf und Härtel, 1902–13), 5:1–3.

EXAMPLE 25-7. Tomás Luis de Victoria, *Conditor alme siderum* (mm. 1–30)

1. Kindly creator of the stars, eternal light of the believers, Christ, redeemer of all, hear
the prayers of the supplicants. 2. Thou who, suffering the destruction of death, the
demise of the people, freed the languishing world, providing a remedy for sin . . .

in traditional fashion—the liturgical tune, but each of the four points of imitation
shows a clear relationship to the borrowed melody, especially in its initial pitches. In
addition, the bassus anticipates in extended values the tenor's presentation of the first
phrase and of the last, where the tenor participates freely in the part-writing before
making its final statement.

In the reduced textures of the fourth stanza the bassus assumes the primary role
of cantus firmus presentation, even though the tenor is present. For the final
strophe, by contrast, Victoria shifted the literal citation of the chant to the cantus,
still in longer values, where its familiar profile emerges all the more clearly from the

four-part sonorities. Imitation predominates in these stanzas as well, much of it clearly derived from, or at least closely related to, the liturgical tune, and the texture is consistently contrapuntal, yielding only briefly in the final section (mm. 22–23) to homophonic declamation (in only two voices) for the beginning of "In saeculorum saecula."

Victoria adhered no less faithfully to tradition in his settings of the Magnificat. The majority are for four voices, two for each of the eight tones, one of them setting the odd-numbered verses of the canticle, the other the even-numbered. There are, in addition, two polychoral works, a *Magnificat primi toni* for double choir (eight voices), and a *Magnificat sexti toni* for triple choir (twelve voices). Like Palestrina's polychoral *Magnificat primi toni* discussed above (pp. 876–79), these works give evidence of the gradual diffusion of composition for *cori spezzati* from its putative origins in Italy's Veneto to the whole of Europe. They also show the strength of the polyphonic tradition for the genre since even in these exceptional works Victoria observes the customary compositional procedures.

This is unmistakably clear from his *Magnificat primi toni*, first published in Rome in 1572 and reedited in Madrid in 1600 (see Example 25-8).[39] Like Palestrina's analogous setting, Victoria's provides polyphony for the entire canticle, excepting only the initial intonation. By contrast, Victoria gave a much larger place in his polyphony to the liturgical tone. In the first verse, for example, it is heard three times, first in the cantus, then in the tenor, and again in the cantus. In subsequent verses, it is not always present at the outset; it yields in verse 4 ("Quia fecit mihi magna") to a point of imitation, which is related nonetheless to the chant intonation, introduced by the altus, and again in verse 5 ("Et misericordia ejus"), where it is not clearly discernible until quoted in the cantus just before the end of the section (mm. 100ff.).

In place of the customary alternation between chant and polyphony, Victoria

39. For a transcription of the entire work in modern score, see Victoria, *Opera omnia*, ed. Pedrell, 3:81-84.

EXAMPLE 25-8. Tomás Luis de Victoria, *Magnificat primi toni* (mm.1–15)

My soul doth magnify the Lord . . .

introduces changes in sonority and texture from verse to verse in a regular pattern. He begins with chorus II by itself, followed by chorus I sustained by a written organ part, then by the two choirs and organ together. The stepwise increase in performing forces enhances the cumulative sonorous effect in a climactic way. Then, as in *alternatim* performance, the pattern is repeated, involving this time verses 4, 5, and 6. The following repetition is abbreviated, involving only chorus II and the full ensemble, thus allowing a final systematic massing of voices and instrument for verses 9, 10, and the Doxology.

Interestingly, there is an alternate version in three parts for verse 5 ("Et misericordia ejus"): a strict canon at the unison for two voices in the cantus range, sustained by an imitative but relatively independent altus. The texture is generally contrapuntal, often imitatively, except for the sections for divided choir where blocks of homophonic declamation are passed back and forth before the voices join together in a more complex webbing of voices to bring the section to a close. Victoria departs from this pattern only for the brief seventh verse ("Deposuit potentes de sede"), which is presented by chorus II in virtually simultaneous declamation. This section also departs from the basic binary mensuration of the work with a shift to a ternary measure, thus matching the beginning of the preceding verse ("Fecit potentiam") in its rhythmic patterns as it does in its homophonic texture.

Victoria's use of the organ in this composition, and in a number of others among the polychoral works published in 1600, warrants comment. Although an organ part is present in this setting of the Magnificat for two verses out of three, as printed it simply duplicates the voice parts of chorus I. The implication, that the use of the instrument did nothing more than provide sonorous enhancement for the voices in those sections, suggests a very limited role for the instrument in the sacred polyphony of the late sixteenth century.

There may well have been some improvisatory embellishment of the part as written. Still, the total absence of securely attributed instrumental music from the repertory ascribed to Palestrina, who began his professional career as an organist, and the apparently restricted place of the organ in the works of Victoria, who finished his career in the same way, are truly puzzling. Such circumstances seem all the more surprising in Victoria's case given the vigorous cultivation of instrumental music in Spain at the time, and the publications of both Continental composers stand in sharp contrast to those of William Byrd, whose involvement with the secular instrumental music of his nation is richly documented.

MASS AND MOTET

Turning to Victoria's Mass composition, the repertory, while substantial, is distinctly modest in size when compared with that of either Palestrina or Lassus. His works in this genre exhibit less variety in traditional procedures for Mass composition reflected in them. Of the twenty polyphonic Masses securely attributed to him, four are based on plainchant; two of these are Requiem Masses, and the other two are for Marian celebrations, the *Missa Ave maris stella* and the *Missa De beata Maria virgine*. The remainder employ to some extent the compositional techniques of the "imitation" (or parody) Mass, and all but four are based on his own compositions.[40] These include the four relatively late works, first published in 1600, in the polychoral manner, three for two choirs of four voices each, the other for three such ensembles.

Among the works in four, five, or six voices the *Missa Quarti toni* is exceptional to a degree in that most of it is freely composed and quotes from its "model," Victoria's *Senex puerum portabat*, only briefly at the end of the Gloria and the Credo.[41] However, Victoria has treated his models with considerable latitude in other instances as well. For example, he opens the Kyrie of his *Missa O magnum mysterium*—a work of remarkable concision—in the conventional manner, quoting the voices of his motet fairly literally and in the same order of entry (from cantus down-

40. These are the *Missa Gaudeamus*, based on Morales's *Jubilate Deo*; the *Missa Pro victoria*, based on Janequin's *La guerre*; the *Missa Simile est regnum celorum*, based on a Guerrero motet; and the *Missa Surge propera*, based on a Palestrina motet. See Robert Stevenson, *The New Grove Dictionary of Music*, 19:707.
41. See Robert Stevenson, "Victoria," *The New Grove Dictionary of Music*, 19:705.

ward through the bassus).[42] Notwithstanding, he begins to tamper with the bor-rowed material almost immediately, shortening the initial duo by a breve, and he never returns to an unequivocal citation from the motet in the entire section, although the ascending fourth used in imitation to open the "Christe" and the cadential phrase for the final "Kyrie" both echo passages in the earlier work.

More striking still is that Victoria begins both the Gloria and the Credo with related passages of homophonic declamation for which only the general idea is to be found in the motet. Similarly, both sections have short segments in a sesquialteral shift to ternary mensuration, again in homophonic style, for which there is little by way of precedent in the model. For the Sanctus Victoria returns to the head motive derived from the motet and shifts to the ternary mensuration for the Hosanna, but neither the latter section nor the Benedictus appears to borrow melodic material or contrapuntal passagework from the model. For the Agnus, which he has expanded to five voices by means of a canon at the unison in the cantus but set in a single sec-tion, Victoria reverts to the ascending fourth first heard in the "Christe," but the link to the model is tenuous at best.

Even more surprising, perhaps, is the relationship of Victoria's *Missa O quam glo-riosum est regnum* to his setting of the Magnificat antiphon upon which it is based (see Example 25-9).[43] Passing over the solemn homophonic opening of his model, the composer took the first two points of imitation (mm. 9–18) for the opening motive of the Kyrie. The "Christe" he derived directly and almost entirely from the

42. For a transcription of Mass and motet in modern score, see, respectively, the *Opera omnia*, ed. Pedrell, 2:69–80, and the *Opera omnia*, ed. Anglès, 2:7–9.
43. For a complete transcription of both works in modern score, see the *Opera omnia*, ed. Anglès, 26:27–29 (the motet), and 30:30–48 (the Mass).

EXAMPLE 25-9. Tomás Luis de Victoria, *O quam gloriosum est regnum* (mm. 1–18, 35–59) and *Missa O quam gloriosum est regnum*, Kyrie (mm. 1–37)

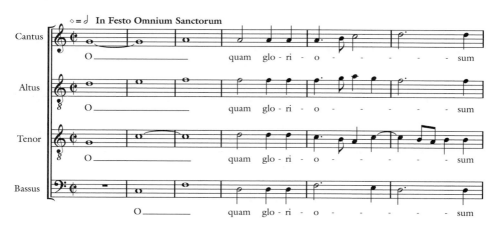

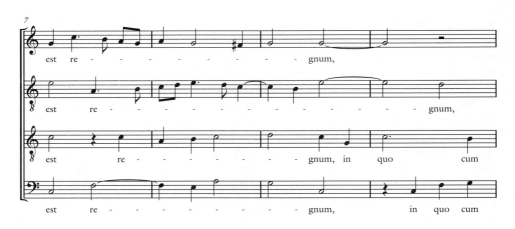

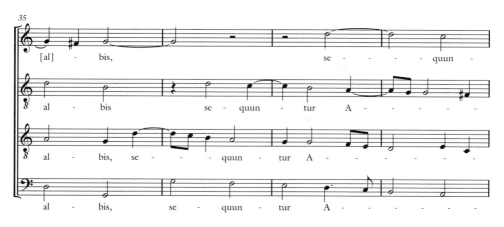

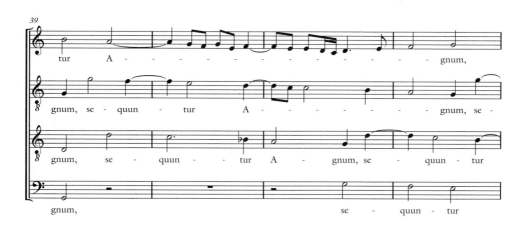

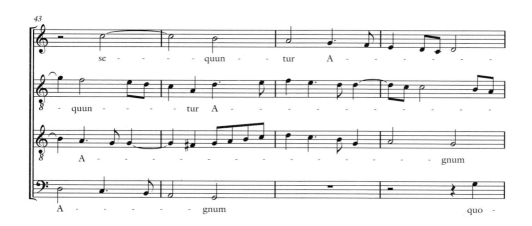

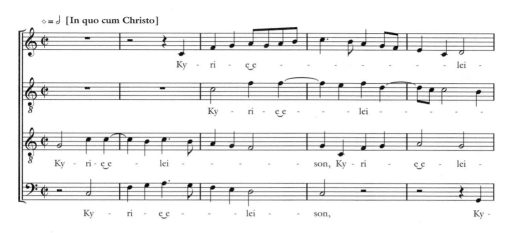

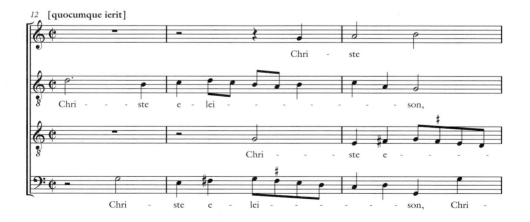

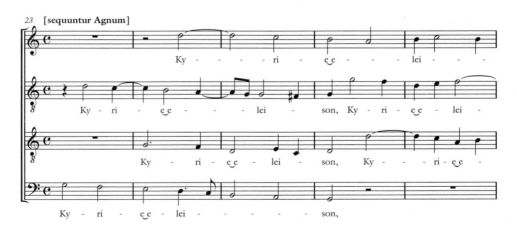

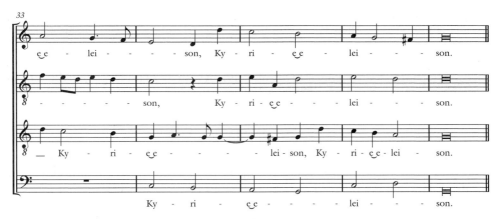

MOTET: O how glorious is the kingdom in which, with Christ, all the saints rejoice; dressed in white robes, they follow the Lamb wherever he shall go.
MASS: Lord, have mercy; Christ, have mercy; Lord, have mercy.

final phrase of his model (mm. 47–56), and he based the second "Kyrie" on its fourth section (mm. 35–46).

Neither the Gloria nor the Credo, which Victoria opens with similar head motives bearing no clear relationship to the motet, make much use of borrowed material. For the Gloria he derived the final phrase of the first subsection (mm. 39–45) from the culminating cadential phrase of the model (mm. 49–56). There may be in addition a reference to the cantus of the motet's second phrase (mm. 19–21) for the words "miserere nobis" (mm. 48–50, 64–66), but without the accompanying counterpoint. Material from the model's fourth phrase (mm. 35–45) is cited a bit less ambiguously at "Quoniam tu solus Dominus, Tu solus altissimus" (mm. 68–79), and the end of the motet's first phrase, including the ascending scalar patterns in the lower three voices that begin the second phrase (mm. 15–20), has been taken over for the final cadence of the section.

In the Credo there is even less material taken directly from the motet. Victoria quoted rather clearly the beginning of the final phrase (mm. 47–50) for "lumen de lumine, Deum verum" (mm. 23–27), but he picked up the end of that segment only at the final cadence of the subsection (mm. 94–100). The conclusion of the Credo, like its opening, points to a traditional pairing with the Gloria, drawing upon the same first imitative phrase of the motet for the final cadence (mm. 138–49), but here Victoria takes the borrowed segment from its beginning (mm. 11–19), thus referring at the same time to the head motive of the first "Kyrie."

References to the model in the Sanctus are more through allusion than direct citation, even at subsectional cadences. In the Agnus, by contrast, after an opening passage unrelated to the head-motive material in any of the other sections of the Mass, Victoria quotes rather clearly first the end of the first imitative phrase of his model (mm. 15–18), then the beginning of the next (mm. 25–32), making of that material the concluding phrases of the Mass (mm. 14–31). Clearly, as with Palestrina's *Missa Nigra sum* (see pp. 881–91), the compositional procedures for the use of derived materials correspond closely to those codified in much detail by Pietro Cerone.

MUSIC FOR HOLY WEEK

Just as Palestrina adapted the use of motet-derived compositional procedures to music for Mass propers with his polyphonic Offertories for the entire liturgical year, so did Victoria apply them to a systematic series of settings for the responsories at Holy Week. Published in Rome in 1585 as the *Officium Hebdomadae Sanctae*, this repertory includes settings for four voices of all of the great responsories sung during the second and third Nocturns at Matins on Maundy Thursday, Good Friday, and Holy Saturday, a total of eighteen.[44]

Typical of these compositions is Victoria's treatment of *Tenebrae factae sunt*, the second responsory sung during the second Nocturn of Matins on Good Friday (see Example 25-10).[45] The respond, including the *repetendum*, is set for four voices, whereas the verse is reduced to three. However, despite this adherence to liturgical form, there is no reference to the plainchant in the polyphony; even the modal orientation is different. Instead of the bright mode 7 chant melody with its tritone relationships between sections and its dramatic shifts to the top of its range for the cries

44. Victoria did not set the responsories sung during the first Nocturn on the last three days of Holy Week in alternation with the Lamentations of Jeremiah that provided the *lectiones*, perhaps because the Lamentations were themselves often sung polyphonically and the answering responsories in contrasting plainchant.

45. For a transcription in modern score of the entire work, see *Opera omnia*, ed. Pedrell, 5:161–63; for the chant, see the *Liber usualis*, 703–4.

EXAMPLE 25-10. Tomás Luis de Victoria, *Tenebre factae sunt* (mm. 1–10, 31–58)

RESPOND: The skies were darkened when the Jews crucified Jesus. And about the ninth
hour Jesus cried with a loud voice, "My God, why hast thou forsaken me?" And,
bowing his head, he gave up the ghost. (Matthew 27:45–50)

VERSE: Jesus, crying with a loud voice, said, "Father, into thy hands I commend my
spirit." (Luke 23:46)

of Jesus, Victoria opted for a Hypophrygian mode in double transposition to a D
final.

Although e-fa is not signed throughout, as is b-fa, it is written in consistently
enough to make the modal implications unmistakable. It first appears in the dramatic opening gesture—a falling fifth answered by a rising minor sixth—that is presented in close imitation by the tenor, cantus I, and cantus II. It also defines the cadences

at the end of the respond and the verse. The final cadence, however, and most of the internal ones are to G, thus corresponding in usage to the many pieces labeled "quarti toni" (mode 4) that close on A.

Syntactic imitation is the basic compositional procedure adopted by Victoria in crafting this motetlike work, but he keeps the textures rather consistently full by the closely spaced entries of the participating voices. Although he does not introduce homophonic declamation outright, he adumbrates its effect for the two passages in which words ascribed to Jesus are sung (in the respond, mm. 19–30, and in the verse, mm. 49–58). In both instances the phrase in question is preceded by a clear cadence and a dramatic moment of total silence, and at least two voices enter together with the biblical quotation. Despite the resulting quasi-homophonic texture, however, at least one of the voices ripples the contrapuntal surface with rhythmic displacements and independent declamation most of the time. Only at the end of the respond (mm. 28–30) do all of the voices move and present their text simultaneously.

Casting a look back, then, it is clear that Victoria and Palestrina moved for the most part in parallel tracks, compositionally speaking. They cultivated the same genres and generic types, observed the same conventions, and made use of the same basic compositional procedures. The stylistic differences between them, however subtle, are of course discernible to both analyst and listener. Still, without question, each represents in his own way a sophisticated synthesis of contrapuntal and structural principles and of stylistic trends whose roots reach back into the fifteenth century. The music of Victoria, like that of his older contemporary, does in fact reflect a stylistic coherence and consistency characteristic of the times that appears to justify the designation of the Renaissance as a period in the history of Western music.

⟶ WILLIAM BYRD (1543–1623) ⟵

In William Byrd's England developments in musical genres and styles followed a rather different trajectory from that to be observed on the Continent during the second half of the sixteenth century. This was undoubtedly due in large measure to the profound and lasting effects of the English Reformation. The English church had little use for the vast repertory of liturgical polyphony on Latin texts that was being penned by composers in Catholic regions such as France, Italy, and Spain and that poured forth from the presses that were thriving in centers such as Antwerp, Lyons, Paris, Rome, Venice, Madrid, and even Nuremberg. Conversely, the insistence on the use of the English vernacular for communal worship brought into existence new compositional types such as the anthem that, while clearly related to the Latin motet, had no long historical tradition upon which to draw. In addition, the relative isolation that was the natural consequence of England's insular geography was reinforced by the political tension between the British Isles and their Catholic neighbors across the channel.

Byrd's place of birth and that of his earliest musical training are as yet unknown,

FIGURE 25-2. Portrait of William Byrd: engraving by Van der Gucht.

but there is reason to believe that he was schooled at least in part in London. At some point he became a student of Thomas Tallis (ca. 1505–85), a distinguished organist and composer who became a gentleman of the chapel royal as early as 1542–44.[46] In 1563, at about twenty years of age, Byrd began his professional career—as Palestrina had done earlier—as organist and master of the choristers (the English term for choirboys) in what may have been his native region, in his case at Lincoln Cathedral. There he remained until December 1572, when he took up his duties as gentleman of the chapel royal, to which he had been named already two years earlier (see Figure 25-2). These included an appointment as joint organist of the chapel together with his former mentor, Tallis, and kept him resident in the city until the early 1590s.[47]

In 1575 Byrd and Tallis, working as partners, secured a patent for the printing and sale of polyphonic music and lined paper. They initiated their commerce with a volume of Latin motets for five to eight voices comprising works by both under the title *Cantiones, quae ab argumento sacrae vocantur*, a curious circumlocution—"motets called sacred because of their texts"—used perhaps because of some uneasiness with the publication of compositions more appropriate for Catholic worship than for the English church. Despite a dedication to Queen Elizabeth, and her apparent acceptance of it, the venture was not a commercial success. Not until some twelve years later, in 1587, did Byrd renew the attempt to establish music publishing as a viable industry on English soil, this time in collaboration with the printer Thomas East. Their initial offering, the *Psalmes, Sonets and Songs* of 1588, was in this instance well received and was followed by a fair number of other prints given over primarily or entirely to the music of Byrd.

Two additional collections of Latin motets appeared in relatively short order, the *Liber primus sacrarum cantionum* for five voices of 1589 and the *Liber secundus sacrarum cantionum* for five and six voices of 1591. There were also two more collections of secular music on English texts, the *Songs of Sundrie Nature* for three to

46. For a concise biography of the composer, see Joseph Kerman, "Byrd, William," *The New Grove Dictionary of Music*, 3:537–52.
47. A lively portrait of the English capital at this time has been drawn by Craig Monson, "Elizabethan London," in *The Renaissance: From the 1470s to the End of the Sixteenth Century*, ed. Iain Fenlon, Man and Music, vol. 2 (Englewood Cliffs, N.J.: Prentice Hall, 1989), 304–40.

six voices of 1589 and the *Psalmes, Songes and Sonnets . . . fit for Voyces or Viols* for three to six voices of 1611. Three settings for the Ordinary of the Latin Mass, one each for four, three, and five voices (in that order) appeared between 1592 and 1595. This was followed by Byrd's monumental repertory of Mass Propers, which he published in two collections, the *Gradualia ac cantiones sacrae* for three to five voices in 1605 and the *Gradualia seu cantionum sacrarum, liber secundus* for four to six voices in 1607.[48]

MUSIC FOR KEYBOARD AND INSTRUMENTAL CONSORT

One should perhaps add to this printed repertory a pair of keyboard collections in manuscript: *My Ladye Nevells Booke*, dated 1591, which includes forty-two pieces of Byrd's keyboard music, and the somewhat later *Fitzwilliam Virginal Book*, copied 1609–10, in which his name is attached to sixty-seven works.[49] It is certainly by his substantial contribution to the instrumental repertory of sixteenth-century England that Byrd differs most sharply from his immediate contemporaries who figure in this discussion—Palestrina, Victoria, and Lassus—and many others as well. Not a single independent instrumental work in any of the established genres is attributed to any one of them. Byrd, by contrast, is known as a prolific composer of music for both instrumental consort and solo keyboard. He is in fact seen by many scholars as the veritable founder of what has emerged as an English virginal school.

In that connection he has already been drawn into the discussion of variations for keyboard for his *The Carman's Whistle* (see Example 24-23 and pp. 846–48), one of fourteen sets of variations that bear his name.[50] There are, in addition, thirteen pieces written over a "ground" (a repeating pattern in the bass). Two of them are pavane-galliard pairs based on the well-traveled *passamezzo* patterns (one the *antico*, the other the *moderno*; see pp. 838–42).[51] In fact, dance music—stylized pieces intended primarily for the pleasure of the player and eventual listeners (as opposed to music for dancing)—constitutes one of the largest and most impressive segments of Byrd's keyboard repertory. In addition to another eighteen pavane-galliard "suites," he wrote a fair number of miscellaneous single dances, mostly pavanes, galliards, and *almans*, but including *corantos, voltas*, and a jig as well.[52]

Byrd's keyboard and consort repertories intersect in two very different genres.

---

48. See the list of works compiled by Joseph Kerman, "Byrd," *The New Grove Dictionary of Music*, 3:545–52.

49. Concerning this collection see John Caldwell, "Sources of Keyboard Music to 1660," *The New Grove Dictionary of Music*, 17:732, who cites further references.

50. Concerning Byrd's keyboard variations, see Oliver Neighbor, *The Consort and Keyboard Music of William Byrd* (Berkeley: University of California Press, 1978), 144–63.

51. For a systematic discussion of Byrd's use of the "ground," see Neighbor, *Consort and Keyboard Music of William Byrd*, 114–43.

52. Concerning Byrd's dance music, see Neighbor, *Consort and Keyboard Music of William Byrd*, 176–220 and 164–74; in the latter chapter Neighbor also deals with intabulations and descriptive pieces in the tradition of Janequin's *La guerre*.

On the one hand are the cantus firmus settings of liturgical melodies—hymns, antiphons, and the Miserere—that had their origins in the *alternatim* practice for organ and plainchant choir (see pp. 793–98); these survived to a degree early on as genres, even though they no longer served any practical need. To these may be added the group of *In nomines,* of which Byrd has left us six or seven.[53] On the other hand are the fantasias in which the contrapuntal practices of the motet are usually carried over into the instrumental genre (see pp. 865–66).[54] With the fantasias for consort, moreover, there is a further intersection with Byrd's English songs, many of which appear to have been based on compositions originally written for viol consort (see pp. 710–13 and Example 20-4).

Byrd is also credited with half a dozen pieces in the related genre of the *praeludium* (five of them for keyboard). Here one sees both the more recent imitative style and the older, toccatalike manner that had earlier been a hallmark of pieces so designated (see pp. 856–63). Byrd used a consistently imitative manner in his Prelude in A, a relatively short piece included in the *Fitzwilliam Virginal Book,* where it retains the original preludial function indicated by its name (I:394). By contrast, the virtuosic combination of chords and running passages typical of an earlier stage in the history of this genre is exemplified by two other pieces included in the same collection, the Prelude in C and the Prelude in G (I:83 and II:40, respectively).

MASS AND MOTET

As for Byrd's sacred music, his seminal role in the development of the verse anthem, a genre that appears to be largely of his creation, has already engaged our attention. His service music, written to accommodate the newly created English liturgy of the Anglican church, tends to be remarkably terse and consistently severe in style. As a rule the declamation is strictly syllabic and the texture almost uniformly homophonic. The only notable exceptions are to be seen in the music of the Great Service, particularly that for Matins and Vespers, as, for example, his setting of the Magnificat.[55]

Byrd's music for the Mass of the Roman rite was written following his removal some time after 1591 to Stondon Massey, Essex, near the family seat of his friends and patrons, the Petres, where he apparently lived the rest of his life in quasi-retirement. His move may have been prompted by the desire to become increasingly involved with the Catholic community that had banded together in that area for protection against the possibly dire consequences of accusations of recusancy. He may

---

53. Concerning Byrd's cantus firmus pieces for keyboard and for consort, see Neighbor, *Consort and Keyboard Music of William Byrd,* 101–13, 51–60, and 26–50.

54. Concerning the *fantasias* both for consort and for keyboard, see Neighbor, *Consort and Keyboard Music of William Byrd,* 61–100 and 221–66.

55. For an edition in modern score of this repertory, see William Byrd, *The English Services,* ed. Craig Monson, 2 vols., The Byrd Edition, vols. 10a and 10b (London: Stainer and Bell, 1980–92). A study of this music by Philip Brett, promised in 1978 as volume 2 in the series The Music of William Byrd, to round out the studies of Oliver Neighbor and Joseph Kerman, has yet to appear.

also have been drawn by the opportunity to participate regularly in the clandestine celebration of the Catholic Mass for which these compositions must have been primarily intended.

Compared with the enormous production of polyphonic Ordinaries by composers such as Palestrina, Lassus, or even Victoria, Byrd's output is modest indeed. There was no call for compositions of the kind, obviously, either at Lincoln Cathedral or at the royal English court, nor was there easy access to the repertory then current on the Continent, assuming that Byrd may have been seeking a model for his own work. It is not clear, either, how much he knew of the earlier tradition of polyphonic Mass composition by English composers, even though he modeled the Sanctus of his four-voice Mass on that of Taverner's *Mean Mass*.[56] If he was familiar with Ordinary cycles based either on a preexistent polyphonic work (in the manner of the *missa ad imitationem*) or on chant (whether as a repeating cantus firmus or as a paraphrase of the appropriate liturgical melody), he elected not to follow suit. All three of his Masses are freely composed.

The only clear connection in these works with traditional practices is Byrd's use of the head motive. All sections but the Sanctus begin in recognizably similar ways in both the four-voice and five-voice Masses. In the three-voice Mass the Kyrie, Gloria, and Credo are so linked—a grouping of sections for which there is also historical precedent—as are the Agnus Dei and the Benedictus. In addition, Byrd follows long-established procedures in articulating the structure of the five major sections into smaller units, both by clear cadential closure and by a reduction in the number of voices for selected subsections.

Despite these traditional elements, his compositional procedures in all three works are those that had become fundamental to the style of the Latin motet. In the four-voice Mass he makes fairly consistent use of imitative counterpoint. By contrast he opens the three-voice Mass with strictly homophonic declamation. Generally, however, his counterpoint is characterized by the skillful alternation between the two basic styles in accordance with liturgical function and textual meaning.

At that level, then, it is once again the compositional style traditionally associated with the motet that Byrd has used for both warp and woof of his musical fabric. As we have seen, moreover, motet-derived procedures also define the style of the extraordinary repertory of music for the Propers of the Mass that Byrd published in his *Gradualia* (see pp. 596–602 and Example 17-5). The motet, as creative concept and compositional genre, appears to have been his most significant connection to past English traditions and, perhaps as well, to compositional practices and styles then current on the Continent. As a pair of examples will show, the role of the motet in Byrd's stylistic development is evident not only from that part of his repertory considered thus far but also from his very substantial body of works in that genre.

Miserere mihi, Domine, published with the *Cantiones sacrae* of 1575, reveals

---

56. For details, see Joseph Kerman, *The Masses and Motets of William Byrd* (Berkeley: University of California Press, 1981), 192.

Byrd's mastery of cantus firmus composition and, at the same time, his skill in handling strict imitation (see Example 25-11).[57] The chant upon which it is based, the same antiphon that he had set earlier both for consort and for organ, is first heard in the discantus through the end of its opening incise at the upper octave in even, unembellished semibreves. The tenor then enters in imitation a fourth below (m. 5), but the borrowed chant is quickly truncated in that part as the bassus enters in strict imitation an octave below the original pitch and quotes the liturgical melody in its entirety without interruption (mm. 7–20).

At that point the liturgical melody is repeated in canonic imitation between discantus and superius, which enter a breve apart at the upper fifth and octave, respectively. This time the rhythms are less rigid, with minims, seminimims, and dotted figures in the mix and with a couple of modest decorative flourishes that introduce nonchant tones (mm. 22–23 and 32–33). A minim after the entry of the superius, a second two-voice canon is begun with a countermelody in the tenor secundus, followed a semibreve later by the bassus a fourth below. The second canon is much

57. For a transcription of the entire work in modern score, see William Byrd, *Cantiones sacrae*, ed. Craig Monson, The Byrd Edition, vol. 1 (London: Stainer and Bell, 1977), 240–45; also Sarah Fuller, ed., *The European Musical Heritage 800–1750* (New York: Alfred A. Knopf, 1987), 239–45.

EXAMPLE 25-11. William Byrd, *Miserere mihi, Domine*, antiphon for Sundays at compline (mm. 20–36)

Have mercy upon me, O Lord, and hearken unto my prayer.
CANON: Four parts out of two with two others as wanted.

more flexible than the first both rhythmically and melodically. Nevertheless, like that based on the chant, it is carried out strictly to the end of the piece while countertenor and tenor make their own way through the musical space between the canonic pairs. The result is an elegant, learned contrapuntal setting that any of Byrd's Continental contemporaries would have easily understood and might well have envied.[58]

The richly contrapuntal fabric of *Laudate pueri Dominum*, which also appeared with the *Cantiones sacrae* of 1575, is no less evocative of the best motet composition the Continent could offer (see Example 25-12).[59] Its genesis reveals a curious twist, however, as the version with Latin text is almost certainly an adaptation of an earlier Fantasia in F for viol consort.[60] The motet's instrumental origins are clear from the structure of the composition; it consists of four sections, all overlapping more or less seamlessly, each of which is repeated, the first with slight differences, the remainder quite literally.[61]

58. For another discussion of this piece, see Kerman, *Masses and Motets of William Byrd*, 78–79.
59. For a transcription in modern score of the entire work, see Byrd, *Cantiones sacrae*, ed. Monson, 82–96; also Claude V. Palisca, ed., *Norton Anthology of Western Music*, 1st ed., 2 vols. (New York: Norton, 1980), 1:148–63.
60. See the discussion of this piece by Kerman, *Masses and Motets of William Byrd*, 85–87.
61. The formal order, which can be represented as AA'BBCCDD, is articulated as follows: A (mm. 1–8), A' (mm. 8–16), B (mm. 16–27), B (mm. 27–38), C (mm. 38–50), C (mm. 50–63), D (mm. 63–84), D (mm. 84–103); there is also a cadential tag of half a dozen measures at the end.

EXAMPLE 25-12. William Byrd, *Laudate pueri Dominum* (mm. 1–11, 83–108)

Praise the Lord, O ye servants of the Lord, praise the name of the Lord. [Blessed be the
name of the Lord henceforth and forever. My help cometh from the Lord, which
made heaven and earth.] Do good, O Lord, unto those that be good; and to them
that are upright in their hearts. (Psalm 112:1–2; 120:2; 124:4)

It is a tribute to Byrd's great skill that he was able to match the words to this preexistent musical structure with relatively little awkwardness in the Latin declamation.
Even more remarkably, he saw in the instrumental piece material that lent itself rather
well to effective rhetorical expression. The text is a centonization of verses from three
separate Psalms and closes with a plea for blessings "to those who are good and true."[62]
Such sentiments are not uncommon in the texts of Byrd's motets, many of which can
be construed as having special resonance for recusant Catholics. In this instance Byrd
has used the ostinato-like figures in extended values in the final section of the superius
to present the verse "Bene fac, Domine, bonis et rectis corde" four times. The rhythmic simplicity of the recurring patterns, the high range of the voice, and some internal
repetition of key words ("bonis et rectis corde") all combine to give exceptional
emphasis to what must have been for Byrd a particularly significant segment of his text.

Despite considerable and significant differences of detail, then, there are pervasive connections and essential continuities between Continental genres and styles and
those being cultivated in England as seen in the works of William Byrd. Moreover,
Byrd's adaptation of a fantasia for viols as a Latin motet demonstrates in dramatic
fashion the extent to which the compositional procedures current everywhere dur-

62. The Psalm verses in question are as follows: 4:1–2 (with slight changes); 121:2; and 125:4.

ing the second half of the sixteenth century had become a kind of musical *lingua franca*, permeating to some extent every musical genre, both sacred and secular.

ORLANDE DE LASSUS (1532–94)

If a prolific, versatile composer capable of producing in his lifetime an astonishing number of works in every known genre can be seen as evidence of a stable musical culture with a common understanding of current compositional procedures, then the life and works of Orlande de Lassus clearly demonstrate that the second half of the sixteenth century was a period in the history of Western music that can be so characterized. In this regard it is surely significant as well that Lassus was undoubtedly the most cosmopolitan musical figure of his age, known and admired as no other in all of Europe. Printers in Amsterdam, Paris, Frankfurt, Munich, and Venice published individual collections devoted to his works, referring to him as the *divin Orlande* and *princeps musicorum*. Maximilian II, Holy Roman Emperor, granted him a patent of nobility in 1570, and in 1574 Pope Gregory XIII made him a Knight of the Golden Spur. By comparison, Byrd, Victoria, even Palestrina may appear to the present-day observer as having cast a much more localized shadow, and this despite the fact that Lassus spent the last thirty-eight years of his life solely in the service of the Bavarian ducal court in Munich (see Figure 25-3).[63]

That Lassus was very much at home with the musical traditions of both northern and southern Europe—the Netherlands, France, Italy, and Germany—may be due in large measure to the unusual trajectory of his early career.

FIGURE 25-3. Portrait by Hans Müelich of Orlande de Lassus at age twenty-eight (1560), just after he became *maestro di cappella* at the Bavarian ducal court in Munich (Vienna, Österreichische Nationalbibliothek, MS Mus. 18774, Tenor, f. 36).

63. For a concise biography of the composer and an informative, sensitive discussion of his music, see James Haar, *The New Grove Dictionary of Music*, 10:480–502.

Born near Mons in the Hainaut, he probably began his training as a choirboy in one of the local churches, but his movements can be traced only after he entered the household of Ferrante Gonzaga as a musician, perhaps as early as 1544, when he was but twelve years of age. With Gonzaga, a cadet of the ducal house of Mantua and a *condottiere* in the employ of Emperor Charles V, Lassus traveled through Paris to Mantua and Palermo, arriving in Sicily in late 1545, and thence to Milan, where he may have resided in 1547–49.

Lassus was then for a time in Naples, where he lived in the household of G. B. d'Azzia della Terza, a humanist scholar who brought him into contact with the Neapolitan Accademia de' Sereni. However brief, that encounter gave him an opportunity for some exposure to contemporary currents in Italian literature that must have helped him in achieving mastery as a composer of madrigals. From there he went to Rome, where he served for a time in the household of the archbishop of Florence, Antonio Altoviti. His first ecclesiastical appointment came in early 1553, when, in his twenty-first year, he became *maestro di cappella* at the papal basilica of St. John Lateran (preceding Palestrina in the post by a couple of years).

During the following year he returned to the Netherlands to visit his parents only to discover that they had died during his absence. Little is known of his activities while back in his native regions, but by 1555 he had apparently spent some time in Antwerp, where he became acquainted with the music publishers Tylman Susato and Jean de Laet (see pp. 198–99). Susato brought out in that year the first of many individual prints dedicated solely to Lassus's music. The collection, which comprised madrigals, *villanesche*, chansons, and motets for four voices, is a clear portend of the composer's versatility and of the catholic character of his career. A first volume of his madrigals for five voices was also published by Gardane in Venice in 1555, and in the following year his first book of motets for five and six voices was brought out in Antwerp. Such a flurry of publication in widely separated urban centers by two of the most important music printers of the age suggests that although he was still in his early twenties, his reputation as a composer was growing quickly.

In 1556 he entered the service of Duke Albrecht V of Bavaria (r. 1550–79), whose court was usually resident in Munich. A tenor, he was one of half a dozen singers newly recruited in the Netherlands at the time for the ducal chapel, then under the direction of Ludwig Daser, a reputable composer in his own right in his lifetime. When Daser was retired in 1563, Lassus—who was only thirty-one— assumed the responsibilities of *maestro di cappella*, which he continued to discharge until shortly before his death some thirty years later. Unlike Palestrina and Victoria, then—or even Byrd, given his involvement with music publishing and the peculiar circumstances of a recusant musician in a militantly Protestant country—Lassus was the quintessential court musician.

His long association with the Bavarian court did not isolate him entirely from musical currents in the rest of Europe, however. In 1569 he was very much involved in the wedding festivities of the future Wilhelm V (r. 1579–97), heir to the ducal domains, with Renée of Lorraine, which brought him into contact with the musicians and the repertory of that court. On three separate occasions—in 1571, 1573, and 1574—he visited the royal court of France at the invitation of Charles IX. Between 1574 and 1579 he traveled rather frequently toward Italy with visits to Vienna, Trent, Ferrara, Mantua, Bologna, and Rome. In 1585 he made a pilgrimage to Loreto, stopping along the way at Verona and Ferrara, where he undoubtedly heard some of the latest works created for the extraordinary musical establishment of the Este court.

There was also correspondence with friends and acquaintances, including some of the most important patrons of music of his age. While in Venice in May of 1567, he saw to the printing of his fourth book of madrigals for five voices, which he dedicated to Duke Alfonso d'Este. He then journeyed to Ferrara to deliver the publication personally to the dedicatee. In 1585 he dedicated a volume of madrigals for five voices to the Veronese nobleman Count Mario Bevilacqua, one of the most famous patrons of music of the age whose *ridotto* he may have attended. And in the last year of his life he dedicated his remarkable cycle of spiritual madrigals, based on Luigi Tansillo's *Lagrime di San Pietro*, to Pope Clement VIII.

Like many German princes of his day, Duke Albrecht had a brief flirtation with the Reformation in Germany, but he maintained his fundamental allegiance to Roman Catholicism, sending a delegate to the Council of Trent in 1563. As chapelmaster Lassus was therefore responsible for the celebration of the Catholic liturgy at the court. In that connection instruction of the choirboys was also his charge, at least for a time, as was the copying of music for the use of the musicians of the chapel, and perhaps the acquisition of printed repertory as well.

SECULAR MUSIC AT THE BAVARIAN COURT

At a secular court, however, the musicians of the "chapel" provided music not only for religious services but also for its recreation and its ceremonial life, most notably occasions of state, the reception of visiting dignitaries, hunting parties, and banquets.[64] For events of this sort Lassus directed the so-called *Tafelmusik*, presumably a combination of voices and instruments like that shown in the celebrated miniature by Hans Müelich (see Figure 25-4) This and other similar images pose difficult questions, however. For despite the wide variety of musical genres in which Lassus was fluent, there is never an explicit indication in the music itself concerning the participation of instruments in performance.

Trumpets undoubtedly played fanfares in the traditional manner whenever significant events were to be announced or important personages introduced. According to a description of the wedding festivities of 1568, they were joined for that purpose on occasion by horns, fifes, and drums as well. (Their music was presumably either

---

64. Concerning the role of music at the Bavarian court, and in the city of Munich more generally, see James Haar, "Munich at the Time of Orlande de Lassus," in *The Renaissance: From the 1470s to the End of the Sixteenth Century*, ed. Iain Fenlon (Englewood Cliffs, N.J.: Prentice Hall, 1989), 243–62.

FIGURE 25-4. Lassus hears the Bavarian Court Chapel in a concert of secular music (he stands to the left just behind the duke), miniature by Hans Müelich (Munich, Bayerische Staatsbibliothek, Mus. MS A II, f. 187).

learned by rote or improvised to some extent and has apparently not reached us in notated form.) Wind bands also played for the dancing, again from traditional repertories. In addition, the duke's instrumentalists—whether in consorts of winds or strings or some combination of the two—also performed—during meals, for example—a large repertory of pieces originally written for voices: motets, chansons, and madrigals. They joined with the ducal choir as well for the performance of vocal pieces in the great hall or the ducal chambers, but rarely, it would seem, in the chapel itself.[65]

Though master of the ducal chapel, there is no indication that Lassus was a cleric. He married Regina Wäckinger—the daughter of a court official—in 1558, shortly after his arrival in Munich, and among the children born to this union were two sons, Ferdinand and Rudolph, who also became professional musicians. The age of the church musician who is hired for his professional competence regardless of his ecclesiastical standing had apparently already dawned. In any case, court musicians had long been expected to be as well versed in secular genres as in sacred music. In this regard, as we have seen, Lassus came well prepared, having already published a volume containing chansons, madrigals, and *villanesche* (in addition to a few motets) and a book of madrigals before he joined the ranks of the ducal chapel in 1556.

MADRIGALS AND VILLANESCHE

In the years that followed, between 1557 and 1595, at least nine other prints dedicated to his music alone were given over either partly or entirely to madrigals. The majority of them were for five voices, the most common combination at the time, although pieces for three, four, and six voices were published as well.[66] Some of those collections were reprinted repeatedly, and a fair number of individual pieces were anthologized as well. In all, more than 200 madrigals can be credited to his creative energies, including several multipartite cycles.

Although Lassus was fairly eclectic in his choice of verse, Petrarch looms large, especially in the earliest of his published collections, suggesting a taste for serious, well-written texts. This is confirmed by other poets whose works he elected to set, including Ludovico Ariosto, Gabriele Fiamma, Jacopo Sannazaro, Torquato Tasso, Luigi Tansillo, and Pietro Bembo. That he was able, in the course of his career, to follow the evolution of style within the genre is evident from his response to the new trends of the 1580s. However, he was never in the vanguard with the composers responsible for stylistic change. This is surely not surprising, inasmuch as the Bavarian court was rather far removed from the centers of Italian culture. To the contrary, his sensitivity to late sixteenth-century currents in madrigal composition, despite the periodic nature of his direct contacts with Italian masters, is yet another testament to his versatility and skill.

65. For details, see Haar, "Munich at the Time of Orlande de Lassus," 252–55.
66. For details, see James Haar, "Lassus," *The New Grove Dictionary of Music*, 10:487–90 and 498–99 (the list of works).

Lassus's mastery of madrigal composition is evident already in the earliest of his published collections, and his production in the genre seems to have peaked in the 1560s and early 1570s, after which it fell off quite considerably. His fourth book of madrigals for five voices, published in Venice in 1567, is separated by two decades from the two late collections printed in Munich in 1585 and 1587, though of course many other works appeared in the meantime in the anthologies of the 1560s and 1570s. As to style, works included in these later publications follow very much in the same vein as those of his maiden collections. This is the case for *S'io esca vivo de dubbiosi scogli*, for example, a setting typical for the period of the final strophe and the *invio* of Petrarch's sestina *Chi è fermato di menar sua vita*, printed in Venice by Scotto in his *Corona de madrigali a sei voci . . . Libro primo* of 1579 (see Example 25-13).[67] The six voices specified in the title include in this instance both two high parts (canto and sesto) and two tenors (tenore and quinto), a "classical" combination.

Textures are generally full, as Lassus makes good use of the sonorous possibilities inherent in such a large vocal ensemble. However, he does hold back the entry of

67. For a transcription of the entire madrigal in modern score, see Orlande de Lassus, *Sämtliche Werke*, ed. F. X. Haberl and A. Sandberger, 21 vols. (Leipzig: Breitkopf und Härtel, 1894–1926; reprint, New York: Broude Brothers, 1973), 10:9–13.

EXAMPLE 25-13. Orlande de Lassus, *S'io esca vivo de dubbiosi scogli* (mm. 1–25)

If I escape with my life from the dangerous shoals, and my exile comes to a good end,
then I should want to strike the sail and cast the anchor in some port . . .

sesto and basso during the initial phrase, first bringing them in for the "arrival" to which the second verse refers (m. 10). Elsewhere a reduction in scoring serves both to articulate the text, as for the entry of the third line ("Chi sarei vago," m. 16), and to vary a bit the vocal registers. Declamation is essentially homophonic in the beginning, but the anticipatory entry of the alto to start and of the quinto for the second verse (mm. 9–15) results in a kind of quasi-contrapuntal texture that lends interest to an otherwise chordal presentation of the text. (Rhythmic displacement of one or two voices in a fundamentally homophonic passage to animate the part-writing without unduly obscuring the text, as here, is a device that had been in use at least since Josquin's *Ave Maria, virgo serena*; see pp. 514–18.)

Although the contrapuntal independence of the individual voices steadily increases through this opening pair of phrases, Lassus does not deploy a full-fledged point of imitation until the third verse with the words "di voltar la vela," where it becomes a mimetic gesture, combining with livelier rhythms to suggest the unfurling sail. Also intended as textual illustration, clearly, is the animated melisma for "vivo" ("alive") in the first phrase. Similarly, the magisterial cadence that brings real closure to the verse, "Ed arrive il mio esilio ad un bel fine," underlines the meaning of Petrarch's metaphor with a musical analogue that also gives rhetorical emphasis to the words being sung.

Any doubt in the listener's mind as to the composer's intentions in this passage must surely be dispelled at the end of the next pair of lines, where another strongly marked cadence mirrors the conceit of "dropping anchor in some port." And, as the piece continues to unfold, with musical phrases corresponding faithfully to syntactic entities, each verse has its rhetorical and mimetic gestures, the so-called madrigalisms that are the quintessential characteristic of the genre.

In sharp contrast, both textually and musically, to the sophisticated elegance of such a madrigal, but equally representative of their genre, are Lassus's essays in the more popular realm of the *villanesca* or *villanella*. Typical is the amusing *Matona mia cara*, which was included in the *Libro de villanelle, moresche, et altre canzoni* published in Paris in 1581 (see Example 25-14).[68] With its short-winded strophes of four hexasyllables each, its tortured grammar, its double entendres, and its nonsense refrain, the verses mock the efforts of a German soldier having only a rudimentary grasp of the language to woo an Italian lady.

Here the structure is crystal clear; Lassus marked off the verses with cadential formulae and articulated the individual strophes with the recurring refrain, which he set each time to the same music. The stanzas, by contrast, are a bit different from one to the next, although with some internal repetition of both words and music. Homophonic declamation reigns supreme in the presentation of the text and, together with the composer's emphasis on structural delineation, seems to preclude any significant rhetorical or mimetic gestures.

68. For a transcription of the complete work in modern score, see Lassus, *Sämtliche Werke*, ed. Haberl and Sandberger, 10:93–97.

EXAMPLE 25-14. Orlande de Lassus, *Matona mia cara* (mm. 1–12)

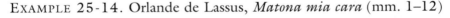

My dear lady, me want to sing song under window, lancer good companion. Don, don, don diridir, don, don, don, don. (Four additional strophes.)

CHANSONS

Lassus's contribution to the printed chanson repertory peaked, like his production of madrigals, in the early 1570s. Ten collections appeared between his initial opus in 1555 and the *Thresor de musique* brought out in Geneva in 1576; these were then followed by a single title, the *Continuation du mellange*, published in Paris in 1584. The total harvest, however, is rather more slender than for the madrigal: about 145 compositions. Cities from which the printed volumes emanated include not only Geneva and Paris but also Antwerp, Louvain, and London, which saw the reprint (now lost) of a 1570 collection fitted out with sacred *contrafacta* in place of the original French texts.

As with his madrigals, the poets whose verse Lassus chose to set to music indicate discriminating tastes and, perhaps more surprising, familiarity with the best French authors of the age. These include Jean Antoine de Baïf, Joachim Du Bellay, Clément Marot, Pierre de Ronsard, and Mellin de Saint-Gelais as well as writers of earlier generations such as Guillaume Crétin and François Villon. Although acquainted with the leading poets of the Pléiade—Baïf, Du Bellay, and Ronsard in particular—he seems never to have become interested in the attempts by the members of the Académie de Poésie et de Musique to impose quantities on the French language corresponding to the prosody of ancient Greek or in the related experiments with *musique mesurée*.

In significant ways many of his chansons are similar in style to those of the generation of Claudin de Sermisy (see pp. 618–29). The majority are for four or, less frequently, five voices, and he adopted for a fair number of them the homophonic, declamatory style favored at the court of Francis I. A striking example is his setting of Ronsard's *Bon jour mon coeur*, first published in Amsterdam in *Le premier livre de chansons . . . a quatre voix* of 1564 (see Example 25-15).[69] With only minor deviations the work's texture and declamation are consistently homophonic, and both prosody and syntax are reflected in the clearly articulated structure of the music.

The rhyming couplet in decasyllables with which the poem begins has been laid out with a rest to mark the caesura after the fourth syllable, a cadence to end the verse, and a musical repetition to mirror the recurring rhyme. Similar procedures are then used throughout the remainder of the piece to divide the text into its constituent lines and syntactic entities while interpreting coherently the author's meaning. Interestingly, Ronsard's poem, which was modeled on a Latin epigram by Marullus and published in his *Nouvelle continuation des Amours* of 1556, has a second strophe, identical in its prosody to the first. It was probably not Lassus's intention that it, too, be sung to his music, but his respect for the structural integrity of

69. For a transcription in modern score of the complete chanson, see Lassus, *Sämtliche Werke*, ed. Haberl and Sandberger, 12:100–101; for an instrumental arrangement by Peter Philips, see J. A. Fuller Maitland and W. Barclay Squire, ed., *The Fitzwilliam Virginal Book*, 2 vols. (London: Breitkopf und Härtel, 1894–99; reprint, New York: Dover, 1963), 1:317–20.

EXAMPLE 25-15. Orlande de Lassus, *Bon jour mon coeur* (mm. 1–16)

Good day my heart, good day my sweet life, good day mine eye, good day my dear friend.
Hey, good day my all beautiful, my daintiness, good day, my delight, my love . . .

the poem is such that it could in fact be adapted to his setting without doing real violence to either its declamation or to its meaning.

Judging from earlier repertory, one might expect Lassus to take a similarly direct compositional approach in those chansons whose diction has a distinctly plebeian flavor. In general, however, he appears to have been inclined to greater contrapuntal variety, as in *Un jeune moine est sorti du couvent*, which narrates the unsuccessful attempt of a young monk to seduce an attractive nun.[70] Although it begins with homophonic declamation, rhythmic displacement of one voice after another quickly puts them out of phase for the pronunciation of the text and begets a more contrapuntal effect. The free part-writing then gives way to a tightly knit point of imitation for the refrain (mm. 22–40), which ends with a repetition of its last five breves and is repeated to conclude each of the two succeeding strophes.

Care of this kind for the prosody, syntax, and meaning of poetry, which is set to music with a sophisticated mix of homophonic texture and contrapuntal play, as just described, is characteristic of Lassus's chansons generally, as it is of the genre through most of the century. In some instances, however, especially for texts of deeper meaning, he also introduced rhetorical and mimetic gestures that had earlier been largely foreign to the chanson. In his composition for Du Bellay's *La nuict froide et sombre*, for example (see Example 25-16),[71] he presents the first five-syllable verse of the poet's *douzain* in a chordal texture and begins with the typical "chanson rhythm," a breve and two semibreves (lightly syncopated). With a few subtle touches, however—the b-fa introduced accidentally in the three lower parts, the suspended dissonance of a fourth (m. 3) and the f♯ of the closing sonority of the phrase—Lassus captures the sombre atmosphere of the poem.

In the third verse, "La terre et les cieux," typically madrigalistic gestures suggest the ascent from earth heavenward with the descending melisma in the tenor followed by an octave leap upward, accompanied by a steadily rising line in the cantus (mm. 8–9). The sweetness of honey, alluded to in the fourth verse, has its musical counterpart in the contrapuntally unnecessary g♯ of the cantus, and in the next phrase a lively scalewise descent through a fourth is treated as a point of imitation to illustrate sleep flowing down from above upon the eyes. Finally, for the second strophe of the poem (mm. 18–34), which contrasts the light and color of newborn day with the cold darkness of night that permeates the first, Lassus has animated the texture, both rhythmically and contrapuntally, in a musical analog to the sense of the text.

In this and other comparable settings, then, Lassus has enriched the compositional vocabulary of the chanson with the expressive gestures typical of the madrigal. He has done so, however, without altering the essential parameters of the genre in any significant way. The concern for clearly articulating poetic forms by means of

70. For a transcription in modern score, see Lassus, *Sämtliche Werke*, ed. Haberl and Sandberger, 12:89–93.

71. For a transcription of the entire piece in modern score, see *Sämtliche Werke*, ed. Haberl and Sandberger, 12:34–35.

EXAMPLE 25-16. Orlande de Lassus, *La nuict froide et sombre* (mm. 1–22)

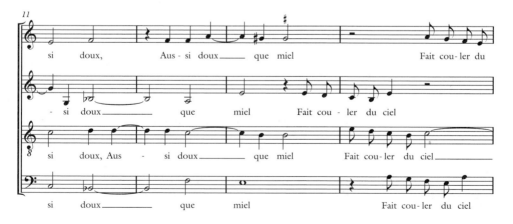

The cold and somber night, running with a dark shadow o'er the earth and the heavens, as sweetly as honey makes sleep flow from above upon the eyes. Then the day, following, leading to labor, exposes its light [and with a diverse hue carpets and composes this great universe].

matching musical structures that is so much a part of the chanson's historical traditions is still very much evident in his own contributions to the repertory of the late sixteenth century.

POLYPHONIC GERMAN SONGS

Naturally enough, Lassus came to the composition of German-texted works long after he had established his reputation as a master of the secular genres of both Italy and France. French was his native tongue, after all, and he began to learn Italian while still an adolescent. By contrast, although he eventually learned to speak and write German well, he appears not to have known it before accepting the offer to join the chapel of the Bavarian court. Not that the ducal chapel was lacking in repertory of this sort. Ludwig Senfl, who distinguished himself as a composer of *Tenor-lieder*, had finished his career in Munich, and there were published collections by Ott, Forster, and others. In any case, following time-honored precedent, some twenty-eight of his chansons were given contrafact texts in German.

His first publication of Lieder came only with the *Neue teütsche Liedlein* for five voices, printed in 1567 in Munich. This was followed by two more, similar collections in 1572 and 1576, indicating a rather measured pace in setting German texts. After a hiatus of nearly a decade, two more Lieder prints appeared in 1583, one for four voices, the other for five. His settings in three parts for twenty-five Psalms based on the Ulenberg translations of 1582 came in 1588, and the last collection containing German-texted works, the *Neue teutsche und etliche Frantzösische Gesäng* for six voices, was published in Munich in 1590. Counting the Psalms, his German repertory numbers about ninety pieces, including some very extensive multipartite Lieder. This is a relatively modest total for Lassus but a very substantial musical corpus nonetheless.

Striking in this repertory, if not surprising given the pervasive influence of the Protestant Reformation in Germany, is the large place given over to religious and devotional works. At least a dozen of these set traditional texts, and melodies, including the venerable *Leise, Christ ist erstanden.*[72] These Lassus has treated in the customary German manner with the well-known tune as a cantus firmus in mostly even values in an inner voice. This is true not only of the sometimes ancient melodies from the German Catholic past but also of the more recent ones associated with the Reformation.

All of the three-voice Psalm settings make use of tunes published in song books of the mid-sixteenth century, for example. Perhaps because of the modest format adopted for these works, and their consistently contrapuntal character, Lassus varies considerably his placement of the borrowed melody. It is at times in its traditional place in the tenor but even more often in cantus or bassus. On occasion it migrates from part to part, and in some pieces imitative treatment of the preexistent material at the beginning of a phrase leaves momentary doubt as to the voice that is meant to carry it through.[73]

As for the works that were freely composed, those in four parts are often very similar in style to the chanson. Many begin with a brief point of imitation that then yields rather quickly to quasi-homophony or a lightly contrapuntal texture. Yet others introduce homophonic declamation from the outset and then turn to greater rhythmic independence for the individual voices, or voice pairs, thus ending the isochronous presentation of the text. Lassus uses both of these approaches, and

72. See the list given by Adolf Sandberger in Lassus, *Sämtliche Werke*, ed. Haberl and Sandberger, 20:xvi.
73. Concerning the source of the Psalm tunes and their placement in Lassus's settings, see Lassus, *Sämtliche Werke*, ed. Haberl and Sandberger, 20:xvii–xviii; transcriptions of these pieces are in the same volume, pp. 61–80.

numerous other variants of the basic compositional procedures involved, in his multipartite setting of the hymnlike *Die Gnad kombt oben her* that opens the 1583 print (see Examples 25-17a and 25-17b).[74]

He has written a brief, wholly autonomous section for each of its twelve strophes, and together they constitute a veritable catalogue of the various types of part-writing he deploys for Lieder of this kind. He opens the initial strophe (Example 25-17a), and the work, with a closely spaced point of imitation for the first verse and, after a clearly marked cadence, homophonic declamation for the second. Thereafter, beginning with the delayed entry for the third verse in the tenor, the counterpoint unfolds more freely in a quasi-contrapuntal manner with an occasional hint of imita-

74. For a transcription in modern score of the entire work, see Lassus, *Sämtliche Werke*, ed. Haberl and Sandberger, 20:4–17.

EXAMPLE 25-17a. Orlande de Lassus, *Die Gnad kombt oben her*, strophe 1 (mm. 1–14)

Grace comes from above, given to us by the Lord God. Whoever does the same willingly, him will God protect; that have I truly experienced in my youth.

tion (as in mm. 12–13 between cantus and tenor). By contrast, he begins the fifth strophe, *Joseph verkauffet ist* (Example 25-17b), with a homophonic phrase for the first verse, after which he pairs the voices rhythmically, with cantus and altus together leading the way and tenor and bassus following in similar fashion till the end of the piece.

EXAMPLE 25-17b. Orlande de Lassus, *Joseph verkauffet ist*, strophe 5 (mm. 1–10)

Joseph was cunningly sold by his brothers, but God preserved him; he was to rule a land.
That did he truly experience in his youth. (Seven additional strophes.)

Many of the Lieder in five parts are very much like their four-voice counterparts, especially the drinking and the Maying songs. Some of these dissolve midway into a kind of patter, as in *Ist keiner hie*,[75] where the rhythmical declamation of "jo, jo, jo" interrupts the hitherto contrapuntal fabric of the piece with a stylized imitation of a noisy wine guzzler. Similarly, in *Der wein, der schmeckt mir also wol*,[76] which opens like *Joseph verkauffet ist* with a passage in simultaneous declamation, the "frisch auf" that is tossed antiphonally back and forth between the cantus and the four lower voices has a similar effect.

Other songs in the five-voice repertory, and even more so those for six voices, especially when based on religious or devotional texts, tend to be more like the madrigal or even the motet in their facture. In these compositions, which tend also to be among the lengthiest, Lassus has made more consistent use of imitative counterpoint and introduced greater variety into his musical textures; it is as though the more serious material called for weightier, more learned compositional procedures.

This is evident already in his setting of Martin Luther's prayer *Vater unser im himmelreich*, which has pride of place at the beginning of the *Neue teütsche Liedlein* of 1567. The traditional treatment of the tune to which it was usually sung as a cantus firmus, handed back and forth contrapuntally between tenor and bassus, the opening point of imitation based upon it, and the sophisticated nature of the part-writing generally all point clearly to the motet as a stylistic model.

Affinity with the motet is even more strongly marked in Lassus's setting of Psalm

75. See Lassus, *Sämtliche Werke*, ed. Haberl and Sandberger, 18:8–10.
76. See Lassus, *Sämtliche Werke*, ed. Haberl and Sandberger, 18:11–13.

129, *De profundis*, in Ulenberg's verse translation, *Ich ruff zu dir, mein Herr und Gott*, first of all in its sheer scope (see Example 25-18).[77] Each of the five strophes of the German poem is set as a separate *pars* or *Theil*. The Psalm tune is imbedded into each one as a tenor cantus firmus, mostly in even minims and semibreves, and often echoed in one or more of the other voices as well. It is in fact the basis for the point of imitation that opens both the first and the fifth parts. In the latter instance, it is heard first in diminution in the cantus, then taken up in its more usual rhythms in each of the other voices in turn, except for the altus. As in this beginning, the textures are overwhelmingly contrapuntal; nowhere in the entire Psalm has Lassus resorted to the kind of untrammeled homophony that is so frequently encountered in the more chansonlike Lieder.

It is clear that Lassus acquainted himself fully with the traditions associated in the sixteenth century with the *tenorlied*. However, it is no less evident that he brought to his cultivation of the genre his own earlier experience with the secular genres of

---

77. For a transcription in modern score of the entire composition, see Lassus, *Sämtliche Werke*, ed. Haberl and Sandberger, 20:88–98.

EXAMPLE 25-18. Orlande de Lassus, *Ich ruff zu dir* (Psalm 129), fifth part (mm. 1–13)

For with the Lord there is mercy, his grace has neither measure nor bounds; with him is
plenteous redemption. And he shall redeem Israel from all his iniquities.

France and Italy. The melding of genres was the result, just as it was in his handling
of chanson and madrigal.

MUSIC FOR MASS

Turning to Lassus's sacred music, the liturgical rituals regularly observed by the
court included a morning service, which was centered upon the celebration of
the Mass. The Ordinary was evidently sung in polyphony on a daily basis, even when
the service was expedited to allow the nobility an early departure for the hunt and
an especially concise setting, known as the *Jäger Mass* (or *Missa Venatorum*), was
heard. Many of the sixty or so Masses securely attributed to Lassus must have been
composed in that connection. Very few of these works are based on plainchant cantus firmi; there are three simply designated *de feria* (for weekdays) in addition to the
three Requiem Masses for which the incorporation of the liturgical melodies in the
setting of their texts was traditional. The majority are based on preexistent polyphonic works *ad imitationem*, not only motets (mostly his own) but also madrigals
by Sebastiano Festa, Jacques Arcadelt, Cipriano de Rore, and Palestrina, and chan-

sons by Claudin de Sermisy, Pierre Certon, Nicolas Gombert, Adrian Willaert, and Clemens (non Papa), among others.

Lassus took his models, then, from composers of previous generations as well as from his immediate contemporaries and mined the chanson repertories of both French and Netherlandish masters. His compositional procedures were also those that had been largely codified by earlier composers. A representative example is his *Missa ad imitationem moduli Susanne un jour* for five voices, first published in 1563 (see Example 25-19a).[78] The model is Lassus's own *chanson spirituelle*, which recounts the misadventure of the chaste heroine with two lustful and unscrupulous old men. Curiously, Lassus's setting of this text was based in turn on a severely homophonic one ascribed to Didier Lupi Second, whose tenor he integrated as tenor I into his imitative counterpoint for five voices (see Example 25-19b).[79]

Lassus opens his Mass with a fairly faithful quotation of the first two half-phrases of the chanson (mm. 1–10 in both). In the model this is followed by a second phrase (mm. 10–14) and a repeat of the entire first section, corresponding to the recurring rhyme scheme for the second pair of verses (mm. 14–28). In the Lupi Second setting the repeat is literal, simply signaled by the usual sign, whereas Lassus has intro-

78. For a transcription of the entire piece in modern score, see Orlande de Lassus, *Messen*, ed. Siegfried Hermelink, *Sämtliche Werke*, neue Reihe, vol. 4 (Kassel: Bärenreiter, 1964): 121–54.
79. Concerning the origins of both text and music, see Kenneth Levy, "'Susanne un jour'; The History of a Sixteenth-Century Chanson," *Annales musicologiques* 1 (1953): 375–408; for a transcription of Lassus's chanson in modern score, see Lassus, *Sämtliche Werke*, ed. Haberl and Sandberger, 14:29–33.

EXAMPLE 25-19a. Orlande de Lassus, *Missa Susanne un jour*, Kyrie (mm. 1–7, 18–26)

Lord, have mercy.

Example 25-19b. Orlande de Lassus, *Susanne un jour* (mm. 1–14)

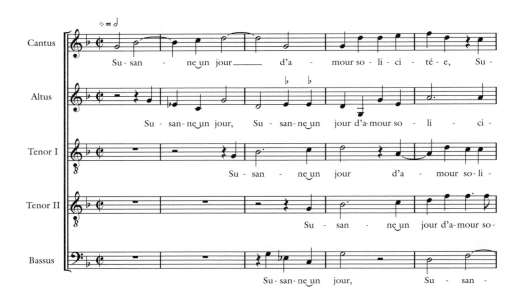

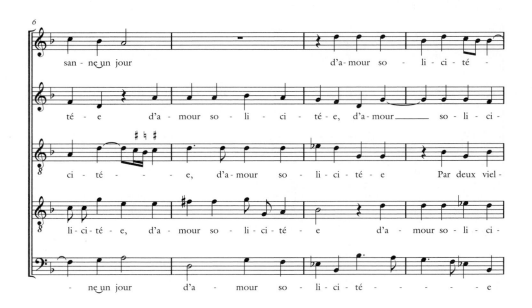

Susanne, solicited one day for love by two old men who coveted her beauty, [was sad and troubled at heart to see the assault made on her chastity].

duced some modest changes. For the first "Kyrie" Lassus has compressed that design, introducing the varied repetition, with even more substantial alterations (mm. 10–22), before going on to the second phrase of chanson (mm. 10–14 and 24–28) to conclude the subsection of the Mass (mm. 22–26) with the cadential material used to articulate the two opening sections of the chanson.

As the closing figure of the first "Kyrie" Lassus also refers in the superius to the next phrase of his model (mm. 28–29) with a leap from g up to d' and a step up a semitone to e'-fa and back. The continuation of that phrase of the chanson (mm. 33–36) then provides the musical substance for the "Christe," a tightly imitative trio for tenor I, altus, and superius. Skipping over the short cadential phrase of this model, its fourth (mm. 36–38), Lassus begins the second "Kyrie" with material from the first truly homophonic passage of the chanson (mm. 38–42) but as the motive for a point of imitation, then continues quoting his model quite closely through to the end. He also repeats the final half-phrase of the chanson (mm. 53–58) to round out the form in a manner characteristic of the genre generally but not in fact present in his model.

All of the essential structural patterns and compositional procedures traditionally associated with Mass composition by the end of the century—as described, for example by Cerone (see pp. 590–91)—are deployed throughout the remaining sections of the Mass in much the same manner as in the Kyrie. The initial point of imitation in the chanson becomes a head motive, introducing each of the main sections of the Ordinary. In the Sanctus it is treated a bit more freely than before, however, and in the Agnus Dei the rising figure that Lassus borrowed from Lupi Second disappears, giving way to his own countermelody in descending thirds. Similarly, the repeated cadential material at the end of the Kyrie is brought back to close each of the subsequent sections except the Sanctus, but, as might be expected, the final quotation in the Agnus Dei is considerably varied.

Lassus also divides the longer texts in all the usual places, reducing the textures for some subsections as well in the traditional way. He breaks the Gloria, for example, just before the "Qui tollis," which he presents in homophonic declamation as was so often done. In the Credo, he casts the "Crucifixus" as a trio, this time for bassus, altus, and superius, and bases it on the opening figures of the model. He returns to full voicing and homophonic declamation to initiate the "Et iterum," in which contrapuntal and chordal textures alternate with some regularity. The Sanctus, too, he treats as a traditional tripartite structure, with the "Benedictus" reduced to a trio for superius, altus, and tenor I and the sonorous "Hosanna" repeated to bring the section to a brilliant close. The Agnus Dei is here a single section, as it was in Victoria's *Missa Quam gloriosum est regnum*, suggesting once again the possibility of alternation with plainsong. In sum, Lassus's intimate knowledge of and adherence to established canons for Mass composition are evident on every page of this admirable work.

HYMNS AND CANTICLES

The large repertory of hymns and Magnificats credited to Lassus indicates that on feast days, in addition to the morning service, he was expected to provide the court chapel with polyphonic music for a solemn observance of Vespers as well. Unlike his Magnificats, all of which were published, his settings of hymns for the major feasts of the liturgical year has survived as a cycle only in a series of manuscripts, most of them prepared for the court chapel and all now either in the Bavarian State Library in Munich or in the Archives of the city's Metropolitan Chapter.

These pieces reveal their strong ties to the polyphonic hymn traditions in a variety of ways. All were conceived for *alternatim* performance, usually with the first stanza sung in plainchant and the last in polyphony. All were written for either four or five voices with internal strophes scored for reduced forces in the customary manner. And all make use of the liturgical melody as a kind of cantus firmus, carried most often in a tenor part. Turning yet again to the Advent hymn *Conditor alme siderum*, Lassus's treatment of it for five voices exemplifies both his approach to the genre and his adherence to established practices (see Example 25-20).[80]

Following the opening strophe in plainsong, the second stanza begins with a point of imitation derived from the chant in superius, tenor I, and tenor II, while the other two parts each have an independent countermelody. Lassus quotes the hymn

---

80. For a transcription of the complete work in modern score, see Orlande de Lassus, *Das Hymnarium aus dem Jahre 1580–81*, ed. Marie-Louise Göllner, *Sämtliche Werke*, neue Reihe, vol. 18 (Kassel: Bärenreiter, 1980), 14–17.

EXAMPLE 25-20. Orlande de Lassus, *Conditor alme siderum* (mm. 1–15)

1. Con - di - tor al - me si - de - rum. Ae - ter - na lux cre - den - ti - um,

Chri - ste re - dem - ptor o - mni - um Ex - au - di pre - ces sup - pli - cum.

Superius — 2. Qui con - do - lens in - te - ri - tu, mor - tis pe - ri - re se -

Altus — 2. Qui con - do - lens in - te - ri - tu, mor - tis pe - ri -

Tenor I — 2. Qui con - do - lens in - te - ri - tu, mor - tis pe -

Tenor II — 2. Qui con - do - lens in - te - ri - tu, mor - tis pe - ri - re se - cu -

Bassus — 2. Qui con - do - lens in - te - ri - tu, mor - tis pe - ri -

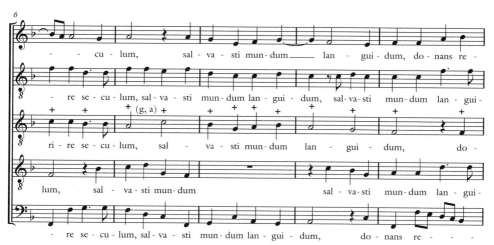

- cu - lum, sal - va - sti mun - dum lan - gui - dum, do - nans re -

ri - re se - cu - lum, sal - va - sti mun - dum lan - gui - dum, sal - va - sti mun - dum lan - gui -

(g, a)
ri - re se - cu - lum, sal - va - sti mun - dum lan - gui - dum, do -

lum, sal - va - sti mun - dum sal - va - sti mun - dum lan - gui -

ri - re se - cu - lum, sal - va - sti mun - dum lan - gui - dum, do - nans re -

1. Kindly creator of the stars, eternal light of the believers, Christ, redeemer of all, hear the prayers of the supplicants. 2. Thou who, suffering the destruction of death, the demise of the people, freed the languishing world, providing a remedy for sin.

tune faithfully in tenor I through to the end of the strophe, and his imitation of it in the two other voices causes the familiar melody to permeate to a considerable degree the contrapuntal fabric. The fourth stanza is an imitative duo for superius and altus (to which a third part was later added in one of the sources), derived almost entirely from the liturgical chant. In the final strophe, for which Lassus returns to the full complement of five voices, he begins again with a point of imitation based on the plainsong, this time heard in each of the parts in turn. Tenor I continues to carry it in the manner of a traditional cantus firmus nonetheless, as the other voices continue to echo the chant, though with increasing freedom, until the final cadence.

In sharp contrast to this single cycle of Vespers hymns are the numerous settings of the Magnificat securely ascribed to Lassus, an astounding total of 102 compositions.[81] No other composer of the age approaches such prolific production in the genre. Even Palestrina, his closest rival in terms of sheer numbers, is credited with only 35, about a third as many. The earliest of Lassus's essays in this genre may be the set for four voices published in 1587 (presumably long after they were composed) by Leroy and Ballard in Paris, *Octo cantica divae Mariae Virginis . . . Magnificat secundum octo modos seu tonos*. As indicated by the title, this is a cycle of eight Magnificat settings, one on each of the liturgical tones.

Among the most widely disseminated of the forty settings dating from the reign of Albrecht V, approximately 1565–79, were those included in the first collection to

81. Concerning the Magnificats attributed to Lassus, see Orlande de Lassus, *Magnificat*, ed. James Erb, *Sämtliche Werke*, neue Reihe, vol. 13 (Kassel: Bärenreiter, 1980), i ff. (also the prefaces to vols. 14–17).

be printed, the *Magnificat Octo Tonorum Sex, Quinque et Quatuor Vocum*, published by Theodor Gerlach in Nuremberg in 1567. It comprises three complete cycles based on the eight traditional tones, one for four, another for five, and a third for six voices. All are intended for *alternatim* performance with only the even-numbered verses set polyphonically. Taking his lead, presumably, from well-established tradition, Lassus also varied the contrapuntal textures in his settings for five and six voices by reducing the scoring for some of the internal verses, as he did for his hymns.

In addition, he emphasized the liturgical function of these works by his treatment of the traditional tone. He often laid it out like a cantus firmus and—although he let it lapse occasionally—he usually placed it either in the tenor (its traditional carrier) or, less frequently, in the superius. Surprisingly, perhaps, these twenty-four relatively modest compositions account for the greatest number of source concordances in all of his vast repertory of Magnificat settings.

Lassus's treatment of the Marian canticle is much less traditional in those he began to compose shortly before 1580, the beginning of the reign of Wilhelm V. In his later years Lassus began to base his Magnificat settings on preexistent polyphonic works, adapting to the genre the compositional procedures that had previously been adopted for polyphonic Masses *ad imitationem*. As for his Masses, so for these settings of the canticle, Lassus took as his models motets, madrigals, and chansons, many of his own creation.

Among the earliest of the pieces upon which he drew for this purpose were two motets by Josquin Desprez; otherwise the masters selected for imitation were generally the same as for his Masses, Cipriano de Rore, Alessandro Striggio, Claudin de Sermisy, and Nicolas Gombert in particular. About two-thirds of his Magnificats—sixty-two pieces in all—are of this new type. Although they did not circulate nearly so widely as those he wrote earlier in his career, they mark a clear departure from the traditional parameters for the genre, an innovatory trend for which he seems to be largely responsible. The innovation, however, involves compositional procedures that were by then deeply rooted in tradition.

Lassus approached in similar fashion his settings for *Nunc dimittis*, the Canticle of Simeon sung at the end of Compline, of which a much tinier repertory has survived. Of the thirteen compositions considered authentic—all of which are found only in manuscript sources—five (all for four voices) are based on a liturgical tone, two on the fourth, and one each on the fifth, the seventh, and the eighth.[82] If Lassus's intention was to provide a cycle including a setting for each of the liturgical tones, either he did not complete it or some pieces have been lost. The remaining eight works are based on polyphonic models, five on madrigals, two on motets, and another on the same chanson that Lassus used in his Mass composition, *Susanne un jour*.

As a subcategory of the motet, *Nunc dimittis* settings also represent an innovation. There are only six among the motets of Palestrina and one by Victoria. Lassus's

---

82. See, for example, the *Liber usualis*, 271 and 784.

approach, however, is once again anchored in traditional procedures and styles; he simply transferred those that defined the Magnificat as a genre in the late sixteenth century to another canticle of similar structure and liturgical function.[83]

MUSIC FOR LENT AND HOLY WEEK

Aside from the polyphonic litanies ascribed to Lassus, of which fourteen sets survive, and some lessons and responsories for Christmastide, the remainder of the extensive repertory of sacred polyphony that he prepared for liturgical use is for special observances during Lent and Holy Week. His *Seven Penitential Psalms* for five voices, published in Munich in 1584 (but composed considerably earlier and copied into the beautifully illuminated MS A II of the Bavarian State Library) were probably heard in the ducal chapel during Lent. Pope Innocent III (1198–1216) had prescribed the recitation of the Penitential Psalms for ordinary weekday services during Lent, and Pius V designated Fridays after Lauds as the appropriate time. Although these texts also had an important place in private devotions, there can be little doubt that Lassus's compositions were conceived for liturgical use.

To begin, he imbedded a liturgical Psalm tone in each of them in the traditional manner of a cantus firmus. This he did systematically, starting with the first tone for Psalm 6 (the first of the seven to be recited) and proceeding numerically through the traditional modal system to end with the eighth in the Psalm-motet *Laudate Dominum de Coelis*, which was obviously added to round out the set and provide an example of each mode. In addition, the Psalms are divided into sections verse by verse, just as they are in plainchant recitation, and include the Doxology required for liturgical use.

Conceptually, however, they are not unlike Lassus's *Ich ruff zu dir*, his setting of Psalm 129 in German translation. The similarities are especially clear if one compares the devotional work in the vernacular with Lassus's treatment of its Latin counterpart, *De profundis clamavi*, the sixth Penitential Psalm (see Example 25-21).[84] Just as the traditional hymn melody runs through the entire devotional Lied, so is the sixth Psalm tone present as a cantus firmus in all ten sections of the Latin Psalm. The tenor carries the borrowed melody for the most part in both works, but Lassus quotes the psalm tone in the bassus in verse 5, at the lower fourth (implying a C final) in verse 6, in the superius in verse 7, and in the altus a fifth higher (again implying C) in verse 8. What is more, the reiterated pitches of the recitation formula inevitably limit the composer's contrapuntal options rather more severely than the tuneful Lied, and the texture of the Latin setting tends to be generally less imitative and more declamatory than its German counterpart.

---

83. Lassus's settings of the *Nunc dimittis* have been edited by Peter Bergquist in Orlande de Lassus, *Cantica, Responsorien und andere Musik für die Officia, Sämtliche Werke*, neue Reihe, vol. 24 (Kassel: Bärenreiter, 1993).

84. For a transcription in modern score of all eight works, see Orlande de Lassus, *The Seven Penitential Psalms and Laudate Dominum de caelis*, ed. Peter Bergquist, 2 vols., Recent Researches in the Music of the Renaissance, vols. 86–87 (Madison: A-R Editions, 1990); for *De profundis clamavi*, see 221–35.

EXAMPLE 25-21. Orlande de Lassus, *De profundis clamavi* (Psalm 129), verse 1 (mm. 1–13)

Out of the depths have I cried unto thee, O Lord. Lord, hear my voice.

In addition, Lassus has used reduced scoring for internal sections of *De profundis* for sonorous variety in a manner that recalls traditional approaches to the Latin hymn and the Magnificat, both liturgically related genres. By contrast, such reductions are not used in *Ich ruff zu dir*. Verse 4, "Quia apud te propitiato est," is written for a trio of low voices (altus, tenor, and bassus), whereas verse 7, "Quia apud Dominum misericordia" is for three higher ones (superius, altus, and tenor). The latter reduction, moreover, is followed by a systematic increase in the number of voices verse by verse to the end, from four (verse 8), to five (verse 9), to six (verse 10). The two settings are clearly not sisters, then, but they are closely related, perhaps as cousins.

Even more closely analogous to Lassus's *De profundis* is Willaert's setting of the same text (see pp. 557–560). Willaert, too, makes reference (although much less literally) to the Psalm tone, and both masters articulate the Psalm verse by verse (Willaert with the antiphonal effect of his divided choir) and include the Doxology as an integral part of the composition. In addition, although both rely on many of the same motet-related compositional procedures for these pieces, they are truly Psalm settings, not merely Psalm-motets.

Music by Lassus for Holy Week includes a comprehensive set of Passions, one from each of the Gospels, suggesting that they were probably sung polyphonically at the appropriate moment during Mass in the ducal chapel. There is also a substantial body of compositions for Matins for the final three days before Easter Sunday. He set systematically the Lamentations of Jeremiah that provide the Lections for the first Nocturn on all three days in two separate versions, one for four voices, known only from a manuscript source, and the other for five, which was published in 1585. He also composed music for the Responsories sung during the second and third Nocturns on those same three days, all of them for four voices and also transmitted only in manuscript.

Lassus's treatment of these responsories is analogous in essential ways to the approach taken by Victoria to the same chants. This is evident from a comparison of Lassus's setting of *Tenebrae factae sunt*, the second responsory sung during the second Nocturn on Good Friday, with that by Victoria (see pp. 912–15) and suggests that a polyphonic tradition for this subgenre of the motet was already rather well established by the 1580s. Like his Spanish contemporary, surprisingly, Lassus had no recourse to the chant but set the respond, the *repetendum*, and the verse as separate sections with a reduction in scoring for the verse. Victoria decreased the voices from four to three, with the third delaying its entry until the fifth breve of the section; Lassus decreased them from four directly to a duo (to which a third voice was later added, probably not by the author).

More significantly, there is a slight but discernible change in texture in both compositions at the verse. Both composers open the respond in a quasi-homophonic style that is then gradually animated contrapuntally, culminating in some imitative phrases toward the end. The verses, by contrast, consist of a series of points of imitation, carried through fairly systematically to the end of the section. In addition, the part-writing is itself a bit different, more fleeting in character, adumbrating a further distinction between choral and soloistic styles. Although both sets probably came into existence in the early 1580s, at a time when even indirect contact between the two composers would have been unlikely, the similarities between their respective settings of the responsory texts seem almost too substantial to be coincidental.

MOTETS

Turning to Lassus's motets, finally, one is again confronted with an enormous and varied repertory, well over 500 compositions in all. They range in scope and style from the textless duos of 1577 and three-voice Latin pieces—many probably written with didactic intent—to elaborate ceremonial motets like *Princeps Marte potens, Guilelmus*. Written in connection with Wilhelm V's marriage to Renée of Lorraine in 1568, it is in a brilliant, declamatory style, culminating, after eight brief *partes* for four voices, in a ninth for double choir.[85]

In addition, Lassus wrote playful, humorous works on Latin texts, like the very compendious *Laudent Deum cythara* (only thirteen breves in length), which names and imitates the performance styles of lutes (*cythara*), voices (*chori vox*), horns (*cornu*), and organs (*organa*).[86] He also put to music his share of classical and classicizing texts; these include the ever popular lament of Dido, *Dulces exuviae*,[87] which he cast in solemn, syllabic homophony (except for a middle section in sesquialtera proportion in which imitative counterpoint illustrates shifting fortune), and the *Prophetiae Sibyllarum*,[88] with its striking combination of homophonic declamation and unpredictable accidentals.

However, the vast majority of Lassus's motets are based on the more traditional liturgical and devotional texts, many of which were set time and again by the composers of his age: antiphons (especially the beloved Marian chants), Psalms, canticles, Gospel and Epistle readings, and the like. And in this large and varied repertory Lassus deployed in one way or another all the compositional procedures that had been developed over the preceding century and a half and that have been under discussion in this chapter. He did it with such skill and power, moreover, that, in the words of Samuel Quickelberg, humanist scholar and physician at the Bavarian court, the subject and the words of his compositions were as if brought before the eyes of the listener.[89]

A famous and much-discussed example is the motet *In me transierunt irae tuae*

---

85. For *Marte potens*, see Lassus, *Sämtliche Werke*, ed. Haberl and Sandberger 1:61–67.
86. See Lassus, *Sämtliche Werke*, ed. Haberl and Sandberger, 3:58.
87. See Lassus, *Sämtliche Werke*, ed. Haberl and Sandberger, 11:57–59.
88. For an edition in modern score, see Orlande de Lassus, *Prophetiae Sibyllarum*, ed. Reinhold Schlötterer, *Sämtliche Werke*, neue Reihe, vol. 21 (Kasel: Bärenreiter, 1990), or the older edition by Hans Joachim Therstappen, *Das Chorwerk*, vol. 48 (Berlin: Kallmeyer, 1937).
89. See Gustave Reese, *Music in the Renaissance* (New York: Norton, 1959), 513, for the complete citation, which reads, in part, "He expressed [the text] so aptly with lamenting and plaintive melody, adapting it where necessary to the subject and the words, expressing the power of the different emotions, [and] presenting the subject as if acted before the eyes."

(see Example 25-22),[90] taken as a model by Joachim Burmeister in his *Musica Poetica* of 1606 for his exposition of "rhetorical" figures in music.[91] The text for Lassus's setting is centonized from arbitrarily selected verses from two separate Psalms (87:17 and 37:10, 18, and 22), appropriately chosen, it would seem, for their intensely emotional tone. Despite his pedantic approach (and a questionable application of terminology), Burmeister does provide an inventory of Lassus's compositional procedures

90. For an edition of the piece in modern score, see Lassus, *Sämtliche Werke*, ed. Haberl and Sandberger, 9:49–52.
91. In this connection, see Claude V. Palisca, "*Ut oratoria musica*: The Rhetorical Basis of Musical Mannerism," in *The Meaning of Mannerism*, ed. F. W. Robinson and S. G. Nichols (Hanover, N.H.: University Press of New England, 1972), 37–65. Also in *Studies in the History of Italian Music and Music Theory*, ed. Claude V. Palisca (New York: Oxford University Press, 1994).

EXAMPLE 25-22. Orlande de Lassus, *In me transierunt*

Thy wrath hath swept over me, and thy terrors have confounded me; my heart is disturbed, and my strength fails me; my sorrow is ever before me. Do not forsake me, O Lord, my God, neither be thou far from me.

that is almost contemporaneous with his musical works. The most noteworthy of the "figures" of musical rhetoric, as defined by Burmeister (and illustrated by Lassus), are as follows:[92]

1. a motive introduced imitatively by two or more voices and carried through several successive entries (*fuga realis*);
2. contrary motion between contrapuntal lines (*hypallage*);
3. the musical delineation of textual meaning in such a way that the music seems to acquire life (*hypotyposis*);[93]
4. a repetition of a single motive in stepwise progression (*climax*, i.e., a sequence);
5. a pairing of voices, either contrapuntally or homophonically (*anadiplosis*);
6. a point of imitation (*fuga*) using fewer than the full complement of voices (*anaphora*);
7. the juxtaposition of contrasting groups of voices, as in an antiphonal exchange (*mimesis*);
8. the introduction of semitones not belonging to the mode of the composition in a manner apt to arouse an emotion (*pathopoeia*);
9. a melodic passage that exceeds the normal range of the mode (*hypobole*);
10. the introduction of homophonic declamation (*noema*);

92. Some examples of Lassus's use of the "figures" described by Burmeister have been keyed to Example 25-22 with the numbers of the following list.
93. Burmeister appears to be attempting to describe here what we might refer to as a madrigalism.

11. a reiteration of the principal cadence or close (*supplementum*);
12. a climactic repetition of the consonances used with a single phrase of text (*auxesis*).[94]

Burmeister's neologisms have not been seen before (and they have not come into common use), but the enumeration of compositional devices has much in common with that outlined earlier for Josquin's *Ave Maria, virgo serena* (see pp. 514–18).

CONCLUSIONS

In the works of these four masters of the late sixteenth century—Palestrina, Victoria, Byrd, and Lassus—are found representative examples of all of the musical genres that were being cultivated at the time, both vocal and, thanks to Byrd, instrumental. Their compositions also embody a complete array of the musical styles that had been slowly and carefully codified and refined over more than a century and a half, from the 1420s on. The very substantial common ground among them, with respect both to genres and to musical styles, gives ample evidence to the careful observer and listener of a grand synthesis of the theoretical principles, the mensural usage, and the contrapuntal practices upon which their music is based. For a brief moment it would be known as an *ars perfecta*, but even as it reached its zenith, the winds of change were beginning to blow. Ere long music such as theirs would be referred to as the *stile antico*, the ancient style. But even today it remains a remarkable monument to their creative energies and to the vibrant musical culture of a fascinating period of history.

---

94. Not cited by Burmeister in conjunction with this example but mentioned elsewhere are the stark use of dissonance (*parrhesia*) and the common suspension (*syncopa*).

APPENDIX

1

The Conceptualization of Music
in the Renaissance

INTRODUCTION

If the music of the fifteenth and sixteenth centuries is to be understood as part of the general historical and cultural context framed for the present study, it must be approached on a practical level by means of the basic concepts and technical tools that were then in common use. The scholar wishing to integrate music into the larger historical picture must attempt to discover, as in other areas of reflective and artistic activity, in what manner and to what extent it is bound up with the intellectual currents and the philosophical and esthetic attitudes of the times. The musical perceptions and the specialized vocabulary of the present age are not necessarily well suited to an analysis of musical style focused on traits and developments that have historical significance for an earlier period. It is in fact possible to argue that their use to that end has often led to erroneous interpretations of such matters in one sense or another.

Certain stylistic features of the music of the Renaissance have been discussed by present-day authors in terms that would undoubtedly have baffled the musicians of the period. The observations that can be made by the anachronistic adoption of analytical techniques developed for use with the tonal music of the eighteenth century, and even more recent repertories, may have their teleological interest. However, they usually fail to reveal the compositional presuppositions and processes that served the musicians of the fifteenth and sixteenth centuries. Conversely, stylistic characteristics that were important for that era have all too frequently been overlooked or misunderstood because of assumptions and expectations based on later periods.

The passage of time brings ineluctable change, and in none of the arts has the transformation of style been more rapid or more decisive than for music. This has been especially true over the past three centuries or so as originality has become an increasingly essential criterion of artistic and esthetic merit. As a result, both the musical concepts and the esthetic values of the past have become increasingly foreign to the present and its music ever more inaccessible to the analytical tools of the modern workshop. It should be abundantly clear from the attempts made thus far to define and explicate the musical style of the Renaissance that its true historical significance and its original esthetic sense become evident only when viewed—insofar as the present state of musical scholarship will allow—from the conceptual matrix that produced it.[1]

In this regard, of course, music does not differ essentially from literature and the visual arts. Whatever the levels and varieties of esthetic experience of which we are currently capable, and whatever the affinities or actual connections between the artistic procedures of the past and some of those now in use, if any work of art is to be understood in historical terms, it must first be restored to its initial intellectual and technical context. As Erwin Panofsky observed:

> The objects of art history . . . can only be characterized in a terminology that is as reconstructive [of the past] as the experience of the art historian: it must describe the stylistic peculiarities, neither as measurable or otherwise determinable data, nor as stimuli of subjective reactions, but as that which bears witness to artistic "intentions." Now "intentions" can only be formulated in terms of alternatives: a situation has to be supposed in which the maker of the work had more than one possibility of procedure, that is to say, in which he found himself confronted with a problem of choice between various modes of emphasis.[2]

These comments are obviously pertinent to the history of music where artistic "intentions," as defined by Panofsky, can only be discovered—if indeed they have remained recoverable—in the light of alternatives actually available for deliberate, conscious use by the musician, whether in the compositional process or in the common conventions of performance.[3]

In approaching the music of the Renaissance, then, two difficult tasks confront us. We must identify, on the one hand, the musical concepts and practical procedures

1. The philosophical and methodological questions touched upon in the foregoing paragraph are much too complex to allow a detailed discussion of them in the present context. For a number of probing arguments and pertinent bibliographical references, see, for example, Bernhard Meier's *The Modes of Renaissance Polyphony*, trans. Ellen Beebe, 23–34 and *passim*; Perkins, "Mode and Structure in the Masses of Josquin," *Journal of the American Musicological Society* 26 (1973), 189–202; and "Modal Strategies in Okeghem's *Missa Cuiusvis Toni*," in *Music Theory and the Exploration of the Past*, ed. Christopher Hatch and David W. Bernstein (Chicago: University of Chicago Press, 1993), 59–71.

2. Erwin Panofsky, "The History of Art as a Humanistic Discipline," in *Meaning in the Visual Arts* (Garden City, N.Y.: Doubleday Anchor Books, 1955), 20f. Much of this essay is applicable to the problems under discussion here.

3. It is undeniable, of course, that certain creative processes recede, with frequent use, from the levels of conscious choice to those that might be characterized as "intuitive" or "instinctive." However, the only useful premise for the historian in such cases is that every phase of artistic activity, whether in composition or performance, can be traced ultimately to a principle once learned or a procedure that required at some point thought and practice. Experience has shown, moreover, that these connections can usually be established.

to which both the composer and the performer may have had recourse. In other words, we must determine the manner in which the basic elements of style were conceived and, given the contemporary modes of understanding, how they were most generally manipulated. And we must ascertain, on the other hand, insofar as we are able, how sounding music was perceived by the listener of the age.

This kind of understanding can be achieved to some extent through a recognition of the skills, conventions, and attitudes that informed the musical experience for an audience of the fifteenth or sixteenth century. However, the questions raised in the process are much more difficult to answer than those of a more practical nature, in part because of the subjective factors involved in musical perception, in part because evidence concerning the effects actually produced in the hearer is rather scanty. The theoretical treatises, so rich in technical explanations and conceptual insights, say little about the auditor's reactions, real or supposed, and the music itself still less. Even contemporary accounts of performances heard are often less than illuminating. We shall begin, then, with the more factual and objective aspect of the problem, where the ground is somewhat firmer under foot.

It should be noted first of all that the fundamental principles, the specialized vocabulary, and even the practical skills of the musician of the Renaissance had been forged piece by piece during the Middle Ages, not only for chant but also for polyphony. Their continued use in the fifteenth and sixteenth centuries thus formed an important link with the past, both conceptually and stylistically. It is, in fact, largely by tracing modifications in the theoretical treatment of traditional concepts and in their application to composition and performance that significant shifts in style can be identified and in some measure defined. Then, as now, the basic elements of the musical systems used in the Western world were essentially three: the scale (or gamut), upon which melodic construction is based; the mensuration (or meter), upon which rhythmic organization depends; and the counterpoint (or "harmony"), by which is meant here the principles and procedures governing the simultaneous combination of pitches and, therefore, in a larger sense, the weaving together of melodic lines. Let us examine each of these as it seems to have been understood by the musicians of the period.

⟶ THE TRADITIONAL SCALE ⟵

The scale that came into common use during the Middle Ages was one of three general types known to the ancient Greeks. It was designated by them the *diatonic* in contradistinction to those that were called *chromatic* or *enharmonic* because of differences that will be explained in due course. This diatonic scale consisted (and still consists) of a series of eight pitches bounded by the interval of an octave and repeated one or more times in order to fill the musical space to be organized. The octave was so named because of the eight steps or degrees traditionally contained within it, and its size was determined, as it had been by the Greeks, by the mathematical ratio of

2:1. This measurement referred to a string vibrating under tension, specifically to the pitch produced by its full length, on the one hand, and to that made by its division exactly in half, on the other.[4] The audible result is a characteristic blend of the two pitches so consonant, so "harmonious" in nature, that one seems to duplicate the other and is distinguishable from it only by its register.

Following the Greek tradition still, the octave was composed in turn of a tetrachord (or fourth) and a pentachord (or fifth), each of which also gets its name from the number of pitches or degrees encompassed within it. These smaller intervals were likewise defined by string ratios, the fifth by 3:2 (the pitch of the whole string compared to that produced by two-thirds of its length), the fourth by 4:3 (the whole string compared to three-fourths of its length). They are similarly identifiable to the ear by a characteristic blending of their two pitches that was perceived to diminish in its degree of euphony or consonance as the numbers by which the intervals are measured increase in size.

In addition to forming the octave when combined conjunctly (that is, by means of a pitch common to both), the latter two intervals also provided the basis for the division of the entire scale into its contiguous degrees. The fifth exceeds the fourth by an amount measurable in the string ratio of 9:8, which produces in the manner already indicated the small interval commonly designated as a tone.[5] The Greeks found this fact reason enough for employing the 9:8 interval to locate within the mathematically determined boundaries of the fourth and the fifth the intermediate scale degrees. The fourth can contain two such tones, producing a total of four pitches, and the fifth three, for a total of five pitches, but in either case there remains another, smaller musical interval not quite half the size of a tone. This segment of musical space was generally termed a semitone, and its inclusion in the musical systems of the Western world, although inevitable in view of the modes of thought that brought it about, disturbed rather disconcertingly their otherwise highly rational order.

The intervals discussed thus far, from octave to tone, were all perceived to be interrelated by the ancient Greeks and, consequently, by the medieval theorists who relied on the digest of their teachings attributed to Anicius Manlius Severinus Boethius (ca. 480–ca. 524).[6] The connections between them were held to be evident not only in a practical, musical sense but also in the mathematical proportions by which they were defined. These ratios are all of a type characterized by the ancients

---

4. In order to produce accurately the musical intervals under discussion here, the ratios given must be applied to vibrating strings of exactly the same thickness under the same degree of tension; hence the common device of dividing a single string according to the proportions indicated, as was done with the medieval monochord.

5. The word "tone" has been and may still be used with a variety of meanings; for example, in addition to designating the interval described, it can denote a pitch, a mode, and a melodic formula such as a Psalm tone. The signification intended is usually clear from the context in works dealing with the Middle Ages and the Renaissance, but the reader should be aware of the possibility of confusion.

6. The work in question is his *De institutione musica*; see Calvin Bower, "Boethius," *The New Grove Dictionary of Music*, 2:844f.

as superparticular because the larger term exceeds the smaller by only one of its aliquot parts. They consist, as we have seen, in small whole numbers that increase in a regular arithmetical progression as the intervals decrease in size from octave to fifth to fourth. There is, consequently, a reasonable, one might even say a predictable, leap in the numerical sequence from 4 to 9 in moving from the fourth to the tone: the highest number previously used is slightly more than doubled for an interval not quite half so large.[7]

With the semitone, however, as if by some caprice of natural law, the hitherto orderly progression is suddenly shattered. The interval is a remainder of sorts, very nearly half as large as the tone but with no rational mathematical connection to it. Its size, when expressed in terms of string ratios, requires the surprisingly large and awkward numbers of 256:243. Further, the tiny interval by which two semitones fall short of a tone—the so-called Pythagorean comma—is not only inaudible to most ears but also requires (in terms of string lengths) the even more unwieldy ratio of 531,441:524,288. Finally, because the semitone in question cannot divide a diatonic tone into two equal halves, its introduction into the scale as an irregular division of that interval resulted in another semitone of slightly larger size, consisting of the space remaining in a tone so divided and equal to the semitone of 256:243 plus the comma, often designated a major semitone. As we shall see, this acoustical phenomenon was to cause severe problems for the tuning of instruments in the fifteenth and sixteenth centuries once a division of the tones of the gamut into a continuous series of semitones had become fairly commonplace.

Despite this apparent aberration in an otherwise orderly system, the philosophers of ancient Greece, beginning with Pythagoras (ca. 582–ca. 507 B.C.), believed that the numerical relationships inherent in the diatonic scale were a veritable manifestation, both easily audible and rationally measurable, of the order governing the universe. This cosmological conviction was already unmistakably explicit in the writings of Plato (427?–347 B.C.), whose influence was to loom so large in the formation of attitudes toward the arts not only during the Middle Ages but with renewed strength during the Renaissance as well. In his *Timaeus*, for example, the distribution of the World Soul through the newly created Universe is described as having been done proportionately by using only those ratios contained within a diatonic scale extended through several octaves of musical space.[8] Elsewhere Plato applied this concept of musical order to the human soul as an explanation of the manner in which its various powers and virtues can function together independently yet "harmoniously."[9]

Thereafter, ideas of this nature were worked out in great detail by the Pythagorean and Platonic philosophers of ancient Greece and widely disseminated wherever classi-

7. Although the complexity of the calculations involved may be imperfectly appreciated by doing so, it is possible to observe that 9 is 2¼ times 4 and that the fourth is nearly 2½ times as large as the tone.

8. An account of that creation, together with an explanation of its musical implications, is found in Beekman Cannon, Alvin Johnson, and William Waite, *The Art of Music* (New York: Thomas E. Crowell, 1960), 9–12.

9. In *The Republic*, IV.443.c–e.

cal culture was known. Their currency was undiminished and their validity unquestioned still in the second century A.D., when Ptolemy of Alexandria (after 83–161) presented them systemically and with characteristic clarity in his treatises. It was primarily on Ptolemy that Boethius drew in writing his *De musica*, which transmitted to the Latin Middle Ages the Greek doctrine of harmonics. Since Boethius was well acquainted with Plato as well, he naturally gave due credence to the concept that musical proportions underlie good order in both the cosmos and the soul.

It was in fact Boethius who coined the Latin terms by which the Pythagorean view was to be known to the Western world all through the Middle Ages and beyond: the musical harmony of the spheres in the Platonic cosmos he called *musica mundana*, the harmony of the soul *musica humana*. Clearly distinguished from these two was a third category, *musica instrumentalis*, by which Boethius designated the music produced by human voices and instruments. For him the sounding art, however pleasant to the ear, was important primarily as a recognizable reflection of universal order that provided a quantifiable basis for cosmological speculation. Still, the diatonic scale, as a practical entity, was solidly grounded in a philosophical system that was widely known and accepted in the West all through the Renaissance.

The Greeks also had other ways of organizing their musical microcosm that they considered to be as much a part of the cosmological scheme of things as the diatonic scale. In all of these the basic structural unit was the tetrachord, and the intervals of the fourth, fifth, and octave (as determined by the string ratios given) provided the fixed points in musical space. One system was distinguished from another in the division of the tetrachord by the placement of its two movable intermediary pitches. As was mentioned, the two principal classes of tetrachord formation, besides the diatonic, were the chromatic and the enharmonic.

In its chromatic division the tetrachord contained a semiditone (a single interval larger than the tone by a semitone) and two semitones; in the enharmonic division it included a ditone (a single interval equal in size to two tones) and two tiny intervals, each half the size of a semitone and dubbed a *diesis*. For each of these general classifications there were also distinct varieties that differed slightly from one another in the string ratios actually used to determine the intervals separating the four pitches of the tetrachord.[10]

Despite this broad spectrum of scale structures from which to choose, medieval theorists seem to have had no practical use for any except the diatonic system constructed by means of the venerable Pythagorean ratios. The reasons for this may have been in part historical. The Greeks believed the diatonic scale to be the oldest, and they recognized that the chromatic and especially the enharmonic divisions of the tetrachord were rather recondite. Some of their scale divisions—subspecies of the main diatonic and chromatic types—may even have been the invention of their harmonists with no basis at all in musical practice. It is possible, then, that the diatonic

---

10. Ptolemy, for example, discusses two divisions for the enharmonic tetrachord, one of which he rejects, gives two acceptable ways of dividing the chromatic tetrachord, and cites four different types of diatonic tetrachords.

division of sonorous space was perceived during the Middle Ages in the light of Platonic views to be mathematically and philosophically superior to all others. However, considering the pragmatic orientation of much medieval writing on music, the most compelling motive for the widespread adoption of the diatonic scale and its quasi-exclusive use in the West over a period of centuries was more likely a close correspondence to the musical realities of liturgical plainchant.

Since the Pythagorean tones and semitones were nearest in size to the intervals used in the sacred monophony of the Christian church, it is not surprising that the chromatic and enharmonic scales, which could not have been easily reconciled to the requirements of the most substantial and significant musical repertory then in existence, were long neglected or ignored. Still, they were not forgotten. In the sixteenth century humanistic scholarship, with its emphasis on the culture of classical Greece, "rediscovered" its musical systems, gained a renewed understanding of them, and prompted in turn practical experiments with the types that had not been current. Some of these efforts produced little more than short-lived curiosities with no discernible influence on the development of musical style, but others were to have a profound effect on the use of accidentals in the contrapuntal practice of the late Renaissance.

If Pythagorean tuning was entirely adequate for the monophony of the early Middle Ages, it lent itself much less well to the complexities of polyphony, especially that involving instruments with a scale of fixed pitches and relatively frequent subdivision of the tone into semitones. Consequently, the increasing emphasis given to polyphonic composition from the twelfth century on generated increasingly pressing reasons for turning to some of the alternate tunings of the tetrachord that had been postulated in classical times for the diatonic scale. In time, renewed consideration was even given the work of Aristoxenus (fl. 4th century B.C.), a student of Aristotle whose methods had been vigorously attacked by harmonists of the Pythagorean school, including Ptolemy and Boethius.

Aristoxenus's fault, in the view of his critics, was to use a simple fractional division of the tone in tuning the tetrachord instead of relying on string ratios of the sacrosanct superparticular variety. Such a procedure was regarded by the Pythagoreans as a mathematical impossibility. As Hellenistic humanism came of age, however, and the Aristoxenian view came to be better understood, it was found to offer a starting point for various types of "tempered" tunings that were tried, starting in the sixteenth century, to alleviate problems of intonation in instrumental polyphony. Most notable among these attempts were meantone temperament, which continued in general use for keyboard instruments for upwards of two centuries, and equal temperament—the division of the octave into twelve equal semitones—which has subsequently come to reign supreme.[11]

---

11. The very notion of tempered tuning implies, nevertheless, the Pythagorean ratios; they had become the established framework within which the tempering of certain intervals was adopted. We are concerned here with the difficult problems of tuning only insofar as they affect or reflect the development of musical style during the Renaissance; but for an overview of the matter, see Mark Lindley, "Temperaments," *The New Grove Dictionary of Music*, 18:660–74.

As formulated in prototypical fashion, however—as for example in the *Dialogus de musica* by an anonymous theorist incorrectly identified as Odo, probably early in the eleventh century—the diatonic scale utilized for singing plainchant was strictly Pythagorean in structure. The intervals were measured in the traditional manner by the monochord, and the proportions were those we have come to know: 2:1 for the octave, 3:2 for the fifth, 4:3 for the fourth, 9:8 for the tone, and (although usually unspecified because it was produced as a kind intervallic remainder) 256:243 for the semitone. The total span of musical space so organized exceeded by just one tone the two-octave diatonic scale that was traditional with the Greek harmonists, their "greater perfect system." And with the exception of that additional tone placed at the bottom of the register, the sequence of intervals—tones and semitones—was precisely the same.

As Boethius (and others) had done earlier, the unknown author of the *Dialogus* designated each step of his monochord, and hence of his scale, with a letter of the alphabet, but with one very significant improvement. For duplications of the seven initial pitches at the octave he used the same series of letters, changing only their form to indicate the register in which a scale degree lies, instead of giving each of them a different letter, as had been done previously. The simple principle of octave duplication proved to be so eminently practical in assigning letter names to points on the scale that it is still in use today. The resulting sequence of pitches can be diagrammed as in Figure A-1.[12]

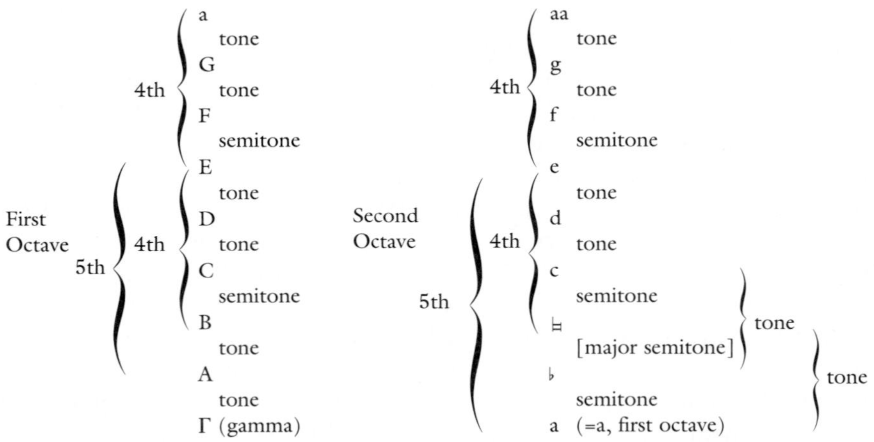

Figure A-1. The medieval gamut.

12. The theorist's prescriptions for generating this scale have been translated into English by Oliver Strunk, ed., *Source Readings in Music History*, rev. ed., ed. Leo Treitler (New York: Norton, 1998), 199–204. The theorist is there identified with Odo of Cluny, who lived in the first half of the tenth century, but more recent scholarship has questioned that identification; see Michel Huglo, "Odo," *The New Grove Dictionary of Music*, 13:503–4.

In the second octave of this scale the step "b" has two positions: one (b-fa) a semitone above the a immediately below, the other (b-mi) a semitone below the c immediately above. The latter corresponds to the arrangement of the lower octave, and the alternative placement disturbs the sequence of intervals as found there. However, this anomaly, like the structure of the diatonic scale generally, can be traced to Greek tradition. In addition to the two-octave system, in which each half consisted of two conjunct tetrachords with a tone added below as shown in Figure A-1 (from A to aa), the ancient harmonists also used a smaller structure. This "lesser perfect system," as it was called, has a single tetrachord added conjunctly above the lower octave. Because the same sequence of tones and semitones was maintained in each of its three constituent tetrachords, the resultant scale (from A to d by way of b-fa in Figure A-1) necessitated the insertion of an additional pitch just a semitone above a.

If the two systems were combined as a single scale by medieval theorists, it was probably once again not simply the consequence of following, perhaps too literally, the model provided by Boethius but rather in response to the requirements of plainchant. The liturgical repertory as codified during the Middle Ages made abundant use of both pitches. That they were regarded as alternate locations for the same scale degree is evident from the use of a single letter to designate them both. There was, nonetheless, a practical need to distinguish between them, and this was satisfied by signing the lower of the two with a rounded outline ♭ and calling it round or soft b, whereas the higher one was written with a squared outline and known as square or hard ♮.

Even though these two pitches were not to be construed in the medieval scheme of things as contiguous degrees of the scale, the practical result of their simultaneous inclusion in the diatonic system was to divide the tone from a to ♮ into two semitones of unequal dimension. The smaller interval (from a to ♭) corresponded in size (like that from ♮ to c) to the Pythagorean ratio of 256:243 and was generally known as the minor semitone, whereas the larger (from ♭ to ♮) exceeded it by a comma and was referred to as the major semitone. By the fourteenth century, presumably in the main as a result of the intensive cultivation of polyphony, a similar division of the tone was being effected elsewhere in the scale, beginning with the corresponding location in the lower octave between A and B. The degree to be altered had only to be lowered to within a minor semitone of the one just below or raised to within a minor semitone of the one just above—that is, shifted to a position analogous to that occupied by ♭ with respect to a on the one hand or like that occupied by ♮ with respect to c on the other.

In principle such an alteration could have been applied to any pitch within the system and in any register. In practice, however, the norms of melodic construction and the rules of counterpoint observed during the Renaissance tended to limit additional downward inflections to the scale degrees e and a, with an occasional example of d or even g, and upward inflections to f and c or, more rarely, g or d, and to restrict as well the range in which they occurred. (The reasons for these restraints will become clear as the principles regulating melodic writing and contrapuntal composition are explained.)

Alterations of this nature, which were not provided for in the diatonic system, were nonetheless understood—like ♭ and ♮—as alternate locations for the scale degrees to which they were applied. In order to indicate their use, then—when in fact a written sign was deemed necessary—the appropriate form of "b" was placed before the note to be affected, the soft one for an inflection downward, the hard one for an inflection upward. The former (♭) has been so used virtually without change in either its shape or its meaning ever since, whereas the latter had become somewhat stylized by the end of the fourteenth century, when it usually appeared in the more familiar form (♯) that is still current.[13] However, in many instances the Renaissance composer, or his copyist, assumed that the reasons for altering a given pitch would be perfectly clear to the performer from the musical context and consequently gave no explicit signal for the change.

Such an assumption was based on the existence of certain basic principles that every trained musician would have known, but there is good evidence that the rules were not always understood and applied in precisely the same manner. It is no surprise, then, that modern scholars often disagree on their application as well. There is little difficulty, as a rule, as long as a presumed inflection is reasonably routine. But when it comes to more exceptional usage—the very cases that are of greatest historical interest and most significant, as a rule, for the development of style—there can be considerable ambiguity as to the inflections actually implied and, as a result, legitimate differences of opinion as to what was intended.

For the medieval musician any deviation from the diatonic scale as it was laid out by our eleventh-century theorist was "accidental" in the best Aristotelian sense of the word. A reflection of that view is still to be seen in the use of the very term to designate the symbols of inflection and, by extension, the pitches that they produce. Because these "accidentals" were so regarded and, as we have seen, had no regular place in the diatonic system (unlike the two "b"s), they were designated *musica ficta* or *falsa*—that is, fictive or feigned scale degrees. Eventually they were to find a permanent place in the musical systems of the Western world, but this did not begin to happen until very late in the sixteenth century when the Renaissance was fast giving way to a new age.

Even though accidentals had by then become an increasingly prominent feature of polyphonic composition, they continued to be excluded by the theorists from the musical systems upon which that kind of composition was based. This was not simply because of the authoritative nature of the diatonic model, which could be traced

---

13. As those acquainted with the technical vocabulary of music generally in use will recognize, the soft or round "♭" is now called a flat because of the direction of the inflection it signs, and the hard or square "♮" is termed a sharp for similar reasons. There is yet another symbol in current use, the so-called natural sign (♮). Its form clearly derives from that of the square b, but its present meaning—that a sharp or a flat previously given is to be canceled—is a modern invention that was not known during the Renaissance.

not only to medieval practice but also to the writings of the Greek harmonists. Presumably, the newly acquired understanding of the chromatic and enharmonic divisions of the tetrachord, as formulated by Greek harmonists, *could* have been used as the basis for a thoroughgoing revision of the scales that were in actual use. That this was not done was probably due in large measure to the continuous use, all through the Middle Ages and the Renaissance, of the system of modes developed very early on in connection with the liturgical chant. The medieval modes were rooted entirely in the diatonic scale and apparently posited in theory no accidental scale degrees. Consequently, it was not until the secularization of musical culture was sufficiently advanced as to allow a gradual replacement of the church modes with the present major-minor system that the diatonic scale was subjected to any significant change.

The scale used during the fifteenth and sixteenth centuries, then, was essentially that codified by the beginning of the eleventh century. It was, however, more extended. By the thirteenth century a fifth was regularly added to the traditional double octave at the upper register, and the resulting pitches were signed, by analogy with those found in the octave below, bb (both round and square), cc, dd, and ee. The different forms of the letters, which had been introduced by the anonymous medieval author to distinguish among the three-octave registers wholly or partially included in the expanded system, were not always maintained by the theorists of later centuries. Rather, at some point a descriptive adjective was used to specify the octave meant: excluding the degree *gamma*, which was known as *gravissimus*, the individual pitches of the lower octave (from A to G) were called *grava*; those of the upper octave (from a to g) *acuta*; and those in the added fifth (from aa to ee) *superacuta*.

This expansion of the diatonic scale to a total of twenty degrees or steps appears to have occurred in conjunction with the codification of the staff and the hexachord system, to be discussed shortly, and may in fact have resulted in part from one or both of these developments. Once the three structures became interlocked in the manner described below, most theorists were content to let the diatonic system stand without further additions. Thus when Tinctoris wrote his *Expositio manus* in the 1470s, the scale on which he based his work encompassed only the two octaves and a sixth from Γ to ee, and the same was true of Zarlino nearly a century later when he was preparing the *Istitutioni harmoniche* of 1558. When it came to composition, however, those limits were not always strictly observed. Already in the fifteenth century Okeghem made use of an entire fifth below Γ (in his *Missa Fors seulement*), while his contemporary Busnoys extended the upward range to a fourth above ee (in his chanson *Pour entretenir mes amours*). Significantly, a considerable expansion of the musical space effectively utilized in composition and performance was one of the signal achievements of the musicians of the Renaissance.[14]

14. For some interesting reflections upon this aspect of Renaissance music, see Edward E. Lowinsky, "The Concept of Physical and Musical Space in the Renaissance," *Papers of the American Musicological Society*, Annual Meeting, 1941 (Minneapolis, Minn.: Richmond, 1946), 57–84.

⌒⊃ THE STAFF ⊂⌒

One of the most ingenious achievements in the history of medieval music was undoubtedly the invention of notation. No other culture has developed a system of signs capable of conveying to the performer the intentions of the composer with sufficient accuracy and in enough detail to allow a fairly faithful transmission of a given composition over distance and even through time. Without it both polyphony and plainchant would have remained in the realm of improvisatory art and, therefore, virtually impossible to reconstruct historically. What is more, the stylistic development of Western music, which has depended to such a great degree upon a written record as a standard of historical comparison and a source of inspiration, would necessarily have been much different. The first step in the fashioning of that historically crucial system was the invention of symbols for indicating pitch, at least in a relative sense. Little by little the notational attempts of the early Middle Ages evolved into a flexible, concise representation of the degrees of the diatonic scale. It came to be called the staff (or stave), because of its form, and it proved to be of such sound design that it has continued in use practically unchanged to the present day.

Its structure was based, simply enough, on the establishment of a fixable correlation between the degrees of the diatonic system and a conveniently usable segment of visual space on a leaf of writing material. This was accomplished by locating the scale degrees to be shown along a vertical continuum at points determined with reference to a horizontal line of orientation. In its application such a method depended in turn upon an arbitrary association, made very early on, between grave pitches (those having low rates of vibration) and spatial depth, on the one hand, and between acute pitches (those with high rates of vibration) and height, on the other. The simple notions involved have become with time so widely accepted—and the resulting notational "picture" has itself so firmly shaped our thinking about melody —that one can now speak glibly of "high" pitches and of "low," of melodic "ascents" and "descents," with no danger of being misunderstood and no thought for what is implied historically by the use of such terms.

These conventions for the spatial representation of pitch, so basic to our notational system, first appeared in attempts to write out completely the music of the liturgy. The neumes, which by then depicted both the direction of the melodic "motion" and the precise number of pitches to be sung (but not the size of the intervals between them), began to be "heightened" on the page that they might convey more accurately to the eye the path to be followed by the voice.[15] The precision of that procedure was increased still further by adopting the drypoint lines scratched into parchment leaves before the copying of a text was begun as the axis of orientation for the notational symbols. The line itself was taken to stand for a scale degree,

---

15. Concerning the development of chant notation, see Richard Hoppin, *Medieval Music* (New York: Norton, 1978), 57ff.

usually one toward the center of the range to be covered, and the spaces immediately above and below for the steps flanking it in the diatonic system. The scale could then be extended in either direction to accommodate the remaining pitches needed for a given composition by increments proportional to the distance separating the three steps determined by the line. Additional degrees resulting from an extension of the sort were soon made yet more explicit by the placement of other lines parallel to the first with not only the lines themselves but also the intervening spaces each representing a step of the diatonic scale.

About the time of Guido of Arezzo (ca. 990–1050) a staff of four lines came to be the norm. Including lines, interlinear spaces, and—by analogy with the single dry-point line—the two spaces implied by the outer rules, this system encompassed a total of nine scale degrees. Some of these were separated by a whole tone, however, others by only a semitone, whereas the intervals of the staff—from line to space or space to line—were everywhere equidistant. In order to indicate the placement of the two semitones contained in each octave, Guido marked the pitch at its upper limit with a distinctive color: yellow for the letter "c" and red for "f," whether on a line or in a space. At the same time he placed the appropriate letter at the beginning of the staff to coincide with the color by which it was represented. With the help of these two devices Guido identified not only the scale degrees so marked but also, by implication, all others as well.[16]

There remained one ambiguity, however; the lines and spaces of the staff, even with colors and letters to identify the steps so depicted, did not specify by themselves the placement of the semitone with regard to "b." This problem was solved by means of the different forms of the letter that had been devised to distinguish between the two positions that it could occupy within the system. The appropriate symbol—♭ or ♮ —was simply placed before any note on that degree whenever confusion was possible in order to clarify the intervals around it. Perhaps in part because the soft "b" represented a departure from the order of the octave below, in part because it was initially less used, it became customary to sign the scale degree in question only where the lower position was wanted and to assume elsewhere the hard "b" (even though it, too, had to be specified at times). These indications were given not only for individual notes but occasionally, where the lowered "♭" was called for, for entire lines of the staff and even as a "signature" for complete compositions; it then appeared at the beginning of each staff and altered the degree so marked at every occurrence.

Once these two symbols had begun to be used routinely in the manner described, it was seen that they could be used with other scale degrees to indicate accidental pitch inflection. When employed in this way, they generally applied only to individual notes or to short melodic passages, but eventually such accidentals were given in turn as a signature for an entire piece. Already in the fifteenth century flats were spec-

---

16. Guido's explanation of the staff with the refinements of his devising is given in the *Prologus antiphonarii sui*, which has been translated into English by Strunk, ed., *Source Readings*, rev. ed., 211–14.

ified in this manner for "e," "a," and yet other degrees in addition to "b," and beginning with the late sixteenth and early seventeenth centuries, sharps were placed on "f," "c," and even further on in the sequence by fifths so begun.

It may seem odd that "flats" came into current use as a signature much before "sharps," but this was because they came to be regarded as a legitimate means for transposing a hexachord or a modal scale to a different range, as will be explained below, whereas the sharps, which were used primarily in cadential structures as a kind of contrapuntal ornament, were not viewed in a similar light until after the modal system had begun to give way to the first stages of major-minor tonality.

The use of a colored line to identify the crucial scale degrees—those reached by a semitone from below—did not continue for long, but the placement of an "f" or a "c" (and occasionally both) on some line of the staff as a *clef*, that is as a "key" to the scale degrees to be represented thereby, became a convention that is still observed.[17] With the passage of time, presumably to avoid possible confusion, each of the original clef signs was linked to a single step within the system. By the late Middle Ages the one denoted the F of its first octave, the other the c a fifth above (commonly known as "middle" c). Since the range covered by a single piece of music tended to be ever wider, however, the limitations placed on the meaning of those two symbols prompted the adoption of yet others.

The third clef sign to come into common use was the letter g indicating the scale degree a fifth above c. Its initial appearance is difficult to date, but it was still relatively rare in Tinctoris's day. Unlike the other two, it does not lie on the upper side of a semitone in the diatonic scale, and its adoption as a means of identifying the pitches on the staff probably reflects the practical needs and systematizing tendencies of the age; the degree in question is related intervallically to b as the latter is to the F below, the intervening space being a fifth in either case. And g, too, was the starting point for one of the three hexachords in that upper octave. Consequently, when any of these three clefs was placed on a line (as came to be the practice already by the twelfth century) and the staff projected upward or downward to the next, it too fell on a line.

This congruence made possible a continuous projection of the staff from one end of the diatonic scale to the other in the manner illustrated in Figure A-2 to form what is now known as the "great staff." At the low end of the system the gamma was also used on occasion as a clef—perhaps by analogy with its replication two octaves higher—for those relatively rare instances in which the general range spanned a fourth or a fifth below it. As a rule, when this happened, the Greek letter that gave its name to that step was also placed on a line of the staff, but occasionally the "g" clef was simply taken from its regular position two octaves up and pressed into service to indicate *gamma*.

---

17. In the theoretical language of the late Middle Ages and the early Renaissance, as used by Tinctoris, for example, the term *clavis* (plural, *claves*) designated generally the letter names for the degrees of the diatonic scale (see below, Figure A-2).

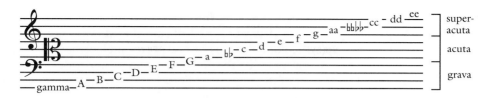

FIGURE A-2. The great staff in the fifteenth century.

With use the letter symbols became stylized to some extent, especially the two that were oldest and most frequently employed. Once their origin is understood, however, the basic form can usually be discerned and the meaning recognized, as Figure A-3 shows.

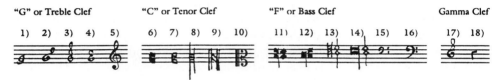

FIGURE A-3. Clef signs used during the fifteenth and sixteenth centuries.

1) Yale University, Beinecke Library, MS 91, The "Mellon Chansonnier" (ca. 1475), f. 5ᵛ: Busnoys, "A une dame."
2) Ibid., f. 11ᵛ: Busnoys, "A qui vens tu."
3) Petrucci, *Missarum Josquin liber secundus* (1505), *Missa Ave maris stella*, Kyrie (superius).
4) Formschneider, Isaac's *Choralis Constantinus* (1550), "Ideo quod nascitur." (Apel, *The Notation of Polyphonic Music*, 169.)
5) Modern
6) Cambrai, Bibliothèque Communale, MS 6 (1430s), f. 4ᵛ: Du Fay, Kyrie. (Apel, *The Notation of Polyphonic Music*, 363.)
7) Oxford, Bodleian Library, MS Canonici Misc. 213 (1420s), f. 73: Du Fay, "Quel fronte signorille." (Apel, *The Notation of Polyphonic Music*, 357.)
8) Petrucci, *Missarum Josquin liber secundus* (1505), *Missa D'ung aultre amer*, "Patrem" (superius).
9) & 10) Modern
11) Paris, Bibliothèque Nationale, MS f. frç. 1584 (ca. 1375), f. 456ᵛ: Machaut, "Dous amis." (Apel, *The Notation of Polyphonic Music*, 357.)
12) Paris, Bibliothèque Nationale, MS ital. 568 (ca. 1400), f. 138: anon., "Benedicamus Domino." (Apel, *The Notation of Polyphonic Music*, 379.)
13) The "Mellon Chansonnier" (cf. no. 1), f. 18ʳ: Busnoys, "Ja que li ne."
14) Petrucci, *Missarum Josquin liber secundus* (1505), *Missa Hercules dux ferrarie*, Kyrie (bassus).
15) Rome, Biblioteca Apostolica Vaticana, MS Chigi C. VIII.234 (1490s), f. 125: Okeghem, *Missa Requiem*, "Rex glorie" (*Collected Works*, ed. Plamenac, vol. 2 plate xiii).
16) Modern
17) MS Chigi C. VIII.234 (cf. no. 15), f. 44: Okeghem, *Missa Fors seulement*, Kyrie (*Collected Works*, ed. Plamenac, vol. 2, plate xi).
18) Florence, Biblioteca Medicea Laurenziana, MS Acquisti e doni 666, The "Medici Codex," f. 93: Mouton, "Peccata mea, Domine."

The span of a ninth covered by the four-line staff corresponded to the ideal range of each of the eight modes that were used during the Middle Ages in the classification (and eventually the composition) of ecclesiastical plainchant. In fact, it frequently exceeded in actual practice the melodic limits of individual pieces, especially from the oldest layers of the repertory. Four lines were usually adequate for the notation of sacred monophony, then, and a staff of that breadth continues to be used for it even today. With the advent of polyphony, however, the separate parts went beyond that modest range much more consistently, especially when written for instruments, and this made necessary some adjustment with the staff itself.

In order to accommodate the scale degrees lying more and more frequently beyond its bounds, two devices inherent in its very nature came gradually into systematic use. The one most often seen was a simple change of clef. Each of the signs could be placed, in principle, on any of the four lines. Accordingly, when the melodic motion would otherwise have taken the notes off the staff, the clef being used at that point could be shifted to the next line, up or down as the circumstances required. Or an adjacent clef was introduced in an appropriate position in its stead, thus moving the problematic passage onto the existing lines and spaces. Clef changes of this kind had in fact been used at times even for the chant. Late medieval compositions not uncommonly spanned as much as an octave and a fourth or a fifth, making some modification indispensable, and yet others of rather modest range were more conveniently adapted to prevailing notational habits in the same manner.

The other solution to the same problem was the temporary addition of a line or two, either above or below the staff as dictated by the direction of the melody. In this way the relation of a small group of notes lying outside the permanent lines of the staff to those located within them could be clearly shown. This simple expedient—the use of what one now calls "ledger lines"—was nothing more than a momentary expansion of the staff to five or more lines. Both the shifting of clefs and the introduction of ledger lines entailed some scribal inconvenience and a certain danger of error, however, whether to the copyist or to the performer. Not surprisingly, then, larger staffs were also tried: five lines as early as the twelfth century for the sacred polyphony of the time and six for the secular music of fourteenth-century Italy (see Figures A-4a and Figure A-4b). But it was the five-line format that had come to prevail generally as the fifteenth century began, and, with remarkable staying power, it has remained the standard up to the present age.

The special requirements of polyphonic composition probably played a major role as well in the development of the great staff, which usually consisted during the Renaissance of ten lines and the eleven resulting spaces (counting the two inferable from its outer rules). Its usefulness lay in its ability to carry the entire diatonic system from *gamma* to ee, thus allowing the composer to represent all of the scale degrees available to him across the entire musical range then currently employed. A staff of this structure (illustrated in Figure A-2), with its three constituent octaves descrip-

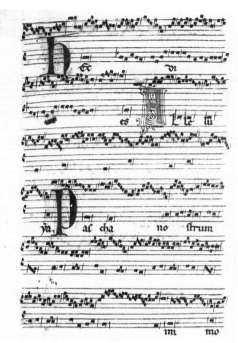

FIGURE A-4a. Twelfth-century setting of the Gradual and Alleluia for Easter showing a four-line staff for the chant and a five-line staff for the duplum (Florence, Biblioteca Laurenziana, MS Pluteus 29.1, f. 92ʳ).

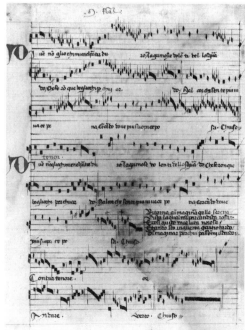

FIGURE A-4b. Landini's *ballata Divennon gli ochi mie*, showing the typical six-line staff (Florence, National Library, MS Panciatichi 26, f. 39ᵛ).

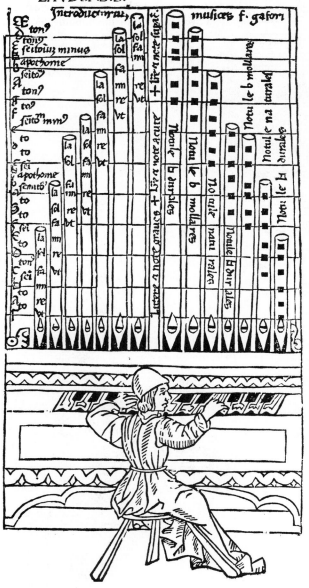

THEORICA MVSICE FRANCHINI GAFVRI LAVDENSIS.

tively labeled in the usual manner, appeared frequently as a didactic illustration in the treatises of fifteenth-century theorists, including Gaffurius and Tinctoris, whose formulations of it may be seen in Figures A-5a and A-5b.

At some point, however, the great staff began to be used in a practical way as a basic score for the composition of polyphony. By sketching simultaneously on such a system all of the voices or parts to a piece, the composer could see at a glance the relationships among them, both horizontally and vertically, which is to say both melodically and contrapuntally. It is not clear when this came to be current practice. The technical procedure in question may well have developed in the second half of the fifteenth century along with an imitative style of composition, but it cannot be documented earlier than about the 1530s. From then on, in any case, the ten-line staff obviously came to be widely used for composition by the masters of contrapuntal polyphony.[18]

FIGURE A-5a. Woodcut from the title page of Gaffurius's *Theorica musice.*

18. See Figure A-2 and pp. 514–18.

HEXACHORDS AND SOLMIZATION

One of the practical difficulties faced by the musicians of the Middle Ages came in correctly placing the semitones of the diatonic scale as they sang the melodies of the liturgy. This led to the invention of one of the most widely used didactic devices to come out of the musical traditions of that age: solmization by hexachords. Like the present design of the staff, the fundamental notions of the hexachordal system go back to the early 1100s and the fertile mind of Guido of Arezzo. He discovered in the initial pitch of the successive lines of a hymn in honor of John the Baptist an ascending scale of six contiguous degrees—hence the name "hexachord," meaning literally six strings or the sounds produced by them. To identify the individual steps of this pattern, he adopted the syllable to which each was sung in the hymn: *ut, re, mi, fa, sol,* and *la* (see Figure A-6). Four of the five intervals separating these pitches were a tone in size, but exactly at the center, between *mi* and *fa,* was a semitone.

Guido's choice was ingenious because a hexachord of that exact composition can be formed at three different locations within the diatonic octave, each a fourth distant from the next: starting from g (with a square ♭), from c (with the "natural" sequence of pitches illustrated by the hymn), and from f (with a round ♭). It was possible, nonetheless, to distinguish among them by means of the special "properties" cited:[19] the hexachord starting from g was described as "hard" (*durum*) because of the square or hard ♭ needed to yield a semitone between *mi* and *fa*; the one built on c was termed "natural" because it was derived without change from the degrees of the diatonic system; and the one from f was called "soft" (*mollis*) because of

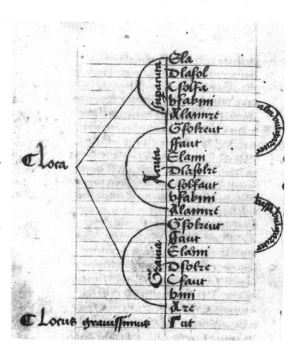

FIGURE A-5b. Diagram from Tinctoris's *Expositio manus*, showing the great staff as represented in the fifteenth century (Brussels, Royal Library, MS II. 4147, f. 2ᵛ).

19. The technical term used in the fifteenth and sixteenth centuries was either the Latin word *proprietas* or one of its vernacular derivatives.

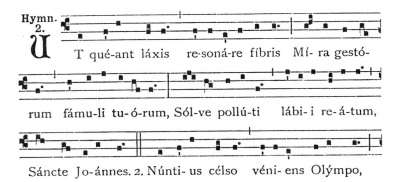

FIGURE A-6. The hymn *Ut queant laxis* (cf. the *Liber usualis*, p. 1504).

the round or soft ♭ required, again, for the proper placement of the semitone.

It was possible, therefore, to begin with the lowest step of the diatonic scale—*gamma*—and to "deduce" seven complete hexachords (known to the theorists by the Latin term *deductiones*). Because they were generated successively, they were also overlapping. Consequently, the degrees of the scale—with the exception of the first three and the last—could all be construed in at least two and sometimes three separate hexachords of different properties. The resulting system provided for each degree of the diatonic system three distinct means of identification, making it possible for each of the twenty steps it then contained to know the intervals by which it was approached and left in either direction. Each of the traditional locations on the staff was designated first of all by its letter name (in Latin, *clavis*) with the octave to which it belonged indicated at times by the form given to its symbol; to this was added the syllable or syllables (*voces*) used for its "solmization"[20] in all of the pertinent "deductions"; and if the range required further specification, the appropriate adjective—*gravis, acutus,* or *superacutus*—could be given as well (see Figure A-7). The singer could then negotiate with security any portion of

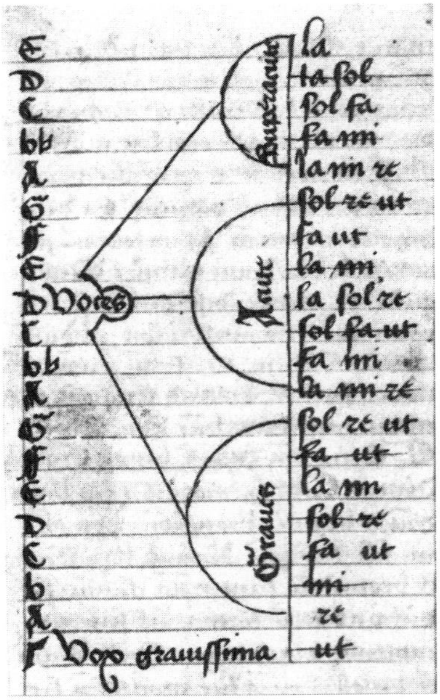

FIGURE A-7. The diatonic system as depicted in Tinctoris's *Expositio manus* (Brussels, Royal Library, MS II.4147, f. 4ʳ).

20. The word itself, like "sol-fa," the Latin *solfisatio*, or the Italian *solfeggio*, is obviously derived from the syllables used in the process.

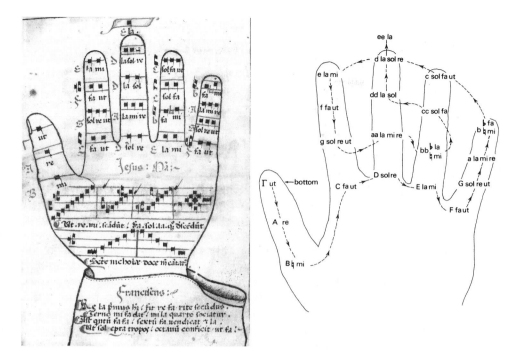

FIGURE A-8. The Guidonian hand as depicted in a Mantuan manuscript (Oxford, Bodleian Library, MS Can. Liturg. 216, f. 168ʳ), and a diagram showing how it was used to trace the scale (cf. *The New Grove Dictionary of Music*, 17:458).

the total gamut (to use for the entire scale the name derived from its first degree, *gamma-ut*). This was accomplished by means of a simple procedure known as "mutation"—that is, by shifting from one hexachord to another whenever the range or a change in the placement of the semitone required it.

To help the singer to learn and to recall readily the letter names and the apposite solmization syllables for the twenty degrees of the diatonic system, the traditional mnemonic device was the hand—usually the left with the palm held forward. Starting at the tip of the thumb with *gamma-ut*, and proceeding in a clockwise direction from the exterior inward, the articulations and ends of the fingers were each assigned a scale degree. Since there are nineteen such locations (*loca*) in the hand, all the steps of the system could thus be accommodated except the last, e-la, which was simply placed in space above the index finger (see Figure A-8).

The fifteenth and sixteenth centuries produced a significant number of practical treatises, written in all sizes for professional and amateur alike, that begin with a diagram and an explanation of the Guidonian hand. This suggests persuasively that complete mastery of the diatonic system—with its letter names, solmization syllables, and range designations—continued to be regarded all through the period as an indispensable initial step in the acquisition of musical skills. Tinctoris says so explicitly, moreover, at the conclusion of his own detailed treatment of the topic: "I exhort the young to study [the hand] earnestly as the foundation of music. For, as all sound reason teaches, where there is no foundation, one cannot build. Thus it is that without a knowledge of the hand, no one can distinguish himself in music."[21]

The attention given to this aspect of a musician's training during the Renaissance is to be explained not only by the uninterrupted use of traditional plainchant in the celebration of the Christian liturgy but also by the usefulness of solmization in the performance of polyphony, both vocal and instrumental. The same gamut was used for both, of course; consequently, the hexachordal system served as well for one as for the other in maintaining the fundamental intervallic order of the diatonic scale.

At the same time, however, it offered a ready tool for altering the traditional sequence of tones and semitones by accidental inflection. As has been seen, the desired placement of b—either a semitone above a or a semitone below c—was effected by selecting the appropriate hexachord: the hard one built on g for b-mi or the soft one on f for b-fa. Similarly, if a semitone was wanted at a point in the diatonic system where it did not regularly occur, it could be introduced by simply construing the two notes to be so related with the syllables *mi* and *fa* and locating the surrounding intervals in accordance with the pattern invariably followed in every hexachord. Or, conversely, the solmization could be "deduced" from a scale degree traditionally not so used in order to produce the semitone (*mi-fa* or *fa-mi*) where it was required.

It is not certain, once again, when procedures of this kind first came into common use. By the 1480s, however, the possibilities had been thoroughly explored. They were systematized to some extent by the Spanish theorist Bartolomeo Ramos of Pareia, who was working in Bologna at the time. In order to provide solmization for the accidentals most frequently heard in the music of his day, Ramos posited two additional series of deductions. These were to be used in conjunction with that ascribed to Guido, and each of them was constructed on identical principles (see Figure A-9).[22] One of these was generated from FF (a step below *gamma-ut*) with two subsequent starting points, each a fourth above the last as in the Guidonian system.

Although it takes its point of departure from outside the hand, the first hexachord of this series duplicates in its octave repetitions the soft hexachords of the traditional scheme. By contrast the other two sets of deductions, which begin from b♭ and e♭, respectively, introduce accidentals on both the latter degree and on a♭, neither of which is found in the diatonic scale. The other series of deductions was construed from A-*re* (a step above *gamma-ut*) and proceeded likewise by fourths with hexa-

21. See Tinctoris, *Expositio manus*, ed. Albert Seay, Corpus scriptorum de musica, vol. 22, no. 1 ([Rome]: American Institute of Musicology, 1975), 56.

22. See Bartolomeo Ramos de Pareia, *Musica practica* (Bologna, 1482) and the English translation by Clement A. Miller, Musicological Studies and Documents 44 (Stuttgart-Neuhausen: American Institute of Musicology, 1993), 77.

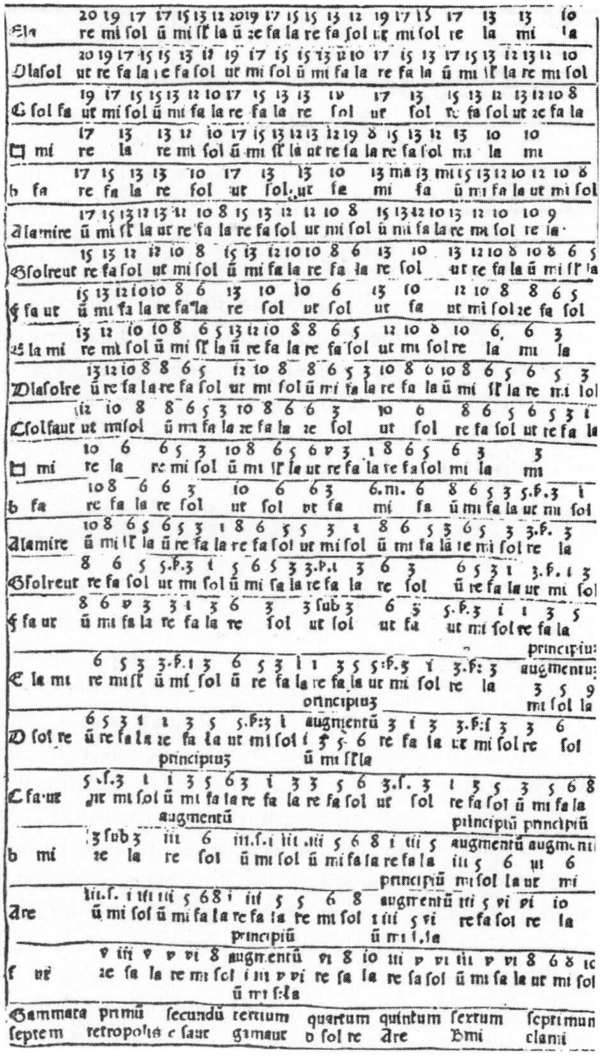

chords also starting from d and g. The last, like the hexachords on f in the preceding supplementary series, is a duplication of the Guidonian system, coinciding in this instance with its hard hexachords. But the first two deductions require—in order that *mi* and *fa* might lie each time just a semitone apart—the accidentals c♯ and f♯, respectively, neither of which is in Guido's hand.

Ramos did not systematize any further hexachordal deductions. As it was, his two supplementary sequences made possible the formation of a hexachord on each of the seven steps of the diatonic octave—if one is willing to accept both b♭ and e♭ in lieu of the uninflected *claves*—and provided for a semitone division of some sort for each of the tones contained within it. Since his additions constituted rational and familiar procedures for dealing with the accidentals that were most often applied in the polyphony of the fifteenth century, Ramos may have seen no need to add yet others. It should be noted, however, that the process he had thus begun could be extended—theoretically at least—to the entire diatonic scale.

FIGURE A-9. Diagram showing the three sequences of deductions from Ramos's treatise *Musica practica*.

If one were to continue from e♭ upward by perfect fourths, generating each time a new hexachord (and allowing octave substitutions where needed to stay within the established range), flats would have to be added in turn to d, g, c, and f. Similarly, if one were to proceed from a downward by fourths (again with the requisite octave repetitions), sharps would have to be applied successively to g, d, a, e, and b. In this manner, then, both a flat and a sharp could have been supplied for each degree of the diatonic octave.

In actuality, however, most of these accidentals were rarely if ever used in the music of the Renaissance. Late in the sixteenth century both the number and the frequency of accidentals increased dramatically in the secular repertory. Not until then was one likely to hear flats on more than two or three different degrees or sharps on more than one or two in the course of a single work. Not that the possibilities inherent in Ramos's formulation of the hexachord system had not been wholly grasped by theorists and composers alike. There are occasional but instructive indications—works of an exceptional nature such as Willaert's celebrated canon *Quidnam ebrietas*[23]—that the fullest implications of the hexachordal system, as reflected in Ramos's extension of the practice of solmization, had been clearly seen. If great restraint was long shown in exploiting its more radical possibilities, it may have been because of an enduring attachment to a system of modes based entirely on the diatonic gamut, which was more ancient and venerable still than the Guidonian hand.

THE MODES: THEORY AND PRACTICE

By the fifteenth century the system of modes associated with the music of the Western world had become fraught with complex subtleties.[24] This was true not so much of the relatively simple concepts by which modes were defined and explained by the theorists as it was of the diverse practical ramifications stemming from centuries of usage. For the notion of mode appears to be as ancient as the repertory of liturgical melody with which it evolved and to which it owes in significant measure its remarkable longevity. In the treatises on music written during the ninth century, when medieval theorists first gave serious practical consideration to such problems, the modes were treated primarily as a system of classification. They were a means of grouping chants with melodic profiles that were similar at points crucial for their recognition and of distinguishing the general type so constituted from others within the total corpus of sacred chants.

The modes may reflect at that point a stage in the history of plainsong when the melodies were transmitted orally and sung from memory—a time, in other words, when they were for the most part essentially formulaic in character. The Latin word most commonly used for mode during the Middle Ages was, in fact, *tonus*, the very term used to designate, then as now, the melodic formulae adapted to the singing of Psalms, canticles, and other texts of similar nature. These formulae or tones shared certain basic structural principles, but each was nevertheless distinctive by virtue of clearly recognizable traits such as the scale degree (or degrees) used as the final note;

23. See, for example, Joseph S. Levitan, "Adrian Willaert's Famous Duo *Quidnam ebrietas*," *Tijdschrift der Vereeniging voor Nederlandsche Muziekgeschiedenis* 15 (1939): 166–233, and cf. Edward E. Lowinsky, "Adrian Willaert's Chromatic Duo Re-examined," *Tijdschrift voor Muziekwetenschap* 18 (1956): 1–36.
24. For a comprehensive history of modal concepts and practices, both in Western music and in a broader cultural perspective, see Harold S. Powers, "Mode," *The New Grove Dictionary of Music*, 12:376–450.

FIGURE A-10. The *cantiunculae* of Johannes Affligemensis.

the pattern of tones and semitones immediately above and below that final; characteristic melodic phrases that recur in predictable ways, especially as intonations and cadential figures; and the consistent use of specific scale degrees (measured from the final) as starting, pivotal, and cadential points in typical melodic lines and as a note to be reiterated—a tenor or *tuba*—in declaiming lengthy texts.[25]

It is perhaps not surprising, then, that the theorists of the ninth century—starting with Aurelian of Réôme and Regino of Prüm, who were among the first to address the problem—present the familiar melodic patterns as prototypical formulae sung to syllables of unknown meaning or to didactic aphorisms (see Figure A-10).[26]

25. Concerning a number of the tones that exemplify these features, see Hoppin, *Medieval Music*, 79–84; cf. Gustave Reese, *Music in the Middle Ages* (New York: Norton, 1940), 172–85.
26. See Johannes Affligemensis, *De musica cum tonario*, chap. 11, "ad demostrandam plenius troporum cognitionem, cantiunculas," ed. Joseph Smits van Waesberge, Corpus scriptorum de musica 1 ([Rome]: American Institute of Musicology, 1950), 86. The melodic formulae in question, the venerable *Noeane* tunes and their Latin counterparts, are also cited by Reese, *Music in the Middle Ages*, 172–74.

They served in that context generally to introduce a *tonary*, as in the case of Johannes Affligemensis, from whose treatise Figure A-10 is taken, that is a classification of the principal chants in current use according to the model to which they most closely conformed. The importance of such catalogues was diminished considerably over the next two centuries by the development of a notational system that was both reasonably specific and easily used.

Nonetheless, the musical features deriving from the ancient types upon which the tonaries had been based were embodied in the plainsong repertory as recognizable modal norms. These melodic conventions continued to be observed despite the changes introduced as the traditional melodies were codified in written form (or perhaps, in some instances, because of them). As a result, a feeling for what was typical of a given mode persisted as long as the chant remained in daily use, as it did in much of western Europe until late in the sixteenth century, and provided the basis for the initial training given every musician.

Shortly after the earliest tonaries began to appear, the first tentative efforts were made to rationalize and explain the modes systematically by drawing upon the concepts of Greek theory. During the Middle Ages these were not known in Europe from original sources but had been transmitted to the Latin west by authors such as Martianus Capella (fl. early fifth century) and Boethius. Consequently, the writers who tried to reconcile those ancient doctrines with the everyday realities of the chant some 400 years later approached the received texts from a much different frame of reference. They either unwittingly misread their sources or simply extracted from them that which they found somehow pertinent to their own needs, ignoring all that could not be understood or put to practical use. This was clearly the case with the various authors of the collection of treatises known as the *Alia musica*. Perhaps because the concept was foreign to their experience they failed to perceive, for example, that the Greek *tonoi* were all composed of the same two-octave system and that they differed from one another only in the position each occupied in sonorous space (in a manner not unlike our major and minor scales).

They found much more relevant to their own musical practice the Greek notion of *species*, definable as the sequence of tones and semitones within the consonant intervals of superparticular proportion (i.e., fourths, fifths, and octaves). Since the harmonists constructed their diatonic system of tetrachords, each comprising two tones and a semitone, it was possible to arrange the four constituent scale degrees and the sequence of three intervals separating them in three different ways: either the semitone could be placed below the two tones, or between them, or above them. These three configurations were referred to by the Greek theorists, and by those who followed them, as species of fourth. Similarly, when a tone was combined with a tetrachord, producing a fifth comprising three tones and a semitone, those four intervals could be combined in four ways differing as to the placement of the semitone and resulting, consequently, in four species of fifth. And when fourth and fifth were construed together as an octave, seven separate configurations or species became possible (see Figure A-11).

Three species of fourth   Four species of fifth

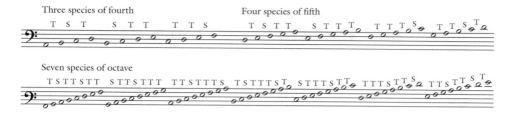

Seven species of octave

FIGURE A-11.   The species of fourth, fifth, and octave in the diatonic system.

The Hellenistic theorists used the concept of species in relating their eight *tonoi* to a fixed point of reference (the thetic *mese*, the central degree of the Dorian *tonos*), to the two-octave scale constructed around it, and to each other. In the process they assigned to each of the eight complete octaves of the greater perfect system the name of the *tonos* having the same octave species within the segment of its overall range that corresponded to the central octave of the Dorian *tonos*. Despite the complexities involved, the ninth-century authors of the *Alia musica* recognized that each of the eight modes associated with liturgical plainchant could be seen, ideally, as defined by a characteristic species of octave located either above or around its final. They perceived, in addition, that the lowest of these modal octaves coincided, by and large, with the first diatonic octave of the greater perfect system. And they apparently concluded that the eight modes familiar to them through the chant could be identified with the eight *tonoi* of the harmonists.

Having gone that far, it was but a short step to match the Greek names for their *tonoi* (and the corresponding octave species) with the eight modes then in use. This they did—not without some violence to the older system—in ascending order as follows: Hypodorian, Hypophrygian, Hypolydian, Hypomixolydian, Dorian, Phrygian, Lydian, and Mixolydian.[27]

This newly borrowed nomenclature for the modes thus took its place beside two others that had already been long in use. The more ancient, it would seem, paired the modes under ordinal numbers taken from the Greek and applied consecutively to the four regular finals of the chant—D, E, F, and G—once again in ascending order. In this scheme the first pair of modes were called *Protus,* and they were followed in turn, two by two, by *Deuterus, Tritus,* and *Tetrardus.* The individual modes of a pair were then further distinguished by their range with respect to the final.

If the musical space to be organized was the octave immediately above the final, the mode was called authentic; if that space spanned not only the fifth above the final but also the fourth below it, it was termed plagal. These names, although never lost to Western theorists, were replaced in common use by an ordinal system using the numerals consecutively from one through eight—initially with their Latin names—

27. The rather tortuous process by which the concepts of Greek theory began to be assimilated to the practical distinctions of the chant has been followed, with all due caution, by Jacques Chailley in the introduction to his edition of the *Alia musica* (Paris: Centre de documentation universitaire, 1965), 3–56.

with each odd number designating an authentic mode and the following even number its plagal companion. Thus *primus, tertius, quintus,* and *septimus* denoted the authentic modes on D, E, F, and G respectively, while *secundus, quartus, sextus,* and *octavus* indicated the corresponding plagals.

A further refinement in the theoretical definition of the modal system used in Europe during the Middle Ages was added in the eleventh century by Hermann the Lame (1013–54), a monk at the Benedictine monastery of Reichenau (which was located on an island in the Lake of Constance). Working from the notions of final and range, which have always been basic to any definition of mode, Hermann adopted the concept of species to systematize the relationship between them. He observed that modes sharing a final, despite their differences in range and octave species, also shared the same species of fourth and fifth. In the characteristic octave of each member of the pair, the fifth was common, and the fourths, although an octave apart, were otherwise identical.

Beginning with the modes closing on D, Hermann numbered consecutively their constituent species of consonance. The order he followed was arbitrary, but it corresponded to that adopted for the modes themselves; the fourth from A to D and the fifth from D to a, from which the plagal of the first modal pair was formed, were designated as the first of their respective species. Mode 1 could thus be seen to consist of the first species of fifth, starting from the final, with the first species of fourth added conjunctly above it, and mode 2, conversely, as having the first species of fourth added conjunctly below. The remaining modes were then defined in the same manner. The second pair was construed as comprising the second species of fifth (E to b) with the second species of fourth above it (b to e) for mode 3 and below it (B to E) for mode 4. Similarly, the third pair was conceived as spanning the third species of fifth (F to c) with the third species of fourth above (c to f) for mode 5 and below (C to F) for mode 6.

The modes on G could be constructed in much the same manner; however, they posed particular problems. There remained a fourth species of fifth (G to d), unused elsewhere, that could be seen as characteristic of both the authentic and plagal forms based upon it. But that fifth was combined with a fourth (d to g above for mode 7 and D to g below for mode 8) having the same sequence of tones and semitones as that from A to D. Its species was therefore the first as in modes 1 and 2. Moreover, mode 8 also shared with the authentic mode on D the selfsame range. As a result, the two could be distinguished only by the location of the final and the division of the characteristic octave, which made the mode either authentic (1) or plagal (8) (see Figure A-12).

It is not certain how widely Hermann's treatise was known during the Middle Ages; it has survived the passing centuries in only two manuscript copies. However, the orderly theoretical system he created by defining the eight traditional modes in terms of their finals and their characteristic species of fifth and fourth obviously gained considerable currency over a relatively wide geographical area. When Marchetto da Padova (fl. 1305–26) penned his treatise on plainchant, the *Lucidarium musicae*

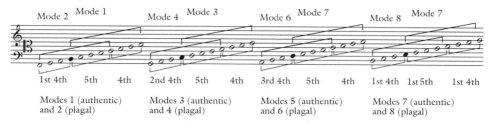

FIGURE A-12. The eight traditional modes as defined by their final (the black note) and their characteristic species of fifth and fourth.

planae, in the second decade of the fourteenth century, he described the modes very much in Hermann's terms.[28]

More than a century and a half later, when Tinctoris set down his compendious guide to the modes, the *De natura et proprietate tonorum*, it was once again by means of the species of fourth and fifth that he defined the characteristic range of the modes with respect to their finals.[29] In fact, although Tinctoris was separated from Hermann by more than four centuries and worked mainly in Italian rather than in Teutonic regions, his theoretical formulation of the modes does not differ in its essentials from that of the earlier writer.

To a large extent, of course, the modal system thus conceived was an idealized fiction. It constituted an abstract structure of such regularity that it could scarcely begin to account for the bewildering variety of musical practice that originated in the early medieval period. When the doctrine of the modes was formulated, much of the plainchant of the Christian liturgy, especially that of its most ancient layers, did not lend itself to easy classification in the terms provided. Despite obvious efforts at normalization during the later Middle Ages, moreover, many of those chants still failed in the fifteenth century to conform fully to the theoretical patterns proposed by Tinctoris. As an informed observer he could not help but note the "irregular" finals, the ranges that were either smaller or larger than the characteristic octave of the normative pattern, the accidental alteration of the prescribed species of fifth or fourth, or even some combination of "deviations" of the sort.[30]

28. The treatise has been published in an excellent edition by Jan Herlinger with original Latin and English translation on facing pages, *The Lucidarium of Marchetto of Padua* (Chicago: University of Chicago Press, 1985). Concerning Marchetto and the dating of his theoretical works, see also Nino Pirrotta, "Marchettus de Padua and the Italian Ars Nova," *Musica disciplina* 9 (1955): 57–71, and F. Alberto Gallo, "Marchetto da Padova," *The New Grove Dictionary of Music*, 11:661–62.

29. Tinctoris's tract on the modes, which was completed in 1476, is available in an English translation by Albert Seay, *Concerning the Nature and Propriety of Tones* (Colorado Springs: Colorado College Music Press, 1967). For the Latin editions of the work, see Heinrich Hüschen, "Tinctoris," *The New Grove Dictionary of Music*, 18:839.

30. Note that even the formulaic melodies provided by Johannes Affligemensis as didactic models for the eight traditional modes (see Figure A-10) do not make use of the entire octave range associated with them—after the fact—by the theorists. Rather, they define those modes melodically in terms of their final, their tenor or *tuba*, and the characteristic range between and around those two scale degrees (the *repercussio*).

By contrast, the chants written *after* the modes began to be defined by their species often reflect to a markedly greater degree the structural uniformities that such a system implied. For the late Middle Ages there is considerable evidence that this theoretical formulation came to serve more and more as a theory of melody rather than merely as a means of classifying existing pieces. Composers apparently began to recognize that the characteristic species of fifth and fourth could be used as the basic components of linear writing. They saw that the scale degrees marking their outer limits constituted ready-made pivotal points and cadential goals for melodic motion as well as practical boundaries for a normative range.

As the liturgical repertory became increasingly fixed, moreover, and compositional activity was directed more and more to polyphony, it would seem that modal theory was applied with ever greater consistency to melodic facture in the latter domain as well. By the fifteenth century chant composition had virtually ceased, as the theorists surely knew, and polyphony was increasingly independent of melodies borrowed or derived from the liturgy. Consequently, some of the treatises written during the fifteenth century and dealing with the modes may have been conceived primarily as a guide to the composer of polyphony. Tinctoris tells us specifically that this was the case for his *De natura et proprietate tonorum*,[31] and a good many of his observations and reflections, like those of his immediate contemporaries such as Gaffurius and Ramos, have the practical significance that was obviously intended only if understood in that light.

As with the earlier chant repertory, however, the definition of the modes by final, range, and species alone—whether for classification or as melodic theory—could not account for the complexities that had become an integral part of the melodic style of the late Middle Ages and early Renaissance, in chant and polyphony alike. Quite clearly, provided the modal frame of reference was first established with sufficient clarity, it was considered possible, perhaps even desirable, to depart from it in some manner in the course of a musical work. Provision was made theoretically, therefore, to account for such irregularities by allowing a certain number of departures from the norm in the three basic criteria of modal determination.

Among the most venerable and most oft-cited of these exceptions were those concerning range. Already in the anonymous writings of the eleventh century once attributed to Odo, it was observed that the authentic modes regularly included the step below the final in addition to the octave above it. Similarly, the plagal modes were allowed not only one degree below the characteristic fourth at the bottom of their ambitus but also a step above the fifth at the top. By the time Tinctoris was writing, in the second half of the fifteenth century, a step beyond the octave was considered normal for all eight of the modes. In the authentic members of each pair it

---

31. In chapter 19, for example, which concerns the scale degrees most suitable to initiate a melody in each of the modes, he declares, "The foregoing I say primarily with respect to the beginning of composed songs (*cantuum compositorum*), which I have had first and foremost in mind in undertaking to write this treatise." See the translation by Albert Seay, *Concerning the Nature and Propriety of Tones*, 20, for the context; the reader should be warned, however, that Seay's English translation must be used with caution.

was still added below the final, whereas in their plagal counterparts it was placed at the top of the ambitus. An additional step was also permitted in either case "by license" beyond the one considered normal. In other words, an authentic mode could go as much as a third (minor or major) below the final and a plagal mode as much as a third above its characteristic fifth without necessarily being considered as exceeding its normative range.[32]

However, if the total range utilized spanned the full octave above the final and a fourth below it—thus encompassing the characteristic octaves of both the authentic and the plagal forms of the pair—the mode could be classified as *mixed*.[33] Tinctoris considered, in addition, whether such a mixture was to be designated as authentic mixed (with its plagal) or as plagal mixed (with its authentic), and he asserted that the statistical prevalence of one octave or the other should determine such a judgment. His view of the problem in this instance, as in so many others, reflects a reliance on pragmatic methods that was rather rare for a man of his day. He was clearly quite willing to classify a melody modally according to the manner in which it behaved most of the time, regardless of its novel or peculiar features. He was held, nonetheless, by the strong medieval roots of the venerable intellectual tradition in which he worked. This is evident from an observation he made in closing the discussion of modal mixtures. He declares that where authentic and plagal elements were evenly balanced, the former should be preferred in the determination of mode not only because the authentic ones were the more ancient but also because the odd numbers by which they were identified were more "noble" than the even.

Other departures from the ideal range of the modes, as theoretically defined, could be accommodated by the concepts of perfection, imperfection, and pluperfection. The "perfect" mode, as defined by Tinctoris, made use of the entire ambitus assigned to it—that is, the characteristic octave plus a degree or two below the final for the authentic modes and a degree or two above the fifth at the upper end for the plagals. It became "imperfect" if it failed to ascend or descend to the outer limits allowed and "pluperfect" if it exceeded those bounds. As Tinctoris observed, moreover, these distinctions could be applied not only to the ambitus overall but to each of its extremes as well, making possible a total of nine different permutations in the description or the treatment of modal range. The mode could thus be characterized as perfect, imperfect, or pluperfect with respect to its ascent or to its descent only, or to both together, according to the scale degrees actually used.

Four of those nine combinations could be difficult to classify as authentic or plagal, however, because of similarities in range between the two basic types that could arise in certain cases from imperfection. For example, an authentic mode imperfect

---

32. See *De natura et proprietate tonorum*, chaps. 20 and 21 (pp. 21–23 in Seay's translation).

33. *De natura et proprietate tonorum*, chap. 23 (pp. 23–24 in Seay's translation). Seay has translated modal mixture (*mixtio tonorum*) as "mingling of tones" and modal commixture (*commixtio tonorum*)—to be discussed shortly—as "mixture of tones." Since this choice of terms tends to confuse the sense of the original Latin, it seemed preferable to retain here the most direct English equivalents for Tinctoris's technical language.

in ascent and perfect in descent might span exactly the same scale degrees as a plagal mode perfect in ascent but imperfect in descent. In like manner, an authentic mode imperfect in ascent and perfect in descent could cover precisely the same range as a plagal mode imperfect in both directions. Furthermore, an authentic mode imperfect in ascent and descent alike could be identical in total ambitus to a plagal mode that was perfect in ascent but imperfect in descent or imperfect, like the authentic mode it resembled, at both extremes.

Where uncertainty was possible, Tinctoris opted for statistical prevalence as the deciding factor. The mode was to be determined from the segment of the range that was predominant, and, once again, where authentic and plagal elements were of equal weight, the former were to be given precedence because of the inherent superiority traditionally assumed for the authentic modes. Tinctoris also recognized that the mixed modes could be either perfect or pluperfect—but not imperfect, obviously. He considered only two such combinations, however: perfect in ascent and pluperfect in descent or, conversely, perfect in descent and pluperfect in ascent. This would suggest that he considered a mixed mode pluperfect at both ends of its ambitus as exceeding in fact either the practical realities or—with respect to most voices and a number of instruments—the technical possibilities for music making in the fifteenth century.

In discussing ambital imperfection, Tinctoris also dealt with those melodies that can be modally ambiguous because they are entirely contained within the fifth above the final. For instances of this kind the theorist proposed two useful criteria. If, on the one hand, the melodic motion gave particular prominence to the fourth above the final—which in three cases out of four is of the species characteristic of the modal pair associated with it—the mode was to be considered plagal. On the other hand, where such an emphasis was not clearly marked, the mode could be determined with reference to what Tinctoris called the *corda* (or *chorda*), defined as the third scale degree above the final. A melody could be classified as authentic if its range lay primarily above that point or plagal if, to the contrary, the ambitus was located mostly below it, and the usual precedence was given to the former in cases of approximate equality.[34]

Somewhat less bewildering than the various concessions made in Tinctoris's theory of the modes for departures from a normative range, but no less significant, were those concerned with a deviation from the species of fourth or fifth customarily associated with a given final. Some of these "irregularities" were rooted in the melodic idioms of liturgical plainchant and were consequently in common usage long before the fifteenth century; others were the direct result of polyphonic practice and were therefore of much more recent date. In either case accidental inflection of the diatonic scale degrees was a principal means of altering the species. Accidentals were

---

34. *De natura et proprietate tonorum*, Chaps. 26–42 (pp. 26–35 in Seay's translation). It will be noted that for the finals on D and F, the *corda* corresponds to the plagal *repercussa*; see the discussion below, pp. 1008–10.

introduced in monophonic music, such as the chant, primarily to avoid a melodic *tritone* (a sequence of three consecutive tones), whether by step or by leap, because it was difficult to sing and the effect it produced was harsh to the medieval ear. Since such a progression occurs naturally in the diatonic scale only between F and b-mi, it was possible to eliminate it simply by using the lower position for the latter step (b-fa), thus reducing the discordant interval to an acceptable perfect fourth.

The tritone between F and b-mi tended to assume particular prominence in modes 5 and 6, where F is the final and consequently an important pivotal and cadential point. As a result, "b" was sung *fa* more frequently in the modes of that pair than in any other. By the fifteenth century it had become usual, in fact, to provide works closing on F with a b-fa (flat) signature, indicating that the lowered b was to be used throughout. This was almost always done in polyphonic composition and often in the monophonic repertories as well. But regardless of the mode, the melodic tritone was generally to be avoided wherever it might occur, as Tinctoris made unequivocally clear.[35]

In addition, a b-fa was not unusual in chants with a final on D, perhaps because the frequent use of melodic figures rising just one degree above a implied the tritone, whereas b-fa was rarely to be seen in melodies ending regularly on E or G. Accidental alteration was comparatively more common in polyphonic composition than it was in the monophonic genres generally, whatever the modal final. Still, the relative frequency of b-fa in polyphony seems to have corresponded as a rule to the natural proclivities of the liturgical melodies of the corresponding mode, especially in the fifteenth and early sixteenth centuries. In most instances alterations of this kind were of short duration; they could thus be viewed as genuinely "accidental" in the Aristotelian sense of the term, having no lasting effect upon the species of fourth or fifth characteristic of a given mode. With modes 5 and 6, however, the regular use of b-fa converted the fifth above the final from the third species, which was prescribed for the pair on F, to the fourth species, which traditionally belonged to the pair on G. If the resulting confusion was tolerated, it was undoubtedly because the melodic tritone was seen as a greater problem. Moreover, it was still possible to distinguish modes 5 and 6 with b-fa from modes 7 and 8 on the basis of the latter's virtually exclusive use of b-mi and a different species of fourth, as Tinctoris himself observed.[36]

Yet other accidental alterations came about in polyphonic composition as a result of the rules and conventions of counterpoint. In some instances the effect was the same as that produced by the melodic factors already mentioned. For example, two scale degrees building a melodic tritone (such as F and b-mi) were not usually allowed to sound simultaneously in separate parts either. As we shall see, the resulting combination was considered dissonant—whether heard as an augmented fourth or a diminished fifth[37]—and was generally avoided by lowering the offending mi by

---

35. *De natura et proprietate tonorum*, chap. 8 (pp. 11–13 in Seay's translation).
36. *De natura et proprietate tonorum*, chap. 11 (p. 14 in Seay's translation).
37. Concerning the concepts of consonance and dissonance and the classification of the various intervals under those two headings, see below, pp. 1037–45.

a semitone to fa. The introduction of a signed flat for b eliminated the troublesome intervals that could arise with reference to F, both horizontally and vertically. However, even that procedure could not banish the tritone entirely from the scale; it simply shifted the difficult interval to another location. With b as *fa* a new tritone was formed in ascent to e of the natural diatonic system. The latter could be avoided in turn, of course, by lowering the e, and this was done fairly often in works where b was consistently given as fa (i.e., with a flat), either for melodic or for contrapuntal reasons.

However, each additional flat generated another tritone in the diatonic scale, thus making it possible—in principle, at least—to join flat to flat in pyramidal fashion, proceeding for example from e♭ to a♭, from a♭ to d♭, and even from d♭ to g♭. A progression of this kind leading so far away from the traditional diatonic gamut is rarely to be seen, or even inferred, in the music of the Renaissance, and its presence was usually charged with symbolic or rhetorical significance, as we shall have occasion to observe.[38] Nevertheless, each additional flat altered anew the characteristic species of the prevailing mode, and that mutation could either be introduced intentionally to modify the modal frame of reference, or it could be treated as necessary but transitory—that is, truly "accidental"—hence construed as of little consequence for modal determination.

The most common type of alteration resulting from the conventions of polyphonic composition seems to have been regarded for the most part in the latter light and hence employed generally without serious concern for the momentary changes in modal species that it produced. The prevailing locus for accidentals of this kind was the cadence. There, in contrapuntal usage dating back to the fourteenth century, the sequence of intervallic combinations considered to be optimal for closing a phrase was effected by approaching the final note in one or two of the parts by a semitone—usually from below but in certain contexts from above as well—even when the scale degree needed to do so was not found in the natural diatonic system.[39] This meant, for example, when the circumstances required, raising f to f♯ when followed by g, c to c♯ when followed by d, and even g to g♯ when followed by a.

Because the placement of cadential accidentals was highly predictable, they could easily be supplied by a knowledgeable performer. It was generally assumed that the singers and players should and would make the alterations that had become customary in cadential passages and, consequently, that those changes did not have to be specified by the notation. As a result, the altered species of fourth or fifth so produced was rarely if ever part of the notational picture. This suggests that cadential sharps—as opposed to flats given as a signature, for example—carried no real significance in determining or identifying the mode to which a work otherwise belonged. When discussed by theorists of the times, moreover, accidentals of this variety were usually des-

38. An example is the celebrated motet *Absalon, fili mi*; see the discussion of the work above, pp. 535–37. For a more radical view, which posits such shifts as much more common in the actual performance of certain works from the period, see Margaret Bent, "Diatonic Ficta," *Early Music History* 4 (1984): 1–48.
39. For a discussion of the contrapuntal procedures involved, see below, pp. 1045–55.

ignated by the term *musica ficta* (or *falsa*), indicating that unlike b-fa—and in the case of modal transposition, to be discussed shortly, other flatted scale degrees as well—they had no real place in the diatonic system or the Guidonian hand.

Considerably more significant, from a modal point of view, was the intentional temporary replacement of the characteristic species associated with the final of a work by those linked instead with another modal pair. This could be accomplished in the course of a composition either by introducing a flat (or eventually a sharp) into a phrase of some duration in the manner already described or by giving melodic emphasis to a fourth, a fifth, or an entire octave properly belonging to another final. The result in either case was usually a clear juxtaposition of the readily distinguishable melodic characteristics of two or more different modes, which Tinctoris called *commixture.* In his discussion of it the theorist was concerned, as always, with the means for determining whether the various species of fourth and fifth so combined were to be identified with the authentic or the plagal forms of the modes to which they belonged. He suggested as a general rule that a fifth should be construed as representing the authentic, a fourth the plagal member of the pair in question.

When the fourth was added directly above the fifth, however, so that the overall ambitus corresponded more or less to that of an authentic mode, both elements could be designated as authentic; conversely, when the fourth was located directly beneath the fifth so that the range approximated that of a plagal mode, both intervals could be identified as plagal. These possibilities Tinctoris illustrated in Example A-1, which shows at the same time the nature of commixture as he understood it. The precedence customarily granted to the authentic modes is again evident here from the fact that the theorist specifically raised the possibility of a fifth combined with the fourth of another mode placed both above and below it, asserting that in such cases all but the lower fourth should be classed as authentic.[40]

40. See *De natura et proprietate tonorum*, chaps. 13–17 for Tinctoris's discussion of these problems (pp. 15–19 in Seay's translation). The difficulties of precise modal determination in instances of commixture are reflected in what appears to be a small inconsistency. In the example at the end of chap. 15 Tinctoris shows mode 8 commixed with the fourths characteristic of the modes on F and E respectively, both of which he identifies as authentic.

EXAMPLE A-1. Commixture, as illustrated in Tinctoris, *De natura et proprietate tonorum*, chap. 15 (the slurs indicate neumes in the original notation)

Mode 3 commixed with Mode 7

Mode 4 commixed with Mode 6

Tinctoris also observed that commixture was introduced at times out of necessity and at others intentionally, presumably for artistic or esthetic reasons.[41] To illustrate the sort of compositional constraints that could result in a change of species, he wrote out a short contrapuntal exercise in two parts in which a flat was required to avoid sounding B-mi against F-fa. This is as close as he comes in any context to defining the distinction, which has been made in these pages, between an alteration that is "accidental" with respect to the governing mode, and consequently without substantial significance for its determination, and an intentional shift in the points of modal reference, however it may have been achieved.

That his formulation and the latter notion are rooted in the same conceptual framework is nonetheless strongly suggested by the fact that the alteration was usually left to the performer when it was "accidental" or "necessary," whereas the change of modal species was generally notationally specific or otherwise entirely unambiguous when it was "voluntary." It should be noted, in addition, that commixtures of the latter type—like the striking departures from the diatonic scale by means of successive flats, cited earlier—began to assume symbolic and rhetorical meaning ever more frequently from the fifteenth century on.

Deviations from the third criterion of modal definition—the location of the final—were also recognized as possible. They could be accomplished by simply replacing any of the four traditional finals with one of a number of alternate scale degrees that could function in its place. Once again, some of these "irregular" finals were well established in the usage of the chant, while others seem to have made their appearance only with the emerging cultivation of polyphony. Among those used in medieval monophony were a-la/mi/re and c-sol/fa/ut, both of which appear as the concluding note for a number of melodies, some of them from the earliest layers of the repertory.

When so employed, however, they were not regarded as legitimate, independent finals capable in either case of carrying a distinct pair of modes. Rather, they were assimilated to the regular finals found a fifth lower in the gamut—to D and F, respectively—and their melodies classed with those of modes 1 and 2, on the one hand, or modes 5 and 6, on the other. The original reasons for doing so have long been lost to history, but the practice was maintained without meaningful exception until well into the sixteenth century. It could be justified theoretically by the scalar affinities that link any two steps in the diatonic system located a perfect fifth apart; the sequence of tones and semitones above, below, or around two degrees at that distance is invariably the same through the interval of a sixth.[42]

41. *De natura et proprietate tonorum*, chap. 18, "Quod commixtio toni interdum fit necessitate, ac interdum voluntate" (pp. 19–20 in Seay's translation).

42. When b was construed as *mi*, the sixth in question corresponded to the hexachord on either C or G. Not surprisingly, then, these similarities in scalar order were noted by such important medieval theorists as the eleventh-century anonymous author of the *Dialogus de musica* and by Guido, who saw in them a reason for the practice of assigning chants ending on a to modes 1 and 2 and those terminating on c to modes 5 and 6. The former's treatment of the matter is found in Strunk, ed., *Source Readings*, 114–16, while Guido's more extensive and systematic discussion appears in his principal work, *Micrologus*, chaps. 7–8. For an English translation of the latter by Warren Babb, see *Hucbald, Guido, and John on Music*, ed. Claude V.

In the two cases at hand the scalar configuration around D is repeated for a, starting a tone below and extending through the fifth above, and the one around F is duplicated for c from the fourth below to the third above. In other words, considered as finals, D and a share the same species of fifth, while F and c have in common their species of fourth. Furthermore, if b-flat is introduced into the scales of the two regular finals—as was done by the fifteenth century with notable frequency in the modes on D and with increasing consistency in the pair on F—the two octaves become entirely identical. A similar relationship was seen to exist between E and B, which have the same intervallic sequence from the third below to the fourth above. But since b-mi was rarely used as a final in any repertory and virtually never in the polyphony of the fifteenth and sixteenth centuries, that observation was apparently of no practical significance (see Figure A-13).

FIGURE A-13. The intervallic affinities between finals and confinals: (1) D and a; (2) E and b-mi; (3) F and c (the semitone in the melodic sequence, marked ⌐, falls each time just below the clef sign).

Because of these affinities, and because the fifth step of every modal scale formed, with its final, the limits for the species of fourth and fifth by which the modes were defined, that scale degree was designated the *confinal*.[43] And because of its relationship to the final and its significant position in the theoretical construct of the modal scale, the confinal came to be the degree, besides the final, most often cited by theorists as a possible goal for internal cadences. It was also the one most frequently used for that purpose in actual practice.

In time the humanist-theorist Heinrich Glarean (1488–1563), who based his work, typically, on a study of the Hellenistic harmonists, attempted to establish a and c (and their octave transpositions) as regular finals in their own right, each with its own identifiable species of octave scale, and to expand thereby the number of modes from eight to twelve.[44] The resulting revision of the traditional modal system was eventually accepted in some quarters, most notably by the influential Venetian theorist Gioseffo Zarlino (ca. 1517–90). Numerous others saw no need for Glarean's

Palisca (New Haven: Yale University Press, 1978), 63–65. The matters touched on here are lucidly discussed in connection with the development of theoretical thought during the early Middle Ages by Richard Crocker, "Hermann's Major Sixth," *Journal of the American Musicological Society* 25 (1972): 19–37.

43. For a discussion of the confinals see, for example, Franchinus Gaffurius, *Practica musicae*, bk. 1, chap. 8 (in the English translation by Clement Miller, pp. 50–51).

44. Concerning Glarean's activity and influence as a theorist, see Clement Miller, *The New Grove Dictionary of Music*, 7:422–24.

innovations, however, and adhered stubbornly to the venerable and consecrated usage based on four finals and eight modes.[45]

Provision was also made for the introduction of irregular finals by means of signed accidental flats, including not only b-fa but also others outside the Guidonian hand. A signed flat had the effect of transposing intact the species of fourth and fifth characteristic of a given mode to a new final and hence to another ambitus, as a rule either a fourth higher or to some octave transposition of the resulting scale degrees. In his characteristically systematic fashion Tinctoris proposed two alternate positions for each of the four regular finals. His discussion must be prescriptive as much as descriptive, however, for some of those transpositions are relatively common while others are rarely if ever seen.

The first of the two he put forward for the modes closing regularly on D shifted the final to G by means of a signed flat for B in all registers; it was also the transposition most often used in the polyphony of the fifteenth and sixteenth centuries. In some repertories it is seen no less frequently than the traditional close. Much rarer, but also used on occasion, was the transposition of modes 1 and 2 to a final on C by means of signed flats on both B and E.

The Phrygian modes were used relatively little for polyphonic composition in either the fifteenth or the sixteenth century, and the traditional final on E is more uncommon still. Tinctoris nonetheless suggested two alternate locations for it: the first on A with a signed B-fa, and the second on D with E flatted as well. The latter may never have been used in actual practice for an entire work, but the former does serve as a final in a substantial number of pieces. Some of these have signed flats for B a good deal of the time, although hardly ever as a running signature, but many more show no written accidentals at all, even when the mode is specified in the source as the third or the fourth. The species of fourth was the same in both scales, regardless, but without the B-fa the transposed Phrygian pair lost the characteristic semitone above the final on A. This may have been tolerated because the subsequent stepwise progression up to the confinal comprised the dreaded tritone.

Moreover, since many melodies skipped over the second degree of the modal scale a good deal of the time, the discrepancy with the proper species of fifth could not always be readily detected. Still, the net result was to replace the second species of fifth, which was associated with the modes on E, with the first, which was characteristic of the modes on D. Confusion was therefore possible as to the proper modal classification of works closing on A. Either they could be assimilated to the modes of the Dorian pair or to those of the Phrygian. A careful examination of the remaining criteria—range and species—and of the general melodic profile is usually indispensable to a convincing determination. Even so, baffling ambiguities sometimes remain, as, for example, when a modal commixture juxtaposes references to the species belonging to both regular finals. And in numerous instances the uncertainty gener-

---

45. See the discussion of polyphonic collections that were arranged according to mode, for example, pp. 549–54, and cf. Harold Powers, "Tonal Types and Modal Categories in Renaissance Polyphony," *Journal of the American Musicological Society* 34 (1981): 458–70.

ated by such means appears to have been intentionally introduced—like a number of the procedures already cited—for expressive purposes.

The transpositions adduced by Tinctoris for the modes on F also constitute a special case. Because a B-fa signature had become customary with the Lydian pair, it was possible to duplicate their species exactly from C by simply eliminating the flat. Like the Dorian pair, then, modes 5 and 6 were transposed a fifth higher to the regular confinal, which had already been employed as an irregular final in liturgical monophony. And since the transposition could be made in the latter instance with no change of species, Tinctoris set it alongside those produced by the addition of flats and provided for it a theoretical justification that he did not even attempt for the use of A as an alternate final for modes 1 and 2.

For the second irregular close in the Lydian modes he followed his usual pattern, placing it a fourth above F on b-fa and prescribing for it a flat signature on E in addition to the one on B that was habitual for the regular ambitus. Of the two irregular finals, the one on C was by far the more used. Its frequent appearance in the polyphony of the period may have led the theorist to include it in his systematization of alternate closes even though it did not quite fit the model he used elsewhere. The close on B-flat is much more unusual, but it, too, is to be found.

The transpositions for the modes regularly on G follow once again the procedure adopted for those on D and E; the shift is upward by a fourth (or, of course, downward by a fifth), each time with the addition of a flat to the signature. The first displacement, to C by means of a B-flat, is not common in the polyphonic repertories of the fifteenth and sixteenth centuries, but it does occur. The second, however, with F as a final and both B- and E-flat as a signature, was simply not used.[46]

As has been observed repeatedly in the foregoing discussion, the various special categories that served to justify and to classify deviations from the final, the range, or the species considered to be normative for any of the eight traditional modes—when defined as an ideal theoretical structure—were made necessary first of all by the melodic realities of the liturgical chant. Although Tinctoris usually illustrated his treatises with examples of his own composition, he could just as easily have turned for the same purpose to sacred melodies familiar to any contemporary reader: to the graduals, for example, for chants closing on irregular finals and imperfect as to range; to the sequences to exemplify ambital extensions that could be construed in some cases as modally pluperfect, in others as mixed; or to virtually any segment of the repertory for examples of commixture.

For the composer of the fifteenth and sixteenth centuries, however, the plainchant represented a good deal more than simply a very large collection of pieces, many of which were modally exceptional. More importantly, it provided entire families of melodic prototypes for the musical realization of modal concepts. Whether the chants were strictly formulaic, like the various tones for Psalms and canticles, or only loosely so, like the different groups of related antiphons, the musician could learn from them how to intone a phrase, how to spin it out to accommodate a

46. See *De natura et proprietate tonorum*, chaps. 44–50 (pp. 36–39 in Seay's translation); though it may have escaped my attention, I know of no piece of the period in which such a signature is found.

lengthy segment of text, and how to bring it to some sort of cadential close. In other words, to paraphrase Tinctoris's definition of mode, the chants exemplified the manner in which one shaped the beginning, the middle, and the close of any melody.[47]

That the chant was in fact so regarded and so used would appear from a remark made by Tinctoris in a chapter that deals with the scale degrees considered appropriate for beginning a melody in each of the modes. The theorist asserts that "certain persons . . . after they had looked through all the openings of simple Gregorian chant with the greatest diligence, assigned to each mode a certain number of beginnings."[48] Tinctoris thus describes what seems to have been a systematic search for the statistically normative, and the results obtained, as he transmitted them, were later listed with very little change by a number of his younger contemporaries, such as Gaffurius and Aaron.

The scale degrees usable for melodic closure were also prescribed by Tinctoris and other theorists of the period, who began, usually, with the final and confinal of the mode and went on to those that were most frequently used for internal cadences in the chant. It is interesting to note that these degrees coincided by and large with those most generally found at the beginning of a phrase. And it is significant that they were also the same as those used to close the cadential formulae that were the one partially variable element in traditional psalmody, the difference tones.[49]

However, the chant provided a good deal more than just practical guidance concerning the scale steps that could serve in any given mode as starting or closing points for a melodic phrase. Offering as it did a vast repertory of melodic formulae that could be used to begin or end a phrase, it shaped in a decisive way the composer's sense of melodic design and his stylistic judgment. These could influence his approach to polyphonic composition, of course, and most generally did. It was not only the intonation or the closure of the line that could be so affected but the very substance of it as well. As has been mentioned, the tones for the Psalms and the canticles were built around a scale degree used in reiteration for declamatory purposes, and this degree was variously called the *tenor*, *tuba*, *dominant*, or *repercussa*.

In the authentic modes on D, F, and G this reciting note was a fifth above the final and hence the same as the confinal; consequently, the interval between them, variously termed *phrasis* or *repercussio*, was identical with the species of fifth characteristic of the mode. In the plagal modes on D and F the *repercussa* was a third lower and thus fell on the degree designated the *corda* by Tinctoris. In these instances, where the constituent intervals of the psalmody and the theoretical structure of the modes corresponded so closely, *repercussio* and characteristic species tend to reinforce

47. *De natura et proprietate tonorum*, chap. 1: "De diffinitione, numero, institutione, et appellatione tonorum: . . . Tone (that is mode), then, is nothing other than the manner (*modus*) in which the beginning, the middle, and the end of a given song are ordered."
48. *De natura et proprietate tonorum*, chap. 19.
49. There were usually several such tones (or *differentiae*) for each of the Psalm tones, which made it possible to adjust the close of the Psalm or canticle to the opening of the accompanying antiphon; see Hoppin, *Medieval Music*, 83, and the pertinent discussion by Perkins, "Mode and Structure," *Journal of the American Musicological Society* 26 (1973): 198–202.

one another. The final, the upper confinal, and—in the plagal modes especially—the *corda* became the pitches of reference for the melodic line, points upon which to begin and end and around which to turn as it rises and falls.

In the remaining modes this is not the case, however. With the final on E, if the reciting note were placed in strict analogy with the other authentic modes, it would fall on b-mi. Perhaps because of the ambiguous character of that scale degree (with its two positions a semitone apart), perhaps because of the latent presence of the melodic tritone, b-mi was rejected for that purpose and the *tuba* raised a semitone to c. This created a *repercussio* that spanned the interval of a sixth and that could therefore be confused from its second step upward with that of the fifth Psalm tone. Since the *tuba* of the corresponding plagal tone was nonetheless a third lower, it fell upon a and gave rise to a *repercussio* encompassing the fourth between the final E and that degree. The species of this fourth was the one characteristic of the mode, but the *repercussio* was the same upward from the second degree as that of the sixth tone. Similarly, the *tuba* of the eighth tone would normally have been b-mi, a third below its authentic counterpart, but once again the troublesome step was replaced by c. This resulted in a *repercussio* that covered a fourth with the same sequence of tones and semitones as the species characteristic of the modes on F and thus created an additional source of possible confusion (see Figure A-14).

FIGURE A-14. Final (○), repercussa (●), and repercussio (—) in the eight tones or modes.

In these three modes, then—the third, fourth, and eighth—two sets of pivotal scale degrees were available to the composer: one provided by the final and its regular confinal and *corda*, the other by the final and its traditional *repercussa*.[50] The skillful composer could select one or the other, according to the nature of the work being written, or he could make use of both at once. He could then explore the relationships between them and, at the same time, with other modes whose basic intervallic structures—the characteristic species of fourth and fifth and the *repercussio* in particular—shared with them melodically significant scale degrees.[51]

50. That the *repercussio* was an important melodic entity, even when it did not correspond to the characteristic species of the mode, is clear not only from its prominence in the didactic formulae of Johannis Affligemensis, where it is perhaps most to be expected (see Figure A-10), but also from the short chants composed by Tinctoris to illustrate modes 3 and 4, where c and a, respectively, figure conspicuously in the line (see Example A-1).

51. *Repercussa* and *repercussio* are defined and their role in polyphonic composition of the sixteenth century is discussed at length by Bernard Meier, *The Modes of Classical Vocal Polyphony*, trans. Ellen Beebe (New York: Broude Brothers, 1988), chap. 2 (pp. 29ff.). For further discussion of the practical implications of the complex relationships among the finals, confinals, and *repercussiones* in the modal usage of the fifteenth century (and beyond), see Perkins, "Modal Strategies in Okeghem's *Missa Cuiusvis Toni*," in *Music Theory and the Exploration of the Past*, ed. Hatch and Bernstein (Chicago: University of Chicago Press, 1993), 59–71.

In the light of such subtle complexities it is perhaps not difficult to understand why Tinctoris continued to be read as an important authority on the modes until late in the sixteenth century, as the evidence clearly indicates. There was, of course, no reason to question the basic criteria—final, range, and species—by which he defined the traditional *toni*. They accommodated and helped to rationalize the regular functions of the modal scale degrees as these were used to define and to organize the melodic space occupied by liturgical plainchant. And, in addition, they were solidly rooted in the Hellenistic tradition that was to assume ever greater importance in the course of the sixteenth century as the influence of the humanists became increasingly marked. At the same time, however, Tinctoris provided a conceptual framework for dealing with the less systematic elements of the melodic structures deriving from the well-established practice of the chant.

Despite the number and diversity of his categories, which can easily bewilder the uninitiated, and the ambiguities of overlapping classifications, to which he himself drew attention, his modal doctrine made it possible to account for the "irregularities" of any melody then existent. More importantly for the polyphonic composition of his age, it could also serve as a justification and a guide for departures from the recognized norms, thus providing considerable leeway in the invention of new melodies. For Tinctoris these two primary aspects of mode, the conceptual and the practical, were apparently not only reconcilable but also complementary, inextricably bound up one with another. Consequently, he attempted to deal with all the troublesome problems that inevitably arose in adapting the abstract notions of mode to the practical realities of classifying a chant or writing a good melodic line for a polyphonic piece.

The theorists who followed Tinctoris most directly in time—Gaffurius, for example, with whom he had contact between 1478 and 1480 while both men were living in Naples—continued to work in much the same vein. They took into account both the conceptual system based upon final, range, and species and the varied melodic patterns characteristic of liturgical monophony in its many forms and guises. But with time the immediacy of the plainchant repertory, and consequently its significance, gradually began to diminish. The manifold pressures of secularizing trends in society and a growing dissatisfaction among reformers of all stripes with certain aspects of the liturgy and its music inevitably took their toll.

The single-minded preoccupation of humanist scholars with the culture of classical Greece and Rome led to a critical new stance toward the Latin of the Middle Ages and toward the arbitrary treatment of the syllabic quantities of classical convention to be seen in the musical settings of the chant. By the early 1560s disaffection with certain of the texts and their musical declamation became sufficiently generalized, even among the clergy of the Roman church, that the "barbarisms" perceived by detractors of medieval liturgy figured in the deliberations of the Council of Trent. In 1577 they prompted a papal commission to revise the traditional repertory and to purge it of its defects.[52]

52. For a discussion of the actions taken by the council and by Pope Gregory XIII, see Reese, *Music in the Renaissance*, 448–51 and 458.

Even as the authority of the chant was on the wane, the classicizing tendencies of the humanists fostered a renewed interest in the music of Greek antiquity and, in particular, the cosmological and intellectual traditions associated with it. This brought about a growing understanding of the writings of the Hellenistic harmonists. A more rigorous study was made of the musical systems of antiquity as compared with those proposed by the writers of the fourteenth and fifteenth centuries. In this process the "irregularities" allowed by the theorists of the then recent past—those due primarily to the concessions made to the musical practice of the chant—were viewed in a more critical light.

As a result, the theorists most strongly influenced by humanistic scholarship, writers such as Glarean and Zarlino, were inclined to take a more systematic approach to the treatment of mode than their fifteenth-century predecessors. In both their basic premises and in the consequent constructs they sought closer conformity to the models of classical antiquity. In their hands modal theory was regularized and—to the extent to which the subtleties and complexities deriving from the chant were eliminated in doing so—simplified. These trends came to be reflected in turn in the polyphonic composition of the sixteenth century; the modes were treated also there in a more systematic fashion with fewer idiosyncrasies of the kind inspired by the melodic profiles of sacred monophony.

It should be borne in mind, however, that the fundamental concepts upon which the modal systems of the Renaissance were based were never called into serious question while the age lasted. In the seventeenth century, by contrast, a striking change in the predominant musical style and a decisive secularization of the musical culture of the West set in motion a radical revision of the theoretical principles of the fifteenth and sixteenth centuries. At the same time a melodic method of composition began to give way across the board to a more chordal one, and the distinctive scales of the individual modes yielded to the simplifications of the major-minor system. Nonetheless, even as the sixteenth century waned, strongly conservative trends among certain composers and theorists of the late Renaissance encouraged adherence not only to the modal systems of the second half of the fifteenth century but also to the melodic paradigms embodied in liturgical chant.

The Notation and Mensuration of Polyphony

The symbols that served for the notation of polyphonic music during the fifteenth and sixteenth centuries were derived, like so many other aspects of the musical practice of the Renaissance, from the plainchant of the medieval Christian church. The process of adoption began in earnest in the twelfth century, when the square note shapes that are still in general use for the chant first became current over much of western Europe. The first graphic forms to be given rhythmic significance for polyphonic purposes were apparently the *neumes*, in which two or more pitches were grouped as a single figure. The most important symbols from our present perspective, however, and the easiest to deal with, are those that stood for individual scale degrees, of which three were taken over early on for polyphonic composition. When used for the chant, the two principal shapes were designated *virga* and *punctum*, while a third, a diamond-shaped version of the latter, was originally found only in neumes and consequently had no distinctive name of its own.[53]

Toward the beginning of the thirteenth century each of these figures came to be associated by convention with one of the durational values utilized in the system of rhythmic modes. In this context the note forms assumed the names of the metrical units for which they stood, and the terminology—like the very concept of modal rhythm—was borrowed from the treatises on the meters of classical poetry that were current at the time.[54] Thus the *virga* became a *longa*, the shorter *punctum* a *brevis*, and the rhomboid note, which was briefer still in duration, was called a *semibrevis* (see Figure A-15).

FIGURE A-15. Note forms of the thirteenth century given specific rhythmic significance.

The rhythmic modes were essentially ternary in nature, at least as they were codified by the theorists of the Continental tradition, and the same was true of the mensural systems that grew out of them. As expounded by Franco of Cologne around mid-thirteenth century, the theory of mensural notation prescribed a division of the *modus*, the basic unit of the modal patterns represented notationally by the long, into three *tempora* or breves, and the division of the *tempus*, represented by the breve, into three semibreves.[55] This triune temporal organization of musical sonorities made use of two concepts that must have caused musicians considerable difficulty during the Middle Ages and the Renaissance, judging from the practical problems they continue to pose for editors and performers of the present day: these are the notions of *perfection* and *alteration*.

The notational unit was considered "perfect" if it was ternary in nature, such as a long of three breves or a breve of three semibreves.[56] It could be "imperfected," however, if deprived of a third of its total duration, as, for example, when followed

53. For a concise discussion of the development of chant notation, see Hoppin, *Medieval Music*, 57–62.
54. Concerning the rhythmic modes and their notation, see Hoppin, *Medieval Music*, 221–31.
55. Franco's treatise on mensuration, *Ars cantus mensurabilis*, to which reference is made in the following discussion, is available in part in an English translation by Strunk, ed., *Source Readings*, rev. ed., 227–45.
56. The concept of "perfection" had both philosophical and theological implications for the medieval theorist. In the philosophical sense it was defined as comprising the three parts necessary for completion: a beginning, a middle, and an end. And from a theological point of view comparisons with the traditional Christian concept of the Trinity were undoubtedly inevitable.

or preceded by a note of the next smallest value. In effect the notes were subsumed to the governing metrical unit—the perfection—in ternary groupings according to the context. An uninterrupted series of either longs or breves was invariably construed as consecutive perfections: each long was equal to three breves, and each breve equal to three semibreves. However, if longs were mixed with single breves or breves with single semibreves, the shorter notes could imperfect the longer, assuming a third of their overall value and thus leaving the perfection intact.

A correct interpretation of mixed values—longs with breves and breves with semibreves—was further complicated by the practice of *alteration*. When two breves fell between longs, or two semibreves between breves, they were regularly construed together as a perfection (that is, a ternary unit). This was done by doubling the "proper" duration of the second of the two; it thus became *altera*, literally "other" or altered in the sense the word has taken in English. As a result, an imperfect long had the same total duration as an altered breve, and an imperfect breve was of the same length as an altered semibreve (see Figure A-16). Obviously, the illustrations

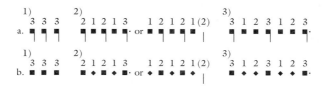

FIGURE A-16. Perfection (1), imperfection (2), and alteration (3) in the thirteenth century (the numerals over the notes indicate, respectively [a] the number of tempora or breve units, and [b] the number of semibreves represented by each figure).

given here show only the simplest and clearest uses made of the notational practices in question. The composer was free to mix these three primary note values in whatever way his artistic purpose required so long as he observed the conventions of the notational and rhythmic systems within which he worked.

Not surprisingly, the resulting note patterns were in many instances subject to differing rhythmic resolutions, and the theorists—even those who thought as systematically and carefully as Franco—could not hope to provide rules for every possible contingency. Some of the ambiguities were eventually clarified by the application of a notational device that came into general use in the thirteenth century: the dot or *punctus* (in the Latin terminology of the Middle Ages). Its primary function was to mark a clear division between the perfections as they were to be construed in performance. By means of the dot, for example, it was possible to change the meaning of the combination of notes that ordinarily called for alteration so that imperfection was required instead. The practice was so helpful that by the end of the thirteenth century a dot was commonly placed at the end of every tempus. The result was a degree of clarity at that notational level comparable in effect to the bar line (which is its modern equivalent). Unfortunately, that happy state of affairs did not endure.

The basic rules governing perfection, imperfection, and alteration grew directly out of the recurring metric and notational patterns of the rhythmic modes—as is evident from Figure A-16, line a. Nevertheless, even when all trace of the modes had finally disappeared from the mensural practice of European polyphony—and with it the underlying rationale for both imperfection and alteration—the notational conventions associated with them had become so firmly entrenched in the thinking of theorists and composers alike that they continued to be observed until late in the sixteenth century.

FROM NEUMES TO LIGATURES

The same was also true of a much more striking peculiarity of mensural notation: the continuing use of the *ligature*. As was mentioned, the neumes of liturgical chant were taken over directly for polyphonic composition and were the first notational symbols to be systematically invested with metrical significance. In their mensural context the neumes were known by a name that identified their essential characteristic of form, the ligation of two or more notes into a single figure. Because ligatures were employed initially to denote the regular patterns of alternating longs and breves that characterized the rhythmic modes, those were the durational values that came to be associated with them in mensural practice from the thirteenth century on.

The rationale upon which that connection rested presupposed "correct" or normative forms for both the beginning and the ending of each of the neumes that was adapted for use in the mensural system. If, on the one hand, the ligature began in the manner considered "proper" for neumes of the type from which it derived—that is, with a descending stroke on its left side when the second scale degree represented was lower than the first and no stroke at all when the second note was higher—it was described as having *propriety*, and the first note was, by convention, a breve. If, on the other hand, the ligature was completed according to the notational practices observed for chant neumes—that is, with the final note square in shape and immediately to the right of the penultimate note when lower in pitch or directly above when higher—it was said to have perfection, and the final note was read as a long. Any notes between the first and the last were then construed as breves (see Figure A-17).

It was possible, however, to reverse the meaning of the opening and closing notes

FIGURE A-17. Ligatures with propriety and perfection. (The durational values signified are indicated by B[reve] and L[ong]. Note that a descending diagonal stroke always represents just two notes, one each at its upper and lower ends.)

of the ligature, either each one separately or both at once. If the normal figure began improperly—that is, without the descending stroke on the left when the first two notes were in descent or with one added when they were in ascent—the ligature was considered to be without propriety, and the initial note was read as a long. Similarly, if the ligature finished with a diagonal bar in descent or with the last note turned out to the right in ascent, it was clearly incomplete and therefore said to be without perfection, and the final figure was then taken to be a breve. The notes between the first and the last were unaffected by these changes and so continued to be construed as breves, however many there were.

There was one other way of transforming the beginning of a ligature and, consequently, its mensural meaning. Its propriety was not simply removed but actually reversed by the placement of an ascending stroke to the left side of the initial figure. When this was done, the ligature was identified as having "opposite propriety," and the first two notes were then read as semibreves (see Figure A-18). This unusual lig-

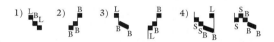

FIGURE A-18. Ligatures without propriety (1), without perfection (2), without propriety and without perfection (3), and with opposite propriety (4) (the durational values intended are indicated by L[ong], B[reve], and S[emibreve]).

ature—the only one in which values other than a long or a breve can be included—originated as an ornamental division of the initial breve within the patterns of modal rhythm. For this reason the semibreves were invariably introduced as a pair, and the remaining notes of the ligature, if there were more than two, were read in the usual way (see the exemplification of thirteenth-century usage in Figure A-19).

In light of the close connection between the rhythmic modes and the mensural significance assigned to the neume forms in their various transmutations, it is not surprising that all of the notational conventions governing perfection, imperfection, or alteration were applied in the same manner to ligatures. Curiously, it was not until after mid-thirteenth century—when modal rhythms were fading from the developing polyphonic style—that Franco of Cologne standardized the meaning of the ligatures for all contexts. And, stranger still, once that usage had been codified theoretically, it remained current and without change for more than three centuries despite the intervening shifts in style and notational practice.

Also standardized by Franco, and with almost equally durable results, was the meaning of the symbols that had come to indicate silence in a polyphonic composition: the *rests*. Obviously, pauses in the production of musical sonorities could be conveniently measured only in the same values as the notes themselves. Their presence was indicated in the twelfth century by a vertical line drawn across the staff. At first the duration of the rest was not apparent from the symbol itself and had to be deduced from the context. Subsequently, the extent of the rest began to be shown

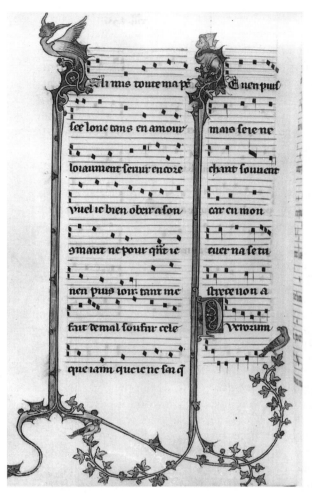

FIGURE A-19. The thirteenth-century motet *J'ai mis toute ma pensee/Je n'en puis mais/Puerorum* showing typical Franconian notation (Montpellier, Faculty of Medicine, MS H196, f. 275ᵛ).

by the length of the stroke with the lines of the staff serving as a ready-made rule. A single space was equated with the duration of the breve. A long rest could then be indicated by a vertical line of two or three spaces, depending upon the number of *tempora* it was to last. The duration of an altered breve, similarly, was shown by a line spanning two spaces, and the semibreve rest by a short stroke filling either one or two thirds of the space in which it was placed, according to that portion of a sounding breve for which it was to stand (see Figure A-20).[57] At that stage in the development of our notational system the total duration of any rest could be made entirely explicit. By contrast the corresponding note forms still carried some ambiguities that could be resolved only from the context. Consequently, rests were not subject to either imperfection or alteration in Franco's mensural system, and that continued to be the case even when subsequent change in notational practice necessitated additional symbols to designate rests for an increasing number of smaller values.

Longs   Breves   Semibreves

FIGURE A-20. Rests in Franco's mensural system.

57. See Strunk, ed., *Source Readings*, rev. ed., 237.

THE INNOVATIONS OF THE FOURTEENTH CENTURY

Around 1320 some important changes to Franco's mensural system were formulated and rationalized by a pair of theorists then working in Paris, Jean de Muris and Philippe de Vitry. Their emphasis on innovation is clear from the titles given to their treatises. Both mention an *ars nova*, meaning, in that context, a new science and practice of notation. In their writings the break with the past was twofold. On the one hand, the number of notational levels or degrees was expanded to include both longer and shorter notes. On the other, an imperfect (binary) division of the larger values was finally recognized as a legitimate mensural practice alongside the perfect (ternary) one.

A note twice the length of a perfect long had in fact already made its appearance in the modal notation of the twelfth century. It was like the long as to shape in that it carried a descending tail on the right side but was made distinguishable from it by a lateral extension of its rectangular head. As a separately identifiable form it eventually acquired a name of its own, *maxima*, indicating that it was the largest notational entity in use. In the theoretical formulation of the early fourteenth century this extended long could be not only *duplex*—that is, equal to two proper longs as it had been from the twelfth century on—but also *triplex*, or equal to three of them.

At the other end of the mensural spectrum a division of the breve into more than three semibreves, which made its appearance toward the end of the thirteenth century, led to as many as nine semibreves in the space of a *tempus*. As a consequence, when the breve was split not only into three but also into four, five, and more smaller notes, the semibreves so produced were necessarily of different lengths. Initially the relative duration of these notes had to be construed by rule,[58] but eventually the shortest of them was given an ascending tail to distinguish it from the others and came to be designated by the descriptive term *semibrevis minima* (soon shortened to *minima* alone). This note assumed particular significance. Because the longer note values were of varying lengths determined by the context, the minim became the standard unit of measure, a metrical constant by which the total duration of all other notes could be calculated and related to one another (see Figure A-21).[59]

With the addition of the *maxima* and the minim to the durational values available to the composer, it became possible to organize musical meters at four separate levels. The level represented by the modal rhythms of the twelfth century, designated *modus*, concerned the division of the long into its constituent breves. Like the other degrees, it could be either imperfect, with the long divisible into two breves, or perfect, with the long divisible into three. The tempus, represented by the breve, could also be either imperfect or perfect (divisible into either two or three equal semibreves). With the addition to *modus* of two levels using smaller notes, however,

---

58. See, for example, Philippe de Vitry, *Ars nova* in the English translation by Leon Plantinga, *Journal of Music Theory* 5 (1961): 204ff.
59. Cf. Strunk, ed., *Source Readings*, rev. ed., 267.

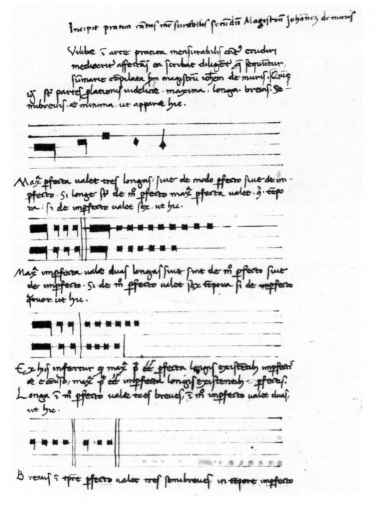

FIGURE A-21.   The beginning of Jean de Muris's *Libellus cantus mensurabilis* (Siena, Biblioteca Comunale, MS L V 30, f. 33ʳ).

the duration of the *tempus*, or breve, had become considerably greater than it had been earlier.

The same principles of mensural order were likewise extended to the more recently added levels of division. The *maxima* could be either imperfect or perfect (composed of either two or three equal longs), and the mensural degree thus created was known as *maximodus* (or *modus maximarum*) by analogy with the one that followed. The fourth—and last—level of division regulated the subdivision of the semibreve into its newly defined component minims. Once again the division could be either binary or ternary (imperfect or perfect). Because it had to do with the manner in which the semibreves were to be read—that is, "brought forth" in performance—this mensural degree was known as *prolatio* (from the Latin verb *profero*). Its perfect division was at times also called major, its imperfect one minor (the terminology originated with de Vitry), and the distinction is a useful one since it can help to keep the various mensural degrees clearly separate. Figure A-22 illustrates the possibilities at each of these levels.

In theory, at least, it was possible to have all four of these levels present in any

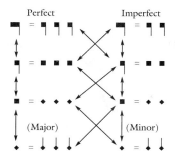

FIGURE A-22. Levels of mensural organization according to Johannes de Muris and Philippe de Vitry (the solid lines show the various combinations possible from one level to the next).

musical composition, but it was rare in practice to have more than two or three. As a rule, *modus* and *maximodus* are to be found only in the large isorhythmic structures of the fourteenth and early fifteenth centuries, primarily in the lower instrumental parts of motets and mass movements. Even there *maximodus* is frequently treated more as a theoretical convention than as a meaningful mensural reality. This was undoubtedly in large part because the longs and, more particularly, the *maximae* had become by then so extended in duration that the rhythmic patterns in which they figured could not easily be aurally perceived (if at all).

There is good evidence that the brisk succession of longs and breves that had characterized the modal rhythms in their earliest stages had been replaced in de Vitry's time by similar rhythmic patterns written in semibreves and minims (see Figure A-23). This meant, of course, that *maximae*, longs, and breves had gradually

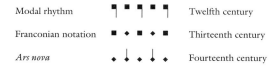

FIGURE A-23. Approximate tempo relationships between the twelfth and the fourteenth centuries as shown by the different note values used for similar rhythmic patterns).

slowed over the intervening centuries until their duration was roughly three times what it once had been. If these values continued to be used in the more traditional forms of composition, it was not merely because they were an integral part of the stylistic conception of the genres involved, historically speaking; it was also because they embodied in their rhythmic interrelationships—at a relatively high level of abstraction—the most essential of the musical proportions upon which Platonic cosmology was based, especially 3:2 and 2:1.

The variety of numerical proportions that could be exploited by composers of the fourteenth century was possible in good measure because—as Figure A-22 shows—

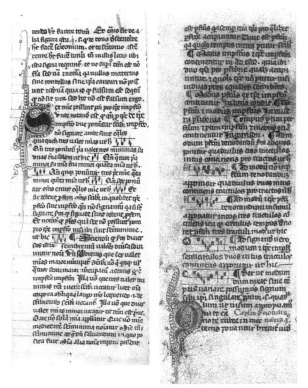

Figure A-24. Two details from Philippe de Vitry's *Ars nova* showing semibreves and minims (in the first column) and the various mensural signs for *modus* and *tempus* that the author put forward for practical use (Rome, Biblioteca Vaticana, MS Barberini 307, ff. 19ʳ and 20ʳ).

each of the four levels of division could be combined with the next in four different ways. Those actually present in a composition could thus be all ternary, all binary, or a mixture of the two. The combinations most frequently employed in the early fourteenth century, especially for the upper, texted parts, have come to be known as Philippe de Vitry's four prolations: (1) perfect tempus with major prolation; (2) perfect tempus with minor prolation; (3) imperfect tempus with major prolation; and (4) imperfect tempus with minor prolation.

Although copyists (and composers?) tended until well into the fifteenth century to leave the performer to his own devices, obliging him to construe the mensural patterns in a musical composition from the notation used to represent them, the theorists, from de Vitry on, proposed a series of signs to make them specific. For *tempus*, perfection was to be symbolized by a closed circle and imperfection by an incomplete circle or semicircle. Major prolation was to be shown by a dot centered in the circle or semicircle indicating *tempus*, minor prolation by its absence (see Figure A-24).[60]

By the second half of the fifteenth century these mensural signatures had begun to appear in the practical sources with increasing regularity. The suggestions made by the theorists for signing *modus* and *maximodus* were, by contrast, virtually ignored. Instead of relying upon more abstract symbols for these degrees, it became customary to construe them from the long rests, which were almost invariably present in a work where *modus* or *maximodus* was operative. (The rests could be used as a signa-

60. See Hoppin, *Medieval Music*, 354f.

ture, moreover, even when they did not function as an indication of silence.) If the signifying stroke traversed three spaces of the staff, the *modus* was perfect; if only two spaces, then it was imperfect. Similarly, if the long rests were grouped by threes, perfect *maximodus* was implied; and if by twos, then imperfect *maximodus* (see Figure A-25). But whether the various levels of mensural organization utilized in a piece of

FIGURE A-25. The use of rests to signify *modus* and/or *maximodus*: (1) perfect *maximodus* and perfect *modus*; (2) perfect *maximodus* and imperfect *modus*; (3) imperfect *maximodus* and perfect *modus*; and (4) imperfect *maximodus* and imperfect *modus*.

music were signed or not, it was possible to indicate an internal change by the notational device called coloration—initially the replacement of the black ink in which the notes were generally drawn by red—and eventually, in special cases, by other colors such as blue (see Figure A-26).

In all of the ternary mensurations the rules for perfection, imperfection, and alteration continued to apply, whether the notes were written separately or in ligature, much as they had from the late thirteenth century on. Dots, too, were retained in a number of contexts to mark off the units of perfection and to divide them from one another according to the wishes of the composer. The dot also assumed a role in the imperfect mensurations, however, unlike the procedures for perfection and alteration, which had no place there. It became, in a binary context, a sign of addition, increasing the

FIGURE A-26. Cantus of an anonymous Credo in canon showing the use of black, red, and blue inks for the notation (London, British Library, MS 57950 ["Old Hall Manuscript"], f. 62ᵛ). Red notes show up here as a lighter color; blue ink was used for the "Et resurrexit," staves 4–7.

duration of the note to which it was affixed by half. Its effect may be seen, of course, as the creation of a "perfected" note within an imperfect mensuration, and this additive function is the only one it has retained in the notation of the present day.

FRENCH AND ITALIAN PRACTICE COMPARED

The mensural system based on the theoretical works of de Muris and de Vitry, which became current in French territories in the course of the fourteenth century, was not the only one in use at the time, however. A related practice, which was distinctive in several significant respects, was adopted by Italian composers of polyphony. Their mensural conventions were first formulated in writing by the theorist Marchetto da Padova, again shortly before 1320. After dealing with such traditional matters as the meaning of note forms, rests, and ligatures, which were for the Italians basically the same as for the French, Marchetto concerned himself primarily with the division of the breve. This he rationalized on three successive levels. On the first of these the breve was divided, if perfect, into three semibreves, and if imperfect into two. Significantly, these semibreves were theoretically all of the same length. As a result, the semibreve of the first division provided the temporal standard by which the relative value of all other notes could be determined; it functioned in this respect like the minim of the French system.

The second division could be once again either perfect or imperfect. When the breve was ternary, a perfect division on the second level could produce up to nine of the shortest possible semibreves (also known as minims in this context), and the Italians referred to it, therefore, as *novenaria*. When the second division of the perfect breve was binary, the total number of minims possible was only six, and this pattern was designated *senaria perfecta*, the qualifier indicating that the minims were to be construed in three pairs. When the breve was binary, a perfect second division also produced up to six minims, this time in two groups of three, and it was consequently known as *senaria imperfecta*. (The Italians also called it *senaria perfecta italica* because their composers were partial to it in the fourteenth century; *senaria imperfecta* they also termed *gallica* because of its persistent prominence in the French music of the period.) An imperfect second division of a binary breve, finally, resulted in a maximum of only four minims and was identified as *quaternaria*.

The four combinations of perfect and imperfect divisions on the two levels described thus far correspond, as to number though not as to relative duration, to the four prolations ascribed to Philippe de Vitry. In addition, the Italians had a third division of the brevis that had no counterpart in French mensural practice. This provided for splitting the ternary breve into as many as twelve minims, a mensuration known to the Italians as *duodenaria*, and the binary breve into as many as eight minims, which was called *octonaria* (see Figure A-27).[61] Other distinctive features of Italian mensural notation included the systematic use of dots of division to mark off

61. Marchetto describes these divisions in his *Pomerium*, the relevant portions of which have been translated into English by Strunk, ed., *Source Readings*, rev. ed., 251–61.

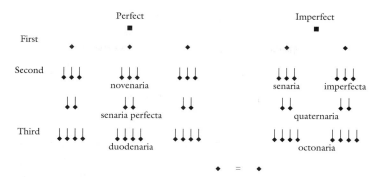

FIGURE A-27. Three divisions of the breve according to Marchetto da Padova.

the brevis units (as in the French notation of the late thirteenth century), a descending tail for semibreves of more than normal length (roughly an Italian equivalent for the dot of addition), and the adoption of the initial letter of the appropriate mensural designation as a mensural signature (instead of a symbol as in the north). Curiously, all these traits eventually disappeared from the notational practice of Renaissance Europe.

Much more significant, historically, was the proportional nature of the Italian mensural system. This is because of what now appears to be its far-reaching impact on the development of musical style in the late fourteenth and early fifteenth centuries. Unlike French mensural doctrine, in which the minim was constant, the theoretical formulation of Marchetto took as its standard of measure the semibreve of the first division. Consequently, the minims of the second and third divisions were not all of the same length. Quite to the contrary, they could be related to one another proportionately by the small superparticular ratios that were so important to all theoretical systems rooted in Greek thought. In the Italian repertories of the fourteenth century, different mensurations were used both simultaneously and, even more typically, successively in the same work. Thus the minims of *duodenaria* and *octonaria*, which were equal in length among themselves, stood in a proportion of 4:3 with those of *novenaria* and *senaria imperfecta*, respectively, and in a proportion of 2:1 with those of *senaria perfecta* and *quaternaria*. Similarly, the minims of *novenaria* and *senaria imperfecta*, which were likewise equal in length among themselves, were in a proportion of 3:2 with those of *senaria perfecta* and *quaternaria*, respectively.[62]

By the second half of the fourteenth century, when musicians of north and south began to be drawn together in and around the papal court at Avignon, French composers clearly came to be fascinated by the rhythmic possibilities offered by such a system. Ironically, even as a recognizably autonomous polyphonic style was disappearing from the Italian peninsula as a result of growing French musical influence

62. This interpretation of the tempo relationships within the Italian mensural system of the fourteenth century differs in some major points from that proposed by Hoppin, *Medieval Music*, 435–37.

there, the northerners found ways of assimilating into their compositional practice the proportional relationships inherent in Italian mensural usage. In so doing they did not abandon the constant minim postulated by the French theorists of the fourteenth century. Rather, they adapted an imaginative variety of notational devices, for which there were numerous models in their own tradition, to the proportional relationships that they wished to borrow from the Italians.

These included, first of all, the use of coloration—red ink in place of black at the time—with its traditional meaning. In repertories of the late fourteenth and early fifteenth centuries, such as those contained in the Chantilly and Modena manuscripts,[63] its presence usually signaled a shift from imperfect *tempus* with major prolation (which continued to be the preferred mensuration of the French through the turn of the century) to perfect *tempus* with minor prolation. This produced a pseudo-proportion, in a sense—as it did later when transferred to the next higher mensural level—since the minim remained constant. The division of the brevis into six minims was merely construed as three groups of two rather than as two groups of three, and that was entirely feasible notationally without coloration. In other instances, however, where coloration was used to signal a shift to a ternary meter in the place of a binary one, the result was to divide the note affected by three instead of by two. This introduced a true sesquialteral proportion and an acceleration of the note values at the next lower level.

More useful for indicating mathematical proportions in mensural relationships were yet other means of altering the visual aspect of the notes without tampering with their traditional shapes. It was possible to void the note forms, for example, drawing them only in outline, and in either red or black, depending upon the intended meaning. In addition to such experiments with colored and voided notes, composers tried stemming the otherwise ambiguous semibreves in various ways, adding both ascending and descending strokes simultaneously, for instance (creating a note type known as the *dragma*), capping certain stems with flags or hooks (usually to show a subdivision of the minim), and drawing them at unusual angles from the diamond-shaped head rather than vertically from its upper or lower point.

Numerals, either alone or written in pairs as a proportion, were also used to show the rhythmic relationships between certain note types from one section of a piece to the next. Even the—by then—traditional mensural signatures were made to signify proportional notations through modifications in their disposition or overall appearance. The circle of temporal perfection was given, in certain instances, two or three internal dots or was bisected by a straight line, while the semicircle was reversed with the break in its arc to the left side and, eventually, cut through with a line as well.

Some of these changes in notes and related symbols assumed fairly soon a standardized meaning that was generally understood. Coloration has already been mentioned as one such device for which the traditional significance was never fundamentally altered. To this we may add the reversal of the semicircle, which came to stand (usually) for a proportion of 4:3 at the level of the minim or the semibreve, and the

---

63. These collections have been succinctly described by Hoppin, *Medieval Music,* 472–75.

stroke of bisection applied to circle and semicircle alike, which represented from the outset a halving of the note values actually written. More often, however, these notational novelties were rather idiosyncratic in nature; they betray an undeniable love of complexity for its own sake, both rhythmically and notationally. Not only are the compositions in which they appear a challenge for the most skillful performers, but the notation itself is also frequently more intricate and complicated than it need be.

Still, it is usually possible, even now, to determine from their context the musical sense of the notational procedures adopted for a given work. Since the three or four parts that were conventional for the period had to proceed together in some recognizable order, the principles governing their rhythmic coordination vertically are generally discoverable by transcription in score. For fourteenth-century performers, however, who had to work from indi-

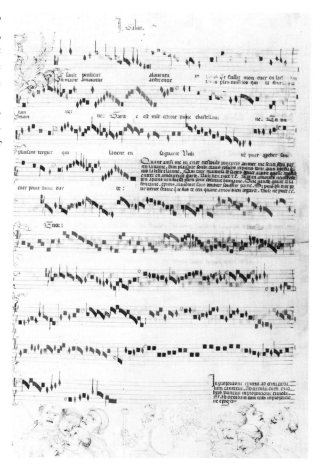

FIGURE A-28. Galiot's *Le sault perilleux* showing a verbal canon at the end of the last staff (Chantilly, Musée Conde, MS 1047 ["Chantilly Codex"], f. 37).

vidual parts, the difficulties were often so considerable that composers provided verbal instructions or *canons* to help them unravel idiosyncratic or experimental usage. These directions were usually written in Latin but were occasionally formulated in the vernacular as well. In time the canons themselves came to be treated as part of the challenge to the performer, and at that point one often finds them in the form of a puzzle or an enigma instead of a straightforward explanation (see Figure A-28).[64]

64. Most of the unusual notational devices cited in the foregoing discussion, including the use of a verbal *canon*, are illustrated by Jacob Senleches's *La harpe de melodie*, no. 69 in Hoppin's *Anthology of Medieval Music*, a facsimile of which appears on the jacket of that collection.

Both the unusual rhythmic complexity characteristic of this late fourteenth-century repertory and the growing arsenal of note values apparently engendered by it suggest that the traditional notes of longer duration—from the *maxima* to the semibreve—continued to slow gradually in comparison with earlier practice. Symptomatic of this unrelenting trend were the devices tried in order to retain for the composer the note forms needed to indicate rhythmic patterns as rapid as any that had been used, or that might be attempted. One of these was the splitting of the minim into smaller values called, by analogy with established terminology, *semiminims*. The other was the utilization of the conventional mensural orders but at an accelerated *tempo* or rate of speed. Both procedures are to be found in the repertory of the "Chantilly Codex," which was probably copied in the 1390s.

The various formal transformations used to impart to the minim a highly flexible range of rhythmic meanings have already been cited, but these appear side by side with mensural usage in which subdivision of the minim is entirely avoided. The latter style of notation was generally achieved by replacing the note values most commonly used with those of the next higher order and then giving them in performance roughly half of their usual duration. For example, the characteristic ternary movement of major prolation written in semibreves and minims was notated instead in perfect tempus with breves and semibreves that were performed at approximately twice their usual speed.

Such a substitution was explicitly indicated in a significant number of compositions by a stroke of diminution through the customary mensural sign (e.g., Φ or ¢) or by simultaneous juxtaposition with another part notated in the conventional manner. In other instances, however, the only evidence for a performance in diminution lies with the nature of the rhythmic figures employed by the composer.[65] This distinction apparently reflects regional differences in notational practice. Continental composers—especially, it would seem, those trained in the French tradition—were inclined to make use of mensural signs or some such indication of diminution in performance. The English, by contrast, generally omitted any overt signal that the duration of the notes written was to be reduced.[66]

The northern masters who tried one or the other of the two procedures described to assure a sufficient range of short rhythmic values for compositional purposes, might have followed Italian models in either case even though the latters' notational solutions were in a sense diametrically opposite. The innovative spirit that characterized mensural practice toward the end of the fourteenth century clearly encouraged experimentation with a variety of means for modifying or transforming the tradi-

65. The notational changes under consideration have been carefully examined by Ursula Günther in a pair of articles available only in German: "Die Anwendung der Diminution in der Handschrift Chantilly 1047," *Archiv für Musikwissenschaft* 17 (1960): 1–21; and idem, "Der Gebrauch des tempus perfectum diminutum in der Handschrift Chantilly 1047," *Archiv für Musikwissenschaft* 17 (1960): 277–97.
66. This aspect of English notational practice has been discussed briefly by Charles Hamm, *A Chronology of the Works of Guillaume Dufay Based on a Study of Mensural Practice* (Princeton: Princeton University Press, 1964), 94–95.

tional systems, regardless of their origins. It may be, however, that the creation of the semiminim, or at least the coining of the term by which it was known, posed a philosophical problem for those who were knowledgeable in such matters, as many theorists and composers appear to have been. Because a *minima* was, by definition, the least of the notational values, it would be argued that it could not be subdivided into still smaller units.

Such was the position to which Tinctoris adhered even though he was writing in the 1470s when both semiminims and their further division by half—producing notes known as *fusae*—were in common use, as his own examples show. He posited only five notes of "fixed value," from the maxima to the minim, and the latter he declared to be "incomposite" and "indivisible." The addition of coloration and flagged stems to the basic shape of this note—processes used to create discrete new note forms to signify the successive subdivisions of the minim—Tinctoris construed rather as proportional indications that could be applied to the note without changing its name or its essential nature.[67]

FROM BLACK TO VOID NOTATION

The fifteenth century brought with it important changes in mensural usage. However, the most striking of these was purely graphic in nature; the solid note forms, which had previously been the norm, came to be regularly drawn in outline only. The result was what has come to be known as "void" or "white" mensural notation. This transformation seems to have been linked to the increasing popularity of paper as a writing material to replace the traditional parchment, which was considerably more expensive. The voided forms required less ink and thus caused fewer blots on the paper page, but they also facilitated the copyist's task and speeded his work.

Whatever the reasons for its adoption, the new method of notation made its appearance early in the fifteenth century as a fully developed system. (It is found already in the MS Canonici Misc. 213 of the Bodleian Library in Oxford with dates from 1422 on.) By mid-century it reigned supreme virtually everywhere, but its introduction left untouched the conventions for writing notes in ligature and the venerable traditions concerning perfection, imperfection, and alteration. The note forms that resulted from the change are shown in Figure A-29 together with the corresponding symbols for silence, which had also undergone some modifications in the course of the fourteenth century. The reader will notice that if the rhomboid heads

67. This philosophical stance was maintained by Tinctoris with unswerving consistency through all of the short treatises in which he deals with the various aspects of mensural notation: see, for example, *De notis et pausis*, Cap. 2, "De notis certi valoris," and Cap. 7, "De minima" (where he asserts that the use of the term "semiminim" is an error); *De regulari valore notarum*, Cap. 32, "De valore minime"; and *Proportionale musices*, Cap. 5, "De genere multiplici." (The Latin text may be found in Johannis Tinctoris, *Opera theoretica*, Corpus scriptorum de musica, 22, edited by Albert Seay, 1:110–11 and 137, and 2a:15; also in Coussemaker, *Scriptorum de musica medii aevi* IV, pp. 41, 41, 53, and 156. Günther ("Gebrauch des tempus perfectum diminutum," 296–97) also suggests that the use of larger values in diminution may have been adopted in order to avoid the necessity of splitting the minim.

Maxima   Long   Breve   Semibreve   Minim   Semiminim   Fusa

FIGURE A-29. The notes and rests of white mensural notation.

used during the fifteenth and sixteenth centuries are rounded, as they were ever more frequently toward the end of that time, the semibreve corresponds to the modern whole note, the minim to the half note, the semiminim to the quarter notes, and the fusa to the eighth note. Similarly, aside from the long and the *maxima*, which have long been out of current use, the rests have retained their essential shape over the past four centuries with only minor modifications. The one exception is the semiminim rest, which is to be seen in the form illustrated in Figure A-29 only in French music printed in a traditional style.

Coloration, too, was used with void notation as it had been earlier, but with solid black ink replacing red as the sign of mensural change. Coloration continued to indicate, as it had since its appearance in the fourteenth century, a shift to a ternary division of a note that was regularly imperfect under the prevailing mensuration or, conversely, a binary division of a note that would otherwise have been perfect. The latter most commonly occurred from approximately the 1430s on in compositions written in perfect *tempus* (O), which began to be preferred to major prolation at about the same time as void notation started displacing black. It served in that context as a sign that perfect breves in groups of two were to be replaced by imperfect breves in groups of three, just as earlier it had signaled the substitution of the perfect semibreves of major prolation (especially in imperfect *tempus*) by an equivalent number of imperfect semibreves (compare Example A-2 and Figure A-30). The result was the same—the creation of a pseudo-proportion in the replacement of two ternary note values with three binary ones of the same overall duration—but at the next higher mensural level.

The opposite effect is most frequently to be observed in works notated in imper-

EXAMPLE A-2. Jean de Okeghem, *L'autre d'antan* (mm. 1–6)

L'aul- tre d'an - tan   l'au - trier pas - sa...

Tenor

Contra-
tenor

NOTE: Blackening in the original notation is indicated here by corner brackets.

FIGURE A-30. Okeghem's *L'autre d'antan* showing the use of coloration (blackening) with void mensural notation (New Haven, Yale University, Beinecke Library, MS 91 ["Mellon Chansonnier"], ff. 25ᵛ–26).

fect *tempus* and minor prolation with diminution (₵), which came to be increasingly prevalent in the second half of the fifteenth century. Under that sign the coloration of breves, semibreves, and minims introduced a perfect division of the breve. At the same time the blackening introduced a true sesquialtera proportion with the regularly voided notes, substituting three blackened semibreves (or their equivalent) for two white ones. A rhythmic shift of this nature was generally used in the 1460s and 1470s for short passages of a more or less ornamental nature (compare Example A-3 and Figure A-31), but by the turn of the century it appeared ever more frequently through an entire section—however brief—of a musical composition, where it usually provided not only rhythmic variety but also a means of structural articulation.[68]

   The proportional meaning of coloration in both of these notational conventions was extended to yet a third; blackened notes came also to be used as an alternate means of writing dotted rhythms. For example, a dotted semibreve followed by a

68. See, as an illustration, Josquin's *Ave Maria*, mm. 94–109, Example 15-1 above.

EXAMPLE A-3. Johannes Tinctoris, *O Virgo, miserere mei* (mm. 8–9)

NOTE: Blackening in the original notation is indicated here by corner brackets.

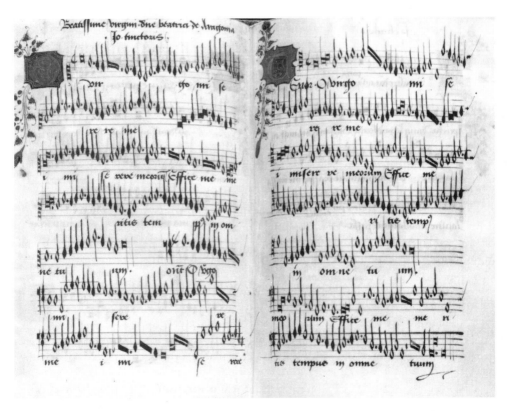

FIGURE A-31. Johannes Tinctoris , *O Virgo, miserere mei*, from the "Mellon Chansonnier" (New Haven, Yale University, Beinecke Library, MS 91, ff. 24ᵛ–25), showing the use of coloration (blackening) with void mensural notation.

minim could be represented instead by a blackened breve and semibreve with no change in rhythmic significance. Similarly, a dotted minim followed by a semiminim could be notated just as clearly by a blackened semibreve and minim (even though the latter was, of course, indistinguishable from the semiminim it replaced). That the two configurations stood for identical rhythms is clear from the many instances in which one of the dotted figures in question is given in the conventional way in one source and with blackened notes in another. The two notational forms are even found side by side in a single copy of a piece in which such a figure is either imitated or repeated.

The proportion conveyed by coloration used in this manner was duple in nature rather than sesquialteral as in the usage previously described; that is, a blackened note (breve or semibreve) of four units replaced one of three, and the difference was made discernible by the adoption of note values at the next higher level. The historical reasons for this practice have yet to be made clear, but the theorists of the fifteenth century coined a distinctive term for it—minor color—by which it continues to be known.

INTEGRAL AND DIMINISHED MENSURATIONS

As noted earlier, the fifteenth century brought with it changing preferences as to the mensurations most commonly used for the main body of a musical composition. Although all four of de Vitry's prolations made frequent appearances, imperfect *tempus* with major prolation seems to have been the one most in use in the late 1300s and early 1400s. In the 1420s some composers tried replacing it with perfect *tempus* in diminution (O), perhaps, as has been suggested, as a way of avoiding the semiminim in the face of a continuing tendency to slow the movement of the basic note values. Such diminution was not always specified by a stroke through the mensural sign, however, especially in the works of English composers.

Since the English presence on the continent in the 1420s during the second main drive of the Hundred Years' War included musicians and composers, it may have been primarily through their influence that a tradition was established for using perfect *tempus* (signed with O in the usual manner) at a faster tempo than would have resulted from a strict adherence to minim equivalence with respect to imperfect *tempus* and major prolation (C) according to de Vitry's notational system. In any case, by the 1430s *tempus perfectum* occurred ever more frequently as a basic mensuration but at a tempo that was distinctly more rapid than was to have been expected if the principles of fourteenth-century French theory had prevailed. This is clear from the fact that major prolation, which was rapidly becoming an archaic curiosity, began to assume in certain contexts (especially where it was used simultaneously with perfect *tempus*) a proportional meaning that required augmentation of its note values by two.

At the same time, the relation between perfect *tempus* (O) and its diminution (Ø) began to change. Whereas the latter had originally indicated a doubling of the basic movement, it continued to do so, apparently, only when the two mensurations were simultaneously combined. Moreover, by the 1430s they are found ever more infrequently in vertical juxtaposition. Rather, they tend to be used in alternation, and when they succeed one another in the same work, the tempo ratio between them is much more difficult to determine. Some scholars have proposed a continuing proportional relationship in accordance with the numerical bases of the prevailing cosmology. But they conclude from the evidence of musical style that the ratio was no longer strictly 2:1, suggesting instead that the tempo for the diminished mensuration was accelerated only by a third.[69] It is even possible that the stroke of diminution lost its proportional meaning entirely and came to signify only an appropriate quickening of the tempo.[70]

This somewhat idiosyncratic convention presumably posed no serious problems for those who witnessed its development and understood its meaning. However, within a generation or two, when perfect *tempus* began in turn to fall into disuse, so did the memory of the altered proportional relationship between perfect tempus and its diminished form. When the performing tradition established pragmatically in this manner was finally forgotten, what remained was the theoretical concept of indicating diminution by half with a vertical stroke through the mensural sign. The result was a source of conflicting mensural usage and interpretation that generated considerable confusion among theorists of the sixteenth century and that continues to pose vexing problems for scholars and performers of our own age.[71]

A clearer and more durable tradition was that in which major prolation came to be regularly construed as a sign of augmentation. Its persistence is probably to be explained by its early and ongoing association with the celebrated *L'homme armé* melody as a cantus firmus for polyphonic settings of the Ordinary of the Mass. This anomalous mensural device is to be seen in some of the earliest known examples, the *L'homme armé* masses by Busnoys and Okeghem, and a more or less continuous chain of compositions on the same tune, many of which were obviously written as technical showpieces in emulation of earlier works.

This tradition extended from the 1460s to the end of the sixteenth century and beyond, keeping the practice in relatively constant use. Consequently, prolation continued to be widely accepted as a sign of augmentation. Its use for that purpose per-

---

69. See Charles Hamm, *A Chronology of the Works of Guillaume Dufay*, 64–66. The relationship between the two mensurations can be described as sesquialteral in a sense; the ternary breve of the diminished form was apparently equated with an imperfect breve of perfect (or imperfect) *tempus*, i.e., ¢ ≡ · = c (or ○) ≡ . However, such a comparison, in which dissimilar note values were juxtaposed (in this case perfect and imperfect breves), violated a basic working rule of the fourteenth-century composer and is not to be found in the repertory of proportional devices of which he made use.

70. This interpretation is argued most persuasively by Alexander Blachly, "Mensuration and Tempo in Fifteenth-Century Music, Cut Signatures in Theory and Practice" (Ph.D. diss., Columbia University, 1995), chap. 2, "The Evolving Meaning of Cut Signatures in the Fifteenth Century," 116–54.

71. See, for example, Alejandro Planchart, "The Relative Speed of *Tempora* in the Period of Dufay," *Royal Musical Association Research Chronicle* 17 (1981): 33–51; and Anna Maria Busse Berger, *Mensuration and Proportion Signs: Origin and Evolution* (Oxford: Clarendon Press, 1988).

sisted despite a general trend among later Renaissance theorists to return—in the absence of an intellectual tradition to codify and rationalize the liberties that had been taken with de Vitry's system—to the minim equivalence that had characterized it originally.

There was no need, after all, to perpetuate the irregular mensural practices of the mid-fifteenth century. The stroke of diminution was easily used and readily understood. In combination with coloration it provided simple means for introducing the basic proportional changes that were most prevalent in contemporary musical styles. And if that was not sufficient, the fifteenth- or sixteenth-century master could always have recourse to the elaborate system of proportions that had been worked out by Tinctoris and presented with customary clarity in his *Proportionale musices*. The possibilities for which the theorist provided there go well beyond the requirements of ordinary usage and reflect a fascination with systematic numerical relationships that would have done credit to Boethius and to his sources, the Hellenistic harmonists.[72]

As has been indicated, the mensuration in most common use around 1430 was perfect *tempus* with minor prolation (O). In the decades that followed diminished imperfect *tempus*, signed in the usual way with a semicircle and a stroke (¢), was adopted with ever greater frequency. It appeared at first alongside the integral mensurations as an element of proportional variety, then, little by little, as a replacement for them. By the end of the century it had largely displaced perfect *tempus* as the predominant mensural order in polyphonic composition. Here, as well, the reduction in notational duration denoted by the stroke of diminution can be shown to be literally by half only when integral and diminished mensurations come together vertically. When diminished imperfect *tempus* began to be used by itself, however, a proportional interpretation of the acceleration in tempo it was meant to signify probably became progressively and increasingly rare.[73]

How was it possible for a mensuration that had arisen as a proportional diminution, dependent for its meaning on the integral mensural orders to which it referred, to come into quasi-exclusive use as a replacement for them? The answer lies with the concept of the *tactus* or beat. The notion of beating time to mark off recurring rhythmic patterns was not new to the fifteenth century. It can be traced to Latin antiquity when the *plausus* was used to regulate the meters of quantitative poetry, and it was linked to music already by Augustine (354–430). It has been argued that the first metrical system to be codified for Western polyphony, that of the rhythmic modes, was in fact dependent, whether directly or indirectly, upon the latter's *De musica*, in which both poetic meters and the *plausus* are discussed in detail.[74]

72. In addition to the Latin text, which has been edited by Coussemaker and by Seay, there is an English translation of this treatise by Seay in the *Journal of Music Theory* 1 (1957): 22–75.

73. See, in this connection as well, Alexander Blachly, "Mensuration and Tempo in Fifteenth-Century Music," 116ff.

74. The connection between Augustine's *De musica* and the rhythmic modes was first examined in detail by William G. Waite, *The Rhythm of Twelfth-Century Polyphony* (New Haven: Yale University Press, 1954), 13–55.

It is far from clear, however, what role, if any, the beating of a recurring metrical unit played in the musical performance of the Middle Ages. Since most polyphony was soloistic until the early years of the fifteenth century, it seems unlikely that the ostentatious beating of the rhythms would have been necessary to coordinate the efforts of the musicians involved. With the beginnings of choral polyphony around 1430, however, the need to maintain an ensemble of individual voices singing in parts may have led to the systematic use of a regularly recurring beat as a means of doing so.[75]

The practice is first explained by Ramos de Pareia in his *Musica practica* of 1482, in a manner suggesting that it was already a well-established convention. It is mentioned again by Adam of Fulda in his *De musica* of circa 1490 and by Franchinus Gaffurius in his *Practica musicae* of 1496. In each case the *tactus* is tied to the regular pulse of the heart and described as consisting of two separate motions—like the rise and fall of the ancient *plausus*—corresponding to the diastole and the systole of the regularly beating organ. Although contemporaneous discussions of the *tactus* are rarely lacking in some element of ambiguity, it seems reasonably clear, from these and other writers, that the complete beat was used to measure the semibreve in perfect *tempus* (O) and the breve in diminished imperfect *tempus* (₵).[76] Once the latter had been linked in this manner to the *tactus*, the presence of an integral mensuration was no longer required as a standard of reference. The diminished mensuration could stand by itself and the duration of its notational units determined by the *tactus*.

The tempo was thus linked in theory to the "normal" rate of the human pulse, but it is difficult to know to what extent the heartbeat was literally used to regulate the *tactus*. The tradition upon which that connection was founded was clearly a venerable one, and it may have been transmitted by the theorists of the fifteenth century simply out of respect for their ancient authorities—regardless of its practical value for performance. Nonetheless, Gaffurius, for one, takes some pains to explain that the pulse to be taken as a guide to tempo should be that of a healthy person, breathing regularly or quietly. His precision suggests that the heartbeat may in fact have served on occasion as a convenient point of reference for the conscientious choirmaster. In fact, he would have had little else to hand; mechanical devices designed for the purposes, such as were invented much later on, were entirely unknown at the time. The unit of measure was undoubtedly approximate at best, however, since the normal pulse rate can vary anywhere from some sixty beats per minute, or less, to seventy-two, or more. Still, it could give the Renaissance musician a general idea concerning the proper tempo for a given work and, if used with all due caution, can help the musician or scholar of the present day in much the same way.

75. In this regard, see Manfred Bukofzer, "The Beginnings of Choral Polyphony," *Studies in Medieval and Renaissance Music* (New York: Norton, 1950), 176–89. Bukofzer does not consider the role of the *tactus* in the development of choral ensembles, however.
76. See, for example, Gaffurius, *Practica musicae*, trans. Clement Miller ([Rome]: American Institute of Musicology, 1968), bk. 2, chaps. 1–3.

The almost exclusive predominance of the imperfect mensuration in its diminished form is nonetheless difficult to explain. It may have come about at least in part as a means of avoiding the semiminim, whether for the philosophical reasons already discussed or for practical ones. The voided notes required less ink and consequently, if they were to be copied by hand, less of the scribe's time. Moreover, as has been observed, there was less danger of blotting and damaging a carefully written page. It may be, however, that the notational convention in question was encouraged to some degree as well by the developing rhythmic style of the late fifteenth century. As is clear from the discussion of works dating from that period in the foregoing text, the ternary mensurations such as imperfect *tempus* with major prolations and, later on, perfect *tempus* tend to set up an unmistakable musical meter. The regularly recurring pattern of beats in threes creates a metrical framework that determines the expectations of the listener and gives meaning to the rhythms by which the prevailing mensuration is exemplified. And once the mensural pattern has been established, it can either be confirmed by the unfolding rhythms or obscured and even contradicted. In short, the ternary meter determined in good measure the rhythms that came to be characteristic of the style; there would have been little reason for the marked preference accorded it otherwise.

By contrast, the binary mensurations are much more neutral from a rhythmic point of view. This is especially true where the unit of beat—the *tactus*—can be identified with the breve, thereby eliminating any implication of a metrical organization at some higher level, such as was present with major prolation or perfect *tempus*. In such cases it became possible to treat meter and rhythm separately and to alternate binary and ternary groupings with little thought for the mensuration. It should not surprise us, then, to discover that in some compositions of the early sixteenth century—such as the *frottole*—although written as usual under the sign for diminished imperfect *tempus*, the rhythms are clearly and resolutely ternary. Whatever the reasons for its adoption, the use of diminished imperfect *tempus* took a tenacious hold on Western practice. Once it had come to predominate, it persisted in the sacred repertory (with little more than an occasional shift to a ternary proportion for variety's sake) until the end of the sixteenth century.

In secular music, it is true, another mensural convention made its appearance in the 1540s. Italian madrigals began to be written during that decade under the sign for imperfect *tempus* without the bisecting vertical stroke. These were characterized, as one would expect, by a much larger number of semiminims and fusae than were generally used in the diminished mensuration and were consequently described as composed *a note nere* or *cromatici* (that is "with black notes" or "colored").[77] Compositions of this kind were very much the exception at the time, however, and remained relatively rare until considerably later in the century.

---

77. See Reese, *Music in the Renaissance*, 320ff., and cf. above, p. 1021.

COUNTERPOINT AND HARMONY

Although the term "harmony" has assumed a technical, musical meaning in the vocabulary of the twentieth century, it continues to be used as well with the general sense that it had for the ancient Greeks. For them harmony was the joining together of disparate elements in such a way that there was agreement or concord, producing somehow an orderly whole from the separate parts, and it was this definition that led them, first of all, to connect it with music. In a musical context it came to mean the combination of sounds or pitches that can be perceived to blend or agree and thus fall pleasantly on the ear. This presupposed aural perceptions and esthetic judgments that appear to have been initially rather pragmatic and somewhat arbitrary in nature. When Pythagoras discovered, however, that it was possible to explain the variable degrees of euphony or asperity resulting from the combined pitches of different intervals in terms of the mathematical proportions by which they were formed, the concept of harmony took on a new dimension. It became, as a result, an essential component of Greek cosmological thought that was usually presented and illustrated by means of its sonorous manifestations. Thus, as we have seen, the harmony of the human soul, like that of the universal creation itself, was defined by small superparticular ratios with inherently musical implications: 2:1 for the octave, 3:2 for the fifth, 4:3 for the fourth, and 9:8 for the whole tone.

As the period we now know as the Renaissance began, these ideas were still current among both philosophers and musicians. Moreover, as humanist scholars recovered the works of Plato and Aristotle and made them available to a wider public in Latin translation, the general notion of harmony became all the more closely linked with its musical connotations. In a strictly musical sense, meanwhile, harmony continued to denote the simultaneous joining of pitches that strike the ear as agreeable. Tinctoris defined it as "a certain pleasant quality arising from sound fittingly combined,"[78] and Zarlino used the term frequently with much the same meaning. Like his predecessors, the Venetian theorist referred constantly to the twofold nature of the concept of harmony: to the sensually perceptible and agreeable impression of concord, on the one hand, and to its inherently proportional and hence numerically demonstrable nature, on the other.[79]

In the musical traditions of the West harmony was made audible in polyphonic music, and by the fifteenth century written polyphony was commonly referred to as counterpoint. The term derived, according to Tinctoris, from the expression *punctus contra punctum*[80] and thus designated (and designates still) the compositional process in which one notational symbol is written to sound synchronously with

---

78. Tinctoris, *Terminorum musicae diffinitorium*, s.v. *armonia*, "Armonia est amoenitas quaedam ex convenienti sono causata."
79. Zarlino, *Le Istitutioni harmoniche* (Venice, 1558, etc.), pt. 3, *passim*. See the English translation by Guy A. Marco and Claude V. Palisca, *The Art of Counterpoint* (New Haven: Yale University Press, 1968).
80. Tinctoris, *De arte contrapuncti*, bk. 1, chap. 1.

another, literally "note against note." Even though the medieval tradition for improvised polyphony was apparently kept alive in one form or another well into the sixteenth century, such a definition implies that the compositional process was begun in the abstract with the notation of rational choices of pitch and duration. Once in written form the conception of the creative imagination could then be realized as a sounding entity by any appropriate group of performers. In practical terms, then, and simply stated, counterpoint was understood to be musical composition.

During the Middle Ages, when polyphony was still an important component of the repertory, it was described and explained to the novice as the combination of only two pitches at once, resulting in two closely related melodic lines. Because that approach was so sound didactically, it was retained long after most composition was regularly for three, four, and more parts. All through the Renaissance, starting well before Tinctoris and continuing well beyond Zarlino, instruction in counterpoint began with writing in two parts. And this didactic pattern held through the fifteenth and sixteenth centuries, even though the theorists who wrote about such matters attempted ever more systematically to deal with the complications that stemmed from the addition of a third or fourth part to the compositional structure.

Also medieval in its origins was the classification of intervals adopted during the Renaissance. In fact, the underlying concepts adopted at the time for the teaching of counterpoint (and accepted even now whenever "tonal" harmony is taught) go back to the theories of the Greek harmonists. During the fifteenth and sixteenth centuries musical intervals were classified generally as either consonant or dissonant; consonances were perceived to possess harmonious qualities that were audible to human sense, whereas dissonances were deemed to lack them. Further distinctions were made among the specific intervals of these two primary categories in relation to their individual characteristics. To the trained ear each of the consonances produces a characteristic (and aurally identifiable) level and quality of agreement. Similarly, each of the dissonances has its own distinctive and recognizable degree of discord. Accordingly, each of the intervals of the notational system was located on a sonorous continuum that stretched from the most consonant on the one extreme to the most dissonant on the other. The practical result was the establishment of a hierarchy of intervals, each of which could fill certain compositional functions in accordance with the usage that had become conventional.

CONSONANCE

The most venerable of the consonances, obviously, and consequently the first to be rationalized for use in counterpoint, were those identified by the Greek harmonists as arising from small superparticular ratios. Of these it was the octave whose two pitches seemed to blend most completely, as if the one were simply a duplication of the other in a different register. Its special sonorous quality could be explained in part by its ratio; in addition to being the first superparticular, the octave was represented by the smallest of the ratios classified by Boethius as multiple. The fifth, by comparison, was considered (with its 3:2 ratio) to be slightly, but discernibly, less consonant and the fourth (at 4:3) even further removed in its euphonious impression on the listener. The aural judgments concerning the relative consonance of these intervals were thus supported, once again, by the mathematical evidence; the ratio increased by one unit each time as the level of agreement between the pitches so represented diminished by a roughly analogous amount. Notwithstanding the differences among them, all three intervals were designated perfect consonances, perhaps, as Zarlino suggested,[81] because they were the only ones found suitable from the early Middle Ages on for both opening and, more importantly, closing or "perfecting" a piece of counterpoint.[82]

Interestingly, it seems to have been the significance attributed to these three intervals as a result of their recognition by the Greek harmonists that has maintained their special status as "perfect" consonances down to the present day. The strength of that tradition is especially striking with respect to the fourth, for by the early fourteenth century it was considered to be insufficiently consonant to create a pleasant effect if sounded alone. Its use was consequently restricted essentially to those contexts in which it was heard above another compatible consonance, such as a fifth or a third. And when it was allowed to sound as the lowest interval in a sonority of three or more pitches, it was generally considered and treated as a dissonance.

The unison—two musical sounds sharing the same pitch—was not considered to be an interval, strictly speaking, since there is no measurable distance between its parts (as certain theorists were at great pains to point out). However, in counterpoint it was treated very much like the octave, filling all of its contrapuntal functions, because its aural effect was perceived to be very much the same. The agreement of its two pitches was not to be doubted, clearly, even if their relationship was not "harmonious" in the usual sense of the word.

The thirds, both major (consisting of two whole tones) and minor (consisting of a tone plus a semitone), were admitted to the medieval family of consonances not long after the perfect concords themselves. This was done initially on purely pragmatic grounds; the intervals in question were found to make an agreeable impression in counterpoint and were thus designated as consonant even though no arithmetical demonstration was adduced at the time to confirm the judgment of the senses.

The sixths by contrast, again both major (consisting of a perfect fifth plus a whole tone) and minor (comprising a perfect fifth plus a semitone) were not so readily accepted. It was not until the fourteenth century that both of them came to be classed consistently with the consonances, once more for strictly practical reasons.

But if the essentially euphonious character and the contrapuntal usefulness of both thirds and sixths were eventually recognized in the manner described, none of them was held to be suitable by itself as a final sonority or, usually, as an initial one

81. Zarlino, *Le Istitutioni harmoniche*, bk. 3, chap. 39.
82. The use of the term "perfection" to refer to the end or completion of a piece, a notational figure, or a mensural order was a consistent feature of the musical theory and practice of the Middle Ages.

either. Rather, their role came to be the separation and mediation of perfect consonances in order to provide greater variety and richer sonorities for the counterpoint. And the differences in consonant quality and contrapuntal function that distinguished them from the perfect consonances were indicated by their general designation as imperfect consonances.

Not until mid-sixteenth century was an attempt made to provide mathematical—and hence philosophical and cosmological—justification for the conventional classification of thirds and sixths as imperfect consonances. It was Zarlino who did so by borrowing one of the divisions of the diatonic tetrachord proposed by the second-century Greek harmonist Ptolemy. This allowed him to define the major third with the proportion of 5:4 and the minor third with that of 6:5 by extending the superparticular series by which consonances were measured from four to six.

This could not be done without tampering with the venerable structure of the medieval scale, however, which may be why this numerical rationalization of the thirds as consonances had not been taken up by some enterprising theorist much earlier. A major third of the size indicated required the introduction of a whole tone with a ratio of 10:9 alongside the traditional one in a ratio of 9:8, and the minor third combined a 9:8 tone with a major semitone in the superparticular ratio of 16:15 (instead of the customary unwieldy measurement of 256:243). Compared with the medieval gamut, the resulting redistribution of sonorous space among the scale degrees of the octave was considerable, as Figure A-32 shows (and compare Figure A-33).[83] In addition, the 10:9 whole tone, when divided by the major semitone of 16:15, yielded a smaller interval that was also superparticular, a minor semitone that could be represented by the ratio 25:24. The division of the 9:8 whole tone, on the other hand, did not produce such rational results.

What is more, Zarlino was unable to do for the sixths what he did for the thirds. His proposed division of the scale did not produce for either of them a rational measurement under a superparticular ratio. Consequently, the classification of the sixths as imperfect consonances continued to be primarily a matter of conventional usage.

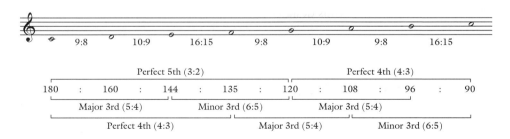

FIGURE A-32. Zarlino's division of the octave.

83. See *Le Istitutioni harmoniche*, bk. 1, chap. 15, and bk. 2, chap. 39, and cf. Claude Palisca, "Zarlino," *The New Grove Dictionary of Music*, 20:646–47.

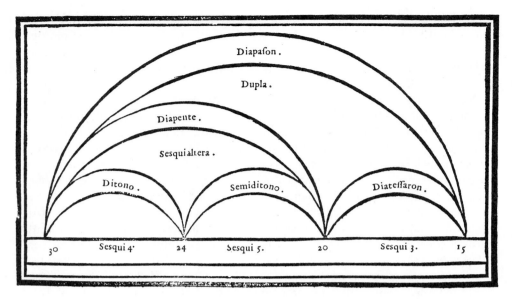

FIGURE A-33.   Zarlino's division of the octave into a fifth (consisting of a major and a minor third) and a fourth, showing his proportions for each of these intervals, from *Le Istitutioni harmoniche*, 1558 edition, bk. 2, chap. 39.

The theorist attempted to justify their traditional status by describing them as a conjunction of two smaller consonances—the perfect fourth and the minor third for the minor sixth, the perfect fourth and the major third for the major sixth. He also pointed out that their numerical ratios, although superpartient rather than superparticular (and hence of a type that did not usually produce harmony), could be expressed by the relatively small numbers of 5:3 for the major sixth and 8:5 for its minor sister.

For the minor sixth, therefore, Zarlino even found it necessary to go beyond his self-imposed limit of the *senaria* (the number 6) within which Zarlino professed to find the source of all truly harmonic intervallic relationships. At the same time, he was obliged to recognize that there were those in his day who questioned whether the sixths were in fact truly consonant,[84] and they did become surprisingly rare in some repertories of the late sixteenth century in view of their traditional place among the consonances.

There were problems, then, with the scalar structure propounded by Zarlino that limited its practical usefulness and prevented its widespread adoption. In addition, more pragmatic attempts had begun considerably earlier to temper Pythagorean tuning in such a way that polyphony accompanied by and played upon keyboards and other instruments of relatively fixed pitch not sound bad (i.e., "out of tune"). By Zarlino's time that process was already well advanced, and his ideas did not signifi-

84. See Zarlino, *Le Istitutioni harmoniche*, bk. 1, chap. 16.

cantly alter its course. But they do reflect in their own way the widely recognized need to adjust the medieval scale to the special requirements of polyphonic composition.

His theoretical system of consonance was a magnificent intellectual achievement nonetheless, and it was recognized as such by his contemporaries, even those who differed with him in matters of detail. It is particularly significant to us now as an indication of the vigorous revival of the Greek conception of "harmony" in the musical thought of sixteenth-century humanists. That a man of Zarlino's broad learning and considerable intelligence would make such a thoroughgoing effort to ground the contrapuntal practice of his day in a mathematically determined cosmology derived from the ancient Greeks is eloquent evidence of the extent to which those ideas were still believed, revered, and given practical application.

FROM DYADS TO CHORDAL SONORITIES

In the light of that trend a subtle conceptual shift in the treatment of consonance (due in large part to the increasing cultivation of compositions for three or four voices) was to have important implications. Many of the smaller intervals, when combined, produce sonorities that are consonant throughout, as both theorists and composers must have realized from the very outset of polyphonic practice. By the fifteenth century, however, it was becoming increasingly common to think of these composite sonorities not as combinations of smaller consonances but rather as a larger consonance divided into its concordant constituents for harmonious effect. From that perspective it was not difficult to view the concurrently sounding pitches resulting from such a division as a kind of chordal entity. Whether the process of generating such clusters of mutually consonant pitches was described as one of addition, as it was by Tinctoris, or as one of division, as it was by Gaffurius, depended upon the point of view of the theorist, but the practical result was the same.

For example, two pitches (a dyad in modern parlance) that form an octave can be divided by a third one to sound with its outer limits both a fifth and a fourth. Similarly, the sixth can be divided to produce with its defining pitches a third and a fourth. In either case the fourth could stand in principle either above or below the other interval. But by the fifteenth century it was avoided in most contexts as the lowest sounding interval because, as has been noted, the resulting sonority was judged insufficiently euphonious. The fifth could also be divided, finally, to form a pair of thirds, the one major and the other minor, and the quality of the resulting sonority is determined by which type of third lies at the bottom (see Figure A-34).

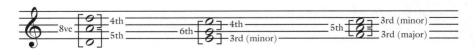

FIGURE A-34.   The division and combination of consonant intervals.

Other divisions (or combinations) were possible only by joining to these intervals one or more additional octaves and duplicating the operations already described.

It was Zarlino, once again, who rationalized mathematically this process of intervallic division. As he observed, the division of the octave with the unacceptable fourth at the bottom could be represented numerically by the insertion of an *arithmetic* mean between the extreme terms of the larger interval, as in Figure A-35a. In

FIGURE A-35. Arithmetic (a and c) and harmonic (b and d) divisions of the octave and the fifth.

order to have the fifth below, however, a division by the *harmonic* mean was required (Figure A-35b). In like manner the division of the fifth with the minor third as the lower of the two could be effected in Zarlino's system with the arithmetic mean (Figure A-35c), whereas the harmonic mean was needed to place the major third below (Figure A-35d).[85]

That the harmonic division was preferable to the arithmetic one must have seemed self-evident to Zarlino, first of all in view of the traditional mathematical demonstrations with which he worked. And he clearly found confirmation for that assumption in his own aural judgment and that of his contemporaries. This led him to conclude that the natural order of the consonances was the numerical one. In his view, then, the most "harmonious" way to combine them was with the largest interval (that represented by the smallest number) at the bottom and the smaller ones added above in order of decreasing size (and increasingly larger ratios). For him, consequently, the most perfect harmony consisted of an octave in the lowest register to which were added successively a fifth, a fourth, a major third, and a minor third to produce the sonority shown in Figure A-36.[86]

In the compositional process it was not always possible, obviously, to arrange the intervals in this configuration, even when it involved the six or more parts required to form the five consonances of the harmonic sequence. Nearly half the degrees of the scale (d, e, a), when taken as a starting point, yield the minor third before the

85. The various types of mean were a component of Boethian arithmetic and were defined by Zarlino in terms clearly derived from the Greek tradition (*Le Istitutioni harmoniche*, pt. 1, bk. 1, chaps. 36–39). Briefly, the arithmetical mean is the average of the two extremes, as, for example, 7 between 6 and 8; the harmonic mean is that in which the ratio of the differences between each of the extremes and the mean is the same as the ratio between the extremes themselves, as, for example, in Figure A-35b where $6-4$ ($=2$) : $4-3$ ($=1$) as 6:3 (that is 2:1). The Swiss humanist and music theorist Glarean, upon whose *Dodecachordon* of 1547 Zarlino modeled his modal system, had earlier used the arithmetic and harmonic divisions of the octave to rationalize the distinction between the plagal and authentic versions of the two modes sharing the same final and to account for the superiority traditionally attributed to the latter. See bk. 2, and Clement Miller's English translation ([Rome]: American Institute of Musicology, 1965).

86. See Zarlino, *Le Istitutioni harmoniche*, bk. 3, chap. 61. It is interesting to note that the overtones or partials of a given fundamental pitch (known as the harmonic series) are produced in exactly this sequence.

FIGURE A-36. Zarlino's ideal harmony.

major one, and both major and minor sixths as well as dissonances of various kinds may find their place in the counterpoint. It was Zarlino's opinion, however, that the natural order—with the larger intervals below the smaller ones—was to be observed as consistently as possible, whether the composer was writing for as few as three voices or for a good many more. That contrapuntal ideal seems to have acquired wide currency among composers of the late sixteenth century, who evidently preferred counterpoint in five and six parts to the more modest format of three or four that had been customary until then. This was presumably because it made possible the vertical accumulation of consonance required for the rich sonorous structures that Zarlino found most acceptable, giving precedence to the "harmony" of thirds and fifths rather than sixths and discords.

DISSONANCE

Dissonances arose from those intervals for which no small or tidy numerical proportion could be adduced, and their lack of harmonious agreement was thought to be as evident to the ear as their lack of arithmetic rationality was to the mind. All dissonances were not held to be the same, however; they were also divided between two separate categories. On the one hand were those that occurred naturally in the traditional gamut but that had nothing in common with the perfect consonances: these were the seconds and the sevenths. On the other hand were those dissonances that have the appearance, notationally, of a perfect consonance but not the requisite superparticular measurement (hence not the proper number of tones and semitones): these were known as "false" concords.

Seconds and sevenths, like imperfect consonances, can be either minor or major, depending upon their size. The two pitches defining the minor second span the small interval of a semitone, whereas those of the major second are a whole tone apart. Similarly, the minor seventh is only a minor third larger than a perfect fifth and a whole tone smaller than the octave, whereas the major seventh exceeds the perfect fifth by a major third and is only a semitone smaller than the octave. Like the consonant pairs of fourth and fifth or third and sixth, the two pairs of dissonant intervals are complementary.[87] They also filled analogous contrapuntal functions. The seconds figure in progressions contracting to the unison and the sevenths in those expanding to the octave, especially in cadential passages. All of them were perceived to be roughly equal in their level of dissonance, but a slightly greater degree of asper-

87. That is, they combine to make an octave. This is true of a perfect fourth combined with a perfect fifth, a major third with a minor sixth, a minor third with a major sixth, and, similarly, a major second with a minor seventh and a minor second with a major seventh.

ity was attributed to the intervals separated from the nearest perfect consonance by only a semitone: the minor second and the major seventh.

The false concords have the same size on the staff as one of the perfect consonances but are either larger or smaller by a semitone than the consonant intervals to which they correspond. Two of them occurred in the diatonic scale of the Middle Ages: the augmented fourth or tritone, and the imperfect or diminished fifth. The tritone is notated like a perfect fourth but exceeds it by a semitone (as between F and b-mi), thus encompassing three whole tones (hence its name). Similarly, the diminished fifth is noted like its perfect counterpart but is a semitone smaller (as between b-mi and f). Presumably because they were native to the traditional scale, composers occasionally treated them like consonances in certain contexts. Purists like Tinctoris censured such usage, but other theorists, such as Zarlino, explained instead how they could be handled without offending unduly the sensitive listener.[88]

It was possible, in addition, to introduce false concords into the counterpoint by means of accidentals: not only tritones and diminished fifths where they would not otherwise occur but also diminished fourths, augmented fifths, and augmented or diminished octaves and unisons. Although never approved by the theorists,[89] tritones and diminished fifths so generated were, it would seem, also occasionally tolerated in composition where consonance was usually required, presumably by analogy with those occurring in the unaltered diatonic scale.[90] By contrast the remaining "false" concords were categorically banned from counterpoint, regardless of the context, and their effect was considered so harsh that they were generally—but perhaps not entirely—avoided even where other types of dissonance were quite acceptable.[91] The spectrum of discord, then, as defined by the theorists of the fifteenth and sixteenth centuries and exemplified in the musical composition of the period can be represented as in Figure A-37.[92]

As will be clear from the foregoing discussion, the harmony of the fifteenth and sixteenth centuries was essentially intervallic in nature. Whether dealing with consonance or dissonance, the theorists and composers of the period usually conceived of them in terms of the distance between individual pairs of pitches. Even in the more or less habitual cultivation of counterpoint for a large number of voices—five, six, and more—the composite sonorities that consistently and inevitably occurred con-

88. Compare Tinctoris, *Art of Counterpoint*, bk. 2, chap. 33, with Zarino, *Le Istitutioni harmoniche*, bk. 3, chap. 30.
89. See, for example, Tinctoris, *Art of Counterpoint*, bk. 2, chap. 34, and cf. the chapter by Zarlino cited in note 88.
90. See, for example, Tinctoris, *Art of Counterpoint*, bk. 2, chap. 34, and cf. the chapter by Zarlino cited in note 88. As the examples given by Tinctoris will show, there is some ambiguity as to what was intended in many instances where a tritone or a diminished fifth may have been introduced accidentally because these intervals frequently occur at cadences where the accidentals were not generally written but left to the performer.
91. In a few clearly cadential passages (in compositions from mid- to late-sixteenth century) the counterpoint occasionally suggests that the composer may actually have intended that performers introduce an augmented octave (such as c against c♯).
92. As noted above, a perfect fourth spans two tones and a semitone, the perfect fifth three tones and a semitone, and the octave is as large as the two combined.

FIGURE A-37. Dissonance as defined during the Renaissance—(1) the natural dissonances: (a) minor second, (b) major second, (c) minor seventh, (d) major seventh; (2) "false" diatonic concords: (a) tritone, (b) diminished fifth; (3) "false" accidental concords (a) tritone, (b) diminished fifth, (c) diminished fourth, (d) augmented fifth, (e) diminished unison, (f) augmented unison, (g) diminished octave, (h) augmented octave.

tinued to be described and explained either as a division of the larger consonant intervals into smaller ones or the simultaneous juxtaposition of several small consonances to construct the larger ones. The concept of a "triad" of pitches a third apart that somehow retains its identity even when its components are "inverted"—rearranged so that the fifth of the initial order gives way to a sixth consisting of a third and a fourth or vice versa—was yet to be imagined.

Zarlino, who is usually credited with having provided a theoretical basis for the triadic idea, was himself working very much within the traditional theoretical framework. His primary purpose was to rationalize the division of the fifth into thirds in order to account for the euphonious character of the sonority most frequently employed in the counterpoint of his period. At the same time, he was able to provide an explanation of sorts for the distinctive sonorous quality produced by the two possible collocations of the smaller intervals. This should not surprise us, however. Except for certain types of instrumental music,[93] the concept of "triad," or even of "chord" (in the present sense), was patently unnecessary and in fact not even particularly useful for composition in the contrapuntal style that predominated in the European tradition from early in the fifteenth century until late in the sixteenth. Not until the monodic ideal of northern Italian solo song began to prevail, early in the seventeenth century, as the preferred approach to composition were conditions generally favorable for triadic formulations. The polarization of melody and harmony in that style, with the latter usually provided essentially by a single chord-playing instrument, made it not only possible but also convenient to conceptualize the various vertical sonorities as permutations of a unit of three pitches, and it was precisely at that point, historically, that the idea of the triad was born.[94]

THE RULES FOR COUNTERPOINT

By the fifteenth century a certain number of conventions for the writing of counterpoint had been widely established. Some of these were recognized so generally that

93. See, for example, Miguel A. Roig Francolí, "Playing in Consonances: A Spanish Renaissance Technique of Chordal Improvisation," *Early Music* 13 (1995): 461–71.
94. See Joel Lester, "Root-Position and Inverted Triads in Theory around 1600," *Journal of the American Musicological Society* 27 (1974): 110–19.

theorists saw fit to formulate them as "rules"; both Tinctoris and Gaffurius, for example, set forth a series of eight such precepts.[95] Although their respective canons are not entirely identical, there is considerable overlap between them. Moreover, other writers, both earlier and later, invariably touched upon the same few basic principles of composition in one way or another. Even so, few of the rules were without exception. Some depended, for the rigor with which they were observed, on the number of parts and the relationships among them; others were more in the nature of artistic and esthetic guidelines than of rigidly prescriptive or proscriptive dicta.

As has been noted, the rules were conceived initially for composition in two parts, and they were applied most strictly when the counterpoint is simple—that is, when it proceeds note against note with no rhythmic deviation from voice to voice. The addition of another part or parts, or the introduction of florid counterpoint—in which the separate melodic lines are rhythmically independent from one another—involves more complex problems and necessitated some adaptation of the traditional rules.

It was generally agreed that the perfect consonances were the only intervals appropriate for opening or closing a piece of counterpoint. But because perfection was customarily construed to mean "completion," those intervals were held to be more essential for closure than for inception. If a composition were to begin with a rest in one or more voices, for example, then imperfect consonance was permissible. Exceptions were not so readily made at the end, however. There perfect consonance was the rule, and it was used in practice with great regularity even in counterpoint for three or more voices until late in the sixteenth century. Only with the predilection for rich, full harmonies that began to prevail in the late fifteenth century did the fifth begin to be divided into a pair of thirds in the final sonority. The shift was gradual, however, and began with the secular repertory, where license with tradition was more readily tolerated.

Despite the superior status attributed to the perfect consonances and the pride of place given them in composition, there was one serious restriction placed on their use. Two (or more, of course) of the same type were not to be sounded consecutively in parallel motion. For example, two fifths or two octaves were not to be taken one directly after the other. It was possible only to repeat them; as long as the pitches remained constant, a number of fifths or octaves could be struck in succession without giving offense, even if the separate parts moved to exchange notes. But when a given part was in motion, another was not to follow it in parallel perfect consonances. Such usage was rigorously proscribed in two-part counterpoint by the theorists and was carefully avoided most of the time, regardless of the number of voices in play (see Figure A-38).

The stated preference was for contrary motion between the voices—that is, to

95. Tinctoris presented his rules as separate chapters in bk. 3 of *Art of Counterpoint*; Gaffurius compressed his into a single chapter (3) of his *Practica musicae*, bk. 3. The compositional principles discussed in the following pages have been drawn primarily from these two sources with confirmation for the sixteenth century coming from Zarlino, *Le Istitutioni harmoniche*, bk. 3.

FIGURE A-38. Contrapuntal progressions proscribed by convention: (1) parallel fifths and (2) parallel octaves, ascending and descending in two- and three-part writing.

counter descent in one part with ascent in another. That was an ideal that could be realized in two-part writing most of the time. When a third part was added, however, it had to move in the same direction as one of the other two, introducing either similar or parallel motion (in the same direction but by different intervals, as seen in Figure A-38, 1c and 2a, respectively). Or it could remain stationary, producing oblique motion (as in Figure A-38, 2b). With each additional part the possible combinations of ascending and descending motion increase (even though some of them could at times remain stationary), as does the complexity of the contrapuntal problems. Still, as Zarlino observed,[96] the most successful solutions to them were thought to be those in which at least two of the parts moved in opposite directions, and a random perusal of virtually any composition from the period will show how often that procedure was adopted.

Not only the direction but also the size of the melodic motion in the various lines of the counterpoint was a matter of concern to the composer. The melodic ideal was a line that proceeded as much as possible by step (conjunctly) rather than by leap (disjunctly), to favor melodic movement by tone and by semitone over the use of larger intervals. By so doing it became possible to satisfy yet another requirement of good counterpoint, to move as smoothly as possible from any given consonant sonority to the one nearest to it. This was more readily done in florid counterpoint than in the simple note-against-note variety, for obvious reasons. It was also easier with two parts than with three, four, or more; the greater the number of voices, the more difficult it is to maintain stepwise motion in all of them. When some compromise becomes necessary—or expedient at the very least—leaps are rarely introduced in the topmost part (the superius or cantus) or in the tenor. Rather, they are introduced in the contratenor altus (which traditionally lay between them) or—more frequently—in the contratenor bassus beneath.[97]

In the course of the fifteenth century these four parts came to be the standard for polyphonic composition, in part undoubtedly because they correspond to the overlapping ranges covered by the different registers of the human voice. Zarlino characterized them as "elemental," pointing out that when yet other parts were added, they simply duplicated these four as to range. They were therefore designated by the same terms (for example tenor 2, altus 2, etc.).

96. Zarlino, *Le Istitutioni harmoniche*, bk. 3, chap. 66.
97. The terms used to designate the four parts that came to be basic for all polyphonic music of the Renaissance are, obviously, the Latin antecedents of the Italian words now in common use: soprano, alto, tenor, and bass (from top to bottom).

Zarlino also indicated the somewhat hierarchical relationship among them by comparing them to the four elements of ancient science: earth, water, air, and fire. The bassus, as he observed, tended to move at a more deliberate pace than the other parts and more often by leap with very little in the way of ornamental figures and divisions. Consequently, it provided a foundation of sorts for the rest of the counterpoint. From the pitches sounded in the bassus were construed the combinations of consonant intervals generated among the parts: the harmonies. For although the bassus usually followed both cantus and tenor in order of composition,[98] all the pitches above it had to be concordant with it. In that significant sense it sustained and stabilized the other voices.

The superius or cantus, by contrast, was the most rapid of the parts, the most conjunctly written, and the most frequently ornamented. Those characteristics, combined with its higher range, caused it to be the most easily heard and followed. It was thus able to push itself into the listener's auditory foreground and take precedence over its more discreet companions. The altus, although it partook at times of the qualities of the superius in its rapidity of movement and stepwise character, was the last to be added, historically, to the conventional quartet, and the first to be dropped when three parts were preferred for either composition or performance.[99]

The most venerable of the parts was the tenor, first of all because of its longstanding role as the bearer of preexistent melodic material, whether chant or secular song. This made it the starting point for a good deal of the counterpoint written between the twelfth and the fifteenth centuries. Its original function as a cantus firmus, and the long musical tradition behind it, continue to be reflected in compositional practice all through the fifteenth and sixteenth centuries. It is to be seen in the precedence given the tenor in the writing of counterpoint. It is likewise apparent in the special status assigned it (according to Zarlino, amongst others) in determining the modal orientation of polyphonic music. Definition of mode was to be accomplished through a judicious choice of the pitches used in the tenor to initiate and to close the successive phrases of a work and of the consonant intervals placed above and/or below it, especially in cadential passages. It was therefore essentially by his handling of the tenor that the Renaissance composer was able to comply with another important rule of counterpoint: that its melodic lines and vertical sonorities be consistent with the fundamental characteristics of the mode selected for its composition.

In simple counterpoint consonant intervals alone were allowed between the

98. See Zarlino, *Le Istitutioni harmoniche*, bk. 3, chap. 58. It is widely believed that by the early sixteenth century the compositional process was "simultaneous," as Edward Lowinsky first suggested in his article "On the Use of Scores by Sixteenth-Century Musicians," *Journal of the American Musicological Society* 1 (1948): 17–23. However, even in a canonic or an imitative style where the composer was obliged to plan each part with an eye to what the other had done and would have to do, the lines of a given phrase or segment seem to have been composed one after the other, and Zarlino stated that one began as a rule with the tenor and proceeded from there to the superius, the bassus, and finally to the altus.
99. For example, the reduction of a vocal composition in four parts as a lute tablature was often facilitated by simply dropping the altus part from the very outset; see above, pp. 818–23.

voices, at least in principal. Dissonance could be introduced only when the writing was florid—that is, with a number of pitches struck successively in one part against a single note sustained in the other. As a result, the treatment of dissonance came to be tied to the duration of the pitches sounded and regulated by means of the mensuration and the *tactus*.[100] In the second half of the fifteenth century, when Tinctoris and Gaffurius were writing, a dissonance was not to last any longer, as a rule, than half the *tactus* unit—a minim under integral mensurations (O and C) and a semibreve under the diminished ones (Ø and ₵). The theorists noted, however, that their colleague-composers were not always so careful. By mid-sixteenth century, when Zarlino was writing, the tolerance for dissonance had apparently decreased. He himself was willing to allow it a maximum duration of only half of one of the two beats of the *tactus*—a semiminim under the integral mensurations (when they were used) and a minim in the diminished ones.

The placement of the dissonance was seen to be as important as its duration, moreover. The discordant effect was judged to be more obtrusive if allowed to coincide with either of the beats of the tactus, and especially the first. It was usually avoided in that position, therefore, but more systematically in the sixteenth century than in the fifteenth. It became customary, as well, to precede and to follow dissonance with consonance, particularly in those instances where the dissonance did fall with the beat. Discord was to be approached and resolved conjunctly as well, although some acceptable conventions for leaving a dissonant note by leap did develop in time. In fact, by the second half of the sixteenth century the treatment of dissonance generally came to be so careful and, in many ways, so uniform that it was possible for later theorists to codify systematically that usage, describing and naming each of the discordant configurations found in the counterpoint.[101]

At the time, however, the only dissonant figure to be so identified was the syncope, a note begun in a consonant context in one *tactus* and suspended through as much as the first beat of the next, where the other part or parts move to form a dissonance against it, as in Example A-4. (Obviously, the syncope can be used with only

EXAMPLE A-4. Examples of cadential formation showing the typical use of a dissonant syncope from Zarlino's *Le istitutioni harmoniche*, bk. 3, chap. 53

---

100. Concerning mensuration and *tactus*, see pp. 1031–35.
101. See, for example, the study by Knud Jeppesen, *The Style of Palestrina and the Dissonance* (Oxford: Oxford University Press, 1927).

consonant intervals as well, but that is of no concern to us here.) The early recognition and codification of this particular use of dissonance was obviously due to its repeated occurrence in cadential patters, where it resolves—almost invariably as here—first to an imperfect consonance and then to a perfect one. Resolution to consonance was of course a necessity for every dissonant sonority. As Zarlino observed, counterpoint was conceived as consisting primarily of consonance and only "accidentally" of dissonance,[102] but if properly handled, the discords could be most useful. They facilitated greatly the conjunct motion that was held to be so desirable and, in the process, added their own spicy charm to the counterpoint.

In all of this the composer was to strive for a pleasing variety in his use of contrapuntal procedures and devices. The esthetic ideal so expressed was in fact important enough that it was formulated by Tinctoris as one of his eight rules for composition. Zarlino, too, went to considerable pains to explain how it could be achieved.[103] In two-part writing it meant separating the perfect consonances with imperfect ones and also varying the latter as to type. When three or more parts were involved, it was necessary to alternate the arithmetic division of the fifth with the harmonic and to include a judicious mix of sixths—preferably divided as well—and dissonant intervals. Literal repetitions were to be avoided, as Tinctoris explicitly stated in yet another of his rules,[104] although sequential writing was admissible and came to be much used. Other techniques were found as well for varying the counterpoint when some element of repetition was either inevitable, as in the quotation of liturgical chant, or, for some reason, desirable.

As will appear from the preceding discussion, the "rules of counterpoint," as they were called, set forth normative procedures for polyphonic composition. Their conventions touched not only upon the problems of combining in harmonious sonorities two or more separate and independent lines but upon many other matters as well. These included the preferred style of melodic writing, the relationships among the parts rhythmically and even stylistically (as well as vertically), the maintenance of modal integrity, and the articulation of formal structures, to cite only some of the most important. Such matters were treated during the Middle Ages rather autonomously in musical terms, but it became increasingly important in the course of the fifteenth and sixteenth centuries that when a text was set, all of these conventions be somehow appropriately adapted to the sense and import of the words.

Usually this was managed by choosing skillfully among the compositional procedures that were generally acceptable, as when dissonance was introduced in connection with "harsh" conceits.[105] However, the very existence of rules and conventions made it possible to honor them in the breach, to violate them intentionally as a means of expressing or illustrating certain words and ideas. The use of parallel per-

102. Zarlino, *Le Istitutioni harmoniche*, bk. 3, chap. 27.
103. See Tinctoris, *Art of Counterpoint*, bk. 3, chap. 8, and Zarlino, *Le Istitutioni harmoniche*, bk. 3 chaps. 32–38 and *passim*.
104. Tinctoris, *Art of Counterpoint*, bk. 3, chap. 6.
105. See Zarlino, *Le Istitutioni harmoniche*, bk. 3, chaps. 26 and 66.

fect consonances, the "improper" or excessive introduction, prolongation, and resolution of dissonance, and obvious departures from modal norms are just a few of the
compositional "faults" that came to be so employed. In sum, the history of the music
of the Renaissance could easily be written, without distorting unduly the known
facts, as an account of increasing sensitivity to textual significance as displayed by successive generations of composers and the ever more imaginative and subtle means
they invented to convey to the listener verbal meanings and moods.[106]

CADENCES, ACCIDENTALS, AND CONTRAPUNTAL ARTIFICE

Every verbal text has its grammar, syntax, and formal structure, however loosely or
prosaically it may have been put together. The elements of which it is composed—
phrases, clauses, and periods—can be articulated, when necessary, by the traditional
marks of punctuation: commas, semicolons, periods, and the like. This was as true
during the Renaissance as it is today, although the usage of the fifteenth century was
much less consistent and considerably more arbitrary than it had become by the end
of the sixteenth, to say nothing of the present. Music, too, had by then acquired a
syntax, one consciously derived from and closely analogous to that of speech, and it
had its own form of punctuation as well. The phrases and periods of which it was
constructed were set off from one another by the cadences.

The simplest of cadential components, and the earliest to appear in the musical
traditions of the West, was melodic. A recognizable formula was used to take the
musical phrase to rest upon one of the scale degrees traditionally assigned a function
of closure within a given mode: the final, confinal, or reciting pitch, for example. The
Psalm tones with their *differentiae* exemplify some of the clearest and most highly
formalized of such cadential patterns, but those and others of a similar nature were
very much a part of all liturgical chant.[107] In a repertory so closely tied to the declamation of sacred and ceremonial texts, some means of melodic punctuation was
clearly to be expected. However, the extent to which the variable degrees of closure
possible in verbal structures were provided with a corresponding musical articulation
through the choice of cadential pitches and/or formulae remains one of the
admirable achievements of Christian plainsong.

Similarly, one of the most significant and characteristic accomplishments of
Western polyphony was the invention of contrapuntal formulae with recognizable
cadential functions analogous to those found in monophony and capable, like the
melodic cadences upon which they were modeled, of different levels of articulation
and nuances of closure.

Like so much in the polyphonic tradition of the Renaissance, the contrapuntal
cadence derived its framework from two-part writing. The basic formula was simplicity itself, consisting initially of only two sonorities, a perfect consonance (required

106. One might in fact describe in these terms the exhaustive study by Don Harrán, *Word-Tone Relations
in Musical Thought* ([Rome]: American Institute of Musicology, 1968).
107. See Hoppin, *Medieval Music*, 81–83 and 77.

for completion) preceded by the imperfect consonance nearest to it. In a two-part context the clearest cadential indication could be given by the octave or, if need be, the unison, since both involved but a single scale degree. For example, an internal phrase could close to the confinal of the mode the concluding passage to the final, and the melodic cadences leading to those scale degrees could be reinforced by a conventional contrapuntal formula. The fifth was also possible as a cadential interval, but its two scale degrees made the note of closure more ambiguous in a two-voice context and thus weakened the sense of cadential finality.

In the course of the fifteenth century it became increasingly common—in florid counterpoint where it was allowed—to introduce the imperfect consonance of the penultimate sonority with a discord, usually a dissonant syncope (as in Example A-4). This produced a sequence of intervals that progressed from the sharpest asperity permitted to the most complete concord deemed possible. So frequently was this formula employed, from the generation of Dunstable and Du Fay on, that when Zarlino was writing in mid-sixteenth century, the preparatory dissonance had become an integral part of the cadential structure. He was led, as a result, to describe the cadence as a sequence of three sonorities rather than two, even in simple counterpoint where dissonance was not used.[108]

There was one other cadential convention that appears to have been observed ever more consistently in the course of the fifteenth century, one that called in certain circumstances for the introduction of accidentals. As has been noted, the rules of counterpoint required that with only two parts a perfect consonance be approached, whenever possible, in contrary motion from the imperfect one nearest to it.[109] This meant that a unison was best approached from a minor third, a fifth from a major third or a minor sixth, and an octave from a major sixth, and that one of the two voices moved to its cadential final by semitone. When the cadence closed to an octave or a unison on E, F, C, or even B♭, this occurred naturally because the required intervals were contained within the diatonic gamut (as may be seen from Example A-4). With a close to D, G, or A, however—all of which were common enough—the third before the unison was normally major and the sixth before the octave regularly minor.

In order to give these imperfect consonances the desired proximity to the perfect ones to which they were to move, one of their constituent pitches was shifted "accidentally" to within a semitone of the cadential final of the phrase. This was usually done by raising the scale degree below it to "mi" (with a sharp), resulting in a pattern like that in closes on F and C. The desired effect could also be achieved by lowering the step above the cadential final with a flat in imitation of natural cadences to the final E. (These procedures are illustrated in Examples A-5a and b.) The best evidence suggests that these alterations were made with a good deal of consistency. But because they were usually left to the performer and rarely notated until late in the sixteenth century, there is sometimes room for doubt as to whether or not the con-

---

108. See Zarlino, *Le Istitutioni harmoniche*, bk. 3, chap. 53, for a fairly detailed and informative discussion of the cadence in polyphonic music.
109. See Gaffurius, *Practica musicae*, bk. 3, chap. 3.

EXAMPLE A-5. Cadential types for two, three, and four voices in the music of the fifteenth and sixteenth centuries: (a) and (b) two-part cadences with accidental alteration needed; (c) three-part cadence with parallel fourths; (d) three-part cadence with octave leap; (e) three-part cadence with cadential final in the third voice; (f) four-part cadence commonly used for closure

a) Du Fay, *Nuper rosarum,* mm. 25–26.

b) Okeghem, *Missa Caput,* Agnus, m. 10.

c) Du Fay, *Conditor alme,* mm. 12–13 and 4–5.

d) Du Fay, *Adieu ces bons vins,* mm. 24–25.

e) Busnoys, *A une damme,* mm. 16–17.

f) Anon., *Orsu car' Signori,* m. 7.

ventional accidental would have been applied, especially where some other contrapuntal rule would be broken as a result.

The addition of a third, fourth, or yet other parts to the counterpoint complicated the cadential formula, but the increased difficulty of handling a greater number of voices was offset by the advantage of an expanded range of possibilities for articulation and closure. The supplementary parts could be used either to reinforce the punctuating power of the cadential structure or to mitigate it, bridging the break in the counterpoint and introducing the following phrase. Both functions made use of a combination of melodic, harmonic, and rhythmic devices.

Reinforcement of closure resulted from duplicating the cadential final or from dividing the octave formed on that scale degree at the fifth, thus sounding only perfect consonances. Similarly, melodic and rhythmic activity in all parts could be brought to a point of repose—however temporary. In the song repertory of the fifteenth century, for example, where a three-voice format was the rule, the third part could proceed to the fifth above the cadential final from the requisite major third, approaching its concluding scale degree from the semitone below in parallel fourths with the uppermost voice. That formula, which made its appearance already in the counterpoint of the fourteenth century, occurred naturally in cadences to F. Elsewhere it required an accidental to expand either the third or the sixth or both to their major form in the penultimate sonority (as in Example A-5c).

When the third part was below the voices of the cadential pair rather than between them, it could reach the fifth above the final by an octave leap upward (as in Example A-5d). This was, at the time, a somewhat more "modern" solution that was apparently employed with increasing frequency as the highly characteristic sound of semitone motion in parallel fourths came to be regarded as slightly archaic. Or the third part could be taken up a fourth or down a fifth from the penultimate sonority to the last so that it duplicated the scale degree of the cadential final. So handled, it formed, instead of the fifth, either a unison with the tenor or an octave below it (as in Example A-5e).

When a fourth part was added to the cadential structure, it was generally used simply to fill out the three-part formula by dividing the octave of the concluding sonority at the fifth. This was done all the more readily since the appropriate scale degree could be reached at the penultimate and had only to be repeated (as in Example A-5f). By the end of the fifteenth century this formula had become the prototype for cadential structures in all Renaissance polyphony written for four voices or more. It has continued to provide the basis for cadential progressions in tonal music up to the present time, even though the musical events involved were radically reinterpreted long ago. For the period that concerns us here, however, the two-part progression from imperfect to perfect consonance remained the essential framework of the cadence, regardless of how many other parts were added or how the underlying formula was varied and embellished.[110]

The characteristic melodic patterns of the structural voices, which were usually superius and tenor, could be inverted or exchanged, and their cadential functions could also be assumed by other parts, including altus and bassus. In addition, the suspended dissonance from which the superius usually moved into the cadential resolution was often ornamented in a variety of ways (as in Examples A-5c, d, and e), especially in the repertory of the fifteenth century. The result was to signal closure even more clearly by giving the most prominent part a highly stylized melodic and rhythmic profile that was immediately recognizable to any listener.

By dint of repeated use both the melodic formula of the superius and the melodic motion by fourths and fifths typical of the lowest voice—of which some scholars have occasionally made a good deal more than is warranted—also acquired over time cadential significance, and this connotation could then be invoked to suggest articulation even when the basic contrapuntal framework was otherwise incomplete. Neither, however, came to be the primary structural element in the cadential patterns of the period. Rather, the two-part progression from dissonance to imperfect consonance to perfect continued to be the conceptual and practical matrix of the cadence throughout the fifteenth and sixteenth centuries; it continued to so function within

---

110. For an informative discussion of the development of cadential structures (from which some rather questionable conclusions were nonetheless drawn), see Don M. Randel, "Emerging Triadic Tonality in the Fifteenth Century," *Musical Quarterly* 57 (1971): 73–86. A more recent account, and historically informed from a different viewpoint, is Peter Urquhart, "False Concords in Busnoys," *Proceedings of the Busnoys Conference* (London: Oxford University Press, in press).

the compositional fabric independently of other, related conventions and never lost its place to some other principle of cadential organization.

It was, in fact, the cadential autonomy of the two-part formula that made it possible to utilize the remaining voice or voices to modify or diminish its powers of articulation. Rhythmic and melodic factors, as well as harmonic movement, could be brought into play not only to reinforce but also to attenuate the sense of closure and provide a measure of continuity with the following phrase. If one or more of the parts maintained its motion through the conventional formula (as in Example A-6a), cadential repose was never quite achieved, and the usual interruption of the contrapuntal flow was diminished to that extent. Rhythmic continuity through the cadence could be enhanced in turn with the introduction of a new melodic phrase, overlapping the cadence and generating its own forward motion. This procedure was particularly useful for imitative writing where the entries of the various parts necessarily came one after the other (as in Example A-6b) and could help to bridge the cadential articulations.

Perhaps the most effective way of tempering cadential closure was by sounding imperfect consonance together with the perfect intervals required for completion, a device that Zarlino termed "avoiding the cadence."[111] The feeling of finality was not badly disturbed if the imperfect consonance was the third above the cadential final, especially when the latter scale degree was doubled in the bassus at the octave below (as in Example A-6c). That is why, as has been observed, the thirds generated by the

EXAMPLE A-6.   The attenuation of closure in cadential formulae: (a) rhythmic continuation; (b) overlapping of phrases; (c) use of imperfect consonance; (d) avoiding the cadence with imperfect consonance between the cadential final and the bassus

a) Obrecht, *Missa Caput*, Agnus Dei, mm. 4–6.

b) Arcadelt, *Missa Noe noe*, Kyrie II, mm. 5–6.

c) De Rore, *Datemi pace*, mm. 9–10.

d) Arcadelt, *Missa Noe noe*, Kyrie I, mm. 23–25.

111.   The expression he used was "fuggir la cadenza"; see Zarlino, *Le Istitutioni harmoniche*, bk. 3, chaps. 53 and 54.

division of the fifth in the final cadential sonority eventually came to be used routinely toward the end of the sixteenth century. However, if it was the bassus that formed the imperfect consonance, especially a sixth with the cadential final, the articulating effect was very sensibly diminished, or at least postponed, until the bassus came to rest at the bottom of an acceptable perfect consonance (as in Example A-6d).

Each of these means, separately or in combination, could be used in a surprising variety of ways to achieve the balance between cadential articulation and forward impetus required by the syntax of the text or, in instrumental music, the structure of the counterpoint. In the works discussed in the body of this study are numerous examples showing how skillfully and effectively that could be done.

As has been mentioned, the cadence was undoubtedly the contrapuntal context in which accidental alteration of the diatonic scale degrees occurred most frequently. There were other situations in which it was called for as well, however. On the one hand were those individual lines spanning or otherwise throwing into relief the melodic tritone. That offensive interval was obviated whenever possible, both melodically and harmonically, usually by applying a flat at its upper limit (as in Example A-7).

On the other hand were the harmonies where false concords could arise either from the degrees of the diatonic scale or from accidentals already introduced into the counterpoint for some other reason. In most such instances the inadmissible interval was also avoided by the use of a flat (as in Example A-8).[112] Toward mid-sixteenth century fastidious ears had become so sensitive to the harsh sound of the false concords that they were usually avoided when possible even in cross-relation, divided between successive sonorities.[113]

The writing of counterpoint, finally, involved a good deal more than just observ-

EXAMPLE A-7.   Du Fay, *Adieu ces bons vins* (mm. 5–7); b-fa, which is present in the fifteenth-century source, is introduced in the cantus to avoid a melodic tritone between b' and f

112. Note that in the cadence of Example A-8, m. 6, as in those of Example A-6b, m. 5 and A-6c, m. 9, the accidental assumed in order to have a major sixth forming the structural framework of the traditional formula generates a diminished fifth with the part above. Although there can be some doubt as to whether or not the accidental would have been used in this context, the evidence of both theorists and sources suggests that the false concord was usually tolerated here because the conventions for cadential articulation were so compelling; see Peter Urquhart, "False Concords in Busnoys."
113. See Zarlino, *Le Istituzioni harmoniche*, bk. 3, chap. 30.

EXAMPLE A-8. Isaac, *Innsbruck, ich muss dich lassen* (mm. 4–7): the b-fa signature necessitates an E♭ in both tenor and bassus (as given by the source) to avoid the possibility of an augmented fourth between tenor and altus, a diminished fifth between altus and bassus, and eventually an imperfect octave between tenor and bassus

ing the rules: correctly aligning the consonant intervals in sufficiently varied sequences, treating the dissonances properly, and providing the appropriate level of cadential articulation for the syntactic components of the whole. It meant, as well, mastering the considerable repertory of learned compositional procedures that had become, by the fifteenth century, a traditional part of the polyphonic style: imitation, for example, both free and strict or canonic; double or invertible counterpoint, with and without imitative structures; and the preparation of a cantus firmus with a variety of mensural and proportional permutations, to cite but a few. Each of these could be employed separately or in combination with others, and by his handling of them the composer could display both his understanding of the theory pertaining to his craft and his skill with the technical procedures of composition.

The ideal was to manage both as artfully as possible, to execute the most complicated contrapuntal structures with seeming ease while responding appropriately on the one hand to the philosophical implications of the audible "harmony" he was able to create and on the other to the meaning of the text being set. As Zarlino observed, "that which is done well against constraints is much more praiseworthy than that which is done well when no difficulty is involved."[114] That view of composition seems to have informed the better part of the musical repertory that has come down to us from the fifteenth and sixteenth centuries.

---

114. Zarlino, *Le Istitutioni harmoniche*, bk. 3, chap. 55.

The Princely Houses of England During the 100 Years' War

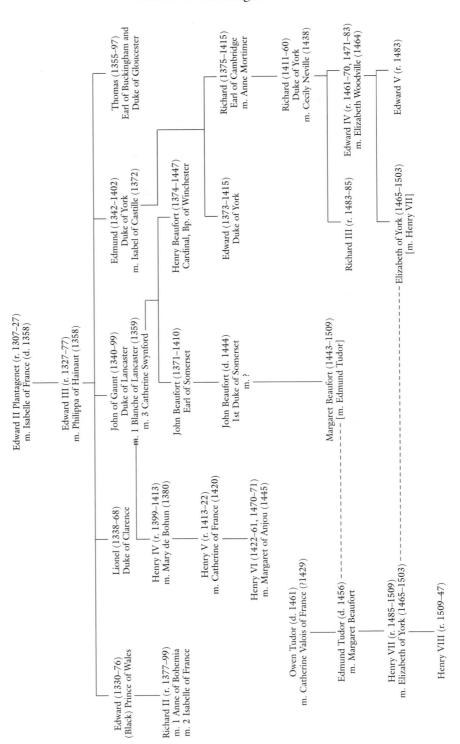

The Princely Houses of France During the 100 Years' War

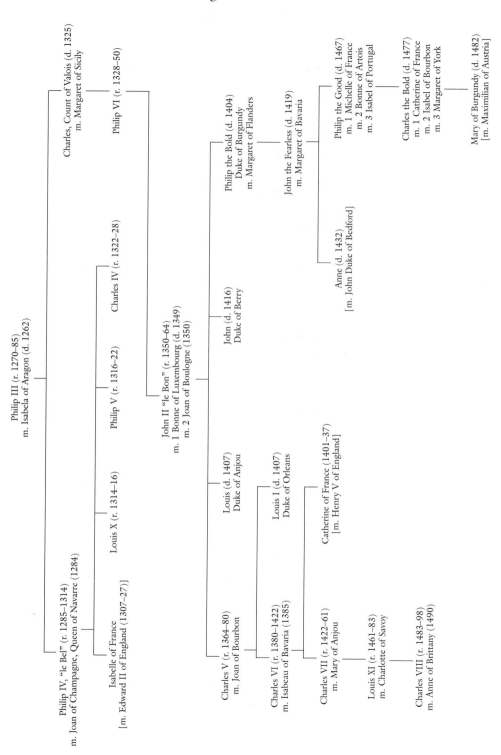

Bibliography

Adkins, Cecil. "Legrense." *The New Grove Dictionary of Music and Musicians*, 10:614–15.

Adler, Guido, et al., eds. *Sechs Trienter Codices: Geistliche und weltliche Kompositionen des XV. Jahrhunderts*, Denkmaler der Tonkunst in Oesterreich, Jahrgang VII (vols. 14–15); XI/1 (vol. 22); XIX/1 (vol. 38), XXVII/1 (vol. 53); XXXI (vol. 61). Vienna, 1900–24. Reprint, Graz: Akademische Druck- und Verlagsanstalt, 1959.

Agnel, Aimé. "Certon, Pierre." *The New Grove Dictionary of Music*, 4:80–82.

Albrect, Hans. "Formschneider." *Die Musik in Geschichte und Gegenwart*, 4:651.

Allmand, Christopher. *The Hundred Years War: England and France at War c. 1300–c. 1450.* Cambridge: Cambridge University Press, 1988.

Allsen, J. Michael. "Style and Intertextuality in the Isorhythmic Motet, 1400–1440." Ph.D. diss., University of Wisconsin, Madison, 1992.

Anglès, Higinio, and José Romeu Figueras, eds. *La música en la Corte de los Reyes Católicos: Cancionero Musical de Palacio (Siglos XV–XVI).* 3 vols. Monumentos de la Música Española, vols. 5, 10, and 14. Barcelona: Consejo Superior de Investigaciones Científicas, Instituto Español de Musicología, 1947–65.

Anglo, Sydney. "Le Camp du Drap d'Or et les entrevues d'Henri VIII et Charles Quint." In *Fêtes et cérémonies au temps de Charles Quint.* Paris: Centre National de la Recherche Scientifique, 1960.

Antico, Andrea, ed. *Canzoni, sonetti, strambotti et frottole, libro tertio*, ed. Alfred Einstein. Smith College Archives, no. 4. Northampton, Mass.: Smith College, 1941.

———. *Frottole intabulate da sonare organi, Libro primo.* Rome, 1517. Reprint, Bologna: Arnaldo Forni, 1970.

Apel, Willi, ed. *Keyboard Music of the Fourteenth and Fifteenth Centuries.* Corpus of Early Keyboard Music 1. [Rome]: American Institute of Musicology, 1963.

Arbeau, Thoinot. *Orchésographie, Méthode et théorie en forme de discours et tablature pour apprendre a danser, battre le tambour en toute sorte & diversité de batteries, Iouër du fifre & atigot, tirer des armes & escrimer, avec autres honnestes exercices fort convenables à la Ieunesse.* Langres, 1588. Reprint, Geneva: Minkoff, 1972.

Arcadelt, Jacques. *Opera omnia*, ed. Albert Seay. 10 vols. Corpus mensurabilis musicae 31. [Rome]: American Institute of Musicology, 1965–71.

Arnold, Denis. "Music at a Venetian Confraternity in the Renaissance." *Acta musicologica* 37 (1965): 62–72.

———. "Villanella." *The New Grove Dictionary of Music*, 19:771.

———. "Villotta." *The New Grove Dictionary of Music*, 19:778–79.

Arnold, Denis, and Elsie M. Arnold. "Monteverdi, Claudio." *The New Grove Dictionary of Music*, 12:514–34.

Arnold, Denis, and Thomas W. Bridges. "Merulo, Claudio." *The New Grove Dictionary of Music*, 12:193–94.

Arnold, Elsie M. "Gabrieli, Andrea." *The New Grove Dictionary of Music*, 7:60.

Atlas, Allan. "Gematria, Marriage Numbers, and Golden Sections in Dufay's 'Revellies Vous.'" *Acta musicologica* 59 (1987): 111–26.

———. "Lebel, Firmin." *The New Grove Dictionary of Music*, 10:578.

———. "Mallapert, Robin." *The New Grove Dictionary of Music*, 11:586.

———. *Music at the Aragonese Court of Naples*. Cambridge: Cambridge University Press, 1985.

Atlas, Allan, ed. *The Cappella Giulia Chansonnier*. 2 vols. Musicological Studies, vol. 27. Brooklyn: Institute of Medieval Music, 1975–76.

Attaingnant, Pierre. *Transcriptions of Chansons for Keyboard (1531)*, ed. Albert Seay. Corpus mensurabilis musicae 20. [Rome]: American Institute of Musicology, 1961.

Augustijn, Cornelis. *Erasmus: His Life, Works, and Influence*, trans. J. C. Grayson. Toronto: University of Toronto Press, 1991.

Babb, Warren, trans. *Hucbald, Guido, and John on Music*, ed. Claude V. Palisca. New Haven: Yale University Press, 1978.

Bain, Susan. "Phalèse." *The New Grove Dictionary of Music*, 14:617–20.

———. "Plantin, Christopher." *The New Grove Dictionary of Music*, 14:851.

———. "Susato, Tylman." *The New Grove Dictionary of Music*, 18:378–79.

Baines, Anthony C. "Cornett." *The New Grove Dictionary of Music*, 4:788–93.

———. "Shawm." *The New Grove Dictionary of Music*, 17:237–43.

———. "Shawm." *The New Grove Dictionary of Musical Instruments*, 3:364–70.

Baini, Giuseppe. *Memorie storico-critiche della vita e delle opere di Giovanni Pierluigi da Palestrina*. Rome, 1828. Reprint, Hildesheim: G. Olms, 1966.

Bank, J. A., ed. *A. Fevin, Missa Ave Maria ad modulum Josquini Pratensis, 4 vocum inaequalium*. Amsterdam: Annie Bank, n.d.

Barbier, Jacques, ed. *Jacques Moderne, Musicque de Joye*. Collection Ricercar, vol. 1. Tours: Centre d'Études Supérieures de la Renaissance, l'Université François Rabelais, 1993.

Barnes, Clifford. "Vaudeville." *The New Grove Dictionary of Music*, 19:564–65.

Baron, John H. "Air de cour." *The New Grove Dictionary of Music*, 1:183.

Becker, Otto F. "The Maitrise in Northern France and Burgundy during the Fifteenth Century." Ph.D. diss., George Peabody College for Teachers, 1967.

Bent, Margaret. "Cooke, J[ohn]." *The New Grove Dictionary of Music*, 4:712.

———. "Diatonic Ficta." *Early Music History* 4 (1984): 1–48.

———. "Dunstable, John." *The New Grove Dictionary of Music*, 5:720–25.

———. "Old Hall MS." *The New Grove Dictionary of Music*, 13:526–29.

———. "Power, Leonel." *The New Grove Dictionary of Music*, 15:174–79.

———. "Pycart." *The New Grove Dictionary of Music*, 14:720.

————. "Roy Henry." *The New Grove Dictionary of Music*, 16:285.

Bente, Martin. "Senfl, Ludwig." *The New Grove Dictionary of Music*, 17:131–37.

Benthem, Jaap van. "Lazarus versus Absalom: About Fiction and Fact in the Netherlands Motet." *Tijdschrift van de Vereniging voor Nederlandse Muziekgeschiedenis* 37 (1989): 54–82.

Bergin, Thomas G., and Jennifer Speake, eds. *Encyclopedia of the Renaissance*. New York: Market House Books, 1987.

Bernoulli, Eduard, ed. *Chansons und Tänze*. Munich: C. Kuhn, 1914.

Bernstein, Jane A., ed. *The Sixteenth-Century Chanson*. Vol. 6, *Pierre Certon*. New York: Garland, 1990.

Bernstein, Lawrence F. "A Canonic Chanson in a German Manuscript: *Faulte d'argent* and Josquin's Approach to the Chanson for Five Voices." In *Von Isaac bis Bach: Studien zur älteren deutschen Musikgeschichte: Festschrift Martin Just zum 60. Geburtstag*, ed. Frank Heidlberger, Wolfgang Osthoff, and Reinhard Wiesend. Kassel: Bärenreiter, 1991.

Bianconi, Lorenzo. "Gesualdo, Carlo." *The New Grove Dictionary of Music*, 7:313–24.

Binchoys, Gilles. *Die Chansons von Gilles Binchois (1400–1460)*, ed. Wolfgang Rehm. Musikalische Denkmäler, vol. 2. Mainz: Schott's Söhne, 1957.

Blachly, Alexander. "Mensuration and Tempo in Fifteenth-Century Music." Ph.D. diss., Columbia University, 1995.

Blackburn, Bonnie. "Two 'Carnival Songs' Unmasked." *Musica disciplina* 35 (1981): 121–78.

Blackburn, Bonnie, Edward Lowinsky, and Clement Miller, eds. *A Correspondence of Renaissance Musicians*. Oxford: Oxford University Press, 1991.

Block, Adrienne F. *The Early French Parody Noël*. 2 vols. Studies in Musicology, no. 36, ed. George Buelow. Ann Arbor: UMI Research Press, 1983.

Bloxam, M. Jennifer. "Plainsong and Polyphony for the Blessed Virgin: Notes on Two Masses by Jacob Obrecht." *Journal of Musicology* 12 (1994): 51–75.

Böker-Heil, Norbert. "Lied." *The New Grove Dictionary of Music*, 10:831–34.

Bonime, Stephen. "Anne de Bretagne (1477–1514) and Music: An Archival Study." Ph.D. diss., Bryn Mawr College, 1975.

Boorman, Stanley. "Longueval." *The New Grove Dictionary of Music*, 11:221.

Borren, Charles Van den. *Polyphonia sacra*. Burnham, Buckshire: The Plainsong and Medieval Music Society, 1932. Reprint, University Park: Pennsylvania State University Press, 1963.

Bouquet, Marie-Thérèse. "La Cappella Musicale dei Duchi di Savoia." *Rivista italiana di musicologia* 3 (1968): 233–85.

Bower, Calvin. "Boethius." *The New Grove Dictionary of Music*, 2:844–85.

Bowers, Roger. "London." *The New Grove Dictionary of Music*, 11:151–52.

Bowers, Roger, and Paul Doe. "Taverner, John." *The New Grove Dictionary of Music*, 18:598–602.

Bowles, Edmund A. "*Haut* and *Bas*: The Grouping of Musical Instruments in the Middle Ages." *Musica disciplina* 8 (1954): 115ff.

————. *Musikleben im 15. Jahrhundert*. Musikgeschichte in Bildern, vol. 3, no. 8. Leipzig: VEB Deutscher Verlag für Musik, 1977.

Bradshaw, Murray C. *The Falsobordone*. Musicological Studies and Documents 34. [Rome]: American Institute of Musicology, 1978.

————. "Falsobordone." *The New Grove Dictionary of Music*, 6:375–76.

Braun, Werner. "Walter, Johann." *The New Grove Dictionary of Music*, 20:188–89.

Brauner, Mitchell P. "The Catalogue of Raffaele Panuzzi and the Repertory of the Papal Chapel in the Fifteenth and Sixteenth Centuries." *Journal of Musicology* 8 (1990): 427–43.

Bridges, Thomas W. "Gardane." *The New Grove Dictionary of Music,* 7:158–59.

———. "Giunta." *The New Grove Dictionary of Music,* 7:415–17.

———. "Scotto, Ottaviano." *The New Grove Dictionary of Music,* 17:85–87.

Brobeck, John T. "Musical Patronage in the Royal Chapel of France under Francis I (r. 1515–1547)." *Journal of the American Musicological Society* 48 (1995): 187–239.

Brothers, Lester D. "On Music and Meditation in the Renaissance: Contemplative Prayer and Josquin's Miserere." *Journal of Musicological Research* 12 (1992): 157–87.

Brothers, Thomas. "Vestiges of the Isorhythmic Tradition in Mass and Motet, ca. 1450–1475." *Journal of the American Musicological Society* 44 (1991): 1–56.

Brown, Alan. "Galliard." *The New Grove Dictionary of Music,* 7:105–7.

———. "Pavan." *The New Grove Dictionary of Music,* 14:311–13.

———. "Piva." *The New Grove Dictionary of Music,* 14:793–94.

Brown, Howard Mayer. "Carpentras." *The New Grove Dictionary of Music,* 3:820.

———. "Chanson." *The New Grove Dictionary of Music,* 4:135–45.

———. "The Chanson Spirituelle, Jacques Buus, and Parody Technique." *Journal of the American Musicological Society* 15 (1962): 145–73.

———. "Crecquillon." *The New Grove Dictionary of Music,* 5:26–29.

———. "Févin, Antoine de." *The New Grove Dictionary of Music,* 6:515–17.

———. "The Genesis of a Style: The Parisian Chanson, 1500–1530." In *Chanson and Madrigal, 1480–1530,* ed. James Haar. Isham Library Papers, vol. 2. Cambridge, Mass.: Harvard University Press, 1964.

———. *Instrumental Music Printed before 1600: A Bibliography.* Cambridge, Mass.: Harvard University Press, 1965.

———. "Instruments and Voices in the Fifteenth-Century Chanson." In *Current Thought in Musicology,* ed. John W. Grubbs. Austin: University of Texas Press, 1976.

———. "Janequin, Clément." *The New Grove Dictionary of Music,* 9:491–94.

———. "The Mirror of Man's Salvation: Music in Devotional Life about 1500." *Renaissance Quarterly* 43 (1990): 744–73.

———. "Mouton, Johannes." *The New Grove Dictionary of Music,* 12:659–60.

———. *Music in the French Secular Theater of the Fifteenth Century.* Cambridge, Mass.: Harvard University Press, 1963.

———. "Richafort." *The New Grove Dictionary of Music,* 15:839–40.

———. Review of *The Castle of Fair Welcome: Courtly Songs of the Later Fifteenth Century,* Gothic Voices, directed by Christopher Page, *Early Music* 15 (1987): 277–79.

———. "A Rondeau with a One-Line Refrain Can Be Sung." *Ars lyrica* 3 (1986): 23–35.

Brown, Howard M., ed. *A Florentine Chansonnier from the Time of Lorenzo the Magnificent.* 2 vols. Monuments of Renaissance Music 7. Chicago: University of Chicago Press, 1983.

———. *Theatrical Chansons of the Fifteenth and Early Sixteenth Centuries.* Cambridge, Mass.: Harvard University Press, 1962.

Brunner, Horst. "Meistergesang." *The New Grove Dictionary of Music,* 12:73–79.

Bukofzer, Manfred. "The Beginnings of Choral Polyphony." In *Studies in Medieval and Renaissance Music.* New York: Norton, 1950.

———. "*Caput*: A Liturgico-Musical Study." In *Studies in Medieval and Renaissance Music.* New York: Norton, 1950.

Burckhardt, Jacob. *The Civilization of the Renaissance in Italy*. 2 vols. New York: Harper and Brothers, 1958.

Busnoys, Antoine. *Collected Works*, ed. Richard Taruskin. 2 vols. Masters and Monuments of the Renaissance 5: Part 2, *Latin-texted Works*; Part 3, *Commentary*. New York: Broude Trust, 1990.

Busse-Berger, Anna Maria. *Mensuration and Proportion Signs: Origin and Evolution*. Oxford: Clarendon Press, 1988.

Byrd, William. *Cantiones sacrae*, ed. Craig Monson. The Byrd Edition, vol. 1. London: Stainer and Bell, 1977.

———. *The Collected Vocal Works of William Byrd*. Vol. 12, *Psalmes, Sonets, and Songs (1588)*, ed. Edmund H. Fellowes. London: Stainer and Bell, 1948.

———. *The Collected Works of William Byrd*. Vol. 13, *Songs of Sundrie Natures (1589)*, ed. Edmund H. Fellowes, rev. Philip Brett. London: Stainer and Bell, 1940.

———. *The English Services*, ed. by Craig Monson. The Byrd Edition, vols. 10a and 10b. London: Stainer and Bell, 1980–92.

Cabezón, Antonio de. *Collected Works*, ed. Charles G. Jacobs. 3 vols. Brooklyn: Institute of Mediaeval Music, 1967–86.

———. *Obras de música para tecla, arpa y vihuela*, ed. Higinio Anglès. 3 vols. Monumentos de música española, vols. 27–29. Barcelona: Consejo Superior de Investigaciones Científicas, Instituto Español de Musicología, 1966.

Caldwell, John. "Browne, John." *The New Grove Dictionary of Music*, 3:345.

———. "Canzona." *The New Grove Dictionary of Music*, 3:743–45.

———. "Davy, Richard." *The New Grove Dictionary of Music*, 5:285–86.

———. "Ricercar." *The New Grove Dictionary of Music*, 15:836.

———. "Sources of Keyboard Music to 1660." *The New Grove Dictionary of Music*, 17:718–33.

Cannon, Beekman, Alvin Johnson, and William Waite. *The Art of Music*. New York: Thomas Y. Crowell, 1960.

Carpenter, Nan Cooke. *Music in the Medieval and Renaissance Universities*. Norman: University of Oklahoma Press, 1958.

Carpentras: see Genet, Elzéar.

Cartwright, Julia. *Isabella d'Este, Marchioness of Mantua, 1474–1539: A Study of the Renaissance*. 2 vols. New York: E. P. Dutton, 1903.

Castiglione, Baldassare. *The Courtier*. 1528.

Cattin, Giulio. "Le composizioni musicali del Ms. Pavia Aldini 361." In *L'Ars nova italiana del trecento*, ed. F. Alberto Gallo. 2 vols. Certaldo: Commune di Certaldo, 1968.

Cattin, Giulio, ed. *Italian Laude and Latin Unica in MS Capetown, Grey 3.b.12*. [Rome]: American Institute of Musicology, 1977.

Cattin, Giulio, F. Facchin, and Maricarmen Gómez, eds. *French Sacred Music*. Polyphonic Music of the Fourteenth Century, vols. 23A–23B. Monaco: Editions l'Oiseau Lyre, 1989–92.

Cavazzoni, Girolamo. *Intavolatura, cioe recercari, canzoni, himni, magnificati* (1542), ed. Oscar Mischiati. Orgelwerke, vol. 1. Mainz: Schott & Söhne, 1959.

Cazeaux, Isabelle. "Sermisy, Claudin de." *The New Grove Dictionary of Music*, 17:171–72.

Census-Catalogue of Manuscript Sources of Polyphonic Music, 1400–1550, ed. Charles Hamm and Herbert Kellman. 5 vols. Neuhausen-Stuttgart: American Institute of Musicology, 1979–88.

Chailley, Jacques. *Alia musica*. Paris: Centre de documentation universitaire, 1965.

Charles, Sidney R., ed. *The Music of the Pepys MS 1236.* Corpus mensurabilis musicae 40. [Rome]: American Institute of Musicology, 1967.

Chartier, F.-L. *L'ancien chapitre de Notre-Dame de Paris et sa maîtrise.* Paris, 1897. Reprint, Geneva: Minkoff, 1971.

Chew, Geoffrey. "Song." *The New Grove Dictionary of Music,* 17:515–17.

Clemens, Jacobus (non Papa). *Opera omnia,* ed. K. Ph. Bernet Kempers. 21 vols. Corpus mensurabilis musicae 4. [Rome]: American Institute of Musicology, 1951–76.

Clerval, J.-A. *L'ancienne maîtrise de Notre-Dame de Chartres.* Paris, 1899. Reprint, Geneva: Minkoff, 1972.

Closson, Ernest, ed. *Le manuscrit dit des basses danses de la Bibliothèque de Bourgogne.* Brussels: Société des Bibliophiles et Iconophiles de Belgique, 1912.

Cohen, Judith. *The Six Anonymous L'homme armé Masses in Naples, Biblioteca Nazionale, MS VI E40.* Musicological Studies and Documents 21. [Rome]: American Institute of Musicology, 1968.

Cohen, Judith, ed. *Anonymous L'homme armé Masses in Naples, Biblioteca Nazionale, MS VI E40.* Corpus mensurabilis musicae 85. Neuhausen-Stuttgart: American Institute of Musicology, 1981.

Colette, Armand-Romain. *Histoire de la maîtrise de Rouen.* Rouen, 1892. Reprint, Geneva: Minkoff, 1972.

Compère, Loyset. *Opera omnia,* ed. Ludwig Finscher. 5 vols. Corpus mensurabilis musicae 15. [Rome]: American Institute of Musicology, 1958–72.

Cornago, Johannes. *Complete Works,* ed. Rebecca L. Gerber. Recent Researches in the Music of the Middle Ages and the Early Renaissance, vol. 15. Madison: A-R Editions, 1984.

Cotgrave, Randle. *A Dictionarie of the French and English Tongues.* London, 1611. Reprint, Columbia: University of South Carolina Press, 1968.

Coussemaker, Charles E. H. de. *Scriptorum de musica medii aevi.* 4 vols. Paris, 1864–76.

Crawford, David. "Savoy." *The New Grove Dictionary of Music,* 16:528.

Crocker, Richard. "Hermann's Major Sixth." *Journal of the American Musicological Society* 20 (1972): 19–37.

Croll, Gerhard. "Weerbeke, Gaspar van." *The New Grove Dictionary of Music,* 20:290–92.

Crook, David. *Orlando di Lasso's Imitation Magnificats for Counter-Reformation Munich.* Princeton: Princeton University Press, 1994.

Cumming, Julie. "The Emergence of the Renaissance Motet." Paper read at the annual meeting of the American Musicological Society, Pittsburgh, 1992.

Cummings, Anthony M. "Toward an Interpretation of the Sixteenth-Century Motet." *Journal of the American Musicological Society* 34 (1981): 43–59.

Curtis, Gareth R. K. "Brussels, Bibliothèque Royale MS 5557, and the Texting of Dufay's 'Ecce ancilla domini' and 'Ave regina celorum' Masses." *Acta musicologica* 51 (1979): 73–86.

Cusick, Suzanne G. "Balletto." *The New Grove Dictionary of Music,* 2:92–94.

——. "Dorico, Valerio." *The New Grove Dictionary of Music,* 5:576–77.

——. "Gendering Modern Music: Thoughts on the Monteverdi–Artusi Controversy." *Journal of the American Musicological Society* 46 (1993): 1–25.

Cuyler, Louise E. "Ducis, Benedictus." *The New Grove Dictionary of Music,* 5:671.

D'Accone, Frank A. "Alcune note sulle Compagnie Fiorentine dei Laudesi durante il quattrocento." *Rivista italiana di musicologia* 10 (1975): 86–114.

——. "Canti carnascialeschi." *The New Grove Dictionary of Music,* 3:721–23.

————. "Le Compagnie dei Laudesi in Firenze durante l'ars nova." In *L'Ars nova italiana del trecento* 2, ed. F. Alberto Gallo. Certaldo: Commune di Certaldo, [1970].

————. "The Performance of Sacred Music in Italy during Josquin's Time, c. 1475–1525." In *Josquin des Prez*, ed. Edward E. Lowinsky and Bonnie J. Blackburn. London: Oxford University Press, 1976.

————. "Pisano [Pagoli], Bernardo." *The New Grove Dictionary of Music*, 14:772.

Dalza, Joan Ambrosio. *Intabulatura de Lauto Libro Quarto* (Venice, 1508). Reprint, Geneva: Minkoff, 1980.

Dart, Thurston, and Richard Marlow. "Tregian, Francis." *The New Grove Dictionary of Music*, 19:126–27.

Dart, Thurston, and John Morehen. "Tablature." *The New Grove Dictionary of Music*, 18:506–15.

Davison, Archibald T., and Willi Apel, eds. *Historical Anthology of Music*. 2 vols. Cambridge, Mass.: Harvard University Press, 1962.

Davison, Nigel. "*Absalom fili mi* Reconsidered." *Tijdschrift van de Vereniging voor Nederlandse Muziekgeschiedenis* 46 (1996): 42–56.

Davison, Nigel, ed. *Neun englische Madrigale zu 5 und 6 Stimmen*. Das Chorwerk, vol. 132. Wolfenbüttel: Möseler, 1983.

————. *Vier Motetten*. Das Chorwerk, vol. 91. Wolfenbüttel: Möseler, 1964.

DeFord, Ruth I. "The Influence of the Madrigal on Canzonetta Texts of the Late Sixteenth Century." *Acta musicologica* 59 (1987): 127–51.

De Silva, Andreas. *Opera omnia*, ed. Winfried Kirsch. 2 vols. Corpus mensurabilis musicae 49. [Rome]: American Institute of Musicology, 1970–77.

Dietrich, Sixt. *Hymnen*, ed. Hermann Zenck and Wilibald Gurlitt. Das Erbe deutscher Musik, vol. 23, 1942. Reprint, St. Louis: Concordia Publishing House, 1960.

Disertori, Benvenuto, ed. *Le frottole per canto e liuto intabulate de Franciscus Bossinensis*. Istituzioni e monumente dell'arte musicale italiana, new ser., vol. 3. Milan: Ricordi, 1964.

Dobbins, Frank. "Baïf, Antoine." *The New Grove Dictionary of Music*, 2:34.

————. "Bourgeois, Loys." *The New Grove Dictionary of Music*, 3:111–13.

————. "Marot, Clément." *The New Grove Dictionary of Music*, 11:695–96.

————. "Mornable, Antoine." *The New Grove Dictionary of Music*, 12:585–86.

————. "Saint-Gelais, Mellin." *The New Grove Dictionary of Music*, 16:390–91.

————. "Valois." *The New Grove Dictionary of Music*, 19:508–9.

Doe, Paul. "Psalm." *The New Grove Dictionary of Music*, 15:332.

————. "Tallis, Thomas." *The New Grove Dictionary of Music*, 18:541–48.

————. "Tye, Christopher." *The New Grove Dictionary of Music*, 19:297–300.

Donà, Mariangela. "Milan." *The New Grove Dictionary of Music*, 12:290–300.

Droz, Eugénie, and Geneviève Thibaut, eds. *Trois chansonniers français*. Paris, 1927. Reprint, New York: Da Capo Press, 1978.

Du Chatel, Françoise. *Damoiselle Christine de Pizan, veuve de Me. Etienne de Castel, 1364–1431*. Paris: Picard, 1972.

Ducrot, Ariane. "Histoire de la Cappella Giulia au XVIe siècle." *Mélanges d'archéologie et d'histoire* 75 (1963): 1:179–240 and 2:467–559.

Du Fay, Guillaume. *Chansons: Forty-Five Settings in Original Notation from Oxford, Bodelian Library MS Canonici 213*, ed. Ross W. Duffin. Miami: Ogni Sorte Editions, 1983.

————. *Opera omnia*, ed. Heinrich Besseler. 6 vols. [Rome]: American Institute of Musicology, 1947–66.

Dunning, Albert. "Calvin [Cauvin], Jean." *The New Grove Dictionary of Music*, 3:630–32.

———. *Die Staatsmotette, 1480–1555*. Utrecht: A. Oosthoek, 1970.

Dunstable, John. *Complete Works*, ed. Manfred Bukofzer. Musica Britannica 8 (1953); with revisions and additions by Margaret Bent, Ian Bent, and Brian Trowell. London: Stainer and Bell, 1970.

Eberlain, Roland. "The Faenza Codex: Music for Organ or Lute?" *Early Music* 20 (1992): 461–66.

Edwards, Warwick. "Songs without Words by Josquin and His Contemporaries." In *Music in Medieval and Early Modern Europe: Patronage, Sources, and Texts*, ed. Iain Fenlon. Cambridge: Cambridge University Press, 1981.

———. "Sources of Instrumental Ensemble Music to 1630." *The New Grove Dictionary of Music*, 17:702ff.

Einstein, Alfred. "Andrea Antico's *Canzoni novi* of 1510." *Musical Quarterly* 37 (1951): 330–39.

———. *The Italian Madrigal*. 3 vols. Princeton: Princeton University Press, 1949.

Einstein, Alfred, ed. *The Golden Age of the Madrigal*. New York: G. Schirmer, 1942.

Eitner, Robert. *Das deutsche Lied des XV. und XVI. Jahrhunderts*. 2 vols. Berlin, 1876–80. Reprint, New York: AMS Press, 1975.

Elders, Willem. "Clemens (non Papa)." *The New Grove Dictionary of Music*, 4:476–80.

———. "G. Dufay's Concept of Fauxbourdon." *Revue belge de musicologie* 43 (1989): 173–95.

Elton, G. R., ed. *The Reformation, 1520–1559*. Vol. 2 of *The New Cambridge Modern History*. Cambridge: Cambridge University Press, 1976.

Encyclopédie illustrée du Pays de Vaud. Vol. 6, *Les arts: Architecture, peinture, littérature, musique*. Lausanne: Imprimeries Réunies, 1976.

"Euphony in the Fifteenth Century." In *Report of the Twelfth Congress of the International Musicological Society, Berkeley, 1977*, ed. Daniel Heartz and Bonnie Wade. Kassel: Bärenreiter, 1981.

Fallows, David. "Binchois." *The New Grove Dictionary of Music*, 2:709.

———. *Dufay*. London: J. M. Dent, 1982.

———. "Dunstable, Bedyngham, and *O rosa bella*." *Journal of Musicology* 12 (1994): 287–305.

———. "Fifteenth-Century Tablatures for Plucked Instruments: A Summary, a Revision, and a Suggestion." *Lute Society Journal* 19 (1977): 7–33.

———. "French as a Courtly Language in Fifteenth-Century Italy." *Renaissance Studies* 3 (1989): 429–41.

———. "A Glimpse of the Lost Years: Spanish Polyphonic Song, 1450–70." In *New Perspectives in Music: Essays in Honor of Eileen Southern*, ed. Samuel A. Floyd Jr. Warren, Mich.: Harmonie Park Press, 1992.

———. "Josquin and Milan." *Plainsong and Medieval Music* 5 (1996): 69–80.

———. "The Life of Johannes Regis, ca. 1425 to 1496." *Revue belge de musicologie* 43 (1989): 143–72.

———. "The Performing Ensembles in Josquin's Sacred Music." *Tijdschrift van de Vereniging voor Nederlandse Muziekgeschiedenis* 35 (1985): 32–66.

———. "Ruf." *The New Grove Dictionary of Music*, 16:318.

———. "Specific Information on the Ensembles for Composed Polyphony, 1400–1474." In *Studies in the Performance of Late Medieval Music*, ed. Stanley Boorman. Cambridge: Cambridge University Press, 1983.

————. "'Trained and Immersed in All Musical Delights': Towards a New Picture of Busnoys." In *Continuities and Transformations in Musical Culture, 1450–1500: Assessing the Legacy of Antoine Busnoys.* London: Oxford University Press, 1998.

Faugues, Guillaume. *Collected Works of Faugues,* ed. George C. Schuetze Jr. Gesamtausgaben 1. Brooklyn: Institute of Medieval Music, 1960.

————. *Opera omnia Faugues: Facsimile,* ed. George C. Schuetze Jr. Publications of Mediaeval Musical Manuscripts, vol. 7. Brooklyn: Institute of Mediaeval Music, 1959.

Federhofer, Hellmut. "Fux, Johann." *The New Grove Dictionary of Music,* 7:43–46.

Feldman, Martha. *City Culture and the Madrigal at Venice.* Berkeley: University of California Press, 1995.

Fellerer, Karl Gustav. "Cecilian Movement." *The New Grove Dictionary of Music,* 4:47–48.

Ferguson, Wallace K. *Europe in Transition.* Boston: Houghton Mifflin Co., 1962.

————. *The Renaissance.* New York: Holt, Rinehart and Winston, 1940.

————. *The Renaissance in Historical Thought.* Cambridge, Mass.: Riverside Press, 1948.

Festa, Costanzo. *Hymni per totum annum, 3, 4, 5, 6 vocibus,* ed. Glen Haydon. Monumenta polyphoniae italicae, vol. 3. Rome: Pontificio Istituto di Musica Sacra, 1958.

————. *Opera omnia,* ed. Alexander Main and Albert Seay. 8 vols. Corpus mensurabilis musicae 25. [Rome]: American Institute of Musicology, 1977.

Field, Christopher D. S. "Fantasia." *The New Grove Dictionary of Music,* 6:380–88.

Finck, Heinrich. *Ausgewählte Werke,* ed. Lothar Hoffmann-Erbrecht and Helmut Lomnitzer. 2 vols. Das Erbe deutscher Musik, vols. 57 and 70. Frankfurt: C. F. Peters, 1962–81.

Fischer, Kurt von. "Passion." *The New Grove Dictionary of Music,* 14:276–82.

Flotzinger, Rudolf, ed. *Das Lautenbüchlein des Jakob Thurner.* Graz: Akademische Druck- und Verlaganstalt, 1971.

Forney, Kristine K. "Music, Ritual, and Patronage at the Church of Our Lady, Antwerp." *Early Music History* 7 (1987): 1–57.

————. "Sixteenth-Century Antwerp." In *The Renaissance: From the 1470s to the End of the Sixteenth Century,* ed. Iain Fenlon. Man and Music, vol. 2. Englewood Cliffs, N.J.: Prentice Hall, 1989.

Francoli, Miguel A. Roig. "Playing in Consonances: A Spanish Renaissance Technique of Chordal Improvisation." *Early Music* 23 (1995): 461–71.

Fromson, Michèle. "Themes of Exile in Willaert's *Musica nova.*" *Journal of the American Musicological Society* 47 (1994): 442–87.

Frye, Walter. *Opera omnia,* ed. Sylvia Kenney. Corpus mensurabilis musicae 19. [Rome]: American Institute of Musicology, 1960.

Fuller, Sarah, ed. *The European Musical Heritage, 800–1750.* New York: Alfred A. Knopf, 1987.

Funck, Heinz, ed. *Deutsche Lieder des 15. Jahrhunderts.* Das Chorwerk, vol. 45. Wolfenbüttel: Kallmeyer, 1937.

Gaetano, Pietro. "Oratio de origine et dignitate musices." Venice, Museo Correr (Italian National Library), MS Ciconia 906.

Gaffurius, Franchinus. *Practica musicae,* trans. Clement A. Miller. Musicological Studies and Documents 20. [Rome]: American Institute of Musicology, 1969.

Gaillard, Paul-André. "Bèze, Théodore." *The New Grove Dictionary of Music,* 2:669.

————. "Goudimel, Claude." *The New Grove Dictionary of Music,* 7:578–79.

Gallico, Claudio. *Un canzoniere musicale italiano del cinquecento.* Biblioteca (Historiae musicae cultores), vol. 13. Florence: Olschki, 1961.

Gallo, Alberto. "Marchetto da Padova." *The New Grove Dictionary of Music*, 11:661–62.

Garey, Howard. "Can a Rondeau with a One-Line Refrain Be Sung?" *Ars lyrica* 2 (1983): 9–21.

———. "The Variable Structure of the Fifteenth-Century Rondeau." In *The Sixth Lacus Forum*. Columbia, S.C.: Hornbeam Press, 1979.

Garside, Charles Jr. *Zwingli and the Arts*. New Haven: Yale University Press, 1966.

Gastoué, A., ed. *Le manuscrit de musique du Trésor d'Apt*. Publications de la Société Française de Musicologie, ser. 1, vol. 10. Paris: E. Droz, 1936.

Gaudemet, Jean. "Les institutions ecclésiastiques en France du milieu du XIIe au début du XIVe siècle." In *Histoire des institutions françaises au moyen age*, vol. 3, *Institutions ecclésiastiques*, ed. Ferdinand Lot and Robert Fawtier. Paris: Presses universitaires de France, 1962.

Gavaldá, Miguel Querol. *Cancionero musical de la Colombina*. Monumentos de la música española, vol. 33. Barcelona: Consejo Superior de Investigaciones Científicas, Instituto Español de Musicología, 1971.

Genet, Elzéar [Carpentras]. *Opera omnia*, ed. Albert Seay. 5 vols. Corpus mensurabilis musicae 58. [Rome]: American Institute of Musicology, 1972–73.

Gerber, Rudolf, ed. *Deutsche Meister des 15. Jahrhunderts: 12 Hymnen*. Das Chorwerk, vol. 32. Wolfenbuttel: Kallmeyer, 1935.

———. *Der Mensuralkodex des Nikolaus Apel*. 2 vols. Das Erbe deutscher Music, vols. 32–33. Kassel: Bärenreiter Verlag, 1956.

———. *Sacrorum hymnorum liber primus*. Das Erbe deutscher Musik, vols. 21, 25. Leipzig: Fr. Kistner and C. V. W. Siegel, 1942–43. Reprint, idem, 1961.

Gérold, Théodore, ed. *Le manuscrit de Bayeux, texte et musique d'un recueil de chansons du XVe siècle*. Strasbourg: University of Strasbourg, 1921.

Ghisi, Federico. "Carnival Songs and the Origins of the Intermezzo Giocoso." *Musical Quarterly* 25 (1939): 325–33.

Giesbert, F. J., ed. *Pariser Tanzbuch aus dem Jahre 1530*. Mainz: B. Schotts Söhne, n.d.

Giustiniani, Vicenzo. *Il Desiderio*, trans. and ed. by Carol MacClintock. Musicological Studies and Documents 9. [Rome]: American Institute of Musicology, 1962.

Glarean, Heinrich. *Dodecachordon* (1547), trans. Clement A. Miller. 2 vols. Musicological Studies and Documents 6. [Rome]: American Institute of Musicology, 1965.

Glixon, Jonathan. "Music at the Venetian *scuole grandi*, 1440–1540." In *Music in Medieval and Modern Europe*, ed. Iain Fenlon. Cambridge: Cambridge University Press, 1981.

———. "The Polyphonic Laude of Innocentius Dammonis." *Journal of Musicology* 8 (1990): 19–53.

Göllner, Marie Louise. "Berg." *The New Grove Dictionary of Music*, 2:539–40.

———. "Petreius." *The New Grove Dictionary of Music*, 14:586.

Göllner, Theodor. "Mass." *The New Grove Dictionary of Music*, 11:783.

Gombosi, Otto, ed. *Compositione di Meser Vincenzo Capirola: Lute-Book (circa 1517)*. Neuilly-sur-Seine: La Société de Musique d'Autrefois, 1955.

Gomez-Muntané, Maria del Carmen. *La música en la casa real Catalano-Aragonesa, 1336–1442*. 2 vols. Barcelona: Antoni Bosch, 1979.

Gossett, Philip. "Techniques of Unification in Early Cyclic Masses and Mass Pairs." *Journal of the American Musicological Society* 19 (1966): 205–31.

Goudimel, Claude. *Oeuvres complètes*, ed. Henri Gagnebin, Rudolf Häusler, and Eleanor Lawry. 14 vols. Brooklyn: Institute of Medieval Music, 1967–83.

Greenberg, Noah, and Paul Maynard, eds. *An Anthology of Early Renaissance Music*. New York: Norton, 1975.

Greer, David. "Cornysh, William." *The New Grove Dictionary of Music*, 4:795–96.

———. "Henry VIII." *The New Grove Dictionary of Music*, 8:485–86.

Grendler, Paul F. *Schooling in Renaissance Italy: Literacy and Learning, 1300–1600*. Baltimore: Johns Hopkins University Press, 1989.

Griffiths, Ann, and Joan Rimmer. "Harp." *The New Grove Dictionary of Music*, 8:194–97.

———. "Harp." *The New Grove Dictionary of Musical Instruments*, 2:134–38.

Günther, Ursula. "Die Anwendung der Diminution in der Handschrift Chantilly 1047." *Archiv für Musikwissenschaft* 17 (1960): 1–21.

———. "Der Gebrauch des *tempus perfectum diminutum* in der Handschrift Chantilly 1047." *Archiv für Musikwissenschaft* 17 (1960): 277–97.

Gushee, Lawrence. "Jehan des Murs." *The New Grove Dictionary of Music*, 9:587–90.

Gutiérrez-Denhoff, Martella. *Der Wolfenbütteler Chansonnier, Wolfenbüttel, Herzog August Bibliothek, Codex Guelf. 287 Extrav.: Untersuchungen zu Repertoire und Ueberlieferung einer Musikhandschrift des 15. Jahrhunderts und ihres Umkreises*. Wolfenbütteler Forschungen, vol. 29. Wiesbaden: Otto Harrassowitz, 1958.

Gutiérrez-Denhoff, Martella, ed. *Der Wolfenbütteler Chansonnier, Wolfenbüttel, Herzog August Bibliothek, Codex Guelf. 287 Extrav.* Musikalische Denkmäler, vol. 10. Mainz: B. Schotts Söhne, 1988.

Haar, James. "*Altro non è 'l mio amor*." In *Words and Music: The Scholar's View, A Medley of Problems and Solutions Compiled in Honor of A. Tillman Merritt*, ed. Laurence Berman. Cambridge, Mass.: Harvard University Press, 1972.

———. "Bembo, Pietro." *The New Grove Dictionary of Music*, 2:459–60.

———. "Cosimo Bartoli on Music." *Early Music History* 8 (1988): 37–79.

———. "The Early Madrigal: A Re-appraisal of Its Sources and Its Character." In *Music in Medieval and Early Modern Europe: Patronage, Sources, and Texts*, ed. Iain Fenlon. Cambridge: Cambridge University Press, 1981.

———. "Munich at the Time of Orlande de Lassus." In *The Renaissance: From the 1470s to the End of the Sixteenth Century*, ed. Iain Fenlon. Man and Music, vol. 2. Englewood Cliffs, N.J.: Prentice Hall, 1989.

———. "Lassus, Orlande de." *The New Grove Dictionary of Music*, 10:480–502.

———. "The *Note Nere* Madrigal." *Journal of the American Musicological Society* 18 (1965): 22–41.

———. "Popularity in the Sixteenth-Century Madrigal: A Study of Two Instances." In *Studies in Musical Sources and Style: Essays in Honor of Jan LaRue*, ed. Eugene K. Wolf and Edward H. Roesner. Madison: A-R Editions, 1990.

———. "A Sixteenth-Century Attempt at Music Criticism." *Journal of the American Musicological Society* 36 (1983): 191–209.

———. "Towards a Chronology of the Madrigals of Arcadelt." *Journal of Musicology* 5 (1987): 28–54.

Haggh, Barbara. "The Celebration of the *Recollectio festorum Beatae Mariae Virginis*, 1457–1987." In *Atti del XIV Congresso della Società Internazionale di Musicología (Bologna, 1987)*, ed. Angelo Pampilio. 3 vols. Turin: Edizioni di Torino, 1990.

Hamm, Charles. "A Catalogue of Anonymous English Music in Fifteenth-Century Continental Manuscripts." *Musica disciplina* 22 (1968): 47–76.

———. *A Chronology of the Works of Guillaume Dufay Based on a Study of Mensural Practice*. Princeton Studies in Music, vol. 1. Princeton: Princeton University Press, 1964.

———. "Dufay, Guillaume." *The New Grove Dictionary of Music*, 5:674–87.

———. "Manuscript Structure in the Dufay Era." *Acta musicologica* 34 (1962): 166–84.

———. "The Reson Mass." *Journal of the American Musicological Society* 18 (1965): 5–21.

Hamm, Charles, and Jerry Call. "Sources, MS." *The New Grove Dictionary of Music*, 17:668.

Hanen, Martha K., ed. *The Chansonnier El Escorial IV.a.24.* 3 vols. Musicological Studies, vol. 36. Henryville, Penn.: Institute of Mediaeval Music, 1983.

Hanning, Barbara Russano. "Guarini, Giambattista." *The New Grove Dictionary of Music,* 7:770–72.

Harrán, Don. "Frottola." *The New Grove Dictionary of Music*, 6:867–73.

———. "Verse Types in the Early Madrigal." *Journal of the American Musicological Society* 22 (1969): 27–53.

Harris, David G. T. "Musical Education in Tudor Times." *Proceedings of the Musical Association* 65 (1938–39): 109–36.

Harrison, Frank L. "The Eton Manuscript." *Annales musicologiques* 1 (1953): 168–75.

———. *Music in Medieval Britain.* 2d. ed. London: Routledge and Kegan Paul, 1963.

Harrison, Frank L., ed. *The Eton Choirbook.* 3 vols. Musica Britannica, vols. 10–12. London: Stainer and Bell, 1956–61.

Harwood, Ian, and Diane Poulton. "Lute." *The New Grove Dictionary of Music*, 11:344–63.

———. "Lute." *The New Grove Dictionary of Musical Instruments*, 2:553–74.

Hay, Denys. *The Church in Italy in the Fifteenth Century.* Cambridge: Cambridge University Press, 1977.

———. *The Italian Renaissance in Its Historical Background.* Cambridge: Cambridge University Press, 1961.

———. "Schools and Universities." In *The Reformation, 1520–1559*, vol. 2 of *The New Cambridge Modern History*, ed. G. R. Elton. Cambridge: Cambridge University Press, 1975.

Heartz, Daniel. "Attaingnant." *The New Grove Dictionary of Music* 1:673–76.

———. "Basse danse." *The New Grove Dictionary of Music*, 2:257–59.

———. "Branle." *The New Grove Dictionary of Music*, 3:201–4.

———. "Calata." *The New Grove Dictionary of Music*, 3:612.

———. *Pierre Attaingnant, Royal Printer of Music.* Berkeley: University of California Press, 1969.

———. "*Voix de ville*: Between Humanist Ideals and Musical Realities." *Words and Music: The Scholar's View, A Medley of Problems and Solutions Compiled in Honor of A. Tillman Merritt,* ed. Laurence Berman. Cambridge, Mass.: Harvard University Press, 1972.

Heartz, Daniel, ed. *Preludes, Chansons, and Dances for Lute.* Neuilly-sur-Seine: La Société de Musique d'Autrefois, 1964.

———. *Keyboard Dances from the Earlier Sixteenth Century.* Corpus of Early Keyboard Music 8. [Rome]: American Institute of Musicology, 1965.

Hewitt, Helen, ed. *Ottaviano Petrucci, Canti B numero cinquanta.* Monuments of Renaissance Music, vol. 2. Chicago: University of Chicago Press, 1967.

Hewitt, Helen, and Isabel Pope, eds. *Harmonice musices odhecaton A.* Cambridge, Mass.: Mediaeval Academy of America, 1942.

Hewitt, Leslie, ed. *A Fifteenth-Century Song Book.* Early Music in Facsimile, vol. 1. Leeds: Boethius Press, 1973.

Higgins, Paula. "Music and Musicians at the Sainte-Chapelle of the Bourges Palace, 1405–1500." In *Atti del XIV Congresso della Società Internazionale di Musicología (Bologna, 1987)*, ed. Angelo Pompilio. 3 vols. Torino: EDT, 1990.

Higgins, Paula, ed. *Chansonnier Nivelle de la Chaussée, Bibliothèque Nationale, Paris, Res. Vmc. ms. 57, ca 1460.* Geneva: Minkoff, 1984.

Hoffmann-Erbrecht, Lothar. "Finck, Heinrich." *The New Grove Dictionary of Music*, 6:559–62.

———. "Stolzer, Thomas." *The New Grove Dictionary of Music*, 18:170–72.

Honneger, Marc, and Frank Dobbins. "Lupi, Second." *The New Grove Dictionary of Music*, 11:336.

Hoppin, Richard H. *Anthology of Medieval Music.* New York: Norton, 1978.

———. *Medieval Music.* New York: Norton, 1978.

Houdoy, Jules. *Histoire artistique de la cathédrale de Cambrai.* Lille, 1880. Reprint, Geneva: Minkoff, 1972.

Hughes, Andrew. "Mass Pairs in the Old Hall and Other English Manuscripts." *Revue belge de musicologie* 19 (1965): 15–27.

Hughes, Andrew, and Margaret Bent, eds. *The Old Hall Manuscript.* 3 vols. [Rome]: American Institute of Musicology, 1969–73.

Huglo, Michel. "Antiphon." *The New Grove Dictionary of Music*, 1:480.

———. "Odo." *The New Grove Dictionary of Music*, 13:503–4.

Hüschen, Heinrich. "Tinctoris." *The New Grove Dictionary of Music*, 18:837f.

Ingram, Jeannine S. "Salve regina." *The New Grove Dictionary of Music*, 16:435f.

Isaac, Heinrich. *Choralis Constantinus, Book III*, ed. Louise Cuyler. Ann Arbor: University of Michigan Press, 1950.

Jacobs, Charles. "Luis de Milán." *The New Grove Dictionary of Music*, 12:300–1.

———. "Valderrábano, Enríquez de." *The New Grove Dictionary of Music*, 19:489–90.

———. "Venegas de Henestrosa, Luis." *The New Grove Dictionary of Music*, 19:602–3.

Jacobson, David Christopher. "Thomas Morley and the Italian Madrigal Tradition: A New Perspective." *Journal of Musicology* 14 (1996): 80–91.

Janequin, Clément. *Chansons polyphoniques*, ed. Tilman Merritt and François Lesure. 6 vols. Monaco: Editions de l'Oiseau Lyre, 1965–71.

Jeans, Susi. "Bull, John." *The New Grove Dictionary of Music*, 3:438–45.

Jeppesen, Knud. *Counterpoint: The Polyphonic Vocal Style of the Sixteenth Century*, trans. Glen Haydon. New York: Prentice Hall, 1951.

———. *La Frottola: Bermerkungen zur Bibliographie der ältesten weltlichen Notendrucke in Italien.* 3 vols. Acta Jutlandica, vols. 41–43. Copenhagen: Munksgaard, 1968–69.

———. "Laude." *Die Musik in Geschichte und Gegenwart*, 8:313–14.

———. "Problems of the *Pope Marcellus Mass*: Some Remarks on the *Missa Papae Marcelli* by Giovanni Pierluigi da Palestrina." In Giovanni Pierluigi da Palestrina, *Pope Marcellus Mass*, ed. Lewis Lockwood. New York: Norton, 1975.

———. *The Style of Palestrina and the Dissonance.* Oxford: Oxford University Press, 1927.

Jeppesen, Knud, ed. *Der Kopenhagener Chansonnier.* Copenhagen, 1927. Reprint, New York: Da Capo Press, 1965.

Jeppesen, Knud, and V. Brøndal, eds. *Die mehrstimmige italienische Laude um 1500.* Leipzig: Breitkopf und Härtel, 1935.

Johannes Afflighemensis. *De musica cum tonario*, ed. Joseph Smits van Waesberge. Corpus scriptorum de musica 1. [Rome]: American Institute of Musicology, 1950.

Johnson, Alvin. "Rore, Cipriano de." *The New Grove Dictionary of Music*, 16:185–90.

Josquin Desprez. *Werken*, ed. Albert Smijers et al. *Missen*, 4 vols.; *Motetten*, 5 vols.; *Wereldlijke Werken*, 2 vols. Amsterdam: Vereniging voor Nederlandse Musiekgeschiedenis, 1921–56.

Karp, Theodore C. "Some Chant Models for Isaac's *Choralis Constantinus*." In *Beyond the*

Moon: Festschrift Luther Dittmer, ed. Bryan Gillingham and Paul Merkley. Ottowa: Institute of Mediaeval Music, 1990.

Kast, Paul. "Remarques sur la musique et les musiciens de la chapelle de François I au Camp du Drap d'Or." In *Fêtes et cérémonies au temps de Charles Quint*. Paris: Editions du Centre National de la Recherche Scientifique, 1960.

Kastner, Macario Santiago. "Cabezón, Antonio de." *The New Grove Dictionary of Music*, 3:572–74.

Kaye, Philip. *The Sacred Music of Gilles Binchois*. London: Oxford University Press, 1992.

Kellman, Herbert. "Alamire." *The New Grove Dictionary of Music*, 1:192–93.

———. "Josquin and the Courts of the Netherlands and France: The Evidence of the Sources." In *Josquin des Prez, Proceedings of the International Josquin Festival-Conference*, ed. Edward E. Lowinsky and Bonnie Blackburn. London: Oxford University Press, 1977.

———. "The Origins of the Chigi Codex: The Date, Provenance, and Original Ownership of Rome, Biblioteca Vaticana, Chigiana, C.VIII.234." *Journal of the American Musicological Society* 11 (1958): 6–19.

Kelly, Thomas Forest, ed. *Plainsong in the Age of Polyphony*. Cambridge: Cambridge University Press, 1992.

Kenney, Sylvia. *Walter Frye and the Contenance Angloise*. New Haven: Yale University Press, 1964.

Kerman, Joseph. "Byrd, William." *The New Grove Dictionary of Music*, 3:537–52.

———. *The Elizabethan Madrigal*. New York: American Musicological Society, 1962.

———. *The Motets and Masses of William Byrd*. Berkeley: University of Califorina Press, 1981.

Keyl, Stephen. "*Tenorlied, Discantlied*, Polyphonic Lied: Voices and Instruments in German Secular Polyphony of the Renaissance." *Early Music* 20 (1992): 434–45.

Kirkendale, Warren. "Ciceronians versus Aristotelians on the Ricercar as Exordium from Bembo to Bach." *Journal of the American Musicological Society* 32 (1979): 1–44.

Kirsch, Winfried. "Magnificat." *The New Grove Dictionary of Music*, 11:495–97.

———. "De Silva, Andreas." *The New Grove Dictionary of Music*, 5:389.

———. *Die Quellen der mehrstimmigen Magnificat- und Te Deum-Vertonungen bis zur Mitte des 16. Jahrhunderts*. Tutzing: Schneider, 1966.

Knighton, Tess. "The *a cappella* Heresy in Spain: An Inquisition into the Performance of the *Cancionero* Repertory." *Early Music* 20 (1992): 561–81.

———. "The Spanish Court of Ferdinand and Isabella." In *The Renaissance: From the 1470s to the End of the Sixteenth Century*, ed. Iain Fenlon. Man and Music, vol. 2. Englewood Cliffs, N.J.: Prentice Hall, 1989.

Korrick, Leslie. "Instrumental Music in the Early Sixteenth-Century Mass: New Evidence." *Early Music* 18 (1990): 359–70.

Kreyszig, Walter K. "Franchino Gaffurio als Vermittler der Musiklehre des Altertums und des Mittelalters: Zur Identifizierung griechischer und lateinischer Quellen in der *Theorica Musice* (1492)." *Acta musicologica* 65 (1993): 134–50.

Kristeller, Paul O. *Renaissance Thought: The Classic, Scholastic, and Humanistic Strains*. New York: Harper and Row, 1961.

———. *Renaissance Thought II*. New York: Harper and Row, 1965.

Lafontaine, Henry Cart de. *The King's Musick*. London, 1909. Reprint, New York: Da Capo Books, 1973.

La Rue, Pierre de. *Liber missarum: Première transcription moderne*, ed. A. Tirabassi. Malines: Dessain, 1941.

Lassus, Orlande de. *Sämtliche Werke*, ed. F. X. Haberl and A. Sandberger. 21 vols. Leipzig: Breitkopf und Härtel, 1894–1926; reprint, New York: Broude Brothers, 1973.

———. *Cantica, Responsorien und andere Musik für die Officia*, ed. Peter Bergquist. Sämtliche Werke, neue Reihe, vol. 24. Kassel: Bärenreiter, 1993.

———. *Das Hymnarium aus dem Jahre 1580–81*, ed. Marie Louise Göllner. Sämtliche Werke, neue Reihe, vol. 18. Kassel: Bärenreiter, 1980.

———. *Magnificat*, ed. James Erb. Sämtliche Werke, neue Reihe, vol. 13. Kassel: Bärenreiter, 1980.

———. *Messen*, ed. Siegfried Hermelink. Sämtliche Werke, neue Reihe, vol. 4. Kassel: Bärenreiter, 1964.

———. *Prophetiae Sibyllarum*, ed. Reinhold Schlötterer. Sämtliche Werke, neue Reihe, vol. 21. Kassel: Bärenreiter, 1990.

———. *Prophetiae Sibyllarum*, ed. Hans Joachim Therstappen. Das Chorwerk, vol. 48. Berlin: Kallmeyer, 1937.

———. *The Seven Penitential Psalms and Laudate Dominum de caelis*, ed. Peter Bergquist. 2 vols. Recent Researches in the Music of the Renaissance, vols. 86–87. Madison: A–R Editions, 1990.

Laurencie, Lionel de la, Adrienne Mairy, and Geneviève Thibaut, eds. *Chansons au luth et airs de cour français du XVIe siècle*. Paris: Publications de la Société Française de Musicologie, 1934.

Lawry, Eleanor. "Some Observations on Goudimel's Psalm Settings." In *Libraries, History, Diplomacy, and the Performing Arts: Essays in Honor of Carleton Sprague Smith*, ed. Israel J. Katz, Malena Kuss, and Richard J. Wolfe. Stuyvesant, N.Y.: Pendragon Press, 1991.

Ledbetter, Steven. "Marenzio, Luca de." *The New Grove Dictionary of Music*, 11:667.

Leech-Wilkinson, Daniel. "Il libro di appunti di un suonatore di tromba del quindicesimo secolo." *Rivista italiana di musicologia* 16 (1981): 16–39.

Legrense (Johannes Gallicus). *The Manner of Singing* (*Ritus canendi*), ed. Albert Seay. Colorado Springs: Critical Texts, USA, 1981.

Le Huray, Peter. "Anthem." *The New Grove Dictionary of Music*, 1:454–59.

———. *Music and the Reformation in England, 1549–1660*. London: Oxford University Press, 1967.

———. "Service." *The New Grove Dictionary of Music*, 17:188–91.

———. "Some Thoughts about Cantus Firmus Composition." In *Byrd Studies*, ed. Alan Brown and Richard Tarbet. Cambridge: Cambridge University Press, 1992.

Le Huray, Peter, ed. *The Treasury of English Church Music*, vol. 2 [1545–1650]. London: Blandford, 1965.

Le Jeune, Claude. *Airs a III. IIII. V. et VI Parties* (1607), ed. D. P. Walker. 4 vols. [Rome]: American Institute of Musicology, 1951–59.

Lemarignier, Jean-François. "Les institutions ecclésiastiques en France de la fin du Xe au milieu du XIIe siècle." In *Histoire des institutions françaises au moyen age*, vol. 3, *Institutions ecclésiastiques*, ed. Ferdinand Lot and Robert Fawtier. Paris: Presses universitaires de France, 1962.

Lester, Joel. "Root-Position and Inverted Triads in Theory around 1600." *Journal of the American Musicological Society* 27 (1974): 110–19.

Leuchtmann, Horst, and Robert Münster. "Munich." *The New Grove Dictionary of Music*, 12:781.

Leverett, Adelyn Peck. "Song Masses in the Trent Codices: The Austrian Connection." *Early Music History* 14 (1995): 205–56.

Levitan, Joseph S. "Adrian Willaert's Famous Duo, *Quidnam ebrietas.*" *Tijdschrift der Vereeniging voor Nederlandsche Muziekgeschiedenis* 15 (1939): 166–223.

Levy, Kenneth. "'Susanne un jour': The History of a Sixteenth-Century Chanson." *Annales musicologiques* 1 (1953): 375–408.

Lewis, Mary. *Antonio Gardane, Venetian Music Printer, 1538–1569: A Descriptive Bibliographical and Historical Study.* Garland Reference Library of the Humanities, vol. 718. New York: Garland, 1988.

Lhéritier, Jean. *Opera omnia*, ed. Leeman L. Perkins. 2 vols. Corpus mensurabilis musicae 48. [Rome]: American Institute of Musicology, 1969.

Liber usualis Missae et Officii pro dominicis et festis cum cantu gregoriano, ex editione Vaticana adamussim excerpto. Paris: Desclée et Socii, 1960.

Lindley, Mark. "Temperaments." *The New Grove Dictionary of Music*, 18:660–74.

Linker, Robert W., and Gwynn S. McPeek. "The Bergerette Form in the Laborde Chansonnier: A Musico-Literary Study." *Journal of the American Musicological Society* 7 (1954): 113–20.

Lipphardt, Walther. "Leisen und Rufe." *Die Musik in Geschichte und Gegenwart*, 16:1108.

Litterick, Louise. "On Italian Instrumental Ensemble Music in the Late Fifteenth Century." In *Music in Medieval and Early Modern Europe: Patronage, Sources, and Texts*, ed. Iain Fenlon. Cambridge: Cambridge University Press, 1981.

Little, Meredith Ellis. "Saltarello." *The New Grove Dictionary of Music*, 16:430–32.

Llorens, José M. "Alba, Alonso." *The New Grove Dictionary of Music*, 1:195.

———. *Capellae Sixtinae Codices.* Studi e testi, vol. 202. Vatican City: Biblioteca Apostolica Vaticana, 1960.

Lockwood, Lewis. "Aspects of the L'homme armé Tradition." *Proceedings of the Royal Music Association* 100 (1973–74): 97–122.

———. "Borromeo, Carlo." *The New Grove Dictionary of Music*, 3:67–68.

———. "Felix namque." *The New Grove Dictionary of Music*, 6:458.

———. "Ferrara." *The New Grove Dictionary of Music*, 6:486–87.

———. "Jean Mouton and Jean Michel: New Evidence on French Music and Musicians in Italy, 1505–1520." *Journal of the American Musicological Society* 32 (1979): 191–246.

———. "Martini." *The New Grove Dictionary of Music*, 11:726–27.

———. "Mass." *The New Grove Dictionary of Music*, 11:786.

———. *Music in Renaissance Ferrara, 1400–1505: The Creation of a Musical Center in the Fifteenth Century.* Cambridge, Mass.: Harvard University Press, 1984.

———. "On 'Parody' as Term and Concept in Sixteenth-Century Music." In *Aspects of Medieval and Renaissance Music: A Birthday Offering to Gustave Reese*, ed. Jan La Rue et al. New York: Norton, 1966.

———. "Renaissance." *The New Grove Dictionary of Music*, 15:736–41.

———. "A View of the Early Sixteenth-Century Parody Mass." In *Queen's College Twenty-Fifth Anniversary Festschrift*, ed. Albert Mell. Flushing, N.Y.: Queen's College Press, 1964.

Lockwood, Lewis, and Jessie Ann Owens. "Palestrina." *The New Grove Dictionary of Music*, 14:118–37.

———. "Willaert, Adrian." *The New Grove Dictionary of Music*, 20:421–28.

Loft, Abram. "Musicians' Guild and Union: A Consideration of the Evolution of Protective Organization among Musicians." Ph.D. diss., Columbia University, 1950.

Lowinsky, Edward E. "Adrian Willaert's Chromatic Duo Re-examined." *Tijdschrift voor Muziekwetenschap* 18 (1956): 1–36.

————. "The Concept of Physical and Musical Space in the Renaissance." *Papers of the American Musicological Society*, Annual Meeting, 1941. Minneapolis, Minn.: Richmond, 1946.

————. "Early Scores in Manuscript." *Journal of the American Musicological Society* 12 (1960): 126–73.

————. "Music in the Culture of the Renaissance." In *Renaissance Essays*, ed. Paul O. Kristeller and Philip P. Wiener. 2 vols. Library of the History of Ideas, vol. 9. Rochester: University of Rochester Press, 1992.

————. "On the Use of Scores by Sixteenth-Century Musicians." *Journal of the American Musicological Society* 1 (1948): 17–23.

Lowinsky, Edward E., ed. *The Medici Codex of 1518: A Choirbook of Motets Dedicated to Lorenzo de' Medici, Duke of Urbino*. 3 vols. Monuments of Renaissance Music, vols. 3–5. Chicago: University of Chicago Press, 1968.

MacClintock, Carol. "Wert, Giaches de." *The New Grove Dictionary of Music*, 20:351.

Macey, Patrick. "Galeazzo Maria Sforza and Musical Patronage in Milan: Compère, Weerbeke, and Josquin." *Early Music History* 15 (1996): 149–214.

————. "*Infiamma il mio cor*: Savonarolan *Laude* by and for Dominican Nuns in Tuscany." In *The Crannied Wall: Women, Religion, and the Arts in Early Modern Europe*, ed. Craig A. Monson. Ann Arbor: University of Michigan Press, 1992.

————. "Josquin's 'Little' Ave Maria: A Misplaced Motet from the Vultum tuum Cycle?" *Tijdschrift van de Vereniging voor Nederlandse Muziekgeschiedenis* 39 (1989): 38–53.

————. "Josquin's *Miserere mei Deus*: Context, Structure, and Influence." Ph.D. diss., University of California, Berkeley, 1985.

————. "The Lauda and the Cult of Savonarola." *Renaissance Quarterly* 46 (1992): 439–83.

————. "Some New Contrafacta for *Canti Carnascialeschi* and *Laude* in Late Quattrocento Florence." In *La musica a Firenze al tempo di Lorenzo il Magnifico*, ed. Piero Gargiulo. Florence: Olschki, 1993.

Macy, Laura. "Speaking of Sex: Metaphor and Performance in the Italian Madrigal." *Journal of Musicology* 14 (1996): 1–34.

Main, Alexander. "Festa, Costanzo." *The New Grove Dictionary of Music*, 6:501–4.

————. "Maximilian's Second-hand Funeral Motet." *Musical Quarterly* 47 (1962): 172–89.

Maitland, J. A. Fuller, and W. Barclay Squire, eds. *The Fitzwilliam Virginal Book*. 2 vols. London: Breitkopf und Härtel, 1894–99; reprint, New York: Dover, 1963.

Maniates, Maria. "Combinative Chansons in the Dijon Chansonnier." *Journal of the American Musicological Society* 23 (1970): 228–81.

Maniates, Maria, ed. *The Combinative Chanson: An Anthology*. Recent Researches in the Music of the Renaissance, vol. 77. Madison: A–R Editions, 1989.

Mann, Alfred, and J. Kenneth Wilson. "Canon." *The New Grove Dictionary of Music*, 3:689–93.

Marchetto da Padova. *The Lucidarium of Marchetto of Padua*, ed. Jan Herlinger. Chicago: University of Chicago Press, 1985.

Marenzio, Luca. *Sämtliche Werke*, ed. Alfred Einstein. 2 vols. Publikationen älterer Musik, vol. 6. Leipzig: Breitkopf und Härtel, 1929–31.

Marinis, Tammaro de. *La Biblioteca Napoletana dei Re d'Aragona*. 4 vols. Milan: Ulrico Hoepli, 1947–52.

Marix, Jeanne. *Histoire de la musique et des musiciens de la cour de Bourgogne*. Strasbourg: Heitz, 1939. Reprint, Geneva: Minkoff, 1972.

Marix, Jeanne, ed. *Les musiciens de la cour de Bourgogne au XVe siècle.* Paris: Droz, 1937.

Marshall, Robert L. "Chorale." *The New Grove Dictionary of Music,* 4:312–16.

Massenkeil, Günther, ed. *Mehrstimmige Lamentationen aus der ersten Hälfte des 16. Jahrhunderts.* Musikalischer Denkmäler der Akademie der Wissenschaft und der Literatur, vol. 6. Mainz: Schott's Söhne, 1965.

————. "Lamentations." *The New Grove Dictionary of Music,* 10:410–12.

Mattfeld, Victor H. "Rhau, Georg." *The New Grove Dictionary of Music,* 15:787–89.

Matthews, Lora, and Paul Merkley. "Iudochus de Picardia and Jossequin Lebloitte dit Desprez: The Names of the Singer(s)." *Journal of Musicology* 16 (1998): 223–26.

————. "Josquin Desprez and His Milanese Patrons." *Journal of Musicology* 12 (1994): 434–63.

McGee, Timothy J. "Instruments and the Faenza Codex." *Early Music* 14 (1986): 480–90.

McKinnon, James W. "Fifteenth-Century Northern Book Painting and the *a cappella* Question: An Essay in Iconographic Method." In *Studies in the Performance of Late Mediaeval Music,* ed. Stanley Boorman. Cambridge: Cambridge University Press, 1983.

McPeek, Gwynn S. *The British Museum Manuscript Egerton 3307.* London: Oxford University Press, 1963.

Meier, Bernhard. *The Modes of Classical Vocal Polyphony,* trans. Ellen Beebe. New York: Broude Brothers, 1988.

Mesnard, Pierre. "La Collégiale Saint-Martin à l'époque des Valois." In *Mémorial de l'année martinienne M.DCCCC.LX–M.DCCCC.LXI.* Paris: Librairie J. Vrin, 1962.

Milano, Francesco Canova da. *The Lute Music of Francesco Canova da Milano (1497–1543),* ed. Arthur J. Ness. 2 vols. Harvard Publications in Music, vols. 3–4. Cambridge, Mass.: Harvard University, Department of Music, 1970.

Miller, Clement A. "Early Gaffuriana: New Answers." *Musical Quarterly* 56 (1970): 380–82.

————. "Glarean." *The New Grove Dictionary of Music,* 7:422–24.

Minor, Andrew C. "Corteccia." *The New Grove Dictionary of Music,* 4:807–8.

Miskimin, Harry A. *The Economy of Early Renaissance Europe, 1300–1460.* Cambridge: Cambridge University Press, 1975.

Mixter, Keith. "Johannes de Lymburgia." *The New Grove Dictionary of Music,* 9:666–67.

Monson, Craig. "Elizabethan London." In *The Renaissance: From the 1470s to the End of the Sixteenth Century,* ed. Iain Fenlon. Man and Music, vol. 2. Englewood Cliffs, N.J.: Prentice Hall, 1989.

Morales, Cristóbal de. *Opera omnia,* ed. Higinio Anglès. 8 vols. Monumentos de la música española, vols. 11, 13, 15, 17, 20, 21, 24, and 34. Barcelona: Consejo Superior de Investigaciones Científicas, Instituto Español de Musicología, 1952–71.

More, Sir Thomas. *Utopia.* In *Three Renaissance Classics,* ed. Burton A. Milligan. New York: Charles Scribner's Sons, 1953.

Morehen, John. "The Engish Anthem Text, 1549–1660." *Journal of the Royal Music Association* 117 (1992): 62–85.

Morley, Thomas. *First Book of Madrigals to Four Voices* (1594/1600). Vol. 2 of *The English Madrigal School,* ed. Edmund H. Fellowes. London: Stainer and Bell, 1921.

Morton, Robert. *The Collected Works,* ed. Allan Atlas. New York: Broude Brothers, 1981.

Mouton, Jean. *Fünf Motetten,* ed. Paul Kast. Das Chorwerk, vol. 76. Wolfenbüttel: Möseler, 1959.

————. *Opera omnia,* ed. Andrew Minor and Thomas G. MacCracken. 4 vols. Corpus mensurabilis musicae 43. Neuhausen-Stuttgart: Hänssler Verlag, 1967–.

Narváez, Luys de. *Los seys libros del Delphin*, ed. Emilio Pujol. Monumentos de música española, vol. 3. Barcelona: Consejo Superior de Investigaciones Científicas, Instituto Español de Musicología, 1945.

Neighbour, Oliver. *The Consort and Keyboard Music of William Byrd*. Berkeley: University of California Press, 1978.

The New Columbia Encyclopedia, ed. William H. Harris and Judith S. Levy. New York: Columbia University Press, 1975.

Newcomb, Anthony. *The Madrigal at Ferrara, 1579–1597*. 2 vols. Princeton: Princeton University Press, 1980.

Nieuwenhuizen, J. Van den. "De koralen, de zangers en de zangmeesters van de Antwerpse O.-L.-Vrouwekerk tijdens de 15e eeuw." In *Antwerps Katedraalkoor, Gouden Jubileum Gedenkboek*. Antwerp: Choraelhuys, 1978.

Noble, Jeremy. "Josquin Desprez." *The New Grove Dictionary of Music*, 9:719–38.

Noblitt, Thomas. "The Ambrosian *motetti missales* Repertory." *Musica disciplina* 22 (1968): 77–103.

———. "Die Datierung der Handschrift Mus. MS. 3154 der Staatsbibliothek München." *Die Musikforschung* 27 (1974): 36–56.

———. "The Earliest Plenary Mass for Easter." In *From Ciconia to Sweelinck, Donum Natalicium Willem Elders*, ed. Albert Clement and Eric Jas. Chloe: Beihefte zum Daphnis, vol. 21. Amsterdam: Editions Rodopi, 1995.

Nugent, George. "Anti-Protestant Music for Sixteenth-Century Ferrara." *Journal of the American Musicological Society* 43 (1990): 228–91.

———. "Gombert." *The New Grove Dictionary of Music*, 7:512–16.

———. "Jacquet of Mantua." *The New Grove Dictionary of Music*, 9:456–58.

Oboussier, Philippe. "Parsons, John." *The New Grove Dictionary of Music*, 14:248.

———. "Parsons, William." *The New Grove Dictionary of Music*, 14:249–50.

Obrecht, Jacob. *Opera omnia editio altera*, ed. Albert Smijers and Marcus Van Crevel. 9 vols. Amsterdam: Vereniging voor Nederlandse Muziekgeschiedenis, 1953–59.

———. *Werken*, ed. Johannes Wolf. 26 vols. Vereeniging voor Noord-Nederlands Muziekgeschiedenis. Amsterdam: G. Albach, 1908–21.

Okeghem, Johannes. *Collected Works*, ed. Dragan Plamenac. 2d ed. 2 vols. New York: American Musicological Society, 1959–66.

———. *Collected Works*, ed. Richard Wexler and Dragan Plamenac. Vol. 3, *Motets and Chansons*. Philadelphia: American Musicological Society, 1992.

———. *Masses and Mass Sections*, ed. Jaap van Benthem. 3 vols. Utrecht: Koninklijke Vereniging voor Nederlandse Muziekgeschiedenis, 1994–.

Orden, Kate van. "Sexual Discourse in the Parisian Chanson: A Libidinous Aviary." *Journal of the American Musicological Society* 48 (1995): 1–41.

Osborn, James M. "Whythorne, Thomas." *The New Grove Dictionary of Music*, 20:393–94.

Osthoff, Helmut. *Josquin Desprez*. 2 vols. Tutzing: Schneider, 1962–65.

Owens, Jessie Ann. "Music Historiography and the Definition of 'Renaissance.'" *Notes* 47 (1990): 305–30.

Packer, Dorothy S. "Collections of Chaste Chansons for the Devout Home (1613–1633)." *Acta musicologica* 61 (1989): 175–216.

Page, Christopher. "The English *a cappella* Heresy." In *Companion to Medieval and Renaissance Music*, ed. by Tess Knighton and David Fallows. London: J. M. Dent and Sons, 1992.

————. "Machaut's 'Pupil' Deschamps on the Performance of Music: Voices or Instruments in the Fourteenth-Century Chanson?" *Early Music* 5 (1977): 484–91.

————. "The Performance of Songs in Late-Medieval France: A New Source." *Early Music* 10 (1982): 441–50.

Palestrina, Giovanni Pierluigi da. *Le opere complete*, ed. Raffaele Casimiri et al. 34 vols. Rome: Edizione Fratelli Scalera, 1939–52.

————. *Pope Marcellus Mass*, ed. Lewis Lockwood. Norton Critical Scores. New York: Norton, 1975.

Palisca, Claude V. "The Artusi–Monteverdi Controversy." In *The New Monteverdi Companion*, ed. Denis Arnold and Nigel Fortune. London: Faber and Faber, 1985.

————. "Diruta, Girolamo." *The New Grove Dictionary of Music*, 5:485–87.

————. *Humanism in Italian Renaissance Musical Thought*. New Haven: Yale University Press, 1985.

————. "The Impact of the Revival of Learning on Music Theory." In *Report of the Twelfth Congress of the International Musicological Society, Berkeley, 1977*, ed. Daniel Heartz and Bonnie Wade. Kassel: Barenreiter, 1981.

————. "*Ut oratoria musica*: The Rhetorical Basis of Musical Mannerism." In *The Meaning of Mannerism*, ed. F. W. Robinson and S. G. Nichols. Hanover, N. H.: University Press of New England, 1972. Also in *Studies in the History of Italian Music and Music Theory*, ed. Claude V. Palisca. New York: Oxford University Press, 1994.

Palisca, Claude V., ed. *Norton Anthology of Western Music*. 2 vols. New York: Norton, 1980; 2d ed., 1988; 3d ed., 1996.

Panofsky, Erwin. *Gothic Architecture and Scholasticism*. New York: Meridian Books, 1957.

————. *Meaning in the Visual Arts*. Garden City, N.Y.: Doubleday Anchor Books, 1955.

————. *Renaissance and Renascences in Western Art*. New York: Harper and Row, 1972.

Pareia, Ramos de. *Musica practica*, ed. Johannes Wolf. Leipzig: Breitkopf und Härtel, 1901.

Paris, Gaston, and Auguste Gevaert, eds. *Chansons du XVe siècle*. Paris: Société des Anciens Textes Français, 1875; reissued 1935.

Pas, Justin de. *Ménestrels et écoles de ménestrels à Saint-Omer*. Saint-Ouen, 1903. Reprint, Geneva: Minkoff, 1972.

Pelnar, Ivana, and Christoph Petzsch. "Oswald von Wolkenstein." *The New Grove Dictionary of Music*, 14:15–19.

Pendle, Karin. "Women in Music, ca. 1450–1600." In *Women and Music: A History*, ed. Karin Pendle. Bloomington: Indiana University Press, 1991.

Perkins, Leeman L. "Conflicting Attributions and Anonymous Chansons in the 'Busnoys' Sources of the Fifteenth Century (Appendix 1)." In *Continuities and Transformations in Musical Culture, 1450–1500: Assessing the Legacy of Antoine Busnoys*, ed. Paula Higgins. London: Oxford University Press, 1998.

————. "Lhéritier, Jean." *The New Grove Dictionary of Music*, newly revised edition, ed. Stanley Sadie. London: Macmillan, 1998.

————. "The L'homme armé Masses of Busnoys and Okeghem: A Comparison." *Journal of Musicology* 3 (1984): 363–96.

————. "Modal Species and Mixtures in a Fifteenth-Century Chanson Repertory." In *Modality in the Music of the Fourteenth and Fifteenth Centuries*, ed. Ursula Günther, Ludwig Finscher, and Jeffrey Dean. Musicological Studies and Documents 49. Neuhausen-Stuttgart: Hänssler-Verlag, 1996.

————. "Modal Strategies in Okeghem's *Missa Cuiusvis toni*." In *Music Theory and the*

Exploration of the Past, ed. Christopher Hatch and David W. Bernstein. Chicago: University of Chicago Press, 1993.

———. "Mode and Structure in the Masses of Josquin." *Journal of the American Musicological Society* 26 (1973): 189–239.

———. "Modern Methods, Received Opinion, and the Chansonnier." Review of *Der Wolfenbütteler Chansonnier, Wolfenbüttel, Herzog August Bibliothek, Codex Guelf. 287 Extrav.*, by Martella Gutiérrez-Denhoff. *Music and Letters* 69 (1988): 356–64.

———. "Musical Patronage at the Royal Court of France under Charles VII and Louis XI (1422–83)." *Journal of the American Musicological Society* 37 (1984): 507–66.

———. "Ockeghem." *The New Grove Dictionary of Music*, 13:489–96.

———. "Toward a Theory of Text–Music Relations in the Music of the Renaissance." To be published in the Proceedings of the First International Conference on Binchois, Graduate School and University Center of the City University of New York, October 31–November 1, 1995.

———. "Toward a Typology of the 'Renaissance' Chanson." *Journal of Musicology* 6 (1988): 441–47.

Perkins, Leeman L., and Howard Garey, eds. *The Mellon Chansonnier*. 2 vols. New Haven: Yale University Press, 1979.

Perroy, Edouard. *The Hundred Years War*. Bloomington: Indiana University Press, 1962.

Picker, Martin. "Antico." *The New Grove Dictionary of Music*, 1:467–69.

———. "Busnois." *The New Grove Dictionary of Music*, 3:504–8.

———. "The Habsburg Courts, 1477–1530." In *The Renaissance: From the 1470s to the End of the Sixteenth Century*, ed. Iain Fenlon. Man and Music, vol. 2. Englewood Cliffs, N.J.: Prentice Hall, 1989.

———. "Habsburg." *The New Grove Dictionary of Music*, 8:12.

———. "Petrucci, Ottaviano." *The New Grove Dictionary of Music*, 14:595–97.

Picker, Martin, ed. *The Chanson Albums of Marguerite of Austria*. Berkeley: University of California Press, 1965.

———. *Fors seulement: Thirty Compositions for Three to Five Voices or Instruments from the Fifteenth and Sixteenth Centuries*. Recent Researches in the Music of the Middle Ages and the Early Renaissance, vol. 14. Madison: A–R Editions, 1981.

Pidoux, Pierre. *Le psautier huguenot du XVIe siècle: Mélodies et documents*. 2 vols. Basel: Bärenreiter, 1962.

Pirrotta, Nino. "Marchettus de Padua and the Italian ars nova." *Musica disciplina* 9 (1955): 57–71.

———. *Music and Culture in Italy from the Middle Ages to the Baroque*. Cambridge, Mass.: Harvard University Press, 1984.

———. *Music and Theater from Poliziano to Monteverdi*. Cambridge, Mass.: Harvard University Press, 1981.

Pirrotta, Nino, and Raoul Meloncelli. "Rome." *The New Grove Dictionary of Music*, 16:155–56.

Pisano, Bernardo. *Collected Works*, ed. Frank D'Accone. Corpus mensurabilis musicae 32. [Rome]: American Institute of Musicology, 1966.

Plamenac, Dragan, ed. *Dijon Bibliothèque Publique manuscrit 517*. Publications of Mediaeval Musical Manuscripts, no. 12. Brooklyn: Institute of Medieval Music, n.d.

Planchart, Alejandro E. "Fifteenth-Century Masses: Notes on Performance and Chronology." *Studi musicali* 10 (1981): 3–29.

———. "Notes on Guillaume Du Fay's Last Works." *Journal of Musicology* 13 (1995): 55–72.

———. "Parts with Words and without Words: The Evidence for Multiple Texts in Fifteenth-Century Masses." In *Studies in the Performance of Late Mediaeval Music*, ed. Stanley Boorman. Cambridge: Cambridge University Press, 1983.

———. "The Relative Speed of Tempora in the Period of Dufay." *Royal Musical Association Research Chronicle* 17 (1981): 33–51.

Planchart, Alejandro, ed. *Missae Caput*, Collegium Musicum, vol. 5. New Haven: Yale University, 1964.

Pogue, Samuel F. "Ballard." *The New Grove Dictionary of Music*, 2:83–86.

———. "Du Chemin." *The New Grove Dictionary of Music*, 5:670f.

———. *Jacques Moderne, Lyons Music Printer of the Sixteenth Century*. Geneva: Librairie Droz, 1969.

———. "Moderne." *The New Grove Dictionary of Music*, 12:452–53.

Poindexter, Adele. "Chapel." *The New Grove Dictionary of Music*, 4:148–51.

Polk, Keith. "Municipal Wind Music in Flanders in the Late Middle Ages." *Brass and Woodwind Quarterly* 2 (1969): 1–15.

Poole, Edmund. "Printing and Publishing of Music." *The New Grove Dictionary of Music*, 15:232–53.

Pope, Isabel. "Musical and Metrical Form of the Villancico." *Annales musicologiques* 2 (1954): 189–214.

———. "The Secular Compositions of Johannes Cornago." In *Miscelánea en homenaje a Monseñor Higinio Anglés*, 2 vols. Barcelona: Consejo Superior de Investigaciones Científicas, 1958–61.

———. "Cornago." *The New Grove Dictionary of Music*, 4:779–80.

———. "Encina, Juan del." *The New Grove Dictionary of Music*, 6:159–61.

———. "Oriola, Pietro." *The New Grove Dictionary of Music*, 13:822.

———. "Triana, Juan de." *The New Grove Dictionary of Music*, 19:137.

———. "Urreda." *The New Grove Dictionary of Music*, 19:467–68.

Pope, Isabel, and Masakata Kanazawa, eds. *The Musical Manuscript Montecassino 871: A Neapolitan Repertory of Sacred and Secular Music of the Late Fifteenth Century*. Oxford: Clarendon Press, 1978.

Power, Leonel. *Complete Works*, ed. Charles Hamm. 2 vols. [Rome]: American Institute of Musicology, 1969–76.

Powers, Harold S. "Mode." *The New Grove Dictionary of Music*, 12:376–450.

———. "Tonal Types and Modal Categories in Renaissance Polyphony." *Journal of the American Musicology Society* 34 (1981): 428–70.

Powley, E. Harrison. "Il trionfo di Dori: A Critical Edition," 3 vols. Ph.D. diss., University of Rochester, Eastman School of Music, 1975.

———. *"Il trionfo di Dori": The 29 Madrigals of the 1592 Collection for Mixed Voices*, Renaissance Voices. New York: Gaudia Music and Arts, 1990.

Prizer, William. *Courtly Pastimes: The Frottole of Marchetto Cara*. Studies in Musicology, vol. 33. Ann Arbor: UMI Research Press, 1980.

———. "Ludovico Milanese." *The New Grove Dictionary of Music*, 11:306.

———. "Lutenists at the Court of Mantua in the Late Fifteenth and Early Sixteenth Centuries." *Journal of the Lute Society of America* 13 (1980): 5–34.

———. "Music and Ceremonial in the Low Countries." *Early Music History* 5 (1985): 113–53.

———. "Music at the Court of the Sforza: The Birth and Death of a Musical Center." *Musica disciplina* 43 (1989): 141–93.

⸻. "North Italian Courts, 1460–1540." In *The Renaissance: From the 1470s to the End of the Sixteenth Century*, ed. Iain Fenlon. Man and Music, vol. 2. Englewood Cliffs, N.J.: Prentice Hall, 1989.

⸻. "Tromboncino, Bartolomeo." *The New Grove Dictionary of Music*, 19:161–63.

Prizer, William, ed. *Libro primo de la croce (Rome: Pasoti and Dorico, 1526): Canzoni, frottole, and capitoli*. Madison: A–R Editions, 1978.

Prizer, William, and John Stevens. "Lauda spirituale." *The New Grove Dictionary of Music*, 10:538–43.

Prunières, Henry. "La musique de chambre et de l'écurie sous le règne de François 1er (1516–47)." *L'année musicale* 1 (1911): 215–51.

Quadris, Johannes de. *Opera*, ed. Giulio Cattin. Antiquae musicae italicae: Monumenta veneta sacra, vol. 2. Bologna: Bardolino, 1972.

Rachum, Ilan, ed. *The Renaissance: An Illustrated Encyclopedia*. London: Octopus Books, 1979.

Ramos de Pareia, Bartolomeo. *Musica practica* (Bologna, 1482). Reprint, Bologna: Arnaldo Forni, 1969.

⸻. *Musica practica*, trans. Clement A. Miller. Musicological Studies and Documents 44. Stuttgart-Neuhausen: American Institute of Musicology, 1993.

Randel, Don M. "Emerging Triadic Tonality in the Fifteenth Century." *Musical Quarterly* 57 (1971): 73–86.

Rashdall, Hastings. *The Universities of Europe in the Middle Ages*, ed. F. M. Powicke and A. B. Emden. 3 vols. Oxford: Oxford University Press, 1936. 2d ed., Oxford: Clarendon Press, 1987–.

Rastall, Richard. "The Minstrels of the English Royal Households, 25 Edward I–1 Henry VIII: An Inventory." *Royal Musical Association Research Chronicle* 4 (1964): 1–41.

Razzi, Giovanni (Serafino), ed. *Libro primo delle laudi spirituali*. Venice, 1563. Reprint, Bologna: Arnaldo Forni, 1969.

Reaney, Gilbert. "Machaut." *The New Grove Dictionary of Music*, 11:428–36.

⸻. "The Manuscript Oxford, Bodleian Library, Canonici Misc. 213." *Musica disciplina* 9 (1955): 73–104.

⸻. "Zacar." *The New Grove Dictionary of Music*, 20:609–10.

Reaney, Gilbert, ed. *Polyphonic Music of the Early Fifteenth Century*. 7 vols. Corpus mensurabilis musicae 11. [Rome]: American Institute of Musicology, 1955.

Reese, Gustave. *Music in the Middle Ages*. New York: Norton, 1940.

⸻. *Music in the Renaissance*. New York: Norton, 1959.

Reese, Gustave, and Theodore Karp. "Monophony in a Group of Renaissance Chansonniers." *Journal of the American Musicological Society* 5 (1952): 8–12.

Reese, Gustave, and Jeremy Noble. "Josquin Desprez." *The New Grove Dictionary of Music*, 9:713–38.

Regis, Johannes. *Opera omnia*, ed. C. Lindenburg. Corpus mensurabilis musicae 9. [Rome]: American Institute of Musicology, 1956.

Remnant, Mary. "Fiddle." *The New Grove Dictionary of Music*, 6:527–33.

⸻. "Gittern." *The New Grove Dictionary of Music*, 7:409–12.

Reynolds, Christopher A. "Musical Careers, Ecclesiastical Benefices, and the Example of Johannes Brunet." *Journal of the American Musicological Society* 37 (1984): 49–97.

⸻. "The Origins of San Pietro B 80 and the Development of a Roman Sacred Repertory." *Early Music History* 1 (1981): 257–304.

———. *Papal Patronage and the Music of St. Peter's, 1380–1513.* Berkeley: University of California Press, 1995.

———. "Rome: A City of Rich Contrast." In *The Renaissance: From the 1470s to the End of the Sixteenth Century,* ed. Iain Fenlon. Man and Music, vol. 2. Englewood Cliffs, N.J.: Prentice Hall, 1989.

Reynolds, Christopher, ed. *Vatican City, Biblioteca Apostolica Vaticana, San Pietro B 80.* Renaissance Music in Facsimile, vol. 23. New York: Garland Publishing, 1986.

Riedel, Johannes, ed. *Leise Settings of the Renaissance and Reformation.* Recent Researches in the Music of the Renaissance, vol. 35. Madison: A-R Editions, 1980.

Rifkin, Joshua. "Compère, Loyset." *The New Grove Dictionary of Music,* 4:595–98.

———. "Problems of Authorship in Josquin: Some Impolitic Observations, with a Postscript on *Absalon, fili mi.*" In *Proceedings of the International Josquin Symposium, Utrecht 1989,* ed. Willem Elders and Frits de Haen. Utrecht: Vereniging voor Nederlandse Muziekgeschiedenis, 1991.

Ringman, Heribert, ed. *Das Glogauer Liederbuch.* 2 vols. Das Erbe deutscher Musik, vols. 4 and 8. Kassel: Bärenreiter, 1936.

Rippa [Ripa da Mantova], Alberto da. *Oeuvres d'Albert de Rippe,* ed. Jean-Michel Vaccaro. 3 vols. Choeur des Muses, Corpus des luthistes français. Paris: Centre National de la Recherche Scientifique, 1972–75.

Rokseth, Yvonne, ed. *Deux livres d'orgues parus chez Pierre Attaingnant en 1531.* Publications de la Société Française de Musicologie, ser. 1, vol. 1. Paris: La Société Française de Musicologie, 1925.

———. *Treize motets et un prélude pour orgue parus chez Attaingnant en 1531.* Publications de la Société Française de Musicologie, ser. 1, vol. 5. Paris: La Société Française de Musicologie, 1930.

Rore, Cipriano de. *Opera omnia,* ed. Bernhard Meier. 8 vols. Corpus mensurabilis musicae 14. [Rome]: American Institute of Musicology, 1959–77.

Ros-Fabregas, Emilio. "The Manuscript Barcelona, Biblioteca de Catalunya, M. 454: Study and Edition in the Context of the Iberian and Continental Manuscript Traditions." 2 vols. Ph.D. diss., City University of New York, 1992.

Ross, James, and Mary McLaughlin, eds. *The Portable Renaissance Reader.* New York: Viking Press, 1953.

Rubin, Patricia Lee. *Giorgio Vasari: Art and History.* New Haven: Yale University Press, 1994.

Rubsamen, Walter H. "The Earliest French Lute Tablature." *Journal of the American Musicological Society* 21 (1968): 286–99.

———. "From Frottola to Madrigal." In *Chanson and Madrigal, 1480–1530,* ed. James Haar. Cambridge, Mass.: Harvard University Press, 1964.

———. "Villotta." *Die Musik in Geschichte und Gegenwart,* 13:1647.

Rumbold, Ian. "The Compilation and Ownership of Munich, Clm 14274." *Early Music History* 2 (1982): 161–235.

Sage, Jack. "Canción." *The New Grove Dictionary of Music,* 3:679.

———. "Cancionero." *The New Grove Dictionary of Music,* 3:679–81.

Salmen, Walter. "Geisslerlieder." *The New Grove Dictionary of Music,* 7:220.

———. "The Social Status of the Musician in the Middle Ages." In *The Social Status of the Professional Musician from the Middle Ages to the Nineteenth Century.* New York: Pendragon Press, 1983.

Salmen, Walter, and Christoph Petzsch, eds. *Das Lochamer Liederbuch.* Denkmäler der Tonkunst in Bayern, new ser., special vol. 2. Wiesbaden: Breitkopf und Härtel, 1972.

Sanders, Ernest. "Isorhythm." *The New Grove Dictionary of Music*, 9:351–54.

———. "Motet." *The New Grove Dictionary of Music*, 12:617–25.

———. "Sources, MS." *The New Grove Dictionary of Music*, 17:657–61.

Sandon, Nicholas. "Fayrfax, Robert." *The New Grove Dictionary of Music*, 6:443–45.

Satowski, Leon G. *Giorgio Vasari: Architect and Courtier.* Princeton: Princeton University Press, 1993.

Schletterer, Hans M. *Geschichte der Hofcappelle der französischen Könige.* Berlin: R. Damköhler, 1884.

Schrade, Leo. "News on the Chant Cycles of the *Ordinarium missae*." *Journal of the American Musicological Society* 8 (1955): 66–69.

———. "Renaissance: The Historical Conception of an Epoch." in *Twentieth-Century Views of Music History*, ed. William Hays. New York: Charles Scribner's Sons, 1972.

Schuler, Manfred. "Dietrich, Sixt." *The New Grove Dictionary of Music*, 5:469–70.

———. "Hofhaimer, Paul." *The New Grove Dictionary of Music*, 8:631–32.

Schwab, Heinrich W. "Stadtpfeifer." *The New Grove Dictionary of Music*, 18:50–52.

Seay, Albert. "Arcadelt, Jacques." *The New Grove Dictionary of Music*, 1:546–48.

———. "Hothby." *The New Grove Dictionary of Music*, 8:729–30.

Seebass, Tilman. "The Visualisation of Music through Pictorial Imagery and Notation in Late Mediaeval France." In *Studies in the Performance of Late Mediaeval Music*, ed. Stanley Boorman. Cambridge: Cambridge University Press, 1983.

Senfl, Ludwig. *Sämtliche Werke*, ed. Arnold Geering and Wilhelm Altwegg. 4 vols. Das Erbe deutscher Musik, vols. 5, 10, 13, and 15. Wolfenbüttel: Möseler, 1927–62.

———. *Sämtliche Werke*, continuation. 11 vols. (including Das Erbe deutscher Music, vols. 5, 10, 13, and 15). Bern: Swiss Musicological Society and Swiss Composers' Society, 1927.

Sermisy, Claudin de. *Opera omnia*, ed. Gaston Allaire and Isabelle Cazeaux. 6 vols. Corpus mensurabilis musicae 52. [Rome]: American Institute of Musicology, 1970–86.

Seward, Desmond. *The Hundred Years War: The English in France, 1337–1453.* New York: Atheneum, 1978.

Sherr, Richard. *Papal Music Manuscripts in the Late Fifteenth and Early Sixteenth Centuries.* Renaissance Manuscript Studies, vol. 5. Stuttgart-Neuhausen: American Institute of Musicology, 1996.

Singer, Gerhard. "Zacconi." *The New Grove Dictionary of Music*, 20:611–12.

Sire, H. J. A. *The Knights of Malta.* New Haven: Yale University Press, 1994.

Slavin, Dennis. "In Support of 'Heresy': Manuscript Evidence for the *a cappella* Performance of Early Fifteenth-Century Songs." *Early Music* 19 (1991): 179–90.

Slim, H. Colin. "Cavazzoni, Girolamo." *The New Grove Dictionary of Music*, 4:35–36.

———. "Cavazzoni, Marc Antonio." *The New Grove Dictionary of Music*, 4:36–37.

———. "Segni, Julio." *The New Grove Dictionary of Music*, 17:105–6.

———. "Parabosco, Girolamo." *The New Grove Dictionary of Music*, 14:173–74.

———. "Verdelot, Philippe." *The New Grove Dictionary of Music*, 19:631–34.

Slim, H. Colin, ed. *A Gift of Madrigals and Motets.* 2 vols. Chicago: University of Chicago Press, 1972.

———. *Ten Altus Parts at Oscott College, Sutton Coldfield.* N.p., [1978].

———. *Musica nova.* Monuments of Renaissance Music, vol. 1. Chicago: University of Chicago Press, 1964.

Smijers, Albert. "Meerstemmige muziek van de Illustre Lieve Vrouwe Broederschap te 's-Hertogenbosch." *Tijdschrift van de Vereniging voor Nederlandse Muziekgeschiedenis* 16 (1946): 1–30 and 63–106.

——. "Music of the Illustrious Confraternity of Our Lady at 's-Hertogenbosch from 1330–1600." In *Papers Read by Members of the American Musicological Society (1939).*

Smith, Hopkinson K. "Narváez, Luys de." *The New Grove Dictionary of Music,* 13:39.

Snow, Robert. "The Mass-Motet Cycle: A Mid-Fifteenth-Century Experiment." In *Essays in Musicology in Honor of Dragan Plamenac,* ed. Gustave Reese and Robert J. Snow. Pittsburgh: University of Pittsburgh Press, 1969.

Southern, Eileen. *The Buxheim Organ Book.* Brooklyn: Institute of Mediaeval Music, 1963.

——. "Foreign Music in German Manuscripts of the Fifteenth Century." *Journal of the American Musicological Society* 21 (1968): 258–85.

Sparks, Edgar H. *Cantus Firmus in Mass and Motet, 1420–1520.* Berkeley: University of California Press, 1963.

Stäblein, Bruno. "Lamentatio." *Die Musik in Geschichte und Gegenwart,* 8:133–42.

Staehelin, Martin. "Buxheimer Orgelbuch." *Die Musik in Geschichte und Gegenwart,* 2d ed., Sachteil, 2 (1995): 285–88.

——. "Isaac." *The New Grove Dictionary of Music,* 9:329–37.

——. "La Rue, Pierre de." *The New Grove Dictionary of Music,* 10:473–76.

——. *Die Messe Heinrich Isaacs.* 3 vols. Publikationen der Schweizerischen Musikforschenden Gesellschaft, ser. 2, vol. 28. Bern: Paul Haupt, 1977.

Starr, Pamela. "Roman Light on Johannes Regis." *Revue belge de musicologie* 49 (1995): 27–38.

——. "Rome as the Center of the Universe: Papal Grace and Music Patronage." *Early Music History* 11 (1992): 223–62.

Steib, Murray. "A Composer Looks at His Model: Polyphonic Borrowing in Masses from the Late Fifteenth Century." *Tijdschrift van de Vereniging voor Nederlandse Muziekgeschiedenis* 46 (1966): 5–41.

——. "Imitation and Elaboration: The Use of Borrowed Material in Masses from the Late Fifteenth Century." Ph.D. diss., University of Chicago, 1992.

Steiner, Ruth. "Benedicamus Domino." *The New Grove Dictionary of Music,* 2:471.

——. "Te Deum." *The New Grove Dictionary of Music,* 18:641–43.

——. "Trope." *The New Grove Dictionary of Music,* 19:172–87.

Stephan, Wolfgang. *Die burgundisch-niederländische Motette zur Zeit Ockeghems.* Kassel: Bärenreiter, 1937. Reprint, idem, 1973.

Stevens, John. "Carol." *The New Grove Dictionary of Music,* 3:806.

Stevens, John, ed. *Medieval Carols.* 2d ed. Musica Britannica, vol. 4. London: Stainer and Bell, 1958.

——. *Music at the Court of Henry VIII.* Musica Britannica, vol. 18. London: Stainer and Bell, 1962.

Stevens, John, and William F. Prizer. "Lauda." *The New Grove Dictionary of Music,* 10:539–43.

Stevenson, Robert. "Anchieta, Juan de." *The New Grove Dictionary of Music,* 1:394.

——. "Escobar, Pedro de." *The New Grove Dictionary of Music,* 6:243–44.

——. "Guerrero." *The New Grove Dictionary of Music,* 7:787–89.

——. "Morales, Cristóbal de." *The New Grove Dictionary of Music,* 12:556.

——. "Mudarra, Alonso." *The New Grove Dictionary of Music,* 12:757–58.

——. "Peñalosa, Francisco de." *The New Grove Dictionary of Music,* 14:347–48.

————. "Spain." *The New Grove Dictionary of Music*, 17:785–88.

————. *Spanish Cathedral Music in the Golden Age*. Berkeley: University of California Press, 1961.

————. *Spanish Music in the Age of Columbus*. The Hague: Nijhoff, 1960.

————. "Victoria, Tomás Luis de." *The New Grove Dictionary of Music*, 19:704–9.

Straeten, Edmond vander. *La musique aux Pays-bas*. Brussels, 1867–88. Reprint, New York: Dover, 1969.

Strohm, Reinhard. *Music in Late Medieval Bruges*. Oxford: Clarendon Press, 1985.

————. *The Rise of European Music, 1380–1500*. Cambridge: Cambridge University Press, 1993.

Strunk, Oliver, ed. *Source Readings in Music History*. New York: Norton, 1950.

————, ed. *Source Readings in Music History*, rev. ed., general ed. Leo Treitler. New York: Norton, 1998.

Symonds, John Addington. *Renaissance in Italy*. New York: Henry Holt and Co., 1888.

Tarr, Edward H. "Trumpet." *The New Grove Dictionary of Music*, 19:214–17.

————. "Trumpet." *The New Grove Dictionary of Musical Instruments*, 3:641–43.

Taruskin, Richard, ed. *Coment peult avoir joye/Wohlauf gut Gesellvon hinnen*. RS 1. Miami: Ogni Sorte Editions, 1978.

————. *D'ung aultre amer*. RS 6. Miami: Ogni Sorte Editions, 1983.

————. *Een vrolic wesen*. RS 2. Miami: Ogni Sorte Editions, 1979.

————. *In mynen zin*. RS 8. Miami: Ogni Sorte Editions, 1984.

————. *J'ai pris amours*. RS 5. Miami: Ogni Sorte Editions, 1982.

————. *L'homme armé*. RS 4. Miami: Ogni Sorte Editions, 1980.

————. *O Venus bant*. RS 3. Miami: Ogni Sorte Editions, 1979.

————. *T'andernaken*. RS 7. Miami: Ogni Sorte Editions, 1981.

Temperley, Nicholas. "Psalms, Metrical." *The New Grove Dictionary of Music*, 15:358–62 and 367–69.

Thomas, Jennifer S. "Modern Myopia and the Renaissance Motet." *Abstracts of Papers Read*, Sixtieth Annual Meeting of the American Musicological Society, Minneapolis, October 29, 1994.

Tinctoris, Johannes. *The Art of Counterpoint*, trans. Albert Seay. Musicological Studies and Documents, vol. 5. [Rome]: American Institute of Musicology, 1961.

————. *Concerning the Nature and Propriety of Tones*, ed. Albert Seay. Colorado Springs: Colorado College Music Press, 1967.

————. *De arte contrapuncti*, ed. Albert Seay. Corpus scriptorum de musica, vol. 22, no. 8. [Rome]: American Institute of Musicology, 1975–78.

————. *De natura et proprietate tonorum*, ed. Albert Seay. Corpus scriptorum de musica, vol. 22, no. 2. [Rome]: American Institute of Musicology, 1975.

————. *De notis et pausis*, ed. Albert Seay. Corpus scriptorum de musica, vol. 22, no. 3. [Rome]: American Institute of Musicology, 1975.

————. *Expositio manus*, ed. Albert Seay. Corpus scriptorum de musica, vol. 22, no. 1. [Rome]: American Institute of Musicology, 1975.

————. *Proportionale musices*, ed. Albert Seay. Corpus scriptorum de musica, vol. 22, no. 10. [Rome]: American Institute of Musicology, 1978. English translation by Albert Seay, "The *Proportionale musices* of Johannes Tinctoris." *Journal of Music Theory* 1 (1957): 22–75.

————. *Terminorum musicae diffinitorium* (1495), ed. Carl Parrish. New York: Free Press of Glencoe, 1963.

Tomlinson, Gary. *Monteverdi and the End of the Renaissance*. Oxford: Clarendon Press, 1987.

Torrefranca, Fausto. *Il segreto del Quattrocento: Musiche ariose e poesia popolaresca*. Milan: Hoepli, 1939.

Trowell, Brian. "Faburden." *The New Grove Dictionary of Music*, 6:350–54.

———. "Fauxbourdon." *The New Grove Dictionary of Music*, 6:433–38.

———. "Frye." *The New Grove Dictionary of Music*, 6:876–79.

———. "Sight, Sighting." *The New Grove Dictionary of Music*, 17:307.

Urquhart, Peter. "False Concords in Busnoys." In *Continuities and Transformations in Musical Culture, 1450–1500: Assessing the Legacy of Antoine Busnoys*, ed. Paula Higgins. London: Oxford University Press, in press.

Vale, Malcolm G. A. *Charles VII*. Berkeley: University of California Press, 1974.

Vanderwerf, Hendrik. "Estampie." *The New Grove Dictionary of Music*, 6:254–58.

Vatican City, Biblioteca Apostolica Vaticana, MS Chigiana C VIII 23. New York: Garland, 1987.

Vaughan, Richard. *Valois Burgundy*. Hamden, Conn.: Archon Books, 1975.

Verdelot, Philippe. *Madrigals for Four and Five Voices*, ed. Jessie Ann Owens. 3 vols. Sixteenth-Century Madrigal, vols. 28–30. New York: Garland, 1989.

Victoria, Tomas Luis de. *Opera omnia*, ed. Higinio Anglès. 4 vols. Monumentos de la música española, vols. 25, 27, 30, 31. Barcelona: Consejo Superior de Investigaciones Científicas, 1965–68.

———. *Opera omnia*, ed. Felipe Pedrell. 8 vols. Leipzig: Breitkopf und Härtel, 1902–13.

Viti, Paolo, ed. *Leonardo Bruni, cancelliere della Repubblica di Firenze: Convegno di Studi*. Atti di Convegni, Istituto di Studi sul Rinascimento, vol. 18. Florence: Olschki, 1990.

Vitry, Philippe de. *Ars nova*, trans. Leon Plantinga. *Journal of Music Theory* 5 (1961): 204–23.

Waesberghe, Joseph Smits van. "Een 15e Eeuws Muziekboek van de Stadsminstrelen van Maastricht?" In *Renaissance-Muziek, 1400–1600: Donum natalicium René Bernard Lenaerts*, ed. Jozef Robijns. Louvain: Katholieke Universiteit Seminarie voor Muziekwetenschap, 1969.

Wagner, David L., ed. *The Seven Liberal Arts*. Bloomington: Indiana University Press, 1983.

Walker, Thomas. "Castrato." *The New Grove Dictionary of Music*, 3:875.

Wallner, Bertha A., ed. *Das Buxheimer Orgelbuch*. Documenta musicologica, vol. 2. Kassel: Bärenreiter, 1955.

———. *Das Buxheimer Orgelbuch*. 3 vols. Das Erbe deutscher Musik, vols. 37–39. Kassel: Bärenreiter, 1958.

Walter, Johann. *Sämtliche Werke*, ed. Otto Schröder. 6 vols. Kassel: Bärenreiter, 1953–73.

Ward, John M. "Fuenllana, Miguel de." *The New Grove Dictionary of Music*, 7:6.

Ward, Lynn Halpern. "The *motetti missales* Repertory Reconsidered." *Journal of the American Musicological Society* 39 (1986): 491–523.

Ward, Tom R. "Hymn." *The New Grove Dictionary of Music*, 8:841–45.

———. "Libert." *The New Grove Dictionary of Music*, 10:718.

———. "The Polyphonic Office Hymn and the Liturgy of Fifteenth-Century Italy." *Musica disciplina* 26 (1972): 166–69.

———. "The Structure of the Manuscript Trent 92-I." *Musica disciplina* 29 (1975): 127–47.

Warlock (alias Heseltine), Peter, ed. *The Oxford Choral Songs from the Old Masters*. London: Oxford University Press, 1927.

Warmington, Flynn. "A Very Fine Troop of Bastards?: Provenance, Date, and Busnois's Role in Brussels 5557." *Abstracts of Papers, American Musicological Society, Annual Meeting Philadelphia, 1984*, p. 11.

Weaver, Robin A. "Zwingli, Ulrich." *The New Grove Dictionary of Music*, 20:725–26.

Weaver, Robin A., and Ann Bond. "Luther, Martin." *The New Grove Dictionary of Music*, 11:365–71.

Wegman, Rob C. "Another 'Imitation' of Busnois's *Missa L'homme armé*." *Journal of the Royal Musical Society* 114 (1989): 189–202.

———. *Born for the Muses: The Life and Masses of Jacob Obrecht*. Oxford: Clarendon Press, 1994.

———. "Music and Musicians at the Guild of Our Lady in Bergen op Zoom, c. 1470–1510." *Early Music History* 9 (1989): 175–249.

———. "New Data concerning the Origins and Chronology of Brussels, Koninklijke Bibliotheek, Manuscript 5557." *Tijdschrift van de Vereniging voor Nederlandse Muziekgeschiedenis* 36 (1986): 5–25.

Weinmann, Karl. *Johannes Tinctoris und sein unbekannter Traktat "De inventione et usu musicae."* Tutzing: Schneider, 1961.

Werbeke, Gaspar van. *Messe e mottetti*, ed. Giampiero Tintori. Milan: Veneranda Fabbrica del Duomo di Milano, 1963.

Wert, Giaches de. *Opera omnia*, ed. Carol MacClintock and Melvin Bernstein. 17 vols. Corpus mensurabilis musicae 24. [Rome]: American Institute of Musicology, 1961–77.

Wess, Joan. "Dalza." *The New Grove Dictionary of Music*, 5:169.

Westrup, Jack. "England." *The New Grove Dictionary of Music*, 6:172.

Wilbye, John. *The Second Set of Madrigales to 3, 4, 5, and 6 parts apt for Voyals and Voyces* (London, 1609). Vol. 7 of *The English Madrigalists*, ed. Edmund H. Fellowes (rev. Thurston Dart). London: Stainer and Bell, 1966.

Willaert, Adriano. *Opera omnia*, ed. Hermann Zenck and Walter Gerstenberg. 15 vols. Corpus mensurabilis musicae 3. [Rome]: American Institute of Musicology, 1950–77.

Wilson, Blake. *Music and Merchants: The Laudesi Companies of Republican Florence*. Oxford: Clarendon Press, 1992.

Wolf, Johannes, ed. *Newe deudsche geistliche Gesenge* (Wittenberg, 1544). Denkmäler deutscher Tonkunst, 1. Folge, vol. 34. Leipzig: Breitkopf und Härtel, 1908.

Wolff, Christoph. "Germany." *The New Grove Dictionary of Music*, 8:268–69.

———. "Paumann." *The New Grove Dictionary of Music*, 14:308–9.

Woodfill, Walter L. *Musicians in English Society from Elizabeth to Charles I*. Princeton: Princeton University Press, 1953.

Woodley, Ronald. "Johannes Tinctoris: A Review of the Documentary Biographical Evidence." *Journal of the American Musicological Society* 34 (1981): 217–48.

———. "The Printing and Scope of Tinctoris' Fragmentary Treatise *De inventione et usu musicae*." *Early Music History* 5 (1985): 239–68.

———. "Tinctoris's Translations of the Golden Fleece Statutes: A Text and a (Possible) Context." *Early Music History* 8 (1988): 173–244.

Woodward, William Harrison. *Studies in Education during the Age of the Renaissance, 1400–1600*. New York: Teachers College Press, 1976.

Wright, Craig. "Burgundy." *The New Grove Dictionary of Music and Musicians*, 3:464–68.

———. "Dufay at Cambrai: Discoveries and Revisions." *Journal of the American Musicological Society* 28 (1975): 194–99.

———. "Dufay's *Nuper rosarum flores*, King Solomon's Temple, and the Veneration of the Virgin." *Journal of the American Musicological Society* 47 (1994): 395–441.

————. "Grenon." *The New Grove Dictionary of Music*, 7:702.

————. *Music at the Court of Burgundy, 1364–1419: A Documentary History*. Brooklyn: Institute of Mediaeval Music, 1979.

————. "Musiciens à la cathédrale de Cambrai." *Revue de musicologie* 62 (1976): 204–28.

————. "Performance Practices at the Cathedral of Cambrai, 1475–1550." *Musical Quarterly* 64 (1978): 295–328.

Zarlino, Gioseffo. *Le istitutioni harmoniche*. Venice, 1558. Reprint, New York: Broude Brothers, 1965.

Credits

Fig. 1-1. Alinari/Art Resource, NY. Andrea del Castagno (1410–1457). Portrait of Petrarch. Uffizi, Florence, Italy.

Fig. 1-2. Alinari/Art Resource, NY. Andrea del Castagno (1410–1457). Portrait of Giovanni Boccaccio. Uffizi, Florence, Italy.

Fig. 1-3. Alinari/Art Resource, NY. Signorelli, Luca. Portrait of Dante. Duomo, Orvieto, Italy.

Fig. 1-4. Alinari/Art Resource, NY. Giotto di Bondone (1266–1336). "Madonna Enthroned" ("Ognissanti Madonna"). Uffizi, Florence, Italy.

Fig. 1-5. Portrait of Erasmus by Hans Holbein. Musée du Louvre.

Fig. 1-7. By Permission of the British Library, MSS. Harley 6525, f. 1.

Fig. 1-8. Universitat de València, Biblioteca General i Històrica.

Fig. 1-9. Biblioteca Comunale Laudense, Museo Civico, Lodì.

Fig. 1-10. Alinari/Art Resource, NY. Basilica of S. Marco. View of the Piazza. Venice. San Marco, Venice, Italy.

Fig. 2-1. Österreichische Nationalbibliothek, Wien.

Fig. 2-2. Chantilly, Musée Condé. Giraudon.

Fig. 2-4. Courtesy of Craig Wright, from his "Performance Practices at the Cathedral of Cambrai 1474–1550, *Musical Quarterly* 64 (1978); 302.

Fig. 2-5. Bibliothèque municipale de Tours.

Fig. 2-6. Lille, Musée des Beaux-Arts.

Fig. 3-1. Copyright Bibliotheca Regia.

Fig. 3-2. Boston Athenaeum: woodcut illustration, title page to Volume 1 of Pierre Attaingnant's "Primus liber viginti missarum musicalium," 1532.

Fig. 3-3. By Permission of the British Library, Add. MSS. 35324, f. 31v.

Fig. 3-4. Cliché Bibliothèque nationale de France.

Fig. 3-5. Graphische Sammlung Albertina, Wien.

Fig. 3-6. Cliché Bibliothèque nationale de France.

Fig. 3-7. Centre Hospitalier Universitaire Dijon, Hôpital Général de Dijon.

Fig. 3-8. Cliché Bibliothèque nationale de France, Bibliothèque de l'Arsenal.

Fig. 3-9. "Jardin d'amour à la cour de Philippe III le Bon." Châteaux de Versailles et de Trianon. © Photo RMN—Gérard Blot.

Fig. 3-10. Copyright Bibliotheca Regia.

Fig. 3-11a. Photo Courtesy of The Newberry Library, Chicago.

Fig. 3-11b. Staatsbibliothek zu Berlin—Preussischer Kulturbesitz, Musikabteilung mit Mendelssohn-Archiv.

Fig. 3-12. By Permission of the British Library.

Fig. 3-13. Bayerische Staatsbibliothek, München, Mus. Ms. A II S. 186.

Fig. 4-1. Österreichische Nationalbibliothek, Wien.

Fig. 4-2. Staatsbibliothek zu Berlin—Preussischer Kulturbesitz, Handschriftenabteilung.

Fig. 4-3. Institut de France—Musée Jacquemart-André. "Les Funérails" from "Le livre d'Heures" by Maréchal de Boucicaut.

Fig. 4-4. Österreichische Nationalbibliothek, Wien.

Fig. 4-5. Stadtbibliothek Nürnberg.

Fig. 4-6. By Permission of the British Library, K.1.c.16.

Fig. 4-7. By Permission of the British Library, Add. MSS. 18851, f. 184v.

Fig. 4-8. Giraudon/Art Resource, NY. Memling, Hans (1425/40–1494). Musical angels (detail). Koninklijk Museum voor Schone Kunsten, Antwerp, Belgium.

Fig. 4-9. Alinari/Art Resource, NY. Bellini, Gentile. Procession in the Piazza San Marco. Accademia, Venice, Italy.

Fig. 5-1. Biblioteca Apostolica Vaticana, MS Cappella Giulia XII 2, ff. 47v, 48.

Fig. 5-2. Bibliothèque Municipale de Dijon, Ms. 517 ff. 28v, 29.

Fig. 5-3. Photo Courtesy of The Newberry Library, Chicago.

Fig. 5-4. Biblioteca Comunale Manfrediana, Faenza.

Fig. 5-5. Bayerische Staatsbibliothek, München, Mus. Ms. 3725 f. 128v.

Fig. 5-6. Photo Courtesy of The Newberry Library, Chicago.

Fig. 5-7. Österreichische Nationalbibliothek, Wien.

Fig. 5-8. Bayerische Staatsbibliothek, München, Cgm 810 ff. 62v,63r.

Fig. 5-9. By Permission of the British Library, MSS. Royal 8 G vii, ff. 56v, 57.

Fig. 5-11. By Permission of the British Library, K.9.a.12.

Fig. 5-12. Herzog August Bibliothek Wolfenbüttel: 2.2.8.2 Musica.

Fig. 6-1. Staatsbibliothek zu Berlin—Preussischer Kulturbesitz, Handschriftenabteilung.

Fig. 6-2. By courtesy of the National Portrait Gallery, London.

Fig. 6-3. By Permission of the British Library, Add. MSS. 18850, f. 256v, detail.

Fig. 6-4. By Permission of the British Library, Add. MSS. 57950, ff. 55v, 56.

Fig. 6-5. By permission of the Syndics of Cambridge University Library.

Fig. 6-6. Copyright by the Dean and Chapter of Worcester.

Fig. 7-1. Constable Publishers, taken from *The Hundred Years War* by Desmond Seward.

Fig. 7-2. Constable Publishers, taken from *The Hundred Years War* by Desmond Seward.

Fig. 7-4. Giraudon/Art Resource, NY. John Plantagenet, Duke of Bedford, battling the French. Miniature from "Abrege de la chronique" by Enguerrand de Monstrelet. Ms. fr. 2680, f. 35. France, 16th c., Bibliotheque Nationale, Paris, France.

Fig. 7-5. Constable Publishers, taken from *The Hundred Years War* by Desmond Seward.

Fig. 7-6. Portrait of King Charles VII of France by Jean Fouquet. Musée du Louvre. © Photo RMN.

Fig. 7-7. Cliché Bibliothèque nationale de France.

Fig. 7-8. Staatliche Museen zu Berlin—Preussischer Kulturbesitz, Gemäldegalerie.

Fig. 7-9. By Permission of the British Library, MSS. Harley 4425, f. 12v.

Fig. 7-10. Cliché Bibliothèque nationale de France.

Fig. 7-11. Firenze, Biblioteca Medicea Laurenziana, Ms. Acq. Doni 666, c. 125v (e poi 126r). Su concessione del Minestero per i Beni Culturali e Ambientali. E' vietata ogni ulteriore riproduzione con qualsiasi mezzo.

Fig. 8-1. Biblioteca Apostolica Vaticana, Chigi Codex VIII, ff. 281v, 282.

Fig. 9-1. Biblioteca Estense Universitaria, Modena, Alfa. X. 1. 11 le carte 13v e 14.

Fig. 10-1. Biblioteca Apostolica Vaticana, Chigi Codex VIII, ff. 106v, 107.

Fig. 11-2. Museo Nazionale di San Martino, Naples, Ministero per i Beni Culturali e Ambientali.

Fig. 11-3. Alinari/Art Resource, NY. Perugino, Pietro (1445/50–1523). Christ delivering the keys to Saint Peter. Sistine Chapel, Vatican Palace, Vatican State.

Fig. 11-4. Cliché Bibliothèque nationale de France.

Fig. 11-5. Portrait of Isabella d'Este by Leonardo da Vinci. Musée du Louvre, D.A.G. ©Photo RMN—M. Bellot.

Fig. 11-6. Bayerische Staatsbibliothek, München, Rar. 878-3 f. 63v.

Fig. 11-7. Copyright © The British Museum.

Fig. 12-1. Biblioteca Estense Universitaria, Modena, Alfa. M. 1. 12 le carte 17v e 18r.

Fig. 12-2. Anonymous, "Cum autem venissem," from Razzi's Libro primo of 1563, pp. 115–16, as printed by Forni in Bologna, 1969, Bibliotheca Musica Bononiensis, Collana diretta de Giuseppe Vecchi dell' Università degli Studi di Bologna, Sezione IV N. 51. Arnaldo Forni Editore S.R.L.

Fig. 13-2. Portrait of Oswald von Wolkenstein in Liederhandschrift B, Innsbruck, University Library, MS. B, 1432 (A-Iu).

Fig. 14-2. Chantilly, Musée Condé. Giraudon.

Fig. 14-3. Österreichische Nationalbibliothek, Wien.

Fig. 17-1. Kimbell Art Museum, Fort Worth, Texas.

Fig. 17-2. Biblioteca Apostolica Vaticana, Cappella Sistina, Cod. 16.

Fig. 17-3. "Passio Christi secundum IV Evangelistas" (Iohannis Kaliveda canonici Olomuncensis 1525), f. 1, Regional Archives Opava, Branch Offfice in Olomouc, Collection of Manuscripts, C.O. 89.

Fig. 18-1. Giraudon/Art Resource, NY. Bontemps, Pierre. Battle at Marignano, 1548. Detail from the Tomb of Francis I and Claude of France. Royal Abbey Church, St. Denis, France.

Fig. 19-1. Biblioteca Nazionale Centrale di Firenze, Ms. Magl. XIX 166 cc. 2v–4r.

Fig. 19-2. Staatliche Museen zu Berlin—Preussischer Kulturbesitz, Gemäldegalerie.

Fig. 19-3. By Permission of the British Library.

Fig. 19-4. Bayerische Staatsbibliothek, München, Mus. Ms. B S. 304.

Fig. 20-1. By Permission of the British Library, MSS. Royal 2 A xvi (miniature), f. 63v.

Fig. 21-1. Alinari/Art Resource, NY. Cranach, Lucas the Elder. Portrait of Martin Luther. Uffizi, Florence, Italy.

Fig. 21-2. Snark/Art Resource, NY. Anonymous. Engraving of John Calvin in his study. Bibliothèque Nationale, Paris, France.

Fig. 22-1. By Permission of the British Library, Add. MSS. 28550, f. 43v.

Fig. 22-2. Staatliches Institut für Musikforschung, Musikinstrumenten-Museum/Preussischer Kulturbesitz.

Fig. 22-3. Scène de roman, Le Concert, vers 1420, Arras, série de 5 tapisseries. Musée des Arts décoratifs, Paris. Photo Laurent-Sully JAULMES. Toutes droits réservés.

Index

A **boldface** page number indicates the primary discussion or definition of the entry word. *Italics* refer to illustrations or music examples.